Lecture Notes in Computer Science   13678

More information about this series at https://link.springer.com/bookseries/558

Shai Avidan · Gabriel Brostow ·
Moustapha Cissé · Giovanni Maria Farinella ·
Tal Hassner (Eds.)

Computer Vision – ECCV 2022

17th European Conference
Tel Aviv, Israel, October 23–27, 2022
Proceedings, Part XVIII

 Springer

Editors
Shai Avidan
Tel Aviv University
Tel Aviv, Israel

Gabriel Brostow (iD)
University College London
London, UK

Moustapha Cissé
Google AI
Accra, Ghana

Giovanni Maria Farinella (iD)
University of Catania
Catania, Italy

Tal Hassner (iD)
Facebook (United States)
Menlo Park, CA, USA

ISSN 0302-9743 ISSN 1611-3349 (electronic)
Lecture Notes in Computer Science
ISBN 978-3-031-19796-3 ISBN 978-3-031-19797-0 (eBook)
https://doi.org/10.1007/978-3-031-19797-0

This Springer imprint is published by the registered company Springer Nature Switzerland AG
The registered company address is: Gewerbestrasse 11, 6330 Cham, Switzerland

Foreword

Organizing the European Conference on Computer Vision (ECCV 2022) in Tel-Aviv during a global pandemic was no easy feat. The uncertainty level was extremely high, and decisions had to be postponed to the last minute. Still, we managed to plan things just in time for ECCV 2022 to be held in person. Participation in physical events is crucial to stimulating collaborations and nurturing the culture of the Computer Vision community.

There were many people who worked hard to ensure attendees enjoyed the best science at the 16th edition of ECCV. We are grateful to the Program Chairs Gabriel Brostow and Tal Hassner, who went above and beyond to ensure the ECCV reviewing process ran smoothly. The scientific program includes dozens of workshops and tutorials in addition to the main conference and we would like to thank Leonid Karlinsky and Tomer Michaeli for their hard work. Finally, special thanks to the web chairs Lorenzo Baraldi and Kosta Derpanis, who put in extra hours to transfer information fast and efficiently to the ECCV community.

We would like to express gratitude to our generous sponsors and the Industry Chairs, Dimosthenis Karatzas and Chen Sagiv, who oversaw industry relations and proposed new ways for academia-industry collaboration and technology transfer. It's great to see so much industrial interest in what we're doing!

Authors' draft versions of the papers appeared online with open access on both the Computer Vision Foundation (CVF) and the European Computer Vision Association (ECVA) websites as with previous ECCVs. Springer, the publisher of the proceedings, has arranged for archival publication. The final version of the papers is hosted by SpringerLink, with active references and supplementary materials. It benefits all potential readers that we offer both a free and citeable version for all researchers, as well as an authoritative, citeable version for SpringerLink readers. Our thanks go to Ronan Nugent from Springer, who helped us negotiate this agreement. Last but not least, we wish to thank Eric Mortensen, our publication chair, whose expertise made the process smooth.

October 2022

Rita Cucchiara
Jiří Matas
Amnon Shashua
Lihi Zelnik-Manor

Preface

Welcome to the proceedings of the European Conference on Computer Vision (ECCV 2022). This was a hybrid edition of ECCV as we made our way out of the COVID-19 pandemic. The conference received 5804 valid paper submissions, compared to 5150 submissions to ECCV 2020 (a 12.7% increase) and 2439 in ECCV 2018. 1645 submissions were accepted for publication (28%) and, of those, 157 (2.7% overall) as orals.

846 of the submissions were desk-rejected for various reasons. Many of them because they revealed author identity, thus violating the double-blind policy. This violation came in many forms: some had author names with the title, others added acknowledgments to specific grants, yet others had links to their github account where their name was visible. Tampering with the LaTeX template was another reason for automatic desk rejection.

ECCV 2022 used the traditional CMT system to manage the entire double-blind reviewing process. Authors did not know the names of the reviewers and vice versa. Each paper received at least 3 reviews (except 6 papers that received only 2 reviews), totalling more than 15,000 reviews.

Handling the review process at this scale was a significant challenge. To ensure that each submission received as fair and high-quality reviews as possible, we recruited more than 4719 reviewers (in the end, 4719 reviewers did at least one review). Similarly we recruited more than 276 area chairs (eventually, only 276 area chairs handled a batch of papers). The area chairs were selected based on their technical expertise and reputation, largely among people who served as area chairs in previous top computer vision and machine learning conferences (ECCV, ICCV, CVPR, NeurIPS, etc.).

Reviewers were similarly invited from previous conferences, and also from the pool of authors. We also encouraged experienced area chairs to suggest additional chairs and reviewers in the initial phase of recruiting. The median reviewer load was five papers per reviewer, while the average load was about four papers, because of the emergency reviewers. The area chair load was 35 papers, on average.

Conflicts of interest between authors, area chairs, and reviewers were handled largely automatically by the CMT platform, with some manual help from the Program Chairs. Reviewers were allowed to describe themselves as senior reviewer (load of 8 papers to review) or junior reviewers (load of 4 papers). Papers were matched to area chairs based on a subject-area affinity score computed in CMT and an affinity score computed by the Toronto Paper Matching System (TPMS). TPMS is based on the paper's full text. An area chair handling each submission would bid for preferred expert reviewers, and we balanced load and prevented conflicts.

The assignment of submissions to area chairs was relatively smooth, as was the assignment of submissions to reviewers. A small percentage of reviewers were not happy with their assignments in terms of subjects and self-reported expertise. This is an area for improvement, although it's interesting that many of these cases were reviewers hand-picked by AC's. We made a later round of reviewer recruiting, targeted at the list of authors of papers submitted to the conference, and had an excellent response which helped provide enough emergency reviewers. In the end, all but six papers received at least 3 reviews.

The challenges of the reviewing process are in line with past experiences at ECCV 2020. As the community grows, and the number of submissions increases, it becomes ever more challenging to recruit enough reviewers and ensure a high enough quality of reviews. Enlisting authors by default as reviewers might be one step to address this challenge.

Authors were given a week to rebut the initial reviews, and address reviewers' concerns. Each rebuttal was limited to a single pdf page with a fixed template.

The Area Chairs then led discussions with the reviewers on the merits of each submission. The goal was to reach consensus, but, ultimately, it was up to the Area Chair to make a decision. The decision was then discussed with a buddy Area Chair to make sure decisions were fair and informative. The entire process was conducted virtually with no in-person meetings taking place.

The Program Chairs were informed in cases where the Area Chairs overturned a decisive consensus reached by the reviewers, and pushed for the meta-reviews to contain details that explained the reasoning for such decisions. Obviously these were the most contentious cases, where reviewer inexperience was the most common reported factor.

Once the list of accepted papers was finalized and released, we went through the laborious process of plagiarism (including self-plagiarism) detection. A total of 4 accepted papers were rejected because of that.

Finally, we would like to thank our Technical Program Chair, Pavel Lifshits, who did tremendous work behind the scenes, and we thank the tireless CMT team.

October 2022

Gabriel Brostow
Giovanni Maria Farinella
Moustapha Cissé
Shai Avidan
Tal Hassner

Organization

General Chairs

Rita Cucchiara   University of Modena and Reggio Emilia, Italy
Jiří Matas   Czech Technical University in Prague, Czech Republic
Amnon Shashua   Hebrew University of Jerusalem, Israel
Lihi Zelnik-Manor   Technion – Israel Institute of Technology, Israel

Program Chairs

Shai Avidan   Tel-Aviv University, Israel
Gabriel Brostow   University College London, UK
Moustapha Cissé   Google AI, Ghana
Giovanni Maria Farinella   University of Catania, Italy
Tal Hassner   Facebook AI, USA

Program Technical Chair

Pavel Lifshits   Technion – Israel Institute of Technology, Israel

Workshops Chairs

Leonid Karlinsky   IBM Research, Israel
Tomer Michaeli   Technion – Israel Institute of Technology, Israel
Ko Nishino   Kyoto University, Japan

Tutorial Chairs

Thomas Pock   Graz University of Technology, Austria
Natalia Neverova   Facebook AI Research, UK

Demo Chair

Bohyung Han   Seoul National University, Korea

Social and Student Activities Chairs

Tatiana Tommasi   Italian Institute of Technology, Italy
Sagie Benaim   University of Copenhagen, Denmark

Diversity and Inclusion Chairs

Xi Yin   Facebook AI Research, USA
Bryan Russell   Adobe, USA

Communications Chairs

Lorenzo Baraldi   University of Modena and Reggio Emilia, Italy
Kosta Derpanis   York University & Samsung AI Centre Toronto,
                             Canada

Industrial Liaison Chairs

Dimosthenis Karatzas   Universitat Autònoma de Barcelona, Spain
Chen Sagiv   SagivTech, Israel

Finance Chair

Gerard Medioni   University of Southern California & Amazon,
                             USA

Publication Chair

Eric Mortensen   MiCROTEC, USA

Area Chairs

Lourdes Agapito   University College London, UK
Zeynep Akata   University of Tübingen, Germany
Naveed Akhtar   University of Western Australia, Australia
Karteek Alahari   Inria Grenoble Rhône-Alpes, France
Alexandre Alahi   École polytechnique fédérale de Lausanne,
                             Switzerland
Pablo Arbelaez   Universidad de Los Andes, Columbia
Antonis A. Argyros   University of Crete & Foundation for Research
                             and Technology-Hellas, Crete
Yuki M. Asano   University of Amsterdam, The Netherlands
Kalle Åström   Lund University, Sweden
Hadar Averbuch-Elor   Cornell University, USA

Hossein Azizpour	KTH Royal Institute of Technology, Sweden
Vineeth N. Balasubramanian	Indian Institute of Technology, Hyderabad, India
Lamberto Ballan	University of Padova, Italy
Adrien Bartoli	Université Clermont Auvergne, France
Horst Bischof	Graz University of Technology, Austria
Matthew B. Blaschko	KU Leuven, Belgium
Federica Bogo	Meta Reality Labs Research, Switzerland
Katherine Bouman	California Institute of Technology, USA
Edmond Boyer	Inria Grenoble Rhône-Alpes, France
Michael S. Brown	York University, Canada
Vittorio Caggiano	Meta AI Research, USA
Neill Campbell	University of Bath, UK
Octavia Camps	Northeastern University, USA
Duygu Ceylan	Adobe Research, USA
Ayan Chakrabarti	Google Research, USA
Tat-Jen Cham	Nanyang Technological University, Singapore
Antoni Chan	City University of Hong Kong, Hong Kong, China
Manmohan Chandraker	NEC Labs America, USA
Xinlei Chen	Facebook AI Research, USA
Xilin Chen	Institute of Computing Technology, Chinese Academy of Sciences, China
Dongdong Chen	Microsoft Cloud AI, USA
Chen Chen	University of Central Florida, USA
Ondrej Chum	Vision Recognition Group, Czech Technical University in Prague, Czech Republic
John Collomosse	Adobe Research & University of Surrey, UK
Camille Couprie	Facebook, France
David Crandall	Indiana University, USA
Daniel Cremers	Technical University of Munich, Germany
Marco Cristani	University of Verona, Italy
Canton Cristian	Facebook AI Research, USA
Dengxin Dai	ETH Zurich, Switzerland
Dima Damen	University of Bristol, UK
Kostas Daniilidis	University of Pennsylvania, USA
Trevor Darrell	University of California, Berkeley, USA
Andrew Davison	Imperial College London, UK
Tali Dekel	Weizmann Institute of Science, Israel
Alessio Del Bue	Istituto Italiano di Tecnologia, Italy
Weihong Deng	Beijing University of Posts and Telecommunications, China
Konstantinos Derpanis	Ryerson University, Canada
Carl Doersch	DeepMind, UK

Matthijs Douze	Facebook AI Research, USA
Mohamed Elhoseiny	King Abdullah University of Science and Technology, Saudi Arabia
Sergio Escalera	University of Barcelona, Spain
Yi Fang	New York University, USA
Ryan Farrell	Brigham Young University, USA
Alireza Fathi	Google, USA
Christoph Feichtenhofer	Facebook AI Research, USA
Basura Fernando	Agency for Science, Technology and Research (A*STAR), Singapore
Vittorio Ferrari	Google Research, Switzerland
Andrew W. Fitzgibbon	Graphcore, UK
David J. Fleet	University of Toronto, Canada
David Forsyth	University of Illinois at Urbana-Champaign, USA
David Fouhey	University of Michigan, USA
Katerina Fragkiadaki	Carnegie Mellon University, USA
Friedrich Fraundorfer	Graz University of Technology, Austria
Oren Freifeld	Ben-Gurion University, Israel
Thomas Funkhouser	Google Research & Princeton University, USA
Yasutaka Furukawa	Simon Fraser University, Canada
Fabio Galasso	Sapienza University of Rome, Italy
Jürgen Gall	University of Bonn, Germany
Chuang Gan	Massachusetts Institute of Technology, USA
Zhe Gan	Microsoft, USA
Animesh Garg	University of Toronto, Vector Institute, Nvidia, Canada
Efstratios Gavves	University of Amsterdam, The Netherlands
Peter Gehler	Amazon, Germany
Theo Gevers	University of Amsterdam, The Netherlands
Bernard Ghanem	King Abdullah University of Science and Technology, Saudi Arabia
Ross B. Girshick	Facebook AI Research, USA
Georgia Gkioxari	Facebook AI Research, USA
Albert Gordo	Facebook, USA
Stephen Gould	Australian National University, Australia
Venu Madhav Govindu	Indian Institute of Science, India
Kristen Grauman	Facebook AI Research & UT Austin, USA
Abhinav Gupta	Carnegie Mellon University & Facebook AI Research, USA
Mohit Gupta	University of Wisconsin-Madison, USA
Hu Han	Institute of Computing Technology, Chinese Academy of Sciences, China

Bohyung Han   Seoul National University, Korea
Tian Han   Stevens Institute of Technology, USA
Emily Hand   University of Nevada, Reno, USA
Bharath Hariharan   Cornell University, USA
Ran He   Institute of Automation, Chinese Academy of
                               Sciences, China
Otmar Hilliges   ETH Zurich, Switzerland
Adrian Hilton   University of Surrey, UK
Minh Hoai   Stony Brook University, USA
Yedid Hoshen   Hebrew University of Jerusalem, Israel
Timothy Hospedales   University of Edinburgh, UK
Gang Hua   Wormpex AI Research, USA
Di Huang   Beihang University, China
Jing Huang   Facebook, USA
Jia-Bin Huang   Facebook, USA
Nathan Jacobs   Washington University in St. Louis, USA
C. V. Jawahar   International Institute of Information Technology,
                               Hyderabad, India
Herve Jegou   Facebook AI Research, France
Neel Joshi   Microsoft Research, USA
Armand Joulin   Facebook AI Research, France
Frederic Jurie   University of Caen Normandie, France
Fredrik Kahl   Chalmers University of Technology, Sweden
Yannis Kalantidis   NAVER LABS Europe, France
Evangelos Kalogerakis   University of Massachusetts, Amherst, USA
Sing Bing Kang   Zillow Group, USA
Yosi Keller   Bar Ilan University, Israel
Margret Keuper   University of Mannheim, Germany
Tae-Kyun Kim   Imperial College London, UK
Benjamin Kimia   Brown University, USA
Alexander Kirillov   Facebook AI Research, USA
Kris Kitani   Carnegie Mellon University, USA
Iasonas Kokkinos   Snap Inc. & University College London, UK
Vladlen Koltun   Apple, USA
Nikos Komodakis   University of Crete, Crete
Piotr Koniusz   Australian National University, Australia
Philipp Kraehenbuehl   University of Texas at Austin, USA
Dilip Krishnan   Google, USA
Ajay Kumar   Hong Kong Polytechnic University, Hong Kong,
                               China
Junseok Kwon   Chung-Ang University, Korea
Jean-Francois Lalonde   Université Laval, Canada

Ivan Laptev	Inria Paris, France
Laura Leal-Taixé	Technical University of Munich, Germany
Erik Learned-Miller	University of Massachusetts, Amherst, USA
Gim Hee Lee	National University of Singapore, Singapore
Seungyong Lee	Pohang University of Science and Technology, Korea
Zhen Lei	Institute of Automation, Chinese Academy of Sciences, China
Bastian Leibe	RWTH Aachen University, Germany
Hongdong Li	Australian National University, Australia
Fuxin Li	Oregon State University, USA
Bo Li	University of Illinois at Urbana-Champaign, USA
Yin Li	University of Wisconsin-Madison, USA
Ser-Nam Lim	Meta AI Research, USA
Joseph Lim	University of Southern California, USA
Stephen Lin	Microsoft Research Asia, China
Dahua Lin	The Chinese University of Hong Kong, Hong Kong, China
Si Liu	Beihang University, China
Xiaoming Liu	Michigan State University, USA
Ce Liu	Microsoft, USA
Zicheng Liu	Microsoft, USA
Yanxi Liu	Pennsylvania State University, USA
Feng Liu	Portland State University, USA
Yebin Liu	Tsinghua University, China
Chen Change Loy	Nanyang Technological University, Singapore
Huchuan Lu	Dalian University of Technology, China
Cewu Lu	Shanghai Jiao Tong University, China
Oisin Mac Aodha	University of Edinburgh, UK
Dhruv Mahajan	Facebook, USA
Subhransu Maji	University of Massachusetts, Amherst, USA
Atsuto Maki	KTH Royal Institute of Technology, Sweden
Arun Mallya	NVIDIA, USA
R. Manmatha	Amazon, USA
Iacopo Masi	Sapienza University of Rome, Italy
Dimitris N. Metaxas	Rutgers University, USA
Ajmal Mian	University of Western Australia, Australia
Christian Micheloni	University of Udine, Italy
Krystian Mikolajczyk	Imperial College London, UK
Anurag Mittal	Indian Institute of Technology, Madras, India
Philippos Mordohai	Stevens Institute of Technology, USA
Greg Mori	Simon Fraser University & Borealis AI, Canada

Vittorio Murino	Istituto Italiano di Tecnologia, Italy
P. J. Narayanan	International Institute of Information Technology, Hyderabad, India
Ram Nevatia	University of Southern California, USA
Natalia Neverova	Facebook AI Research, UK
Richard Newcombe	Facebook, USA
Cuong V. Nguyen	Florida International University, USA
Bingbing Ni	Shanghai Jiao Tong University, China
Juan Carlos Niebles	Salesforce & Stanford University, USA
Ko Nishino	Kyoto University, Japan
Jean-Marc Odobez	Idiap Research Institute, École polytechnique fédérale de Lausanne, Switzerland
Francesca Odone	University of Genova, Italy
Takayuki Okatani	Tohoku University & RIKEN Center for Advanced Intelligence Project, Japan
Manohar Paluri	Facebook, USA
Guan Pang	Facebook, USA
Maja Pantic	Imperial College London, UK
Sylvain Paris	Adobe Research, USA
Jaesik Park	Pohang University of Science and Technology, Korea
Hyun Soo Park	The University of Minnesota, USA
Omkar M. Parkhi	Facebook, USA
Deepak Pathak	Carnegie Mellon University, USA
Georgios Pavlakos	University of California, Berkeley, USA
Marcello Pelillo	University of Venice, Italy
Marc Pollefeys	ETH Zurich & Microsoft, Switzerland
Jean Ponce	Inria, France
Gerard Pons-Moll	University of Tübingen, Germany
Fatih Porikli	Qualcomm, USA
Victor Adrian Prisacariu	University of Oxford, UK
Petia Radeva	University of Barcelona, Spain
Ravi Ramamoorthi	University of California, San Diego, USA
Deva Ramanan	Carnegie Mellon University, USA
Vignesh Ramanathan	Facebook, USA
Nalini Ratha	State University of New York at Buffalo, USA
Tammy Riklin Raviv	Ben-Gurion University, Israel
Tobias Ritschel	University College London, UK
Emanuele Rodola	Sapienza University of Rome, Italy
Amit K. Roy-Chowdhury	University of California, Riverside, USA
Michael Rubinstein	Google, USA
Olga Russakovsky	Princeton University, USA

Mathieu Salzmann   École polytechnique fédérale de Lausanne,
                                     Switzerland
Dimitris Samaras   Stony Brook University, USA
Aswin Sankaranarayanan   Carnegie Mellon University, USA
Imari Sato   National Institute of Informatics, Japan
Yoichi Sato   University of Tokyo, Japan
Shin'ichi Satoh   National Institute of Informatics, Japan
Walter Scheirer   University of Notre Dame, USA
Bernt Schiele   Max Planck Institute for Informatics, Germany
Konrad Schindler   ETH Zurich, Switzerland
Cordelia Schmid   Inria & Google, France
Alexander Schwing   University of Illinois at Urbana-Champaign, USA
Nicu Sebe   University of Trento, Italy
Greg Shakhnarovich   Toyota Technological Institute at Chicago, USA
Eli Shechtman   Adobe Research, USA
Humphrey Shi   University of Oregon & University of Illinois at
                                     Urbana-Champaign & Picsart AI Research,
                                     USA
Jianbo Shi   University of Pennsylvania, USA
Roy Shilkrot   Massachusetts Institute of Technology, USA
Mike Zheng Shou   National University of Singapore, Singapore
Kaleem Siddiqi   McGill University, Canada
Richa Singh   Indian Institute of Technology Jodhpur, India
Greg Slabaugh   Queen Mary University of London, UK
Cees Snoek   University of Amsterdam, The Netherlands
Yale Song   Facebook AI Research, USA
Yi-Zhe Song   University of Surrey, UK
Bjorn Stenger   Rakuten Institute of Technology
Abby Stylianou   Saint Louis University, USA
Akihiro Sugimoto   National Institute of Informatics, Japan
Chen Sun   Brown University, USA
Deqing Sun   Google, USA
Kalyan Sunkavalli   Adobe Research, USA
Ying Tai   Tencent YouTu Lab, China
Ayellet Tal   Technion – Israel Institute of Technology, Israel
Ping Tan   Simon Fraser University, Canada
Siyu Tang   ETH Zurich, Switzerland
Chi-Keung Tang   Hong Kong University of Science and
                                     Technology, Hong Kong, China
Radu Timofte   University of Würzburg, Germany & ETH Zurich,
                                     Switzerland
Federico Tombari   Google, Switzerland & Technical University of
                                     Munich, Germany

James Tompkin	Brown University, USA
Lorenzo Torresani	Dartmouth College, USA
Alexander Toshev	Apple, USA
Du Tran	Facebook AI Research, USA
Anh T. Tran	VinAI, Vietnam
Zhuowen Tu	University of California, San Diego, USA
Georgios Tzimiropoulos	Queen Mary University of London, UK
Jasper Uijlings	Google Research, Switzerland
Jan C. van Gemert	Delft University of Technology, The Netherlands
Gul Varol	Ecole des Ponts ParisTech, France
Nuno Vasconcelos	University of California, San Diego, USA
Mayank Vatsa	Indian Institute of Technology Jodhpur, India
Ashok Veeraraghavan	Rice University, USA
Jakob Verbeek	Facebook AI Research, France
Carl Vondrick	Columbia University, USA
Ruiping Wang	Institute of Computing Technology, Chinese Academy of Sciences, China
Xinchao Wang	National University of Singapore, Singapore
Liwei Wang	The Chinese University of Hong Kong, Hong Kong, China
Chaohui Wang	Université Paris-Est, France
Xiaolong Wang	University of California, San Diego, USA
Christian Wolf	NAVER LABS Europe, France
Tao Xiang	University of Surrey, UK
Saining Xie	Facebook AI Research, USA
Cihang Xie	University of California, Santa Cruz, USA
Zeki Yalniz	Facebook, USA
Ming-Hsuan Yang	University of California, Merced, USA
Angela Yao	National University of Singapore, Singapore
Shaodi You	University of Amsterdam, The Netherlands
Stella X. Yu	University of California, Berkeley, USA
Junsong Yuan	State University of New York at Buffalo, USA
Stefanos Zafeiriou	Imperial College London, UK
Amir Zamir	École polytechnique fédérale de Lausanne, Switzerland
Lei Zhang	Alibaba & Hong Kong Polytechnic University, Hong Kong, China
Lei Zhang	International Digital Economy Academy (IDEA), China
Pengchuan Zhang	Meta AI, USA
Bolei Zhou	University of California, Los Angeles, USA
Yuke Zhu	University of Texas at Austin, USA

Todd Zickler   Harvard University, USA
Wangmeng Zuo   Harbin Institute of Technology, China

Technical Program Committee

Davide Abati
Soroush Abbasi
  Koohpayegani
Amos L. Abbott
Rameen Abdal
Rabab Abdelfattah
Sahar Abdelnabi
Hassan Abu Alhaija
Abulikemu Abuduweili
Ron Abutbul
Hanno Ackermann
Aikaterini Adam
Kamil Adamczewski
Ehsan Adeli
Vida Adeli
Donald Adjeroh
Arman Afrasiyabi
Akshay Agarwal
Sameer Agarwal
Abhinav Agarwalla
Vaibhav Aggarwal
Sara Aghajanzadeh
Susmit Agrawal
Antonio Agudo
Touqeer Ahmad
Sk Miraj Ahmed
Chaitanya Ahuja
Nilesh A. Ahuja
Abhishek Aich
Shubhra Aich
Noam Aigerman
Arash Akbarinia
Peri Akiva
Derya Akkaynak
Emre Aksan
Arjun R. Akula
Yuval Alaluf
Stephan Alaniz
Paul Albert
Cenek Albl

Filippo Aleotti
Konstantinos P.
  Alexandridis
Motasem Alfarra
Mohsen Ali
Thiemo Alldieck
Hadi Alzayer
Liang An
Shan An
Yi An
Zhulin An
Dongsheng An
Jie An
Xiang An
Saket Anand
Cosmin Ancuti
Juan Andrade-Cetto
Alexander Andreopoulos
Bjoern Andres
Jerone T. A. Andrews
Shivangi Aneja
Anelia Angelova
Dragomir Anguelov
Rushil Anirudh
Oron Anschel
Rao Muhammad Anwer
Djamila Aouada
Evlampios Apostolidis
Srikar Appalaraju
Nikita Araslanov
Andre Araujo
Eric Arazo
Dawit Mureja Argaw
Anurag Arnab
Aditya Arora
Chetan Arora
Sunpreet S. Arora
Alexey Artemov
Muhammad Asad
Kumar Ashutosh

Sinem Aslan
Vishal Asnani
Mahmoud Assran
Amir Atapour-Abarghouei
Nikos Athanasiou
Ali Athar
ShahRukh Athar
Sara Atito
Souhaib Attaiki
Matan Atzmon
Mathieu Aubry
Nicolas Audebert
Tristan T.
  Aumentado-Armstrong
Melinos Averkiou
Yannis Avrithis
Stephane Ayache
Mehmet Aygün
Seyed Mehdi
  Ayyoubzadeh
Hossein Azizpour
George Azzopardi
Mallikarjun B. R.
Yunhao Ba
Abhishek Badki
Seung-Hwan Bae
Seung-Hwan Baek
Seungryul Baek
Piyush Nitin Bagad
Shai Bagon
Gaetan Bahl
Shikhar Bahl
Sherwin Bahmani
Haoran Bai
Lei Bai
Jiawang Bai
Haoyue Bai
Jinbin Bai
Xiang Bai
Xuyang Bai

Bowen Cai
Mu Cai
Qin Cai
Ruojin Cai
Weidong Cai
Weiwei Cai
Yi Cai
Yujun Cai
Zhiping Cai
Akin Caliskan
Lilian Calvet
Baris Can Cam
Necati Cihan Camgoz
Tommaso Campari
Dylan Campbell
Ziang Cao
Ang Cao
Xu Cao
Zhiwen Cao
Shengcao Cao
Song Cao
Weipeng Cao
Xiangyong Cao
Xiaochun Cao
Yue Cao
Yunhao Cao
Zhangjie Cao
Jiale Cao
Yang Cao
Jiajiong Cao
Jie Cao
Jinkun Cao
Lele Cao
Yulong Cao
Zhiguo Cao
Chen Cao
Razvan Caramalau
Marlène Careil
Gustavo Carneiro
Joao Carreira
Dan Casas
Paola Cascante-Bonilla
Angela Castillo
Francisco M. Castro
Pedro Castro

Luca Cavalli
George J. Cazenavette
Oya Celiktutan
Hakan Cevikalp
Sri Harsha C. H.
Sungmin Cha
Geonho Cha
Menglei Chai
Lucy Chai
Yuning Chai
Zenghao Chai
Anirban Chakraborty
Deep Chakraborty
Rudrasis Chakraborty
Souradeep Chakraborty
Kelvin C. K. Chan
Chee Seng Chan
Paramanand Chandramouli
Arjun Chandrasekaran
Kenneth Chaney
Dongliang Chang
Huiwen Chang
Peng Chang
Xiaojun Chang
Jia-Ren Chang
Hyung Jin Chang
Hyun Sung Chang
Ju Yong Chang
Li-Jen Chang
Qi Chang
Wei-Yi Chang
Yi Chang
Nadine Chang
Hanqing Chao
Pradyumna Chari
Dibyadip Chatterjee
Chiranjoy Chattopadhyay
Siddhartha Chaudhuri
Zhengping Che
Gal Chechik
Lianggangxu Chen
Qi Alfred Chen
Brian Chen
Bor-Chun Chen
Bo-Hao Chen

Bohong Chen
Bin Chen
Ziliang Chen
Cheng Chen
Chen Chen
Chaofeng Chen
Xi Chen
Haoyu Chen
Xuanhong Chen
Wei Chen
Qiang Chen
Shi Chen
Xianyu Chen
Chang Chen
Changhuai Chen
Hao Chen
Jie Chen
Jianbo Chen
Jingjing Chen
Jun Chen
Kejiang Chen
Mingcai Chen
Nenglun Chen
Qifeng Chen
Ruoyu Chen
Shu-Yu Chen
Weidong Chen
Weijie Chen
Weikai Chen
Xiang Chen
Xiuyi Chen
Xingyu Chen
Yaofo Chen
Yueting Chen
Yu Chen
Yunjin Chen
Yuntao Chen
Yun Chen
Zhenfang Chen
Zhuangzhuang Chen
Chu-Song Chen
Xiangyu Chen
Zhuo Chen
Chaoqi Chen
Shizhe Chen

Xiaotong Chen

Xiaozhi Chen

Dian Chen

Defang Chen

Dingfan Chen

Ding-Jie Chen

Ee Heng Chen

Tao Chen

Yixin Chen

Wei-Ting Chen

Lin Chen

Guang Chen

Guangyi Chen

Guanying Chen

Guangyao Chen

Hwann-Tzong Chen

Junwen Chen

Jiacheng Chen

Jianxu Chen

Hui Chen

Kai Chen

Kan Chen

Kevin Chen

Kuan-Wen Chen

Weihua Chen

Zhang Chen

Liang-Chieh Chen

Lele Chen

Liang Chen

Fanglin Chen

Zehui Chen

Minghui Chen

Minghao Chen

Xiaokang Chen

Qian Chen

Jun-Cheng Chen

Qi Chen

Qingcai Chen

Richard J. Chen

Runnan Chen

Rui Chen

Shuo Chen

Sentao Chen

Shaoyu Chen

Shixing Chen

Shuai Chen

Shuya Chen

Sizhe Chen

Simin Chen

Shaoxiang Chen

Zitian Chen

Tianlong Chen

Tianshui Chen

Min-Hung Chen

Xiangning Chen

Xin Chen

Xinghao Chen

Xuejin Chen

Xu Chen

Xuxi Chen

Yunlu Chen

Yanbei Chen

Yuxiao Chen

Yun-Chun Chen

Yi-Ting Chen

Yi-Wen Chen

Yinbo Chen

Yiran Chen

Yuanhong Chen

Yubei Chen

Yuefeng Chen

Yuhua Chen

Yukang Chen

Zerui Chen

Zhaoyu Chen

Zhen Chen

Zhenyu Chen

Zhi Chen

Zhiwei Chen

Zhixiang Chen

Long Chen

Bowen Cheng

Jun Cheng

Yi Cheng

Jingchun Cheng

Lechao Cheng

Xi Cheng

Yuan Cheng

Ho Kei Cheng

Kevin Ho Man Cheng

Jiacheng Cheng

Kelvin B. Cheng

Li Cheng

Mengjun Cheng

Zhen Cheng

Qingrong Cheng

Tianheng Cheng

Harry Cheng

Yihua Cheng

Yu Cheng

Ziheng Cheng

Soon Yau Cheong

Anoop Cherian

Manuela Chessa

Zhixiang Chi

Naoki Chiba

Julian Chibane

Kashyap Chitta

Tai-Yin Chiu

Hsu-kuang Chiu

Wei-Chen Chiu

Sungmin Cho

Donghyeon Cho

Hyeon Cho

Yooshin Cho

Gyusang Cho

Jang Hyun Cho

Seungju Cho

Nam Ik Cho

Sunghyun Cho

Hanbyel Cho

Jaesung Choe

Jooyoung Choi

Chiho Choi

Changwoon Choi

Jongwon Choi

Myungsub Choi

Dooseop Choi

Jonghyun Choi

Jinwoo Choi

Jun Won Choi

Min-Kook Choi

Hongsuk Choi

Janghoon Choi

Yoon-Ho Choi

Yukyung Choi
Jaegul Choo
Ayush Chopra
Siddharth Choudhary
Subhabrata Choudhury
Vasileios Choutas
Ka-Ho Chow
Pinaki Nath Chowdhury
Sammy Christen
Anders Christensen
Grigorios Chrysos
Hang Chu
Wen-Hsuan Chu
Peng Chu
Qi Chu
Ruihang Chu
Wei-Ta Chu
Yung-Yu Chuang
Sanghyuk Chun
Se Young Chun
Antonio Cinà
Ramazan Gokberk Cinbis
Javier Civera
Albert Clapés
Ronald Clark
Brian S. Clipp
Felipe Codevilla
Daniel Coelho de Castro
Niv Cohen
Forrester Cole
Maxwell D. Collins
Robert T. Collins
Marc Comino Trinidad
Runmin Cong
Wenyan Cong
Maxime Cordy
Marcella Cornia
Enric Corona
Huseyin Coskun
Luca Cosmo
Dragos Costea
Davide Cozzolino
Arun C. S. Kumar
Aiyu Cui
Qiongjie Cui

Quan Cui
Shuhao Cui
Yiming Cui
Ying Cui
Zijun Cui
Jiali Cui
Jiequan Cui
Yawen Cui
Zhen Cui
Zhaopeng Cui
Jack Culpepper
Xiaodong Cun
Ross Cutler
Adam Czajka
Ali Dabouei
Konstantinos M. Dafnis
Manuel Dahnert
Tao Dai
Yuchao Dai
Bo Dai
Mengyu Dai
Hang Dai
Haixing Dai
Peng Dai
Pingyang Dai
Qi Dai
Qiyu Dai
Yutong Dai
Naser Damer
Zhiyuan Dang
Mohamed Daoudi
Ayan Das
Abir Das
Debasmit Das
Deepayan Das
Partha Das
Sagnik Das
Soumi Das
Srijan Das
Swagatam Das
Avijit Dasgupta
Jim Davis
Adrian K. Davison
Homa Davoudi
Laura Daza

Matthias De Lange
Shalini De Mello
Marco De Nadai
Christophe De
    Vleeschouwer
Alp Dener
Boyang Deng
Congyue Deng
Bailin Deng
Yong Deng
Ye Deng
Zhuo Deng
Zhijie Deng
Xiaoming Deng
Jiankang Deng
Jinhong Deng
Jingjing Deng
Liang-Jian Deng
Siqi Deng
Xiang Deng
Xueqing Deng
Zhongying Deng
Karan Desai
Jean-Emmanuel Deschaud
Aniket Anand Deshmukh
Neel Dey
Helisa Dhamo
Prithviraj Dhar
Amaya Dharmasiri
Yan Di
Xing Di
Ousmane A. Dia
Haiwen Diao
Xiaolei Diao
Gonçalo José Dias Pais
Abdallah Dib
Anastasios Dimou
Changxing Ding
Henghui Ding
Guodong Ding
Yaqing Ding
Shuangrui Ding
Yuhang Ding
Yikang Ding
Shouhong Ding

Haisong Ding
Hui Ding
Jiahao Ding
Jian Ding
Jian-Jiun Ding
Shuxiao Ding
Tianyu Ding
Wenhao Ding
Yuqi Ding
Yi Ding
Yuzhen Ding
Zhengming Ding
Tan Minh Dinh
Vu Dinh
Christos Diou
Mandar Dixit
Bao Gia Doan
Khoa D. Doan
Dzung Anh Doan
Debi Prosad Dogra
Nehal Doiphode
Chengdong Dong
Bowen Dong
Zhenxing Dong
Hang Dong
Xiaoyi Dong
Haoye Dong
Jiangxin Dong
Shichao Dong
Xuan Dong
Zhen Dong
Shuting Dong
Jing Dong
Li Dong
Ming Dong
Nanqing Dong
Qiulei Dong
Runpei Dong
Siyan Dong
Tian Dong
Wei Dong
Xiaomeng Dong
Xin Dong
Xingbo Dong
Yuan Dong

Samuel Dooley
Gianfranco Doretto
Michael Dorkenwald
Keval Doshi
Zhaopeng Dou
Xiaotian Dou
Hazel Doughty
Ahmad Droby
Iddo Drori
Jie Du
Yong Du
Dawei Du
Dong Du
Ruoyi Du
Yuntao Du
Xuefeng Du
Yilun Du
Yuming Du
Radhika Dua
Haodong Duan
Jiafei Duan
Kaiwen Duan
Peiqi Duan
Ye Duan
Haoran Duan
Jiali Duan
Amanda Duarte
Abhimanyu Dubey
Shiv Ram Dubey
Florian Dubost
Lukasz Dudziak
Shivam Duggal
Justin M. Dulay
Matteo Dunnhofer
Chi Nhan Duong
Thibaut Durand
Mihai Dusmanu
Ujjal Kr Dutta
Debidatta Dwibedi
Isht Dwivedi
Sai Kumar Dwivedi
Takeharu Eda
Mark Edmonds
Alexei A. Efros
Thibaud Ehret

Max Ehrlich
Mahsa Ehsanpour
Iván Eichhardt
Farshad Einabadi
Marvin Eisenberger
Hazim Kemal Ekenel
Mohamed El Banani
Ismail Elezi
Moshe Eliasof
Alaa El-Nouby
Ian Endres
Francis Engelmann
Deniz Engin
Chanho Eom
Dave Epstein
Maria C. Escobar
Victor A. Escorcia
Carlos Esteves
Sungmin Eum
Bernard J. E. Evans
Ivan Evtimov
Fevziye Irem Eyiokur
    Yaman
Matteo Fabbri
Sébastien Fabbro
Gabriele Facciolo
Masud Fahim
Bin Fan
Hehe Fan
Deng-Ping Fan
Aoxiang Fan
Chen-Chen Fan
Qi Fan
Zhaoxin Fan
Haoqi Fan
Heng Fan
Hongyi Fan
Linxi Fan
Baojie Fan
Jiayuan Fan
Lei Fan
Quanfu Fan
Yonghui Fan
Yingruo Fan
Zhiwen Fan

Zicong Fan
Sean Fanello
Jiansheng Fang
Chaowei Fang
Yuming Fang
Jianwu Fang
Jin Fang
Qi Fang
Shancheng Fang
Tian Fang
Xianyong Fang
Gongfan Fang
Zhen Fang
Hui Fang
Jiemin Fang
Le Fang
Pengfei Fang
Xiaolin Fang
Yuxin Fang
Zhaoyuan Fang
Ammarah Farooq
Azade Farshad
Zhengcong Fei
Michael Felsberg
Wei Feng
Chen Feng
Fan Feng
Andrew Feng
Xin Feng
Zheyun Feng
Ruicheng Feng
Mingtao Feng
Qianyu Feng
Shangbin Feng
Chun-Mei Feng
Zunlei Feng
Zhiyong Feng
Martin Fergie
Mustansar Fiaz
Marco Fiorucci
Michael Firman
Hamed Firooz
Volker Fischer
Corneliu O. Florea
Georgios Floros

Wolfgang Foerstner
Gianni Franchi
Jean-Sebastien Franco
Simone Frintrop
Anna Fruehstueck
Changhong Fu
Chaoyou Fu
Cheng-Yang Fu
Chi-Wing Fu
Deqing Fu
Huan Fu
Jun Fu
Kexue Fu
Ying Fu
Jianlong Fu
Jingjing Fu
Qichen Fu
Tsu-Jui Fu
Xueyang Fu
Yang Fu
Yanwei Fu
Yonggan Fu
Wolfgang Fuhl
Yasuhisa Fujii
Kent Fujiwara
Marco Fumero
Takuya Funatomi
Isabel Funke
Dario Fuoli
Antonino Furnari
Matheus A. Gadelha
Akshay Gadi Patil
Adrian Galdran
Guillermo Gallego
Silvano Galliani
Orazio Gallo
Leonardo Galteri
Matteo Gamba
Yiming Gan
Sujoy Ganguly
Harald Ganster
Boyan Gao
Changxin Gao
Daiheng Gao
Difei Gao

Chen Gao
Fei Gao
Lin Gao
Wei Gao
Yiming Gao
Junyu Gao
Guangyu Ryan Gao
Haichang Gao
Hongchang Gao
Jialin Gao
Jin Gao
Jun Gao
Katelyn Gao
Mingchen Gao
Mingfei Gao
Pan Gao
Shangqian Gao
Shanghua Gao
Xitong Gao
Yunhe Gao
Zhanning Gao
Elena Garces
Nuno Cruz Garcia
Noa Garcia
Guillermo
    Garcia-Hernando
Isha Garg
Rahul Garg
Sourav Garg
Quentin Garrido
Stefano Gasperini
Kent Gauen
Chandan Gautam
Shivam Gautam
Paul Gay
Chunjiang Ge
Shiming Ge
Wenhang Ge
Yanhao Ge
Zheng Ge
Songwei Ge
Weifeng Ge
Yixiao Ge
Yuying Ge
Shijie Geng

Zhengyang Geng
Kyle A. Genova
Georgios Georgakis
Markos Georgopoulos
Marcel Geppert
Shabnam Ghadar
Mina Ghadimi Atigh
Deepti Ghadiyaram
Maani Ghaffari Jadidi
Sedigh Ghamari
Zahra Gharaee
Michaël Gharbi
Golnaz Ghiasi
Reza Ghoddoosian
Soumya Suvra Ghosal
Adhiraj Ghosh
Arthita Ghosh
Pallabi Ghosh
Soumyadeep Ghosh
Andrew Gilbert
Igor Gilitschenski
Jhony H. Giraldo
Andreu Girbau Xalabarder
Rohit Girdhar
Sharath Girish
Xavier Giro-i-Nieto
Raja Giryes
Thomas Gittings
Nikolaos Gkanatsios
Ioannis Gkioulekas
Abhiram
  Gnanasambandam
Aurele T. Gnanha
Clement L. J. C. Godard
Arushi Goel
Vidit Goel
Shubham Goel
Zan Gojcic
Aaron K. Gokaslan
Tejas Gokhale
S. Alireza Golestaneh
Thiago L. Gomes
Nuno Goncalves
Boqing Gong
Chen Gong

Yuanhao Gong
Guoqiang Gong
Jingyu Gong
Rui Gong
Yu Gong
Mingming Gong
Neil Zhenqiang Gong
Xun Gong
Yunye Gong
Yihong Gong
Cristina I. González
Nithin Gopalakrishnan
  Nair
Gaurav Goswami
Jianping Gou
Shreyank N. Gowda
Ankit Goyal
Helmut Grabner
Patrick L. Grady
Ben Graham
Eric Granger
Douglas R. Gray
Matej Grcić
David Griffiths
Jinjin Gu
Yun Gu
Shuyang Gu
Jianyang Gu
Fuqiang Gu
Jiatao Gu
Jindong Gu
Jiaqi Gu
Jinwei Gu
Jiaxin Gu
Geonmo Gu
Xiao Gu
Xinqian Gu
Xiuye Gu
Yuming Gu
Zhangxuan Gu
Dayan Guan
Junfeng Guan
Qingji Guan
Tianrui Guan
Shanyan Guan

Denis A. Gudovskiy
Ricardo Guerrero
Pierre-Louis Guhur
Jie Gui
Liangyan Gui
Liangke Gui
Benoit Guillard
Erhan Gundogdu
Manuel Günther
Jingcai Guo
Yuanfang Guo
Junfeng Guo
Chenqi Guo
Dan Guo
Hongji Guo
Jia Guo
Jie Guo
Minghao Guo
Shi Guo
Yanhui Guo
Yangyang Guo
Yuan-Chen Guo
Yilu Guo
Yiluan Guo
Yong Guo
Guangyu Guo
Haiyun Guo
Jinyang Guo
Jianyuan Guo
Pengsheng Guo
Pengfei Guo
Shuxuan Guo
Song Guo
Tianyu Guo
Qing Guo
Qiushan Guo
Wen Guo
Xiefan Guo
Xiaohu Guo
Xiaoqing Guo
Yufei Guo
Yuhui Guo
Yuliang Guo
Yunhui Guo
Yanwen Guo

Akshita Gupta
Ankush Gupta
Kamal Gupta
Kartik Gupta
Ritwik Gupta
Rohit Gupta
Siddharth Gururani
Fredrik K. Gustafsson
Abner Guzman Rivera
Vladimir Guzov
Matthew A. Gwilliam
Jung-Woo Ha
Marc Habermann
Isma Hadji
Christian Haene
Martin Hahner
Levente Hajder
Alexandros Haliassos
Emanuela Haller
Bumsub Ham
Abdullah J. Hamdi
Shreyas Hampali
Dongyoon Han
Chunrui Han
Dong-Jun Han
Dong-Sig Han
Guangxing Han
Zhizhong Han
Ruize Han
Jiaming Han
Jin Han
Ligong Han
Xian-Hua Han
Xiaoguang Han
Yizeng Han
Zhi Han
Zhenjun Han
Zhongyi Han
Jungong Han
Junlin Han
Kai Han
Kun Han
Sungwon Han
Songfang Han
Wei Han

Xiao Han
Xintong Han
Xinzhe Han
Yahong Han
Yan Han
Zongbo Han
Nicolai Hani
Rana Hanocka
Niklas Hanselmann
Nicklas A. Hansen
Hong Hanyu
Fusheng Hao
Yanbin Hao
Shijie Hao
Udith Haputhanthri
Mehrtash Harandi
Josh Harguess
Adam Harley
David M. Hart
Atsushi Hashimoto
Ali Hassani
Mohammed Hassanin
Yana Hasson
Joakim Bruslund Haurum
Bo He
Kun He
Chen He
Xin He
Fazhi He
Gaoqi He
Hao He
Haoyu He
Jiangpeng He
Hongliang He
Qian He
Xiangteng He
Xuming He
Yannan He
Yuhang He
Yang He
Xiangyu He
Nanjun He
Pan He
Sen He
Shengfeng He

Songtao He
Tao He
Tong He
Wei He
Xuehai He
Xiaoxiao He
Ying He
Yisheng He
Ziwen He
Peter Hedman
Felix Heide
Yacov Hel-Or
Paul Henderson
Philipp Henzler
Byeongho Heo
Jae-Pil Heo
Miran Heo
Sachini A. Herath
Stephane Herbin
Pedro Hermosilla Casajus
Monica Hernandez
Charles Herrmann
Roei Herzig
Mauricio Hess-Flores
Carlos Hinojosa
Tobias Hinz
Tsubasa Hirakawa
Chih-Hui Ho
Lam Si Tung Ho
Jennifer Hobbs
Derek Hoiem
Yannick Hold-Geoffroy
Aleksander Holynski
Cheeun Hong
Fa-Ting Hong
Hanbin Hong
Guan Zhe Hong
Danfeng Hong
Lanqing Hong
Xiaopeng Hong
Xin Hong
Jie Hong
Seungbum Hong
Cheng-Yao Hong
Seunghoon Hong

Yi Hong
Yuan Hong
Yuchen Hong
Anthony Hoogs
Maxwell C. Horton
Kazuhiro Hotta
Qibin Hou
Tingbo Hou
Junhui Hou
Ji Hou
Qiqi Hou
Rui Hou
Ruibing Hou
Zhi Hou
Henry Howard-Jenkins
Lukas Hoyer
Wei-Lin Hsiao
Chiou-Ting Hsu
Anthony Hu
Brian Hu
Yusong Hu
Hexiang Hu
Haoji Hu
Di Hu
Hengtong Hu
Haigen Hu
Lianyu Hu
Hanzhe Hu
Jie Hu
Junlin Hu
Shizhe Hu
Jian Hu
Zhiming Hu
Juhua Hu
Peng Hu
Ping Hu
Ronghang Hu
MengShun Hu
Tao Hu
Vincent Tao Hu
Xiaoling Hu
Xinting Hu
Xiaolin Hu
Xuefeng Hu
Xiaowei Hu

Yang Hu
Yueyu Hu
Zeyu Hu
Zhongyun Hu
Binh-Son Hua
Guoliang Hua
Yi Hua
Linzhi Huang
Qiusheng Huang
Bo Huang
Chen Huang
Hsin-Ping Huang
Ye Huang
Shuangping Huang
Zeng Huang
Buzhen Huang
Cong Huang
Heng Huang
Hao Huang
Qidong Huang
Huaibo Huang
Chaoqin Huang
Feihu Huang
Jiahui Huang
Jingjia Huang
Kun Huang
Lei Huang
Sheng Huang
Shuaiyi Huang
Siyu Huang
Xiaoshui Huang
Xiaoyang Huang
Yan Huang
Yihao Huang
Ying Huang
Ziling Huang
Xiaoke Huang
Yifei Huang
Haiyang Huang
Zhewei Huang
Jin Huang
Haibin Huang
Jiaxing Huang
Junjie Huang
Keli Huang

Lang Huang
Lin Huang
Luojie Huang
Mingzhen Huang
Shijia Huang
Shengyu Huang
Siyuan Huang
He Huang
Xiuyu Huang
Lianghua Huang
Yue Huang
Yaping Huang
Yuge Huang
Zehao Huang
Zeyi Huang
Zhiqi Huang
Zhongzhan Huang
Zilong Huang
Ziyuan Huang
Tianrui Hui
Zhuo Hui
Le Hui
Jing Huo
Junhwa Hur
Shehzeen S. Hussain
Chuong Minh Huynh
Seunghyun Hwang
Jaehui Hwang
Jyh-Jing Hwang
Sukjun Hwang
Soonmin Hwang
Wonjun Hwang
Rakib Hyder
Sangeek Hyun
Sarah Ibrahimi
Tomoki Ichikawa
Yerlan Idelbayev
A. S. M. Iftekhar
Masaaki Iiyama
Satoshi Ikehata
Sunghoon Im
Atul N. Ingle
Eldar Insafutdinov
Yani A. Ioannou
Radu Tudor Ionescu

Umar Iqbal
Go Irie
Muhammad Zubair Irshad
Ahmet Iscen
Berivan Isik
Ashraful Islam
Md Amirul Islam
Syed Islam
Mariko Isogawa
Vamsi Krishna K. Ithapu
Boris Ivanovic
Darshan Iyer
Sarah Jabbour
Ayush Jain
Nishant Jain
Samyak Jain
Vidit Jain
Vineet Jain
Priyank Jaini
Tomas Jakab
Mohammad A. A. K. Jalwana
Muhammad Abdullah Jamal
Hadi Jamali-Rad
Stuart James
Varun Jampani
Young Kyun Jang
YeongJun Jang
Yunseok Jang
Ronnachai Jaroensri
Bhavan Jasani
Krishna Murthy Jatavallabhula
Mojan Javaheripi
Syed A. Javed
Guillaume Jeanneret
Pranav Jeevan
Herve Jegou
Rohit Jena
Tomas Jenicek
Porter Jenkins
Simon Jenni
Hae-Gon Jeon
Sangryul Jeon

Boseung Jeong
Yoonwoo Jeong
Seong-Gyun Jeong
Jisoo Jeong
Allan D. Jepson
Ankit Jha
Sumit K. Jha
I-Hong Jhuo
Ge-Peng Ji
Chaonan Ji
Deyi Ji
Jingwei Ji
Wei Ji
Zhong Ji
Jiayi Ji
Pengliang Ji
Hui Ji
Mingi Ji
Xiaopeng Ji
Yuzhu Ji
Baoxiong Jia
Songhao Jia
Dan Jia
Shan Jia
Xiaojun Jia
Xiuyi Jia
Xu Jia
Menglin Jia
Wenqi Jia
Boyuan Jiang
Wenhao Jiang
Huaizu Jiang
Hanwen Jiang
Haiyong Jiang
Hao Jiang
Huajie Jiang
Huiqin Jiang
Haojun Jiang
Haobo Jiang
Junjun Jiang
Xingyu Jiang
Yangbangyan Jiang
Yu Jiang
Jianmin Jiang
Jiaxi Jiang

Jing Jiang
Kui Jiang
Li Jiang
Liming Jiang
Chiyu Jiang
Meirui Jiang
Chen Jiang
Peng Jiang
Tai-Xiang Jiang
Wen Jiang
Xinyang Jiang
Yifan Jiang
Yuming Jiang
Yingying Jiang
Zeren Jiang
ZhengKai Jiang
Zhenyu Jiang
Shuming Jiao
Jianbo Jiao
Licheng Jiao
Dongkwon Jin
Yeying Jin
Cheng Jin
Linyi Jin
Qing Jin
Taisong Jin
Xiao Jin
Xin Jin
Sheng Jin
Kyong Hwan Jin
Ruibing Jin
SouYoung Jin
Yueming Jin
Chenchen Jing
Longlong Jing
Taotao Jing
Yongcheng Jing
Younghyun Jo
Joakim Johnander
Jeff Johnson
Michael J. Jones
R. Kenny Jones
Rico Jonschkowski
Ameya Joshi
Sunghun Joung

Felix Juefei-Xu
Claudio R. Jung
Steffen Jung
Hari Chandana K.
Rahul Vigneswaran K.
Prajwal K. R.
Abhishek Kadian
Jhony Kaesemodel Pontes
Kumara Kahatapitiya
Anmol Kalia
Sinan Kalkan
Tarun Kalluri
Jaewon Kam
Sandesh Kamath
Meina Kan
Menelaos Kanakis
Takuhiro Kaneko
Di Kang
Guoliang Kang
Hao Kang
Jaeyeon Kang
Kyoungkook Kang
Li-Wei Kang
MinGuk Kang
Suk-Ju Kang
Zhao Kang
Yash Mukund Kant
Yueying Kao
Aupendu Kar
Konstantinos Karantzalos
Sezer Karaoglu
Navid Kardan
Sanjay Kariyappa
Leonid Karlinsky
Animesh Karnewar
Shyamgopal Karthik
Hirak J. Kashyap
Marc A. Kastner
Hirokatsu Kataoka
Angelos Katharopoulos
Hiroharu Kato
Kai Katsumata
Manuel Kaufmann
Chaitanya Kaul
Prakhar Kaushik

Yuki Kawana
Lei Ke
Lipeng Ke
Tsung-Wei Ke
Wei Ke
Petr Kellnhofer
Aniruddha Kembhavi
John Kender
Corentin Kervadec
Leonid Keselman
Daniel Keysers
Nima Khademi Kalantari
Taras Khakhulin
Samir Khaki
Muhammad Haris Khan
Qadeer Khan
Salman Khan
Subash Khanal
Vaishnavi M. Khindkar
Rawal Khirodkar
Saeed Khorram
Pirazh Khorramshahi
Kourosh Khoshelham
Ansh Khurana
Benjamin Kiefer
Jae Myung Kim
Junho Kim
Boah Kim
Hyeonseong Kim
Dong-Jin Kim
Dongwan Kim
Donghyun Kim
Doyeon Kim
Yonghyun Kim
Hyung-Il Kim
Hyunwoo Kim
Hyeongwoo Kim
Hyo Jin Kim
Hyunwoo J. Kim
Taehoon Kim
Jaeha Kim
Jiwon Kim
Jung Uk Kim
Kangyeol Kim
Eunji Kim

Daeha Kim
Dongwon Kim
Kunhee Kim
Kyungmin Kim
Junsik Kim
Min H. Kim
Namil Kim
Kookhoi Kim
Sanghyun Kim
Seongyeop Kim
Seungryong Kim
Saehoon Kim
Euyoung Kim
Guisik Kim
Sungyeon Kim
Sunnie S. Y. Kim
Taehun Kim
Tae Oh Kim
Won Hwa Kim
Seungwook Kim
YoungBin Kim
Youngeun Kim
Akisato Kimura
Furkan Osman Kınlı
Zsolt Kira
Hedvig Kjellström
Florian Kleber
Jan P. Klopp
Florian Kluger
Laurent Kneip
Byungsoo Ko
Muhammed Kocabas
A. Sophia Koepke
Kevin Koeser
Nick Kolkin
Nikos Kolotouros
Wai-Kin Adams Kong
Deying Kong
Caihua Kong
Youyong Kong
Shuyu Kong
Shu Kong
Tao Kong
Yajing Kong
Yu Kong

Jan E. Lenssen
Vincent Lepetit
Thomas Leung
María Leyva-Vallina
Xin Li
Yikang Li
Baoxin Li
Bin Li
Bing Li
Bowen Li
Changlin Li
Chao Li
Chongyi Li
Guanyue Li
Shuai Li
Jin Li
Dingquan Li
Dongxu Li
Yiting Li
Gang Li
Dian Li
Guohao Li
Haoang Li
Haoliang Li
Haoran Li
Hengduo Li
Huafeng Li
Xiaoming Li
Hanao Li
Hongwei Li
Ziqiang Li
Jisheng Li
Jiacheng Li
Jia Li
Jiachen Li
Jiahao Li
Jianwei Li
Jiazhi Li
Jie Li
Jing Li
Jingjing Li
Jingtao Li
Jun Li
Junxuan Li
Kai Li

Kailin Li
Kenneth Li
Kun Li
Kunpeng Li
Aoxue Li
Chenglong Li
Chenglin Li
Changsheng Li
Zhichao Li
Qiang Li
Yanyu Li
Zuoyue Li
Xiang Li
Xuelong Li
Fangda Li
Ailin Li
Liang Li
Chun-Guang Li
Daiqing Li
Dong Li
Guanbin Li
Guorong Li
Haifeng Li
Jianan Li
Jianing Li
Jiaxin Li
Ke Li
Lei Li
Lincheng Li
Liulei Li
Lujun Li
Linjie Li
Lin Li
Pengyu Li
Ping Li
Qiufu Li
Qingyong Li
Rui Li
Siyuan Li
Wei Li
Wenbin Li
Xiangyang Li
Xinyu Li
Xiujun Li
Xiu Li

Xu Li
Ya-Li Li
Yao Li
Yongjie Li
Yijun Li
Yiming Li
Yuezun Li
Yu Li
Yunheng Li
Yuqi Li
Zhe Li
Zeming Li
Zhen Li
Zhengqin Li
Zhimin Li
Jiefeng Li
Jinpeng Li
Chengze Li
Jianwu Li
Lerenhan Li
Shan Li
Suichan Li
Xiangtai Li
Yanjie Li
Yandong Li
Zhuoling Li
Zhenqiang Li
Manyi Li
Maosen Li
Ji Li
Minjun Li
Mingrui Li
Mengtian Li
Junyi Li
Nianyi Li
Bo Li
Xiao Li
Peihua Li
Peike Li
Peizhao Li
Peiliang Li
Qi Li
Ren Li
Runze Li
Shile Li

Sheng Li
Shigang Li
Shiyu Li
Shuang Li
Shasha Li
Shichao Li
Tianye Li
Yuexiang Li
Wei-Hong Li
Wanhua Li
Weihao Li
Weiming Li
Weixin Li
Wenbo Li
Wenshuo Li
Weijian Li
Yunan Li
Xirong Li
Xianhang Li
Xiaoyu Li
Xueqian Li
Xuanlin Li
Xianzhi Li
Yunqiang Li
Yanjing Li
Yansheng Li
Yawei Li
Yi Li
Yong Li
Yong-Lu Li
Yuhang Li
Yu-Jhe Li
Yuxi Li
Yunsheng Li
Yanwei Li
Zechao Li
Zejian Li
Zeju Li
Zekun Li
Zhaowen Li
Zheng Li
Zhenyu Li
Zhiheng Li
Zhi Li
Zhong Li

Zhuowei Li
Zhuowan Li
Zhuohang Li
Zizhang Li
Chen Li
Yuan-Fang Li
Dongze Lian
Xiaochen Lian
Zhouhui Lian
Long Lian
Qing Lian
Jin Lianbao
Jinxiu S. Liang
Dingkang Liang
Jiahao Liang
Jianming Liang
Jingyun Liang
Kevin J. Liang
Kaizhao Liang
Chen Liang
Jie Liang
Senwei Liang
Ding Liang
Jiajun Liang
Jian Liang
Kongming Liang
Siyuan Liang
Yuanzhi Liang
Zhengfa Liang
Mingfu Liang
Xiaodan Liang
Xuefeng Liang
Yuxuan Liang
Kang Liao
Liang Liao
Hong-Yuan Mark Liao
Wentong Liao
Haofu Liao
Yue Liao
Minghui Liao
Shengcai Liao
Ting-Hsuan Liao
Xin Liao
Yinghong Liao
Teck Yian Lim

Che-Tsung Lin
Chung-Ching Lin
Chen-Hsuan Lin
Cheng Lin
Chuming Lin
Chunyu Lin
Dahua Lin
Wei Lin
Zheng Lin
Huaijia Lin
Jason Lin
Jierui Lin
Jiaying Lin
Jie Lin
Kai-En Lin
Kevin Lin
Guangfeng Lin
Jiehong Lin
Feng Lin
Hang Lin
Kwan-Yee Lin
Ke Lin
Luojun Lin
Qinghong Lin
Xiangbo Lin
Yi Lin
Zudi Lin
Shijie Lin
Yiqun Lin
Tzu-Heng Lin
Ming Lin
Shaohui Lin
SongNan Lin
Ji Lin
Tsung-Yu Lin
Xudong Lin
Yancong Lin
Yen-Chen Lin
Yiming Lin
Yuewei Lin
Zhiqiu Lin
Zinan Lin
Zhe Lin
David B. Lindell
Zhixin Ling

Zhan Ling
Alexander Liniger
Venice Erin B. Liong
Joey Litalien
Or Litany
Roee Litman
Ron Litman
Jim Little
Dor Litvak
Shaoteng Liu
Shuaicheng Liu
Andrew Liu
Xian Liu
Shaohui Liu
Bei Liu
Bo Liu
Yong Liu
Ming Liu
Yanbin Liu
Chenxi Liu
Daqi Liu
Di Liu
Difan Liu
Dong Liu
Dongfang Liu
Daizong Liu
Xiao Liu
Fangyi Liu
Fengbei Liu
Fenglin Liu
Bin Liu
Yuang Liu
Ao Liu
Hong Liu
Hongfu Liu
Huidong Liu
Ziyi Liu
Feng Liu
Hao Liu
Jie Liu
Jialun Liu
Jiang Liu
Jing Liu
Jingya Liu
Jiaming Liu

Jun Liu
Juncheng Liu
Jiawei Liu
Hongyu Liu
Chuanbin Liu
Haotian Liu
Lingqiao Liu
Chang Liu
Han Liu
Liu Liu
Min Liu
Yingqi Liu
Aishan Liu
Bingyu Liu
Benlin Liu
Boxiao Liu
Chenchen Liu
Chuanjian Liu
Daqing Liu
Huan Liu
Haozhe Liu
Jiaheng Liu
Wei Liu
Jingzhou Liu
Jiyuan Liu
Lingbo Liu
Nian Liu
Peiye Liu
Qiankun Liu
Shenglan Liu
Shilong Liu
Wen Liu
Wenyu Liu
Weifeng Liu
Wu Liu
Xiaolong Liu
Yang Liu
Yanwei Liu
Yingcheng Liu
Yongfei Liu
Yihao Liu
Yu Liu
Yunze Liu
Ze Liu
Zhenhua Liu

Zhenguang Liu
Lin Liu
Lihao Liu
Pengju Liu
Xinhai Liu
Yunfei Liu
Meng Liu
Minghua Liu
Mingyuan Liu
Miao Liu
Peirong Liu
Ping Liu
Qingjie Liu
Ruoshi Liu
Risheng Liu
Songtao Liu
Xing Liu
Shikun Liu
Shuming Liu
Sheng Liu
Songhua Liu
Tongliang Liu
Weibo Liu
Weide Liu
Weizhe Liu
Wenxi Liu
Weiyang Liu
Xin Liu
Xiaobin Liu
Xudong Liu
Xiaoyi Liu
Xihui Liu
Xinchen Liu
Xingtong Liu
Xinpeng Liu
Xinyu Liu
Xianpeng Liu
Xu Liu
Xingyu Liu
Yongtuo Liu
Yahui Liu
Yangxin Liu
Yaoyao Liu
Yaojie Liu
Yuliang Liu

Yongcheng Liu
Yuan Liu
Yufan Liu
Yu-Lun Liu
Yun Liu
Yunfan Liu
Yuanzhong Liu
Zhuoran Liu
Zhen Liu
Zheng Liu
Zhijian Liu
Zhisong Liu
Ziquan Liu
Ziyu Liu
Zhihua Liu
Zechun Liu
Zhaoyang Liu
Zhengzhe Liu
Stephan Liwicki
Shao-Yuan Lo
Sylvain Lobry
Suhas Lohit
Vishnu Suresh Lokhande
Vincenzo Lomonaco
Chengjiang Long
Guodong Long
Fuchen Long
Shangbang Long
Yang Long
Zijun Long
Vasco Lopes
Antonio M. Lopez
Roberto Javier
    Lopez-Sastre
Tobias Lorenz
Javier Lorenzo-Navarro
Yujing Lou
Qian Lou
Xiankai Lu
Changsheng Lu
Huimin Lu
Yongxi Lu
Hao Lu
Hong Lu
Jiasen Lu

Juwei Lu
Fan Lu
Guangming Lu
Jiwen Lu
Shun Lu
Tao Lu
Xiaonan Lu
Yang Lu
Yao Lu
Yongchun Lu
Zhiwu Lu
Cheng Lu
Liying Lu
Guo Lu
Xuequan Lu
Yanye Lu
Yantao Lu
Yuhang Lu
Fujun Luan
Jonathon Luiten
Jovita Lukasik
Alan Lukezic
Jonathan Samuel Lumentut
Mayank Lunayach
Ao Luo
Canjie Luo
Chong Luo
Xu Luo
Grace Luo
Jun Luo
Katie Z. Luo
Tao Luo
Cheng Luo
Fangzhou Luo
Gen Luo
Lei Luo
Sihui Luo
Weixin Luo
Yan Luo
Xiaoyan Luo
Yong Luo
Yadan Luo
Hao Luo
Ruotian Luo
Mi Luo

Tiange Luo
Wenjie Luo
Wenhan Luo
Xiao Luo
Zhiming Luo
Zhipeng Luo
Zhengyi Luo
Diogo C. Luvizon
Zhaoyang Lv
Gengyu Lyu
Lingjuan Lyu
Jun Lyu
Yuanyuan Lyu
Youwei Lyu
Yueming Lyu
Bingpeng Ma
Chao Ma
Chongyang Ma
Congbo Ma
Chih-Yao Ma
Fan Ma
Lin Ma
Haoyu Ma
Hengbo Ma
Jianqi Ma
Jiawei Ma
Jiayi Ma
Kede Ma
Kai Ma
Lingni Ma
Lei Ma
Xu Ma
Ning Ma
Benteng Ma
Cheng Ma
Andy J. Ma
Long Ma
Zhanyu Ma
Zhiheng Ma
Qianli Ma
Shiqiang Ma
Sizhuo Ma
Shiqing Ma
Xiaolong Ma
Xinzhu Ma

Gautam B. Machiraju
Spandan Madan
Mathew Magimai-Doss
Luca Magri
Behrooz Mahasseni
Upal Mahbub
Siddharth Mahendran
Paridhi Maheshwari
Rishabh Maheshwary
Mohammed Mahmoud
Shishira R. R. Maiya
Sylwia Majchrowska
Arjun Majumdar
Puspita Majumdar
Orchid Majumder
Sagnik Majumder
Ilya Makarov
Farkhod F.
    Makhmudkhujaev
Yasushi Makihara
Ankur Mali
Mateusz Malinowski
Utkarsh Mall
Srikanth Malla
Clement Mallet
Dimitrios Mallis
Yunze Man
Dipu Manandhar
Massimiliano Mancini
Murari Mandal
Raunak Manekar
Karttikeya Mangalam
Puneet Mangla
Fabian Manhardt
Sivabalan Manivasagam
Fahim Mannan
Chengzhi Mao
Hanzi Mao
Jiayuan Mao
Junhua Mao
Zhiyuan Mao
Jiageng Mao
Yunyao Mao
Zhendong Mao
Alberto Marchisio

Diego Marcos
Riccardo Marin
Aram Markosyan
Renaud Marlet
Ricardo Marques
Miquel Martí i Rabadán
Diego Martin Arroyo
Niki Martinel
Brais Martinez
Julieta Martinez
Marc Masana
Tomohiro Mashita
Timothée Masquelier
Minesh Mathew
Tetsu Matsukawa
Marwan Mattar
Bruce A. Maxwell
Christoph Mayer
Mantas Mazeika
Pratik Mazumder
Scott McCloskey
Steven McDonagh
Ishit Mehta
Jie Mei
Kangfu Mei
Jieru Mei
Xiaoguang Mei
Givi Meishvili
Luke Melas-Kyriazi
Iaroslav Melekhov
Andres Mendez-Vazquez
Heydi Mendez-Vazquez
Matias Mendieta
Ricardo A. Mendoza-León
Chenlin Meng
Depu Meng
Rang Meng
Zibo Meng
Qingjie Meng
Qier Meng
Yanda Meng
Zihang Meng
Thomas Mensink
Fabian Mentzer
Christopher Metzler

Gregory P. Meyer
Vasileios Mezaris
Liang Mi
Lu Mi
Bo Miao
Changtao Miao
Zichen Miao
Qiguang Miao
Xin Miao
Zhongqi Miao
Frank Michel
Simone Milani
Ben Mildenhall
Roy V. Miles
Juhong Min
Kyle Min
Hyun-Seok Min
Weiqing Min
Yuecong Min
Zhixiang Min
Qi Ming
David Minnen
Aymen Mir
Deepak Mishra
Anand Mishra
Shlok K. Mishra
Niluthpol Mithun
Gaurav Mittal
Trisha Mittal
Daisuke Miyazaki
Kaichun Mo
Hong Mo
Zhipeng Mo
Davide Modolo
Abduallah A. Mohamed
Mohamed Afham
    Mohamed Aflal
Ron Mokady
Pavlo Molchanov
Davide Moltisanti
Liliane Momeni
Gianluca Monaci
Pascal Monasse
Ajoy Mondal
Tom Monnier

Aron Monszpart
Gyeongsik Moon
Suhong Moon
Taesup Moon
Sean Moran
Daniel Moreira
Pietro Morerio
Alexandre Morgand
Lia Morra
Ali Mosleh
Inbar Mosseri
Sayed Mohammad
    Mostafavi Isfahani
Saman Motamed
Ramy A. Mounir
Fangzhou Mu
Jiteng Mu
Norman Mu
Yasuhiro Mukaigawa
Ryan Mukherjee
Tanmoy Mukherjee
Yusuke Mukuta
Ravi Teja Mullapudi
Lea Müller
Matthias Müller
Martin Mundt
Nils Murrugarra-Llerena
Damien Muselet
Armin Mustafa
Muhammad Ferjad Naeem
Sauradip Nag
Hajime Nagahara
Pravin Nagar
Rajendra Nagar
Naveen Shankar Nagaraja
Varun Nagaraja
Tushar Nagarajan
Seungjun Nah
Gaku Nakano
Yuta Nakashima
Giljoo Nam
Seonghyeon Nam
Liangliang Nan
Yuesong Nan
Yeshwanth Napolean

Dinesh Reddy
    Narapureddy
Medhini Narasimhan
Supreeth
    Narasimhaswamy
Sriram Narayanan
Erickson R. Nascimento
Varun Nasery
K. L. Navaneet
Pablo Navarrete Michelini
Shant Navasardyan
Shah Nawaz
Nihal Nayak
Farhood Negin
Lukáš Neumann
Alejandro Newell
Evonne Ng
Kam Woh Ng
Tony Ng
Anh Nguyen
Tuan Anh Nguyen
Cuong Cao Nguyen
Ngoc Cuong Nguyen
Thanh Nguyen
Khoi Nguyen
Phi Le Nguyen
Phong Ha Nguyen
Tam Nguyen
Truong Nguyen
Anh Tuan Nguyen
Rang Nguyen
Thao Thi Phuong Nguyen
Van Nguyen Nguyen
Zhen-Liang Ni
Yao Ni
Shijie Nie
Xuecheng Nie
Yongwei Nie
Weizhi Nie
Ying Nie
Yinyu Nie
Kshitij N. Nikhal
Simon Niklaus
Xuefei Ning
Jifeng Ning

Yotam Nitzan
Di Niu
Shuaicheng Niu
Li Niu
Wei Niu
Yulei Niu
Zhenxing Niu
Albert No
Shohei Nobuhara
Nicoletta Noceti
Junhyug Noh
Sotiris Nousias
Slawomir Nowaczyk
Ewa M. Nowara
Valsamis Ntouskos
Gilberto Ochoa-Ruiz
Ferda Ofli
Jihyong Oh
Sangyun Oh
Youngtaek Oh
Hiroki Ohashi
Takahiro Okabe
Kemal Oksuz
Fumio Okura
Daniel Olmeda Reino
Matthew Olson
Carl Olsson
Roy Or-El
Alessandro Ortis
Guillermo Ortiz-Jimenez
Magnus Oskarsson
Ahmed A. A. Osman
Martin R. Oswald
Mayu Otani
Naima Otberdout
Cheng Ouyang
Jiahong Ouyang
Wanli Ouyang
Andrew Owens
Poojan B. Oza
Mete Ozay
A. Cengiz Oztireli
Gautam Pai
Tomas Pajdla
Umapada Pal

Simone Palazzo
Luca Palmieri
Bowen Pan
Hao Pan
Lili Pan
Tai-Yu Pan
Liang Pan
Chengwei Pan
Yingwei Pan
Xuran Pan
Jinshan Pan
Xinyu Pan
Liyuan Pan
Xingang Pan
Xingjia Pan
Zhihong Pan
Zizheng Pan
Priyadarshini Panda
Rameswar Panda
Rohit Pandey
Kaiyue Pang
Bo Pang
Guansong Pang
Jiangmiao Pang
Meng Pang
Tianyu Pang
Ziqi Pang
Omiros Pantazis
Andreas Panteli
Maja Pantic
Marina Paolanti
Joao P. Papa
Samuele Papa
Mike Papadakis
Dim P. Papadopoulos
George Papandreou
Constantin Pape
Toufiq Parag
Chethan Parameshwara
Shaifali Parashar
Alejandro Pardo
Rishubh Parihar
Sarah Parisot
JaeYoo Park
Gyeong-Moon Park

Hyojin Park
Hyoungseob Park
Jongchan Park
Jae Sung Park
Kiru Park
Chunghyun Park
Kwanyong Park
Sunghyun Park
Sungrae Park
Seongsik Park
Sanghyun Park
Sungjune Park
Taesung Park
Gaurav Parmar
Paritosh Parmar
Alvaro Parra
Despoina Paschalidou
Or Patashnik
Shivansh Patel
Pushpak Pati
Prashant W. Patil
Vaishakh Patil
Suvam Patra
Jay Patravali
Badri Narayana Patro
Angshuman Paul
Sudipta Paul
Rémi Pautrat
Nick E. Pears
Adithya Pediredla
Wenjie Pei
Shmuel Peleg
Latha Pemula
Bo Peng
Houwen Peng
Yue Peng
Liangzu Peng
Baoyun Peng
Jun Peng
Pai Peng
Sida Peng
Xi Peng
Yuxin Peng
Songyou Peng
Wei Peng

Weiqi Peng
Wen-Hsiao Peng
Pramuditha Perera
Juan C. Perez
Eduardo Pérez Pellitero
Juan-Manuel Perez-Rua
Federico Pernici
Marco Pesavento
Stavros Petridis
Ilya A. Petrov
Vladan Petrovic
Mathis Petrovich
Suzanne Petryk
Hieu Pham
Quang Pham
Khoi Pham
Tung Pham
Huy Phan
Stephen Phillips
Cheng Perng Phoo
David Picard
Marco Piccirilli
Georg Pichler
A. J. Piergiovanni
Vipin Pillai
Silvia L. Pintea
Giovanni Pintore
Robinson Piramuthu
Fiora Pirri
Theodoros Pissas
Fabio Pizzati
Benjamin Planche
Bryan Plummer
Matteo Poggi
Ashwini Pokle
Georgy E. Ponimatkin
Adrian Popescu
Stefan Popov
Nikola Popović
Ronald Poppe
Angelo Porrello
Michael Potter
Charalambos Poullis
Hadi Pouransari
Omid Poursaeed

Shraman Pramanick
Mantini Pranav
Dilip K. Prasad
Meghshyam Prasad
B. H. Pawan Prasad
Shitala Prasad
Prateek Prasanna
Ekta Prashnani
Derek S. Prijatelj
Luke Y. Prince
Véronique Prinet
Victor Adrian Prisacariu
James Pritts
Thomas Probst
Sergey Prokudin
Rita Pucci
Chi-Man Pun
Matthew Purri
Haozhi Qi
Lu Qi
Lei Qi
Xianbiao Qi
Yonggang Qi
Yuankai Qi
Siyuan Qi
Guocheng Qian
Hangwei Qian
Qi Qian
Deheng Qian
Shengsheng Qian
Wen Qian
Rui Qian
Yiming Qian
Shengju Qian
Shengyi Qian
Xuelin Qian
Zhenxing Qian
Nan Qiao
Xiaotian Qiao
Jing Qin
Can Qin
Siyang Qin
Hongwei Qin
Jie Qin
Minghai Qin

Yipeng Qin
Yongqiang Qin
Wenda Qin
Xuebin Qin
Yuzhe Qin
Yao Qin
Zhenyue Qin
Zhiwu Qing
Heqian Qiu
Jiayan Qiu
Jielin Qiu
Yue Qiu
Jiaxiong Qiu
Zhongxi Qiu
Shi Qiu
Zhaofan Qiu
Zhongnan Qu
Yanyun Qu
Kha Gia Quach
Yuhui Quan
Ruijie Quan
Mike Rabbat
Rahul Shekhar Rade
Filip Radenovic
Gorjan Radevski
Bogdan Raducanu
Francesco Ragusa
Shafin Rahman
Md Mahfuzur Rahman
    Siddiquee
Hossein Rahmani
Kiran Raja
Sivaramakrishnan
    Rajaraman
Jathushan Rajasegaran
Adnan Siraj Rakin
Michaël Ramamonjisoa
Chirag A. Raman
Shanmuganathan Raman
Vignesh Ramanathan
Vasili Ramanishka
Vikram V. Ramaswamy
Merey Ramazanova
Jason Rambach
Sai Saketh Rambhatla

Clément Rambour
Ashwin Ramesh Babu
Adín Ramírez Rivera
Arianna Rampini
Haoxi Ran
Aakanksha Rana
Aayush Jung Bahadur
    Rana
Kanchana N. Ranasinghe
Aneesh Rangnekar
Samrudhdhi B. Rangrej
Harsh Rangwani
Viresh Ranjan
Anyi Rao
Yongming Rao
Carolina Raposo
Michalis Raptis
Amir Rasouli
Vivek Rathod
Adepu Ravi Sankar
Avinash Ravichandran
Bharadwaj Ravichandran
Dripta S. Raychaudhuri
Adria Recasens
Simon Reiß
Davis Rempe
Daxuan Ren
Jiawei Ren
Jimmy Ren
Sucheng Ren
Dayong Ren
Zhile Ren
Dongwei Ren
Qibing Ren
Pengfei Ren
Zhenwen Ren
Xuqian Ren
Yixuan Ren
Zhongzheng Ren
Ambareesh Revanur
Hamed Rezazadegan
    Tavakoli
Rafael S. Rezende
Wonjong Rhee
Alexander Richard

Christian Richardt
Stephan R. Richter
Benjamin Riggan
Dominik Rivoir
Mamshad Nayeem Rizve
Joshua D. Robinson
Joseph Robinson
Chris Rockwell
Ranga Rodrigo
Andres C. Rodriguez
Carlos Rodriguez-Pardo
Marcus Rohrbach
Gemma Roig
Yu Rong
David A. Ross
Mohammad Rostami
Edward Rosten
Karsten Roth
Anirban Roy
Debaditya Roy
Shuvendu Roy
Ahana Roy Choudhury
Aruni Roy Chowdhury
Denys Rozumnyi
Shulan Ruan
Wenjie Ruan
Patrick Ruhkamp
Danila Rukhovich
Anian Ruoss
Chris Russell
Dan Ruta
Dawid Damian Rymarczyk
DongHun Ryu
Hyeonggon Ryu
Kwonyoung Ryu
Balasubramanian S.
Alexandre Sablayrolles
Mohammad Sabokrou
Arka Sadhu
Aniruddha Saha
Oindrila Saha
Pritish Sahu
Aneeshan Sain
Nirat Saini
Saurabh Saini

Takeshi Saitoh
Christos Sakaridis
Fumihiko Sakaue
Dimitrios Sakkos
Ken Sakurada
Parikshit V. Sakurikar
Rohit Saluja
Nermin Samet
Leo Sampaio Ferraz
    Ribeiro
Jorge Sanchez
Enrique Sanchez
Shengtian Sang
Anush Sankaran
Soubhik Sanyal
Nikolaos Sarafianos
Vishwanath Saragadam
István Sárándi
Saquib Sarfraz
Mert Bulent Sariyildiz
Anindya Sarkar
Pritam Sarkar
Paul-Edouard Sarlin
Hiroshi Sasaki
Takami Sato
Torsten Sattler
Ravi Kumar Satzoda
Axel Sauer
Stefano Savian
Artem Savkin
Manolis Savva
Gerald Schaefer
Simone Schaub-Meyer
Yoni Schirris
Samuel Schulter
Katja Schwarz
Jesse Scott
Sinisa Segvic
Constantin Marc Seibold
Lorenzo Seidenari
Matan Sela
Fadime Sener
Paul Hongsuck Seo
Kwanggyoon Seo
Hongje Seong

Dario Serez
Francesco Setti
Bryan Seybold
Mohamad Shahbazi
Shima Shahfar
Xinxin Shan
Caifeng Shan
Dandan Shan
Shawn Shan
Wei Shang
Jinghuan Shang
Jiaxiang Shang
Lei Shang
Sukrit Shankar
Ken Shao
Rui Shao
Jie Shao
Mingwen Shao
Aashish Sharma
Gaurav Sharma
Vivek Sharma
Abhishek Sharma
Yoli Shavit
Shashank Shekhar
Sumit Shekhar
Zhijie Shen
Fengyi Shen
Furao Shen
Jialie Shen
Jingjing Shen
Ziyi Shen
Linlin Shen
Guangyu Shen
Biluo Shen
Falong Shen
Jiajun Shen
Qiu Shen
Qiuhong Shen
Shuai Shen
Wang Shen
Yiqing Shen
Yunhang Shen
Siqi Shen
Bin Shen
Tianwei Shen

Xi Shen
Yilin Shen
Yuming Shen
Yucong Shen
Zhiqiang Shen
Lu Sheng
Yichen Sheng
Shivanand Venkanna
  Sheshappanavar
Shelly Sheynin
Baifeng Shi
Ruoxi Shi
Botian Shi
Hailin Shi
Jia Shi
Jing Shi
Shaoshuai Shi
Baoguang Shi
Boxin Shi
Hengcan Shi
Tianyang Shi
Xiaodan Shi
Yongjie Shi
Zhensheng Shi
Yinghuan Shi
Weiqi Shi
Wu Shi
Xuepeng Shi
Xiaoshuang Shi
Yujiao Shi
Zenglin Shi
Zhenmei Shi
Takashi Shibata
Meng-Li Shih
Yichang Shih
Hyunjung Shim
Dongseok Shim
Soshi Shimada
Inkyu Shin
Jinwoo Shin
Seungjoo Shin
Seungjae Shin
Koichi Shinoda
Suprosanna Shit

Palaiahnakote
  Shivakumara
Eli Shlizerman
Gaurav Shrivastava
Xiao Shu
Xiangbo Shu
Xiujun Shu
Yang Shu
Tianmin Shu
Jun Shu
Zhixin Shu
Bing Shuai
Maria Shugrina
Ivan Shugurov
Satya Narayan Shukla
Pranjay Shyam
Jianlou Si
Yawar Siddiqui
Alberto Signoroni
Pedro Silva
Jae-Young Sim
Oriane Siméoni
Martin Simon
Andrea Simonelli
Abhishek Singh
Ashish Singh
Dinesh Singh
Gurkirt Singh
Krishna Kumar Singh
Mannat Singh
Pravendra Singh
Rajat Vikram Singh
Utkarsh Singhal
Dipika Singhania
Vasu Singla
Harsh Sinha
Sudipta Sinha
Josef Sivic
Elena Sizikova
Geri Skenderi
Ivan Skorokhodov
Dmitriy Smirnov
Cameron Y. Smith
James S. Smith
Patrick Snape

Mattia Soldan
Hyeongseok Son
Sanghyun Son
Chuanbiao Song
Chen Song
Chunfeng Song
Dan Song
Dongjin Song
Hwanjun Song
Guoxian Song
Jiaming Song
Jie Song
Liangchen Song
Ran Song
Luchuan Song
Xibin Song
Li Song
Fenglong Song
Guoli Song
Guanglu Song
Zhenbo Song
Lin Song
Xinhang Song
Yang Song
Yibing Song
Rajiv Soundararajan
Hossein Souri
Cristovao Sousa
Riccardo Spezialetti
Leonidas Spinoulas
Michael W. Spratling
Deepak Sridhar
Srinath Sridhar
Gaurang Sriramanan
Vinkle Kumar Srivastav
Themos Stafylakis
Serban Stan
Anastasis Stathopoulos
Markus Steinberger
Jan Steinbrener
Sinisa Stekovic
Alexandros Stergiou
Gleb Sterkin
Rainer Stiefelhagen
Pierre Stock

Ombretta Strafforello
Julian Straub
Yannick Strümpler
Joerg Stueckler
Hang Su
Weijie Su
Jong-Chyi Su
Bing Su
Haisheng Su
Jinming Su
Yiyang Su
Yukun Su
Yuxin Su
Zhuo Su
Zhaoqi Su
Xiu Su
Yu-Chuan Su
Zhixun Su
Arulkumar Subramaniam
Akshayvarun Subramanya
A. Subramanyam
Swathikiran Sudhakaran
Yusuke Sugano
Masanori Suganuma
Yumin Suh
Yang Sui
Baochen Sun
Cheng Sun
Long Sun
Guolei Sun
Haoliang Sun
Haomiao Sun
He Sun
Hanqing Sun
Hao Sun
Lichao Sun
Jiachen Sun
Jiaming Sun
Jian Sun
Jin Sun
Jennifer J. Sun
Tiancheng Sun
Libo Sun
Peize Sun
Qianru Sun

Shanlin Sun
Yu Sun
Zhun Sun
Che Sun
Lin Sun
Tao Sun
Yiyou Sun
Chunyi Sun
Chong Sun
Weiwei Sun
Weixuan Sun
Xiuyu Sun
Yanan Sun
Zeren Sun
Zhaodong Sun
Zhiqing Sun
Minhyuk Sung
Jinli Suo
Simon Suo
Abhijit Suprem
Anshuman Suri
Saksham Suri
Joshua M. Susskind
Roman Suvorov
Gurumurthy Swaminathan
Robin Swanson
Paul Swoboda
Tabish A. Syed
Richard Szeliski
Fariborz Taherkhani
Yu-Wing Tai
Keita Takahashi
Walter Talbott
Gary Tam
Masato Tamura
Feitong Tan
Fuwen Tan
Shuhan Tan
Andong Tan
Bin Tan
Cheng Tan
Jianchao Tan
Lei Tan
Mingxing Tan
Xin Tan

Zichang Tan
Zhentao Tan
Kenichiro Tanaka
Masayuki Tanaka
Yushun Tang
Hao Tang
Jingqun Tang
Jinhui Tang
Kaihua Tang
Luming Tang
Lv Tang
Sheyang Tang
Shitao Tang
Siliang Tang
Shixiang Tang
Yansong Tang
Keke Tang
Chang Tang
Chenwei Tang
Jie Tang
Junshu Tang
Ming Tang
Peng Tang
Xu Tang
Yao Tang
Chen Tang
Fan Tang
Haoran Tang
Shengeng Tang
Yehui Tang
Zhipeng Tang
Ugo Tanielian
Chaofan Tao
Jiale Tao
Junli Tao
Renshuai Tao
An Tao
Guanhong Tao
Zhiqiang Tao
Makarand Tapaswi
Jean-Philippe G. Tarel
Juan J. Tarrio
Enzo Tartaglione
Keisuke Tateno
Zachary Teed

Ajinkya B. Tejankar
Bugra Tekin
Purva Tendulkar
Damien Teney
Minggui Teng
Chris Tensmeyer
Andrew Beng Jin Teoh
Philipp Terhörst
Kartik Thakral
Nupur Thakur
Kevin Thandiackal
Spyridon Thermos
Diego Thomas
William Thong
Yuesong Tian
Guanzhong Tian
Lin Tian
Shiqi Tian
Kai Tian
Meng Tian
Tai-Peng Tian
Zhuotao Tian
Shangxuan Tian
Tian Tian
Yapeng Tian
Yu Tian
Yuxin Tian
Leslie Ching Ow Tiong
Praveen Tirupattur
Garvita Tiwari
George Toderici
Antoine Toisoul
Aysim Toker
Tatiana Tommasi
Zhan Tong
Alessio Tonioni
Alessandro Torcinovich
Fabio Tosi
Matteo Toso
Hugo Touvron
Quan Hung Tran
Son Tran
Hung Tran
Ngoc-Trung Tran
Vinh Tran

Phong Tran
Giovanni Trappolini
Edith Tretschk
Subarna Tripathi
Shubhendu Trivedi
Eduard Trulls
Prune Truong
Thanh-Dat Truong
Tomasz Trzcinski
Sam Tsai
Yi-Hsuan Tsai
Ethan Tseng
Yu-Chee Tseng
Shahar Tsiper
Stavros Tsogkas
Shikui Tu
Zhigang Tu
Zhengzhong Tu
Richard Tucker
Sergey Tulyakov
Cigdem Turan
Daniyar Turmukhambetov
Victor G. Turrisi da Costa
Bartlomiej Twardowski
Christopher D. Twigg
Radim Tylecek
Mostofa Rafid Uddin
Md. Zasim Uddin
Kohei Uehara
Nicolas Ugrinovic
Youngjung Uh
Norimichi Ukita
Anwaar Ulhaq
Devesh Upadhyay
Paul Upchurch
Yoshitaka Ushiku
Yuzuko Utsumi
Mikaela Angelina Uy
Mohit Vaishnav
Pratik Vaishnavi
Jeya Maria Jose Valanarasu
Matias A. Valdenegro Toro
Diego Valsesia
Wouter Van Gansbeke
Nanne van Noord

Simon Vandenhende
Farshid Varno
Cristina Vasconcelos
Francisco Vasconcelos
Alex Vasilescu
Subeesh Vasu
Arun Balajee Vasudevan
Kanav Vats
Vaibhav S. Vavilala
Sagar Vaze
Javier Vazquez-Corral
Andrea Vedaldi
Olga Veksler
Andreas Velten
Sai H. Vemprala
Raviteja Vemulapalli
Shashanka
    Venkataramanan
Dor Verbin
Luisa Verdoliva
Manisha Verma
Yashaswi Verma
Constantin Vertan
Eli Verwimp
Deepak Vijaykeerthy
Pablo Villanueva
Ruben Villegas
Markus Vincze
Vibhav Vineet
Minh P. Vo
Huy V. Vo
Duc Minh Vo
Tomas Vojir
Igor Vozniak
Nicholas Vretos
Vibashan VS
Tuan-Anh Vu
Thang Vu
Mårten Wadenbäck
Neal Wadhwa
Aaron T. Walsman
Steven Walton
Jin Wan
Alvin Wan
Jia Wan

Jun Wan
Xiaoyue Wan
Fang Wan
Guowei Wan
Renjie Wan
Zhiqiang Wan
Ziyu Wan
Bastian Wandt
Dongdong Wang
Limin Wang
Haiyang Wang
Xiaobing Wang
Angtian Wang
Angelina Wang
Bing Wang
Bo Wang
Boyu Wang
Binghui Wang
Chen Wang
Chien-Yi Wang
Congli Wang
Qi Wang
Chengrui Wang
Rui Wang
Yiqun Wang
Cong Wang
Wenjing Wang
Dongkai Wang
Di Wang
Xiaogang Wang
Kai Wang
Zhizhong Wang
Fangjinhua Wang
Feng Wang
Hang Wang
Gaoang Wang
Guoqing Wang
Guangcong Wang
Guangzhi Wang
Hanqing Wang
Hao Wang
Haohan Wang
Haoran Wang
Hong Wang
Haotao Wang

Hu Wang
Huan Wang
Hua Wang
Hui-Po Wang
Hengli Wang
Hanyu Wang
Hongxing Wang
Jingwen Wang
Jialiang Wang
Jian Wang
Jianyi Wang
Jiashun Wang
Jiahao Wang
Tsun-Hsuan Wang
Xiaoqian Wang
Jinqiao Wang
Jun Wang
Jianzong Wang
Kaihong Wang
Ke Wang
Lei Wang
Lingjing Wang
Linnan Wang
Lin Wang
Liansheng Wang
Mengjiao Wang
Manning Wang
Nannan Wang
Peihao Wang
Jiayun Wang
Pu Wang
Qiang Wang
Qiufeng Wang
Qilong Wang
Qiangchang Wang
Qin Wang
Qing Wang
Ruocheng Wang
Ruibin Wang
Ruisheng Wang
Ruizhe Wang
Runqi Wang
Runzhong Wang
Wenxuan Wang
Sen Wang

Shangfei Wang
Shaofei Wang
Shijie Wang
Shiqi Wang
Zhibo Wang
Song Wang
Xinjiang Wang
Tai Wang
Tao Wang
Teng Wang
Xiang Wang
Tianren Wang
Tiantian Wang
Tianyi Wang
Fengjiao Wang
Wei Wang
Miaohui Wang
Suchen Wang
Siyue Wang
Yaoming Wang
Xiao Wang
Ze Wang
Biao Wang
Chaofei Wang
Dong Wang
Gu Wang
Guangrun Wang
Guangming Wang
Guo-Hua Wang
Haoqing Wang
Hesheng Wang
Huafeng Wang
Jinghua Wang
Jingdong Wang
Jingjing Wang
Jingya Wang
Jingkang Wang
Jiakai Wang
Junke Wang
Kuo Wang
Lichen Wang
Lizhi Wang
Longguang Wang
Mang Wang
Mei Wang

Min Wang
Peng-Shuai Wang
Run Wang
Shaoru Wang
Shuhui Wang
Tan Wang
Tiancai Wang
Tianqi Wang
Wenhai Wang
Wenzhe Wang
Xiaobo Wang
Xiudong Wang
Xu Wang
Yajie Wang
Yan Wang
Yuan-Gen Wang
Yingqian Wang
Yizhi Wang
Yulin Wang
Yu Wang
Yujie Wang
Yunhe Wang
Yuxi Wang
Yaowei Wang
Yiwei Wang
Zezheng Wang
Hongzhi Wang
Zhiqiang Wang
Ziteng Wang
Ziwei Wang
Zheng Wang
Zhenyu Wang
Binglu Wang
Zhongdao Wang
Ce Wang
Weining Wang
Weiyao Wang
Wenbin Wang
Wenguan Wang
Guangting Wang
Haolin Wang
Haiyan Wang
Huiyu Wang
Naiyan Wang
Jingbo Wang

Jinpeng Wang
Jiaqi Wang
Liyuan Wang
Lizhen Wang
Ning Wang
Wenqian Wang
Sheng-Yu Wang
Weimin Wang
Xiaohan Wang
Yifan Wang
Yi Wang
Yongtao Wang
Yizhou Wang
Zhuo Wang
Zhe Wang
Xudong Wang
Xiaofang Wang
Xinggang Wang
Xiaosen Wang
Xiaosong Wang
Xiaoyang Wang
Lijun Wang
Xinlong Wang
Xuan Wang
Xue Wang
Yangang Wang
Yaohui Wang
Yu-Chiang Frank Wang
Yida Wang
Yilin Wang
Yi Ru Wang
Yali Wang
Yinglong Wang
Yufu Wang
Yujiang Wang
Yuwang Wang
Yuting Wang
Yang Wang
Yu-Xiong Wang
Yixu Wang
Ziqi Wang
Zhicheng Wang
Zeyu Wang
Zhaowen Wang
Zhenyi Wang

Zhenzhi Wang
Zhijie Wang
Zhiyong Wang
Zhongling Wang
Zhuowei Wang
Zian Wang
Zifu Wang
Zihao Wang
Zirui Wang
Ziyan Wang
Wenxiao Wang
Zhen Wang
Zhepeng Wang
Zi Wang
Zihao W. Wang
Steven L. Waslander
Olivia Watkins
Daniel Watson
Silvan Weder
Dongyoon Wee
Dongming Wei
Tianyi Wei
Jia Wei
Dong Wei
Fangyun Wei
Longhui Wei
Mingqiang Wei
Xinyue Wei
Chen Wei
Donglai Wei
Pengxu Wei
Xing Wei
Xiu-Shen Wei
Wenqi Wei
Guoqiang Wei
Wei Wei
XingKui Wei
Xian Wei
Xingxing Wei
Yake Wei
Yuxiang Wei
Yi Wei
Luca Weihs
Michael Weinmann
Martin Weinmann

Congcong Wen
Chuan Wen
Jie Wen
Sijia Wen
Song Wen
Chao Wen
Xiang Wen
Zeyi Wen
Xin Wen
Yilin Wen
Yijia Weng
Shuchen Weng
Junwu Weng
Wenming Weng
Renliang Weng
Zhenyu Weng
Xinshuo Weng
Nicholas J. Westlake
Gordon Wetzstein
Lena M. Widin Klasén
Rick Wildes
Bryan M. Williams
Williem Williem
Ole Winther
Scott Wisdom
Alex Wong
Chau-Wai Wong
Kwan-Yee K. Wong
Yongkang Wong
Scott Workman
Marcel Worring
Michael Wray
Safwan Wshah
Xiang Wu
Aming Wu
Chongruo Wu
Cho-Ying Wu
Chunpeng Wu
Chenyan Wu
Ziyi Wu
Fuxiang Wu
Gang Wu
Haiping Wu
Huisi Wu
Jane Wu

Jialian Wu
Jing Wu
Jinjian Wu
Jianlong Wu
Xian Wu
Lifang Wu
Lifan Wu
Minye Wu
Qianyi Wu
Rongliang Wu
Rui Wu
Shiqian Wu
Shuzhe Wu
Shangzhe Wu
Tsung-Han Wu
Tz-Ying Wu
Ting-Wei Wu
Jiannan Wu
Zhiliang Wu
Yu Wu
Chenyun Wu
Dayan Wu
Dongxian Wu
Fei Wu
Hefeng Wu
Jianxin Wu
Weibin Wu
Wenxuan Wu
Wenhao Wu
Xiao Wu
Yicheng Wu
Yuanwei Wu
Yu-Huan Wu
Zhenxin Wu
Zhenyu Wu
Wei Wu
Peng Wu
Xiaohe Wu
Xindi Wu
Xinxing Wu
Xinyi Wu
Xingjiao Wu
Xiongwei Wu
Yangzheng Wu
Yanzhao Wu

Yawen Wu
Yong Wu
Yi Wu
Ying Nian Wu
Zhenyao Wu
Zhonghua Wu
Zongze Wu
Zuxuan Wu
Stefanie Wuhrer
Teng Xi
Jianing Xi
Fei Xia
Haifeng Xia
Menghan Xia
Yuanqing Xia
Zhihua Xia
Xiaobo Xia
Weihao Xia
Shihong Xia
Yan Xia
Yong Xia
Zhaoyang Xia
Zhihao Xia
Chuhua Xian
Yongqin Xian
Wangmeng Xiang
Fanbo Xiang
Tiange Xiang
Tao Xiang
Liuyu Xiang
Xiaoyu Xiang
Zhiyu Xiang
Aoran Xiao
Chunxia Xiao
Fanyi Xiao
Jimin Xiao
Jun Xiao
Taihong Xiao
Anqi Xiao
Junfei Xiao
Jing Xiao
Liang Xiao
Yang Xiao
Yuting Xiao
Yijun Xiao

Yao Xiao
Zeyu Xiao
Zhisheng Xiao
Zihao Xiao
Binhui Xie
Christopher Xie
Haozhe Xie
Jin Xie
Guo-Sen Xie
Hongtao Xie
Ming-Kun Xie
Tingting Xie
Chaohao Xie
Weicheng Xie
Xudong Xie
Jiyang Xie
Xiaohua Xie
Yuan Xie
Zhenyu Xie
Ning Xie
Xianghui Xie
Xiufeng Xie
You Xie
Yutong Xie
Fuyong Xing
Yifan Xing
Zhen Xing
Yuanjun Xiong
Jinhui Xiong
Weihua Xiong
Hongkai Xiong
Zhitong Xiong
Yuanhao Xiong
Yunyang Xiong
Yuwen Xiong
Zhiwei Xiong
Yuliang Xiu
An Xu
Chang Xu
Chenliang Xu
Chengming Xu
Chenshu Xu
Xiang Xu
Huijuan Xu
Zhe Xu

Jie Xu
Jingyi Xu
Jiarui Xu
Yinghao Xu
Kele Xu
Ke Xu
Li Xu
Linchuan Xu
Linning Xu
Mengde Xu
Mengmeng Frost Xu
Min Xu
Mingye Xu
Jun Xu
Ning Xu
Peng Xu
Runsheng Xu
Sheng Xu
Wenqiang Xu
Xiaogang Xu
Renzhe Xu
Kaidi Xu
Yi Xu
Chi Xu
Qiuling Xu
Baobei Xu
Feng Xu
Haohang Xu
Haofei Xu
Lan Xu
Mingze Xu
Songcen Xu
Weipeng Xu
Wenjia Xu
Wenju Xu
Xiangyu Xu
Xin Xu
Yinshuang Xu
Yixing Xu
Yuting Xu
Yanyu Xu
Zhenbo Xu
Zhiliang Xu
Zhiyuan Xu
Xiaohao Xu

Yanwu Xu
Yan Xu
Yiran Xu
Yifan Xu
Yufei Xu
Yong Xu
Zichuan Xu
Zenglin Xu
Zexiang Xu
Zhan Xu
Zheng Xu
Zhiwei Xu
Ziyue Xu
Shiyu Xuan
Hanyu Xuan
Fei Xue
Jianru Xue
Mingfu Xue
Qinghan Xue
Tianfan Xue
Chao Xue
Chuhui Xue
Nan Xue
Zhou Xue
Xiangyang Xue
Yuan Xue
Abhay Yadav
Ravindra Yadav
Kota Yamaguchi
Toshihiko Yamasaki
Kohei Yamashita
Chaochao Yan
Feng Yan
Kun Yan
Qingsen Yan
Qixin Yan
Rui Yan
Siming Yan
Xinchen Yan
Yaping Yan
Bin Yan
Qingan Yan
Shen Yan
Shipeng Yan
Xu Yan

Yan Yan
Yichao Yan
Zhaoyi Yan
Zike Yan
Zhiqiang Yan
Hongliang Yan
Zizheng Yan
Jiewen Yang
Anqi Joyce Yang
Shan Yang
Anqi Yang
Antoine Yang
Bo Yang
Baoyao Yang
Chenhongyi Yang
Dingkang Yang
De-Nian Yang
Dong Yang
David Yang
Fan Yang
Fengyu Yang
Fengting Yang
Fei Yang
Gengshan Yang
Heng Yang
Han Yang
Huan Yang
Yibo Yang
Jiancheng Yang
Jihan Yang
Jiawei Yang
Jiayu Yang
Jie Yang
Jinfa Yang
Jingkang Yang
Jinyu Yang
Cheng-Fu Yang
Ji Yang
Jianyu Yang
Kailun Yang
Tian Yang
Luyu Yang
Liang Yang
Li Yang
Michael Ying Yang

Yang Yang
Muli Yang
Le Yang
Qiushi Yang
Ren Yang
Ruihan Yang
Shuang Yang
Siyuan Yang
Su Yang
Shiqi Yang
Taojiannan Yang
Tianyu Yang
Lei Yang
Wanzhao Yang
Shuai Yang
William Yang
Wei Yang
Xiaofeng Yang
Xiaoshan Yang
Xin Yang
Xuan Yang
Xu Yang
Xingyi Yang
Xitong Yang
Jing Yang
Yanchao Yang
Wenming Yang
Yujiu Yang
Herb Yang
Jianfei Yang
Jinhui Yang
Chuanguang Yang
Guanglei Yang
Haitao Yang
Kewei Yang
Linlin Yang
Lijin Yang
Longrong Yang
Meng Yang
MingKun Yang
Sibei Yang
Shicai Yang
Tong Yang
Wen Yang
Xi Yang

Xiaolong Yang
Xue Yang
Yubin Yang
Ze Yang
Ziyi Yang
Yi Yang
Linjie Yang
Yuzhe Yang
Yiding Yang
Zhenpei Yang
Zhaohui Yang
Zhengyuan Yang
Zhibo Yang
Zongxin Yang
Hantao Yao
Mingde Yao
Rui Yao
Taiping Yao
Ting Yao
Cong Yao
Qingsong Yao
Quanming Yao
Xu Yao
Yuan Yao
Yao Yao
Yazhou Yao
Jiawen Yao
Shunyu Yao
Pew-Thian Yap
Sudhir Yarram
Rajeev Yasarla
Peng Ye
Botao Ye
Mao Ye
Fei Ye
Hanrong Ye
Jingwen Ye
Jinwei Ye
Jiarong Ye
Mang Ye
Meng Ye
Qi Ye
Qian Ye
Qixiang Ye
Junjie Ye

Sheng Ye
Nanyang Ye
Yufei Ye
Xiaoqing Ye
Ruolin Ye
Yousef Yeganeh
Chun-Hsiao Yeh
Raymond A. Yeh
Yu-Ying Yeh
Kai Yi
Chang Yi
Renjiao Yi
Xinping Yi
Peng Yi
Alper Yilmaz
Junho Yim
Hui Yin
Bangjie Yin
Jia-Li Yin
Miao Yin
Wenzhe Yin
Xuwang Yin
Ming Yin
Yu Yin
Aoxiong Yin
Kangxue Yin
Tianwei Yin
Wei Yin
Xianghua Ying
Rio Yokota
Tatsuya Yokota
Naoto Yokoya
Ryo Yonetani
Ki Yoon Yoo
Jinsu Yoo
Sunjae Yoon
Jae Shin Yoon
Jihun Yoon
Sung-Hoon Yoon
Ryota Yoshihashi
Yusuke Yoshiyasu
Chenyu You
Haoran You
Haoxuan You
Yang You

Quanzeng You
Tackgeun You
Kaichao You
Shan You
Xinge You
Yurong You
Baosheng Yu
Bei Yu
Haichao Yu
Hao Yu
Chaohui Yu
Fisher Yu
Jin-Gang Yu
Jiyang Yu
Jason J. Yu
Jiashuo Yu
Hong-Xing Yu
Lei Yu
Mulin Yu
Ning Yu
Peilin Yu
Qi Yu
Qian Yu
Rui Yu
Shuzhi Yu
Gang Yu
Tan Yu
Weijiang Yu
Xin Yu
Bingyao Yu
Ye Yu
Hanchao Yu
Yingchen Yu
Tao Yu
Xiaotian Yu
Qing Yu
Houjian Yu
Changqian Yu
Jing Yu
Jun Yu
Shujian Yu
Xiang Yu
Zhaofei Yu
Zhenbo Yu
Yinfeng Yu

Zhuoran Yu
Zitong Yu
Bo Yuan
Jiangbo Yuan
Liangzhe Yuan
Weihao Yuan
Jianbo Yuan
Xiaoyun Yuan
Ye Yuan
Li Yuan
Geng Yuan
Jialin Yuan
Maoxun Yuan
Peng Yuan
Xin Yuan
Yuan Yuan
Yuhui Yuan
Yixuan Yuan
Zheng Yuan
Mehmet Kerim Yücel
Kaiyu Yue
Haixiao Yue
Heeseung Yun
Sangdoo Yun
Tian Yun
Mahmut Yurt
Ekim Yurtsever
Ahmet Yüzügüler
Edouard Yvinec
Eloi Zablocki
Christopher Zach
Muhammad Zaigham
  Zaheer
Pierluigi Zama Ramirez
Yuhang Zang
Pietro Zanuttigh
Alexey Zaytsev
Bernhard Zeisl
Haitian Zeng
Pengpeng Zeng
Jiabei Zeng
Runhao Zeng
Wei Zeng
Yawen Zeng
Yi Zeng

Yiming Zeng
Tieyong Zeng
Huanqiang Zeng
Dan Zeng
Yu Zeng
Wei Zhai
Yuanhao Zhai
Fangneng Zhan
Kun Zhan
Xiong Zhang
Jingdong Zhang
Jiangning Zhang
Zhilu Zhang
Gengwei Zhang
Dongsu Zhang
Hui Zhang
Binjie Zhang
Bo Zhang
Tianhao Zhang
Cecilia Zhang
Jing Zhang
Chaoning Zhang
Chenxu Zhang
Chi Zhang
Chris Zhang
Yabin Zhang
Zhao Zhang
Rufeng Zhang
Chaoyi Zhang
Zheng Zhang
Da Zhang
Yi Zhang
Edward Zhang
Xin Zhang
Feifei Zhang
Feilong Zhang
Yuqi Zhang
GuiXuan Zhang
Hanlin Zhang
Hanwang Zhang
Hanzhen Zhang
Haotian Zhang
He Zhang
Haokui Zhang
Hongyuan Zhang

Hengrui Zhang
Hongming Zhang
Mingfang Zhang
Jianpeng Zhang
Jiaming Zhang
Jichao Zhang
Jie Zhang
Jingfeng Zhang
Jingyi Zhang
Jinnian Zhang
David Junhao Zhang
Junjie Zhang
Junzhe Zhang
Jiawan Zhang
Jingyang Zhang
Kai Zhang
Lei Zhang
Lihua Zhang
Lu Zhang
Miao Zhang
Minjia Zhang
Mingjin Zhang
Qi Zhang
Qian Zhang
Qilong Zhang
Qiming Zhang
Qiang Zhang
Richard Zhang
Ruimao Zhang
Ruisi Zhang
Ruixin Zhang
Runze Zhang
Qilin Zhang
Shan Zhang
Shanshan Zhang
Xi Sheryl Zhang
Song-Hai Zhang
Chongyang Zhang
Kaihao Zhang
Songyang Zhang
Shu Zhang
Siwei Zhang
Shujian Zhang
Tianyun Zhang
Tong Zhang

Tao Zhang
Wenwei Zhang
Wenqiang Zhang
Wen Zhang
Xiaolin Zhang
Xingchen Zhang
Xingxuan Zhang
Xiuming Zhang
Xiaoshuai Zhang
Xuanmeng Zhang
Xuanyang Zhang
Xucong Zhang
Xingxing Zhang
Xikun Zhang
Xiaohan Zhang
Yahui Zhang
Yunhua Zhang
Yan Zhang
Yanghao Zhang
Yifei Zhang
Yifan Zhang
Yi-Fan Zhang
Yihao Zhang
Yingliang Zhang
Youshan Zhang
Yulun Zhang
Yushu Zhang
Yixiao Zhang
Yide Zhang
Zhongwen Zhang
Bowen Zhang
Chen-Lin Zhang
Zehua Zhang
Zekun Zhang
Zeyu Zhang
Xiaowei Zhang
Yifeng Zhang
Cheng Zhang
Hongguang Zhang
Yuexi Zhang
Fa Zhang
Guofeng Zhang
Hao Zhang
Haofeng Zhang
Hongwen Zhang

Hua Zhang
Jiaxin Zhang
Zhenyu Zhang
Jian Zhang
Jianfeng Zhang
Jiao Zhang
Jiakai Zhang
Lefei Zhang
Le Zhang
Mi Zhang
Min Zhang
Ning Zhang
Pan Zhang
Pu Zhang
Qing Zhang
Renrui Zhang
Shifeng Zhang
Shuo Zhang
Shaoxiong Zhang
Weizhong Zhang
Xi Zhang
Xiaomei Zhang
Xinyu Zhang
Yin Zhang
Zicheng Zhang
Zihao Zhang
Ziqi Zhang
Zhaoxiang Zhang
Zhen Zhang
Zhipeng Zhang
Zhixing Zhang
Zhizheng Zhang
Jiawei Zhang
Zhong Zhang
Pingping Zhang
Yixin Zhang
Kui Zhang
Lingzhi Zhang
Huaiwen Zhang
Quanshi Zhang
Zhoutong Zhang
Yuhang Zhang
Yuting Zhang
Zhang Zhang
Ziming Zhang

Zhizhong Zhang
Qilong Zhangli
Bingyin Zhao
Bin Zhao
Chenglong Zhao
Lei Zhao
Feng Zhao
Gangming Zhao
Haiyan Zhao
Hao Zhao
Handong Zhao
Hengshuang Zhao
Yinan Zhao
Jiaojiao Zhao
Jiaqi Zhao
Jing Zhao
Kaili Zhao
Haojie Zhao
Yucheng Zhao
Longjiao Zhao
Long Zhao
Qingsong Zhao
Qingyu Zhao
Rui Zhao
Rui-Wei Zhao
Sicheng Zhao
Shuang Zhao
Siyan Zhao
Zelin Zhao
Shiyu Zhao
Wang Zhao
Tiesong Zhao
Qian Zhao
Wangbo Zhao
Xi-Le Zhao
Xu Zhao
Yajie Zhao
Yang Zhao
Ying Zhao
Yin Zhao
Yizhou Zhao
Yunhan Zhao
Yuyang Zhao
Yue Zhao
Yuzhi Zhao

Bowen Zhao
Pu Zhao
Bingchen Zhao
Borui Zhao
Fuqiang Zhao
Hanbin Zhao
Jian Zhao
Mingyang Zhao
Na Zhao
Rongchang Zhao
Ruiqi Zhao
Shuai Zhao
Wenda Zhao
Wenliang Zhao
Xiangyun Zhao
Yifan Zhao
Yaping Zhao
Zhou Zhao
He Zhao
Jie Zhao
Xibin Zhao
Xiaoqi Zhao
Zhengyu Zhao
Jin Zhe
Chuanxia Zheng
Huan Zheng
Hao Zheng
Jia Zheng
Jian-Qing Zheng
Shuai Zheng
Meng Zheng
Mingkai Zheng
Qian Zheng
Qi Zheng
Wu Zheng
Yinqiang Zheng
Yufeng Zheng
Yutong Zheng
Yalin Zheng
Yu Zheng
Feng Zheng
Zhaoheng Zheng
Haitian Zheng
Kang Zheng
Bolun Zheng

Haiyong Zheng
Mingwu Zheng
Sipeng Zheng
Tu Zheng
Wenzhao Zheng
Xiawu Zheng
Yinglin Zheng
Zhuo Zheng
Zilong Zheng
Kecheng Zheng
Zerong Zheng
Shuaifeng Zhi
Tiancheng Zhi
Jia-Xing Zhong
Yiwu Zhong
Fangwei Zhong
Zhihang Zhong
Yaoyao Zhong
Yiran Zhong
Zhun Zhong
Zichun Zhong
Bo Zhou
Boyao Zhou
Brady Zhou
Mo Zhou
Chunluan Zhou
Dingfu Zhou
Fan Zhou
Jingkai Zhou
Honglu Zhou
Jiaming Zhou
Jiahuan Zhou
Jun Zhou
Kaiyang Zhou
Keyang Zhou
Kuangqi Zhou
Lei Zhou
Lihua Zhou
Man Zhou
Mingyi Zhou
Mingyuan Zhou
Ning Zhou
Peng Zhou
Penghao Zhou
Qianyi Zhou

Shuigeng Zhou
Shangchen Zhou
Huayi Zhou
Zhize Zhou
Sanping Zhou
Qin Zhou
Tao Zhou
Wenbo Zhou
Xiangdong Zhou
Xiao-Yun Zhou
Xiao Zhou
Yang Zhou
Yipin Zhou
Zhenyu Zhou
Hao Zhou
Chu Zhou
Daquan Zhou
Da-Wei Zhou
Hang Zhou
Kang Zhou
Qianyu Zhou
Sheng Zhou
Wenhui Zhou
Xingyi Zhou
Yan-Jie Zhou
Yiyi Zhou
Yu Zhou
Yuan Zhou
Yuqian Zhou
Yuxuan Zhou
Zixiang Zhou
Wengang Zhou
Shuchang Zhou
Tianfei Zhou
Yichao Zhou
Alex Zhu
Chenchen Zhu
Deyao Zhu
Xiatian Zhu
Guibo Zhu
Haidong Zhu
Hao Zhu
Hongzi Zhu
Rui Zhu
Jing Zhu

Jianke Zhu
Junchen Zhu
Lei Zhu
Lingyu Zhu
Luyang Zhu
Menglong Zhu
Peihao Zhu
Hui Zhu
Xiaofeng Zhu
Tyler (Lixuan) Zhu
Wentao Zhu
Xiangyu Zhu
Xinqi Zhu
Xinxin Zhu
Xinliang Zhu
Yangguang Zhu
Yichen Zhu
Yixin Zhu
Yanjun Zhu
Yousong Zhu
Yuhao Zhu
Ye Zhu
Feng Zhu
Zhen Zhu
Fangrui Zhu
Jinjing Zhu
Linchao Zhu
Pengfei Zhu
Sijie Zhu
Xiaobin Zhu
Xiaoguang Zhu
Zezhou Zhu
Zhenyao Zhu
Kai Zhu
Pengkai Zhu
Bingbing Zhuang
Chengyuan Zhuang
Liansheng Zhuang
Peiye Zhuang
Yixin Zhuang
Yihong Zhuang
Junbao Zhuo
Andrea Ziani
Bartosz Zieliński
Primo Zingaretti

Nikolaos Zioulis
Andrew Zisserman
Yael Ziv
Liu Ziyin
Xingxing Zou
Danping Zou
Qi Zou

Shihao Zou
Xueyan Zou
Yang Zou
Yuliang Zou
Zihang Zou
Chuhang Zou
Dongqing Zou

Xu Zou
Zhiming Zou
Maria A. Zuluaga
Xinxin Zuo
Zhiwen Zuo
Reyer Zwiggelaar

Contents – Part XVIII

Dynamic Dual Trainable Bounds for Ultra-low Precision Super-Resolution Networks

Yunshan Zhong[1,2], Mingbao Lin[3], Xunchao Li[2], Ke Li[3], Yunhang Shen[3], Fei Chao[1,2], Yongjian Wu[3], and Rongrong Ji[1,2(✉)]

[1] Institute of Artificial Intelligence, Xiamen University, Xiamen, China
zhongyunshan@stu.xmu.edu.cn, {fchao,rrji}@xmu.edu.cn
[2] MAC Lab, School of Informatics, Xiamen University, Xiamen, China
lixunchao@stu.xmu.edu.cn
[3] Tencent Youtu Lab, Shanghai, China
littlekenwu@tencent.com

Abstract. Light-weight super-resolution (SR) models have received considerable attention for their serviceability in mobile devices. Many efforts employ network quantization to compress SR models. However, these methods suffer from severe performance degradation when quantizing the SR models to ultra-low precision (*e.g.*, 2-bit and 3-bit) with the low-cost layer-wise quantizer. In this paper, we identify that the performance drop comes from the contradiction between the layer-wise symmetric quantizer and the highly asymmetric activation distribution in SR models. This discrepancy leads to either a waste on the quantization levels or detail loss in reconstructed images. Therefore, we propose a novel activation quantizer, referred to as Dynamic Dual Trainable Bounds (DDTB), to accommodate the asymmetry of the activations. Specifically, DDTB innovates in: 1) A layer-wise quantizer with trainable upper and lower bounds to tackle the highly asymmetric activations. 2) A dynamic gate controller to adaptively adjust the upper and lower bounds at runtime to overcome the drastically varying activation ranges over different samples. To reduce the extra overhead, the dynamic gate controller is quantized to 2-bit and applied to only part of the SR networks according to the introduced dynamic intensity. Extensive experiments demonstrate that our DDTB exhibits significant performance improvements in ultra-low precision. For example, our DDTB achieves a 0.70 dB PSNR increase on Urban100 benchmark when quantizing EDSR to 2-bit and scaling up output images to ×4. Code is at https://github.com/zysxmu/DDTB.

Keywords: Super-resolution · Network quantization · Dual trainable bounds · Dynamic gate controller

Supplementary Information The online version contains supplementary material available at https://doi.org/10.1007/978-3-031-19797-0_1.

1   Introduction

Single image super-resolution (SISR) is a classic yet challenging research topic in low-level computer vision. It aims to construct a high-resolution (HR) image from a given low-resolution (LR) image. Recent years have witnessed the revolution of deep convolutional neural networks (DCNN), which leads to many state-of-the-arts [5, 24, 47] in SISR task.

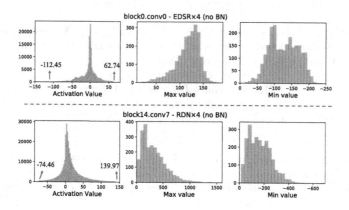

Fig. 1. The first column shows the activation histograms. The second and third columns show the maximum and minimum activation values of different samples. We perform experiments with EDSR [24] and RDN [47] on DIV2K [38] dataset.

When looking back on the development of DCNN in SISR, we find that the record-breaking performance is accompanied by a drastically increasing model complexity. SRCNN [5], the first work to integrate DCNN to SR, has only three convolutional layers with a total of 57K parameters. Then, EDSR [24] constructs a 64-layer CNN with 1.5M parameters. Equipped with a residual dense block, RDN [47] introduces 151 convolutional layers with 22M parameters. Also, it requires around 5,896G float-point operations (FLOPs) to produce only one 1920 × 1080 image (upscaling factor ×4). On the one hand, the high memory footprint and computation cost of DCNN-based SR models barricade their deployment on many resource-hungry platforms such as smartphones, wearable gadgets, embedding devices, *etc*. On the other hand, SR is particularly popular on these devices where the photograph resolution must be enhanced after being taken by the users. Therefore, compressing DCNN-based SR models has gained considerable attention from both academia and industries. In recent years, a variety of methodologies are explored to realize practical deployment [8, 10, 20, 25].

By discretizing the full-precision weights and activations within the DCNN, network quantization has emerged as one of the most promising technologies. It reduces not only memory storage for lower-precision representation but computation cost for more efficient integer operations. Earlier studies mostly focus on high-level vision tasks, such as classification [7, 20, 26, 27, 35, 48] and segmentation [44, 45]. A direct extension of these methods to SR networks has been proved infeasible since low-vision networks often have different operators with

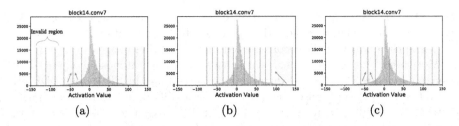

Fig. 2. Example of "quantization unfitness" using RDN [47] on DIV2K [38]. The orange bar denotes the quantization levels. The red arrows show the quantization level of activations. (a) Two quantization levels are wasted on the region without activations. (b) High-magnitude activations are quantized to a small quantization level. (c) The distribution of the quantization levels from dual bounds in our DDTB. (Color figure online)

these high-level networks [23]. Consequently, excavating specialized quantization methods for DCNN-based SR models recently has aroused increasing attention in the research community. For example, PAMS [23] designs a layer-wise quantizer with a learnable clipping to tackle the large ranges of activations, but severe performance degradation occurs in ultra-low precision settings (*e.g.*, 2-bit and 3-bit) as shown in Sec. 4.2. A recent study DAQ [11] adopts a channel-wise distribution-aware quantization scheme. Despite the progress, the performance improvement comes at the cost of considerable overhead from normalizing and de-normalizing feature maps, as well as the expensive per-channel quantizer. Therefore, existing studies are stuck in either heavy extra costs or severe performance drops when performing ultra-low precision quantization.

In this paper, we realize that the inapplicability of existing studies comes from the contradiction between the layer-wise symmetric quantizer and the asymmetric activation distribution in DCNN-based SR models. Specifically, it has been a wide consensus [9,24,46,47] that removing batch normalization (BN) layers increases the super-resolution performance since low-level vision is sensitive to the scale information of images while BN reduces the range flexibility of activations. However, the removal of BN leads to highly asymmetric activation distribution, as well as diverse maximum and minimum activations for different input samples. Illustrative examples with EDSR [24] and RDN [47] are given in Fig. 1. Despite some previous works equip SR networks with BN layers, they have to compensate for the performance drops by other strategies. For example, SRResNet [22] constructs a highway that propagates the activations of the first convolutional layer to the outputs of every other block, which again leads to activation distributions like Fig. 1.

Although these abnormal activation distributions benefit a full-precision SR network, they are unfriendly to the quantized version which often constructs a symmetric quantizer with only one clipping bound to perform network quantization, resulting in the issue of "quantization unfitness". Figure 2 illustrates a toy example. With an asymmetric activation distribution, a large clipping wastes two quantization levels on the region without any activation items, while a small clipping quantizes large-magnitude activations to a small quantization level which leads to large quantization error and causes details loss in high-resolution images. Thus, an adaptive quantizer to the activation distribution is crucial to the quality of the reconstructed high-resolution images.

Motivated by the above analysis, in this paper, we propose dynamic dual trainable bounds (DDTB) to quantize the activations in SR models. DDTB innovates in: 1) A layer-wise quantizer with trainable upper and lower bounds to tackle the highly asymmetric activations; 2) A dynamic gate controller to adaptively adjust the upper and lower bounds based on different input samples at runtime for overcoming the drastically varying activation ranges over different samples. To minimize the extra costs on computation and storage, the dynamic gate is quantized to 2-bit and applied to part of the network based on the dynamic intensity in each layer. We also introduce an initializer for DDTB. Specifically, we first use the activation statistics from the full-precision network instead of the quantized version to initialize the upper and lower bounds. Then, the dynamic gate controller is trained individually towards its target output of 1 for all inputs in the early several epochs. Combing with the proposed initializer, DDTB provides significant performance improvements, especially when SR models are quantized to the case of ultra-low bits. For instance, compared with the state-of-the-art, our DDTB achieves performance gains by 0.70dB PSNR on Urban100 benchmark [12] when quantizing EDSR×4 [24] to 2-bit.

2   Related Work

2.1   Single Image Super Resolution

Owing to the strength of deep convolutional neural networks, DCNN-based SR methods have gained great performance boosts and dominated the field of SISR. SRCNN [5] is the first to construct an end-to-end CNN-based mapping between the low- and high-resolution images. By increasing the network depth, VDSR [17] manifests significant performance improvements. Nevertheless, the increasing depth also weakens the capacity of overcoming the gradient vanishing problem and retaining image detail. Consequently, the skip-connection based blocks, such as the residual block [22] and the dense block [39], have become a basic component of the SR models [24,47]. Also, many other complex network structures like channel attention mechanism [30,46] and non-local attention [32,33] are also integrated into SR for a better performance. With the increasing popularity of CNNs on resource-hungry devices, developing efficient SR models has aroused much attention recently. Most works in this area are indicated to devising lightweight network architectures. For example, DRCN [18] and DRRN [37] adopt the recursive structure to increase the network depth while mitigating the model parameters. To escape from the expensive up-sampling operator, FSRCNN [6] introduces a de-convolutional layer while ESPCN [36] devises a sub-pixel convolution module. Many others resort to enhance the efficiency of intermediate feature representation [1,13,21,28]. However, these computation savings are very limited compared to costs from the full-precision convolution.

2.2 Quantized SR Models

As a promising technique to compress SR models, network quantization has received ever-growing attention [11,15,23,29,41,43]. Ma *et al.* [29] pioneered 1-bit quantization over the weights of SR model. Performance drops severely if binarizing the activations as well. To remedy this issue, the structure of SR models is often adjusted. For example, BAM [43] and BTM [15] introduce multiple feature map aggregations and skip connection layers. Except for 1-bit quantization, other ultra-low quantization precision such as 2-bit, 3-bit and 4-bit is discussed in many studies as well. To handle the unstable activation ranges, Li [23] proposed a symmetric layer-wise linear quantizer that adopts a trainable clipping bound to clamp the abnormal activations. As for weights, the same symmetric quantizer is adopted but the clipping variable is simply set to the maximum magnitude of the weights. Moreover, the quantized model is enhanced by the structured knowledge transfer from its full-precision counterpart. Wang *et al.* [41] chose to quantize all layers of SR models and perform both weights and activations quantization using a symmetric layer-wise quantizer equipped with a trainable clipping variable. DAQ [11] observes that each channel has non-zero distributions and the activation values also vary drastically to the input image. Based on this observation, a channel-wise distribution-aware quantizer is adopted where the activations are normalized before discretizing and de-normalized after convolution.

3 Methodology

3.1 Preliminaries

Previous low-bit SR adopt a symmetric quantizer to perform quantization upon the premise of activations and weights with a symmetric distribution. Specifically, denoting b as the bit-width, $\boldsymbol{x}$ as weights or activations, α as the clipping bound, the symmetric linear quantizer is defined as:

$$\bar{\boldsymbol{x}} = round\Big(\frac{clip(\boldsymbol{x}, \alpha)}{s}\Big) \cdot s, \tag{1}$$

where $clip(\boldsymbol{x}, \alpha) = min\big(max(\boldsymbol{x}, -\alpha), \alpha\big)$, $\bar{\boldsymbol{x}}$ is the de-quantized value of $\boldsymbol{x}$, $round(\cdot)$ rounds its input to the nearest integer and $s = \frac{2\alpha}{2^{b-1}-1}$ is the scaling factor that projects a floating-point number to a fixed-point integer. An appropriate α is crucial to the quantization performance since it not only eliminates outlier but refers to retaining details in the reconstructed images.

3.2 Our Insights

Despite the progress, the performance of earlier low-bit SR quantization methods [11,23,41] remains an open issue when quantizing the full-precision counterpart to ultra-low precision with a layer-wise quantizer. After an in-depth analysis, we attribute the poor performance to the contradiction between the layer-wise symmetric quantizer and the asymmetric activation distribution in SR models.

Concretely, we observe the activations from different SR models. Figure 1 shows the histograms, maximum and minimum of activations collected from the pre-trained EDSR [24] and RDN [47]. From the first column of Fig. 1, we realize that the activations of SR models are highly asymmetric in an irregular state. For example, the magnitude of the minimum activation is almost twice that of the maximum activation in EDSR. A similar phenomenon can be observed in RDN. Furthermore, as the second and third columns of Fig. 1 shows, the maximum and minimum of activations also vary drastically for different samples. Such an asymmetric activation distribution mostly results from the removal of BN layers in modern SR networks since BN reduces the scale information of images which however is crucial to SR tasks. Despite some studies retain BN layers, however, other remedies have to be taken to regain the performance. For example, SRResNet [22] propagates outputs of the first layer to the outputs of all following blocks, which causes asymmetric distributions as well. It is natural that the symmetric quantizer in existing studies cannot well fit the symmetric activation distributions, which we term as "quantization unfitness" in this paper.

To be specific, using only one clipping bound fails to handle the symmetric activations, whatever the value of α. To demonstrate this, we quantize the activations of RDN [47] to 3-bit using the quantizer in Eq. (1). As shown in Fig. 2(a), the lack of activations along the negative axis direction causes a waste of two quantization levels if α is set to a large value such as the maximum of the activation magnitude. The wastes are more severe as the bit-width goes down. Taking the activations in Fig. 2(a) as an example, we observe 37.5% are wasted in 3-bit quantization, while it increases sharply to 50% in 2-bit quantization. When it comes to a small α such as the absolute value of the minimum of activation magnitude, as illustrated in Fig. 2(b), though avoiding the waste on quantization levels, only the small-magnitude activations are covered, leading to large quantization error since many high-magnitude activations are quantized to a small quantization level, *i.e.*, α. Recall that SR models are sensitive to the scale information of images. Consequently, representing the large full-precision activations with a small quantization level inevitably brings about detail loss in the reconstructed high-resolution images, leading to significant quality degradation. Similar observations can be found if the same clipping bound is applied to all the input images since the maximum and minimum activations over different images also drastically vary as illustrated in Fig. 1. Thus, an appropriate quantizer is vital to the performance of quantized SR models.

3.3   Our Solutions

In the following, we first detail dynamic dual trainable bounds (DDTB) specifically designed to quantize activations of SR models. Then, we elaborate on our initializer for DDTB. Finally, we describe the quantizer for weights. The overall computational graph is presented in Fig. 3(a).

Activation Quantization. Our DDTB consists of two parts: 1) A layer-wise quantizer with a trainable upper bound and a trainable lower bound; 2) A dynamic gate controller with adaptive upper and lower bounds to the inputs.

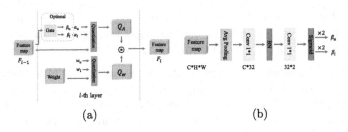

Fig. 3. (a) Computational graph in the l-th quantized convolutional layer. (b) Structure of the dynamic gate controller.

Dual Trainable Bounds: As mentioned in Sect. 3.2, only using one clipping variable to clamp the asymmetric activations leads to the "quantization unfitness" problem. To address this, we introduce two trainable clipping variables of α_u and α_l to respectively determine the upper bound and the lower bound of the activations. Equipped with these two dual trainable clipping variables, the quantized integer q for the input x can be obtained as:

$$q = round\left(\frac{clip(x, \alpha_l, \alpha_u)}{s}\right) + Z, \tag{2}$$

where $clip(x, \alpha_l, \alpha_u) = min\left(max(x, \alpha_l), \alpha_u\right)$, $Z = round(\frac{-\alpha_l}{s})$ is a zero-point integer corresponding to the real value 0. Accordingly, the scaling factor s is calculated as: $s = \frac{\alpha_u - \alpha_l}{2^b - 1}$. Finally, the de-quantized value $\bar{a}$ is:

$$\bar{a} = (q - Z) \cdot s. \tag{3}$$

Combining Eq. (2) and Eq. (3) completes our activation quantizer. As depicted in Fig. 2(c), the quantization levels generated by this quantization scheme well fit the activations when α_u and α_l are set to the maximum and minimum of activations, respectively. In order to accommodate samples with drastically varying ranges, we employ the stochastic gradient descent to adaptively learn α_u and α_l by minimizing the finally loss function. Denoting the clipped activations as $\tilde{a} = min(max(a, \alpha_l), \alpha_u)$, $\frac{\partial \bar{a}}{\partial \tilde{a}}$ is set to 1 by using the straight-through estimator (STE) [4]. Then, the gradients of α_u, α_l can be calculated as:

$$\frac{\partial \bar{a}}{\partial \alpha_u} = \frac{\partial \bar{a}}{\partial \tilde{a}} \frac{\partial \tilde{a}}{\partial \alpha_u} \overset{STE}{\approx} \begin{cases} 1, & a \geq \alpha_u \\ 0, & a \leq \alpha_u \end{cases}, \quad \frac{\partial \bar{a}}{\partial \alpha_l} = \frac{\partial \bar{a}}{\partial \tilde{a}} \frac{\partial \tilde{a}}{\partial \alpha_l} \overset{STE}{\approx} \begin{cases} 0, & a \geq \alpha_l \\ 1, & a \leq \alpha_l \end{cases}. \tag{4}$$

With the dual α_l and α_u, "quantization unfitness" can be alleviated. Note that, early study [16] also introduces two trainable parameters to determine the quantization range. This paper differs in: 1) [16] utilizes the center and radius of the quantization region to parameterize the quantization range while we explicitly introduce the upper and lower bounds. 2) [16] requires an expensive transformation to normalize activations to a fixed range before performing quantization.

3) Though trainable, the final quantization range is consistent with different inputs. Thus, we design a dynamic gate controller to provide an instance-wise quantization range adaptive to different inputs as illustrated in the next section.

Dynamic Gate Controller: Though the trainable upper and lower bounds partially alleviate the "quantization unfitness" problem, it is still suboptimal if only applying the same pair of (α_l, α_u) for different inputs since their activation ranges also dramatically vary as shown in Fig. 1. To address this issue, we devise a dynamic gate controller to adapt (α_l, α_u) to every input sample at runtime. Figure 3(b) depicts the structure of our gate controller, which is composed of a series of consequently stacked operators including two convolutional layers, a BN layer, a ReLU function, and a sigmoid function multiplied by 2. It takes the feature maps from the SR model as inputs and outputs two scaling coefficients β_l and β_u for each sample. Then, β_l and β_u are respectively used to re-scale the lower bound α_l and the upper bound α_u, results of which serve as the final clipping bounds of the corresponding input images as shown in Fig. 3(a). Denoting the $\alpha'_u = \beta_u \cdot \alpha_u$ and $\alpha'_l = \beta_l \cdot \alpha_l$, the clipped activations $\tilde{a}$ now can be reformulated as: $\tilde{a} = min(max(a, \alpha'_l), \alpha'_u)$. Similar to Eq. (4), the gradient is:

$$\frac{\partial \tilde{a}}{\partial \alpha'_u} = \frac{\partial \tilde{a}}{\partial \tilde{a}} \frac{\partial \tilde{a}}{\partial \alpha'_u} \overset{STE}{\approx} \begin{cases} 1, & a \geq \alpha'_u \\ 0, & a \leq \alpha'_u \end{cases}, \quad \frac{\partial \tilde{a}}{\partial \alpha'_l} = \frac{\partial \tilde{a}}{\partial \tilde{a}} \frac{\partial \tilde{a}}{\partial \alpha'_l} \overset{STE}{\approx} \begin{cases} 0, & a \geq \alpha'_l \\ 1, & a \leq \alpha'_l \end{cases}. \quad (5)$$

Then, the gradients of β_u, β_l, α_u, α_l can be obtained by the chain rule.

Our gate controller enables the clipping bounds adaptive to each of the input samples, with which the gate outputs are dynamically correlated at runtime. However, the extra costs on computation and storage of the gate controller are expensive, causing a contradiction with our motive to reduce the complexity of SR models. Thus, we reduce the its complexity from two perspectives: 1) We quantize the weights and activations of the gate to a 2-bit using the quantizer defined by Eq. (2) and Eq. (3). The clipping bounds are set as the maximum and minimum of the weights/activations. We empirically find that such a simple setting is sufficient. During the inference phase, the BN layer in gate controller can be folded into the previous convolutional layer [41] and the extra floating-point operations are very cheap. 2) We choose to apply our dynamic gate controller to some layers of the SR model. Concretely, we define the dynamic intensity in the l-th layer as $DI^l = V^l_{max} + V^l_{min}$, where V^l_{max} and V^l_{min} are variances of the maximum activations and minimum activations. The overhead is trivial as it forwards the training data to the full-precision network only once and can be completed offline. It is intuitive that a larger DI^l indicates a more dynamic activation range. Thus, we apply the dynamic gate to these layers with the top-$P\%$ largest dynamic intensity, where the gate ratio P is a hyper-parameter.

DDTB Initializer. One common way to initialize the α_u and α_l is to use the activation statistics such as the maximum and minimum values in the quantized network. However, for ultra-low bit cases, quantization error accumulates drastically, leading to unreliable statistics in deep layers. Instead, we derive the activation statistics by feeding a patch of images to the full-precision network, and then use the M-th and $(100 - M)$-th percentiles of obtained activations to initialize the α_u and α_l, which are more stable even in the ultra-low bit situation since the full-precision network is not challenged by the quantization error issue.

In addition, we observe that the β_u and β_l are either too small or too large in the early training phase due to the random initialization of gate weights, which obstacles the learning of α_u and α_l, and leads to inferior performance. Therefore, in the first K training epochs, we do not apply β_u and β_l to scaling α_u, α_l, and the gate is trained individually to push its outputs close to 1 whatever the inputs. After K epochs, we then apply β_u and β_l which start from a stable initial value, i.e., around 1. Then, the dynamic gate controller and the clipping variables are jointly trained to accommodate the drastically varying activation ranges. In all our experiments, we set $K = 5$.

Weight Quantization. The symmetric quantizer is also adopted to quantize weights in previous works. We suggest utilizing the asymmetric quantizer to quantize the weights. Similar to our activation quantization, an upper bound w_u and a lower bound w_l are used to clip the weight range: $\tilde{w} = min(max(\boldsymbol{w}, w_l), w_u)$. The quantized integer and de-quantized value can be obtained similar to Eq. (2) and Eq. (3). This quantization scheme is also compatible with the symmetric case when $w_u = -w_l$. In all our experiments, w_u is set to the 99-th percentile and w_u is set to 1-th percentile of the full-precision weights since we observe no performance gains if setting them to trainable parameters.

3.4   Training Loss

Following PAMS [23], we use L_1 loss and L_{SKT} loss in all the experiments. Denoting $D = \{I^i_{LR}, I^i_{HR}\}^N_{i=1}$ as the training dataset with N pairs of LR and HR images. The L_1 loss and L_{SKT} loss are defined as:

$$L_1 = \frac{1}{N} \sum_{i=1}^{N} \|I^i_{LR} - I^i_{HR}\|_1, \tag{6}$$

$$L_{SKT} = \frac{1}{N} \sum_{i=1}^{N} \|\frac{F'_S(I^i_{LR})}{\|F'_S(I^i_{LR})\|_2} - \frac{F'_T(I^i_{LR})}{\|F'_T(I^i_{LR})\|_2}\|_2, \tag{7}$$

where $F'_S(I^i_{LR})$ and $F'_T(I^i_{LR})$ are structure features of I^i_{LR} from the quantized network and the full-precision network, respectively. The structure feature can be calculated by $F'(I^i_{LR}) = \sum_{c=1}^{N} |F_c(I^i_{LR})|^2 \in \mathbb{R}^{H \times W}$, where $F(I^i_{LR}) \in \mathbb{R}^{C \times H \times W}$ is the feature map after the last layer in the high-level feature extractor. Then, the overall loss function L is:

$$L = L_1 + \lambda L_{SKT}. \tag{8}$$

where $\lambda = 1,000$ in all our experiments.

Table 1. PSNR/SSIM comparisons between existing low-bit SR methods and our DDTB in quantizing EDSR [24] of scale 4 and scale 2 to the low-bit format. Results of the full-precision model are displayed below the dataset name.

Model	Dataset	Bit	Dorefa [49]	TF Lite [14]	PACT [3]	PAMS [23]	DDTB(Ours)
EDSR ×4	Set5 [2]	2	29.90/0.850	29.96/0.851	30.03/0.854	29.51/0.835	**30.97/0.876**
	32.10/0.894	3	30.76/0.870	31.05/0.877	30.98/0.876	27.25/0.780	**31.52/0.883**
		4	30.91/0.873	31.54/0.884	31.32/0.882	31.59/0.885	**31.85/0.889**
	Set14 [22]	2	27.08/0.744	27.12/0.745	27.21/0.747	26.79/0.734	**27.87/0.764**
	28.58/0.781	3	27.66/0.759	27.92/0.765	27.87/0.764	25.24/0.673	**28.18/0.771**
		4	27.78/0.762	28.20/0.772	28.07/0.769	28.20/0.773	**28.39/0.777**
	BSD100 [31]	2	26.66/0.704	26.68/0.705	26.73/0.706	26.45/0.696	**27.09/0.719**
	27.56/0.736	3	26.97/0.716	27.12/0.721	27.09/0.719	25.38/0.644	**27.30/0.727**
		4	27.04/0.719	27.31/0.727	27.21/0.724	27.32/0.728	**27.44/0.732**
	Urban100 [12]	2	24.02/0.705	24.03/0.705	24.12/0.708	23.72/0.688	**24.82/0.742**
	26.04/0.785	3	24.59/0.732	24.85/0.743	24.82/0.741	22.76/0.641	**25.33/0.761**
		4	24.73/0.739	25.28/0.760	25.05/0.751	25.32/0.762	**25.69/0.774**
EDSR ×2	Set5 [2]	2	36.12/0.952	36.23/0.952	36.58/0.955	35.30/0.946	**37.25/0.958**
	37.93/0.960	3	37.13/0.957	37.33/0.957	37.36/0.958	36.76/0.955	**37.51/0.958**
		4	37.22/0.958	37.64/0.959	37.57/0.958	37.67/0.958	**37.72/0.959**
	Set14 [22]	2	32.09/0.904	32.14/0.904	32.38/0.907	31.63/0.899	**32.87/0.911**
	33.46/0.916	3	32.73/0.910	32.98/0.912	32.99/0.912	32.50/0.907	**33.17/0.914**
		4	32.82/0.911	33.24/0.914	33.20/0.914	33.20/0.915	**33.35/0.916**
	BSD100 [31]	2	31.03/0.884	31.07/0.885	31.26/0.887	30.66/0.879	**31.67/0.893**
	32.10/0.899	3	31.57/0.892	31.76/0.894	31.77/0.894	31.38/0.889	**31.89/0.896**
		4	31.63/0.893	31.94/0.896	31.93/0.897	31.94/0.897	**32.01/0.898**
	Urban100 [12]	2	28.71/0.886	28.77/0.886	29.22/0.894	28.11/0.875	**30.34/0.910**
	31.71/0.925	3	30.00/0.906	30.48/0.912	30.57/0.912	29.50/0.898	**31.01/0.919**
		4	30.17/0.908	31.11/0.919	31.09/0.919	31.10/0.919	**31.39/0.922**

4   Experiments

4.1   Implementation Details

All the models are trained on the training set of DIV2K including 800 images [38], and tested on four standard benchmarks including Set5 [2], Set14 [22], BSD100 [31] and Urban100 [12]. Two upscaling factors of ×2 and ×4 are evaluated. The quantized SR models include EDSR [24], RDN [47], and SRResNet [22]. We quantize them to 4, 3, and 2-bit and compare with the SOTA competitors including DoReFa [49], Tensorflow Lite (TF Lite) [14], PACT [3], and PAMS [23]. The PSNR and SSIM [42] over the Y channel are reported.

The full-precision models and compared quantization methods are implemented based on their open-source code. For the quantized models, following PAMS [23], we quantize both weights and activations of the high-level feature extraction module. The low-level feature extraction and reconstruction modules are set to the full-precision[1]. The batch size is set to 16 and the optimizer is Adam [19] with $\beta_1 = 0.9$, $\beta_2 = 0.999$ and $\epsilon = 10^{-8}$. We set the initial learning rate to 10^{-4} and halve it every 10 epochs. For EDSR, the gate ratio P is set to 30 and the initialization coefficient M is 99. As for RDN, P and M are 50 and

---

[1] Results of fully quantized SR models are provided in the supplementary material.

Table 2. PSNR/SSIM comparisons between existing low-bit SR methods and our DDTB in quantizing RDN [47] of scale 4 and scale 2 to the low-bit format. Results of the full-precision model are displayed below the dataset name.

Model	Dataset	Bit	Dorefa [49]	TF Lite [14]	PACT [3]	PAMS [23]	DDTB(Ours)
RDN ×4	Set5 [2]	2	29.90/0.849	29.93/0.850	28.78/0.820	29.73/0.843	**30.57/0.867**
	32.24/0.896	3	31.24/0.881	30.13/0.854	31.30/0.879	29.54/0.838	**31.49/0.883**
		4	31.51/0.885	31.08/0.874	31.93/0.890	30.44/0.862	**31.97/0.891**
	Set14 [22]	2	27.08/0.743	27.11/0.744	26.33/0.717	26.96/0.739	**27.56/0.757**
	28.67/0.784	3	28.02/0.769	27.21/0.744	28.06/0.767	26.82/0.734	**28.17/0.772**
		4	28.21/0.773	27.98/0.764	28.44/0.778	27.54/0.753	**28.49/0.780**
	BDS100 [31]	2	26.65/0.703	26.64/0.703	26.16/0.681	26.57/0.700	**26.91/0.714**
	27.63/0.738	3	27.20/0.724	26.71/0.705	27.21/0.722	26.47/0.696	**27.30/0.728**
		4	27.30/0.727	27.16/0.720	27.46/0.732	26.87/0.710	**27.49/0.735**
	Urban100 [12]	2	23.99/0.702	23.99/0.703	23.38/0.672	23.87/0.696	**24.50/0.728**
	26.29/0.792	3	25.07/0.754	24.27/0.713	25.17/0.754	23.83/0.692	**25.35/0.764**
		4	25.36/0.764	25.25/0.755	25.83/0.779	24.52/0.726	**25.90/0.783**
RDN ×2	Set5 [2]	2	36.20/0.952	36.12/0.951	36.55/0.954	35.45/0.946	**36.76/0.955**
	38.05/0.961	3	37.44/0.958	36.38/0.953	37.39/0.958	35.25/0.942	**37.61/0.959**
		4	37.61/0.959	36.83/0.955	37.82/0.959	36.53/0.953	**37.88/0.960**
	Set14 [22]	2	32.14/0.904	32.08/0.903	32.34/0.905	31.67/0.899	**32.54/0.908**
	33.59/0.917	3	33.08/0.914	32.46/0.907	33.08/0.914	31.52/0.893	**33.26/0.915**
		4	33.23/0.915	32.72/0.910	33.47/0.916	32.39/0.905	**33.51/0.917**
	BSD100 [31]	2	31.06/0.885	31.01/0.884	31.21/0.886	30.69/0.879	**31.44/0.890**
	32.20/0.900	3	31.87/0.896	31.34/0.888	31.86/0.896	30.62/0.874	**31.91/0.897**
		4	31.98/0.897	31.63/0.892	32.09/0.898	31.27/0.885	**32.12/0.899**
	Urban100 [12]	2	28.81/0.888	28.72/0.885	29.15/0.892	28.14/0.874	**29.77/0.903**
	32.13/0.927	3	30.96/0.918	29.83/0.903	30.97/0.918	28.30/0.873	**31.10/0.920**
		4	31.33/0.922	30.49/0.912	31.69/0.925	29.70/0.898	**31.76/0.926**

95. For SRResNet, $P = 10$ and $M = 99$. The total training epochs are set to 60. The training images are pre-processed by subtracting the mean RGB. During training, random horizontal flip and vertical rotation are adopted to augment data. All experiments are implemented with PyTorch [34].

4.2   Experimental Results

Table 1, Table 2, and Table 3 respectively show the quantitative results of EDSR, RDN, and SRResNet on different datasets. Details are discussed below.

Evaluation on EDSR. In the case of 4-bit, our DDTB outperforms the advanced PAMS by a large margin. For instance, for 4-bit EDSR×4, DDTB obtains 0.37 dB PSNR gains on Urban100. More noticeable improvements can be observed when performing ultra-low bit quantization. For instance, our DDTB obtains performance gains by 0.94 dB, 0.66 dB, 0.36 dB, and 0.70 dB on Set5, Set14, BSD100, and Urban100 when quantizing EDSR×4 to 2-bit.

Evaluation on RDN. When quantizing the model to 4-bit, our DDTB slightly outperforms the existing SOTA of PACT. When it comes to ultra-low bit, the superior performance is in particular obvious. In detail, for 2-bit RDN×4, the performance gains of our DDTB are 0.64 dB, 0.45 dB, 0.26 dB, and 0.51 dB on Set5, Set14, BSD100, and Urban100.

Evaluation on SRResNet. The results of SRResNet also manifest that the performance gains of our DDTB are more prominent with ultra-low precision. For 2-bit SRResNet×4, our DDTB improves the performance by 0.65 dB, 0.47 dB, 0.30 dB, and 0.69 dB on Set5, Set14, BSD100, and Urban100, while the performance gains are 1.15 dB, 0.79 dB, 0.67 dB, and 1.80 dB for 2-bit SRResNet×2.

Table 3. PSNR/SSIM comparison between existing low-bit SR methods and our DDTB in quantizing SRResNet [22] of scale 4 and scale 2 to the low-bit format. Results of the full-precision model are displayed below the dataset name.

Model	Dataset	Bit	Dorefa [49]	TF Lite [14]	PACT [3]	PAMS [23]	DDTB(Ours)
SRResNet ×4	Set5 [2]	2	30.25/0.860	30.33/0.861	30.86/0.874	30.25/0.861	**31.51/0.887**
	32.07/0.893	3	30.34/0.862	31.58/0.886	31.62/0.887	31.68/0.888	**31.85/0.890**
		4	30.32/0.861	31.82/0.890	31.85/0.890	31.88/0.891	**31.97/0.892**
	Set14 [22]	2	27.33/0.749	27.39/0.751	27.76/0.761	27.36/0.750	**28.23/0.773**
	28.50/0.780	3	27.39/0.751	28.24/0.773	28.25/0.773	28.27/0.774	**28.39/0.776**
		4	27.41/0.751	28.40/0.777	28.38/0.775	28.41/0.777	**28.46/0.778**
	BSD100 [31]	2	26.78/0.708	26.80/0.709	27.03/0.717	26.79/0.709	**27.33/0.728**
	27.52/0.735	3	26.81/0.709	27.31/0.726	27.33/0.727	27.34/0.728	**27.44/0.731**
		4	26.82/0.709	27.42/0.730	27.41/0.730	27.45/0.732	**27.48/0.733**
	Urban100 [12]	2	24.17/0.711	24.21/0.713	24.68/0.733	24.19/0.713	**25.37/0.762**
	25.86/0.779	3	24.24/0.714	25.33/0.759	25.39/0.761	25.46/0.765	**25.64/0.770**
		4	24.26/0.714	25.62/0.780	25.61/0.769	25.68/0.773	**25.77/0.776**
SRResNet ×2	Set5 [2]	2	35.27/0.946	35.34/0.946	36.31/0.953	34.75/0.942	**37.46/0.958**
	37.89/0.960	3	35.30/0.946	37.50/0.958	37.42/0.958	37.52/0.958	**37.67/0.959**
		4	35.39/0.946	37.69/0.959	37.65/0.959	37.71/0.959	**37.78/0.960**
	Set14 [22]	2	31.54/0.899	31.61/0.899	32.23/0.905	31.31/0.896	**33.02/0.913**
	33.40/0.916	3	31.56/0.899	33.05/0.913	32.92/0.911	33.09/0.914	**33.24/0.915**
		4	31.63/0.899	33.26/0.915	33.24/0.915	33.26/0.915	**33.32/0.916**
	BSD100 [31]	2	30.61/0.879	30.66/0.879	31.11/0.885	30.48/0.877	**31.78/0.895**
	32.08/0.898	3	30.62/0.879	31.81/0.894	31.70/0.893	31.85/0.896	**31.95/0.897**
		4	30.67/0.880	31.99/0.897	31.96/0.897	31.99/0.897	**32.03/0.898**
	Urban100 [12]	2	27.98/0.871	28.04/0.872	28.77/0.885	27.86/0.868	**30.57/0.913**
	31.60/0.923	3	27.99/0.871	30.64/0.913	30.43/0.910	30.69/0.914	**31.15/0.919**
		4	28.06/0.872	31.25/0.920	31.19/0.919	31.20/0.920	**31.40/0.921**

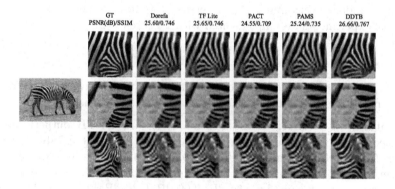

Fig. 4. Reconstructed results of 2-bit EDSR×4

Qualitative Visualizations. Figure 4 exhibits the qualitative visualizations of 2-bit EDSR[2]. Compared with others methods, the reconstructed HR image of our DDTB provides sharper edges and richer details.

---

[2] More qualitative visualizations are presented in the supplementary material.

Above results demonstrate the effectiveness of our DDTB and also verify the correctness of our motivation in designing an appropriate quantizer adaptive to the activation distribution. Moreover, it is worth noticing that DDTB provides stable improvements over different SR models and bit-widths. For example, PAMS obtains the best results among the compared methods when quantizing EDSR×4 to 4-bit, but it was outperformed by TF Lite in 3-bit and PACT in 2-bit. In contrast, DDTB achieves the best results in all these three bit-widths. Such stability further illustrates the advanced generalization of DDTB.

Table 4. Complexity analysis. The number in brackets indicates the parameters in the high-level feature extraction module. We compute BOPs by generating a 1920 × 1080 image (upscaling factor ×4). Results of 2-bit are displayed and more can be found in the supplementary.

Model	Bit	Params	Gate Params(*ratio*)	BOPs	Gate BOPs(*ratio*)
EDSR [24]	32	1.52 M	0	532T	0
EDSR_DDTB	2	0.41 M(0.08 M)	0.6%	219T	0.0000013%
RDN [47]	32	22.3 M	0	6038T	0
RDN_DDTB	2	1.76 M(1.42 M)	2.8%	239T	0.0000066%
SRResNet [22]	32	1.543 M	0	591T	0
SRResNet_DDTB	2	0.44 M(0.07 M)	0.1%	278T	0.0000002%

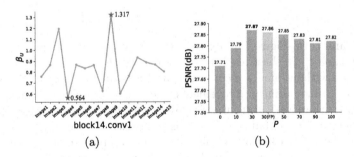

(a)   (b)

Fig. 5. (a) The β_u in 2-bit EDSR×4. (b) Influence of the gate ratio P in 2-bit EDSR×4.

4.3   Model Analysis

To measure the complexity of the quantized network, we use the parameters and Bit-Operations (BOPs) [40] as the metric. BOPs are the number of multiplication operations multiplied by the bit-widths of two operands. As shown in Table 4, DDTB significantly reduces the model size and computation cost. And the extra computation cost and size of our dynamic gate controller are negligible. Note that, the full-precision low-level feature extraction and reconstruction modules occupy most of the memory and computation costs when quantizing the network to the case of ultra-low bit. Figure 5(a) displays the β_u values of 15 randomly selected test images. We select the results of 2-bit EDSR×4. It can be seen that the β_u of different images varies a lot, which proves that the dynamic gate controller can well adjust the clipping bounds adaptive to the input images.

4.4 Ablation Study

This section conducts the ablation study of our DDTB. All experiments are conducted with 2-bit EDSR×4.

Table 5. Effect of different components in our methods. "DW": dual bounds for weight quantization. "DI": DDTB initializer. The PSNR/SSIM are reported.

Components			Results			
DDTB	DW	DI	Set5 [2]	Set14 [22]	BSD100 [31]	Urban100 [12]
PAMS [23]			29.51/0.835	26.79/0.734	26.45/0.696	23.72/0.688
✓			30.00/0.853	27.15/0.745	26.69/0.705	24.06/0.707
	✓		29.82/0.846	27.02/0.741	26.62/0.702	23.98/0.702
	✓	✓	30.19/0.852	27.30/0.747	26.76/0.703	24.19/0.711
✓		✓	30.23/0.858	27.33/0.750	26.78/0.709	24.23/0.714
✓	✓		30.80/0.871	27.68/0.760	26.99/0.717	24.64/0.735
✓	✓	✓	**30.97/0.876**	**27.87/0.764**	**27.09/0.719**	**24.82/0.742**

Gate Parameters. Figure 5(b) exhibits the results of different gate ratio P on Set14 [22] dataset. The best result is observed when the P is set to 30. Compared with the case without our gate controller, its PSNR increases by 0.16 dB. Using more layers cannot bring improvements and even does slight damage to the performance. Moreover, using the full-precision gate does not provide better results, which indicates that a 2-bit gate is sufficient. To reduce search overhead, we find the best P on the model of scale 4 and apply it to the corresponding model of scale 2. Though not optimal, it is sufficient to show SOTA performance.

Components. We use PAMS as the baseline to show the effect of different components including dynamic dual training bounds (DDTB) for activation quantization, dual bounds for weight quantization, and DDTB initializer (DI). Table 5 shows the experimental results. When DDTB and DW are individually added, the performance increases compared with the baseline. The DDTB significantly boosts the baseline which proves its ability to fit the asymmetric activation distribution. By combining the initializer, the performance continues to increase. When all of them are applied, the best performance can be obtained.

5   Conclusion

This paper presents a novel quantization method, termed Dynamic Dual Trainable Bounds (DDTB) to solve the asymmetric activation distribution in the DCNN-based SR model. Our DDTB introduces trainable upper and lower bounds, to which a dynamic gate controller is applied in order to adapt to the input sample at runtime. The gate is represented in a 2-bit format and only applied to part of the network to minimize the extra overhead. Moreover, we design a special DDTB initializer for stable training. Our DDTB shows its superiority over many competitors with different quantized SR models on many benchmarks, especially when performing ultra-low precision quantization.

Acknowledgements. This work was supported by the National Science Fund for Distinguished Young Scholars (No.62025603), the National Natural Science Foundation of China (No. U21B2037, No. 62176222, No. 62176223, No. 62176226, No. 62072386, No. 62072387, No. 62072389, and No. 62002305), Guangdong Basic and Applied Basic Research Foundation (No.2019B1515120049), and the Natural Science Foundation of Fujian Province of China (No.2021J01002).

References

1. Ahn, N., Kang, B., Sohn, K.A.: Fast, accurate, and lightweight super-resolution with cascading residual network. In: Proceedings of the European Conference on Computer Vision (ECCV), pp. 252–268 (2018)
2. Bevilacqua, M., Roumy, A., Guillemot, C., Morel, M.L.A.: Low-complexity single-image super-resolution based on nonnegative neighbor embedding. In: British Machine Vision Conference (BMVC) (2012)
3. Choi, J., Wang, Z., Venkataramani, S., Chuang, P.I.J., Srinivasan, V., Gopalakrishnan, K.: Pact: parameterized clipping activation for quantized neural networks. arXiv preprint arXiv:1805.06085 (2018)
4. Courbariaux, M., Hubara, I., Soudry, D., El-Yaniv, R., Bengio, Y.: Binarized neural networks: training deep neural networks with weights and activations constrained to+ 1 or-1. arXiv preprint arXiv:1602.02830 (2016)
5. Dong, C., Loy, C.C., He, K., Tang, X.: Learning a deep convolutional network for image super-resolution. In: Proceedings of the European Conference on Computer Vision (ECCV), pp. 184–199 (2014)
6. Dong, C., Loy, C.C., Tang, X.: Accelerating the super-resolution convolutional neural network. In: Proceedings of the European Conference on Computer Vision (ECCV), pp. 391–407 (2016)
7. Esser, S.K., McKinstry, J.L., Bablani, D., Appuswamy, R., Modha, D.S.: Learned step size quantization. In: Proceedings of the International Conference on Learning Representations (ICLR) (2020)
8. Han, S., Pool, J., Tran, J., Dally, W.J., et al.: Learning both weights and connections for efficient neural network. In: Proceedings of the Advances in Neural Information Processing Systems (NeurIPS), pp. 1135–1143 (2015)
9. Haris, M., Shakhnarovich, G., Ukita, N.: Deep back-projection networks for super-resolution. In: Proceedings of the IEEE/CVF Conference on Computer Vision and Pattern Recognition (CVPR), pp. 1664–1673 (2018)

10. Hinton, G., Vinyals, O., Dean, J.: Distilling the knowledge in a neural network. arXiv preprint arXiv:1503.02531 (2015)
11. Hong, C., Kim, H., Baik, S., Oh, J., Lee, K.M.: DAQ: channel-wise distribution-aware quantization for deep image super-resolution networks. In: Proceedings of the IEEE/CVF Winter Conference on Applications of Computer Vision (WACV), pp. 2675–2684 (2022)
12. Huang, J.B., Singh, A., Ahuja, N.: Single image super-resolution from transformed self-exemplars. In: Proceedings of the IEEE/CVF Conference on Computer Vision and Pattern Recognition (CVPR), pp. 5197–5206 (2015)
13. Hui, Z., Gao, X., Yang, Y., Wang, X.: Lightweight image super-resolution with information multi-distillation network. In: Proceedings of the 27th ACM international conference on multimedia (ACM MM), pp. 2024–2032 (2019)
14. Jacob, B., et al.: Quantization and training of neural networks for efficient integer-arithmetic-only inference. In: Proceedings of the IEEE/CVF Conference on Computer Vision and Pattern Recognition (CVPR), pp. 2704–2713 (2018)
15. Jiang, X., Wang, N., Xin, J., Li, K., Yang, X., Gao, X.: Training binary neural network without batch normalization for image super-resolution. In: Proceedings of the AAAI Conference on Artificial Intelligence (AAAI), pp. 1700–1707 (2021)
16. Jung, S., et al.: Learning to quantize deep networks by optimizing quantization intervals with task loss. In: Proceedings of the IEEE/CVF Conference on Computer Vision and Pattern Recognition (CVPR), pp. 4350–4359 (2019)
17. Kim, J., Lee, J.K., Lee, K.M.: Accurate image super-resolution using very deep convolutional networks. In: Proceedings of the IEEE/CVF Conference on Computer Vision and Pattern Recognition (CVPR), pp. 1646–1654 (2016)
18. Kim, J., Lee, J.K., Lee, K.M.: Deeply-recursive convolutional network for image super-resolution. In: Proceedings of the IEEE/CVF Conference on Computer Vision and Pattern Recognition (CVPR), pp. 1637–1645 (2016)
19. Kingma, D.P., Ba, J.: Adam: a method for stochastic optimization. In: Proceedings of the International Conference on Learning Representations (ICLR) (2014)
20. Krishnamoorthi, R.: Quantizing deep convolutional networks for efficient inference: a whitepaper. arXiv preprint arXiv:1806.08342 (2018)
21. Lai, W.S., Huang, J.B., Ahuja, N., Yang, M.H.: Deep laplacian pyramid networks for fast and accurate super-resolution. In: Proceedings of the IEEE/CVF Conference on Computer Vision and Pattern Recognition (CVPR), pp. 624–632 (2017)
22. Ledig, C., et al.: Photo-realistic single image super-resolution using a generative adversarial network. In: Proceedings of the IEEE/CVF Conference on Computer Vision and Pattern Recognition (CVPR), pp. 4681–4690 (2017)
23. Li, H., et al.: PAMS: quantized super-resolution via parameterized max scale. In: Vedaldi, A., Bischof, H., Brox, T., Frahm, J.-M. (eds.) ECCV 2020. LNCS, vol. 12370, pp. 564–580. Springer, Cham (2020). https://doi.org/10.1007/978-3-030-58595-2_34
24. Lim, B., Son, S., Kim, H., Nah, S., Mu Lee, K.: Enhanced deep residual networks for single image super-resolution. In: Proceedings of the IEEE/CVF Conference on Computer Vision and Pattern Recognition Workshops (CVPRW), pp. 136–144 (2017)
25. Lin, M., et al.: HRank: filter pruning using high-rank feature map. In: Proceedings of the IEEE/CVF Conference on Computer Vision and Pattern Recognition (CVPR), pp. 1529–1538 (2020)
26. Lin, M., et al.: Rotated binary neural network. In: Proceedings of the Advances in Neural Information Processing Systems (NeurIPS), pp. 7474–7485 (2020)

27. Liu, Z., Shen, Z., Savvides, M., Cheng, K.-T.: ReActNet: towards precise binary neural network with generalized activation functions. In: Vedaldi, A., Bischof, H., Brox, T., Frahm, J.-M. (eds.) ECCV 2020. LNCS, vol. 12359, pp. 143–159. Springer, Cham (2020). https://doi.org/10.1007/978-3-030-58568-6_9

28. Luo, X., Xie, Y., Zhang, Y., Qu, Y., Li, C., Fu, Y.: LatticeNet: towards lightweight image super-resolution with lattice block. In: Proceedings of the European Conference on Computer Vision (ECCV), pp. 272–289 (2020)

29. Ma, Y., Xiong, H., Hu, Z., Ma, L.: Efficient super resolution using binarized neural network. In: Proceedings of the IEEE/CVF Conference on Computer Vision and Pattern Recognition Workshops (CVPRW), pp. 694–703 (2019)

30. Magid, S.A., et al.: Dynamic high-pass filtering and multi-spectral attention for image super-resolution. In: Proceedings of the IEEE/CVF International Conference on Computer Vision (ICCV), pp. 4288–4297 (2021)

31. Martin, D., Fowlkes, C., Tal, D., Malik, J.: A database of human segmented natural images and its application to evaluating segmentation algorithms and measuring ecological statistics. In: Proceedings of the IEEE/CVF International Conference on Computer Vision (ICCV), pp. 416–423 (2001)

32. Mei, Y., Fan, Y., Zhou, Y.: Image super-resolution with non-local sparse attention. In: Proceedings of the IEEE/CVF Conference on Computer Vision and Pattern Recognition (CVPR), pp. 3517–3526 (2021)

33. Mei, Y., Fan, Y., Zhou, Y., Huang, L., Huang, T.S., Shi, H.: Image super-resolution with cross-scale non-local attention and exhaustive self-exemplars mining. In: Proceedings of the IEEE/CVF Conference on Computer Vision and Pattern Recognition (CVPR), pp. 5690–5699 (2020)

34. Paszke, A., et al.: PyTorch: an imperative style, high-performance deep learning library. In: Proceedings of the Advances in Neural Information Processing Systems (NeurIPS), pp. 8026–8037 (2019)

35. Rastegari, M., Ordonez, V., Redmon, J., Farhadi, A.: XNOR-Net: ImageNet classification using binary convolutional neural networks. In: Leibe, B., Matas, J., Sebe, N., Welling, M. (eds.) ECCV 2016. LNCS, vol. 9908, pp. 525–542. Springer, Cham (2016). https://doi.org/10.1007/978-3-319-46493-0_32

36. Shi, W., et al.: Real-time single image and video super-resolution using an efficient sub-pixel convolutional neural network. In: Proceedings of the IEEE/CVF Conference on Computer Vision and Pattern Recognition (CVPR), pp. 1874–1883 (2016)

37. Tai, Y., Yang, J., Liu, X.: Image super-resolution via deep recursive residual network. In: Proceedings of the IEEE/CVF Conference on Computer Vision and Pattern Recognition (CVPR), pp. 3147–3155 (2017)

38. Timofte, R., Agustsson, E., Van Gool, L., Yang, M.H., Zhang, L.: NTIRE 2017 challenge on single image super-resolution: methods and results. In: Proceedings of the IEEE/CVF Conference on Computer Vision and Pattern Recognition Workshops (CVPRW), pp. 114–125 (2017)

39. Tong, T., Li, G., Liu, X., Gao, Q.: Image super-resolution using dense skip connections. In: Proceedings of the IEEE/CVF Conference on Computer Vision and Pattern Recognition (CVPR), pp. 4799–4807 (2017)

40. Van Baalen, M., et al.: Bayesian bits: unifying quantization and pruning. In: Proceedings of the Advances in Neural Information Processing Systems (NeurIPS), pp. 5741–5752 (2020)

41. Wang, H., Chen, P., Zhuang, B., Shen, C.: Fully quantized image super-resolution networks. In: Proceedings of the 29th ACM International Conference on Multimedia (ACM MM), pp. 639–647 (2021)

42. Wang, Z., Bovik, A.C., Sheikh, H.R., Simoncelli, E.P.: Image quality assessment: from error visibility to structural similarity. IEEE Trans. Image Process. (TIP) **13**(4), 600–612 (2004)
43. Xin, J., Wang, N., Jiang, X., Li, J., Huang, H., Gao, X.: Binarized neural network for single image super resolution. In: Vedaldi, A., Bischof, H., Brox, T., Frahm, J.-M. (eds.) ECCV 2020. LNCS, vol. 12349, pp. 91–107. Springer, Cham (2020). https://doi.org/10.1007/978-3-030-58548-8_6
44. Xu, X., et al.: Quantization of fully convolutional networks for accurate biomedical image segmentation. In: Proceedings of the IEEE/CVF Conference on Computer Vision and Pattern Recognition (CVPR), pp. 8300–8308 (2018)
45. Zhang, R., Chung, A.C.: MedQ: lossless ultra-low-bit neural network quantization for medical image segmentation. Med. Image Anal. **73**, 102200 (2021)
46. Zhang, Y., Li, K., Li, K., Wang, L., Zhong, B., Fu, Y.: Image super-resolution using very deep residual channel attention networks. In: Proceedings of the European Conference on Computer Vision (ECCV), pp. 286–301 (2018)
47. Zhang, Y., Tian, Y., Kong, Y., Zhong, B., Fu, Y.: Residual dense network for image super-resolution. In: Proceedings of the IEEE/CVF Conference on Computer Vision and Pattern Recognition (CVPR), pp. 2472–2481 (2018)
48. Zhong, Y., et al.: IntraQ: Learning synthetic images with intra-class heterogeneity for zero-shot network quantization. In: Proceedings of the IEEE/CVF Conference on Computer Vision and Pattern Recognition (CVPR), pp. 12339–12348 (2022)
49. Zhou, S., Wu, Y., Ni, Z., Zhou, X., Wen, H., Zou, Y.: DoReFa-Net: training low bitwidth convolutional neural networks with low bitwidth gradients. arXiv preprint arXiv:1606.06160 (2016)

OSFormer: One-Stage Camouflaged Instance Segmentation with Transformers

Jialun Pei[1], Tianyang Cheng[2], Deng-Ping Fan[3(✉)], He Tang[2],
Chuanbo Chen[2], and Luc Van Gool[3]

[1] School of Computer Science and Technology, HUST, Wuhan, China
[2] School of Software Engineering, HUST, Wuhan, China
[3] Computer Vision Lab, ETH Zurich, Zurich, Switzerland
dengpfan@gmail.com

Abstract. We present **OSFormer**, the first one-stage transformer
framework for camouflaged instance segmentation (CIS). OSFormer is
based on two key designs. First, we design a **location-sensing transformer** (LST) to obtain the location label and instance-aware parameters by introducing the location-guided queries and the blend-convolution
feed-forward network. Second, we develop a **coarse-to-fine fusion**
(CFF) to merge diverse context information from the LST encoder and
CNN backbone. Coupling these two components enables OSFormer to
efficiently blend local features and long-range context dependencies for
predicting camouflaged instances. Compared with two-stage frameworks,
our OSFormer reaches 41% AP and achieves good convergence efficiency
without requiring enormous training data, *i.e.*, only 3,040 samples under
60 epochs. Code link: https://github.com/PJLallen/OSFormer.

Keywords: Camouflage · Instance segmentation · Transformer

1 Introduction

Camouflage is a powerful and widespread means of avoiding detection or recognition that stems from biology [51]. In nature, camouflage objects have evolved a
suite of concealment strategies to deceive perceptual and cognitive mechanisms of
prey or predators, such as background matching, self-shadow concealment, oblit-
erative shading, disruptive coloration, and distractive markings [11,48]. These
defensive behaviors make camouflaged object detection (COD) a very challenging
task compared to generic object detection [5,32,42,44,50]. COD is dedicated to
distinguishing camouflaged objects with a high degree of intrinsic similarity with
backgrounds [16]. It is essential to use computer vision models to assist human
visual and perceptual systems for COD, such as polyp segmentation [17,28], lung
infection segmentation [18], wildlife protection, and recreational art [10].

Thanks to the build of large-scale and standard benchmarks like
COD10K [16], CAMO [31], CAMO++ [30], and NC4K [37], the performance

---

J. Pei and T. Cheng—Equal contributions.

© The Author(s), under exclusive license to Springer Nature Switzerland AG 2022
S. Avidan et al. (Eds.): ECCV 2022, LNCS 13678, pp. 19–37, 2022.
https://doi.org/10.1007/978-3-031-19797-0_2

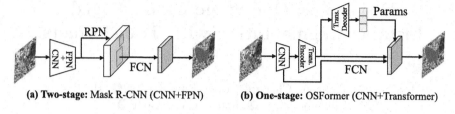

(a) **Two-stage:** Mask R-CNN (CNN+FPN)   (b) **One-stage:** OSFormer (CNN+Transformer)

Fig. 1. Framework comparisons of Mask R-CNN [23] and the proposed OSFormer.

of COD has received significant progress. However, COD only separates camouflaged objects from the scene at region-level while ignoring further instance-level identification. Recently, Le *et al.* [30] presented a new camouflaged instance segmentation (CIS) benchmark and a camouflage fusion learning framework. Capturing camouflaged instances can provide more clues (*e.g.*, semantic category, the number of objects) in real-world scenarios, thus CIS is more challenging.

Compared to generic instance segmentation [23], CIS needs to be performed in more complex scenarios with high feature similarity and results in class-agnostic masks. Moreover, various instances may display different camouflage strategies in a scene, and they may combine to form mutual camouflage. These derived ensemble camouflages make the CIS task even more daunting. When humans gaze at a heavily camouflaged scene, the visual system will instinctively sweep across a series of local scopes throughout the whole scene to search for valuable clues [38,45]. Inspired by this visual mechanism, we present a novel location-aware CIS approach that meticulously captures crucial information at all positions (*i.e.*, *local context*) in a *global perspective* and directly generates camouflaged instance masks (*i.e.*, *one-stage* model).

Thanks to the rise of the transformer [52] in the visual domain, we can employ self-attention and cross-attention to capture long-range dependencies and build global content-aware interactions [5]. Although the transformer model has shown strong performance on some dense prediction tasks [22,53,54,60], it requires embracing large-scale training data and longer training epochs. However, there is currently only limited instance-level training data available as a brand-new downstream task. To this end, we propose a **location-sensing transformer (LST)** based on [65] to achieve faster convergence and higher performance with fewer training samples. To dynamically yield location-guided queries for each input image, we grid the multi-scale global features output from the LST encoder into a set of feature patches with varying local information. Compared to zero initialization of object queries in vanilla DETR [5], the proposed location-guided queries can lead to focus on location-specific features and interact with global features through cross-attention to gain the instance-aware embeddings. This design effectively speeds up convergence and significantly improves detecting camouflaged instances. To enhance local perception and the correlation between neighboring tokens, we introduce convolution operations into the standard feed-forward network [52], which we term blend-convolution feed-forward network

(BC-FFN). Therefore, our LST-based model can seamlessly integrate local and global context information and efficiently provide location-sensitive features for segmenting camouflaged instances.

In addition, we design a **coarse-to-fine fusion (CFF)** to integrate multi-scale low- and high-level features successively derived from ResNet [24] and LST to bring out the shared mask feature. Since the edges of the camouflaged instances are difficult to capture, a reverse edge attention (REA) module is embedded in our CFF module to enhance the sensitivity to edge features. Finally, inspired by [25], we introduce the dynamic camouflaged instance normalization (DCIN) to generate the masks by uniting the high-resolution mask feature and the instance-aware embeddings. Based on those mentioned above two novel designs, *i.e.*, LST and CFF, we provide a new one-stage framework **OSFormer** for camouflaged instance segmentation (Fig. 1). To the best of our knowledge, OSFormer is the first work to explore the transformer-based framework for the CIS task. Our **contributions** are as follows:

1. We propose **OSFormer**, the first one-stage transformer-based framework designed for the camouflage instance segmentation task. It is a flexible framework that can be trained in an end-to-end manner.
2. We present a **location-sensing transformer (LST)** to dynamically seize instance clues at different locations. Our LST contains an encoder with the blend-convolution feed-forward network to extract multi-scale global features and a decoder with the proposed location-guided queries to bring the instance-aware embeddings. The proposed LST structure converges quickly with limited *i.e.*, about 3,000 images, training data.
3. A novel **coarse-to-fine fusion (CFF)** is proposed to get the high-resolution mask features by fusing multi-scale low- and high-level features from the backbone and LST block. In this module, reverse edge attention (REA) is embedded to highlight the edge information of camouflaged instances.
4. Extensive experiments show that OSFormer performs well for the challenging CIS task, **outperforming** 11 popular instance segmentation approaches by a large margin, *e.g.*, *8.5% AP improvement* on the COD10K test set.

2   Related Work

Camouflaged Object Detection. This category of the models aims to identify objects that blend in the surrounding scene [20]. Earlier studies mainly employed low-level handcrafted contrast features and certain heuristic priors (*e.g.*, color [27], texture [2,47] and motion boundary [41]) to build camouflaged object detection (COD) models. With the popularity of deep learning architecture and the release of large-scale pixel-level COD datasets [16,31], the performance of COD has been improved by leaps and bounds in the past two years. Deep learning methods [39,43,61,64] utilize CNNs to extract high-level informative features to search and locate camouflaged objects, and then design an FCN-based decoder to purify features to predict camouflaged maps. For instance, Mei *et al.*[39] presented a positioning and focus network (PFNet) to mimic the process of predation in nature. PFNet first leverages the positioning module to locate the potential targets and use the focus module to refine the ambiguous regions. Zhai et al.[63] adopted a mutual graph learning strategy to train the regions and edges of camouflaged objects interactively. Afterward, Lyu et al.[37] proposed a ranking network that simultaneously localizes, segments, and ranks concealed objects for better prediction. Recently, a novel uncertainty-guided transformer-based model proposed by Yang et al.[62] is designed to infer uncertain regions with Bayesian learning. The COD task ignores the instance-level predicted maps essential for actual application scenarios despite the rapid development. Thus, we are dedicated to advancing the COD task from region-level to instance-level.

Generic Instance Segmentation. Existing works can be roughly summarized as the top-down and bottom-up patterns. The former model performs a classic detect-then-segment design that first detects ROIs by bounding boxes and then segment pixel-level instances locally [49]. The typical model is Mask R-CNN [23], which extends Faster R-CNN [44] by adding a mask branch to predict instance-level masks. On this basis, Mask Scoring R-CNN [26] introduces a MaskIoU head to assess the quality of the instance mask. To enhance the feature pyramid and shorten the information flow, PANet [35] creates a bottom-up path augmentation. Furthermore, Chen et al. [7] proposed Hybrid Task Cascade (HTC) to interweave detection and segmentation features for joint processing. Different from the above-mentioned two-stage models, YOLACT [3] is a real-time one-stage framework that embraces two parallel tasks: producing non-local prototype masks and predicting a set of mask coefficients.

In contrast to the top-down manner, the bottom-up methods first learn instance-aware holistic embeddings and then identify each specific instance with clustering operations [8,34]. Bai et al.[1] proposed an end-to-end boundary-aware deep model derived from the classical watershed transform. SSAP [21] can jointly learn the pixel-level semantic class and instance differentiating by an instance-aware pixel-pair affinity pyramid. However, the performance of previous bottom-up models is inferior to top-down models because of the suboptimal pixel grouping. To this end, Tian et al.[49] presented a dynamic instance-aware network that directly outputs instance masks in a fully convolutional paradigm. The simpler strategy is efficient and performs favorably against Mask R-CNN-like frameworks. Furthermore, SOLO [56,57] detects the center location of instances by semantic categories and decouples the mask prediction into the dynamic kernel feature learning. Inspired by this strategy, we design a location-aware network based on the transformer to dynamically perceive camouflaged instances.

Vision Transformer. Transformer [52] was born out of natural language processing and has been successfully extended to the field of computer vision [15]. The core idea of the transformer encoder-decoder architecture is a self-attention mechanism that builds long-range dependencies and captures global context information from an input sequence. Recently, Carion et al. proposed DETR [5], which combined transformer with CNN backbone to aggregate object-related information and provided a group of object queries to output the final set of predictions. Despite DETR pioneering a novel and concise paradigm, it still suffers from the high computational cost and the slow convergence. Considering

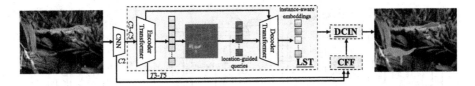

Fig. 2. OSFormer includes the location-sensing transformer (LST), coarse-to-fine fusion (CFF) module, and dynamic camouflaged instance normalization (DCIN) module.

these issues, many efforts focused on how to develop a more efficient DETR architecture [12,13,65]. Zhu et al. [65] introduced a deformable attention layer embedded in the self-attention module to reduce the computational cost and training schedule. UP-DETR [13] leveraged a novel unsupervised pretext task to pre-train the transformer of DETR for accelerating convergence. However, most existing transformer models are adapted to vision tasks with many training data. Therefore, for downstream tasks with only small datasets, fully utilizing the performance of transformer is an urgent issue to be solved. To this end, we present an efficient location-sensing transformer (LST) based on the deformable DETR [65] for CIS. The proposed transformer converges easily on the CIS task with only 3,040 training samples.

3   OSFormer

Architecture. The proposed OSFormer comprises four essential components: (1) a CNN backbone to extract object feature representation, (2) a location-sensing transformer (LST) that utilizes the global feature and location-guided queries to produce the instance-aware embeddings. (3) a coarse-to-fine fusion (CFF) to integrate multi-scale low- and high-level features and yield a high-resolution mask feature, and (4) a dynamic camouflaged instance normalization (DCIN) that is applied to predict the final instance masks. We illustrate the whole architecture in Fig. 2.

3.1   CNN Backbone

Given an input image $I \in \mathbb{R}^{H \times W \times 3}$, we use multi-scale features $\{Ci\}_{i=2}^{5}$ from the CNN backbone (*i.e.*, ResNet-50 [24]). To reduce the computational cost, we directly flatten and concatenate the last three feature maps ($C3, C4, C5$) into a sequence X_m with 256 channels as input to the proposed LST encoder (Sect. 3.2). For $C2$ feature, we feed it into our CFF (Sect. 3.3) module as high-resolution low-level feature to capture more camouflaged instance cues.

3.2   Location-Sensing Transformer

Although the transformer can better extract global information by the self-attention layer, it requires large-scale training samples and high computational

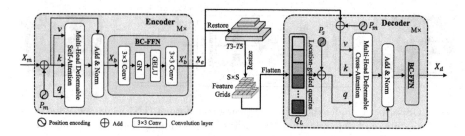

Fig. 3. Structure of our location-sensing transformer.

cost to support. Due to the limited data size of CIS, our goal is to design an efficient architecture that can converge faster and achieve competitive performance. In Fig. 3, we present our location-sensing transformer (LST).

LST Encoder. Unlike DETR [5] with only a single-scale low-resolution feature input to the transformer encoder, our LST encoder receive multi-scale features X_m to obtain rich information. Following deformable self-attention layers [65] to better capture local information and enhance the correlation between neighboring tokens, we bring the convolution operations into the feed-forward network, named blend-convolution feed-forward network (BC-FFN). First, the feature vector is restored to the spatial dimension depending on the shape of Ci. Then, a convolution layer with the kernel size of 3×3 is performed to learn the inductive biases. Finally, we add a group normalization (GN) and a $GELU$ activation to form our feed-forward network. After a 3×3 convolution layer, we flatten the features back into a sequence. Compared to mix-FFN [60], our BC-FFN contains no MLP operations and residual connections. Unlike [59] that designs a convolutional token embedding at the beginning of each stage and employs depth-wise separable convolution operation in the transformer block, we only bring two convolution layers in BC-FFN. Specifically, given an input feature X_b, the process of *BC-FFN* can be formulated as:

$$X_b' = Conv^3(GELU(GN(Conv^3(X_b)))), \tag{1}$$

where $Conv^3$ is a 3×3 convolution operation. Overall, a LST encoder layer is described as follows:

$$X_e = \text{BC-FFN}(LN((X_m + P_m) + MDAttn(X_m + P_m))), \tag{2}$$

where P_m is denoted as the position encodings. *MDAttn* and *LN* represent multi-head deformable self-attention and layer normalization, respectively.

Location-Guided Queries. Object queries play a critical role in the transformer architecture [5], which are used as the initial input to the decoder and attain the output embeddings through the decoder layers. However, one of the reasons for the slow convergence of the vanilla DETR is that object queries are zero-initialized. To this end, we propose location-guided queries

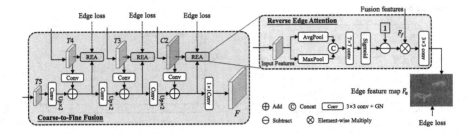

Fig. 4. Structure of our coarse-to-fine fusion.

that take advantage of multi-scale feature maps $Ti, i = 3, 4, 5$ from the LST encoder[1]. It is noteworthy that each query in DETR concentrates on specific areas. Inspired by SOLO [56], we first resize the restored feature maps $T3$-$T5$ to the shape of $S_i \times S_i \times D, i = 1, 2, 3$. Then, we divide the resized features into $S_i \times S_i$ feature grids and flatten them to produce our location-guided queries $Q \in \mathbb{R}^{L \times D}, L = \sum_{i=1}^{3} S_i^2$. In this situation, the proposed location-guided queries can utilize learnable local features in different locations to optimize the initialization and efficiently aggregate the features in the camouflaged areas. Compared to the zero or random initialization [5,65], this query generation strategy improves the efficiency of query iterations in the transformer decoder and accelerates the training convergence. For more discussion, please refer to Sect. 4.2.

LST Decoder. The LST decoder is essential to interact with the global features produced by the LST encoder and location-guided queries for producing the instance-aware embeddings. Spatial position encoding is also added to our location-guided queries Q_L and the encoder memory X_e. After that, they are fused by the deformable cross-attention layer. Unlike the general transformer decoder, we directly use cross-attention without self-attention because the proposed queries already contain learnable global features. BC-FFN is also employed after deformable attention operations, similar to the LST encoder. Given location-guided queries Q_L, the pipeline of our LST decoder is summarized as:

$$X_d = \text{BC-FFN}(LN((Q_L + P_s) + MDCAttn((Q_L + P_s), (X_e + P_m)))), \quad (3)$$

where P_s represents the position encoding based on the feature grids. *MDCAttn* is denoted as the multi-head deformable cross-attention operation. X_d is the output embeddings for instance-aware representation. Finally, X_d is restored to feed into the following DCIN module (Sect. 3.4) for predicting masks.

---

[1] We split and restore the X_e to the 2D representations $T3 \in \mathbb{R}^{\frac{H}{8} \times \frac{W}{8} \times D}$, $T4 \in \mathbb{R}^{\frac{H}{16} \times \frac{W}{16} \times D}$, and $T5 \in \mathbb{R}^{\frac{H}{32} \times \frac{W}{32} \times D}$.

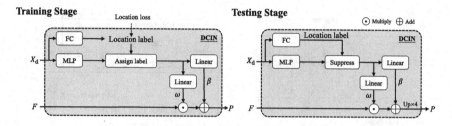

Fig. 5. Structure of our dynamic camouflaged instance normalization.

3.3   Coarse-to-Fine Fusion

As a bottom-up transformer-based model, OSFormer strives to utilize multi-level global features output from the LST encoder to result in a shared mask feature representation. To merge diverse context information, we also fuse the low-level feature $C2$ from the CNN backbone as a complement to yield a unified high-resolution feature map $F \in \mathbb{R}^{\frac{H}{4} \times \frac{W}{4} \times D}$. The detailed structure of the proposed coarse-to-fine fusion (CFF) is shown in Fig. 4. We take the multi-level features $C2, T3, T4$, and $T5$ as input for cascade fusion. Starting from $T5$ at 1/32 scale of input, a 3×3 convolution, GN, and 2× bilinear upsampling are passed and added with the higher-resolution feature ($T4$ with 1/16 scale). After fusing $C2$ with a 1/4 scale, the feature proceeds through a 1×1 convolution, GN, and RELU operations to generate the mask feature F. Note that each input feature reduces the channels from 256 to 128 after the first convolution and then is increased to 256 channels at the final output.

Considering that the edge features of camouflage appear more challenging to capture, we design a reverse edge attention (REA) module embedded in CFF to supervise the edge features during the iterative process. Unlike the previous reverse attention [9,17], our REA operates on the edge features rather than the predicted binary masks. In addition, the edge labels used for supervision are obtained by erosion of instance mask labels without any manual labeling. Inspired by the Convolutional Block Attention [58], the input features are operated by both average-pooling ($AvgPool$) and max-pooling ($MaxPool$). Then, we concatenate and forward them to a 7×7 convolution and a sigmoid function. Afterward, we reverse the attention weight and apply them to the fusion feature F_f by element-wise multiplication. Lastly, we use a 3×3 convolution to predict the edge feature. Assuming that the input feature is Ti, the whole process of each REA module can be formulated as follows:

$$F_e = Conv^3(F_f \otimes (1 - Sigmoid(Conv^7([AvgPool(Ti); MaxPool(Ti)])))), \quad (4)$$

where $Conv^7$ represents the 7×7 convolution layer, and [;] denotes concatenation on the channel axis. In a word, the proposed CFF provides a shared mask feature F to feed into the DCIN to predict the final camouflaged per-instance mask.

3.4 Dynamic Camouflaged Instance Normalization

Inspired by the instance normalization operation in the style transfer domain [25, 46], we introduce a dynamic camouflaged instance normalization (DCIN) to predict final masks. When DCIN receives the output embeddings $X_d \in \mathbb{R}^{S^2 \times D}$ from the LST decoder, a fully-connected layer (FC) is employed to gain the location label. In parallel, a multi-layer perceptron (MLP) is used to gain the instance-aware parameters with a size of D (i.e., 256). We assign positive and negative locations according to the ground truth in the training stage. The instance-aware parameters of the positive location are applied to generate the segmentation mask. In the testing stage, we utilize the confidence value of the location label to filter (See Suppress in Fig. 5) ineffective parameters (e.g., Threshold > 0.5). Subsequently, two linear layers are operated on the filtered location-aware parameters to attain affine weights $\omega \in \mathbb{R}^{N \times D}$ and biases $\beta \in \mathbb{R}^{N \times 1}$, respectively. Finally, they are used together with the shared mask feature $F \in \mathbb{R}^{\frac{H}{4} \times \frac{W}{4} \times D}$ to predict the camouflaged instances, which can be described as:

$$P = U_{\times 4}(\omega F + \beta), \tag{5}$$

where $P \in \mathbb{R}^{H \times W \times N}$ is the predicted masks. N is the number of predicted instances. $U_{\times 4}$ is an upsampling operation by a factor of 4. In the end, the Matrix NMS [57] is applied to get the final instances.

3.5 Loss Function

During the training, the total loss function can be written as:

$$L_{total} = \lambda_{edge} L_{edge} + \lambda_{loc} L_{loc} + \lambda_{mask} L_{mask}, \tag{6}$$

where L_{edge} is the edge loss to supervise edges from different levels in our CFF. The edge loss can be defined as $L_{edge} = \sum_{j=1}^{J} L_{dice}^{(j)}$, where J represents the total number of levels of edge features for supervision, which can be seen in Fig. 4. λ_{edge} is the weight for edge loss that is set to 1 by default. Since the CIS task is category-agnostic, we use the confidence of the existence of camouflages in each location (L_{loc}) compared to the classification confidence in generic instance segmentation. In addition, L_{loc} is implemented by Focal loss [32] and L_{mask} is computed by Dice loss [40] for segmentation. λ_{loc} and λ_{mask} are set to 1 and 3 respectively to balance the total loss.

4 Experiments

4.1 Experimental Settings

Datasets. As a brand-new challenging CIS task, few task-specific datasets so far. Comfortingly, Fan et al. contributed a COD dataset [16], namely COD10K, which simultaneously provides high-quality instance-level annotations for training CIS models. Concretely, COD10K contains 3,040 camouflaged images with instance-level labels for training and 2,026 images for testing. Recently, Le *et al.*[30] provided a larger CIS dataset called CAMO++, which includes a total of 5,500 samples with hierarchically pixel-wise annotation. Furthermore, Lyu *et al.*[37] introduced a CIS test set with 4,121 images, called NC4K. We use the instance-level annotations in COD10K to train the proposed OSFormer and evaluate it on the COD10K and NC4K test set.

Evaluation Metrics. We adopt COCO-style evaluation metrics including AP_{50}, AP_{75}, and AP scores [33] to evaluate segmentation results. In contrast to the mAP metric in instance segmentation, each camouflaged instance detected from concealed regions is class-agnostic. Therefore, we only need to consider the existence of camouflaged instances while ignoring the mean value of the category.

Technical Details. Our OSFormer is implemented in PyTorch on a single RTX 3090 GPU and trained with Stochastic Gradient Descent. For fair comparisons, we adopt wisely used ResNet-50 backbone [24] that is initialized from the pre-trained weights of ImageNet [14]. If not specially mentioned, other backbones used in our experiments are also pre-trained on ImageNet. During training, all our models are trained for 90K iterations (60 epochs) with a batch size of 2 and a base learning rate of 2.5e−4 with a warm-up of 1K iterations. Then, the learning rate is divided by 10 at 60K and 80K, respectively. In addition, the weight decay is set to 10^{-4} and the momentum is 0.9. The input images are resized such that the size of the shortest side is from 480 to 800 while the longest side is at most 1,333. We also use the scale jittering augmentation for data augmentation. In our LST, S_1, S_2, and S_3 are set to 36, 24, and 16, respectively. Note that the dimension of the features is kept at 256 throughout the whole process of BC-FFN. We embed a total of six encoder layers stacked sequentially. To reach better performance, we only repeat the LST decoder layer three times to aggregate camouflaged cues relevant to queries.

4.2   Ablation Studies

We conduct a series of ablation studies on the instance-level COD10K dataset [16] to validate the effectiveness of our OSFormer and determine the hyper-parameters. The ablation experiments mainly consist of the following aspects: layers of encoder and decoder in LST, number of multi-scale feature inputs, location-guided queries designs, feature fusion in the CFF module, backbone architecture, real-time settings, and contributions of different components.

Layers of Encoder and Decoder in LST. The depth of the transformer is a key factor influencing the performance and efficiency of transformer-based models. We attempt multiple combinations of different numbers of encoder and decoder layers in our LST to optimize the performance of OSFormer. As shown in Table 1, the first three rows indicate that three layers are insufficient to maximize the performance of OSFormer. In addition, we observe that LST is more sensitive to the encoder than the decoder. The highest value of AP is reached when the number of encoder and decoder layers are 6 and 3, respectively. When more

Table 1. Effect of the different number of encoder and decoder layers in our LST.

Encoder	Decoder	AP	AP_{50}	AP_{75}	FPS
1	3	37.0	68.0	35.4	**21.8**
3	1	39.2	69.1	38.5	20.0
3	3	39.4	70.2	39.3	18.8
3	6	38.9	68.6	37.9	17.2
6	3	**41.0**	**71.1**	40.8	14.5
6	6	40.6	70.3	**41.2**	13.4
9	6	40.7	70.6	40.4	11.3

Table 2. Ablations for different combinations of multi-scale features input to our LST.

Scales	Number	AP	AP_{50}	AP_{75}	Params	Memory
$C3$-$C5$	3	**41.0**	**71.1**	**40.8**	**46.58M**	**6.4G**
$C2$-$C5$	4	39.9	70.5	38.7	46.80M	9.3G
$C3$-$C6$	4	40.8	70.6	40.9	47.39M	6.7G
$C2$-$C6$	5	40.2	69.9	40.3	47.62M	17.7G

layers are added, the accuracy is not further improved, and the inference time drops to under 14 *fps*. As a result, we adopt 6 encoder layers and 3 decoder layers as our default setting to balance performance and efficiency.

Number of Multi-scale Feature Inputs. We utilize multi-level features extracted from the ResNet-50 as input of our LST. To more accurately capture camouflages at different scales while maintaining model efficiency, we combine different numbers of features in the backbone, including $C3$-$C5$, $C2$-$C5$, $C3$-$C6$, and $C2$-$C6$. In Table 2, we observe that the combination of $C3$-$C5$ achieves a strong performance with the lowest number of parameters and training memory.

Location-Guided Queries Designs. Object queries are essential in the transformer architecture for dense prediction tasks. To validate the effectiveness of our location-guided queries, we compare two typical object query designs, including zero-initialized in vanilla DETR [5] and learnable input embeddings in deformable DETR [65]. We set the number of queries uniformly to the default number of multi-scale feature grids for fair comparisons. Other settings in the proposed OSFormer remain unchanged. In a nutshell, object queries in transformer decoder comprise two parts: query features and query position embeddings. In the vanilla DETR, an all-zero matrix added by a set of learnable position embeddings is taken as object queries through the decoder to generate the corresponding output embeddings. In contrast, the deformable DETR is directly initialized by learnable embeddings as query features and is coupled with learnable position embeddings. As seen in Table 3, our location-guided queries are significantly superior to other query designs. It illustrates that inserting super-

Table 3. Comparison of different query designs on the proposed OSFormer.

Queries	AP	AP$_{50}$	AP$_{75}$
Zero-Initialized [5]	34.7	64.1	33.1
Learnable Embeddings [65]	35.0	64.8	33.2
Location-Guided Queries (**Ours**)	**41.0** $_{+6.0}$	**71.1** $_{+6.3}$	**40.8** $_{+7.6}$

Table 4. Comparison of different feature combinations input to our CFF module.

Features	AP	AP$_{50}$	AP$_{75}$
Single $T2$	38.0	69.2	36.8
$C2, C3, C4, C5$	35.4	64.3	34.6
$C2, C3, C4, T5$	40.0	69.7	40.1
$C2, C3, T4, T5$	39.5	69.9	39.0
$T2, T3, T4, T5$	40.0	70.1	40.0
$C2, T3, T4, T5$	**41.0**	**71.1**	**40.8**

vised global features in queries is crucial to regressing different camouflage cues and locating instances efficiently. Furthermore, we compare the learning ability of three strategies. We find that our location-guided queries scheme has a faster convergence rate at the early training stage, and the final convergence is also better than the other two models. It also demonstrates that location-guided queries are efficient to exploit global features to capture camouflaged information at different locations by cross-attention mechanism.

Feature Fusion in CFF. In the proposed CFF module, the multi-scale input features directly impact the quality of the mask feature F operated by fusing. To explore the optimal fusion scheme from ResNet-50 and LST encoder, we conduct different combinations in Table 4. Using only a single-scale feature $T2$ without multi-scale fusion is not promising. The result of the 2nd row illustrates that fusing only the backbone features is inefficient. In the end, we attain the optimal results by feeding $C2, T3, T4$, and $T5$ into the CFF module. It can be explained that the features from our LST encoder have more detailed global information. Furthermore, the feature $C2$ is also required to provide some low-level features as a supplement. In addition, we visualize the features at each scale input to the CFF module and the mask feature F in Fig. 6.

Backbone Networks. In this experiment, we use different backbone networks *i.e.*, ResNet-50 [24], ResNet-101 [24], PVTv2-B2-Li [55], and Swin-T [36], to train our OSFormer. All of them are pre-trained on ImageNet [14]. From Table 5, we observe that OSFormer only with the ResNet-50 can achieve 41% AP scores. Moreover, using a more powerful backbone can further stimulate the potential of our method that further improves to 47.7% AP.

Table 5. Performance of OSFormer with different backbone networks.

Backbone Networks	AP	AP_{50}	AP_{75}	FPS
ResNet-50 [24] (**Default**)	41.0	71.1	40.8	**14.5**
ResNet-101 [24]	42.0	71.3	42.8	12.9
PVTv2-B2-Li [55]	47.2	74.9	**49.8**	13.2
Swin-T [36]	**47.7**	**78.6**	49.3	12.6

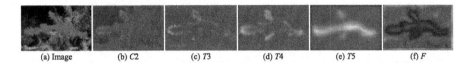

| (a) Image | (b) $C2$ | (c) $T3$ | (d) $T4$ | (e) $T5$ | (f) F |

Fig. 6. Visualizations of feature maps. (a) The input image overlapped with ground-truth; (b)-(e) is the input features of CFF produced from the CNN backbone and our LST encoder; (f) is the mask feature F output from CFF.

Real-Time Settings. To improve the application value of OSFormer, we provide a real-time version named OSFormer-550. Concretely, we resize the input shorter side to 550 while reducing the LST encoder layers to 3. As shown in Table 6, despite the value of AP dropping to 36.0%, the inference time is increased to $25.8 fps$, and the number of parameters and FLOPs is also significantly improved. We hope OSFormer-550 can be extended to more real-life scenarios.

Table 6. Performance of OSFormer with real-time setting.

Models	Backbones	AP	AP_{50}	FPS	Params	FLOPs
OSFormer (**Default**)	ResNet-50	**41.0**	**71.1**	14.5	46.6 M	324.7G
OSFormer-550	ResNet-50	36.0	65.3	**25.8**	**42.4 M**	**138.7G**

Contributions of Different Components. We conduct extensive ablation studies on the COD10K test set [16], including LST encoder (Encoder), location-guided queries (LGQ), blend-convolution FFN (BC-FFN), coarse-to-fine fusion (CFF) and reverse edge attention (REA). We adopt a control variable manner, where we only ablate the current module while keeping the other parts as default settings. When validating the LGQ, we use the learnable embeddings [65] as an alternative. Similarly, BC-FFN is replaced by the vanilla FFN [52]. For the CFF module, we directly use a single-scale feature $T2$ as the output of CFF. As shown in Table 8, without Encoder, the value of AP directly dropped by about 7%. It indicates that the LST encoder is essential to extract high-level global features. Furthermore, the 2nd row validates the effectiveness of LGQ design again. Note that BC-FFN plays a vital role in the encoder and decoder of LST because 3×3 convolution layers can strengthen the local correlation of global features

Table 7. Ablation studies for different components in our OSFormer.

Encoder	LGQ	BC-FFN	CFF	REA	AP	AP_{50}	AP_{75}
	✓	✓	✓	✓	33.7	63.4	32.0
✓		✓	✓	✓	34.7	64.1	33.1
✓	✓		✓	✓	37.2	67.3	35.8
✓	✓	✓			38.0	69.2	36.8
✓	✓	✓	✓		39.3	69.7	38.5
✓	✓	✓	✓	✓	**41.0**	**71.1**	**40.8**

Table 8. Quantitative comparisons with 11 representative methods.

	Methods	Backbones	Params	FLOPs	COD10K-Test AP	AP_{50}	AP_{75}	NC4K-Test AP	AP_{50}	AP_{75}
	Mask R-CNN [23]	ResNet-50	43.9 M	186.3G	25.0	55.5	20.4	27.7	58.6	22.7
	Mask R-CNN [23]	ResNet-101	62.9 M	254.5G	28.7	60.1	25.7	36.1	68.9	33.5
	MS R-CNN [26]	ResNet-50	60.0 M	198.5G	30.1	57.2	28.7	31.0	58.7	29.4
	MS R-CNN [26]	ResNet-101	79.0 M	251.1G	33.3	61.0	32.9	35.7	63.4	34.7
Two-Stage	Cascade R-CNN [4]	ResNet-50	71.7 M	334.1G	25.3	56.1	21.3	29.5	60.8	24.8
	Cascade R-CNN [4]	ResNet-101	90.7 M	386.7G	29.5	61.0	25.9	34.6	66.3	31.5
	HTC [7]	ResNet-50	76.9 M	331.7G	28.1	56.3	25.1	29.8	59.0	26.6
	HTC [7]	ResNet-101	95.9 M	384.3G	30.9	61.0	28.7	34.2	64.5	31.6
	BlendMask [6]	ResNet-50	35.8 M	233.8G	28.2	56.4	25.2	27.7	56.7	24.2
	BlendMask [6]	ResNet-101	54.7 M	302.8G	31.2	60.0	28.9	31.4	61.2	28.8
	Mask Transfiner [29]	ResNet-50	44.3 M	**185.1G**	28.7	56.3	26.4	29.4	56.7	27.2
	Mask Transfiner [29]	ResNet-101	63.3 M	253.7G	31.2	60.7	29.8	34.0	63.1	32.6
	YOLACT [3]	ResNet-50	–	–	24.3	53.3	19.7	32.1	65.3	27.9
	YOLACT [3]	ResNet-101	–	–	29.0	60.1	25.3	37.8	70.6	35.6
	CondInst [49]	ResNet-50	**34.1 M**	200.1G	30.6	63.6	26.1	33.4	67.4	29.4
	CondInst [49]	ResNet-101	53.1 M	269.1G	34.3	67.9	31.6	38.0	71.1	35.6
	QueryInst [19]	ResNet-50	–	–	28.5	60.1	23.1	33.0	66.7	29.4
One-Stage	QueryInst [19]	ResNet-101	–	–	32.5	65.1	28.6	38.7	72.1	37.6
	SOTR [22]	ResNet-50	63.1 M	476.7G	27.9	58.7	24.1	29.3	61.0	25.6
	SOTR [22]	ResNet-101	82.1 M	549.6G	32.0	63.6	29.2	34.3	65.7	32.4
	SOLOv2 [57]	ResNet-50	46.2 M	318.7G	32.5	63.2	29.9	34.4	65.9	31.9
	SOLOv2 [57]	ResNet-101	65.1 M	394.6G	35.2	65.7	33.4	37.8	69.2	36.1
	OSFormer (Ours)	ResNet-50	46.6 M	324.7G	41.0	71.1	40.8	42.5	72.5	42.3
	OSFormer (Ours)	ResNet-101	65.5 M	398.2G	**42.0**	**71.3**	**42.8**	**44.4**	**73.7**	**45.1**

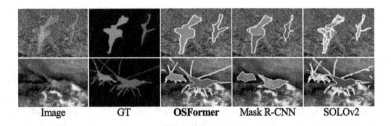

| Image | GT | **OSFormer** | Mask R-CNN | SOLOv2 |

Fig. 7. Qualitative comparison of OSFormer with Mask R-CNN and SOLOv2.

from self-attention. Moreover, the CFF efficiently fuses multi-scale features and enhances the edges of camouflaged instances by embedding REA. By integrating all modules, OSFormer reaches best performance.

4.3   Comparisons with Cutting-Edge Methods

We compare our OSFormer with several famous instance segmentation models (*i.e.*, two-stage and one-stage models) retrained on the instance-level COD10K [16] dataset. We uniformly adopt official codes for fair comparisons to train each model and evaluate them on the COD10K and NC4K [37] test set. In addition, we also show the results based on different backbones *i.e.*, ResNet-50, ResNet-101, with the ImageNet [14] pre-trained weights.

Quantitative Comparisons. As shown in Table 7, although the CIS task is challenging, our OSFormer still performs favorably against other competitors across all metrics. In particular, the AP score of OSFormer is higher than that of the second-ranked SOLOv2 [57] by a large margin ($\sim$8.5%) using ResNet-50. The desirable result should be attributed to our LST because it provided higher-level global features and interacted with camouflage clues in different locations in the LST decoder. By leveraging a more powerful backbone, *i.e.*, Swin-T, OSFormer can continue to boost the performance to 47.7% AP (Table 5). According to the parameters and FLOPs in Table 7, it also demonstrates that our OSFormer achieves better performance without adding extra parameters.

Qualitative Comparisons. To validate the effectiveness of OSFormer, we also exhibit two representative visualization results in Fig. 7. Specifically, the top sample suggests that OSFormer can comfortably distinguish camouflages in the case of multiple instances. The bottom result shows that our method excels at capturing slender boundaries, which can be attributed to the enhancement of edge features by our REA module. Overall, compared to the visualization results from other famous methods, OSFormer has the capability to overcome more challenging cases and achieve good performance.

5   Conclusion

We contributed a novel location-aware one-stage transformer framework, called
OSFormer, for camouflaged instance segmentation (CIS). OSFormer embraces
an efficient location-sensing transformer to capture global features and dynamically regress the location and body of the camouflaged instances. As the first
one-stage bottom-up CIS framework, we further designed a coarse-to-fine fusion
to integrate multi-scale features and highlight the edge of camouflages to produce
the global features. Extensive experimental results show that OSFormer performs
favorably against all other well-known models. Furthermore, OSFormer requires
only about 3,000 images to train, and it converges rapidly. It is easily and flexibly
extended to other downstream vision tasks with smaller training samples.

References

1. Bai, M., Urtasun, R.: Deep watershed transform for instance segmentation. In:
    IEEE CVPR (2017)
2. Bhajantri, N.U., Nagabhushan, P.: Camouflage defect identification: a novel app-
    roach. In: IEEE ICIT (2006)
3. Bolya, D., Zhou, C., Xiao, F., Lee, Y.J.: Yolact: Real-time instance segmentation.
    In: IEEE CVPR (2019)
4. Cai, Z., Vasconcelos, N.: Cascade r-cnn: high quality object detection and instance
    segmentation. IEEE TPAMI **43**(5), 1483–1498 (2019)
5. Carion, N., Massa, F., Synnaeve, G., Usunier, N., Kirillov, A., Zagoruyko, S.: End-
    to-end object detection with transformers. In: Vedaldi, A., Bischof, H., Brox, T.,
    Frahm, J.-M. (eds.) ECCV 2020. LNCS, vol. 12346, pp. 213–229. Springer, Cham
    (2020). https://doi.org/10.1007/978-3-030-58452-8_13
6. Chen, H., Sun, K., Tian, Z., Shen, C., Huang, Y., Yan, Y.: Blendmask: Top-down
    meets bottom-up for instance segmentation. In: IEEE CVPR (2020)
7. Chen, K., et al.: Hybrid task cascade for instance segmentation. In: IEEE CVPR
    (2019)
8. Chen, L.C., Papandreou, G., Kokkinos, I., Murphy, K., Yuille, A.L.: Deeplab:
    Semantic image segmentation with deep convolutional nets, atrous convolution,
    and fully connected crfs. IEEE TPAMI **40**(4), 834–848 (2017)
9. Chen, S., Tan, X., Wang, B., Hu, X.: Reverse attention for salient object detection.
    In: Ferrari, V., Hebert, M., Sminchisescu, C., Weiss, Y. (eds.) ECCV 2018. LNCS,
    vol. 11213, pp. 236–252. Springer, Cham (2018). https://doi.org/10.1007/978-3-
    030-01240-3_15
10. Chu, H.K., Hsu, W.H., Mitra, N.J., Cohen-Or, D., Wong, T.T., Lee, T.Y.: Cam-
    ouflage images. ACM TOG **29**(4), 51–61 (2010)
11. Cuthill, I.: Camouflage. JOZ **308**(2), 75–92 (2019)
12. Dai, X., Chen, Y., Yang, J., Zhang, P., Yuan, L., Zhang, L.: Dynamic detr: End-
    to-end object detection with dynamic attention. In: IEEE CVPR (2021)
13. Dai, Z., Cai, B., Lin, Y., Chen, J.: Up-detr: Unsupervised pre-training for object
    detection with transformers. In: IEEE CVPR (2021)
14. Deng, J., Dong, W., Socher, R., Li, L.J., Li, K., Fei-Fei, L.: Imagenet: A large-scale
    hierarchical image database. In: IEEE CVPR (2009)

15. Dosovitskiy, A., et al.: An image is worth 16×16 words: Transformers for image recognition at scale. In: ICLR (2021)
16. Fan, D.P., Ji, G.P., Sun, G., Cheng, M.M., Shen, J., Shao, L.: Camouflaged object detection. In: IEEE CVPR (2020)
17. Fan, D.-P., et al.: PraNet: Parallel reverse attention network for polyp segmentation. In: Martel, A.L., Abolmaesumi, P., Stoyanov, D., Mateus, D., Zuluaga, M.A., Zhou, S.K., Racoceanu, D., Joskowicz, L. (eds.) MICCAI 2020. LNCS, vol. 12266, pp. 263–273. Springer, Cham (2020). https://doi.org/10.1007/978-3-030-59725-2_26
18. Fan, D.P., et al.: Inf-net: Automatic covid-19 lung infection segmentation from ct images. IEEE TMI **39**(8), 2626–2637 (2020)
19. Fang, Y., et al.: Instances as queries. In: IEEE CVPR (2021)
20. Fennell, J.G., Talas, L., Baddeley, R.J., Cuthill, I.C., Scott-Samuel, N.E.: The camouflage machine: Optimizing protective coloration using deep learning with genetic algorithms. Evolution **75**(3), 614–624 (2021)
21. Gao, N., et al.: Ssap: Single-shot instance segmentation with affinity pyramid. In: IEEE CVPR (2019)
22. Guo, R., Niu, D., Qu, L., Li, Z.: Sotr: Segmenting objects with transformers. In: IEEE ICCV (2021)
23. He, K., Gkioxari, G., Dollár, P., Girshick, R.: Mask r-cnn. In: IEEE ICCV (2017)
24. He, K., Zhang, X., Ren, S., Sun, J.: Deep residual learning for image recognition. In: IEEE CVPR (2016)
25. Huang, X., Belongie, S.: Arbitrary style transfer in real-time with adaptive instance normalization. In: IEEE ICCV (2017)
26. Huang, Z., Huang, L., Gong, Y., Huang, C., Wang, X.: Mask scoring r-cnn. In: IEEE CVPR (2019)
27. Huerta, I., Rowe, D., Mozerov, M., Gonzàlez, J.: Improving background subtraction based on a casuistry of colour-motion segmentation problems. In: Iberian PRIA (2007)
28. Ji, G.-P., et al.: Progressively normalized self-attention network for video polyp segmentation. In: de Bruijne, M., et al. (eds.) MICCAI 2021. LNCS, vol. 12901, pp. 142–152. Springer, Cham (2021). https://doi.org/10.1007/978-3-030-87193-2_14
29. Ke, L., Danelljan, M., Li, X., Tai, Y.W., Tang, C.K., Yu, F.: Mask transfiner for high-quality instance segmentation. In: IEEE CVPR (2022)
30. Le, T.N., et al.: Camouflaged instance segmentation in-the-wild: Dataset, method, and benchmark suite. IEEE TIP **31**, 287–300 (2022)
31. Le, T.N., Nguyen, T.V., Nie, Z., Tran, M.T., Sugimoto, A.: Anabranch network for camouflaged object segmentation. CVIU **184**, 45–56 (2019)
32. Lin, T.Y., Goyal, P., Girshick, R., He, K., Dollár, P.: Focal loss for dense object detection. In: IEEE ICCV (2017)
33. Lin, T.-Y., et al.: Microsoft COCO: Common objects in context. In: Fleet, D., Pajdla, T., Schiele, B., Tuytelaars, T. (eds.) ECCV 2014. LNCS, vol. 8693, pp. 740–755. Springer, Cham (2014). https://doi.org/10.1007/978-3-319-10602-1_48
34. Liu, S., Jia, J., Fidler, S., Urtasun, R.: Sgn: Sequential grouping networks for instance segmentation. In: IEEE ICCV (2017)
35. Liu, S., Qi, L., Qin, H., Shi, J., Jia, J.: Path aggregation network for instance segmentation. In: IEEE CVPR (2018)
36. Liu, Z., et al.: Swin transformer: Hierarchical vision transformer using shifted windows. In: IEEE CVPR (2021)
37. Lyu, Y., et al.: Simultaneously localize, segment and rank the camouflaged objects. In: IEEE CVPR (2021)

38. Matthews, O., Liggins, E., Volonakis, T., Scott-Samuel, N., Baddeley, R., Cuthill, I.: Human visual search performance for camouflaged targets. J. Vis. **15**(12), 1164–1164 (2015)

39. Mei, H., Ji, G.P., Wei, Z., Yang, X., Wei, X., Fan, D.P.: Camouflaged object segmentation with distraction mining. In: IEEE CVPR (2021)

40. Milletari, F., Navab, N., Ahmadi, S.A.: V-net: Fully convolutional neural networks for volumetric medical image segmentation. In: IEEE 3DV (2016)

41. Mondal, A.: Camouflaged object detection and tracking: A survey. IJIG **20**(04), 2050028 (2020)

42. Redmon, J., Divvala, S., Girshick, R., Farhadi, A.: You only look once: Unified, real-time object detection. In: IEEE CVPR (2016)

43. Ren, J., et al.: Deep texture-aware features for camouflaged object detection. In: IEEE TCSVT (2021)

44. Ren, S., He, K., Girshick, R., Sun, J.: Faster r-cnn: Towards real-time object detection with region proposal networks. In: NeurIPS (2015)

45. Sandon, P.A.: Simulating visual attention. J. Cogn. Neurosci. **2**(3), 213–231 (1990)

46. Sofiiuk, K., Barinova, O., Konushin, A.: Adaptis: Adaptive instance selection network. In: IEEE CVPR (2019)

47. Song, L., Geng, W.: A new camouflage texture evaluation method based on wssim and nature image features. In: ICMT (2010)

48. Stevens, M., Merilaita, S.: Animal camouflage: current issues and new perspectives. PTRS B: BS **364**(1516), 423–427 (2009)

49. Tian, Z., Shen, C., Chen, H.: Conditional convolutions for instance segmentation. In: Vedaldi, A., Bischof, H., Brox, T., Frahm, J.-M. (eds.) ECCV 2020. LNCS, vol. 12346, pp. 282–298. Springer, Cham (2020). https://doi.org/10.1007/978-3-030-58452-8_17

50. Tian, Z., Shen, C., Chen, H., He, T.: Fcos: Fully convolutional one-stage object detection. In: IEEE ICCV (2019)

51. Troscianko, J., Nokelainen, O., Skelhorn, J., Stevens, M.: Variable crab camouflage patterns defeat search image formation. Commun. Biol. **4**(1), 1–9 (2021)

52. Vaswani, A., et al.: Attention is all you need. In: NeurIPS (2017)

53. Wang, H., Zhu, Y., Adam, H., Yuille, A., Chen, L.C.: Max-deeplab: End-to-end panoptic segmentation with mask transformers. In: IEEE CVPR (2021)

54. Wang, W., et al.: Pyramid vision transformer: A versatile backbone for dense prediction without convolutions. In: IEEE CVPR (2021)

55. Wang, W., et al.: Pvtv 2: Improved baselines with pyramid vision transformer. In: CVMJ (2022)

56. Wang, X., Kong, T., Shen, C., Jiang, Y., Li, L.: SOLO: Segmenting objects by locations. In: Vedaldi, A., Bischof, H., Brox, T., Frahm, J.-M. (eds.) ECCV 2020. LNCS, vol. 12363, pp. 649–665. Springer, Cham (2020). https://doi.org/10.1007/978-3-030-58523-5_38

57. Wang, X., Zhang, R., Kong, T., Li, L., Shen, C.: Solov2: Dynamic and fast instance segmentation. In: NeurIPS (2020)

58. Woo, S., Park, J., Lee, J.-Y., Kweon, I.S.: CBAM: Convolutional block attention module. In: Ferrari, V., Hebert, M., Sminchisescu, C., Weiss, Y. (eds.) ECCV 2018. LNCS, vol. 11211, pp. 3–19. Springer, Cham (2018). https://doi.org/10.1007/978-3-030-01234-2_1

59. Wu, H., et al.: Cvt: Introducing convolutions to vision transformers. In: IEEE CVPR (2021)

60. Xie, E., Wang, W., Yu, Z., Anandkumar, A., Alvarez, J.M., Luo, P.: Segformer: Simple and efficient design for semantic segmentation with transformers. In: NeurIPS (2021)
61. Yan, J., Le, T.N., Nguyen, K.D., Tran, M.T., Do, T.T., Nguyen, T.V.: Mirrornet: Bio-inspired camouflaged object segmentation. IEEE Access **9**, 43290–43300 (2021)
62. Yang, F., et al.: Uncertainty-guided transformer reasoning for camouflaged object detection. In: IEEE CVPR (2021)
63. Zhai, Q., Li, X., Yang, F., Chen, C., Cheng, H., Fan, D.P.: Mutual graph learning for camouflaged object detection. In: IEEE CVPR (2021)
64. Zhu, J., Zhang, X., Zhang, S., Liu, J.: Inferring camouflaged objects by texture-aware interactive guidance network. In: AAAI (2021)
65. Zhu, X., Su, W., Lu, L., Li, B., Wang, X., Dai, J.: Deformable detr: Deformable transformers for end-to-end object detection. In: ICLR (2020)

Highly Accurate Dichotomous Image Segmentation

Xuebin Qin[1], Hang Dai[1], Xiaobin Hu[2], Deng-Ping Fan[3]([✉]),
Ling Shao[4], and Luc Van Gool[3]

[1] MBZUAI, Abu Dhabi, UAE
xuebin@ualberta.ca, hang.dai@mbzuai.ac.ae
[2] Tencent Youtu Lab, Shanghai, China
xiaobin.hu@tum.de
[3] ETH Zurich, Zurich, Switzerland
dengpfan@gmail.com, vangool@vision.ee.ethz.ch
[4] Terminus Group, Beijing, China
ling.shao@ieee.org

Abstract. We present a systematic study on a new task called dichotomous image segmentation (DIS), which aims to segment highly accurate objects from natural images. To this end, we collected the first large-scale DIS dataset, called **DIS5K**, which contains 5,470 high-resolution (*e.g.*, 2K, 4K or larger) images covering *camouflaged*, *salient*, or *meticulous objects* in various backgrounds. DIS is annotated with extremely fine-grained labels. Besides, we introduce a simple intermediate supervision baseline (**IS-Net**) using both feature-level and mask-level guidance for DIS model training. IS-Net outperforms various cutting-edge baselines on the proposed DIS5K, making it a general self-learned supervision network that can facilitate future research in DIS. Further, we design a new metric called human correction efforts (**HCE**) which approximates the number of mouse clicking operations required to correct the false positives and false negatives. HCE is utilized to measure the gap between models and real-world applications and thus can complement existing metrics. Finally, we conduct the largest-scale benchmark, evaluating 16 representative segmentation models, providing a more insightful discussion regarding object complexities, and showing several potential applications (*e.g.*, background removal, art design, 3D reconstruction). Hoping these efforts can open up promising directions for both academic and industries. Project page: https://xuebinqin.github.io/dis/index.html.

Keywords: Dichotomous image segmentation · High resolution · Metric

We would like to thank Jiayi Zhu for his efforts in re-organizing the dataset and codes.

Supplementary Information The online version contains supplementary material available at https://doi.org/10.1007/978-3-031-19797-0_3.

Fig. 1. Sample images from our DIS5K dataset. Zoom-in for best view.

1   Introduction

Currently, the annotation accuracy of computer vision datasets that drive a tremendous amount of Artificial Intelligence (AI) models satisfy the requirements of machine perceiving systems to some extent. However, AI has entered an era of demanding highly accurate outputs from computer vision algorithms to support delicate human-machine interaction. Compared with classification [14,37,71] and detection [27,28,66], segmentation can provide more geometrically accurate target descriptions for wide applications, *e.g.*, image editing [29], AR/VR [62], medical image analysis [68], robot manipulation [7], *etc.*

These applications can be grouped as "light" (*e.g.*, image editing and analysis) and "heavy" (*e.g.*, human-machine interaction), based on their immediate affects on real-world objects. The "light" ones (Fig. 1), which usually allows post-corrections, are relatively tolerant to the segmentation errors. While, in the "heavy" ones, the segmentation deflects or failures are more likely to cause physic damages on objects or injuries (sometimes fatal) of humans. Hence, *highly accurate* and *robust* models are needed. Now, most of the segmentation models are still less applicable in those "heavy" applications due to the accuracy and robustness issues. Hence, **our goal** is to address the "heavy" and "light" applications in a general framework, called *dichotomous image segmentation (DIS)*, which aims to segment highly accurate objects.

Existing segmentation tasks mainly focus on objects with specific characteristics, *e.g.*, salient [77,80,92], camouflaged [22,38,72], meticulous [43,88] or specific categories [36,44,53,68,70]. They have the same input/output formats, and the exclusive mechanisms are barely used for segmenting specific targets in their models, which means they are usually dataset-dependent. Thus, we propose to formulate **a category-agnostic DIS task defined on non-conflicting annotations for accurately segmenting objects with different structure complexities, regardless of their characteristics**. Compared with semantic segmentation [13,16,45,61,101], the proposed DIS task mainly focuses on images with single or a few targets, from which getting richer accurate details of each target is more feasible. Therefore, we provide four **contributions**:

i) A large-scale, extendable DIS dataset, **DIS5K**, contains 5,470 high-resolution images paired with highly accurate binary segmentation masks.
ii) A novel baseline **IS-Net** built with intermediate supervision reduces overfitting by enforcing direct high-dimensional feature synchronization.

iii) A newly designed human correction efforts (**HCE**) metric measures the barriers between model predictions and real-world applications by counting the human interventions needed to correct the faulty regions.

iv) Based on the new DIS5K, we establish the complete DIS **benchmark**, making ours the most extensive DIS investigation. We compared our IS-Net with 16 cutting-edge segmentation models and showed promising performance.

2 Related Work

Tasks and Datasets of image segmentation are closely related in deep learning era. Some of the segmentation tasks like [11,20,43,44,53,70,80,88], are even directly built upon the datasets. Their problem formulations are exactly the same: $P = F(\theta, I)$, where I and P are the input image and the binary map output, respectively. However, the relevance between most of these tasks are rarely studied, which restricts their trained models from being generalized to wider applications. Besides, the datasets used in different tasks are not exclusive, which shows a unified task for *dichotomous image segmentation* (DIS) is possible. **Models.** are often struggling with the conflicts between stronger representative capabilities and higher risks of over-fitting. To obtain more representative features, FCN-based models [47], Encoder-Decoder [3,68], Coarse-to-Fine [81], Predict-Refine [64,77], Vision Transformer [99] and so on are developed. Besides, many real-time models are designed [23,35,41,56,57,90,95] to balance the performance and the time costs. Other methods, such as weights regularization [30], dropout [73], dense supervision [39,63,85], and hybrid loss [48,64,97], focus on alleviating the over-fitting. Dense supervision is one of the most effective ways for reducing the over-fitting. However, supervising the side outputs from the intermediate deep features may not be the best option because the supervision is weakened by the conversion from multi-channel deep features to single-channel side outputs. **Evaluation Metrics** can be categorized as *region-based* (*e.g.*, IoU or Jaccard index [1], F-measure [12,67] or Dice's coefficient [75], weighted F-measure [50]), *boundary-based* (*e.g.*, CM [55], boundary F-measure [15,51,54,60,64,69,94], boundary IoU [9], boundary displacement error (BDE) [25], Hausdorff distances [4,5,32]), *structure-based* (*e.g.*, S-measure [18], E-measure [19,21]), *confidence-based* (*e.g.*, MAE [59]), *etc.* They mainly measure the consistencies between the predictions and the ground truth from mathematical or cognitive perspectives. But the costs of synchronizing the predictions against the requirements in real-world applications are not well studied.

3 Proposed DIS5K Dataset

3.1 Data Collection and Annotation

Data Collection. To address the dataset issue (see §2), we build a highly accurate DIS dataset named **DIS5K**. We first manually collected over 12,000 images

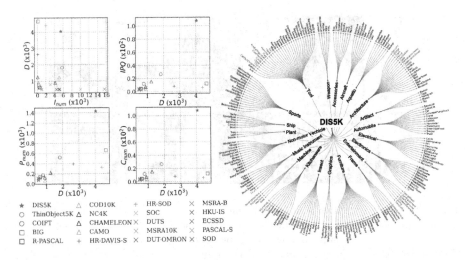

Fig. 2. Left: Correlations between different complexities. **Right**: Categories and groups of our DIS5K dataset. Zoom-in for better view. Please refer to §3.1 for details.

from Flickr[1] based on our pre-designed keywords[2]. Then, according to the structural complexities of the objects, we obtained 5,470 images covering 225 categories (Fig. 2) in 22 groups. Note that the adopted selection strategy is similar to Zhou et al. [100]. Most selected images only contain single objects to obtain rich and highly accurate structures and details. Meanwhile, the segmentation and labeling confusions caused by the co-occurrence of multiple objects from different categories are avoided to the greatest extent. Specifically, the image selection criteria can be summarized as follows:

- Cover more categories while reducing the number of "redundant" samples with simple structures, which other existing datasets have already covered.
- Enlarge the intra-category dissimilarities (See §2.3 of the supplementary (SM)) of the selected categories by adding more diversified intra-category images (Fig. 3-f).
- Include more categories with complicated structures, *e.g.*, *fence, stairs, cable, bonsai, tree, etc.*, which are common in our lives but not well-labeled (Fig. 3-a) or neglected by other datasets due to labeling difficulties.

Therefore, the labeled targets in our DIS5K are mainly the *"foreground objects of the images defined by the pre-designed keywords"* regardless of their characteristics *e.g.*, *salient, common, camouflaged, meticulous, etc.*

---

[1] Images with the license of "Commercial use & mods allowed".
[2] Since the long-term goal of this research is to facilitate the "safe" and "efficient" interaction between the machines and our living/working environments, these keywords are mainly related to the common targets (*e.g.*, bicycle, chair, bag, cable, tree, *etc.*) in our daily lives.

Fig. 3. Qualitative comparisons of different datasets. (a) and (b) indicate that our DIS5K provides more accurate labels. (c) shows one sample from COD10K [22], of which the structural complexity is caused by occlusion. (d) illustrates the synthetic ThinObject5K [43] dataset. (e) and (f) demonstrate that DIS5K has a larger diversity of intra-categorical structure complexities.

Data Annotation. Each image of DIS5K is manually labeled with pixel-wise accuracy using GIMP[3]. The average per-image labeling time is ∼30 min and some images cost up to 10 h. It is worth mentioning that some of our labeled ground truth (GT) masks are visually close to the image matting GT. The labeled targets, including transparent and translucent, are binary masks with one pixel's highest accuracy. Here, the DIS task is category-agnostic while our DIS5K is collected based on pre-designed keywords/categories, which seems contradictory. The reasons are threefold. (1) The keywords greatly facilitate the retrieval and organization of the large-scale dataset. (2) To achieve the goal of category-agnostic segmentation, diversified samples are needed. Collecting samples based on their categories is a reasonable way to guarantee the diversities' lower bound of the dataset. The diversities' upper bound of our DIS5K is determined by the diversified characteristics (*e.g.*, textures, structures, shapes, contrasts, complexities, *etc.*) of a large number of samples, guaranteeing the robustness and generalization of the category-agnostic segmentation. (3) There are no perfect datasets, so re-organizing or further extension of the existing datasets is usually necessary for different real-world applications. The category information will significantly facilitate tracing the collected and to-be-collected samples. Therefore, the category-based data collection is not contradictory but internally consistent with the goal of DIS task.

3.2 Data Analysis

For deeper insights into DIS dataset, we compare our DIS5K against 19 other related datasets including: (1) nine salient object detection (SOD) datasets:

---

[3] https://www.gimp.org/.

Table 1. Data analysis of existing datasets. See §3.2 for details.

Task	Dataset	Number	Image Dimension			Object Complexity		
		I_{num}	$H \pm \sigma_H$	$W \pm \sigma_W$	$D \pm \sigma_D$	$IPQ \pm \sigma_{IPQ}$	$C_{num} \pm \sigma_C$	$P_{num} \pm \sigma_P$
SOD	SOD [55]	300	366.87 ± 72.35	435.13 ± 72.35	578.28 ± 0.00	4.74 ± 3.89	2.25 ± 1.76	122.79 ± 62.97
	PASCAL-S [42]	850	387.63 ± 64.65	467.82 ± 61.46	613.22 ± 32.00	3.39 ± 2.46	5.14 ± 11.72	102.76 ± 70.09
	ECSSD [87]	1000	311.11 ± 56.27	375.45 ± 47.70	492.75 ± 19.78	3.26 ± 2.62	1.69 ± 1.42	107.54 ± 53.09
	HKU-IS [40]	4447	292.42 ± 51.13	386.64 ± 37.42	488.00 ± 29.44	4.41 ± 4.28	2.21 ± 2.07	114.05 ± 55.06
	MSRA-B [46]	5000	321.94 ± 56.33	370.86 ± 50.84	496.42 ± 22.53	2.89 ± 3.67	1.77 ± 2.25	102.04 ± 56.50
	DUT-OMRON [89]	5168	320.93 ± 54.35	376.78 ± 46.02	499.50 ± 22.97	4.08 ± 6.20	2.27 ± 3.54	71.09 ± 59.60
	MSRA10K [11]	10000	324.51 ± 56.26	370.27 ± 50.25	497.57 ± 22.79	2.54 ± 2.62	4.07 ± 17.94	101.95 ± 63.24
	DUTS [80]	15572	322.1 ± 53.69	375.48 ± 47.03	499.35 ± 21.95	3.37 ± 4.28	2.62 ± 4.73	84.78 ± 57.74
	SOC [17]	3000	480.00 ± 0.00	640.00 ± 0.00	800.00 ± 0.00	4.44 ± 3.57	13.69 ± 30.41	151.72 ± 154.83
HRS	HR-SOD [92]	2010	2713.12 ± 1043.7	3111.81 ± 1407.56	4465.46 ± 1631.03	5.85 ± 12.60	6.33 ± 16.65	319.32 ± 264.20
	HR-DAVIS-S [60]	92	1299.13 ± 440.77	2309.57 ± 783.59	2649.87 ± 899.05	7.84 ± 5.69	15.60 ± 29.51	389.58 ± 309.29
COD	CAMO [38]	250	564.22 ± 402.12	693.89 ± 578.53	905.51 ± 690.12	3.97 ± 4.47	1.48 ± 1.18	65.21 ± 40.99
	CHAMELEON [72]	76	741.80 ± 452.25	981.08 ± 464.88	1239.98 ± 629.19	15.25 ± 51.43	10.28 ± 48.03	222.45 ± 332.22
	NC4K [22]	4121	529.61 ± 158.16	709.19 ± 198.90	893.23 ± 223.94	7.28 ± 11.28	4.32 ± 9.44	125.43 ± 123.76
	COD10K [22]	5066	737.37 ± 185.65	963.85 ± 222.73	1224.53 ± 239.40	15.28 ± 71.84	17.18 ± 183.87	214.12 ± 857.83
SMS	R-PASCAL [10]	501	384.34 ± 64.69	469.66 ± 60.04	612.19 ± 36.32	4.44 ± 6.91	7.30 ± 8.73	139.31 ± 104.60
	BIG [10]	150	2801.11 ± 889.78	3672.43 ± 1128.90	4655.81 ± 1312.44	11.94 ± 31.43	31.69± 71.94	157.05 ± 710.20
TOS	COIFT [43]	280	488.27 ± 92.25	600.40 ± 78.66	782.73 ± 30.45	11.88 ± 12.5	4.01 ± 3.98	173.14 ± 74.54
	ThinObject5K [43]	5748	1185.59 ± 909.53	1325.06 ± 958.43	1823.03 ± 1258.49	20.11 ± 52.25	19.13 ± 210.07	519.14 ± 1325.51
DIS	**DIS5K (Ours)**	5470	2513.37 ± 1053.40	3111.44 ± 1339.51	4041.93 ± 1649.20	107.60 ± 320.69	106.84 ± 436.88	1427.82 ± 3326.72

SOD [55], PASCAL-S [42], ECSSD [87], HKU-IS [40], MSRA-B [46], DUT-OMRON [89], MSRA10K [11], DUTS [80], and SOC [17]; (2) two high-resolution salient object detection (HR-SOD) datasets: HR-SOD [92] and HR-DAVIS-S [60,92]; (3) four camouflaged object detection (COD) datasets: CAMO [38], CHAMELEON [72], COD10K [22], and NC4K [49]; (4) two semantic segmentation (SMS)[4] datasets: R-PASCAL [10,16] and BIG [10]; (5) two thin object segmentation (TOS) datasets: COIFT [43] and ThinObject5K [43]. The comparisons are conducted mainly from the following three perspectives: *image number*, *image dimension*, and *object complexity* as illustrated in Table 1.

Image Dimension is crucial to segmentation tasks because of its significant impacts on accuracy, efficiency, and computational costs. The mean (H, W, D) and standard deviations $(\sigma_H, \sigma_W, \sigma_D)$ of the image height, width and diagonal length are provided in Table 1. The BIG dataset has the largest average image dimensions, but it only contains 150 images. HR-SOD has slightly greater dimensions than ours, its complexity is low. The average dimensions of our DIS5K are almost eight times larger than those of the SOD and COD datasets. Besides, the targets in COD datasets are mainly animals and insects, which restricts its applications in diversified tasks.

Object Complexity is described by three metrics including the *isoperimetric inequality quotient* (IPQ) [58,82,88], the *number of object contours* (C_{num}) and the *number of dominant points* P_{num}. The IPQ mainly describes the overall structure complexity as $IPQ = \frac{L^2}{4\pi A}$, where L and A denote the object perimeter and the region area, respectively. It is designed to differentiate objects with elongated components and thin concave structures from close-to-convex objects.

---

[4] It is worth noting that only R-PASCAL and the BIG datasets are included here because they target highly accurate segmentation, and most of their images contain one or two objects, which is comparable to the listed tasks and datasets.

The C_{num} is used to represent the topological complexity in contour level for observing the objects consisting of many (small) contours which usually have minor influences on the IPQ. To describe the object complexity at a finer level, we employ P_{num} to count the number of the dominant points [65] along the object boundaries. Therefore, the complexities of the small jagged segments along the boundaries, which usually cannot be accurately measured by IPQ and C_{num}, can be well-evaluated with P_{num}. Essentially, P_{num} is the total number of the polygon corners needed for approximating the segmentation masks, which also directly reflects the human labeling costs. Thus, it is then adapted to our Human Correction Efforts (HCE) metric (§5) for evaluating the prediction quality.

Discussion. Table 1 and Fig. 2 (Left) illustrate the computed metrics. Our DIS5K is around 20 (up to 50) times more complicated than the SOD datasets in terms of average IPQ. Although CHAMELEON, COD10K, BIG, COIFT, and ThinObject5K have higher average IPQ against the SOD datasets, they are still much less complicated than ours. The average C_{num} and its standard deviation of DIS5K are over 100 and 400. This indicates the objects in DIS5K contain more detailed structures that are comprised of multiple contours. The average P_{num} of DIS5K is over 1400, which is almost five and three times greater than those of HR-SOD and the synthetic ThinObject5K, respectively. These three complexity measurements are complementary to provide a comprehensive analysis of the object complexities. The large standard deviations in Table 1 demonstrate the great diversities of DIS5K from different perspectives. Refer to the SM for more results. Figure 3-a shows an observation tower from DUT-OMRON. Similar object (b) has also been included in our DIS5K, which has higher labeling accuracy and structural complexity. Figure 3-c shows a sample from COD10K where the relatively higher structure complexity than that of SOD datasets is partially caused by the labeled occlusions, which are not the structural complexity of the target itself. A sample, where a set of the barbell is floating in the sky, from the synthesized ThinObject5K dataset is shown in Fig. 3-d. Synthesizing images is a common way for generating training sets in image matting [86,91]. But the synthesized images are usually different from the real ones, which leads to biases in predictions. Figure 3-e & f demonstrate the larger diversity of intra-categorical structure complexities of our DIS5K.

3.3   Dataset Splitting

We split 5,470 images in DIS5K into three subsets: DIS-TR (3,000), DIS-VD (470), and DIS-TE (2,000) for training, validation, and testing. The categories in DIS-TR and those in DIS-VD and DIS-TE are mainly consistent. Since our dataset's object shapes and structure complexities are diversified, the 2000 images of DIS-TE are further split into four subsets with ascending shape complexities for a more comprehensive evaluation. Specifically, we first rank the 2,000 testing images in ascending order according to the multiplication ($IPQ \times P_{num}$) of their structure complexities IPQ and boundary complexities P_{num}. Then, DIS-TE is split into four subsets (*i.e.*, DIS-TE1~DIS-TE4) with 500 images in each subset to represent four testing difficulty levels.

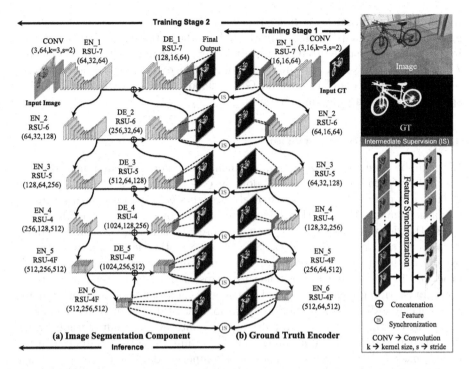

Fig. 4. Our IS-Net: (a) shows the image segmentation component, (b) illustrates the ground truth encoder built upon the intermediate supervision (IS) component.

4   Proposed IS-Net Baseline

Overview. As shown in Fig. 4, our IS-Net consists of a ground truth (GT) encoder, a image segmentation component, and a newly proposed intermediate supervision strategy. The **GT encoder** (27.7 MB) is designed to encode the GT masks into high-dimensional spaces and then used to enforce intermediate supervision on the segmentation component. While, the **image segmentation component** (176.6 MB) is expected to have the capability of capturing fine structures and handle large size e.g., 1024×1024, inputs with affordable memory and time costs. In the following experiment, we choose U^2-Net [63] as the image segmentation component because of its strong capability in capturing fine structures. Note that other segmentation models, such as transformer backbone, are also compatible with our strategy.

Technique Details. U^2-Net was originally designed for small size (320×320) SOD image. Because of its GPU memory costs, it cannot be used directly for handling large size (e.g., 1024×1024) inputs. We adapt the architecture of U^2-Net by adding an input convolution layer before its first encoder stage. The input convolution layer is set as a plain convolution layer with a kernel size of 3×3 and stride of 2. Given an input image with a shape of $I^{1024 \times 1024 \times 3}$, the input convolution layer first transforms it to a feature map $f^{512\times512\times64}$ and this feature map is then directly fed to the original U^2-Net, where the input channel is changed to 64 correspondingly. Compared with directly feeding $I^{1024\times1024\times3}$ to U^2-Net, the input convolution layer helps the whole network reduce three quarters of the overall GPU memory overhead while maintaining spatial information in feature channels.

4.1   Intermediate Supervision

DIS can be seen as a mapping in segmentation models from image domain $\mathcal{I} \in \mathbb{R}^{H\times W\times3}$ to segmentation GT domain $\mathcal{G} \in \mathbb{R}^{H\times W\times1}$: $\mathcal{G} = F(\theta, \mathcal{I})$, where F indicates the model that uses learnable weights θ to map inputs from image to mask domain. Most of the models are easy to over-fit on the training set. Thus, the deep supervision has been proposed to supervise the intermediate outputs of a given deep network [39]. In [63,85], the dense supervisions are usually applied to the side outputs, which are single-channel probability maps produced by convolving the last feature maps of particular deep layers. However, transforming high-dimensional features to single-channel probability maps is essentially a dimension reduction operation, inevitably losing critical cues.

   To avoid this issue, we propose a novel intermediate supervision training strategy. Given an input image $I^{H\times W\times3}$ and its corresponding segmentation mask $G^{W\times H\times1}$, we first train a self-supervised GT encoder to extract the high-dimensional features by "over-fitting" the training ground truth using a lightweight deep model F_{gt}, Fig. 4-b, as $\underset{\theta_{gt}}{\arg\min} \sum_{d=1}^{D} BCE(F_{gt}(\theta_{gt}, G)_d, G)$, where θ_{gt} indicates the model weights, BCE is the binary cross entropy loss and D denotes the number of the intermediate feature maps.

   After obtaining the GT encoder F_{gt}, its weights θ_{gt} are frozen for generating the "ground truth" high-dimensional intermediate deep features by: $f_D^G = F_{gt}^-(\theta_{gt}, G), D = \{1, 2, 3, 4, 5, 6\}$, where F_{gt}^- represents the F_{gt} without the last convolution layers for generating the probability maps. F_{gt}^- is to supervise those corresponding features f_D^I from the segmentation model F_{sg}. In the image segmentation component F_{sg} (Fig. 4-a), the image I is transformed to a set of high-dimensional intermediate feature maps f_D^I before producing the probability maps. Each feature map f_d^I has the same dimension with its corresponding GT intermediate feature map f_d^G: $f_D^I = F_{sg}^-(\theta_{sg}, I), D = \{1, 2, 3, 4, 5, 6\}$, where θ_{sg} denotes the weights of the segmentation model. Then, the intermediate supervision (IS) via *feature synchronization* on the deep intermediate features can be conducted by the following high-dimensional feature consistency loss: $L_{\text{fs}} = \sum_{d=1}^{D} \lambda_d^{fs} \left\| f_d^I - f_d^G \right\|^2$, where λ_d^{fs} denotes the weight of each FS loss. The training process of the segmentation model F_{sg} can be formulated as the following optimization problem: $\underset{\theta_{sg}}{\arg\min}(L_{\text{fs}} + L_{\text{sg}})$, where L_{sg} indicates the BCE loss of the side outputs of F_{sg}: $L_{\text{sg}} = \sum_{d=1}^{D} \lambda_d^{sg} BCE(F_{sg}(\theta_{sg}, I), G)$, where λ_d^{sg} represents the hyperparameter to weight each side output loss.

Fig. 5. Feature maps produced by the last layer of the EN_2 stage of our GT encoder. "21", "23", "29" and "37" are the indices (start with 1) of the corresponding channels in the feature map.

Figure 5 illustrates the feature maps from the stage 2 in Fig. 4, EN_2, of the GT encoder. We can see the diversified characteristics of the input mask are encoded into different channels. For example, the 21st channel encodes both the fine and large structures close to the original mask. While the 23rd, 29th, and 37th channels encode the middle size structures (seat, wheels), delicate structures (brake cables and spokes), large size region (the overall shape of the bicycle), respectively. These diversified features of the GT can provide stronger regularizations and more comprehensive supervisions for reducing the risks of over-fitting.

5   Proposed HCE Metric

Given a predicted segmentation probability map $P \in \mathbb{R}^{W \times H \times 1}$ and its corresponding GT mask $G \in \mathbb{R}^{W \times H \times 1}$, the existing metrics, *e.g.*, IoU, boundary IoU [9], F-measure [2], boundary F-measure [15,64], and MAE [59], usually evaluate the quality of the prediction P by calculating the scores based on the mathematical or cognitive consistency (or inconsistency) between P and G. In other words, these metrics describe how significant the "gap" is between P and G. However, evaluating the costs of filling the "gap" is more important than measuring the magnitude of the "gap" in many applications.

Therefore, we propose a novel evaluation metric, Human Correction Efforts (HCE), which measures the human efforts required in correcting faulty predictions to satisfy specific accuracy requirements in real-world applications. According to our labeling experiences, there are mainly two frequently used operations: (1) points selection along target boundaries to formulate polygons and (2) region selection based on similar pixel intensities inside the region. Both operations correspond to one mouse clicking. Therefore, the HCE here is quantified by the number of mouse clicking. To correct a faulty predicted mask, the operators need to manually sample dominant points along the erroneously predicted targets' boundaries or regions for correcting both False Positive (FP) and False Negative (FN) regions. As shown in Fig. 6, the FNs and FPs can be categorized into two classes, according to their adjacent regions: FN_N (N=TN+FP), FN_{TP}, FP_P (P=TP+FN) and FP_{TN}. To correct the FN_N regions, its boundaries adjacent to the TN need to be manually labeled with dominant points (Fig. 6-b). Similarly, to correct the FP_P regions, we only need to label its boundaries

48   X. Qin et al.

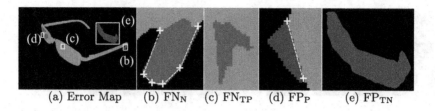

(a) Error Map   (b) FN_N   (c) FN_TP   (d) FP_P   (e) FP_TN

Fig. 6. Faulty regions to be corrected. Refer to §5 for details.

Input: P, G, $\gamma = 5$, *epsilon* = 2.0
Output: HCE_γ
1 G_{ske} = skeletonize (G);
2 $P_{or}G$, TP = or (P, G), and (P,G);
3 FN, FP = $(G - TP)$, $(P - TP)$;
4 **for** *(i = 0; i ≤ γ; i + +)* **do**
5 | $P_{or}G$ = erode $(P_{or}G, disk (1))$;
6 **end**
7 FN', FP' = and $(FN, P_{or}G)$, and $(FP, P_{or}G)$;
8 **for** *(i = 0; i ≤ γ; i + +)* **do**
9 | FN' = dilate $(FN', disk (1))$;
10 | FN' = and $(FN', not\ P)$;
11 | FP' = dilate $(FP', disk (1))$;
12 | FP' = and $(FP', not\ G)$;
13 **end**
14 FN', FP' = and (FN, FN'), and (FP, FP');
15 FN' = or $(FN', xor (G_{ske}, and (TP, G_{ske})))$;
16 HCE_γ = compute_HCE $(FN', FP', TP, epsilon)$

Algorithm 1: Relax HCE.

---

adjacent to the TP regions (Fig. 6-d). The FN_TP regions (Fig. 6-c) enclosed by TP and the FP_TN regions (Fig. 6-e) enclosed by TN can be easily corrected by one-click region selection. Therefore, the HCE for correcting the faulty regions in Fig. 6 (b-e) is 10 (six and two clicks needed in (b) and (d), one click needed in (c) and one click needed in (e)). The dominant point selection operations and the region selection operations are approximated by DP Algorithm [65] based on the contours obtained by OpenCV findContours [74] function and the connected regions labeling algorithm [24,84], respectively, in the evaluation stage.

Relax HCE. Some applications may be tolerant to certain minor prediction errors. Therefore, the HCE is extended by taking the error tolerance γ into consideration (HCE_γ). The key idea is to relax the FP and FN regions by excluding the small FP and FN components using erosion [31] and dilation [31]. Given a segmentation map P, its GT mask G, the error tolerance (*e.g.*, $\gamma = 5$, which denotes the size of the to-be-ignored small faulty regions), the *epsilon* of DP algorithm, the HCE_γ is calculated as Algorthim 1. Note that the erosion operation can remove all the thin and fine components of $P_{or}G$. However, some thin components (*e.g.*, thin cables, nets) are critical in describing the targets, and they need to be retained. To this end, the skeleton of the GT mask is extracted by [93] and combined with the relaxed FN' mask for retaining these structures.

Table 2. Quantitative evaluation on DIS5K validation and test sets. R = ResNet [33]. R2 = Res2Net [26]. S-813 = STDC813 [23], E-B1 = EffinetB1 [76].

Dataset	Metric	UNet [68]	BASNet [64]	GateNet [98]	F³Net [83]	GCPANet [8]	U²Net [63]	SINetV2 [20]	PFNet [52]	PSPNet [96]	DLV3+ [6]	HRNet [79]	BSV1 [90]	ICNet [95]	MBV3 [34]	STDC [28]	HySM [50]	IS-Net
Attr.	Backbone	-	R-34	R-50	R-50	R-50	-	R2-50	R-50	R-50	R-50	-	R-18	R-18	MBV3	S-813	E-B1	-
	Size (MB)	121.4	348.6	515.0	102.5	268.7	176.3	108.5	186.6	196.1	161.8	264.4	47.6	46.5	21.5	48.4	49.8	176.6
	Time (ms)	3.87	10.71	12.69	14.23	11.04	19.73	18.69	17.16	8.08	8.68	40.5	6.07	4.93	8.86	6.17	24.06	19.49
	Input Size	512^2	320^2	384^2	352^2	320^2	320^2	352^2	416^2	512^2	513^2	1024^2	1024×1024	1024×1024	1024^2	512×1024	411×1024	1024^2
DIS-VD	$maxF_\beta\uparrow$	.692	.731	.678	.685	.648	.748	.665	.691	.691	.660	.726	.662	.697	.714	.696	.784	.791
	$F_\beta^w\uparrow$	.586	.641	.574	.595	.542	.656	.584	.604	.603	.568	.641	.548	.609	.642	.613	.640	.717
	$M\downarrow$	.113	.094	.110	.107	.118	.090	.110	.106	.102	.114	.095	.116	.102	.092	.103	.096	.074
	$S_\alpha\uparrow$	.745	.788	.723	.733	.718	.781	.727	.740	.744	.716	.767	.728	.747	.758	.740	.773	.813
	$E_\phi^m\uparrow$	.785	.816	.783	.800	.765	.823	.798	.811	.802	.796	.824	.767	.811	.841	.817	.814	.856
	$HCE_\gamma\downarrow$	1337	1402	1493	1567	1555	1413	1568	1606	1588	1520	1560	1660	1503	1625	1598	1324	1116
DIS-TE1	$maxF_\beta\uparrow$	.625	.688	.620	.640	.598	.694	.644	.646	.645	.601	.688	.595	.631	.669	.648	.695	.740
	$F_\beta^w\uparrow$	.514	.595	.517	.549	.495	.601	.558	.552	.557	.506	.579	.474	.535	.595	.562	.597	.662
	$M\downarrow$	.106	.084	.099	.095	.103	.083	.094	.094	.089	.102	.088	.108	.095	.083	.090	.082	.074
	$S_\alpha\uparrow$	.716	.754	.701	.721	.705	.760	.727	.722	.725	.694	.742	.698	.716	.740	.723	.761	.787
	$E_\phi^m\uparrow$	.750	.801	.766	.783	.750	.801	.791	.796	.791	.772	.797	.741	.784	.818	.798	.803	.820
	$HCE_\gamma\downarrow$	233	220	230	244	271	224	274	253	267	234	262	288	234	374	249	205	149
DIS-TE2	$maxF_\beta\uparrow$	.703	.755	.702	.712	.673	.756	.700	.720	.724	.681	.747	.680	.716	.743	.720	.759	.799
	$F_\beta^w\uparrow$	.597	.668	.598	.620	.570	.668	.618	.633	.636	.587	.664	.564	.627	.672	.636	.667	.728
	$M\downarrow$	.107	.084	.102	.097	.109	.085	.099	.096	.092	.105	.087	.111	.098	.093	.092	.085	.070
	$S_\alpha\uparrow$	.755	.796	.737	.755	.735	.798	.753	.761	.763	.729	.784	.740	.759	.777	.759	.794	.823
	$E_\phi^m\uparrow$	.796	.836	.804	.815	.796	.833	.823	.829	.828	.813	.840	.761	.826	.856	.834	.832	.858
	$HCE_\gamma\downarrow$	474	480	501	542	574	490	503	567	586	516	555	621	512	600	556	451	340
DIS-TE3	$maxF_\beta\uparrow$	.748	.785	.726	.743	.699	.798	.730	.751	.747	.717	.794	.710	.752	.772	.745	.792	.830
	$F_\beta^w\uparrow$	.644	.696	.620	.656	.590	.707	.641	.664	.657	.623	.700	.595	.654	.702	.662	.701	.758
	$M\downarrow$	.098	.083	.103	.092	.109	.079	.096	.092	.092	.102	.080	.109	.091	.078	.090	.079	.064
	$S_\alpha\uparrow$	.780	.798	.747	.773	.748	.809	.766	.774	.749	.749	.805	.757	.780	.794	.771	.811	.836
	$E_\phi^m\uparrow$	.827	.856	.815	.848	.801	.858	.840	.854	.843	.833	.869	.801	.852	.880	.855	.857	.883
	$HCE_\gamma\downarrow$	883	948	972	1059	1055	965	1006	1082	1111	999	1049	1146	1001	1136	1081	887	687
DIS-TE4	$maxF_\beta\uparrow$	.759	.780	.729	.721	.670	.795	.699	.731	.725	.715	.772	.710	.749	.736	.731	.782	.827
	$F_\beta^w\uparrow$	.659	.693	.625	.633	.559	.705	.616	.647	.630	.621	.687	.598	.683	.684	.663	.693	.753
	$M\downarrow$	.102	.091	.109	.107	.127	.087	.113	.107	.107	.111	.092	.114	.099	.098	.102	.091	.072
	$S_\alpha\uparrow$	.784	.794	.743	.782	.723	.807	.744	.763	.758	.744	.792	.755	.776	.770	.762	.802	.830
	$E_\phi^m\uparrow$	.821	.848	.803	.825	.767	.847	.824	.839	.815	.820	.851	.778	.848	.841	.842	.870	.870
	$HCE_\gamma\downarrow$	3218	3601	3854	3760	3678	3653	3693	3803	3926	3759	3864	3699	3690	3817	3819	3331	2888
Overall DIS-TE (1-4)	$maxF_\beta\uparrow$	.708	.752	.694	.704	.660	.761	.693	.712	.710	.678	.743	.674	.711	.729	.710	.757	.799
	$F_\beta^w\uparrow$	.603	.663	.590	.614	.554	.670	.608	.624	.620	.584	.658	.558	.622	.658	.628	.665	.726
	$M\downarrow$	.103	.096	.103	.100	.112	.083	.101	.097	.095	.105	.087	.110	.095	.085	.094	.084	.070
	$S_\alpha\uparrow$	.759	.783	.732	.750	.728	.791	.747	.756	.755	.729	.781	.737	.758	.770	.754	.792	.819
	$E_\phi^m\uparrow$	.799	.835	.797	.819	.776	.835	.822	.827	.819	.810	.840	.778	.825	.850	.832	.834	.858
	$HCE_\gamma\downarrow$	1202	1313	1339	1401	1395	1333	1411	1427	1442	1432	1432	1513	1359	1457	1426	1218	1016

6 DIS5K Benchmark

As discussed above, our DIS5K is built from scratch to cover highly diversified objects with very different geometrical structures and image characteristics. One of the most important reasons is to exclude the existing datasets' possible biases (to specific image or object characteristics). Therefore, its diversities (*e.g.*, resolutions, image characteristics, object complexities, labeling accuracy) and distributions differ from the existing datasets. All models are trained, validated, and tested on DIS-TR, DIS-VD, and DIS-TE, respectively, to provide a fair comparison. Currently, cross-dataset evaluations [78] are not conducted mainly because their labeling accuracy is not consistent with ours.

Metrics. To provide relatively comprehensive and unbiased evaluations, six different metrics, including maximal F-measure ($F_\beta^{mx}\uparrow$) [2], weighted F-measure ($F_\beta^w\uparrow$) [50], mean absolute error ($M\downarrow$) [59], structural measure ($S_\alpha\uparrow$) [18], mean enhanced alignment measure ($E_\phi^m\uparrow$) [19,21] and our human correction efforts ($HCE\gamma\downarrow$), are used to evaluate the performance from different perspectives.

Competitors. We compared our IS-Net with 16 popular models designed for different segmentation tasks, including (i) popular medical image segmentation model, U-Net [68]; (ii) salient object detection models such as BASNet [64], GateNet [98], F³Net [83], GCPA [8] and U²-Net [63]; (iii) models designed for COD like SINet-V2[20] and PFNet [52]; (iv) semantic segmentation models: PSP-Net [96], DeepLab-V3+ [6] and HRNet [79]; (v) real-time semantic segmentation

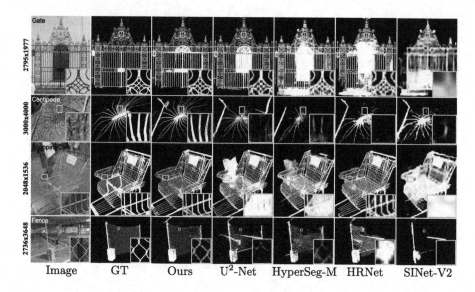

Fig. 7. Qualitative comparisons of IS-Net with four baselines.

models: BiSeNetV1 [90], ICNet [95], MobileNet-V3-Large [34], STDC [23] and HyperSegM [56]. All models are re-trained using DIS-TR set (on Tesla V100 or RTX A6000) and the time costs in Table 2 are all tested on RTX A6000.

6.1   Quantitative Evaluation

Compared with the 16 SOTA models, our IS-Net achieves the most competitive performance across all metrics (see Table 2). We observe that the performance of different models may be partially related to the spatial size of the model input and their feature maps. Most of the segmentation models introduce the classification backbones to construct their encoder-decoder architectures. However, backbones like ResNet-50 [33] starts with an input convolution layer (stride of two) followed by a pooling operation (stride of two) to reduce the spatial size of the feature maps, which leads to the loss of much spatial information and significant performance degradation. When the shape of the to-be-segmented target is close to convex, the degradation is less significant. However, many objects in DIS5K are non-convex, and they have very complicated and fine structures. It requires the models to keep the spatial information as much as possible, which is challenging to most models.

6.2   Qualitative Evaluation

Figure 7 presents qualitative comparisons between our approach and four SOTA baselines. Our model achieves promising results on the diverse scenes no matter that they are salient (gate), camouflaged (centipede), thin (shopping cart) or

Table 3. Ablation studies on our DIS-VD set.

Settings	F_β^{mx} ↑	F_β^w ↑	M ↓	S_α ↑	E_ϕ^m ↑	HCE_γ ↓
U^2-Net 320^2 (baseline)	.748	.656	.090	.781	.823	1413
U^2-Net 512^2	.769	.677	.085	.789	.826	1146
U^2-Net 1024^2	.764	.667	.088	.792	.820	1085
U^2-Net 1024^2 (**Adp**)	**.776**	**.695**	**.080**	**.804**	**.844**	**1076**
Adp+Last-1(L_2)	.777	.695	.080	.799	.840	1115
Adp+Last-2(L_2)	.778	.704	.079	.803	.847	**1049**
Adp+Last-3(L_2)	.788	.708	.079	**.812**	.845	1078
Adp+Last-4(L_2)	.782	.703	.079	.807	.849	1063
Adp+Last-5(L_2)	.788	**.715**	**.074**	.811	**.853**	1059
Adp+Last-6(L_2)	**.790**	.710	**.074**	.810	.852	1056
Adp+Last-6(KL)	.770	.684	.084	.794	.837	1092
Adp+Last-6(L_1)	.770	.686	.080	.797	.837	1144
Adp+Last-6(L_2) (shared outconv)	.745	.646	.094	.779	.813	1191
Adp+Last-6(L_2,sd(1))	.786	.706	.076	.807	.844	1086
Adp+Last-6(L_2,sd(58))	.790	.709	.078	.812	.848	**1085**
Adp+Last-6(L_2,sd(472))	.790	.712	.075	.812	.852	1071
Adp+Last-6(L_2,sd(5289)) (**IS-Net**)	**.791**	**.717**	**.074**	**.813**	**.856**	1116

meticulous (fence) objects, demonstrating the generalization capability of our IS-Net baseline.

6.3   Ablation Study

To validate the effectiveness of our adaptation on recent SOTA model *e.g.*, U^2-Net and our newly proposed intermediate supervision strategy, we conduct comprehensive ablation studies.

Input Size. As can be seen in Table 3, a larger input size can improve the performance of U^2-Net. However, it also increases the GPU memory costs so that we need to reduce the batch size (3 on Tesla V100, 32 GB) when the input size is 1024×1024, which degrades the performance. Our simple and effective variant (*i.e.*, Adp, 4rd row) addresses this memory issue and improves the performance.

Supervision on Different Decoder Stages. In Table 3, Last-S means the intermediate supervision is applied on the last S decoder stages. As shown, applying intermediate supervisions on the Last-6 stage gives relatively better performance, which is used as our default setting.

Different Loss. The results of different losses show that L_2 is better than KL divergence and $L1$. Besides, sharing the "outconvs", which transform the deep feature maps to the segmentation probability maps, of the GT encoders and the segmentation decoders leads to negative impacts.

Random Seeds. To study the influences of random weights initialization, we trained the same GT encoder multiple times with weights initialized by different random seeds. As seen, although the performance produced by different random seeds are different, their variations are minor, and all of them are better than that of the models (U^2-Net and Adp) trained without our intermediate supervision strategy. Since the model from seed 5289 ranks the 1st on five out of six overall metrics, we use this model as our IS-Net.

7 Conclusions

We have systematically studied the highly accurate dichotomous image segmentation (DIS) task from both the application and the research perspective. To prove that the task is solvable, we have built a new challenging **DIS5K** dataset, introduced a simple and effective intermediate supervision network, called IS-Net, to achieve high-quality segmentation results in real-time, and designed a novel Human Correction Efforts (**HCE**) metric by considering the shape complexities for applications. With an extensive ablation study and comprehensive benchmarking, we obtained that our newly formulated DIS task is solvable.

References

1. Jaccard index. https://en.wikipedia.org/wiki/Jaccard_index. (Accessed 21 Sep 2021)
2. Achanta, R., Hemami, S., Estrada, F., Susstrunk, S.: Frequency-tuned salient region detection. In: CVPR (2009)
3. Badrinarayanan, V., Kendall, A., Cipolla, R.: Segnet: A deep convolutional encoder-decoder architecture for image segmentation. IEEE TPAMI **39**(12), 2481–2495 (2017)
4. Birsan, T., Tiba, D.: One hundred years since the introduction of the set distance by dimitrie pompeiu. In: IFIP SMO (2005)
5. Blumberg, H.: Hausdorff's Grundzüge der Mengenlehre. Bull. Am. Math. Soc. **27**(3), 116–129 (1920)
6. Chen, L.-C., Zhu, Y., Papandreou, G., Schroff, F., Adam, H.: Encoder-decoder with atrous separable convolution for semantic image segmentation. In: Ferrari, V., Hebert, M., Sminchisescu, C., Weiss, Y. (eds.) ECCV 2018. LNCS, vol. 11211, pp. 833–851. Springer, Cham (2018). https://doi.org/10.1007/978-3-030-01234-2_49
7. Chen, S., Ma, X., Lu, Y., Hsu, D.: Ab initio particle-based object manipulation. In: Shell, D.A., Toussaint, M., Hsieh, M.A. (eds.) RSS (2021)
8. Chen, Z., Xu, Q., Cong, R., Huang, Q.: Global context-aware progressive aggregation network for salient object detection. In: AAAI (2020)
9. Cheng, B., Girshick, R., Dollár, P., Berg, A.C., Kirillov, A.: Boundary IoU: Improving object-centric image segmentation evaluation. In: CVPR (2021)
10. Cheng, H.K., Chung, J., Tai, Y.W., Tang, C.K.: Cascadepsp: Toward class-agnostic and very high-resolution segmentation via global and local refinement. In: CVPR (2020)
11. Cheng, M., Mitra, N.J., Huang, X., Torr, P.H.S., Hu, S.: Global contrast based salient region detection. IEEE TPAMI **37**(3), 569–582 (2015)
12. Chinchor, N.: MUC-4 evaluation metrics. In: MUC (1992)
13. Cordts, M., et al.: The cityscapes dataset for semantic urban scene understanding. In: CVPR (2016)
14. Deng, J., Dong, W., Socher, R., Li, L.J., Li, K., Fei-Fei, L.: Imagenet: A large-scale hierarchical image database. In: CVPR (2009)

15. Ehrig, M., Euzenat, J.: Relaxed precision and recall for ontology matching. In: K-CapW (2005)
16. Everingham, M., Van Gool, L., Williams, C.K., Winn, J., Zisserman, A.: The pascal visual object classes (voc) challenge. IJCV **88**(2), 303–338 (2010)
17. Fan, D.-P., Cheng, M.-M., Liu, J.-J., Gao, S.-H., Hou, Q., Borji, A.: Salient objects in clutter: Bringing salient object detection to the foreground. In: Ferrari, V., Hebert, M., Sminchisescu, C., Weiss, Y. (eds.) ECCV 2018. LNCS, vol. 11219, pp. 196–212. Springer, Cham (2018). https://doi.org/10.1007/978-3-030-01267-0_12
18. Fan, D.P., Cheng, M.M., Liu, Y., Li, T., Borji, A.: Structure-measure: A new way to evaluate foreground maps. In: ICCV (2017)
19. Fan, D.P., Gong, C., Cao, Y., Ren, B., Cheng, M.M., Borji, A.: Enhanced-alignment measure for binary foreground map evaluation. In: IJCAI (2018)
20. Fan, D.P., Ji, G.P., Cheng, M.M., Shao, L.: Concealed object detection. In: IEEE TPAMI (2021)
21. Fan, D.P., Ji, G.P., Qin, X., Cheng, M.M.: Cognitive vision inspired object segmentation metric and loss function. In: SSI, vol. 6 (2021)
22. Fan, D.P., Ji, G.P., Sun, G., Cheng, M.M., Shen, J., Shao, L.: Camouflaged object detection. In: CVPR (2020)
23. Fan, M., et al.: Rethinking bisenet for real-time semantic segmentation. In: CVPR (2021)
24. Fiorio, C., Gustedt, J.: Two linear time union-find strategies for image processing. TCS **154**(2), 165–181 (1996)
25. Freixenet, J., Muñoz, X., Raba, D., Martí, J., Cufí, X.: Yet another survey on image segmentation: Region and boundary information integration. In: Heyden, A., Sparr, G., Nielsen, M., Johansen, P. (eds.) ECCV 2002. LNCS, vol. 2352, pp. 408–422. Springer, Heidelberg (2002). https://doi.org/10.1007/3-540-47977-5_27
26. Gao, S.H., Cheng, M.M., Zhao, K., Zhang, X.Y., Yang, M.H., Torr, P.: Res2net: A new multi-scale backbone architecture. IEEE TPAMI **43**(2), 652–662 (2019)
27. Girshick, R.: Fast r-cnn. In: ICCV (2015)
28. Girshick, R.B., Donahue, J., Darrell, T., Malik, J.: Rich feature hierarchies for accurate object detection and semantic segmentation. In: CVPR (2014)
29. Goferman, S., Zelnik-Manor, L., Tal, A.: Context-aware saliency detection. IEEE TPAMI **34**(10), 1915–1926 (2012)
30. Goodfellow, I., Bengio, Y., Courville, A.: Deep Learning. MIT Press (2016). http://www.deeplearningbook.org
31. Haralick, R.M., Sternberg, S.R., Zhuang, X.: Image analysis using mathematical morphology. IEEE TPAMI PAMI **9**(4), 532–550 (1987)
32. Hausdorff, F.: Grundzüge der Mengenlehre. Leipzig: Veit, ISBN 978-0-8284-0061-9 Reprinted by Chelsea Publishing Company in 1949, Germany (1914)
33. He, K., Zhang, X., Ren, S., Sun, J.: Deep residual learning for image recognition. In: CVPR (2016)
34. Howard, A., et al.: Searching for mobilenetv3. In: ECCV (2019)
35. Hu, P., Caba, F., Wang, O., Lin, Z., Sclaroff, S., Perazzi, F.: Temporally distributed networks for fast video semantic segmentation. In: CVPR (2020)
36. Ke, Z., et al.: Is a green screen really necessary for real-time portrait matting? arXiv: 2011.11961 (2020)
37. Krizhevsky, A., Sutskever, I., Hinton, G.E.: Imagenet classification with deep convolutional neural networks. In: NeurIPS (2012)
38. Le, T.N., Nguyen, T.V., Nie, Z., Tran, M.T., Sugimoto, A.: Anabranch network for camouflaged object segmentation. CVIU **184**, 45–56 (2019)

39. Lee, C.Y., Xie, S., Gallagher, P., Zhang, Z., Tu, Z.: Deeply-supervised nets. In: AISTATS (2015)

40. Li, G., Yu, Y.: Visual saliency based on multiscale deep features. In: CVPR (2015)

41. Li, H., Xiong, P., Fan, H., Sun, J.: Dfanet: Deep feature aggregation for real-time semantic segmentation. In: CVPR (2019)

42. Li, Y., Hou, X., Koch, C., Rehg, J.M., Yuille, A.L.: The secrets of salient object segmentation. In: CVPR (2014)

43. Liew, J.H., Cohen, S., Price, B., Mai, L., Feng, J.: Deep interactive thin object selection. In: WACV (2021)

44. Lin, S., Yang, L., Saleemi, I., Sengupta, S.: Robust high-resolution video matting with temporal guidance. arXiv: 2108.11515 (2021)

45. Lin, T.-Y.: Microsoft COCO: common objects in context. In: Fleet, D., Pajdla, T., Schiele, B., Tuytelaars, T. (eds.) ECCV 2014. LNCS, vol. 8693, pp. 740–755. Springer, Cham (2014). https://doi.org/10.1007/978-3-319-10602-1_48

46. Liu, T., et al.: Learning to detect a salient object. IEEE TPAMI **33**(2), 353–367 (2011)

47. Long, J., Shelhamer, E., Darrell, T.: Fully convolutional networks for semantic segmentation. In: CVPR (2015)

48. Luc, P., Couprie, C., Chintala, S., Verbeek, J.: Semantic segmentation using adversarial networks. arXiv preprint arXiv:1611.08408 (2016)

49. Lv, Y., Zhang, J., Dai, Y., Li, A., Liu, B., Barnes, N., Fan, D.P.: Simultaneously localize, segment and rank the camouflaged objects. In: CVPR (2021)

50. Margolin, R., Zelnik-Manor, L., Tal, A.: How to evaluate foreground maps. In: CVPR (2014)

51. Martin, D.R., Fowlkes, C.C., Malik, J.: Learning to detect natural image boundaries using local brightness, color, and texture cues. IEEE TPAMI **26**(5), 530–549 (2004)

52. Mei, H., Ji, G.P., Wei, Z., Yang, X., Wei, X., Fan, D.P.: Camouflaged object segmentation with distraction mining. In: CVPR (2021)

53. Mnih, V.: Machine Learning for Aerial Image Labeling. Ph.D. thesis, University of Toronto (2013)

54. Mnih, V., Hinton, G.E.: Learning to detect roads in high-resolution aerial images. In: Daniilidis, K., Maragos, P., Paragios, N. (eds.) ECCV 2010. LNCS, vol. 6316, pp. 210–223. Springer, Heidelberg (2010). https://doi.org/10.1007/978-3-642-15567-3_16

55. Movahedi, V., Elder, J.H.: Design and perceptual validation of performance measures for salient object segmentation. In: CVPRW (2010)

56. Nirkin, Y., Wolf, L., Hassner, T.: Hyperseg: Patch-wise hypernetwork for real-time semantic segmentation. arXiv preprint arXiv:2012.11582 (2020)

57. Orsic, M., Kreso, I., Bevandic, P., Segvic, S.: In defense of pre-trained imagenet architectures for real-time semantic segmentation of road-driving images. In: CVPR (2019)

58. Osserman, R.: The isoperimetric inequality. BAM **84**(6), 1182–1238 (1978)

59. Perazzi, F., Krähenbühl, P., Pritch, Y., Hornung, A.: Saliency filters: Contrast based filtering for salient region detection. In: CVPR (2012)

60. Perazzi, F., et al.: A benchmark dataset and evaluation methodology for video object segmentation. In: CVPR (2016)

61. Qi, L., et al.: Open-world entity segmentation. arXiv preprint arXiv:2107.14228 (2021)

62. Qin, X., et al.: Boundary-aware segmentation network for mobile and web applications. arXiv preprint arXiv:2101.04704 (2021)

63. Qin, X., Zhang, Z., Huang, C., Dehghan, M., Zaiane, O.R., Jagersand, M.: U2-net: Going deeper with nested u-structure for salient object detection. PR **106**, 107404 (2020)

64. Qin, X., Zhang, Z., Huang, C., Gao, C., Dehghan, M., Jagersand, M.: Basnet: Boundary-aware salient object detection. In: CVPR (2019)

65. Ramer, U.: An iterative procedure for the polygonal approximation of plane curves. CGIP **1**(3), 244–256 (1972)

66. Ren, S., He, K., Girshick, R., Sun, J.: Faster r-cnn: Towards real-time object detection with region proposal networks. In: NeurIPS (2015)

67. van Rijsbergen, C.J.: Information retrieval. London: Butterworths (1979).http://www.dcs.gla.ac.uk/Keith/Preface.html (1979)

68. Ronneberger, O., Fischer, P., Brox, T.: U-Net: Convolutional networks for biomedical image segmentation. In: Navab, N., Hornegger, J., Wells, W.M., Frangi, A.F. (eds.) MICCAI 2015. LNCS, vol. 9351, pp. 234–241. Springer, Cham (2015). https://doi.org/10.1007/978-3-319-24574-4_28

69. Saito, S., Yamashita, T., Aoki, Y.: Multiple object extraction from aerial imagery with convolutional neural networks. EI **2016**(10), 1–9 (2016)

70. Shen, X., et al.: Automatic portrait segmentation for image stylization. In: CGF (2016)

71. Simonyan, K., Zisserman, A.: Very deep convolutional networks for large-scale image recognition. In: ICLR (2015)

72. Skurowski, P., Abdulameer, H., Błaszczyk, J., Depta, T., Kornacki, A., Kozieł, P.: Animal camouflage analysis: Chameleon database. Unpublished Manuscript (2018)

73. Srivastava, N., Hinton, G.E., Krizhevsky, A., Sutskever, I., Salakhutdinov, R.: Dropout: a simple way to prevent neural networks from overfitting. JMLR **15**(1), 1929–1958 (2014)

74. Suzuki, S., Abe, K.: Topological structural analysis of digitized binary images by border following. CVGIP **30**(1), 32–46 (1985)

75. Sørensen, T.J.: A method of establishing groups of equal amplitude in plant sociology based on similarity of species content and its application to analyses of the vegetation on Danish commons. I kommission hos E. Munksgaard, Denmark, København (1948)

76. Tan, M., Le, Q.: Efficientnet: Rethinking model scaling for convolutional neural networks. In: ICML, pp. 6105–6114 (2019)

77. Tang, L., Li, B., Zhong, Y., Ding, S., Song, M.: Disentangled high quality salient object detection. In: ICCV (2021)

78. Torralba, A., Efros, A.A.: Unbiased look at dataset bias. In: CVPR (2011)

79. Wang, J., et al.: Deep high-resolution representation learning for visual recognition. In: IEEE TPAMI (2019)

80. Wang, L., et al.: Learning to detect salient objects with image-level supervision. In: CVPR (2017)

81. Wang, T., et al.: Detect globally, refine locally: A novel approach to saliency detection. In: CVPR (2018)

82. Watson, A.B.: Perimetric complexity of binary digital images. Math. J. **14**, 1–40 (2012)

83. Wei, J., Wang, S., Huang, Q.: F^3net: Fusion, feedback and focus for salient object detection. In: AAAI (2020)

84. Wu, K., Otoo, E.J., Shoshani, A.: Optimizing connected component labeling algorithms. In: Fitzpatrick, J.M., Reinhardt, J.M. (eds.) MI (2005)

85. Xie, S., Tu, Z.: Holistically-nested edge detection. In: ICCV (2015)
86. Xu, N., Price, B., Cohen, S., Huang, T.: Deep image matting. In: CVPR (2017)
87. Yan, Q., Xu, L., Shi, J., Jia, J.: Hierarchical saliency detection. In: CVPR (2013)
88. Yang, C., Wang, Y., Zhang, J., Zhang, H., Lin, Z., Yuille, A.: Meticulous object segmentation. arXiv preprint arXiv:2012.07181 (2020)
89. Yang, C., Zhang, L., Lu, H., Ruan, X., Yang, M.H.: Saliency detection via graph-based manifold ranking. In: CVPR (2013)
90. Yu, C., Wang, J., Peng, C., Gao, C., Yu, G., Sang, N.: BiSeNet: bilateral segmentation network for real-time semantic segmentation. In: Ferrari, V., Hebert, M., Sminchisescu, C., Weiss, Y. (eds.) ECCV 2018. LNCS, vol. 11217, pp. 334–349. Springer, Cham (2018). https://doi.org/10.1007/978-3-030-01261-8_20
91. Yu, H., Xu, N., Huang, Z., Zhou, Y., Shi, H.: High-resolution deep image matting. arXiv preprint arXiv:2009.06613 (2020)
92. Zeng, Y., Zhang, P., Zhang, J., Lin, Z., Lu, H.: Towards high-resolution salient object detection. In: CVPR, pp. 7234–7243 (2019)
93. Zhang, T.Y., Suen, C.Y.: A fast parallel algorithm for thinning digital patterns. Commun. ACM **27**(3), 236–239 (1984)
94. Zhang, Z., Liu, Q., Wang, Y.: Road extraction by deep residual u-net. GRSL **15**(5), 749–753 (2018)
95. Zhao, H., Qi, X., Shen, X., Shi, J., Jia, J.: ICNet for real-time semantic segmentation on high-resolution images. In: Ferrari, V., Hebert, M., Sminchisescu, C., Weiss, Y. (eds.) ECCV 2018. LNCS, vol. 11207, pp. 418–434. Springer, Cham (2018). https://doi.org/10.1007/978-3-030-01219-9_25
96. Zhao, H., Shi, J., Qi, X., Wang, X., Jia, J.: Pyramid scene parsing network. In: CVPR (2017)
97. Zhao, J.X., Liu, J.J., Fan, D.P., Cao, Y., Yang, J., Cheng, M.M.: Egnet: Edge guidance network for salient object detection. In: ICCV (2019)
98. Zhao, X., Pang, Y., Zhang, L., Lu, H., Zhang, L.: Suppress and balance: A simple gated network for salient object detection. In: Vedaldi, A., Bischof, H., Brox, T., Frahm, J.-M. (eds.) ECCV 2020. LNCS, vol. 12347, pp. 35–51. Springer, Cham (2020). https://doi.org/10.1007/978-3-030-58536-5_3
99. Zheng, S., et al.: Rethinking semantic segmentation from a sequence-to-sequence perspective with transformers. In: CVPR (2021)
100. Zhou, B., Lapedriza, A., Khosla, A., Oliva, A., Torralba, A.: Places: A 10 million image database for scene recognition. IEEE TPAMI **40**(6), 1452–1464 (2017)
101. Zhou, B., Zhao, H., Puig, X., Fidler, S., Barriuso, A., Torralba, A.: Scene parsing through ade20k dataset. In: CVPR (2017)

Boosting Supervised Dehazing Methods via Bi-level Patch Reweighting

Xingyu Jiang[1], Hongkun Dou[1], Chengwei Fu[1], Bingquan Dai[1], Tianrun Xu[2], and Yue Deng[1($\boxtimes$)]

[1] School of Astronautics, Beihang University, Beijing, China
ydeng@buaa.edu.cn
[2] North China University of Technology, Beijing, China

Abstract. Natural images can suffer from non-uniform haze distributions in different regions. However, this important fact is hardly considered in existing supervised dehazing methods, in which all training patches are accounted for equally in the loss design. These supervised methods may fail in making promising recoveries on some regions contaminated by heavy hazes. Therefore, for a more reasonable dehazing losses design, the varying importance of different training patches should be taken into account. Such rationale is exactly in line with the process of human learning that difficult concepts always require more practice in learning. To this end, we propose a bi-level dehazing (BILD) framework by designing an internal loop for weighted supervised dehazing and an external loop for training patch reweighting. With simple derivations, we show the gradients of BILD exhibit natural connections with policy gradient and can thus explain the BILD objective by the rewarding mechanism in reinforcement learning. The BILD is not a new dehazing method per se, it is better recognized as a flexible framework that can seamlessly work with general supervised dehazing approaches for their performance boosting.

Keywords: Single image dehazing · Bi-level optimization · Visual importance · Deep learning

1 Introduction

Image dehazing has been widely discussed in the computer vision community and is vital for subsequent high-level tasks including image classification [23] and object detection [9]. Conventional dehazing algorithms can be categorized into prior-based approaches [20,47] and data-driven approaches (*a.k.a.* supervised approaches) [34,35,45]. Prior-based dehazing models are mainly built upon the basic atmospheric scattering model [30,31] with various physical assumptions imposed on image statistics. These prior-based models are more interpretable but

Supplementary Information The online version contains supplementary material available at https://doi.org/10.1007/978-3-031-19797-0_4.

can easily fail in real-world images where the assumed prior does not hold. Data-driven methods [12,26,43] tackle the dehazing problem from the view of supervised learning. Early supervised dehazing approaches [8,23] mainly contribute to designing learnable parametrized functions (*e.g.* a neural network) to replace some important modules (*e.g.* transmission maps) in the traditional atmospheric scattering model. Recent works [26,32] show the potential to conduct supervised dehazing in an end-to-end manner by directly learning the hazy-to-clear mapping. Compared with the prior-based dehazing models, these data-driven approaches can better approximate the complex structure of the high-dimensional image manifold and hence achieve better performances on real-world images.

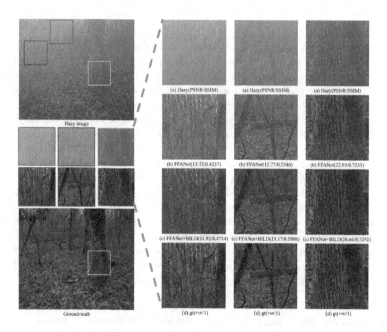

Fig. 1. The left shows non-uniform haze distributions in different regions. The degradation degree of red, blue and yellow patches varies from severe to mild. Compared with equally additive loss design (*e.g.* L1 loss in FFANet [32]), BILD framework performs much better in restoring dense-haze regions from both visualization and quantitative evaluations via PSNR/SSIM. (Color figure online)

In the benchmark supervised dehazing protocol, large hazy images are always cropped into patches for subsequent dehazing learning [11,12,26,32]. Such patch-level dehazing implementation can enhance the diversity of training samples, reduce the demands of hardware memory and improve the flexibility for parallelized training [7,46]. Then, these patch-level losses are equally accumulated to define the image-level loss. While this equally accumulated loss is extensively used in existing works, we still suspect its reasonableness in the context of image dehazing. The haze distributions of real-world scenes are highly non-uniform

[1,3], making the cropped image patches vary greatly in degradation degrees (see the left column of Fig. 1). When dehazing all patches with the same efforts, even the SOTA method (FFANet [32]) cannot effectively restore the seriously contaminated patch from heavy haze (see the (b) row of Fig. 1). Accordingly, the heterogeneity of these training patches should not be overlooked and their unique importances should be properly discriminated in the loss design.

To address the aforementioned challenges, we introduce a simple patch reweighting strategy by assigning different importance weights to different patches. In this way, the image-level loss is becoming a weighted summation of the individual losses from its containing patches. Such patch-level reweighting is intuitive and exactly mimic the behaviour of human learning, that people always invest more learning efforts on valuable matters [37,39,42]. As a whole, we design a bi-level dehazing(BILD) framework to enable automatically patch reweighting by monitoring the learned dehazing performances on some out-of-sample data. In details, the internal loop of BILD is trained for weighted supervised dehazing with in-sample training patches; and the external loop utilizes out-of-sample patches from validation set for training patch reweighting. The in-sample training and out-of-sample validating strategy can ultimately enhance the generalization ability of the trained dehazing machines.

With simple derivatives, we further bridge our BILD model with the policy gradient and interpret its objective function from max-entropy reinforcement learning [18]. The dehazing performances of the same algorithm can be non-trivially improved by BILD (as observed from the (c) row in Fig. 1), especially for those hard patches. While only the FFANet [32] was used as a showcase here, we emphasized that the BILD is general enough to improve other supervised dehazing methods, by simply integrating their respective objectives into BILD's internal loop.

We summarize the main contributions as three-fold:

- We propose bi-level dehazing (BILD)—a general framework that is compatible with various supervised dehazing approaches for performance boosting, especially in restoring seriously degraded regions.
- We introduce the reweighting and validating concepts into dehazing tasks for improving their generalizations in dehazing new images with non-uniform haze distributions.
- We uncover the natural connections of our BILD model with max-entropy reinforcement learning, enhancing the interpretability of the whole learning process from the novel view of agent-environment interactions.

2 Related Work

Single Image Dehazing. All along, single image dehazing is viewed as a highly ill-posed problem, which requires extra prior information or constraints. To tackle this problem, existing single image dehazing methods can be divided into two categories: the prior-based methods [6,20,28,47] and the data-driven methods [11,33–36].

Most prior-based approaches employ novel physical assumptions (*e.g.* DCP [20], CAP [47], NLD [6]) to estimate the transmission map and ambient light[5] in atmospheric scattering model [30,31], which can explicitly recover a clear image from haze. For instance, He *et al.* [20] notice pixels (at least one channel) tend to zero on non-sky regions. Berman *et al.* [6] observe pixel colors of the whole scene can be well clustered to hundreds of distinct colors. These prior-based methods show nice statistical properties in specific scenes, but can easily fail in real-world images where the physical assumptions do not hold.

Recently, data-driven supervised dehazing methods have been proposed to overcome shortcomings of traditional prior-based methods, with advances in deep learning and the establishment of large-scale datasets[1,2,24]. Early supervised dehazing approaches [8,23,45] design learnable neural networks to estimate the transmission map and ambient light. In [8], DehazeNet designs a three-layer CNN with BReLU activation function to estimate transmission map. Recent works trigger a great impact on supervised dehazing by learning the hazy-to-clear mapping in an end-to-end manner. The GridDehazeNet [26] designs an attention-based multi-scale network to directly recover haze-free images and introduces perception loss in objective. In [43], AECRNet develops an autoencoder-like dehazing network with a novel contrastive regularization. Although great advances have been made in network architecture and loss design, samples of different importances are equally accounted in loss computation. In this work, by introducing the idea of visual importance, we design a weighted loss function based on traditional L1/L2 loss and employ bi-level optimization strategy to optimize it.

Bi-level Optimization. Bi-level optimization is committed to optimizing another set of parameters other than target network parameters, which describes higher-level elements related to training neural networks [37]. Wu *et al.* [44] trains a task scheduler for sequential learning to better assist the main task. Wang *et al.*[42] uses bi-level optimization to help with data selection. Sun *et al.* [39] designs an efficient data sampling schedule for learning a robust sampling strategy. In addition, the bi-level optimization can also be used to optimize the graph structure and embedding [14], ensemble model [25,27], data auto-augment [10,29,41] and search network structure [4,15]. In this work, inspired by the idea of maximum entropy in reinforcement learning [17,19], we design the entropy regular term in external loop to alleviate the phenomenon of weight concentration in one batch, which can enhance the stability of training process. To our best knowledge, we are the first paper to combine bi-level optimization with visual importance in the field of image restoration and our BILD framework can boost the performance of supervised dehazing methods well beyond SOTA.

3   Bi-level Dehazing Framework

3.1   Patch Reweighting

In supervised dehazing training, small patches x are cropped from the large hazy image and are fed into an arbitrary dehazing neural network $f_d(\cdot; \theta)$ parametrized by θ. The dehazing performance on this single patch can be quantified by counting the differences between the dehazed image with its corresponding ground truth clean image y under some proper loss L, e.g. the L_1 norm:

$$\ell(x, y; \theta) = L(f_d(x; \theta), y) \tag{1}$$

Then, these single-patch-losses are equally accumulated forming the global loss function J_e on the training set $\mathcal{D}_t$:

$$J_e(\mathcal{D}_t; \theta) = \mathop{\mathbb{E}}_{(x,y) \sim \mathcal{D}_t} \ell(x, y; \theta) \tag{2}$$

The additive loss J_e implies that different patches are treated equally in training, although they can suffer from very different degrees of degradation or with very diverse pixel distributions. While J_e has already been a benchmark loss function used in most existing supervised dehazing methods, we still consider it is not ideal for the discussed dehazing tasks because the haze distribution on the same scene can be highly heterogeneous (see Fig. 1). Therefore, the values of different training samples should be properly weighted and exploited in the loss design. To this end, we introduce a more reasonable dehazing loss by the intuitive reweighting mechanism:

$$J_w(\mathcal{D}_t; \phi, \theta) = \mathop{\mathbb{E}}_{(x,y) \sim \mathcal{D}_t} w(x, y; \phi) \ell(x, y; \theta) \tag{3}$$

where $w(x, y; \phi) = f_w(x, y; \phi)$ is the output of the weighting neural network $f_w(\cdot; \phi)$ with (x, y) as input. We remark here that although we have fully emphasized the importance of patch reweighting, the underlying weighting mechanism is still unknown. For instance, for two patches that vary in backgrounds and illuminations, there is no concrete prior to inform us which patch should be weighed heavier than the other in the loss function. Accordingly, rather than heuristic weighting, we opt to adopt the parametrized weighting mechanism that can automatically assess the importance of each training patch through a learnable neural network $f_w(\cdot; \psi)$.

3.2 Bi-level Dehazing Framework

While the aforementioned parametrized weighting concept is simple, it yields a highly under-determined and non-convex objective function coupled with two unknown neural networks. Without extra constraints, the direct minimization of $J_w(\mathcal{D}_t; \phi, \theta)$ on the training set can easily lead to a trivial solution. In this case, the reweighting neural network $f_w(\cdot; \psi)$ may intend to assign (near) zero weights to all patches and hence totally mute the functions of the dehazing network (see the multiplications between the weight term and dehazing loss term in J_w in Eq. 3). To avoid such trivial solution, extra constraints or guiding information should be imposed to restrict the feasibility of the learned results. In this work, inspired by recent works [16,37,39,41,42], we consider enforcing the feasibility of the learned results by monitoring the dehazing networks' performances on

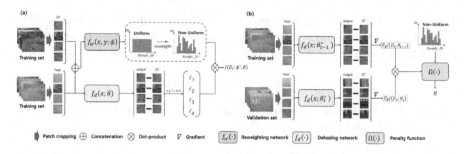

Fig. 2. The optimization process of the BILD framework, which consists of two loops. (a) The computational flow of internal weighted supervised dehazing loop. Patches from training set are fed into reweighting and dehazing network, respectively, to generate patch-wise weights and reconstruction loss of restored images and ground-truth. Then, the dot-product of the two outputs yields the objective function of internal loop. (b) The computational flow of external patch reweighting loop. Patches from training and validation set are respectively fed into dehazing networks of two consecutive iterations to obtain the gradient of reconstruction loss($e.g.$ L1 loss). Then, the combination of the saved gradient and penalty function constitutes the key reward for external loop updating(see Eq. 6 and 7)

a new validation set $\mathcal{D}_v, \mathcal{D}_t \cap \mathcal{D}_v = \varnothing$ (see related ablation study in Sect. 4.3). With this objective, the whole learning process is subject to the following bi-level dehazing (BILD) optimization:

$$\min_{\phi} \quad J_e\left(\mathcal{D}_v; \theta^*(\phi)\right) + \alpha \Omega(\boldsymbol{w})$$
$$\text{s.t. } \theta^*(\phi) = \arg\min_{\theta} J_w\left(\mathcal{D}_t; \phi, \theta\right) \tag{4}$$

The above bi-level optimization is composed of the internal loop in the constraint and the external loop in the objective function. The internal loop minimizes the empirical error of the training set under guidances of the patch-wise weight provided by the external loop. The external loop trades off the generalization error and penalty term with a hyper-parameter α. The generalization error is obtained by evaluating the current suboptimal dehazing network on the keep-out validation data and the penalty term quantify the structure of $\boldsymbol{w}$ with a function $\Omega(\boldsymbol{w})$, where $\boldsymbol{w} = [w(x_0, y_0; \phi), w(x_1, y_1; \phi), \cdots, w(x_n, y_n; \phi)]^\top$ and n is the number of training patches in a batch. The most intuitive penalty function can be used here is the entropy term that encourages the learned patch-wise weight not only to concentrate on a small number of training patches.

The primary advantage of building up the external loop is to enhance our dehazing models' generalization ability outside the training samples. Loosely speaking, the external loop learns to generate a set of reasonable weights $w(\cdot; \phi)$ that can guide the internal optimization converging to better solutions with enhanced generalization ability. The enhanced generalization ability covers two angles including better generalization to out-of-sample new images (granted by the validating mechanism in the external loop) and better generalization to various training patches (granted by the weighting mechanism in the internal loop).

The parameter (θ) is only involved in the internal loop and can be easily updated with typical gradient descending approaches on a sampled batch with n patches,

$$\theta_t \leftarrow \theta_{t-1} - \eta_1 \nabla_\theta \sum_{i=0}^{n} w(x_i, y_i; \phi) \ell(x_i, y_i; \theta) \tag{5}$$

The major difficulty of the BILD optimization stems from the external loop to learn parameter ϕ for the reweighting neural network. As witnessed in Eq. 4, ϕ is coupled into θ and its gradient can be derived by applying the chain rule(detailed derivation is available in supplement):

$$\nabla_\phi \left(J_e \left(\mathcal{D}_v; \theta_t \right) + \alpha \Omega(\boldsymbol{w}) \right)$$

$$= -\sum_i \nabla_\phi \log w \left(x_i, y_i; \phi \right)$$

$$\cdot \underbrace{ w \left(x_i, y_i; \phi \right) \left[\nabla_\theta J_e \left(\mathcal{D}_v; \theta_t \right)^\top \nabla_\theta \ell \left(x_i, y_i; \theta_{t-1} \right) - \alpha \frac{\partial \Omega(\boldsymbol{w})}{\partial w(x_i, y_i; \phi)} \right] }_{R_i} \tag{6}$$

The above equation is an approximate solution for external loop updating. The R_i can be regarded as the feedback of internal dehazing loop to patch reweighting neural network(As is shown in Fig. 2b). Here, we use entropy $\mathcal{H}(\boldsymbol{w})$ as the regular term $\Omega(\boldsymbol{w})$, preventing over concentration of sample weight. Thus, we get the update rule of ϕ,

$$\phi_t \leftarrow \phi_{t-1} + \eta_2 \sum_{i=0}^{n} \frac{1}{n} R_i \cdot \nabla_\phi \log w \left(x_i, y_i; \phi \right) \tag{7}$$

According to the updating rules based on Eq. 5 and 7, we alternately optimize two sets of parameters as in Algorithm 1. It is worth noting that BILD can be used to improve various supervised dehazing network or be integrated with other alternative losses, which will be extended in the experimental part.

3.3   Relationship with RL

The updating rule for ϕ in Eq. 7 resembles the general form of policy gradient approaches used in REINFORCE Algorithm[38, 40]. Then, we can interpret the coupled bi-level optimization from the view of reinforcement learning. In this context, the iterative interactions between the external and internal loops are well illustrated as agent-environment interactions. In detail, the external patch reweighting network is an agent, learning to perform actions (generating weights) to the environment. After getting the action from the agent, three sequential implementations will be activated in the environment including 1) updating the

---

Algorithm 1: Bi-level dehazing framework

Input: Parameters of dehazing network θ; parameters of reweighting network ϕ; trainset $\mathcal{D}_t$; validset $\mathcal{D}_v$

Output: θ^*

1 **for** *epoch* = 1 *to max_epoch_nums* **do**
2   **for** $\mathcal{B}$ *in* $\mathcal{D}_t$ **do**
3   Crop $\mathcal{B}$ randomly into $\{x_i, y_i\}_{i=1,2,\cdots,n}$
4   Fix ϕ and update θ via Eq. 5
5   Evaluation on $\mathcal{D}_v$ and calculate R_i
6   Fix θ and update ϕ via Eq. 7
7   **end**
8 **end**

---

dehazing neural network with the guidance of the current action (weight), 2) evaluate the updated dehazing net on the validation set and 3) generate the reward R by synchronizing the training performance, validating performance and the quality of the current action by the formulation defined in Eq. 6. As observed from the first term in reward R_i, the environment intends to feedback a positive reward when the inner product between $\nabla_\theta J_e(\mathcal{D}_v; \theta_t)$ (from validation set) and $\nabla_\theta \ell(x_i, y_i; \theta_{t-1})$ (defined on training set) is close enough and vice versa(see Eq. 6). Moreover, when using the entropy $\mathcal{H}(\cdot)$ to realize the penalty $\Omega(\cdot)$ in R_i, we retain the same reward penalty mechanism as defined in the maximum entropy reinforcement learning [17,19] that can encourage the actor to explore more adequately in the action space.

4 Experimental Results

4.1 Training, Validation and Testing Dataset

We evaluate the proposed framework on both synthetic datasets and real-world datasets against the state-of-the-art methods. The RESIDE [24] is a widely used synthetic dataset, which contains both indoor and outdoor synthetic images. To evaluate the effectiveness of our framework on synthetic hazy scenes, the RESIDE dataset is divided into three parts: training, validation and testing, respectively in indoor and outdoor datasets. For training, we randomly select 5000 indoor hazy/clear pairs from Indoor Training Set (ITS) and 5000 outdoor pairs from Outdoor Training Set (OTS). For validation, we hold out 10% of the training part. For testing, Synthetic Objective Testing Set (SOTS) is adopted, which contains 500 indoor and 500 outdoor hazy images. As for real-world hazy scenes, O-HAZE [2] and NH-HAZE [1,3] datasets are adopted and each dataset provides training sets, validation sets and testing sets. More details can be found in the supplement.

Table 1. Quantitative evaluations on the synthetic datasets and real-world datasets in terms of PSNR and SSIM.

Method	SOTS [24]				O-HAZE [2]		NH-HAZE [1]	
	Indoor		Outdoor					
	PSNR↑	SSIM↑	PSNR↑	SSIM↑	PSNR↑	SSIM↑	PSNR↑	SSIM↑
(TPAMI'10) DCP [20]	16.62	0.8179	19.13	0.8148	15.87	0.6310	12.36	0.4448
(ICCV'13) BCCR [28]	17.04	0.7853	15.51	0.7914	14.43	0.5825	13.12	0.4831
(TIP'15) CAP [47]	18.97	0.8148	18.14	0.7585	15.36	0.5785	12.39	0.3753
(TPAMI'18) NLD [6]	17.29	0.7767	17.97	0.8194	15.34	0.5891	12.23	0.4823
(TIP'16) DehazeNet [8]	20.56	0.7954	–	–	–	–	–	–
(ICCV'17) AODNet [23]	19.04	0.8215	22.43	0.9022	18.07	0.6517	16.93	0.5717
(ICCV'19) GridDehazeNet [26]	28.22	0.9691	27.53	0.9583	22.11	0.7097	17.22	0.5921
(CVPR'20) MSBDN [12]	28.66	0.9515	26.94	0.9107	22.99	0.6927	17.97	0.6072
(AAAI'20) FFANet [32]	31.44	0.9728	30.50	0.9718	24.13	0.7438	18.04	0.6236
DehazeNet + BILD	21.15	0.8509	–	–	–	–	–	–
AODNet + BILD	19.53	0.8303	24.44	0.9216	20.81	0.6706	17.36	0.5779
GridDehazeNet + BILD	28.87	0.9765	27.93	0.9649	22.43	0.7242	17.97	0.6075
MSBDN + BILD	29.69	0.9596	27.03	0.9113	23.54	0.6954	18.14	0.6201
FFANet + BILD	32.14	0.9747	31.22	0.9760	24.91	0.7552	19.13	0.6439

4.2 Implementation Details

Our BILD framework consists of internal and external networks and is optimized by alternative training. Adam optimizer with β_1 and β_2 equal to 0.9 and 0.999 is used to train the two networks with a batch size of 10, respectively. The initial learning rate of the interal network is set as 10^{-4} with the external network set as 10^{-1}. The training epoch is set to 150 in total. All training models are trained on training set and verified on validation set. We choose the best model on the validation as the final model to evaluate its performance on the test set. All experiments are implemented by PyTorch 1.7.1 with one NVIDIA 3090 GPU.

Considering image sizes of different datasets and GPU memory, following [12, 32] work: for RESIDE dataset, which image size is 640×480, we randomly crop size 240×240 patches as networks' input; for O-HAZE and NH-HAZE, where image size is 1600×1200 or even 4599×3632, we randomly crop size 800×800 as input. Following [46] work, due to GridDehazeNet, FFA, MSBDN cannot process 4K images in O-HAZE, we adopt the downsample-dehazing-upsample (DDU) [46] strategy to solve this problem. Also for DCP [20], the window size is set to 15×15 for less time cost [46]. See supplementary materials for network architecture and more details.

4.3 Performance Results and Ablation Analysis

We evaluate the proposed BILD framework against SOTA methods based on the physics prior and supervised data-driven learning. The metrics PSNR and SSIM are adopted and all dehazing methods are retrained on the selected training, validation and testing datasets.

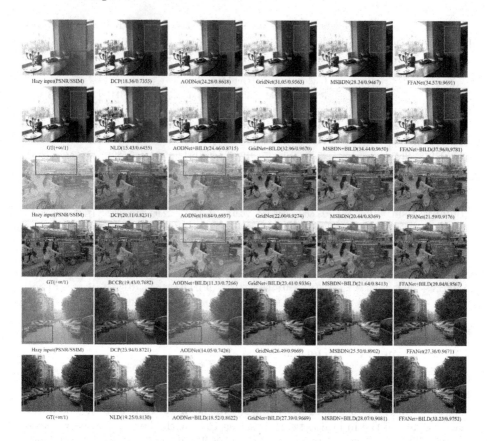

Fig. 3. Visual comparisons on the SOTS dataset. More examples can be found in supplement. Zoom in for best view.

Results on Synthetic Dataset. The first four columns of Table 1 show the quantitative results on SOTS [24]. Our BILD framework improves the performances of SOTA methods to varying degrees. As shown, FFANet + BILD obtains the highest PSNR and GridDehazeNet + BILD obtains the highest SSIM on the indoor part. Meanwhile, FFANet + BILD obtains the highest PSNR and SSIM on the outdoor part. We also compare the qualitative results(see Fig. 3). We can observe that physics-prior dehazing methods (DCP [20], BCCR [28], CAP[47] and NLD [6]) tend to over-darken or over-enhance the hazy image and are unable to remove dense haze. Compared to physics-prior methods, the supervised dehazing methods achieve better visual quality. However, the quality of DehazeNet is greatly affected by the estimation of ambient light and others (e.g. GridDehazeNet, MSBDN and FFANet) cannot remove haze uniformly: some regions close to the ground-truth but some regions still remain hazy. Our method restores the hazy images more uniformly and removes haze more thoroughly at patch-level(see red box in Fig. 3).

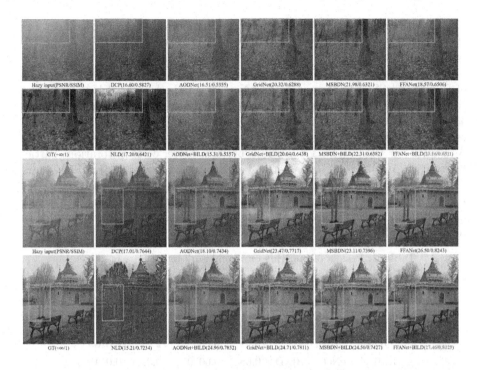

Fig. 4. Visual comparisons on the O-HAZE dataset. Zoom in for best view.

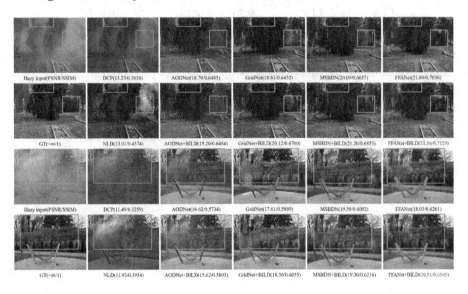

Fig. 5. Visual comparisons on the NH-HAZE dataset. Zoom in for best view.

Results on Real-World Dataset. The last four columns of Table 1 demonstrate the quantitative results on the O-HAZE [2] and NH-HAZE dataset [1]. As shown, on O-HAZE dataset [2], our FFANet + BILD framework obtains the highest PSNR and SSIM and achieves the gain with 0.78 dB and 0.0114 in terms of PSNR and SSIM compared to FFANet [32] method. On NH-HAZE dataset [1], our FFANet + BILD framework obtains the highest PSNR and SSIM and achieves the gain with 1.09 dB and 0.0203 in terms of PSNR and SSIM compared to FFANet [32] method. The qualitative results are presented in Figs. 4 and 5. As shown, our BILD + SOTA methods perform better color restoration (particularly with AODNet [23]) and better patch-level haze removal (see Figs. 4 and 5). The physics-prior methods (DCP [20], BCCR [28], CAP [47] and NLD [6]) and AODNet [23] suffer from serious color distortion. Besides, GridDehazeNet [26], MSBDN [12] and FFANet [32] still have some residual haze in dense-haze regions(see red box in Figs. 4 and 5).

Table 2. Results of applying our framework into SOTA methods.

Method	SOTS-indoor [24]		O-HAZE [2]	
	PSNR	SSIM	PSNR	SSIM
DehazeNet + BILD	↑0.59	↑0.0555	–	–
AODNet + BILD	↑0.49	↑0.0088	↑2.74	↑0.0189
GridDehazeNet + BILD	↑0.65	↑0.0079	↑0.32	↑0.0145
MSBDN + BILD	↑1.03	↑0.0081	↑0.55	↑0.0027
FFANet + BILD	↑0.70	↑0.0019	↑0.78	↑0.0114

Ablation Analysis of BILD. We apply the BILD framework to various SOTA methods to evaluate its effectiveness [8,23,26,32]. As presented in Table 2, our BILD framework can improve the performance of SOTA methods to varying degrees. Furthermore, the BILD framework cannot increase the additional parameters for the internal supervised dehazing network, since the external patch reweighing network is just used for training and can be removed for testing.Experiment results also show that the BILD framework can further increase supervised dehazing network training efficiency for performance boosting, as shown in Fig. 6.

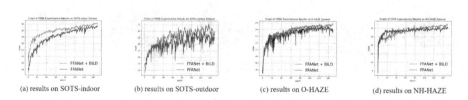

(a) results on SOTS-indoor   (b) results on SOTS-outdoor   (c) results on O-HAZE   (d) results on NH-HAZE

Fig. 6. Graph of PSNR with/without BILD framework during training process.

Table 3. Comparison of the effectiveness with training set and validation set in external loop.

Method	SOTS: indoor	
	PSNR	SSIM
AODNet [23]	19.04	0.8215
GridDehazeNet [26]	28.22	0.9691
MSBDN [12]	28.66	0.9515
FFANet [32]	31.44	0.9728
AODNet + training set	19.33	0.8239
GridDehazeNet + training set	28.68	0.9704
MSBDN + training set	28.92	0.9518
FFANet + training set	31.53	0.9739
AODNet + validation set	19.53	0.8303
GridDehazeNet + validation set	28.87	0.9765
MSBDN + validation set	29.69	0.9596
FFANet + validation set	32.14	0.9747

We meanwhile consider the effect of validation set in external patch reweighting loop. For better comparisons, we design the corresponding ablation experiments: 1) without external reweighting loop(see the first four rows in Table 3), 2) with external reweighting loop but objective function is defined on training set(see the middle four rows in Table 3) and 3) with external reweighting loop and objective function is defined on validation set (see the last four rows in Table 3). We conduct the same training setting for all experiments and considering the volume of data, we integrate the validation set into the training set for the experiments of "BILD + training set". The results are summarized in Table 3. Our "BILD + validation set" outperforms "BILD + training set" and baseline, which shows the effectiveness with validation set in external loop.

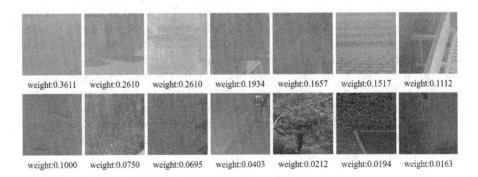

weight:0.3611   weight:0.2610   weight:0.2610   weight:0.1934   weight:0.1657   weight:0.1517   weight:0.1112

weight:0.1000   weight:0.0750   weight:0.0695   weight:0.0403   weight:0.0212   weight:0.0194   weight:0.0163

Fig. 7. The experimental results of patch reweighting. More examples can be found in supplement.

4.4   Patch Reweighting and Additional Experiment

Figure 7 illustrates the learned importance of each patch generated by the external patch reweighing loop. In general, the dense-haze patches have more learning weights and the light-haze patches have less learning weights, which is in line with our intention. Meanwhile, experimental results show that the complex background and illumination will also encourage more learning weight (see Fig. 7).

Table 4. Results of applying our framework on full ITS dataset.

Method	full-indoor[24]	
	PSNR	SSIM
(ICCV'19) GridDehazeNet [26]	32.16	0.9836
(ECCV'20) FDU [13]	32.68	0.9760
(CVPR'20) MSBDN [12]	33.79	0.9840
(CVPR'20) KDDN [21]	34.72	0.9845
(AAAI'20) FFANet [32]	36.39	0.9886
(CVPR'21)AECRNet [43]	37.17	0.9901
FFANet + BILD	38.58	0.9921

Considering the training time cost and empirical partition ratio of training, validation and testing sets [22,42], we select a subset from RESIDE dataset [24] for supervised dehazing, which may suffer from overfitting of the training set. As a complement, we conduct additional experiments on full ITS dataset [24] to evaluate the effectiveness of our BILD framework, in which FFANet is adopted as the supervised dehazing network. Experimental results show our BILD framework achieves the best performance compared with SOTA methods(see Table 4).

5   Conclusion

In this paper, we propose a bi-level supervised dehazing framework(*e.g.* BILD), which is composed of two mutually coupled loops. The internal loop solves the weighted supervised dehazing optimization with the known patch-wise weights provided by the external loop. The external loop evaluates the current dehazing network (obtained from internal loop) on validated samples and, accordingly, generates a new set of structured weights to guide the supervised dehazing in the internal loop. The combination of the two alternative loops strengthens the robustness of supervised dehazing process. The BILD framework is compatible with general supervised dehazing methods and extensive experiments demonstrate our BILD framework boosts the performances of SOTA methods to varying degrees on synthetic and real-world datasets.

Acknowledgement. This research is supported by National Natural Science Foundation of China (Grant No.62031001, Grant No.61971020), National Key Research and Development Program of China (No.2020AAA0105502).

References

1. Ancuti, C.O., Ancuti, C., Timofte, R.: NH-HAZE: an image dehazing benchmark with non-homogeneous hazy and haze-free images. In: CVPRW (2020)
2. Ancuti, C.O., Ancuti, C., Timofte, R., Vleeschouwer, C.D.: O-haze: a dehazing benchmark with real hazy and haze-free outdoor images. In: CVPRW (2018)
3. Ancuti, C.O., Ancuti, C., Vasluianu, F.A., Timofte, R., et al.: NTIRE 2020 challenge on nonhomogeneous dehazing. In: CVPRW (2020)
4. Baker, B., Gupta, O., Naik, N., Raskar, R.: Designing neural network architectures using reinforcement learning. arXiv preprint arXiv:1611.02167 (2016)
5. Berman, D., Treibitz, T., Avidan, S.: Air-light estimation using haze-lines. In: ICCP, pp. 1–9 (2017)
6. Berman, D., Treibitz, T., Avidan, S.: Single image dehazing using haze-lines. IEEE TPAMI **42**(3), 720–734 (2018)
7. Bochkovskiy, A., Wang, C.Y., Liao, H.Y.M.: Yolov4: Optimal speed and accuracy of object detection. arXiv preprint arXiv:2004.10934 (2020)
8. Cai, B., Xu, X., Jia, K., Qing, C., Tao, D.: Dehazenet: An end-to-end system for single image haze removal. IEEE TIP **25**(11), 5187–5198 (2016)
9. Chen, Y., Li, W., Sakaridis, C., Dai, D., Van Gool, L.: Domain adaptive faster r-cnn for object detection in the wild. In: CVPR, pp. 3339–3348 (2018)
10. Cubuk, E.D., Zoph, B., Mane, D., Vasudevan, V., Le, Q.V.: Autoaugment: Learning augmentation strategies from data. In: CVPR, pp. 113–123 (2019)
11. Deng, Z., et al.: Deep multi-model fusion for single-image dehazing. In: ICCV, pp. 2453–2462 (2019)
12. Dong, H., Pan, J., Xiang, L., Hu, Z., Zhang, X., Wang, F., Yang, M.H.: Multi-scale boosted dehazing network with dense feature fusion. In: CVPR, pp. 2157–2167 (2020)
13. Dong, J., Pan, J.: Physics-based feature dehazing networks. In: Vedaldi, A., Bischof, H., Brox, T., Frahm, J.-M. (eds.) ECCV 2020. LNCS, vol. 12375, pp. 188–204. Springer, Cham (2020). https://doi.org/10.1007/978-3-030-58577-8_12
14. Franceschi, L., Niepert, M., Pontil, M., He, X.: Learning discrete structures for graph neural networks. In: ICML, pp. 1972–1982 (2019)
15. Gao, Y., Yang, H., Zhang, P., Zhou, C., Hu, Y.: Graphnas: Graph neural architecture search with reinforcement learning. arXiv preprint arXiv:1904.09981 (2019)
16. Grazzi, R., Franceschi, L., Pontil, M., Salzo, S.: On the iteration complexity of hypergradient computation. In: ICML, pp. 3748–3758 (2020)
17. Haarnoja, T., Tang, H., Abbeel, P., Levine, S.: Reinforcement learning with deep energy-based policies. In: ICML, pp. 1352–1361 (2017)
18. Haarnoja, T., Zhou, A., Abbeel, P., Levine, S.: Soft actor-critic: Off-policy maximum entropy deep reinforcement learning with a stochastic actor. In: ICML, pp. 1861–1870 (2018)
19. Haarnoja, T., et al.: Soft actor-critic algorithms and applications. arXiv preprint arXiv:1812.05905 (2018)
20. He, K., Sun, J., Tang, X.: Single image haze removal using dark channel prior. IEEE TPAMI **33**(12), 2341–2353 (2010)
21. Hong, M., Xie, Y., Li, C., Qu, Y.: Distilling image dehazing with heterogeneous task imitation. In: CVPR, pp. 3462–3471 (2020)
22. Kohavi, R., et al.: A study of cross-validation and bootstrap for accuracy estimation and model selection. In: IJCAI, pp. 1137–1145 (1995)

23. Li, B., Peng, X., Wang, Z., Xu, J., Feng, D.: Aod-net: All-in-one dehazing network. In: ICCV, pp. 4770–4778 (2017)
24. Li, B., et al.: Benchmarking single-image dehazing and beyond. IEEE TIP **28**(1), 492–505 (2019)
25. Liu, R., Liu, J., Jiang, Z., Fan, X., Luo, Z.: A bilevel integrated model with data-driven layer ensemble for multi-modality image fusion. IEEE TIP **30**, 1261–1274 (2020)
26. Liu, X., Ma, Y., Shi, Z., Chen, J.: Griddehazenet: Attention-based multi-scale network for image dehazing. In: ICCV, pp. 7314–7323 (2019)
27. Liu, Z., Wei, P., Jiang, J., Cao, W., Bian, J., Chang, Y.: Mesa: Boost ensemble imbalanced learning with meta-sampler. In: NeurIPS, vol. 33 (2020)
28. Meng, G., Wang, Y., Duan, J., Xiang, S., Pan, C.: Efficient image dehazing with boundary constraint and contextual regularization. In: ICCV, pp. 617–624 (2013)
29. Mounsaveng, S., Laradji, I., Ben Ayed, I., Vázquez, D., Pedersoli, M.: Learning data augmentation with online bilevel optimization for image classification. In: WACV, pp. 1691–1700 (2021)
30. Narasimhan, S.G., Nayar, S.K.: Chromatic framework for vision in bad weather. In: CVPR, pp. 598–605 (2000)
31. Narasimhan, S.G., Nayar, S.K.: Vision and the atmosphere. IJCV **48**(3), 233–254 (2002)
32. Qin, X., Wang, Z., Bai, Y., Xie, X., Jia, H.: Ffa-net: Feature fusion attention network for single image dehazing. In: AAAI, pp. 11908–11915 (2020)
33. Qu, Y., Chen, Y., Huang, J., Xie, Y.: Enhanced pix2pix dehazing network. In: CVPR, pp. 8160–8168 (2019)
34. Ren, W., Liu, S., Zhang, H., Pan, J., Cao, X., Yang, M.-H.: Single image dehazing via multi-scale convolutional neural networks. In: Leibe, B., Matas, J., Sebe, N., Welling, M. (eds.) ECCV 2016. LNCS, vol. 9906, pp. 154–169. Springer, Cham (2016). https://doi.org/10.1007/978-3-319-46475-6_10
35. Ren, W., Ma, L., Zhang, J., Pan, J., Cao, X., Liu, W., Yang, M.H.: Gated fusion network for single image dehazing. In: CVPR, pp. 3253–3261 (2018)
36. Shao, Y., Li, L., Ren, W., Gao, C., Sang, N.: Domain adaptation for image dehazing. In: CVPR, pp. 2808–2817 (2020)
37. Shu, J., et al.: Meta-weight-net: Learning an explicit mapping for sample weighting. arXiv preprint arXiv:1902.07379 (2019)
38. Silver, D., Lever, G., Heess, N., Degris, T., Wierstra, D., Riedmiller, M.: Deterministic policy gradient algorithms. In: ICML, pp. 387–395 (2014)
39. Sun, M., Dou, H., Li, B., Yan, J., Ouyang, W., Cui, L.: Autosampling: Search for effective data sampling schedules. In: ICML, pp. 9923–9933 (2021)
40. Sutton, R.S., McAllester, D.A., Singh, S.P., Mansour, Y.: Policy gradient methods for reinforcement learning with function approximation. In: NeurIPS, pp. 1057–1063 (2000)
41. Tian, K., Lin, C., Sun, M., Zhou, L., Yan, J., Ouyang, W.: Improving auto-augment via augmentation-wise weight sharing. arXiv preprint arXiv:2009.14737 (2020)
42. Wang, X., Pham, H., Michel, P., Anastasopoulos, A., Carbonell, J., Neubig, G.: Optimizing data usage via differentiable rewards. In: ICML, pp. 9983–9995 (2020)
43. Wu, H., et al.: Contrastive learning for compact single image dehazing. In: CVPR, pp. 10551–10560 (2021)
44. Wu, X., et al.: Temporally correlated task scheduling for sequence learning. In: ICML, pp. 11274–11284 (2021)
45. Zhang, H., Patel, V.M.: Densely connected pyramid dehazing network. In: CVPR, pp. 3194–3203 (2018)

46. Zheng, Z., et al.: Ultra-high-definition image dehazing via multi-guided bilateral learning. In: CVPR, pp. 16180–16189 (2021)
47. Zhu, Q., Mai, J., Shao, L.: A fast single image haze removal algorithm using color attenuation prior. IEEE TIP **24**(11), 3522–3533 (2015)

Flow-Guided Transformer for Video Inpainting

Kaidong Zhang[1], Jingjing Fu[2(✉)], and Dong Liu[1]

[1] University of Science and Technology of China, Hefei, China
richu@mail.ustc.edu.cn, dongeliu@ustc.edu.cn
[2] Microsoft Research Asia, Beijing, China
jifu@microsoft.com

Abstract. We propose a flow-guided transformer, which innovatively leverage the motion discrepancy exposed by optical flows to instruct the attention retrieval in transformer for high fidelity video inpainting. More specially, we design a novel flow completion network to complete the corrupted flows by exploiting the relevant flow features in a local temporal window. With the completed flows, we propagate the content across video frames, and adopt the flow-guided transformer to synthesize the rest corrupted regions. We decouple transformers along temporal and spatial dimension, so that we can easily integrate the locally relevant completed flows to instruct spatial attention only. Furthermore, we design a flow-reweight module to precisely control the impact of completed flows on each spatial transformer. For the sake of efficiency, we introduce window partition strategy to both spatial and temporal transformers. Especially in spatial transformer, we design a dual perspective spatial MHSA, which integrates the global tokens to the window-based attention. Extensive experiments demonstrate the effectiveness of the proposed method qualitatively and quantitatively. Codes are available at https://github.com/hitachinsk/FGT.

Keywords: Video inpainting · Optical flow · Transformer

1 Introduction

Video inpainting aims at filling the corrupted regions in a video with reasonable and spatiotemporally coherent content [2]. Its application includes but not limited to watermark removal [34], object removal [15], video retargeting [22], and video stabilization [31]. High-quality video inpainting is challenging because it requires spatiotemporal consistency of the restored video. Directly applying image inpainting methods [20,26,27,33,37,38,51,53,54] is sub-optimal, because they mainly refer the content within one frame but fail to utilize the complementary content across the whole video.

Supplementary Information The online version contains supplementary material available at https://doi.org/10.1007/978-3-031-19797-0_5.

(a) GT & mask   (b) FFM   (c) FGVC   (d) Ours

(e) GT flow   (f) DFGVI   (g) FGVC   (h) Ours

Fig. 1. Performance comparison on frame synthesis (top row) and flow completion (bottom row) between our method and some state-of-the-art baselines [14,29,50]. Our method achieves significant performance improvement against the compared baselines and obtains more coherent results.

Transformer [43] has sparked the computer vision community. Its outstanding long-range modeling capacity makes it naturally suitable for video inpainting, as video inpainting relies on the content propagation across frames spatiotemporally to fill the corrupted regions with high fidelity. Previous works [28,29,55] modify transformer for video inpainting task, and achieve unprecedented performance. However, these works still suffer from inaccurate attention retrieval. They mainly utilize the appearance features in transformer, but ignore the object integrity exposed by the motion fields, which indicates the relevant regions.

Recently, several works [14,50,57] propose to complete optical flows for video inpainting. As discussed in DFGVI [50], optical flows are much easier to complete because they contain far less complex patterns than frames. Since the relative motion magnitude between foreground objects and background are different, the contents with similar motion pattern are more likely to be relevant. Therefore, the motion discrepancy of optical flows can serve as a strong instructor to guide the attention retrieval for more relevant content. Inspired by this, we propose a novel flow-guided transformer to synthesize the corrupted regions with the motion guidance from completed flows. Our method contains two parts: the first is a flow completion network designed to complete the corrupted flows, and the second is the flow-guided transformer proposed to synthesize the corrupted frames under the guidance of the completed flows.

During flow completion, we observe that the flows in a local temporal window are more correlated than the distant ones, because motion fields are likely to be maintained in a short temporal window. Therefore, we propose to exploit the correlation of complementary features of optical flows in a local temporal window, which is different from the simply stacking strategy in DFGVI [50] and the single flow completion method in FGVC [14]. We integrate spatial-temporal decoupled P3D blocks [39] to a simple U-Net [40], which completes the target flow based on the local reference flows. Furthermore, we propose a novel edge loss to supervise the completion quality in the edge regions without introducing additional computation cost during inference. Compared with previous counterparts [14,50], our method can complete more accurate flows.

Under guidance of the completed optical flows, we propagate the content from the valid regions to the corrupted regions, and then synthesize the rest corrupted content in the video frames with the flow-guided transformer. Following previous transformer-based video inpainting methods [28,29,55], we sample video frames from the whole video and inpaint these frames simultaneously. Given that the optical flows are locally correlated, we decouple the spatial and temporal attention in transformer and only integrate optical flows into spatial transformers. In temporal transformer, we perform multi-head self-attention (MHSA) spatiotemporally, while in spatial transformer, we only perform MHSA within the tokens coming from the same frame. Considering that the completed flows are not perfect and the content with different appearance may have similar motion patterns, we propose a novel flow-reweight module to control the impact of flow tokens based on the interaction between frame and flow tokens adaptively.

To improve the efficiency of our transformer, we introduce window partition strategy [9,30,52] in the flow-guided transformer. In temporal transformer, as the temporal offset between distant frames may be large, small temporal window size cannot include abundant temporal relevant tokens. As a result, we perform MHSA in a large window to exploit rich spatiotemporal tokens. In spatial transformer, after flow guidance integration, we restrict the attention within a smaller window based on local smoothness prior of natural images. However, simple window attention ignores the possible correlated content at the distant location. To relieve such problem, we extract the tokens from the whole token map globally and integrate these global tokens to the key and value. In such manner, the queries can not only retrieve the fine-grained local tokens, but also attend to the global content. We refer this design as dual perspective spatial MHSA.

We conduct extensive experiments to validate the effectiveness of different components of our method. As shown in Fig. 1, our method remarkably outperforms previous baselines in terms of visualization results on frame synthesis and flow completion. In summary, our contributions are:

- We propose a flow-guided transformer to integrate the completed optical flow into the transformer for more accurate attention retrieval in video inpainting.
- We design a novel flow completion network with local flow features exploitation, which outperforms previous methods significantly.
- We introduce window partition strategy in the video inpainting transformer and propose the dual perspective spatial MHSA to enrich the local window attention with global content.

2   Related Work

Traditional Methods. Traditional video inpainting methods [2,12,15,16,31, 34] explore the geometry relationship (e.g. homography or optical flows) between the corrupted regions of the target frames and the valid regions of the reference frames for content synthesis with high fidelity. Huang et al. [19] design a set of energy equation to optimize optical flow reconstruction and frame synthesis interactively and achieve unprecedented video inpainting quality.

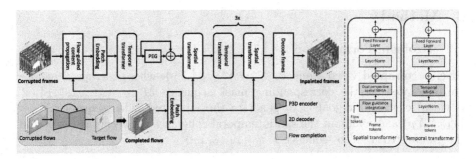

Fig. 2. Our method consists of two steps. Firstly, we adopt the **L**ocal **A**ggregation **F**low **C**ompletion network (LAFC) to complete the corrupted target flow, and then propagate the content among the video frames with the completed flows. Secondly, we synthesize the rest corrupted regions with **F**low-**G**uided **T**ransformer (FGT). PEG: Position embedding generator.

Deep Learning Based Methods. Deep learning based methods can be divided into two categories, the first one [14,50] aims to complete the missing optical flows to capture the motion correlation between the valid regions and the corrupted regions. Our method also includes the flow completion component, but we only exploit the complementary flow features in a local window for more efficient and accurate flow completion.

The second category targets on directly synthesizing the corrupted regions from video frames. Some works adopt 3D CNN [7,44] or channel shift [8,21,59] to model the complementary features between local frames. Several methods integrate recurrent [22,25] or attention [24,35] mechanism into CNN-based networks to expand the temporal receptive field. Inspired by the spatiotemporal redundancy in videos, Zhang et al. [56] and Ouyang et al. [36] adopt internal learning to perform long range propagation for video inpainting. Currently, Zeng et al. [55] and Liu et al. [28,29] design specific transformer [43] to retrieve similar features in a considerable temporal receptive field for high-quality video inpainting. Our method is also built upon transformer, but differently we improve the attention retrieval accuracy with the completed flows.

Transformer in Vision. Due to the outstanding long range feature capture ability, transformer [43] has been introduced to various computer vision tasks, such as basic architecture design [9,30,52], image classification [3,11,13,48], object detection [6,32], action detection [46], segmentation [45], etc. We revisit the design of transformer in video inpainting and propose several strategies to improve efficiency while maintaining competitive performance, including spatial-temporal decomposition and the combination of local and global tokens.

3 Method

3.1 Problem Formulation

Given a corrupted video sequence $X := \{X_1, ..., X_T\}$, whose corrupted regions are annotated by the corresponding mask sequence $M := \{M_1, ..., M_T\}$. T is video length. Our goal is to generate the inpainted video sequence $\hat{Y} := \{\hat{Y}_1, ..., \hat{Y}_T\}$ and maintain the spatiotemporal coherence between our result and the ground truth video sequence $Y := \{Y_1, ..., Y_T\}$.

3.2 Network Overview

As shown in Fig. 2, our network consists of a **L**ocal **A**ggregation **F**low **C**ompletion network (LAFC) for flow completion and a **F**low-**G**uided **T**ransformer (FGT) to synthesize the corrupted regions. For a given masked video sequence X, we extract its forward and backward optical flows $\tilde{F}_f$ and $\tilde{F}_b$ and utilize LAFC to complete each optical flow with its local references. Based on completed flows, we propagate the content across video frames. As for the rest corrupted regions, we adopt FGT to synthesize them.

3.3 Local Aggregation Flow Completion Network

Local Flow Aggregation. The motion direction and velocity of objects vary overtime, and the correlation between distant optical flows may be degraded severely. Fortunately, the variance of motion in short time is a gradual process, which means optical flows in a short temporal window are highly correlated, and they are reliable references for more accurate flow completion.

3D convolution block [42] is suitable to capture the local relevant content spatiotemporally. However, the parameter and computation overhead of 3D convolution block are large, which increases the difficulty for network optimization. Considering efficiency, we adopt P3D block [39] instead to decouple the local flow feature aggregation along temporal and spatial dimension. We insert P3D blocks to the encoder of LAFC and add skip connection [40] to exploit the local correlation between flows. Considering that LAFC completes forward and backward optical flows in the same manner, we denote both F_f and F_b as F for simplicity. Given a corrupted flow sequence, we utilize Laplacian filling to obtain the initialized flows $\tilde{F}=\{\tilde{F}_{t-ni}, ..., \tilde{F}_t, ..., \tilde{F}_{t+ni}\}$, where $\tilde{F}_t$ is the target corrupted flow, i is the temporal interval between consecutive flows, and the length of the flow sequence is $2n + 1$. The initialized flow sequence $\tilde{F}$ are fed to the LAFC to complete the target flow $\tilde{F}_t$. We denote the input of m-th P3D block as $\tilde{f}^m$, and the output as $\tilde{f}^{m+1}$. The local feature aggregation process can be formulated as.

$$\tilde{f}^{m+1} = \text{TC}(\text{SC}(\tilde{f}^m)) + \tilde{f}^m \qquad (1)$$

where TC represents 1D temporal convolution, and SC is the 2D spatial convolution. We keep the temporal resolution unchanged except the final P3D block in the encoder and the P3D blocks inserted in the skip connection. In these blocks, we shrink the temporal resolution of the flow sequence to obtain the aggregated flow features of the target flow. Finally, a 2D decoder is utilized to obtain the completed target optical flow $\hat{F}_t$.

Edge Loss. In general, flow fields are piece-wise smooth, which means the flow gradients are considerable small except motion boundaries [14]. The edges in flow maps inherently contain crucial salient features that may benefit the reconstruction of object boundaries. Nevertheless, the flow completion in edge regions is a tough task, as there is no specified guidance to edge recovery. Therefore, we design a novel edge loss in LAFC to supervise the completion quality in edge regions of $\hat{F}_t$ explicitly, which can improve the flow completion quality without introducing additional computation overhead during inference.

For the completed target flow $\hat{F}_t$, we extract the edges with a small projection network P_e and calculate the binary cross entropy loss with the edges that extracted from the ground truth F_t with Canny edge detector [5].

$$L_e = \mathrm{BCE}(\mathrm{Canny}(F_t), P_e(\hat{F}_t)) \qquad (2)$$

where L_e is the edge loss. We utilize four convolution layers with residual connection [17] to formulate P_e.

Loss Function. We adopt L1 loss to penalize $\hat{F}_t$ in the corrupted and the valid regions, respectively. To improve the smoothness of $\hat{F}_t$, we impose first and second order smoothness loss to $\hat{F}_t$.

What's more, we also warp the corresponding ground truth frames with $\hat{F}_t$ to penalize the regions with large warp error. We adopt the L1 loss to supervise the warping quality, and expel the occlusion regions with forward-backward consistency check of ground truth optical flows for more accurate loss calculation. The loss function of LAFC is the combination of the loss terms discussed above, and the detailed formulas are provided in the supplementary material.

3.4   Flow-Guided Transformer for Video Inpainting

After flow completion, we propagate the content from valid regions to corrupted regions throughout the whole video to fill-in the corrupted regions that can be connected with the valid regions. The rest corrupted regions are filled with our designed flow-guided transformer (FGT). FGT takes multiple corrupted frames into consideration and synthesize these frames simultaneously. Since the motion discrepancy of completed optical flows to some extent reveals the shape and location of foreground objects and background, we integrate such information to FGT to indicate the relevant regions inside a single frame. Due to the degraded correlation between distant optical flows, the traditional all-pair interaction between tokens from distant frames may not be suitable for flow guidance integration. Therefore, we decouple MHSA along the temporal and spatial dimension, and we only integrate the flow content to the spatial MHSA.

In both spatial and temporal transformer blocks, we introduce specific designs for efficiency and performance balance. In temporal transformer, we adopt large

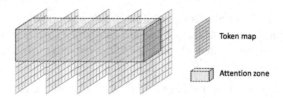

Fig. 3. The temporal MHSA in the temporal transformer. We split non-overlapped large windows (zones) for each token map, and perform MHSA inside the cube formed by the corresponding position in each token map. The windows are shown with different colors. In this figure, we illustrate the 2×2 zone.

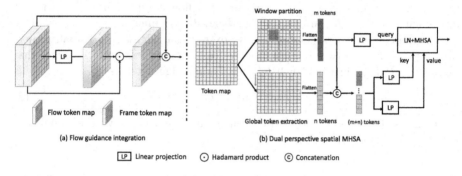

Fig. 4. Illustration of flow guidance integration and dual perspective spatial MHSA in the spatial transformer.

window to compensate the reference offset between distant frames. In spatial transformer, we divide each token map into small window based on the local smoothness prior of natural images, and supply the key and value with the condensed global tokens to perform spatial MHSA in dual perspective from local and global views.

As shown in Fig. 2, given the frame sequence $\hat{X}$ after flow-guided content propagation, we crop $\hat{X}$ and completed flows into patches and project them to frame tokens TI with an encoder. The completed flows are also projected to flow tokens TF. We refer such process as "patch embedding". We design interleaved temporal and spatial transformer blocks to process TI, and enrich the frame tokens with TF in each spatial transformer block before dual perspective spatial MHSA. As for positional embedding, we follow CVPT [10] to adopt depth-wise convolution [18] after the first transformer block for video inpainting in flexible resolutions, while the pre-defined trainable positional embedding of previous works [29] can only process the videos at certain resolution.

Temporal Transformer. In temporal transformer, attention retrieval is performed to the tokens across different frames. Since the content shifts along temporal dimension, it is reasonable to apply large size window to compensate the reference offset. Liu et al. [28] also demonstrate the all-pair attention strategy is unnecessary in video inpainting. Therefore, we divide each token maps in TI into non-overlap cubes with large window size (denoted as "zone") along height and width dimension and perform MHSA within the cubes, as shown in Fig. 3.

Flow Guidance Integration. The motion discrepancy between different objects and background exposed by optical flows indicates the content relationship. The tokens with similar motion magnitude are more likely to be relevant. Therefore, we utilize the completed optical flows to guide the attention process in FGT.

As discussed in Sect. 3.3, optical flows are locally correlated. Therefore, we only exploit the optical flows in the spatial transformer. A straightforward way is to concatenate TI and TF along channel dimension directly before spatial MHSA. However, there are two problems in this way. First, the completed flows are not perfect. The distorted flows may mislead the judgement about relevant regions. Second, the appearance patches may vary a lot within objects, while the corresponding motion patterns may still be similar, which is likely to confuse the attention retrieval process. In order to ease these problems, we propose a flow-reweight module to control the impact of flow tokens TF with respect to the interaction between TF and TI, as shown in Fig. 4(a). We formulate the flow-reweight module as.

$$\hat{TF}_t^j = TF_t^j \odot \text{MLP}(\text{Concat}(TI_t^j, TF_t^j)) \tag{3}$$

where Concat is the concatenation operation. MLP represents the MLP layers, and $\hat{TF}_t^j$ represents the t-th reweighted flow token map in j-th spatial transformer. Finally, we concatenate $\hat{TF}_t^j$ and TI_t^j to obtain the flow-enhanced tokens TK_t^j to enhance spatial MHSA.

Dual Perspective Spatial MHSA. We introduce window partition to spatial MHSA for efficiency. According to the local smoothness prior of natural images, the tokens are more correlated to their neighbors. Hence, we adopt relative small window size in spatial transformer. Given the t-th frame token map processed by j-th transformer $TK_t^j \in \mathbb{R}^{H \times W \times C}$, where H, W and C represent the height, width and channel size. Window partition divides TK_t^j into several $h \times w$ non-overlapped windows, and MHSA is performed inside each window, respectively. However, if the window contains numerous tokens projected from corrupted regions, the attention accuracy would be deteriorated due to the lack of valid content. Therefore, we integrate global tokens to spatial MHSA. We adopt depth-wise convolution [18] to condense TK_t^j to global tokens, and supply them to each window. Given the kernel size k and downsampling rate s (also known as stride), the global tokens are generated as.

$$TG_t^j = \text{DC}(TK_t^j, k, s) \tag{4}$$

where TG_t^j represents the extracted global tokens and DC is the depth-wise convolution. The query $Q_t^j(d)$, key $K_t^j(d)$ and value $V_t^j(d)$ of the d-th window in TK_t^j are generated as.

$$
\begin{aligned}
Q_t^j(d) &= \text{MLP}(\text{LN}(TK_t^j(d))) \\
K_t^j(d) &= \text{MLP}(\text{LN}(\text{Concat}(TK_t^j(d), TG_t^j))) \\
V_t^j(d) &= \text{MLP}(\text{LN}(\text{Concat}(TK_t^j(d), TG_t^j)))
\end{aligned} \tag{5}
$$

where $TK_t^j(d)$ represents the d-th window in TK_t^j, and LN is layer normalization [1]. After we obtain $Q_t^j(d)$, $K_t^j(d)$ and $V_t^j(d)$, we apply spatial MHSA to process them. The dual perspective spatial MHSA is illustrated in Fig. 4(b).

Note that the global tokens are shared by all the windows. In each spatial transformer, if we adopt all-pair attention retrieval for MHSA, each token will retrieve $H \times W$ tokens. While the token number for retrieval in our dual perspective spatial MHSA is ($\lceil \frac{H}{s} \rceil \times \lceil \frac{W}{s} \rceil + h \times w$). It is easy to derive that when $s \geq \lceil \sqrt{\frac{HW}{HW-hw}} \rceil$, the referenced token number will be smaller than the token number in all-pair attention retrieval.

Recently, focal transformer [52] has also adopted the combination of local and global attention in transformer. Compared with [52], our method decouples the global token size and the window shape, which is more flexible than the sub-window pooling strategy in focal transformer.

Loss Function. We adopt the reconstruction loss in the corrupted and the valid regions together with the T-Patch GAN loss [7] to supervise the training process. We use hinge loss as the adversarial loss. We provide the detailed loss formulas in the supplementary material.

4 Experiments

4.1 Settings

We adopt Youtube-VOS [49] and DAVIS [4] datasets for evaluation. Youtube-VOS contains 4453 videos and DAVIS contains 150 videos. We adopt the training set of Youtube-VOS to train our networks. As for Youtube-VOS, we evaluate the trained models on its testset. Since DAVIS contains densely annotated masks on its training set, we adopt its training set to evaluate our method.

Following the previous work [14], we choose PSNR, SSIM [47] and LPIPS [58] as our evaluation metrics. Meanwhile, we adopt end-point-error (EPE) to evaluate the flow completion quality. We compare our method with state-of-the-art baselines, including VINet [22], DFGVI [50], CPN [24], OPN [35], 3DGC [7], STTN [55], FGVC [14], TSAM [59], DSTT [28] and FFM [29].

4.2 Implementation Details

In our experiments, We utilize RAFT [41] to extract optical flows. In flow completion network, the flow interval and input flow number are both set to 3. The flow locating in middle of the local temporal window is treated as the target flow for completion. We adopt gradient propagation [14] as our flow-guided content propagation strategy, and the detailed procedure will be provided in the supplementary material. As for FGT, we keep the patch embedding method the same as FFM [29] for fair comparisons. We utilize the forward optical flows in the flow guidance integration module. FGT adopts 8 transformer blocks in total (4 temporal and 4 spatial transformer blocks). In the temporal transformer, we adopt 2×2 zone division for temporal MHSA. In the spatial transformer, the downsampling rate of the global

Table 1. Quantitative results on the Youtube-VOS and DAVIS datasets. The best and second best numbers for each metric are indicated by red and blue fonts, respectively. ↓ means lower is better, while ↑ means higher is better. "FGT" represents we adopt our proposed flow-guided transformer to fill all the pixels in the corrupted regions without flow-guided content propagation.

| Method | Youtube-VOS | | | DAVIS | | | | | |
| | | | | Square | | | Object | | |
	PSNR↑	SSIM↑	LPIPS↓	PSNR↑	SSIM↑	LPIPS↓	PSNR↑	SSIM↑	LPIPS↓
VINet [22]	29.83	0.955	0.047	28.32	0.943	0.049	28.47	0.922	0.083
DFGVI [50]	32.05	0.965	0.038	29.75	0.959	0.037	30.28	0.925	0.052
CPN [24]	32.17	0.963	0.040	30.20	0.953	0.049	31.59	0.933	0.058
OPN [35]	32.66	0.965	0.039	31.15	0.958	0.044	32.40	0.944	0.041
3DGC [7]	30.22	0.961	0.041	28.19	0.944	0.049	31.69	0.940	0.054
STTN [55]	32.49	0.964	0.040	30.54	0.954	0.047	32.83	0.943	0.052
TSAM [59]	31.62	0.962	0.031	29.73	0.951	0.036	31.50	0.934	0.048
DSTT [28]	33.53	0.969	0.031	31.61	0.960	0.037	33.39	0.945	0.050
FFM [29]	33.73	0.970	0.030	31.87	0.965	0.034	34.19	0.951	0.045
FGT	34.04	0.971	0.028	32.60	0.965	0.032	34.30	0.953	0.040
FGVC [14]	33.94	0.972	0.026	32.14	0.967	0.030	33.91	0.955	0.036
Ours	34.53	0.976	0.024	33.41	0.974	0.023	34.96	0.966	0.029

token is 4, while the window size is 8. We adopt Adam optimizer [23] to train our networks. The training iteration is 280K for LAFC and 500K for FGT. The initial learning rate is 1e-4, which is divided by 10 after 120K iterations for LAFC and 300K iterations for FGT. For ablation studies, following FFM [29], we train FGT for 250K iterations, and the learning rate is divided by 10 after 200K iterations. We perform ablation studies on DAVIS dataset.

4.3   Quantitative Evaluation

During inference, the resolution of videos is set to 432×256. We generate square masksets with continuous motion trace for Youtube-VOS and DAVIS datasets. The average size of the masks in the square maskset is $\frac{1}{16}$ of the whole frame. We shuffle DAVIS object maskset randomly and corrupt frames with these masks to evaluate video inpainting performance upon object masks. For fair comparisons among flow-based video inpainting methods, we utilize the same optical flow extractor for DFGVI [50], FGVC [14] and our method.

We report the quantitative evaluation results of our method and other baselines in Table 1. Our method outperforms previous baselines by a significant margin on all three metrics, which means the restored videos from our method enjoy less distortion and better perceptual quality than previous counterparts. What's more, if we fill the corrupted region purely with FGT, we can still outperform previous transformer-based video inpainting baselines [28,29,55].

4.4   Qualitative Comparisons

We compare the qualitative results between our method and five recent baselines [14,28,29,55,59] under the square mask, object mask and object removal

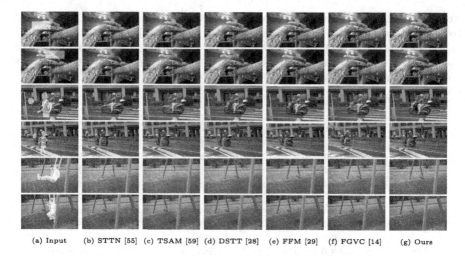

(a) Input   (b) STTN [55]   (c) TSAM [59]   (d) DSTT [28]   (e) FFM [29]   (f) FGVC [14]   (g) Ours

Fig. 5. Qualitative comparison between our method and some recent baselines [14, 28, 29, 55, 59]. From top to bottom, every two rows display inpainting results of square mask set, object mask set, and object removal, respectively.

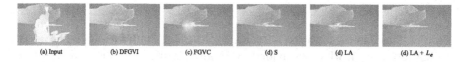

(a) Input   (b) DFGVI   (c) FGVC   (d) S   (d) LA   (d) LA + L_e

Fig. 6. Comparison of flow results between DFGVI [50], FGVC [14], and several variants of our method. S: single flow completion, LA: Flow completion with local aggregation, L_e: Edge loss.

settings. The results are shown in Fig. 5. Compared with these baselines, our method enjoys outstanding visual quality. Our method can complete more accurate optical flows, which describes the motion trajectory with high fidelity. Therefore, our method enjoys less distortion in the content propagation stage than FGVC [14]. What's more, the completed optical flows provide accurate object clusters. Such information leads to more accurate attention retrieval and naturally produce better visual quality. We will provide more video inpainting results in the supplementary materials.

4.5   Ablation Studies

Model Analysis. We compare our method with (1) FGVC and (2) FGVC+ FGT to justify the design of our method over flow completion and image inpainting baseline [53]. The results in Table 2(a) demonstrate the effectiveness of our method in both flow completion and frame synthesis. In Table 2(b), we compare FGT with different transformer baselines. Since FLOPs in video inpainting is related to the number of frames processed simultaneously, we assume the processed frame number is 20, which is a common practice in STTN [55] and FFM [29]. "FGT(all-pair)"

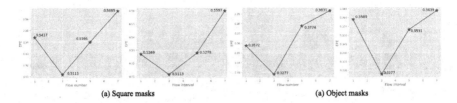

(a) Square masks   (a) Object masks

Fig. 7. EPE results with varying flow number (when flow interval is 3) or varying flow interval (when flow number is 3) on both square and object mask sets.

Table 2. Model analysis We report the analysis of the method variants and the comparison of the efficiency between FGT and other baselines.

(a) Analysis about method variants.

Method	Square			Object		
	PSNR↑	SSIM↑	LPIPS↓	PSNR↑	SSIM↑	LPIPS↓
FGVC [14]	32.14	0.967	0.030	33.91	0.955	0.034
FGVC+FGT	32.49	0.968	0.027	34.58	0.956	0.031
LAFC+FGT	**33.41**	**0.974**	**0.023**	**34.96**	**0.966**	**0.029**

(b) Efficiency analysis.

Method	FLOPs (per frame)	Params	Speed
STTN [55]	477.91 G	16.56 M	0.22 s
FFM [29]	579.82 G	36.59 M	0.30 s
FGT (all-pair)	703.22 G	42.31 M	–
FGT	455.91 G	42.31 M	0.39 s

means we adopt all-pair attention in FGT, which consumes much more computation overhead compared with FGT. If we adopt flow-guided content propagation, we can obtain better video inpainting quality, but the speed will degrade to 2.11s/frame, which indicates the performance-efficiency trade-off in our method. We provide detailed run-time analysis in the supplementary material.

Local Flow Aggregation and Edge Loss for Flow Completion. We report the end-point-error (EPE) of single flow completion (replace the P3D blocks with vanilla convolution blocks), local aggregation for flow completion without and with edge loss, together with two baselines [14,50] in Table 3. With the introduction of local aggregation and edge loss, our method achieves substantial improvement. The subjective results are shown in Fig. 6. With local aggregation, our method can exploit the complementary flow features in a local temporal window, which is beneficial to complete accurate flow shape. With edge loss, our method can synthesize optical flows with clearer motion boundaries. Finally, we report the influence of flow number and flow interval w.r.t. EPE in Fig. 7. When the flow number or interval is too small, the target flow cannot utilize abundant references for accurate flow completion, which undermines the performance. When the flow number or interval is large, the flow completion performance deteriorates gradually, which reveals the distant flows contribute less to flow completion relative to local flows.

Flow Guidance Integration and Dual Perspective Spatial MHSA. In this part, we adopt the transformer to synthesize all the pixels in the corrupted regions for fair comparisons across different settings. We evaluate the effectiveness of the dual perspective tokens, the completed flow guidance and the flow-reweight module in spatial MHSA, and report the corresponding results in Table 4.

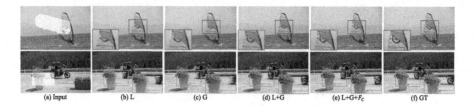

Fig. 8. Qualitative comparison of different components in the dual perspective transformer. L: Local window attention. G: Global tokens. F_c: Flow guidance with flow-reweight module.

Table 3. Ablation study about flow completion. S: single flow completion, LA: Flow completion with local aggregation, L_e: Edge loss.

Maskset	EPE↓				
	DFGVI [50]	FGVC [14]	S	LA	LA + L_e
Square	1.161	0.633	0.546	0.524	0.511
Object	1.053	0.491	0.359	0.338	0.328

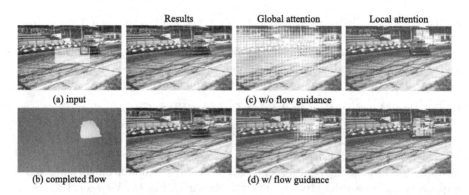

Fig. 9. Attention map visualization of our transformer model with/without the flow guidance. The red square in (a) indicates the location of the chosen query token for visualization. (Color figure online)

The quantitative results demonstrate the effectiveness of our proposed method. Compared with attention with only local or global tokens, the combination of these two perspective tokens achieves significant performance boost. With the introduction of the completed flow tokens and the flow-reweight module, the performance of our model boosts further. When we remove the flow-reweight module, the performance degrades, which demonstrates the necessity to introduce flow guidance and control its impact during attention retrieval.

The qualitative comparisons between different components in our flow-guided transformer are shown in Fig. 8. We can observe the substantial improved visual quality on dual perspective attention and the introduction of flow guidance. The

Table 4. Ablation study about the spatial transformer. W: Local window partition. G: Global tokens. F_C: Completed flow tokens. RF: Flow-reweight module.

W	G	F_C	RF	Square			Object		
				PSNR↑	SSIM↑	LPIPS↓	PSNR↑	SSIM↑	LPIPS↓
✓	–	–	–	31.37	0.957	0.038	32.98	0.945	0.051
–	✓	–	–	31.42	0.958	0.040	33.10	0.945	0.050
✓	✓	–	–	31.62	0.959	0.038	33.25	0.946	0.048
✓	✓	✓	–	31.54	0.958	0.039	33.12	0.945	0.049
✓	✓	✓	✓	31.87	0.961	0.036	33.52	0.947	0.045

combination of global and local tokens enlarges the attention retrieval space while maintaining the local smoothness simultaneously. As for flow guidance, we visualize the local and global attention maps in Fig. 9. The red square in Fig. 9(a) indicates the query token. With flow guidance, our transformer tends to query the tokens with similar motion pattern (e.g. tokens in car region), which leads to clearer object boundary for video inpainting in higher quality.

5 Conclusion

In this work, we propose a flow-guided transformer for video inpainting, which introduces a novel way to leverage the motion discrepancy from optical flows to instruct the attention retrieval in transformer. We decouple the attention module along spatial and temporal dimension to facilitate the integration of the completed flows. We propose the flow-reweight module to control the impact of the flows in the attention retrieval process. What's more, in both temporal and spatial transformer blocks, we design specific window partition strategy for better efficiency while maintaining the competitive performance. Besides the proposed flow-guided transformer, We design a flow completion network to exploit the complementary features of the optical flows in a local temporal window, and introduce edge loss to supervise the reconstruction of flows for clear motion boundaries. The high-quality completed flows benefit the content propagation and flow-guided transformer. Extensive experiments demonstrate the effectiveness of our proposed method.

Acknowledgment. This work was supported by the Natural Science Foundation of China under Grants 62036005, 62022075, and 62021001, and by the Fundamental Research Funds for the Central Universities under Contract No. WK3490000006.

References

1. Ba, J.L., Kiros, J.R., Hinton, G.E.: Layer normalization (2016)
2. Bertalmio, M., Bertozzi, A.L., Sapiro, G.: Navier-stokes, fluid dynamics, and image and video inpainting. In: CVPR, vol. 1, pp. 355–362 (2001)

3. Bhojanapalli, S., Chakrabarti, A., Glasner, D., Li, D., Unterthiner, T., Veit, A.: Understanding robustness of transformers for image classification. In: ICCV, pp. 10231–10241 (October 2021)

4. Caelles, S., et al.: The 2018 DAVIS challenge on video object segmentation. arXiv preprint arXiv:1803.00557 (2018)

5. Canny, J.: A computational approach to edge detection. TPAMI PAMI **8**(6), 679–698 (1986). https://doi.org/10.1109/TPAMI.1986.4767851

6. Carion, N., Massa, F., Synnaeve, G., Usunier, N., Kirillov, A., Zagoruyko, S.: End-to-end object detection with transformers. In: Vedaldi, A., Bischof, H., Brox, T., Frahm, J.-M. (eds.) ECCV 2020. LNCS, vol. 12346, pp. 213–229. Springer, Cham (2020). https://doi.org/10.1007/978-3-030-58452-8_13

7. Chang, Y.L., Liu, Z.Y., Lee, K.Y., Hsu, W.: Free-form video inpainting with 3D gated convolution and temporal PatchGAN. In: ICCV, pp. 9066–9075 (2019)

8. Chang, Y.L., Liu, Z.Y., Lee, K.Y., Hsu, W.: Learnable gated temporal shift module for deep video inpainting. In: BMVC (2019)

9. Chu, X., et al.: Twins: Revisiting the design of spatial attention in vision transformers. In: NeurIPS (2021)

10. Chu, X., et al.: Conditional positional encodings for vision transformers. arXiv: 2102.10882 (2021). https://arxiv.org/pdf/2102.10882.pdf

11. Dosovitskiy, A., et al.: An image is worth 16 × 16 words: Transformers for image recognition at scale. In: ICLR (2021). https://openreview.net/forum?id=YicbFdNTTy

12. Ebdelli, M., Le Meur, O., Guillemot, C.: Video inpainting with short-term windows: Application to object removal and error concealment. TIP **24**(10), 3034–3047 (2015). https://doi.org/10.1109/TIP.2015.2437193

13. Fan, H., Xiong, B., Mangalam, K., Li, Y., Yan, Z., Malik, J., Feichtenhofer, C.: Multiscale vision transformers. In: ICCV, pp. 6824–6835 (October 2021)

14. Gao, C., Saraf, A., Huang, J.-B., Kopf, J.: Flow-edge guided video completion. In: Vedaldi, A., Bischof, H., Brox, T., Frahm, J.-M. (eds.) ECCV 2020. LNCS, vol. 12357, pp. 713–729. Springer, Cham (2020). https://doi.org/10.1007/978-3-030-58610-2_42

15. Granados, M., Tompkin, J., Kim, K., Grau, O., Kautz, J., Theobalt, C.: How not to be seen - object removal from videos of crowded scenes. Comput. Graph. Forum **31**(2pt1), 219–228 (2012). https://doi.org/10.1111/j.1467-8659.2012.03000.x

16. Granados, M., Kim, K.I., Tompkin, J., Kautz, J., Theobalt, C.: Background inpainting for videos with dynamic objects and a free-moving camera. In: Fitzgibbon, A., Lazebnik, S., Perona, P., Sato, Y., Schmid, C. (eds.) ECCV 2012. LNCS, vol. 7572, pp. 682–695. Springer, Heidelberg (2012). https://doi.org/10.1007/978-3-642-33718-5_49

17. He, K., Zhang, X., Ren, S., Sun, J.: Deep residual learning for image recognition. In: CVPR, pp. 770–778 (2016)

18. Howard, A.G., et al.: Mobilenets: Efficient convolutional neural networks for mobile vision applications. arXiv preprint arXiv:1704.04861 (2017)

19. Huang, J.B., Kang, S.B., Ahuja, N., Kopf, J.: Temporally coherent completion of dynamic video. TOG **35**(6), 196:1–11 (2016)

20. Iizuka, S., Simo-Serra, E., Ishikawa, H.: Globally and locally consistent image completion. TOG **36**(4), 107:1–14 (2017)

21. Ke, L., Tai, Y.W., Tang, C.K.: Occlusion-aware video object inpainting. In: ICCV (2021)

22. Kim, D., Woo, S., Lee, J.Y., Kweon, I.S.: Deep video inpainting. In: CVPR, pp. 5792–5801 (2019)

23. Kingma, D.P., Ba, J.: Adam: A method for stochastic optimization. In: ICLR (2014)

24. Lee, S., Oh, S.W., Won, D., Kim, S.J.: Copy-and-paste networks for deep video inpainting. In: ICCV, pp. 4413–4421 (2019)

25. Li, A., et al.: Short-term and long-term context aggregation network for video inpainting. In: Vedaldi, A., Bischof, H., Brox, T., Frahm, J.-M. (eds.) ECCV 2020. LNCS, vol. 12349, pp. 728–743. Springer, Cham (2020). https://doi.org/10.1007/978-3-030-58548-8_42

26. Liao, L., Xiao, J., Wang, Z., Lin, C.W., Satoh, S.: Image inpainting guided by coherence priors of semantics and textures. In: CVPR, pp. 6539–6548 (June 2021)

27. Liu, G., Reda, F.A., Shih, K.J., Wang, T.-C., Tao, A., Catanzaro, B.: Image inpainting for irregular holes using partial convolutions. In: Ferrari, V., Hebert, M., Sminchisescu, C., Weiss, Y. (eds.) ECCV 2018. LNCS, vol. 11215, pp. 89–105. Springer, Cham (2018). https://doi.org/10.1007/978-3-030-01252-6_6

28. Liu, R., et al.: Decoupled spatial-temporal transformer for video inpainting (2021)

29. Liu, R., et al.: Fuseformer: Fusing fine-grained information in transformers for video inpainting. In: ICCV (2021)

30. Liu, Z., et al.: Swin transformer: Hierarchical vision transformer using shifted windows. In: ICCV, pp. 10012–10022 (October 2021)

31. Matsushita, Y., Ofek, E., Ge, W., Tang, X., Shum, H.Y.: Full-frame video stabilization with motion inpainting. TPAMI **28**(7), 1150–1163 (2006). https://doi.org/10.1109/TPAMI.2006.141

32. Misra, I., Girdhar, R., Joulin, A.: An end-to-end transformer model for 3d object detection. In: ICCV, pp. 2906–2917 (Oct 2021)

33. Nazeri, K., Ng, E., Joseph, T., Qureshi, F., Ebrahimi, M.: Edgeconnect: Structure guided image inpainting using edge prediction. In: ICCVW (Oct 2019)

34. Newson, A., Almansa, A., Fradet, M., Gousseau, Y., Pérez, P.: Video inpainting of complex scenes. SIAM J. Imag. Sci. **7**(4), 1993–2019 (2014)

35. Oh, S.W., Lee, S., Lee, J.Y., Kim, S.J.: Onion-peel networks for deep video completion. In: ICCV, pp. 4403–4412 (2019)

36. Ouyang, H., Wang, T., Chen, Q.: Internal video inpainting by implicit long-range propagation. In: ICCV (2021)

37. Pathak, D., Krähenbühl, P., Donahue, J., Darrell, T., Efros, A.: Context encoders: Feature learning by inpainting. In: CVPR, pp. 2536–2544 (2016)

38. Peng, J., Liu, D., Xu, S., Li, H.: Generating diverse structure for image inpainting with hierarchical VQ-VAE. In: CVPR, pp. 10775–10784 (2021)

39. Qiu, Z., Yao, T., Mei, T.: Learning spatio-temporal representation with pseudo-3d residual networks. In: ICCV, pp. 5533–5541 (2017)

40. Ronneberger, O., Fischer, P., Brox, T.: U-Net: Convolutional networks for biomedical image segmentation. In: Navab, N., Hornegger, J., Wells, W.M., Frangi, A.F. (eds.) MICCAI 2015. LNCS, vol. 9351, pp. 234–241. Springer, Cham (2015). https://doi.org/10.1007/978-3-319-24574-4_28

41. Teed, Z., Deng, J.: RAFT: Recurrent all-pairs field transforms for optical flow. In: Vedaldi, A., Bischof, H., Brox, T., Frahm, J.-M. (eds.) ECCV 2020. LNCS, vol. 12347, pp. 402–419. Springer, Cham (2020). https://doi.org/10.1007/978-3-030-58536-5_24

42. Tran, D., Bourdev, L., Fergus, R., Torresani, L., Paluri, M.: Learning spatiotemporal features with 3d convolutional networks. In: CVPR, pp. 4489–4497 (2015)

43. Vaswani, A., et al.: Attention is all you need. In: NeurIPS, vol. 30 (2017)

44. Wang, C., Huang, H., Han, X., Wang, J.: Video inpainting by jointly learning temporal structure and spatial details. In: AAAI, vol. 33, pp. 5232–5239 (2019)

45. Wang, H., Zhu, Y., Adam, H., Yuille, A., Chen, L.C.: Max-deeplab: End-to-end panoptic segmentation with mask transformers. In: CVPR, pp. 5463–5474 (2021)
46. Wang, X., et al.: Oadtr: Online action detection with transformers. In: ICCV, pp. 7565–7575 (Oct 2021)
47. Wang, Z., Bovik, A.C., Sheikh, H.R., Simoncelli, E.P.: Image quality assessment: From error visibility to structural similarity. TIP **13**(4), 600–612 (2004)
48. Wu, H., et al.: Cvt: Introducing convolutions to vision transformers. In: ICCV, pp. 22–31 (Oct 2021)
49. Xu, N., et al.: Youtube-vos: A large-scale video object segmentation benchmark. arXiv preprint arXiv:1809.03327 (2018)
50. Xu, R., Li, X., Zhou, B., Loy, C.C.: Deep flow-guided video inpainting. In: CVPR, pp. 3723–3732 (2019)
51. Xu, S., Liu, D., Xiong, Z.: E2I: Generative inpainting from edge to image. In: TCSVT (2020)
52. Yang, J., et al.: Focal attention for long-range interactions in vision transformers. In: NeurIPS (Dec 2021). https://www.microsoft.com/en-us/research/publication/focal-self-attention-for-local-global-interactions-in-vision-transformers/
53. Yu, J., Lin, Z., Yang, J., Shen, X., Lu, X., Huang, T.S.: Generative image inpainting with contextual attention. In: CVPR, pp. 5505–5514 (2018)
54. Yu, J., Lin, Z., Yang, J., Shen, X., Lu, X., Huang, T.S.: Free-form image inpainting with gated convolution. In: ICCV, pp. 4471–4480 (2019)
55. Zeng, Y., Fu, J., Chao, H.: Learning joint spatial-temporal transformations for video inpainting. In: Vedaldi, A., Bischof, H., Brox, T., Frahm, J.-M. (eds.) ECCV 2020. LNCS, vol. 12361, pp. 528–543. Springer, Cham (2020). https://doi.org/10.1007/978-3-030-58517-4_31
56. Zhang, H., Mai, L., Xu, N., Wang, Z., Collomosse, J., Jin, H.: An internal learning approach to video inpainting. In: ICCV, pp. 2720–2729 (2019)
57. Zhang, K., Fu, J., Liu, D.: Inertia-guided flow completion and style fusion for video inpainting. In: CVPR, pp. 5982–5991 (June 2022)
58. Zhang, R., Isola, P., Efros, A.A., Shechtman, E., Wang, O.: The unreasonable effectiveness of deep features as a perceptual metric. In: CVPR, pp. 586–595 (2018)
59. Zou, X., Yang, L., Liu, D., Lee, Y.J.: Progressive temporal feature alignment network for video inpainting. In: CVPR (2021)

Shift-Tolerant Perceptual Similarity Metric

Abhijay Ghildyal[✉] and Feng Liu

Portland State University, Portland, OR 97201, USA
{abhijay,fliu}@pdx.edu

Abstract. Existing perceptual similarity metrics assume an image and its reference are well aligned. As a result, these metrics are often sensitive to a small alignment error that is imperceptible to the human eyes. This paper studies the effect of small misalignment, specifically a small shift between the input and reference image, on existing metrics, and accordingly develops a shift-tolerant similarity metric. This paper builds upon LPIPS, a widely used learned perceptual similarity metric, and explores architectural design considerations to make it robust against imperceptible misalignment. Specifically, we study a wide spectrum of neural network elements, such as anti-aliasing filtering, pooling, striding, padding, and skip connection, and discuss their roles in making a robust metric. Based on our studies, we develop a new deep neural network-based perceptual similarity metric. Our experiments show that our metric is tolerant to imperceptible shifts while being consistent with the human similarity judgment. Code is available at https://tinyurl.com/5n85r28r.

Keywords: Perceptual similarity metric · Image quality assessment

1 Introduction

Image similarity measurement is a common task for many computer vision and computer graphics applications. General similarity metrics like PSNR and RMSE, however, do not match the human visual perception well when assessing the similarity between two images. Therefore, many dedicated image similarity metrics, such as Structural Similarity (SSIM) and its variations [30–32,35], were developed in order to more closely reflect human perception. However, manually crafting a perceptual similarity metric remains a challenging task as it involves the complex human cognitive judgment [22,28,30,37].

Recently, learning-based image similarity metrics have been developed, which learn from a large set of labeled data and predict similarity between images that correlates well with human perception [3,5,6,16,25,37]. Among them, the Learned Perceptual Image Patch Similarity metric (LPIPS) by Zhang *et al.*, is a widely adopted metric and used in computer graphics and vision literature [37].

This paper studies how similarity metrics work on a pair of images that are not perfectly aligned. For instance, a tiny one-pixel translation in the image pair, is imperceptible to humans. But, *will such a visually imperceptible misalignment compromise any existing similarity metrics?* PSNR and RMSE assume pixel-wise registration, naturally making them sensitive

S. Avidan et al. (Eds.): ECCV 2022, LNCS 13678, pp. 91–107, 2022.
https://doi.org/10.1007/978-3-031-19797-0_6

even to a one-pixel misalignment. Our study found that learned metrics, such as LPIPS are also sensitive to a tiny misalignment. Figure 1 shows such an example via a two-alternative forced choice test, in which we asked viewers *"which of the two distorted images, I_0 or I_1, is more similar to the reference image I_{ref}?"* Then, we shifted I_0 and I_1 by one pixel and obtained opinions again. None of the participants flipped from I_0 to I_1 or vice versa, which is intuitive as a one-pixel shift is imperceptible to viewers. But existing metrics, such as MS-SSIM and LPIPS, flipped judgment after the one-pixel shift.

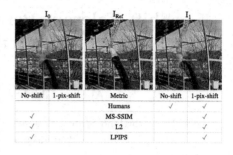

No-shift	1-pix-shift	Metric	No-shift	1-pix-shift
		Humans	✓	✓
✓		MS-SSIM		✓
✓		L2		✓
✓		LPIPS		✓

Fig. 1. Whether I_0 and I_1 are shifted by 1 pixel or not, viewers always consider I_1 more similar to I_{ref} than I_0; but existing similarity metrics often switch their predictions after the shift.

Our problem is related to the recent work on making deep neural networks shift invariant [13,15,19,29,36,39]. Recently, Azulay and Weiss found that an image classifier can change its top-1 prediction if the image is translated by only one pixel [2]. Their results showed that after translating an image by one pixel, the classifier made a different top-1 prediction for 30% of the 1000 validation images. Zhang introduced anti-aliasing filters into a deep neural network to make the feature extraction network shift-equivariant, which in terms makes the whole network shift-invariant for the down streaming tasks [36]. Compared to these works, our problem is different in that 1) a perceptual similarity metric takes two images as input instead of working on a single input image, and 2) only one of the two images is shifted, thus introducing imperceptible misalignment instead of shifting the two images simultaneously.

This paper aims to develop a shift-tolerant perceptual similarity metric that correlates well with the human judgment on the similarity between images while being robust against imperceptible misalignment between them. We build our metric upon LPIPS, a deep neural network-based metric widely adopted for its close correlation with human perception. We investigate a variety of elements that can be incorporated into a deep neural network to make it resistant to an imperceptible misalignment. These elements include anti-aliasing filters, striding, pooling, padding, placement of anti-aliasing, etc. Based on our findings on these elements, we develop a shift-tolerant perceptual similarity metric that not only is more consistent with human perception but also is significantly more resistant to imperceptible misalignment between a pair of images than existing metrics.

In the remainder of this paper, we first report our study, verifying that viewers are not sensitive to small amounts of shifts between two images when comparing them, in Sect. 3. We then benchmark existing similarity metrics and show that they are sensitive to imperceptible shifts between a pair of images in Sect. 4. We study several important elements that make a deep neural network-based similarity metric both tolerant to imperceptible shifts and consistent with human perception of visual similarity in Sect. 5. We finally report our experiments that thoroughly evaluate our new perceptual similarity metric by comparing it to state-of-the-art metrics and through detailed ablation studies in Sect. 6.

2   Related Work

Visual similarity metrics are commonly used to compare two images or evaluate the performance of many image and video processing, editing and synthesis algorithms. While there are already many established metrics for these tasks, such as PSNR, MSE, SSIM and its variations [30–32], there is still a gap between their prediction and the human's judgment. This section provides a brief overview of the recent advances in learned perceptual similarity metrics that aim to bridge the gap mentioned above.

In their influential work, Zhang *et al.* reported that features from a deep neural network can be used to measure the similarity between two images that is more consistent with the human perception than other commonly used metrics [37]. Accordingly, they developed LPIPS, a perceptual metric learned from a large collection of labelled data. Specifically, LPIPS uses a pre-trained network for image classification tasks or learns a neural network to compute the features for each of the two images or patches, and also learns to aggregate the feature distances into a similarity score. Since its debut, LPIPS has been widely used as a perceptual quality metric. On a related note, the computer vision and graphics community also calculate the difference between the deep features of two images as a loss function to train deep neural networks for image enhancement and synthesis. Such a loss function, often called perceptual loss, enables the neural networks to learn to generate perceptually pleasing images [7,14,18,24,26,38].

Kettunen *et al.* developed the E-LPIPS metric that adopts the LPIPS network and uses randomly transformed samples to calculate expected LPIPS distance over them [16]. They showed that E-LPIPS is robust against the Expectation Over Transformation attack [1]. Different from LPIPS, Prashnani *et al.* use the differences between features to generate patch-wise errors and corresponding weights, via two different fully-connected networks [25]. Their final similarity score is a weighted average of the patch-wise distances. Czolbe *et al.* developed a similarity metric based on Watson's perceptual model [33], by replacing discrete cosine transform with discrete fourier transform [5]. They posit that their metric is robust against small translations and is sensitive to large translations.

In an earlier work, Wang and Simoncelli [31] improved SSIM [30] by replacing the spatial correlation measures with phase correlations in wavelet subbands which made the metric less sensitive to geometric transformations. Ma *et al.* [21] developed a geometric transformation invariant method (GTI-CNN). Our work is closely related to theirs, as GTI-CNN is a similarity metric invariant to the misalignment between a pair of images. In their method, Ma *et al.* train a fully convolutional neural network to extract deep features from each image and calculate the mean squared error between them as final similarity [21]. They showed that training the network directly on aligned samples leads to a metric sensitive to misalignment, which is consistent with what we found in our study. They reported that augmenting the training samples with small misalignment can make the learned metric significantly more resistant to the misalignment. Compared to this method, our work focuses on designing a deep neural network architecture robust to misalignment without any data augmentation. Bhardwaj *et al.* followed the understanding of the physiology of the human visual system and developed a fully convolutional neural network that generates a multi-scale probabilistic representation of an input image and then calculates the symmetric Kullback-Leibler divergences between such representations of two images to measure their similarity [3]. They found their similarity metric, perceptual information metric (PIM), robust against small shifts between a pair of images. While benchmarking existing metrics, our study also finds that PIM is most robust against small shifts among all metrics tested. We posit that the robustness of PIM partially comes from training on neighboring video frames that might already have small shifts among them, thus effectively serving as data augmentation, as done by Ma *et al.* [21]. We consider these as orthogonal efforts in developing a robust metric. As shown in our study, our metric is more consistent with human judgment and more robust against imperceptible misalignment than these methods, except PIM, to which ours is comparable, although our metric is trained on aligned samples directly without any data augmentation.

Our work is most related to deep image structure and texture similarity (DISTS) metric by Ding *et al.* [6]. They used global feature aggregation to make DISTS robust against mild geometric transformations. They also replaced the max pooling layers with l_2 pooling layers [11] in their VGG backbone network for anti-aliasing and found that blurring the input with l_2 pooling makes their network more robust against small shifts. Gu *et al.* [9] found that existing metrics like LPIPS do not perform well with images generated by GAN-based restoration algorithms. They attributed it to the small misalignment between the GAN results and the ground truth. Therefore, they used l_2 pooling [6,11] and *BlurPool* [36] to improve LPIPS. They found that both can improve LPIPS while *BlurPool* performs better. Compared to these two recent papers, our paper systematically investigates a broad range of neural network elements besides *BlurPool*. By integrating these elements, we develop a perceptual similarity metric both robust against small shifts and consistent with the human visual similarity judgment. Our method outperforms existing metrics and a variety of recently developed learned metrics. Integrating multiple network elements together makes our metric better than individual ones.

3 Human Perception of Small Shifts

As commonly expected, shifting one image by a few pixels will not alter human similarity judgment on a pair of images [3,34]. We conducted a user study to verify this common belief. Our hypothesis is that *it is difficult for people to detect a small shift in images*. In our study, we randomly chose 50 images from the MS-COCO test dataset [20] and divided them into 10 groups, each with 5 images. For each image in Group n with $n \in [0, 10)$, we cropped a 256×256 patch as a reference image and shifted the cropping window by n pixels to produce its shifted version. Since we always cropped the reference from the same location, we had an n-pixel shifted version for each of the 50 images, and thus in total, we have 500 pairs of images in our study. For each participant, we randomly sampled 50 pairs from the 500, with 5 pairs for each 0–9 pix-shift. The 50 pairs were presented one at a time, with the two images placed side by side. The position of the reference image, right, or left, is randomized to avoid biases. We asked our participants to judge whether a pair of images are the same or not.

To maintain the quality of our study and avoid boring the users, we only presented 50 samples to each user. Interestingly, humans managed to detect the shift for a 2 pixel shift in 50% of cases. We attribute this partially to the fact that the users were informed that there might or might not be a shift between a pair of images. While this might bias participants, such that their sensitivity to the shifts is likely increased, we found it helpful to obtain a more informative understanding of the human perception of small shifts; otherwise, participants tended to overly overlook the difference between a pair of images. Specifically, in our pilot study, we found that users were very confused when we asked them if a pair of images looked the same or not. Many of them thought if we were asking them to compare high-level features such as objects in the two images or if there were some artifacts in one of the pair of images.

We recruited 32 participants for our study. They have a wide range of professional backgrounds, including computer science, business, medicine, arts, and education, and most of them are 20 to 35 years old. To ensure the quality of this user study, we removed the responses from two participants who failed to pass a validation test. If a participant identified a pair of images with 0-pixel shift as *different* or a pair of images with 9-pixel shift as *the same* for more than two-thirds of the time in the study, we exclude all responses from that participant. In total, 30 participants passed our validation test. We obtained responses to 1500 trials in total, with 150 responses for each of the n-pixel shifts.

Finally, we report the user responses in Table 1. When the amount of shift is small, participants find it difficult to detect the shift. Samples with 1- and 2-pixel shifts were considered the same in 80.7% and 56.0% of the responses, respectively. As expected, shifts become easier to detect as the size of shifts increases. But even pairs with a 5-pixel shift were still not identified in 26.7% of the responses. We further analyzed the variability in user responses per sample, grouping them by the amount

Table 1. Human perception of small shifts. Image pairs with 1- and 2-pixel shift are deemed the same in 80.7% and 56.0% of the responses, resp. The avg. of std. in responses per sample indicates that users were more doubtful about image pairs with 2–5 pixel shift.

Pixel shift	Number of user responses			Avg. of std. in user
	Said Yes (Same)	Said No (Shifted)	Yes%	responses per sample
0	140	10	93.3%	0.09 ± 0.17
1	121	29	80.7%	0.19 ± 0.23
2	84	66	56.0%	0.34 ± 0.21
3	52	98	34.7%	0.24 ± 0.23
4	52	98	34.7%	0.30 ± 0.24
5	40	110	26.7%	0.23 ± 0.24
6	35	115	23.3%	0.21 ± 0.24
7	31	119	20.7%	0.12 ± 0.20
8	27	123	18.0%	0.18 ± 0.23
9	15	135	10.0%	0.13 ± 0.21

of pixel-shift. As observed in Table 1, with no or only a 1-pixel shift, users were consistently sure that the images in each pair were the same. Similarly, users could consistently detect the large shift (6 to 9 pixels). However, for a 2 to 5-pixel shift, we observed that users were doubtful whether images were shifted or not, indicated by the high variation in responses. As shown in our study, even after being informed about the possible shifts, participants still had difficulty detecting small shifts. This verifies our hypothesis that it is difficult for people to detect a small shift in images. In addition, we use this data and test the consistency of various metrics with the sensitivity of human perception to pixel shifts in Sect. 6. The test results provide further evidence that our metric is more consistent with human perception.

4   Effect of Small Shifts on Similarity Metrics

To understand how existing similarity metrics handle small shifts between a pair of images, we benchmarked representative metrics, including off-the-shelf metrics, such as L2 and SSIM, and the recent deep learning-based metrics. We derived a new dataset from the Berkeley-Adobe Perceptual Patch Similarity Dataset (BAPPS) [37]. The original BAPPS data consists of 36,344 samples, each with a reference I_r, and two distorted images I_1 and I_2. They cover a wide range of common distortions, including traditional, CNN-based, and from algorithms such as superresolution, frame interpolation, deblurring, and colorization. Please refer to [37] for more details. For each sample in the BAPPS dataset, we shifted the distorted images horizontally by k pixels where $k \in \{1, 2, 3\}$. To avoid any boundary artifacts from shifting, we cropped each shifted image I_i as follows.

$$\hat{I}_i = I_i[\, 0 : h, \ k : (w + k - 3)] \tag{1}$$

where w and h are the original sizes. In this way, all the images in our test were of size $(w - 3) \times h$ without regard to the amount of shift, which eliminates the effect of image sizes when we test how the amount of shift affects the performance. The references are cropped to the same size as the distorted images, but no shifts were applied. In addition, we also cropped all the images in each original sample to the size of $(w - 3) \times h$ to make the shifted sample and the original sample the same size to avoid the effect of the image size on a similarity metric in our late experiments.

Table 2. Accuracy (2AFC) and shift-tolerance (r_{rf}) of various metrics on the BAPPS val. dataset. 2AFC score is computed on the BAPPS data resized to 64 × 64 while r_{rf} scores are obtained from its shifted version of size 64 × 61.

Network	2AFC	r_{rf}		
		1pixel	2pixel	3pixel
L2	62.91	12.27	23.07	28.83
SSIM [30]	63.08	13.08	25.50	32.74
CW-SSIM [31]	60.55	11.33	18.28	23.22
E-LPIPS [16]	69.23	8.72	10.67	12.34
GTI-CNN [21]	63.74	9.37	12.32	16.25
DISTS [6]	68.89	5.57	8.20	10.07
PIM-1 [3]	69.45	1.63	3.06	4.39
PIM-5 [3]	69.47	2.28	3.56	5.19
LPIPS (Alex) [37]	69.83	6.79	8.90	9.70
LPIPS (Alex)[a,b,c]	**70.04**	9.25	9.34	11.55
LPIPS (Alex) ours[b,c]	69.83	3.48	4.75	6.84

(a, b) Retrained from scratch. (b) Trained on image patches of size 64 using author's (c) setup.

No shift was introduced to the original samples. A 3-pixel shift in our setting is equivalent to shifting 1.2% of the pixels for the images of size 256×256 pixels.

When evaluating a metric, we apply it to both the original sample from BAPPS and its corresponding shift, i.e., for each sample, we obtain two pairs of similarity scores, (s_1, s_2) and $(\hat{s}_1, \hat{s}_2)$. (s_1, s_2) are the similarity scores between I_1 and its reference I_r, and I_2 and I_r, respectively. $(\hat{s}_1, \hat{s}_2)$ are the corresponding pair of similarity scores for the shifted sample. Each pair of scores indicates which of the two distorted images is more similar to the reference according to the metric. We count the number of samples for which the similarity rank flipped when a sample was shifted and compute the rank-flip rate as follows.

$$r_{rf} = \frac{1}{N} \sum_{l=1}^{N} (s_1^l < s_2^l) \neq (\hat{s}_1^l < \hat{s}_2^l) \tag{2}$$

where r_{rf} is the rank-flip rate and N is the number of samples. r_{rf} evaluates how robust a metric is against the small shift between a pair of images.

For all learned metrics involved in this study, we used the trained models shared by their authors. While the image size in BAPPS is 256×256, some models were trained on 64×64 resized images. Thus, we conducted studies on these two sizes separately to provide fair comparisons. We report the results in Tables 2 and 3. All scores are obtained by averaging over examples in each distortion category in BAPPS and then averaging over all the categories. The two-alternative forced choice (2AFC) scores were obtained from the original BAPPS dataset that indicates how a metric's prediction correlates with the human opinion [37]. The rank-flip rate (r_{rf}) is calculated from the shifted dataset. It shows how robust a metric is to the shift between a distorted image and its reference. As reported in Table 3, learned metrics match human perception better than

Table 3. Accuracy (2AFC) and shift-tolerance (r_{rf}) across various metrics on the BAPPS val. dataset. 2AFC score is computed on the original BAPPS data of size 256×256 while r_{rf} is obtained from its shifted version of size 256×253.

Network	2AFC	r_{rf}		
		1pixel	2pixel	3pixel
L2	62.92	3.59	7.55	10.82
SSIM [30]	61.41	3.16	7.20	13.73
CW-SSIM [31]	61.48	3.91	6.88	9.47
MS-SSIM [32]	62.54	2.22	5.83	10.66
PIEAPP Sparse [25]	64.20	2.83	3.19	3.81
PIEAPP Dense [25]	64.15	2.97	1.37	3.33
PIM-1 [3]	67.45	0.79	1.70	2.52
PIM-5 [3]	67.38	1.01	1.88	2.96
GTI-CNN [21]	63.87	3.95	4.91	7.88
DISTS [6]	68.83	2.85	2.89	4.03
E-LPIPS [16]	68.22	5.84	5.86	5.77
LPIPS (Alex) [37]	68.59	2.81	3.41	3.84
LPIPS (Alex) [a,b,c]	70.54	2.58	3.59	3.53
LPIPS (Alex) ours[b,c]	70.39	0.66	1.24	1.79
LPIPS (Alex) [a,b,c]	**70.65**	2.87	3.92	3.74
LPIPS (Alex) ours[b,c]	70.48	**0.57**	**1.06**	**1.50**

(a) Retrained from scratch. (b) Trained on patches of size 256 using author's (c)/our (d) setup.

non-learned ones such as L2, SSIM, CW-SSIM and MS-SSIM. However, even these learned metrics are sensitive to small shifts except for the recent PIM [3]. Compared to these existing metrics except PIM, our metrics are more consistent with human perception as per 2AFC and more robust against small shifts. Overall, our method is comparable to PIM. Our method outperforms PIM on images of size 256×256 (Table 3) but does not work as well as it on smaller images

(Table 2). As discussed in Sect. 2, PIM is trained on neighboring video frames that often contain small shifts, which makes it robust against the imperceptible shifts. Our work is orthogonal to PIM as we investigate neural network elements to build a robust similarity metric. Hence, we purposely trained our metrics on the BAPPS dataset without any data augmentation.

5   Elements of Shift-Tolerant Metrics

Some recent papers reported that training a deep neural network using samples with shifted images through either data augmentation or neighboring video frames can make a learned similarity metric robust against small shifts between a pair of images [3, 21]. This paper aims to solve this problem from a different perspective; we investigate how one can design a deep neural network resistant to small shifts. We select the LPIPS network architecture as our baseline framework as it correlates with the human visual similarity judgment well [37]. To make this paper self-complete, we briefly describe the LPIPS framework. As illustrated in Fig. 2, LPIPS uses a

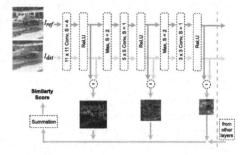

Fig. 2. LPIPS framework. The same feature extraction network (AlexNet) is used to extract feature embeddings from I_{dst} and I_{ref}. The difference between these embeddings is calculated at different levels and is combined together as the similarity between I_{dst} and I_{ref}.

backbone network, such as AlexNet [17] or VGG [27], to extract multi-level feature embeddings from a distorted image I_{dst} or its reference image I_{ref}. We denote the resulting feature embeddings as F_{dst} and F_{ref}, respectively. It then calculates the difference between F_{dst} and F_{ref} at all the levels and linearly combines the embedding difference at different levels into a final similarity/difference score, denoted as $d(F_{dst}, F_{ref})$. The combination coefficients and the feature extraction network are learned or fine-tuned.

Below we discuss how various neural network elements affect a similarity metric and how they can be improved to handle imperceptible shifts between a pair of images. Our focus is to develop a feature extraction network to generate feature embeddings from a pair of images that 1) are invariant to imperceptible shifts and 2) lead to a metric that correlates well with the human judgments.

Reducing Stride. Striding is widely used in a deep neural network to reduce the input size. For instance, AlexNet has a strided convolution (stride = 4) in its first convolutional layer (*conv-1*) and many max pooling operators with stride = 2 in the rest of the network. However, it is commonly known that striding with size >1 leads to the sampling rate falling well below the Nyquist rate, which causes aliasing artifacts. In their experiments with image classification tasks, [2] showed that AlexNet without any subsampling is significantly less sensitive to translations and also maintains its accuracy. Similarly, we also investigate the reduction of the stride size in the convolutional layers in the LPIPS framework to make it more resistant to imperceptible shifts at no expense of its consistency with the human visual similarity perception.

Anti-aliasing. Convolution is the most common operator for a deep convolutional neural network. A pure convolutional operator is shift-equivariant instead of being shift-invariant [23]. Shift equivariance makes a learned similarity metric sensitive to small shifts as small shifts between two images I_{dst} and I_{ref} will be transferred to the shifts between their feature embeddings F_{dst} and F_{ref}, which will in term drastically increase the distance between the feature embeddings $d(F_{dst}, F_{ref})$ as shown in Fig. 3(b). Downsampling in a neural network improves its shift invariance. Typically, downsampling can be

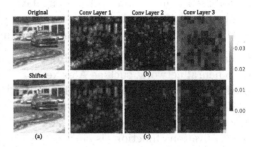

Fig. 3. Feature embedding difference maps at different levels. (a) an input image and its one-pixel shifted version. (b) difference maps between embeddings extracted by the original AlexNet. (c) difference maps between embeddings extracted by AlexNet augmented with anti-aliased strided convolution and pooling layers.

achieved by a strided convolutional operator or a strided pooling operator with stride n ($n > 1$). However, as discussed earlier in Reducing Stride, striding introduces aliasing. While reducing stride size lessens aliasing, it prevents the network from reducing the feature size.

To keep the benefit of downsampling while reducing stride, [36] invented a *BlurPool* operator. Take max pooling with stride n as an example. Such a max pooling operator can be decomposed into two steps: max pooling with stride 1, followed by a downsampling operator with stride n. To reduce the aliasing artifacts, [36] followed the pre-filtering idea for anti-aliasing and replaced this max pooling operator with a sequence of three operators: a max pooling with stride 1, a Gaussian filter, and a downsampling operator with stride n. The last two operators are combined into as a single operator, called *BlurPool*. Similarly, a convolution operator with stride n can be replaced with its anti-aliased version as a convolution operator with stride b and *BlurPool* with stride n/b. [36] found that replacing the original convolutional and pooling layers in a feature extraction neural network with their *BlurPool* versions helps generate feature embeddings that make the downstreaming tasks more shift invariant. *BlurPool* uses a fixed Gaussian filter for blurring and may lose some spatial features that are important attributes defining the quality of an image. [39] developed an adaptive anti-aliasing filter by learning a low-pass filter that is more content-aware. In this paper, we replace the strided convolution layers or pooling layers in the LPIPS framework with *BlurPool* or adaptive anti-aliasing filters to make it invariant to imperceptible shifts among images in a pair. Figure 3(c) shows that while anti-aliased convolution and pooling layers cannot make the feature network completely shift-invariant, they significantly reduce the difference between the feature embeddings from a pair of shifted images.

Location of Anti-aliasing. In a deep neural network, such as AlexNet used in LPIPS, a convolution layer is usually followed by an activation function. According to Zhang [36], the activation function is inserted between the stride-reduced convolutional layer and *BlurPool*, as illustrated in Fig. 4(a). Vasconcelos *et al.* [29] created variants of the anti-aliased strided convolution by placing the anti-aliasing filter at different

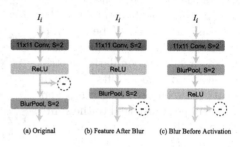

Fig. 4. Alternative positions of *BlurPool*.

locations, specifically, before or after the convolution operation. They found that some variants can lead to stronger learned inductive priors. But, will they provide significant improvements in shift tolerance? We build upon their findings and design variations of the anti-aliased strided convolutions. Specifically, we modify AlexNet *conv-1* as illustrated in Fig. 4 and explain the variants below.

Original. As shown in Fig. 4(a), we follow the original design of *BlurPool* and put it after *ReLU* [36]. For anti-aliasing, the stride size of *conv-1* is reduced from 4 to 2 and the *BlurPool* layer has a stride of 2 so that the total stride of 4 is preserved in this anti-aliased version. We take the output of *ReLU* as the feature embedding to calculate the similarity.

Feature After Blur. In the above design, the feature embedding is used before *BlurPool*. This effectively reduces the anti-aliasing effect on the feature embeddings although the reduced stride size in *conv-1* still offers some level of anti-aliasing. Therefore, we investigated a variation of the anti-aliased convolution by taking the output of *BlurPool* as the feature embedding to be used for similarity calculation, as illustrated in Fig. 4 (b).

Blur Before Activation. Vasconcelos *et al.* [29] suggested that blurring after the non-linearity, as done in Fig. 4(a) and (b), prevents high frequency from getting passed on to subsequent layers. Following their findings, we adopted their design by placing *BlurPool* before *ReLU* to keep the high-frequency information from *ReLU*, as shown in Fig. 4(c).

Border Handling. Islam *et al.* reported that feature embeddings extracted by a CNN encode absolute position information [13]. This has an important implication for a learning-based similarity metric that feature embeddings from a CNN are position-dependent and are not shift-invariant. They found that zero padding can relieve this bound-

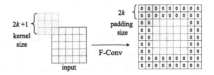

Fig. 5. Full convolution applies every value of the filter to each value of an image. Hence, the input needs to be padded first with size $2k$ for a filter with size $2k + 1$ [15].

ary problem for computer vision tasks that are sensitive to spatial information. Kayhan & Gemert further proposed the concept of full convolution (F-Conv), in which every element of the filter needs to be applied to every pixel in the input image [15]. They implemented F-Conv as a regular convolutional operator with zero padding of $2k$ where $2k + 1$ is the filter kernel size as illustrated in Fig. 5. Note, F-Conv will make the output of an un-strided convolution operator $2k$ larger than the input. They reported that F-Conv is least sensitive to the absolute position of the objects for image classification tasks. Inspired by these works, we replace the regular convolution operators with F-Conv in the LPIPS framework and increase the padding size in *BlurPool* operators to achieve better shift-invariance.

Pooling. Max pooling is well known for being more shift invariant than average pooling. We investigate whether its anti-aliased version, *MaxBlurPool* (described earlier in Anti-aliasing) is also more shift invariant than *AvgBlurPool*, the anti-aliased version of average pooling when used in the LPIPS framework. Average pooling in its original form already supports anti-aliasing. We follow [36] and implement *AvgBlurPool* with a stride of n as Gaussian filtering followed by downsampling with a factor of n.

Strided-Skip Connections. Skip connection is widely used to speedup neural network training and obtain a high quality model. We investigate whether skip connection helps improve shift invariance of a learned similarity metric. As discussed in [29], a strided skip connection introduces aliasing for the same reason discussed earlier in Anti-aliasing. We therefore explore anti-aliased strided skip connections, as shown in Fig. 6.

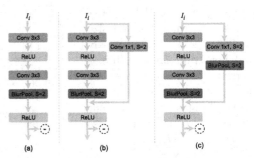

Fig. 6. Anti-aliased skipped connection. (a) VGG-like network with AvgBlurPool, (b) with skip connection, and (c) with anti-aliased skip.

6 Experiments

We built upon the LPIPS framework and incorporated the elements discussed in Sect. 5 to investigate how these elements help develop a similarity metric that is consistent with the human visual similarity judgment and is robust against imperceptible shifts. We first compare our metrics to both off-the-shelf metrics, such as SSIM and MS-SSIM, and the recent learned similarity metrics. We then conduct ablation studies to evaluate how these elements work.

Comparisons to Existing Metrics. In Sect. 4, we derived a shifted dataset from the BAPPS dataset and compared our metrics to existing metrics [3,6,16, 21,25,30,32,37]. In our experiments, we adopt the 2AFC score to evaluate how consistent a metric is with human judgment, and the rank-flipping rate, r_{rf}, to evaluate how robust it is against small shifts. As shown in Tables 2 and 3, our metrics are both more consistent with human visual similarity judgment and more robust against imperceptible shifts than most of them, except a recent metric PIM [3], to which our method is comparable. PIM achieves shift robustness by training on neighboring video frames that often have small shifts. We work on an orthogonal solution by investigating neural network elements to make the learned metric robust and thus only train our metrics on the examples without any shift through data augmentation. We further evaluated the metrics on the perceptual validation dataset from the Challenge on Learned Image Compression [4]. The results in Table 4 are consistent with previous results, i.e., our method outperforms all others in terms of accuracy and is more shift-robust than others except PIM, which is similarly robust to ours.

Ablation Studies. We now examine how individual network elements affect our metrics. In these studies, we trained all our metrics using the original BAPPS training set on their original size of 256×256. We purposely did not train on the shifted version of the dataset to focus on neural network element designs. To train our metrics, we used the loss function: $MSE(s, h)$, where $s = s_1/(s_1 + s_2)$, s_1 and s_2

Table 4. Experiments on the CLIC dataset.

Network	Accuracy(%)	No. of rank flips		
		1pixel	2pixel	3pixel
L2	58.16	833	2102	2214
SSIM [30]	60.00	349	931	1109
PIEAPP [25]	75.44	91	134	158
E-LPIPS [16]	74.44	212	251	317
DISTS [6]	75.63	28	36	50
PIM-1 [3]	73.79	13	22	33
LPIPS(Alex) [37]	73.68	90	108	121
LPIPS(Alex)[a,b,c]	76.53	59	51	62
LPIPS(Alex) ours[b,c]	**76.97**	17	**14**	**21**

(a) Retrained from scratch. (b) Trained on image patches of size 64 using author's (c) setup.

are the predicted similarity scores of I_1 and I_2 to their corresponding reference, and h is the human score. We trained our metrics using the same settings as [37] except we used a lower dropout rate of 0.01. We tested all our metrics on the shifted dataset to obtain the rank-flipping rate. To obtain the 2AFC scores, we ran our metrics on full-size images (with no shift) of the original BAPPS dataset to verify whether our metrics sacrifice consistency with human visual similarity judgment to be robust against imperceptible shifts.

We first examine elements discussed in Sect. 5 individually. We use AlexNet as the backbone feature extraction network with the LPIPS framework as it provides the best result among other backbone networks [37]. As reported in Table 5, anti-aliasing via *BlurPool* can greatly improve LPIPS's robustness against imperceptible shifts. Reducing stride size in its strided convolutional layer (*conv-1*) also helps making it significantly more robust at little

Table 5. Effect of (1) anti-aliasing (AA) via *BlurPool*, (2) F-Conv, (3) reduced stride, & (4) adaptive-AA[§] [39] on learned metrics.

AA (BlurPool) Reflection-Pad		F-Conv	Stride in conv-1	2AFC	r_{rf}		
1	2				1pixel	2pixel	3pixel
✓			4	70.65	2.87	3.92	3.74
			2	70.53	1.85	2.22	2.58
	✓		2	**70.67**	1.46	1.82	2.25
		✓	4	70.57	2.78	3.92	3.91
	✓	✓	2	70.52	1.77	2.15	2.48
			2	70.54	1.84	2.28	2.34
	✓		1	70.42	0.66	**1.13**	1.83
	✓	✓	1	70.44	**0.63**	1.14	**1.68**
✓[§]			2	70.57	2.63	3.36	3.16
	✓[§]		2	70.63	2.80	3.57	3.39
	✓[§]	✓	2	70.52	2.95	4.13	3.93

expense of the 2AFC score. Combining *BlurPool* with reducing stride size makes the network even more robust against imperceptible shifts and more consistent with human judgment based on the 2AFC score. A larger reflection padding size also helps as it reduces the position information encoded in the feature embeddings from the image boundaries, as discussed in Sect. 5. However, F-Conv, also designed to reduce the boundary issue, does not help. While the learned *BlurPool* [39] helps, it is not as effective as the original version for our task of making a robust similarity metric.

We test on different backbone feature networks, including VGG-16 [27], ResNet-18 [10], and SqueezeNet [12]. While reducing the stride size is effective, not all networks have a strided convolution layer. Hence, we focus on *BlurPool* applied to pooling layers. As shown in Table 6, *BlurPool* significantly improves the robustness of other backbone networks as well. What is interesting is the effect of the padding size within these backbone networks. While a larger padding size improves 2AFC, it does not make shift-invariance better for VGG-16 and ResNet-18.

Table 6. Anti-aliasing via *BlurPool* can significantly improve shift-tolerance and often improve 2AFC scores consistently for different backbone networks.

Network	AA (BlurPool) Reflection-Pad		2AFC	r_{rf}		
	1	2		1pixel	2pixel	3pixel
VGG-16			70.03	3.01	3.76	3.44
	✓		70.05	**0.66**	**1.08**	**1.44**
		✓	**70.07**	**0.66**	1.12	1.82
ResNet-18			69.86	2.67	3.35	3.77
	✓		69.95	**0.82**	**1.51**	**2.19**
		✓	**70.14**	1.07	1.81	2.38
Squeeze			69.61	7.41	7.58	10.35
	✓		69.24	**2.03**	3.06	3.93
		✓	**69.44**	2.10	**2.48**	**3.42**

For them, the anti-aliased *conv* layers have a stride size of 1, which leads to minor boundary issues. We conjecture that this makes a larger padding size unnecessary.

We also examine the effect of the location of *BlurPool* within AlexNet. As reported in Table 7, the original version (Fig. 4(a)) works best when the stride size is 2 in *conv-1*. With a smaller stride size, it does not work as well as Blur Before

Table 7. Effect of *BlurPool* locations within an anti-aliased strided convolution (Fig. 4).

Anti-Alias (BlurPool)	Stride in *Conv-1*	BlurPool Location	2AFC	r_{rf}		
				1pixel	2pixel	3pixel
✓	2	Original	**70.67**	**1.46**	**1.82**	**2.25**
✓	2	FeatAfterBlur	70.55	1.73	1.84	2.49
✓	2	BlurBeforeAct	70.50	2.06	2.02	2.74
✓	1	Original	70.42	0.66	1.13	1.83
✓	1	FeatAfterBlur	**70.52**	0.69	1.11	1.60
✓	1	BlurBeforeAct	70.48	**0.57**	**1.06**	**1.50**

Activation (Fig. 4(c)). This is in part consistent with what was found by Vasconcelos *et al.* [29]. In the original design, *BlurPool* is placed after the activation layer for anti-aliasing at the expense of the reduction of the high-frequency information from the activation layer. With the need for anti-aliasing due to a larger stride size, this trade-off works out. However, when stride size is 1, the need for anti-aliasing is reduced; therefore, it is more helpful to place *BlurPool* before the activation layer to avoid the loss of high-frequency information. Thus, Blur Before Activation works better when the stride size is 1. We also observed that *MaxBlurPool* has better shift tolerance but lower 2AFC scores (accuracy) than *AvgBlurBool*. Moreover, using anti-aliased strided-skip connections leads to higher accuracy with a negligible drop in shift tolerance.

Just Noticeable Differences (JND). We conducted the following experiment to study how consistent our shift-tolerant perceptual similarity metric is with the human perception results reported in Table 1. In our study reported in Table 1, we had asked our participants if the two images, which may be shifted by a few pixels, were the same or not. Using these responses, we perform a just noticeable difference test. We use only those samples which have at least 3 human responses. There were 301 such samples, and the mean number of samples per pixel-shift (0 to 9) is 30.1 with a standard deviation of 1.6 (maximum 33 and minimum 28). Following Zhang *et al.* [37], we rank the pairs by a perceptual similarity metric and compute the area under the precision/recall curve

Table 8. Consistency of perceptual similarity metrics with the sensitivity of human perception to pixel shifts.

Metric	JND mAP%
SSIM [30]	0.722
LPIPS (Alex) [37]	0.757
LPIPS (Alex)[a,b,c]	0.740
LPIPS (Alex) **ours**[b,c]	0.771
LPIPS (VGG) [37]	0.770
LPIPS (VGG)[a,b,c]	0.769
LPIPS (VGG) **ours**[b,c]	**0.775**
DISTS [6]	0.766
PIM-1 [3]	0.773

(a) Retrained from scratch. (b) Trained on image patches of size 64 using author's (c) setup.

(mAP) [8,37]. The results in Table 8 show that our shift-tolerant LPIPS metrics follow the sensitivity of human perception to pixel shifts more accurately than their vanilla versions. The accuracy of PIM-1 and DISTS is comparable to ours.

Summary. Among the network elements we investigated, anti-aliased strided convolution, anti-aliased pooling, and reduction of stride size are most effective to develop a perceptual similarity metric that is robust against imperceptible shifts. These findings are consistent across a variety of backbone network architectures. A larger padding size helps reduce the position information due to the boundary issues encoded in the feature embeddings. Anti-aliased skip connection can help improve accuracy but with little effect on shift invariance. The position of *BlurPool* matters. It should be placed before the activation layer if its precedent convolution uses a small stride size.

7   Conclusion

This paper reported our investigation on how to design a deep neural network as a learned perceptual image similarity metric that is both consistent with the human visual similarity judgment and robust against the imperceptible shift among a pair of images. We discussed various neural network elements, such as anti-aliased strided convolution, anti-aliased pooling, the placement of *BlurPool*, stride size, and skip connection, and studied their effect on a similarity metric. We found that using anti-aliasing strided convolutions and pooling operators and reducing stride size help to make a learned similarity metric shift-invariant. Our experiments show that by integrating these elements into a neural network, we are able to develop a learned metric that is more robust against imperceptible shifts and more consistent with the human visual similarity judgment.

Acknowledgments. Figure 1 uses frames from https://www.youtube.com/watch?v=jW7pFhkVNYY under a Creative Commons license.

References

1. Athalye, A., Carlini, N., Wagner, D.: Obfuscated gradients give a false sense of security: circumventing defenses to adversarial examples. In: International Conference on Machine Learning. vol. 80, pp. 274–283 (2018)
2. Azulay, A., Weiss, Y.: Why do deep convolutional networks generalize so poorly to small image transformations? J. Mach. Learn. Res. **20**(184), 1–25 (2019)
3. Bhardwaj, S., Fischer, I., Ballé, J., Chinen, T.: An unsupervised information-theoretic perceptual quality metric. In: Advances in Neural Information Processing Systems, pp. 13–24 (2020)
4. CLIC: Workshop and challenge on learned image compression (2021). http://www.compression.cc/2021/
5. Czolbe, S., Krause, O., Cox, I., Igel, C.: A loss function for generative neural networks based on Watson's perceptual model. In: Advances in Neural Information Processing Systems, pp. 2051–2061 (2020)
6. Ding, K., Ma, K., Wang, S., Simoncelli, E.P.: Image quality assessment: Unifying structure and texture similarity. IEEE Trans. Pattern Anal. Mach. Intell., 1 (2020)
7. Dosovitskiy, A., Brox, T.: Generating images with perceptual similarity metrics based on deep networks. In: Advances in Neural Information Processing Systems, pp. 658–666 (2016)
8. Everingham, M., Van Gool, L., Williams, C.K., Winn, J., Zisserman, A.: The PASCAL Visual Object Classes Challenge 2007 (VOC2007) Results. Int. J. Comput. Vision **88**(2), 303–338 (2010)

9. Jinjin, G., Haoming, C., Haoyu, C., Xiaoxing, Y., Ren, J.S., Chao, D.: PIPAL: a large-scale image quality assessment dataset for perceptual image restoration. In: Vedaldi, A., Bischof, H., Brox, T., Frahm, J.-M. (eds.) ECCV 2020. LNCS, vol. 12356, pp. 633–651. Springer, Cham (2020). https://doi.org/10.1007/978-3-030-58621-8_37

10. He, K., Zhang, X., Ren, S., Sun, J.: Deep residual learning for image recognition. In: IEEE Conference on Computer Vision and Pattern Recognition, pp. 770–778 (2016)

11. Hénaff, O.J., Simoncelli, E.P.: Geodesics of learned representations. In: International Conference on Learning Representations (2016)

12. Iandola, F.N., Han, S., Moskewicz, M.W., Ashraf, K., Dally, W.J., Keutzer, K.: Squeezenet: Alexnet-level accuracy with 50x fewer parameters and <0.5mb model size. arXiv/1602.07360 (2016)

13. Islam, M.A., Jia, S., Bruce, N.D.B.: How much position information do convolutional neural networks encode? In: International Conference on Learning Representations (2020)

14. Johnson, J., Alahi, A., Fei-Fei, L.: Perceptual losses for real-time style transfer and super-resolution. In: Leibe, B., Matas, J., Sebe, N., Welling, M. (eds.) ECCV 2016. LNCS, vol. 9906, pp. 694–711. Springer, Cham (2016). https://doi.org/10.1007/978-3-319-46475-6_43

15. Kayhan, O.S., Gemert, J.C.v.: On translation invariance in CNNs: convolutional layers can exploit absolute spatial location. In: IEEE Conference on Computer Vision and Pattern Recognition, pp. 14262–14273 (2020)

16. Kettunen, M., Härkönen, E., Lehtinen, J.: E-LPIPS: robust perceptual image similarity via random transformation ensembles. arXiv/1906.03973 (2019)

17. Krizhevsky, A., Sutskever, I., Hinton, G.E.: ImageNet classification with deep convolutional neural networks. In: Advances in Neural Information Processing Systems, pp. 1106–1114 (2012)

18. Ledig, C., et al.: Photo-realistic single image super-resolution using a generative adversarial network. arXiv/1609.04802 (2016)

19. Lee, J., Yang, J., Wang, Z.: What does CNN shift invariance look like? a visualization study. In: Bartoli, A., Fusiello, A. (eds.) ECCV 2020. LNCS, vol. 12539, pp. 196–210. Springer, Cham (2020). https://doi.org/10.1007/978-3-030-68238-5_15

20. Lin, T.-Y., Maire, M., Belongie, S., Hays, J., Perona, P., Ramanan, D., Dollár, P., Zitnick, C.L.: Microsoft COCO: common objects in context. In: Fleet, D., Pajdla, T., Schiele, B., Tuytelaars, T. (eds.) ECCV 2014. LNCS, vol. 8693, pp. 740–755. Springer, Cham (2014). https://doi.org/10.1007/978-3-319-10602-1_48

21. Ma, K., Duanmu, Z., Wang, Z.: Geometric transformation invariant image quality assessment using convolutional neural networks. In: IEEE International Conference on Acoustics, Speech and Signal Processing, pp. 6732–6736 (2018)

22. Medin, D.L., Goldstone, R.L., Gentner, D.: Respects for similarity. Psychol. Rev. 100(2), 254 (1993)

23. Nair, V., Hinton, G.E.: Rectified linear units improve restricted boltzmann machines. In: International Conference on Machine Learning, pp. 807–814 (2010)

24. Niklaus, S., Mai, L., Liu, F.: Video frame interpolation via adaptive separable convolution. In: IEEE International Conference on Computer Vision, pp. 261–270 (2017)

25. Prashnani, E., Cai, H., Mostofi, Y., Sen, P.: Pieapp: perceptual image-error assessment through pairwise preference. In: IEEE Conference on Computer Vision and Pattern Recognition, pp. 1808–1817 (2018)

26. Sajjadi, M.S.M., Schölkopf, B., Hirsch, M.: EnhanceNet: single image super-resolution through automated texture synthesis. arXiv/1612.07919 (2016)
27. Simonyan, K., Zisserman, A.: Very deep convolutional networks for large-scale image recognition. In: International Conference on Learning Representations (2015)
28. Tversky, A.: Features of similarity. Psychol. Rev. **84**(4), 327 (1977)
29. Vasconcelos, C., Larochelle, H., Dumoulin, V., Romijnders, R., Roux, N.L., Goroshin, R.: Impact of aliasing on generalization in deep convolutional networks. In: IEEE International Conference on Computer Vision (2021)
30. Wang, Z., Bovik, A.C., Sheikh, H.R., Simoncelli, E.P.: Image quality assessment: from error visibility to structural similarity. IEEE Trans. Image Process. **13**(4), 600–612 (2004)
31. Wang, Z., Simoncelli, E.P.: Translation insensitive image similarity in complex wavelet domain. In: IEEE International Conference on Acoustics, Speech, and Signal Processing, vol. 2, pp. ii–573 (2005)
32. Wang, Z., Simoncelli, E.P., Bovik, A.C.: Multiscale structural similarity for image quality assessment. In: Asilomar Conference on Signals, Systems & Computers, vol. 2, pp. 1398–1402. IEEE (2003)
33. Watson, A.B.: DCT quantization matrices visually optimized for individual images. In: Human vision, visual processing, and digital display IV, vol. 1913, pp. 202–216. International Society for Optics and Photonics (1993)
34. Xiao, C., Zhu, J.Y., Li, B., He, W., Liu, M., Song, D.: Spatially transformed adversarial examples. In: International Conference on Learning Representations (2018)
35. Zhang, L., Zhang, L., Mou, X., Zhang, D.: Fsim: a feature similarity index for image quality assessment. IEEE Trans. Image Process. **20**(8), 2378–2386 (2011)
36. Zhang, R.: Making convolutional networks shift-invariant again. In: International Conference on Machine Learning, pp. 7324–7334 (2019)
37. Zhang, R., Isola, P., Efros, A.A., Shechtman, E., Wang, O.: The unreasonable effectiveness of deep features as a perceptual metric. In: IEEE Conference on Computer Vision and Pattern Recognition, pp. 586–595 (2018)
38. Zhu, J.-Y., Krähenbühl, P., Shechtman, E., Efros, A.A.: Generative visual manipulation on the natural image manifold. In: Leibe, B., Matas, J., Sebe, N., Welling, M. (eds.) ECCV 2016. LNCS, vol. 9909, pp. 597–613. Springer, Cham (2016). https://doi.org/10.1007/978-3-319-46454-1_36
39. Zou, X., Xiao, F., Yu, Z., Lee, Y.J.: Delving deeper into anti-aliasing in convnets. In: British Machine Vision Conference (2020)

Perception-Distortion Balanced ADMM Optimization for Single-Image Super-Resolution

Yuehan Zhang[1], Bo Ji[1], Jia Hao[2], and Angela Yao[1]($\boxtimes$)

[1] National University of Singapore, Singapore, Singapore
{zyuehan,jibo,ayao}@comp.nus.edu.sg
[2] HiSilicon Technologies, Shanghai, China
hao.jia@huawei.com

Abstract. In image super-resolution, both pixel-wise accuracy and perceptual fidelity are desirable. However, most deep learning methods only achieve high performance in one aspect due to the perception-distortion trade-off, and works that successfully balance the trade-off rely on fusing results from separately trained models with ad-hoc post-processing. In this paper, we propose a novel super-resolution model with a low-frequency constraint (LFc-SR), which balances the objective and perceptual quality through a single model and yields super-resolved images with high PSNR and perceptual scores. We further introduce an ADMM-based alternating optimization method for the non-trivial learning of the constrained model. Experiments showed that our method, without cumbersome post-processing procedures, achieved the state-of-the-art performance. The code is available at https://github.com/Yuehan717/PDASR.

Keywords: Image super-resolution · Perception-distortion trade-off · Constrained optimization

1 Introduction

Single image super-resolution (SISR) recovers a high-resolution (HR) image from a low-resolution (LR) input. There are two types of quality assessments for super-resolved images: objective quality, evaluated by PSNR and SSIM, and perceptual quality, based on metrics such as NRQM [25] and LPIPS [47]. SISR methods aiming at high objective quality [5,14,15,23,31,33,50,51] achieve high PSNR values, but the results look blurry. Another line of research focuses on improving perceptual quality [19,26,29,34,44,49], which produces HR images that are visually shaper, but have lower PSNR scores and unrealistic patterns (see comparisons in Fig. 1).

Supplementary Information The online version contains supplementary material available at https://doi.org/10.1007/978-3-031-19797-0_7.

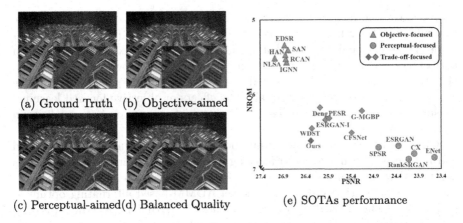

(a) Ground Truth   (b) Objective-aimed

(c) Perceptual-aimed (d) Balanced Quality

(e) SOTAs performance

Fig. 1. (a)–(d) are ground truth from Urban100 [12] and ×4 super-resolved images. Note that (b) produced by NLSA [31] is blurry in detailing, while (c) from RankSR-GAN [49] has unnatural patterns; our balanced approach in (d) mitigates both types of artifacts. (e) is performance of state-of-the-art ×4 SISR models on Urban100. Higher PSNR and NRQM scores indicate better objective and perceptual quality. Our method reaches state-of-the-art while being single-shot.

An ideally reconstructed image is similar to the ground truth HR image, with limited distortion *and* high perceptual quality, where distortion refers to a drop in objective quality. However, most deep learning methods can achieve high performance in only one of the two qualities. This perception-distortion (PD) trade-off is rooted in the supervised training process of SISR methods. Since perception and distortion measurements are incoherent with each other, optimization in one direction naturally leads to sacrifice in the other [2,9]. A recently emerging line of work seeks to balance or improve both the objective and perceptual quality of SISR images [6,7,20,32,36,41–44]. Some researchers have studied the trade-off problem through model optimization [20,32,36,41,43]. However, they have only focused on traversing the PD trade-off instead of improving both the objective and perceptual quality. Others bypassed the optimization incoherence and merged the models or model outputs trained separately for the two objectives via post-processing [6,7,42,44]. Some methods [6,7] achieved excellent results, but their post-processing can be computationally costly.

Previous studies have aligned image quality with different image frequency subbands. Low-frequency (LF) information captures the overall scene structure [35,54], while high-frequency (HF) details are critical to achieving high perceptual quality [19,54]. This observation has been leveraged to reconstruct details in single-image SR [37,54] and suppress misalignment in real-world video SR [45]. However, it has not been used to explicitly balance the objective and perceptual quality in model optimization.

This paper present a new low-frequency constrained SISR model (LFc-SR) model that improves both objective and perceptual quality. The model has two stages: stage one focuses on super-resolution for objective quality, while stage two subsequently refines the image for perceptual quality (see Fig. 2). At our model's core is a similarity constraint that keeps the low-frequency subbands of both stages similar during optimization. The constraint allows the optimization of perceptual quality to be oriented towards the high-frequency bands while ensuring that the overall scene retains the effects of objective-focused learning. As such, our method yields images with high performance on both qualities in a one-shot manner.

Our key novelty is in our formulation of LFc-SR training as constrained multi-objective optimization. Enforcing constraints within deep learning is non-trivial with challenges to find satisfying solutions. To cooperate the low-frequency constraint, we designed a novel ADMM-based alternating optimization method. The alternating direction method of multipliers (ADMM) was originally introduced as a tool for convex optimization problems, decomposing the constrained optimization into solvable substeps [3]. However, it has also been widely applied to non-convex problems, including deep neural network training [13,21,22,38,48,52]. While finding the optimum for non-convex problems is not guaranteed, ADMM often finds satisfying approximations. We refer to our optimization method as PD-ADMM, as it aims at mitigating the perception-distortion (PD) trade-off.

To summarize our contributions in this paper:

1. We propose LFc-SR, a novel SISR model trained with a low-frequency constraint, to balance the perception-distortion trade-off.
2. We propose a novel formulation of SISR as a constrained multi-objective optimization problem and show how to incorporate an ADMM-based method (PD-ADMM) for solutions that balance the perception-distortion trade-off.
3. Our LFc-SR model learned with the PD-ADMM optimization scheme yields HR images with high objective and perceptual quality. The proposed one-shot model requires significantly less computational expense than competing trade-off methods that rely on heavy post-processing.

2   Related Work

2.1   Objective Quality versus Perceptual Quality

SISR methods designed for objective quality are deep neural networks that use pixel-wise losses, such as L_1 and MSE. Starting with the CNN-based SRCNN [8], later variants leverage residual [14,19,23], dense [40,51], and attention mechanisms [5,31,33]. These works strongly focus on architecture design and achieve high PSNR and SSIM scores. However, their results are blurry and evaluated poorly on perceptual metrics, especially at larger scaling factors like ×4.

Many SISR methods often incorporate GANs [19,26,29,34,44,49] and combine the adversarial loss with a content loss to improve the perceptual quality. Common content losses include the VGG [19] and contextual loss [29]. GAN-based models yield sharper lines and more high-frequency details. They achieve high scores on perceptual measures such as LPIPS [47] and NRQM [25], attributed to implicit distribution learning. At the same time, these methods suffer from unrealistic artifacts resulting from adversarial training.

2.2 Perception-Distortion Trade-off

Most state-of-the-art methods perform well either in objective or perceptual quality, but not in both. This trade-off phenomenon was explored by Blau *et al.* [2]; they attributed it to the incoherence between distortion and perception measurements. Some methods have tried to control the compromise between the two qualities. One solution was to fuse either two models [44] or model outputs [6,7,42] trained separately for objective and perceptual quality. The most notable of these post-processing works is WDST [7], which, like our work, set out to take separate frequency band considerations. A significant difference between our work and WDST is that WDST merges wavelet channels from the outputs of two separately trained networks, whereas our method is one-shot with a single model. Moreover, as WDST relies on a style-transfer [10] for the fusion, their inference procedure is computationally expensive and time-consuming, as the output channels are iteratively merged at test time. Our one-shot inference consumes significantly less computational resources and is much more efficient.

In addition to post-processing, another line of balancing approaches focuses on the training strategy. They balance the loss terms [41] or introduce a controlling factor as training inputs [20,32,36,43]. For example, Vasu *et al.* [41] directly added MSE, VGG, and adversarial loss together and weighted them in different proportions. CFSNet [43] achieved a test-time transition between perceptual and objective quality by using an extra input factor α in their training strategy. These approaches create a smooth transition between the two qualities; but do not attempt to improve both of them. In contrast, our method focuses on the training strategy *and* improves both qualities.

3 Method

3.1 Revisiting the Multi-objective SR Formulation

SISR recovers a high-resolution image $Y \in \mathbb{R}^{H \times W}$, given an input low-resolution image $X \in \mathbb{R}^{h \times w}$ via a neural network G, *i.e.* $Y = G(X)$. Here, $h \times w$ and $H \times W$ are input and output image heights and widths respectively. As it is challenging to gather real-world pairs of images in low- and high-resolution, X is typically generated from a ground truth high-resolution image $\hat{Y}$ via a downsampling function, *i.e.* $X = f_{\downarrow}(\hat{Y})$. Bicubic downsampling is a commonly used $f_{\downarrow}(\cdot)$, with standard downsampling factors of $\times 2$ or $\times 4$, *e.g.* $H = 2 \times h, W = 2 \times w$.

Considering both distortion and perception, a simple way to learn $G(\cdot)$ is by weighting different loss terms L_O and L_P with weights λ_O and λ_P[1] for objective

---

[1] Throughout the paper, we will use O and P (either subscript or superscript) to denote objective- and perception-focused items respectively.

and perceptual quality respectively, *i.e.*

$$L_G = \lambda_O \cdot L_O(Y) + \lambda_P \cdot L_P(Y). \tag{1}$$

However, this does not achieve a good PD trade-off because of the incoherence between perception and distortion losses [2]. Specifically, minimizing L_O (*i.e.* with MSE, L_1) leads to low expectation of pixel-wise error, whereas L_P (*i.e.* adversarial loss combined with contextual loss) targets distribution-based learning for sharp results [2]. It is therefore common for methods seeking a good trade-off to learn two separate networks and fuse the results via post-processing, *i.e.*

$$Y = F(Y^O, Y^P), \quad \text{where} \quad Y^O = G_O(X), \text{ and } Y^P = G_P(X), \tag{2}$$

where G_O and G_P are two separately trained models and F is some fusion module. F can be quite complex and computationally expensive. For example, in Deng [6] and WDST [7], F is a style transfer module applied during inference.

Inspired by previous research in human perception [16,54] and the direct link between low- and high-frequency information to objective and perceptual quality [7,19], we take a frequency-banded approach. A naïve formulation is to separate the learning objectives for the low- and high-frequency bands, *i.e.*

$$Y = G(X), \quad \text{where} \quad L_G = \lambda_O \cdot L_O(T_{LF}(Y)) + \lambda_P \cdot L_P(T_{HF}(Y)). \tag{3}$$

In this formulation, the network G is learned by applying a weighted loss on the low-pass and high-pass decomposed subbands of the output Y, based on the respective transformations T_{LF} and T_{HF}. Like previous works [7,24,53], we used the discrete wavelet transform with a Haar wavelet basis for decomposing the image into frequency subbands. Supervising a network based on the loss of Eq. (3) assumes that the different frequency bands can be optimized independently, which is not the case. A hard separation increases the difficulty of learning, especially for high-frequency bands $T_{HF}(Y)$, as L_P includes an adversarial loss and is, from our observations, unstable and prone to training collapse.

3.2   Low-Frequency Constrained SR (LFc-SR)

Due to the lack of independence, we contend that the optimization of each objective, be it objective or perceptual, must observe the entire band of image frequencies. Our solution to encourage stable learning of high-frequency information of Y while maintaining objective quality is to allow a separate (early stage) output Y' for the objective quality. Specifically, we partitioned the model G into two stages, where $G = \{\mathcal{G}_O, \mathcal{G}_P\}$ (see Fig. 2), *i.e.*

$$Y' = \mathcal{G}_O(X), \quad Y = \mathcal{G}_P(Y') \quad s.t. \quad T_{LF}(Y) = T_{LF}(Y'), \tag{4}$$

where $\mathcal{G}_O(\cdot)$ represents the first objective-focused stage of G and Y' is a super-resolved image with high objective quality. $\mathcal{G}_P(\cdot)$ is the perception-focused stage targeting a further improvement on high-frequency detailing that takes Y' as

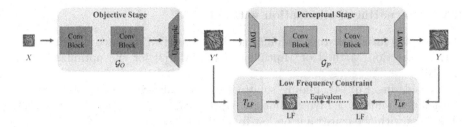

Fig. 2. Proposed two-stage model with a low-frequency constraint. The first stage learns high-fidelity LF subbands to yield high objective quality. The second stage focuses on the distribution learning of HF subbands to improve perceptual quality for the overall image. Discrete Wavelet Transform (DWT) decreases the spatial size of each channel without information loss, and Inverse Discrete Wavelet Transform (iDWT) recovers the spatial resolution (see Sect. 4.1 for details). The two stages are trained with the low-frequency constraint to encourage the similarity of the LF subbands of the two outputs.

input. To encourage the final output Y to maintain high objective quality, we placed a constraint that the low-frequency subbands of Y should be equal to those of Y', which in practice encourages the two to be similar.

The two stages accordingly have different loss functions. Outputs from $\mathcal{G}_O$ are supervised by a L_1 loss:

$$L_O = L_1(Y', \hat{Y}) \tag{5}$$

where $\hat{Y}$ is the ground truth for the training input X. For $\mathcal{G}_P$, we used the contextual loss [29] together with adversarial training for high perceptual quality. The contextual loss approximates KL-divergence between the deep features of super-resolved and ground-truth images, and we refer to Mechrez et al. [29,30] for further details. The overall loss function for $\mathcal{G}_P$ is as follows:

$$L_P = \lambda_{CX} \cdot L_{CX}(Y, \hat{Y}) + \lambda_D \cdot L_1(f_\downarrow(Y), f_\downarrow(\hat{Y})) + \lambda_{Gen} \cdot L_{Gen}(Y), \tag{6}$$

where L_{CX} is the contextual loss and $f_\downarrow(\cdot)$ estimates the low-resolution counterparts of HR images. The L_1 loss here is, as introduced in Mechrez et al. [30], to boost the spatial structure similarity with the contextual loss, and L_{Gen} represents the generator loss used in adversarial training.

A straightforward way to implement the equivalence constraint in Eq. (4) is to apply a L_1 regularizer on the outputs of two stages, and the total loss is as following:

$$\lambda_O \cdot L_O + \lambda_P \cdot L_P + \lambda_r \cdot \|\mathrm{T}_{LF}(Y) - \mathrm{T}_{LF}(Y')\|_1. \tag{7}$$

Theoretically, regularization will also encourage LF similarity. However, minimizing Eq. (7) requires a difficult-to-achieve balance between L_O, L_P [4] and the selection of a good λ_r. To bypass this difficulty, we interpret Eq. (4) as a multi-objective optimization problem with a combinatorial constraint. ADMM is an established algorithm for solving such constrained optimizations and in the next section, we outline PD-ADMM, our ADMM-based optimization method.

3.3   Alternating Optimization with ADMM

We designed an alternating training method, PD-ADMM, based on the Alternating Direction Method of Multipliers (ADMM) [3] for the optimization of LFc-SR.

Considering Eq. (4), finding solutions for the LFc-SR model is actually a constrained multi-objective optimization problem, *i.e.* there are two different objectives with the constraint on low-frequency coherency:

$$\min \ L_P + L_O \quad s.t. \ \mathrm{T}_{LF}(Y) = \mathrm{T}_{LF}(Y'), \tag{8}$$

where L_P and L_O are loss functions in Sect. 3.2, and the constraint is the same as that in Eq. (4). Since the model parameters are variables in this optimization, we express Eq. (8) as functions of θ_P and θ_O, the parameters of $\mathcal{G}_P$ and $\mathcal{G}_O$:

$$\min_{\theta_P, \theta_O} \ P(\theta_P) + O(\theta_O) \quad s.t. \ \mathrm{LF}_\mathrm{p}(\theta_P) = \mathrm{LF}_\mathrm{O}(\theta_O), \tag{9}$$

where $P(\theta_P)$ measures the perceptual error of the perceptual stage output, and $O(\theta_O)$ measures the objective error of the objective stage; $\mathrm{LF_P}(\theta_P) = \mathrm{T_{LF}}(\mathcal{G}_P(Y'; \theta_P))$ and $\mathrm{LF_O}(\theta_O) = \mathrm{T_{LF}}(\mathcal{G}_O(X; \theta_O))$ represent the low-frequency subbands of outputs from the perceptual- and objective-focused stage.

The augmented Lagrangian function of Eq. (9) is:

$$\begin{aligned}
\mathcal{L}(\theta_P, \theta_O, u) = {} & P(\theta_P) + O(\theta_O) + u^T(\mathrm{LF_P}(\theta_P) - \mathrm{LF_O}(\theta_O)) \\
& + \frac{\rho}{2} \|\mathrm{LF_P}(\theta_P) - \mathrm{LF_O}(\theta_O)\|_2^2.
\end{aligned} \tag{10}$$

where u is the Lagrangian multiplier, and ρ is the penalty parameter. It is often easier to express the above function in the scaled form by defining $u = \rho s$ [13,21,48], resulting in

$$\mathcal{L}(\theta_P, \theta_O, s) = P(\theta_P) + O(\theta_O) + \frac{\rho}{2} \|\mathrm{LF_P}(\theta_P) - \mathrm{LF_O}(\theta_O) + s\|_2^2 - \frac{\rho}{2} \|s\|_2^2. \tag{11}$$

ADMM solves Eq. (11) by a *decomposition* into three iterative sub-steps:

$$\theta_P^{k+1} = \operatorname*{argmin}_{\theta_P} \mathcal{L}(\theta_P, \theta_O^k, s^k) \tag{12a}$$

$$\theta_O^{k+1} = \operatorname*{argmin}_{\theta_O} \mathcal{L}(\theta_P^{k+1}, \theta_O, s^k) \tag{12b}$$

$$s^{k+1} = s^k + \mathrm{LF_P}(\theta_P^{k+1}) - \mathrm{LF_O}(\theta_O^{k+1}) \tag{12c}$$

The first two steps are equivalent to:

$$\operatorname*{argmin}_{\theta_P} P(\theta_P) + \frac{\rho}{2} \|\mathrm{LF_P}(\theta_P) - \mathrm{LF_O}(\theta_O) + s\|_2^2 \tag{13a}$$

$$\operatorname*{argmin}_{\theta_O} O(\theta_O) + \frac{\rho}{2} \|\mathrm{LF_P}(\theta_P) - \mathrm{LF_O}(\theta_O) + s\|_2^2, \tag{13b}$$

where the first term of each minimization function is the loss function of the perception-focused stage or objective-focused stage, *i.e.* L_P or L_O discussed in Sect. 3.2. The second terms are special L_2 regularizers applied to variable s and the low-frequency subbands of the outputs from the two stages. Thus, we can solve these two sub-problems through a deep model optimization algorithm, such as Stochastic Gradient Descent. Based on above analysis through ADMM, our training algorithm for the LFc-SR model consists of three alternating steps and is concluded by dual variable updates in Eq. (12c) after optimizing the perceptual- and objective-focused stage through Eq. (13a) and Eq. (13b).

4   Experiments

4.1   Settings

Dataset and Evaluation: We used the DIV2K dataset [39] for training and validation, We evaluated on standard benchmarks: Set5 [1], Set14 [46], BSD100 [27], Urban100 [12] and Manga109 [28]. To measure objective quality, we computed the PNSR and SSIM on the image's Y channel with Matlab functions. For perceptual quality, we used the no-reference metric NRQM [25] and the full-reference metric LPIPS [47] for a comprehensive treatment. We provide visual comparisons in Fig. 4 and Fig. 5 to show the qualitative efficacy of our method.

Image Decomposition: We used the discrete wavelet transform (DWT) to decompose our image into frequency subbands. DWT is an invertible frequency transformation common in image processing [11, 24, 53]. It decomposes the image into four half-resolution channels, LL, HL, LH and HH, including low- (L) or high- (H) frequency subbands of height and width dimension. DWT can be applied on LL iteratively. We used the LL channel from a 1-level Haar DWT of the image as the LF information in Eq. (9). Other transformations are also feasible, and we experimented with Gaussian blur as an ablation. For downsampling function $f_\downarrow(\cdot)$ in Eq. (6), we also used DWT for convenience; we used the LL channel from a 2-level DWT for ×4 super-resolution.

Model Architecture: We tested our method for ×4 super-resolution. For $\mathcal{G}_O$, we directly adopted the architecture of HAN [33], which finish upscaling the images into high resolution. $\mathcal{G}_P$ starts with DWT and ends with inverse DWT (iDWT), saving training time by losslessly reducing the spatial resolution of processed feature maps. Between the two transformations are 15 Res-clique blocks designed by Zhong *et al.* [53]. For the architecture and loss calculation of discriminator for adversarial training, we adopted what was used in SRGAN [19]. More details are in the Supplementary.

Training Details: We took RGB patches of size 36×36 as inputs and trained the model with the ADAM optimizer [18] using the settings $\beta_1 = 0.9$, $\beta_2 = 0.999$, and $\epsilon = 10^{-8}$ on a minibatch of 16. The two stages were pretrained with L_1 loss jointly for 400 epochs. The initial learning rate was 10^{-4} and decay rates were 0.1 every 100 epochs. We subsequently trained the model using the proposed PD-ADMM algorithm with a penalty factor $\rho = 10^{-4}$ and initialized s with 0.

We trained the whole model for another 200 epochs with an initial learning rate of 5×10^{-5} and decreasing to one-eighth after 20, 50, 70, 100, and 140 epochs.

4.2 Comparison with State-of-the-Art Methods

Quantitative Comparison with Trade-off Methods: We first compare our method with existing methods aiming to balance objective and perceptual quality. These include CFSNet [43], G-MGBP [32], PESR [42], ESRGAN with network interpolation [44], Deng [6], and WDST [7]. We note, however, that both Deng and WDST rely on image style transfer [10] for post-processing, which requires much more computational power and impractical inference runtimes (see detailed discussion on inference complexity in Sect. 4.2). Hence, a fair comparison with them is impossible. Nevertheless, as shown in Table 1, our method still reaches comparable performance to WDST and surpasses all other methods.

Table 1. Comparison with other PD trade-off state-of-the-art models aiming at both objective and perceptual quality on $\times 4$ super-resolution. We color the best performance in red and second best in blue. We separate Deng [6] and WDST [7] as they rely on three orders of magnitude higher computational power and a fair comparison with other listed methods is impossible. For reference, we set the best performance of Deng and WDST that surpass all other methods to **bold**. Higher PSNR, SSIM, NRQM score and *lower* LPIPS score mean better performance.

Dateset	Metric	Deng [6]	WDST [7]	G-MGBP [32]	PESR [42]	ESRGAN [44]	CFSNet [43]	Ours
Set5 [1]	PSNR	31.14	31.46	30.87	30.76	31.11	31.00	31.79
	SSIM	0.8917	**0.8929**	0.8807	0.8915	0.8839	0.8894	0.8910
	NRQM	7.0022	**7.5180**	7.3155	7.1344	7.0724	7.4820	7.3462
	LPIPS	–	0.0868	0.1003	0.0884	0.0841	0.1020	0.0776
Set14 [17]	PSNR	27.77	**28.07**	27.56	27.57	27.53	27.61	27.87
	SSIM	0.8325	**0.8356**	0.8206	0.8322	0.8228	0.8280	0.8282
	NRQM	7.5575	7.6827	7.5042	7.5301	7.5936	7.6074	7.7957
	LPIPS	–	0.1658	0.1757	0.1612	0.1539	0.1754	0.1423
BSD100 [27]	PSNR	26.46	26.82	26.59	26.33	26.44	26.46	26.84
	SSIM	0.7048	**0.7085**	0.6926	0.6980	0.7002	0.6991	0.7010
	NRQM	8.4452	**8.5948**	8.1790	8.3298	8.3034	8.3770	8.4406
	LPIPS	–	0.2140	0.2238	0.2045	0.1903	0.2129	0.187
Urban100 [12]	PSNR	25.96	26.26	25.15	25.88	26.08	25.38	26.28
	SSIM	0.9620	**0.9649**	0.9495	0.9610	0.9624	0.9546	0.9636
	NRQM	6.4317	6.4556	6.2190	6.3190	6.1762	6.5140	6.6220
	LPIPS	–	0.1604	0.1775	0.1402	0.1519	0.1506	0.1235
Manga109 [28]	PSNR	–	–	29.07	28.77	29.72	29.49	30.20
	SSIM	–	–	0.8815	0.9795	0.9772	0.9789	0.9804
	NRQM	–	–	6.4073	6.6071	6.3909	6.5344	6.6532
	LPIPS	–	–	0.0779	0.0634	0.0610	0.0719	0.0627

Quantitative Comparison with Single-Focused Methods: We further compare our method with single-focused state-of-the-art methods. Quantitatively comparing our balanced method with methods that only consider one type of quality is non-trivial. Due to the PD trade-off, our method will be inferior to the single-focused method in its optimized direction while surpassing it in the other. We thus make the comparison on a PD trade-off plane [2]. We generate a curve on the plane by interpolating the outputs from the state-of-the-art objective-focused and perceptual-focused methods. The interpolated image Y is produced through the following function:

$$Y = \alpha \cdot Y^O + (1 - \alpha) \cdot Y^P, \tag{14}$$

where Y^O is an HR image super-resolved by objective-focused model, Y^P is the perceptual-focused counterpart and the value of α is in $[0, 1]$. Freirich *et al.* [9] found this interpolation curve to be an optimal PD trade-off boundary achievable using single-focused estimators. Methods that sit in the region below the curve are better than those on or above the curve in terms of PD trade-off. In Fig. 3, we plot the curve between the best estimators, NLSA [31] and RankSRGAN [49], and show that our method is the only one below the estimated trade-off boundary considering all single-focused state-of-the-art methods on the plane.

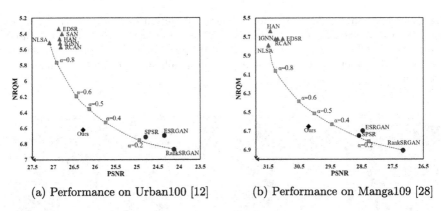

(a) Performance on Urban100 [12]   (b) Performance on Manga109 [28]

Fig. 3. Comparison with single-focused start-of-the-art SR methods on Urban100 [12] and Manga109 [28] datasets for ×4 super-resolution. We plot the curve by interpolating results from the best objective estimator [31] and the best perceptual estimator [49] on the plane. Our model can reach a better balance than the trade-off boundary approximated by single-focused state-of-the-art methods, as it sits well below the boundary.

Qualitative Results: We compare image samples generated from our method with those from NLSA [31], RankSRGAN [49] and WDST [7] on BSD100 [27] and Urban100 [12] in Fig. 4. Our method generates clear structures with fewer artifacts compared to single-focused methods and more realistic high-frequency details than WDST does. We provide frequency subbands comparison in Fig. 5. While single-focused methods only achieve good results at one of the subbands, our method learns both low- and high-frequency information effectively.

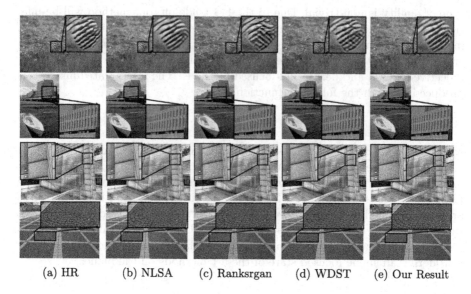

(a) HR   (b) NLSA   (c) Ranksrgan   (d) WDST   (e) Our Result

Fig. 4. Image sample comparison for ×4 super-resolution on BSD100 [27] *(first two rows)* and Urban100 [12] *(thrid and forth rows)* dataset. NLSA [31] is objective-focused, RankSRGAN [49] is perceptual-focused, while WDST [7] and our method are balanced approaches. Our method retains relatively sharp detailing without introducing unnatural artifacts.

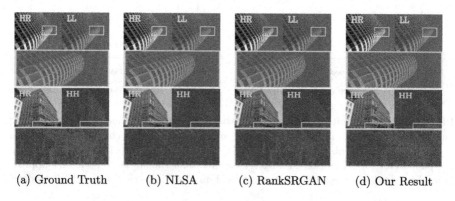

(a) Ground Truth   (b) NLSA   (c) RankSRGAN   (d) Our Result

Fig. 5. Visual comparison of low- and high-frequency subbands for ×4 super-resolution by NLSA [31], RankSRGAN [49] and our method. We visualize the LL *(first row)* and HH *(second row)* wavelet channels for low- and high-frequency comparison. *Within each image*, we show the HR image *(top left)*, wavelet channel *(top right)* and the zoom-in region of the wavelet channel under them. NLSA generates high-fidelity low-frequency information but lacks high-frequency detailing in the HH channel; RankSRGAN produces twisted structures in the LL channel but can reconstruct more high-frequency information. Our method predicts both high-fidelity LL channel and abundant high-frequency detailing.

Inference Complexity: A significant advantage of our method is that it is one-shot. We directly optimize a single model and bypass the complex fusing of two outputs, unlike competing work WDST [7] and its predecessor, Deng [6]. Central to their inference is an image style transfer procedure [10], which requires thousands of iterations to update the initial input signal towards a fused wavelet channel or image. In contrast, our method super-resolves the LR image through a single model in a one-shot manner. We used a 24 GB NVIDIA RTX A5000 GPU for running the models. Table 2 provides a quantitative comparison of the computational complexity, including the FLOPs and runtime for ×4 super-resolution of a 128 × 128 LR input. Our model's FLOPs and runtime are three orders of magnitude lower than WDST, assuming only 1000 iterations of updates for WDST (the actual number of updates is usually much more).

Table 2. Comparison of the inference complexity of our method and WDST [7] for ×4 super-resolution of a 128 × 128 LR image. The SR model super-resolves LR inputs and gives HR images, while post-processing further process super-resolved images. Our model's FLOPs and runtime are three orders of magnitude less than WDST. We refer to the supplementary material for detailed analysis.

Method	Values	SR model	Post-processing	All
WDST	FLOPs	50.6 M	$\approx 37448.1\,\text{M}$	$\approx 37500.3\,\text{M}$
	Run-time	0.918 s	$\approx 1152\,\text{s}$	$\approx 1153\,\text{s}$
Ours	FLOPs	26.8 M	–	26.8 M
	Run-time	0.566 s	–	0.566 s

4.3   Ablation Studies

Verification of Low-Frequency Constraint and ADMM Optimization: In this experiment, we kept a constant architecture as described in Sect. 4.1. Then we implemented the equivalence constraint through the second-stage regularizer in Eq. (7) and trained the models with different weights λ_r for the regularizer. Figure 6 shows the performance of regularizer-based methods on the PD trade-off plane, together with our PD-ADMM method; for each hyperparameter setting, we also illustrate the LF difference between the two stages' outputs, *i.e.* Y' and Y, with a circle. The more different the two stages, the larger the circle. Compared to the no-constraint version ($\lambda_r = 0$), both using PD-ADMM and adding the low-frequency constraint yield higher LF similarity. Figure 7 also provides visual evidence of the efficacy of adding the low-frequency constraint. The increase of λ_r results in higher LF similarity, transitioning from better perceptual quality to better objective quality. However, the model optimized by PD-ADMM achieves a superior balance of perceptual- and objective-quality to this transition.

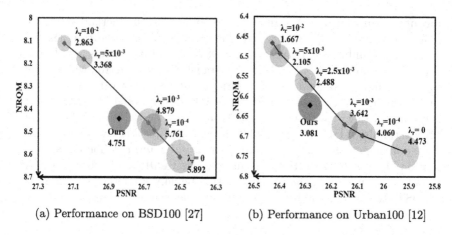

(a) Performance on BSD100 [27]   (b) Performance on Urban100 [12]

Fig. 6. Comparison with regularizer-based method on BSD100 [27] and Urban100 [12]. λ_r is the weight of regularizer; numbers below λ_r are mean absolute error (MAE) of low-frequency subbands between outputs of two stages. A lower value means a higher similarity. Our method achieves appropriate LF similarity and better balance than the curve plot by regularizer-based models.

Stage Order and Constrained Subband: This experiment validates the reconstruction ordering of frequency subbands in our proposed model. Without changing model architecture, we exchanged the optimization objectives of the two stages and converted the equivalence constraint to HF subbands extracted by DWT. Representing our original method as the O-P model, this swapped P-O model completes perceptual-focused reconstruction first, and then optimizes LF subbands while keeping HF equivalence to the first stage. We also optimized the P-O model through PD-ADMM. Borrowing the comparison with single-focused models in Sect. 4.2, we plotted the results of our original model and P-O model on a PD trade-off plane with the trade-off boundary. As shown in Fig. 8, the

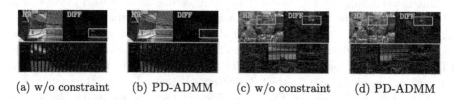

(a) w/o constraint   (b) PD-ADMM   (c) w/o constraint   (d) PD-ADMM

Fig. 7. Visualization of *difference* in low-frequency subband compared to the ground-truth for ×4 super-resolution. Each image shows the HR result *(top left)*, grayscale map of difference of the LL channel between the variant and the ground truth *(top right)*, and the zoom-in region of the grayscale map. The darker the map, the better. Limiting the change of the LF subband keeps higher accuracy of the LF information while learning the HF information at the perceptual stage.

performance of the order-exchanged model is dominated by the objective optimization and fails to achieve a good PD trade-off.

Low-frequency Subbands Extraction: To verify that our results are not dependent on specific frequency decomposition method, *i.e.* the DWT, we applied Gaussian blur on the outputs from the two stages to extract the LF subbands that should satisfy the equivalence constraint in PD-ADMM. Experimentally, we applied convolution with a 21×21 Gaussian kernel with $\sigma = 3$ to extract the LF information. As shown in Fig. 8, models with DWT and with Gaussian Blur (GB) have extremely close positions on the PD trade-off plane, and both of them are under the PD trade-off boundary introduced in Sect. 4.2. It shows that using different extraction methods can reach similar PD balances. We chose DWT for our model because of its popularity in image frequency analysis.

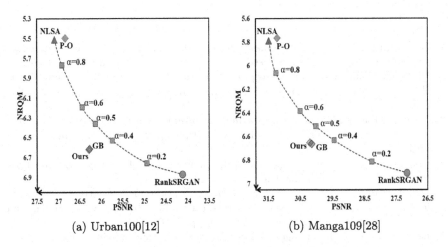

(a) Urban100[12]   (b) Manga109[28]

Fig. 8. Comparison between our model and its two variants. The order-exchanged version *(P-O)* optimizes HF subband for perceptual quality first. Its performance is close to the top-left corner and above the estimated trade-off boundary, *i.e.* it fails to balance the perceptual and objective quality. The other variant *(GB)* implements the low-frequency constraint of LFc-SR by Gaussian Blur rather than DWT used in our original model. The close performance of two models shows that our constraint design does not rely on a specific extraction method.

5   Conclusion and Limitations

In this paper, we learned a SISR model for both objective and perceptual quality. We proposed LFc-SR, a two-stage model trained with a low-frequency constraint to implicitly optimize low- and high-frequency bands for objective and perceptual quality in a successive way. The training of LFc-SR is formulated as a constrained multi-objective optimization problem. We designed PD-ADMM, an alternating algorithm, to solve for a solution that balances the perception-distortion trade-off. Our method is effective compared with other PD trade-off related methods and single-focused models without the expense of heavy fusion procedure.

Despite being more efficient than trade-off related fusion methods, our method is still far from optimal compared with some efficiency-oriented SISR models. Due to the successive processing in stages, some parts of the two-stage model may extract similar information and cause redundancy. However, such a design also offers the potential to reuse information efficiently, which we will leave for future work.

Acknowledgement. This research is supported by Singapore Ministry of Education (MOE) Academic Research Fund Tier 1 T1251RES1819.

References

1. Bevilacqua, M., Roumy, A., Guillemot, C., Alberi-Morel, M.L.: Low-complexity single-image super-resolution based on nonnegative neighbor embedding (2012)
2. Blau, Y., Michaeli, T.: The perception-distortion tradeoff. In: Proceedings of the IEEE Conference on Computer Vision and Pattern Recognition, pp. 6228–6237 (2018)
3. Boyd, S., Parikh, N., Chu, E.: Distributed Optimization and Statistical Learning via the Alternating Direction Method of Multipliers. Now Publishers Inc, Norwell (2011)
4. Chen, T.: A Fast Reduced-Space Algorithmic Framework for Sparse Optimization. Ph.D. thesis, Johns Hopkins University (2018)
5. Dai, T., Cai, J., Zhang, Y., Xia, S.T., Zhang, L.: Second-order attention network for single image super-resolution. In: Proceedings of the IEEE/CVF Conference on Computer Vision and Pattern Recognition, pp. 11065–11074 (2019)
6. Deng, X.: Enhancing image quality via style transfer for single image super-resolution. IEEE Sig. Process. Lett. **25**(4), 571–575 (2018)
7. Deng, X., Yang, R., Xu, M., Dragotti, P.L.: Wavelet domain style transfer for an effective perception-distortion tradeoff in single image super-resolution. In: Proceedings of the IEEE/CVF International Conference on Computer Vision, pp. 3076–3085 (2019)
8. Dong, C., Loy, C.C., He, K., Tang, X.: Image super-resolution using deep convolutional networks. IEEE Trans. Pattern Anal. Mach. Intell. **38**(2), 295–307 (2015)
9. Freirich, D., Michaeli, T., Meir, R.: A theory of the distortion-perception tradeoff in Wasserstein space. Adv. Neural Inf. Process. Syst. **34**, 25661–25672 (2021)
10. Gatys, L.A., Ecker, A.S., Bethge, M.: Image style transfer using convolutional neural networks. In: Proceedings of the IEEE Conference on Computer Vision and Pattern Recognition, pp. 2414–2423 (2016)
11. Guo, T., Seyed Mousavi, H., Huu Vu, T., Monga, V.: Deep wavelet prediction for image super-resolution. In: Proceedings of the IEEE Conference on Computer Vision and Pattern Recognition Workshops, pp. 104–113 (2017)
12. Huang, J.B., Singh, A., Ahuja, N.: Single image super-resolution from transformed self-exemplars. In: Proceedings of the IEEE Conference on Computer Vision and Pattern Recognition, pp. 5197–5206 (2015)

13. Kiaee, F., Gagné, C., Abbasi, M.: Alternating direction method of multipliers for sparse convolutional neural networks. arXiv preprint arXiv:1611.01590 (2016)
14. Kim, J., Lee, J.K., Lee, K.M.: Accurate image super-resolution using very deep convolutional networks. In: Proceedings of the IEEE Conference on Computer Vision and Pattern Recognition, pp. 1646–1654 (2016)
15. Kim, J., Lee, J.K., Lee, K.M.: Deeply-recursive convolutional network for image super-resolution. In: Proceedings of the IEEE Conference on Computer Vision and Pattern Recognition, pp. 1637–1645 (2016)
16. Kim, J., Lee, S.: Deep learning of human visual sensitivity in image quality assessment framework. In: Proceedings of the IEEE Conference on Computer Vision and Pattern Recognition, pp. 1676–1684 (2017)
17. Kim, K.I., Kwon, Y.: Single-image super-resolution using sparse regression and natural image prior. IEEE Trans. Pattern Anal. Mach. Intell. **32**(6), 1127–1133 (2010)
18. Kingma, D.P., Ba, J.: Adam: a method for stochastic optimization. arXiv preprint arXiv:1412.6980 (2014)
19. Ledig, C., et al.: Photo-realistic single image super-resolution using a generative adversarial network. In: Proceedings of the IEEE Conference on Computer Vision and Pattern Recognition, pp. 4681–4690 (2017)
20. Lee, H., Kim, T., Son, H., Baek, S., Cheon, M., Lee, S.: Smoother network tuning and interpolation for continuous-level image processing. arXiv preprint arXiv:2010.02270 (2020)
21. Leng, C., Dou, Z., Li, H., Zhu, S., Jin, R.: Extremely low bit neural network: squeeze the last bit out with ADMM. In: Thirty-Second AAAI Conference on Artificial Intelligence (2018)
22. Li, C., Chen, C., Zhang, B., Ye, Q., Han, J., Ji, R.: Deep spatio-temporal manifold network for action recognition. arXiv preprint arXiv:1705.03148 (2017)
23. Lim, B., Son, S., Kim, H., Nah, S., Mu Lee, K.: Enhanced deep residual networks for single image super-resolution. In: Proceedings of the IEEE Conference on Computer Vision and Pattern Recognition Workshops, pp. 136–144 (2017)
24. Liu, P., Zhang, H., Zhang, K., Lin, L., Zuo, W.: Multi-level wavelet-CNN for image restoration. In: Proceedings of the IEEE Conference on Computer Vision and Pattern Recognition Workshops, pp. 773–782 (2018)
25. Ma, C., Yang, C.Y., Yang, X., Yang, M.H.: Learning a no-reference quality metric for single-image super-resolution. Comput. Vis. Image Underst. **158**, 1–16 (2017)
26. Ma, C., Rao, Y., Cheng, Y., Chen, C., Lu, J., Zhou, J.: Structure-preserving super resolution with gradient guidance. In: Proceedings of the IEEE/CVF Conference on Computer Vision and Pattern Recognition, pp. 7769–7778 (2020)
27. Martin, D., Fowlkes, C., Tal, D., Malik, J.: A database of human segmented natural images and its application to evaluating segmentation algorithms and measuring ecological statistics. In: Proceedings of 8th International Conference Computer Vision, vol. 2, pp. 416–423, July 2001
28. Matsui, Y., et al.: Sketch-based manga retrieval using manga109 dataset. Multimedia Tools Appl. **76**(20), 21811–21838 (2016). https://doi.org/10.1007/s11042-016-4020-z
29. Mechrez, R., Talmi, I., Shama, F., Zelnik-Manor, L.: Maintaining natural image statistics with the contextual loss. In: Jawahar, C.V., Li, H., Mori, G., Schindler, K. (eds.) ACCV 2018. LNCS, vol. 11363, pp. 427–443. Springer, Cham (2019). https://doi.org/10.1007/978-3-030-20893-6_27

30. Mechrez, R., Talmi, I., Zelnik-Manor, L.: The contextual loss for image transformation with non-aligned data. In: Proceedings of the European Conference on Computer Vision (ECCV), pp. 768–783 (2018)
31. Mei, Y., Fan, Y., Zhou, Y.: Image super-resolution with non-local sparse attention. In: Proceedings of the IEEE/CVF Conference on Computer Vision and Pattern Recognition, pp. 3517–3526 (2021)
32. Navarrete Michelini, P., Zhu, D., Liu, H.: Multi-scale recursive and perception-distortion controllable image super-resolution. In: Proceedings of the European Conference on Computer Vision (ECCV) Workshops (2018)
33. Niu, B., et al.: Single image super-resolution via a holistic attention network. In: Vedaldi, A., Bischof, H., Brox, T., Frahm, J.-M. (eds.) ECCV 2020. LNCS, vol. 12357, pp. 191–207. Springer, Cham (2020). https://doi.org/10.1007/978-3-030-58610-2_12
34. Park, S.J., Son, H., Cho, S., Hong, K.S., Lee, S.: SRFeat: single image super-resolution with feature discrimination. In: Proceedings of the European Conference on Computer Vision (ECCV), pp. 439–455 (2018)
35. Ramamonjisoa, M., Firman, M., Watson, J., Lepetit, V., Turmukhambetov, D.: Single image depth prediction with wavelet decomposition. In: Proceedings of the IEEE/CVF Conference on Computer Vision and Pattern Recognition, pp. 11089–11098 (2021)
36. Shoshan, A., Mechrez, R., Zelnik-Manor, L.: Dynamic-net: Tuning the objective without re-training for synthesis tasks. In: Proceedings of the IEEE/CVF International Conference on Computer Vision, pp. 3215–3223 (2019)
37. Singh, V., Mittal, A.: WDN: a wide and deep network to divide-and-conquer image super-resolution. IEEE J. Sel. Top. Sign. Process. **15**(2), 264–278 (2020)
38. Takapoui, R., Moehle, N., Boyd, S., Bemporad, A.: A simple effective heuristic for embedded mixed-integer quadratic programming. Int. J. Control **93**(1), 2–12 (2020)
39. Timofte, R., Agustsson, E., Van Gool, L., Yang, M.H., Zhang, L.: NTIRE 2017 challenge on single image super-resolution: Methods and results. In: Proceedings of the IEEE Conference on Computer Vision and Pattern Recognition Workshops, pp. 114–125 (2017)
40. Tong, T., Li, G., Liu, X., Gao, Q.: Image super-resolution using dense skip connections. In: Proceedings of the IEEE International Conference on Computer Vision, pp. 4799–4807 (2017)
41. Vasu, S., Thekke Madam, N., Rajagopalan, A.: Analyzing perception-distortion tradeoff using enhanced perceptual super-resolution network. In: Proceedings of the European Conference on Computer Vision (ECCV) Workshops (2018)
42. Vu, T., Luu, T.M., Yoo, C.D.: Perception-enhanced image super-resolution via relativistic generative adversarial networks. In: Proceedings of the European Conference on Computer Vision (ECCV) Workshops (2018)
43. Wang, W., Guo, R., Tian, Y., Yang, W.: CFSNet: toward a controllable feature space for image restoration. In: Proceedings of the IEEE/CVF International Conference on Computer Vision, pp. 4140–4149 (2019)
44. Wang, X., et al.: ESRGAN: Enhanced super-resolution generative adversarial networks. In: Proceedings of the European Conference on Computer Vision (ECCV) Workshops (2018)
45. Yang, X., Xiang, W., Zeng, H., Zhang, L.: Real-world video super-resolution: a benchmark dataset and a decomposition based learning scheme. In: Proceedings of the IEEE/CVF International Conference on Computer Vision, pp. 4781–4790 (2021)

46. Zeyde, R., Elad, M., Protter, M.: On single image scale-up using sparse-representations. In: Boissonnat, J.-D., et al. (eds.) Curves and Surfaces 2010. LNCS, vol. 6920, pp. 711–730. Springer, Heidelberg (2012). https://doi.org/10.1007/978-3-642-27413-8_47
47. Zhang, R., Isola, P., Efros, A.A., Shechtman, E., Wang, O.: The unreasonable effectiveness of deep features as a perceptual metric. In: Proceedings of the IEEE Conference on Computer Vision and Pattern Recognition, pp. 586–595 (2018)
48. Zhang, T., et al.: A systematic DNN weight pruning framework using alternating direction method of multipliers. In: Proceedings of the European Conference on Computer Vision (ECCV), pp. 184–199 (2018)
49. Zhang, W., Liu, Y., Dong, C., Qiao, Y.: Ranksrgan: Generative adversarial networks with ranker for image super-resolution. In: Proceedings of the IEEE/CVF International Conference on Computer Vision, pp. 3096–3105 (2019)
50. Zhang, Y., Li, K., Li, K., Wang, L., Zhong, B., Fu, Y.: Image super-resolution using very deep residual channel attention networks. In: Proceedings of the European Conference on Computer Vision (ECCV), pp. 286–301 (2018)
51. Zhang, Y., Tian, Y., Kong, Y., Zhong, B., Fu, Y.: Residual dense network for image super-resolution. In: Proceedings of the IEEE Conference on Computer Vision and Pattern Recognition, pp. 2472–2481 (2018)
52. Zhao, P., Liu, S., Wang, Y., Lin, X.: An ADMM-based universal framework for adversarial attacks on deep neural networks. In: Proceedings of the 26th ACM International Conference on Multimedia, pp. 1065–1073 (2018)
53. Zhong, Z., Shen, T., Yang, Y., Lin, Z., Zhang, C.: Joint sub-bands learning with clique structures for wavelet domain super-resolution. Adv. Neural Inf. Process. Syst. 31, 165–175 (2018)
54. Zhou, Y., Deng, W., Tong, T., Gao, Q.: Guided frequency separation network for real-world super-resolution. In: Proceedings of the IEEE/CVF Conference on Computer Vision and Pattern Recognition Workshops, pp. 428–429 (2020)

VQFR: Blind Face Restoration with Vector-Quantized Dictionary and Parallel Decoder

Yuchao Gu[1,2], Xintao Wang[2], Liangbin Xie[2,5], Chao Dong[4,5], Gen Li[3], Ying Shan[2], and Ming-Ming Cheng[1(✉)]

[1] TMCC, CS, Nankai University, Tianjin, China
cmm@nankai.edu.cn
[2] ARC Lab, Tencent PCG, Beijing, China
[3] Platform Technologies, Tencent Online Video, Beijing, China
[4] Shanghai AI Laboratory, Beijing, China
[5] Shenzhen Institute of Advanced Technology, Chinese Academy of Sciences, Beijing, China
https://github.com/TencentARC/VQFR/

Abstract. Although generative facial prior and geometric prior have recently demonstrated high-quality results for blind face restoration, producing fine-grained facial details faithful to inputs remains a challenging problem. Motivated by the classical dictionary-based methods and the recent vector quantization (VQ) technique, we propose a VQ-based face restoration method – VQFR. VQFR takes advantage of high-quality low-level feature banks extracted from high-quality faces and can thus help recover realistic facial details. However, the simple application of the VQ codebook cannot achieve good results with faithful details and identity preservation. Therefore, we further introduce two special network designs. 1). We first investigate the compression patch size in the VQ codebook and find that the VQ codebook designed with a proper compression patch size is crucial to balance the quality and fidelity. 2). To further fuse low-level features from inputs while not "contaminating" the realistic details generated from the VQ codebook, we proposed a parallel decoder consisting of a texture decoder and a main decoder. Those two decoders then interact with a texture warping module with deformable convolution. Equipped with the VQ codebook as a facial detail dictionary and the parallel decoder design, the proposed VQFR can largely enhance the restored quality of facial details while keeping the fidelity to previous methods.

Keywords: Blind face restoration · Vector quantization · Parallel decoder

X. Wang—Project lead.
Y. Gu—is an intern in ARC Lab, Tencent PCG.

Supplementary Information The online version contains supplementary material available at https://doi.org/10.1007/978-3-031-19797-0_8.

1   Introduction

Blind face restoration aims at recovering low-quality (LQ) faces with unknown degradations, such as noise [40], blur [21,29], down-sampling [9,25], *etc.* This task becomes more challenging in real-world scenarios, where there are more complicated degradations, diverse face poses and expressions. Previous works typically exploit face-specific priors, including geometric priors [5,6,39], generative priors [33,37] and reference priors [8,23,24]. Specifically, geometric priors usually consist of facial landmarks [6], face parsing maps [5,6] and facial component heatmaps [39]. They could provide global guidance for restoring accurate face shapes, but do not help generate realistic details. Besides, geometric priors are estimated from degraded images and thus become inaccurate for inputs with severe degradations. These properties motivate researchers to find better priors.

Recent works [33,37] begin to investigate generative priors in face restoration and achieve superior performance. They usually leverage the powerful generation ability of a pre-trained face generative adversarial network (*e.g.*, Style-GAN [18,19]) to generate realistic textures. These methods typically project the degraded images back into the GAN latent space, and then decode high-quality (HQ) faces with the pre-trained generator. Although GAN-prior-based methods achieve decent overall restoration quality at first glance, they still fail to produce fine-grained facial details, especially the fine hair and delicate facial components (see examples in Fig. 1). This can be partially attributed to the imperfect latent space of the well-trained GAN model. Reference-based methods explore the high-quality guided faces [8,24] or facial component dictionary [23] to solve face restoration problems. DFDNet [23] is a representative method, which does not need to access the faces of the same identity. It explicitly establishes

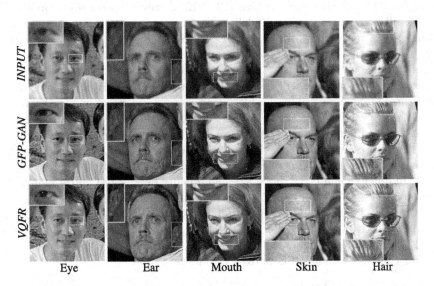

Fig. 1. Comparisons of restoration quality between GFP-GAN [33] and VQFR. Our VQFR can restore high-quality facial details on various facial regions and keep the fidelity as well, while GFP-GAN lacks realistic fine details. (**Zoom in for best view**)

a high-quality "texture bank" for several facial components and then replaces degraded facial components with the nearest HQ facial components in the dictionary. Such a discrete replacement operation directly bridges the gap between the low-quality facial components and high-quality ones, thus having the potential to provide decent facial details. However, the facial component dictionary in DFDNet still has two weaknesses. 1) It offline generates the facial component dictionary with a pre-trained VGGFace [3] network, which is optimized for the recognition task but is sub-optimal for restoration. 2) It only focuses on several facial components (i.e., eyes, nose, and mouth), but does not include other important areas, such as hair and skin.

The limitations of the facial component dictionary motivate us to explore Vector Quantized (VQ) codebook, a dictionary constructed for all facial areas. The proposed face restoration method – VQFR, takes advantage of both dictionary-based methods and GAN training, yet does not require any geometric or GAN prior. Compared to the facial component dictionary [23], the VQ codebook could provide a more comprehensive low-level feature bank that is not restricted to limited facial components. It is also learned in an end-to-end manner by the face reconstruction task. Besides, the mechanism of vector quantization makes it more robust for diverse degradations. Nevertheless, it is not easy to achieve good results simply by applying the VQ codebook. We further introduce two special network designs, which allow VQFR to surpass previous methods in both detail generation and identity preserving.

First, to generate realistic details, we find that it is crucial to select a proper compression patch size f, which indicates "how large a patch is represented" by an atom of the codebook. As shown in Fig. 2, a larger f could lead to better visual quality but worse fidelity. After a comprehensive investigation, we suggest using $f = 32$ for the input image size 512×512. However, such a selection is only a trade-off between quality and fidelity. The expression and identity could also change a lot even with a proper compression patch size (see Fig. 2). A straightforward solution is to fuse low-level features from input into different decoder layers, just like in GFP-GAN [33]. Although the input features could bring more fidelity information, they will also "contaminate" the realistic details generated from the VQ codebook. This problem leads to our second network design – a parallel decoder. Specifically, the parallel decoder structure consists of a texture decoder and a main decoder. The texture decoder only receives information from the latent representations from the VQ codebook, while the main decoder warps the features from the texture decoder to match the information from degraded input. In order to eliminate the loss of high-quality details and better match the degraded faces, we further adopt a texture warping module with deformable convolution [43] in the main decoder. Equipped with the VQ codebook as a facial dictionary and the parallel decoder design, we can achieve more high-quality facial details while reserving the fidelity for face restoration.

Our contributions are summarized as follows:

1. We propose the VQ dictionary of HQ facial details for face restoration. Our analysis of the VQ codebook shows the potential and limitations of the VQ

codebook, together with the importance of the compression patch sizes in face restoration.

2. A parallel decoder is proposed to gradually fuse input features and texture features from VQ codebooks, which keeps the fidelity without sacrificing HQ facial details.

3. Extensive experiments with quantitative and qualitative comparisons show VQFR largely surpasses previous works in restoration quality while keeping high fidelity.

2 Related Work

Blind Face Restoration

Early works explore different facial priors in face restoration. Those priors can be categorized into three types: geometric priors [5,6,39], generative priors [33,37] and reference priors [8,23,24]. The geometric priors include facial landmark [6], face parsing maps [5,6] and facial component heatmaps [39]. Those priors are estimated from degraded images and thus become inaccurate for inputs with severe degradations. Besides, the geometric structures cannot provide sufficient information to recover facial details. In this work, we do not explicitly integrate geometric priors, but we use landmark distance to estimate restoration fidelity.

Recent works investigate the generative priors to provide facial details and achieve decent performance. In the early arts, GAN inversion methods [14,26] aim to find the closest latent vector in the GAN space given an input image. Within this category, PULSE [26] iteratively optimizes the latent code of a pre-trained StyleGAN [18]. mGANprior [14] simultaneously optimize several codes to promote its reconstruction. Recent works GFP-GAN [33] and GPEN [37] extract fidelity information from inputs and then leverage the pre-trained GAN as a decoder, which achieves a good balance between visual quality and fidelity. Those methods still fail to produce fine-grained facial details. We conjecture that StyleGAN constructs a continuous latent space, and thus GAN-prior methods easily project degraded faces into a suboptimal latent code.

Reference priors [8,23,24] typically rely on reference images of the same identity. To address this issue, DFDNet [23] constructs an offline facial component dictionary [23] with VGGFace [3] for face recognition. It then conducts discrete replacement, *i.e.*, replacing the degraded facial components with high-quality ones in the dictionary by the nearest search. With the facial component dictionary, DFDNet [23] restores better facial components. However, it still has two limitations: 1) The dictionary is offline generated with a recognition model, which is sub-optimal for face restoration. 2) It only builds on several facial components (*i.e.*, eyes, nose and mouth), leaving other facial regions like skin and hair untouched. In this work, we explore the VQ codebook as a facial dictionary, which can be end-to-end trained by a reconstruction objective and provide realistic facial details. Recent RestoreFormer [34] also exploits the VQ codebook, but their work mainly discusses the diverse cross-attention mechanism for LQ latent and HQ code interaction. It does not explore deeply in VQ codebook while we show the dilemma between fidelity and realness when using the VQ codebook of different scales. Moreover, restoreformer does not exploit the input feature of larger resolution and thus results in limited restoration fidelity. Instead, we explore the parallel decoder to achieve realness and fidelity simultaneously.

Vector-Quantized Codebook

The vector-quantized codebook is first introduced in VQ-VAE [31]. With this codebook, the encoder network outputs are discrete rather than continuous, and the prior encapsulated in the codebook is learned rather than static. The following works propose different improvements to codebook learning. VQVAE2 [28] introduces a multi-scale codebook for better image generation. VQGAN [11] trains the codebook with the adversarial objective and thus the codebook can achieve high perceptual quality. To improve the codebook usage, some works [22,38] explore training techniques like L2-normalization or periodically re-initialization. Such a VQ codebook is a patch tokenizer and can be adopted in multiple tasks, like image generation [4,11,38], multi-modal generation [35]

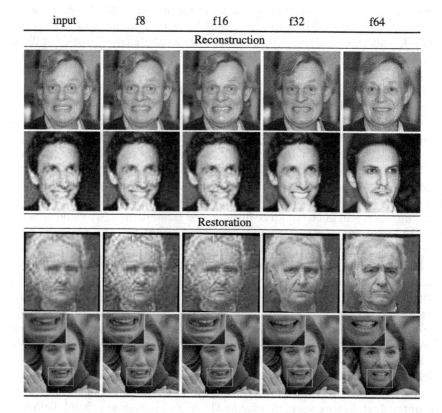

Fig. 2. Reconstruction and restoration results based on codebook with compression patch size $f = \{8, 16, 32, 64\}$. In the reconstruction experiment, we analyze the HQ reconstruction (row 1) and LQ reconstruction (row 2) based on pretrained HQ codebook. In the restoration experiment, we visualized the restoration result of faces of large degradation (row 3) and small degradation (row 4), respectively.

and large-scale pretraining [1,10]. Different from previous works that use the VQ codebook to get token features, we explore the potential of the VQ codebook as an HQ facial details dictionary.

3 Methodology

We describe the proposed VQFR framework in this section. Our goal is to restore high-quality faces with realistic facial details while reserving the fidelity of degraded faces. To achieve this goal, VQFR explores two key ingredients: Vector-Quantized (VQ) dictionary and parallel decoder. The overview of VQFR framework is illustrated in Fig. 3. VQFR contains an encoder, a parallel decoder and a pretrained HQ codebook. We first learn a VQ codebook from only HQ faces with an encoder-decoder structure by the vector-quantization technique [11,31]. Then, a degraded face is encoded to a compact latent representation with a downsampling factor f. At each spatial location of this latent representation, we replace the latent vector with its nearest code in the HQ codebook. After that, the substituted latent representation is then decoded back to the image space, *i.e.*, restored image with high-quality facial details.

The remaining parts are arranged as follows: In Sect. 3.1, we first analyze the potential and limitation of vector-quantization technique as a texture dictionary in face restoration task. Then we introduce the parallel decoder to promote the fidelity while maintaining the rich high-quality facial details in Sect. 3.2. In Sect. 3.3, we describe the overall training objective of VQFR framework.

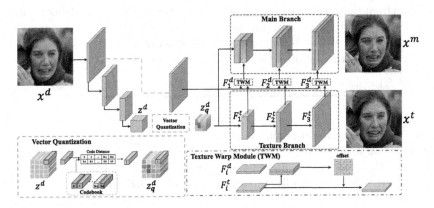

Fig. 3. Overview of VQFR framework. It consists of an encoder to map degraded face into latent and a parallel decoder to exploit the HQ code and input feature. The encoder and decoder are bridged by vector quantization model and a pretrained HQ codebook to replace the encoded latent to HQ code.

3.1 Vector-Quantized Codebook

Preliminary. The Vector-Quantized (VQ) codebook is first introduced in VQVAE [31], which aims to learn discrete priors to encode images. The following work VQGAN [11] proposes a perceptual codebook by further using perceptual loss [17] and adversarial training objectives [16]. We briefly describe the VQGAN model with its codebook in this section, and more details can be found in [11]. VQGAN is comprised of an encoder E, a decoder G and a codebook $\mathcal{Z} = \{z_k\}_{k=1}^{K}$ with K discrete codes. For an input image $x \in \mathbb{R}^{H \times W \times 3}$, the encoder E maps the image x to its spatial latent representation $\hat{z} = E(x) \in \mathbb{R}^{h \times w \times n_z}$, where n_z is the dimension of latent vectors. The vector-quantized representation $z_{\mathbf{q}}$ is then obtained by applying element-wise quantization $\mathbf{q}(\cdot)$ of each spatial code $\hat{z}_{ij} \in \mathbb{R}^{n_z}$ onto its closest codebook entry z_k:

$$z_{\mathbf{q}} = \mathbf{q}(\hat{z}) := \left(\arg \min_{z_k \in \mathcal{Z}} \| \hat{z}_{ij} - z_k \| \right) \in \mathbb{R}^{h \times w \times n_z}. \tag{1}$$

The decoder G maps the quantized representation $z_{\mathbf{q}}$ back to the image space, and the overall reconstruction $\hat{x} \approx x$ can be formulated as:

$$\hat{x} = G(z_{\mathbf{q}}) = G\left(\mathbf{q}(E(x))\right). \tag{2}$$

The encoder E maps images of size $H \times W$ into discrete codes of size $H/f \times W/f$, where f denotes the downsampling factor. It can be regarded as compressing each $f \times f$ patch in the image x into one code. In other words, for each code in $z_{\mathbf{q}}$, f also denotes the corresponding spatial size in the original image x. We name this downsampling factor f as the *compression patch size* in our paper.

Since the quantization operation in Equ. (2) is discrete and non-differentiable, VQGAN adopts straight-through gradient estimator [2], which simply copies the gradients from the decoder to the encoder. Thus, the model and codebook can be trained end-to-end via the loss function $\mathcal{L}_{vq}$. VQGAN also employs perceptual loss and adversarial loss to encourage reconstructions with better perceptual quality. The full training objective of VQGAN and its codebook is:

$$\mathcal{L}(E, G, \mathcal{Z}) = \underbrace{\|x - \hat{x}\|_1 + \|\mathrm{sg}[E(x)] - z_{\mathbf{q}}\|_2^2 + \beta\|\mathrm{sg}[z_{\mathbf{q}}] - E(x)\|_2^2}_{\mathcal{L}_{vq}} + \mathcal{L}_{per} + \mathcal{L}_{adv},$$

$$\tag{3}$$

where $\|x - \hat{x}\|_1$ is the reconstruction loss and $\mathrm{sg}[\cdot]$ denotes stop gradient operation. The codebook is updated by $\|\mathrm{sg}[E(x)] - z_{\mathbf{q}}\|_2^2$. $\beta\|\mathrm{sg}[z_{\mathbf{q}}] - E(x)\|_2^2$ is the commitment loss [31] to reduce the discrepancy between the encoded latent vectors and codes, where β is the commitment weight and set to 0.25 in all experiments.

Analysis. In order to better understand the potential and limitations of VQ codebooks for face restoration, we conduct several preliminary experiments and draw the following observations.

Observation 1. *Degradations in LQ faces can be removed by VQ codebooks trained only with HQ faces, when we adopt a proper compression patch size f.*

Following [11] and Equ. (3), we first train VQGAN with perceptual codebooks on HQ faces using different compression patch sizes $f = \{8, 16, 32, 64\}$. All our experiments are conducted on 512×512 input faces. The illustration of training architectures is shown in Fig. 4. We then examine the reconstruction quality for different compression patch sizes f. Note that the reconstruction output is expected to be the same as the input. As shown in row 1 of Fig. 2, the reconstruction quality of HQ faces is as expected. The reconstruction quality of HQ faces exhibits a reasonable trend: a smaller compression patch size f will lead to more faithful outputs. After that, we are curious whether the codebook trained only on HQ faces can also reconstruct LQ faces. We use LQ faces as inputs and examine the outputs. Interestingly, we can observe that under the compression patch sizes $f = 32$, the degradation in LQ faces can be removed (see row 2 in Fig. 2). This is because the codebook trained only on HQ faces has almost no degradation-related codes. During reconstruction, the vector quantization operation can replace the "degraded" vectors of inputs with the "clean" codes in codebooks.

Such a phenomenon shows the potential of the VQ codebook. However, it only happens with a large compression patch size f, as the codebook with a small compression patch size cannot well distinguish the degradations and detailed textures. In the extreme, for $f = 1$ with each pixel having a quantized code, both the degradation and detailed textures can be well recovered by a combination of codebook entries. On the other hand, a too large compression patch size (e.g., $f = 64$) will result in a significant change in identity, even it could also reconstruct "clean" face images.

Observation 2. *When training for the restoration task, there is also a trade-off between improved detailed textures and fidelity changes.*

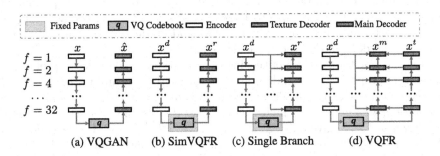

Fig. 4. Illustration of the architecture variants. (a) The VQGAN structure is used in codebook training. (b) The SimVQFR structure. (c) Single branch decoder. (d) The proposed parallel decoder.

We then investigate the VQ codebooks in face restoration, *i.e.*, training with LQ-HQ pairs as most face restoration works do [33]. Based on the trained model for reconstruction, we then fix the VQ codebooks, and finetune the encoder and decoder with LQ-HQ pairs (the training details are the same as that in Sect. 4.1). We denote this simple VQ model for face restoration as SimVQFR. We can observe from Fig. 2 that there is still a trade-off between improved detailed textures and fidelity changes. The key influential factor is the compression patch size f. With a small f (*i.e.*, $\{8, 16\}$), the SimVQFR model fails to remove degradations and cannot recover sufficient detailed textures. While with a large f (*i.e.*, $\{32, 64\}$), the textures are largely improved but the fidelity (*i.e.*, expression and identity) also changes a lot by the codebook.

Our Choice. Based on the above analysis, we can conclude that the VQ codebook, as a texture dictionary, has its value in generating high-quality facial textures and removing input degradations. However, there is a trade-off between the improved detailed textures and fidelity changes. The key influential factor is the compression patch size f. In order to better leverage the strength of generating high-quality facial textures, we choose the compression patch size $f = 32$ for 512×512 input faces. The left problem is how to preserve the fidelity with the VQ codebook of $f = 32$. We will present our parallel decoder solution to address this problem in Sect. 3.2.

3.2   Parallel Decoder

The VQ codebook with the compression patch size of $f = 32$ can be used as a texture bank to provide realistic facial details, but it also brings the problem of fidelity changes. From the results in Fig. 2, we can find that the position of facial components and the facial lines are changed, making the expression and identity largely deviate from the inputs. A straightforward solution is to integrate the feature information from degraded inputs to help improve the fidelity. However, simply fusing input features into the decoder with a single branch (as shown in Fig. 4) will lead to inferior details (see Fig. 8). In other words, such a single branch fusion strategy tends to corrupt the generated high-quality details. Though input features can bring more fidelity information, these features also contain input degradations. During feature propagation, *i.e.*, the upsampling process from small spatial size to large spatial size, the intermediate features will largely be influenced by input features, and gradually contain fewer high-quality facial details from the VQ codebook.

To overcome the dilemma of keeping the realistic facial details and promoting fidelity, we propose a parallel decoder structure with a texture warping module. The core idea of the parallel decoder (Fig. 4) is to decouple the two goals of face restoration, *i.e.*, generating high-quality facial details and keeping the fidelity. As shown in Fig. 3, given a degraded face $x^d \in \mathbb{R}^{H \times W \times 3}$, we first encode it to the latent vector z^d by $z^d = E(x^d)$. The encoder consists of several residual blocks and downsampling operations. Then we replace the code z^d with the HQ codebooks by Equ. (1) to get the quantized code $z_{\mathbf{q}}^d$. Since the quantized code $z_{\mathbf{q}}^d$ is from the HQ codebook, it contains HQ facial details without degradations. In order to keep its realistic textures, we use a texture decoder G_t to decode it back to image space $x^t = G_t(z_{\mathbf{q}}^d)$. We denote the multi-level feature of the texture branch as $F^t = \{F_i^t\}$. Since the texture branch only decodes from the HQ code, F^t can keep realistic facial details.

The main branch decoder G_m aims to generate faces x^m with high fidelity while having the realistic facial details from the texture decoder G_t. As illustrated in Fig. 3, the main branch decoder G_m warps the texture feature F^t based on the input feature extracted from degraded inputs at multiple spatial levels. We use the input feature with the largest spatial resolution as it retains the richest fidelity information of degraded faces. We then directly downsample the input feature to different resolution levels to get the multi-level features of degraded faces $F^d = \{F_i^d\}$.

For the i-th resolution level, we first warp F_i^t with high-quality facial details towards F_i^d by a texture warping module, which will be described later. After that, we fuse the warped feature F_i^w and the upsampled feature from F_{i-1}, to get the F_i feature in the main decoder. The process can be formulated as:

$$F_i^w = TWM(F_i^d, F_i^t), \qquad F_i = Conv(Concat(Upsample(F_{i-1}), F_i^w)), \qquad (4)$$

where TWM is the texture warping module. Our parallel decoder shares the same spirits as reference-based restoration [24]. In our case, the features from the texture decoder serve as the reference features containing high-quality details. Unlike reference-based restoration, our method does not require extra high-quality images with rich textures. Instead, the parallel decoder learns the main feature and "reference" feature jointly.

Texture Warping Module (TWM). The texture warping module aims to warp realistic facial details to match the fidelity of degraded inputs, especially the position of facial components and expressions. There are two inputs of TWM, one is the input feature F^d and the other is the texture feature F^t. As analyzed above, the texture features are decoded from the HQ codebook and have high-quality facial details. But their fidelity probably deviates from inputs. Therefore, we adopt a deformable convolution [43] to better warp the realistic facial details F^t towards the input feature F^d. Specifically, we first concatenate those two features to generate offsets. Then the offset is used in the deformable convolution to warp the texture features to match the fidelity of input, which can be formulated as:

$$offset = Conv(Concat(F_i^d, F_i^t)), \qquad F_i^w = Dconv(F_i^t, offset), \qquad (5)$$

where $Dconv$ denotes the deformable convolution. We also adopt a separable convolution with a large kernel size to model large position offsets between texture features and input features.

3.3 Model Objective

The training objective of VQFR consists of 1) pixel reconstruction loss that constraints the restored outputs close to the corresponding HQ faces; 2) code alignment loss that forces the codes of LQ inputs to match the codes of the corresponding HQ inputs; 3) perceptual loss to improve the perceptual quality in feature space; and 4) adversarial loss for restoring realistic textures. We denote the degraded face as x^d, decoder restored results as $x^r = \{x^t, x^m\}$ and the ground truth HQ image as x^h. The loss definitions are as follows.

Pixel Reconstruction Loss. We use the widely-used L1 loss in the pixel space as the reconstruction loss, which is denoted as: $\mathcal{L}_{pix} = \|x^r - x^h\|_1$. Empirically, we find that with the input feature of degraded faces, the pixel reconstruction loss has a negative impact on facial details. Therefore, we discard pixel reconstruction loss in the main decoder.

Code Alignment Loss. The code alignment loss aims to improve the performance of matching the codes of LQ images with codes of HQ images.

We adopt the L2 loss to measure the distance, which can be formulated as: $\mathcal{L}_{code} = \|z^d - z_{\mathsf{q}}^h\|_2^2$, where z_{q}^h is the ground truth code obtained from encoding HQ face to the quantized code by pretrained VQGAN.

Perceptual Loss. We use the widely used perceptual loss [17,41] for both two decoder outputs: $\mathcal{L}_{per} = \|\phi(x^r) - \phi(x^h)\|_1 + \lambda_{style}\|Gram(\phi(x^r)) - Gram(\phi(x^h))\|_1$, where ϕ is the pretrained VGG-16 [30] network and $Gram$ means the Gram matrix [13]. The former term measures the content distance and the latter term measures the style difference between the restoration results and the corresponding HQ images.

Adversarial Loss. We employ the global discriminator D_g in SWAGAN [12] to encourage VQFR to favor the solutions in the natural image manifold and generate realistic textures. In order to increase the local quality of facial details, we further adopt the local discriminator D_l of PatchGAN [16] in our training. The objectives of the global and local discriminators are defined as

$$\mathcal{L}_{adv}^{global} = -\mathbb{E}_{x^r}[\texttt{softplus}(D_g(x^r))], \mathcal{L}_{adv}^{local} = \mathbb{E}_{x^r}[\log D_l(x^h) + \log(1 - D_l(x^r))]. \quad (6)$$

Total Objective. The total training objective is the combination of above losses:

$$\mathcal{L}_{total} = \lambda_{pix}\mathcal{L}_{pix} + \lambda_{code}\mathcal{L}_{code} + \lambda_{per}\mathcal{L}_{per} + \lambda_{global}\mathcal{L}_{adv}^{global} + \lambda_{local}\mathcal{L}_{adv}^{local}, \quad (7)$$

where the λ_{pix}, λ_{code}, λ_{per}, λ_{global} and λ_{local} are scale factors of corresponding loss.

4   Experiments

4.1   Implementation and Evaluation Settings

Implementation. We implement the VQGAN and VQFR with six resolution levels, i.e., $\{1, 2, 4, 8, 16, 32\}$. For the VQ codebook, we use 1024 codebook entries

Table 1. Quantitative comparison on the **CelebA-Test** dataset for blind face restoration. Red and blue indicates the best and second best performance.

Methods	LPIPS↓	FID↓	NIQE ↓	Deg.↓	LMD.↓	PSNR↑	SSIM↑
Input	0.4866	143.98	13.440	47.94	3.76	25.35	0.6848
Wan et al. [32]	0.4826	67.58	5.356	43.00	2.92	24.71	0.6320
HiFaceGAN [36]	0.4770	66.09	4.916	42.18	3.16	24.92	0.6195
DFDNet [23]	0.4341	59.08	4.341	40.31	3.31	23.68	0.6622
PSFRGAN [5]	0.4240	47.59	5.123	39.69	3.41	24.71	0.6557
mGANprior [14]	0.4584	82.27	6.422	55.45	411.72	24.30	0.6758
PULSE [26]	0.4851	67.56	5.305	69.55	7.35	21.61	0.6200
GFP-GAN [33]	0.3646	42.62	4.077	34.60	2.41	25.08	0.6777
VQFR (ours)	0.3515	41.28	3.693	35.75	2.43	24.14	0.6360

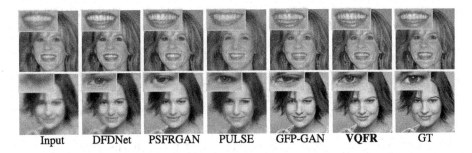

Input   DFDNet   PSFRGAN   PULSE   GFP-GAN   **VQFR**   GT

Fig. 5. Qualitative comparisons on the **CelebA-Test**. VQFR is able to restore high-quality facial details in various facial components, *e.g.*, eyes and mouth.

with 256 channels in all experiments. In order to increase the codebook usage, we follow [22] and periodically re-initialize the codebook with k-means clustering. More implementation details are provided *in the supplementary*.

In the first stage of codebook training, we adopt ADAM [20] optimizer with a learning rate of $1e-4$. The training iteration is set to 800K with a batch size of 16. For the second stage training for restoration, the loss weights are set to $\lambda_{pix}=\lambda_{code}=\lambda_{per}=1$, $\lambda_{style}=2000$ and the adversarial loss weights are set to $\lambda_{local}=\lambda_{global}=0.5$. We train VQFR for 200K iterations by ADAM optimizer with the learning rate of $1e-5$.

Training Datasets. The VQFR is trained on the FFHQ dataset [18] including 70,000 high-quality faces. The images are resized to 512^2 during training. Following the common practice in [23,24,33], we use the following degradation model to synthesize training pairs: $x = [(y \circledast k_\sigma) \downarrow_r +n_\delta]_{\mathrm{JPEG}_q}$, where σ, r, δ and q are randomly sampled from $\{0.2:10\}$, $\{1:8\}$, $\{0:15\}$ and $\{60:100\}$, respectively.

Testing Datasets. Following the practice in GFP-GAN [33], we conduct experiments on the synthetic dataset *CelebA-Test* and three real-world datasets - *LFW-Test*, *CelebChild-Test* and *WebPhoto-Test*. These datasets have diverse and complicated degradations. All these datasets have no overlap with the training dataset.

Evaluation Metrics. Our evaluation metrics contain two widely-used non-reference perceptual metrics: FID [15] and NIQE [27]. We also measure the pixel-wise metrics (PSNR and SSIM) and perceptual metric (LPIPS [42]) for benchmarking CelebA-Test with Ground-Truth (GT). We follow previous work [33] to use the embedding angle of ArcFace [7] as the identity metric, which is denoted by 'Deg.'. In order to better measure the fidelity with accurate facial positions and expressions, we further adopt landmark distance (LMD) as the fidelity metric. More details are provided *in the supplementary*.

Table 2. Quantitative comparison on the *real-world* **LFW**, **CelebChild**, **WebPhoto**. Red and <u>blue</u> indicates the best and second best performance.

Dataset	LFW-Test		CelebChild		WebPhoto	
Methods	FID↓	NIQE ↓	FID↓	NIQE ↓	FID↓	NIQE ↓
Input	137.56	11.214	144.42	9.170	170.11	12.755
Wan *et al.* [32]	73.19	5.034	115.70	4.849	100.40	5.705
HiFaceGAN [36]	64.50	4.510	113.00	4.855	116.12	4.885
DFDNet [23]	62.57	4.026	111.55	4.414	100.68	5.293
PSFRGAN [5]	51.89	5.096	107.40	4.804	88.45	5.582
mGANprior [14]	73.00	6.051	126.54	6.841	120.75	7.226
PULSE [26]	64.86	5.097	102.74	5.225	86.45	5.146
GFP-GAN [33]	49.96	<u>3.882</u>	111.78	<u>4.349</u>	<u>87.35</u>	<u>4.144</u>
VQFR (ours)	<u>50.64</u>	3.589	<u>105.18</u>	3.936	75.38	3.607

4.2   Comparisons with State-of-the-art Methods

We compare our VQFR with several state-of-the-art face restoration methods: Wan *et al.* [32], HiFaceGAN [36], DFDNet [23], PSFRGAN [5], mGANprior [14], PULSE [26] and GFP-GAN [33].

Synthetic CelebA-Test. From the quantitative results in Table. 1, VQFR achieves the lowest LPIPS, implying that VQFR generates the restored faces with the closest perceptual quality to ground-truth. VQFR also achieves the best FID and NIQE, with a large improvement over GFP-GAN, demonstrating that results of VQFR are closer to real faces and have more realistic details. For fidelity, VQFR can achieve comparable landmark distance and identity degree to GFP-GAN, showing that it can recover accurate facial expressions and detail positions.

Qualitative results are presented in Fig. 5. Thanks to the VQ codebook design, VQFR generates high-quality facial components like eyes and mouth as well as other facial regions. VQFR also maintains the fidelity with the help of the parallel decoder.

Real-World LFW, CelebChild, and WedPhoto-Test. We evaluate VQFR on three real-world test datasets to test the generalization ability. Table. 2 shows the quantitative results. It is observed that VQFR largely improves the realness and perceptual quality of all three real-world datasets. PULSE [26] achieves a higher perceptual quality on CelebChild, but its fidelity is severely affected. From the qualitative results in Fig. 6, the face restored by VQFR is of the most high quality on different facial regions.

4.3   Ablation Study

Importance of Input Features from Degraded Faces. The SimVQFR model directly uses the VQ codebook without exploiting input features. As

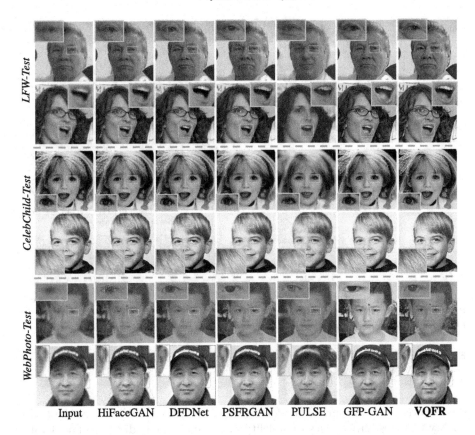

Fig. 6. Qualitative comparisons on three real-world datasets. **Zoom in for best view.**

shown in Fig. 7(a), though it can achieve high perceptual quality (low FID and NIQE), its landmark distance is large, indicating the low fidelity. After incorporating the input features of degraded faces, the fidelity improves significantly. From the visualization of Fig. 8(a), we can observe that the facial lines of SimVQFR are deviated from LQ faces, resulting in an expression change. Such a phenomenon can also be observed in the examples in Fig. 3, where the texture decoder output changes the woman's expression apparently.

Importance of Parallel Decoder. When comparing Variant 1 and Variant 2, the NIQE (which favors high-quality details) of Variants 1 is higher and clearly inferior to Variant 2 (Fig. 7 (a)). From the visualization in Fig. 8(b), we observe that, in Variant 1 without the parallel decoder, the eyes and hair lose high-frequency details and are biased to degraded ones. While with the parallel decoder, the details are clearer and more realistic.

Texture Warping Module. As shown in Fig. 7 (a), Variant 2 does not have a TWM module and directly utilizes concatenation fusion of texture features and input features of degraded features. It lacks the ability to dynamically adjust

Models	Configurations			CelebA-Test		
	Inp Feat.	Para Dec.	TWM	FID↓	NIQE↓	LMD↓
SimVQFR				40.51	3.844	2.96
Variant 1	✓			39.64	4.019	2.36
Variant 2	✓	✓		42.61	3.714	2.48
VQFR	✓	✓	✓	41.28	3.693	2.43

(a) Ablation results on CelebA-Test. *Inp Feat.*: input feature of degraded faces; *Para Dec.*: parallel decoder; *TWM*: texture warping module.

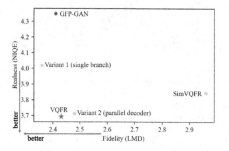

(b) Visualization of the balance between realness of fidelity of different configurations.

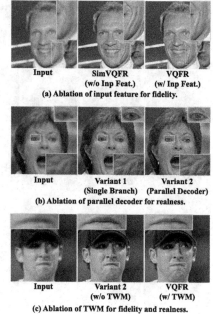

Input   SimVQFR   VQFR
(w/o Inp Feat.) (w/ Inp Feat.)
(a) Ablation of input feature for fidelity.

Input   Variant 1   Variant 2
(Single Branch) (Parallel Decoder)
(b) Ablation of parallel decoder for realness.

Input   Variant 2   VQFR
(w/o TWM) (w/ TWM)
(c) Ablation of TWM for fidelity and realness.

Fig. 7. Quantitative ablation studies of key designs in VQFR.

Fig. 8. Qualitative ablation studies of key designs on VQFR.

the features with warping. Therefore, Variant 2 without TWM keeps the high-quality textures but changes the fidelity, as it cannot well adjust the fine details and expression. From the visualization of Fig. 8(c), the TWM module helps accurately warp the high-quality facial details to better match the degraded input.

5 Conclusion

In this paper, we propose the vector-quantized (VQ) dictionary of high-quality facial details for face restoration. Our analysis of the VQ codebook shows the potential and limitations of the VQ codebook. In order to keep the fidelity without the loss of high-quality facial details, a parallel decoder is further proposed to gradually fuse input features and texture features from VQ codebooks. Equipped with the VQ codebook as a dictionary and the parallel decoder, our proposed vector-quantized face restoration (VQFR) can produce high-quality facial details while preserving fidelity. Extensive experiments show that our methods surpass previous works on both synthetic and real-world datasets.

Acknowledgement. This work is funded by the National Key Research and Development Program of China Grant No.2018AAA0100400 and NSFC (NO. 62176130). And this work is partially supported by National Natural Science Foundation of China (61906184, U1913210), and the Shanghai Committee of Science and Technology, China (Grant No. 21DZ1100100).

References

1. Bao, H., Dong, L., Wei, F.: Beit: bert pre-training of image transformers. arXiv preprint arXiv:2106.08254 (2021)
2. Bengio, Y., Léonard, N., Courville, A.: Estimating or propagating gradients through stochastic neurons for conditional computation. arXiv preprint arXiv:1308.3432 (2013)
3. Cao, Q., Shen, L., Xie, W., Parkhi, O.M., Zisserman, A.: Vggface2: a dataset for recognising faces across pose and age. In: 2018 13th IEEE International Conference on Automatic Face & Gesture Recognition (FG 2018), pp. 67–74. IEEE (2018)
4. Chang, H., Zhang, H., Jiang, L., Liu, C., Freeman, W.T.: Maskgit: masked generative image transformer. arXiv preprint arXiv:2202.04200 (2022)
5. Chen, C., Li, X., Yang, L., Lin, X., Zhang, L., Wong, K.Y.K.: Progressive semantic-aware style transformation for blind face restoration. In: Proceedings of the IEEE/CVF Conference on Computer Vision and Pattern Recognition, pp. 11896–11905 (2021)
6. Chen, Y., Tai, Y., Liu, X., Shen, C., Yang, J.: FSRNet: end-to-end learning face super-resolution with facial priors. In: Proceedings of the IEEE Conference on Computer Vision and Pattern Recognition, pp. 2492–2501 (2018)
7. Deng, J., Guo, J., Xue, N., Zafeiriou, S.: ArcFace: additive angular margin loss for deep face recognition. In: Proceedings of the IEEE/CVF Conference on Computer Vision and Pattern Recognition, pp. 4690–4699 (2019)
8. Dogan, B., Gu, S., Timofte, R.: Exemplar guided face image super-resolution without facial landmarks. In: Proceedings of the IEEE/CVF Conference on Computer Vision and Pattern Recognition Workshops (2019)
9. Dong, C., Loy, C.C., He, K., Tang, X.: Learning a deep convolutional network for image super-resolution. In: Fleet, D., Pajdla, T., Schiele, B., Tuytelaars, T. (eds.) ECCV 2014. LNCS, vol. 8692, pp. 184–199. Springer, Cham (2014). https://doi.org/10.1007/978-3-319-10593-2_13
10. Dong, X., et al.: PeCo: perceptual codebook for bert pre-training of vision transformers. arXiv preprint arXiv:2111.12710 (2021)
11. Esser, P., Rombach, R., Ommer, B.: Taming transformers for high-resolution image synthesis. In: Proceedings of the IEEE/CVF Conference on Computer Vision and Pattern Recognition, pp. 12873–12883 (2021)
12. Gal, R., Hochberg, D.C., Bermano, A., Cohen-Or, D.: SWAGAN: a style-based wavelet-driven generative model. ACM Trans. Graph. (TOG) 40(4), 1–11 (2021)
13. Gatys, L.A., Ecker, A.S., Bethge, M.: Image style transfer using convolutional neural networks. In: Proceedings of the IEEE Conference on Computer Vision and Pattern Recognition, pp. 2414–2423 (2016)
14. Gu, J., Shen, Y., Zhou, B.: Image processing using multi-code GAN prior. In: Proceedings of the IEEE/CVF Conference on Computer Vision and Pattern Recognition, pp. 3012–3021 (2020)
15. Heusel, M., Ramsauer, H., Unterthiner, T., Nessler, B., Hochreiter, S.: GANs trained by a two time-scale update rule converge to a local nash equilibrium. Adv. Neural Inf. Process. Syst. 30 (2017)
16. Isola, P., Zhu, J.Y., Zhou, T., Efros, A.A.: Image-to-image translation with conditional adversarial networks. In: Proceedings of the IEEE Conference on Computer Vision and Pattern Recognition, pp. 1125–1134 (2017)

17. Johnson, Justin, Alahi, Alexandre, Fei-Fei, Li.: Perceptual losses for real-time style transfer and super-resolution. In: Leibe, Bastian, Matas, Jiri, Sebe, Nicu, Welling, Max (eds.) ECCV 2016. LNCS, vol. 9906, pp. 694–711. Springer, Cham (2016). https://doi.org/10.1007/978-3-319-46475-6_43

18. Karras, T., Laine, S., Aila, T.: A style-based generator architecture for generative adversarial networks. In: Proceedings of the IEEE/CVF Conference on Computer Vision and Pattern Recognition, pp. 4401–4410 (2019)

19. Karras, T., Laine, S., Aittala, M., Hellsten, J., Lehtinen, J., Aila, T.: Analyzing and improving the image quality of StyleGAN. In: Proceedings of the IEEE/CVF Conference on Computer Vision and Pattern Recognition, pp. 8110–8119 (2020)

20. Kingma, D.P., Ba, J.: Adam: a method for stochastic optimization. arXiv preprint arXiv:1412.6980 (2014)

21. Kupyn, O., Budzan, V., Mykhailych, M., Mishkin, D., Matas, J.: DeblurGAN: blind motion deblurring using conditional adversarial networks. In: Proceedings of the IEEE Conference on Computer Vision and Pattern Recognition, pp. 8183–8192 (2018)

22. Łańcucki, A., et al.: Robust training of vector quantized bottleneck models. In: 2020 International Joint Conference on Neural Networks (IJCNN), pp. 1–7. IEEE (2020)

23. Li, Xiaoming, Chen, Chaofeng, Zhou, Shangchen, Lin, Xianhui, Zuo, Wangmeng, Zhang, Lei: Blind face restoration via deep multi-scale component dictionaries. In: Vedaldi, Andrea, Bischof, Horst, Brox, Thomas, Frahm, Jan-Michael. (eds.) ECCV 2020. LNCS, vol. 12354, pp. 399–415. Springer, Cham (2020). https://doi.org/10.1007/978-3-030-58545-7_23

24. Li, X., Liu, M., Ye, Y., Zuo, W., Lin, L., Yang, R.: Learning warped guidance for blind face restoration. In: Proceedings of the European Conference on Computer Vision (ECCV), pp. 272–289 (2018)

25. Lim, B., Son, S., Kim, H., Nah, S., Mu Lee, K.: Enhanced deep residual networks for single image super-resolution. In: Proceedings of the IEEE Conference on Computer Vision and Pattern Recognition Workshops, pp. 136–144 (2017)

26. Menon, S., Damian, A., Hu, S., Ravi, N., Rudin, C.: Pulse: self-supervised photo upsampling via latent space exploration of generative models. In: Proceedings of the IEEE/CVF Conference on Computer Vision and Pattern Recognition, pp. 2437–2445 (2020)

27. Mittal, A., Soundararajan, R., Bovik, A.C.: Making a "completely blind" image quality analyzer. IEEE Sig. Process. Lett. **20**(3), 209–212 (2012)

28. Razavi, A., Van den Oord, A., Vinyals, O.: Generating diverse high-fidelity images with VQ-VAE-2. Adv. Neural Inf. Process. Syst. **32** (2019)

29. Shen, Z., Lai, W.S., Xu, T., Kautz, J., Yang, M.H.: Deep semantic face deblurring. In: Proceedings of the IEEE Conference on Computer Vision and Pattern Recognition, pp. 8260–8269 (2018)

30. Simonyan, K., Zisserman, A.: Very deep convolutional networks for large-scale image recognition. arXiv preprint arXiv:1409.1556 (2014)

31. Van Den Oord, A., Vinyals, O., et al.: Neural discrete representation learning. Adv. Neural Inf. Process. Syst. **30** (2017)

32. Wan, Z., et al.: Bringing old photos back to life. In: proceedings of the IEEE/CVF Conference on Computer Vision and Pattern Recognition, pp. 2747–2757 (2020)

33. Wang, X., Li, Y., Zhang, H., Shan, Y.: Towards real-world blind face restoration with generative facial prior. In: Proceedings of the IEEE/CVF Conference on Computer Vision and Pattern Recognition, pp. 9168–9178 (2021)

34. Wang, Z., Zhang, J., Chen, R., Wang, W., Luo, P.: RestoreFormer: high-quality blind face restoration from undegraded key-value pairs. arXiv preprint arXiv:2201.06374 (2022)
35. Wu, C., et al.: Nüwa: Visual synthesis pre-training for neural visual world creation. arXiv preprint arXiv:2111.12417 (2021)
36. Yang, L., et al.: HiFaceGAN: face renovation via collaborative suppression and replenishment. In: Proceedings of the 28th ACM International Conference on Multimedia, pp. 1551–1560 (2020)
37. Yang, T., Ren, P., Xie, X., Zhang, L.: Gan prior embedded network for blind face restoration in the wild. In: Proceedings of the IEEE/CVF Conference on Computer Vision and Pattern Recognition, pp. 672–681 (2021)
38. Yu, J., et al.: Vector-quantized image modeling with improved VQGAN. arXiv preprint arXiv:2110.04627 (2021)
39. Yu, X., Fernando, B., Ghanem, B., Porikli, F., Hartley, R.: Face super-resolution guided by facial component heatmaps. In: Proceedings of the European Conference on Computer Vision (ECCV), pp. 217–233 (2018)
40. Zhang, K., Zuo, W., Chen, Y., Meng, D., Zhang, L.: Beyond a gaussian denoiser: residual learning of deep CNN for image denoising. IEEE Trans. Image Process. **26**(7), 3142–3155 (2017)
41. Zhang, R., Isola, P., Efros, A.A., Shechtman, E., Wang, O.: The unreasonable effectiveness of deep features as a perceptual metric. In: CVPR (2018)
42. Zhang, R., Isola, P., Efros, A.A., Shechtman, E., Wang, O.: The unreasonable effectiveness of deep features as a perceptual metric. In: Proceedings of the IEEE Conference on Computer Vision and Pattern Recognition, pp. 586–595 (2018)
43. Zhu, X., Hu, H., Lin, S., Dai, J.: Deformable convnets v2: more deformable, better results. In: Proceedings of the IEEE/CVF Conference on Computer Vision and Pattern Recognition, pp. 9308–9316 (2019)

Uncertainty Learning in Kernel Estimation for Multi-stage Blind Image Super-Resolution

Zhenxuan Fang[1], Weisheng Dong[1(✉)], Xin Li[2], Jinjian Wu[1], Leida Li[1], and Guangming Shi[1]

[1] School of Artificial Intelligence, Xidian University, Xi'an, China
zxfang@stu.xidian.edu.cn, {wsdong,jinjian.wu}@mail.xidian.edu.cn,
{ldli,gmshi}@xidian.edu.cn
[2] Lane Department of CSEE, West Virginia University, Morgantown, WV, USA
xin.li@mail.wvu.edu

Abstract. Conventional wisdom in blind super-resolution (SR) first estimates the unknown degradation from the low-resolution image and then exploits the degradation information for image reconstruction. Such sequential approaches suffer from two fundamental weaknesses - i.e., the lack of robustness (the performance drops when the estimated degradation is inaccurate) and the lack of transparency (network architectures are heuristic without incorporating domain knowledge). To address these issues, we propose a joint Maximum a Posteriori (MAP) approach for estimating the unknown kernel and high-resolution image simultaneously. Our method first introduces uncertainty learning in the latent space when estimating the blur kernel, aiming at improving the robustness to the estimation error. Then we propose a novel SR network by unfolding the joint MAP estimator with a learned Laplacian Scale Mixture (LSM) prior and the estimated kernel. We have also developed a novel approach of estimating both the scale prior coefficient and the local means of the LSM model through a deep convolutional neural network (DCNN). All parameters of the MAP estimation algorithm and the DCNN parameters are jointly optimized through end-to-end training. Extensive experiments on both synthetic and real-world images show that our method achieves state-of-the-art performance for the task of blind image SR.

1 Introduction

Single image super-resolution (SISR) is a typical low-level vision problem that aims to reconstruct the high-resolution (HR) image from its low-resolution (LR) observation. Since the pioneering work of applying convolutional neural networks to SR (SRCNN) [10], extensive deep learning-based methods [11,17,26,30,34,38,52,53] have been developed and achieved impressive performance. Most existing methods are based on the assumption that the degradation is known and predefined

---

Supplementary Information The online version contains supplementary material available at https://doi.org/10.1007/978-3-031-19797-0_9.

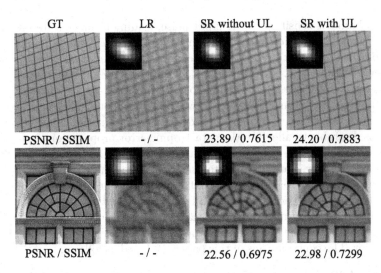

GT	LR	SR without UL	SR with UL
PSNR / SSIM	- / -	23.89 / 0.7615	24.20 / 0.7883
PSNR / SSIM	- / -	22.56 / 0.6975	22.98 / 0.7299

Fig. 1. SR results produced by the multi-stage network, the corresponding estimated blur kernels with or without uncertainty learning (UL) are illustrated on the top left.

(e.g., bicubic downsampling), so numerous training data can be manually synthesized and used to train powerful networks. However, these methods will suffer a dramatic performance drop when the degradation involved in the test image is different from the assumption. To tackle this problem, several methods have been proposed [50,51] by taking the blur kernel as an additional input of the network to utilize the degradation prior knowledge. Recently, [42,43] only focused on exploiting the internal information of the test images, also known as zero-shot SR. However, the above methods need to provide the blur kernels of test images, so kernel estimation [4,37] is crucial before these non-blind SR methods, but if the estimated kernel deviates from the ground truth, the kernel mismatch will lead to undesired artifacts [15].

Generally, the degradation processes of real-world LR images are probably complicated and unknown [7,15], so studying the problem of blind SR is particularly valuable. Most early blind SR methods are model-based [3,18,20,47], they exploit internal self-similarity and edge prior to estimate the underlying blur kernels of LR images before performing SR. But their optimization procedures are usually time-consuming due to complex and iterative computation. Deep learning-based iterative kernel correction (IKC) [15] uses the SR result to correct the estimated kernel in an iterative manner, where the estimation is integrated into reconstruction by spatial feature transform (SFT) layers [48]. An unsupervised degradation representation learning scheme was proposed in [46] by contrastive learning based on the assumption that the degradation is invariant within the same image but varies from image to image.

However, these methods have several obvious limitations. First, accurate estimation is often impossible - due to the ill-posed nature of inverse problems, there exist multiple candidates of the kernel for a single LR input [15]. Meanwhile, the estimated kernel is sensitive to the input noise, leading to inaccurate estimation results. Second, the fusion modules such as [51] will face the domain interference problem because it directly concatenates the degradation representations with image features [46]. Meanwhile, the SR networks are designed based on the black-box principle, making it difficult for interpretation or optimization.

The motivation behind this work is twofold. On the one hand, we advocate a joint optimization of kernel estimation and image reconstruction. Such end-to-end training is desirable to alleviate the catastrophic error propagation in sequential approaches. On the other hand, it is desirable to quantify the uncertainty of kernel estimation so that we can incorporate such ambiguity into the process of image reconstruction. In this paper, we first introduce data uncertainty learning with kernel estimation. Instead of using fixed feature maps in the estimation network, the feature (mean) and uncertainty (variance) are learned simultaneously. Then we propose a transparent blind SR method with learned Laplacian Scale Mixture (LSM) prior. The contributions of this paper are listed as follows.

- The blind SR problem is formulated as a joint Maximum a Posteriori (MAP) approach for estimating the blur kernel and reconstructing the HR image. Then we propose a novel multi-stage SR network by converting the MAP estimator with a learned LSM prior and estimated kernel into a multi-stage deep network, all parameters in the MAP estimator are optimized in an end-to-end manner.
- To improve the performance and robustness of kernel estimation, we introduce uncertainty learning to the kernel estimation network. Both the feature (mean) and uncertainty (variance) in the latent space of the blur kernel are learned, which is proved can produce more accurate kernel than deterministic model.
- Extensive experimental results on both synthetic and real-world datasets show that the proposed method outperforms existing state-of-the-art blind SR methods, especially in the presence of heavy noise contamination. Subjective evaluation of SR images is also convincingly in favor of our method.

2   Related Work

2.1   Blind Image Super-Resolution

Blind SR assumes that the blur kernels of test images are unknown. Previous model-based methods [20,21] are time-consuming because most of them involve complicated optimization procedures. In [37], an optimal kernel can be recovered by utilizing the internal patch recurrence property in an image. With the development of deep learning, CNN-based blind SR methods become more popular [15,24,27,32,33,35,44,46]. IKC method [15] performs blind SR by using the intermediate reconstruction results to iteratively correct the estimation of blur kernels. Luo et al. [35] proposed a deep alternating network (DAN) by concatenating the estimator and restorer module alternately. By utilizing the degenerative similarity of small patches in an image, [46] introduces an unsupervised contrastive learning scheme to extract various degradation representations for further reconstruction. Recently, [27] proposed a blind SR framework based on kernel-oriented adaptive local adjustment of SR features. MANet [32] proposes a kernel estimation framework using the mutual affine convolution layer.

2.2 Uncertainty in Deep Learning

The uncertainty in deep learning can be divided into two categories [9]: epistemic/model uncertainty and aleatoric/data uncertainty. The former describes how much the model is uncertain about its predictions. The latter refers to the noise inherent in the observation data. Many works [2,6,16,25] have been studied to model the uncertainty in deep learning tasks, including image classification, image segmentation, and face recognition. By introducing uncertainty, they have improved the performance and robustness of deep networks. GAMA [31] analyses the effect of aleatoric/data uncertainty on SISR reconstruction by decreasing the loss attenuation of large variance pixels. Recently, [39] proposed a novel uncertainty-driven loss (UDL) to enforce the network concentrating more on the pixels with large variance, which is beneficial for better reconstruction of texture and edge regions.

2.3 LSM Model for Image Restoration

As a probability model, the Laplacian Scale Mixture (LSM) model is an analogy to the classical Gaussian scale mixture model, which has been used for various image restoration tasks [23,40,41]. The early work [14] proposed a class of sparse coding models that utilizes a LSM prior to model dependencies among coefficients. In [22], the LSM distribution has also been used to model impulse noise and remove mixture noise effectively. [12] propose a novel robust tensor approximation framework for the LSM modeling of three-dimensional data. Different from the existing LSM model for image restoration with manually selected scale priors, we use the DCNNs to learn both the scale prior and local means in the LSM model. Through end-to-end training, all parameters are learned jointly.

3   Method

3.1   Problem Formulation

The widely accepted degradation model assumes that the LR image is produced by downsampling HR image after the convolution with blur kernel, which can be mathematically expressed as $y = (x * k) \downarrow_s + n$, where x is the original HR image, y is the degraded LR image, $*$ denotes the convolution with blur kernel k, $\downarrow_s$ is the s-fold downsampling operation and n denotes the additional noise. The matrix-vector form can be formulated as

$$y = \mathbf{A}x + n, \tag{1}$$

where $\mathbf{A} = \mathbf{DH}$ denotes the degradation operator ($\mathbf{H}$ is the blur matrix constructed from the kernel k and $\mathbf{D}$ is the downsampling matrix). Then blind SR refers to the process of estimating $\mathbf{H}$ and recovering x from y and $\mathbf{H}$, which is a highly ill-posed inverse problem. We formulate it as a maximum a posteriori (MAP) estimation problem

$$p(\mathbf{H}, x|y) = p(\mathbf{H}|y)\, p(x|\mathbf{H}, y). \tag{2}$$

Take logarithms on both sides of the equation

$$\log p(\mathbf{H}, x|y) \propto \log p(\mathbf{H}|y) + \log p(y|\mathbf{H}, x) + \log p(x). \tag{3}$$

Then solving the MAP problem can be expressed as

$$(\mathbf{H}^*, x^*) = \underset{\mathbf{H},x}{\operatorname{argmax}} \log p(\mathbf{H}|y) + \log p(y|\mathbf{H}, x) + \log p(x). \tag{4}$$

The above optimization problem can be converted into two subproblems

$$\mathbf{H}^* = \underset{\mathbf{H}}{\operatorname{argmax}} \log p(\mathbf{H}|y), \tag{5a}$$

$$x^* = \underset{x}{\operatorname{argmax}} \log p(y|\mathbf{H}, x) + \log p(x). \tag{5b}$$

Their specific meanings are clear: Eq. (5a) denotes the estimation of blur kernel and Eq. (5b) denotes reconstructing HR image from LR image and the estimated kernel.

3.2 Uncertainty Learning in Kernel Estimation

For the estimation of blur kernel, there exist some inevitable errors in the prediction results due to noise interference and the ill-posed nature. To properly take the uncertainty of the prediction into account, we introduce uncertainty learning (UL) to the process of blur kernel estimation. For the likelihood term $p(\mathbf{H}|y)$ in Eq. (5a), we propose to model it by the following Gaussian distribution,

$$p(\mathbf{H}|y) \sim \mathcal{N}(k|\mu(y), \sigma^2(y)), \tag{6}$$

where $\mu(y)$ and $\sigma^2(y)$ denote the mappings from y to the posterior distribution parameters (μ and σ) of k. However, it is difficult to calculate the mappings explicitly. As shown in Fig. 2(a), we parameterize the two mappings into deep networks, - i.e. $\mu = f_{\Theta_1}(y), \sigma = f_{\Theta_2}(y)$, where Θ_1 and Θ_2 represent the parameters of mean and variance branches respectively. Specifically, the LR image y is input into a DCNN to extract the feature maps of the underlying blur kernel. Then the features go through two 3×3 convolution layers to learn the mean and variance of prediction result simultaneously. From another perspective, μ can be interpreted as the identity mapping of the blur kernel and σ is the uncertainty of the predicted μ. Then we generate an equivalent sampling representation z through re-parameterization method [29]

$$z = \mu + \epsilon\sigma, \quad \epsilon \sim \mathcal{N}(0, \mathbf{I}), \tag{7}$$

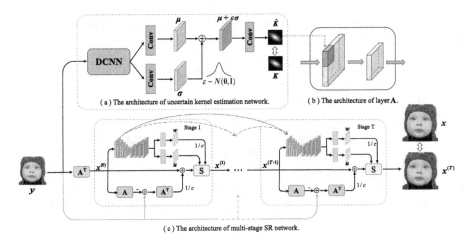

(a) The architecture of uncertain kernel estimation network.

(b) The architecture of layer **A**.

(c) The architecture of multi-stage SR network.

Fig. 2. Overview of the proposed KULNet for blind SR. The architectures of (a) the uncertain kernel estimation network, (b) the layer **A**, which contains a convolution layer with the estimated kernel and a downsampling layer, (c) the multi-stage SR network.

where ϵ denotes a random noise sampled from the normal distribution. Since μ is corrupted by σ during the training period, z is not a deterministic point embedding anymore. However, we notice that the model tends to predict small σ for all samples to suppress the instable components if there are no constraints on the embeddings. Similar to [6], we adopt the Kullback-Leibler (KL) divergence regularization term to enforce $\mathcal{N}\left(\mu, \sigma^2\right)$ to be close to the standard normal distribution $\mathcal{N}(\mathbf{0}, \mathbf{I})$,

$$
\begin{aligned}
\mathcal{L}_{kl} &= KL\left[\mathcal{N}\left(\mu, \sigma^2\right) \| \mathcal{N}(\mathbf{0}, \mathbf{I})\right] \\
&= -\frac{1}{2}\left(1 + \log \sigma^2 - \mu^2 - \sigma^2\right).
\end{aligned}
\tag{8}
$$

Then the sampled embedding z is input to the final convolution layer to obtain the kernel estimation.

3.3 Multi-stage SR Network

LSM Model for SR. To solve Eq. (5b), we note that $p(y|\mathbf{H}, x)$ is the likelihood term and $p(x)$ is the prior distribution of x. The likelihood term can be generally modeled by a Gaussian distribution

$$
p(y|\mathbf{H}, x) = \frac{1}{\sqrt{2\pi}\sigma_n} \exp\left(-\frac{\|y - \mathbf{D}\mathbf{H}x\|_2^2}{2\sigma_n^2}\right).
\tag{9}
$$

For the prior term $p(x)$ of the HR image, we propose to characterize each pixel x_i with a *nonzero-mean* Laplacian distribution of variance $2\theta_i^2$ and mean u_i

$$
p\left(x_i|\theta_i\right) = \frac{1}{2\theta_i} \exp\left(-\frac{|x_i - u_i|}{\theta_i}\right).
\tag{10}
$$

With the assumption that x_i and θ_i are independent, we can model $\boldsymbol{x}$ with the following LSM model

$$p(\boldsymbol{x}) = \prod_i p\left(x_i\right), \ p\left(x_i\right) = \int_0^\infty p\left(x_i|\theta_i\right) p\left(\theta_i\right) d\theta_i, \tag{11}$$

where the scale prior $p(\theta_i)$ can be modeled by a general energy function - e.g., $p\left(\theta_i\right) \propto \exp\left(-J\left(\theta_i\right)\right)$. Then Eq. (5b) is equivalent to a bivariate estimation problem - i.e.,

$$(\boldsymbol{x}^*, \boldsymbol{\theta}^*) = \underset{\boldsymbol{x}, \boldsymbol{\theta}}{\operatorname{argmax}} \log p(\mathbf{H}, \boldsymbol{y}|\boldsymbol{x}) + \log p(\boldsymbol{x}|\boldsymbol{\theta}) + \log p(\boldsymbol{\theta}). \tag{12}$$

By substituting the Gaussian likelihood term of Eq. (9), the prior terms of Eq. (10) into the MAP estimator Eq. (12), we can obtain the following objective function

$$(\boldsymbol{x}^*, \boldsymbol{\theta}^*) = \underset{\boldsymbol{x}, \boldsymbol{\theta}}{\operatorname{argmin}} \frac{1}{2}\|\boldsymbol{y} - \mathbf{DH}\boldsymbol{x}\|_2^2 + \sum_{i=1}^N \frac{\sigma_n^2}{\theta_i}|x_i - u_i| + \Omega(\boldsymbol{\theta}), \tag{13}$$

where $\Omega(\boldsymbol{\theta}) = \sigma_n^2 \sum_{i=1}^N \log \theta_i + \sigma_n^2 J(\boldsymbol{\theta})$, then the SR problem can be solved by alternating optimizing $\boldsymbol{x}$ and $\boldsymbol{\theta}$. For the $\boldsymbol{x}$-subproblem, with fixed $\boldsymbol{\theta}$, we can solve $\boldsymbol{x}$ by

$$\boldsymbol{x}^* = \underset{\boldsymbol{x}}{\operatorname{argmin}} \frac{1}{2}\|\boldsymbol{y} - \mathbf{DH}\boldsymbol{x}\|_2^2 + \sum_{i=1}^N w_i|x_i - u_i|, \tag{14}$$

where $w_i = \sigma_n^2/\theta_i$. Inspired by recent advances in image denoising [13,38], the mean u_i can be predicted by a deep denoising module, i.e. $u_i = f(x_i)$, where $f(\cdot)$ denotes a denoiser. Then Eq. (14) can be solved by the iterative shrinkage-thresholding algorithm [8] as

$$\boldsymbol{x}^{(t+1)} = \mathcal{S}_{\boldsymbol{\tau}^{(t)}, \boldsymbol{u}^{(t)}} \left(\boldsymbol{x}^{(t)} + \frac{1}{c}\mathbf{A}^\top \left(\boldsymbol{y} - \mathbf{A}\boldsymbol{x}^{(t)}\right) \right), \tag{15}$$

where $\mathbf{A} = \mathbf{DH}$, $\mathbf{A}^\top = \mathbf{H}^\top \mathbf{D}^\top$ and c is chosen to ensure convergence. $\mathcal{S}_{\boldsymbol{\tau}^{(t)}, \boldsymbol{u}^{(t)}}(\cdot)$ denotes a generalized shrinkage operator with threshold $\boldsymbol{\tau}^{(t)} = \frac{w^{(t)}}{c}$ and $\boldsymbol{u}^{(t)}$, which is defined by

$$\mathcal{S}_{\boldsymbol{\tau}, \boldsymbol{u}}(\boldsymbol{t}) = \begin{cases} \boldsymbol{t} + \boldsymbol{\tau}, & \boldsymbol{t} < \boldsymbol{u} - \boldsymbol{\tau} \\ \boldsymbol{u}, & \boldsymbol{u} - \boldsymbol{\tau} \le \boldsymbol{t} \le \boldsymbol{u} + \boldsymbol{\tau} \\ \boldsymbol{t} - \boldsymbol{\tau}, & \boldsymbol{t} > \boldsymbol{u} + \boldsymbol{\tau} \end{cases} \tag{16}$$

Similarly, the $\boldsymbol{\theta}$-subproblem is equivalent to solve the $\boldsymbol{w}$-subproblem. With a fixed $\boldsymbol{x}$, we have

$$\boldsymbol{w}^* = \underset{\boldsymbol{w}}{\operatorname{argmin}} \sum_{i=1}^N w_i|x_i - u_i| + \Omega(\boldsymbol{w}). \tag{17}$$

Iterative algorithms [40] can be used to solve $\boldsymbol{w}$, which depends on a hand-crafted prior $p(\boldsymbol{\theta})$ in $\Omega(\boldsymbol{w})$ - e.g., Jeffrey's prior. Instead of using a fixed prior, we propose to estimate $\boldsymbol{w}^{(t)}$ from $\boldsymbol{x}^{(t)}$ using a universal DCNN-based denoiser [13,38].

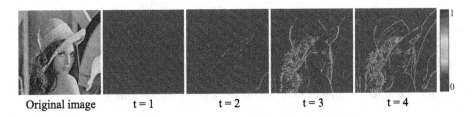

Original image   t = 1   t = 2   t = 3   t = 4

Fig. 3. The visualization of the learned regularization parameter w estimated in 4 stages.

Multi-stage Network for SR. Despite the theoretical rigor, alternatively solving x and w requires many iterations to converge and need a hand-crafted prior $p(\theta)$. Meanwhile, all parameters and the denoiser can not be jointly optimized. To address these issues, we replace all variables in Eq. (15) with a common expression containing x, so that x and w can be jointly optimized in a unified framework.

$$x^{(t+1)} = \mathcal{S}_{\frac{\mathcal{G}_w(x^{(t)})}{c},\mathcal{G}_u(x^{(t)})}\left(x^{(t)} + \frac{1}{c}\mathbf{A}^\top\left(y - \mathbf{A}x^{(t)}\right)\right), \qquad (18)$$

where $\mathcal{G}_w(\cdot)$ denotes the CNN generator for estimating w, and the mean u is also predicted by a generator - i.e., $u^{(t)} = \mathcal{G}_u(x^{(t)})$. Note that the blur kernel $\mathbf{H}$ in $\mathbf{A}$ has been estimated from y by our uncertain kernel estimation network. Similar to [13], we can unfold the iterative optimization in Eq. (18) into a multi-stage network implementation.

Network Architecture. The architecture of the proposed multi-stage SR network is shown in Fig. 2(c). All modules in the network strictly correspond to the steps in the optimization process, the network executes T iterations of Eq. (18). The input LR image $y \in \mathbb{R}^{C \times H \times W}$ first goes through a convolution (Conv) layer parameterized by the degradation matrix $\mathbf{A}^\top$ for an initial estimate $x^{(0)} \in \mathbb{R}^{C \times sH \times sW}$, s denotes the scale factor. For the upper branch, $x^{(t)}$ is fed to a U-Net followed by two generators to estimate the weight $w^{(t)}$ and mean $u^{(t)}$. The lightweight U-net consists of five encoding blocks (EBs) and four decoding blocks (DBs), each EB and DB contain two Conv layers with ReLU activation function. The average pooling and bilinear interpolation layer are used to downsample and upsample the feature maps. The channel number of the output features in 5 EBs and 4 DBs are set to 32, 64, 64, 128, 128, 128, 64, 64, and 32, respectively. The weight and mean generator both contain three Conv layers. The estimated weight w in each stage are visualized (with normalization) in Fig. 3, we can see that w is sparse and helps the network concentrate more and more on high-frequency edges and textures.

To leverage information of multiple stages, we use long connections to concatenate previous features with current features, leading to more faithful reconstruction of the missing high-frequency information. As illustrated in Fig. 2(b), the layers $\mathbf{A}$ and $\mathbf{A}^\top$ are designed for a specific blur kernel $\mathbf{H}$ obtained by our uncertain kernel estimation network. For Gaussian degradation, $\mathbf{A} = \mathbf{DH}$, where $\mathbf{H}$ and $\mathbf{D}$ denote the Gaussian blur matrix and the downsampling matrix respectively. In layer $\mathbf{A}$, the input feature maps are convoluted with the estimated blur kernel $\mathbf{H}$ and then downsampled via bicubic interpolation. Similarly, the layer $\mathbf{A}^\top = \mathbf{H}^\top \mathbf{D}^\top$ corresponds to first upsample the LR image and then put the upsampled image into a transpose convolution layer with the blur kernel. Module $\boldsymbol{S}$ denotes a shrinkage operator with threshold $\boldsymbol{w}$ and $\boldsymbol{u}$.

3.4   Network Training

We combine the above uncertain kernel estimation network and multi-stage SR network into a whole training framework, called Kernel Uncertianty Learning network (KULNet). For the kernel estimation network, we use a combination loss of the $\mathcal{L}_1$ loss between the estimated kernel $\hat{\boldsymbol{K}}$ and the GT kernel $\boldsymbol{K}$ ($\mathcal{L}_e = \frac{1}{m}\sum_{i=1}^m \|\hat{\boldsymbol{K}}_i - \boldsymbol{K}_i\|_1$) and the KL loss in Eq. (8), denoted by $\mathcal{L}_K = \mathcal{L}_e + \lambda\mathcal{L}_{kl}$, where λ is set to be 0.001. For the SR network, all parameters of each stage are shared except c. The $\mathcal{L}_1$ loss function is adopted to train the proposed deep network, written as

$$\mathcal{L}_1 = \frac{1}{m}\sum_{i=1}^m \|\mathcal{F}(\boldsymbol{y}_i) - \boldsymbol{x}_i\|_1, \tag{19}$$

where m denotes the total number of the training samples, $\boldsymbol{y}_i$ and $\boldsymbol{x}_i$ denote the i-th pair of LR and HR image patches, and $\mathcal{F}(\boldsymbol{y}_i)$ denotes the SR image by the network. The total loss is described as $\mathcal{L}_{total} = \mathcal{L}_K + \mathcal{L}_1$. The ADAM optimizer [28] is used to train the network with setting $\beta_1 = 0.9$, $\beta_2 = 0.999$ and $\epsilon = 10^{-8}$. The learning rate is set as 2×10^{-4}. The parameters of the convolutional layers are initialized by the Xavier initialization [19]. We implement the proposed method by PyTorch and train the network using an Nvidia RTX 2080Ti GPU.

4   Experimental Results

4.1   Datasets and Settings

Following [15,46], the training set consists of 3450 HR images, including 800 images in DIV2K [1] and 2650 images in Flickr2K [45]. The LR training patches are generated by Gaussian blur and bicubic downsampling with a size of 48×48. Four standard benchmark datasets: Set5 [5], Set14 [49], BSD100 [36] and Urban100 [21] are used for testing. We train our network on the general degradation with anisotropic Gaussian kernels and noises, the Gaussian kernels are generated by randomly selecting the kernel width determined by a diagonal covariance matrix with $\sigma_1, \sigma_2 \sim U(0.2, 4)$ and a random rotation angle $\theta \sim U(0, \pi)$, the range of noise level is set to $[0, 25]$. The kernel size is fixed to 21×21. For evaluation, 9 typical blur kernels in [46] and different noise levels are used to generate the test images. Performances in terms of PSNR and SSIM metrics are conducted on the Y channel of YCbCr space.

Fig. 4. The visualization of anisotropic blur kernels used for testing.

Table 1. MAE ($\downarrow$) results of the estimated kernels by kernel estimation network with or without Uncertainty Learning (UL).

Kernel estimation	Noise	1	2	3	4	5	6	7	8	9	Average
w/o UL	0	0.252	0.174	0.204	0.167	0.151	0.226	0.181	0.157	0.195	0.190
	10	0.259	0.183	0.218	0.186	0.171	0.240	0.201	0.183	0.216	0.206
	20	0.269	0.202	0.251	0.235	0.223	0.271	0.251	0.267	0.302	0.252
w/UL	0	**0.191**	**0.120**	**0.181**	**0.140**	**0.095**	**0.208**	**0.168**	**0.098**	**0.117**	**0.146**
	10	**0.212**	**0.141**	**0.186**	**0.143**	**0.110**	**0.210**	**0.170**	**0.119**	**0.145**	**0.160**
	20	**0.239**	**0.152**	**0.189**	**0.148**	**0.119**	**0.217**	**0.176**	**0.136**	**0.169**	**0.172**

Table 2. PSNR results produced by the proposed multi-stage network with ($\checkmark$) or without ($\times$) Uncertainty Learning (UL).

Scale	UL	Set5			Set14			BSD100			Urban100		
Noise		0	10	20	0	10	20	0	10	20	0	10	20
×2	$\times$	33.78	30.76	29.27	30.55	28.21	27.10	29.87	27.56	26.54	27.75	25.82	24.93
	$\checkmark$	**34.36**	**31.03**	**29.54**	**30.93**	**28.42**	**27.27**	**30.43**	**27.69**	**26.62**	**28.16**	**26.10**	**25.08**
×3	$\times$	31.77	29.72	28.08	28.39	27.24	26.20	27.72	26.67	25.77	25.88	24.95	24.22
	$\checkmark$	**32.27**	**29.91**	**28.34**	**28.92**	**27.53**	**26.45**	**28.17**	**26.83**	**25.88**	**26.26**	**25.19**	**24.31**
×4	$\times$	30.39	28.80	27.34	27.49	26.52	25.53	26.82	25.97	25.15	24.86	24.15	23.49
	$\checkmark$	**30.79**	**29.07**	**27.56**	**27.81**	**26.76**	**25.74**	**27.02**	**26.12**	**25.27**	**25.07**	**24.36**	**23.62**

4.2   Comparing UL with Deterministic Network

In the proposed kernel estimation network, uncertainty learning is used to improve the robustness to the degraded images. To demonstrate the effectiveness of uncertainty learning, we modify the network into a deterministic model by removing the Conv layer of variance σ and the Gaussian sampling operation. The KL loss is also excluded during training. The test images are generated by applying the blur kernels to the datasets followed by subsampling of scale factors 2, 3 and 4, then added with additive Gaussian noise. The visualization of the 9 anisotropic blur kernels used for testing is shown in Fig. 4.

We first compare the mean absolute error (MAE) of the blur kernels estimated by our uncertain network and the modified deterministic network. As shown in Table 1, by introducing uncertainty learning, we can estimate more accurate kernels with lower error compared with deterministic network. Note that when the LR image is disturbed by large noise, the deterministic network suffer an obvious performance drop. And our uncertain network can handle the noise inherent in the observation data well, thus produces more stable results robustly. We further verify the blind SR performance of the multi-stage network with two kinds of kernel estimations. Table 2 and Fig. 1 prove that our multi-stage network can produce higher PSNR results and shaper edges due to more accurate estimation of blur kernels.

4.3   Comparison with State-of-the-Art Methods

We have compared our method with several recent state-of-the-art blind SR methods, including ZSSR [42], IKC [15], DASR [46], KOALAnet [27] and MANet [32]. For a fair comparison, the results are generated by the official codes released by authors or directly cited from the original papers; all models are trained under the same training settings. Since IKC model was trained under a noise-free isotropic setting, we also retrained it under an anisotropic blur kernel setting with noise.

Quantitative and Visual Comparison. Following [46], anisotropic blur kernels (as illustrated in Fig. 4) and different noise levels are used to evaluate the performance. The average PSNR results of the test methods for blind SR are reported in Table 3. Since zero-shot method ZSSR (blur kernel estimated by KernelGAN [4]) only leverages the internal information of test images, it has a relatively limited performance. We noticed that the image noise is preserved and magnified significantly after SR by ZSSR, so it is only tested under a noise-free setting. It can be seen that MANet slightly outperforms KOALAnet. And we have achieved some superior advantages over the other methods, especially at higher noise levels and scale factors. We compare the blind SR visualization results produced by different methods in Fig. 5, the specific blur kernel used for generating the LR image is displayed on the upper left. The LR images with a scale factor of 4 are added with Gaussian noise of level 10. It is obvious that the proposed method can reconstruct more high-frequency details and sharper edges than other methods.

Computational Complexity Comparison. We have further compared the proposed network with other methods in terms of computational complexity. The total number of parameters of each deep network are listed in Table 4. We can see that the MANet contains the largest number of parameters over three times of the proposed network, as its RRDB-SFT architecture is very deep. Since we enforce the DCNNs in each stage to share the same parameters, the total number of parameters of the proposed multi-stage network is much smaller. Though there are $T = 4$ stages in the proposed network, the running time is similar to that of MANet. This is because the feature maps in the U-Net structure are gradually downsampled, thus the computational complexity can be much reduced.

4.4   Results on Real-World Images

We also conduct experiments on real-world images to demonstrate the generalization property and effectiveness of our method. We have only compared the visualization results of different methods, as there is no ground-truth. All models are trained on the anisotropic setting with noise, since real-world degradation is complicated. As shown in Fig. 6, our method can produce more natural and visually more pleasant results than other methods.

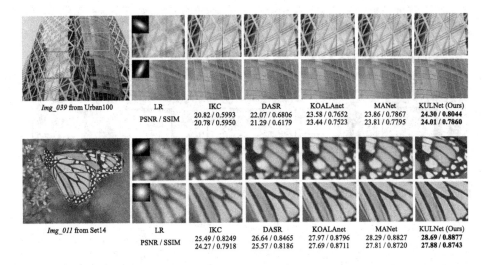

| Img_039 from Urban100 | LR
PSNR / SSIM | IKC
20.82 / 0.5993
20.78 / 0.5950 | DASR
22.07 / 0.6806
21.29 / 0.6179 | KOALAnet
23.58 / 0.7652
23.44 / 0.7523 | MANet
23.86 / 0.7867
23.81 / 0.7795 | KULNet (Ours)
24.30 / 0.8044
24.01 / 0.7860 |

| Img_011 from Set14 | LR
PSNR / SSIM | IKC
25.49 / 0.8249
24.27 / 0.7918 | DASR
26.64 / 0.8465
25.57 / 0.8186 | KOALAnet
27.97 / 0.8796
27.69 / 0.8711 | MANet
28.29 / 0.8827
27.81 / 0.8720 | KULNet (Ours)
28.69 / 0.8877
27.88 / 0.8743 |

Fig. 5. Visual comparison to other methods. The blur kernels are illustrated on the top left. Noise levels are set to 0 and 10 for scale factor ×2 and ×4, respectively.

Table 3. Quantitative comparison of the SOTA blind SR methods and the proposed method on various datasets and noise levels.

Method	Scale	Set5			Set14			BSD100			Urban100		
Noise		0	10	20	0	10	20	0	10	20	0	10	20
KernelGAN [4]+ZSSR [42]	×2	26.94	–	–	23.96	–	–	23.17	–	–	21.69	–	–
IKC [15]		27.89	27.62	26.86	26.29	25.90	25.26	26.03	25.67	25.12	23.84	23.35	22.82
DASR [46]		29.89	28.13	27.18	27.25	26.06	25.41	26.97	25.78	25.21	24.58	23.54	22.98
KOALAnet [27]		33.96	30.59	29.05	30.53	27.98	26.87	29.77	27.23	26.28	27.56	25.59	24.52
MANet [32]		33.99	30.77	29.28	30.61	28.22	27.11	29.85	27.48	26.49	27.64	25.71	24.76
KULNet (Ours)		**34.36**	**31.03**	**29.54**	**30.93**	**28.42**	**27.27**	**30.43**	**27.69**	**26.62**	**28.16**	**26.10**	**25.08**
IKC [15]	×3	28.40	27.01	26.00	26.42	25.32	24.54	26.20	25.20	24.56	23.59	23.24	22.35
DASR [46]		29.40	27.54	26.43	26.92	25.68	24.89	26.65	25.42	24.76	24.23	23.45	22.57
MANet [32]		31.78	29.65	28.10	28.50	27.22	26.18	27.79	26.64	25.74	25.42	24.62	23.85
KULNet (Ours)		**32.27**	**29.91**	**28.34**	**28.92**	**27.53**	**26.45**	**28.17**	**26.83**	**25.88**	**26.26**	**25.19**	**24.31**
KernelGAN [4]+ZSSR [42]	×4	23.85	–	–	22.55	–	–	21.37	–	–	19.12	–	–
IKC [15]		27.91	26.51	25.52	26.06	24.92	24.19	25.80	24.83	24.21	23.26	22.47	21.90
DASR [46]		30.33	27.29	25.94	27.31	25.48	24.54	26.77	25.16	24.42	24.34	22.98	22.28
KOALAnet [27]		30.36	28.56	27.13	27.35	26.19	25.33	26.72	25.73	24.95	24.37	23.76	23.01
MANet [32]		30.38	28.73	27.31	27.41	26.46	25.50	26.78	25.96	25.16	24.49	23.91	23.23
KULNet (Ours)		**30.79**	**29.07**	**27.56**	**27.81**	**26.76**	**25.74**	**27.02**	**26.12**	**25.27**	**25.07**	**24.36**	**23.62**

Table 4. Complexity comparison with other methods. The average running time is measured on the Set14 dataset for ×4.

Method	IKC	DASR	KOALAnet	MANet	Ours
#Params	5.2M	5.8 M	6.2 M	14.3 M	3.9 M
Run Time(ms/image)	568	96	991	157	176
PSNR(dB)	24.92	25.48	26.29	26.46	26.76

| Real-world image | DASR | KOALAnet | MANet | KULNet (Ours) |

Fig. 6. Visualization results of different methods on real-world images upscaled by ×4.

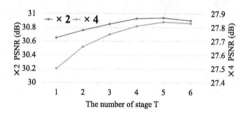

Fig. 7. Ablation study on the effect of the number of stage T.

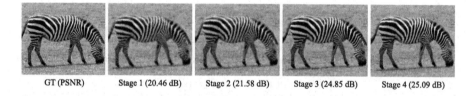

| GT (PSNR) | Stage 1 (20.46 dB) | Stage 2 (21.58 dB) | Stage 3 (24.85 dB) | Stage 4 (25.09 dB) |

Fig. 8. Intermediate visual results of different stages for ×4 blind SR.

4.5   Ablation Study

We conduct several ablation studies to verify the impacts of different modules in the proposed network, including the number of stages, the value of hyperparameter λ and the effect of dense connections.

Figure 7 shows the ×2 and ×4 PSNR results on Set14 produced by the proposed method with different number of stages, we can draw a conclusion that increasing the stage number T leads to better results. We set $T = 4$ in our implementation, targeting a good trade-off between SR performance and computational complexity. Moreover, we have shown the intermediate image comparison results of different stages in Fig. 8, from which we can see that more high-frequency information has been recovered along with the increasing number of stages during the process of SR reconstruction.

Table 5. Results trained with different value of hyperparameter λ.

λ	0	0.0001	0.001	0.01	0.1	1
Set14	26.49	26.67	26.76	26.71	26.15	25.89
BSD100	25.95	26.01	26.12	26.05	25.62	25.43

We have studied the influence of KL divergence regularization term by adjusting the value of hyperparameter λ. The PSNR results on Set14 and BSD100 are shown in Table 5. As the previous analysis has shown, if there are no constraints on mean and variance ($\lambda = 0$), the network tends to predict small σ for all samples, thus there exists almost no uncertainty in the network, the results are also similar to the deterministic networks in Sect. 4.2. As λ increasing, uncertainty learning can effectively improve the performance. When the KL constraint is too strong ($\lambda = 1$), the network will predict large variance for all samples, making the mean μ deviate from the original feature maps. Here we set λ as 0.001.

Finally, we have conducted an ablation study on the proposed network with or without dense connections. The PSNR results increase 0.13 dB on the Set14 dataset for a scale factor of 4, justifying the effectiveness of dense connections to KULNet.

5   Conclusions

In this paper, we formulate the blind SR problem as a joint maximum a posteriori probability (MAP) problem for estimating the unknown kernel and high-resolution image simultaneously. To improve the robustness of the kernel estimation network, we introduce uncertainty learning in the latent space instead of using deterministic feature maps. Then we propose a novel multi-stage SR network by unfolding the MAP estimator with the learned LSM prior and the estimated kernel. Both the scale prior coefficient and the local means of the LSM model are estimated through deep convolutional neural networks. All parameters of the MAP estimation algorithm and the DCNN parameters are jointly optimized through end-to-end training. Extensive experimental results on both synthetic and real datasets demonstrate that the proposed method outperforms existing state-of-the-art methods. Future research directions include the extension of this work to spatially varying blur kernels and the generalization study to more real-world test images.

Acknowledgement. This work was supported in part by the National Key R&D Program of China under Grant 2018AAA0101400 and the Natural Science Foundation of China under Grant 61991451, Grant 61632019, Grant 61621005, and Grant 61836008.

References

1. Agustsson, E., Timofte, R.: Ntire 2017 challenge on single image super-resolution: dataset and study. In: Proceedings of the IEEE Conference on Computer Vision and Pattern Recognition Workshops, pp. 126–135 (2017)
2. Badrinarayanan, V., Kendall, A., Cipolla, R.: SegNet: a deep convolutional encoder-decoder architecture for image segmentation. IEEE Trans. Pattern Anal. Mach. Intell. **39**(12), 2481–2495 (2017)
3. Begin, I., Ferrie, F.: Blind super-resolution using a learning-based approach. In: Proceedings of the 17th International Conference on Pattern Recognition, 2004. ICPR 2004, vol. 2, pp. 85–89. IEEE (2004)
4. Bell-Kligler, S., Shocher, A., Irani, M.: Blind super-resolution kernel estimation using an internal-GAN. In: NeurIPS, pp. 284–293 (2019)
5. Bevilacqua, M., Roumy, A., Guillemot, C., Alberi-Morel, M.L.: Low-complexity single-image super-resolution based on nonnegative neighbor embedding (2012)
6. Chang, J., Lan, Z., Cheng, C., Wei, Y.: Data uncertainty learning in face recognition. In: Proceedings of the IEEE/CVF Conference on Computer Vision and Pattern Recognition, pp. 5710–5719 (2020)
7. Cornillere, V., Djelouah, A., Yifan, W., Sorkine-Hornung, O., Schroers, C.: Blind image super-resolution with spatially variant degradations. ACM Trans. Graph. (TOG) **38**(6), 1–13 (2019)
8. Daubechies, I., Defrise, M., De Mol, C.: An iterative thresholding algorithm for linear inverse problems with a sparsity constraint. Commun. Pure Appl. Math. J. Issued Courant Inst. Math. Sci. **57**(11), 1413–1457 (2004)
9. Der Kiureghian, A., Ditlevsen, O.: Aleatory or epistemic? does it matter? Struct. Saf. **31**(2), 105–112 (2009)
10. Dong, C., Loy, C.C., He, K., Tang, X.: Learning a deep convolutional network for image super-resolution. In: Fleet, D., Pajdla, T., Schiele, B., Tuytelaars, T. (eds.) ECCV 2014. LNCS, vol. 8692, pp. 184–199. Springer, Cham (2014). https://doi.org/10.1007/978-3-319-10593-2_13
11. Dong, C., Loy, C.C., Tang, X.: Accelerating the super-resolution convolutional neural network. In: Leibe, B., Matas, J., Sebe, N., Welling, M. (eds.) ECCV 2016. LNCS, vol. 9906, pp. 391–407. Springer, Cham (2016). https://doi.org/10.1007/978-3-319-46475-6_25
12. Dong, W., Huang, T., Shi, G., Ma, Y., Li, X.: Robust tensor approximation with laplacian scale mixture modeling for multiframe image and video denoising. IEEE J. Sel. Top. Sig. Process. **12**(6), 1435–1448 (2018)
13. Dong, W., Wang, P., Yin, W., Shi, G., Wu, F., Lu, X.: Denoising prior driven deep neural network for image restoration. IEEE Trans. Pattern Anal. Mach. intell. **41**(10), 2305–2318 (2018)
14. Garrigues, P., Olshausen, B.: Group sparse coding with a laplacian scale mixture prior. In: Advances in Neural Information Processing Systems, vol. 23 (2010)
15. Gu, J., Lu, H., Zuo, W., Dong, C.: Blind super-resolution with iterative kernel correction. In: Proceedings of the IEEE/CVF Conference on Computer Vision and Pattern Recognition, pp. 1604–1613 (2019)
16. Gu, Y., Jin, Z., Chiu, S.C.: Active learning combining uncertainty and diversity for multi-class image classification. IET Comput. Vis. **9**(3), 400–407 (2015)
17. Haris, M., Shakhnarovich, G., Ukita, N.: Deep back-projection networks for super-resolution. In: Proceedings of the IEEE Conference on Computer Vision and Pattern Recognition, pp. 1664–1673 (2018)

18. He, H., Siu, W.C.: Single image super-resolution using gaussian process regression. In: CVPR 2011, pp. 449–456. IEEE (2011)
19. He, K., Zhang, X., Ren, S., Sun, J.: Delving deep into rectifiers: surpassing human-level performance on ImageNet classification. In: Proceedings of the IEEE International Conference on Computer Vision, pp. 1026–1034 (2015)
20. He, Y., Yap, K.H., Chen, L., Chau, L.P.: A soft map framework for blind super-resolution image reconstruction. Image Vis. Comput. **27**(4), 364–373 (2009)
21. Huang, J.B., Singh, A., Ahuja, N.: Single image super-resolution from transformed self-exemplars. In: Proceedings of the IEEE Conference on Computer Vision and Pattern Recognition, pp. 5197–5206 (2015)
22. Huang, T., Dong, W., Xie, X., Shi, G., Bai, X.: Mixed noise removal via laplacian scale mixture modeling and nonlocal low-rank approximation. IEEE Trans. Image Process. **26**(7), 3171–3186 (2017)
23. Huang, T., Dong, W., Yuan, X., Wu, J., Shi, G.: Deep gaussian scale mixture prior for spectral compressive imaging. In: Proceedings of the IEEE/CVF Conference on Computer Vision and Pattern Recognition, pp. 16216–16225 (2021)
24. Jo, Y., Oh, S.W., Vajda, P., Kim, S.J.: Tackling the ill-posedness of super-resolution through adaptive target generation. In: Proceedings of the IEEE/CVF Conference on Computer Vision and Pattern Recognition, pp. 16236–16245 (2021)
25. Kendall, A., Gal, Y.: What uncertainties do we need in bayesian deep learning for computer vision? In: NeurIPS (2017)
26. Kim, J., Lee, J.K., Lee, K.M.: Accurate image super-resolution using very deep convolutional networks. In: Proceedings of the IEEE Conference on Computer Vision and Pattern Recognition, pp. 1646–1654 (2016)
27. Kim, S.Y., Sim, H., Kim, M.: Koalanet: blind super-resolution using kernel-oriented adaptive local adjustment. In: Proceedings of the IEEE/CVF Conference on Computer Vision and Pattern Recognition, pp. 10611–10620 (2021)
28. Kingma, D.P., Ba, J.: Adam: a method for stochastic optimization. arXiv preprint arXiv:1412.6980 (2014)
29. Kingma, D.P., Welling, M.: Auto-encoding variational bayes. In: ICLR (2014)
30. Ledig, C., et al.: Photo-realistic single image super-resolution using a generative adversarial network. In: Proceedings of the IEEE Conference on Computer Vision and Pattern Recognition, pp. 4681–4690 (2017)
31. Lee, C., Chung, K.S.: Gram: gradient rescaling attention model for data uncertainty estimation in single image super resolution. In: 2019 18th IEEE International Conference On Machine Learning And Applications (ICMLA), pp. 8–13. IEEE (2019)
32. Liang, J., Sun, G., Zhang, K., Van Gool, L., Timofte, R.: Mutual affine network for spatially variant kernel estimation in blind image super-resolution. In: Proceedings of the IEEE/CVF International Conference on Computer Vision, pp. 4096–4105 (2021)
33. Liang, J., Zhang, K., Gu, S., Van Gool, L., Timofte, R.: Flow-based kernel prior with application to blind super-resolution. In: Proceedings of the IEEE/CVF Conference on Computer Vision and Pattern Recognition, pp. 10601–10610 (2021)
34. Lim, B., Son, S., Kim, H., Nah, S., Mu Lee, K.: Enhanced deep residual networks for single image super-resolution. In: Proceedings of the IEEE Conference on Computer Vision and Pattern Recognition Workshops, pp. 136–144 (2017)
35. Luo, Z., Huang, Y., Li, S., Wang, L., Tan, T.: Unfolding the alternating optimization for blind super resolution. arXiv preprint arXiv:2010.02631 (2020)

36. Martin, D., Fowlkes, C., Tal, D., Malik, J.: A database of human segmented natural images and its application to evaluating segmentation algorithms and measuring ecological statistics. In: Proceedings Eighth IEEE International Conference on Computer Vision. ICCV 2001, vol. 2, pp. 416–423. IEEE (2001)
37. Michaeli, T., Irani, M.: Nonparametric blind super-resolution. In: Proceedings of the IEEE International Conference on Computer Vision, pp. 945–952 (2013)
38. Ning, Q., Dong, W., Shi, G., Li, L., Li, X.: Accurate and lightweight image super-resolution with model-guided deep unfolding network. IEEE J. Sel. Top. Sig. Process. **15**(2), 240–252 (2020)
39. Ning, Q., Dong, W., Shi, G., Li, L., Li, X.: Uncertainty-driven loss for single image super-resolution. In: NeurIPS (2021)
40. Ning, Q., Dong, W., Wu, F., Wu, J., Lin, J., Shi, G.: Spatial-temporal gaussian scale mixture modeling for foreground estimation. In: Proceedings of the AAAI Conference on Artificial Intelligence, vol. 34, pp. 11791–11798 (2020)
41. Shi, G., Huang, T., Dong, W., Wu, J., Xie, X.: Robust foreground estimation via structured gaussian scale mixture modeling. IEEE Trans. Image Process. **27**(10), 4810–4824 (2018)
42. Shocher, A., Cohen, N., Irani, M.: "Zero-shot" super-resolution using deep internal learning. In: Proceedings of the IEEE Conference on Computer Vision and Pattern Recognition, pp. 3118–3126 (2018)
43. Soh, J.W., Cho, S., Cho, N.I.: Meta-transfer learning for zero-shot super-resolution. In: Proceedings of the IEEE/CVF Conference on Computer Vision and Pattern Recognition, pp. 3516–3525 (2020)
44. Tao, G., et al.: Spectrum-to-kernel translation for accurate blind image super-resolution. Adv. Neural Inf. Process. Syst. **34**, 22643–22654 (2021)
45. Timofte, R., Agustsson, E., Van Gool, L., Yang, M.H., Zhang, L.: Ntire 2017 challenge on single image super-resolution: methods and results. In: Proceedings of the IEEE Conference on Computer Vision and Pattern Recognition Workshops, pp. 114–125 (2017)
46. Wang, L., et al.: Unsupervised degradation representation learning for blind super-resolution. In: Proceedings of the IEEE/CVF Conference on Computer Vision and Pattern Recognition, pp. 10581–10590 (2021)
47. Wang, Q., Tang, X., Shum, H.: Patch based blind image super resolution. In: Tenth IEEE International Conference on Computer Vision (ICCV'05) Volume 1, vol. 1, pp. 709–716. IEEE (2005)
48. Wang, X., Yu, K., Dong, C., Loy, C.C.: Recovering realistic texture in image super-resolution by deep spatial feature transform. In: Proceedings of the IEEE Conference on Computer Vision and Pattern Recognition, pp. 606–615 (2018)
49. Zeyde, R., Elad, M., Protter, M.: On single image scale-up using sparse-representations. In: Boissonnat, J.-D., et al. (eds.) Curves and Surfaces 2010. LNCS, vol. 6920, pp. 711–730. Springer, Heidelberg (2012). https://doi.org/10.1007/978-3-642-27413-8_47
50. Zhang, K., Gool, L.V., Timofte, R.: Deep unfolding network for image super-resolution. In: Proceedings of the IEEE/CVF Conference on Computer Vision and Pattern Recognition, pp. 3217–3226 (2020)
51. Zhang, K., Zuo, W., Zhang, L.: Learning a single convolutional super-resolution network for multiple degradations. In: Proceedings of the IEEE Conference on Computer Vision and Pattern Recognition, pp. 3262–3271 (2018)

52. Zhang, Y., Li, K., Li, K., Wang, L., Zhong, B., Fu, Y.: Image super-resolution using very deep residual channel attention networks. In: Proceedings of the European Conference on Computer Vision (ECCV), pp. 286–301 (2018)
53. Zhang, Y., Tian, Y., Kong, Y., Zhong, B., Fu, Y.: Residual dense network for image super-resolution. In: Proceedings of the IEEE Conference on Computer Vision and Pattern Recognition, pp. 2472–2481 (2018)

Learning Spatio-Temporal Downsampling for Effective Video Upscaling

Xiaoyu Xiang[1]([✉]) [ID], Yapeng Tian[2] [ID], Vijay Rengarajan[1] [ID],
Lucas D. Young[1] [ID], Bo Zhu[1] [ID], and Rakesh Ranjan[1] [ID]

[1] Meta Reality Labs, Menlo Park, USA
{xiangxiaoyu,apvijay,bozhufrl,rakeshr}@fb.com, lucasyoung482@gmail.com
[2] University of Texas at Dallas, Richardson, USA
tianyapeng92@gmail.com

Abstract. Downsampling is one of the most basic image processing operations. Improper spatio-temporal downsampling applied on videos can cause aliasing issues such as moiré patterns in space and the wagon-wheel effect in time. Consequently, the inverse task of upscaling a low-resolution, low frame-rate video in space and time becomes a challenging ill-posed problem due to information loss and aliasing artifacts. In this paper, we aim to solve the space-time aliasing problem by learning a spatio-temporal downsampler. Towards this goal, we propose a neural network framework that jointly learns spatio-temporal downsampling and upsampling. It enables the downsampler to retain the key patterns of the original video and maximizes the reconstruction performance of the upsampler. To make the downsamping results compatible with popular image and video storage formats, the downsampling results are encoded to uint8 with a differentiable quantization layer. To fully utilize the space-time correspondences, we propose two novel modules for explicit temporal propagation and space-time feature rearrangement. Experimental results show that our proposed method significantly boosts the space-time reconstruction quality by preserving spatial textures and motion patterns in both downsampling and upscaling. Moreover, our framework enables a variety of applications, including arbitrary video resampling, blurry frame reconstruction, and efficient video storage.

Keywords: Downsampling · Anti-aliasing · Video upscaling

1 Introduction

Resizing is one of the most commonly used operations in digital image processing. Due to the limit of available memory and transfer bandwidth in compact devices, *e.g.* mobile phones and glasses, the high resolutions, high frame rate videos captured by such devices trade off either spatial or temporal resolution [1,82]. While

---

Supplementary Information The online version contains supplementary material available at https://doi.org/10.1007/978-3-031-19797-0_10.

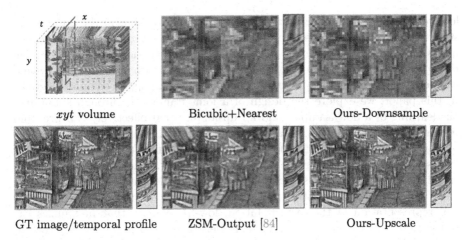

xyt volume	Bicubic+Nearest	Ours-Downsample

GT image/temporal profile	ZSM-Output [84]	Ours-Upscale

Fig. 1. *Effect of learned downsampling and upscaling for space-time reconstruction.* Compared to previous methods, the outputs of our learned downsampler maintain better spatial-temporal patterns, thus leading to more visually-appealing reconstruction results with better space-time consistency.

nearest-neighbor downsampling is the standard operation to perform such reduction in space and time, it is not the best option: it folds over high-frequency information in the downsampled frequency domain, leading to aliasing as indicated by the Nyquist theorem [60]. One way to avoid aliasing is to deliberately smudge high-frequency information by allowing more space and time to capture a single sample, *i.e.* by optical blur [26,52] and motion blur [11,31,64], respectively. These spatial and temporal anti-aliasing filters band-limit frequencies, making it possible to reconstruct fine details during post-capture. Pre-designed anti-aliasing filters can be employed with the downsampler during capture time; for instance, using an optical low-pass filter [67] for spatial blur, and computational cameras such as the flutter shutter [51] camera for temporal blur.

To design the optimal filter for a specific task, it is natural to incorporate the downstream performance in the loop, where the weights of the downsampling filter are updated by the objective function of the task [69]. Kim *et al.* [28] inverts the super-resolution network as a downscaling encoder. Zhang *et al.* [91] proposes to add blur layers before each downsampling operation, and Zou *et al.* [94] adaptively predicts filter weights for each spatial location.

For the video restoration task, a major benefit of pre-designing the downsampler is to allow the co-design of an upsampler that recovers missing high-frequency details. While traditional methods mainly focus on upsampling – super-resolution (SR) in the case of space, and video frame interpolation (VFI) in the case of time – they assume the downsampler to be a trivial module. The low-resolution (LR) images for SR tasks are usually acquired by bicubic downsampling. For temporal reconstruction tasks like VFI, the low-fps (frames per second) frames are acquired by nearest-neighbor sampling, which keeps one frame per interval. Obviously, these operations are not optimal - the stride in time will lead to temporal aliasing artifacts. This independent tackling of the upsampling stage makes solving the inverse problem harder, and it is typical to employ heavy priors on texture and motion, which results in hallucination of lost details. On the other hand, jointly handling upsampling together with downsampling would enable better performance in retaining and recovering spatio-temporal details. In this paper, we explore the design of a joint framework through simultaneous learning of a downsampler and an upsampler that effectively captures and reconstructs high-frequency details in both space and time.

Based on the above observations, we propose a unified framework that jointly learns spatio-temporal downsampling and upsampling, which works like an autoencoder for low-fps, low-resolution frames. To handle the ill-posed space-time video super-resolution problem, we first make the downsampler to find the optimal representation in the low-resolution, low-fps domain that maximizes the restoration performance. Moreover, considering the downsampled representation should be stored and transmitted in the common image and video data formats, we quantize them to be uint8 with a differentiable quantization layer that enables end-to-end training. Finally, the downsampled frames are upscaled by our upsampler. To improve the reconstruction capability, we devise space-time pixel-shuffle and deformable temporal propagation modules to better exploit the space-time correspondences.

The main contributions of our paper are summarized as follows: (1) We provide a new perspective for space-time video downsampling by learning it jointly with upsampling, which preserves better space-time patterns and boosts restoration performance. (2) We observe that naive 3D convolution cannot achieve high reconstruction performance, and hence, we propose the deformable temporal propagation and space-time pixel-shuffle modules to realize a highly effective model design. (3) Our proposed framework exhibits great potential to inspire the community. We discuss the following applications: video resampling with arbitrary ratio, blurry frame reconstruction, and efficient video storage.

2   Related Works

2.1   Video Downsampling

Spatial. Spatial downsampling is a long-standing research problem in image processing. Classical approaches, such as the box, nearest, bicubic, and Lasnczos [13,27,53], usually design image filters to generate low resolution (LR) images by removing high frequencies and mitigating aliasing. Since most visual details exist in the high frequencies, they are also removed during downsampling. To address the problem, a series of structure and detail-preserving image downscaling methods [30,48,79] are proposed. Although these approaches can produce visually appealing LR images, they cannot guarantee that upscaling methods can restore the original high resolution (HR) images due to aliasing and non-uniform structure deformation in the downscaled LR images. To boost the restoration quality, [66,80] proposed to learn a downsampler network. Pioneering research [73,74] demonstrates that it is possible to design filters that allow for reconstructing the high-resolution input image with minimum error.

The key is to add a small amount of optical blurring before sampling. Inspired by this, we propose to automatically learn the best blurring filters during downsampling for more effective visual upscaling.

Temporal. A simple way to downsample along the temporal dimension is to increase the exposure time of a frame and capture the scene motion via blur. The loss of texture due to averaging is traded off for the ability to embed motion information in a single frame. Blur-to-video methods [2,22,23,50,62,90] leverage motion blur and recover the image sequence, constraining the optimization with spatial sharpness and temporal smoothness. To regularize the loss of texture during capture, Yuan et al. [88] use a long and short exposure pair for deblurring, while Rengarajan et al. [54] exploit the idea to reconstruct high-speed videos. Coded exposure methods replace the box-filter averaging over time with a broadband filter averaging by switching the shutter on and off multiple times with varying on-off durations within a single exposure period. This results in better reconstruction owing to the preservation of high-frequency details over space. Raskar et al. [51] use such a coded exposure camera for deblurring, while Holloway et al. [18] recover a high-speed video from a coded low frame rate video. Our work contributes an extension of this previous work by learning the optimal temporal filters during downsampling for restoring sharp high-fps videos.

2.2 Video Upscaling

Video Super-Resolution. The goal of video super-resolution (VSR) is to restore HR video frames from their LR counterparts. Due to the existence of visual motion, the core problem to solve in VSR is how to temporally align neighboring LR frames with the reference LR frame. Optical flow methods seek to compute local pixel shifts and capture motions. Thus, a range of VSR approaches [7,17,58,70,76,87] use optical flow to estimate motion and then perform motion compensation with warping. However, optical flow is generally limited in handling large motions, and flow warping can introduce artifacts into aligned frames. To avoid computing optical flow, implicit temporal alignment approaches, such dynamic upsampling filters [24], recurrent propagation [19,20,32,34,35], and deformable alignment [8,9,71,77] are utilized to handle complex motions.

Video Frame Interpolation. Video frame interpolation (VFI) aims to synthesize intermediate video frames in between the original frames and upscale the temporal resolution of videos. Meyer et al. [40] utilizes phase information to assist frame interpolation. [25,39] proposed an encoder-decoder framework to directly predict intermediate video frames. Niklaus et al. [45,46] utilizes a spatially-adaptive convolution kernel for each pixel for synthesizing missing frames. Similar to VSR, optical flow is also adopted in VFI approaches [3,4,21,38,44,65] to explicitly handle motions.

Space-Time Video Super-resolution. The pioneering work to extend SR to both space and time domains was proposed by Shechtman et al. [61]. Compared with VSR and VFI tasks, STVSR is even more ill-posed since pixels are missing along both spatial and temporal axes. To constrain the problem, early

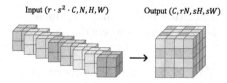

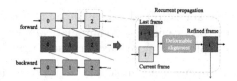

Fig. 2. *Space-Time Pixel-Shuffle.* It rearranges elements with shape $(r \cdot s^2 \cdot C, N, H, W)$ into the shape (C, rN, sH, sW), which enables efficient sub-pixel convolutions in space and time (xyt) dimensions.

Fig. 3. *Deformable temporal modeling* with recurrent temporal propagation: at each step, we model the correspondence between the last output and the current input with deformable alignment to refine the current frame.

approaches [42,59,61,68] usually exploited space-time local smoothness priors. Very recently, deep learning-based STVSR frameworks [14,16,29,83–86] have been developed. These methods directly interpolate the missing frame features and then upsample all frames in space. Like the video frame-interpolation methods, the input frames are anchors of timestamps, which limits the upscale ratio in the temporal dimension. Unlike these methods, we aim to freely resize the space-time volume with arbitrary scale ratios in this work.

3   Space-Time Anti-Aliasing (STAA)

We first explain the intuition behind STAA: treating video as spatio-temporal xyt volume and leveraging the characteristic spatio-temporal patterns for video reconstruction. Towards this end, we propose efficiently utilizing the spatio-temporal patterns in upscaling with space-time pixel-shuffle. However, naively regarding time as an additional dimension beyond space has a limitation: the pixel (x, y) at the i-th frame is usually not related to the same (x, y) at the $i + k$-th frame. To tackle this problem, we model the temporal correspondences with deformable sampling.

3.1   Intuition

To tackle the aliasing problem, previous methods insert low-pass filters either in space or time. However, we noticed that the space and time dimensions of an xyt volume are not independent: as shown in Fig. 1, the temporal profiles xt and yt display similar patterns as the spatial patches. In an ideal case where the 2D objects move with a constant velocity, the temporal profile will appear as a downsampled version of the object [49,59], as illustrated in Fig. 5. This space-time patch recurrence makes it possible to aid the reconstruction of the under-sampled dimension with abundant information from other dimensions. Based upon this observation, we adopt a 3D low-pass filter on both space and time to better utilize the correspondences across dimensions. Accordingly, our upsampler network also adopts the 3D convolutional layers as the basic building block due to its capability of jointly handling the spatio-temporal features.

3.2   Module Design

Space-Time Pixel-Shuffle. Pixel-shuffle [63] is a widely-used operation in single image super-resolution (SISR) for efficient subpixel convolution. It has two advantages: the learned upscaling filter can achieve the optimal performance; computational complexity is reduced by rearranging the elements in LR feature maps. Inspired by its success in SISR, we extend it to space-time. Figure 2 illustrates the shuffling operation: for an input tensor with shape $(r \cdot s^2 \cdot C, N, H, W)$, the elements are shuffled periodically into the shape (C, rN, sH, sW).

Naive Deconvolution Is Insufficient. If we simply regard the space-time upscaling as the reverse process of the downsampling, then conceptually, a deconvolution should be enough to handle this process. To investigate this idea, we build a small network using 3D convolutions and the aforementioned space-time pixel-shuffle layers with a style of ESPCN [63]. Although this network does converge, it only improves the PSNR by ~0.5 dB compared with trilinear upscaling the xyt cube – such improvement is too trivial to be considered effective, particularly when compared to the success of ESPCN in SISR.

Enhance Temporal Modeling Capacity. As noted above, this suboptimal result was expected due to the lost correspondences between the i-th and $i + k$-th frames. Thus, 3D convolution alone cannot guarantee a good reconstruction performance due to its relatively small field of view. Understanding "what went where" [81] is the fundamental problem for video tasks. Such correspondence is even more critical in our framework: our STAA downsampler encodes the motion by dispersing the space feature along the temporal dimension. Correspondingly, during the reconstruction stage, the supporting information can come from neighboring frames. Motivated by this, we devise a deformable module to build temporal correspondences and enhance the model's capability to handle dynamic scenes: for a frame at time i, it should look at adjoining $i - k, \ldots i + k$ frames and refine the current feature by aggregating the relevance. For efficient implementation, we split the information propagation into forward and backward directions, where the temporal correspondence is built and passed recurrently per direction, as shown in Fig. 3. The refined features from both forward and backward passes are aggregated to yield the output. Hence, the difficulty of perceiving long-range information within the 3D convolutional receptive field is alleviated.

4   Joint Downscaling and Upscaling Framework

Our framework architecture is shown in Fig. 4: given a sequence of video frames $V = \{I_i\}_1^{rN}$ where each I_i is an RGB image of dimensions $sW \times sH$ (r and s as scale factors), our goal is to design (a) a downsampler which would produce $V_\downarrow = \{D(I_i)\}_1^N$ where each $D(I_i)$ has the dimensions $W \times H$, and, (b) an upsampler which would produce $\widetilde{V} = \{U(D(I_i))\}_1^{rN}$ where, in the perfect case, $V = \widetilde{V}$.

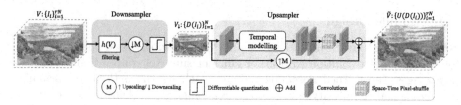

Fig. 4. Our training framework functions as an auto-encoder in which we train the downsampler D (encoder), and the upsampler U (decoder) jointly in an end-to-end manner.

4.1   Downsampler

Our downsampler consists of a 3D low pass filter $h(\cdot)$ followed by a downsampling operation by striding. Given a sequence of input frames $V = \{I_i\}_1^{TN}$ that needs to be downsampled, we first convolve it with the filter h as follows: $h(V)[t,x,y] = \sum_{i,j,k\in\Omega} h[i,j,k] \cdot V[t-i, x-j, y-k]$.

To ensure that the learned filters are low-pass, we add a softmax layer to regularize the weight values within the range $[0,1]$ and the sum to be 1. We then use striding to produce our desired downsampled frames in both space and time. An ideal anti-aliasing filter should restrict the bandwidth to satisfy the Nyquist theorem without distorting the in-band frequencies.

Analysis of Learned Filters. We present a study based on the frequency domain analysis of spatio-temporal images to compare different types of low-pass filters. We analyze the canonical case of a single object moving with uniform velocity. The basic setup is shown in the first column of Fig. 5, where the top row shows the static object and the bottom row shows the xyt volume corresponding to the motion. Figs. 5(a) to (f) show the temporal profiles xt corresponding to the 1D scanline (marked in red) for various scenarios/filters in the top row and their corresponding Fourier domain plots in the bottom row. Please check the supplementary material for more details about how the Fourier plots are calculated and what the spectra components represent.

In Fig. 5, (a) is a space-time diagram for a static scene (zero velocity), so there is no change along the time (vertical) dimension. In (b), we can see that the motion causes a time-varying effect, which results in shear along the spatial x direction. This shows the coupling of spatial and temporal dimensions. Applying just the nearest-neighbor downsampling in time leads to severe aliasing, as shown by duplication of streaks in (c) bottom row. Thus, the plain downsampling method leads to temporal pattern distortions. Characteristic spatio-temporal patterns relate to events in the video [10,47,89]. Thus, good downsampling methods should also retain the "textures" in time dimension.

Figures 5(d), (e), and (f) show the images and frequency plots for the case of applying Gaussian, box, and our STAA low pass filters, respectively, first, followed by nearest-neighbor downsampling. The convolution with these filters causes blurring across space and time dimensions, as shown in the images, and since convolution corresponds to frequency domain multiplication, we can see

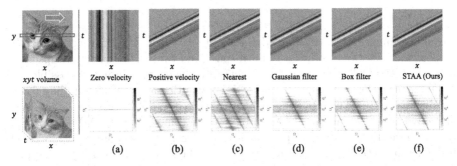

Fig. 5. Space-time and Fourier domain plots for a moving object. (Color figure online)

the benefits of these filters visually in the frequency domain plots. The Gaussian filter reduces the subbands and high spatiotemporal frequencies in (d). The Box filter along the temporal dimension, which is used to describe the motion blur [6,15,56], destroys spatial details and attenuates certain temporal frequencies, which causes post-aliasing [41] during reconstruction. Our proposed STAA filter attenuates high frequencies and the subbands like the Gaussian filter does, but at the same time, it preserves more energy in the main spectra component, as shown in (f). This characteristic ensures the prefiltered image maintains a good spatio-temporal texture, thus benefiting the reconstruction process.

Connection to Coded Exposure. Traditional motion blur caused by long exposure can be regarded as filtering with a temporal box filter. While long exposure acts as a natural form of filtering during the capture time itself, the box filter is not the best filter for alias-free reconstruction [41]. Hence, coded exposure methods "flutter" the shutter in a designed sequence to record the motion without completely smearing the object across the spatial dimension to recover sharp high-frame-rate images and videos [18,51]. Our learned downsampler can be regarded as a learned form of the coded exposure: considering the temporal kernel size as an exposure window, we aggregate the pixels at each time step to preserve an optimal space-time pattern for better reconstruction.

Differentiable Quantization Layer. The direct output of our downsampler is a floating-point tensor, while in practical applications, images are usually encoded as 8-bit RGB (uint8) format. Quantization is needed to make our downsampled frames compatible with popular image storage and transmission pipelines. However, this operation is not differentiable. The gap between float and discrete integer causes training unstable and a drop in performance. To bridge the gap, we adopt a differentiable quantization layer that enables end-to-end training [5]. More details can be found in *supplementary material.*

4.2   Upsampler

Given a sequence of downsampled frames, $V_\downarrow = \{D(I_i)\}_{i=1}^N$, the upsampler U aims to increase the resolution in both space and time. The estimated upscaled video $\widetilde{V} = \{U(D(I_i))\}_{i=1}^{rN}$ should be as close to the original input as possible.

To achieve this purpose, we choose 3D convolution as our basic building block for the upsampler. The input sequence is converted to the feature domain $\mathcal{F}$ by a 3D convolution. We adopt a deformable temporal modeling (DTM) subnetwork to aggregate the long-range dependencies recurrently. It takes the last aggregated frame feature $DTM(f_{i-1})$ at time step $i-1$ and the current feature f_i as inputs, outputting the current aggregated feature:

$$DTM(f_i) = T(f_i, DTM(f_{i-1})), \tag{1}$$

where f_i is the frame feature at time step i, and T denotes a general function that finds and aligns the corresponding information to the current feature. We adopt the deformable sampling function [12,93] as T to capture such correspondences. To fully exploit the temporal information, we implement a bidirectional DTM that aggregates the refined features from both forward and backward passes.

The refined sequence is then passed to the reconstruction module that is composed of 3D convolutions. To fully explore the hierarchical features from these convolutional layers, we organize them into residual dense blocks [92]. It densely connects the 3D convolution layers into local groups and fuses the features of different layers. Following the previous super-resolution networks [36], no BatchNorm layer is used in our reconstruction module. Finally, a space-time pixel-shuffle layer is adopted to rearrange the features with a periodic shuffling across the xyt volume [57].

We denote the output just after the space-time pixel-shuffle as $F(V_\downarrow)$, where $F(\cdot)$ is all the previous operations for upscaling the input $V_\downarrow$. To help the main network focus on generating high-frequency information, we bilinearly upscale the input sequence and add it to the reconstructed features as the final output:

$$U(V_\downarrow) = V_\downarrow \uparrow_M + F(V_\downarrow). \tag{2}$$

This long-range skip-connection allows the low-frequency information of the input to bypass the major network and makes the major part of the network predict the residue. It "lower-bounds" the reconstruction performance and increases the convergence speed of the network.

5   Experiments

We use the Peak Signal-to-Noise-Ratio (PSNR) and Structural Similarity Index (SSIM) [78] metrics to evaluate video restoration. We also compare the number of parameters (million, M) to evaluate model efficiency. Please find our datasets and implementation details in the *supplementary materials*.

Table 1. Comparisons with SOTA cascaded video frame interpolation (VFI) and super-resolution (VSR), and space-time super-resolution (STVSR) methods.

Upscale rate time/space	Downsampler time/space	Reconstruction Method VFI	VSR	Params/M	Vimeo-90k PSNR	SSIM	Vid4 PSNR	SSIM
2×/1×	Nearest/-	XVFI [65]	–	5.7	34.76	0.9532	29.21	0.9496
		FLAVR [25]	–	42.1	36.73	0.9632	29.83	0.9585
	STAA	Ours		15.9	**45.01**	**0.9912**	**39.78**	**0.9926**
1×/4×	-/Bicubic	–	BasicVSR++ [9]	7.3	35.91	0.9383	26.24	0.8214
		–	VRT [33]	35.6	36.35	0.9420	26.39	0.8248
		–	RVRT [34]	10.8	36.30	0.9417	26.44	0.8285
	STAA	Ours		15.9	**37.35**	**0.9629**	**30.10**	**0.9517**
2×/4×	Nearest/Bicubic	XVFI [65]	BasicVSR++ [9]	5.7+7.3	32.41	0.9123	24.90	0.7726
		FLAVR [25]	BasicVSR++ [9]	42.1+7.3	32.74	0.9119	24.79	0.7678
		ZSM [83]		11.1	33.48	0.9178	24.82	0.7763
		TMNet [86]		12.3	33.66	0.9200	24.90	0.7803
		STDAN [75]		8.3	33.59	0.9192	24.91	0.7832
	STAA	Ours		16.0	**34.53**	**0.9426**	**27.31**	**0.9173**

5.1 Comparison with State-of-the-Art Methods

We compare the performance of reconstructing a video in space and time with SOTA VFI, VSR and STVSR methods. For two input frames, previous VFI methods generate one interpolated frame along with the two inputs, while our STAA generates four upsampled ones. For an apples-to-apples comparison, we only calculate the PSNR/SSIM of the synthesized frames. Quantitative results on Vimeo-90k [87] and Vid4 [37] are shown in Table 1.

Our method outperforms the previous methods by a large margin on all datasets and settings. For temporal upscaling, adopting the STAA downsampling and upscaling exceeds the second-best method by 8.28 dB on Vimeo-90k and 9.95 dB on Vid4, which validates the importance of anti-aliasing in the temporal dimension. For $s \times 4$ spatial upscaling, the STAA pipeline exceeds the SOTA VSR method under bicubic degradation by 1 dB on Vimeo-90k. For the challenging case of 4× space/2× time, our method still demonstrates remarkable improvement by 2.4 dB on the Vid4 and more than 1 dB on the Vimeo-90k datasets. Such significant improvement brought by the co-design of downsampling filter and upscaling network provides a new possibility for improving current video restoration methods.

5.2 Ablation Studies

Downsampler. To verify the effectiveness of our learned downsampling filter, we compare the reconstruction performance by switching downsamplers. Since the reconstruction capability of the same upsampler architecture is unchanged, a better reconstruction result means that the downsampler produces a better space-time representation. We compare our method with other learned downsampling networks: CAR [66] and PASA [94] (see Table 2). Since the existing

Table 2. Comparison of spatial downsamplers ($1 \times t$, $4 \times s$).

Downsampler	Params/M	GFLOPs/MP	PSNR	SSIM
CAR [66]	9.896	2305.77	35.96	0.9400
PASA [94]	0.003	6.144	35.37	0.9524
Ours	**0.002**	**0.081**	**37.35**	**0.9629**

Table 3. Quantitative comparison of downsampling filters ($2 \times t$, $2 \times s$). The best two results are highlighted in red and blue, respectively.

Time	Space	PSNR	SSIM
Nearest	Bicubic	28.88	0.9073
Gaussian		37.44	0.9679
$STAA_{no}$		39.44	0.9775
$STAA_{soft}$		40.40	0.9812
$STAA_{quant}$		40.42	0.9811
$STAA_{ada}$		38.13	0.9720

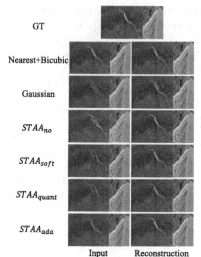

GT

Nearest+Bicubic

Gaussian

$STAA_{no}$

$STAA_{soft}$

$STAA_{quant}$

$STAA_{ada}$

Input   Reconstruction

Fig. 6. Visual comparison at $2 \times t/2 \times s$ setting in the left table.

methods only perform spatial down+upsampling learning, we set $t = 1$ and $s = 4$. Our STAA filter has significantly fewer number of parameters and computational cost compared with the other two methods while demonstrating better performance in terms of reconstruction PSNR and SSIM.

We compare with other 3d downsampling filters in Table 3. The nearest-bicubic downsampling, which is adopted by previous video reconstruction tasks, provides the worst representation among all. For the $2 \times t/2 \times s$ setting, the reconstruction network cannot converge to global optimal. Although it is still the dominant setting, it cannot handle the temporal-aliasing issue and might hinder the development of video reconstruction methods. Pre-filtering with a 3D Gaussian blur kernel can alleviate the aliasing problem, which exceeds the nearest-neighbor downsampling in time and the bicubic downsampling in space. Still, the Gaussian filter cannot produce the optimal spatio-temporal textures. Compared with these classical methods, our STAA filters improve the reconstruction performance by a large margin, as shown in the last four rows. We believe that our proposed STAA downsampler has the potential to serve as a new benchmark for video reconstruction method design and inspire the community from multiple perspectives.

We visualize the downsampled frames and their corresponding reconstruction results in Fig. 6. For nearest-bicubic downsampled results, the temporal profile has severe aliasing. In comparison, the anti-aliasing filters make the downsampled frames "blurry" to embed the motion information.

Constraints of the Encoded Frames. The classical downsampling filters, *e.g.*, nearest and Gaussian, can generate downsampled frames that resemble the

Table 4. Ablation of upsampler design.

Naive 3D Conv	3D RDB	DTM	Params/M	GFlops/MP	PSNR	SSIM
✓			0.3	3.2	28.67	0.8536
	✓		11.0	114.4	31.35	0.9016
		✓	5.3	51.7	31.55	0.9032
	✓	✓	16.0	164.7	32.00	0.9109

Table 5. Upsampling methods.

Method	3D deconv	Up+3Dconv	ST-pixelshuffle
PSNR	34.53	31.69	**34.56**
SSIM	0.9409	0.9025	**0.9413**

input's appearance. However, in our auto-encoder framework, there is actually no guarantee that the encoded frames look like the original input. A straightforward way is to use the classical downsampled results as supervision, but it might impede the downsampler from learning the optimal spatio-temporal representation. So we turn to regularize the downsampling filter with following experiments: (1) *no*: no constraints; (2) *soft*: use the softmax to regularize the weights; (3) *quant*: add the differentiable quantization layer; (4) *ada*: dynamically generate filters for each spatial location according to the input content (also with softmax).

From the last four rows of Table 3, all STAA filters outperform the classical ones for reconstruction. The filter without any constraint is not necessary to be low-pass. Besides, it may cause color shifts in the encoded frames. Constraining the filter weights with softmax can alleviate color shifts and improve the reconstruction results due to anti-aliasing. Still, the moving regions are encoded as the color difference. Adding the quantization layer does not cause performance degradation, which validates the effectiveness of our differentiable implementation. Making the filter weights conditioned on the input content creates visually pleasing LR frames. However, the reconstruction performance degrades, probably because the changing weights of the downsampling filter confuse the upsampler.

Comparing different downsampling settings, we observe that our STAA is more robust to temporal downsampling than previous methods. Specifically, the reconstruction quality is correlated to the logarithm of the percentage of pixels in the downsampling representation. More discussions are in our *Appendix*.

Effectiveness of Proposed Modules. In Table 4, we compare the video reconstruction results and the computational cost with different modules of the upsampler. We check the FLOPs per million pixels (MP) using the open-source tool fvcore [55]. From the first row, we can observe that naive 3D convolution performs bad. Changing it to a more complex 3D residual-dense block (RDB) improves the performance by 2.68 dB, with a rapid increase of the computational cost. Although this network still cannot explicitly find the temporal correspondence, the deeper structure enlarges the perceiving area, thus enabling capturing dependencies with large displacement. In the third row, adopting deformable temporal modeling (DTM) shows a great performance improvement with relatively low computational cost, which validates the importance of aggregating the displaced information across space and time. Such spatio-temporal aggregated features can be effectively utilized by the 3D CNN, resulting in improved PSNR and SSIM results (see the last row).

Fig. 7. Our methods enable smooth frame rate conversion with arbitrary rates, *e.g.* 20 fps (top row) to 24 fps (bottom row). We plot a timeline in the middle and mark the timestamp of each frame. The generated frames have natural motion transition and vivid textures, *e.g.* water flow, reflection, and refraction.

In Table 5, we compare our space-time pixel-shuffle (ST-pixelshuffle) with two other upscaling methods: 3D deconvolution, and trilinear upscaling + 3D convolution. Our proposed space-time pixel-shuffle achieves the best performance in terms of PSNR and SSIM.

5.3　Applications

The STAA downsampler can be used to reduce the resolution and frame rate of a video for efficient video transmission. The learned upsampler can also be applied to process natural videos with a simple modification. Besides, our upsampler network can also reconstruct crisp clean frames from a blurry sequence.

Video Resampling. The space-time pixel-shuffle module makes it possible to change the frame rate with arbitrary ratios while keeping the motion patterns. Previous VFI methods can only synthesize new frames in-between two inputs. Anchored by the input timestamps, their scale ratio can only be integers. ffm-peg [72] change frame rate by dropping or duplication at a certain interval, which changes the motion pattern of the original timestamps and cannot generate smooth results. Another option is to use frame blending to map the intermediate motion between keyframes while creating fuzzy and ghosting artifacts. Some softwares adopt optical flow warping, which can synthesize better results than the above two methods. Still, it cannot handle large motions or morph.

Our upsampler can maintain the space-time patterns when upscaling the temporal dimension at any given ratio: we show an example of converting 20 fps to 24 fps ($1.2 \times t$) in Fig. 7, which does synthesize the correct motion at the non-existent time steps, leading to smoother visual results. Our temporal modeling module can map long-range dependencies among the input frames, and together with the space-time convolutional layers, can reconstruct sharp and crisp frames.

Blurry Frame Reconstruction. As discussed in Sect. 4.1, motion blur is a temporal low-pass filter. It is a real-world case of our STAA filter: the temporal kernel size is the exposure time window, and the weights at each time step are equal. Hence, there is a good reason to believe that our designed upsampler

| Overlaid inputs | Output: 0 | Output: 1 | Output: 2 | Output: 3 |

Fig. 8. Our upsampler can also be used for reconstructing sharp and crisp details from videos with motion-blur. The left column shows the overlaid two LR blurry inputs, and the right four columns are our reconstruction results with 2× in time and 4× in space, which recover shapes and textures from motion blur.

can be applied on blurry frame reconstruction, which turns the low-resolution blurry sequence into a high frame-rate and high-resolution clean sequence. We trained our upsampler with a $4 \times s, 2 \times t$ upscale setting using the REDS-blur [43] data. We show the restoration images in Fig. 8. Even when the motion is rather large and the object texture is badly smeared, our upsampler does a good job in reconstructing the shape and structures at the correct timestep.

Efficient Video Storage. Since the downsampler output is still in the same color space and data type (*e.g.* 8-bit RGB) as the input, it can be processed by any existing encoding and compression algorithms for storage and transmission without extra elaborations. Especially, the downsampled frames still preserve the temporal connections implying their compatibility with video codecs.

6 Conclusions

In this paper, we propose to learn a space-time downsampler and upsampler jointly to optimize the intermediate downsampled representations and ultimately boost video reconstruction performance. The downsampler includes a learned 3D low-pass filter for spatio-temporal anti-aliasing and a differentiable quantization layer ensuring the downsampled frames are encoded in uint8. For the upsampler, we propose the space-time pixel-shuffle to enable upscaling the xyt volume at any given ratio. We further exploit the temporal correspondences between consecutive frames by explicit temporal modeling. Due to the advantages of these designs, our framework outperforms state-of-the-art works in VSR and VFI by a large margin. Moreover, we demonstrate that our proposed upsampler can be used for highly accurate arbitrary frame-rate conversion, generating high-fidelity motion and visual details at the new timestamps for the first time. Our network can also be applied to blurry frame reconstruction and efficient video storage. We believe that our approach provides a new perspective on space-time video super-resolution tasks and has a broad potential to inspire novel methods for future works such as quantization-aware image/video reconstruction, restoration-oriented video compression, and hardware applications such as coded exposure and optical anti-aliasing filter.

References

1. Allebach, J., Wong, P.W.: Edge-directed interpolation. In: IEEE International Conference on Image Processing, vol. 3, pp. 707–710. IEEE (1996)
2. Argaw, D.M., Kim, J., Rameau, F., Kweon, I.S.: Motion-blurred video interpolation and extrapolation. In: AAAI Conference on Artificial Intelligence (2021)
3. Bao, W., Lai, W.S., Ma, C., Zhang, X., Gao, Z., Yang, M.H.: Depth-aware video frame interpolation. In: IEEE Conference on Computer Vision and Pattern Recognition, pp. 3703–3712 (2019)
4. Bao, W., Lai, W.S., Zhang, X., Gao, Z., Yang, M.H.: Memc-net: Motion estimation and motion compensation driven neural network for video interpolation and enhancement. IEEE Trans. Pattern Anal. Mach. Intell. **43**, 933–948 (2019)
5. Bengio, Y., Léonard, N., Courville, A.: Estimating or propagating gradients through stochastic neurons for conditional computation. arXiv preprint arXiv:1308.3432 (2013)
6. Brooks, T., Barron, J.T.: Learning to synthesize motion blur. In: IEEE Conference on Computer Vision and Pattern Recognition, pp. 6840–6848 (2019)
7. Caballero, J., et al.: Real-time video super-resolution with spatio-temporal networks and motion compensation. In: IEEE Conference on Computer Vision and Pattern Recognition, pp. 4778–4787 (2017)
8. Chan, K.C., Wang, X., Yu, K., Dong, C., Loy, C.C.: Understanding deformable alignment in video super-resolution. arXiv preprint arXiv:2009.07265 4(3), 4 (2020)
9. Chan, K.C., Zhou, S., Xu, X., Loy, C.C.: Basicvsr++: improving video super-resolution with enhanced propagation and alignment. arXiv preprint arXiv:2104.13371 (2021)
10. Cooper, M., Liu, T., Rieffel, E.: Video segmentation via temporal pattern classification. IEEE Trans. Multimedia **9**(3), 610–618 (2007)
11. Dachille, F., Kaufman, A.: High-degree temporal antialiasing. In: Proceedings Computer Animation, pp. 49–54. IEEE (2000)
12. Dai, J., et al.: Deformable convolutional networks. In: IEEE International Conference on Computer Vision, pp. 764–773 (2017)
13. Duchon, C.E.: Lanczos filtering in one and two dimensions. J. Appl. Meteorol. Climatol. **18**(8), 1016–1022 (1979)
14. Dutta, S., Shah, N.A., Mittal, A.: Efficient space-time video super resolution using low-resolution flow and mask upsampling. In: IEEE Conference on Computer Vision and Pattern Recognition, pp. 314–323 (2021)
15. Egan, K., Tseng, Y.T., Holzschuch, N., Durand, F., Ramamoorthi, R.: Frequency analysis and sheared reconstruction for rendering motion blur. ACM Trans. Graph. **28**(3), 93–1 (2009)
16. Haris, M., Shakhnarovich, G., Ukita, N.: Space-time-aware multi-resolution video enhancement. In: IEEE Conference on Computer Vision and Pattern Recognition, pp. 2859–2868 (2020)
17. Haris, M., Shakhnarovich, G., Ukita, N.: Recurrent back-projection network for video super-resolution. In: IEEE Conference on Computer Vision and Pattern Recognition, pp. 3897–3906 (2019)

18. Holloway, J., Sankaranarayanan, A.C., Veeraraghavan, A., Tambe, S.: Flutter shutter video camera for compressive sensing of videos. In: International Conference on Computational Photography, pp. 1–9. IEEE (2012)
19. Huang, Y., Wang, W., Wang, L.: Video super-resolution via bidirectional recurrent convolutional networks. IEEE Trans. Pattern Anal. Mach. Intell. **40**(4), 1015–1028 (2017)
20. Isobe, T., Jia, X., Gu, S., Li, S., Wang, S., Tian, Q.: Video super-resolution with recurrent structure-detail network. In: Vedaldi, A., Bischof, H., Brox, T., Frahm, J.-M. (eds.) ECCV 2020. LNCS, vol. 12357, pp. 645–660. Springer, Cham (2020). https://doi.org/10.1007/978-3-030-58610-2_38
21. Jiang, H., Sun, D., Jampani, V., Yang, M.H., Learned-Miller, E., Kautz, J.: Super slomo: high quality estimation of multiple intermediate frames for video interpolation. In: IEEE Conference on Computer Vision and Pattern Recognition, pp. 9000–9008 (2018)
22. Jin, M., Hu, Z., Favaro, P.: Learning to extract flawless slow motion from blurry videos. In: IEEE Conference on Computer Vision and Pattern Recognition, pp. 8112–8121 (2019)
23. Jin, M., Meishvili, G., Favaro, P.: Learning to extract a video sequence from a single motion-blurred image. In: IEEE Conference on Computer Vision and Pattern Recognition, pp. 6334–6342 (2018)
24. Jo, Y., Wug Oh, S., Kang, J., Joo Kim, S.: Deep video super-resolution network using dynamic upsampling filters without explicit motion compensation. In: IEEE Conference on Computer Vision and Pattern Recognition, pp. 3224–3232 (2018)
25. Kalluri, T., Pathak, D., Chandraker, M., Tran, D.: Flavr: Flow-agnostic video representations for fast frame interpolation. arXiv preprint arXiv:2012.08512 (2020)
26. Keelan, B.: Handbook of image quality: characterization and prediction. CRC Press (2002)
27. Keys, R.: Cubic convolution interpolation for digital image processing. IEEE Trans. Acoust. Speech Signal Process. **29**(6), 1153–1160 (1981)
28. Kim, H., Choi, M., Lim, B., Mu Lee, K.: Task-aware image downscaling. In: Ferrari, V., Hebert, M., Sminchisescu, C., Weiss, Y. (eds.) ECCV 2018. LNCS, vol. 11208, pp. 419–434. Springer, Cham (2018). https://doi.org/10.1007/978-3-030-01225-0_25
29. Kim, S.Y., Oh, J., Kim, M.: Fisr: deep joint frame interpolation and super-resolution with a multi-scale temporal loss. In: AAAI Conference on Artificial Intelligence, pp. 11278–11286 (2020)
30. Kopf, J., Shamir, A., Peers, P.: Content-adaptive image downscaling. ACM Trans. Graph. **32**(6), 1–8 (2013)
31. Korein, J., Badler, N.: Temporal anti-aliasing in computer generated animation. In: Annual Conference on Computer Graphics and Interactive Techniques. pp. 377–388 (1983)
32. Li, Y., Jin, P., Yang, F., Liu, C., Yang, M.H., Milanfar, P.: Comisr: Compression-informed video super-resolution. In: Proceedings of the IEEE/CVF International Conference on Computer Vision. pp. 2543–2552 (2021)
33. Liang, J., Cao, J., Fan, Y., Zhang, K., Ranjan, R., Li, Y., Timofte, R., Van Gool, L.: Vrt: A video restoration transformer. arXiv preprint arXiv:2201.12288 (2022)
34. Liang, J., Fan, Y., Xiang, X., Ranjan, R., Ilg, E., Green, S., Cao, J., Zhang, K., Timofte, R., Van Gool, L.: Recurrent video restoration transformer with guided deformable attention. arXiv preprint arXiv:2206.02146 (2022)

35. Lim, B., Lee, K.M.: Deep recurrent resnet for video super-resolution. In: Asia-Pacific Signal and Information Processing Association Annual Summit and Conference. pp. 1452–1455. IEEE (2017)

36. Lim, B., Son, S., Kim, H., Nah, S., Mu Lee, K.: Enhanced deep residual networks for single image super-resolution. In: IEEE Conference on Computer Vision and Pattern Recognition Workshops. pp. 136–144 (2017)

37. Liu, C., Sun, D.: A bayesian approach to adaptive video super resolution. In: IEEE Conference on Computer Vision and Pattern Recognition. pp. 209–216. IEEE (2011)

38. Liu, Z., Yeh, R.A., Tang, X., Liu, Y., Agarwala, A.: Video frame synthesis using deep voxel flow. In: IEEE International Conference on Computer Vision, pp. 4463–4471 (2017)

39. Long, G., Kneip, L., Alvarez, J.M., Li, H., Zhang, X., Yu, Q.: Learning image matching by simply watching video. In: Leibe, B., Matas, J., Sebe, N., Welling, M. (eds.) ECCV 2016. LNCS, vol. 9910, pp. 434–450. Springer, Cham (2016). https://doi.org/10.1007/978-3-319-46466-4_26

40. Meyer, S., Wang, O., Zimmer, H., Grosse, M., Sorkine-Hornung, A.: Phase-based frame interpolation for video. In: IEEE Conference on Computer Vision and Pattern Recognition, pp. 1410–1418 (2015)

41. Mitchell, D.P., Netravali, A.N.: Reconstruction filters in computer-graphics. ACM Siggraph Comput. Graph. **22**(4), 221–228 (1988)

42. Mudenagudi, U., Banerjee, S., Kalra, P.K.: Space-time super-resolution using graph-cut optimization. IEEE Trans. Pattern Anal. Mach. Intell. **33**(5), 995–1008 (2010)

43. Nah, S., Baik, S., Hong, S., Moon, G., Son, S., Timofte, R., Lee, K.M.: Ntire 2019 challenge on video deblurring and super-resolution: Dataset and study. In: IEEE Conference on Computer Vision and Pattern Recognition Workshops, June 2019

44. Niklaus, S., Liu, F.: Context-aware synthesis for video frame interpolation. In: IEEE Conference on Computer Vision and Pattern Recognition, pp. 1701–1710 (2018)

45. Niklaus, S., Mai, L., Liu, F.: Video frame interpolation via adaptive convolution. In: IEEE Conference on Computer Vision and Pattern Recognition, pp. 670–679 (2017)

46. Niklaus, S., Mai, L., Liu, F.: Video frame interpolation via adaptive separable convolution. In: IEEE International Conference on Computer Vision, pp. 261–270 (2017)

47. Niyogi, S.A., Adelson, E.H.: Analyzing gait with spatiotemporal surfaces. In: IEEE Workshop on Motion of Non-rigid and Articulated Objects, pp. 64–69. IEEE (1994)

48. Oeztireli, A.C., Gross, M.: Perceptually based downscaling of images. ACM Trans. Graph. **34**(4), 1–10 (2015)

49. Zuckerman, L.P., Naor, E., Pisha, G., Bagon, S., Irani, M.: Across scales and across dimensions: temporal super-resolution using deep internal learning. In: Vedaldi, A., Bischof, H., Brox, T., Frahm, J.-M. (eds.) ECCV 2020. LNCS, vol. 12352, pp. 52–68. Springer, Cham (2020). https://doi.org/10.1007/978-3-030-58571-6_4

50. Purohit, K., Shah, A., Rajagopalan, A.: Bringing alive blurred moments. In: IEEE Conference on Computer Vision and Pattern Recognition, pp. 6830–6839 (2019)

51. Raskar, R., Agrawal, A., Tumblin, J.: Coded exposure photography: Motion deblurring using fluttered shutter. ACM Trans. Graph. **25**(3), 795–804 (2006)

52. Ray, S.: Scientific photography and applied imaging. Routledge (1999)

53. Reinhard, E., Heidrich, W., Debevec, P., Pattanaik, S., Ward, G., Myszkowski, K.: High dynamic range imaging: acquisition, display, and image-based lighting. Morgan Kaufmann (2010)
54. Rengarajan, V., Zhao, S., Zhen, R., Glotzbach, J., Sheikh, H., Sankaranarayanan, A.C.: Photosequencing of motion blur using short and long exposures. In: IEEE Conference on Computer Vision and Pattern Recognition Workshops, pp. 510–511 (2020)
55. Research, M.: fvcore (2019). https://github.com/facebookresearch/fvcore
56. Rim, J., Kim, G., Kim, J., Lee, J., Lee, S., Cho, S.: Realistic blur synthesis for learning image deblurring. arXiv preprint arXiv:2202.08771 (2022)
57. Rogozhnikov, A.: Einops: clear and reliable tensor manipulations with einstein-like notation. In: International Conference on Learning Representations (2021)
58. Sajjadi, M.S., Vemulapalli, R., Brown, M.: Frame-recurrent video super-resolution. In: IEEE Conference on Computer Vision and Pattern Recognition, pp. 6626–6634 (2018)
59. Shahar, O., Faktor, A., Irani, M.: Space-time super-resolution from a single video. IEEE (2011)
60. Shannon, C.: Communication in the presence of noise. Proc. IRE **37**(1), 10–21 (1949). https://doi.org/10.1109/jrproc.1949.232969
61. Shechtman, E., Caspi, Y., Irani, M.: Increasing space-time resolution in video. In: Heyden, A., Sparr, G., Nielsen, M., Johansen, P. (eds.) ECCV 2002. LNCS, vol. 2350, pp. 753–768. Springer, Heidelberg (2002). https://doi.org/10.1007/3-540-47969-4_50
62. Shen, W., Bao, W., Zhai, G., Chen, L., Min, X., Gao, Z.: Blurry video frame interpolation. In: IEEE Conference on Computer Vision and Pattern Recognition, pp. 5114–5123 (2020)
63. Shi, W., Caballero, J., Huszár, F., Totz, J., Aitken, A.P., Bishop, R., Rueckert, D., Wang, Z.: Real-time single image and video super-resolution using an efficient sub-pixel convolutional neural network. In: IEEE Conference on Computer Vision and Pattern Recognition, pp. 1874–1883 (2016)
64. Shinya, M.: Spatial anti-aliasing for animation sequences with spatio-temporal filtering. In: Annual Conference on Computer Graphics and Interactive Techniques, pp. 289–296 (1993)
65. Sim, H., Oh, J., Kim, M.: Xvfi: extreme video frame interpolation. In: IEEE International Conference on Computer Vision (2021)
66. Sun, W., Chen, Z.: Learned image downscaling for upscaling using content adaptive resampler. IEEE Trans. Image Process. **29**, 4027–4040 (2020)
67. Suzuki, T.: Optical low-pass filter (Jan 1987)
68. Takeda, H., Van Beek, P., Milanfar, P.: Spatiotemporal video upscaling using motion-assisted steering kernel (mask) regression. In: Mrak, M., Grgic, M., Kunt, M. (eds.) High-Quality Visual Experience, pp. 245–274. Springer, Heidelberg (2010). https://doi.org/10.1007/978-3-642-12802-8_10
69. Talebi, H., Milanfar, P.: Learning to resize images for computer vision tasks. In: IEEE International Conference on Computer Vision, pp. 497–506, October 2021
70. Tao, X., Gao, H., Liao, R., Wang, J., Jia, J.: Detail-revealing deep video super-resolution. In: IEEE International Conference on Computer Vision, pp. 4472–4480 (2017)
71. Tian, Y., Zhang, Y., Fu, Y., Xu, C.: Tdan: Temporally-deformable alignment network for video super-resolution. In: IEEE Conference on Computer Vision and Pattern Recognition, pp. 3360–3369 (2020)

72. Tomar, S.: Converting video formats with ffmpeg. Linux J. **2006**(146), 10 (2006)
73. Trentacoste, M., Mantiuk, R., Heidrich, W.: Blur-aware image downsampling. In: Computer Graphics Forum, vol. 30, pp. 573–582. Wiley Online Library (2011)
74. Triggs, B.: Empirical filter estimation for subpixel interpolation and matching. In: IEEE International Conference on Computer Visio, vol. 2, pp. 550–557. IEEE (2001)
75. Wang, H., Xiang, X., Tian, Y., Yang, W., Liao, Q.: Stdan: deformable attention network for space-time video super-resolution. arXiv preprint arXiv:2203.06841 (2022)
76. Wang, L., Guo, Y., Lin, Z., Deng, X., An, W.: Learning for video super-resolution through hr optical flow estimation. In: Jawahar, C.V., Li, H., Mori, G., Schindler, K. (eds.) ACCV 2018. LNCS, vol. 11361, pp. 514–529. Springer, Cham (2019). https://doi.org/10.1007/978-3-030-20887-5_32
77. Wang, X., Chan, K.C., Yu, K., Dong, C., Change Loy, C.: EDVR: video restoration with enhanced deformable convolutional networks. In: IEEE Conference on Computer Vision and Pattern Recognition Workshops (2019)
78. Wang, Z., Bovik, A.C., Sheikh, H.R., Simoncelli, E.P.: Image quality assessment: from error visibility to structural similarity. IEEE Trans. Image Process. **13**(4), 600–612 (2004)
79. Weber, N., Waechter, M., Amend, S.C., Guthe, S., Goesele, M.: Rapid, detail-preserving image downscaling. ACM Trans. Graph. **35**(6), 1–6 (2016)
80. Wei, Y., Chen, L., Song, L.: Video compression based on jointly learned downsampling and super-resolution networks. In: 2021 International Conference on Visual Communications and Image Processing (VCIP), pp. 1–5. IEEE (2021)
81. Wills, J., Agarwal, S., Belongie, S.: What went where [motion segmentation]. In: IEEE Conference on Computer Vision and Pattern Recognition (2003)
82. Xiang, X., Lin, Q., Allebach, J.P.: Boosting high-level vision with joint compression artifacts reduction and super-resolution. In: International Conference on Pattern Recognition. IEEE (2020)
83. Xiang, X., Tian, Y., Zhang, Y., Fu, Y., Allebach, J.P., Xu, C.: Zooming slow-mo: fast and accurate one-stage space-time video super-resolution. In: IEEE Conference on Computer Vision and Pattern Recognition, pp. 3370–3379 (2020)
84. Xiang, X., Tian, Y., Zhang, Y., Fu, Y., Allebach, J.P., Xu, C.: Zooming slowmo: an efficient one-stage framework for space-time video super-resolution. arXiv preprint arXiv:2104.07473 (2021)
85. Xiao, Z., Xiong, Z., Fu, X., Liu, D., Zha, Z.J.: Space-time video super-resolution using temporal profiles. In: ACM International Conference on Multimedia, pp. 664–672 (2020)
86. Xu, G., Xu, J., Li, Z., Wang, L., Sun, X., Cheng, M.M.: Temporal modulation network for controllable space-time video super-resolution. In: IEEE Conference on Computer Vision and Pattern Recognition, pp. 6388–6397 (2021)
87. Xue, T., Chen, B., Wu, J., Wei, D., Freeman, W.T.: Video enhancement with task-oriented flow. Int. J. Comput. Vision **127**(8), 1106–1125 (2019)
88. Yuan, L., Sun, J., Quan, L., Shum, H.Y.: Image deblurring with blurred/noisy image pairs. ACM Trans. Graph. **26**(3) (2007)
89. Zelnik-Manor, L., Irani, M.: Event-based analysis of video. In: IEEE Conference on Computer Vision and Pattern Recognition, vol. 2, pp. II-II. IEEE (2001)
90. Zhang, K., Luo, W., Stenger, B., Ren, W., Ma, L., Li, H.: Every moment matters: Detail-aware networks to bring a blurry image alive. In: ACM International Conference on Multimedia, pp. 384–392 (2020)

91. Zhang, R.: Making convolutional networks shift-invariant again. In: International Conference on Machine Learning, pp. 7324–7334. PMLR (2019)
92. Zhang, Y., Tian, Y., Kong, Y., Zhong, B., Fu, Y.: Residual dense network for image super-resolution. In: IEEE Conference on Computer Vision and Pattern Recognition, pp. 2472–2481 (2018)
93. Zhu, X., Hu, H., Lin, S., Dai, J.: Deformable convnets v2: more deformable, better results. In: IEEE Conference on Computer Vision and Pattern Recognition, pp. 9308–9316 (2019)
94. Zou, X., Xiao, F., Yu, Z., Lee, Y.: Delving deeper into anti-aliasing in convnets. In: British Machine Vision Conference (2020)

Learning Local Implicit Fourier Representation for Image Warping

Jaewon Lee[1], Kwang Pyo Choi[2], and Kyong Hwan Jin[1](✉)

[1] Daegu Gyeongbuk Institute of Science and Technology (DGIST), Daegu, Korea
{ljw3136,kyong.jin}@dgist.ac.kr
[2] Samsung Electronics, Suwon-si, Korea
kp5.choi@samsung.com

Abstract. Image warping aims to reshape images defined on rectangular grids into arbitrary shapes. Recently, implicit neural functions have shown remarkable performances in representing images in a continuous manner. However, a standalone multi-layer perceptron suffers from learning high-frequency Fourier coefficients. In this paper, we propose a local texture estimator for image warping (LTEW) followed by an implicit neural representation to deform images into continuous shapes. Local textures estimated from a deep super-resolution (SR) backbone are multiplied by locally-varying Jacobian matrices of a coordinate transformation to predict Fourier responses of a warped image. Our LTEW-based neural function outperforms existing warping methods for asymmetric-scale SR and homography transform. Furthermore, our algorithm well generalizes arbitrary coordinate transformations, such as homography transform with a large magnification factor and equirectangular projection (ERP) perspective transform, which are not provided in training. Our source code is available at https://github.com/jaewon-lee-b/ltew.

Keywords: Image warping · Implicit neural representation · Fourier features · Jacobian · Homography transform · Equirectangular projection (ERP)

1 Introduction

Our goal is to deform images defined on rectangular grids into continuous shapes, referred to as image warping. Image warping is widely used in various computer vision and graphic tasks, such as image editing [11,12], optical flow [43], image alignment [7,21,23,38], and omnidirectional vision [2,3,5,14,28]. A conventional approach [21,24] applies an inverse coordinate transformation to interpolate the missing RGB value in the input space. However, interpolation-based methods cause jagging and blurring artifacts in output images. Recently, SRWarp [42]

Supplementary Information The online version contains supplementary material available at https://doi.org/10.1007/978-3-031-19797-0_11.

S. Avidan et al. (Eds.): ECCV 2022, LNCS 13678, pp. 182–200, 2022.
https://doi.org/10.1007/978-3-031-19797-0_11

paved the way to reshape images with high-frequency details by adopting a deep single image super-resolution (SISR) architecture as a backbone.

SISR is a particular case of image warping [42]. A goal of SISR is to reconstruct a high-resolution (HR) image from its degraded low-resolution (LR) counterpart. Recent lines of research in solving SISR are to extract deep feature maps using advanced architectures [8,29,30,32,48,51,52] and upscale them to HR images at the end of a network [10,19,27,39,50]. Even though deep SISR methods reconstruct visually clear HR images, directly applying them to our problem is limited since each local region of a warped image is stretched with different scale factors [17]. By reconsidering the warping problem as a spatially-varying SR task, SRWarp [42] shed light on deforming images with sharp edges. However, interpolation-based SRWarp shows limited performance in generalizing to a large-scale representation which is out of training range.

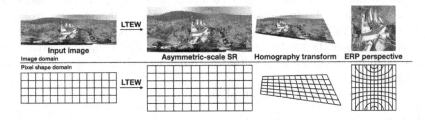

Fig. 1. Implicit neural representation for image warping.

Recently, implicit neural functions have attracted significant attention in representing signals, such as image [10,27], video [9], signed distance [36], occupancy [33], shape [22], and view synthesis [34,41], in a continuous manner. A multi-layer perceptron (MLP) parameterizes such an implicit neural representation [40,44] and takes coordinates as an input. Inspired by the recent implicit function success, LIIF [10] well generalizes to a large-scale rectangular SR beyond a training distribution. However, one shortcoming of implicit neural functions [37,44] is that a standalone MLP with ReLUs is biased towards learning low-frequency content. To alleviate this spectral bias problem, Local Texture Estimator (LTE) [27] estimates Fourier features for an HR image from its LR counterpart motivated by Fourier analysis. While LTE achieved arbitrary-scale rectangular SR with high-frequency details, LTE representation fails to evaluate a frequency response for image warping due to its spatially-varying nature.

Given an image $I^{IN} : X \mapsto \mathbb{R}^3$ and a differentiable and invertible coordinate transformation $f : X \mapsto Y$, we propose a local texture estimator for image warping (LTEW) followed by an implicit neural function representing $I^{WARP} : Y \mapsto \mathbb{R}^3$, as in Fig. 1. Our algorithm leverages both Fourier features estimated from an input image and the Jacobian of coordinate transformation. In geometry, the determinant of the Jacobian indicates a local magnification ratio. Hence, we multiply spatially-varying Jacobian matrices to Fourier features for each pixel before our MLP represents $\mathbf{I}^{\mathbf{WARP}}$. Furthermore, we point out that a spatially-varying prior for pixel shape is essential in enhancing a representational power of neural functions. The pixel shape described by orientation and curvature is numerically computed by gradient terms of given coordinate transformation.

We demonstrate that our proposed LTEW with a deep SISR backbone [48, 51, 52] surpasses existing warping methods [24, 42, 46] for both upscaling and homography transform. While previous warping techniques [42, 46] employ convolution and polynomial interpolation as a resampling module, our LTEW-based implicit neural function takes continuous coordinates as an input. Therefore, our proposed algorithm effectively generalizes in continuously representing $\mathbf{I}^{\mathbf{WARP}}$, especially for homography transforms with a substantial magnification factor ($\times 4$-$\times 8$), which is not provided during a training phase. We further pay attention to omni-directional imaging (ODI) [2, 3, 5, 14, 28] to verify the generalization ability of our algorithm. With the rapid advancement in virtual reality (VR), ODI has become crucial for product development. Equirectangular projection (ERP) is widely used in imaging pipelines of a head-mounted display (HMD) [20]. As a result of projection from spherical grids to rectangular grids, pixels are sparsely located near high latitudes. Since the proposed LTEW learns spatially-varying properties, our method qualitatively outperforms other warping methods in projecting perspective without extra training.

To summarize, the contributions of our work include:

- We propose a continuous neural representation for image warping by taking advantage of both Fourier features and spatially-varying Jacobian matrices of coordinate transformations.
- We claim that a spatially-varying prior for pixel shape described by orientation and curvature is significant in improving the representational capacity of the neural function.
- We demonstrate that our LTEW-based implicit neural function outperforms the existing warping methods for upscaling and homography transform, and unseen coordinate transformations.

2   Related Works

Image Warping. Image warping is a popular technique for various computer vision and graphics tasks, such as image editing [11, 12], optical flow estimation [43], and image alignment [7, 21, 23, 38]. A general technique for image warping [21] is finding a spatial location in input space and applying an interpolation kernel to calculate missing RGB values. Even though an interpolation-based image warping is differentiable and an easy-to-implement framework, an output image suffers from jagging and blurring artifacts [42]. Recently, SRWarp [42] proposed an arbitrary image transformation framework by interpreting an image warping task as a spatially-varying SR problem. SRWarp shows noticeable performance gain in arbitrary SR, including homography transform using an adaptive warping layer. However, the generalization ability of SRWarp is limited for unseen transformations, like a homography transform with a large magnification factor.

Implicit Neural Representation (INR). Motivated from the fact that neural network is a universal function approximator [18], INR is widely applied to represent continuous-domain signals. Conventionally, the memory requirement for data is quadratically (2D) or cubically (3D) proportional to signal resolution. In contrast, INR is a memory-efficient framework to store continuous signals since storage size is proportional to the number of model parameters rather than signal resolution. Recently, local INR [10,22,27] has been proposed to enhance the spatial resolution of input signals in an arbitrary manner. By using both feature maps from a deep neural encoder and relative coordinates (or *local grid* in [22,28]), such approaches are capable of generalizing to unseen tasks, which are not given during training. Inspired by previous works, our proposed LTEW utilizes Fourier features from a deep neural backbone and local grids to represent warped images under arbitrary coordinate transformations.

Spectral Bias. Early works [37,44] have shown that INR parameterized by a standalone MLP with a ReLU activation fails to capture high-frequency details of signals. Dominant approaches for resolving this spectral bias problem are substituting ReLUs with a periodic function [40], projecting input coordinates into a high-dimensional Fourier [4,27,34,44] or spline [47] feature space, and multiplying sinusoidal or Gabor filters [16]. Recently, LTE [27] achieved arbitrary-scale SR using INR by estimating Fourier information from an LR image. Unlike previous attempts [34,44], Fourier feature space in LTE representation [27] is data-driven and characterizes texture maps in 2D space. However, considering a spatially-varying SR issue in image warping, directly applying LTE is limited to characterize the Fourier space of warped images.

Deep SISR. After ESPCN [39] has proposed a memory-efficient upsampling layer based on sub-pixel convolution, advanced deep vision backbones, such as residual block [30], densely connected residual block [48,52], channel attention [51], second-order attention [13], holistic attention [35], non-local network [32], are jointly employed to reconstruct high-quality images. Recently, by taking advantage of inductive bias in self-attention mechanism [15,31], general-purpose image restoration backbones [8,29] remarkably outperform convolution-based architectures using a large dataset. Despite their compelling representational power, we have to train and store several models for each scale factor. Current approaches [10,19,27,46,50] for arbitrary-scale SR are utilizing a dynamic filter network [19,46], INR [10,27], or transformer [50]. Unlike the previous arbitrary-scale SR methods, our LTEW represents images under arbitrary coordinate transformations, like homography transform, with only a single network.

Omnidirectional Image (ODI). In a new era of VR, omnidirectional vision [2, 3,5,14,28] becomes playing a crucial role in product development. While natural images are represented in the Euclidean space, ODIs are defined on the spherical coordinates. A common methods to project ODIs to the 2D plane is an ERP to be consistent with imaging pipelines in HMD [20]. One limitation of an ERP projected ODIs is that non-uniform spatial resolving power leads to severe spatial distortion near boundaries [28]. To handle this varying pixel densities across

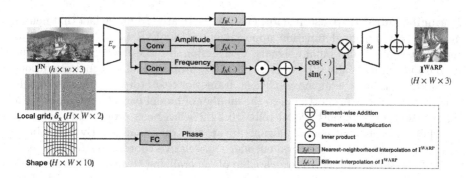

Fig. 2. A flowchart of our proposed Local Texture Estimator Warp (LTEW).

latitudes, Deng *et al.* [14] proposed a hierarchically adaptive network. Since our proposed LTEW utilizes Jacobian matrices of given coordinate transformation to learn spatially-varying property for image warping, the distortion caused by varying pixel densities can be safely projected without extra training.

3   Problem Formulation

Given an image $\mathbf{I}^{\mathbf{IN}} : X \mapsto \mathbb{R}^3$, and a differentiable and invertible coordinate transformation $f : X \mapsto Y$, our goal is to formulate an implicit neural representation of an $\mathbf{I}^{\mathbf{WARP}} : Y \mapsto \mathbb{R}^3$ for image warping. The set $X \triangleq \{\mathbf{x}|\mathbf{x} \in \mathbb{R}^2\} : [0, h) \times [0, w)$ is an input coordinate space, and $Y \triangleq \{\mathbf{y}|\mathbf{y} = f(\mathbf{x}) \in \mathbb{R}^2\} : [0, H) \times [0, W)$ is an output coordinate space. In practice, warping changes an image resolution to preserve the density of pixels (In Fig. 2: $h \times w \to H \times W$). Note that neural representation parameterized by an MLP with ReLU activations fails to capture high-frequency details of signals [34,37,40,44]. Recently, LTE [27] achieved arbitrary-scale SR for symmetric scale factors by estimating essential Fourier information. However, concerning the spatially-varying nature of warping problems [6], frequency responses of an input and a deformed image are inconsistent for each location. Therefore, we formalize a Local Texture Estimator Warp (LTEW), a frequency response estimator for image warping, by considering both Fourier features of an input image and spatially-varying property of coordinate transformations. We show that our LTEW is a generalized form of the LTE, allowing a neural representation to be biased towards learning high-frequency components while manipulating images under arbitrary coordinate transformations. In addition, we present shape-dependent phase estimation to enrich the information in output images.

3.1   Learning Fourier Information for Local Neural Representation

In local neural representation [10,22], a neural representation g_θ is parameterized by an MLP with trainable parameters θ. A decoding function g_θ predicts RGB value for a query point $\mathbf{y} = f(\mathbf{x}) \in Y \subseteq \mathbb{R}^2$ as

$$\mathbf{I^{WARP}}[\mathbf{y}; \Theta] = \sum_{j \in \mathcal{J}} w_j g_\theta(\mathbf{z}_j, \mathbf{y} - f(\mathbf{x}_j)) \qquad (1)$$

$$\text{where } \mathbf{z} = E_\varphi(\mathbf{I^{IN}}), \qquad (2)$$

$\Theta = [\theta, \varphi]$, $\mathcal{J}$ is a set $\{j | j = [f^{-1}(\mathbf{y}) + [\frac{m}{w}, \frac{n}{h}], [m, n] \in [-1, 1]\}$ [10,21], w_j is a local ensemble coefficient [10,22,27], $\mathbf{z}_j \in \mathbb{R}^C$ indicates a latent variable for a index j, and $\mathbf{x}_j \in X \subseteq \mathbb{R}^2$ is a coordinate of $\mathbf{z}_j$.

Recent works [37,44] have shown that a standard MLP structure suffers from learning high-frequency content. Lee *et al.* [27] modified the local neural representation in Eq. (1) to overcome this spectral bias problem as

$$\mathbf{I^{WARP}}[\mathbf{y}; \Theta, \psi] = \sum_{j \in \mathcal{J}} w_j g_\theta(h_\psi(\mathbf{z}_j, \mathbf{y} - f(\mathbf{x}_j)) \qquad (3)$$

where h_ψ is a Local Texture Estimator (LTE). LTE $(h_\psi(\cdot))$ contains two estimators;(1) an amplitude estimator $(h_a(\cdot) : \mathbb{R}^C \mapsto \mathbb{R}^{2D})$ (2) a frequency estimator $(h_f(\cdot) : \mathbb{R}^C \mapsto \mathbb{R}^{2 \times D})$. Specifically, an estimating function $h_\psi(\cdot, \cdot) : (\mathbb{R}^C, \mathbb{R}^2) \mapsto \mathbb{R}^{2D}$ is defined as

$$h_\psi(\mathbf{z}_j, \boldsymbol{\delta_y}) = \mathbf{A}_j \odot \begin{bmatrix} \cos(\pi < \mathbf{F}_j, \boldsymbol{\delta_y} >) \\ \sin(\pi < \mathbf{F}_j, \boldsymbol{\delta_y} >) \end{bmatrix}, \qquad (4)$$

$$\text{where } \mathbf{A}_j = h_a(\mathbf{z}_j), \ \mathbf{F}_j = h_f(\mathbf{z}_j), \qquad (5)$$

$\boldsymbol{\delta_y} = \mathbf{y} - f(\mathbf{x}_j)$ is a local grid, $\mathbf{A}_j \in \mathbb{R}^{2D}$ is an amplitude vector, $\mathbf{F}_j \in \mathbb{R}^{2 \times D}$ indicates a frequency matrix for an index j, $< \cdot, \cdot >$ is an inner product, and $\odot$ denotes element-wise multiplication. However, this formulation fails to represent warped images since $\mathbf{F}_j$ is a frequency response of an input image $\mathbf{I^{IN}}$, which is different from that of a warped image $\mathbf{I^{WARP}}$ [6]. In the following, we generalize LTE by considering a spatially-varying property of coordinate transformations.

3.2   Learning Fourier Information with Coordinate Transformations

We linearize the given coordinate transformation f into affine transformations. A linear approximation of the local grid $\boldsymbol{\delta_y}$ near a point $\mathbf{x}_j$ is computed as

$$\begin{aligned} \boldsymbol{\delta_y} = \mathbf{y} - f(\mathbf{x}_j) &= f(\mathbf{x}) - f(\mathbf{x}_j) \\ &= \{f(\mathbf{x}_j) + \mathbf{J}_f(\mathbf{x}_j)(\mathbf{x} - \mathbf{x}_j) + \mathcal{O}(\mathbf{x}^2)\} - f(\mathbf{x}_j) \\ &\simeq \mathbf{J}_f(\mathbf{x}_j)(\mathbf{x} - \mathbf{x}_j) = \mathbf{J}_f(\mathbf{x}_j)\boldsymbol{\delta_x} \end{aligned} \qquad (6)$$

where $\mathbf{J}_f(\mathbf{x}_j) \in \mathbb{R}^{2 \times 2}$ is the Jacobian matrix of coordinate transformation f at $\mathbf{x}_j$, $\mathcal{O}(\mathbf{x}^2)$ means terms of order $\mathbf{x}^2$ and higher, and $\boldsymbol{\delta_x} = \mathbf{x} - \mathbf{x}_j$ is a local grid in input space X. By the affine theorem [6] and Eq. (6), a frequency response $\mathbf{F}'_j$ of a warped image $\mathbf{I^{WARP}}$ near a point $f(\mathbf{x}_j)$ is approximated as follows:

$$\mathbf{F}'_j \simeq \mathbf{J}_f^{-T}(\mathbf{x}_j)\mathbf{F}_j. \qquad (7)$$

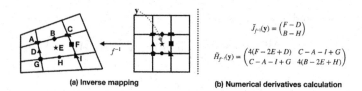

$$\tilde{J}_{f^{-1}}(\mathbf{y}) = \begin{pmatrix} F - D \\ B - H \end{pmatrix}$$

$$\tilde{H}_{f^{-1}}(\mathbf{y}) = \begin{pmatrix} 4(F - 2E + D) & C - A - I + G \\ C - A - I + G & 4(B - 2E + H) \end{pmatrix}$$

(a) Inverse mapping   (b) Numerical derivatives calculation

Fig. 3. Numerical Jacobian matrix and Hessian tensor for shape representation.

From Eq. (6) and Eq. (7), we generalize the estimating function in Eq. (4) as:

$$h_\psi(\mathbf{z}_j, \boldsymbol{\delta_y}, f) = \mathbf{A}_j \odot \begin{bmatrix} \cos(\pi < \mathbf{F}'_j, \boldsymbol{\delta_y} >) \\ \sin(\pi < \mathbf{F}'_j, \boldsymbol{\delta_y} >) \end{bmatrix} \tag{8}$$

$$\simeq \mathbf{A}_j \odot \begin{bmatrix} \cos(\pi < \mathbf{J}_f^{-T}(\mathbf{x}_j)\mathbf{F}_j, \mathbf{J}_f(\mathbf{x}_j)\boldsymbol{\delta_x} >) \\ \sin(\pi < \mathbf{J}_f^{-T}(\mathbf{x}_j)\mathbf{F}_j, \mathbf{J}_f(\mathbf{x}_j)\boldsymbol{\delta_x} >) \end{bmatrix} \tag{9}$$

$$= \mathbf{A}_j \odot \begin{bmatrix} \cos(\pi < \mathbf{F}_j, \boldsymbol{\delta_x} >) \\ \sin(\pi < \mathbf{F}_j, \boldsymbol{\delta_x} >) \end{bmatrix} \tag{10}$$

$$= h_\psi(\mathbf{z}_j, \boldsymbol{\delta_x}). \tag{11}$$

When comparing Eq. (4) and Eq. (11), we see that LTEW representation is capable of extracting Fourier information for warped images by utilizing the local grid in input coordinate space $\boldsymbol{\delta_x}$ instead of $\boldsymbol{\delta_y}$.

3.3   Shape-Dependent Phase Estimation

For SISR tasks within symmetric scale factors, the pixel shape of upsampled images is square and spatially invariant. However, when it comes to image warping, pixels in resampled images are able to have arbitrary shapes and spatially-varying, as described in Fig. 3.(a). To address this issue, we represent the pixel shape $\mathbf{s(y)} \in \mathbb{R}^{12}$ ($\mathbb{R}^4$ is for pixel orientation, and $\mathbb{R}^8$ is for pixel curvature) with a gradient of coordinate transformation for a point $\mathbf{y}$ as

$$\mathbf{s(y)} = [\tilde{\mathbf{J}}_{f^{-1}}(\mathbf{y}), \tilde{\mathbf{H}}_{f^{-1}}(\mathbf{y})] \tag{12}$$

where $[\cdot, \cdot]$ refers to the concatenation after flattening, $\tilde{\mathbf{J}}_{f^{-1}}(\mathbf{y}) \in \mathbb{R}^{2\times2}$ and $\tilde{\mathbf{H}}_{f^{-1}}(\mathbf{y}) \in \mathbb{R}^{2\times2\times2}$ denote the numerical Jacobian matrix, indicating an orientation of pixel, and the numerical Hessian tensor, specifying the degree of curvature, respectively. For shape representation, we apply an inverse coordinate transformation to a query point and its eight nearest points ($\mathbf{y} + [\frac{m}{W}, \frac{n}{H}]$ with $[m, n] \in [-1, 0, 1]$) and compute the difference to calculate numerical derivatives as described in Fig. 3(b). Let us assume that given coordinate transformation f is in class C^2, which means $f_{x_1 x_2} = f_{x_2 x_1}$. Hence; we use only six elements in $\tilde{\mathbf{H}}_{f^{-1}}(\mathbf{y})$ for shape representation.

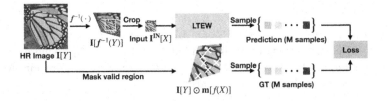

Fig. 4. Training strategy for Local Texture Estimator Warp (LTEW).

Phase in Eq. (13) includes the information of edge locations or the shape of pixels [27]. Therefore, we redefine the estimating function in Eq. (11) as:

$$h_\psi(\mathbf{z}_j, \boldsymbol{\delta}_\mathbf{x}, s(\mathbf{y})) = \mathbf{A}_j \odot \begin{bmatrix} \cos\{\pi(< \mathbf{F}_j, \boldsymbol{\delta}_\mathbf{x} > + h_p(s(\mathbf{y})))\} \\ \sin\{\pi(< \mathbf{F}_j, \boldsymbol{\delta}_\mathbf{x} > + h_p(s(\mathbf{y})))\} \end{bmatrix} \quad (13)$$

where $h_p(\cdot) : \mathbb{R}^{10} \mapsto \mathbb{R}^D$ is a phase estimator.

Lastly, we add a bilinear interpolated image $\mathbf{I}_B[\mathbf{y}] = \boldsymbol{f}_B(\mathbf{I^{IN}}) \simeq \mathbf{I^{IN}}(f^{-1}(\mathbf{y}))$ to stabilize network convergence and aid LTEW in learning high-frequency details [25]. Thus, the local neural representation of a warped image $\mathbf{I^{WARP}}$ with the proposed LTEW is formulated as follows:

$$\mathbf{I^{WARP}}[\mathbf{y}; \Theta, \psi] = \mathbf{I}_B[\mathbf{y}] + \sum_{j \in \mathcal{J}} w_j g_\theta(h_\psi(\mathbf{z}_j, f^{-1}(\mathbf{y}) - \mathbf{x}_j, s(\mathbf{y}))) \quad (14)$$

4   Methods

4.1   Architecture Details

Our LTEW-based image warping network consists of an encoder (E_φ), the LTEW (h_ψ, a purple shaded region in Fig. 2), and a decoder (g_θ). An encoder (E_φ) is designed with a deep SR network, such as EDSR [30], RCAN [51], RRDB [48], without upscaling modules. A decoder (g_θ) is a 4-layer MLP with ReLUs, and its hidden dimension is 256. Our LTEW (h_ψ) takes a local grid ($\boldsymbol{\delta}_\mathbf{x}$), shape (s), and feature map (z) as input, and includes an amplitude estimator (h_a), a frequency estimator (h_f), and a phase estimator (h_p). An amplitude and a frequency estimator are implemented with 3×3 convolution layer having 256 channels, and a phase estimator is a single linear layer with 128 channels. We assume that a warped image has the same texture near point $f(\mathbf{x}_j)$. Hence, we find estimated Fourier information ($\mathbf{A}_j, \mathbf{F}_j$) at $\mathbf{x}_j$ using the nearest-neighborhood interpolation. Then, estimated phase is added to an inner product between the local grid ($\boldsymbol{\delta}_\mathbf{x}$) and estimated frequencies, as in Eq. (13). Before the decoder (g_θ) resamples images, we multiply amplitude and sinusoidal activation output.

4.2   Training Strategy

We have two batches with a size B: (1) Image batch $\{I_1, I_2, \ldots, I_B\}$, $I_i[Y] \in \mathbb{R}^{H \times W \times 3}$. (2) Coordinate transformation batch $\{f_1, f_2, \ldots, f_B\}$, where each f_i : $X \mapsto Y$ is differentiable and invertible. For an input image preparation, we first apply an inverse coordinate transformation as:

$$\{I_1[f_1^{-1}(Y)], I_2[f_2^{-1}(Y)], \ldots, I_B[f_B^{-1}(Y)]\} \tag{15}$$

where $I_i[f_i^{-1}(Y)] \in \mathbb{R}^{h_i \times w_i \times 3}$. While avoiding void pixels, we crop input images $I_i^{crop}[f_i^{-1}(Y)] \in \mathbb{R}^{h \times w \times 3}$, where $h \leq \min(\{h_i\}), w \leq \min(\{w_i\})$. For a ground truth (GT) preparation, we randomly sample M query points among valid coordinates for an i-th batch element as: $\{\mathbf{y}_1^i, \mathbf{y}_2^i, \ldots, \mathbf{y}_M^i\}$, where $\mathbf{y}_j^i \in \mathbb{R}^2$. Then, we evaluate our LTEW for each query point with cropped input images to compute loss as in Fig. 4 by comparing with following GT batch:

$$\begin{pmatrix} I_1[\mathbf{y}_1^1] & \cdots & I_B[\mathbf{y}_1^B] \\ \vdots & \ddots & \\ I_1[\mathbf{y}_M^1] & & I_B[\mathbf{y}_M^B] \end{pmatrix} \tag{16}$$

where $I_i[\mathbf{y}_j^i]$ is an RGB value.

For asymmetric-scale SR, each scale factor s_x, s_y is randomly sampled from $\mathcal{U}(0.25, 1)$. For homography transform, we randomly sample inverse coordinate transformation from the following distribution, dubbed *in-scale*:

$$\begin{pmatrix} 1 & h_x & 0 \\ h_y & 1 & 0 \\ 0 & 0 & 1 \end{pmatrix} \begin{pmatrix} \cos\theta & \sin\theta & 0 \\ -\sin\theta & \cos\theta & 0 \\ 0 & 0 & 1 \end{pmatrix} \begin{pmatrix} s_x & 0 & 0 \\ 0 & s_y & 0 \\ 0 & 0 & 1 \end{pmatrix} \begin{pmatrix} 1 & 0 & t_x \\ 0 & 1 & t_y \\ p_x & p_y & 1 \end{pmatrix} \tag{17}$$

where $h_x, h_y \sim \mathcal{U}(-0.25, 0.25)$ are for sheering, $\theta \sim \mathcal{N}(0, 0.15^{\circ 2})$ is for rotation, $s_x, s_y \sim \mathcal{U}(0.35, 0.5)$ are for scaling, $t_x \sim \mathcal{U}(-0.75W, 0.125W)$, $t_y \sim \mathcal{U}(-0.75H, 0.125H)$, $p_x \sim \mathcal{U}(-0.6W, 0.6W)$, $p_y \sim \mathcal{U}(-0.6H, 0.6H)$ are for projection. We evaluate our LTEW for unseen transformations to verify the generalization ability. For asymmetric-scale SR and homography transform, untrained coordinate transformations are sampled from $s_x, s_y \sim \mathcal{U}(0.125, 0.25)$, dubbed *out-of-scale*, other parameter distributions for $h_x, h_y, \theta, t_x, t_y, p_x, p_y$ remain the same.

5   Experiments

5.1   Dataset and Training

We use a DIV2K dataset [1] of an NTIRE 2017 challenge [45] for training. For optimization, we use an L1 loss [30] and an Adam [26] with $\beta_1 = 0.9, \beta_2 = 0.999$. Networks are trained for 1000 epochs with batch size 16. The learning rate is initialized as 1e-4 and reduced by 0.5 at [200, 400, 600, 800]. Due to the page limit, evaluation details are provided in the supplementary.

5.2   Evaluation

Asymmetric-Scale SR. We compare our LTEW for asymmetric-scale SR to RCAN [51], MetaSR [19], ArbSR [46] within *in-scale* in Table 1, Fig. 5 and *out-of-scale* in Table 2, Fig. 6. For RCAN [51], we first upsample LR images by a factor of 4 and resample using bicubic interpolation. For MetaSR [19], we first upsample input images by a factor of $\max(s_x, s_y)$ and downsample using a bicubic method as in [46]. Except for the case of Set14 ($\times 3.5$, $\times 2$) and B100 ($\times 1.5$, $\times 3$), LTEW outperforms existing methods within asymmetric scale factors in performance and visual quality for all scale factors and all datasets.

Homography Transform. We compare our LTEW for homography transform to RRDB [48] and SRWarp [42] in Table 3, Fig. 7, Fig. 8. For RRDB [48], we super-sample input images by a factor of 4 and transform using bicubic resampling as in [42]. We see that our LTEW surpasses existing homography transform methods in mPSNR and visual quality for both *in-scale* and *out-of-scale*

Table 1. Quantitative comparison with state-of-the-art methods for **asymmetric-scale SR** within **in-scale** on benchmark datasets (PSNR (dB)). Red and blue colors indicate the best and the second-best performance, respectively.

Method	Set5			Set14			B100			Urban100		
	×1.5 ×4	×1.5 ×3.5	×1.6 ×3.05	×4 ×2	×3.5 ×2	×3.5 ×1.75	×4 ×1.4	×1.5 ×3	×3.5 ×1.45	×1.6 ×3	×1.6 ×3.8	×3.55 ×1.55
Bicubic	30.01	30.83	31.40	27.25	27.88	27.27	27.45	28.86	27.94	25.93	24.92	25.19
RCAN [51]	34.14	35.05	35.67	30.35	31.02	31.21	29.35	31.30	29.98	30.72	28.81	29.34
MetaSR-RCAN [19]	34.20	35.17	35.81	30.40	31.05	31.33	29.43	31.26	30.09	30.73	29.03	29.67
Arb-RCAN [46]	34.37	35.40	36.05	30.55	31.27	31.54	29.54	31.40	30.22	31.13	29.36	30.04
LTEW-RCAN (ours)	34.45	35.46	36.12	30.57	31.21	31.55	29.62	31.40	30.24	31.25	29.57	30.21

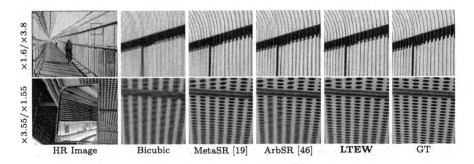

HR Image   Bicubic   MetaSR [19]   ArbSR [46]   **LTEW**   GT

Fig. 5. Qualitative comparison to other **asymmetric-scale SR** within **in-scale**. RCAN [51] is used as an encoder for all methods.

Table 2. Quantitative comparison with state-of-the-art methods for **asymmetric-scale SR** within **out-of-scale** on benchmark datasets (PSNR (dB)). Red and blue colors indicate the best and the second-best performance, respectively.

Method	Set5			Set14			B100			Urban100		
	×3 ×8	×3 ×7	×3.2 ×6.1	×8 ×4	×7 ×4	×7 ×3.5	×8 ×2.8	×3 ×6	×7 ×2.9	×3.2 ×6	×3.2 ×7.6	×7.1 ×3.1
Bicubic	25.69	26.35	26.84	24.27	24.62	24.79	24.67	25.58	24.98	22.55	21.92	22.15
RCAN [51]	29.00	30.01	30.46	26.48	26.94	27.11	26.06	27.19	26.47	25.52	24.50	24.84
MetaSR-RCAN [19]	28.75	29.74	30.38	26.32	26.85	27.03	26.07	27.15	26.45	25.50	24.47	24.84
Arb-RCAN [46]	28.37	29.35	30.08	26.06	26.63	26.84	25.91	27.14	26.40	25.36	24.12	24.61
LTEW-RCAN (ours)	29.26	30.16	30.64	26.60	27.06	27.25	26.25	27.28	26.62	25.85	24.79	25.18

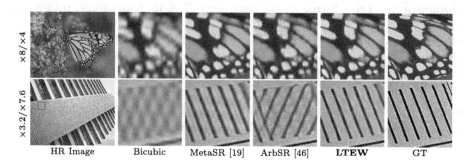

Fig. 6. Qualitative comparison to other **asymmetric-scale SR** within **out-of-scale**. RCAN [51] is used as an encoder for all methods.

Table 3. Quantitative comparison with state-of-the-art methods for **homography transform** within **in-scale** (*isc*) and **out-of-scale** (*osc*) on DIV2KW and benchmarkW datasets (mPSNR (dB)). Red and blue colors indicate the best and the second-best performance, respectively.

Method	DIV2KW		Set5W		Set14W		B100W		Urban100W	
	isc	*osc*	*isc*	*osc*	*isc*	*osc*	*isc*	*osc*	*isc*	*osc*
Bicubic	27.85	25.03	35.00	28.75	28.79	24.57	28.67	25.02	24.84	21.89
RRDB [48]	30.76	26.84	37.40	30.34	31.56	25.95	30.29	26.32	28.83	23.94
SRWarp-RRDB [42]	31.04	26.75	37.93	29.90	32.11	25.35	30.48	26.10	29.45	24.04
LTEW-RRDB (ours)	31.10	26.92	38.20	31.07	32.15	26.02	30.56	26.41	29.50	24.25

ERP Perspective Projection. We train our LTEW to perform homography transform and apply an unseen transformation: ERP perspective projection, to validate the generalization ability. Since we are not able to obtain high-quality GT for ERP perspective projection (due to JPEG compression artifact), we visually compare our method to RRDB [48] and SRWarp [42] in Fig. 9. For RRDB [48], we upsample input ERP images by a factor of 4 and interpolate them in a bicubic manner. Resolution of input ERP images is 1664 × 832. As pointed out in [14], considering HMD's limited hardware resources, storing and transmitting

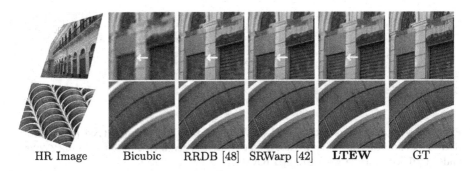

HR Image   Bicubic   RRDB [48]   SRWarp [42]   **LTEW**   GT

Fig. 7. Qualitative comparison to other **homography transform** within **in-scale**. RRDB [48] is used as an encoder for all methods.

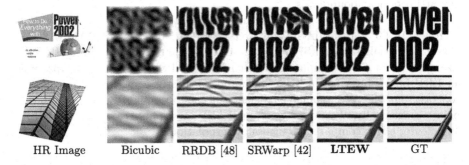

HR Image   Bicubic   RRDB [48]   SRWarp [42]   **LTEW**   GT

Fig. 8. Qualitative comparison to other **homography transform** within **out-of-scale**. RRDB [48] is used as an encoder for all methods.

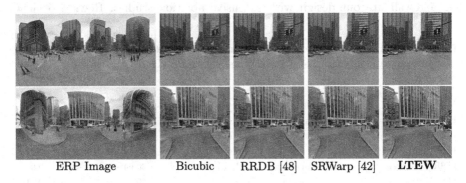

ERP Image   Bicubic   RRDB [48]   SRWarp [42]   **LTEW**

Fig. 9. Qualitative comparison to other **warping** for **ERP perspective projection**. RRDB [48] is used as an encoder for all methods.

ERP images in full resolution is impractical. Therefore, we downsample HR ERP images by a factor of 4 and then project images to a size of 832×832 with a field of view (FOV) $120°$. From Fig. 9, we observe that RRDB [48] is limited in capturing high-frequency details, and SRWarp [42] shows artifacts

ERP Image (8190px × 2529px)   LTEW   Bicubic **LTEW**

Fig. 10. Visual demonstration of LTEW for **HR ERP perspective projection**. RRDB [48] and SRWarp [42] are not able to evaluate given ERP size (8190px×2529px) under CPU-computing with 512 GB RAM.

near boundaries. In contrast, our proposed LTEW captures fine details without any artifacts near boundaries.

In Fig. 10, we project an HR ERP image with size 8190×2529 to 4095×4095 with a FOV $90°$ on the Intel Xeon Gold 6226R@2.90 GHz and RAM 512 GB. Note that RRDB [48] and SRWarp [42] are not able to evaluate given HR ERP size even under CPU-computing. Both RRDB and SRWarp need to upsample an ERP image by a factor of 4, consuming a massive amount of memory. In contrast, our LTEW is memory-efficient since we are able to query evaluation points sequentially. We notice that our LTEW is capable of restoring sharper and clearer edges compared to bicubic interpolation.

5.3   Ablation Study

In Table 4, we explore other arbitrary-scale SR methods [10,50] for image warping and validate our design with extensive ablation studies. Rows 1–5 show

Table 4. Quantitative ablation study for **homography transform** within **in-scale** (*isc*) and **out-of-scale** (*osc*) on DIV2KW dataset (mPSNR (dB)). EDSR-baseline [30] is used as an encoder.

Method	Amp	Long	N_{F_j}	Act	Jacob	Hess	*isc*	*osc*
LIIF $(-c)$ [10]	Concat			ReLU	✗	✗	30.65(−0.28)	26.73(+0.00)
LIIF [10] + Eq. (12)	Concat			ReLU	✓	✓	30.74(−0.09)	26.66(−0.07)
LIIF [10] + Eq. (12) + [40]	Concat			sin	✓	✓	30.49(−0.34)	26.52(−0.21)
ITSRN $(-token)$ [50]	Transformer			ReLU	✗	✗	30.64(−0.19)	26.69(−0.04)
ITSRN [50] + Eq. (12)	Transformer			ReLU	✓	✓	30.74(−0.09)	26.52(−0.21)
LTEW $(-A)$	✗	✓	256	ReLU	✓	✓	30.77(−0.06)	26.66(−0.07)
LTEW $(-L)$	✓	✗	256	ReLU	✓	✓	30.79(−0.04)	26.67(−0.06)
LTEW $(-F)$	✓	✓	128	ReLU	✓	✓	30.80(−0.03)	26.70(−0.03)
LTEW $(-P_J, -P_H, +c$ [27]$)$	✓	✓	256	ReLU	$(2r_x, 2/r_y)$		25.23(−5.60)	25.91(−0.82)
LTEW $(-P_J, -P_H)$	✓	✓	256	ReLU	✗	✗	30.69(−0.14)	**26.76**(+0.03)
LTEW $(-P_J)$	✓	✓	256	ReLU	✗	✓	30.70(−0.13)	26.72(−0.01)
LTEW $(-P_H)$	✓	✓	256	ReLU	✓	✗	30.80(−0.03)	26.73(+0.00)
LTEW + [40]	✓	✓	256	sin	✓	✓	30.80(−0.03)	26.71(−0.02)
LTEW	✓	✓	256	ReLU	✓	✓	**30.83**(+0.00)	26.73(+0.00)

that Fourier features provide performance gain compared to concatenation [10], transformer [50] or periodic activation [40]. Since [10,50] are designed to perform rectangular SR, we retrain them after modifying *cell* in [10] (rows 2–3) and *token* in [50] (row 5) to our shape term as Eq. (12).

In rows 6–8, we remove an amplitude estimator (row 6), long skip connection (row 7), and reduce the number of estimated frequencies (row 8). We see that each component consistently enhances mPSNR of LTEW for both *in-scale* and *out-of-scale*. In row 9, we test LTEW with spatially-invariant cell as [27], specifically $r_\mathbf{x} = 2w/W, r_\mathbf{y} = 2h/H$. It causes a significant mPSNR drop for both *in-scale* and *out-of-scale*. From rows 10–12, we observe that both the Jacobian and Hessian shapes are significant in improving mPSNR only for *in-scale*. Inspired by [49], we hypothesize that INR performs superior interpolating unseen coordinates but relatively poorly extrapolating untrained shapes. Extrapolation for untrained shapes will be investigated in future work.

5.4   Fourier Feature Space

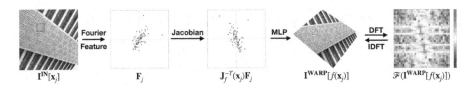

Fig. 11. Visualization of Fourier feature space from LTEW.

In Fig. 11, we visualize estimated Fourier feature space from LTEW and the discrete Fourier transform (DFT) of a warped image for validation. We first scatter estimated frequencies to 2D space and set the color according to magnitude. We observe that our LTEW (h_ψ) extracts Fourier information ($\mathbf{F}_j$) for an input image at $\mathbf{x}_j$ ($\mathbf{I^{IN}}[\mathbf{x}_j]$). By observing pixels inside an encoder's receptive field (RF), LTEW estimates dominant frequencies and corresponding Fourier coefficients for RF-sized local patches of an input image. Before our MLP (g_θ) represents $\mathbf{I^{WARP}}[f(\mathbf{x}_j)]$, the Fourier space ($\mathbf{F}_j$) is transformed by the Jacobian matrix $\mathbf{J}_f^{-T}(\mathbf{x}_j)$ and matched to a frequency response of an output image at $f(\mathbf{x}_j)$ ($\mathcal{F}(\mathbf{I^{WARP}}[f(\mathbf{x}_j)])$). We observe that LTEW utilizing the local grid in output space ($\delta_\mathbf{y}$) instead of $\delta_\mathbf{x}$ diverges during training. We hypothesize that representing $\mathbf{I^{WARP}}[f(\mathbf{x}_j)]$ with frequencies ($\mathbf{F}_j$) of an input image makes the overall training procedure unstable. This indicates that a spatially-varying Jacobian matrix $\mathbf{J}_f^{-T}(\cdot)$ for the given coordinate transformation f is significant in predicting accurate frequency responses of warped images. By estimating Fourier response in latent space instead of directly applying DFT to input images, we avoid extracting undesirable frequencies due to aliasing, as discussed in [27].

5.5 Discussion

In Table 5, we compare model complexity and symmetric-scale SR performance of our LTEW for both *in-scale* and *out-of-scale* to other warping methods: ArbSR [46] and SRWarp [42]. Note that ArbSR [46] and SRWarp [42] are learned to perform asymmetric-scale SR and homography transform. Following [27], we use $\max(\mathbf{s}, \mathbf{s}_{tr})$ instead of $\mathbf{s}$ in Eq. (13) for phase estimation. We see that LTEW significantly outperforms exiting warping methods for *out-of-scale*, achieving competitive quality to [42,46] for *in-scale*. A local ensemble [10,22,27] in LTEW, preventing blocky artifacts, makes the model more complex than ArbSR [46]. SRWarp [42] blends ×1, ×2, and ×4 features, leading to increased model complexity than LTEW, which uses only an ×1 feature map.

Table 5. Quantitative comparison with state-of-the-art warping methods for **symmetric-scale SR** on B100 dataset (PSNR (dB)). RCAN [51] and RRDB [48] are used as encoders. Computation time and memory consumption are measured with an 256 × 256-sized input for an ×2 task on NVIDIA RTX 3090 24 GB.

Method	Training task	#Params.	Runtime	Memory	in-scale			out-of-scale	
					×2	×3	×4	×6	×8
Arb-RCAN [46]	Asymmetric -scale SR	16.6 M	**160 ms**	**1.39 GB**	**32.39**	**29.32**	27.76	25.74	24.55
LTEW-RCAN (ours)		**15.8 M**	283 ms	1.77 GB	32.36	29.30	**27.78**	**26.01**	**24.95**
SRWarp-RRDB [42]	Homography transform	18.3 M	328 ms	2.34 GB	32.31	29.27	**27.77**	25.33	24.45
LTEW-RRDB (ours)		**17.1 M**	**285 ms**	**1.79 GB**	32.35	29.29	27.76	**25.98**	**24.95**

6 Conclusions

In this paper, we proposed the continuous neural representation by learning Fourier characteristics of images warped by the given coordinate transformation. Particularly, we found that shape-dependent phase estimation and long skip connection enable MLP to predict signals more accurately. We demonstrated that the LTEW-based neural function outperforms existing warping techniques for asymmetric-scale SR and homography transform. Moreover, our method effectively generalizes untrained coordinate transformations, specifically *out-of-scale* and ERP perspective projection.

Acknowledgement. This work was partly supported by the National Research Foundation of Korea (NRF) grant funded by the Korea government (MSIT) (No. 2021R1A4A1028652), the DGIST R&D Program of the Ministry of Science and ICT (No. 22-IJRP-01) and Institute of Information & communications Technology Planning & Evaluation (IITP) grant funded by the Korea government (MSIT) (No. IITP-2021-0-02068).

References

1. Agustsson, E., Timofte, R.: NTIRE 2017 challenge on single image super-resolution: dataset and study. In: Proceedings of the IEEE Conference on Computer Vision and Pattern Recognition (CVPR) Workshops, July 2017
2. Arican, Z., Frossard, P.: Joint registration and super-resolution with omnidirectional images. IEEE Trans. Image Process. **20**(11), 3151–3162 (2011)
3. Bagnato, L., Boursier, Y., Frossard, P., Vandergheynst, P.: Plenoptic based super-resolution for omnidirectional image sequences. In: 2010 IEEE International Conference on Image Processing, pp. 2829–2832 (2010)
4. Benbarka, N., Höfer, T., Riaz, H.u.M., Zell, A.: Seeing implicit neural representations as fourier series. In: Proceedings of the IEEE/CVF Winter Conference on Applications of Computer Vision (WACV), pp. 2041–2050, January 2022
5. Boomsma, W., Frellsen, J.: Spherical convolutions and their application in molecular modelling. In: Guyon, I., Luxburg, U.V., Bengio, S., Wallach, H., Fergus, R., Vishwanathan, S., Garnett, R. (eds.) Advances in Neural Information Processing Systems, vol. 30. Curran Associates, Inc. (2017)
6. Bracewell, R., Chang, K.Y., Jha, A., Wang, Y.H.: Affine theorem for two-dimensional Fourier transform. Electron. Lett. **29**(3), 304–304 (1993)
7. Chan, K.C., Wang, X., Yu, K., Dong, C., Loy, C.C.: BasicVSR: the Search for Essential Components in Video Super-Resolution and Beyond. In: Proceedings of the IEEE/CVF Conference on Computer Vision and Pattern Recognition (CVPR), pp. 4947–4956, June 2021
8. Chen, H., et al.: Pre-trained image processing transformer. In: Proceedings of the IEEE/CVF Conference on Computer Vision and Pattern Recognition (CVPR), pp. 12299–12310 (June 2021)
9. Chen, H., He, B., Wang, H., Ren, Y., Lim, S.N., Shrivastava, A.: NeRV: neural representations for videos. In: Ranzato, M., Beygelzimer, A., Dauphin, Y., Liang, P., Vaughan, J.W. (eds.) Advances in Neural Information Processing Systems, vol. 34, pp. 21557–21568. Curran Associates, Inc. (2021)
10. Chen, Y., Liu, S., Wang, X.: Learning continuous image representation with local implicit image function. In: Proceedings of the IEEE/CVF Conference on Computer Vision and Pattern Recognition (CVPR), pp. 8628–8638, June 2021
11. Chiang, M.C., Boult, T.: Efficient super-resolution via image warping. Image Vis. Comput. **18**(10), 761–771 (2000)
12. Chiang, M.C., Boult, T.: Efficient image warping and super-resolution. In: Proceedings Third IEEE Workshop on Applications of Computer Vision. WACV1996, pp. 56–61 (1996)
13. Dai, T., Cai, J., Zhang, Y., Xia, S.T., Zhang, L.: Second-order attention network for single image super-resolution. In: Proceedings of the IEEE/CVF Conference on Computer Vision and Pattern Recognition (CVPR), June 2019
14. Deng, X., Wang, H., Xu, M., Guo, Y., Song, Y., Yang, L.: LAU-Net: Latitude adaptive upscaling network for omnidirectional image super-resolution. In: Proceedings of the IEEE/CVF Conference on Computer Vision and Pattern Recognition (CVPR), pp. 9189–9198, June 202
15. Dosovitskiy, A., et al.: An image is worth 16×16 words: transformers for image recognition at scale. In: 9th International Conference on Learning Representations, ICLR 2021, Virtual Event, Austria, 3–7 May 2021. OpenReview.net (2021)
16. Fathony, R., Sahu, A.K., Willmott, D., Kolter, J.Z.: Multiplicative filter networks. In: 9th International Conference on Learning Representations, ICLR 2021, Virtual Event, Austria, May 3–7, 2021. OpenReview.net (2021)

17. Greene, N., Heckbert, P.S.: Creating raster omnimax images from multiple perspective views using the elliptical weighted average filter. IEEE Comput. Graphics Appl. **6**(6), 21–27 (1986)
18. Hornik, K., Stinchcombe, M., White, H.: Multilayer feedforward networks are universal approximators. Neural Netw. **2**(5), 359–366 (1989)
19. Hu, X., Mu, H., Zhang, X., Wang, Z., Tan, T., Sun, J.: Meta-SR: a magnification-arbitrary network for super-resolution. In: Proceedings of the IEEE/CVF Conference on Computer Vision and Pattern Recognition (CVPR), June 2019
20. Huang, M., Shen, Q., Ma, Z., Bovik, A.C., Gupta, P., Zhou, R., Cao, X.: Modeling the perceptual quality of immersive images rendered on head mounted displays: resolution and compression. IEEE Trans. Image Process. **27**(12), 6039–6050 (2018)
21. Jaderberg, M., Simonyan, K., Zisserman, A., kavukcuoglu, K.: Spatial Transformer Networks. In: Cortes, C., Lawrence, N., Lee, D., Sugiyama, M., Garnett, R. (eds.) Advances in Neural Information Processing Systems, vol. 28. Curran Associates, Inc. (2015)
22. Jiang, C.M., Sud, A., Makadia, A., Huang, J., Niessner, M., Funkhouser, T.: Local implicit grid representations for 3D scenes. In: IEEE/CVF Conference on Computer Vision and Pattern Recognition (CVPR), June 2020
23. Jiang, W., Trulls, E., Hosang, J., Tagliasacchi, A., Yi, K.M.: COTR: correspondence transformer for matching across images. In: Proceedings of the IEEE/CVF International Conference on Computer Vision (ICCV), pp. 6207–6217, October 2021
24. Keys, R.: Cubic convolution interpolation for digital image processing. IEEE Trans. Acoust. Speech Signal Process. **29**(6), 1153–1160 (1981)
25. Kim, J., Lee, J.K., Lee, K.M.: Accurate image super-resolution using very deep convolutional networks. In: Proceedings of the IEEE Conference on Computer Vision and Pattern Recognition (CVPR), June 2016
26. Kingma, D.P., Ba, J.: Adam: a method for stochastic optimization. In: Bengio, Y., LeCun, Y. (eds.) 3rd International Conference on Learning Representations, ICLR 2015, San Diego, CA, USA, 7–9 May, 2015, Conference Track Proceedings (2015)
27. Lee, J., Jin, K.H.: Local Texture Estimator for Implicit Representation Function. In: Proceedings of the IEEE/CVF Conference on Computer Vision and Pattern Recognition (CVPR). pp. 1929–1938 (June 2022)
28. Lee, Y., Jeong, J., Yun, J., Cho, W., Yoon, K.J.: SpherePHD: applying CNNs on a spherical PolyHeDron representation of 360deg images. In: Proceedings of the IEEE/CVF Conference on Computer Vision and Pattern Recognition (CVPR), June 2019
29. Liang, J., Cao, J., Sun, G., Zhang, K., Van Gool, L., Timofte, R.: SwinIR: image restoration using swin transformer. In: Proceedings of the IEEE/CVF International Conference on Computer Vision (ICCV) Workshops, pp. 1833–1844, October 2021
30. Lim, B., Son, S., Kim, H., Nah, S., Mu Lee, K.: Enhanced deep residual networks for single image super-resolution. In: Proceedings of the IEEE Conference on Computer Vision and Pattern Recognition (CVPR) Workshops, July 2017
31. Liu, Z., et al.: Swin transformer: hierarchical vision transformer using shifted windows. In: Proceedings of the IEEE/CVF International Conference on Computer Vision (ICCV), pp. 10012–10022, October 2021
32. Mei, Y., Fan, Y., Zhou, Y.: Image super-resolution with non-local sparse attention. In: Proceedings of the IEEE/CVF Conference on Computer Vision and Pattern Recognition (CVPR), pp. 3517–3526 (June 2021)

33. Mescheder, L., Oechsle, M., Niemeyer, M., Nowozin, S., Geiger, A.: Occupancy networks: learning 3D reconstruction in function space. In: Proceedings of the IEEE/CVF Conference on Computer Vision and Pattern Recognition (CVPR), June 2019

34. Mildenhall, B., Srinivasan, P.P., Tancik, M., Barron, J.T., Ramamoorthi, R., Ng, R.: NeRF: representing scenes as neural radiance fields for view synthesis. In: Vedaldi, A., Bischof, H., Brox, T., Frahm, J.-M. (eds.) ECCV 2020. LNCS, vol. 12346, pp. 405–421. Springer, Cham (2020). https://doi.org/10.1007/978-3-030-58452-8_24

35. Niu, B.: Single image super-resolution via a holistic attention network. In: Vedaldi, A., Bischof, H., Brox, T., Frahm, J.-M. (eds.) ECCV 2020. LNCS, vol. 12357, pp. 191–207. Springer, Cham (2020). https://doi.org/10.1007/978-3-030-58610-2_12

36. Park, J.J., Florence, P., Straub, J., Newcombe, R., Lovegrove, S.: DeepSDF: learning continuous signed distance functions for shape representation. In: Proceedings of the IEEE/CVF Conference on Computer Vision and Pattern Recognition (CVPR), June 2019

37. Rahaman, N., et al.: On the spectral bias of neural networks. In: Chaudhuri, K., Salakhutdinov, R. (eds.) Proceedings of the 36th International Conference on Machine Learning. Proceedings of Machine Learning Research, vol. 97, pp. 5301–5310. PMLR, 09–15 Jun 2019

38. Sajjadi, M.S.M., Vemulapalli, R., Brown, M.: Frame-recurrent video super-resolution. In: Proceedings of the IEEE Conference on Computer Vision and Pattern Recognition (CVPR), June 2018

39. Shi, W., et al.: Real-time single image and video super-resolution using an efficient sub-pixel convolutional neural network. In: Proceedings of the IEEE Conference on Computer Vision and Pattern Recognition (CVPR), June 2016

40. Sitzmann, V., Martel, J., Bergman, A., Lindell, D., Wetzstein, G.: Implicit neural representations with periodic activation functions. In: Larochelle, H., Ranzato, M., Hadsell, R., Balcan, M.F., Lin, H. (eds.) Advances in Neural Information Processing Systems, vol. 33, pp. 7462–7473. Curran Associates, Inc. (2020)

41. Sitzmann, V., Zollhoefer, M., Wetzstein, G.: Scene Representation Networks: Continuous 3D-Structure-Aware Neural Scene Representations. In: Wallach, H., Larochelle, H., Beygelzimer, A., d' Alché-Buc, F., Fox, E., Garnett, R. (eds.) Advances in Neural Information Processing Systems. vol. 32. Curran Associates, Inc. (2019)

42. Son, S., Lee, K.M.: SRWarp: generalized image super-resolution under arbitrary transformation. In: Proceedings of the IEEE/CVF Conference on Computer Vision and Pattern Recognition (CVPR), pp. 7782–7791, June 2021

43. Sun, D., Yang, X., Liu, M.Y., Kautz, J.: PWC-Net: CNNs for optical flow using pyramid, warping, and cost volume. In: Proceedings of the IEEE Conference on Computer Vision and Pattern Recognition (CVPR), June 2018

44. Tancik, M., et al.: Fourier features let networks learn high frequency functions in low dimensional domains. In: Larochelle, H., Ranzato, M., Hadsell, R., Balcan, M.F., Lin, H. (eds.) Advances in Neural Information Processing Systems, vol. 33, pp. 7537–7547. Curran Associates, Inc. (2020)

45. Timofte, R., Agustsson, E., Van Gool, L., Yang, M.H., Zhang, L.: NTIRE 2017 challenge on single image super-resolution: methods and results. In: Proceedings of the IEEE Conference on Computer Vision and Pattern Recognition (CVPR) Workshops, July 2017

46. Wang, L., Wang, Y., Lin, Z., Yang, J., An, W., Guo, Y.: Learning a single network for scale-arbitrary super-resolution. In: Proceedings of the IEEE/CVF International Conference on Computer Vision (ICCV), pp. 4801–4810, October 2021

47. Wang, P.S., Liu, Y., Yang, Y.Q., Tong, X.: Spline positional encoding for learning 3D implicit signed distance fields. In: Zhou, Z.H. (ed.) Proceedings of the Thirtieth International Joint Conference on Artificial Intelligence, IJCAI-21, pp. 1091–1097. International Joint Conferences on Artificial Intelligence Organization (8 2021), main Track

48. Wang, X., Yu, K., Wu, S., Gu, J., Liu, Y., Dong, C., Qiao, Yu., Loy, C.C.: ESR-GAN: enhanced super-resolution generative adversarial networks. In: Leal-Taixé, L., Roth, S. (eds.) ECCV 2018. LNCS, vol. 11133, pp. 63–79. Springer, Cham (2019). https://doi.org/10.1007/978-3-030-11021-5_5

49. Xu, K., Zhang, M., Li, J., Du, S.S., Kawarabayashi, K., Jegelka, S.: How neural networks extrapolate: from feedforward to graph neural networks. In: 9th International Conference on Learning Representations, ICLR 2021, Virtual Event, Austria, 3–7 May, 2021. OpenReview.net (2021)

50. Yang, J., Shen, S., Yue, H., Li, K.: Implicit transformer network for screen content image continuous super-resolution. In: Ranzato, M., Beygelzimer, A., Dauphin, Y., Liang, P., Vaughan, J.W. (eds.) Advances in Neural Information Processing Systems, vol. 34, pp. 13304–13315. Curran Associates, Inc. (2021)

51. Zhang, Y., Li, K., Li, K., Wang, L., Zhong, B., Fu, Y.: Image super-resolution using very deep residual channel attention networks. In: Ferrari, V., Hebert, M., Sminchisescu, C., Weiss, Y. (eds.) ECCV 2018. LNCS, vol. 11211, pp. 294–310. Springer, Cham (2018). https://doi.org/10.1007/978-3-030-01234-2_18

52. Zhang, Y., Tian, Y., Kong, Y., Zhong, B., Fu, Y.: Residual dense network for image super-resolution. In: Proceedings of the IEEE Conference on Computer Vision and Pattern Recognition (CVPR), June 2018

SepLUT: Separable Image-Adaptive Lookup Tables for Real-Time Image Enhancement

Canqian Yang[1], Meiguang Jin[2], Yi Xu[1(✉)], Rui Zhang[1], Ying Chen[2], and Huaida Liu[2]

[1] MoE Key Lab of Artificial Intelligence, AI Institute,
Shanghai Jiao Tong University, Shanghai, China
{charles.young,xuyi,zhang_rui}@sjtu.edu.cn
[2] Alibaba Group, Hangzhou, China
{meiguang.jmg,yingchen,liuhuaida.lhd}@alibaba-inc.com

Abstract. Image-adaptive lookup tables (LUTs) have achieved great success in real-time image enhancement tasks due to their high efficiency for modeling color transforms. However, they embed the complete transform, including the color component-independent and the component-correlated parts, into only a single type of LUTs, either 1D or 3D, in a coupled manner. This scheme raises a dilemma of improving model expressiveness or efficiency due to two factors. On the one hand, the 1D LUTs provide high computational efficiency but lack the critical capability of color components interaction. On the other, the 3D LUTs present enhanced component-correlated transform capability but suffer from heavy memory footprint, high training difficulty, and limited cell utilization. Inspired by the conventional divide-and-conquer practice in the image signal processor, we present SepLUT (separable image-adaptive lookup table) to tackle the above limitations. Specifically, we separate a single color transform into a cascade of component-independent and component-correlated sub-transforms instantiated as 1D and 3D LUTs, respectively. In this way, the capabilities of two sub-transforms can facilitate each other, where the 3D LUT complements the ability to mix up color components, and the 1D LUT redistributes the input colors to increase the cell utilization of the 3D LUT and thus enable the use of a more lightweight 3D LUT. Experiments demonstrate that the proposed method presents enhanced performance on photo retouching benchmark datasets than the current state-of-the-art and achieves real-time processing on both GPUs and CPUs.

C. Yang and M. Jin—Equal contribution.
Work partially done during an internship of C. Yang at Alibaba Group.

Supplementary Information The online version contains supplementary material available at https://doi.org/10.1007/978-3-031-19797-0_12.

S. Avidan et al. (Eds.): ECCV 2022, LNCS 13678, pp. 201–217, 2022.
https://doi.org/10.1007/978-3-031-19797-0_12

1 Introduction

The lookup table (LUT) is a promising data structure to efficiently conduct specific transforms by replacing expensive runtime computation with cheap array caching and indexing. It precomputes the outputs of a function over a sampled domain of inputs and evaluates the same function via efficient lookup and interpolation operations. LUTs are widely used to optimize color transforms in the image signal processor (ISP), a crucial component in the camera imaging pipeline and many display devices. To transform sensor signals into human-perceptible digital images, typical ISP follows the divide-and-conquer principle to utilize two types of LUTs, of 1D and 3D, for handling different transforms [15]. 1D LUTs are suitable for *component-independent transforms* that require no interaction between three color components, such as white-balancing, gamma correction, brightness adjustment, and contrast stretching. 3D LUTs further enable the mixture of different color components, thus supporting more sophisticated *component-correlated transforms*, like adjustments in hue and saturation.

The high effectiveness and efficiency of LUTs motivate recent advances in deep learning to propose learnable, image-adaptive LUTs for enhanced real-time image enhancement [1,11,14,17,18,21,25,26,30,32,35]. However, these methods encode a complete color transform to only a single type of LUTs, either 1D or 3D, but neglecting the limited capability of a single module to model component-independent and component-correlated transformations simultaneously. Such a paradigm limits the expressiveness of these methods. Specifically, methods based on 1D LUTs lack the critical model capability of interacting component information as they work on each color component independently. Though the methods based on 3D LUTs are able to handle both component-independent and component-correlated transforms, they model these two transforms in a coupled manner, which increases the capability requirement of the model. The reason owns to the lack of a prior component-independent transform that can rescale the input image range into a normalized and perceptually uniform color space for the 3D LUTs. Therefore, the 3D LUTs rely on increasing their sizes for adaption to the diversity of input color ranges. For example, [32,35] adopt 33-point 3D LUTs, while the ISP typically employs 17-point or even 9-point 3D LUTs [15]. The large LUT size introduces massive parameters, resulting in heavy memory burden and high training difficulty. Besides, adopting a relatively large LUT size will lead to insufficient cell utilization of the 3D LUTs since the colors appearing in a single input image usually occupy only a tiny sub-space of the entire color space, causing redundancy of the model capacity.

To simultaneously improve the model's expressiveness and efficiency, we propose a novel framework called separable image-adaptive lookup tables (SepLUT). It decouples a single color transform into component-independent and component-correlated sub-transforms instantiated as 1D and 3D LUTs, respectively. The idea is directly motivated by the common practice in ISP, where 1D and 3D LUTs play their roles in conjunction. As illustrated in Fig. 1, we follow the paradigm of dynamic neural functions [6] to employ a CNN backbone network on a downsampled, fixed-resolution version of the input image for predicting the

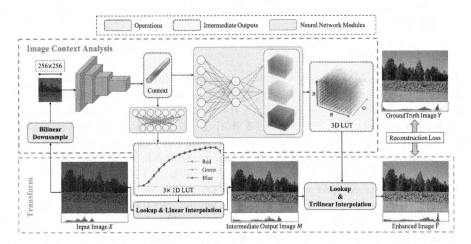

Fig. 1. Framework of the proposed method. Our method employs a lightweight CNN network to analyze the image context from a down-sampled, fixed-resolution version of the input image. The image context is used to guide the generation of a 3× 1D LUT and a 3D LUT in an image-adaptive fashion. The original input image is afterward enhanced by the cascade of the predicted 1D and 3D LUTs. Best viewed in color. (Color figure online)

parameters of a 3× 1D LUT and a 3D LUT. The two generated LUTs are then applied to the original input image sequentially – the 3× 1D LUT rescales each color channel to adaptively adjust the brightness/contrast, followed by the 3D LUT to mix up three color components for manipulation on hue and saturation. The advantages are two-fold. On the one hand, the 3D LUTs can complement the 1D LUTs with color components interaction. On the other, the 1D LUTs can redistribute the input colors into specific ranges of the following 3D LUTs, which increase the cell utilization of the 3D LUTs, thus reducing the redundant capacity and enabling the usage of smaller sizes. Furthermore, the consistency between the input and output spaces of a LUT allows trivial LUT quantization that provides significant lightweight property to the proposed method.

The contributions of this paper are three-fold: (1) We present a novel viewpoint of separating a single color transform into two sub-transforms, *i.e.*, the component-independent transform and the component-correlated transform. (2) We propose a general framework that adopts a cascade of 1D and 3D LUTs to instantiate the above two sub-transforms, making them facilitate each other and present overall lightweight property, high efficiency, and enhanced expressiveness. (3) We demonstrate the efficiency and effectiveness of the proposed method via extensive experiments on publicly available benchmark datasets.

2   Related Works

2.1   Lookup Tables

A lookup table (LUT) defines a table of values addressed by a set of indices. It usually serves as an effective and efficient representation of a univariate or multivariate function $y = f(x_1, \ldots, x_n), n = 1, 2, \ldots$ by enumerating all possible input combinations $\{(x_1, \ldots, x_n)\}$ and storing the corresponding output values y. The function can afterward be evaluated using only the memory access and interpolation, without performing the computation again. Therefore, LUTs are commonly used in computer systems [20,29], especially some embedded devices [15], to accelerate computation. The simplest LUT is the 1D LUT indexed by a single variable ($n = 1$), which utilizes linear interpolation to generate values of specific indices that are not an element of the table. Another frequently-used LUTs are the 3D LUTs indexed by a triplet of three independent variables ($n = 3$), which require more complicated interpolation techniques such as the trilinear [28] and the tetrahedral [16] interpolations. According to [15], most of the modules in the practical ISP systems are implemented using either 1D or 3D LUTs due to their high efficacy and suitability for modeling color transforms.

Learnable LUTs. The high efficiency and wide usage of the LUTs in ISP also attract efforts in deep learning-based image enhancement to learning more powerful LUTs via data-driven approaches. Previous works [1,11,14,17,18,21, 25,26,30] mainly focus on learning 1D LUTs to mimic the color adjustment curves in popular image enhancement software such as Photoshop and Lightroom. They regress either a set of the control points of the curve, or the coefficients of some hand-crafted functions (*e.g.*, polynomial function). However, these methods usually suffer from the lack of correlation between color channels. Recently, [32,35] extended those 1D LUT-based methods into using 3D LUTs. They predict 3D LUTs with adaption to different image contents by learning several image-independent basis 3D LUTs and combining them using image-dependent weights. The 3D LUTs consider the relationship between color channels and thus provide higher expressiveness to model more complicated color transforms. However, the large model capacity of the 3D LUTs requires massive learnable parameters, making these methods suffer from heavy memory/storage footprints. In contrast to previous works based on a single kind of LUTs, we present a more general framework that considers the conjunction of both types of LUTs, thus providing an advanced solution to the above limitations.

2.2   Image Enhancement

Existing learning-based image enhancement methods can be roughly categorized into two paradigms, *i.e.*, the fully convolutional network-based methods, and the color transform-based methods. The first paradigm [4,5,8,24,34,36] is to train a fully convolutional network (FCN) that directly regresses the enhanced image from the input in a dense prediction fashion. However, these methods

Table 1. Architecture of the backbone network, where m is a hyper-parameter that serves as a channel multiplier controlling the width of each convolutional layer.

Id	Layer	Output shape
0	Bilinear Resize	$3 \times 256 \times 256$
1	Conv3×3, LeakyReLU	$m \times 128 \times 128$
2	InstanceNorm	$m \times 128 \times 128$
3	Conv3×3, LeakyReLU	$2\,m \times 64 \times 64$
4	InstanceNorm	$2m \times 64 \times 64$
5	Conv3×3, LeakyReLU	$4\,m \times 32 \times 32$
6	InstanceNorm	$4m \times 32 \times 32$
7	Conv3×3, LeakyReLU	$8\,m \times 16 \times 16$
8	InstanceNorm	$8m \times 16 \times 16$
9	Conv3×3, LeakyReLU	$8\,m \times 8 \times 8$
10	Dropout (0.5)	$8\,m \times 8 \times 8$
11	AveragePooling	$8\,m \times 2 \times 2$
12	Reshape	$32m$

Table 2. Architecture of the 1D LUT generator, where S_o is the size (number of elements) of the 1D LUTs. "FC" denotes the fully-connected layer.

Id	Layer	Output shape
0	FC	$3\,S_o$
1	Reshape	$3 \times S_o$
2	Sigmoid	$3 \times S_o$

Table 3. Architecture of the 3D LUT generator, where S_t is the size (number of elements along each dimension) of the 3D LUT.

Id	Layer	Output shape
0	FC	K
1	FC	$3\,S_t^3$
2	Reshape	$3 \times S_t \times S_t \times S_t$

are still far from practical applications due to their heavy computational burdens and limited feasible input resolutions. In contrast, the second paradigm decouples the color transformations from the heavy CNN model for real-time and high-resolution processing. Specifically, these methods employ CNNs on a low-resolution, fixed-size version of the input image to predict image-adaptive parameters of some specific color transform functions. Typical color transform functions include affine transformation matrices [3,9,23,31], curve-based functions [1,11,14,17,18,21,25,26,30], multi-layer perceptrons (MLPs) [12] and 3D LUTs [32,35]. These learned transform functions can adapt to different input image contents and present high runtime efficiency. Some of them are also flexible and scalable on arbitrary input resolutions. Therefore, our work also follows this line of the color transform-based scheme and builds a novel framework with a cascade of 1D and 3D LUTs for real-time image enhancement.

3   Methods

3.1   Overall Framework

Figure 1 shows an overview of the proposed image enhancement framework, which follows the popular paradigm of dynamic neural functions. Specifically, a lightweight CNN network is employed as the backbone network on the input image to extract global context that will serve as the guide to generate image content-dependent color transform functions. The form of the color transform functions is designed as a cascade of a 3× 1D LUT and a 3D LUT, aiming to handle the component-independent and component-correlated transforms in a decoupled and sequential manner. Afterward, the generated functions enhance the quality of the input through efficient lookup and interpolation operations.

3.2   Global Image Context Analysis: Backbone Network

The backbone CNN network is central to achieving image-adaptiveness in the proposed framework. It is responsible for predicting the parameters of the subsequent 1D and 3D LUTs according to the image content through analyzing the input image $X \in [0,1]^{3 \times H \times W}$. Since both the 1D and 3D LUTs in our method are designed for global color transform, the backbone network only needs to capture a coarse understanding of the input image. Therefore, a low-resolution version (e.g., 256 × 256) of the input image is sufficient and can substantially reduce the computational cost to a fixed level. The detailed architecture of the CNN backbone network is listed in Table 1, where m is a hyper-parameter controlling the channel width of each convolutional layer. The backbone network adopts 5 strided convolutional layers to downsample the input image into 1/32 resolution. At the end of the network are an average pooling layer and a reshape operation that further convert the feature maps into a compact vector representation $E \in \mathbb{R}^{32\,m}$. The vector representation captures some global attributes of the input image and will be fed into the subsequent modules as the guide to generate image content-dependent LUT parameters.

3.3   Component-Independent Transform: 1D Lookup Tables

The component-independent transform aims to redistribute the input colors into a more perceptually uniform space that can increase the cell utilization of the following 3D LUT. In this paper, we propose to adopt the 3× 1D LUT for the above purpose, where three individual 1D LUTs are predicted for each color channel, respectively. The elements $\{T_{1D}^c\}_{c \in \{r,g,b\}}$ of the 1D LUTs are conditioned on the image context E to achieve image-adaptiveness, formulated as:

$$\{T_{1D}^r, T_{1D}^g, T_{1D}^b\} = g_{1D}(E), \tag{1}$$

where $T_{1D}^c \in [0,1]^{S_o}$ denotes a 1D LUT of S_o values for the channel $c \in \{r,g,b\}$. g_{1D} is the 1D LUT generator module that takes E as input and predicts all output values, whose architecture is detailed in Table 2. Note that the *sigmoid* layer is used to normalize the elements in the 1D LUTs into a valid range. Once the 1D LUTs are predicted, the component-independent transform can be performed on each pixel separably via simple linear interpolation:

$$M[c,h,w] = \mathrm{linear\_interpolate}(T_{1D}^c, X[c,h,w]), \tag{2}$$

where $M \in [0,1]^{3 \times H \times W}$ denotes the intermediate image transformed by the 1D LUTs. $h \in \mathbb{I}_0^{H-1}$ and $w \in \mathbb{I}_0^{W-1}$ are indices to traverse the image[1].

---

[1] $\mathbb{I}_s^t$ denotes the integer set starting from s and ending at t, i.e., $\mathbb{I}_s^t = \{s, \ldots, t\}$.

Intuitively, directly applying histogram equalization, a conventional technique in image processing to adjust image contrast, is another alternative as the component-independent transform to increase the distribution uniformity of each color component. However, histogram equalization maximizes the entropy of the image statically by mapping the input color ranges to an *exact uniform* distribution, which is not intelligent and not always necessary in the scenario of image enhancement. Instead, by adopting the data-driven approach to learn the 1D LUTs, our method is expected to be image-adaptive for the network and each input image. The quantitative comparisons can be found in Table 4.

3.4   Component-Correlated Transform: 3D Lookup Tables

After the previous component-independent transform, the component-correlated transform aims at mixing and interacting different color channels to achieve more sophisticated color transforms, such as alteration in hue and saturation. Considering the balance between expressiveness and efficiency, we choose the 3D LUTs to formulate such a transformation from a triplet to one another. A typical 3D LUT defines a 3D grid of S_t^3 elements, where S_t denotes the number of values along each color dimension. Similar to Sect. 3.3, all the S_t^3 elements in the 3D LUT should be automatically predicted by the neural network to consider the adaption to the diversity of various input images. Such an objective formulates a mapping from the image context E to a $3S_t^3$-dimension parameter space:

$$T_{3D} = g_{3D}(E), \qquad (3)$$

where $T_{3D} \in [0,1]^{3 \times S_t \times S_t \times S_t}$ denotes a 3D LUT of size S_t. g_{3D} is the 3D LUT generator module. To prevent the involvement of significant memory burden and training difficulty, we consider the *rank factorization* to decompose the complete mapping in Eq. (3) into two sub-mappings h_1 and h_2:

$$g_{3D} = h_1 \circ h_2, \ h_1 : \mathbb{R}^{32m} \to \mathbb{R}^K, \ h_2 : \mathbb{R}^K \to \mathbb{R}^{3S_t^3}. \qquad (4)$$

h_1 and h_2 can be instantiated with two respective fully-connected (FC) layers. Compared with a single FC layer, such a strategy reduces the number of parameters from $32m \times 3S_t^3$ to $K \times (32m + 3S_t^3)$, making the transform more feasible and easier to optimize. The detailed architecture can be found in Table 3.

Given the predicted 3D LUT T_{3D}, the final enhanced image $\hat{Y} \in [0,1]^{3 \times H \times W}$ can be derived via a simple trilinear interpolation:

$$\hat{Y}[c, h, w] = \text{trilinear\_interpolate}(T_{3D}, M[c, h, w]). \qquad (5)$$

3.5   Efficient Implementation via Quantization

Our method can also benefit from the model quantization technique to further reduce the memory and storage footprints. Specifically, the FC layers in the LUT generators (Tables 2 and 3) are equivalent to learning several image-independent basis LUTs encoded as the learnable parameters. The input to the FC layer serves as the image-dependent coefficients that linearly combine the basis LUTs into the final LUT. Note that the output of the LUT is simply a linear combination of the elements in the LUT and falls into the color space that can be naturally quantized. Therefore, thanks to the semantic consistency between the parameter space and the output space, the trained parameters of the LUT generators can be naturally quantized to lower-bit representation during the testing time without significant performance decline. It is worth noting that it is not trivial for other image enhancement methods to benefit from the model quantization techniques due to their inconsistency between parameter and output spaces. More complicated model quantization approaches are required but would introduce cumbersome training protocols or substantially hurt the performance. Besides, since the LUTs and the input image can be quantized into fixed-point representation (*e.g.*, 8-bit integer), we can also replace the floating-point computation with the fixed-point counterpart in the lookup and interpolation procedure for further speedup, as shown in Table 5.

4   Experiments

4.1   Datasets

The publicly available MIT-Adobe FiveK [2] and PPR10K [22] datasets are adopted to evaluate the proposed method. The FiveK dataset contains 5,000 RAW images with five manually retouched ground truths (A/B/C/D/E). Version C is selected in our experiments. We use the commonly used settings [5,35] to split the dataset into 4,500 image pairs for training and the remaining 500 image pairs for testing. The 480P version of the dataset is used to speed up the training process, while the testing is conducted on both 480P and original 4K resolutions. The PPR10K dataset contains a larger scale of 11,161 RAW portrait photos with 3 versions of groundtruths (a/b/c). We follow the setting in [22] to utilize all three retouched versions as the groundtruth in different experiments and split the dataset into 8,875 pairs for training and 2,286 pairs for testing. Experiments are conducted on the 360P verison of the dataset. Following [35], experiments are organized on two typical application scenarios, *photo retouching*, and *tone mapping*. The former task retouches the input image in the same sRGB format, whereas the latter transforms the 16-bit CIE XYZ input images into 8-bit sRGB. We conduct both tasks on the FiveK dataset, but only the retouching task on PPR10K as done in [22]. As for the data augmentation strategies, we follow the settings in [35] and [22] to ensure a fair comparison.

4.2   Implementation Details

Tables 1 to 2 show the instantiations of modules in the proposed method. The parameters of the backbone network are randomly initialized as in [10]. To make a fair comparison, we also conduct experiments using the ResNet-18 [13] backbone network (initialized with ImageNet-pretrained [7] weights) on the PPR10K

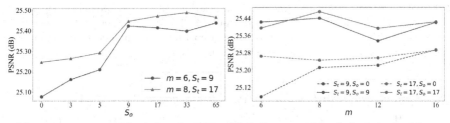

(a) Different sizes (S_o) of the 1D LUT.   (b) Different widths (m) of the backbone.

Fig. 2. Ablation studies on different sizes of the 1D LUT (a) and different widths of the backbone network (b). $S_o = 0$ indicates models with only 3D LUTs.

dataset, as done in [22]. As for the LUT generators, inspired by [35], we initialize the 3D LUT generator to predict an identity mapping at the early training stage to speed up the training convergence. The mean square error (MSE) loss is adopted to train the proposed method in an end-to-end manner. We do not introduce any other constraint or loss function to the predicted 1D and 3D LUTs, willing that they can be image-adaptive for the network and input image itself, not for any hand-crafted priors. We implement our method based on PyTorch 1.8.1 [27]. The standard Adam optimizer [19] is adopted to train the proposed method, with the mini-batch size set to 1 and 16 on FiveK and PPR10K, respectively. All models are trained for 400 epochs with a fixed learning rate of 1×10^{-4} on an NVIDIA Tesla V100 GPU. K in Eq. (4) is set to 3 and 5 for FiveK and PPR10K respectively, whereas S_o and S_t are set according to the purposes of the experiments. We provide them in the following sections.

4.3   Ablation Studies

In this section, we conduct several ablation studies on the retouching task with the FiveK dataset (480P) to verify the key components of the proposed method.

Size of Lookup Tables. (1) **3D LUT:** We explore the effects of the size of the 3D LUT by varying S_t in the absence of the 1D LUT ($S_o = 0$) and $m = 8$. The experiments on the FiveK dataset (480P) for the photo retouching task show that, with only the 3D LUT, decreasing the LUT size S_t (from 33, 17 to 9) can significantly reduce the number of parameters (from 385K, 106K to 69K) without a substantial performance drop (from 25.27 dB, 25.24 dB to 25.21 dB). Such a phenomenon suggests the capacity redundancy of the 3D LUT. Therefore, considering the balance between performance and model size, we select $S_t = 9$ and $S_t = 17$ as the default settings in this paper. (2) **1D LUT:** We also investigate the effects of different sizes of the 1D LUT when the size of the 3D LUT is fixed. As shown in Fig. 2a, increasing the size of the 1D LUT improves the performance continuously and saturates after it exceeds that of the 3D LUT. A possible reason is that the precision of the 3D LUT serves as a bottleneck and will cancel the additional quantization granularity introduced by the 1D LUT.

Table 4. Ablation study on different instantiations of the component-independent transform. The results on the FiveK dataset (480P) for the photo retouching task are listed. "HE" is the abbreviation of Histogram Equalization. The ↑ and ↓ symbols indicate the larger or the smaller is better, respectively.

Strategies	$m = 6, S_t = S_o = 9$			$m = 8, S_t = S_o = 17$		
	PSNR ↑	SSIM ↑	#Params ↓	PSNR ↑	SSIM ↑	#Params ↓
HE	21.75	0.848	42.0 K	21.76	0.847	106.7 K
1D LUT	25.32	0.918	43.7 K	25.41	0.917	111.1 K
3× 1D LUT	25.42	0.921	47.2 K	25.47	0.921	119.8 K

Table 5. Effects of the quantization technique. The runtimes are measured on 480P input using an Intel(R) Xeon(R) Platinum 8163 CPU, whereas the memory footprints are represented by the number of the equivalent parameters.

Method	PSNR↑		CPU Runtime ↓		#Params↓		
	Ori.	Quant.	Ori.	Quant.	Ori.	Quant.	Rel.
3D-LUT [35]	25.28	25.25	17.35	15.52	593.5 K	332.5 K	43.98%↓
$m = 6, S_t = S_o = 9$	25.42	25.35	25.34	15.65	47.2 K	37.9 K	19.59%↓
$m = 8, S_t = S_o = 17$	25.47	25.43	25.64	16.21	119.8 K	76.3 K	36.34%↓

Capacity of the Backbone. Since the backbone network is responsible for providing a coarse analysis of the input image to guide the generation of the 1D and 3D LUTs, its capacity requirement should be correlated with the capacity or the size of the LUTs. For verification, we ablate the width of the backbone network by varying the hyper-parameter m under the same setting of the LUT sizes (S_o and S_t) and report the results in Fig. 2b. The ablation results indicate that increasing the width of the backbone does not guarantee enhanced performance but might increase the capacity redundancy and the training difficulty. Besides, a larger LUT size is inclined to require a stronger backbone network. Considering the trade-off between the performance and the memory footprint, we adopt $m = 6$ and $m = 8$ for $S_t = 9$ and $S_t = 17$, respectively.

Instantiation of the Component-Independent Transform. In this section, we compare several variants to investigate the proper instantiation of the transform, including the histogram equalization (HE) transform, a learnable 1D LUT, and a learnable 3× 1D LUT. Table 4 demonstrates that the 3× 1D LUT performs the best under two different model settings. The results show that the fixed and hand-crafted mechanism of uniforming the input color distribution cannot adapt to different image contents and distinct retouching styles. Hence it does not guarantee advanced performance on the image enhancement task. The learnable 1D LUTs avoid the above issues by end-to-end optimization, and the 3× 1D LUT provides more flexibility and intelligence than the single 1D LUT.

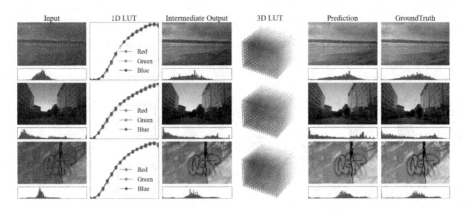

Fig. 3. Illustration of the pair of images, the corresponding histograms, the predicted LUTs, the intermediate transformed output and the final prediction. Images are selected from the FiveK [2] dataset (480P). Best viewed on screen. (Color figure online)

Quantization on Lookup Tables. As described in Sect. 3.5, we quantify the parameters in both 1D and 3D LUT generators from 32-bit floats to 8-bit integers. The results in Table 5 show that such quantization can significantly reduce the storage/memory footprints with only a slight performance drop. It is worth noting that the above results are obtained by directly quantizing the trained model without any finetuning or quantization-aware training strategy, demonstrating the flexibility of the proposed method. Besides, the LUT quantization enables the fixed-point arithmetic, which decreases the CPU inference time of our approach from about 25ms to 16ms. We also apply quantization and fixed-point arithmetic to another 3DLUT-based method [35] and find a similar phenomenon. The proposed framework benefits more from the fixed-point arithmetic in terms of runtime since both the 1D and 3D LUT transforms can be optimized, while [35] only includes the 3D LUT transform.

4.4   Analysis

To help draw an intuitive understanding of the behavior of the image-adaptive LUTs, we illustrate the intermediate outputs as shown in Fig. 3. It can be observed that the 1D LUT is inclined to adaptively stretch the input brightness and image contrast, making them in a state more similar to those of the ground truth. Afterward, the 3D LUT is responsible for altering the hue and enhancing the saturation. Besides, to provide quantitative analysis, we also calculate and analyze some statistics of a series of trained models, including the color distribution and the cell utilization of the 3D LUTs, as detailed in follows.

Distribution of Each Color Component. To quantitatively investigate the effects of the 1D LUTs on the color distribution, we compare the histogram

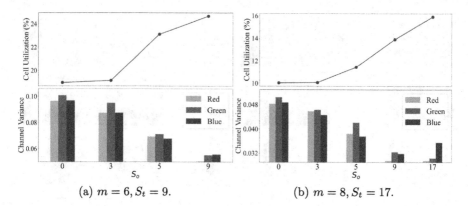

Fig. 4. Effects of the 1D LUT on the utilization of the 3D LUT (the top row) and the distribution of each color channel (the bottom row). Best viewed in color.

Fig. 5. Qualitative comparisons for **photo retouching** on the **FiveK** dataset (4K) [2]. The corresponding error maps are placed at the top-right of each image, where brighter colors indicate larger errors. Best viewed on screen. (Color figure online)

uniformity of images M transformed by the 1D LUTs of different sizes. The histogram uniformity, to some extent, indicates the level of image contrast and can be approximated by the variance of the image histogram. The bottom row of Fig. 4 shows the results averaged on the FiveK dataset. As the size of the 1D LUT (S_o) increases, the per-channel histogram variance of the image decreases, showing the progressive increase of the uniformity of the color distribution. The phenomenon is in line with our expectation that the 1D LUT would adjust the image contrast into a more uniform distribution in an image-adaptive manner.

Cell Utilization of 3D Lookup Tables. A typical 3D LUT discretizes the entire 3D color space into a grid of cells. Unfortunately, when transforming a single input image, those cells are only partially utilized as the input rarely contains all possible colors. For example, the cell utilization of [35], which can be regarded as a special case of our framework that adopts a single 33-point 3D LUT, is only about 5.53%. To investigate the effects of the 1D LUT on the cell utilization of the 3D LUT, we count for each image the percentage of the cells that have valid pixels falling in. The results averaged on the FiveK dataset are

Table 6. Quantitative comparisons on the **FiveK** dataset [2] for **photo retouching**. "–" means the result is not available due to insufficient GPU memory. "*" indicates that the results are adopted from the original paper (some are absent ("/")) due to the unavailable source code. The best and second results are in bold and underlined, respectively.

Method	#Params	480 p			Full resolution (4K)		
		PSNR	SSIM	ΔE_{ab}	PSNR	SSIM	ΔE_{ab}
UPE [31]	927.1K	21.88	0.853	10.80	21.65	0.859	11.09
DPE [5]	3.4M	23.75	0.908	9.34	–	–	–
HDRNet [9]	483.1K	24.66	0.915	8.06	24.52	0.921	8.20
CSRNet [12]	36.4K	25.17	0.921	7.75	24.82	0.924	7.94
3D-LUT [35]	593.5K	25.29	0.920	7.55	25.25	0.930	7.59
SA-3DLUT [32]*	4.5M	**25.50**	/	/	/	/	/
Ours-S	47.2K	25.42	<u>0.921</u>	**7.51**	<u>25.40</u>	<u>0.931</u>	**7.52**
Ours-L	119.8K	<u>25.47</u>	**0.921**	<u>7.54</u>	**25.43**	**0.932**	<u>7.56</u>

Table 7. Quantitative comparisons on the **FiveK** dataset (480p) [2] for the **tone mapping**.

Method	480 p		
	PSNR	SSIM	ΔE_{ab}
UPE [31]	21.56	0.837	12.29
DPE [5]	22.93	0.894	11.09
HDRNet [9]	24.52	0.915	8.14
CSRNet [12]	25.19	0.921	7.63
3D-LUT [35]	25.07	0.920	7.55
Ours-S	<u>25.42</u>	<u>0.920</u>	<u>7.43</u>
Ours-L	**25.43**	**0.922**	**7.43**

Table 8. Quantitative comparisons on the **PPR10K** dataset (360p) [22] for **photo retouching**, where a, b, and c denote the groundtruths retouched by three experts

GT	Metric	3D-LUT [35]	Ours-S	Ours-L
a	PSNR	25.64	<u>26.19</u>	**26.28**
	ΔE_{ab}	6.96	<u>6.71</u>	**6.59**
b	PSNR	24.70	<u>25.17</u>	**25.23**
	ΔE_{ab}	7.71	<u>7.50</u>	**7.49**
c	PSNR	25.18	<u>25.51</u>	**25.59**
	ΔE_{ab}	7.58	**7.48**	<u>7.51</u>

reported in the top row of Fig. 4. The 1D LUT is able to activate more cells to increase the model capability of the 3D LUT, and such ability becomes stronger as the 1D LUT becomes preciser (with larger S_o).

4.5 Comparisons with State-of-the-Arts

Quantitative and Qualitative Comparisons. For comparisons with *state-of-the-art* real-time methods, we select two typical settings for our approach, namely $m = 6, S_o = S_t = 9$ and $m = 8, S_o = S_t = 17$, denoted as *Ours-S* and *Ours-L*, respectively. Tables 6, 7 and 8 report the quantitative comparisons in terms of PSNR, SSIM [33], and the L_2-distance in CIE LAB color space (ΔE_{ab}). The results of the selected methods are obtained via using their publicly avail-

Table 9. Running time (in millisecond) comparisons on different input resolutions. "–" means the result is not available due to insufficient GPU memory. The "*" symbol indicates that the results are adopted from the original paper (some are absent ("/")) due to the unavailable source code.

Resolution	GPU				CPU
	480P	720P	4K	8K	480P
UPE [31]	4.27	6.77	56.88	249.77	126.37
DPE [5]	7.21	–	–	–	553.36
HDRNet [9]	3.49	5.59	56.07	241.90	130.94
CSRNet [12]	3.09	8.80	77.10	308.78	349.61
SA-3DLUT [32]*	2.27	2.34	4.39	/	/
3D-LUT [35]	1.02	1.06	1.14	2.35	15.52
Ours-S	1.08	1.09	1.18	2.23	15.65
Ours-L	1.10	1.12	1.20	2.35	16.21

able codes and default configurations. The proposed method outperforms others considerably with even fewer parameters. Note that in Table 6, SA-3DLUT [32] achieves slightly better performance than our method but at the cost of a significant model size increase (about 37 times) and speed decrease (about 3 times, see Table 9). We also provide some visual comparisons in Fig. 5, where our method produces more visually pleasing results than others. For example, while the enhanced images of other methods suffer from incorrect brightness or hazy ill-effects, those of our approach present enhanced contrast and sufficient saturation. Please refer to the supplementary materials for more qualitative results.

Real-Time Performance Comparisons. To demonstrate the practicality of the proposed method, we evaluate the inference time on 100 images and report the average. Each image is tested 100 times on different resolutions including 480P (640×480), 720P (1280×720), 4K (3840×2160) and 8K (7680×4320). The time measure is conducted on a machine with an Intel(R) Xeon(R) Platinum 8163 CPU and an NVIDIA Tesla V100 GPU. As listed in Table 9, our method exceeds the requirement of real-time processing by a large margin on both GPUs and CPUs. The high efficiency of our approach mainly benefits from two factors. First, the downsampled, fixed-resolution input fed to the CNN network makes its computational cost fixed and insensitive to the input resolution. Second, the LUT transform is highly efficient as it is parallelizable on GPUs and can benefit from the fixed-point arithmetic on CPUs.

5   Conclusion

In this paper, we present a novel framework called SepLUT that simultaneously takes advantage of two different types of LUTs, both 1D and 3D, for real-time image enhancement. It separates a single color transform into component-independent and component-correlated sub-transforms. Extensive experiments demonstrate that such a scheme helps sufficiently exert the capabilities of both types of LUTs and presents several promising properties, including enhanced expressiveness, high efficiency, and light memory footprints. The feasibility of the proposed method reflects that the principle of divide-and-conquer can reduce the capability requirements and ease the optimization of each sub-module, which can significantly increase efficiency. Besides, a proper module decomposition can also benefit from the capability complement between the sub-modules and even achieve enhanced overall performance.

Acknowledgements. Yi Xu is supported in part by National Natural Science Foundation of China (62171282, 111 project BP0719010, STCSM 18DZ2270700) and Shanghai Municipal Science and Technology Major Project (2021SHZDZX0102).

References

1. Bianco, S., Cusano, C., Piccoli, F., Schettini, R.: Personalized image enhancement using neural spline color transforms. IEEE Trans. Image Process. (TIP) **29**, 6223–6236 (2020)
2. Bychkovsky, V., Paris, S., Chan, E., Durand, F.: Learning photographic global tonal adjustment with a database of input/output image pairs. In: Proceedings of the IEEE/CVF Conference on Computer Vision and Pattern Recognition (CVPR), pp. 97–104 (2011)
3. Chai, Y., Giryes, R., Wolf, L.: Supervised and unsupervised learning of parameterized color enhancement. In: Proceedings of the IEEE/CVF Winter Conference on Applications of Computer Vision (WACV). pp. 992–1000 (2020)
4. Chen, C., Chen, Q., Xu, J., Koltun, V.: Learning to see in the dark. In: Proceedings of the IEEE/CVF Conference on Computer Vision and Pattern Recognition (CVPR). pp. 3291–3300 (2018)
5. Chen, Y.S., Wang, Y.C., Kao, M.H., Chuang, Y.Y.: Deep photo enhancer: unpaired learning for image enhancement from photographs with gans. In: Proceedings of the IEEE/CVF Conference on Computer Vision and Pattern Recognition (CVPR), pp. 6306–6314 (2018)
6. De Brabandere, B., Jia, X., Tuytelaars, T., Van Gool, L.: Dynamic filter networks. In: Proceedings of the 30th International Conference on Neural Information Processing Systems (NeurIPS), pp. 667–675 (2016)
7. Deng, J., Dong, W., Socher, R., Li, L.J., Li, K., Fei-Fei, L.: Imagenet: a large-scale hierarchical image database. In: Proceedings of the IEEE/CVF Conference on Computer Vision and Pattern Recognition (CVPR), pp. 248–255 (2009)
8. Deng, Y., Loy, C.C., Tang, X.: Aesthetic-driven image enhancement by adversarial learning. In: Proceedings of the 26th ACM International Conference on Multimedia (ACMMM), pp. 870–878 (2018)
9. Gharbi, M., Chen, J., Barron, J.T., Hasinoff, S.W., Durand, F.: Deep bilateral learning for real-time image enhancement. ACM Trans. Graph. (TOG) **36**(4), 1–12 (2017)
10. Glorot, X., Bengio, Y.: Understanding the difficulty of training deep feedforward neural networks. In: Proceedings of the Thirteenth International Conference on Artificial Intelligence and Statistics, vol. 9, pp. 249–256. PMLR (2010)

11. Guo, C., Li, C., Guo, J., Loy, C.C., Hou, J., Kwong, S., Cong, R.: Zero-reference deep curve estimation for low-light image enhancement. In: Proceedings of the IEEE/CVF Conference on Computer Vision and Pattern Recognition (CVPR). pp. 1780–1789 (2020)

12. He, J., Liu, Y., Qiao, Yu., Dong, C.: Conditional sequential modulation for efficient global image retouching. In: Vedaldi, A., Bischof, H., Brox, T., Frahm, J.-M. (eds.) ECCV 2020. LNCS, vol. 12358, pp. 679–695. Springer, Cham (2020). https://doi.org/10.1007/978-3-030-58601-0_40

13. He, K., Zhang, X., Ren, S., Sun, J.: Deep residual learning for image recognition. In: Proceedings of the IEEE/CVF Conference on Computer Vision and Pattern Recognition (CVPR), pp. 770–778 (2016)

14. Hu, Y., He, H., Xu, C., Wang, B., Lin, S.: Exposure: a white-box photo post-processing framework. ACM Trans. Graph. (TOG) **37**(2), 1–17 (2018)

15. Karaimer, H.C., Brown, M.S.: A software platform for manipulating the camera imaging pipeline. In: Leibe, B., Matas, J., Sebe, N., Welling, M. (eds.) ECCV 2016. LNCS, vol. 9905, pp. 429–444. Springer, Cham (2016). https://doi.org/10.1007/978-3-319-46448-0_26

16. Kasson, J.M., Nin, S.I., Plouffe, W., Hafner, J.L.: Performing color space conversions with three-dimensional linear interpolation. J. Electron. Imaging **4**(3), 226–250 (1995)

17. Kim, H.-U., Koh, Y.J., Kim, C.-S.: Global and local enhancement networks for paired and unpaired image enhancement. In: Vedaldi, A., Bischof, H., Brox, T., Frahm, J.-M. (eds.) ECCV 2020. LNCS, vol. 12370, pp. 339–354. Springer, Cham (2020). https://doi.org/10.1007/978-3-030-58595-2_21

18. Kim, H., Choi, S.M., Kim, C.S., Koh, Y.J.: Representative color transform for image enhancement. In: Proceedings of the IEEE/CVF International Conference on Computer Vision (ICCV), pp. 4459–4468 (2021)

19. Kingma, D.P., Ba, J.: Adam: A method for stochastic optimization. In: Bengio, Y., LeCun, Y. (eds.) International Conference on Learning Representations (ICLR) (2015)

20. Kwok, W., Haghighi, K., Kang, E.: An efficient data structure for the advancing-front triangular mesh generation technique. Commun. Numer. Methods Eng. **11**(5), 465–473 (1995)

21. Li, C., Guo, C., Ai, Q., Zhou, S., Loy, C.C.: Flexible piecewise curves estimation for photo enhancement. arXiv preprint arXiv:2010.13412 (2020)

22. Liang, J., Zeng, H., Cui, M., Xie, X., Zhang, L.: Ppr10k: a large-scale portrait photo retouching dataset with human-region mask and group-level consistency. In: Proceedings of the IEEE/CVF Conference on Computer Vision and Pattern Recognition (CVPR), pp. 653–661 (2021)

23. Liu, E., Li, S., Liu, S.: Color enhancement using global parameters and local features learning. In: Proceedings of the Asian Conference on Computer Vision (ACCV), pp. 202–216 (2020)

24. Moran, S., Marza, P., McDonagh, S., Parisot, S., Slabaugh, G.: Deeplpf: deep local parametric filters for image enhancement. In: Proceedings of the IEEE/CVF Conference on Computer Vision and Pattern Recognition (CVPR), pp. 12823–12832 (2020)

25. Moran, S., McDonagh, S., Slabaugh, G.: Curl: neural curve layers for global image enhancement. In: International Conference on Pattern Recognition (ICPR), pp. 9796–9803 (2021)

26. Park, J., Lee, J.Y., Yoo, D., Kweon, I.S.: Distort-and-recover: color enhancement using deep reinforcement learning. In: Proceedings of the IEEE/CVF Conference on Computer Vision and Pattern Recognition (CVPR), pp. 5928–5936 (2018)
27. Paszke, A., et al.: Pytorch: an imperative style, high-performance deep learning library. In: Advances in Neural Information Processing Systems (NeurIPS), vol. 32, pp. 8024–8035 (2019)
28. Selan, J.: Using lookup tables to accelerate color transformations. GPU Gems **2**, 381–392 (2005)
29. Sharif, M.H.: High-performance mathematical functions for single-core architectures. J. Circuits Syst. Comput. **23**(04), 1450051 (2014)
30. Song, Y., Qian, H., Du, X.: Starenhancer: learning real-time and style-aware image enhancement. In: Proceedings of the IEEE/CVF International Conference on Computer Vision (ICCV), pp. 4126–4135 (2021)
31. Wang, R., Zhang, Q., Fu, C.W., Shen, X., Zheng, W.S., Jia, J.: Underexposed photo enhancement using deep illumination estimation. In: Proceedings of the IEEE/CVF Conference on Computer Vision and Pattern Recognition (CVPR), pp. 6849–6857 (2019)
32. Wang, T., et al.: Real-time image enhancer via learnable spatial-aware 3d lookup tables. In: Proceedings of the IEEE/CVF International Conference on Computer Vision (ICCV), pp. 2471–2480 (2021)
33. Wang, Z., Bovik, A.C., Sheikh, H.R., Simoncelli, E.P.: Image quality assessment: from error visibility to structural similarity. IEEE Trans. Image Process. (TIP) **13**(4), 600–612 (2004)
34. Wei, C., Wang, W., Yang, W., Liu, J.: Deep retinex decomposition for low-light enhancement. In: British Machine Vision Conference (BMVC), p. 155 (2018)
35. Zeng, H., Cai, J., Li, L., Cao, Z., Zhang, L.: Learning image-adaptive 3d lookup tables for high performance photo enhancement in real-time. IEEE Trans. Pattern Anal. Mach. Intell. (TPAMI) (2020)
36. Zhang, Y., Zhang, J., Guo, X.: Kindling the darkness: a practical low-light image enhancer. In: Proceedings of the 27th ACM International Conference on Multimedia (ACMMM), pp. 1632–1640 (2019)

Blind Image Decomposition

Junlin Han[1,2]($\boxtimes$), Weihao Li[1], Pengfei Fang[1,2], Chunyi Sun[2], Jie Hong[1,2], Mohammad Ali Armin[1], Lars Petersson[1], and Hongdong Li[2]

[1] Data61-CSIRO, Sydney, Australia
junlin.han@data61.csiro.au
[2] Australian National University, Canberra, Australia

Abstract. We propose and study a novel task named **B**lind **I**mage **D**ecomposition (BID), which requires separating a superimposed image into constituent underlying images in a blind setting, that is, both the source components involved in mixing as well as the mixing mechanism are unknown. For example, rain may consist of multiple components, such as rain streaks, raindrops, snow, and haze. Rainy images can be treated as an arbitrary combination of these components, some of them or all of them. How to decompose superimposed images, like rainy images, into distinct source components is a crucial step toward real-world vision systems. To facilitate research on this new task, we construct multiple benchmark datasets, including mixed image decomposition across multiple domains, real-scenario deraining, and joint shadow/reflection/watermark removal. Moreover, we propose a simple yet general **B**lind **I**mage **De**composition Network (BIDeN) to serve as a strong baseline for future work. Experimental results demonstrate the tenability of our benchmarks and the effectiveness of BIDeN.

Codes and datasets are available at GitHub.

Keywords: Image decomposition · Low-level vision · Rain removal

1 Introduction

Various computer vision and computer graphics tasks [1,2,15,23,26,28,37,40,44, 98] can be viewed as image decomposition, which aims to separate a superimposed image into distinct components/layers with only a single observation. For example, foreground-background segmentation [3,16,50,52,69] aims at decomposing a holistic image into foreground objects and background stuff. Image dehazing [5,31,47] can be treated as decomposing a hazy image into a haze-free image and a haze map (medium transmission map, atmosphere light). Shadow removal [8,13,18,38,38,44] decomposes a shadow image into a shadow-free image and a shadow mask. Other tasks like transparency separation [17,46,56,91], watermark removal [7,53], image deraining [51,65,79,82,86,95], texture separation [26], underwater image restoration [22,29], image desnowing [55,68], stereo

Supplementary Information The online version contains supplementary material available at https://doi.org/10.1007/978-3-031-19797-0_13.

mixture decomposition [92], 3D intrinsic mixture image decomposition [2], fence removal [14,54,80], flare removal [4,78] are covered in image decomposition.

Vanilla image decomposition tasks come with a fixed and known number of source components, and the number is most often set to two [23,26,40,43,44,86, 98]. Such a setting does capture some basic real-world cases. However, real-world scenarios are more complex. Consider autonomous driving on rainy days, where the visual perception quality is degraded by different forms of precipitation and the co-occurring components, shown in Fig. 1. Some natural questions emerge: Can a vision system assume precipitations to be of a specific form? Should a vision system assume raindrops always exist or not? Shall a vision system assume the haze or snow comes along with rain or not? These questions are particularly important based on their relevance in real-world applications. The answer to these questions should be *NO*. A comprehensive vision system is supposed to be robust with the ability to handle many possible circumstances [48,61,72]. Yet, with the previous setting in deraining [49,51,57,65,67,82,87–90,93,94] there remains a gap toward sophisticated real-world scenarios.

Fig. 1. Example of raining cases. Rain exists in different formats such as rain streak and raindrop. Snow and haze often co-occur during raining. BID setting treats rainy images as an arbitrary combination of these components. Deraining under the BID setting becomes more challenging yet more overarching

This paper aims at addressing the aforementioned gap, as a step toward robust real-world vision systems. We propose a task that: (1) does not fix the number of source components, (2) considers the presence and varying intensities of source components, and (3) amalgamates every source component as potential combinations. To disambiguate with previous tasks, we refer to our proposed task as *Blind Image Decomposition (BID)*. This name is inspired by the Blind Source Separation (BSS) task in the field of signal processing.

The task format is straightforward. We no longer set the number of source components to a fixed value. Instead, we set a maximum number of potential source components, where each component can be arbitrarily part of the mix. Let 'A', 'B', 'C', 'D', 'E' denote five source components and 'a', 'b', 'c', 'd', 'e' denote images from the corresponding source components. The mixed image can be either 'a', 'd', 'ab', 'bc', 'abd', 'ade', 'acde', 'abcde' ⋯, with up to 31 possible combinations in total. Given any of the 31 possible combinations as input, a BID method is required to predict and reconstruct the individual source components involved in mixing.

As different components can be arbitrarily involved in the mixing, no existing datasets support such a training protocol. Thus, we construct three benchmark datasets, they are: (I) mixed image decomposition across multiple domains, (II) real-scenario deraining, and (III) joint shadow/reflection/watermark removal.

To perform multiple BID tasks, we design a simple yet flexible model, dubbed BIDeN (Blind Image Decomposition Network). BIDeN is a generic model that supports diverse BID tasks with distinct objectives. BIDeN is based on the framework of GANs (Generative Adversarial Networks) [25], and we explore some critical design choices of BIDeN to present a general model. Designed for a more challenging BID setting, BIDeN still outperforms the current state-of-the-art image decomposition model [23,98] and shows competitive results compared to models designed for specific tasks. Lastly, a comprehensive ablation study is conducted to analyze the design choices of BIDeN.

2   Related Work

Image Decomposition. This task is a general task covering numerous computer vision and computer graphics tasks. Double-DIP [23] couples multiple DIPs [74] to decompose images into their basic components in an unsupervised manner. Deep Generative Priors [37] employs a likelihood-based generative model as a prior, performing the image decomposition task. Deep Adversarial Decomposition (DAD) [98] proposed a unified framework for image decomposition by employing three discriminators. A crossroad L1 loss is introduced to support pixel-wise supervision when domain information is unknown. Different from the conventional image decomposition task that usually aims to solve a particular degradation, in the BID setting, we treat degraded images as an arbitrary combination of individual components, and aim to solve sophisticated compound degradation in a unified framework.

Blind Source Separation. BSS [9,20,21,34,35], also known as the "cocktail party problem", is an important research topic in the field of signal processing. Blind refers to a setting where sources and mixing mechanism are both unknown. The task requires performing the separation of a mixture signal into the constituent underlying source signals with limited prior information. A representative algorithm is the Independent Component Analysis (ICA) [35,45,63]. The BID task shares common properties with BSS, where the blind settings are similar but not identical. The setting of BID assumes an unknown number of source components involved in the mixing and unknown mixing mechanisms. With such a setting, the number of source components involved in mixing is also unknown. However, the domain information of each source component is considered known as the goal of BID is to advance real-world vision systems. The setting of including known domain information can be better applied to computer vision tasks. For instance, the goal of the shadow removal task is to

separate a shadow image into a shadow-free image and a shadow mask, where
the domain information is clear.

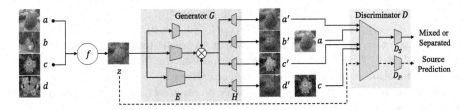

Fig. 2. The architecture of the Blind Image Decomposition Network (BIDeN). We
show an example, where $N = 4$, $L = 2$, $x = \{a, b, c, d\}$, and $I = \{1, 3\}$. a, c are
selected then passed to the mixing function f, and outputs the mixed input image z,
which is $f(a, c)$ here. The generator consists of an encoder E with three branches and
multiple heads H. $\bigotimes$ denotes the concatenation operation. Depth and receptive field
of each branch are different to capture multiple scales of features. Each specified head
points to the corresponding source component, and the number of heads varies with
the maximum number of source components N. All reconstructed images (a', c') and
their corresponding real images (a, c) are sent to an unconditional discriminator. The
discriminator also predicts the source components involved in the mixing of the input
image z. The outputs from other heads (b', d') do not contribute to the optimization

Generative Adversarial Networks. GANs [25] include two key components,
a generator, and a discriminator, where the generator is trying to generate realistic samples while the discriminator is trying to identify real samples and generated samples. The adversarial training mechanism helps the output from the
generator match the distribution of real data. GANs are especially successful in
image generation tasks [41,85] and image-to-image translation tasks [30,36,97].
GANs are also a common tool for image decomposition tasks, where GANs
have been successfully employed in image deraining [65,86], transparency separation [56,91], and image dehazing [47].

3   Blind Image Decomposition Formulation

Given a set of N $(N \geq 2)$ source components, *i.e.*, image domains, denoted by
$\mathcal{X} = \{X_m\}_{m=1}^N$. Each source component X_m contains some images x_m, $x_m \in$
X_m. L $(1 \leq L \leq N)$ source components are randomly selected from $\mathcal{X}$. Let
$I = \{I_j\}_{j=1}^L$ indicate the index set for the selected source components, where $I_j \in$
$\{1, ..., N\}$. Hence, the selected source components are denoted by $\{X_{I_j}\}_{j=1}^L$. Each
selected source component X_{I_j} contains some images x_{I_j}. With a predetermined
mixing function f, the mixed image z is given by $z = f(\{x_{I_j}\}_{j=1}^L)$. The mixed
image z can be identical to a single image when $L = 1$. The BID task requires
the BID method to find a function g to separate z, as $g(z) = \{x'_{I_j}\}_{j=1}^L$. Each
reconstructed image x'_{I_j} is close to its corresponding image x_{I_j}. That is, given
a mixed image as input, the task requires the BID method to: (1) predict the

source components involved in mixing, (2) reconstruct images preserving the fidelity of the corresponding images involved in mixing.

For the example shown in Fig. 2, where $N = 4$, $\mathcal{X} = \{A, B, C, D\}$, $x = \{a, b, c, d\}$, L can be $1, 2, 3, 4$, z can be $a, b, c, d, f(a, b), f(a, c), f(a, d), f(b, c), f(b, d), f(c, d), f(a, b, c), f(a, b, d), f(a, c, d), f(b, c, d), f(a, b, c, d)$. Let $L = 2$ and $I = \{1, 3\}$. Given $z = f(a, c)$ as the input, knowing there are four different source components A, B, C, D without any other information, the task requires the method to find a function g, so that $g(f(a, c)) = a', c'$, where $a' \rightarrow a$ and $c' \rightarrow c$. Also, the method should correctly predict the source components involved in the mixing, that is, predicting $I = \{1, 3\}$.

The BID task is challenging for the following reasons: (1) When N increases, the number of possible z increases rapidly. The BID setting forces the method to deal with $2^N - 1$ possible combinations. For instance, when N increases to 8, there are 255 variants of z. (2) The task requires the method to predict the source components involved in the mixing. Source components are difficult to be predicted when N is large and L varies a lot. (3) The mixing mechanism, or the mixing function f, is unknown to the method. The mixing function f varies with different source components and can be non-linear/complex in specific circumstances, such as rendering raindrop images, adding shadows or reflections to images. (4) As L increases, each source component contributes a decreasing amount of information to z, making the task highly ill-posed.

4   Blind Image Decomposition Network

To perform diverse BID tasks, a unified framework is required. Inspired by the success of image-to-image translation models [30,36,97], we design our Blind Image Decomposition Network (BIDeN) as follows. Figure 2 presents an overall architecture of BIDeN when the maximum number of source components is four.

The generator G consists of two parts: a multi-scale encoder E and multiple heads H. We design a multi-scale encoder containing three branches to capture multiple scales of features. This design is beneficial to the reconstruction of source components. We concatenate different scales of features and send them to multiple heads, where the number of heads is identical to the maximum number of source components. Each head is specific to reconstructing a particular kind of source component. Such multiple-head domain-specific autoencoders have been adopted particularly in inverse rendering task [28,77].

The discriminator D consists of two branches and most weights are shared. The reconstructed images and corresponding real images are sent to the discriminator branch D_S (Separation) individually. The function of D_S is similar to a typical discriminator, $i.e.$, classifying whether the input to D_S is generated or real to direct the generator generating realistic images. The discriminator branch D_P (Prediction) predicts the source components involved in the mixed image z, with a confidence threshold of zero. A successful prediction unveils the correct index set of the selected source components I.

Taking the example of Fig. 2, we name four heads as H_A, H_B, H_C, and H_D. For an input $f(a, c)$, H_A and H_C aim to reconstruct a', c', so that $a' \rightarrow a$ and

$c' \to c$ while H_B, H_D are free to output anything or are simply turned off. We employ adversarial loss [25], perceptual loss [39], L1/L2 loss, and binary cross-entropy loss. The details of the objective function are expressed below.

4.1   Objective

We employ the adversarial loss [25] to encourage the generator G to output well separated and realistic images, regardless of the source components. For the function $g(z) = \{x'_{I_j}\}_{j=1}^L$, the GAN loss is expressed as:

$$
\begin{aligned}
\mathcal{L}_{\text{GAN}}(G, D_S) = {} & \mathbb{E}_x \left[\log D_S(x)\right] \\
& + \mathbb{E}_z \left[\log \left(1 - D_S(G(z))\right)\right],
\end{aligned}
\tag{1}
$$

where G behaves as g. It tries to separate the input mixed image z and reconstruct separated outputs x'_{I_j}, while D_S attempts to distinguish between $G(z)$ and real samples x_{I_j}. Note x inside Eqs. 1–5 denotes x_{I_j}. We employ the LSGAN [58] loss and the Markovian discriminator [36].

The reconstructed images x'_{I_j} should be separated, as well as to be near the corresponding x_{I_j} in a distance sense. Hence, we employ perceptual loss (VGG loss) [39] and L1/L2 loss. They are formalized as:

$$
\mathcal{L}_{\text{VGG}}(G) = \mathbb{E}_{x,z}[\textstyle\sum_l \lambda_l \left[\|\Phi_l(x) - \Phi_l(G(z))\|_1\right]],
\tag{2}
$$

$$
\mathcal{L}_{\text{L1}}(G) = \mathbb{E}_{x,z} \left[\|x - G(z)\|_1\right],
\tag{3}
$$

$$
\mathcal{L}_{\text{L2}}(G) = \mathbb{E}_{x,z} \left[\|x - G(z)\|_2^2\right],
\tag{4}
$$

where Φ is a trained VGG19 [71] network, Φ_l denotes a specific layer, and λ_l denotes the weights for the l-th layer. The choice of layers and weights is identical to pix2pixHD [76]. We use L2 loss for masks and L1 loss for other source components. For simplification, we denote L1/L2 loss as $\mathcal{L}_{\text{L}}$.

For the source prediction task, we find that the discriminator performs better than the generator. The goal of the discriminator is to classify between reconstructed samples and real samples. It naturally learns an embedding. Such an embedding is beneficial even when the input is a mixed image z. The discriminator D is capable of performing an additional source prediction task. Thus we design a source prediction branch D_P. The binary cross-entropy loss is employed for the source prediction task:

$$
\begin{aligned}
\mathcal{L}_{\text{BCE}}(D_P) = {} & \mathbb{E}_z[-\sum_{m=1}^{N} [GT(z)_m \log(D_P(z)_m) \\
& + (1 - GT(z)_m) \log(1 - D_P(z)_m)]],
\end{aligned}
\tag{5}
$$

where N denotes the maximum number of source components, GT denotes the binary label of the source components involved in the mixing of input image z. D_P is the source prediction branch of the discriminator.

Our final objective function is:

$$\mathcal{L}(G, D_S, D_P) = \lambda_{\text{GAN}}\mathcal{L}_{\text{GAN}}(G, D_S) + \lambda_{\text{VGG}}\mathcal{L}_{\text{VGG}}(G)$$
$$+ \lambda_{\text{L}}\mathcal{L}_{\text{L}}(G) + \lambda_{\text{BCE}}\mathcal{L}_{\text{BCE}}(D_P). \tag{6}$$

We set $\lambda_{\text{GAN}}, \lambda_{\text{VGG}}, \lambda_{\text{L}}, \lambda_{\text{BCE}}$ to be 1, 10, 30, 1 respectively. This setting is a generic setting that is applied to all tasks.

4.2 Training Details

Throughout all experiments, we use the Adam optimizer [42] with $\beta_1 = 0.5$ and $\beta_2 = 0.999$ for both G, D. BIDeN is trained for 200 epochs with a learning rate of 0.0003. The learning rate starts to decay linearly after half of the total epochs. We use a batch size of 1 and instance normalization [73]. All training images are loaded as 286×286 then cropped to 256×256 patches. Horizontal flip is randomly applied. At test time, we load test images in a 256×256 resolution. More details on the training settings, the architecture, the number of parameters, and training speed are provided in the supplementary material. The training details of all baselines are also provided there.

5   Blind Image Decomposition Tasks

We construct benchmark datasets from different views to support practical usages of BID. For each benchmark dataset, we involve multiple source components that may occur together. To explore the generality of BIDeN and the tenability of constructed datasets, we test BIDeN on three new challenging datasets. BIDeN is trained under the BID setting, which is more difficult than the conventional image decomposition setting. During training, mixed images are randomly synthesized. At test time, the input mixed images are fixed. As BID is a novel task not previously investigated, no existing baselines are available for comparison. For different tasks, we choose different evaluation strategies and baselines.

Throughout all tasks, BIDeN is trained under the BID setting, that is, BIDeN is facing more challenging requirements than other baselines. Also, BIDeN is a generic model designed to perform all kinds of BID tasks. These two constraints limit the performance of BIDeN. We compare BIDeN to other baselines designed for specific tasks, where BIDeN is still able to show very competitive results on all tasks. All qualitative results are ***randomly picked***. Additional task settings, discussion on the order of mixing, dataset construction details, results, including the detailed case results of BIDeN, are provided in the supplementary material.

5.1   Task I: Mixed Image Decomposition Across Multiple Domains

Dataset. This dataset contains eight different image domains, *i.e.*, source components. Each domain has approximately 2500 to 3000 images in the training set, and the test set contains 300 images for each domain. Image domains are

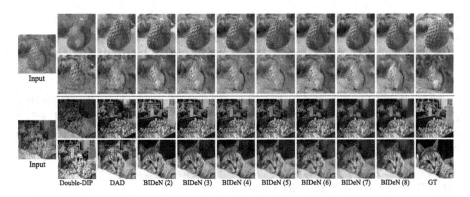

Fig. 3. Qualitative results of Task I (Mixed image decomposition across multiple domains). We train BIDeN 7 times, setting different maximum numbers of source components (2–8). Double-DIP fails to separate the mixed input. DAD shows blurry, non-clean results while the results shown by BIDeN are well-separated and visually satisfying. When BIDeN is trained on a greater maximum number of source components, the quality of the results drops progressively as expected

designed to be big and inclusive to cover multiple categories, like animal, fruit, vehicle, instead of being comparatively small domains such as horse, cat, car. The eight domains are Fruit (2653), Animal (2653), Flower (2950), Furniture (2582), Yosemite (2855), Vehicle (2670), Vegetable (2595), and CityScape (2975). CityScape and Flower are selected from the CityScape [11] dataset and the VGG flower [62] dataset. The remaining six image domains are mainly gathered from Flicker using the corresponding keyword, except for Yosemite, which also combines the Summer2Winter dataset from CycleGAN [97]. The order of the eight domains is randomly shuffled. The mixing mechanism is linear mix.

Table 1. Quantitative results on Task I (Mixed image decomposition across multiple domains). The testing condition is identical, using Fruit (A) + Animal (B) mixture as inputs. N in BIDeN (N) denotes the maximum number of source components. Double-DIP [23] performs poorly. Under a more challenging BID setting, BIDeN (2,3,4) still outperforms DAD [98] overall, suggesting the superiority of BIDeN. Please refer to Appendices for detailed case results

Method	Fruit (A)			Animal (B)			Acc (AB) ↑	Acc (All) ↑	Model size
	PSNR ↑	SSIM ↑	FID ↓	PSNR ↑	SSIM ↑	FID ↓			
Double-DIP [23]	13.14	0.49	257.80	13.11	0.39	221.76	–	–	–
DAD [98]	17.59	0.72	137.66	17.52	0.62	126.32	0.996	–	669.0 MB
BIDeN (2)	20.07	0.79	62.99	19.89	0.69	69.35	1.0	0.957	144.9 MB
BIDeN (3)	19.04	0.75	74.68	18.75	0.61	88.23	0.836	0.807	147.1 MB
BIDeN (4)	18.19	0.73	79.03	18.03	0.58	97.16	0.716	0.733	149.3 MB
BIDeN (5)	17.66	0.71	81.17	17.27	0.54	114.40	0.676	0.603	151.5 MB
BIDeN (6)	17.28	0.69	85.64	16.57	0.51	118.00	0.646	0.483	153.7 MB
BIDeN (7)	16.70	0.68	97.26	16.54	0.49	126.66	0.413	0.310	155.9 MB
BIDeN (8)	16.49	0.67	105.61	15.79	0.45	191.29	0.383	0.278	158.1 MB

Experiments and Results. We compare BIDeN to Double-DIP [23] and DAD [98]. DAD is trained on the first two domains (Fruit, Animal) with mixed input only. For BIDeN, we train it 7 times under the BID setting, varying from 2 domains to 8 domains. At test time, we evaluate the separation results on Fruit + Animal mixture with PSNR, SSIM [96], and FID [32].

Table 1 and Fig. 3 present the results of Task I. In terms of PSNR/SSIM, BIDeN outperforms Double-DIP by a large margin and outperforms DAD when N is less than 5. For FID, BIDeN shows preferable results than DAD even when $N = 7$, showing the superiority of BIDeN.

5.2   Task II: Real-Scenario Deraining

We design two sub-tasks, real-scenario deraining in driving (Task II.A) and real-scenario deraining in general (Task II.B).

Task II.A: Real Scenario Deraining in Driving

Dataset. Based on the CityScape [11] dataset, we construct our real-scenario deraining in driving dataset. We use the test set from the original CityScape dataset as our training set (2975), and the validation set from the original CityScape dataset as our test set (500). The test set for all source components contains a fixed number of 500 images. We use three different masks, including rain streak (1620), raindrop (3500), and snow (3500). These masks cover different intensities. For haze, we use the corresponding transmission maps (2975 × 3) with three different intensities acquired from Foggy CityScape [70]. The masks for rain streak are acquired from Rain100L and Rain100H [82] while the masks for snow are selected from Snow100K [55]. For raindrop masks, we model the droplet shape and property using the metaball model [6]. The locations, numbers, and sizes of raindrops are randomly sampled. Paired refraction maps are generated using refractive model [10,64]. The mixing mechanism for this dataset is based on physical imaging models [10,31,55,64,82].

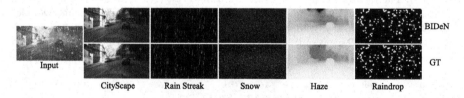

Fig. 4. CityScape, masks (Rain Streak, Snow, Raindrop), and transmission map (Haze) generated by BIDeN for case (6), rain streak + snow + moderate haze + raindrop. All generated images are perceptually faithful and visually close to the ground truth (GT)

Task II.B: Real Scenario Deraining in General

Experiments and Results. We train BIDeN, MPRNet [84], Restormer [83], and RCDNet [75] under the BID setting. For all baselines, we do not require the

Table 2. Results of BIDeN on Task II.A (Real-scenario deraining in driving). We employ PSNR and SSIM metrics for both CityScape images, masks, and transmission maps. We report the results for 6 test cases as presented in Fig. 1, the 6 cases are (1): rain streak, (2): rain streak + snow, (3): rain streak + light haze, (4): rain streak + heavy haze, (5): rain streak + moderate haze + raindrop, (6) rain streak + snow + moderate haze + raindrop. Note that only haze is divided into light/moderate/heavy intensities. Both training set and test set of Rain Streak, Snow, and Raindrop already consist of different intensities

Method	CityScape		Rain Streak		Snow		Haze		Raindrop		Acc ↑
	PSNR↑	SSIM↑	PSNR↑	SSIM↑	PSNR↑	SSIM↑	PSNR↑	SSIM↑	PSNR↑	SSIM↑	
BIDeN (1)	30.89	0.932	32.13	0.924	-	-	-	-	-	-	0.998
BIDeN (2)	29.34	0.899	29.24	0.846	25.77	0.692	-	-	-	-	0.996
BIDeN (3)	28.62	0.919	31.48	0.914	-	-	30.77	0.960	-	-	0.994
BIDeN (4)	26.77	0.898	30.57	0.897	-	-	33.73	0.957	-	-	0.998
BIDeN (5)	27.11	0.898	30.54	0.898	-	-	30.52	0.952	20.20	0.908	0.994
BIDeN (6)	26.44	0.870	28.31	0.823	24.79	0.658	29.83	0.948	21.47	0.893	0.998

prediction of the source component and the generation of masks. Thus, BIDeN is still trained with a more challenging requirement. We report the results for 6 cases, as the examples presented in Fig. 1. Note that only haze is divided into light/moderate/heavy intensities. Both training set and test set of rain streak, snow, and raindrop already contain different intensities. We report the results in SSIM and PSNR for CityScape images, masks, and transmission maps. For all 6 cases, we report the detailed results of BIDeN in Table 2. BIDeN shows excellent

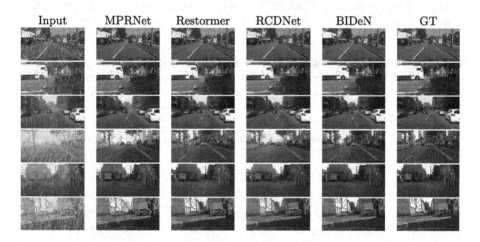

Fig. 5. Results of Task II.A (Real-scenario deraining in driving). Row 1–6 presents 6 cases as presented in Table 2. Baselines performs well at case (1) and they effectively removes rain streak but is not strong at removing other components. BIDeN is more robust at the removal of all components. BIDeN generates artifact-free, visually pleasing results while all baselines leaves some components that are not completely removed, especially when hazy intensity is moderate or heavy, as shown in case (4), (5), and (6)

Table 3. Comparison on task II.A (Real-scenario deraining in driving) between MPR-Net [84], RCDNet [75], and BIDeN. MPRNet and Rostormer shows superior results for case (1) and case (2). In contrast, BIDeN is better at other cases. For the details of 6 test cases, please refer to Table 2 and Fig. 1

Case	Input		MPRNet		Restormer		RCDNet		BIDeN	
	PSNR↑	SSIM↑	PSNR↑	SSIM↑	PSNR↑	SSIM↑	PSNR↑	SSIM↑	PSNR↑	SSIM↑
(1)	25.69	0.786	33.39	0.945	34.29	0.951	32.38	0.937	30.89	0.932
(2)	18.64	0.564	30.52	0.909	30.60	0.917	28.45	0.892	29.34	0.899
(3)	17.45	0.712	23.98	0.900	23.74	0.905	27.14	0.911	28.62	0.919
(4)	11.12	0.571	18.54	0.829	20.33	0.853	19.67	0.865	26.77	0.898
(5)	14.05	0.616	21.18	0.846	22.17	0.859	24.23	0.889	27.11	0.898
(6)	12.38	0.461	20.76	0.812	21.24	0.821	22.93	0.846	26.44	0.870

quantitative results on accuracy. For the PSNR/SSIM metrics on all source components, BIDeN performs well except for the raindrop masks. An example of all components generated by BIDeN is shown in Fig. 4. Table 3 and Fig. 5 presents the comparison between BIDeN and baselines. For better visualization, we resize the resolution of visual examples to match the original CityScape resolution.

Dataset. The training set contains 3661 natural images as rain-free images, where 861 images are adopted from the training set of [65], 1800 images are borrowed from the training set of Rain1800 [82], and the rest 1000 images are selected from the training set of Snow100K [55]. We adopt identical rain streak, snow, and raindrop masks from Task II.A. The test set contains real images only, including rain streak (185, from [49]), raindrop (249, from [65]) and snow (1329, from [55]) images.

Table 4. Quantitative results of Task II.B (Real-scenario deraining in general). * indicates the BID setting. For all methods and testing cases, models trained under the BID setting performs better than the conventional image decomposition setting

Method	Rain Streak		Raindrop		Snow	
	NIQE ↓	BRISQUE ↓	NIQE ↓	BRISQUE ↓	NIQE ↓	BRISQUE ↓
Input	4.86	27.84	5.61	24.85	4.74	22.68
MPRNet	4.14	28.72	4.94	29.42	4.60	25.93
MPRNet*	4.34	28.00	4.81	25.86	4.24	24.55
BIDeN	4.71	25.39	5.39	22.94	4.97	22.64
BIDeN*	4.31	26.55	4.71	21.22	4.28	22.40

Experiments and Results. We aim to validate whether models trained on the synthetic dataset can generalize to real testing samples and whether the BID training setting generalizes better than the conventional image decomposition setting. We train BIDeN and MPRNet under the BID setting as well as the conventional image decomposition setting with identical training recipes, that is, the training recipes used in Task II.A. For the conventional image decomposition setting, models are trained on a large-scale synthetic dataset [84] (13712 pairs). We report the quantitative results with no-reference metrics, NIQE [60] and BRISQUE [59].

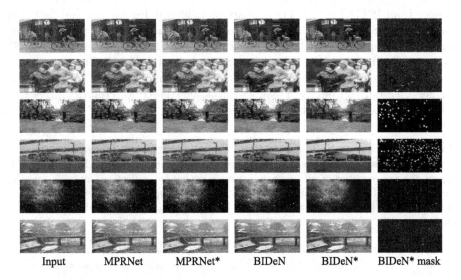

| Input | MPRNet | MPRNet* | BIDeN | BIDeN* | BIDeN* mask |

Fig. 6. Qualitative results of Task II.B (Real-scenario deraining in general). * indicates the BID setting. Rows 1–2, 3–4, and 5–6 presents the results of real rain streak, raindrop, and snow images, respectively. For all cases, models trained under the BID setting are more robust in restoring real-world images

All trained models are evaluated with real-world images. Results are presented in Table 4 and Fig. 6. With only 26.6% training data and iterations, both BIDeN and MPRNet models trained under the BID setting are more robust in restoring real images, showing the generality and robustness of the BID setting in real-world scenarios.

5.3   Task III: Joint Shadow/Reflection/Watermark Removal

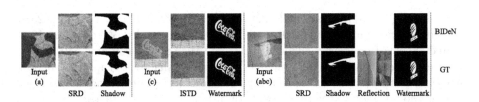

Fig. 7. Images and masks (Shadow, Watermark) produced by BIDeN for three cases, (a), (c), and (abc). All generated masks are faithful to the ground truth (GT)

Dataset. This task is designed to jointly perform multiple tasks with uncertainty in one go. Once a model is trained on this dataset under the BID setting, the model is capable of performing multiple tasks. We construct two versions for this dataset, Version one (V1) is based on ISTD [76], and Version two (V2) is based on SRD [12,66]. We use paired shadow masks, shadow-free images, and shadow images from ISTD/SRD. ISTD consists of 1330 training images and 540 test images while SRD contains 2680 training images and 408 testing images. The algorithm for adding reflection to images is acquired from [91], we select 3120 images from the reflection subset [91] as the reflection layer. The watermark generation algorithm as well as the paired watermark masks, RGB watermark images are acquired from LVM [53], we select 3000 paired watermark images and masks from the training set of LVW [53] (Fig. 7).

Table 5. Results of Task III (Joint shadow/reflection/watermark removal). We employ RMSE↓ to measure shadow region, non-shadow region, and all region. For BIDeN, we report the performance of all cases. a,b,c denotes shadow, reflection, and watermark, respectively. BIDeN (ab) is the result of BIDeN tested on shadow + reflection inputs. Results for all baselines are reported by [12,19]. The generality of BIDeN and the challenging BID training setting limit the performance of BIDeN

Method	Version one (V1), ISTD				Version two (V2), SRD			
	Shadow	Non-Shadow	All	Acc	Shadow	Non-Shadow	All	Acc
Bilateral [81]	19.82	14.83	15.63	–	23.43	22.26	22.57	–
Regions [27]	18.95	7.46	9.30	–	29.89	6.47	12.60	–
Interactive [24]	14.98	7.29	8.53	–	19.58	4.92	8.73	–
DSC [33]	9.48	6.14	6.67	–	10.89	4.99	6.23	–
DHAN [12]	8.14	6.04	6.37	–	8.94	4.80	5.67	–
Auto-Exposure [19]	7.77	5.56	5.92	–	8.56	5.75	6.51	–
CANet [8]	8.86	6.07	6.15	–	7.82	5.88	5.98	–
BIDeN (a)	11.55	10.24	10.45	0.359	12.06	7.47	8.73	0.919
BIDeN (ab)	12.96	10.77	11.12	0.661	14.10	8.16	9.79	0.911
BIDeN (ac)	11.89	10.23	10.50	0.694	13.29	8.08	9.51	0.943
BIDeN (abc)	13.20	10.76	11.16	0.929	15.28	8.85	10.62	0.936
BIDeN (b)	–	–	10.85	0.559	–	–	8.01	0.891
BIDeN (c)	–	–	10.20	0.461	–	–	7.92	0.914
BIDeN (bc)	–	–	10.77	0.727	–	–	8.71	0.879

Following the data split of ISTD and SRD, both V1 and V2 share 2580 reflection layer images and 2460 watermark images/masks. V1 contains 1330 paired shadow-free images/shadow masks and the test set contains 540 images for every source component. V2 includes 2680 paired shadow-free images/shadow masks and the test set contains 408 images for every source component. Note that we do not require the reconstruction of reflection layer images.

Experiments and Results. We mainly compare the shadow removal results to multiple shadow removal baselines, including [8,12,19,24,27,33,81]. We train

BIDeN under the BID setting. The trained BIDeN is capable of dealing with all combinations between shadow/reflection/watermark removal tasks. At test time, we report the results for all cases. We employ the root mean square error (RMSE) in LAB color space, following [12,19].

The quantitative results for Task III are reported in Table 5. Constrained by the generality of BIDeN and the challenging BID training setting, BIDeN does not show superior quantitative results compared to other baselines designed for the shadow removal task only. Please refer to the supplementary material for qualitative results.

6   Ablation Study and Analysis

We perform ablation experiments to analyze the effectiveness of each component inside BIDeN. Evaluation is performed on Task I (Mixed image decomposition across multiple domains). We set the maximum number of source components to be 4 throughout all ablation experiments. The results are shown in Table 6.

Table 6. Ablation study on the design choices of BIDeN. (I) Single-scale encoder. (II) No adversarial loss. (III) No perceptual loss. (IV) No L1/L2 loss. (V) No binary cross-entropy loss. (VI) Source prediction branch inside the generator. (VII) No weights sharing between two branches of discriminator. (VIII) Zeroed loss

Ablation	Fruit (A) PSNR↑	Animal (B) PSNR↑	Acc (AB) ↑	Acc (All) ↑
I	17.26	17.05	0.730	0.732
II	17.95	17.41	0.566	0.616
III	16.67	16.34	0.706	0.722
IV	15.56	13.65	0.733	0.753
V	18.04	17.98	0.0	0.06
VI	18.19	17.97	0.634	0.698
VII	18.13	17.98	0.520	0.609
VIII	15.68	15.64	0.716	0.683
BIDeN	**18.19**	**18.03**	**0.716**	**0.733**

Multi-scale Encoder (I). We present the results of using a single-scale encoder to replace the multi-scale encoder. BIDeN yields better performance when the multi-scale encoder is employed, which validates the effectiveness of our design.

Choice of Losses (II, III, IV, V). BIDeN consists of four different losses, we show that removing either one of the losses leads to a performance drop.

Source Prediction Branch (VI, VII). We move the prediction branch D_P to the generator. This change degrades the performance, showing that the source prediction task is better to be performed by the discriminator. We report the results for a variant where D_P does not share weights with the separation branch D_S. The performance of this variant is worse than vanilla BIDeN, indicating that the embedding learned by D_S is beneficial to D_P.

Zeroed Loss (VIII). Taking the example of Fig. 2, four heads are H_A, H_B, H_C, and H_D. By default, BIDeN ignores the outputs from H_B and H_D. Here, we encourage the outputs from H_B and H_D to be zero pixels. Such a zeroed loss forces the generator to perform the source prediction task implicitly, however, the results after applying zeroed loss are not comparable to default BIDeN.

7   Conclusion

We believe BID is a novel computer vision task advancing real-world vision systems. We form a solid foundation for the future study and we invite the community to further explore its potential, including discovering interesting areas of application, developing novel methods, extending the BID setting, and constructing benchmark datasets. We expect more application areas related to image decomposition, especially in image deraining, to apply the BID setting.

References

1. Alayrac, J.B., Carreira, J., Zisserman, A.: The visual centrifuge: model-free layered video representations. In: Proceedings of the IEEE/CVF Conference on Computer Vision and Pattern Recognition, pp. 2457–2466 (2019)
2. Alhaija, H.A., et al.: Intrinsic autoencoders for joint deferred neural rendering and intrinsic image decomposition. In: 2020 International Conference on 3D Vision (3DV), pp. 1176–1185. IEEE (2020)
3. Alpert, S., Galun, M., Brandt, A., Basri, R.: Image segmentation by probabilistic bottom-up aggregation and cue integration. IEEE Trans. Pattern Anal. Mach. Intell. **34**(2), 315–327 (2011)
4. Asha, C., Bhat, S.K., Nayak, D., Bhat, C.: Auto removal of bright spot from images captured against flashing light source. In: 2019 IEEE International Conference on Distributed Computing, VLSI, Electrical Circuits and Robotics (DISCOVER), pp. 1–6. IEEE (2019)
5. Berman, D., Avidan, S., et al.: Non-local image dehazing. In: Proceedings of the IEEE Conference on Computer Vision and Pattern Recognition, pp. 1674–1682 (2016)
6. Blinn, J.F.: A generalization of algebraic surface drawing. ACM Trans. Graph. (TOG) **1**(3), 235–256 (1982)
7. Chen, X., et al.: ReFit: a unified watermark removal framework for deep learning systems with limited data. In: Proceedings of the 2021 ACM Asia Conference on Computer and Communications Security, pp. 321–335 (2021)
8. Chen, Z., Long, C., Zhang, L., Xiao, C.: CaNet: a context-aware network for shadow removal. In: ICCV, pp. 4743–4752 (2021)
9. Cichocki, A., Amari, S.I.: Adaptive Blind Signal and Image Processing: Learning Algorithms and Applications. Wiley, Hoboken (2002)

10. Cohen, J., Olano, M., Manocha, D.: Appearance-preserving simplification. In: Proceedings of the 25th Annual Conference on Computer Graphics and Interactive Techniques, pp. 115–122 (1998)

11. Cordts, M., et al.: The cityscapes dataset for semantic urban scene understanding. In: Proceedings of the IEEE Conference on Computer Vision and Pattern Recognition, pp. 3213–3223 (2016)

12. Cun, X., Pun, C.M., Shi, C.: Towards ghost-free shadow removal via dual hierarchical aggregation network and shadow matting GAN. In: Proceedings of the AAAI Conference on Artificial Intelligence, vol. 34, pp. 10680–10687 (2020)

13. Ding, B., Long, C., Zhang, L., Xiao, C.: ArGAN: attentive recurrent generative adversarial network for shadow detection and removal. In: Proceedings of the IEEE/CVF International Conference on Computer Vision, pp. 10213–10222 (2019)

14. Du, C., Kang, B., Xu, Z., Dai, J., Nguyen, T.: Accurate and efficient video defencing using convolutional neural networks and temporal information. In: 2018 IEEE International Conference on Multimedia and Expo (ICME), pp. 1–6. IEEE (2018)

15. Fadili, M.J., Starck, J.L., Bobin, J., Moudden, Y.: Image decomposition and separation using sparse representations: an overview. Proc. IEEE $98(6)$, 983–994 (2009)

16. Faktor, A., Irani, M.: Co-segmentation by composition. In: Proceedings of the IEEE International Conference on Computer Vision, pp. 1297–1304 (2013)

17. Fan, Q., Yang, J., Hua, G., Chen, B., Wipf, D.: A generic deep architecture for single image reflection removal and image smoothing. In: Proceedings of the IEEE International Conference on Computer Vision, pp. 3238–3247 (2017)

18. Finlayson, G.D., Drew, M.S., Lu, C.: Entropy minimization for shadow removal. Int. J. Comput. Vision $85(1)$, 35–57 (2009)

19. Fu, L., et al.: Auto-exposure fusion for single-image shadow removal. In: Proceedings of the IEEE/CVF Conference on Computer Vision and Pattern Recognition, pp. 10571–10580 (2021)

20. Gai, K., Shi, Z., Zhang, C.: Blindly separating mixtures of multiple layers with spatial shifts. In: 2008 IEEE Conference on Computer Vision and Pattern Recognition, pp. 1–8. IEEE (2008)

21. Gai, K., Shi, Z., Zhang, C.: Blind separation of superimposed images with unknown motions. In: 2009 IEEE Conference on Computer Vision and Pattern Recognition, pp. 1881–1888. IEEE (2009)

22. Galdran, A., Pardo, D., Picón, A., Alvarez-Gila, A.: Automatic red-channel underwater image restoration. J. Vis. Commun. Image Represent. 26, 132–145 (2015)

23. Gandelsman, Y., Shocher, A., Irani, M.: "double-dip": Unsupervised image decomposition via coupled deep-image-priors. In: Proceedings of the IEEE/CVF Conference on Computer Vision and Pattern Recognition, pp. 11026–11035 (2019)

24. Gong, H., Cosker, D.: Interactive shadow removal and ground truth for variable scene categories. In: BMVC, pp. 1–11. Citeseer (2014)

25. Goodfellow, I., et al.: Generative adversarial nets. In: Advances in Neural Information Processing Systems (2014)

26. Gu, S., Meng, D., Zuo, W., Zhang, L.: Joint convolutional analysis and synthesis sparse representation for single image layer separation. In: Proceedings of the IEEE International Conference on Computer Vision, pp. 1708–1716 (2017)

27. Guo, R., Dai, Q., Hoiem, D.: Paired regions for shadow detection and removal. IEEE Trans. Pattern Anal. Mach. Intell. $35(12)$, 2956–2967 (2012)

28. Halperin, T., Ephrat, A., Hoshen, Y.: Neural separation of observed and unobserved distributions. In: International Conference on Machine Learning, pp. 2566–2575. PMLR (2019)

29. Han, J., et al.: Underwater image restoration via contrastive learning and a real-world dataset. arXiv preprint arXiv:2106.10718 (2021)
30. Han, J., Shoeiby, M., Petersson, L., Armin, M.A.: Dual contrastive learning for unsupervised image-to-image translation. In: Proceedings of the IEEE/CVF Conference on Computer Vision and Pattern Recognition Workshops (2021)
31. He, K., Sun, J., Tang, X.: Single image haze removal using dark channel prior. IEEE Trans. Pattern Anal. Mach. Intell. 33(12), 2341–2353 (2010)
32. Heusel, M., Ramsauer, H., Unterthiner, T., Nessler, B., Hochreiter, S.: GANs trained by a two time-scale update rule converge to a local NASH equilibrium. In: Advances in Neural Information Processing Systems (2017)
33. Hu, X., Fu, C.W., Zhu, L., Qin, J., Heng, P.A.: Direction-aware spatial context features for shadow detection and removal. IEEE Trans. Pattern Anal. Mach. Intell. 42(11), 2795–2808 (2019)
34. Hyvärinen, A., Oja, E.: A fast fixed-point algorithm for independent component analysis. Neural Comput. 9(7), 1483–1492 (1997)
35. Hyvärinen, A., Oja, E.: Independent component analysis: algorithms and applications. Neural Netw. 13(4–5), 411–430 (2000)
36. Isola, P., Zhu, J.Y., Zhou, T., Efros, A.A.: Image-to-image translation with conditional adversarial networks. In: Proceedings of the IEEE Conference on Computer Vision and Pattern Recognition, pp. 1125–1134 (2017)
37. Jayaram, V., Thickstun, J.: Source separation with deep generative priors. In: International Conference on Machine Learning, pp. 4724–4735. PMLR (2020)
38. Jin, Y., Sharma, A., Tan, R.T.: DC-ShadowNet: single-image hard and soft shadow removal using unsupervised domain-classifier guided network. In: Proceedings of the IEEE/CVF International Conference on Computer Vision, pp. 5027–5036 (2021)
39. Johnson, J., Alahi, A., Fei-Fei, L.: Perceptual losses for real-time style transfer and super-resolution. In: Leibe, B., Matas, J., Sebe, N., Welling, M. (eds.) ECCV 2016. LNCS, vol. 9906, pp. 694–711. Springer, Cham (2016). https://doi.org/10.1007/978-3-319-46475-6_43
40. Kang, L.W., Lin, C.W., Fu, Y.H.: Automatic single-image-based rain streaks removal via image decomposition. IEEE Trans. Image Process. 21(4), 1742–1755 (2011)
41. Karras, T., Laine, S., Aila, T.: A style-based generator architecture for generative adversarial networks. In: Proceedings of the IEEE/CVF Conference on Computer Vision and Pattern Recognition, pp. 4401–4410 (2019)
42. Kingma, D.P., Ba, J.: Adam: a method for stochastic optimization. International Conference on Learning Representations (ICLR) (2014)
43. Kong, Q., Xu, Y., Wang, W., Jackson, P.J., Plumbley, M.D.: Single-channel signal separation and deconvolution with generative adversarial networks. arXiv preprint arXiv:1906.07552 (2019)
44. Le, H., Samaras, D.: Shadow removal via shadow image decomposition. In: Proceedings of the IEEE/CVF International Conference on Computer Vision, pp. 8578–8587 (2019)
45. Lee, T.W., Lewicki, M.S., Sejnowski, T.J.: Ica mixture models for unsupervised classification of non-Gaussian classes and automatic context switching in blind signal separation. IEEE Trans. Pattern Anal. Mach. Intell. 22(10), 1078–1089 (2000)
46. Li, C., Yang, Y., He, K., Lin, S., Hopcroft, J.E.: Single image reflection removal through cascaded refinement. In: Proceedings of the IEEE/CVF Conference on Computer Vision and Pattern Recognition, pp. 3565–3574 (2020)

47. Li, R., Pan, J., Li, Z., Tang, J.: Single image dehazing via conditional generative adversarial network. In: Proceedings of the IEEE Conference on Computer Vision and Pattern Recognition, pp. 8202–8211 (2018)
48. Li, R., Tan, R.T., Cheong, L.F.: All in one bad weather removal using architectural search. In: Proceedings of the IEEE/CVF Conference on Computer Vision and Pattern Recognition, pp. 3175–3185 (2020)
49. Li, S., et al.: Single image deraining: a comprehensive benchmark analysis. In: CVPR, pp. 3838–3847 (2019)
50. Li, W., Hosseini Jafari, O., Rother, C.: Deep object co-segmentation. In: Jawahar, C.V., Li, H., Mori, G., Schindler, K. (eds.) ACCV 2018. LNCS, vol. 11363, pp. 638–653. Springer, Cham (2019). https://doi.org/10.1007/978-3-030-20893-6_40
51. Li, X., Wu, J., Lin, Z., Liu, H., Zha, H.: Recurrent squeeze-and-excitation context aggregation net for single image deraining. In: Ferrari, V., Hebert, M., Sminchisescu, C., Weiss, Y. (eds.) ECCV 2018. LNCS, vol. 11211, pp. 262–277. Springer, Cham (2018). https://doi.org/10.1007/978-3-030-01234-2_16
52. Lin, S., Ryabtsev, A., Sengupta, S., Curless, B.L., Seitz, S.M., Kemelmacher-Shlizerman, I.: Real-time high-resolution background matting. In: Proceedings of the IEEE/CVF Conference on Computer Vision and Pattern Recognition, pp. 8762–8771 (2021)
53. Liu, Y., Zhu, Z., Bai, X.: WDNet: watermark-decomposition network for visible watermark removal. In: Proceedings of the IEEE/CVF Winter Conference on Applications of Computer Vision, pp. 3685–3693 (2021)
54. Liu, Y.L., Lai, W.S., Yang, M.H., Chuang, Y.Y., Huang, J.B.: Learning to see through obstructions with layered decomposition. In: Proceedings of the IEEE Conference on Computer Vision and Pattern Recognition (2020)
55. Liu, Y.F., Jaw, D.W., Huang, S.C., Hwang, J.N.: DesnowNet: context-aware deep network for snow removal. IEEE Trans. Image Process. **27**(6), 3064–3073 (2018)
56. Ma, D., Wan, R., Shi, B., Kot, A.C., Duan, L.Y.: Learning to jointly generate and separate reflections. In: Proceedings of the IEEE/CVF International Conference on Computer Vision, pp. 2444–2452 (2019)
57. Man, Z., Fu, X., Xiao, Z., Yang, G., Liu, A., Xiong, Z.: Unfolding Taylor's approximations for image restoration. Adv. Neural. Inf. Process. Syst. **34**, 18997–19009 (2021)
58. Mao, X., Li, Q., Xie, H., Lau, R.Y., Wang, Z., Paul Smolley, S.: Least squares generative adversarial networks. In: IEEE International Conference on Computer Vision (ICCV), pp. 2794–2802 (2017)
59. Mittal, A., Moorthy, A.K., Bovik, A.C.: No-reference image quality assessment in the spatial domain. IEEE Trans. Image Process. **21**(12), 4695–4708 (2012)
60. Mittal, A., Soundararajan, R., Bovik, A.C.: Making a "completely blind" image quality analyzer. IEEE Sig. Process. Lett. **20**(3), 209–212 (2012)
61. Nayar, S.K., Narasimhan, S.G.: Vision in bad weather. In: Proceedings of the Seventh IEEE International Conference on Computer Vision, vol. 2, pp. 820–827. IEEE (1999)
62. Nilsback, M.E., Zisserman, A.: A visual vocabulary for flower classification. In: 2006 IEEE Computer Society Conference on Computer Vision and Pattern Recognition (CVPR 2006), vol. 2, pp. 1447–1454. IEEE (2006)
63. Oliveira, P.R., Romero, R.A.: Improvements on ICA mixture models for image pre-processing and segmentation. Neurocomputing **71**(10–12), 2180–2193 (2008)
64. Porav, H., Bruls, T., Newman, P.: I can see clearly now: Image restoration via deraining. In: 2019 International Conference on Robotics and Automation (ICRA), pp. 7087–7093. IEEE (2019)

65. Qian, R., Tan, R.T., Yang, W., Su, J., Liu, J.: Attentive generative adversarial network for raindrop removal from a single image. In: CVPR, pp. 2482–2491 (2018)
66. Qu, L., Tian, J., He, S., Tang, Y., Lau, R.W.: DeShadowNet: a multi-context embedding deep network for shadow removal. In: Proceedings of the IEEE Conference on Computer Vision and Pattern Recognition, pp. 4067–4075 (2017)
67. Quan, R., Yu, X., Liang, Y., Yang, Y.: Removing raindrops and rain streaks in one go. In: Proceedings of the IEEE/CVF Conference on Computer Vision and Pattern Recognition, pp. 9147–9156 (2021)
68. Ren, W., Tian, J., Han, Z., Chan, A., Tang, Y.: Video desnowing and deraining based on matrix decomposition. In: Proceedings of the IEEE Conference on Computer Vision and Pattern Recognition, pp. 4210–4219 (2017)
69. Rother, C., Kolmogorov, V., Blake, A.: " grabcut" interactive foreground extraction using iterated graph cuts. ACM Trans. Graph. (TOG) 23(3), 309–314 (2004)
70. Sakaridis, C., Dai, D., Van Gool, L.: Semantic foggy scene understanding with synthetic data. Int. J. Comput. Vision 126(9), 973–992 (2018)
71. Simonyan, K., Zisserman, A.: Very deep convolutional networks for large-scale image recognition. arXiv preprint arXiv:1409.1556 (2014)
72. Tan, R.T.: Visibility in bad weather from a single image. In: 2008 IEEE Conference on Computer Vision and Pattern Recognition, pp. 1–8. IEEE (2008)
73. Ulyanov, D., Vedaldi, A., Lempitsky, V.: Instance normalization: the missing ingredient for fast stylization. arXiv preprint arXiv:1607.08022 (2016)
74. Ulyanov, D., Vedaldi, A., Lempitsky, V.: Deep image prior. In: Proceedings of the IEEE Conference on Computer Vision and Pattern Recognition, pp. 9446–9454 (2018)
75. Wang, H., Xie, Q., Zhao, Q., Meng, D.: A model-driven deep neural network for single image rain removal. In: Proceedings of the IEEE/CVF Conference on Computer Vision and Pattern Recognition, pp. 3103–3112 (2020)
76. Wang, J., Li, X., Yang, J.: Stacked conditional generative adversarial networks for jointly learning shadow detection and shadow removal. In: Proceedings of the IEEE Conference on Computer Vision and Pattern Recognition, pp. 1788–1797 (2018)
77. Wang, Z., Philion, J., Fidler, S., Kautz, J.: Learning indoor inverse rendering with 3D spatially-varying lighting. In: Proceedings of the IEEE/CVF International Conference on Computer Vision, pp. 12538–12547 (2021)
78. Wu, Y., et al.: How to train neural networks for flare removal. In: Proceedings of the IEEE/CVF International Conference on Computer Vision (2021)
79. Xiao, J., Zhou, M., Fu, X., Liu, A., Zha, Z.J.: Improving de-raining generalization via neural reorganization. In: Proceedings of the IEEE/CVF International Conference on Computer Vision, pp. 4987–4996 (2021)
80. Xue, T., Rubinstein, M., Liu, C., Freeman, W.T.: A computational approach for obstruction-free photography. ACM Trans. Graph. (TOG) 34(4), 1–11 (2015)
81. Yang, Q., Tan, K.H., Ahuja, N.: Shadow removal using bilateral filtering. IEEE Trans. Image Process. 21(10), 4361–4368 (2012)
82. Yang, W., Tan, R.T., Feng, J., Liu, J., Guo, Z., Yan, S.: Deep joint rain detection and removal from a single image. In: 2017 IEEE Conference on Computer Vision and Pattern Recognition (CVPR), pp. 1685–1694 (2017). https://doi.org/10.1109/CVPR.2017.183
83. Zamir, S.W., Arora, A., Khan, S., Hayat, M., Khan, F.S., Yang, M.H.: ReStormer: efficient transformer for high-resolution image restoration. In: CVPR (2022)
84. Zamir, S.W., et al.: Multi-stage progressive image restoration. In: CVPR (2021)

85. Zhang, H., Goodfellow, I., Metaxas, D., Odena, A.: Self-attention generative adversarial networks. In: International Conference on Machine Learning, pp. 7354–7363. PMLR (2019)
86. Zhang, H., Sindagi, V., Patel, V.M.: Image de-raining using a conditional generative adversarial network. IEEE Trans. Circuits Syst. Video Technol. **30**(11), 3943–3956 (2019)
87. Zhang, K., Li, D., Luo, W., Ren, W., Liu, W.: Enhanced spatio-temporal interaction learning for video deraining: a faster and better framework. IEEE Trans. Pattern Anal. Mach. Intell. (2022)
88. Zhang, K., Li, D., Luo, W., Ren, W., Ma, L., Li, H.: Dual attention-in-attention model for joint rain streak and raindrop removal. arXiv preprint arXiv:2103.07051 (2021)
89. Zhang, K., et al.: Beyond monocular deraining: stereo image deraining via semantic understanding. In: Vedaldi, A., Bischof, H., Brox, T., Frahm, J.-M. (eds.) ECCV 2020. LNCS, vol. 12372, pp. 71–89. Springer, Cham (2020). https://doi.org/10.1007/978-3-030-58583-9_5
90. Zhang, K., et al.: Beyond monocular deraining: parallel stereo deraining network via semantic prior. Int. J. Comput. Vision, 1–16 (2022)
91. Zhang, X., Ng, R., Chen, Q.: Single image reflection separation with perceptual losses. In: Proceedings of the IEEE/CVF Conference on Computer Vision and Pattern Recognition, pp. 4786–4794 (2018)
92. Zhong, Y., Dai, Y., Li, H.: Stereo computation for a single mixture image. In: Ferrari, V., Hebert, M., Sminchisescu, C., Weiss, Y. (eds.) ECCV 2018. LNCS, vol. 11213, pp. 441–456. Springer, Cham (2018). https://doi.org/10.1007/978-3-030-01240-3_27
93. Zhou, M., Wang, F., Wei, X., Wang, R., Wang, X.: PID controller-inspired model design for single image de-raining. IEEE Trans. Circuits Syst. II Express Briefs **69**(4), 2351–2355 (2021)
94. Zhou, M., Wang, R.: Control theory-inspired model design for single image de-raining. IEEE Trans. Circuits Syst. II Express Briefs **69**(2), 649–653 (2021)
95. Zhou, M., et al.: Image de-raining via continual learning. In: Proceedings of the IEEE/CVF Conference on Computer Vision and Pattern Recognition, pp. 4907–4916 (2021)
96. Wang, Z., Bovik, A.C., Sheikh, H.R., Simoncelli, E.P.: Image quality assessment: from error visibility to structural similarity. IEEE Trans. Image Process. **13**(4), 600–612 (2004). https://doi.org/10.1109/TIP.2003.819861
97. Zhu, J.Y., Park, T., Isola, P., Efros, A.A.: Unpaired image-to-image translation using cycle-consistent adversarial networks. In: Proceedings of the IEEE International Conference on Computer Vision, pp. 2223–2232 (2017)
98. Zou, Z., Lei, S., Shi, T., Shi, Z., Ye, J.: Deep adversarial decomposition: a unified framework for separating superimposed images. In: Proceedings of the IEEE/CVF Conference on Computer Vision and Pattern Recognition, pp. 12806–12816 (2020)

MuLUT: Cooperating Multiple Look-Up Tables for Efficient Image Super-Resolution

Jiacheng Li[1], Chang Chen[2], Zhen Cheng[1], and Zhiwei Xiong[1(✉)]

[1] University of Science and Technology of China, Hefei, China
{jclee,mywander}@mail.ustc.edu.cn, zwxiong@ustc.edu.cn
[2] Huawei Noah's Ark Lab, Beijing, China
chenchang25@huawei.com

Abstract. The high-resolution screen of edge devices stimulates a strong demand for efficient image super-resolution (SR). An emerging research, SR-LUT, responds to this demand by marrying the look-up table (LUT) with learning-based SR methods. However, the size of a *single* LUT grows *exponentially* with the increase of its indexing capacity. Consequently, the receptive field of a single LUT is restricted, resulting in inferior performance. To address this issue, we extend SR-LUT by enabling the cooperation of ***Multiple*** LUTs, termed MuLUT. Firstly, we devise two novel complementary indexing patterns and construct multiple LUTs in parallel. Secondly, we propose a re-indexing mechanism to enable the hierarchical indexing between multiple LUTs. In these two ways, the total size of MuLUT is *linear* to its indexing capacity, yielding a practical method to obtain superior performance. We examine the advantage of MuLUT on five SR benchmarks. MuLUT achieves a significant improvement over SR-LUT, up to 1.1 dB PSNR, while preserving its efficiency. Moreover, we extend MuLUT to address demosaicing of Bayer-patterned images, surpassing SR-LUT on two benchmarks by a large margin.

Keywords: Image super-resolution · Look-up table · Image demosaicing

1 Introduction

Single-image super-resolution (SR) aims to restore a high-resolution (HR) image with high-frequency details from its low-resolution (LR) observation. Recent methods based on deep neural network (DNN) [10,11,26,34,53,68,69] have made

---

J. Li and C. Chen—Equal contribution.

Supplementary Information The online version contains supplementary material available at https://doi.org/10.1007/978-3-031-19797-0_14.

S. Avidan et al. (Eds.): ECCV 2022, LNCS 13678, pp. 238–256, 2022.
https://doi.org/10.1007/978-3-031-19797-0_14

impressive progress in restoration performance, yet usually at a cost of heavy computational burden. Although this can be alleviated by elaborated model designs or dedicated computing engines (*e.g.*, GPU and NPU), the hardware cost and power consumption still limit the deployment of existing SR methods on edge devices. Therefore, the growing number of high-resolution screens on edge devices (*e.g.*, smartphones and televisions) calls for a practical SR solution.

An emerging research, SR-LUT [23], responds to this demand by replacing the expensive computing with relatively cheap memory access of cached index-value pairs. Different from the existing lightweight SR methods based on dedicated computing engines [2,11,31], SR-LUT utilizes a single look-up table (LUT) to cache the exhaustive values for later retrieval, which are computed in advance by a learned SR network. This contributes to the power efficiency and inference speed. However, in practice, the size of LUT is limited by the on-device memory. For a single LUT, the size grows exponentially as the dimension of indexing entries (*i.e.*, indexing capacity) increases. This imposes a restriction on the indexing capacity as well as the corresponding receptive field (RF) size of the SR network to be cached, which is the main obstacle for performance improvement.

In this paper, we embrace the merits of SR-LUT and propose MuLUT to overcome its intrinsic limitation, by enabling the cooperation of **Mu**ltiple **LUT**s. Firstly, we devise two novel *complementary indexing* patterns and cooperate multiple LUTs in parallel. Correspondingly, we propose a multi-branch network structure to learn and generate SR results for caching. Secondly, we devise a cascaded framework to enable the *hierarchical indexing* between multiple LUTs, where a re-indexing mechanism is proposed to link between LUTs from different hierarchies. In the above two ways, the total size of MuLUT is linear to its indexing capacity, yielding a practical method to obtain superior performance.

Extensive experiments demonstrate a clear advantage of our proposed MuLUT compared with SR-LUT. On five standard SR benchmarks, MuLUT achieves up to 1.1 dB PSNR improvement, approaching the performance of the lightweight FSRCNN model [11]. Meanwhile, MuLUT preserves the efficiency of SR-LUT, for example, the theoretical energy cost is about 100 times less than that of FSRCNN.

Moreover, to evaluate the versatility of MuLUT, we extend MuLUT to address demosaicing of Bayer-patterned images. Although SR-LUT can be directly applied to demosaicing, it yields inferior performance due to the subpixel shift between Bayer-patterned and HR images. Instead, we cooperate multiple LUTs with complementary indexing and hierarchical indexing, addressing this misalignment problem of the single LUT solution. As a result, MuLUT achieves over 6.0 dB PSNR gain compared with SR-LUT on two widely-used benchmarks.

The contributions of this work are summarized as follows:

1) We devise two novel indexing patterns and a corresponding multi-branch network to enable the complementary indexing of multiple LUTs.
2) We devise a cascaded framework with a re-indexing mechanism to enable the hierarchical indexing of multiple LUTs.

3) Extensive experiments on SR demonstrate that MuLUT achieves a significant improvement in performance over SR-LUT while preserving the clear advantage in efficiency over DNNs, showing its practicality for edge devices.
4) We adapt MuLUT to the image demosaicing task and demonstrate its superiority over SR-LUT, showing the versatility of the proposed method.

2   Related Works

Classical SR Methods. Interpolation-based methods, including nearest, bilinear, and bicubic [25], often produce blurry results because the interpolation weights are calculated without considering the local structure inside the image. Examplar-based methods leverage a dataset of LR-HR image patch pairs [13,14,43,59,60], or exploit self-similarity inside the LR image [16,62]. Sparse coding methods learn a compact representation of the patches, showing promising results [44,50,51,63,64]. But, computing the sparse representation of the input patch is time-consuming. Other fast SR methods based on random forests [45], gradient filed sharpening [49], and displacement field [52] are also explored. Nevertheless, these classical SR methods suffer either unsatisfying visual quality or time-consuming computations.

Efficient SR Networks. With the rise of DNN methods, the community has made impressive progress in the task of SR [2,6,8,10,26,34,41,53,56,57,61,65, 68]. However, it comes with a substantial computational burden of numerous floating-point operations. Thus, many efforts for efficient SR are conducted. Researchers elaborately design lightweight networks, including ESPCN [46], FSRCNN [11], CARN-M [2], IMDN [21], and LatticeNet [36], to name a few. General network compression methods like quantization [31,58], neural architecture search [9,30,48], network pruning [33], and AdderNet [7,47] have also been explored for efficient SR. Most recently, Jo *et al.* propose SR-LUT for practical SR [23]. They train a deep SR network with a restricted RF and then cache the output values of the learned SR network to the LUT, which are retrieved to obtain HR predictions at the test time. However, a single LUT yields inferior performance due to the restriction of the dimension of indexing entries, *i.e.*, the RF of the learned SR network. This is proved to be critical for SR [17]. Our method overcomes the intrinsic limitation of SR-LUT by enabling the cooperation of multiple LUTs.

Image Demosaicing. Image demosaicing aims to produce colored observation from linear responses of light sensors inside the camera. It can be viewed as an SR problem with a particular color pattern. Interpolation-based methods like nearest and bilinear can also be used in image demosaicing. However, they tend to produce artifacts in the region with high-frequency signal changes. Classical methods taking advantage of the self-similarity inside the image [3,5,12,67] or relying on an optimization process [18,22,66] are proposed. Recently, DNN methods have been introduced to take advantage of powerful representations learned from large-scale datasets [15,29,54]. However, dedicated computing engines are required to execute numerous floating-point operations in DNNs. We adapt MuLUT to the image demosaicing task and show its versatility.

3   Cooperation of Multiple LUTs for SR

3.1   Preliminary

LUT is a widely-used mapping operator, especially for color manipulation and tone mapping modules in the image processing pipeline [27,37,40]. A LUT is composed of pairs of indexes and values, which play as lookup indexing entries and interpolation candidates at the inference time, respectively. These paired indexing entries and values can be stored in the on-device memory, resulting in high execution efficiency. Recently, Jo *et al.* proposed SR-LUT, adopting LUT to the SR task. As illustrated in Fig. 1a, they firstly train a deep SR network. Then, the output values of the trained SR network are cached into a LUT via traversing all possible inputs. Finally, the HR predictions are obtained by locating LR input pixels and interpolating cached HR values. Due to the exponential growth of LUT size as the dimension of indexing entry increases, the authors impose a restriction on the indexing capacity of LUT, resulting in the limited RF of the SR network to be cached. Although with the rotation ensemble trick, where the input patch is rotated 4 times and the lookup results are ensembled, the RF size of SR-LUT is still limited to 3×3. This limitation leads to inferior performance, since the RF size plays a critical role [17]. As shown in Fig. 1b, with increased RF size, the performance for SR can be significantly improved.

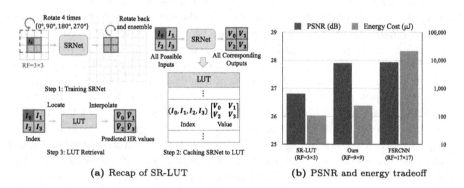

(a) Recap of SR-LUT   **(b)** PSNR and energy tradeoff

Fig. 1. (a) SR-LUT is obtained by caching the output values of a learned deep SR network with a restricted RF. At inference time, the precomputed HR output values are retrieved from the LUT for query LR input pixels. The indexing entries and corresponding HR values of a 4D LUT for $2\times$ SR are marked in blue and green, respectively. The actual receptive area with the rotation ensemble trick are depicted with dashed lines. Please refer to the supplementary material and SR-LUT [23] for more details. (b) By cooperating multiple LUTs, we increase the RF from 3×3 to 9×9, resulting in a significant performance improvement over SR-LUT while preserving its efficiency. The PSNR values are evaluated on Manga109 for $4\times$ SR. (Color figure online)

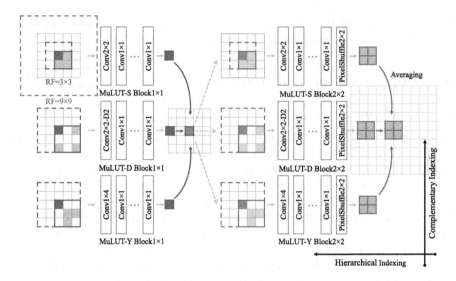

Fig. 2. Overview of MuLUT. Compared with a single LUT, MuLUT is able to greatly increase the RF size (*e.g.*, from 3×3 to 9×9). The MuLUT blocks are trained end-to-end and then cached to multiple LUTs. At inference time, these parallel and cascaded LUTs are retrieved with complementary indexing and hierarchical indexing in exactly the same order as the MuLUT blocks.

3.2   Overview

From the above observation, we propose to increase the indexing capacity by cooperating multiple LUTs, thus addressing the limitation of the RF. Specifically, as illustrated in Fig. 2, we propose two fundamental ways, *i.e.*, complementary indexing and hierarchical indexing, to generalize a single LUT to MuLUT, whose RF can be effectively enlarged by constructing multiple elementary components just like a neural network. To obtain multiple LUTs, we train a MuLUT network, composed of multiple elementary MuLUT blocks. By parallelizing and cascading these MuLUT blocks, the RF and modeling capacity of the MuLUT networks increase, while the total size of cached LUTs grows linearly instead of exponentially. As shown in Fig. 2, the MuLUT network with 3 parallel blocks and 2 cascaded stages increases the RF size from 3×3 to 9×9 (9 times larger), while the total size of these LUTs is less than 4 times a single LUT. In contrast, the full size of a 25D LUT with an equivalent 9×9 RF size is $(2^8)^{25-4} = 2^{168}$ times a 4D LUT. In this way, MuLUT equips with a much larger indexing capacity without introducing the enormous cost of storage and computation.

During training, the MuLUT network is trained in an end-to-end manner. After caching the trained MuLUT network, MuLUT shares exactly the same structure of the original SR network and can be retrieved through complementary indexing and hierarchical indexing. In these two principled ways, we extend SR-LUT both in the width and depth dimensions and empower it to cache more

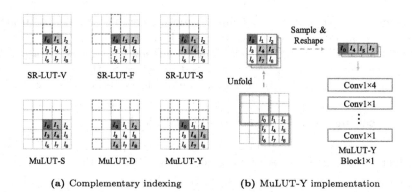

(a) Complementary indexing   (b) MuLUT-Y implementation

Fig. 3. Complementary indexing of multiple LUTs. With the proposed two novel index-ing patterns, MuLUT covers more pixels than different variants of SR-LUT. The cov-ered pixels with the rotation ensemble trick are marked with dashed boxes.

complicated neural networks, taking advantage of both elaborate designs of deep neural networks and the high efficiency of LUT retrieval.

3.3   Parallelizing LUTs with Complementary Indexing

The first way we propose to increase the indexing capacity is parallelizing LUTs with complementary indexing. In SR, the surrounding pixels provide critical information to restore the high-frequency details, making it essential to cover as many as input pixels for SR methods. Thus, we construct multiple LUTs with different indexing patterns in parallel, which are carefully designed to com-plement each other. For 4D LUTs, besides the standard indexing pattern, *i.e.*, MuLUT-S, we devise two novel indexing patterns (MuLUT-D and MuLUT-Y) with complementary covered pixels. As shown in Fig. 3a, the indexing pixels of MuLUT-S, MuLUT-D, and MuLUT-Y are (I_0, I_1, I_3, I_4), (I_0, I_2, I_6, I_8), and (I_0, I_4, I_5, I_7), respectively. Different from the variants of SR-LUT, our comple-mentary design covers the whole 5×5 area with the three types of MuLUT working together. Correspondingly, we propose a MuLUT network with multi-ple branches, where the parallel MuLUT blocks with complementary receptive areas are jointly trained. The cached LUTs, *i.e.*, LUT_S, LUT_D, and LUT_Y, are retrieved in parallel, after which their predictions are averaged. Thus, for anchor I_0, the corresponding HR values $\mathbf{V}$ are obtained by

$$\mathbf{V} = (LUT_S[I_0][I_1][I_3][I_4] + LUT_D[I_0][I_2][I_6][I_8] + LUT_Y[(I_0][I_4][I_5][I_7])/3, \quad (1)$$

where $LUT_*[\cdot]$ denotes the lookup and interpolation process in the LUT retrieval. In practice, the MuLUT-S block and MuLUT-D block can be implemented with standard convolutions, where the MuLUT-D block equips with an entry con-volution with a dilation size of 2. As for MuLUT-Y, we implement it through the process illustrated in Fig. 3b. Precisely, we first unfold the input image by extracting 3×3 patches with a sliding window. Then, we sample and reshape these "Y" shape pixels into 1×4 vectors, which are fed into a standard convolution with a 1×4 kernel. In summary, with complementary indexing of parallel LUTs, more surrounding pixels are involved to better capture the local structures, which help to predict the corresponding high-resolution observations.

3.4   Cascading LUTs with Hierarchical Indexing

The second way we propose to increase the indexing capacity is cascading LUTs with hierarchical indexing. As illustrated in Fig. 4 (left), with cascaded LUTs, we conduct the lookup process in a hierarchical manner. The values $(I_*^{(2)})$ in the previous LUT serve as the indexes of the following LUT. This hierarchical indexing process can be formulated as

$$\mathbf{V} = LUT^{(2)}[LUT^{(1)}[I_*]][LUT^{(1)}[I_*]][LUT^{(1)}[I_*]][LUT^{(1)}[I_*]]. \tag{2}$$

From the perspective of the RF, this cascaded framework is very similar to cascading multiple convolutional layers in a neural network. As shown in Fig. 4 (right), cascading two stages of MuLUT blocks increases the RF size from 3×3 to 4×4. However, the indexes for image data are sampled and stored in the *int8* data type because of the constraint of LUT size, while training neural networks requires gradients in the *float* data type. Thus, we design a LUT re-indexing mechanism to integrate the behavior of hierarchical indexing in the learning process of MuLUT networks. Specifically, as shown in Fig. 4 (right), the prediction values of the previous MuLUT block are quantized to integers in the forward pass while their gradients are retained as floating-point values in the backward pass. This way, the cascaded LUTs are able to reproduce the performance of the cascaded MuLUT blocks. In practice, we adopt the dense connection [19] to help the convergence of MuLUT networks.

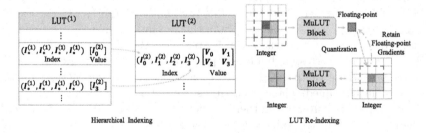

Fig. 4. Hierarchical indexing and LUT re-indexing mechanism. With LUT re-indexing, the behavior of LUT retrieval is involved in the learning process of the network with cascaded stages. Thus, the cascaded LUTs are able to reproduce its performance.

3.5   The LUT-Aware Finetuning Strategy

In SR-LUT [23], due to the constraint of storage, the indexes of a LUT are uniformly sampled to reduce the LUT size, and the nonsampled indexes are

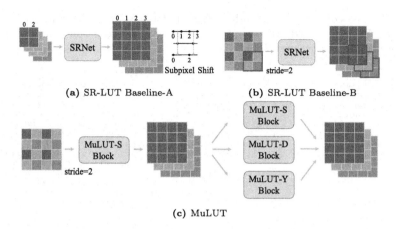

(a) SR-LUT Baseline-A   (b) SR-LUT Baseline-B

(c) MuLUT

Fig. 5. The MuLUT network and SR-LUT baselines for image demosaicing. The cooperation of multiple LUTs enables the flexible design of the processing pipeline.

approximated with nearest neighbors. Also, an interpolation process is performed to compute final predictions from weighted LUT values during LUT retrieval. The aforementioned loss of information causes a performance gap between the SR network and the cached LUT (See Table 4). Thus, we propose a LUT-aware finetuning strategy to address this issue. Specifically, we treat the values stored inside LUTs as trainable parameters and finetune them in a similar process to LUT re-indexing. After finetuning, the values inside LUTs are adapted to the sampling and interpolation process. This strategy is universal and serves as a practical improvement for MuLUT.

4   Extension of MuLUT to Demosaicing

MuLUT enables the flexible design of the processing pipeline for different vision tasks. Here, we take demosaicing Bayer-patterned images as an example. Image demosaicing can be viewed as an SR problem with a particular color pattern. However, there are grave obstacles in adopting SR-LUT to this task. Two straightforward solutions are shown in Fig. 5a and Fig. 5b, respectively. In Baseline-A, the pixels in the bayer pattern are treated as four independent channels, which are processed separately, and then the two green channels are averaged. As shown in Fig. 5a, this solution suffers from a subpixel shift of center points due to the misalignment between the HR pixels and the Bayer-patterned sampled ones. In Baseline-B, at a stride of 2, the 2×2 Bayer-patterned blocks are upsampled into colored patches directly. But the limited RF of SR-LUT leads to the independent processing of these bayer blocks, thus failing to capture the inter-block patterns. In contrast, MuLUT is easy to be adapted to the characteristics of Bayer-patterned images. As shown in Fig. 5c, our MuLUT network resembles three color channels like Baseline-B in the first stage, and then integrates the surrounding pixels with three indexing patterns in the second stage.

Table 1. The comparison with other methods for 4× SR on standard benchmark datasets. With increased RF size, MuLUT achieves a significant improvement in restoration performance over SR-LUT.

PSNR/SSIM	Method	RF size	Set5	Set14	BSDS100	Urban100	Manga109
Interpolation	Nearest	1 × 1	26.25/0.7372	24.65/0.6529	25.03/0.6293	22.17/0.6154	23.45/0.7414
	Bilinear	2 × 2	27.55/0.7884	25.42/0.6792	25.54/0.6460	22.69/0.6346	24.21/0.7666
	Bicubic	4 × 4	28.42/0.8101	26.00/0.7023	25.96/0.6672	23.14/0.6574	24.91/0.7871
LUT	SR-LUT-S [23]	3 × 3	29.82/0.8478	27.01/0.7355	26.53/0.6953	24.02/0.6990	26.80/0.8380
	MuLUT-SDY	5 × 5	30.40/0.8600	27.48/0.7507	26.79/0.7088	24.31/0.7137	27.52/0.8551
	MuLUT-SDY-X2	9 × 9	30.60/0.8653	27.60/0.7541	26.86/0.7110	24.46/0.7194	27.90/0.8633
Sparse coding	NE + LLE [4]	-	29.62/0.8404	26.82/0.7346	26.49/0.6970	23.84/0.6942	26.10/0.8195
	Zeyde et al. [64]	-	26.69/0.8429	26.90/0.7354	26.53/0.6968	23.90/0.6962	26.24/0.8241
	ANR [50]	-	29.70/0.8422	26.86/0.7368	26.52/0.6992	23.89/0.6964	26.18/0.8214
	A+ [51]	–	30.27/0.8602	27.30/0.7498	26.73/0.7088	24.33/0.7189	26.91/0.8480
DNN	FSRCNN [11]	17 × 17	30.72/0.8660	27.61/0.7550	26.98/0.7150	24.62/0.7280	27.90/0.8610
	CARN-M [2]	45 × 45	31.82/0.8898	28.29/0.7747	27.42/0.7305	25.62/0.7694	29.85/0.8993
	RRDB [53]	703 × 703	32.68/0.8999	28.88/0.7891	27.82/0.7444	27.02/0.8146	31.57/0.9185

This multi-stage and multi-branch structure enabled by the cooperation of multiple LUTs addresses the above obstacles of adapting LUT to the task of image demosaicing effectively, showing the versatility of MuLUT.

5 Experiments and Results

5.1 Experimental Settings

Datasets. We train the MuLUT networks on the DIV2K dataset [1], which is widely used in the task of SR. The DIV2K dataset contains 800 training images and 100 validation images with 2K resolution. It covers multiple scenes and encapsulates diverse patches. We evaluate our method with 5 well-recognized benchmark datasets: Set5, Set14, BSDS100 [38], Urban100 [20], and Manga109 [39]. For quantitative evaluation, we report peak signal-to-noise ratio (PSNR) and structural similarity index (SSIM) [55], which are widely used for image quality assessment in terms of restoration fidelity. Besides, we compute the theoretical energy cost following AdderSR [47] to evaluate the efficiency tradeoff of our method as well as other solutions.

Comparison Methods. We compare our method with various single-image SR methods, including interpolation-based methods (nearest neighbor, bilinear, and bicubic interpolation), sparse coding methods (NE + LLE [4], Zeyde et al. [64], ANR [50], and A+ [51]), SR-LUT [23], and DNN methods (FSRCNN [11], CARN-M [2], and RRDB [53]). Besides, to evaluate the efficiency of our method, we also compare the computation cost with the AdderNet [47] version and the quantized versions of VDSR [26] and CARN [2].

Implementation Details. We train MuLUT networks with the Adam optimizer [28] in the cosine annealing schedule [35]. We use the mean-squared error (MSE) loss function as the optimization target. The MuLUT networks are trained for 2×10^5 iterations at a batch size of 32. The cached LUTs are uniformly sampled with the interval 2^4, $i.e.$, from LUT[256][256][256][256] to

LUT[17][17][17][17]. After locating coordinates, the final prediction is obtained with 4D simplex interpolation [23], a 4D equivalent of 3D tetrahedral interpolation [24]. We further finetune the cached LUTs on the same training dataset for 2000 iterations with the proposed LUT-aware finetuning strategy.

5.2 Quantitative Evaluation

Restoration Performance. The quantitative comparisons with other methods are listed in Table 1. The PSNR and SSIM values are computed at the Y-channel in the YCbCr color space. As can be seen, MuLUT boosts the performance of SR-LUT significantly. For example, with 2 cascaded stages and 3 parallel blocks, MuLUT-SDY-X2 improves the PSNR performance of a single LUT up to 1.1 dB on the Manga109 dataset and exceeds FSRCNN in terms of SSIM. With only complementary indexing, MuLUT-SDY increases the RF size from 3×3 to 5×5, boosting the PSNR value by about 0.6 dB on the Set5 dataset. Overall, MuLUT obtains comparable or better performance compared with FSRCNN.

Table 2. The comparison of energy cost and performance for producing a 1280 × 720 HD image through 2× SR. The statistics of operations not involved in a method are leaved blank. A-VDSR denotes the AdderNet version of VDSR [26,47]. A-VDSR-8 bit denotes performing 8 bit quantization for A-VDSR. Our method shows superior performance (0.6–0.8 dB) over SR-LUT, and a clear energy cost advantage (about 100× less) compared with DNN methods, even with their AdderNet and quantized versions.

	int8 Add.	int8 Mul.	int32 Add.	int32 Mul.	float32 Add.	float32 Mul.	Energy cost (pJ)	Set14 PSNR	BSDS100 PSNR	Urban100 PSNR
Bilinear					7.4M	2.8M	**29.8M**	29.15	28.65	25.95
Bicubic					12.0M	10.1M	**53.5M**	30.23	29.53	26.86
SR-LUT-F [23]	13.6M	0.5M	11.8M	19.1M			**61.0M**	31.88	30.77	28.49
SR-LUT-S [23]	19.1M	0.5M	28.6M	22.8M			**74.2M**	31.73	30.64	28.50
MuLUT-SDY	56.9M	0.5M	118.0M	68.0M			**224.3M**	32.35	31.17	29.10
MuLUT-SDY-X2	80.6M	0.9M	109.4M	85.5M			**278.5M**	32.49	31.23	29.31
FSRCNN [11]					6.1G	6.1G	**28.1G**	32.69	31.49	29.87
A-VDSR-8 bit [47]	1224.1G	1.1G					**36.9G**	32.85	31.66	30.07
A-VDSR [47]					1224.1G	1.1G	**1105.6G**	32.93	31.81	30.48
VDSR [26]					612.6G	612.6G	**2817.9G**	33.03	31.90	30.76
A-CARN-1/4 [47]					28.9G	0.1G	**26.3G**	-	-	30.21
CARN-1/4 [47]					14.5G	14.5G	**66.5G**	-	-	30.40
CARN-M [2]					91.2G	91.2G	**419.5G**	33.26	31.92	30.83

Computational Analysis. Following the protocol in AdderSR [47], we estimate the theoretical energy cost of MuLUT. We calculate the statistics of multiplications and additions in different data types needed by each method and estimate their total energy cost. The detailed comparison is listed in Table 2. As can be seen, our method shows superior performance compared with interpolation methods and SR-LUT, while maintaining similar energy cost. For example, MuLUT-SDY-X2 exceeds SR-LUT by 0.6~0.8 dB while maintaining comparable energy cost. On the other hand, MuLUT maintains the clear energy cost advantage over DNN methods, even with their AdderNet and quantized versions. Compared with FSRCNN, A-VDSR-8-bit, and A-CARN-1/4, MuLUT costs about 100× less energy while achieving comparable restoration performance. In summary,

Table 3. Runtime comparison for generating a 1280 × 720 HD image through 4× SR. * denotes that the runtimes of sparse coding methods are from SR-LUT [23], which are tested on a desktop computer. All the other runtimes are measured on a Xiaomi 11 smartphone, among which the DNN methods are implemented in the CPU-version of the PyTorch library [42]. For SR-LUT-S, we test the official implementation provided by the authors. PSNR values are evaluated on Manga109.

	Interpolation			LUT			Sparse Coding*		DNN		
	Nearest	Bilinear	Bicubic	SR-LUT-S	MuLUT-SDY	MuLUT-SDY-X2	ANR	A+	FSRCNN	CARN-M	RRDB
Runtime (ms)	9	20	97	137	228	242	1715	1748	350	3300	23377
PSNR (dB)	23.45	24.21	24.91	26.80	27.52	27.90	26.18	26.91	27.91	29.85	31.57

MuLUT achieves a better performance and efficiency tradeoff, boosting the performance of SR-LUT significantly with similar computation cost.

We also report the running times of different methods in Table 3. As listed, MuLUT maintains the efficiency of SR-LUT, showing a clear advantage compared to sparse coding methods and DNN methods. Note that the CPU computing architecture is not optimized for LUT, which can be embedded into on-device memory such as those of image processors in consumer cameras for low-latency execution. Moreover, MuLUT can be implemented without modern computing libraries like PyTorch, thus having better practicality on edge devices.

5.3   Qualitative Evaluation

We compare the visual quality of our method (MuLUT-SDY-X2) with other methods in Fig. 6. In the first two examples, SR-LUT-S produces notable artifacts, *e.g.*, along the border of the hat (*baby* form Set5). Our method achieves similar visual quality as computation-heavy methods like A+ and FSRCNN. In the last two examples, our method is able to generate sharper edges and obtain better visual quality than A+ and FSRCNN, *e.g.*, the eyebrow of the character (*TetsuSan* from Manga109). To sum up, MuLUT achieves better visual quality than SR-LUT-S and comparable visual quality with A+ and FSRCNN. More visual results are provided in the supplementary material.

5.4   Ablation Studies

We conduct several ablation experiments to verify the effectiveness of MuLUT.

The Effectiveness of Complementary Indexing. We conduct an experiment with combinations of different indexing patterns of parallel LUTs. As listed in Table 4, with MuLUT-S and MuLUT-D working together, MuLUT-SD is able to cover a region of 5 × 5, but not all pixels are covered. Still, it improves the performance of SR-LUT. Further, involving the novel MuLUT-Y with a "Y" shape indexing pattern, the MuLUT-SDY covers all pixels in a 5 × 5 region and improves the performance, showing the effectiveness of complementary indexing.

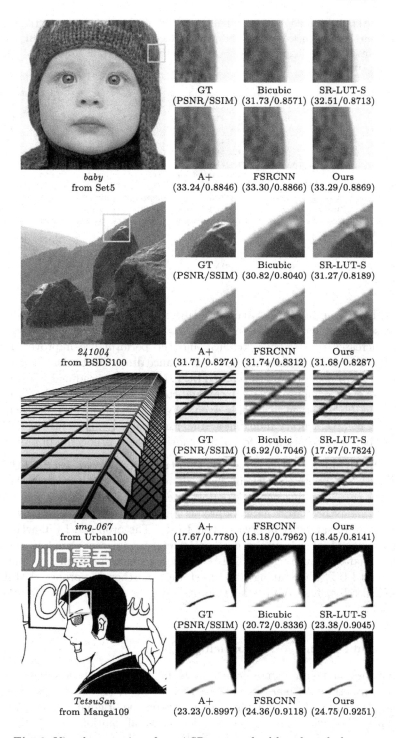

Fig. 6. Visual comparison for ×4 SR on standard benchmark datasets.

Table 4. Ablation studies on MuLUT for 4× SR, where re-index denotes the LUT re-indexing mechanism, net. denotes the performance of corresponding neural network, 4 bit denotes the sampling interval is 2^4 and 3 bit the 2^5, and ft. denotes the LUT-aware finetuning strategy.

PSNR (dB)	Energy (pJ)	LUT size	RF size	Set5	Set14	BSDS100	Urban100	Manga109
SR-LUT-S	72.5M	1.274 MB	3 × 3	29.82	27.01	26.53	24.02	26.80
MuLUT-SD	149.2M	2.549 MB	5 × 5	30.31	27.41	26.75	24.25	27.38
MuLUT-SDY	222.3M	3.823 MB	5 × 5	30.40	27.48	26.79	24.32	27.52
MuLUT-S-X2 w/o re-index	78.0M	1.354 MB	4 × 4	30.11	27.26	26.64	24.15	27.02
MuLUT-S-X2	78.0M	1.354 MB	4 × 4	30.23	27.39	26.70	24.28	27.39
MuLUT-S-X3	83.4M	1.434 MB	5 × 5	30.31	27.42	26.73	24.31	27.54
MuLUT-S-X4	88.9M	1.513 MB	6 × 6	30.40	27.47	26.76	24.36	27.66
SR-LUT-S net	-	-	3 × 3	29.88	27.14	26.57	24.04	26.86
SR-LUT-S (4 bit LUT) w/o ft	72.5M	1.274 MB	3 × 3	29.82	27.01	26.53	24.02	26.80
SR-LUT-S (4 bit LUT) w/ ft	72.5M	1.274 MB	3 × 3	29.94	27.18	26.59	24.09	26.94
SR-LUT-S (3 bit LUT) w/o ft	72.5M	102.5 KB	3 × 3	29.58	26.99	26.49	23.95	26.76
SR-LUT-S (3 bit LUT) w/ ft	72.5M	102.5 KB	3 × 3	29.87	27.13	26.56	24.04	26.85
MuLUT-SDY-X2 net	-	-	9 × 9	30.61	27.61	26.86	24.47	27.93
MuLUT-SDY-X2 w/o ft	233.6M	4.062 MB	9 × 9	30.52	27.55	26.83	24.40	27.83
MuLUT-SDY-X2	233.6M	4.062 MB	9 × 9	30.60	27.60	26.86	24.46	27.90

The Effectiveness of Hierarchical Indexing. We conduct an experiment with cascading different stages of LUTs. As listed in Table 4, cascading more stages increases the RF size steadily, and the performance improves accordingly. Without LUT re-indexing, the performance drops due to the inconsistency between the SR network and the cached LUT. Note that cascading LUTs involves *sub-linear* extra computational burden and storage space, since all LUTs except the ones in the last stage cache only one value for each index entry. Furthermore, with both complementary indexing and hierarchical indexing, MuLUT-SDY-X2 achieves better restoration performance, showing their orthogonal improvement.

The Effectiveness of LUT-Aware Finetuning. We compare SR-LUT and MuLUT-SDY-X2 with or without the LUT-aware finetuning strategy. We also report the corresponding network performance. As can be seen in Table 4, there is a performance drop from network predictions to LUT results, especially for the one with larger sampling intervals (3 bit LUT). The proposed LUT-aware finetuning strategy is able to fill this gap consistently for different sampling intervals. Especially, after finetuning, a 3 bit LUT achieves similar performance compared with a 4 bit LUT, while taking 10× less storage. Further, the proposed MuLUT-SDY-X2 also benefits from the finetuning strategy, showing its effectiveness and universality.

5.5 Results in Image Demosaicing

For the task of image demosaicing, we train baseline methods and MuLUT on the synthetic data pairs from the DIV2K dataset [1], where the mosaiced images are simulated by applying color masks on the original images. We compare our method with bilinear interpolation, classical solutions (D-LMMSE [66], AHD [18], and LSLCD [22]), and DNN (DemosaicNet [15]) on the widely-used

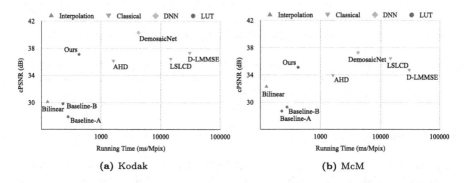

Fig. 7. MuLUT achieves a better performance and efficiency tradeoff, compared with interpolation, classical solutions, single-LUT baselines, and DNN methods. The cPSNR values are average over 3 color channels. The runtimes of classical solutions are from DemosaicNet [15], where they are tested on a desktop computer. The runtimes of other methods are measured on a Xiaomi 11 smartphone. (Color figure online)

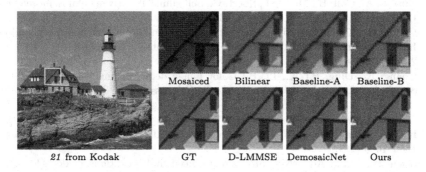

Fig. 8. Visual comparison for image demosaicing on the Kodak dataset.

Kodak dataset [32] and McMaster dataset [67]. As illustrated in Fig. 7a and Fig. 7b, MuLUT improves the performance of SR-LUT baselines by a large margin, e.g., over 6.0 dB on the Kodak dataset, achieving a better performance and efficiency tradeoff. Besides, as shown in Fig. 8, the results of Baseline-A are blurry, and Baseline-B produces noticeable blocking artifacts due to limited RF, while MuLUT obtains comparable visual quality with computation-heavy classical solutions and DNN.

6 Conclusion Remarks

In this work, we propose MuLUT to generalize the SR-LUT by enabling the cooperation of multiple LUTs. Our method overcomes the limitation of the receptive field of a single LUT, empowering LUTs to be constructed like a neural network. Extensive experiments on both image super-resolution and image demosaicing demonstrate that MuLUT achieves significant improvement in restoration performance over SR-LUT while preserving its efficiency. Overall, the proposed

MuLUT shows its versatility to serve as a universal caching framework and an efficient solution to avoid deploying heavy DNNs on edge devices.

Acknowledgments. We acknowledge funding from National Key R&D Program of China under Grant 2017YFA0700800, and National Natural Science Foundation of China under Grants 62131003 and 62021001.

References

1. Agustsson, E., Timofte, R.: NTIRE 2017 challenge on single image super-resolution: dataset and study. In: IEEE Conference on Computer Vision and Pattern Recognition Workshops (CVPRW), pp. 1122–1131 (2017)
2. Ahn, N., Kang, B., Sohn, K.-A.: Fast, accurate, and lightweight super-resolution with cascading residual network. In: Ferrari, V., Hebert, M., Sminchisescu, C., Weiss, Y. (eds.) ECCV 2018. LNCS, vol. 11214, pp. 256–272. Springer, Cham (2018). https://doi.org/10.1007/978-3-030-01249-6_16
3. Buades, A., Coll, B., Morel, J., Sbert, C.: Self-similarity driven color demosaicking. IEEE Trans. Image Process. 18(6), 1192–1202 (2009)
4. Chang, H., Yeung, D., Xiong, Y.: Super-resolution through neighbor embedding. In: IEEE Conference on Computer Vision and Pattern Recognition (CVPR), pp. 275–282 (2004)
5. Chang, K., Ding, P.L.K., Li, B.: Color image demosaicking using inter-channel correlation and nonlocal self-similarity. Sig. Process. Image Commun. 39, 264–279 (2015)
6. Chen, C., Xiong, Z., Tian, X., Zha, Z., Wu, F.: Camera lens super-resolution. In: IEEE Conference on Computer Vision and Pattern Recognition (CVPR), pp. 1652–1660 (2019)
7. Chen, H., et al.: AdderNet: do we really need multiplications in deep learning? In: IEEE Conference on Computer Vision and Pattern Recognition (CVPR), pp. 1465–1474 (2020)
8. Cheng, Z., Xiong, Z., Chen, C., Liu, D., Zha, Z.: Light field super-resolution with zero-shot learning. In: IEEE Conference on Computer Vision and Pattern Recognition (CVPR), pp. 10010–10019 (2021)
9. Chu, X., Zhang, B., Ma, H., Xu, R., Li, Q.: Fast, accurate and lightweight super-resolution with neural architecture search. In: International Conference on Pattern Recognition (ICPR), pp. 59–64 (2020)
10. Dong, C., Loy, C.C., He, K., Tang, X.: Learning a deep convolutional network for image super-resolution. In: Fleet, D., Pajdla, T., Schiele, B., Tuytelaars, T. (eds.) ECCV 2014. LNCS, vol. 8692, pp. 184–199. Springer, Cham (2014). https://doi.org/10.1007/978-3-319-10593-2_13
11. Dong, C., Loy, C.C., Tang, X.: Accelerating the super-resolution convolutional neural network. In: Leibe, B., Matas, J., Sebe, N., Welling, M. (eds.) ECCV 2016. LNCS, vol. 9906, pp. 391–407. Springer, Cham (2016). https://doi.org/10.1007/978-3-319-46475-6_25
12. Duran, J., Buades, A.: Self-similarity and spectral correlation adaptive algorithm for color demosaicking. IEEE Trans. Image Process. 23(9), 4031–4040 (2014)

13. Freeman, W.T., Jones, T.R., Pasztor, E.C.: Example-based super-resolution. IEEE Comput. Graph. Appl. **22**(2), 56–65 (2002)
14. Freeman, W.T., Pasztor, E.C., Carmichael, O.T.: Learning low-level vision. Int. J. Comput. Vis. **40**(1), 25–47 (2000)
15. Gharbi, M., Chaurasia, G., Paris, S., Durand, F.: Deep joint demosaicking and denoising. ACM Trans. Graph. **35**(6), 191:1–191:12 (2016)
16. Glasner, D., Bagon, S., Irani, M.: Super-resolution from a single image. In: IEEE International Conference on Computer Vision (ICCV), pp. 349–356 (2009)
17. Gu, J., Dong, C.: Interpreting super-resolution networks with local attribution maps. In: IEEE Conference on Computer Vision and Pattern Recognition (CVPR), pp. 9199–9208 (2021)
18. Hirakawa, K., Parks, T.W.: Adaptive homogeneity-directed demosaicing algorithm. IEEE Trans. Image Process. **14**(3), 360–369 (2005)
19. Huang, G., Liu, Z., van der Maaten, L., Weinberger, K.Q.: Densely connected convolutional networks. In: IEEE Conference on Computer Vision and Pattern Recognition (CVPR), pp. 2261–2269 (2017)
20. Huang, J., Singh, A., Ahuja, N.: Single image super-resolution from transformed self-exemplars. In: IEEE Conference on Computer Vision and Pattern Recognition (CVPR), pp. 5197–5206 (2015)
21. Hui, Z., Wang, X., Gao, X.: Fast and accurate single image super-resolution via information distillation network. In: IEEE Conference on Computer Vision and Pattern Recognition (CVPR), pp. 723–731 (2018)
22. Jeon, G., Dubois, E.: Demosaicking of noisy Bayer-sampled color images with least-squares Luma-chroma demultiplexing and noise level estimation. IEEE Trans. Image Process. **22**(1), 146–156 (2013)
23. Jo, Y., Kim, S.J.: Practical single-image super-resolution using look-up table. In: IEEE Conference on Computer Vision and Pattern Recognition (CVPR), pp. 691–700 (2021)
24. Kasson, J.M., Nin, S.I., Plouffe, W., Hafner, J.L.: Performing color space conversions with three-dimensional linear interpolation. J. Electron. Imaging **4**(3), 226–250 (1995)
25. Keys, R.: Cubic convolution interpolation for digital image processing. IEEE Trans. Acoust. Speech Sig. Process. **29**, 1153–1160 (1981)
26. Kim, J., Lee, J.K., Lee, K.M.: Accurate image super-resolution using very deep convolutional networks. In: IEEE Conference on Computer Vision and Pattern Recognition (CVPR), pp. 1646–1654 (2016)
27. Kim, S.J., Lin, H.T., Lu, Z., Süsstrunk, S., Lin, S., Brown, M.S.: A new in-camera imaging model for color computer vision and its application. IEEE Trans. Pattern Anal. Mach. Intell. **34**(12), 2289–2302 (2012)
28. Kingma, D.P., Ba, J.: Adam: a method for stochastic optimization. In: International Conference on Learning Representations (ICLR) (2015)
29. Kokkinos, F., Lefkimmiatis, S.: Iterative joint image demosaicking and denoising using a residual denoising network. IEEE Trans. Image Process. **28**(8), 4177–4188 (2019)
30. Lee, R., et al.: Journey towards tiny perceptual super-resolution. In: Vedaldi, A., Bischof, H., Brox, T., Frahm, J.-M. (eds.) ECCV 2020. LNCS, vol. 12371, pp. 85–102. Springer, Cham (2020). https://doi.org/10.1007/978-3-030-58574-7_6
31. Li, H., et al.: PAMS: quantized super-resolution via parameterized max scale. In: Vedaldi, A., Bischof, H., Brox, T., Frahm, J.-M. (eds.) ECCV 2020. LNCS, vol. 12370, pp. 564–580. Springer, Cham (2020). https://doi.org/10.1007/978-3-030-58595-2_34

32. Li, X., Gunturk, B.K., Zhang, L.: Image demosaicing: a systematic survey. In: Electronic Imaging (2008)
33. Li, Y., Gu, S., Zhang, K., Van Gool, L., Timofte, R.: DHP: differentiable meta pruning via hypernetworks. In: Vedaldi, A., Bischof, H., Brox, T., Frahm, J.-M. (eds.) ECCV 2020. LNCS, vol. 12353, pp. 608–624. Springer, Cham (2020). https://doi.org/10.1007/978-3-030-58598-3_36
34. Lim, B., Son, S., Kim, H., Nah, S., Lee, K.M.: Enhanced deep residual networks for single image super-resolution. In: IEEE Conference on Computer Vision and Pattern Recognition Workshops (CVPRW), pp. 1132–1140 (2017)
35. Loshchilov, I., Hutter, F.: SGDR: stochastic gradient descent with warm restarts. In: International Conference on Learning Representations (ICLR) (2017)
36. Luo, X., Xie, Y., Zhang, Y., Qu, Y., Li, C., Fu, Y.: LatticeNet: towards lightweight image super-resolution with lattice block. In: Vedaldi, A., Bischof, H., Brox, T., Frahm, J.-M. (eds.) ECCV 2020. LNCS, vol. 12367, pp. 272–289. Springer, Cham (2020). https://doi.org/10.1007/978-3-030-58542-6_17
37. Mantiuk, R., Daly, S.J., Kerofsky, L.: Display adaptive tone mapping. ACM Trans. Graph. **27**(3), 68 (2008)
38. Martin, D.R., Fowlkes, C.C., Tal, D., Malik, J.: A database of human segmented natural images and its application to evaluating segmentation algorithms and measuring ecological statistics. In: IEEE International Conference on Computer Vision (ICCV), pp. 416–425 (2001)
39. Matsui, Y., et al.: Sketch-based manga retrieval using manga109 dataset. Multim. Tools Appl. **76**(20), 21811–21838 (2017)
40. Mukherjee, J., Mitra, S.K.: Enhancement of color images by scaling the DCT coefficients. IEEE Trans. Image Process. **17**(10), 1783–1794 (2008)
41. Pan, Z., et al.: Towards bidirectional arbitrary image rescaling: joint optimization and cycle idempotence. In: IEEE Conference on Computer Vision and Pattern Recognition (CVPR), pp. 17389–17398 (2022)
42. Paszke, A., et al.: PyTorch: an imperative style, high-performance deep learning library. In: Advances in Neural Information Processing Systems (NeurIPS) (2019)
43. Qiu, G.: Interresolution look-up table for improved spatial magnification of image. J. Vis. Commun. Image Represent. **11**(4), 360–373 (2000)
44. Romano, Y., Isidoro, J., Milanfar, P.: RAISR: rapid and accurate image super resolution. IEEE Trans. Comput. Imaging **3**(1), 110–125 (2017)
45. Schulter, S., Leistner, C., Bischof, H.: Fast and accurate image upscaling with super-resolution forests. In: IEEE Conference on Computer Vision and Pattern Recognition (CVPR), pp. 3791–3799 (2015)
46. Shi, W., et al.: Real-time single image and video super-resolution using an efficient sub-pixel convolutional neural network. In: IEEE Conference on Computer Vision and Pattern Recognition (CVPR), pp. 1874–1883 (2016)
47. Song, D., Wang, Y., Chen, H., Xu, C., Xu, C., Tao, D.: AdderSR: towards energy efficient image super-resolution. In: IEEE Conference on Computer Vision and Pattern Recognition (CVPR), pp. 15648–15657 (2021)
48. Song, D., Xu, C., Jia, X., Chen, Y., Xu, C., Wang, Y.: Efficient residual dense block search for image super-resolution. In: Conference on Artificial Intelligence (AAAI), pp. 12007–12014 (2020)
49. Song, Q., Xiong, R., Liu, D., Xiong, Z., Wu, F., Gao, W.: Fast image super-resolution via local adaptive gradient field sharpening transform. IEEE Trans. Image Process. **27**(4), 1966–1980 (2018)

50. Timofte, R., Smet, V.D., Gool, L.V.: Anchored neighborhood regression for fast example-based super-resolution. In: IEEE International Conference on Computer Vision (ICCV), pp. 1920–1927 (2013)
51. Timofte, R., De Smet, V., Van Gool, L.: A+: adjusted anchored neighborhood regression for fast super-resolution. In: Cremers, D., Reid, I., Saito, H., Yang, M.-H. (eds.) ACCV 2014. LNCS, vol. 9006, pp. 111–126. Springer, Cham (2015). https://doi.org/10.1007/978-3-319-16817-3_8
52. Wang, L., Wu, H., Pan, C.: Fast image upsampling via the displacement field. IEEE Trans. Image Process. **23**(12), 5123–5135 (2014)
53. Wang, X., et al.: ESRGAN: enhanced super-resolution generative adversarial networks. In: Leal-Taixé, L., Roth, S. (eds.) ECCV 2018. LNCS, vol. 11133, pp. 63–79. Springer, Cham (2019). https://doi.org/10.1007/978-3-030-11021-5_5
54. Wang, Y.: A multilayer neural network for image demosaicking. In: IEEE International Conference on Image Processing (ICIP), pp. 1852–1856 (2014)
55. Wang, Z., Bovik, A.C., Sheikh, H.R., Simoncelli, E.P.: Image quality assessment: from error visibility to structural similarity. IEEE Trans. Image Process. **13**(4), 600–612 (2004)
56. Xiao, Z., Fu, X., Huang, J., Cheng, Z., Xiong, Z.: Space-time distillation for video super-resolution. In: IEEE Conference on Computer Vision and Pattern Recognition (CVPR), pp. 2113–2122 (2021)
57. Xiao, Z., Xiong, Z., Fu, X., Liu, D., Zha, Z.: Space-time video super-resolution using temporal profiles. In: ACM Multimedia Conference, pp. 664–672 (2020)
58. Xin, J., Wang, N., Jiang, X., Li, J., Huang, H., Gao, X.: Binarized neural network for single image super resolution. In: Vedaldi, A., Bischof, H., Brox, T., Frahm, J.-M. (eds.) ECCV 2020. LNCS, vol. 12349, pp. 91–107. Springer, Cham (2020). https://doi.org/10.1007/978-3-030-58548-8_6
59. Xiong, Z., Sun, X., Wu, F.: Robust web image/video super-resolution. IEEE Trans. Image Process. **19**(8), 2017–2028 (2010)
60. Xiong, Z., Xu, D., Sun, X., Wu, F.: Example-based super-resolution with soft information and decision. IEEE Trans. Multim. **15**(6), 1458–1465 (2013)
61. Xu, R., Xiao, Z., Yao, M., Zhang, Y., Xiong, Z.: Stereo video super-resolution via exploiting view-temporal correlations. In: ACM Multimedia Conference, pp. 460–468 (2021)
62. Yang, J., Lin, Z., Cohen, S.: Fast image super-resolution based on in-place example regression. In: IEEE Conference on Computer Vision and Pattern Recognition (CVPR), pp. 1059–1066 (2013)
63. Yang, J., Wright, J., Huang, T.S., Ma, Y.: Image super-resolution via sparse representation. IEEE Trans. Image Process. **19**(11), 2861–2873 (2010)
64. Zeyde, R., Elad, M., Protter, M.: On single image scale-up using sparse-representations. In: Curves and Surfaces - 7th International Conference, Avignon, France, 24–30 June 2010, Revised Selected Papers, vol. 6920, pp. 711–730 (2010)
65. Zhang, H., Liu, D., Xiong, Z.: Two-stream action recognition-oriented video super-resolution. In: IEEE International Conference on Computer Vision (ICCV), pp. 8798–8807 (2019)
66. Zhang, L., Wu, X.: Color demosaicking via directional linear minimum mean square-error estimation. IEEE Trans. Image Process. **14**(12), 2167–2178 (2005)
67. Zhang, L., Wu, X., Buades, A., Li, X.: Color demosaicking by local directional interpolation and nonlocal adaptive thresholding. J. Electron. Imaging **20**(2), 023016 (2011)

68. Zhang, Y., Li, K., Li, K., Wang, L., Zhong, B., Fu, Y.: Image super-resolution using very deep residual channel attention networks. In: Ferrari, V., Hebert, M., Sminchisescu, C., Weiss, Y. (eds.) ECCV 2018. LNCS, vol. 11211, pp. 294–310. Springer, Cham (2018). https://doi.org/10.1007/978-3-030-01234-2_18
69. Zhang, Y., Tian, Y., Kong, Y., Zhong, B., Fu, Y.: Residual dense network for image super-resolution. In: IEEE Conference on Computer Vision and Pattern Recognition (CVPR), pp. 2472–2481 (2018)

Learning Spatiotemporal Frequency-Transformer for Compressed Video Super-Resolution

Zhongwei Qiu[1,2(✉)], Huan Yang[3], Jianlong Fu[3], and Dongmei Fu[1,2]

[1] University of Science and Technology Beijing, Beijing, China
qiuzhongwei@xs.ustb.edu.cn, fdm_ustb@ustb.edu.cn
[2] Shunde Graduate School of University of Science and Technology Beijing,
Beijing, China
[3] Microsoft Research, Beijing, China
{huayan,jianf}@microsoft.com

Abstract. Compressed video super-resolution (VSR) aims to restore high-resolution frames from compressed low-resolution counterparts. Most recent VSR approaches often enhance an input frame by "borrowing" relevant textures from neighboring video frames. Although some progress has been made, there are grand challenges to effectively extract and transfer high-quality textures from compressed videos where most frames are usually highly degraded. In this paper, we propose a novel Frequency-Transformer for compressed video super-resolution (FTVSR) that conducts self-attention over a joint space-time-frequency domain. First, we divide a video frame into patches, and transform each patch into DCT spectral maps in which each channel represents a frequency band. Such a design enables a fine-grained level self-attention on each frequency band, so that real visual texture can be distinguished from artifacts, and further utilized for video frame restoration. Second, we study different self-attention schemes, and discover that a "divided attention" which conducts a joint space-frequency attention before applying temporal attention on each frequency band, leads to the best video enhancement quality. Experimental results on two widely-used video super-resolution benchmarks show that FTVSR outperforms state-of-the-art approaches on both uncompressed and compressed videos with clear visual margins. Code are available at https://github.com/researchmm/FTVSR.

Keywords: VSR · Transformer · Frequency learning · Compression

1 Introduction

Video super-resolution (VSR) aims to restore a sequence of high-resolution (HR) frames from its low-resolution (LR) counterparts. It is a fundamental computer

---

This work was done when Z. Qiu was an intern at Microsoft Research.

Supplementary Information The online version contains supplementary material available at https://doi.org/10.1007/978-3-031-19797-0_15.

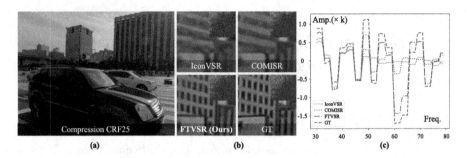

Fig. 1. Comparison of our FTVSR and state-of-the-art VSR methods (IconVSR [2], COMISR [20]) on compressed videos with a compression rate of CRF25. (a) The results of ×4 VSR by FTVSR. (b) Comparison of the zoom-in patches and their DCT-based spectral maps (shown in the top-right corner). FTVSR recovers more high-frequency information than IconVSR and COMISR. (c) Comparison of the Amplitude-Frequency curves on clipped frequency bands of 30 to 80. The proposed FTVSR is superior than other methods to approximate the curve of ground-truth (Best viewed in color) (Color figure online)

vision task, and can benefit a broad range of downstream applications, such as video surveillance [39] and high-definition television [9]. State-of-the-art VSR approaches mainly focus on leveraging temporal information by sliding windows [14,17,29,30] or recurrent structures [2,27,37], and have achieved great success in limited scenarios that usually take uncompressed video frames as inputs.

However, most videos on the internet or in user devices are stored and transmitted in a compressed format. For example, the most widely-used video codec H.264 takes a constant rate factor (CRF) varied from 0 to 51 as its parameter to control the compression rate. As shown in Fig. 1, directly applying the state-of-the-art IconVSR approach [2] to such a compressed scenario failed to generate visually pleasant results. Because the model trained on uncompressed videos often treats the unseen compression artifacts as common textures and magnifies these artifacts during restoration processes. Recent progress has been made by taking into account the compression artifacts in VSR model design. To strength the awareness of compression, a pioneer work, COMISR [20], is proposed to predict detail-aware flow to align high-resolution features and enhance HR images by Laplacian enhancement module. However, there are still large gaps between the generated frame and the ground-truth, as shown in Fig. 1.

To solve the above issues, we propose a novel **F**requency **T**ransformer for compressed **V**ideo **S**uper-**R**esolution (**FTVSR**). The key insight is to transform a compressed video frame into a bunch of frequency-based patch representations by Discrete Cosine Transform (DCT), and design frequency-based attention to enable deep feature fusions across multiple frequency bands. Such a design has the following two key merits: 1) the DCT-based representation treats each frequency band "fairly", so that high-frequency visual details can be well-preserved; 2) the frequency attention enables low-frequency information (e.g., object structure) to guide the generation of high-frequency textures, so that the effect of compression artifacts can be greatly reduced. Besides, to further utilize the spatial and temporal dependencies in videos, we extensively explore different frequency attention mechanisms that combine with space and time attention in a proper manner. Extensive experiments on two widely-used VSR benchmarks demonstrate that the proposed FTVSR significantly outperforms previous methods and achieves new SOTA results. For example, for the setting of $CRF = 25$ in the REDS dataset, the gains of the proposed FTVSR are nearly 1.6 dB and 2.1 dB, compared with the competitive COMISR [20] and IconVSR [2], respectively.

2   Related Work

2.1   Video Super-Resolution

Uncompressed Video Super-Resolution. Modern video super-resolution approaches [2,14,21,27,29,30,36,37] focus on improving the quality of HR sequences by extracting more information from temporal features, which can be categorized into sliding-window and recurrent structure. The approaches [14, 29,30] based on sliding-window structure recover HR frames from adjacent LR frames within a sliding-window. They mainly use 3D convolution [14], optical flow [15,28] or deformable convolution [29,30] to align the temporal features. However, these methods can't utilize the temporal features from long-distance frames. Other approaches [2,11,12,28,37] based recurrent structure usually use a hidden state to transmit temporal information from long-distance frames. BasicVSR and IconVSR [2] achieve significant improvements with bidirectional recurrent structure, which fuses the forward and backward propagation features. Recently, transformer-based approaches [1,18,38] make great success by using different attention [8,40] to capture temporal features. Limited by computational costs, they just can aggregate information from a few adjacent frames. Despite the remarkable progress by these approaches, they are focus on uncompressed videos and usually fail to recover the HR frames from compressed LR frames.

Compressed Video Super-Resolution. Compared with uncompressed VSR, compressed VSR is more difficult due to the lost information and the extra high-frequency artifacts caused by compression. There are three potential solutions to handle the compressed problem: video denoising, training on compressed videos and specific model design for compression. COMISR [20] firstly applies different video denoising [23,24,34] on compressed videos to remove the artifacts and uses state-of-the-art VSR methods [2,18,30] on the denoised LR videos. Experimental results have shown that this pre-process is not working since the degradation kernel used for training VSR is different from the denoising model. COMISR [20] further designs detail-aware module to align high-resolution features and Laplacian module to enhance HR frames with recurrent structure. However, these designs can not distinguish the high-frequency textures from the artifacts since these signals are coupled.

2.2 Frequency Learning

Lot of studies explore to learn in frequency domain, including high-level semantic tasks [6,26,33] and low-level restoration tasks [5,7,19,31]. High-level semantic tasks usually reduce the computational cost by transforming images into frequency domain. Particularly, FcaNet [26] propose frequency channel attention to improve the performance of ResNet on classification task. Many low-level studies explore to restore content details from frequency decomposition perspective. Parts of them [7,19] study decomposing features into different frequency bands by multi-branch CNNs. Typically, OR-Net [19] uses multi-branch CNNs to separate different frequency components and enhances these features with frequency enhancement unit. Another parts [5,31] of them transform images into frequency domain. For example, D^3 [31] designs a dual-domain restoration network to remove artifacts of JPEG compressed images. Moreover, Ehrlich *et al.* [5] designs a Y-channel correction network and a color channel correction network in frequency domain to correct the JPEG artifact. Existing VSR methods are developed in pixel domain, but the video compression problem is generated in frequency domain. Inspired by this, we introduce a frequency-transformer to tackle the compression problems in VSR.

3 Approach

3.1 Problem Formulation

VSR aims to restore the HR videos from its LR counterparts without taking into account video compression. Our focus, compressed VSR, aims to recover the HR frames from its compressed LR frames, which is more difficult. Let $I_{LR} = \{I_{LR}^t | t \in [1, T]\}$ be a compressed LR sequence of height H, width W, and frame length T. The restored super-resolution frames are denoted as $I_{SR} = \{I_{SR}^t | t \in [1, T]\}$ of height αH, width αW, in which α represents the upsampling scale factor. The corresponding HR frames are denoted as $I_{HR} = \{I_{HR}^t | t \in [1, T]\}$.

3.2 Frequency-Based Tokenization

To solve the problem of compressed video super-resolution, we propose to adopt a frequency-based patch representation. Following the previous works [5,6,10] in computer vision, we adopt the widely-used method, DCT, as our operation to transfer an image into frequency domain.

DCT. Discrete Cosine Transform projects an image into a set of cosine components for different 2D frequencies. Given an image patch P of height B and width B, a $B \times B$ DCT block D is generated as:

$$D(u,v) = c(u)c(v) \sum_{x=0}^{B-1} \sum_{y=0}^{B-1} P(x,y) cos[\frac{(2x+1)u\pi}{2B}] cos[\frac{(2y+1)v\pi}{2B}], \quad (1)$$

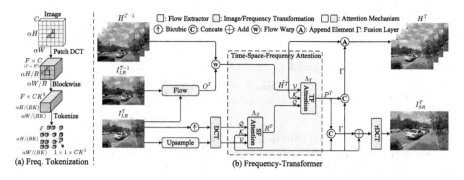

Fig. 2. (a) An RGB image is extracted as frequency tokens of size $C \times K \times K$ by DCT-based frequency tokenization. (b) A Frequency-Transformer with divide time-space-frequency (TSF) attention Λ_{ST}, which achieves best performance in our experiments. Given compressed LR sequence, Frequency-Transformer performs TSF attention on the frequency tokens of video frames and output SR frames with a hidden state H maintained by a recurrent structure. TSF consists of Λ_S attention and Λ_T attention. The Q, K, V of Λ_S are tokens from videos frame sampled I_{LR}^T by bicubic and upsample network, respectively. R^T is the output of Λ_S, further sums with hidden states $\hat{H}^T$ warped from past hidden states by flow O^T, as the K and V of Λ_T attention. P^T is the output of Λ_T, which further used to update hidden state and recover SR frame I_{SR}^T

where x and y are the 2D indexes of pixels. $u \in [0, B-1]$ and $v \in [0, B-1]$ are the 2D indexes of frequencies. $c(\cdot)$ represents normalizing scale factor to enforce orthonormality and $c(u) = \sqrt{\frac{1}{B}}$ if $u = 0$, else $c(u) = \sqrt{\frac{2}{B}}$. The DCT and its inversion are denoted as $\text{DCT}(\cdot)$ and $\text{rDCT}(\cdot)$, respectively.

DCT-Based Frequency Tokenization. Given a LR sequence, we firstly upsample the I_{LR} by a upsampling network $\varphi(\cdot)$. For each frame, we transform each channel of RGB image into frequency domain by applying DCT on the patches of shape $B \times B$ as Eq. 1, which can be formulated as:

$$D_{LR}(u, v) = \text{DCT}(\varphi(I_{LR})), \qquad (2)$$

where $D_{LR}(u, v)$ of shape $T \times F \times C \times \frac{\alpha H}{B} \times \frac{\alpha W}{B}$ represents the transformed 2D spectral map from LR image. T, F, C, $\frac{\alpha H}{B}$ and $\frac{\alpha W}{B}$ represent sequence length, frequency dimensions, image channels, height and width, respectively. The frequency number is $F = B^2$.

For a spectral frame $D_{LR}(u, v)$, we split the frequency dimension to form F visual tokens. The frequency tokens set $\mathcal{T}$ can be represented as:

$$\mathcal{T} = \{\tau_f, f \in [1, F]\}, \qquad (3)$$

where τ_f represents the frequency token in f^{th} frequency, which has a feature size of $C \times \frac{\alpha H}{B} \times \frac{\alpha W}{B}$. This frequency tokenization mechanism brings the information

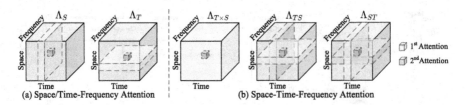

Fig. 3. The visualization of (a) space/time-frequency attention, and (b) space-time-frequency attention. The red cube denotes the query token. The yellow area and green area represent the candidate area for computing attention with query following the order of yellow first and then green (Color figure online)

exchange between different frequency bands and forces neural network treating low-frequency signals and high-frequency signals "fairly", which is beneficial to preserve high-frequency visual details. Combined with frequency attention mechanism in Sect. 3.3, the high-frequency textures can be restored well by the guidance of low-frequency information (e.g., object structure).

In order to capture the frequency relationship between different spatial blocks, the spectral maps are split into a set of blocks with a kernel size of $K \times K$. To further extract temporal information, we extend the same tokenization to all video frames. Therefore, we generate more fine-grained frequency tokens in both space and time dimensions, which can be represented as:

$$\mathcal{T} = \{\tau_{(t,i,f)}, t \in [1, T], i \in [1, N], f \in [1, F]\}, \tag{4}$$

where each token $\tau_{(t,i,f)}$ has a shape of $C \times K \times K$. N represents the generated block number in each frame. Different from traditional vision Transformers [1, 4, 22], which crop image patches and form a set of spatial visual tokens, our tokens are based on different frequency bands. In a nutshell, we generate N blocks for each spectral frame D_{LR}^t, and each block has DCT-based frequency tokens τ of the number of F. The total number of frequency tokens is $T \times N \times F$. Figure 2 (a) presents more details about the whole tokenization process.

3.3   Frequency-Based Attention

The inputs of frequency transformer are DCT-based visual tokens, which have been generated in Sect. 3.2. To better take advantage of temporal information for VSR, the query tokens $\mathcal{Q}$ are extracted from spectral map D_{LR}^T. Keys $\mathcal{K}$ and values $\mathcal{V}$ are extracted from spectral maps $\{D_{LR}^t, t \in [1, T-1]\}$. For a target frame D_{LR}^T, the query, key, and value sets are denoted as:

$$
\begin{aligned}
\mathcal{Q} &= \{\tau_{(T,i,f)}^q, i \in [1, N], f \in [1, F]\}, \\
\mathcal{K} &= \{\tau_{(t,i,f)}^k, t \in [1, T-1], i \in [1, N], f \in [1, F]\}, \\
\mathcal{V} &= \{\tau_{(t,i,f)}^v, t \in [1, T-1], i \in [1, N], f \in [1, F]\},
\end{aligned}
\tag{5}
$$

where $\tau^q_{(T,i,f)}$, $\tau^k_{(t,i,f)}$, and $\tau^v_{(t,i,f)}$ represent the query, key, and value tokens, respectively. Each token is extracted from spectral maps among time, space, and frequency dimensions according to needs of computing different kinds of frequency attention, which will be discussed as follows.

Frequency Attention. The frequency attention aims to capture the relationship between different frequency bands. Given a query token τ^q_f at the fth frequency, the uniform formulation of frequency attention (denoted as Λ) is:

$$\Lambda(\tau^q_f, \tau^k_{\hat{f}}, \tau^v_{\hat{f}}) = \mathrm{SM}(\frac{\tau^q_f \cdot \tau^k_{\hat{f}}}{\sqrt{d^k}})\tau^v_{\hat{f}}, \hat{f} \in [1, F], \tag{6}$$

where SM represents the softmax activation function and d^k denotes the normalization factor. Note that there is a feed forward network (FFN) after frequency attention, which is omitted in this paper. However, computing frequency attention on whole spectral maps is impractical since the feature size of spectral map is different during the process of training and inference. Therefore, we adopt the way of computing frequency attention on spatial blocks of spectral maps. To explore different frequency attention mechanisms combined with time or space attention. As shown in Fig. 3, we propose space-frequency attention, time-frequency attention, and time-space-frequency attention.

Space/Time-Frequency Attention. Space-Frequency (SF) attention computes the frequency attention weights between spatial blocks. The visualization of SF is shown in Fig. 3 (a). For a query token $\tau^q_{(i,f)}$ at the fth frequency in the ith block, the SF attention is $\Lambda_S(\tau^q_{(i,f)}, \tau^k_{(\hat{i},\hat{f})}, \tau^v_{(\hat{i},\hat{f})})$, $\hat{i} \in [1, N], \hat{f} \in [1, F]$, which computes the frequency attention as Eq. 6 in spatial dimension. The inputs of Λ_S are space-frequency tokens $\tau_{(i,f)}$. Since the tokens are extracted from both space and frequency dimensions, $N \times F$ tokens are generated for SF attention.

The Time-Frequency (TF) attention is computed on the blocks with the same spatial position from different video frames. The visualization of TF attention is shown in Fig. 3 (a). Given a query token $\tau^q_{(t,f)}$, the TF attention is $\Lambda_T(\tau^q_{(t,f)}, \tau^k_{(\hat{t},\hat{f})}, \tau^v_{(\hat{t},\hat{f})})$, $\hat{t} \in [1, T-1], \hat{f} \in [1, F]$, which computes frequency attention as Eq. 6 in temporal dimension. The inputs of Λ_T are time-frequency tokens $\tau_{(t,f)}$. Since the tokens are extracted from both time and frequency dimensions, $T \times F$ tokens are generated for TF attention.

Time-Space-Frequency Attention. Both the temporal and spatial information are important for compressed VSR. To further explore the frequency attention in both spatial and temporal dimensions, we propose Time-Space-Frequency (TSF) attention. TSF are the combinations of SF and TF attention. It can be divided into two types: joint SF and TF attention, divided SF and TF attention. The visualizations of TSF are shown in Fig. 3 (b).

Given a query token $\tau_{(t,i,f)}^q$, joint TSF attention is $\Lambda_{T \times S}(\tau_{(t,i,f)}^q, \tau_{(\hat{t},\hat{i},\hat{f})}^k, \tau_{(\hat{t},\hat{i},\hat{f})}^v)$, $\hat{t} \in [1, T-1], \hat{i} \in [1, N], \hat{f} \in [1, F]$, which computes the frequency attention as Eq. 6 in both spatial and temporal dimensions. The inputs of joint TSF attention are time-space-frequency tokens $\tau_{(t,i,f)}$. Since the tokens are extracted among time, space, and frequency dimensions, $T \times N \times F$ tokens are generated for joint TSF.

For divided TSF attention, two types of TSF are designed according to the order of computing TF and SF attention. One of them can be formulated as:

$$
\begin{aligned}
\Lambda_{ST}(\tau_{(t,i,f)}^q, \tau_{(\hat{t},\hat{i},\hat{f})}^k, \tau_{(\hat{t},\hat{i},\hat{f})}^v) &= \Lambda_T(\hat{\tau}_{(t,f)}^q, \tau_{(\hat{t},\hat{f})}, \tau_{(\hat{t},\hat{f})}), \\
where\ \hat{\tau} = \Lambda_S(\tau_{(i,f)}^q, \tau_{(\hat{i},\hat{f})}^k, \tau_{(\hat{i},\hat{f})}^v), \hat{t} &\in [1, T-1], \hat{i} \in [1, N], \hat{f} \in [1, F].
\end{aligned}
\tag{7}
$$

The divided TSF attention Λ_{ST} represents the attention that computes space-frequency attention Λ_S firstly, then computes time-frequency attention Λ_T. In our experiments, Λ_{ST} performs best for frequency transformer. This is because in compressed VSR, degraded frames should be first restored by the space-frequency attention then the recovered textures could be used to benefit temporal learning in the time-frequency attention.

The other one can be formulated as $\Lambda_{TS}(\tau_{(t,i,f)}^q, \tau_{(\hat{t},\hat{i},\hat{f})}^k, \tau_{(\hat{t},\hat{i},\hat{f})}^v)$. The divided TSF attention Λ_{TS} represents the attention that computes time-frequency attention Λ_T firstly, then computes space-frequency attention Λ_S. The computing process of Λ_{TS} is similar with Eq. 7.

3.4   Frequency Transformer

To recover HR sequences, we use the similar recurrent structure as TTVSR [21]. Each HR frame is restored from its LR counterparts and a propagation hidden state H. Given a LR frame I_{LR}^T, the SR frame can be restored as:

$$
\begin{aligned}
I_{SR}^T &= \text{rDCT}(T_{freq}(\mathcal{Q}, \mathcal{K}, \mathcal{V})) \\
&= \text{rDCT}(\Gamma(A_{freq}(\mathcal{Q}, \mathcal{K}, \mathcal{V}), D_{LR}^T) + D_{LR}^T),
\end{aligned}
\tag{8}
$$

where T_{freq} represents the Frequency Transformer. A_{freq} represents the frequency attention used in T_{freq} and $A_{freq} \in \{\Lambda_S, \Lambda_T, \Lambda_{T \times S}, \Lambda_{TS}, \Lambda_{ST}\}$. Γ represents the fusion operation which concatenates the outputs of A_{freq} and D_{LR}^T, then reduces the dimensions of the concatenated features by Linear layer.

For example, a frequency Transformer formed by divided TSF attention Λ_{SF} is shown in Fig. 2 (b). The output P^T of TSF can be formulated as:

$$
\begin{aligned}
P^T &= \Lambda_T(R_T, \hat{H}^T, \hat{H}^T), \\
where\ R^T &= \Lambda_S(\mathcal{Q}_S, \mathcal{K}_S, \mathcal{V}_S), \hat{H}^T = W(H^{T-1}, O^T).
\end{aligned}
\tag{9}
$$

$\hat{H}^T$ represents the hidden states warped from past frames H^{T-1} according to flow O^T. W represents the flow warp operation as [2]. H^T is updated by the output P^T of TSF attention and the DCT-based features D_{LR}^T. $\mathcal{Q}_S$ are extracted from upsampled I_{LR}^T by Bicubic upsampling while $\mathcal{K}$ and $\mathcal{V}$ are extracted from upsampled I_{LR}^T by a upsample neural network. The difference between upsample operations brings the location guidance of the hard-to-recover parts, which should pay more attention to it. $\mathcal{Q}_T$ is the temporal-frequency query tokens for Λ_T. The output P^T of TSF attention Λ_{SF} is used to recover SR frames, which can be formulated as:

$$I_{SR}^T = \text{rDCT}(\Gamma(P^T, D_{LR}^T) + D_{LR}^T). \tag{10}$$

More details about the network structure of our proposed Frequency-Transformer can be found in the supplementary material.

We follow the previous works [2,20], using Charbonnier penalty loss [16], which is applied on each video frames. The total loss $\mathcal{L}$ is the average of frames,

$$\mathcal{L} = \frac{1}{T} \sum_{t=1}^{T} \sqrt{||I_{HR}^t - I_{SR}^t||^2 + \epsilon^2}, \tag{11}$$

where ϵ is a constant value and $\epsilon = 1e - 3$.

4   Experiments

4.1   Implementation Details

During training, the Cosine Annealing scheme and Adam optimizer with $\beta_1 = 0.9$ and $\beta_2 = 0.99$ are used. The initial learning rate of FTVSR is 2×10^4. The batch size is 8 videos. The training frame length is 40 for final results and 10 for ablation study. The input patch size is 64×64 and the SR scale is $4\times$. Data augmentations include random horizontal flips, vertical flips, and rotations. We train FTVSR with 400k iterations for the final model and 100k iterations for quick ablation study. All ablation study are based on the backbone of BasicVSR [2] and final model is based on the backbone of TTVSR [21] for better results. Unless otherwise stated, FTVSR is trained with a ratio of 50% uncompressed videos and 50% compressed videos. The compressed videos are uniformly sampled from different compression rates. During inference, we pad the input images with the edge values to keep they can be transformed into spectral maps by DCT and remove the padding after transforming spectral maps into pixel images by rDCT. We crop images into 4×4 patches for inference since the limitation of CUDA memory.

4.2   Datasets and Evaluation Metrics

Datasets. Following the previous works [1,2], we use REDS [25] and Vimeo-90K [35] for training. The REDS dataset contains 270 videos and each video in has 100 frames with a resolution of 1280×720. For a fair comparison, four sequences as previous works [1,2,18,30] for testing, called REDS4. The Vimeo-90K contains 64,612 sequences for training. Each video contains 7 frames with a resolution of 448×256. Same as previous works [2,20], the testing set of Vimeo-90K is Vid4, which contains four videos. Each video includes 30 to 50 frames.

Table 1. Quantitative comparison on the **compressed** videos of REDS4 [25] for 4× VSR. Each entry shows the PSNR↑/SSIM↑ on RGB channels as [2,20]. Red indicates the best and blue indicates the second best performance (Best viewed in color)

Method	Per clip with compression CRF25				Average of clips with compression		
	Clip_000	Clip_011	Clip_015	Clip_020	CRF15	CRF25	CRF35
DUF [13]	23.46/0.622	24.02/0.686	25.76/0.773	23.54/0.689	25.61/0.775	24.19/0.692	22.17/0.588
FRVSR [27]	24.25/0.631	25.65/0.687	28.17/0.770	24.79/0.694	27.61/0.784	25.72/0.696	23.22/0.579
EDVR [30]	24.38/0.629	26.01/0.702	28.30/0.783	25.21/0.708	28.72/0.805	25.98/0.706	23.36/0.600
TecoGan [3]	24.01/0.624	25.39/0.682	27.95/0.768	24.48/0.686	26.93/0.768	25.46/0.690	22.95/0.589
RSDN [12]	24.04/0.602	25.40/0.673	27.93/0.766	24.54/0.676	27.66/0.768	25.48/0.679	23.03/0.579
MuCAN [18]	24.39/0.628	26.02/0.702	28.25/0.781	25.17/0.707	28.67/0.804	25.96/0.705	23.55/0.600
BasicVSR [2]	24.37/0.628	26.01/0.702	28.13/0.777	25.21/0.709	29.05/0.814	25.93/0.704	23.22/0.596
IconVSR [2]	24.35/0.627	26.00/0.702	28.16/0.777	25.22/0.709	29.10/0.816	25.93/0.704	23.22/0.596
COMISR [20]	24.76/0.660	26.54/0.722	29.14/0.805	25.44/0.724	28.40/0.809	26.47/0.728	23.56/0.599
FTVSR	26.06/0.703	28.71/0.779	30.17/0.839	27.26/0.782	30.51/0.853	28.05/0.776	24.82/0.657

Evaluation Metrics. We use the same metrics peak signal-to-noise ratio (PSNR) and structural similarity index (SSIM) [32] as previous works [1,2,18,30] in our evaluation. In addition, for compression videos, we use the most common setting for H.264 codec at different compression rates (different CRF values). Following previous COMISR [20], we use CRF of 15, 25, and 35 to generate compressed videos. Detailed command for video compression can be found in the supplementary material. We then evaluate FTVSR and report the PSNR and SSIM on these compressed videos with these CRF values.

4.3   Comparison with State-of-the-Art Methods

Evaluation on Compressed Videos. We compare FTVSR with other state-of-the-art methods on REDS [25] and Vid4 [35] datasets. Following the compressed settings as COMISR [20], we compress the videos with several compression rates (CRF15, CRF25, CRF35) and evaluate on the compressed videos in PSNR and SSIM.

For REDS [25] dataset, the results on compressed videos are shown in Table 1 and results of other methods are cited from [20]. For BasicVSR and IconVSR, we finetune them on the compressed videos as the same training settings of [20]. Although recent BasicVSR [2] and IconVSR [2] achieve state-of-the-art results on uncompressed videos, they perform not well on the compressed videos. For example, BasicVSR achieves 25.93dB and 23.22dB in PSNR of compression CRF25 and CRF35. Besides, IconVSR, which performs better than BasicVSR on uncompressed videos, but just obtain 25.93dB and 23.22dB in PSNR of compression CRF25 and CRF35 same as the BasicVSR. This phenomenon indicates that only increases the model capacity has less effect on compression problems.

COMISR [20] alleviates the compression problem to some extent by its special designs for compression, but the gains are small (e.g., 26.47dB and 23.56dB in PSNR with a compression rate of CRF25 and CRF35). However, FTVSR achieves 30.51, 28.05dB, and 24.82dB in PSNR on compressed videos with a

Table 2. Quantitative comparison on the **compressed** video of Vid4 [35] for 4× VSR. Following previous works [2,20], each entry shows the PSNR↑/SSIM↑ on Y-channel. Red and blue indicates the best and second best performances (Best viewed in color)

Method	Per clip with compression CRF25				Average of clips with compression		
	Calendar	City	Foliage	Walk	CRF15	CRF25	CRF35
DUF [13]	21.16/0.634	23.78/0.632	22.97/0.603	24.33/0.771	24.40/0.773	23.06/0.660	21.27/0.515
FRVSR [27]	21.55/0.631	25.40/0.575	24.11/0.625	26.21/0.764	26.01/0.766	24.33/0.655	22.05/0.482
EDVR [30]	21.69/0.648	25.51/0.626	24.01/0.606	26.72/0.786	26.34/0.771	24.45/0.667	22.31/0.534
TecoGan [3]	21.34/0.624	25.26/0.561	23.50/0.592	25.73/0.756	25.25/0.741	23.94/0.639	21.99/0.479
RSDN [12]	21.72/0.650	25.28/0.615	23.69/0.615	25.57/0.747	26.58/0.781	24.06/0.650	21.29/0.483
MuCAN [18]	21.60/0.643	25.38/0.620	23.93/0.599	26.43/0.782	25.85/0.753	24.34/0.661	22.26/0.531
BasicVSR [2]	21.64/0.641	25.45/0.620	23.79/0.586	26.26/0.774	26.56/0.780	24.28/0.656	21.97/0.509
IconVSR [2]	21.67/0.644	25.46/0.621	23.83/0.588	26.26/0.774	26.65/0.782	24.31/0.657	21.97/0.509
COMISR [20]	22.81/0.695	25.94/0.640	24.66/0.656	26.95/0.799	26.43/0.791	24.97/0.701	22.35/0.509
FTVSR	22.97/0.720	26.29/0.670	24.94/0.664	27.30/0.816	27.40/0.811	25.38/0.706	22.61/0.540

Table 3. Evaluation on the **uncompressed** videos of REDS4 [25] and Vid4 [35] for 4× VSR. Each entry shows the PSNR↑/SSIM↑. ∗ represents the FTVSR is trained on only uncompressed videos. † represents FTVSR is trained on both compressed and uncompressed videos, which is a more difficult setting. All other methods are trained on uncompressed videos and evaluated on uncompressed videos

Datasets	TOFlow [35]	DUF [13]	EDVR [30]	COMISR [20]	BasicVSR [2]	IconVSR [2]	**FTVSR**∗	**FTVSR**†
REDS4	27.98/0.799	28.63/0.825	31.09/0.880	29.68/0.868	31.42/0.890	31.67/0.895	31.82/0.896	31.74/0.895
Vid4	25.85/0.766	27.38/0.832	27.85/0.850	27.31/0.840	27.96/0.855	28.04/0.857	28.31/0.860	28.06/0.856

Table 4. Comparison of parameters, FLOPs and PSNR↑/SSIM↑ on the compressed videos with CRF25. FLOPs is computed on one LR frame with the size of 180 × 320 and ×4 upsampling on the REDS4 dataset

Methods	DUF [13]	EDVR [30]	MuCAN [18]	BasicVSR [2]	IconVSR [2]	COMISR [20]	FTVSR
Params(M)	5.8	20.6	13.6	6.3	8.7	6.2	10.8
FLOPs(T)	2.34	2.95	>1.07	0.33	0.51	0.36	0.76
PSNR/SSIM	24.19/0.692	25.98/0.706	25.96/0.705	25.93/0.704	25.93/0.704	26.47/0.728	27.28/0.763

compression rate of CRF15, CRF25, and CRF35, respectively. FTVSR outperforms SOTA COMISR by 1.6dB on the compressed videos in CRF25. The results show that FTVSR has strong capabilities on compression problems.

For Vid4 [35] dataset, the results on compressed videos are shown in Table 2. The results of BasicVSR and IconVSR are obtained by finetuning on compressed videos as [20]. For a fair comparison, we also adopt the same compression settings as COMISR [20]. On compressed videos with a compression rate of CRF 15, 25, and 35, FTVSR achieves 27.40 dB, 25.38 dB, and 22.61 dB in PSNR, respectively. FTVSR outperforms other methods. These results demonstrate the huge potential of FTVSR on the task of compressed VSR.

We also visualize the results of FTVSR and SOTA methods on compressed videos. As shown in Fig. 4, FTVSR performs well on both compressed and

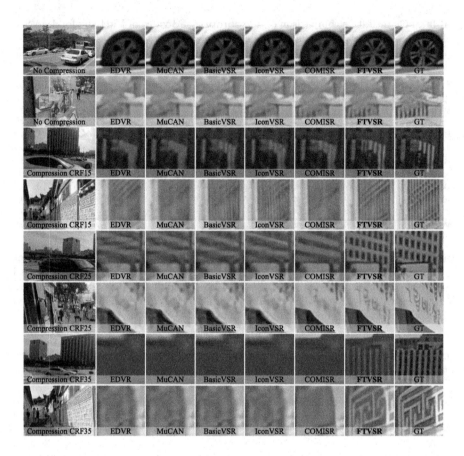

Fig. 4. Visualization results of our FTVSR and other VSR methods on the uncompressed videos and compressed videos with compression rates of CRF 15, 25, and 35

uncompressed video. Especially on the compressed video with CRF25 and CRF35, the visual quality of FTVSR is superior to other methods. An interesting phenomenon is that COMISR performs better than BasicVSR and IconVSR on compressed videos, but poorly on uncompressed videos. However, our FTVSR performs well on both compressed videos and uncompressed videos as shown in Fig. 4. Especially on the cases with a compression rate of CRF35, BasicVSR, IconVSR, and COMISR are failed to recover the texture, but FTVSR still performs well on these cases. It's because frequency attention enables low-frequency information to guide the generation of high-frequency textures.

Evaluation on Uncompressed Videos. To study the potential of FTVSR, we also evaluate FTVSR on the uncompressed videos of the REDS and Vid4 datasets, respectively. For a fair comparison, we compare with SOTA methods

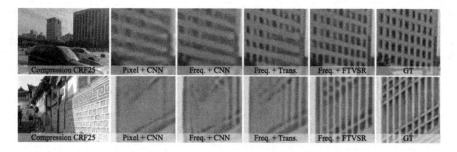

Fig. 5. Visualization results of "Pixel + CNN", "Frequency + CNN", "Frequency + Transformer", and "Frequency + FTVSR" in Table 5

Table 5. Ablation study of FTVSR (PSNR↑/SSIM↑) on the REDS4 dataset

Domain + Backbone	Per clip with compression CRF25				Average of clips with compression		
	Clip_000	Clip_011	Clip_015	Clip_020	CRF15	CRF25	CRF35
Pixel + CNN	24.37/0.628	26.01/0.702	28.13/0.777	25.21/0.709	29.05/0.814	25.93/0.704	23.22/0.596
Frequency + CNN	24.98/0.666	27.11/0.746	29.36/0.818	26.05/0.751	29.20/0.825	26.87/0.745	23.83/0.629
Frequency + Transformer	25.20/0.684	27.53/0.763	29.47/0.828	26.33/0.766	29.51/0.837	27.15/0.759	24.03/0.644
Frequency + FTVSR	25.26/0.609	27.75/0.766	29.62/0.831	26.47/0.772	29.70/0.843	27.28/0.763	24.22/0.646

in two settings: 1) FTVSR*, training only on uncompressed videos, and testing on uncompressed videos. 2) FTVSR†, training on both compressed and uncompressed videos, and testing on uncompressed videos, which is a more difficult setting for evaluating on uncompressed videos since the compressed data brings more noises for VSR model. As shown in Table 3, all results are evaluated on uncompressed videos. The results of other methods are all obtained from their paper and their model is trained on only uncompressed videos as setting 1. For the setting 1 which is fair for our method, FTVSR* outperforms SOTA Icon-VSR [2] in PSNR on both REDS4 and Vid4 datasets. Moreover, for setting 2, FTVSR† achieves 31.74dB in PSNR on REDS4 dataset, which outperforms IconVSR [2] although IconVSR is trained on full clean uncompressed videos. Besides, FTVSR† obtain comparable results on Vid4 dataset. Compared with COMISR [20] that performs well on compressed videos while unsatisfactory on uncompressed videos, FTVSR performs well on both compressed videos and uncompressed videos, even in the difficult setting of that the model is trained on both compressed videos and uncompressed videos.

Comparison of Parameters and FLOPs. The comparisons of parameters and FLOPs are shown in Table 4. The FLOPs are computed with the input of LR frame size 180×320 and conducting $4\times$ upsampling VSR task. Based on BasicVSR, FTVSR outperforms other methods with the comparable parameters and FLOPs. FTVSR adopt a similar architecture as BasicVSR and process HR frames in the frequency domain. The FLOPs are comparable with BasicVSR since the DCT operation reduces the computational costs of FTVSR.

Table 6. Comparisons of different types of frequency attention on the compressed videos of REDS with compression rates of CRF 15, 25, and 35. All the methods in this table are in the frequency domain. "Base" represents the traditional attention without frequency attention mechanism. Each entry shows PSNR↑/SSIM↑

Attention	Base	Λ_S	Λ_T	$\Lambda_{T \times S}$	Λ_{TS}	Λ_{ST}
CRF15	29.51/0.837	29.63/0.840	29.60/0.840	29.61/0.839	29.65/0.841	**29.70/0.843**
CRF25	27.15/0.759	27.23/0.761	27.11/0.760	27.22/0.760	27.24/0.762	**27.28/0.763**
CRF35	24.03/0.644	24.12/0.646	24.05/0.641	24.11/0.644	24.12/0.645	**24.22/0.646**

4.4 Ablation Study

To evaluate the effectiveness of FTVSR, we conduct the ablation study on the REDS4 dataset. As shown in Table 5, We use BasicVSR [2] as baseline, which learns in pixel domain and achieves 29.05 dB, 25.93 dB, 23.22 dB in PSNR on the compressed videos with compression CRF15, CRF25, and CRF35, respectively. The performances are poor compared with its 31.42 dB on uncompressed videos. Then, we transfer images into the frequency domain, which obtains a relative gain of 0.94 dB in PSNR on the compressed videos with CRF25. In the frequency domain, a transformer-based model without frequency attention achieves 27.15 dB in PSNR on the compressed videos with CRF25, which shows that the attention mechanism is beneficial for frequency learning. Replacing the basic transformer by our FTVSR, FTVSR achieves 27.28 dB in PSNR on the compressed videos with CRF25, which shows that the frequency attention is better than traditional attention in the frequency domain. As shown in Fig. 5, FTVSR achieves better visualization results than others.

To evaluate the effectiveness of different frequency attention introduced in Sect. 3.3, we conduct the ablation study on the REDS dataset. As shown in Table 6, "Base" represents a traditional transformer which computes spatial attention in frequency domain. The results of base attention are lower than frequency attention. For the different frequency attentions, space-frequency attention, time-frequency attention, joint time-space-frequency attention and divided time-space-frequency attention ($\{\Lambda_S, \Lambda_T, \Lambda_{T \times S}, \Lambda_{TS}, \Lambda_{ST}\}$), the results in Table 6 show that the divided frequency attention (Λ_{ST}) with an order of space first and time later is better. This is because in compressed VSR, degraded frames should be first restored by the space-frequency attention then the recovered textures could be used to benefit temporal learning in the time-frequency attention.

5 Conclusions

In this paper, we propose a novel spatiotemporal Frequency-Transformer for compressed Video Super-Resolution (FTVSR). To handle the compression issues, we transform compressed video frames into frequency domain and design frequency-based attention to enable the feature fusions across multiple frequency bands. The frequency-based tokenization and frequency attention mechanism enables low-frequency information to guide the generation of high-frequency textures. To utilize spatial and temporal information, we further explore the different types of frequency attention combined with space and time attentions. Experiments on two widely-used VSR datasets show that the proposed FTVSR significantly outperforms previous works and achieves new SOTA results.

Acknowledgment. This work was supported by the Scientific and Technological Innovation of Shunde Graduate School of University of Science and Technology Beijing (No. BK20AE004 and No. BK19CE017).

References

1. Cao, J., Li, Y., Zhang, K., Van Gool, L.: Video super-resolution transformer. arXiv preprint arXiv:2106.06847 (2021)
2. Chan, K.C., Wang, X., Yu, K., Dong, C., Loy, C.C.: BasicVSR: the search for essential components in video super-resolution and beyond. In: CVPR, pp. 4947–4956 (2021)
3. Chu, M., Xie, Y., Mayer, J., Leal-Taixé, L., Thuerey, N.: Learning temporal coherence via self-supervision for gan-based video generation. ACM TOG **39**(4), 75-1 (2020)
4. Dosovitskiy, A., Beyeret al.: An image is worth 16x16 words: transformers for image recognition at scale. arXiv preprint arXiv:2010.11929 (2020)
5. Ehrlich, M., Davis, L., Lim, S.-N., Shrivastava, A.: Quantization guided JPEG artifact correction. In: Vedaldi, A., Bischof, H., Brox, T., Frahm, J.-M. (eds.) ECCV 2020. LNCS, vol. 12353, pp. 293–309. Springer, Cham (2020). https://doi.org/10.1007/978-3-030-58598-3_18
6. Ehrlich, M., Davis, L.S.: Deep residual learning in the jpeg transform domain. In: ICCV, pp. 3484–3493 (2019)
7. Fritsche, M., Gu, S., Timofte, R.: Frequency separation for real-world super-resolution. In: ICCVW, pp. 3599–3608. IEEE (2019)
8. Fu, J., Zheng, H., Mei, T.: Look closer to see better: recurrent attention convolutional neural network for fine-grained image recognition. In: CVPR, pp. 4438–4446 (2017)
9. Goto, T., Fukuoka, T., Nagashima, F., Hirano, S., Sakurai, M.: Super-resolution system for 4k-HDTV. In: ICPR, pp. 4453–4458. IEEE (2014)
10. Gueguen, L., Sergeev, A., Kadlec, B., Liu, R., Yosinski, J.: Faster neural networks straight from JPEG. In: NeurIPS 31 (2018)
11. Haris, M., Shakhnarovich, G., Ukita, N.: Recurrent back-projection network for video super-resolution. In: CVPR, pp. 3897–3906 (2019)
12. Isobe, T., Jia, X., Gu, S., Li, S., Wang, S., Tian, Q.: Video super-resolution with recurrent structure-detail network. In: Vedaldi, A., Bischof, H., Brox, T., Frahm, J.-M. (eds.) ECCV 2020. LNCS, vol. 12357, pp. 645–660. Springer, Cham (2020). https://doi.org/10.1007/978-3-030-58610-2_38
13. Jo, Y., Oh, S.W., Kang, J., Kim, S.J.: Deep video super-resolution network using dynamic upsampling filters without explicit motion compensation. In: CVPR, pp. 3224–3232 (2018)
14. Kim, S.Y., Lim, J., Na, T., Kim, M.: 3DSRnet: video super-resolution using 3D convolutional neural networks. arXiv preprint arXiv:1812.09079 (2018)

15. Kim, T.H., Sajjadi, M.S.M., Hirsch, M., Schölkopf, B.: Spatio-temporal transformer network for video restoration. In: Ferrari, V., Hebert, M., Sminchisescu, C., Weiss, Y. (eds.) ECCV 2018. LNCS, vol. 11207, pp. 111–127. Springer, Cham (2018). https://doi.org/10.1007/978-3-030-01219-9_7
16. Lai, W.S., Huang, J.B., Ahuja, N., Yang, M.H.: Deep Laplacian pyramid networks for fast and accurate super-resolution. In: CVPR, pp. 624–632 (2017)
17. Li, S., He, F., Du, B., Zhang, L., Xu, Y., Tao, D.: Fast spatio-temporal residual network for video super-resolution. In: CVPR, pp. 10522–10531 (2019)
18. Li, W., Tao, X., Guo, T., Qi, L., Lu, J., Jia, J.: MuCAN: multi-correspondence aggregation network for video super-resolution. In: Vedaldi, A., Bischof, H., Brox, T., Frahm, J.-M. (eds.) ECCV 2020. LNCS, vol. 12355, pp. 335–351. Springer, Cham (2020). https://doi.org/10.1007/978-3-030-58607-2_20
19. Li, X., Jin, X., Yu, T., Sun, S., Pang, Y., Zhang, Z., Chen, Z.: Learning omni-frequency region-adaptive representations for real image super-resolution. In: AAAI, vol. 35, pp. 1975–1983 (2021)
20. Li, Y., Jin, P., Yang, F., Liu, C., Yang, M.H., Milanfar, P.: COMISR: compression-informed video super-resolution. In: ICCV (2021)
21. Liu, C., Yang, H., Fu, J., Qian, X.: Learning trajectory-aware transformer for video super-resolution. In: CVPR, pp. 5687–5696 (2022)
22. Liu, Z., et a.: Swin transformer: hierarchical vision transformer using shifted windows. In: ICCV, pp. 10012–10022 (2021)
23. Lu, G., Ouyang, W., Xu, D., Zhang, X., Gao, Z., Sun, M.-T.: Deep Kalman filtering network for video compression artifact reduction. In: Ferrari, V., Hebert, M., Sminchisescu, C., Weiss, Y. (eds.) Computer Vision – ECCV 2018. LNCS, vol. 11218, pp. 591–608. Springer, Cham (2018). https://doi.org/10.1007/978-3-030-01264-9_35
24. Lu, G., Zhang, X., Ouyang, W., Xu, D., Chen, L., Gao, Z.: Deep non-local kalman network for video compression artifact reduction. TIP **29**, 1725–1737 (2019)
25. Nah, S., et a.: Ntire 2019 challenge on video deblurring and super-resolution: dataset and study. In: CVPRW (2019)
26. Qin, Z., Zhang, P., Wu, F., Li, X.: FcaNet: frequency channel attention networks. In: ICCV, pp. 783–792 (2021)
27. Sajjadi, M.S., Vemulapalli, R., Brown, M.: Frame-recurrent video super-resolution. In: CVPR, pp. 6626–6634 (2018)
28. Tao, X., Gao, H., Liao, R., Wang, J., Jia, J.: Detail-revealing deep video super-resolution. In: ICCV, pp. 4472–4480 (2017)
29. Tian, Y., Zhang, Y., Fu, Y., Xu, C.: TDAN: temporally-deformable alignment network for video super-resolution. In: CVPR, pp. 3360–3369 (2020)
30. Wang, X., Chan, K.C., Yu, K., Dong, C., Change Loy, C.: EDVR: video restoration with enhanced deformable convolutional networks. In: CVPRW (2019)
31. Wang, Z., Liu, D., Chang, S., Ling, Q., Yang, Y., Huang, T.S.: D3: deep dual-domain based fast restoration of jpeg-compressed images. In: CVPR, pp. 2764–2772 (2016)
32. Wang, Z., Bovik, A.C., Sheikh, H.R., Simoncelli, E.P.: Image quality assessment: from error visibility to structural similarity. IEEE TIP **13**(4), 600–612 (2004)
33. Xu, K., Qin, M., Sun, F., Wang, Y., Chen, Y.K., Ren, F.: Learning in the frequency domain. In: CVPR, pp. 1740–1749 (2020)
34. Xu, Y., Gao, L., Tian, K., Zhou, S., Sun, H.: Non-local ConvLSTM for video compression artifact reduction. In: ICCV, pp. 7043–7052 (2019)
35. Xue, T., Chen, B., Wu, J., Wei, D., Freeman, W.T.: Video enhancement with task-oriented flow. IJCV **127**(8), 1106–1125 (2019)

36. Yang, F., Yang, H., Fu, J., Lu, H., Guo, B.: Learning texture transformer network for image super-resolution. In: CVPR, pp. 5791–5800 (2020)
37. Yi, P., et al.: Omniscient video super-resolution. In: ICCV, pp. 4429–4438 (2021)
38. Zeng, Y., Yang, H., Chao, H., Wang, J., Fu, J.: Improving visual quality of image synthesis by a token-based generator with transformers. NeurIPS **34**, 21125–21137 (2021)
39. Zhang, L., Zhang, H., Shen, H., Li, P.: A super-resolution reconstruction algorithm for surveillance images. Sig. Process. **90**(3), 848–859 (2010)
40. Zheng, H., Fu, J., Mei, T., Luo, J.: Learning multi-attention convolutional neural network for fine-grained image recognition. In: ICCV, pp. 5209–5217 (2017)

Spatial-Frequency Domain Information Integration for Pan-Sharpening

Man Zhou[1,2], Jie Huang[1], Keyu Yan[1,2], Hu Yu[1], Xueyang Fu[1], Aiping Liu[1], Xian Wei[3], and Feng Zhao[1(✉)] (iD)

[1] University of Science and Technology of China, Hefei, China
{manman,hj0117}@mail.ustc.edu.cn, fzhao956@ustc.edu.cn
[2] Hefei Institute of Physical Science, Chinese Academy of Sciences, Hefei, China
[3] MoE Engineering Research Center of Hardware/Software Co-design Technology
and Application, East China Normal University, Shanghai, China

Abstract. Pan-sharpening aims to generate high-resolution multi-spectral (MS) images by fusing PAN images and low-resolution MS images. Despite its great advances, most existing pan-sharpening methods only work in the spatial domain and rarely explore the potential solutions in the frequency domain. In this paper, we first attempt to address pan-sharpening in both spatial and frequency domains and propose a Spatial-Frequency Information Integration Network, dubbed as SFIIN. To implement SFIIN, we devise a core building module tailored with pan-sharpening, consisting of three key components: spatial-domain information branch, frequency-domain information branch, and dual domain interaction. To be specific, the first employs the standard convolution to integrate the local information of two modalities of PAN and MS images in the spatial domain, while the second adopts deep Fourier transformation to achieve the image-wide receptive field for exploring global contextual information. Followed by, the third is responsible for facilitating the information flow and learning the complementary representation. We conduct extensive experiments to validate the effectiveness of the proposed network and demonstrate the favorable performance against other state-of-the-art methods.

Keywords: Pan-sharpening · Spatial-frequency domain

1 Introduction

Pan-sharpening is the process of super-resolving the low-resolution (LR) multi-spectral (MS) images in the spatial domain to generate the expected high-resolution (HR) MS images, conditioning on the paired high-resolution PAN images. In other words, pan-sharpening is essentially a PAN-guided MS image

---

M. Zhou and J. Huang—Co-first authors contributed equally.
F. Zhao—Corresponding author.

S. Avidan et al. (Eds.): ECCV 2022, LNCS 13678, pp. 274–291, 2022.
https://doi.org/10.1007/978-3-031-19797-0_16

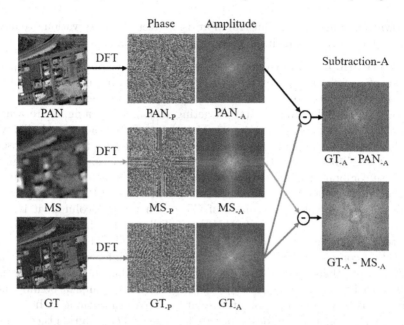

Fig. 1. The frequency domain analysis of discrete Fourier transform (DFT) of PAN image, MS image and the corresponding ground truth (GT) where phase and amplitude are abbreviated as P and A respectively. The middle two columns represent the phase and amplitude components in Fourier space while the last column shows the absolute value of the amplitude subtraction among the connected pairs.

super-resolution problem by learning the non-linear mapping between low- and high-resolution MS images. Both high-spectral and high-spatial images are desirable in the field of remote sensing for a variety of applications such as military systems, environmental monitoring, and mapping services. However, due to the limits of hardware devices, such images can hardly be obtained. To this end, pan-sharpening technique has drawn great attention from both image processing and remote sensing communities.

Inspired by the success of deep neural networks (DNN) over image processing, explosive DNN-based pan-sharpening methods [1,12,33,34] have been developed. The pioneering one refers to PNN [36], which only adapts three-layer convolution operation to account for the MS pan-sharpening learning motivated by the representative super-resolution model SRCNN [9]. Since then, more complicated and deeper architectures have been designed to improve the mapping capability of pan-sharpening. Despite the remarkable progress, existing pan-sharpening methods still suffer from the common limitation. All of them only focus on learning the pan-sharpening function in the spatial domain and rarely explore the potential solutions of pan-sharpening in the frequency domain, which deserves more attention in pan-sharpening. However, pan-sharpening is essentially a PAN-guided MS image super-resolution problem and super-resolution task is tightly coupled to the frequency domain due to the removal of high frequency information during the down-sampling process, illustrated in [14]. Given this observation, we devote considerable effort to pan-sharpening in frequency domain.

Our Motivation. As shown in Fig. 1, we conduct the comprehensive frequency analysis of pan-sharpening by revisiting the properties of phase and amplitude components via discrete Fourier transformation and deepening into their difference of amplitude components. Targeting at pan-sharpening, there are two observations in frequency domain: 1) The phase of PAN is more similar with the phase of GT than that of MS, which is consistent with the spatial observation that PAN has more detailed textures than MS images. As well recognized, the phase component of the Fourier transformation characterizes the structure information. It is therefore natural to leverage the phase of PAN to support that of MS for approximating the phase of GT; 2) In the last column, it is noted that the amplitude difference of PAN and GT lies in low frequency while the amplitude difference of MS and GT lies in both low and high frequency. We can deduce that compared with GT, the missing frequency information of MS can be borrowed from that of PAN. In short, the frequency domain provides the more powerful tool to analyze and observe the degradation of pan-sharpening and it motivates us to explore the potential solution of pan-sharpening in both space and frequency domains. Besides, motivated by spectral convolution theorem [10], we note that learning in frequency information allows the image-wide receptive field that models the global contextual information. Therefore, leveraging the global frequency information complements the local information by pixel values in spatial domain with boosting the information representation and model capability.

Based on above analysis, we introduce a novel perspective for pan-sharpening in this paper. Specifically, we first attempt to address pan-sharpening in both spatial-frequency domain and propose a Spatial-Frequency Information Integration Network, dubbed as SFIIN. To implement SFIIN, the fundamental building module called SFIB is devised, which consists of three key components: spatial-domain information branch, frequency-domain information branch and dual domain information interaction. The spatial branch employs the ordinary convolution to exploit the local information of two modalities of PAN and MS images in spatial domain while the frequency branch is responsible for extracting and transforming the global frequency information via deep Fourier transformation over amplitude and phase components in frequency domain. Motivated by spectral convolution theorem, we argue that the frequency information branch allows the image-wide receptive field that models the global contextual information, thus boosting the model capability. Followed by, the dual domain information interaction is performed to facilitate the information flow and learn the complementary representation in spatial and frequency domain. We conduct extensive experiments to analyze the effectiveness of the proposed network and demonstrate the favorable performance against state-of-the-art methods qualitatively and quantitatively while generalizing well to real-world scenes.

In summary, the contributions of this work are as follows:

- To the best of our knowledge, this is the first attempt to explore the potential solution of pan-sharpening in both spatial and frequency domain. In this paper, a Spatial-Frequency Information Integration Network is proposed and substantially improves the Pan-sharping performance.
- We devise a core building module tailored with pan-sharpening, consisting of three key components: spatial domain information branch, frequency domain information one and dual domain information interaction. It enables the local spatial information and global frequency information to learn the complementary representation, thus boosting the model capability.
- Extensive experiments over different satellite datasets demonstrate that our proposed method performs the best qualitative and quantitative while generalizing well to real-world full-resolution scenes.

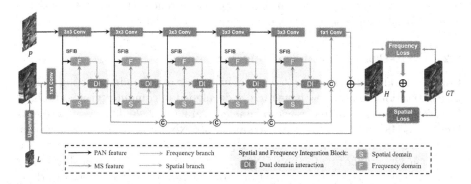

Fig. 2. The framework of our proposed pan-sharpening network. The network is equipped with the core building module SFIB which is tailored with pan-sharpening and consists of three key components: spatial domain information S, frequency domain information F and dual domain interaction DI. Therefore, it is capable of effectively exploring the space and frequency domain information of MS and PAN images. In addition, we design the new loss function in both spatial and frequency domain to better optimize the proposed network.

2   Related Work

2.1   Traditional Pan-Sharpening Methods

Component Substitution (CS), Multi-resolution Analysis (MRA), and Variational Optimization (VO) are the three categories under which traditional pan-sharpening techniques are categorized [38,39]. The principal component analysis (PCA) methods [28,37], Brovey transforms [16], and the Gram-Schmidt (GS) orthogonalization approach [30] are the most used CS techniques. Researchers have also suggested various enhancements to the approaches mentioned above, such as the nonlinear IHS (NIHS) method [15], which reduces the spectrum distortion of IHS, and the GSA method, which has adaptive capabilities for the GS method [2]. These CS algorithms are quite quick to calculate, however the artifacts that are produced in the photos are quite common. When sharpening MS images, MRA approaches produce less spectral distortion than CS methods. Decimated wavelet transform (DWT), high-pass filter fusion (HPF), indusion method [27], Laplacian pyramid (LP) [41], and atrous wavelet transform (ATWT) are examples of common MRA techniques. The first variational method, P+XS pan-sharpening approach [4], makes the assumption that PAN images are created by linearly combining different bands of HRMS images, while upsampled low resolution multi-spectral (LRMS) images are created from fuzzy HRMS images. The pan-sharpening task is then subjected to a variety of constraints, including the dynamic gradient sparsity property (SIRF) [8], the local gradient constraint (LGC) [11], the group low-rank constraint for texture similarity (ADMM) [39], and others. These numerous priors and restrictions, which call for manual parameter setup, can only imperfectly reflect the images' restricted structural relationships, which can also lead to degradation.

2.2 CNN-Based Pan-Sharpening Methods

Convolutional neural networks (CNN), which have strong nonlinear fitting and feature extraction capabilities, have rapidly developed in computer vision and have been frequently used in hyperspectral images [7,13,17,22–26,43] and remote sensing images [48,49,53–57]. Recently, a number of CNN-based techniques have been proposed to support the fusion quality of pan-sharpening [35,46,52]. For instance, Masi et al. [36] are the first to apply CNN to address the problem of pan-sharpening. Even though the structure is straightforward, the results are far superior to those of conventional techniques. Then, Yang et al. [50] then used resblock in [19] to create a deeper convolutional network. In the meantime, Yuan et al. [51] added the multi-scale module into the fundamental CNN design. Later, Cai et al. [5] and Wu et al. [44] had a similar idea: continuously introducing images of various scales into the backbone network. The two methods differ in that the former uses PAN images and the latter MS images. A few model-driven CNN models with obvious physical meaning have recently surfaced. The fundamental concept is to create optimization issues for computer vision tasks using previous knowledge, and then to develop the optimization algorithms into deep neural networks. For instance, to build the unfolding structure for pan-sharpening, Xu et al. [47] constructed two distinct priors of PAN and MS. The model-driven approaches are comprehensible and have obvious physical significance. CNN was updated with an alternative optimization approach by Cao et al. [6]. Variational optimization and deep residual CNN were integrated by Tian et al. [40] and Wu et al. [45].

3   Method

In this section, we will first revisit the properties of Fourier Transformation of images and then present an overview of the proposed pan-sharpening network, illustrated in Fig. 2 and Fig. 3. We further provide details of the fundamental building block of our method, containing three key elements: (a) frequency

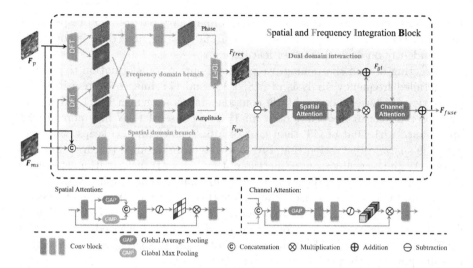

Fig. 3. The detailed flowchart of the proposed core building module SFIB, consisting of three components: frequency domain branch, spatial domain branch and dual domain interaction.

domain information branch for extracting the global frequency information representations via DFT, (b) spatial domain information branch to explore the local information via ordinary convolution, (c) dual domain information interaction to facilitate the information flow and learn the complementary representation. Finally, we deepen into the newly-designed loss functions.

3.1 Fourier Transformation of Images

As recognized, the Fourier transform is widely used to analyze the frequency content of images. For the images of multiple color channels, the Fourier transform is calculated and performed for each channel separately. For simplicity, we eliminate the notation of channels in formulas. Given a image $x \in R^{H \times W \times C}$, the Fourier transform $\mathcal{F}$ converts it to Fourier space as the complex component $\mathcal{F}(x)$, which is expressed as:

$$\mathcal{F}(x)(u, v) = \frac{1}{\sqrt{HW}} \sum_{h=0}^{H-1} \sum_{w=0}^{W-1} x(h, w) e^{-j2\pi(\frac{h}{H}u + \frac{w}{W}v)}, \tag{1}$$

$\mathcal{F}^{-1}(x)$ defines the inverse Fourier transform accordingly. Both the Fourier transform and its inverse procedure can be efficiently implemented with the FFT algorithm in [10]. The amplitude component $\mathcal{A}(x)(u, v)$ and phase component $\mathcal{P}(x)(u, v)$ are expressed as:

$$\mathcal{A}(x)(u, v)) = \sqrt{R^2(x)(u, v)) + I^2(x)(u, v))},$$
$$\mathcal{P}(x)(u, v)) = \arctan[\frac{I(x)(u, v))}{R(x)(u, v))}], \tag{2}$$

where $R(x)$ and $I(x)$ represent the real and imaginary part of $\mathcal{F}(x)$ respectively. In our method, the Fourier transformation and inverse procedure is computed independently on each channel of feature maps.

Targeting at pan-sharpening, we employ Fourier transformation to conduct the detailed frequency analysis of MS, PAN and GT images by revisiting the properties of phase and amplitude components, as shown in Fig. 1. There are two observations in frequency domain: 1) The phase of PAN has more similar appearance with that of GT than that of MS. This claim also keeps consistent with the spatial observation that PAN has the more detailed textures than MS images. With the well-known properties of the Fourier transformation, the phase component characterizes the structure information. 2) The amplitude difference of PAN and GT lies in low frequency while the amplitude difference of MS and GT lies in both low and high frequency. We can deduce that compared with GT, the missing frequency information of MS can be borrowed from that of PAN to restore that of GT. It motivates us to explore the potential solution of pan-sharpening in both spatial and frequency domains.

3.2 Framework

Structure Flow. Based on above analysis, we introduce a novel spatial-frequency information integration-based perspective for pan-sharpening, detailed in Fig. 2. Given PAN image $P \in R^{H \times W \times 1}$ and MS image $L \in R^{H/r \times W/r \times C}$, the network first applies the convolution layer to project the r-times L by Bibubic upsampling into shallow feature representations while P is progressively fed into multiple cascaded convolution to extract the series of informative features. Next, the obtained modality-aware feature maps of MS and PAN are jointly pass through N number of the core building module SFIB with space-frequency information extraction and integration, yielding the effective feature representation. Next, we apply a convolution layer to transform the collected features from all N SFIBs back to image space and then combine with the input L as the output image.

Supervision Flow. Orthogonal to structure design, we also introduce a newly-designed loss functions to enable the network for better optimization, thus reconstructing the more pleasing results in both spatial and frequency domains. As shown in Fig. 2, it consists of two parts: spatial domain loss and frequency domain loss. In contrast to existing methods that usually adopt pixel losses with local guidance in the spatial domain, we additionally propose the frequency domain supervision loss via Fourier transformation that is calculated on the global frequency components. Motivated by spectral convolution theorem, direct emphasis on the frequency content is capable of better reconstructing the global information, thus improving the pan-sharpening performance.

3.3 The Core Building Block

As shown in Fig. 3, the fundamental building block of our method contains three key elements: (a) frequency domain information branch for extracting the global frequency information representation via deep Fourier transform, (b) spatial domain information branch to explore the local information via ordinary convolution, (c) dual domain information interaction to facilitate the information flow and learn the complementary representation.

Frequency Domain Information Branch. In the frequency branch, we first adopt Fourier transform to convert the modality-aware features of MS and PAN images and generate the amplitude and phase components. Suppose that the features of MS and PAN images denote as F_p and F_{ms}, the corresponding Fourier transform is expressed as

$$\mathcal{A}(F_p), \mathcal{P}(F_p) = \mathcal{F}(F_p), \tag{3}$$

$$\mathcal{A}(F_{ms}), \mathcal{P}(F_{ms}) = \mathcal{F}(F_{ms}), \tag{4}$$

where $\mathcal{A}(.)$ and $\mathcal{P}(.)$ indicate the amplitude and phase respectively. Then we uses two groups of independent operation $OA(\cdot)$ and $OP(\cdot)$, consisting of 1×1 convolution and $Relu$ activation function to integrate the corresponding amplitude and phase components for providing the enhanced global frequency representations

$$\mathcal{A}(F) = \mathcal{O}\mathcal{A}(Cat[\mathcal{A}(F_p), \mathcal{A}(F_{ms})]), \tag{5}$$

$$\mathcal{P}(F) = \mathcal{O}\mathcal{P}(Cat[\mathcal{P}(F_p), \mathcal{P}(F_{ms})]), \tag{6}$$

where Cat indicates the concatenation operation by channel dimension. Next, we apply the inverse DFT to transform the fused amplitude and phase components of $\mathcal{A}(F)$ and $\mathcal{P}(F)$ back to spatial domain

$$F_{fre} = F^{-1}(\mathcal{A}(F), \mathcal{P}(F)). \tag{7}$$

According to spectral convolution theorem in Fourier theory, processing information of Fourier space is capable of capturing the global frequency representation in frequency domain. In short, the frequency branch generates the global information representation F_{fre}.

Spatial Domain Information Branch. In contrast, the spatial branch first adopts a residual block [20] with 3×3 convolution layers to integrate information of MS and PAN features and generate the space representation F_{spa} in spatial domain. It is well recognized that the ordinary convolution focuses on learning local representations in spatial domain. In short, the spatial branch provides the local information representation F_{spa}. Based on the above spatial and frequency domain branches, we note that the generated information representation from both branches is complementary. Therefore, interacting and integrating them is beneficial to compensate each other and provide more informative representation.

Dual Domain Information Interaction. The schematic of Dual domain information interaction mainly consists of information compensation and information integration part. **(a) information compensation:** Owing the complementary property of the frequency and spatial representation F_{fre} and F_{spa}, this motivates us to extract the distinguished components of local spatial information

F_{spa} to compensate the global frequency information F_{fre}. Therefore, we first calculate the absolute difference among them and then employ the spatial attention mechanism SA to exploit the inter-spatial dependencies. It outputs the spatial attention map and multiplies it over F_{spa} to select the more informative content, impose it over global frequency representation F_{fre} to the enriched representation F_{gl}

$$F_{gl} = F_{fre} + SA(F_{fre} - F_{spa}) \times F_{spa}. \tag{8}$$

(b) information integration: When obtaining the enhanced global frequency feature F_{gl}, we combine it with the local feature F_{spa} and then perform the channel attention to exploit the inter-channel relationship, thus facilitating the complementary learning and providing the more informative feature representation F_{fuse}. Finally, the residual learning mechanism is adopted by adding the input MS feature F_{ms} to the fused one

$$F_{fuse} = CA([F_{gl}, F_{spa}]) + F_{ms}. \tag{9}$$

Equipped with the core building block, our proposed network is capable of modeling and integrating the global and local information representation by exploring the potential of spatial and frequency dual domains.

3.4 Loss Function

Let H_L and GT denote the network output and the corresponding ground truth respectively. To generate the pleasing pan-sharpening results, we propose a joint spatial-frequency domain loss for supervising the network training. In spatial domain, we adopt the $L1$ loss

$$\mathcal{L}_{spa} = \|H_L - GT\|_1. \tag{10}$$

In frequency domain, we first employ the DFT to convert H_L and GT into Fourier space where the amplitude and phase components are calculated. Then, the $L1$-norms of amplitude difference and phase difference between H_L and GT are summed to produce the total frequency loss

$$\mathcal{L}_{fre} = \|\mathcal{A}(H_L) - \mathcal{A}(GT)\|_1 + \|\mathcal{P}(H_L) - \mathcal{P}(GT)\|_1. \tag{11}$$

Finally, the overall loss function is formulated as follows

$$\mathcal{L} = \mathcal{L}_{spa} + \lambda \mathcal{L}_{fre}, \tag{12}$$

where λ is weight factor and set to 0.1 empirically.

4   Experiments

4.1   Baseline Methods

To demonstrate the efficacy of our proposed method, we compare its performance to that of several representative pansharpening methods: 1) five cutting-edge deep-learning methods, such as PNN [36], PANNET [50], MSDCNN [51], SRPPNN [5], and GPPNN [47]; 2) five promising traditional methods, including SFIM [32], Brovey [16], GS [29], IHS [18], and GFPCA [31].

4.2 Implementation Details

On a personal computer with a single NVIDIA GeForce GTX 2080Ti GPU, the PyTorch framework is used to construct each of our networks. During the training phase, the Adam optimizer will optimize them using four-epoch batches over a total of 2000 iterations. 8×10^{-4} yields the initial value for the learning rate. After 200 epochs, the pace of learning will begin to decrease by a factor of two. Due to the lack of pan-sharpened ground-truth images, we generate the training set by employing the Wald protocol tool [42], as was done in previous studies. Specifically, given the MS image $H \in R^{M \times N \times C}$ and the PAN image $P \in R^{rM \times rN \times b}$, both of them are downsampled with ratio r, and the resulting images are denoted by $L \in R^{M/r \times N/r \times C}$ and $p \in R^{M \times N \times b}$ respectively. In the training set, L and p are regarded as the inputs, whereas H is the ground truth.

We have chosen to assess the worldview II, worldview III, and GaoFen2 satellite image datasets for this study. The PAN images for each database are cropped into patches measuring 128×128 pixels, while the corresponding MS patches are 32×32 pixels. Image quality assessment (IQA) metrics such as the relative dimensionless global error in synthesis (ERGAS) [3], the peak signal-to-noise ratio (PSNR), the structural similarity (SSIM) and SAM [21], are used for performance evaluation. These measures are frequently employed in the pan-sharpening field.

To compare the generalization of models, we create an additional real-world full-resolution dataset of 200 samples over the newly-selected GaoFen2 satellite for evaluation. Specifically, the additional dataset is generated when the full-resolution setting is used to generate the PAN and MS images as aforementioned manner without performing the down-sampling with PAN images of 32×32 and MS images of 128×128 resolutions. Due to the lack of ground-truth MS images, we measure the model's performance using the three commonly-used IQA metrics: the spectral distortion index D_λ, the spatial distortion index D_S, and the quality without reference (QNR).

4.3 Comparison with State-of-the-Art Methods

Evaluation on Reduced-Resolution Scene. Table 1 displays the assessment metrics for three datasets, with the red-highlighted values denoting the best results. On three satellite datasets, it is evidently discovered that our technique outperforms other comparison algorithms in all assessment measures. Specifically, on the WorldView-II, GaoFen2, and WorldView-III datasets, our technique improves PSNR by 0.27 dB, 0.28 dB, and 0.16 dB over the second-best findings, respectively. Similar gains may be observed in the other parameters in addition to PSNR. We greatly outperform the most recent deep learning-based algorithms, demonstrating the viability of the suggested approach.

We also compare the visual results to demonstrate the efficacy of our methodology using typical samples from the WorldView-II and GaoFen2 datasets in Fig. 4 and Fig. 5, respectively. The MSE residual between the pan-sharpened findings and the actual data are shown by the images in the last row. Our model

Table 1. Quantitative comparison. The best values are highlighted by the red bold. The up or down arrow indicates higher or lower metric corresponding to better images.

Method	Worldview II				GaoFen2				Worldview III			
	PSNR↑	SSIM↑	SAM↓	ERGAS↓	PSNR↑	SSIM↑	SAM↓	EGAS↓	PSNR↑	SSIM↑	SAM↓	EGAS↓
SFIM	34.1297	0.8975	0.0439	2.3449	36.9060	0.8882	0.0318	1.7398	21.8212	0.5457	0.1208	8.9730
Brovey	35.8646	0.9216	0.0403	1.8238	37.7974	0.9026	0.0218	1.372	22.5060	0.5466	0.1159	8.2331
GS	35.6376	0.9176	0.0423	1.8774	37.2260	0.9034	0.0309	1.6736	22.5608	0.5470	0.1217	8.2433
IHS	35.2962	0.9027	0.0461	2.0278	38.1754	0.9100	0.0243	1.5336	22.5579	0.5354	0.1266	8.3616
GFPCA	34.5581	0.9038	0.0488	2.1411	37.9443	0.9204	0.0314	1.5604	22.3344	0.4826	0.1294	8.3964
PNN	40.7550	0.9624	0.0259	1.0646	43.1208	0.9704	0.0172	0.8528	29.9418	0.9121	0.0824	3.3206
PANNET	40.8176	0.9626	0.0257	1.0557	43.0659	0.9685	0.0178	0.8577	29.6840	0.9072	0.0851	3.4263
MSDCNN	41.3355	0.9664	0.0242	0.9940	45.6874	0.9827	0.0135	0.6389	30.3038	0.9184	0.0782	3.1884
SRPPNN	41.4538	0.9679	0.0233	0.9899	47.1998	0.9877	0.0106	0.5586	30.4346	0.9202	0.0770	3.1553
GPPNN	41.1622	0.9684	0.0244	1.0315	44.2145	0.9815	0.0137	0.7361	30.1785	0.9175	0.0776	3.2593
Ours	41.7244	0.9725	0.0220	0.9506	47.4712	0.9901	0.0102	0.5462	30.5971	0.9236	0.0741	3.0798

Table 2. Evaluation on the real-world full-resolution scenes from GaoFen2 dataset. The best results are highlighted in **bold**.

Metrics	SFIM	GS	Brovey	IHS	GFPCA	PNN	PANNET	MSDCNN	SRPPNN	GPPNN	Ours
D_λ ↓	0.0822	0.0696	0.1378	0.0770	0.0914	0.0746	0.0737	0.0734	0.0767	0.0782	**0.0681**
D_s ↓	**0.1087**	0.2456	0.2605	0.2985	0.1635	0.1164	0.1224	0.1151	0.1162	0.1253	0.1119
QNR↑	0.8214	0.7025	0.6390	0.6485	0.7615	0.8191	0.8143	0.8251	0.8173	0.8073	**0.8466**

exhibits very slight spectral and spatial aberrations as compared to other competing techniques. It is obvious to draw from the examination of MSE maps. Regarding the MSE residues, it has been observed that our suggested technique is more accurate than previous comparison methods. We can thus state with confidence that our approach outperforms other competing pan-sharpening methods.

Evaluation on Full-Resolution Scene We apply a pre-trained model created using GaoFen2 data to some unused full-resolution GaoFen2 satellite datasets in order to evaluate the performance of our network in the full resolution situation and the generalizability of the model. Table 2 provides an overview of the experimental findings for all approaches. Table 2 shows that our devised technique performs almost at the top of all the indices, which suggests that it has superior generalization capacity than other conventional and deep learning-based methods.

4.4 Parameter Numbers vs Model Performance

In order to conduct a more in-depth analysis of the methods, we will analyze the complexity of the suggested technique by looking at the number of floating-point operations (FLOPs) and the number of parameters (by 10 million) in Table 3. Compared to other deep learning-based methods, our network achieves the highest performance with the fewer parameters and storage space.

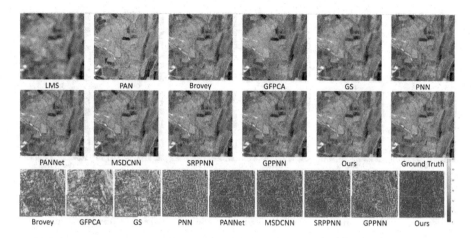

Fig. 4. The visual comparisons between other pan-sharpening methods and our method on WorldView-II satellite.

Table 3. Comparisons of FLOPs (G) and parameters number (M). 'Param' denotes parameters number.

	PNN	PANNET	MSDCNN	SRPPNN	GPPNN	Ours
Param	0.0689	0.0688	0.2390	1.7114	0.1198	0.0871
FLOPs	1.1289	1.1275	3.9158	21.1059	1.3967	1.2558

4.5 Ablation Experiments

We have performed thorough ablation investigations using the WorldView-II satellite dataset of the Pan-sharpening task to examine the contribution of the created modules in our suggested network. The two fundamental designs are, more precisely, the frequency information branch in the core building module and the frequency loss in the optimization function. Additionally, research is done about the quantity of fundamental building modules used in the network. The commonly used IQA measures, such as ERGAS [3], PSNR, SSIM, SCC, Q index, SAM [21], D_λ, D_S, and QNR, are utilized to evaluate all of the experimental data.

The Number of the Core Building Modules. We experiment the suggested network with various numbers of the core building module to examine the influence of the number of the core building modules. Table 4 gives the equivalent quantitative figures K comparison from 1 to 5. It is evident from the findings in Table 4 that as the number of IQAs rises, the model performance has significantly improved at the expense of computation for nearly all of them. Performance and computational complexity were balanced in this work by using the default option of $K = 5$.

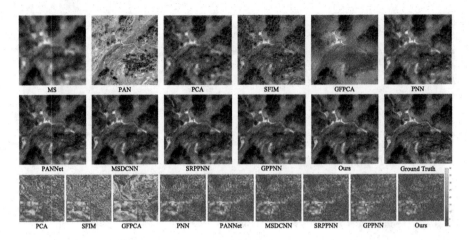

Fig. 5. The visual comparisons between other pan-sharpening methods and our method on GaoFen2 satellite.

Table 4. Average performance comparison on the WorldView-II datasets as the number of SFIB increases. The best performance is shown in red **bold**.

Number (K)	PSNR↑	SSIM ↑	SAM ↓	ERGAS ↓	SCC ↑	Q ↑	D_λ ↓	D_S ↓	QNR ↑
1	41.1343	0.9644	0.0257	1.0218	0.9651	0.7548	0.0639	0.1188	0.8249
2	41.2566	0.9650	0.0249	1.0126	0.9661	0.7554	0.0635	0.1176	0.8264
3	41.4781	0.9677	0.0242	0.9841	0.9696	0.7681	0.0627	0.1170	0.8276
4	41.6287	0.9690	0.0226	0.9527	0.9711	0.7699	0.0618	0.1168	0.8286
5	41.7244	0.9725	0.0220	0.9506	0.9720	0.7751	0.0613	0.1167	0.8290

The Frequency Information Branch. To assess the influence of the frequency information, we merely substitute the spatial information branch in the core building module with the frequency information branch in the first experiment of Table 5. The results in Table 5 show that eliminating it will impair the performance of our network. The global frequency information modeling will be broken if it is deleted, which would worsen the pan-sharpening results.

The Frequency Loss. The newly developed frequency loss intends to clearly highlight the optimization of global frequency information. We erase it in the second trial of Table 5 to test its efficacy. The findings in Table 5 show that deleting it would significantly worsen all metrics, demonstrating its importance to our network.

4.6   Visualization of Feature Maps in Dual Domains

To verify the effect of the designed dual domain information integration mechanism, we deepen into the feature maps of F_{ms}, F_{fre}, F_{spa}, $F_{fre} - F_{spa}$, F_{gl}, F_{fuse}. As illustrated in Sect. 3.3, the frequency feature F_{fre} and the spatial feature F_{spa}

Table 5. Ablation studies comparison on the WorldView-II datasets. The best performance is shown in **bold**.

Config	FSB	FSF	PSNR ↑	SSIM ↑	SAM ↓	ERGAS ↓	SCC ↑	Q ↑	D_λ ↓	D_S ↓	QNR ↑
(I)	✗	✓	41.2664	0.9651	0.0253	1.0117	0.9658	0.7553	0.0633	0.1181	0.8260
(II)	✓	✗	41.6766	0.9698	0.0227	0.9524	0.9747	0.7746	0.0621	0.1174	0.8267
(III)	✓	✓	41.7244	0.9725	0.0220	0.9506	0.9720	0.7751	0.0613	0.1167	0.8290

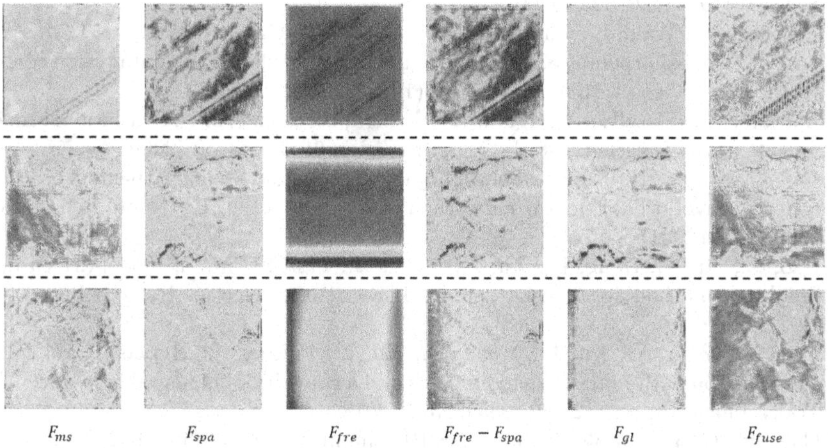

F_{ms} F_{spa} F_{fre} $F_{fre} - F_{spa}$ F_{gl} F_{fuse}

Fig. 6. The Visualization of feature maps in dual domains.

are complementary. In Fig. 6, it is clearly seen that the frequency feature F_{fre} characterizes the global information while the spatial feature F_{spa} focuses on the local content. With integrating them, the response of F_{fuse} is more informative. It demonstrates the powerful capability of the core module.

5 Conclusion

In this paper, we propose a spatial-frequency information integration network for pan-sharpening. To implement the network, we devise a core building module tailored with pan-sharpening to learn the complementary information representation of spatial and frequency domains, thus boosting the model capability. To the best of our knowledge, this is the first attempt to explore the potential solution of pan-sharpening in both spatial-frequency domain. Extensive experiments demonstrate that the proposed network performs favorably against state-of-the-art methods while generalizing well to real-world full-resolution scenes.

Acknowledgements. This work was supported by the Anhui Provincial Natural Science Foundation under Grant 2108085UD12. We acknowledge the support of GPU cluster built by MCC Lab of Information Science and Technology Institution, USTC.

References

1. Addesso, P., Vivone, G., Restaino, R., Chanussot, J.: A data-driven model-based regression applied to panchromatic sharpening. IEEE Trans. Image Process. **29**, 7779–7794 (2020)
2. Aiazzi, B., Baronti, S., Selva, M.: Improving component substitution pansharpening through multivariate regression of ms + pan data. IEEE Trans. Geosci. Remote Sens. **45**(10), 3230–3239 (2007)
3. Alparone, L., Wald, L., Chanussot, J., Thomas, C., Gamba, P., Bruce, L.M.: Comparison of pansharpening algorithms: Outcome of the 2006 grs-s data fusion contest. IEEE Trans. Geosci. Remote Sens. **45**(10), 3012–3021 (2007)
4. Ballester, C., Caselles, V., Igual, L., Verdera, J., Rougé, B.: A variational model for p+ xs image fusion. Int. J. Comput. Vision **69**(1), 43–58 (2006)
5. Cai, J., Huang, B.: Super-resolution-guided progressive pansharpening based on a deep convolutional neural network. IEEE Trans. Geosci. Remote Sens. **59**(6), 5206–5220 (2021)
6. Cao, X., Fu, X., Hong, D., Xu, Z., Meng, D.: PanCSC-net: a model-driven deep unfolding method for pansharpening. IEEE Trans. Geosci. Remote Sens. 1–13 (2021)
7. Cao, X., Zhou, F., Xu, L., Meng, D., Xu, Z., Paisley, J.: Hyperspectral image classification with Markov random fields and a convolutional neural network. IEEE Trans. Image Process. **27**(5), 2354–2367 (2018)
8. Chen, C., Li, Y., Liu, W., Huang, J.: SIRF: simultaneous satellite image registration and fusion in a unified framework. IEEE Trans. Image Process. **24**(11), 4213–4224 (2015)
9. Dong, C., Loy, C.C., He, K., Tang, X.: Image super-resolution using deep convolutional networks. IEEE Trans. Pattern Anal. Mach. Intell. **38**(2), 295–307 (2016)
10. Frigo, M., Johnson, S.G.: FFTW: an adaptive software architecture for the FFT. In: 1988 International Conference on Acoustics, Speech, and Signal Processing. ICASSP-88, vol. 3 (1998)
11. Fu, X., Lin, Z., Huang, Y., Ding, X.: A variational pan-sharpening with local gradient constraints. In: Proceedings of the IEEE/CVF Conference on Computer Vision and Pattern Recognition, pp. 10265–10274 (2019)
12. Fu, X., Wang, W., Huang, Y., Ding, X., Paisley, J.: Deep multiscale detail networks for multiband spectral image sharpening. IEEE Trans. Neural Netw. Learn. Syst. **32**(5), 2090–2104 (2021)
13. Fu, Y., Liang, Z., You, S.: Bidirectional 3D quasi-recurrent neural network for hyperspectral image super-resolution. IEEE J. Sel. Topics Appl. Earth Observ. Remote Sens. **14**, 2674–2688 (2021)
14. Fuoli, D., Gool, L.V., Timofte, R.: Fourier space losses for efficient perceptual image super-resolution (2021)
15. Ghahremani, M., Ghassemian, H.: Nonlinear IHS: a promising method for pan-sharpening. IEEE Geosci. Remote Sens. Lett. **13**(11), 1606–1610 (2016)
16. Gillespie, A.R., Kahle, A.B., Walker, R.E.: Color enhancement of highly correlated images. ii. channel ratio and "chromaticity" transformation techniques - sciencedirect. Remote Sens. Environ. **22**(3), 343–365 (1987)
17. Haut, J.M., Paoletti, M.E., Plaza, J., Li, J., Plaza, A.: Active learning with convolutional neural networks for hyperspectral image classification using a new Bayesian approach. IEEE Trans. Geosci. Remote Sens. **56**(11), 6440–6461 (2018)

18. Haydn, R., Dalke, G.W., Henkel, J., Bare, J.E.: Application of the IHS color trans-form to the processing of multisensor data and image enhancement. Natl. Acad. Sci. USA **79**(13), 571–577 (1982)
19. He, K., Zhang, X., Ren, S., Sun, J.: Deep residual learning for image recognition. In: IEEE Conference on Computer Vision and Pattern Recognition, pp. 770–778 (2016)
20. He, K., Zhang, X., Ren, S., Sun, J.: Deep residual learning for image recognition. In: 2016 IEEE Conference on Computer Vision and Pattern Recognition (CVPR), pp. 770–778 (2016)
21. J. R. H. Yuhas, A.F.G., Boardman, J.M.: Discrimination among semi-arid land-scape endmembers using the spectral angle mapper (SAM) algorithm. In: Pro-ceedings of Summaries Annual JPL Airborne Geoscience Workshop, pp. 147–149 (1992)
22. Jiang, J., Ma, J., Liu, X.: Multilayer spectral-spatial graphs for label noisy robust hyperspectral image classification. IEEE Trans. Neural Netw. Learn. Syst. 1–14 (2020)
23. Jiang, J., Ma, J., Wang, Z., Chen, C., Liu, X.: Hyperspectral image classification in the presence of noisy labels. IEEE Trans. Geosci. Remote Sens. **57**(2), 851–865 (2019)
24. Jiang, J., Sun, H., Liu, X., Ma, J.: Learning spatial-spectral prior for super-resolution of hyperspectral imagery. IEEE Trans. Comput. Imaging **6**, 1082–1096 (2020)
25. Jiang, K., Wang, Z., Yi, P., Jiang, J.: A progressively enhanced network for video satellite imagery superresolution. IEEE Sig. Process. Lett. **25**(11), 1630–1634 (2018)
26. Jiang, K., et al.: GAN-based multi-level mapping network for satellite imagery super-resolution. In: 2019 IEEE International Conference on Multimedia and Expo (ICME), pp. 526–531 (2019)
27. Khan, M.M., Chanussot, J., Condat, L., Montanvert, A.: Indusion: fusion of mul-tispectral and panchromatic images using the induction scaling technique. IEEE Geosci. Remote Sens. Lett. **5**(1), 98–102 (2008)
28. Kwarteng, P., Chavez, A.: Extracting spectral contrast in Landsat thematic map-per image data using selective principal component analysis. Photogramm. Eng. Remote. Sens. **55**(339–348), 1 (1989)
29. Laben, C., Brower, B.: Process for enhancing the spatial resolution of multispectral imagery using pan-sharpening. US Patent 6011875A (2000)
30. Laben, C.A., Brower, B.V.: Process for enhancing the spatial resolution of multi-spectral imagery using pan-sharpening. US Patent 6,011,875 (2000)
31. Liao, W., Xin, H., Coillie, F.V., Thoonen, G., Philips, W.: Two-stage fusion of thermal hyperspectral and visible RGB image by PCA and guided filter. In: Work-shop on Hyperspectral Image and Signal Processing: Evolution in Remote Sensing (2017)
32. Liu., J.G.: Smoothing filter-based intensity modulation: a spectral preserve image fusion technique for improving spatial details. Int. J. Remote Sens. **21**(18), 3461–3472 (2000)
33. Lu, X., Zhang, J., Yang, D., Xu, L., Jia, F.: Cascaded convolutional neural network-based hyperspectral image resolution enhancement via an auxiliary panchromatic image. IEEE Trans. Image Process. **30**, 6815–6828 (2021)
34. Ma, J., Xu, H., Jiang, J., Mei, X., Zhang, X.P.: DDCGAN: a dual-discriminator conditional generative adversarial network for multi-resolution image fusion. IEEE Trans. Image Process. **29**, 4980–4995 (2020)

35. Ma, J., Yu, W., Chen, C., Liang, P., Guo, X., Jiang, J.: Pan-GAN: an unsupervised pan-sharpening method for remote sensing image fusion. Inf. Fusion **62**, 110–120 (2020)
36. Masi, G., Cozzolino, D., Verdoliva, L., Scarpa, G.: Pansharpening by convolutional neural networks. Remote Sens. **8**(7) (2016)
37. Shah, V.P., Younan, N.H., King, R.L.: An efficient pan-sharpening method via a combined adaptive PCA approach and contourlets. IEEE Trans. Geosci. Remote Sens. **46**(5), 1323–1335 (2008)
38. Tian, X., Chen, Y., Yang, C., Gao, X., Ma, J.: A variational pansharpening method based on gradient sparse representation. IEEE Sig. Process. Lett. **27**, 1180–1184 (2020)
39. Tian, X., Chen, Y., Yang, C., Ma, J.: Variational pansharpening by exploiting cartoon-texture similarities. IEEE Trans. Geosci. Remote Sens. 1–16 (2021)
40. Tian, X., Li, K., Wang, Z., Ma, J.: VP-Net: an interpretable deep network for variational pansharpening. IEEE Trans. Geosci. Remote Sens. 1–16 (2021)
41. Vivone, G., et al.: A critical comparison among pansharpening algorithms. IEEE Trans. Geosci. Remote Sens. **53**(5), 2565–2586 (2014)
42. Wald, L., Ranchin, T., Mangolini, M.: Fusion of satellite images of different spatial resolutions: assessing the quality of resulting images. Photogram. Eng. Remote Sens. **63**, 691–699 (1997)
43. Wang, X., Ma, J., Jiang, J.: Hyperspectral image super-resolution via recurrent feedback embedding and spatial-spectral consistency regularization. IEEE Trans. Geosci. Remote Sens. 1–13 (2021)
44. Wu, X., Huang, T.Z., Deng, L.J., Zhang, T.J.: Dynamic cross feature fusion for remote sensing pansharpening. In: Proceedings of the IEEE/CVF International Conference on Computer Vision (ICCV), pp. 14687–14696, October 2021
45. Wu, Z.C., Huang, T.Z., Deng, L.J., Hu, J.F., Vivone, G.: Vo+net: an adaptive approach using variational optimization and deep learning for panchromatic sharpening. IEEE Trans. Geosci. Remote Sens. 1–16 (2021)
46. Xu, H., Ma, J., Shao, Z., Zhang, H., Jiang, J., Guo, X.: SDPNet: a deep network for pan-sharpening with enhanced information representation. IEEE Trans. Geosci. Remote Sens. **59**(5), 4120–4134 (2021)
47. Xu, S., Zhang, J., Zhao, Z., Sun, K., Liu, J., Zhang, C.: Deep gradient projection networks for pan-sharpening. In: IEEE Conference on Computer Vision and Pattern Recognition, pp. 1366–1375, June 2021
48. Yan, K., Zhou, M., Liu, L., Xie, C., Hong, D.: When pansharpening meets graph convolution network and knowledge distillation. IEEE Trans. Geosci. Remote Sens. **60**, 1–15 (2022). https://doi.org/10.1109/TGRS.2022.3168192
49. Yang, G., Zhou, M., Yan, K., Liu, A., Fu, X., Wang, F.: Memory-augmented deep conditional unfolding network for pan-sharpening. In: Proceedings of the IEEE/CVF Conference on Computer Vision and Pattern Recognition (CVPR), pp. 1788–1797, June 2022
50. Yang, J., Fu, X., Hu, Y., Huang, Y., Ding, X., Paisley, J.: PanNet: a deep network architecture for pan-sharpening. In: IEEE International Conference on Computer Vision, pp. 5449–5457 (2017)
51. Yuan, Q., Wei, Y., Meng, X., Shen, H., Zhang, L.: A multiscale and multidepth convolutional neural network for remote sensing imagery pan-sharpening. IEEE J. Sel. Topics Appl. Earth Observ. Remote Sens. **11**(3), 978–989 (2018)
52. Zhang, H., Ma, J.: GTP-PNet: a residual learning network based on gradient transformation prior for pansharpening. ISPRS J. Photogramm. Remote Sens. **172**, 223–239 (2021)

53. Zhou, M., Fu, X., Huang, J., Zhao, F., Liu, A., Wang, R.: Effective pan-sharpening with transformer and invertible neural network. IEEE Trans. Geosci. Remote Sens. **60**, 1–15 (2022). https://doi.org/10.1109/TGRS.2021.3137967

54. Zhou, M., Huang, J., Fang, Y., Fu, X., Liu, A.: Pan-Sharpening with Customized Transformer and Invertible Neural Network. AAAI Press, Palo Alto (2022)

55. Zhou, M., Xiao, Z., Fu, X., Liu, A., Yang, G., Xiong, Z.: Unfolding Taylor's approximations for image restoration. In: NeurIPS (2021)

56. Zhou, M., Yan, K., Huang, J., Yang, Z., Fu, X., Zhao, F.: Mutual information-driven pan-sharpening. In: Proceedings of the IEEE/CVF Conference on Computer Vision and Pattern Recognition (CVPR), pp. 1798–1808 (June 2022)

57. Zhou, M., Yan, K., Pan, J., Ren, W., Xie, Q., Cao, X.: Memory-augmented deep unfolding network for guided image super-resolution. arXiv abs/2203.04960 (2022)

Adaptive Patch Exiting for Scalable Single Image Super-Resolution

Shizun Wang[1], Jiaming Liu[2,4], Kaixin Chen[1], Xiaoqi Li[2,4],
Ming Lu[3(✉)], and Yandong Guo[4]

[1] Beijing University of Posts and Telecommunications, Beijing, China
wangshizun@bupt.edu.cn
[2] Peking University, Beijing, China
[3] Intel Labs China, Beijing, China
lu199192@gmail.com
[4] OPPO Research Institute, Shanghai, China

Abstract. Since the future of computing is heterogeneous, scalability is a crucial problem for single image super-resolution. Recent works try to train one network, which can be deployed on platforms with different capacities. However, they rely on the pixel-wise sparse convolution, which is not hardware-friendly and achieves limited practical speedup. As image can be divided into patches, which have various restoration difficulties, we present a scalable method based on Adaptive Patch Exiting (APE) to achieve more practical speedup. Specifically, we propose to train a regressor to predict the incremental capacity of each layer for the patch. Once the incremental capacity is below the threshold, the patch can exit at the specific layer. Our method can easily adjust the trade-off between performance and efficiency by changing the threshold of incremental capacity. Furthermore, we propose a novel strategy to enable the network training of our method. We conduct extensive experiments across various backbones, datasets and scaling factors to demonstrate the advantages of our method. Code is available at https://github.com/littlepure2333/APE.

Keywords: Single image super-resolution · Scalability · Efficiency

1 Introduction

Super-Resolution (SR) is an important technique and has been widely used in video compression [8], rendering acceleration [20], network streaming [23], medical imaging [18], computational photography [19] and so on. As the development of Deep Neural Networks (DNNs), plenty of DNN-based methods are proposed for Single Image Super-Resolution (SISR) [4,9,13,14,16,27,28]. Existing methods mostly cascade convolutional layers many times to construct deep networks

---

S. Wang and J. Liu—Equal Contribution.

Supplementary Information The online version contains supplementary material available at https://doi.org/10.1007/978-3-031-19797-0_17.

and adopt the pixel-shuffle layer [16] to obtain high-resolution output. The cascaded layers increase the network's capacity of modeling contextual information over larger image regions. Although significant improvements have been made in performance or efficiency over the past few years, the trade-off between performance and efficiency is still under-explored to the best of our knowledge.

Since there are various hardware platforms like CPUs, GPUs, FPGAs and so on, training one scalable network that can be deployed on platforms with different capacities is strongly demanded for future heterogeneous computing. Recently, a pixel-wise adaptive inference method for scalable SISR has been proposed [15]. It learns a predictor to generate the pixel-wise depth map that indicates the target number of layers for each pixel. Sparse convolution guided by the pixel-wise depth map is implemented to achieve speedup. The scalability of [15] is realized by changing the mean average of layers for all pixels. However, although [15] can obtain theoretical FLOPs reduction, the practical speedup is limited since the pixel-wise sparse convolution is not hardware-friendly. Inspired by the fact that image can be divided into patches, which have various restoration difficulties, [10] proposes a general framework that applies appropriate networks to different patches. A module is learned to classify the patches into various restoration difficulties. They train several models with different capacities to super-resolve patches with different difficulties. Although [10] can save up to 50% FLOPS on benchmarking datasets, we observe it has two limitations. Firstly, it applies one fixed network to a certain restoration difficulty, which cannot adjust the trade-off between performance and efficiency as [15]. Secondly, it needs to store one network for each restoration difficulty, heavily increasing the model size.

To solve the above limitations, we present a scalable method based on Adaptive Patch Exiting (APE) for SISR. Our method can train one network to adaptively super-resolve patches with different difficulties. To be more specific, we train a regressor to predict the incremental capacity of each layer for the input patch. The incremental capacity can evaluate the necessity of each layer. Once the incremental capacity is below a threshold, the patch can exit at the specific layer. Our method can easily adjust the trade-off between performance and efficiency by changing the threshold of incremental capacity. On platforms with high computational resources, our method can lower the threshold to utilize more layers for super-resolution. On platforms with low computational resources, our method can raise the threshold to make the patches exit earlier. Therefore, our method is scalable over platforms with different computational resources. Compared with [10], which classifies the patches into certain restoration difficulties, our method enables the scalability by adjusting the threshold. In addition, our method only needs to store one network for all restoration difficulties, significantly reducing the model size.

In order to enable the network training, we further propose a strategy that can jointly train the regressor and SR network. Our strategy first train the multi-exit SR network based on the original network, then we calculate the target incremental capacity of each layer based on the multi-exit SR network. Finally, we jointly train the SR network and regressor to converge.

Our contributions can be concluded as follows:

- We present a novel scalable method for SISR based on adaptive patch exiting, which can be deployed on platforms with different capacities.
- We propose to learn the incremental capacity of each layer instead of patch difficulty, enabling the patch to exit at the optimal layer.
- We introduce an effective joint training strategy to enable the training of incremental capacity regressor and SR network.
- We conduct detailed experiments across various SR backbones and scaling factors to demonstrate the advantages of our method over existing approaches.

2 Related Work

Single Image Super-Resolution. Since the seminal work SRCNN [4], which first applies DNN to SISR, many methods have been proposed. For example, VDSR [9] adopts a very deep neural network to learn the image residual. EDSR [14] analyzes the DNN layers and proposes to remove some redundant layers from SRResNet [11]. RDN [29] uses dense connections that fully utilize the information of preceding layers. RCAN [28] explores the attention mechanism and proposes attentive DNNs to boost the performance. In order to reduce the computational cost, FSRCNN [5] and ESPCN [16] propose to use LR image as input and upscale the feature map at the end of networks. LAPAR [12] presents a method based on linearly-assembled pixel-adaptive regression network, which learns the pixel-wise filter kernel. In addition to methods focusing on network design, many works study the real-world SR problem. RealSR [3] builds a real-world dataset with paired LR-HR images captured by adjusting the focal length. They also present a Laplacian pyramid-based kernel prediction network to recover the HR image. Zero-Shot SR [17] exploits the power of DNN without relying on prior training. They train a small image-specific DNN at test time on examples extracted from the input image itself. Recently, the community also shows the trend of applying techniques like network pruning, quantization, distillation, AutoML to SR. BSRN [21] designs a bit-accumulation mechanism to approximate the full-precision convolution with a value accumulation scheme. Although plenty of DNN-based methods are proposed to improve the performance or efficiency, the scalability problem is still under-explored to the best of our knowledge.

Adaptive Inference. Since the future of computing is heterogeneous, training one scalable network that can be deployed on platforms with different capacities is a very important problem. [26] proposes a simple method that trains a single network executable at different widths, enabling instant and adaptive performance-efficiency trade-off at runtime. [25] further extends the slimmable networks [26] from a predefined widths set to arbitrary width, and generalizes to networks both with and without batch normalization layers. [24] presents a method that trains a single slimmable network to approximate the network performance of different channel configurations, and then searches the optimized channel configurations under different resource constraints. Instead of switching network width, [7] investigates the option that achieves instant and flexible deployment by adaptive bit-widths of weights and activations in the model. [22] trains a set of sub-networks with different widths using different input resolutions to mutually learn multi-scale representations for each sub-network. The performance-efficiency trade-off can be achieved by changing both the network width and input resolution. [2] proposes to train a once-for-all network that supports diverse platforms by decoupling training and search. They can quickly get a specialized sub-network by selecting from the once-for-all network without additional training. Although plenty of methods are proposed for adaptive inference, they mainly focus on high-level vision tasks. The scalability problem of low-level vision tasks is still under-explored as far as we know. Inspired by the fact that different image regions have different restoration difficulties, [15] introduces a lightweight adapter module, which takes image features and resource constraints as input and predicts a pixel-wise depth map. Therefore, only a fraction of the layers in the backbone is performed at a given position according to the predicted depth. While [15] can achieve theoretical FLOPS reduction, the practical speed gain is limited since unstructured sparse convolution is not hardware friendly. [10] also utilizes the properties of different image regions by dividing the images into local patches. They train a module to classify the patches into different difficulties, and apply appropriate model to each difficulty. Although [10] can obtain practical speed gains, it is not scalable under different resource constraints.

3   Method

To apply Adaptive Patch Exiting (APE) to existing SR networks, we modify the original SR networks to multi-exit networks and present the training strategy in Sect. 3.1. We then analyze the performance of each patch at a certain layer, and introduce the incremental capacity to evaluate the necessity of each layer for a patch in Sect. 3.2. Finally, we jointly train the SR network and lightweight regressor in Sect. 3.3. The regressor is used to estimate the incremental capacity at a certain layer. The trained network can achieve the trade-off between performance and efficiency by adjusting the threshold of incremental capacity. The overall pipeline is illustrated in Fig. 1.

3.1   Training Multi-exit SR Networks

Super-resolution aims to recover a High-Resolution (HR) image $\hat{y}$ from a given Low-Resolution (LR) image x. Since the pioneering work [4], most of the SR networks consist of three parts: head, body and tail. The head part H extracts the features f_0 from the LR image:

$$f_0 = H(x; \Theta_h) \qquad (1)$$

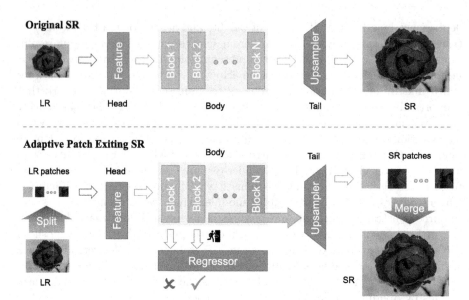

Fig. 1. The pipeline of Adaptive Patch Exiting (APE). Original SR networks take a LR image as input, and forward it through head, body and tail to generate the SR image. Instead, APE first splits the LR image into patches, which are forwarded in parallel. The patches will exit early if the incremental capacity estimated by the regressor is below a given threshold. Finally, the SR patches are merged to the output image.

and the body part B enhances f_0 by cascading N convolutional layers to generate feature f_N:

$$f_N = B(f_0; \Theta_b) \tag{2}$$

Finally, the tail part T takes the enhanced feature f_N to obtain the SR output $\hat{y}$:

$$\hat{y} = T(f_N; \Theta_t) \tag{3}$$

where Θ_h, Θ_b and Θ_t denote the parameters of head, body and tail individually. Typical SISR architectures such as EDSR [14], RCAN [28], VDSR [9] and ECBSR [27] all follow this pipeline. We denote the original SR network as F:

$$\hat{y} = F(x; \Theta_h, \Theta_b, \Theta_t) = T(B(H(x; \Theta_h); \Theta_b); \Theta_t) \tag{4}$$

Without any change to head and tail, we can simply modify the number of repeated layers in the body to change the network capacity. We extract the intermediate feature f_i of the body, where $i \in [1, N]$, to generate the early-exit output:

$$\widehat{y_i} = T(f_i; \Theta_t) \tag{5}$$

The original SR network uses the last layer's feature f_N to generate the output. As the intermediate features of body have the same resolution as last layer's feature, we construct the multi-exit SR network by exit early in the intermediate layers. Different exits require different computational resources. We initialize the multi-exit SR network with the pre-trained model, and all exits' L1 losses are summed up as the multi-exit SR network's reconstruction loss L_m:

$$L_m = \sum_{i=1}^{N} |\hat{y}_i - y| \tag{6}$$

where y represents the HR image and N is the total number of layers. The training details are identical to the setup described in Sect. 4.1.

3.2   Estimating Incremental Capacity

In order to make the multi-exit SR networks scalable, we need to design the signal of early-exit at a certain layer. Therefore, we train a 32-exit EDSR on DIV2K, and randomly sample 32 × 32 LR patches to observe their layer-wise performances. The result is shown in Fig. 2a. A naive method of adaptive inference is to exit early when the performance is exceeding a threshold. However, we observe that there are three types of patches. The first one is named as bottleneck patches, which can achieve satisfying performance with a few layers as shown in Fig. 2b. The second one is called growing patches, which need more layers to achieve good performance as shown in Fig. 2c. The third one is called over-fitting patches as shown in Fig. 2d, which might even achieve worse performance with more layers. In addition, the intervals of these three types are also quite different. The above observation shows that the signal of early-exit should be released when the performance gets saturated, rather than when the performance exceeding a threshold.

We define the early-exit signal I_i as the incremental capacity of ith layer, which measures the performance difference between current layer and previous layer:

$$I_i = \sigma(P_i - P_{i-1}) \tag{7}$$

where σ is the tanh function, P_i is the reconstruction performance of ith layer. As can be seen, the range of I_i is $[-1, 1]$. Higher incremental capacity means more performance gain when forwarding i^{th} layer. When I_i is close to 0, it means the performance get saturated. When I_i is below 0, it indicates the performance will get worse. In this paper, we use the PSNR between SR image and HR image as the reconstruction performance:

$$P_i = PSNR(\hat{y}_i, y) \tag{8}$$

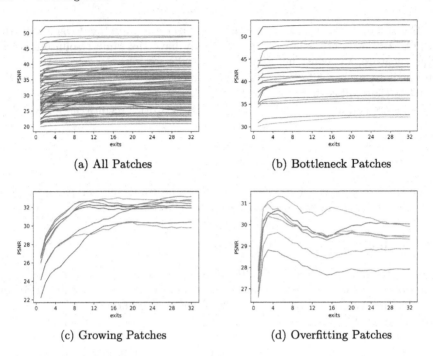

(a) All Patches

(b) Bottleneck Patches

(c) Growing Patches

(d) Overfitting Patches

Fig. 2. Layer-wise PSNR performances of different patches. All patches are of size 32×32 and super-resolved by 32-exit EDSR at $\times 2$ scaling factor. The layer-wise performances of all sampled patches are reported in (a). There are three types of patches according to our observation, which are called bottleneck patches, growing patches, overfitting patches respectively as shown in (b), (c) and (d)

[10] proposes to train a module to classify the patches into different difficulties. However, as we have mentioned above, the relation between network capacity and performance is not monotonic. There are some patches that achieve worse results with more layers. Instead, using the incremental capacity can always correctly measure the saturation of performance and exit at the optimal layer.

During inference, since we cannot get the accurate incremental capacity due to the lack of HR image. Therefore, we propose to train a lightweight regressor R, which takes the feature f_i of each layer in the body as input, to estimate the ith layer's incremental capacity $\hat{I}_i$. All the layers share the same regressor:

$$\hat{I}_i = \sigma(W * g(f_i) + b) \tag{9}$$

The regressor contains a fully-connected layer, where g is global average pooling operation, W and b are the weight and bias of the fully-connected layer. The loss function of the regressor is the L2 loss between $\hat{I}_i$ and ground-truth incremental capacity I_i:

$$L_i = \|\hat{I}_i - I_i\|_2^2 \tag{10}$$

3.3   Jointly Training SR Network and Regressor

To apply APE to a SR network, we train its multi-exit SR network and the regressor jointly. The overall loss consists of all layers' reconstruction loss and the incremental capacity regression loss:

$$L = L_m + \lambda \sum_{i=1}^{N} L_i \tag{11}$$

where λ is a hyper-parameter to balance these two losses, and we set it to 1 for all our experiments. During inference, we split the input image into overlapped patches, and feed all the patches into multi-exit SR network in parallel. Once the incremental capacity of a patch is below a given threshold, the patch can exit early. Increasing the threshold will make patches exit earlier and reduce the computational cost. Finally, the HR patches are merged to obtain the output image.

4   Experiments

4.1   Implementation Details

Training Setup. We use DIV2K dataset [1] to train all the models. The low-resolution images are generated by bicubic downsampling with scaling factors ×2, ×3 and ×4. Following former works, we use the first 800 images as the training set and 10 images (0801–0810) as the validation set. During training, data augmentation including random horizontal flip, random vertical flip and 90° rotation are applied. We train all the models for 300 epochs with learning rate initialed as 1e−4 and decayed to half at 200 epochs. The batch size is 16 and the HR patch size is 192. We use Adam optimizer, where β_1 is set to 0.9 and β_2 is set to 0.999.

Testing Setup. We use DIV2K [1] dataset and DIV8K [6] dataset for testing since the widely-used benchmark datasets are not suitable for large image super-resolution evaluation. Specifically, we choose 100 images (0801–0900) from DIV2K for high-definition (HD) scenario, and 100 images (1401–1500) from DIV8K for ultra high-definition (UHD) scenario. During testing, we first split LR images into patches of size 48 with stride 46 unless otherwise specified. Then the LR patches are super-resolved in parallel, and the parallel size can be tuned to fit the computational resource. Finally, the SR patches are merged to obtain the complete SR images by weighting overlapping areas. The Peak Signal-to-Noise Ratio (PSNR) and Structural Similarity (SSIM) calculated on RGB channels are adopted as the evaluation metrics to measure super-resolution performance. We use FLOPs to evaluate the computational cost and the practical running time is benchmarked on NVIDIA 2080Ti GPUs.

Table 1. Performance evaluation of APE. FLOPs, PSNR and SSIM on DIV2K and DIV8K datasets with scaling factors ×2, ×3, ×4 are reported in the table. To compare the performance of APE with baselines, incremental capacity threshold is set to 0. Therefore, all the patches can exit at the optimal layers.

Method	Scale	DIV2K			DIV8K		
		FLOPS	PSNR	SSIM	FLOPS	PSNR	SSIM
ECBSR	×2	1.38G	33.86 dB	0.9309	1.38G	39.82 dB	0.9649
ECBSR-APE	×2	1.37G	33.87 dB	0.9316	1.37G	39.73 dB	0.9646
VDSR	×2	6.17G	33.63 dB	0.9286	6.17G	39.71 dB	0.9640
VDSR-APE	×2	6.14G	33.62 dB	0.9292	6.15G	39.54 dB	0.9636
RCAN	×2	35.36G	34.09 dB	0.9330	35.36G	40.04 dB	0.9657
RCAN-APE	×2	35.36G	34.36 dB	0.9357	35.36G	40.22 dB	0.9663
EDSR	×2	93.89G	34.21 dB	0.9343	93.89G	39.97 dB	0.9656
EDSR-APE	×2	93.89G	34.46 dB	0.9366	93.89G	40.16 dB	0.9662
ECBSR	×3	1.40G	30.22 dB	0.8606	1.40G	35.36 dB	0.9158
ECBSR-APE	×3	1.40G	30.16 dB	0.8618	1.40G	35.31 dB	0.9159
VDSR	×3	13.88G	29.99 dB	0.8567	13.88G	35.15 dB	0.9133
VDSR-APE	×3	13.88G	29.92 dB	0.8574	13.88G	35.15 dB	0.9138
RCAN	×3	35.80G	30.45 dB	0.8645	35.80G	35.44 dB	0.9171
RCAN-APE	×3	35.74G	30.59 dB	0.8695	35.76G	35.65 dB	0.9192
EDSR	×3	100.77G	30.55 dB	0.8669	100.77G	35.54 dB	0.9178
EDSR-APE	×3	100.77G	30.66 dB	0.8711	100.77G	35.68 dB	0.9197
ECBSR	×4	1.43G	28.29 dB	0.8026	1.43G	33.07 dB	0.8724
ECBSR-APE	×4	1.43G	28.31 dB	0.8036	1.43G	33.05 dB	0.8719
VDSR	×4	24.68G	28.12 dB	0.7974	24.68G	32.88 dB	0.8688
VDSR-APE	×4	24.53G	28.10 dB	0.7991	24.53G	32.83 dB	0.8689
RCAN	×4	36.77G	28.52 dB	0.8077	36.77G	33.25 dB	0.8753
RCAN-APE	×4	36.71G	28.70 dB	0.8138	36.74G	33.38 dB	0.8776
EDSR	×4	115.83G	28.66 dB	0.8112	115.83G	33.30 dB	0.8762
EDSR-APE	×4	115.79G	28.78 dB	0.8158	115.81G	33.39 dB	0.8779

4.2 Evaluation of APE

Performance Results. To evaluate the effectiveness of our method, we apply APE to state-of-the-art SR networks, including ECBSR [27], VDSR [9], EDSR [14] and RCAN [28]. We set the threshold of incremental capacity to 0 and evaluate the performance of APE on DIV2K and DIV8K. As we have mentioned above, there are three types of patches. The over-fitting patches might achieve worse performance with more layers. Therefore, setting the threshold to 0 enables all the patches to exit at the optimal layers. As shown in Table 1, SR networks with APE can achieve comparable or even superior performance compared to original SR networks in terms of PSNR and SSIM. This comparison demonstrates that incremental capacity is a more reasonable metric to evaluate the contribution of each layer.

Table 2. Efficiency evaluation of APE under the same performance as original SR networks. Parameters, body FLOPs, total FLOPs, and practical inference times on DIV2K with scaling factors ×2, ×3, ×4 are reported in the table. Inference time is evaluated on NVIDIA 2080Ti GPUs.

Method	Scale	Param.	PSNR	Body FLOPs	Total FLOPs	Time (ms)
ECBSR	×2	1.0K	33.86 dB	1.36G	1.38G (100%)	244
ECBSR-APE	×2	1.0K	33.82 dB	0.99G	1.01G (73%)	211
VDSR	×2	0.67M	33.63 dB	6.14G	6.17G (100%)	346
VDSR-APE	×2	0.67M	33.61 dB	4.13G	4.16G (67%)	334
RCAN	×2	15.4M	34.09 dB	34.91G	35.36G (100%)	2323
RCAN-APE	×2	15.4M	34.09 dB	8.26G	8.71G (24%)	974
EDSR	×2	40.7M	34.21 dB	87.01G	93.89G (100%)	2133
EDSR-APE	×2	40.7M	34.21 dB	34.07G	40.95G (43%)	733
ECBSR	×3	1.0K	30.21 dB	1.36G	1.40G (100%)	239
ECBSR-APE	×3	1.0K	30.12 dB	1.01G	1.05G (74%)	219
VDSR	×3	0.67M	29.99 dB	13.80G	13.88G (100%)	346
VDSR-APE	×3	0.67M	29.91 dB	11.01G	11.09G (79%)	325
RCAN	×3	15.6M	30.45 dB	34.91G	35.80G (100%)	1040
RCAN-APE	×3	15.6M	30.45 dB	13.57G	14.46G (40%)	627
EDSR	×3	43.7M	30.55 dB	87.01G	100.77G (100%)	1777
EDSR-APE	×3	43.7M	30.55 dB	49.28G	63.04G (62%)	492
ECBSR	×4	1.0K	28.29 dB	1.36G	1.43G (100%)	245
ECBSR-APE	×4	1.0K	28.22 dB	0.85G	0.92G (64%)	196
VDSR	×4	0.67M	28.12 dB	24.55G	24.68G (100%)	345
VDSR-APE	×4	0.67M	28.07 dB	17.75G	17.88G (72%)	303
RCAN	×4	15.6M	28.53 dB	34.91G	36.77G (100%)	620
RCAN-APE	×4	15.6M	28.53 dB	10.53G	12.39G (33%)	350
EDSR	×4	43.1M	28.66 dB	87.01G	115.83G (100%)	1123
EDSR-APE	×4	43.1M	28.67 dB	49.86G	78.68G (67%)	419

Efficiency Results. As for the efficiency of APE, Table 2 shows the detailed computational cost under same performance as original SR networks. Our method adds a lightweight regressor whose FLOPs is negligible. APE can significantly reduce the computational cost of original SR networks across different scaling factors. For example, RCAN-APE only needs 24%, 40%, and 33% of original computational cost on scaling factors ×2, ×3 and ×4. The computational cost of body is significantly reduced by our method, and the computational costs of head and tail stay the same. Overall, our method can nearly halve the computational cost under the same performance.

Scalability Results. We also show the performance-efficiency trade-off results in Fig. 3 to demonstrate the scalability of APE. By controlling the incremental capacity threshold, APE can achieve scalable performance-efficiency trade-off.

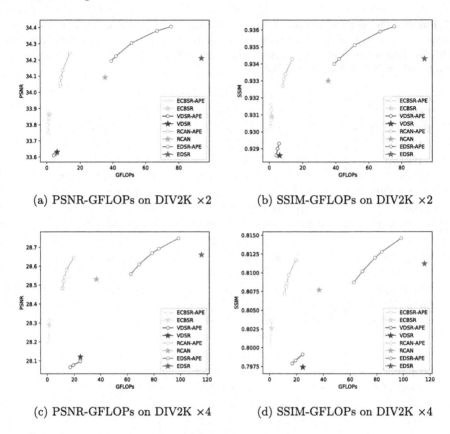

(a) PSNR-GFLOPs on DIV2K ×2   (b) SSIM-GFLOPs on DIV2K ×2

(c) PSNR-GFLOPs on DIV2K ×4   (d) SSIM-GFLOPs on DIV2K ×4

Fig. 3. Quantitative results of performance-efficiency trade-off. We apply APE to ECBSR, VDSR, EDSR and RCAN with scaling factors ×2 and ×4 on DIV2K dataset. Average FLOPs of all 48 × 48 LR patches and PSNR/SSIM calculated on the full image are reported.

Therefore, we can deploy one APE SR network on platforms with different computational resources. For the device with low computational resource, we can raise the threshold to get lower performance and faster inference speed.

Visual Results. Figure 4 shows the qualitative comparison of our method against the original SR networks. As we can see, EDSR-APE and RCAN-APE can achieve same or even better visual results compared with original SR networks. Although we merge the patches to obtain complete SR images, weighting overlapped patches can avoid the stitching artifacts.

Figure 5 visualizes the status of adaptive exiting patches. As can be seen, most patches in smooth regions exit at the early layers since they are easy to be restored. As for patches in complicated regions, they will exit at the later layers. This is consistent with the motivation of applying appropriate networks to various difficulties.

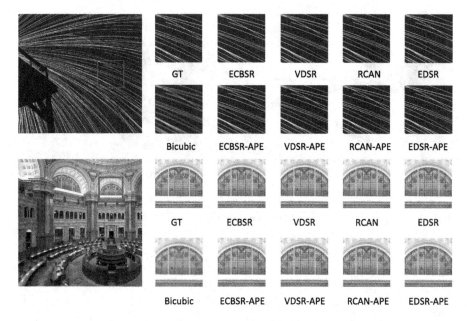

Fig. 4. Qualitative results of APE and original SR networks on DIV2K dataset with ×4 scaling factor.

4.3   Ablation Study

Variants of Exit Interval. We conduct the experiment to study the influence of different exit intervals using EDSR as the backbone. Specifically, EDSR has 32 repeated residual layers in the body. We evaluate the exit intervals of 4, 2 and 1 layers. The results on DIV2K dataset with scaling factors ×2 are shown in Fig. 6. As can be seen, exit interval of 4 layers achieves the best results, indicating that multi-exit SR networks need sufficient learning capacity within each exit.

Variants of Early-Exit Signal. Apart from the proposed incremental capacity (IC), we can also use the absolute performance (AP) of each layer as the early-exit signal to measure the necessity of early-exiting at specific layer. We compare the results of incremental capacity and absolute performance in Fig. 7. As can be seen, compared with absolute performance, incremental capacity can reduce more computational cost, validating that incremental capacity is the better early-exit signal for multi-exit SR networks.

Variants of Patch Size and Stride. Since our method splits an image into patches, we evaluate the performance of different patch sizes and strides. As shown in Table 3, different patch size can achieve similar performance in terms of PSNR and SSIM.

(a) Original image

(b) Adaptive exiting patches

Fig. 5. Visualization of early-exit patches. The number in the patch indicates the exit index of each patch. Best viewed by zooming x4.

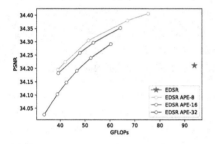

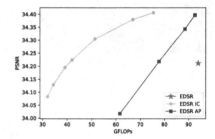

Fig. 6. Variants of exit interval. We show the results of different exit intervals by evaluating EDSR-APE on the DIV2K dataset with scaling factors ×2. APE-n means APE with n exits.

Fig. 7. Variants of early-exit signal. IC denotes incremental capacity, and AP denotes absolute performance. Both are evaluated on DIV2K dataset with ×2 scaling factor.

4.4   Comparison with ClassSR and AdaDSR

We also compare with ClassSR [10] and AdaDSR [15] on DIV2K ×4 using RCAN as the backbone under the same performance in Table 4. We use the published codes of AdaDSR and ClassSR to perform the comparison. ClassSR [10] is a patch-based SR method. It manually designs easy, medium and hard networks by changing the number of channels. A module is trained to classify the patches into easy, medium and hard. ClassSR [10] can reduce the overall computational cost by applying different networks to different patches. However, they need to store all the models with different capacities, heavily increasing the model size. Apart from this, ClassSR classifies the patches into certain restoration difficulties. Therefore, it is not scalable over different computational resources. Instead, our method can easily adjust the trade-off between performance and efficiency to meet different computational resources.

Table 3. Variants of patch size and stride. PSNR and SSIM are evaluated on DIV2K dataset with scaling factor ×4. The numbers in the Patch column indicate (patch size, patch stride).

Method	Patch	PSNR	SSIM
EDSR	–	28.66	0.8112
EDSR-APE	(32, 30)	28.702	0.8136
EDSR-APE	(40, 38)	28.723	0.8151
EDSR-APE	(48, 46)	28.783	0.8158

Table 4. Comparison with AdaDSR and ClassSR, APE achieves fastest inference speed without increasing the model's size. Besides, APE is scalable to different computational resources.

Method	Param	PSNR	Time
RCAN	15.6M	28.526	620 ms
RCAN-APE	15.6M	28.530	350 ms
RCAN-Ada	15.7M	28.535	1644 ms
RCAN-ClassSR	30.1M	28.533	22 s

We also compare with AdaDSR [15], which is based on pixel-wise sparse convolution. It will generate a spatially sparse mask for each layer and sparse convolution is conducted to achieve speedup. However, pixel-wise sparse convolution is not hardware-friendly on modern GPUs, thus there exists a gap between theoretical and practical speedup. As can be seen in Table 4, with similar model size, APE is faster than AdaDSR in practice.

5   Future Work

Although our method can decide the optimal exit for each patch, we still rely on overlapped patches to avoid the stitching artifacts. Therefore, we can further improve the efficiency by adopting non-overlapped patches. Besides, we uniformly split an image into patches, which might not be the optimal solution for image splitting. Finally, applying our method to other low-level vision tasks is also a promising future work.

6   Conclusion

In this paper, we present adaptive patch exiting (APE) for scalable single image super-resolution. Since image patches are structured and have different restoration difficulties, we split an image into patches and train a regressor to predict the incremental capacity of each layer for the input patch. Therefore, the patch can exit at any layer by adjusting the threshold. We also propose a novel joint training strategy to train both the SR network and regressor. Extensive comparisons are conducted across various SR backbones, datasets and scaling factors to demonstrate the effectiveness of our method.

References

1. Agustsson, E., Timofte, R.: Ntire 2017 challenge on single image super-resolution: dataset and study. In: The IEEE Conference on Computer Vision and Pattern Recognition (CVPR) Workshops (2017)

2. Cai, H., Gan, C., Wang, T., Zhang, Z., Han, S.: Once-for-all: train one network and specialize it for efficient deployment. arXiv preprint arXiv:1908.09791 (2019)

3. Cai, J., Zeng, H., Yong, H., Cao, Z., Zhang, L.: Toward real-world single image super-resolution: a new benchmark and a new model. In: Proceedings of the IEEE/CVF International Conference on Computer Vision, pp. 3086–3095 (2019)

4. Dong, C., Loy, C.C., He, K., Tang, X.: Learning a deep convolutional network for image super-resolution. In: Fleet, D., Pajdla, T., Schiele, B., Tuytelaars, T. (eds.) ECCV 2014. LNCS, vol. 8692, pp. 184–199. Springer, Cham (2014). https://doi.org/10.1007/978-3-319-10593-2_13

5. Dong, C., Loy, C.C., Tang, X.: Accelerating the super-resolution convolutional neural network. In: Leibe, B., Matas, J., Sebe, N., Welling, M. (eds.) ECCV 2016. LNCS, vol. 9906, pp. 391–407. Springer, Cham (2016). https://doi.org/10.1007/978-3-319-46475-6_25

6. Gu, S., Lugmayr, A., Danelljan, M., Fritsche, M., Lamour, J., Timofte, R.: DIV8K: diverse 8k resolution image dataset. In: 2019 IEEE/CVF International Conference on Computer Vision Workshop (ICCVW), pp. 3512–3516. IEEE (2019)

7. Jin, Q., Yang, L., Liao, Z.: AdaBits: neural network quantization with adaptive bit-widths. In: Proceedings of the IEEE/CVF Conference on Computer Vision and Pattern Recognition, pp. 2146–2156 (2020)

8. Khani, M., Sivaraman, V., Alizadeh, M.: Efficient video compression via content-adaptive super-resolution. arXiv preprint arXiv:2104.02322 (2021)

9. Kim, J., Kwon Lee, J., Mu Lee, K.: Accurate image super-resolution using very deep convolutional networks. In: Proceedings of the IEEE Conference on Computer Vision and Pattern Recognition, pp. 1646–1654 (2016)

10. Kong, X., Zhao, H., Qiao, Y., Dong, C.: ClassSR: a general framework to accelerate super-resolution networks by data characteristic. In: Proceedings of the IEEE/CVF Conference on Computer Vision and Pattern Recognition, pp. 12016–12025 (2021)

11. Ledig, C., et al.: Photo-realistic single image super-resolution using a generative adversarial network. In: Proceedings of the IEEE Conference on Computer Vision and Pattern Recognition, pp. 4681–4690 (2017)

12. Li, W., Zhou, K., Qi, L., Jiang, N., Lu, J., Jia, J.: LAPAR: linearly-assembled pixel-adaptive regression network for single image super-resolution and beyond. In: Advances in Neural Information Processing Systems, vol. 33 (2020)

13. Li, W., Zhou, K., Qi, L., Jiang, N., Lu, J., Jia, J.: LAPAR: linearly-assembled pixel-adaptive regression network for single image super-resolution and beyond. arXiv preprint arXiv:2105.10422 (2021)

14. Lim, B., Son, S., Kim, H., Nah, S., Mu Lee, K.: Enhanced deep residual networks for single image super-resolution. In: Proceedings of the IEEE Conference on Computer Vision and Pattern Recognition Workshops, pp. 136–144 (2017)

15. Liu, M., Zhang, Z., Hou, L., Zuo, W., Zhang, L.: Deep adaptive inference networks for single image super-resolution. In: Bartoli, A., Fusiello, A. (eds.) ECCV 2020. LNCS, vol. 12538, pp. 131–148. Springer, Cham (2020). https://doi.org/10.1007/978-3-030-66823-5_8

16. Shi, W., et al.: Real-time single image and video super-resolution using an efficient sub-pixel convolutional neural network. In: Proceedings of the IEEE Conference on Computer Vision and Pattern Recognition, pp. 1874–1883 (2016)

17. Shocher, A., Cohen, N., Irani, M.: "Zero-shot" super-resolution using deep internal learning. In: Proceedings of the IEEE Conference on Computer Vision and Pattern Recognition, pp. 3118–3126 (2018)

18. Sui, Y., Afacan, O., Gholipour, A., Warfield, S.K.: Learning a gradient guidance for spatially isotropic MRI super-resolution reconstruction. In: Martel, A.L., et al. (eds.) MICCAI 2020. LNCS, vol. 12262, pp. 136–146. Springer, Cham (2020). https://doi.org/10.1007/978-3-030-59713-9_14

19. Wronski, B., et al.: Handheld multi-frame super-resolution. ACM Trans. Graph. (TOG) **38**(4), 1–18 (2019)

20. Xiao, L., Nouri, S., Chapman, M., Fix, A., Lanman, D., Kaplanyan, A.: Neural supersampling for real-time rendering. ACM Trans. Graph. (TOG) **39**(4), 142–1 (2020)

21. Xin, J., Wang, N., Jiang, X., Li, J., Huang, H., Gao, X.: Binarized neural network for single image super resolution. In: Vedaldi, A., Bischof, H., Brox, T., Frahm, J.-M. (eds.) ECCV 2020. LNCS, vol. 12349, pp. 91–107. Springer, Cham (2020). https://doi.org/10.1007/978-3-030-58548-8_6

22. Yang, T., Zhu, S., Chen, C., Yan, S., Zhang, M., Willis, A.: MutualNet: adaptive ConvNet via mutual learning from network width and resolution. In: Vedaldi, A., Bischof, H., Brox, T., Frahm, J.-M. (eds.) ECCV 2020. LNCS, vol. 12346, pp. 299–315. Springer, Cham (2020). https://doi.org/10.1007/978-3-030-58452-8_18

23. Yeo, H., Chong, C.J., Jung, Y., Ye, J., Han, D.: NEMO: enabling neural-enhanced video streaming on commodity mobile devices. In: Proceedings of the 26th Annual International Conference on Mobile Computing and Networking, pp. 1–14 (2020)

24. Yu, J., Huang, T.: AutoSlim: towards one-shot architecture search for channel numbers. arXiv preprint arXiv:1903.11728 (2019)

25. Yu, J., Huang, T.S.: Universally slimmable networks and improved training techniques. In: Proceedings of the IEEE/CVF International Conference on Computer Vision, pp. 1803–1811 (2019)

26. Yu, J., Yang, L., Xu, N., Yang, J., Huang, T.: Slimmable neural networks. arXiv preprint arXiv:1812.08928 (2018)

27. Zhang, X., Zeng, H., Zhang, L.: Edge-oriented convolution block for real-time super resolution on mobile devices. In: Proceedings of the 29th ACM International Conference on Multimedia, pp. 4034–4043 (2021)

28. Zhang, Y., Li, K., Li, K., Wang, L., Zhong, B., Fu, Y.: Image super-resolution using very deep residual channel attention networks. In: Proceedings of the European conference on computer vision (ECCV), pp. 286–301 (2018)

29. Zhang, Y., Tian, Y., Kong, Y., Zhong, B., Fu, Y.: Residual dense network for image super-resolution. In: Proceedings of the IEEE Conference on Computer Vision and Pattern Recognition, pp. 2472–2481 (2018)

Efficient Meta-Tuning for Content-Aware Neural Video Delivery

Xiaoqi Li[1], Jiaming Liu[1,2], Shizun Wang[3], Cheng Lyu[3],
Ming Lu[4(✉)], Yurong Chen[4], Anbang Yao[4], Yandong Guo[2],
and Shanghang Zhang[1(✉)]

[1] Peking University, Beijing, China
shzhang.pku@gmail.com
[2] OPPO Research Institute, Beijing, China
[3] Beijing University of Posts and Telecommunications, Beijing, China
[4] Intel Labs China, Beijing, China

Abstract. Recently, Deep Neural Networks (DNNs) are utilized to reduce the bandwidth and improve the quality of Internet video delivery. Existing methods train corresponding content-aware super-resolution (SR) model for each video chunk on the server, and stream low-resolution (LR) video chunks along with SR models to the client. Although they achieve promising results, the huge computational cost of network training limits their practical applications. In this paper, we present a method named Efficient Meta-Tuning (EMT) to reduce the computational cost. Instead of training from scratch, EMT adapts a meta-learned model to the first chunk of the input video. As for the following chunks, it fine-tunes the partial parameters selected by gradient masking of previous adapted model. In order to achieve further speedup for EMT, we propose a novel sampling strategy to extract the most challenging patches from video frames. The proposed strategy is highly efficient and brings negligible additional cost. Our method significantly reduces the computational cost and achieves even better performance, paving the way for applying neural video delivery techniques to practical applications. We conduct extensive experiments based on various efficient SR architectures, including ESPCN, SRCNN, FSRCNN and EDSR-1, demonstrating the generalization ability of our work. The code is released at https:// github.com/Neural-video-delivery/EMT-Pytorch-ECCV2022.

Keywords: Neural video delivery · Super-resolution · Meta learning

---

X. Li, J. Liu and S. Wang—Equal contribution.

Supplementary Information The online version contains supplementary material available at https://doi.org/10.1007/978-3-031-19797-0_18.

1   Introduction

With the popularity of High-Definition (HD) display devices, high-resolution videos are strongly demanded by end users. This brings a huge burden to the video delivery infrastructure. As the development of deep learning, several recent works are proposed to reduce the bandwidth of video delivery [13,14,19,29]. The motivation of these works is to stream both the low-resolution videos and content-aware SR models from servers to clients. The clients run the inference of SR models to super-resolve the LR videos. In this manner, high-resolution videos can be delivered under limited Internet bandwidth.

In contrast to existing approaches on Single Image Super-Resolution (SISR) [8,15,18,23,31] and Video Super-Resolution (VSR) [2–4,25], content-aware models utilize the overfitting property of DNNs to achieve higher SR performance. To be more specific, a video is divided into several video chunks, and a corresponding SR model is trained for each chunk. This type of DNN-based video delivery system can achieve better performance even compared with commercial techniques like WebRTC [14].

Although neural video delivery is a promising technique, the huge computational cost of training content-aware SR models limits its practical applications. For example, existing methods [19,29] uniformly divide a 45s/1080P/30FPS video into 5-second chunks, and train the SR models for all chunks. However, even with efficient SR architectures like ESPCN [23], it still takes about 10.2 h to train the content-aware SR models on a high-end NVIDIA V100 GPU. Therefore, reducing the computational cost of network training is crucial for neural video delivery.

In order to pave the way for practical applications, we propose Efficient Meta-Tuning (EMT) in this paper. Instead of training from scratch [19,29], EMT sequentially adapts a meta-learned model to the video chunks, delivering all the content-aware SR models. Compared with random initialization or pre-trained initialization, a meta-learned model can transfer better to different video chunks. We collect a large-scale dataset of diverse video chunks and take each chunk as one specific task. MAML [9] is adopted to train the meta-learned model, whose parameters are shared by all content-aware SR models. For the chunks of the input video, EMT adapts the meta-learned model to the first chunk. As for the following chunks, it can fine-tune the partial parameters of the previous adapted model due to the temporal consistency between neighboring chunks. The partial parameters are selected by gradient masking, which masks a fraction of most significant parameters after a few gradient updates. Since EMT sequentially adapts the meta-learned model, each chunk simply needs to store the selected partial parameters. The current content-aware SR model can be constructed by updating the partial parameters of the previous model. This is important to compress all the models into one shared model and a few private parameters. Compared with CaFM [19], our method is more compact since the meta-learned model is shared by all chunks, while CaFM can only share one model for chunks within the input video.

To further reduce the computational cost, we propose a novel sampling strategy for EMT, which selects the most challenging patches from video frames. Our motivation is that previous adapted SR model already possesses the ability to super-resolve current chunk due to temporal consistency. Therefore, the training efforts of EMT should focus on challenging patches, which cannot be well handled by the previous model. However, performing the evaluation of previous model on all patches of current chunk is time-consuming and brings additional cost. Inspired by video codec, we extract the I-frames from the input video and only perform the evaluation on I-frames. The positions of challenging patches are extracted based on I-frames and propagated to other frames. Since I-frame is very sparse within a video, the computational cost of the evaluation is negligible. On the other side, as the frames between two I-frames are temporally consistent, the propagated positions can extract reasonable patches on the in-between frames. Our sampling strategy is simple yet effective and can further reduce the computational cost of EMT.

Our contributions can be concluded as follows:

- We propose Efficient Meta-Tuning (EMT) for neural video delivery, significantly reducing the cost of training content-aware SR models and achieving even better performance.
- We present a novel challenging patch sampling strategy, which further reduces the cost of EMT. Our strategy improves the convergence of EMT with negligible additional cost.
- We conduct detailed experiments based on various efficient SR architectures to evaluate the advantage and generalization of our method.

2   Related Work

DNN-Based Image Super-Resolution. SRCNN [8] is the first work that introduces DNNs to SR task. Their method consists of three stages, namely feature extraction, non-linear mapping and image reconstruction. With the rapid advance of DNN, plenty of methods are proposed to improve the performance of SISR following the pipeline of SRCNN. For example, VDSR [15] adopts a very deep DNN to predict the image residual instead of HR image. Motivated by ResNet [10], SRResNet [16] introduces Residual Block to the network and improves the SR performance. EDSR [18] modifies the structure of SRResNet by removing the Batch Normalization layer [11], further boosting the SR performance. RCAN [31] introduces the attention mechanism to the networks and presents deeper DNNs for SR. However, RCAN is computationally complicated, which limits its practical usage. To reduce the computational cost, many efficient methods are proposed for SR. ESPCN [23] uses LR image as input and up-samples the feature map by the pixel-shuffle layer to obtain the HR output. LAPAR [17] proposes a method based on linearly-assembled adaptive regression network. All of those methods are external methods, which train one model on large-scale image databases like DIV2K [1] and test on given input images. However, external methods fail to explore the overfitting property of DNNs, which can significantly boost the performance for practical video delivery system.

DNN-Based Video Super-Resolution. Different from image super-resolution, video super-resolution can additionally exploit the neighboring frames for SR. Therefore, temporal alignment plays an essential role and should be thoroughly considered. VESPCN [2] first predicts the motions between neighboring frames, and then performs image warping before feeding neighboring frames into the SR network. However, it is difficult to accurately estimate the optical flow. TOFlow [27] proposes a task-oriented flow designed for specific video processing tasks. They jointly train the motion estimation component and video processing component in a self-supervised manner. DUF [12] solves the problem of accurate explicit motion compensation by training a network to generate dynamic upsampling filters and a residual image. In order to reduce the computational cost of VSR, FRVSR [22] presents a recurrent framework that uses the previous SR result to super-resolve the following frame. Their recurrent framework naturally ensures temporally consistency and reduces the computational cost by warping only one image in each step. All these VSR approaches also belong to external methods that fail to explore the overfitting property of DNN. Apart from this, handling temporal alignment brings huge additional computational and storage costs, which limits their practical applications in resource-limited devices like mobile phone.

Neural Video Delivery. NAS [29] is a promising Internet video delivery framework that integrates DNN for quality enhancement. It can solve the video quality degradation problem under limited Internet bandwidth. NAS can enhance the average Quality of Experience (QoE) by 43.08% using the same bandwidth budget, or saving 17.13% of bandwidth while providing the same user QoE. The main idea is to leverage DNN's overfitting property and use the training accuracy to deliver high SR performance. Many following works are proposed to apply the idea of NAS to different scenarios, like UAV video streaming [26], live streaming [14], 360 video streaming [5,7], volumetric video streaming [30], and mobile video streaming [28], etc. Recent methods [13,19] propose to further reduce the bandwidth budget by sharing most of the parameters over video chunks. Therefore, only a small portion of private parameters are streamed for each video chunk. However, they still need huge computational cost for network training and fail to study the scene conversion for constructing optimal video chunks.

3   Method

3.1   Overview

In this section, we present our method to significantly accelerate the training of content-aware SR models. Our method adapts the meta-learned model to the first chunk of the video, and sequentially adapts partial parameters of the previous model to the following chunks. The partial parameters are selected by gradient masking and the challenging patches are extracted for adaption. The pipeline of our method is illustrated in Fig. 1. We first introduce Efficient Meta-Tuning (EMT) to sequentially deliver the models from a meta-learned model in Sect. 3.2. Then we propose a novel challenging patch sampling strategy to further accelerate EMT in Sect. 3.3.

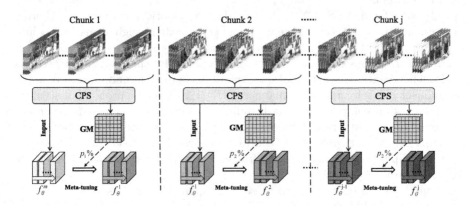

Fig. 1. The pipeline of our method. CPS and GM indicate challenging patch sampling and gradient masking respectively. The selected challenging patches are used to mask the parameters and fine-tune the models.

3.2 Efficient Meta-Tuning

Following former works [19,29], we uniformly divide the input video into chunks, and train the corresponding content-aware SR model for each chunk. [29] proposes to apply deep super-resolution networks to video delivery by training one model for each chunk from scratch. [19] presents a method to compress all the models by one shared model and a few private parameters. However, both methods train the content-aware SR models from scratch, resulting in huge computational cost. Since neighboring chunks are temporally consistent, fine-tuning is much more reasonable compared with training from scratch. Precisely, finding a generic initial model that can not only generalize over diverse video chunks but also adapt rapidly to any specific video chunk, plays a key role in fine-tuning. In order to obtain a better initialization, we adopt MAML [9] to train a meta-learned model. Although MAML has been applied to Zero-Shot SR [21,24] and video frame interpolation [6], it has never been studied in neural video delivery to the best of our knowledge. Compared with random initialization or pretrained initialization, a meta-learned model has better transferability. To obtain the content-aware SR models, we sequentially fine-tune partial parameters of the previous model. In contrast to fine-tuning the whole model, our method can compress the parameters of all models into one shared meta-learned model and a few partial parameters.

Meta-learned Initialization. We take one chunk as a specific task and aim to learn a SR model that can adapt to various chunks. Specifically, we first pretrain the SR model f_θ on DIV2K [1], then we utilize meta learning to optimize the pretrained parameters as illustrated by Algorithm 1. This step enables the SR

Algorithm 1. Meta-Learned Initialization

Input: Initialized SR model f_θ, meta-learning dataset D_N
Output: Meta-learned model f_θ^m
1: **while** not done **do**
2:    Sample n tasks D_n from D_N
3:    **for** $t_i \in D_n$ **do**
4:       Sample pairs (I_{HR}^i, I_{LR}^i) from t_i
5:       Copy $f_{\theta i}$ from the latest f_θ
6:       Evaluate training loss according to Eq. 1
7:       Update parameters according to Eq. 2
8:    **end for**
9:    Calculate $\mathcal{L}_{f_{\theta i}}$ with respect to t_i
10:    Update f_θ according to Eq. 3
11: **end while**
12: **return** Meta-learned model f_θ^m

---

model to converge to a transferable point, which can be rapidly fine-tuned. In order to build a variety of tasks, we collect several video sequences and uniformly divide them into video chunks. Totally, we obtain N chunks for meta-learning, and each chunk is set as the task t_i. The collected dataset is denoted as D_N. We apply bicubic downsampling to the frames and generate LR-HR pairs (I_{LR}^i, I_{HR}^i). Our goal is to optimize f_θ according to each LR-HR pair by minimizing the L1 loss as shown in Eq. 1.

$$\mathcal{L}_f = |f_\theta(I_{LR}) - I_{HR}|_1 \tag{1}$$

During the inner loop (Line 4–7), we conduct one or more gradient updates for the task t_i in each iteration. The temporary model for task t_i is denoted as $f_{\theta i}$. During each inner gradient update, the task-specific parameters are updated according to Eq. 2, where α is the inner learning rate.

$$f_{\theta i} \leftarrow f_{\theta i} - \alpha \nabla_{f_{\theta i}} \mathcal{L}_{f_{\theta i}} \tag{2}$$

As for the outer loop (Line 9–10), we evaluate the loss of $f_{\theta i}$ on each t_i and sum up the losses of all tasks to update the SR model f_θ. For one outer gradient update, it considers the gradients from all tasks. The outer update can be formulated as Eq. 3, where β is the outer learning rate.

$$f_\theta \leftarrow f_\theta - \beta \nabla_{f_\theta} \sum_i \mathcal{L}_{f_{\theta i}} \tag{3}$$

Partial Model Adaption. The meta-learned model f_θ^m is shared by all the video chunks. To obtain the content-aware SR models for the input video, we adapt the meta-learned model to the first chunk, and sequentially fine-tune the partial parameters of previous adapted model. Formally, we denote the content-aware SR model of jth chunk as f_θ^j. For the first chunk, we rapidly fine-tune the meta-learned model f_θ^m to obtain the adapted model f_θ^1. We use the gradient masking to select $p_1\%$ most significant parameters before adapting f_θ^m. As for

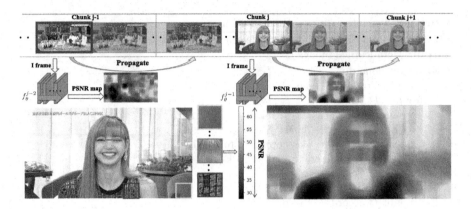

Fig. 2. Illustration of challenging patch sampling. Different colors in PSNR map represent patch's difficult levels for previous chunk's model. 'propagate' arrow indicates the propagation of PSNR map from I frame to its in-between frames.

other chunks, we fine-tune previous model f_θ^{j-1} on j^{th} chunk, delivering the adapted model f_θ^j. We also adopt the gradient masking to select $p_2\%$ most significant parameters before fine-tuning f_θ^{j-1}. It has to be noted that we adopt different percentages for the first chunk and other chunks in this work. Our partial model adaption requires much fewer epochs for both the first chunk and other chunks. Therefore, the computational cost can be greatly reduced compared with training from scratch under the same performance.

Gradient Masking. In order to compress the parameters of content-aware models, we design a simple yet effective strategy to find the $p\%$ most significant parameters. Given a reference model f, we need to find a fraction of parameters before fine-tuning f. Specifically, we adopt a few iterations to update f, obtaining a temporal model $\widehat{f}$. Afterwards, we calculate $|\theta_{\widehat{f}} - \theta_f|$ and choose the $p\%$ parameters that vary most, delivering the parameter mask $M(\theta_f)$.

Once we collect the $p\%$ most significant parameters, we can fine-tune the reference model f and simply update the significant parameters. In this manner, our method only needs to store $p\%$ private parameters of the reference model. When fine-tuning for the first chunk, we choose the meta-learned model f_θ^m as the reference model. For j^{th} chunk of the input video, we choose the previous adapted model f_θ^{j-1} as the reference model.

3.3   Challenging Patch Sampling

Previous adapted SR model already possesses the ability to super-resolve current chunk due to the temporal consistency. Thus it can achieve satisfying results on the majority of regions. However, some hard regions are still challenging for the previous adapted model. Since SR networks are fine-tuned on sampled LR-HR patch pairs, we further present a strategy to sample the $r\%$ most challenging patches for EMT. Our strategy is highly efficient and brings negligible additional cost. Inspired by the video codec, it first locates the positions of challenging patches in I-frames, then propagates the positions to in-between frames as shown in Fig. 2.

Formally, we denote the frames of input video as $I_1, ..., I_T$, where T is the number of frames. The I-frames are denoted as $I_{k_1}, ..., I_{k_M}$, where $k_1, ..., k_M$ are the indices of M I-frames. We also denote the chunk indices of M I-frames as $c_1, ..., c_M$. In order to localize the challenging patches for I_{k_m}, we run the inference of previous adapted model $f_\theta^{c_m-1}$ to super-resolve the downsampled I-frame $I_{k_m}^{LR}$:

$$I_{k_m}^{SR} = f_\theta^{c_m-1}(I_{k_m}^{LR}) \tag{4}$$

We can calculate the PSNR between $I_{k_m}^{SR}$ and I_{k_m} in terms of all possible patches as illustrated by Fig. 2. The time of calculating the PSNR map for 1080P frames is 0.1 s. Therefore, it is time-consuming to produce PSNR maps for all frames. For instance, when dealing with a 45-second video, it usually takes around 135 s to generate PSNR maps for all frames. Instead, we localize the positions of $r\%$ (r = 20) most challenging patches in I_{k_m}, and then extract the patches from frames between I_{k_m} and $I_{k_{m+1}}$ according to the coordinates. As the frames between two I-frames are temporally consistent, the localized positions at I-frame can also choose reasonable patches on the in-between frames. Since I-frame is very sparse within a video, the computational cost is negligible. For a 45-second video, the total time of position localization and patch extraction is 0.7 s. However, the results of EMT using challenging patches are the same as results using all frames to some extent. In this way, the training efforts of EMT focus on challenging patches, resulting in faster convergence.

4   Experiments

In this section, we conduct extensive experiments to show the advantages of our method. The experimental details are given in Sect. 4.1. We first present the comparison with baseline and codec standards in Sect. 4.2, and then compare EMT with other neural video delivery methods in Sect. 4.3. We also conduct comprehensive ablation study to evaluate the contribution of each component in Sect. 4.4. In order to show the generalization ability, we report results across different scaling factors and architectures in Sect. 4.5.

4.1   Experimental Details

For meta-learning, we conduct two gradient updates for each individual task in the inner loop. After updating on all sampled tasks, we conduct one outer gradient update on the SR model. We randomly select training patches with a resolution of 144×144 and set mini-batch size as $16*n$, where n is the number of sampled tasks. Particularly, we set n to 15 and each task consists of 50 frames. We set inner learning rate $\alpha = 0.5e-5$ and outer learning rate $\beta = 1e-3$. We adopt Adam optimizer with $\beta_1 = 0.9$, $\beta_2 = 0.999$, $\epsilon = 10^{-8}$. ESPCN serves as the default architecture, x2 is utilized as the default scaling factor and PSNR is the default metric.

For fine-tuning, we conduct experiments on two video lengths, including 45 s and 2 min. The batch size is 16 and learning rate is $1e - 4$. We set $p_1\%$ as 20% and $p_2\%$ as 1% to compress the parameters as default. We design three settings of our method, including S, M, and L. S and M settings adopt 0.1 epoch and 3 epochs for fine-tuning respectively. As for L setting, we alter $p_1\%$ to 100%. We conduct all the experiments on NVIDIA V100 GPUs.

4.2 Comparison with Baseline and Codec Standards

In this section, we compare our method against the baseline [29] and two codec standards. The baseline uniformly divides a video into chunks and trains one SR model for each chunk from scratch with 300 epochs. We denote the baseline as C_{1-n}. For the two commercial codec standards H.264 and H.265, we use ffmpeg with libx264 codec and libx265 codec to compress the HR videos to lower bit-rate while maintaining the resolution. The compressed videos are of the same storage size as our method (LR videos and SR models). We report three variants of our method under S, M, and L settings. Under the L setting, we aim to show the potential of meta-tuning by updating all the parameters for the first chunk. As shown in Table 1, our method achieves better performance with less time and parameters compared with baseline [29]. Our results with 0.1 epoch already outperform the baseline with 300 epochs. In terms of parameter compression, given a video with n chunks, we compress all models $n * P$ to $1 * p_1\%P + (n - 1) * p_2\%P$. In comparison with H.264 and H.265, our results outperform H.264 and H.265 in most cases as shown in Table 2. We also show the qualitative comparison in Fig. 3. As can be seen, our method can restore better details compared with codec standards.

4.3 Comparison with Neural Video Delivery Methods

In this section, we compare our work with other neural video delivery methods. CaFM [19] uses content-aware models to compress parameters and achieve competitive performance. However, its joint training strategy takes huge computational cost. Therefore, CaFM is not practical for delivering long videos. SRVC [13] also sequentially delivers the content-aware SR models by fine-tuning previous model. However, they fail to generalize on various architectures and have to train from scratch for a new video. Deep Video Compression (DVC) [20] is an end-to-end DNN-based video compression method. We also compare our method with (DVC) at four different bitrate-distortion trade-off operating points $\lambda \in \{256, 512, 1024, 2048\}$ (DVC1, DVC2, DVC3, DVC4). In Fig. 4 and Table 3, we demonstrate the advantages of our method in terms of accuracy, training time, and storage. In Fig. 4, we calculate the average PSNR and storage cost on 45 s videos from VSD4K [19]. Under the same storage, our method outperforms other methods at most circumstances. Though CaFM achieves promising

Table 1. Comparisons with baseline [29]. We show the results of our method under S, M, and L settings. Paras indicates the model parameters and P denotes the parameters of ESPCN. m and h in Time column represent minutes and hours respectively.

	Inter-45 s			Sport-45 s			Game-45 s		
	PSNR	Paras	Time	PSNR	Paras	Time	PSNR	Paras	Time
C_{1-n}	38.95	9P	11.2 h	46.03	9P	11.2 h	35.61	9P	11.2 h
Ours(S)	**39.08**	0.28P	1.2 m	**46.11**	0.28P	1.2 m	**36.32**	0.28P	1.2 m
Ours(M)	39.18	0.28P	7.6 m	46.25	0.28P	7.6 m	36.51	0.28P	7.6 m
Ours(L)	39.56	1.08P	55.5 m	46.41	1.08P	1.76 h	37.09	1.08P	1.64 h
	Dance-45 s			Vlog-45 s			Game-2 min		
	PSNR	Paras	Time	PSNR	Paras	Time	PSNR	Paras	Time
C_{1-n}	43.47	9P	11.2 h	46.20	9P	11.2 h	34.46	24P	11.2 h
Ours(S)	**44.13**	0.28P	1.2 m	**46.48**	0.28P	1.2 m	**34.35**	0.43P	1.2 m
Ours(M)	44.24	0.28P	7.6 m	46.71	0.28P	7.6 m	34.50	0.43P	7.6 m
Ours(L)	44.59	1.08P	1.53 h	46.97	1.08P	48.6 m	35.33	1.23P	56.3 m

Table 2. Comparisons with H.264 and H.265. Under the same storage size, our PSNR results outperform H.264 and H.265 in most cases.

H.264	Inter		Sport		Game		Dance		Vlog	
	45 s	2 min	45 s	2 min	45 s	2 min	45 s	2 min	45 s	2 min
	36.32	44.82	38.29	36.75	37.29	35.13	28.86	29.36	42.37	43.02
H.265	36.78	45.47	39.98	38.44	**38.17**	**36.87**	30.83	31.06	43.35	43.97
Ours(M)	**39.18**	**46.73**	**46.25**	**40.44**	36.51	34.50	**44.24**	**42.74**	**46.71**	**48.66**
Storage(mB)	13.19	35.21	13.65	37.43	13.97	35.17	13.81	36.80	13.83	36.37

results, it takes a huge computational cost. As shown in Table 3, we demonstrate the trade-off between accuracy and training time. Our method shows competitive performance while maintaining low computational cost.

4.4 Ablation Study

Variants of EMT. We intend to evaluate the contribution of each component in EMT. Firstly, we compare our method with pretrained initialization, which is denoted as P_{1-n}. Similar to our meta-learned initialization, P_{1-n} first initializes the SR model on DIV2K, and is normally finetuned on the meta-learning dataset D_N. We replace the meta-learned model of EMT by the normally finetuned model to obtain the results of P_{1-n}. To be mentioned, P_{1-n} still utilizes gradient masking and challenging patch sampling for a fair comparison. Therefore, we are able to evaluate the effectiveness of meta-learned initialization. To evaluate the effectiveness of Challenging Patch Sampling (CPS), we remove the step of patch sampling in our full pipeline and the results are denoted as MT_{1-n}. As shown in

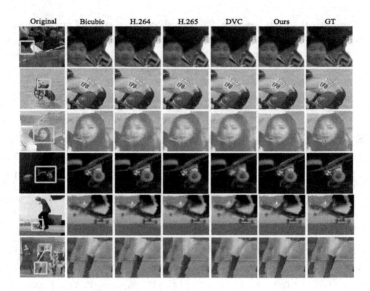

Fig. 3. Qualitative results. This figure shows the qualitative comparison against H.264, H.265 and DVC. Our method can restore better details compared with other methods. Best viewed by zooming x4.

Table 4, in order to achieve the same PSNR, P_{1-n} takes extra cost compared with our meta-learned initialization. Meanwhile, our method outperforms MT_{1-n} in regard to efficiency, demonstrating the effectiveness of CPS.

Variants of Meta Learning. During meta-learning, we randomly sample 15 tasks and each task contains 50 frames. We also study the effect of different numbers of tasks and frames. For the number of tasks, we compare the results of 10, 15 and 20. For the number of frames, we evaluate the results of 10, 50 and 150. As shown in Table 5, all the variants achieve similar results, and the setting of 15 tasks with 50 frames already achieves competitive performance.

Variants of Gradient Masking. We conduct extensive experiments to explore the performance under different variants of gradient masking. Since our method uses different portions of parameters for fine-tuning the first chunk and other chunks. We report the results of $p_1 \in \{10, 20, 30, 100\}$ and $p_2 \in \{0.5, 1, 5, 10\}$. As can be seen from Table 6, we empirically set $p_1 = 20$ and $p_2 = 1$ as our default setting since it can already achieve satisfying results.

4.5 The Generalization of Our Method

Generalization of Various Scaling Factors. We evaluate the generalization ability of EMT using ESPCN as the backbone across scaling factors x2, x3 and x4. As shown in Table 7, EMT outperforms C_{1-n} under various scaling factors, demonstrating the generalization ability of EMT across various scaling factors.

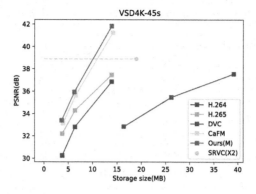

Fig. 4. Comparisons with neural video delivery methods in terms of PSNR and storage.

Table 3. Comparisons with neural video delivery in terms of PSNR and training time. Red and blue indicate the best and the second best results among all methods.

	Inter-45 s		Sport-45 s		Game-45 s		Dance-45 s		Vlog-45s	
	Acc	Time	Acc	Time	Acc	Time	Acc	Time	Acc	Time
C1-n	38.95	11.2 h	46.03	11.2 h	35.61	11.2 h	43.47	11.2 h	46.20	11.2 h
CaFM	38.90	10.2 h	46.12	10.2 h	35.96	10.2 h	43.63	10.2 h	46.45	10.2 h
SRVC	37.26	12.1 m	41.38	12.1 m	33.34	12.1 m	40.87	12.1 m	45.59	12.1 m
DVC1	31.98	35.6 m	35.52	33.6 m	31.76	35.8 m	27.67	34.8 m	37.86	35.3 m
DVC2	34.44	36.1 m	37.45	34.3 m	33.93	36.0 m	32.46	35.2 m	39.92	35.8 m
DVC3	36.60	37.1 m	39.58	34.8 m	36.10	36.5 m	34.40	35.4 m	41.67	36.2 m
DVC4	38.70	38.0 m	41.28	34.8 m	38.10	36.2 m	36.33	35.8 m	43.22	36.4 m
Ours(M)	39.18	7.6 m	46.25	7.6 m	36.51	7.6 m	44.24	7.6 m	46.71	7.6 m

Table 4. Variants of EMT. We show the results of our method under S setting. MT stands for meta-tuning strategy. m and h in Time column represent minutes and hours respectively. P denotes the parameters of SR architecture (ESPCN).

Method	MT	CPS	Inter-45 s			Sport-45 s		
			PSNR	Paras	Time	PSNR	Paras	Time
C_{1-n}	–	–	38.95	9P	11.2 h	46.03	9P	11.2 h
P_{1-n}	–	✓	39.08	0.28P	18.4 m	46.11	0.28P	4.2 m
MT_{1-n}	✓	–	39.08	0.28P	9.7 m	46.11	0.28P	2.7 m
Ours(S)	✓	✓	39.08	0.28P	1.2 m	46.11	0.28P	1.2 m

Table 5. Variants of meta-learning. Ours(S) adopt S setting.

	Task	Frame	Inter-45 s	Sport-45 s	Game-45 s	Vlog-45 s
C_{1-n}	–	–	38.95	46.03	35.61	46.20
Ours(S)	10	50	39.06	46.06	36.25	46.51
Ours(S)	15	50	39.08	46.11	36.32	46.48
Ours(S)	20	50	39.07	46.09	36.22	46.45
Ours(S)	15	10	39.09	45.94	36.34	46.57
Ours(S)	15	50	39.08	46.11	36.32	46.48
Ours(S)	15	150	39.03	46.20	36.39	46.58

Table 6. Variants of gradient masking. Ours(S) adopt S setting.

	p1%	p2 %	Inter-45 s	Sport-45 s	Game-45 s	Vlog-45 s
C1-n	–	–	38.95	46.03	35.61	46.20
Ours(S)	10	1	39.04	46.00	36.28	46.42
Ours(S)	20	1	39.08	46.11	36.32	46.48
Ours(S)	30	1	39.11	46.13	36.33	46.49
Ours(S)	100	1	39.19	46.13	36.35	46.56
Ours(S)	20	0.5	39.08	46.10	36.31	46.47
Ours(S)	20	1	39.08	46.11	36.32	46.48
Ours(S)	20	5	39.09	46.18	36.34	46.53
Ours(S)	20	10	39.11	46.23	36.37	46.57

Table 7. Results of ESPCN on various scaling factors. We show the results of our method under M setting for fine-tuning.

	Inter-45 s			Sport-45 s			Vlog-45 s		
	x2	x3	x4	x2	x3	x4	x2	x3	x4
C_{1-n}	38.95	32.19	28.73	46.03	40.43	37.21	46.20	41.68	39.52
Ours(M)	39.18	32.55	29.05	46.25	40.51	37.22	46.71	42.25	40.08
	Dance-45 s			Game-45 s			City-45 s		
	x2	x3	x4	x2	x3	x4	x2	x3	x4
C_{1-n}	43.47	36.86	35.22	35.61	30.67	28.80	36.44	31.60	29.23
Ours(M)	44.24	37.42	35.88	36.51	31.13	29.01	36.42	31.56	29.16

Generalization of Various Efficient Backbones. In this part, we present the results of our method using different efficient SR backbones. We evaluate our method on 45 s videos and adopt three additional efficient backbones, including SRCNN [8], FSRCNN [8], and EDSR with one residual block in body (EDSR-1). As shown in Table 8, our method also generalizes well to different efficient backbones, validating the generalization ability of our method.

5   Extension to Long Videos

In this section, we extend EMT to long videos beyond 2 min. Since former works [19,29] take too much time to train the content-aware SR models, we only compare with commercial codec standards. Directly applying EMT to long videos may achieve degraded results since the temporal consistency between neighboring chunks is not always true for long videos. Therefore, in order to extend EMT to long videos, we first divide the video frames into groups and apply EMT to each group. To be specific, we extract all the I-frames from the input video and make each group contain 30 I-frames. As shown in Table 9, our method outperforms commercial codec standards even on long videos, showing the great potential of our method.

Table 8. Results of various SR architectures. We show the results of our method under M setting for fine-tuning.

Backbone	Inter-45 s		Sport-45 s		Game-45 s		Dance-45 s		Vlog-45 s	
	C_{1-n}	Ours	C_{1-n}	Ours	C_{1-n}	Ours	C_{1-n}	Ours	C_{1-n}	Ours
SRCNN	39.02	39.06	46.21	46.19	35.37	35.64	43.28	43.92	46.25	46.42
FSRCNN	39.06	39.25	46.29	46.32	35.84	35.90	43.61	44.08	46.09	46.47
EDSR-1	39.17	39.13	45.99	46.02	35.51	35.58	44.04	44.05	46.28	46.28

Table 9. Comparisons with H.264 and H.265 on long videos. We show the results of our method using 3 epochs for fine-tuning. The storage is measured in megabytes.

	Vlog-5 min		Vlog-10 min		Vlog-20 min		vlog-30 min	
	PSNR	Storage	PSNR	Storage	PSNR	Storage	PSNR	Storage
Ours(M)	37.67	18.62	38.33	35.64	38.31	71.19	38.41	145.12
H.264	34.68	18.62	37.15	35.64	35.29	71.19	35.02	145.12
H.265	36.75	18.62	35.78	35.64	37.18	71.19	37.07	145.12

6 Conclusion

To pave the way for practical applications, we propose Efficient Meta-Tuning (EMT) to significantly reduce the computational cost of neural video delivery. Instead of training from scratch, EMT sequentially fine-tunes a meta-learned model to deliver the content-aware SR models of the input video. Gradient masking is introduced to select partial parameters for fine-tuning, compressing all the models into one shared model and a few private parameters. In addition, we also present a sampling strategy to extract the challenging patches for fine-tuning, further reducing the cost of EMT. We conduct detailed comparisons with the commercial codec standards and other neural video delivery methods to demonstrate the advantages of our approach. We hope this paper can inspire future work on neural video delivery.

References

1. Agustsson, E., Timofte, R.: NTIRE 2017 challenge on single image super-resolution: dataset and study. In: The IEEE Conference on Computer Vision and Pattern Recognition (CVPR) Workshops, July 2017
2. Caballero, J., et al.: Real-time video super-resolution with spatio-temporal networks and motion compensation. In: Proceedings of the IEEE Conference on Computer Vision and Pattern Recognition, pp. 4778–4787 (2017)
3. Chan, K.C., Wang, X., Yu, K., Dong, C., Loy, C.C.: BasicVSR: the search for essential components in video super-resolution and beyond. arXiv preprint arXiv:2012.02181 (2020)
4. Chan, K.C., Zhou, S., Xu, X., Loy, C.C.: BasicVSR++: improving video super-resolution with enhanced propagation and alignment. arXiv preprint arXiv:2104.13371 (2021)
5. Chen, J., Hu, M., Luo, Z., Wang, Z., Wu, D.: Sr360: boosting 360-degree video streaming with super-resolution. In: Proceedings of the 30th ACM Workshop on Network and Operating Systems Support for Digital Audio and Video, pp. 1–6 (2020)
6. Choi, M., Choi, J., Baik, S., Kim, T.H., Lee, K.M.: Scene-adaptive video frame interpolation via meta-learning. In: Proceedings of the IEEE/CVF Conference on Computer Vision and Pattern Recognition, pp. 9444–9453 (2020)
7. Dasari, M., Bhattacharya, A., Vargas, S., Sahu, P., Balasubramanian, A., Das, S.R.: Streaming 360-degree videos using super-resolution. In: IEEE INFOCOM 2020-IEEE Conference on Computer Communications, pp. 1977–1986. IEEE (2020)
8. Dong, C., Loy, C.C., He, K., Tang, X.: Learning a deep convolutional network for image super-resolution. In: Fleet, D., Pajdla, T., Schiele, B., Tuytelaars, T. (eds.) ECCV 2014. LNCS, vol. 8692, pp. 184–199. Springer, Cham (2014). https://doi.org/10.1007/978-3-319-10593-2_13
9. Finn, C., Abbeel, P., Levine, S.: Model-agnostic meta-learning for fast adaptation of deep networks. In: International Conference on Machine Learning, pp. 1126–1135. PMLR (2017)
10. He, K., Zhang, X., Ren, S., Sun, J.: Deep residual learning for image recognition. In: Proceedings of the IEEE Conference on Computer Vision and Pattern Recognition, pp. 770–778 (2016)

11. Ioffe, S., Szegedy, C.: Batch normalization: Accelerating deep network training by reducing internal covariate shift. In: International Conference on Machine Learning, pp. 448–456. PMLR (2015)
12. Jo, Y., Oh, S.W., Kang, J., Kim, S.J.: Deep video super-resolution network using dynamic upsampling filters without explicit motion compensation. In: Proceedings of the IEEE Conference on Computer Vision and Pattern Recognition, pp. 3224–3232 (2018)
13. Khani, M., Sivaraman, V., Alizadeh, M.: Efficient video compression via content-adaptive super-resolution. arXiv preprint arXiv:2104.02322 (2021)
14. Kim, J., Jung, Y., Yeo, H., Ye, J., Han, D.: Neural-enhanced live streaming: improving live video ingest via online learning. In: Proceedings of the Annual Conference of the ACM Special Interest Group on Data Communication on the Applications, Technologies, Architectures, and Protocols for Computer Communication, pp. 107–125 (2020)
15. Kim, J., Kwon Lee, J., Mu Lee, K.: Accurate image super-resolution using very deep convolutional networks. In: Proceedings of the IEEE Conference on Computer Vision and Pattern Recognition, pp. 1646–1654 (2016)
16. Ledig, C., et al.: Photo-realistic single image super-resolution using a generative adversarial network. In: Proceedings of the IEEE Conference on Computer Vision and Pattern Recognition, pp. 4681–4690 (2017)
17. Li, W., Zhou, K., Qi, L., Jiang, N., Lu, J., Jia, J.: LAPAR: Linearly-assembled pixel-adaptive regression network for single image super-resolution and beyond. Adv. Neural Inf. Process. Syst. **33**, 20343–20355 (2020)
18. Lim, B., Son, S., Kim, H., Nah, S., Mu Lee, K.: Enhanced deep residual networks for single image super-resolution. In: Proceedings of the IEEE Conference on Computer Vision and Pattern Recognition Workshops, pp. 136–144 (2017)
19. Liu, J., et al.: Overfitting the data: Compact neural video delivery via content-aware feature modulation. In: Proceedings of the IEEE/CVF International Conference on Computer Vision, pp. 4631–4640 (2021)
20. Lu, G., Ouyang, W., Xu, D., Zhang, X., Cai, C., Gao, Z.: DVC: an end-to-end deep video compression framework. In: Proceedings of the IEEE/CVF Conference on Computer Vision and Pattern Recognition, pp. 11006–11015 (2019)
21. Park, S., Yoo, J., Cho, D., Kim, J., Kim, T.H.: Fast adaptation to super-resolution networks via meta-learning. arXiv preprint arXiv:2001.02905 5 (2020)
22. Sajjadi, M.S., Vemulapalli, R., Brown, M.: Frame-recurrent video super-resolution. In: Proceedings of the IEEE Conference on Computer Vision and Pattern Recognition, pp. 6626–6634 (2018)
23. Shi, W., et al.: Real-time single image and video super-resolution using an efficient sub-pixel convolutional neural network. In: Proceedings of the IEEE Conference on Computer Vision and Pattern Recognition, pp. 1874–1883 (2016)
24. Soh, J.W., Cho, S., Cho, N.I.: Meta-transfer learning for zero-shot super-resolution. In: Proceedings of the IEEE/CVF Conference on Computer Vision and Pattern Recognition, pp. 3516–3525 (2020)
25. Wang, X., Chan, K.C., Yu, K., Dong, C., Change Loy, C.: EDVR: video restoration with enhanced deformable convolutional networks. In: Proceedings of the IEEE/CVF Conference on Computer Vision and Pattern Recognition Workshops (2019)
26. Xiao, X., Wang, W., Chen, T., Cao, Y., Jiang, T., Zhang, Q.: Sensor-augmented neural adaptive bitrate video streaming on UAVs. IEEE Trans. Multimedia **22**(6), 1567–1576 (2019)

27. Xue, T., Chen, B., Wu, J., Wei, D., Freeman, W.T.: Video enhancement with task-oriented flow. Int. J. Comput. Vis. **127**(8), 1106–1125 (2019)
28. Yeo, H., Chong, C.J., Jung, Y., Ye, J., Han, D.: Nemo: enabling neural-enhanced video streaming on commodity mobile devices. In: Proceedings of the 26th Annual International Conference on Mobile Computing and Networking, pp. 1–14 (2020)
29. Yeo, H., Jung, Y., Kim, J., Shin, J., Han, D.: Neural adaptive content-aware internet video delivery. In: 13th {USENIX} Symposium on Operating Systems Design and Implementation ({OSDI} 18), pp. 645–661 (2018)
30. Zhang, A., Wang, C., Liu, X., Han, B., Qian, F.: Mobile volumetric video streaming enhanced by super resolution. In: Proceedings of the 18th International Conference on Mobile Systems, Applications, and Services, pp. 462–463 (2020)
31. Zhang, Y., Li, K., Li, K., Wang, L., Zhong, B., Fu, Y.: Image super-resolution using very deep residual channel attention networks. In: Proceedings of the European Conference on Computer Vision (ECCV), pp. 286–301 (2018)

Reference-Based Image Super-Resolution with Deformable Attention Transformer

Jiezhang Cao[1], Jingyun Liang[1], Kai Zhang[1], Yawei Li[1], Yulun Zhang[1(✉)], Wenguan Wang[1], and Luc Van Gool[1,2]

[1] Computer Vision Lab, ETH Zürich, Zürich, Switzerland
{jiezhang.cao,jingyun.liang,kai.zhang,yawei.li,yulun.zhang,
wenguan.wang,vangool}@vision.ee.ethz.ch
[2] KU Leuven, Leuven, Belgium
https://github.com/caojiezhang/DATSR

Abstract. Reference-based image super-resolution (RefSR) aims to exploit auxiliary reference (Ref) images to super-resolve low-resolution (LR) images. Recently, RefSR has been attracting great attention as it provides an alternative way to surpass single image SR. However, addressing the RefSR problem has two critical challenges: (i) It is difficult to match the correspondence between LR and Ref images when they are significantly different; (ii) How to transfer the relevant texture from Ref images to compensate the details for LR images is very challenging. To address these issues of RefSR, this paper proposes a deformable attention Transformer, namely DATSR, with multiple scales, each of which consists of a texture feature encoder (TFE) module, a reference-based deformable attention (RDA) module and a residual feature aggregation (RFA) module. Specifically, TFE first extracts image transformation (*e.g.*, brightness) insensitive features for LR and Ref images, RDA then can exploit multiple relevant textures to compensate more information for LR features, and RFA lastly aggregates LR features and relevant textures to get a more visually pleasant result. Extensive experiments demonstrate that our DATSR achieves state-of-the-art performance on benchmark datasets quantitatively and qualitatively.

Keywords: Reference-based image super-resolution · Correspondence matching · Texture transfer · Deformable attention transformer

1 Introduction

Single image super-resolution (SISR), which aims at recovering a high-resolution (HR) image from a low-resolution (LR) input, is an active research topic due to its high practical values [9,13–16,18,20,21,41,46,49,51]. However, SISR is a highly ill-posed problem since there exist multiple HR images that can degrade to

Supplementary Information The online version contains supplementary material available at https://doi.org/10.1007/978-3-031-19797-0_19.

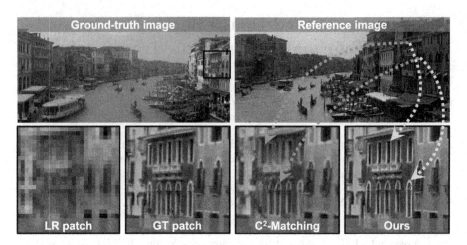

Fig. 1. Comparison with the state-of-the-art RefSR method C^2-Matching [12]. When the brightness of LR and Ref image is different, our method performs better than C^2-Matching [12] in transferring relevant textures from the Ref image to the SR image, which is closer to the ground-truth image.

the same LR image [8,38]. While real LR images usually have no corresponding HR ground-truth (GT) images, one can easily find a high-quality image as a reference (Ref) image with high-frequency details from various sources, such as photo albums, video frames, and web image search, which has similar semantic information (such as content and texture) to the LR image. Such an alternative SISR method is referred to as reference-based super-resolution (RefSR), which aims to transfer HR textures from the Ref images to super-resolved images and has shown promising results over SISR. Although various RefSR methods [12, 27,45,47] have been recently proposed, two challenges remain unsolved for SR performance improvement.

First, it is difficult to match the correspondence between the LR and Ref images especially when their distributions are different. For example, the brightness of the Ref images is different from that of the LR images. Existing methods [48,56] mostly match the correspondence by estimating the pixel or patch similarity of texture features between LR and Ref images. However, such similarity metric is sensitive to image transformations, such as brightness and color of images. Recently, the state-of-the-art (SOTA) method C^2-Matching [12] trains a feature extractor, which demonstrates strong robustness to scale and rotation. However, it neglects to explore the effects of brightness, contrast, and color of images. As a result, this method may transfer inaccurate textures from the Ref image, when the Ref images have different brightness from the LR image, as shown in Fig. 1. Based on the observation and analyses, we can see that the quality of correspondence is affected by the similarity metric and the distribution gap between the LR and Ref images.

On the other hand, some methods [34,57] adopt optical flow or deformable convolutions [3,4,42,59] to align spatial features between the Ref and LR images. However, these methods may find an inaccurate correspondence when the distance between the LR and Ref images is relatively large. With the inaccurate correspondence, their performance would deteriorate seriously since the irrelevant texture cannot provide meaningful details. Therefore, how to accurately match the correspondence between the Ref and LR images is a challenging problem as it affects the quality of super-resolved results.

Second, it is also challenging to transfer textures of the high-quality Ref images to restore the HR images. One representative work CrossNet [57] estimates the flow from the Ref image to the LR image and then warp the features based on the optical flow. However, the optical flow may be inaccurate, since the Ref and LR images could be significantly different. In addition, most existing methods [27,48,56] search the most similar textures and the corresponding position, and then swap the texture features from the Ref image. As a result, these methods may transfer irrelevant textures to the output and have poor SR performance, when the original estimated flow or position is inaccurate. Hence, it is important and necessary to explore a new architecture to adaptively transfer texture and mitigate the impact of inaccurate correspondence in the Ref image.

To address the above two challenges, we propose a novel deformable attention Transformer, namely DATSR, for reference-based image super-resolution. DATSR is built on the U-Net and consists of three basic modules, including texture feature encoders, deformable attention, and residual feature aggregation. Specifically, we first use texture feature encoders to extract multi-scale features with different image transformations. Then, we propose a reference-based deformable attention to discover the multiple relevant correspondences and adaptively transfer the textures. Last, we fuse features and reconstruct the SR images using residual feature aggregation. We conduct extensive comparisons with recent representative SOTA methods on benchmark datasets. The quantitative and visual results demonstrate that our DATSR achieves the SOTA performance.

The main contributions are summarized as follows:

- We propose a novel reference-based image super-resolution with deformable attention transformer (DATSR), which is end-to-end trainable by incorporating Transformer into RefSR. Compared with existing RefSR methods, our DATSR performs more robust correspondence matching and texture transfer and subsequently achieves SOTA performance quantitatively and visually.
- We design a new reference-based deformable attention module for correspondence matching and texture transfer. Different from existing transformer-based methods, our transformer is built on U-Net with multi-scale features and alleviates the resolution gap between Ref and LR images. Moreover, our transformer relieves the correspondence mismatching issue and the impact of distribution gap between LR and Ref images.
- We conduct extensive experiments on benchmark datasets to demonstrate that our DATSR achieves SOTA performance and is also robust to different image transformations (e.g., brightness, contrast and hue). Moreover, we find that our DATSR trained with a single Ref image outperforms existing Multi-RefSR methods trained with multiple Ref images. In addition, our DATSR still shows good performance even in some extreme cases, when the Ref images have no texture information.

2   Related Work

We will briefly introduce two related super-resolution paradigms, including single image super-resolution and reference-based image super-resolution.

Single Image Super-Resolution (SISR). The goal of SISR is to recover high-resolution (HR) images from the low-resolution (LR) images. Recent years have witnessed significant achievements of using deep neural networks to solve SISR [6,55]. SRCNN [6] is the pioneer work of exploiting deep convolutional networks to map LR image into HR image. To further improve SR performance, researchers resort to employing deeper neural networks with attention mechanisms and residual blocks [5,19–23,31,33,36,50,54,55]. However, it is difficult for traditional SISR methods to produce realistic images when the HR textures are highly degraded. To relieve this, some SR methods [11,17,40,43,44,53,58] adopt generative adversarial networks (GANs) to further improve the perceptual quality of the super-resolved outputs.

Reference-Based Image Super-Resolution (RefSR). Different from SISR, RefSR has auxiliary HR images and aims to super-resolves images by transferring HR details of Ref images. Such auxiliary information can be extracted from the reference images which are similar to HR ground-truth images. CrossNet [57] estimates the optical flow (OF) between Ref and LR images and then performs the cross-scale warping and concatenation. Instead of estimating OF, SRNTT [56] calculates the similarity between the LR and Ref images and transfer the texture from the Ref images. Similarly, SSEN [34] proposes a similarity search and extraction network and it is aware of the best matching position and the relevancy of the best match. To improve the performance, TTSR [48] proposes a hard and soft attention for texture transfer and synthesis. Instead of using the features of a classifier, E2ENT^2 [45] transfers texture features by using a SR task-specific features. To improve the efficiency of matching, MASA [27] proposes a coarse-to-fine correspondence matching module and a spatial adaptation module to map the distribution of the Ref features to that of the LR features. Recently, a strong RefSR method C^2-Matching [12] first proposes a contrastive correspondence network to learn correspondence, and then adopts a teacher-student correlation distillation to improve LR-HR matching, and last uses a residual feature aggregation to synthesize HR images.

It should be noted that RefSR can be extended to the case of multiple reference images, called **Multi-RefSR**, which aims to transfer the texture features from multiple Ref images to the SR image. Recently, a content independent multi-reference super-resolution model CIMR-SR [47] is proposed to transfer the HR textures from multiple reference images. To improve the performance, AMRSR [32] proposes an attention-based multi-reference super-resolution network to match the most similar textures from multiple reference images. Different from RefSR, Multi-RefSR can exploit more training information as it has multiple Ref images. In this paper, we mainly study RefSR and train the model with single Ref image. Nevertheless, we still compare our model with the above Multi-RefSR methods to further demonstrate the effectiveness of our DATSR.

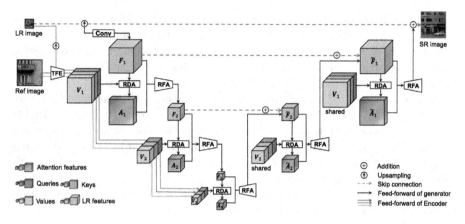

Fig. 2. The architecture of our DATSR network. At each scale, our model consists of texture feature encoders (TFE), a reference-based deformable attention (RDA) module and a residual feature aggregation module (RFA).

3   Proposed Method

Due to the the intrinsic complexity of RefSR, we divide the problem into two main sub-tasks: correspondence matching and texture transfer. To address these, we propose a multi-scale reference-based image SR with deformable Transformer, as shown in Fig. 2. Specifically, we first use TFE to extract multi-scale texture features of Ref and LR images, then propose RDA to match the correspondences and transfer the textures from Ref images to LR images, and last use RFA to aggregate features and generate SR images.

3.1   Texture Feature Encoders

In the RefSR task, it is important to discover robust correspondence between LR and Ref images. However, there are some underlying gaps between LR and Ref images, *i.e.*, the resolution gap and the distribution gap (*e.g.*, brightness, contrast and hue). To address this, we propose texture feature encoders to extract robust features of LR and Ref images. For the resolution gap, we propose to use pre-upsampling in the LR image and extract multi-scale features of LR and Ref images. Specifically, given an LR image X_{LR} and a reference image X_{Ref}, we upsample the LR image to the resolution of the Ref image, denoted as $X_{LR\uparrow}$. Then, we calculate multi-scale features of the LR and Ref images, *i.e.*,

$$Q_l = E_l^q(X_{LR\uparrow}), \quad K_l = E_l^k(X_{Ref}), \quad V_l = E_l^v(X_{Ref}), \tag{1}$$

where E_l^q, E_l^k and E_l^v are feature encoders at the l-th scale. In our architecture, we use three scales in the texture feature encoders. With the help of the multi-scale features in U-Net, we are able to alleviate the resolution gap between the Ref and LR images since they contain the complementary scale information.

For the distribution gap, we augment images with different image transformations (*e.g.*, brightness, contrast and hue) in the training to improve the robustness of our model. In addition to data augmentation, we use contrastive learning to train the encoder be less sensitive to different image transformations, inspired by [12]. To estimate the stable correspondence between $X_{LR\uparrow}$ and X_{Ref}, the feature encoders E_l^q and E_l^k are the same, and the feature encoder E_l^r is pretrained and fixed in the training. In contrast, TTSR [48] directly uses a learnable feature encoder, resulting in limited performance since the textures are changing during training and the correspondence matching is unstable. For C^2-Matching [12], it neglects to improve the robustness to brightness, contrast and hue. To address these, we propose to learn robust multi-scale features Q_l, K_l, V_l, which can be regraded as Query, Key, and Value, and can be used in our attention mechanism conditioned on the LR features.

3.2 Reference-Based Deformable Attention

Existing attention-based RefSR methods (*e.g.*, [48]) tend to suffer from limited performance when the most relevant features between LR and Ref images are inaccurate, *i.e.*, the learned LR features may not well match the Ref features. To address this, we propose a new reference-based attention mechanism, called RefAttention, as shown in Fig. 3. Formally, given Query Q_l, Key K_l, Value V_l, and LR features F_l, the attention feature A_l is defined as follows:

$$A_l = \text{RefAttention}(Q_l, K_l, V_l, F_l) = \mathcal{T}\left(\sigma\left(Q_l^\top K_l\right), V_l, F_l\right). \tag{2}$$

Different from existing attention mechanism [39], our attention is conditioned on the LR features and designed for the RefSR task. In Fig. 3, we denoted by A_l and F_l in the downscaling process, and $\tilde{A}_l$ and $\tilde{F}_l$ in the upscaling process. $\sigma(\cdot)$ is a correspondence matching function to calculate the relevance between the Ref and LR images. Based on the relevance, we propose a texture transfer function $\mathcal{T}(\cdot)$ to transfer the textures from the Ref to the LR image.

Correspondence Matching. The first important sub-task in RefSR is to match correspondences between LR and Ref images. Most existing methods [48,56] are sensitive to different image transformations (*e.g.*, brightness, contrast and hue) and may match inaccurate correspondences. To relieve this issue, we propose a correspondence matching module in our RefAttention, as shown in Fig. 3. Specifically, we estimate the relevance between $X_{LR\uparrow}$ and X_{Ref} by calculating similarity between $Q_l \in \mathbb{R}^{C \times H_1 \times W_1}$ and $K_l \in \mathbb{R}^{C \times H_2 \times W_2}$. First, we unfold Q_l and K_l into patches $Q'_l = [q_1, \ldots, q_{H_1 W_1}] \in \mathbb{R}^{C \times H_1 W_1}$ and $K'_l = [k_1, \ldots, k_{H_2 W_2}] \in \mathbb{R}^{C \times H_2 W_2}$. Then, for the given query q_i in Q', the top K relevant positions in K' can be calculated by normalized inner product,

$$P_i = \left[\sigma\left(Q_l'^\top K_l'\right)\right]_i = \text{TopK}_j\left(\tilde{q}_i \cdot \tilde{k}_j\right), \tag{3}$$

where $\tilde{q}_i = q_i/\|q_i\|$ and $\tilde{k}_j = k_j/\|k_j\|$ are normalized features, and TopK$(\cdot)$ is a function and returns top K relevant positions $P_i = \{p_i^1, \ldots, p_i^K\}$. Here, P_i is

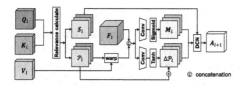 

Fig. 3. The architecture of RDA.   **Fig. 4.** The architecture of RFA.

the i-th element of $\mathcal{P}_l$, and the position p_i^1 is the most relevant position in the Ref image to the i-th position in LR. When $K > 1$, it helps discover multiple correspondences, motivated by KNN [24]. For fair comparisons with other RefSR methods, we set $K = 1$ and exploit the most relevant position in the experiments.

Similarity-Aware Texture Transfer. The second important sub-task in RefSR is to transfer textures from Ref images to LR images based on the matched correspondence. Most existing RefSR methods [48,56] directly swap the most relevant texture from Ref image. However, it may degrade the performance when the most relevant texture is inaccurate. To address this, we propose to improve the deformable convolution (DCN) [4,59] to transfer the texture around every position p_i^k of Ref images. Specifically, let Δp_i^k be the spatial difference between the position p_i and the k-th relevant position p_i^k, *i.e.*, $\Delta p_i^k = p_i^k - p_i$. Then, we calculate a feature at the position p using modified DCN, *i.e.*,

$$A_l(p_i) = \sum_{k=1}^{K} s_i^k \sum_j w_j V_l(p_i + \Delta p_i^k + p_j + \Delta p_j) \, m_j, \qquad (4)$$

where $p_j \in \{(-1,1), (-1,0), \ldots, (1,1)\}$, s_i^k is the cooperative weight to aggregate the K textures from the Ref image, *i.e.*, $s_i^k = \exp(\widetilde{q}_i \cdot \widetilde{k}_{p_i^k}) / \sum_{j \in P_i} \exp(\widetilde{q}_i \cdot \widetilde{k}_j)$, w_j is the convolution kernel weight, Δp_j is the j-th learnable offset of $\Delta \mathcal{P}_l$, and m_j is the j-th learnable mask of M_l, which can be calculated as follows,

$$\begin{cases} \Delta \mathcal{P}_l = r \cdot \text{Tanh}\left(\text{Conv}([F_l; \, \omega(V_l, \mathcal{P}_l)])\right), \\ M_l = \text{Sigmoid}\left(\text{Conv}([F_l; \, \omega(V_l, \mathcal{P}_l)])\right), \end{cases} \qquad (5)$$

where ω is a warping function, $[;]$ is a concatenation operation, Conv is convolutional layers. Sigmoid and Tanh are activation functions, r is the max magnitude which is set as 10 in default, and F_l is the feature of upsampled LR images at the l-th scale. With the help of the mask, we can adaptively transfer textures even if LR and Ref images are significantly different. When the Ref image has irrelevant texture or no information, our model is able to guild whether to transfer the textures in Ref images. In this sense, it can relieve the correspondence mismatching issue. In this paper, we mainly compare with RefSR methods with single Ref image. Thus, we transfer one relevant textures from the Ref image for fair comparison. With the help of our architecture, the proposed RDA module is able to improve the RefSR performance by transferring textures at each scale in both downscaling and upscaling, which is different from C^2-Matching [12].

3.3 Residual Feature Aggregation

To aggregate the multi-scale LR features at different layers and the transferred texture features, we propose a residual feature aggregation module (RFA) to perform feature fusion and extraction. As shown in Fig. 4, RFA consists of CNNs and Swin Transformer layers (STL) [25] which gain much attention in many tasks [2,19,26]. Specifically, we first use a convolution layer to fuse the LR feature F_l and attention features A_l, i.e., $F'_{l+1} = \text{Conv}(F_l, A_l)$, where Conv is convolutional layers. Then, we use Swin Transformer and a residual connection to extract deeper features of the LR and transferred features,

$$F'_{l+1} = \text{STL}(F'_{l+1}) + F_l, \tag{6}$$

where the details of STL are put in the supplementary materials. At the end of RFA, we use another convolutional layer to extract the features of STL, $F_{l+1} = \text{Conv}(F'_{l+1})$. Based on the aggregated features F_L at the last scale, we synthesize SR images with a skip connection as

$$X_{SR} = F_L + X_{LR\uparrow}. \tag{7}$$

3.4 Loss Function

In the training, we aim to i) preserve the spatial structure and semantic information of LR images; ii) discover more texture information of Ref images; iii) synthesize realistic SR images with high quality. To this end, we use a reconstruction loss, a perceptual loss and an adversarial loss, which is the same as [12,48]. The overall loss with the hype-parameters λ_1 and λ_2 is written as:

$$\mathcal{L} = \mathcal{L}_{rec} + \lambda_1 \mathcal{L}_{per} + \lambda_2 \mathcal{L}_{adv}. \tag{8}$$

Reconstruction Loss. In order to make the SR image X_{SR} to be close to the HR ground-truth image X_{HR}, we adopt the following reconstruction loss

$$\mathcal{L}_{rec} = \|X_{HR} - X_{SR}\|_1, \tag{9}$$

where $\| \cdot \|_1$ is the ℓ_1-norm.

Perceptual Loss. To enhance the visual quality of SR images, the perceptual loss is widely used in SR models [12,56]. The perceptual loss is defined as:

$$\mathcal{L}_{per} = \frac{1}{V} \sum_{i=1}^{C} \|\phi_i(X_{HR}) - \phi_i(X_{SR})\|_F, \tag{10}$$

where $\|\cdot\|_F$ is the Frobenius norm, and V and C are the volume and channel number of the feature maps, respectively. The function ϕ_i is the i-th intermediate layer in VGG19 [35], and we use the relu5_1 layer of VGG19 in the experiment.

Adversarial Loss. To improve the visual quality of SR images, many SR methods [17,44] introduce GANs [1,7] which have achieved good performance for SR. Specifically, we use WGAN [1] loss as follows,

$$\mathcal{L}_{adv} = \mathbb{E}_{X_{SR} \sim \mathbb{P}_{SR}}[D(X_{SR})] - \mathbb{E}_{X_{HR} \sim \mathbb{P}_{HR}}[D(X_{HR})], \tag{11}$$

where $D(\cdot)$ is a discriminator, $\mathbb{P}_{SR}$ is the distribution of the generated SR images, and $\mathbb{P}_{HR}$ is the distribution of the real data.

4   Experiments

Datasets. In the experiment, we consider the RefSR dataset, *i.e.*, CUFED5 [56], which consists of a training set and a testing set. The CUFED5 training set contains 11,871 training pairs, and each pair has an original HR image and a corresponding Ref image at the size of 160 × 160. The CUFED5 testing set has 126 input images and each image has 4 reference images with different similarity levels. For fair comparisons, all models are trained on the training set of CUFED5. To evaluate the generalization ability, we test our model on the CUFED5 testing set, Urban100 [10], Manga109 [30], Sun80 [37] and WR-SR [12]. The Sun80 and WR-SR datasets contain 80 natural images, and each paired with one or more reference images. For the Urban100 dataset, we concatenate the LR and random sampled HR images as the reference images. For the Manga109 dataset, we randomly sample HR images as the reference images since there are no the reference images. All experiments are conducted for 4× SR.

Evaluation Metrics. Existing RefSR methods [12, 48, 48] mainly use PSNR and SSIM to compare the performance. Here, PSNR and SSIM are calculated on the Y channel of YCbCr color space. In general, larger PSNR and SSIM correspond to better performance of the RefSR method. In addition, we compare the model size (*i.e.*, the number of trainable parameters) of different models.

Implementation Details. The input LR images are generated by bicubicly downsampling the HR images with scale factor 4. For the encoders and discriminator, we adopt the same architectures as [12]. We use a pre-trained relu1_1, relu2_1 and relu3_1 of VGG19 to extract multi-scale features. we augment the training data with randomly horizontal and vertical flipping or different random rotations of 90°, 180° and 270°. Besides, we also augment the training data by randomly changing different brightness, contrast and hue of an image by using ColorJitter in pytorch. In the training, we set the batch size as 9, *i.e.*, each batch has 9 LR, HR and Ref patches. The size of LR images is 40 × 40, and the size of HR and Ref images is 160 × 160. Following the training of [12], we set the hype-parameters λ_1 and λ_2 as 1×10^{-4} and 1×10^{-6}, respectively. We set the learning rate of the SR model and discriminator as 1×10^{-4}. For the Adam optimizer, we set $\beta_1 = 0.9$ and $\beta_2 = 0.999$. We provide more detailed network architectures and training details in the supplementary material.

4.1   Comparison with State-of-the-Art Methods

We compare with the SISR methods (SRCNN [6], EDSR [22], RCAN [55], SwinIR [19], SRGAN [17], ENet [33], ESRGAN [44], and RankSR-GAN [53]) and RefSR methods (CrossNet [57], SRNTT [56], SSEN [34], TTSR [48], E2ENT2 [45], and MASA [27]). For fair comparisons, the above models are trained on CUFED5 training set, and tested on CUFED5 testing set, Urban100, Manga109, Sun80 and WR-SR. In this experiment, we train our model on two cases only with reconstruction loss (denoted as '-rec'), and with all loss functions.

Table 1. Quantitative comparisons (PSNR and SSIM) of SR models trained with only reconstruction loss (with the suffix '-rec'). We group methods by SISR and RefSR. We mark the best results **in bold**.

SR paradigms	Methods	CUFED5 [56]		Urban100 [10]		Manga109 [30]		Sun80 [37]		WR-SR [12]	
		PSNR	SSIM	PSNR	SSIM	PSNR	SSIM	PSNR	SSIM	PSNR	SSIM
SISR	SRCNN [6]	25.33	0.745	24.41	0.738	27.12	0.850	28.26	0.781	27.27	0.767
	EDSR [22]	25.93	0.777	25.51	0.783	28.93	0.891	28.52	0.792	28.07	0.793
	ENet [33]	24.24	0.695	23.63	0.711	25.25	0.802	26.24	0.702	25.47	0.699
	RCAN [55]	26.06	0.769	25.42	0.768	29.38	0.895	29.86	0.810	28.25	0.799
	SwinIR [19]	26.62	0.790	26.26	0.797	30.05	0.910	30.11	0.817	28.06	0.797
RefSR	CrossNet [57]	25.48	0.764	25.11	0.764	23.36	0.741	28.52	0.793	–	–
	SRNTT-rec [56]	26.24	0.784	25.50	0.783	28.95	0.885	28.54	0.793	27.59	0.780
	TTSR-rec [48]	27.09	0.804	25.87	0.784	30.09	0.907	30.02	0.814	27.97	0.792
	SSEN-rec [34]	26.78	0.791	–	–	–	–	–	–	–	–
	E2ENT^2-rec [45]	24.24	0.724	–	–	–	–	28.50	0.789	–	–
	MASA-rec [27]	27.54	0.814	26.09	0.786	30.24	0.909	30.15	0.815	28.19	0.796
	C^2-Matching-rec [12]	28.24	0.841	26.03	0.785	30.47	0.911	30.18	0.817	28.32	0.801
	DATSR-rec (Ours)	**28.72**	**0.856**	**26.52**	**0.798**	**30.49**	**0.912**	**30.20**	**0.818**	**28.34**	**0.805**

Table 2. Quantitative comparisons (PSNR and SSIM) of SR models trained with all losses. We mark the best results **in bold**.

SR paradigms	Methods	CUFED5 [56]		Urban100 [10]		Manga109 [30]		Sun80 [37]		WR-SR [12]	
		PSNR	SSIM	PSNR	SSIM	PSNR	SSIM	PSNR	SSIM	PSNR	SSIM
SISR	SRGAN [17]	24.40	0.702	24.07	0.729	25.12	0.802	26.76	0.725	26.21	0.728
	ESRGAN [44]	21.90	0.633	20.91	0.620	23.53	0.797	24.18	0.651	26.07	0.726
	RankSRGAN [53]	22.31	0.635	21.47	0.624	25.04	0.803	25.60	0.667	26.15	0.719
RefSR	SRNTT [56]	25.61	0.764	25.09	0.774	27.54	0.862	27.59	0.756	26.53	0.745
	TTSR [48]	25.53	0.765	24.62	0.747	28.70	0.886	28.59	0.774	26.83	0.762
	SSEN [34]	25.35	0.742	–	–	–	–	–	–	–	–
	E2ENT^2 [45]	24.01	0.705	–	–	–	–	28.13	0.765	–	–
	MASA [27]	24.92	0.729	23.78	0.712	27.26	0.847	27.12	0.708	25.74	0.717
	C^2-Matching [12]	27.16	0.805	25.52	0.764	29.73	0.893	29.75	0.799	27.80	0.780
	DATSR (Ours)	**27.95**	**0.835**	**25.92**	**0.775**	**29.75**	**0.893**	**29.77**	**0.800**	**27.87**	**0.787**

Quantitative Comparison. We provide quantitative comparisons of SR models trained with only reconstruction loss and all losses in Tables 1 and 2, respectively. In Table 1, our model has the best PSNR and SSIM on all testing sets and significantly outperforms all SISR and RefSR models. It implies that our Transformer achieves the state-of-the-arts and good generalization performance. For the SISR setting, our method performs better than the state-of-the-art SISR method [19]. It is difficult for these SISR methods to synthesize since the high-frequency information is degraded. In contrast, our model is able to adaptively discover the useful information from a reference image on the Urban100 and Manga109 datasets even if it is a random image. For the RefSR setting, our proposed DATSR significantly outperforms all methods with the help of the cooperative transfer with deformable convolution module.

In Table 2, our DATSR also achieves the much higher PSNR/SSIM values than other RefSR methods with a large margin. Our DATSR trained with adversarial loss reduces PSNR and SSIM but increases the visual quality. Still, it has the best performance over all compared methods. The above quantitative comparison results on different SR paradigms demonstrate the superiority of our Transformer over state-of-the-art SISR and RefSR methods.

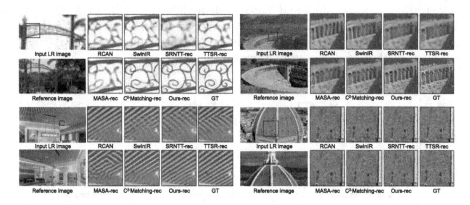

Fig. 5. Qualitative comparisons of SISR and RefSR models trained with the reconstruction loss.

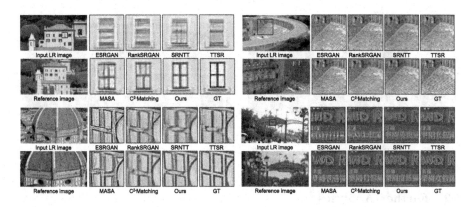

Fig. 6. Qualitative comparisons of SISR and RefSR models trained with all loss.

Qualitative Comparison. The visual results of our method are shown in Figs. 5 and 6. In these figures, our model also achieves the best performance on visual quality when trained with the reconstruction loss and all loss. These results demonstrate that our proposed method is able to transfer more accurate textures from the Ref images to generate SR images with higher quality. When trained with the reconstruction loss, our model can synthesize SR images with sharp structure. Moreover, our method is able to search and transfer meaningful texture in a local regions even if the Ref image is not globally relevant to the input image. When trained with the adversarial loss, our model is able to restore the realistic details in the output images which are very close to the

HR ground-truth images with the help of the given Ref images. In contrast, it is hard for ESRGAN and RankSRGAN to generate realistic images without the Ref images since the degradation is severely destroyed and high frequency details of images are lost. For RefSR methods, our model is able to synthesize more realistic texture from the Ref images than SRNTT [56], TTSR [48], MASA [27], and C^2-Matching [12]. For example, in the top of Fig. 6, our model is able to recover the "window" with sharper edge and higher quality than C^2-Matching, but other methods fail to restore it even if they have a Ref image.

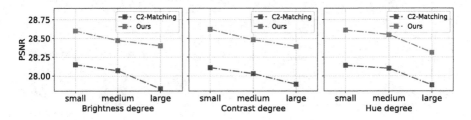

Fig. 7. Robustness to different image transformations. Our DATSR is more robust than C^2-Matching [12] under different image transformations.

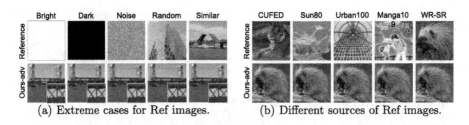

(a) Extreme cases for Ref images.   (b) Different sources of Ref images.

Fig. 8. Investigation on different types of reference images.

4.2   Further Analyses

Robustness to Image Transformations. We analyze the robustness of our model to different kinds of image transformations. Specifically, we use ColorJitter to augment the CUFED5 testing set by randomly change the brightness, contrast and hue of Ref images into three group: small, medium and large. The detailed settings are put in the supplementary materials. In Fig. 7, our model is more robust than C^2-Matching [12] under different image transformations. Note that the medium and large transformations are not included during training but our model still has superior performance.

Effect on Type and Number of Ref Images. We test our model on different Ref images, such as extreme images (*i.e.*, may have only one color or noise without any information) and random images from different testing sets. In Fig. 8, our method has robust performance and high visual quality even if the

Ref images have no useful texture information. In addition, our model has better performance when increasing #Ref images in Fig. 9. Table 3 shows the results of four similarity levels ("L1" to "L4") where L1 is the most relevant level. Our method achieves the best performance across all similarity levels.

Comparisons with Multi-RefSR Methods. We compare our model with multi-RefSR methods, *i.e.*, CIMR-SR [47] and AMRSR [32]. Note that these multi-RefSR methods are trained with a collection of reference images. In Table 4, our model trained with single reference image performs better than CIMR-SR and AMRSR with many reference images, which further demonstrate the superiority of our proposed DATSR.

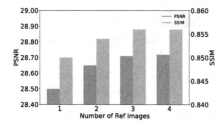

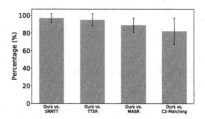

Fig. 9. Effect on #Ref images.

Fig. 10. User study.

Table 3. Performance in terms of different similarity levels on CUFED5 test set.

Similarity levels	L1		L2		L3		L4		Average	
	PSNR	SSIM	PSNR	SSIM	PSNR	SSIM	PSNR	SSIM	PSNR	SSIM
CrossNet [57]	25.48	0.764	25.48	0.764	25.47	0.763	25.46	0.763	25.47	0.764
SRNTT-rec [56]	26.15	0.781	26.04	0.776	25.98	0.775	25.95	0.774	26.03	0.777
TTSR-rec [48]	26.99	0.800	26.74	0.791	26.64	0.788	26.58	0.787	26.74	0.792
C^2-Matching-rec [12]	28.11	0.839	27.26	0.811	27.07	0.804	26.85	0.796	27.32	0.813
DATSR-rec (Ours)	**28.50**	**0.850**	**27.47**	**0.820**	**27.22**	**0.811**	**26.96**	**0.803**	**27.54**	**0.821**

4.3 More Evaluation Results

Perceptual Metric. We further use the perceptual metric LPIPS [52] to evaluate the visual quality of the generated SR images on the CUFED5 and WR-SR testing sets. Recently, this metric is also widely used in many methods [28,29]. In general, smaller LPIPS corresponds to the better performance for RefSR. As shown in Table 5, our model achieves smaller LPIPS than C^2-Matching. Thus, our model generates SR images with better quality than C^2-Matching.

User Study. To further evaluate the visual quality of the SR images, we conduct the user study to compare our proposed method with previous state-of-the-art methods, including SRNTT [56], TTSR [48], MASA [27] and C^2-Matching [12] on the WR-SR testing set. The user study contains 20 users, and each user is given multiple pairs of SR images where one is our result. Then, each user chooses one image with better visual quality. The final percentage is the average user preference of all images. In Fig. 10, over 80% of the users prefer that our results have better quality than existing RefSR methods.

4.4   Discussion on Model Size

To further demonstrate the effectiveness of our model, we also show the comparison of model size (*i.e.*, the number of trainable parameters) with the state-of-the-art model (*i.e.*, C^2-Matching [12]) in Table 6. Our model has a total number of 18.0M parameters and achieves PSNR and SSIM of 28.72 and 0.856, respectively. The results demonstrate that our proposed model outperforms C^2-Matching with a large margin, although our model size is higher than this method. The part of our model size comes from the Swin Transformer in the RFA module. More discussions of other RefSR models are put in the supplementary materials.

Table 4. Comparisons with Multi-RefSR on the CUFED5 testing set.

Methods	CIMR-SR [47]	AMRSR [32]	DATSR-rec
w/ rec. loss	26.35/0.789	28.32/0.839	**28.72/0.856**
w/ all losses	26.16/0.781	27.49/0.815	**27.95/0.835**

Table 5. Comparisons of LPIPS [52] with C^2-Matching.

Methods	CUFED5	WR-SR
C^2-Matching [12]	0.164	0.219
DATSR (Ours)	**0.140**	**0.211**

Table 6. Comparisons of model size and performance with C^2-Matching.

Methods	Params	PSNR	SSIM
TTSR-rec [48]	6.4M	27.09	0.804
C^2-Matching-rec [12]	8.9M	28.24	0.841
DATSR-rec (Ours)	18.0M	**28.72**	**0.856**

Table 7. Ablation study on the RDA and RFA modules.

Methods	PSNR	SSIM
RDA (w/ feature warping)	28.25	0.844
RFA (w/ ResNet blocks)	28.50	0.850
DATSR-rec	**28.72**	**0.856**

4.5   Ablation Study

We first investigate the effectiveness of RDA and RFA in Table 7. Specifically, we replace the texture transfer method in RDA with a feature warping based on the most relevant correspondence, and replace RFA with several convolutional neural networks (CNNs). The model with feature warping or CNNs is worse than original model with RDA or RFA. Therefore, RDA is able to discover more relevant features especially when the correspondence is not inaccurate.

For RFA, our model has better performance than the directly using simple CNNs. Nevertheless, with the help of RDA, training with CNNs still outperforms C^2-Matching with large margin. Therefore, it verifies that the effectiveness of RFA and it is able to aggregate the features at different scales. More discussions on ablation studies are put in the supplementary materials.

5   Conclusion

In this work, we propose a novel reference-based image super-resolution with deformable attention Transformer, called DATSR. Specifically, we use texture feature encoders module to extract multi-scale features and alleviate the resolution and transformation gap between LR and Ref images. Then, we propose reference-based deformable attention module to discover relevant textures, adaptively transfer the textures, and relieve the correspondence mismatching issue. Last, we propose a residual feature aggregation module to fuse features and generate SR images. Extensive experiments verify that DATSR achieves the state-of-the-arts performance as it is robust to different brightness, contrast, and color between LR and Ref images, and still shows good robustness even in some extreme cases, when the Ref images have no useful texture information. Moreover, DATSR trained with a single Ref image has better performance than existing Multi-RefSR methods trained with multiple Ref images.

Acknowledgements. This work was partly supported by Huawei Fund and the ETH Zürich Fund (OK).

References

1. Arjovsky, M., Chintala, S., Bottou, L.: Wasserstein generative adversarial networks. In: International Conference on Machine Learning, pp. 214–223 (2017)
2. Cao, H., ET AL.: Swin-Unet: unet-like pure transformer for medical image segmentation. arXiv preprint arXiv:2105.05537 (2021)
3. Chan, K.C., Zhou, S., Xu, X., Loy, C.C.: BasicVSR++: Improving video super-resolution with enhanced propagation and alignment. In: IEEE Conference on Computer Vision and Pattern Recognition, pp. 5972–5981 (2022)
4. Dai, J., et al.: Deformable convolutional networks. In: IEEE International Conference on Computer Vision, pp. 764–773 (2017)
5. Dai, T., Cai, J., Zhang, Y., Xia, S.T., Zhang, L.: Second-order attention network for single image super-resolution. In: IEEE Conference on Computer Vision and Pattern Recognition, pp. 11065–11074 (2019)
6. Dong, C., Loy, C.C., He, K., Tang, X.: Image super-resolution using deep convolutional networks. IEEE Trans. Pattern Anal. Mach. Intell. **38**(2), 295–307 (2015)
7. Goodfellow, I., et al.: Generative adversarial nets. In: Advances in Neural Information Processing Systems, vol. 27 (2014)
8. Guo, Y., et al.: Closed-loop matters: dual regression networks for single image super-resolution. In: IEEE Conference on Computer Vision and Pattern Recognition, pp. 5407–5416 (2020)
9. Guo, Y., Luo, Y., He, Z., Huang, J., Chen, J.: Hierarchical neural architecture search for single image super-resolution. IEEE Sig. Process. Lett. **27**, 1255–1259 (2020)
10. Huang, J.B., Singh, A., Ahuja, N.: Single image super-resolution from transformed self-exemplars. In: IEEE Conference on Computer Vision and Pattern Recognition, pp. 5197–5206 (2015)
11. Hui, Z., Li, J., Wang, X., Gao, X.: Learning the non-differentiable optimization for blind super-resolution. In: IEEE Conference on Computer Vision and Pattern Recognition, pp. 2093–2102 (2021)

12. Jiang, Y., Chan, K.C., Wang, X., Loy, C.C., Liu, Z.: Robust reference-based super-resolution via c2-matching. In: IEEE Conference on Computer Vision and Pattern Recognition, pp. 2103–2112 (2021)
13. Jo, Y., Kim, S.J.: Practical single-image super-resolution using look-up table. In: IEEE Conference on Computer Vision and Pattern Recognition, pp. 691–700 (2021)
14. Kar, A., Biswas, P.K.: Fast bayesian uncertainty estimation and reduction of batch normalized single image super-resolution network. In: IEEE Conference on Computer Vision and Pattern Recognition, pp. 4957–4966 (2021)
15. Khrulkov, V., Babenko, A.: Neural side-by-side: predicting human preferences for no-reference super-resolution evaluation. In: IEEE Conference on Computer Vision and Pattern Recognition, pp. 4988–4997 (2021)
16. Kong, X., Zhao, H., Qiao, Y., Dong, C.: ClassSR: a general framework to accelerate super-resolution networks by data characteristic. In: IEEE Conference on Computer Vision and Pattern Recognition, pp. 12016–12025 (2021)
17. Ledig, C., et al.: Photo-realistic single image super-resolution using a generative adversarial network. In: IEEE Conference on Computer Vision and Pattern Recognition, pp. 4681–4690 (2017)
18. Li, Z., Yang, J., Liu, Z., Yang, X., Jeon, G., Wu, W.: Feedback network for image super-resolution. In: IEEE Conference on Computer Vision and Pattern Recognition, pp. 3867–3876 (2019)
19. Liang, J., Cao, J., Sun, G., Zhang, K., Van Gool, L., Timofte, R.: SwinIR: image restoration using swin transformer. In: IEEE International Conference on Computer Vision Workshops, pp. 1833–1844 (2021)
20. Liang, J., Lugmayr, A., Zhang, K., Danelljan, M., Van Gool, L., Timofte, R.: Hierarchical conditional flow: a unified framework for image super-resolution and image rescaling. In: Proceedings of the IEEE/CVF International Conference on Computer Vision, pp. 4076–4085 (2021)
21. Liang, J., Sun, G., Zhang, K., Van Gool, L., Timofte, R.: Mutual affine network for spatially variant kernel estimation in blind image super-resolution. In: Proceedings of the IEEE/CVF International Conference on Computer Vision, pp. 4096–4105 (2021)
22. Lim, B., Son, S., Kim, H., Nah, S., Mu Lee, K.: Enhanced deep residual networks for single image super-resolution. In: IEEE Conference on Computer Vision and Pattern Recognition Workshops, pp. 136–144 (2017)
23. Liu, J., Zhang, W., Tang, Y., Tang, J., Wu, G.: Residual feature aggregation network for image super-resolution. In: IEEE Conference on Computer Vision and Pattern Recognition, pp. 2359–2368 (2020)
24. Liu, Q., Liu, C.: A novel locally linear KNN model for visual recognition. In: IEEE Conference on Computer Vision and Pattern Recognition, pp. 9446–9454 (2015)
25. Liu, Z., et al.: Swin transformer: Hierarchical vision transformer using shifted windows. In: IEEE International Conference on Computer Vision, pp. 10012–10022 (2021)
26. Liu, Z., et al.: Video Swin transformer. arXiv preprint arXiv:2106.13230 (2021)
27. Lu, L., Li, W., Tao, X., Lu, J., Jia, J.: MASA-SR: matching acceleration and spatial adaptation for reference-based image super-resolution. In: IEEE Conference on Computer Vision and Pattern Recognition, pp. 6368–6377 (2021)
28. Lucas, A., Lopez-Tapia, S., Molina, R., Katsaggelos, A.K.: Generative adversarial networks and perceptual losses for video super-resolution. IEEE Trans. Image Process. **28**(7), 3312–3327 (2019)

29. Lugmayr, A., Danelljan, M., Timofte, R.: Ntire 2020 challenge on real-world image super-resolution: Methods and results. In: IEEE Conference on Computer Vision and Pattern Recognition Workshops, pp. 494–495 (2020)
30. Matsui, Y., et al.: Sketch-based manga retrieval using manga109 dataset. Multimedia Tools Appl. **76**(20), 21811–21838 (2016). https://doi.org/10.1007/s11042-016-4020-z
31. Mei, Y., Fan, Y., Zhou, Y.: Image super-resolution with non-local sparse attention. In: IEEE Conference on Computer Vision and Pattern Recognition, pp. 3517–3526 (2021)
32. Pesavento, M., Volino, M., Hilton, A.: Attention-based multi-reference learning for image super-resolution. In: IEEE International Conference on Computer Vision, pp. 14697–14706 (2021)
33. Sajjadi, M.S., Scholkopf, B., Hirsch, M.: EnhanceNet: single image super-resolution through automated texture synthesis. In: IEEE International Conference on Computer Vision, pp. 4491–4500 (2017)
34. Shim, G., Park, J., Kweon, I.S.: Robust reference-based super-resolution with similarity-aware deformable convolution. In: IEEE Conference on Computer Vision and Pattern Recognition, pp. 8425–8434 (2020)
35. Simonyan, K., Zisserman, A.: Very deep convolutional networks for large-scale image recognition. In: International Conference on Learning Representations (2015)
36. Song, X., et al.: Channel attention based iterative residual learning for depth map super-resolution. In: IEEE Conference on Computer Vision and Pattern Recognition, pp. 5631–5640 (2020)
37. Sun, L., Hays, J.: Super-resolution from internet-scale scene matching. In: IEEE International Conference on Computational Photography, pp. 1–12 (2012)
38. Ulyanov, D., Vedaldi, A., Lempitsky, V.: Deep image prior. In: IEEE Conference on Computer Vision and Pattern Recognition, pp. 9446–9454 (2018)
39. Vaswani, A., et al.: Attention is all you need. In: Advances in Neural Information Processing Systems, vol. 30 (2017)
40. Wang, L., Kim, T.K., Yoon, K.J.: EventSR: from asynchronous events to image reconstruction, restoration, and super-resolution via end-to-end adversarial learning. In: IEEE Conference on Computer Vision and Pattern Recognition, pp. 8315–8325 (2020)
41. Wang, L., et al.: Exploring sparsity in image super-resolution for efficient inference. In: IEEE Conference on Computer Vision and Pattern Recognition, pp. 4917–4926 (2021)
42. Wang, X., Chan, K.C., Yu, K., Dong, C., Change Loy, C.: EDVR: video restoration with enhanced deformable convolutional networks. In: IEEE Conference on Computer Vision and Pattern Recognition Workshops (2019)
43. Wang, X., Xie, L., Dong, C., Shan, Y.: Real-ESRGAN: training real-world blind super-resolution with pure synthetic data. In: IEEE International Conference on Computer Vision, pp. 1905–1914 (2021)
44. Wang, X., et al.: ESRGAN: enhanced super-resolution generative adversarial networks. In: European Conference on Computer Vision Workshops (2018)
45. Xie, Y., Xiao, J., Sun, M., Yao, C., Huang, K.: Feature representation matters: end-to-end learning for reference-based image super-resolution. In: European Conference on Computer Vision, pp. 230–245 (2020)
46. Xing, W., Egiazarian, K.: End-to-end learning for joint image demosaicing, denoising and super-resolution. In: IEEE Conference on Computer Vision and Pattern Recognition, pp. 3507–3516 (2021)

47. Yan, X., Zhao, W., Yuan, K., Zhang, R., Li, Z., Cui, S.: Towards content-independent multi-reference super-resolution: adaptive pattern matching and feature aggregation. In: European Conference on Computer Vision, pp. 52–68 (2020)
48. Yang, F., Yang, H., Fu, J., Lu, H., Guo, B.: Learning texture transformer network for image super-resolution. In: IEEE Conference on Computer Vision and Pattern Recognition, pp. 5791–5800 (2020)
49. Zhang, K., Liang, J., Van Gool, L., Timofte, R.: Designing a practical degradation model for deep blind image super-resolution. In: IEEE Conference on International Conference on Computer Vision, pp. 4791–4800 (2021)
50. Zhang, K., Liang, J., Van Gool, L., Timofte, R.: Designing a practical degradation model for deep blind image super-resolution. In: Proceedings of the IEEE/CVF International Conference on Computer Vision, pp. 4791–4800 (2021)
51. Zhang, K., Zuo, W., Zhang, L.: FFDNet: toward a fast and flexible solution for CNN-based image denoising. IEEE Trans. Image Process. **27**(9), 4608–4622 (2018)
52. Zhang, R., Isola, P., Efros, A.A., Shechtman, E., Wang, O.: The unreasonable effectiveness of deep features as a perceptual metric. In: IEEE Conference on Computer Vision and Pattern Recognition, pp. 586–595 (2018)
53. Zhang, W., Liu, Y., Dong, C., Qiao, Y.: RankSRGAN: generative adversarial networks with ranker for image super-resolution. In: IEEE International Conference on Computer Vision, pp. 3096–3105 (2019)
54. Zhang, Y., Li, K., Li, K., Fu, Y.: MR image super-resolution with squeeze and excitation reasoning attention network. In: IEEE Conference on Computer Vision and Pattern Recognition, pp. 13425–13434 (2021)
55. Zhang, Y., Li, K., Li, K., Wang, L., Zhong, B., Fu, Y.: Image super-resolution using very deep residual channel attention networks. In: European Conference on Computer Vision, pp. 286–301 (2018)
56. Zhang, Z., Wang, Z., Lin, Z., Qi, H.: Image super-resolution by neural texture transfer. In: IEEE Conference on Computer Vision and Pattern Recognition, pp. 7982–7991 (2019)
57. Zheng, H., Ji, M., Wang, H., Liu, Y., Fang, L.: CrossNet: an end-to-end reference-based super resolution network using cross-scale warping. In: European Conference on Computer Vision, pp. 88–104 (2018)
58. Zhou, R., Susstrunk, S.: Kernel modeling super-resolution on real low-resolution images. In: IEEE International Conference on Computer Vision, pp. 2433–2443 (2019)
59. Zhu, X., Hu, H., Lin, S., Dai, J.: Deformable convnets v2: More deformable, better results. In: IEEE Conference on Computer Vision and Pattern Recognition, pp. 9308–9316 (2019)

Local Color Distributions Prior for Image Enhancement

Haoyuan Wang[✉], Ke Xu, and Rynson W.H. Lau

Department of Computer Science, City University of Hong Kong, Hong Kong,
People's Republic of China
hywang26-c@my.city.edu.hk

Abstract. Existing image enhancement methods are typically designed
to address either the over- or under-exposure problem in the input
image. When the illumination of the input image contains both over-
and under-exposure problems, these existing methods may not work well.
We observe from the image statistics that the local color distributions
(LCDs) of an image suffering from both problems tend to vary across different regions of the image, depending on the local illuminations. Based
on this observation, we propose in this paper to exploit these LCDs as
a prior for locating and enhancing the two types of regions (*i.e.*, over-
/under-exposed regions). First, we leverage the LCDs to represent these
regions, and propose a novel local color distribution embedded (LCDE)
module to formulate LCDs in multi-scales to model the correlations
across different regions. Second, we propose a dual-illumination learning mechanism to enhance the two types of regions. Third, we construct
a new dataset to facilitate the learning process, by following the camera
image signal processing (ISP) pipeline to render standard RGB images
with both under-/over-exposures from raw data. Extensive experiments
demonstrate that the proposed method outperforms existing state-of-
the-art methods quantitatively and qualitatively. Codes and dataset are
in https://hywang99.github.io/lcdpnet/.

1 Introduction

When taking photos, the illumination condition of a scene may not always be
ideal, and the photos may suffer from under-exposure (due to low-light/back-
light) or over-exposure (due to some intense lights inside the image region). Often,
both over- and under-exposures may occur together in the same image due to
unbalanced lighting conditions. The illumination may change significantly, bury-
ing the local image contents in *both* over- and under-exposed regions, as shown in
Fig. 1(a). While photography experts may leverage high-end DSLR cameras and

---

K. Xu and R.W.H. Lau—Joint corresponding authors. This work was led by Rynson
Lau.

Supplementary Information The online version contains supplementary material
available at https://doi.org/10.1007/978-3-031-19797-0_20.

S. Avidan et al. (Eds.): ECCV 2022, LNCS 13678, pp. 343–359, 2022.
https://doi.org/10.1007/978-3-031-19797-0_20

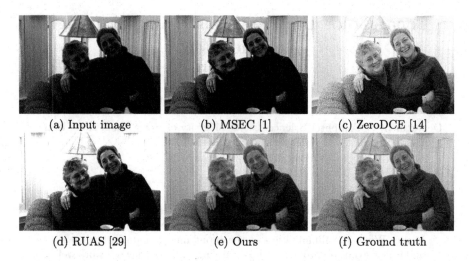

(a) Input image   (b) MSEC [1]   (c) ZeroDCE [14]

(d) RUAS [29]   (e) Ours   (f) Ground truth

Fig. 1. Given an input image (a) with both over-exposure (background windows) and under-exposure (foreground persons), existing methods fail to handle both problems well. While (b) performs better on the background, the foreground is only slightly brightened. Although (c) performs better on the foreground, the background is still over-exposed. (d) slightly brightens the foreground but further over-exposed the background. In contrast, our method (e), which is based on learning local color distributions, can handle both problems well. The textures of the window curtains and the patterns of the clothes can both be seen clearly.

carefully tune them (*e.g.*, the aperture, ISO, and special filters) to alleviate the problem, it requires photography expertise and expensive equipment.

Many methods have been proposed to enhance the quality of images that are captured with poor illumination conditions. A line of methods focus on enhancing the under-exposed images captured in low-light scenes via the Retinex based approach [32], bilateral learning [13], generative adversarial learning [11], deep parametric filtering [22], and self-supervised [14] or semi-supervised learning [38]. Other works [1,4] try to enhance the over-exposed or under-exposed images in one network. All these methods typically assume the scene illumination to be generally uniform, such that an improper exposure would result in either over- or under-exposure. Hence, they tend to adjust the image intensity globally, *i.e.*, either increasing or decreasing the intensity. However, if the illumination of a scene is non-uniform, causing the input image to suffer from both over- and under-exposures as shown in Fig. 1(a), existing methods may not work well. For example, ZeroDCE [14] (c) and RUAS [28] (d) worsen the over-exposure problem at the background regions as they try to enhance the under-exposed foreground persons. On the other hand, while MSEC [1] (b) enhances the foreground slightly, it produces some color distortions around the background windows.

In this paper, we aim to address both over- and under-exposure problems appearing in a single image. The key challenge is how to effectively separate these two types of regions and recover their local illuminations accordingly. We observe that the local color distributions (LCDs), which consist of regional local histogram vectors, can be a reliable prior to address this challenge for two reasons. First, we note that these LCDs in the over- and under-exposed regions show significant divergences and deviate from those in the properly exposed regions. Hence, they can be used to help identify and separate different types of regions. Second, while it may not be reliable to directly infer the true scene lighting from the image with both over- and under-exposures, colors are important cues that are readily available in the image. Modeling the LCDs essentially help estimate the proper local illumination and recover the buried contents. Based on our observation, we propose a novel neural network to jointly tackle the two problems (*i.e.*, both over- and under-exposure problems) with two novel modules: (1) the local color distribution embedded (LCDE) module to formulate LCDs in multi-scales to learn the representations of over- and under-exposed regions as well as their correlations, and (2) the dual-illumination learning mechanism to constrain the learning of the LCDE module, estimate and combine an over-illumination map and an under-illumination map for enhancing the image. In addition, as existing datasets (*e.g.*, [1,5,10,32]) contain mostly images with either over- or under-exposure, we further construct a new image dataset containing $\sim 1,700$ diverse scenes with both over- and under-exposures, to facilitate training and evaluation. We follow the camera ISP pipeline by applying linear transform functions and clipping on the pixel intensity of the input raw images to render sRGB images. As shown in Fig. 1(e), our proposed method based on the LCD prior brightens the under-exposed regions while darkening the over-exposed regions, allowing the textures of the over-exposed window curtains to be revealed as well as the patterns of the under-exposed sweaters that the two persons are wearing to become visible.

Our main contributions of this work can be summarized as follows:

- We propose to exploit the local color distributions (LCDs) to jointly address both over- and under-exposure problems in the input image, and a neural network to leverage the LCDs for locating and enhancing over-/under-exposed regions of the image.
- We propose the LCDE module to formulate multi-scale LCDs in order to learn the representations of over- and under-exposed regions as well as their correlations to the global illumination. We also propose a dual-illumination estimator to combine both over- and under-illumination maps to enhance the input image.
- We construct a new paired dataset consisting of over 1700 images of diverse, non-uniformly illuminated scenes to facilitate the learning process.
- Extensive experiments demonstrate that the proposed method outperforms state-of-the-art methods qualitatively and quantitatively on the popular MSEC [1] and our datasets.

2   Related Work

Image-to-Image Translation-Based Methods. A line of methods enhance under-exposed images by learning different image-to-image translation mappings.

Histogram equalization [25] and gamma correction are the most representative methods. Some methods propose to combine global and local contrast enhancement operators with semantic region detection (*e.g.*, face, building and sky) [19], regional templates [16] or contrast statistics along image boundaries and in textured regions [29].

Recent deep-learning based methods typically learn the mapping functions using high-quality retouched images or images taken using high-end cameras, with bilateral learning [13], intermediate HDR supervision [39], multi-stage restoration [9,41], generative adversarial learning [11,17,18,26], or reinforcement learning [23,40]. Cai *et al.* [4] propose to enhance an under-exposed image by separately modeling the illuminance and detail layers from multiple exposure images. Moran *et al.* [31] propose to learn a set of piece-wise linear scaling curves and apply them in different color spaces for under-exposed image enhancement. Xu *et al.* [36] propose to enhance under-exposed images based on frequency decomposition. In [22], different kinds of local parametric filters are learned for image enhancement. Mahmoud *et al.* [1] propose a coarse-to-fine network to learn color and detail enhancement for addressing either over- or under-exposure.

Retinex-Based Methods. Another line of works are Retinex-based image enhancement methods [3,12,15,32,43,44]. They first decompose the input image into illumination and reflectance layers, and then enhance the illumination layer of the image. Conventional optimization based methods [3,12,15] propose different hand-craft priors for constraining the illumination or reflectance layers. Deep learning based methods [10,28,32,44] learn such intrinsic decomposition from a large amount of data. For example, DeepUPE [32] propose to directly estimate the proper illumination layer from the input under-exposed image via bilateral learning [6]. Most recently, Liu *et al.* [28] propose an architecture search based method to leverage cooperative priors for under-exposed image enhancement.

Limitation of Existing Works. All aforementioned methods typically assume that only either over- or under-exposure problem would appear in a single image. Hence, they tend to brighten the under-exposed images or darken the over-exposed images, but lack the capability to tackle images with both over- and under-exposures. In this paper, we aim to tackle this common shortfall. We first construct a new dataset, and propose a LCD prior guided deep-learning approach for enhancing images containing both over- and under-exposures.

3   Proposed Dataset

To study our problem, we first revisit a recently published large-scale image enhancement dataset, the Multi-Scale Exposure Correction (MSEC) dataset [1]. Although it contains images with different levels of over- or under-exposures, each of the images is either over- or under-exposed. We visualize the luminance intensity mapping between input and reference images in Fig. 2. Figure 2(a) shows that the shapes of the luminance mappings for individual images from the MSEC dataset [1] are either concave or convex. These luminance mappings do not show any non-uniform illumination exhibited from images that suffer from both

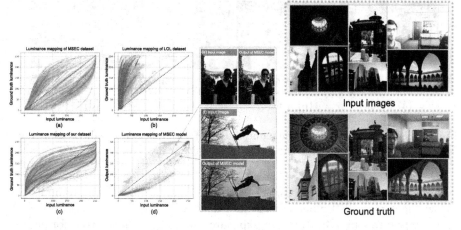

Fig. 2. The input-ground truth luminance mapping curve of (a) MSEC dataset [1], (b) LOL dataset [10], and (c) our dataset. Each cluster represents an image. For a single image, both (a) and (b) contains a single mapping of either brightening or darkening. (d) is the input-output mapping learned by the model trained on the MSEC dataset when given (e, f) as the input.

Fig. 3. Some input-ground truth pairs in our dataset. Our dataset contains images of over 1700 scenes.

over- and under-exposures. Statistics shown in Fig. 2(d) demonstrate that the MSEC model [1] trained on this dataset either brightens or darkens the input image (see Fig. 2(e,f) for illustration). Figure 2(b) shows the statistics of the luminance mappings for the images from the LOL dataset [10], which is a popular low-light image enhancement dataset. We can see that it only allows the learning of under-exposure enhancement. This means that methods trained on the LOL dataset [10] would typically brighten the input images. This demonstrates that a new dataset containing both over- and under-exposures in individual images is desired.

We construct our dataset from the raw images in the MIT Adobe5k dataset [2], which contains 5000 raw and expert-retouched sRGB image pairs for learning the tone mapping process. Since raw images have higher dynamic ranges to preserve scene information than sRGB images and their intensities are linearly proportional to the scene radiance, we generate our input images of both over- and under-exposures from the raw images. We use the expert-retouched sRGB images as our ground truth images. However, we note that not all raw images in this dataset are suitable for generating our images with both over- and under-exposures (*e.g.*, synthesizing over-exposure from a very dark image would likely produce an unrealistic image), and many expert-retouched images contain very dark/bright regions that cannot be used to form our ground truth images.

In order to generate high-quality learning pairs, we formulate the dataset generation pipeline in three steps as: (1) We manually go through all the image pairs in Adobe5k, and remove those pairs whose expert-retouched images contain

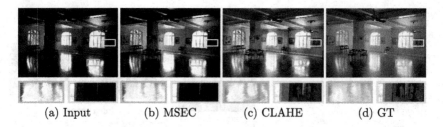

(a) Input   (b) MSEC   (c) CLAHE   (d) GT

Fig. 4. MSEC [1] (b) enhances the input image (a) with a better overall visual quality, while CLAHE [27] (c) produces more faithful details in the local regions.

very dark or very bright regions. (2) For each candidate raw image from (1), we follow the camera ISP pipeline to render an sRGB image with both over- and under-exposures, by adjusting the exposure level with a linear transformation function. (3) For each rendered sRGB image from (2), we ask a volunteer (who is a photographer) to help assess its quality. If the volunteer points out that the rendered image is not realistic or has obvious artifacts (*e.g.*, color bleeding), we feed it back to step (2) to produce another sRGB image for re-assessment. This iterates until we have a good quality image, or after five iterations and we simply discard this pair.

The linear mapping function used in step (2) is:

$$I'(i,j) = \phi \left[k \left(I(i,j) - 0.5 \right) + 0.5 \right], \tag{1}$$

where I is the input raw image whose pixel values range between $[0, 1]$. i, j are the spatial position in the image, and $\phi[\cdot]$ is the clipping operator to drop the overflow value with the upper/lower bounds being 1/0. k is the slope value that represents the scaling factor of the exposure level. We manipulate k to generate images with over- and under-exposures. We apply Eq. 1 on all three channels of the input raw image equally to obtain the final rendered sRGB image. In total, we generate 1,733 pairs of images, which are split into 1,415 for training, 100 for validation, and 218 for testing. Some sample pairs are shown in Fig. 3.

4 Proposed Method

The over- and under-exposed image enhancement task could be formulated as seeking a mapping function F, which maps an 8-bit per channel sRGB image I_x to an enhanced image I_y such that $I_y = F(I_x)$. Instead of directly learning the image-to-image translation model or Retinex-based image-to-illumination mapping model, we propose to learn a *region-aware illumination mapping model* by learning to exploit the multi-scale LCDs and dual-illumination estimation.

4.1 Local Color Distribution (LCD) Pyramid

Directly inferring the true scene lighting from a single image is challenging, especially when the input image contains both over- and under exposures. Instead,

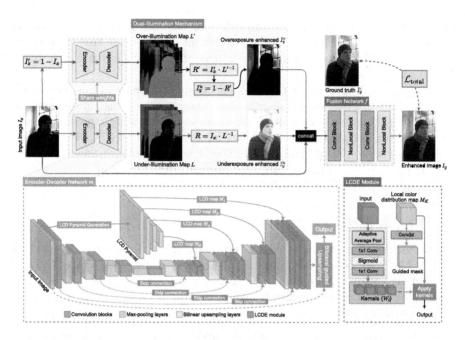

Fig. 5. Overview of our proposed network. It leverages the LCD pyramid with an encoder-decoder architecture for detecting the regions with problematic exposures implicitly, and the for enhancement of the over- and under-exposed regions.

as the color is a key component of scene lighting preserved in the image, we can leverage the local color information to help build representations of regional illuminations. Figure 4(c) shows an example, where the color histogram based method CLAHE [27] recovers more details than the latest deep method MSEC [1] in both over- and under-exposed regions. However, CLAHE [27] tends to produce images of inconsistent colors, due to its lack of global information. We model LCDs based on CLAHE [27], and extend it to be a multi-scale pyramid in our neural network, in order to tackle the inconsistency by learning the local-to-global illumination correlations.

Building the LCD Pyramid. Given an input image I_x of size $h \times w$, whose pixel values range between $[0, 1]$, we split I_x into $N = [h/K] \cdot [w/K]$ patches, where $[\cdot]$ is the closest-integer operator. We define a LCD as the color histogram within a local patch of size $K \times K$. We then use the 4D LCD map M_K to represent the distribution of scale K. We first build a $h \times w$ bilateral grid Γ [7] by splatting the pixel histogram voting along the range dimension, and then we compute M_k using:

$$M_k\left(\left[\frac{i}{K}\right], \left[\frac{j}{K}\right], c, b\right) = \frac{1}{K^2} \sum_{p,q \in \Omega_K(i,j)} \Gamma(p, q, c, b), \qquad (2)$$

where i, j, c are the horizontal, vertical, and channel indices of the image, respectively. b is the index to the histogram bins, which can be computed by $b = [I_x(i,j,c) \cdot B]$. $\Omega_K(i,j)$ returns the indices of the pixels in the $K \times K$ patch that pixel (i,j) belongs to.

By assigning K with different values, we obtain LCD maps at different scales, e.g., M_1 is the pixel-wise color distribution, where the local histogram vector in M_1 is a sparse one-hot vector. When K increases, the locality representation of M_K grows correspondingly. Let K take its value from $\{2^l, l \in N^+\}$. $\mathbf{M} = \{M_K\}$ is then a multi-scale LCD pyramid with different levels of color distribution maps. A LCD pyramid contains regional illumination distributions in multi-scale, as visualized in Fig. 6. It can help differentiate over-/under-exposed regions.

4.2   Proposed Network

Figure 5 shows the overview of the proposed network. It has an encoder-decoder [30] architecture, incorporating the LCDE module to leverage the LCD pyramid for learning the representations of over- and under-exposed regions and the dual-illumination mechanism for adaptive enhancement.

LCDE module. In order to learn adaptive representations for over- and under-exposed regions, we propose the LCDE module to predict the adaptive convolutional kernels with the guidance of the LCD pyramid. Our design of the LCDE module is based on DRconv [8] (originally proposed for high-level image classification and detection tasks). We choose DRconv [8] to exploit its idea of producing region-wise kernels. Unlike DRconv [8] that learn different kernels according to the local semantics, which are not reliable in the over- and under-exposed regions, we learn different kernels according to the local illuminations guided by the local color distributions.

Specifically, the LCDE module has two branches, *i.e.*, the convolution-kernels-generation branch and the guided-mask-prediction branch (bottom right part of Fig. 5). The first branch takes as input the precursor feature map and produces the parameters of n kernels $\{W_1, W_2, ...W_n\}$. The guided-mask-prediction branch inputs the LCD map M_K, and uses it to guide the prediction of a multi-value mask for dividing the spatial feature maps into n regions in order to apply different convolution kernels on different regions. By applying a different convolution kernel on a different region, the multi-scale LCD pyramid guides the network to differentiate regions of different exposures and enhances them separately.

To handle high resolution inputs, we construct this module upon the bilateral upsampling method [6,7] to achieve a fast inference speed.

Dual-Illumination Estimation. To constrain the model to learn the exposure-aware masks, we exploit the Retinex theory in our model. The Retinex based methods (*e.g.*, [32]) typically decompose the input image I_x into an illumination map L and a reflectance map R. By considering the reflectance map R as the enhanced image, DeepUPE [32] generates the under-exposure enhanced result I_y^u with $I_y^u = R = I_x \cdot L^{-1}$. Since the values in L fall within $[0,1]$, the pixel values in the result image are always larger than the those of the input image. Hence, these methods cannot suppress over-exposure. To address this problem, we propose to extend the illumination prediction mechanism of [32] to dual-illumination prediction mechanism by incorporating dual-path learning in [42]. The main idea here is that over-exposures in I_x could be regarded as under-exposures in the reverse image of I_x. By first computing the reverse image I_x' via $I_x' = 1 - I_x$, we can then compute the over-illumination map L' of the input image I_x in addition to the under-illumination map L. Thus, the over-exposure enhanced images I_y^o could be obtained by $I_y^o = 1 - R' = 1 - I_x' \cdot L'^{-1}$, where L' is the over-illumination map of I_x. L and L' are estimated via the encoder-decoder network with the LCDE module. The two enhanced components are then fused by our fusion network to generate the final result.

Fig. 6. The visualization of a LCD pyramid layer, taking an over-/under-exposed image as input. Over-/under-exposed regions are implicitly separated along the channel dimension.

Fig. 7. Inferring the illumination maps helps constrain the learning of the guided mask. Our model implicitly assigns one decoder to each region type for adaptive enhancement.

Fusion Network. The fusion network f takes the two separately enhanced images, I_y^u and I_y^o, and the original image I_x as inputs to regress the final enhanced image. It contains two convolution layers and two non-local [33] blocks. With the non-local blocks, the network is able to capture long-range spatial correlations across pixels. The fusion network fuses the three inputs by predicting a 3-channel weight map to generate the enhanced result I_y.

Given the input image I_x, the whole process of our method to produce I_y is:

$$I_y = f\left(\frac{I_x}{m(I_x)}, \, 1 - \frac{1 - I_x}{m(1 - I_x)}, \, I_x\right), \tag{3}$$

where m represents the encoder-decoder network and f is the fusion network.

Why Would our Model Work? Since the LCDE module applies n different kernels on n regions, each region can be regarded as being assigned with an individual decoder to learn the luminance mapping but without introducing extra computational cost, while all regions share the same encoder for feature extraction (see Fig. 7). In addition, by inferring the illumination maps, it helps constrain the learning of the guided mask in the LCDE module to focus on the exposure levels of these regions.

4.3 Loss Function

We adopt four loss terms to train our model. We apply the widely used MSE term $\mathcal{L}_{\mathrm{mse}}$ to measure the intensity reconstruction errors. To correct the color distortions in the over- and under-exposed regions, we apply the cosine similarity term $\mathcal{L}_{\mathrm{cos}}$ [32,34,35], which measures the color similarity of the reconstructed image and its ground truth in the sRGB color space. In addition, in order to guide the network to estimate the illumination maps, we apply the local smoothness term [32,37] to our dual-illumination estimation process, denoted as $\mathcal{L}_{\mathrm{tv1}}$ and $\mathcal{L}_{\mathrm{tv2}}$, respectively. The local smoothness term aims to preserve the local smoothness characteristics of image illuminations by minimizing their gradient variations. The overall function can be written as:

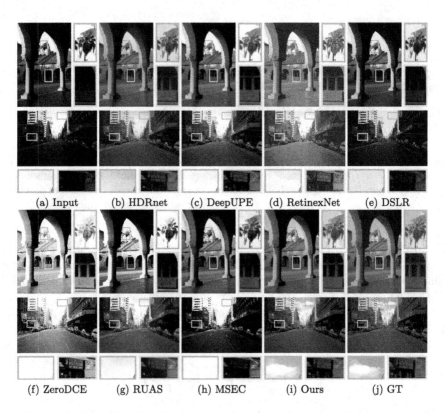

(a) Input   (b) HDRnet   (c) DeepUPE   (d) RetinexNet   (e) DSLR

(f) ZeroDCE   (g) RUAS   (h) MSEC   (i) Ours   (j) GT

Fig. 8. Visual comparison of over-/under-exposed images from our dataset. Our model reconstructs the details in the over-exposed regions (sky and tower) as well as the under-exposed regions (wall and door).

$$\mathcal{L}_{\mathrm{total}} = \lambda_1 \mathcal{L}_{\mathrm{mse}} + \lambda_2 \mathcal{L}_{\mathrm{cos}} + \lambda_3 \mathcal{L}_{\mathrm{tv1}} + \lambda_4 \mathcal{L}_{\mathrm{tv2}}, \tag{4}$$

where λ_1, λ_2, λ_3 and λ_4 are the balancing hyper-parameters. Refer to the Supplemental for more details on the loss functions.

5 Experiments

5.1 Implementation Details

We implement our model using PyTorch [24]. All our experiments are conducted on a single NVIDIA GTX3080 GPU. The parameters of the network are optimized by the ADAM optimizer [20] with $\beta_1 = 0.9, \beta_2 = 0.999$, and the learning rate is $1e^{-4}$. The desired region number is set to $n = 2$, indicating over- and under-exposed regions. The weights for the terms in the loss function in Eq. 4 are $\lambda_1 = 1.0, \lambda_2 = 0.5, \lambda_3 = \lambda_4 = 0.01$. We utilize a 4-scale LCD pyramid and a 4-scale encoder-decoder network in our experiments. We implement the splatting operation in Γ in Eq. 2 using the soft-histogram-voting in [21]. During training, we resize the input images to 512×512 and apply random horizontal and vertical flippings to augment the input data. The model reported in the experiments is implemented based on a plain encoder-decoder network with 218K parameters.

Table 1. Quantitative comparison on the MSEC [1] test set. Best performances are marked in **bold**.

Method	PSNR↑	SSIM↑
HE [25]	16.525	0.696
CLAHE [27]	15.383	0.599
DSLR [17] (Sony)	18.020	0.683
DSLR [17] (BlackBerry)	17.606	0.653
DSLR [17] (iPhone)	15.907	0.622
RetinexNet [10]	11.135	0.605
DeepUPE [32]	13.689	0.632
ZeroDCE [14]	12.058	0.544
MSEC [1]	20.205	0.769
Ours	**22.295**	**0.855**

Table 2. Quantitative comparison on the proposed test set. * indicates that the model is retrained on our proposed training set. Best performances are marked in **bold**.

Method	PSNR↑	SSIM↑	Method	PSNR↑	SSIM↑
HE [25]	15.975	0.684	DSLR$_{Sony}$ [17]	16.991	0.672
ClAHE [27]	16.327	0.642	DSLR$_{BlackBerry}$ [17]	17.215	0.693
LIME [15]	17.335	0.686	DSLR$_{iPhone}$ [17]	18.560	0.712
RetinexNet [10]	16.200	0.630	DSLR* [17]	20.856	0.758
RetinexNet* [10]	19.250	0.704	DeepUPE* [32]	20.970	0.818
MSEC* [1]	20.377	0.779	RUAS [28]	13.927	0.634
MSEC [1]	17.066	0.642	RUAS* [28]	13.757	0.606
ZeroDCE* [14]	12.587	0.653	HDRnet* [13]	21.834	0.818
Ours	**23.239**	**0.842**			

5.2 Comparisons with State-of-the-Art Methods

To verify the effectiveness of our method, we compare our model with the existing exposure correction and image enhancement methods. We select three conventional enhancement methods, including histogram equalization (HE), CLAHE [27] and LIME [15], and seven deep-learning-based methods: ZeroDCE [14], RetinexNet [10], MSEC [1], DSLR [17], HDRnet [13], Deep-UPE [32] and RUAS [28]. We adopt the commonly used Peak Signal-to-Noise Ratio (PSNR) and Structural Similarity (SSIM) as our evaluation metrics.

Quantitative Comparison. Table 1 reports the performance evaluation on the MSEC [1] test set. Both MSEC [1] and ours are trained on the MSEC [1] training set, while other numbers are copied from MSEC [1]. From the table, we can see

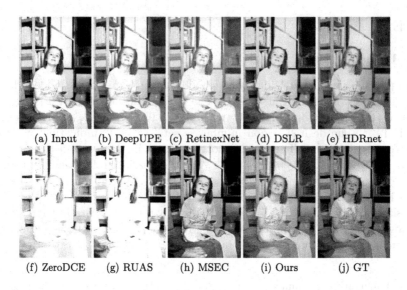

(a) Input   (b) DeepUPE (c) RetinexNet   (d) DSLR   (e) HDRnet

(f) ZeroDCE   (g) RUAS   (h) MSEC   (i) Ours   (j) GT

Fig. 9. Visual comparison of an over-exposed image from our dataset. Our result has the best visual quality.

Table 3. Ablation study.

Method	Ours$_{plain}$	Ours$_{single}$	Ours$_{DRconv}$	Ours$_{mse}$	Ours$_{mse+tv}$	Ours
PSNR↑	21.878	22.198	21.001	21.261	22.421	23.239
SSIM↑	0.783	0.840	0.785	0.793	0.815	0.842

that our method outperforms the second best method (*i.e.*, MSEC [1]) by a large margin. Table 2 further shows the comparison on our proposed test dataset. For a fair comparison, we report the performances of existing deep learning based methods using their pre-trained models as well as the models retrained on our training set. The results show that our method outperforms all existing methods on both PSNR and SSIM metrics.

Visual Comparisons. We visually compare the results of our method with those of the existing methods. Note that all models used in this experiment are retrained on our dataset for a fair comparison. Figure 8 shows two examples containing both over- and under-exposed regions from our dataset, and results of existing methods and ours. We can see that our method can correct both over- and under-exposed regions, and produce more visually pleasing details and colors. We further show comparisons on images with large amount of over-exposed pixels (Fig. 9) or under-exposed pixels (Fig. 10) from our dataset, an image from the MSEC [1] dataset (Fig. 11), and two images from the Internet (Fig. 12). These comparisons generally demonstrate that our method generalizes well to different exposure levels and varying illumination conditions. Refer to the supplemental for more visual comparisons.

5.3 Internal Analysis

Ablation Study. In order to analyze the effectiveness of our proposed module and pipeline, we perform ablation experiments on the network structure. Specifically, we train four different models: **(1)** A plain encoder-decoder (Ours$_{plain}$), **(2)** Add LCDE modules to the decoder of (1) (Ours$_{single}$), **(3)** Add the DRconv blocks [8] to the decoder of (1) (Ours$_{DRconv}$), **(4)** Add dual-illumination estimation to (2) (Ours).

As shown in Table 3, the dual-illumination estimation or the LCDE module significantly increase the performance, which verifies the effectiveness of the dual-illumination learning and the local color distribution prior. The comparison between (2) and (3) shows that the performance gain of our model is mainly due to the LCD pyramid prior instead of regional dynamic convolution. We also perform the ablation study of loss function terms in Table 3. By comparing the

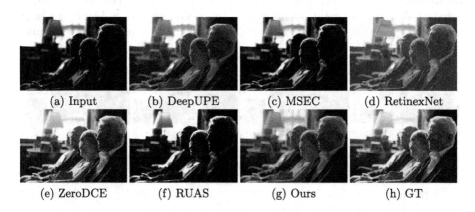

(a) Input	(b) DeepUPE	(c) MSEC	(d) RetinexNet
(e) ZeroDCE	(f) RUAS	(g) Ours	(h) GT

Fig. 10. Visual comparison of an under-exposed image from our dataset. Our result has the best visual quality.

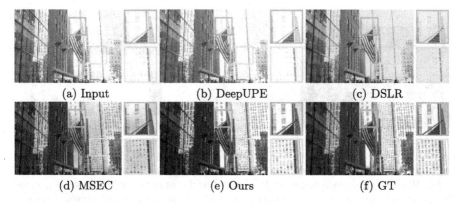

(a) Input	(b) DeepUPE	(c) DSLR
(d) MSEC	(e) Ours	(f) GT

Fig. 11. Visual comparison of an over-exposed image from the MSEC dataset [1]. Our result has the best visual quality and details.

last three columns, we can see that gradually incorporating the local smoothness term $\mathcal{L}_{tv}$ and the cosine similarity term $\mathcal{L}_{cos}$ consistently improves the enhancement performance.

Visualization and Interpretation. We visualize the intermediate results of our network to examine whether the network has the region-aware capability. Figure 13 shows the predicted multi-scale guided mask features by the LCDE module. We expect that under the guidance of LCD pyramid, the input images and feature maps could be divided into different regions by the guided mask according to the exposure level As shown in Fig. 13, the intermediate guided masks of the LCDE module generally divide the pixels into the bright region and dark region when $n = 2$. This indicates that under the guidance of the LCDE module, the network does learn the region-aware adaptive enhancement for input images.

Limitations. Fig. 14 shows two challenging cases that our method may fail to enhance. If an image contains a large under-exposed region (Fig. 14(a)) or a large over-exposed region (Fig. 14(A)), it may be difficult for our model to enhance

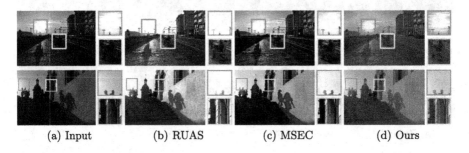

(a) Input   (b) RUAS   (c) MSEC   (d) Ours

Fig. 12. Visual comparison on over-/under-exposed images from the Internet. Our result has the best visual quality.

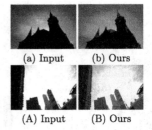

Fig. 13. The visualization of the learned guided mask in multi-scales intermediate LCDE module layers. With the guidance of the LCD pyramid and the constraint of the dual-illumination map, the model learns the guided mask adaptively.

Fig. 14. Failure cases. Our method may fail to enhance images with a large region of under-exposed pixels (building in (b)) or over-exposed pixels (sky in (B)).

the region. As a future work, we would like to explore semantic scene layouts as well as image inpainting techniques to handle this situation.

6 Conclusion

In this paper, we have tackled the image enhancement problem of correcting images with both over- and under-exposed regions. We have proposed a new dataset and designed a new end-to-end model to address the problem. We propose the LCDE module to detect over- and under-exposed regions under the guidance of the local color distributions. We extend the Retinex theory based illumination by proposing the dual-illumination estimator for better detail reconstruction. Extensive experiments show that our method performs favorably against state-of-the-art methods.

Acknowledgments. This project is in part supported by a General Research Fund from RGC of Hong Kong (RGC Ref.: 11205620).

References

1. Afifi, M., Derpanis, K.G., Ommer, B., Brown, M.S.: Learning multi-scale photo exposure correction. In: CVPR (2021)
2. Bychkovsky, V., Paris, S., Chan, E., Durand, F.: Learning photographic global tonal adjustment with a database of input/output image pairs. In: CVPR (2011)
3. Cai, B., Xu, X., Guo, K., Jia, K., Hu, B., Tao, D.: A joint intrinsic-extrinsic prior model for retinex. In: ICCV (2017)
4. Cai, J., Gu, S., Zhang, L.: Learning a deep single image contrast enhancer from multi-exposure images. IEEE TIP **27**(4), 2049–2062 (2018)
5. Chen, C., Chen, Q., Xu, J., Koltun, V.: Learning to see in the dark. In: CVPR (2018)
6. Chen, J., Adams, A., Wadhwa, N., Hasinoff, S.: Bilateral guided upsampling. ACM TOG **35**(6), 1–8 (2016)
7. Chen, J., Paris, S., Durand, F.: Real-time edge-aware image processing with the bilateral grid. ACM TOG **26**(3), 103-es (2007)
8. Chen, J., Wang, X., Guo, Z., Zhang, X., Sun, J.: Dynamic region-aware convolution. In: CVPR (2021)
9. Chen, L., Lu, X., Zhang, J., Chu, X., Chen, C.: HINet: half instance normalization network for image restoration. In: CVPR Workshops (2021)
10. Chen, W., Wenjing, W., Wenhan, Y., Jiaying, L.: Deep Retinex decomposition for low-light enhancement. In: BMVC (2018)
11. Chen, Y., Wang, Y., Kao, M., Chuang, Y.: Deep photo enhancer: unpaired learning for image enhancement from photographs with GANs. In: CVPR (2018)
12. Fu, X., Zeng, D., Huang, Y., Zhang, X., Ding, X.: A weighted variational model for simultaneous reflectance and illumination estimation. In: CVPR (2016)
13. Gharbi, M., Chen, J., Barron, J.T., Hasinoff, S.W., Durand, F.: Deep bilateral learning for real-time image enhancement. In: ACM TOG (2017)
14. Guo, C., et al.: Zero-reference deep curve estimation for low-light image enhancement. In: CVPR (2020)

15. Guo, X., Li, Y., Ling, H.: Lime: low-light image enhancement via illumination map estimation. IEEE TIP **26**(2), 982–993 (2017)
16. Hwang, S.J., Kapoor, A., Kang, S.B.: Context-based automatic local image enhancement. In: ECCV (2012)
17. Ignatov, A., Kobyshev, N., Timofte, R., Vanhoey, K., Van Gool, L.: DSLR-quality photos on mobile devices with deep convolutional networks. In: ICCV (2017)
18. Jiang, Y., et al.: EnlightenGAN: deep light enhancement without paired supervision. IEEE TIP **30**, 2340–2349 (2021)
19. Kaufman, L., Lischinski, D., Werman, M.: Content-aware automatic photo enhancement. In: Computer Graphics Forum (2012)
20. Kingma, P., Ba, J.: Adam: a method for stochastic optimization. arXiv:1412.6980 (2014)
21. Liu, Y.L., et al.: Single-image HDR reconstruction by learning to reverse the camera pipeline. In: CVPR (2020)
22. Moran, S., Marza, P., McDonagh, S., Parisot, S., Slabaugh, G.G.: DeepLPF: deep local parametric filters for image enhancement. In: CVPR (2020)
23. Park, J., Lee, J.Y., Yoo, D., So Kweon, I.: Distort-and-recover: color enhancement using deep reinforcement learning. In: CVPR (2018)
24. Paszke, A., et al.: Automatic differentiation in pytorch. In: NeurIPS Workshops (2017)
25. Pizer, S., et al.: Adaptive histogram equalization and its variations. Graph. Image Process. Comput. Vis. **39**(3), 355–368 (1987)
26. Ren, W., et al.: Low-light image enhancement via a deep hybrid network. IEEE TIP **28**(9), 4364–4375 (2019)
27. Reza, A.M.: Realization of the contrast limited adaptive histogram equalization (CLAHE) for real-time image enhancement. J. VLSI Sig. Process. Syst. Sig. Image Video Technol. **38**(1), 35–44 (2004). https://doi.org/10.1023/B:VLSI.0000028532.53893.82
28. Risheng, L., Long, M., Jiaao, Z., Xin, F., Zhongxuan, L.: Retinex-inspired unrolling with cooperative prior architecture search for low-light image enhancement. In: CVPR (2021)
29. Rivera, R., Ryu, B., Chae, O.: Content-aware dark image enhancement through channel division. IEEE TIP **21**(9), 3967–3980 (2012)
30. Ronneberger, O., Fischer, P., Brox, T.: U-Net: convolutional networks for biomedical image segmentation. In: MICCAI (2015)
31. Sean Moran, Ales Leonardis, G.S.S.M.: Curl: neural curve layers for global image enhancement. arXiv:1911.13175 (2019)
32. Wang, R., Zhang, Q., Fu, C., Shen, X., Zheng, W., Jia, J.: Underexposed photo enhancement using deep illumination estimation. In: CVPR (2019)
33. Wang, X., Girshick, R., Gupta, A., He, K.: Non-local neural networks. In: CVPR (2018)
34. Wei, H., Yifeng, Z., Rui, H.: Low light image enhancement network with attention mechanism and Retinex model. IEEE Access **8**, 74306–74314 (2020)
35. Xu, K., Tian, X., Yang, X., Yin, B., Lau, R.W.H.: Intensity-aware single-image deraining with semantic and color regularization. IEEE TIP **30**, 8497–8509 (2021)
36. Xu, K., Yang, X., Yin, B., Lau, R.W.: Learning to restore low-light images via decomposition-and-enhancement. In: CVPR (2020)
37. Xu, L., Yan, Q., Xia, Y., Jia, J.: Structure extraction from texture via natural variation measure. ACM TOG **31**(6), 1–10 (2012)

38. Yang, W., Wang, S., Fang, Y., Wang, Y., Liu, J.: From fidelity to perceptual quality: a semi-supervised approach for low-light image enhancement. In: CVPR (2020)

39. Yang, X., Xu, K., Song, Y., Zhang, Q., Wei, X., Lau, R.: Image correction via deep reciprocating HDR transformation. In: CVPR (2018)

40. Yu, R., Liu, W., Zhang, Y., Qu, Z., Zhao, D., Zhang, B.: DeepExposure: learning to expose photos with asynchronously reinforced adversarial learning. In: NeurIPS (2018)

41. Zamir, S.W., et al.: Multi-stage progressive image restoration. In: CVPR (2021)

42. Zhang, Q., Nie, Y., Zheng, W.: Dual illumination estimation for robust exposure correction. In: Computer Graphics Forum (2019)

43. Zhang, Q., Yuan, G., Xiao, C., Zhu, L., Zheng, W.S.: High-quality exposure correction of underexposed photos. In: ACM MM (2018)

44. Zhang, Y., Zhang, J., Guo, X.: Kindling the darkness: a practical low-light image enhancer. In: ACM MM (2019)

L-CoDer: Language-Based Colorization with Color-Object Decoupling Transformer

Zheng Chang[1], Shuchen Weng[2], Yu Li[3], Si Li[1(✉)], and Boxin Shi[2]

[1] School of Artificial Intelligence, Beijing University of Posts and
Telecommunications, Beijing, China
{zhengchang98,lisi}@bupt.edu.cn

[2] NERCVT, School of Computer Science, Peking University, Beijing, China
{shuchenweng,shiboxin}@pku.edu.cn

[3] International Digital Economy Academy, Shenzhen, China
liyu@idea.edu.cn

Abstract. Language-based colorization requires the colorized image to be consistent with the user-provided language caption. A most recent work proposes to decouple the language into color and object conditions in solving the problem. Though decent progress has been made, its performance is limited by three key issues. (i) The large gap between vision and language modalities using independent feature extractors makes it difficult to fully understand the language. (ii) The inaccurate language features are never refined by the image features such that the language may fail to colorize the image precisely. (iii) The local region does not perceive the whole image, producing global inconsistent colors. In this work, we introduce transformer into language-based colorization to tackle the aforementioned issues while keeping the language decoupling property. Our method unifies the modalities of image and language, and further performs color conditions evolving with image features in a coarse-to-fine manner. In addition, thanks to the global receptive field, our method is robust to the strong local variation. Extensive experiments demonstrate our method is able to produce realistic colorization and outperforms prior arts in terms of consistency with the caption.

1 Introduction

Image colorization, the task of converting a grayscale image into a plausible color image, has been widely used in black-and-white image restoration, artist assistance, and advertising/film industry. However, automatic image colorization [21,23,30] is inherently an ill-posed problem, as there are multiple reasonable colors suitable for the grayscale image. Thus an interactive supervised signal is

---

Z. Chang and S. Weng—Equal contributions.

Supplementary Information The online version contains supplementary material available at https://doi.org/10.1007/978-3-031-19797-0_21.

S. Avidan et al. (Eds.): ECCV 2022, LNCS 13678, pp. 360–375, 2022.
https://doi.org/10.1007/978-3-031-19797-0_21

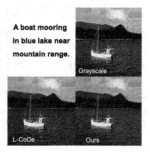

Fig. 1. We demonstrate three typical issues in existing language-based colorization approaches (*e.g.*, L-Code [25]) and how our method improves them correspondingly. **Left:** With modality unification, our method understands the intrinsic color properties behind words, therefore it could colorize images with word that describes abstract appearance (colorful) rather than specific colors (red for tomato and green for salad). **Middle:** The results of our method present more accurate color than previous work (the hat tends to be gray rather than purple), which benefits from the color representation evolving with image features. **Right:** Thanks to the transformer architecture, our method is robust to the locally strong texture variation (upper part of the sea) in grayscale image. (Color figure online)

required to determine the unique solution. Commonly used signals (*e.g.*, user scribble [20,32] and reference example [10,18,28]) require either high-level artistic skill or time-consuming search, while taking language as the guidance of colorization is recently demonstrated to be a friendly way of user interaction for colorization [3,19,25,27].

Language-based colorization requires the colorized results to be consistent with the description of language. Though natural language shows superior potential as the conditions of colorization, the usage of it is the rose among thorns because of the huge semantic chasm between grayscale image and language inputs, which causes color-object coupling and color-object mismatch [3,19,27]. To handle these problems, researchers pay special attention to decoupling language conditions [25]. However, these existing methods [3,19,25,27] have several commonly remaining issues to be solved. *(i)* Large gap between modalities - previous methods leverage different architectures independently to encode two input sources into embedding features (CNN for image and LSTM for caption). There is an inevitable gap between these two types of features, and they are not easy to be fully and precisely unified at a later stage, which prevents the model from understanding the semantics of the language in depth (Fig. 1 left). *(ii)* Inaccurate language representation - by directly taking the outputs of LSTM as conditions to inject into image features, fixed embedding limits the representation power of language, which causes inaccurate colorization (Fig. 1 middle). *(iii)* Local vulnerability - color bleeding occurs when there is a strong variation of texture or luminance in the local context, as the semantics is cued from the local regions in grayscale images (Fig. 1 right).

We for the first time introduce transformer into language-based colorization and propose **L-CoDer**, a **L**anguage based **Co**lorization with color-object **De**coupling transformer, to deal with aforementioned issues as follows: *(i)* Thanks to the color-object decoupling transformer we proposed, both image and decoupled language conditions are unified in one modality as tokens, which is beneficial to understand intrinsic color properties behind the word (Fig. 1 left). *(ii)* Every transformer block extracts and fuses the self-modality and corresponding cross-modality token features so that the language conditions evolve from coarse to fine instead of being kept with fixed semantic, which provides adaptive supervisory signals to generate accurate and plausible colors (Fig. 1 middle). *(iii)* Benefited from the global receptive field of transformer, L-CoDer has stronger robustness to locally strong variation of texture or luminance, which further improves the colorization quality (Fig. 1 right). Our contributions are summarized as:

- We propose the color-object decoupling transformer to deal with the large gap between modalities, inaccurate language representation, and local vulnerability issues that reside in language-based colorization.
- We design the decoupling attention to make images globally and bidirectionally interact with language features while maintaining the decoupled properties of language conditions.
- We organize the decoupled language tokens into a coarse-to-fined representation, which provides adaptive supervisory signals evolving with image features and bringing in accurate and plausible colorized results.

We conduct our experiments in the extended COCO-Stuff dataset [25] and demonstrate that our transformer model achieves state-of-the-art performance with better colorized quality and condition consistency in both quantitative and qualitative results.

2 Related Works

Automatic Colorization. Automatic colorization approaches colorize grayscale image without any external hints, which learns data distribution on large-scale datasets and directly estimate the proper colors. A part of works [4,12,15,30] focus on feature engineering to explore the effective architecture. Some works pay attention to advanced generative models, *e.g.*, VAE [5], GAN [23], cINN [2], and transformer [14]. Recently, to further extract semantic information, prior knowledge is widely introduce into automatic colorization methods, *e.g.*, detection boxes [21], segmentation masks [33], pretrained GAN [26]. However, automatic colorization methods suffer from multi-modal uncertainty and may fail to generate results satisfying users' expectations.

Language-Based Colorization. Language-based colorization is to colorize gray images under the guidance of user-given caption, which is presented by Manjunatha *et al.* [19]. After that, researchers start to explore the way to fuse image and language features spatially by adopting recurrent attentive model [3]. Generating segmentation mask as the side-task is later introduced to jointly optimize the colorization results [27]. A more recent work decouples language conditions into object space and color space, which solves color-object coupling and color-object mismatch problem [25]. Although noticeable progress has been made in the task, the modality differences still largely affect the performance of colorization.

Vision Transformer. Transformer is firstly proposed and demonstrated to make great success in natural language processing (NLP) to model sequence data [22]. Computer vision researchers have find it also performs excellent on various visual computing problems, *e.g.*, classification [9], detection [36], segmentation [34], super resolution [16], inpainting [17], to name a few. Benefit by the generality of transformer, it works well in cross-modality task, like referring segmentation [7], image-text retrieval [13], VQA [35] and text-to-image generation [8,29]. Vision transformer has also been applied to automatic colorization [14], but it remains space for exploration in language-guided interactions.

3   Method

To make this paper self-contained, we first review the language condition decoupling proposed by L-CoDe [25] to clarify the necessity of language decoupling. Next, we present the overview of L-CoDer and elaborate on the detailed designs of modules. In our approach, we address the issues of large gap between modalities, inaccurate language representation, and local vulnerability, which previous methods suffer from. Finally, we introduce the loss functions and training details.

3.1   Language Condition Decoupling for Colorization

Language condition decoupling mainly solves two main problems: *(i)* Color-object coupling: When the specified color and object combination is less observed in the dataset, the model may fail to apply the corresponding color to the object. *(ii)* Color-object mismatch: The model may incorrectly colorize the object whose color is not mentioned in the caption with the color of another object. For example, given language "green bananas on the plate" and a corresponding image, the model without decoupling may fail to colorize bananas with green because the banana object is always combined with yellow (color-object coupling); or it may incorrectly colorize plate with green, which is used to describe the bananas (color-object mismatch).

Instead of encoding caption into a single vector, L-CoDe decouples caption into adjective vectors that represent colors (*e.g.*, green) and noun vectors that describe the object category (*e.g.*, bananas and plate). After that, it predicts the combination of adjective vectors and noun vectors and constructs an object-color corresponding matrix (OCCM). A binary cross entropy (BCE) loss is used to supervise the optimization of predicted OCCM [25], which ensures the word "green" is combined with the word "bananas".

It is required to design unique modules to apply decoupled language conditions into colorization networks. In L-CoDe [25], the attention transfer module is presented for dealing with color-object coupling problem. Specifically, it uses noun vectors to find the corresponding image regions with a standard attention operator, and transfers the correspondence between regions and nouns into the correspondence between regions and adjectives with predicted OCCM. Therefore, regions corresponding to noun vectors are colorized with the adjective vectors in the combination. For avoiding color-object mismatch issue, the soft-gated

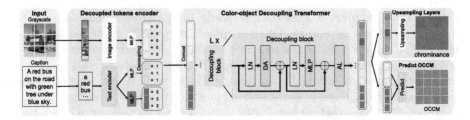

Fig. 2. Framework of L-CoDer. The **decoupled tokens encoder** maps the input grayscale image and language into the same modality, but they are represented in disparate feature spaces: Each word is decoupled as a noun token and an adjective token, and each image patch is encoded as an image token (Sect. 3.3). After concatenating all the tokens, the **color-object decoupling transformer** makes global interaction between tokens of the same or different modalities to supervise the evolution of tokens bidirectionally from coarse to fine with several decoupling blocks (Sect. 3.4). The **decoupling attention** (DA) in decoupling block is presented to avoid color-object coupling and color-object mismatch problems, which makes image tokens interact with decoupled language tokens while maintaining the decoupled properties of language (Sect. 3.5). The **upsampling layers**, composed of a stack of convolutions, are used to convert the image tokens at the finest grain into two missing chrominance channels with user-desired resolution (Sect. 3.6). The OCCM [25] (briefly recalled in Sect. 3.1) is calculated by noun tokens and adjective tokens, which is used to maintain decouple property in decoupling blocks.

injection module is designed. In detail, a soft-gated mask is constructed using the transferred attention maps as input, which guides the injection of decoupled language conditions to ensure that colors are not applied to objects not mentioned in the caption.

However, there remain difficult problems in language-based colorization task, *e.g.*, large gap between modalities, inaccurate language representation, and local vulnerability, which are shown in Fig. 1 from left to right, respectively. Transformer could unify the modality of image and language, dynamically represent language conditions, and have robustness to locally strong variation of texture or luminance, which motivates us to design L-CoDer to solve these problems.

3.2   L-Coder Framework

We illustrate the framework of L-CoDer in Fig. 2. It works in the CIE *Lab* color space, which requires models to generate two missing chrominance channels corresponding to the input grayscale image (as the luminance channel) under the guidance of user-specified language. L-CoDer is composed of a decoupled tokens encoder, a color-object decoupling transformer with decoupling attentions, and several upsampling layers. Two loss functions are used during training: *(i)* the ground truth image as a candidate colorized results, and *(ii)* the ground truth OCCM to constraint the semantic decoupling of object tokens and color tokens. The parameter settings are shown in the supplementary.

3.3   Decoupled Tokens Encoder

This module is proposed to encode both image and language as tokens so that they could be unified in one modality, which helps bridge the large gap between modalities. The decoupling design also avoids color-object coupling and color-object mismatch issues mentioned in Sect. 3.1. The decoupled tokens encoder is composed of an image encoder, a language encoder, and a decoupling module. Given a grayscale image $I \in \mathbb{R}^{H \times W}$ where H and W are the height and width of the input image, the image encoder first repeats the grayscale image for adapting to the input of ViT [9] as $(I, I, I) \in \mathbb{R}^{H \times W \times 3}$, and then reshapes it into N patches as $I_{\mathrm{P}} = [I_{\mathrm{P}}^1, \ldots, I_{\mathrm{P}}^N] \in \mathbb{R}^{N \times P^2 \times 3}$, where (P, P) is the patch resolution and $N = HW/P^2$. After that, image encoder feeds patches into a standard ViT [9] to extract global features and generate image tokens $T_{\mathrm{I}} = [T_{\mathrm{I}}^1, \ldots, T_{\mathrm{I}}^N] \in \mathbb{R}^{N \times C_{\mathrm{I}}}$, where C_{I} is the channel number of image tokens.

We use BERT [6] as our language encoder, which encodes input caption $[w_1, \ldots, w_M]$ into language tokens $T_{\mathrm{L}} = [T_{\mathrm{L}}^1, \ldots, T_{\mathrm{L}}^M] \in \mathbb{R}^{M \times C_{\mathrm{L}}}$, where M is the number of words in the caption and C_{L} is the channel number of language tokens. Note that we build our dictionary based on BERT, so that it includes a large vocabulary and the isolated words never appear in the training dataset will also be assigned with a pretrained embedded vector.

After the image and language are encoded, we decouple language conditions to handle color-object coupling and color-object mismatch problems [25] mentioned in Sect. 3.1. Specifically, we adopt a Multi-Layer Perceptron (MLP) to map image tokens into latent space, and another two MLPs to convert language tokens into object space and color space separately, written as:

$$T_{\mathrm{img}} = f^{\mathrm{img}}(T_{\mathrm{I}}), \qquad T_{\mathrm{obj}} = f^{\mathrm{col}}(T_{\mathrm{L}}), \qquad T_{\mathrm{col}} = f^{\mathrm{col}}(T_{\mathrm{L}}), \qquad (1)$$

where $T_{\mathrm{img}} = [T_{\mathrm{img}}^1, \ldots, T_{\mathrm{img}}^N] \in \mathbb{R}^{N \times C_{\mathrm{s}}}$ are image tokens in latent space, $T_{\mathrm{obj}} = [T_{\mathrm{obj}}^1, \ldots, T_{\mathrm{obj}}^M] \in \mathbb{R}^{M \times C_{\mathrm{s}}}$ are noun tokens represented in object space, and $T_{\mathrm{col}} = [T_{\mathrm{col}}^1, \ldots, T_{\mathrm{col}}^M] \in \mathbb{R}^{M \times C_{\mathrm{s}}}$ are adjective tokens represented in color space, and C_{s} is the number of embedding channels.

Inspired by ViLT [13], we introduce the modal-type embedding vectors $T_{\mathrm{type}} \in \mathbb{R}^{C_{\mathrm{s}}}$ to distinguish token modalities. We add modal-type embedding vectors $[T_{\mathrm{type}}^0, T_{\mathrm{type}}^1, T_{\mathrm{type}}^2]$ to image tokens, noun tokens, and adjective tokens separately:

$$\hat{T}_{\mathrm{img}}^i = T_{\mathrm{img}}^i + T_{\mathrm{type}}^0, \qquad \hat{T}_{\mathrm{obj}}^j = T_{\mathrm{obj}}^j + T_{\mathrm{type}}^1, \qquad \hat{T}_{\mathrm{col}}^j = T_{\mathrm{col}}^j + T_{\mathrm{type}}^2, \qquad (2)$$

where $i \in \{1, \ldots, N\}$ and $j \in \{1, \ldots, M\}$.

3.4   Color-Object Decoupling Transformer

With the color-object decoupling transformer, the semantic of decoupled language tokens evolves with image features from coarse to fine, which avoids inaccurate language representation issue. We show the attention maps at different layers to illustrate the focus of colorization changes with the evolution of tokens

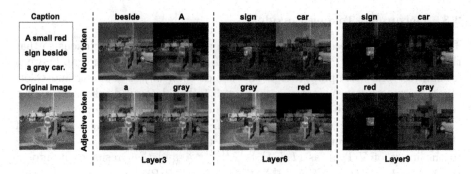

Fig. 3. We show the top-2 most attended words by the color-object decoupling transformer at layers 3, 6, and 9. As the number of layers increases, the model gradually finds the most important noun tokens (sign and car) and adjective tokens (red and gray). Meanwhile, the semantic of tokens evolves towards more accurate representation in a coarse-to-fine manner, *e.g.*, nouns tokens find regions of corresponding objects, and adjective tokens find regions with similar colors. (Color figure online)

in Fig. 3. In addition, thanks to the ability of transformer to capture global dependencies, our method has stronger robustness to locally strong variation of texture or luminance. The Z_{img}^1, Z_{obj}^1, and Z_{col}^1 generated from $\hat{T}_{\text{img}}$, $\hat{T}_{\text{obj}}$, and $\hat{T}_{\text{col}}$ by separate fully connected layers are the initial input of the proposed color-object decoupling transformer, which we introduce in detail next.

The color-object decoupling transformer is made up of L decoupling blocks (depending on the model variant), and each decoupling block contains a decoupling layer (DL) and an adaptive layer (AL). Given the input of the i-th block that includes image tokens Z_{img}^i, and decoupled language tokens Z_{obj}^i and Z_{col}^i, we formulate the process of extraction intermediate feature as:

$$[Z^{i+1}] = \text{AL}(\text{DL}([Z^i])), \qquad i \in \{1,\dots,L\} \qquad (3)$$

where $[Z^i]$ is the abbreviation of $[Z_{\text{img}}^i; Z_{\text{obj}}^i; Z_{\text{col}}^i] \in \mathbb{R}^{(N+2M)\times C_z}$, $Z_{\text{img}}^i \in \mathbb{R}^{N\times C_z}$, $Z_{\text{obj}}^i, Z_{\text{col}}^i \in \mathbb{R}^{M\times C_z}$, and C_z is the channel number.

Decoupling layer (DL) is modified from standard transformer block, which contains an MLP that has two fully connected layers, a decoupling attention (DA) (Sect. 3.5), and a LayerNorm (LN) layer added before MLP and DA. This process is formulated as:

$$[\bar{Z}^i] = \text{DA}\,(\text{LN}([Z^i])) + [Z^i], \qquad i \in \{1,\dots,L\} \qquad (4)$$

$$[\hat{Z}^i] = \text{MLP}(\text{LN}([\bar{Z}^i])) + [\bar{Z}^i]. \qquad i \in \{1,\dots,L\} \qquad (5)$$

The operator of adaptive layer (AL) depends on the modality of tokens. Specifically, for image tokens Z_{img}^i, AL reshapes them into spatial space followed by a convolution operator; but for decoupled language tokens Z_{obj} and Z_{col}, AL performs a fully connected operation, written as:

$$[Z^{i+1}] = [\text{F}_{\text{conv}}(\hat{Z}_{\text{img}}^i); \text{F}_{\text{fc}}([\hat{Z}_{\text{obj}}^i; \hat{Z}_{\text{col}}^i])], \qquad i \in \{1,\dots,L\} \qquad (6)$$

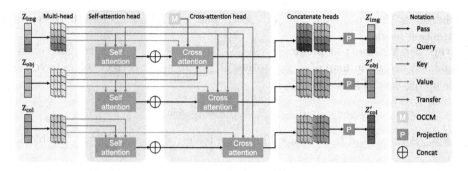

Fig. 4. Illustration of decoupling attention. The tokens are firstly projected into multi-head feature space. Next, tokens in each space are fed into self-attention and cross-attention heads separately to extract high-level semantic. Finally, we concatenate the output of self-attention and cross-attention heads in the multi-head feature space, and project them into common feature space to fuse semantic from various perspectives as the output of decoupling attention.

where F_{conv} is a 3×3 convolution layer and F_{fc} is a fully connected layer. AL is similar to RTSB [16], which is designed to take convolution operator to enhance the translational equivariance of our transformer.

3.5 Decoupling Attention

To maintain the decoupled properties of language conditions, we propose decoupling attention to ensure the interaction between decoupled language tokens and image tokens. As shown in Fig. 4, decoupling attention is composed of H self-attention heads, H cross-attention heads, and a projection layer.

For self-attention heads, tokens of each modality calculate similarity with themselves to extract high-level global features; while for cross-attention heads, tokens cue semantic from other modal tokens: *(i)* We locate objects in image tokens Z_{img} with noun tokens Z_{obj}, and inject color with adjective tokens Z_{col}; *(ii)* Inspired by VLT [7], we integrate features of image tokens Z_{img} into noun tokens Z_{obj} to help understand perspectives and emphasis of the sentence and further improve the accuracy of location; *(iii)* As the image tokens Z_{img} are gradually colorized, we also fuse image features into adjective tokens Z_{col}, which keeps the accuracy of color semantic by adjusting the features of tokens. For each modality, a projection layer is designed to fuse the results of H self-attention heads and H cross-attention heads to output the refined tokens. We formulate the decoupling attention as three steps:

Step 1): For each attention head, we project $[Z_{img}; Z_{obj}; Z_{col}]$ into query, key, and value feature space by fully connected layers, and calculate attention maps to measure the relevance between tokens and themselves (self-attention head) or corresponding tokens of another modality (cross-attention head):

$$A_{i,h}^{slf} = Z_{i,h}^{qry} \times (Z_{i,h}^{key})^\top, \quad \bar{A}_{img,h}^{crs} = Z_{img,h}^{qry} \times (Z_{obj,h}^{key})^\top, \quad A_{j,h}^{crs} = Z_{j,h}^{qry} \times (Z_{img,h}^{key})^\top, \quad (7)$$

where $i \in \{\text{img}, \text{obj}, \text{col}\}$, $j \in \{\text{obj}, \text{col}\}$, and $h \in \{1, \ldots, H\}$ is the index of attention heads.

Step 2): We use the predicted OCCM $M_{\text{occm}} \in \mathbb{R}^{M \times M}$ to transfer cross-modality attention map of object tokens $\bar{A}^{\text{crs}}_{\text{img},h}$ to apply correct colors to corresponding objects position:

$$A^{\text{crs}}_{\text{img},h} = \bar{A}^{\text{crs}}_{\text{img},h} \times M_{\text{occm}}. \tag{8}$$

M_{occm} is calculated by decoupled language tokens Z^{l-1}_{obj} and Z^{l-1}_{col} at last block:

$$M_{\text{occm}} = \text{Norm}(\sigma(Z^{l-1}_{\text{obj}} U (Z^{l-1}_{\text{col}})^\top + Z^{l-1}_{\text{obj}} u), 0.1), \tag{9}$$

where $l \in \{1, \ldots, L\}$ is the index of decoupling blocks, σ is the sigmoid function, $U \in \mathbb{R}^{C_{\text{in}} \times C_{\text{in}}}$, $u \in \mathbb{R}^{C_{\text{in}} \times M}$ are learnable parameters, and $\text{Norm}(A, v)$ is a function to normalize matrix with ℓ_1 normalization after setting elements in matrix A smaller than v as zero. The process of applying OCCM is in the supplementary.

Step 3): We further use the softmax to normalize all attention maps $\hat{A} = \text{Softmax}(A/C_{\text{in}})$, which are used as the soft gate to inject assigned tokens:

$$Z^{\text{slf}}_{i,h} = \hat{A}^{\text{slf}}_{i,h} \times Z^{\text{val}}_{i,h}, \qquad Z^{\text{crs}}_{\text{img},h} = \hat{A}^{\text{crs}}_{\text{img},h} \times Z^{\text{val}}_{\text{col},h}, \qquad Z^{\text{crs}}_{j,h} = \hat{A}^{\text{crs}}_{j,h} \times Z^{\text{val}}_{\text{img},h}. \tag{10}$$

We finally concatenate H self-attention heads and H cross-attention heads and projected them into the high-level feature space:

$$Z'_i = ([Z^{\text{slf}}_{i,0} \ Z^{\text{crs}}_{i,0} \ \ldots \ Z^{\text{slf}}_{i,H} \ Z^{\text{crs}}_{i,H}]) W^{\text{proj}}_i, \qquad i \in \{\text{img}, \text{obj}, \text{col}\} \tag{11}$$

where $W^{\text{proj}}_i \in \mathbb{R}^{C_z \times C_z}$ is the parameter matrix.

3.6 Upsampling Layers

Upsampling layers use colorized image tokens Z^{L+1}_{img} to generate colorful image with user-desired resolution. Specifically, the colorized image tokens are first reshaped into spatial resolution $\hat{Z}_{\text{img}} \in \mathbb{R}^{\sqrt{N} \times \sqrt{N} \times C_z}$, and then fed into a stack of transposed convolutions to upsample the resolution and predict the two chrominance channels. We concatenate the grayscale image I_L and predict two chrominance channels to obtain the colorized result in the CIE *Lab* space, written as:

$$I_{\text{Lab}} = \text{Concat}(I_L, G_{\text{deconv}}(\hat{Z}_{\text{img}})), \tag{12}$$

where G_{deconv} is compose of 4 upsampling blocks with transposed convolution layers to achieve 16 times larger resolution.

3.7 Learning

There are two losses we use to supervise the optimization as L-CoDe [25]: *(i)* a smooth-ℓ_1 loss with $\delta = 1$ to supervise the colorized images:

$$L_\delta(x, y) = \frac{1}{2}(x - y)^2 \mathbb{1}_{\{|x-y| < \delta\}} + \delta(|x - y| - \frac{1}{2}\delta) \mathbb{1}_{\{|x-y| \geq \delta\}}, \tag{13}$$

Table 1. Quantitative comparison result. L-CoDer (ours) performs best in three metrics. Throughout this paper, ↑ (↓) means higher (lower) is better.

Category	Method	PSNR↑	SSIM↑	LPIPS↓
Automatic	CIC [30]	22.156	89.705%	0.224
	DeOldify [1]	21.708	86.451%	0.255
	InstColor [21]	23.914	90.618%	0.194
	ChromaGAN [23]	22.085	84.161%	0.275
Language-based	LBIE [3]	22.092	85.197%	0.265
	ML2018 [19]	21.055	85.333%	0.282
	Xie2018 [27]	21.407	84.016%	0.298
	L-CoDe [25]	24.965	91.657%	0.169
Ablation	W/o decouple	25.014	90.724%	0.173
	W/o evolution	25.141	91.155%	0.167
	W/o bidirection	25.135	91.131%	0.168
	W/o upsample	25.305	91.464%	0.161
Ours	L-CoDer	**25.504**	**91.963%**	**0.159**

and *(ii)* a binary cross entropy loss to optimize last predicted OCCM towards the ground truth matrix:

$$L_{\mathrm{BCE}}(x, y) = -(y \log(x) + (1 - y) \log(1 - x)). \quad (14)$$

We jointly optimize L_δ and L_{BCE} as:

$$L = \alpha L_\delta + \beta L_{\mathrm{BCE}}, \quad (15)$$

where we set $\alpha = 1$ and $\beta = 0.0001$.

We train L-CoDer 40 epochs with batchsize 32 for 12 h on 4 NVIDIA TITAN RTX GPUs. We use AdamW optimizer to minimize our losses with learning rate as 1×10^{-5}, momentum parameters $\beta_1 = 0.99$ and $\beta_2 = 0.999$.

4 Experiments

Dataset. We conduct our experiments on the extended COCO-Stuff dataset proposed in L-CoDe [25], which includes 59K training images and 2.4K evaluation images of 224×224 resolution, with annotated correspondence between objects and colors as the basis for generating ground truth of OCCM.

Evaluation Metrics. Following L-CoDe [25], we report Peak Signal-to-Noise Ratio (PSNR) [11], Structural Similarity Index Measure (SSIM) [24], and Learned Perceptual Image Patch Similarity (LPIPS) [31] to quantify the colorization quality. We further conduct user studies to evaluate whether our results are favored by human observers.

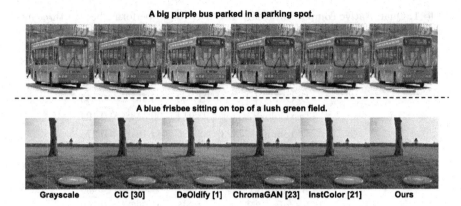

Fig. 5. Comparison with automatic colorization methods. Without the interactive supervised signal, automatic colorization methods cannot change the color of the bus in the top and the frisbee in the bottom, if the users have special request.

Table 2. User study results. Our method outperforms other approaches with the highest scores on both experiments.

Experiment	LBIE [3]	ML2018 [19]	Xie2018 [27]	L-CoDe [25]	Ours
Reality	10.68%	10.56%	15.72%	25.76%	**37.28%**
Corresponding	10.80%	13.56%	22.00%	23.40%	**30.24%**

4.1   Comparisons with State-of-the-Art Methods

We make comparisons with four automatic colorization methods to demonstrate the necessity of language conditions as supervisory signal of colorization task, including CIC [30], Deoldify [1], ChromaGAN [23], and InstColorization [21]. We also make comparisons with another four language-based colorization approaches to show the improvement by overcoming large gap between modalities, inaccurate language representation, and local vulnerability problems, which contains LBIE [3], ML2018 [19], Xie2018 [27], and L-CoDe [25].

Qualitative Comparisons. The automatic methods suffer from multi-modal uncertainty, which degrades the quality of colorized images. We show the comparison with automatic methods in Fig. 5, where the bus and frisbee could be colorized as any reasonable color, so the model cannot figure out the most appropriate color and may not meet the users' requirement. The comparison with language-based approaches is shown in Fig. 6, where we show overall quality improvement, word ontology understanding, accurate color representation, and local variation robustness from top to the bottom separately.

Quantitative Comparisons. We show the quantitative comparison results in Table 1. Our method (L-CoDer) outperforms all compared methods of both automatic and language-based approaches, and achieves the best PSNR, SSIM, and LPIPS scores.

A flat screen monitor shows a brightly colored image on the screen.

The green street sign is above a *stop sign*.

A brown dog, a fence, and a tree.

A toddler in a pink shirt sits on the lap of a woman.

| Grayscale | LBIE [3] | ML2018 [19] | Xie2018 [27] | L-CoDe [25] | Ours |

Fig. 6. Comparison with language-based colorization methods. **First row**: Our method could generate more realistic images. **Second row**: Our method cues intrinsic color property behind words (inferring red from words "stop sign"). **Third row**: Our method colorizes objects with more accurate color (dog with accurate brown). **Fourth row**: Our method shows robustness to locally strong texture variation (correctly colorizing pink shirt near the arm). (Color figure online)

4.2 User Study

We conduct two user study experiments to evaluate whether our colorization results are more favored by human observers rather than other language-based colorization approaches. We perform two experiments following the setting of L-CoDe [25]: *(i)* Reality experiment: Participants are shown a ground truth image and five language-based colorization results, along with a caption that describes the ground truth color image, and asked to choose the result that is most visually pleasing with respect to the ground truth. *(ii)* Corresponding experiment: We randomly replace a word that describes the appearance of objects in the caption with another one, and use the modified caption to re-colorized five results. Shown modified caption and re-colorized results, participants are asked to choose an image that matches best with the given caption.

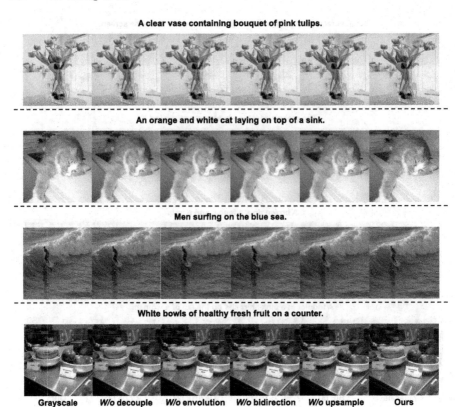

A clear vase containing bouquet of pink tulips.

An orange and white cat laying on top of a sink.

Men surfing on the blue sea.

White bowls of healthy fresh fruit on a counter.

Grayscale   *W/o decouple*   *W/o envolution*   *W/o bidirection*   *W/o upsample*   Ours

Fig. 7. Ablation study with different variants of the proposed method. **First row**: Without decoupling, the stem of flower is colorized with the pink color that describes the petals. **Second row**: Disabling evolution, the cat becomes grayish. **Third row**: Removing bidirection, the saturation of blue sea decreases. **Fourth row**: After removing upsampling layers, the red color of left apple is presented as a square patch. (Color figure online)

In each experiment, there are 100 images randomly selected from the testing set. Experiments are published on Amazon Mechanical Turk (AMT) and each experiment is completed by 25 participants. As shown in Table 2, our method achieves the highest scores in both experiments.

4.3   Ablation Study

We disable various modules to create four baselines to study the impact of our proposed modules. The evaluation scores and synthetic images of the ablation study are shown in Table 1 and Fig. 7.

W/o Decouple. We remove the decoupling module in decoupled tokens encoder, replace decoupling attention with conventional cross attention, and

1896. "Lightship   There is a white
Scotland."   ship with two red
sign on the sea.

1937. "Dad jokes,   Man in blue shirt
the McNallys at   with his family in
dinner. "   front of tan wall.

1940. "Old mine   A   red   house
office. Virginia   surrounded by
City, Nevada."   yellow grass.

Fig. 8. Examples of colorizing legacy photos with user-given captions.

take out all the relevant modules about OCCM. In this way, we meet color-object mismatch problem mentioned in L-CoDe [25] (first row in Fig. 7).

W/o Evolution. We use fixed decoupled tokens as language conditions and inject them into every decoupling block. As the result, the colorized image becomes grayish and color representation becomes inaccurate (second row in Fig. 7).

W/o Bidirection. We modify the decoupling attention by controlling information flow only from decoupled language tokens to image tokens. This strategy prevents language tokens from capturing image semantics, and further interferes with the evolution of language tokens. The colorization results are undersaturated without bidirectional interaction between tokens (third row in Fig. 7).

W/o Upsample. We remove the upsampling layers that are composed of a series of convolutions. Instead, a matrix multiplication is performed to project image tokens into pixels. Then, pixels are reshaped as 2D image. In this ablation, obvious patch artifacts occur (fourth row in Fig. 7).

4.4   Application

We show our application on colorizing legacy black and white photos under the guidance of language in Fig. 8.

5   Conclusion

We propose L-CoDer to deal with language-based colorization task. We introduce transformer into the task for three advantages: *(i)* The input image and language could be unified in one modality as tokens, which narrows the gap between modalities and helps the model understand intrinsic color property behind the word. *(ii)* The semantic of decoupled language tokens is organized coarse-to-fine evolving with image feature, which makes color representation more accurate. *(iii)* The global receptive field of transformer makes our method locally robust, which further improves the colorization quality. We conduct our experiments on the extended COCO-Stuff dataset, and our method achieves significantly higher scores than other compared methods in PSNR, SSIM, and LPIPS metrics.

Limitation. The transformer architecture also brings drawbacks, *e.g.*, when our method is expanded to train the high resolution version, it will require significantly more computing resources and longer training time than CNN-based methods. These could be improved with the development of transformer.

Acknowledgements. This project is supported by National Natural Science Foundation of China under Grant No. 62136001.

References

1. Antic, J.: A deep learning based project for colorizing and restoring old images (and video!). https://github.com/jantic/DeOldify
2. Ardizzone, L., Lüth, C., Kruse, J., Rother, C., Köthe, U.: Guided image generation with conditional invertible neural networks. arXiv preprint arXiv:1907.02392 (2019)
3. Chen, J., Shen, Y., Gao, J., Liu, J., Liu, X.: Language-based image editing with recurrent attentive models. In: CVPR (2018)
4. Cheng, Z., Yang, Q., Sheng, B.: Deep colorization. In: ICCV (2015)
5. Deshpande, A., Lu, J., Yeh, M.C., Jin Chong, M., Forsyth, D.: Learning diverse image colorization. In: CVPR (2017)
6. Devlin, J., Chang, M.W., Lee, K., Toutanova, K.: BERT: pre-training of deep bidirectional transformers for language understanding. In: NAACL (2019)
7. Ding, H., Liu, C., Wang, S., Jiang, X.: Vision-language transformer and query generation for referring segmentation. In: ICCV (2021)
8. Ding, M., et al.: CogView: mastering text-to-image generation via transformers. In: NIPS (2021)
9. Dosovitskiy, A., et al.: An image is worth 16 x 16 words: transformers for image recognition at scale. In: ICLR (2021)
10. He, M., Chen, D., Liao, J., Sander, P.V., Yuan, L.: Deep exemplar-based colorization. ACM TOG **37**(4), 1–16 (2018)
11. Huynh-Thu, Q., Ghanbari, M.: Scope of validity of PSNR in image/video quality assessment. Electron. Lett. **44**(13), 800–801 (2008)
12. Iizuka, S., Simo-Serra, E., Ishikawa, H.: Let there be color!: joint end-to-end learning of global and local image priors for automatic image colorization with simultaneous classification. ACM ToG **35**(4), 1–11 (2016)
13. Kim, W., Son, B., Kim, I.: ViLT: vision-and-language transformer without convolution or region supervision. In: ICML (2021)
14. Kumar, M., Weissenborn, D., Kalchbrenner, N.: Colorization transformer. In: ICLR (2021)
15. Larsson, G., Maire, M., Shakhnarovich, G.: Learning representations for automatic colorization. In: ECCV (2016)
16. Liang, J., Cao, J., Sun, G., Zhang, K., Van Gool, L., Timofte, R.: Swinir: image restoration using swin transformer. In: ICCV (2021)
17. Liu, R., ET AL.: FuseFormer: fusing fine-grained information in transformers for video inpainting. In: ICCV (2021)
18. Lu, P., Yu, J., Peng, X., Zhao, Z., Wang, X.: Gray2colornet: transfer more colors from reference image. In: ACM MM (2020)
19. Manjunatha, V., Iyyer, M., Boyd-Graber, J., Davis, L.: Learning to color from language. In: NAACL (2018)

20. Sangkloy, P., Lu, J., Fang, C., Yu, F., Hays, J.: Scribbler: controlling deep image synthesis with sketch and color. In: CVPR (2017)
21. Su, J.W., Chu, H.K., Huang, J.B.: Instance-aware image colorization. In: CVPR (2020)
22. Vaswani, A., et al.: Attention is all you need. In: NIPS (2017)
23. Vitoria, P., Raad, L., Ballester, C.: ChromaGAN: adversarial picture colorization with semantic class distribution. In: WACV (2020)
24. Wang, Z., Bovik, A.C., Sheikh, H.R., Simoncelli, E.P.: Image quality assessment: from error visibility to structural similarity. TIP **13**(4), 600–612 (2004)
25. Weng, S., Wu, H., Chang, Z.C., Tang, J., Li, S., Shi, B.: L-code: language-based colorization using color-object decoupled conditions. In: AAAI (2022)
26. Wu, Y., Wang, X., Li, Y., Zhang, H., Zhao, X., Shan, Y.: Towards vivid and diverse image colorization with generative color prior. In: ICCV (2021)
27. Xie, Y.: Language-guided image colorization. Master's thesis, ETH Zurich, Departement of Computer Science (2018)
28. Xu, Z., Wang, T., Fang, F., Sheng, Y., Zhang, G.: Stylization-based architecture for fast deep exemplar colorization. In: CVPR (2020)
29. Zhang, H., Koh, J.Y., Baldridge, J., Lee, H., Yang, Y.: Cross-modal contrastive learning for text-to-image generation. In: CVPR (2021)
30. Zhang, R., Isola, P., Efros, A.A.: Colorful image colorization. In: ECCV (2016)
31. Zhang, R., Isola, P., Efros, A.A., Shechtman, E., Wang, O.: The unreasonable effectiveness of deep features as a perceptual metric. In: Proceedings of the IEEE Conference on Computer Vision and Pattern Recognition (CVPR) (2018)
32. Zhang, R., et al.: Real-time user-guided image colorization with learned deep priors. ACM TOG (2017)
33. Zhao, J., Liu, L., Snoek, C.G., Han, J., Shao, L.: Pixel-level semantics guided image colorization. In: BMVC (2018)
34. Zheng, S., et al.: Rethinking semantic segmentation from a sequence-to-sequence perspective with transformers. In: CVPR (2021)
35. Zhou, Y., et al.: TRAR: routing the attention spans in transformer for visual question answering. In: ICCV (2021)
36. Zhu, X., Su, W., Lu, L., Li, B., Wang, X., Dai, J.: Deformable detr: deformable transformers for end-to-end object detection. In: ICLR (2020)

From Face to Natural Image: Learning Real Degradation for Blind Image Super-Resolution

Xiaoming Li[1,5], Chaofeng Chen[2], Xianhui Lin[3], Wangmeng Zuo[1,4(✉)],
and Lei Zhang[5]

[1] Faculty of Computing, Harbin Institute of Technology, Harbin, China
wmzuo@hit.edu.cn
[2] S-Lab, Nanyang Technological University, Singapore, Singapore
[3] DAMO Academy, Alibaba Group, Shenzhen, China
[4] Peng Cheng Lab, Shenzhen, China
[5] Department of Computing, The Hong Kong Polytechnic University,
Hung Hom, Hong Kong
cslzhang@comp.polyu.edu.hk

Abstract. How to design proper training pairs is critical for super-resolving real-world low-quality (LQ) images, which suffers from the difficulties in either acquiring paired ground-truth high-quality (HQ) images or synthesizing photo-realistic degraded LQ observations. Recent works mainly focus on modeling the degradation with handcrafted or estimated degradation parameters, which are however incapable to model complicated real-world degradation types, resulting in limited quality improvement. Notably, LQ face images, which may have the same degradation process as natural images, can be robustly restored with photo-realistic textures by exploiting their strong structural priors. This motivates us to use the real-world LQ face images and their restored HQ counterparts to model the complex real-world degradation (namely ReDegNet), and then transfer it to HQ natural images to synthesize their realistic LQ counterparts. By taking these paired HQ-LQ face images as inputs to explicitly predict the degradation-aware and content-independent representations, we could control the degraded image generation, and subsequently transfer these degradation representations from face to natural images to synthesize the degraded LQ natural images. Experiments show that our ReDegNet can well learn the real degradation process from face images. The restoration network trained with our synthetic pairs performs favorably against SOTAs. More importantly, our method provides a new way to handle the real-world complex scenarios by learning their degradation representations from the facial portions, which can be used to significantly improve the quality of non-facial areas. The source code is available at https://github.com/csxmli2016/ReDegNet.

Keywords: Real world degradation · Blind image super-resolution

---

Supplementary Information The online version contains supplementary material available at https://doi.org/10.1007/978-3-031-19797-0_22.

1   Introduction

It is widely known that Convolutional Neural Networks (CNNs) are proficient in handling the data they have seen, but perform inferior on these deviating from the training sets. This property makes the blind image super-resolution networks difficult to handle the real-world LQ images which are usually corrupted with complex and unsynthesizable degradation. However, building these pairs of real-world LQ and HQ datasets is neither feasible nor practical, because the real-world degradation types are too diverse and some of them are not brought by the imaging system. Figure 1(a) shows a real-world LQ image that is degraded with halftone related artifacts. One can see that the synthetic LQ image (on the top-left of (b)) by the inverse halftoning method [13] is hardly consistent with the complex real-world degradation, which makes these types of restoration methods (*e.g.*, [43]) fail to generate photo-realistic result (see (b)).

To alleviate the difficulties in restoring the real-world LQ images, some works attempt to predict the degradation parameters [16,17,19,20,34] and then handle the LQ input with the non-blind restoration works. However, the real degradation usually combines with various corruption types, each of which has lost its intrinsic characteristics. This inevitably makes these methods sensitive to the prediction errors of the degradation parameters, and consequently makes them fail to handle the real-world LQ image (see (c) in Fig. 1).

Recently, data-driven methods are suggested to design a practical degradation model by handcrafting the complex combinations of blur, downsampling, noise and

Fig. 1. (a): A real-world LQ image. (b)–(g): Restoration comparisons with inverse halftone method [43], RealSR [19], Real-ESRGAN [48], BSRGAN [56], BSRGAN* fine-tuned with halftone degradation [13], and Ours[s] that is specifically trained with the synthetic pairs in (i). (h): Face restoration result by GPEN [53]. (i): Our synthetic LQ sample with the degradation representation from (h).

JPEG compression with random [56] or high orders [48]. Albeit these methods have more diverse degradation types [10,31,57] and show great generalization in handling the real-world LQ images in most cases, they still fail to cover some complex real degradation which cannot be well synthesized (see (d) and (e) in Fig. 1). By incorporating the synthetic halftone degradation [13], BSRGAN* has slight improvement (see (f)), but still contains obvious linearity artifacts.

In contrast, face image has specific and strong structure prior, and can be better restored while exhibiting great generalization ability on real-world LQ images in most cases [27,47,53]. Although the image is corrupted by intractable degradation, the face restoration result is very plausible and photo-realistic (see Fig. 1(h)). Since the face and non-face (natural) regions in an image share the same degradation, once we have known the degradation process on face regions, transferring it to natural HQ images would bring considerable benefits, e.g., we can apply this degradation process on the HQ natural image to synthesize these types of natural image pairs (see (i)) for training restoration network (see (g)).

In this paper, we make the first attempt to explore the **real deg**radation with ReDegNet, which contains (i) learning the real degradation from the pairs of real-world LQ and pseudo HQ face images with DegNet, and (ii) transferring it to HQ natural images to synthesizing their realistic LQ ones with SynNet. As for (i), instead of taking a single LQ image to predict its degradation parameters [19], our DegNet takes the real-world LQ and its pseudo HQ face images as input to generate the degradation representation, which models the degradation process of how the HQ image is degraded to the LQ one. To disentangle the image content and degradation type, we adopt two manners, i.e., a) carefully designed framework by predicting the degradation representation through several fully connected layers to generate the convolution weights which can be regarded as the styles in StyleGANs [22,23], and b) contrastive loss [46] by minimizing the representation distance between the pairs with different content but degraded with the same degradation parameters, and meanwhile maximizing these with the same content but different degradation. This process is fully supervised by the paired LQ/HQ face images. As for (ii), our SynNet synthesizes the realistic LQ natural images with these degradation representations extracted from face images, which can help us to learn the real-world restoration mapping. Note that our method may perform limited on scenarios without faces. By extending the degradation space with face images share the similar degradation, our model would be further improved. The main contributions are summarized as follows:

- We propose the ReDegNet to explore the real degradation from face images by explicitly learning the degradation-aware and content-independent representations which control the degraded image generation.
- We transfer these real-world degradation representations to HQ natural images to generate their realistic LQ ones for supervised real restoration.
- We provide a new manner for handling intractable degraded images by learning their degradation from face regions within them, which can be used for synthesizing these types of LQ natural images for specifically fine-tuning.
- Experimental results demonstrate that our ReDegNet can well learn the degradation representations from face images and can effectively transfer to

natural ones, contributing to the comparable performance on general restoration and superior performance in specific scenarios against the SOTAs.

2 Related Work

2.1 Blind Face Restoration

Different from the complex textures in natural images, the specific structure in face images make it feasible to well handle the real-world LQ face images [5,7, 8,18,24,60]. To alleviate the sensibility for the unknown degradation, reference images or component features are suggested for guiding the blind restoration process [27–29]. Most recently, generative face prior [22,23] based methods [4, 47,53] are proposed to improve and stabilize the restoration quality, which can robustly restore the real-world LQ face images in most scenarios. Their great generalization on face images inspires us to explore the possibility of extending the restoration performance from the local region (*i.e.*, face) to the whole image.

2.2 Degradation Estimation Based Blind Image Super-Resolution

The real-world LQ images are mainly corrupted with unknown degradation parameters, so some works focus on estimating these degradation parameters and then apply non-blind restoration methods to recover it. Bell-Kligler *et al.* [2] firstly propose the image-specific KernelGAN to predict the blur kernels and feed them to ZSSR [41] for non-blind restoration. Gu *et al.* [16] introduce iterative kernel correction method to estimate the blur kernel which further benefits the restoration results. Luo *et al.* [34] alternate the optimization of restoring HQ images with the predicted kernel and estimating the blur kernel with the restored results, both of which can compensate each other. Wang *et al.* [46] suggest a degradation-aware super-resolution network that learn the degradation related parameters to guide the restoration process. However, real-world LQ images usually have high frequency noises or compression artifacts, and these methods are sensitive with them, which brings adverse effect for parameter prediction.

2.3 Data-Driven Based Blind Image Super-Resolution

The main challenge of blind image super-resolution task can be ascribed to the lack of suitable training pairs. So a straightforward way is to collect the real-world LQ and HQ pairs. Cai *et al.* [3] adjust the focal length of the digital cameras to capture the paired LQ/HQ images on the same scene. Wei *et al.* [50] build a larger dataset with a large-scale diverse benchmark by zooming the digital cameras. Except for the cumbersome capturing process, the spatial and brightness misalignment easily leads to uncontrollable errors. Moreover, although these images are realistic, they are more suitable for the specific super-resolution task that has the similar capturing scenarios. These types of collecting data occupies very few of these complex real-world degraded images, resulting in the failure cases when handling other real degradation, *e.g.*, noise or compression.

To alleviate the difficulties in synthesizing real-world LQ images, recent works tend to learn the restoration mapping with unpaired LQ and HQ images. Yuan *et al.* [54] suggest a Cycle-in-Cycle network by firstly mapping the LQ input to noise-free space and then super-resolving it through a pre-trained super-resolution model. Similarly, Lugmayr *et al.* [32] adopt the cycle consistent loss to learn a domain distribution network to generate new LQ/HQ pairs for supervised restoration. Fritsche *et al.* [12] also propose the unsupervised DSGAN model to generate the degraded LQ images with the same characteristics as the original ones. To constitute more realistic LQ images, Ji *et al.* [19] extract the blur kernels via KernelGAN [2] and noise injection through [6,59], which perform on HQ images to simulate the real degradation process. Although these methods achieve great performance in most cases, they still show limited generalization ability in super-resolving real-world LQ images, because 1) the estimated degradation parameters from only a single image is highly ill-posed and they are not enough to infer how the HQ images degraded (Fig. 1(a)), and 2) the real-world LQ images usually suffer from complex degradation, which is challenging to model due to the lack of paired data. In contrast, our ReDegNet adopts the pairs of real-world LQ and pseudo HQ face images to explore the real degradation process.

Another way is to extend the degradation space. Instead of the traditional degradation process that degrades the HQ image with Gaussian blurring, followed by the bicubic downsampling operation, and the injection of Gaussian noise and JPEG compression, Zhang *et al.* [56] propose a practical degradation model with randomly shuffled orders of these operations which tremendously cover the diverse degradation space. Similarly, Wang *et al.* [48] suggest a high order degradation model with several repeated degradation process. Although these two methods show great generalization in handling real-world images, they are still incapable for those images corrupted with complex degradation like the halftone image in Fig. 1(a). Traditional methods remove these continuous noisy dots mainly through filters [26,33,36], look-up-tables [9], dictionary learning [11], or maximum a posteriori estimation [44]. Recent CNN-based inverse halftoning methods [13,43,51,52] and even these estimation or data-driven based methods still fail to generate photo-realistic results on these types of real-world LQ images, which can be ascribed to the difficulties in synthesizing proper LQ images.

3   Methodology

Our ReDegNet aims to learn the real degradation from the pairs of real-world LQ and pseudo HQ face images, and transfer it to natural ones. So it mainly contains two sub-networks, *i.e.*, DegNet for learning the degradation representation Ω, and SynNet for synthesizing the LQ images with the given HQ input and Ω. With the collected real-world LQ face images I_f^{ReaL} and their pseudo HQ ones I_f^{PseH}, the learning process of DegNet ($\mathcal{F}_{Deg}$) and SynNet ($\mathcal{F}_{Syn}$) can be formulated as:

$$\Omega_f^{Rea} = \mathcal{F}_{Deg}\left(I_f^{ReaL}, I_f^{PseH}; \Theta_{Deg}\right), \tag{1}$$

$$\hat{I}_f^L = \mathcal{F}_{Syn}\left(I_f^{PseH}, \Omega_f^{Rea}; \Theta_{Syn}\right), \tag{2}$$

where Θ_{Deg} and Θ_{Syn} are the learnable parameters for DegNet and SynNet.

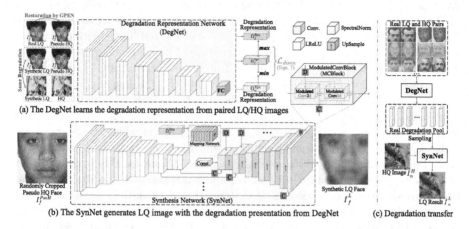

Fig. 2. Overview of our ReDegNet. (a) The DegNet learns the degradation representation. (b) The SynNet synthesizes the LQ image with the degradation presentation Ω from DegNet. $\boxed{D}$ denotes a learned affine transform from Ω that produces a degradation style. $\boxed{C}$ represents the content features that will be degraded by $\boxed{D}$ through modulated convolution. (c) The HQ natural image together with the degradation representation sampled from the face pairs are taken into SynNet to generate their synthetic LQ one.

After jointly end-to-end learning through degradation disentanglement, the synthetic realistic LQ natural images can be obtained in the inference through:

$$\hat{I}_n^L = \mathcal{F}_{Syn}\left(I_n^H, \Omega_f^{Rea}; \Theta_{Syn}\right),\qquad(3)$$

where I_n^H and $\hat{I}_n^L$ are the HQ and the synthetic LQ natural images, respectively. Ω_f^{Rea} can be sampled from these real degradation representations which are extracted from the collected real-world face pairs. The whole framework and each sub-network are illustrated in Fig. 2 and will be introduced in the following.

3.1 Learning Real Degradation from Face Image

Instead of predicting the degradation related representations from only a single LQ image [19,46], we take the LQ and HQ pairs as input to explore the degradation process about how the HQ image is degraded to the LQ one. The degradation representation network (DegNet) shown in Fig. 2(a) is stacked with several convolutional layers, each of which followed by spectral normalization [39] and LeakyReLU activation. A fully convolutional (FC) layer is incorporated in the last to predict the degradation representation vector Ω, which has the size of 1×512. This sub-network is optimized through two terms, *i.e.*, the disentanglement loss in Eq. 7 and the gradient back propagated from the following SynNet.

3.2   Synthesizing the LQ Image

After obtaining the degradation representation vector Ω, the remaining problem is about how to utilize it to control the degradation process. Inspired by the StyleGANs [22,23] that control the style of the generated image with one vector within $\mathcal{W}$ space, we adopt the similar structure to map the degradation representation Ω to $\mathcal{W}$ space through several fully convolutional (FC) layers. Then, instead of feeding the broadcast noise in StyleGAN, the image content of our SynNet is provided by the features of the input HQ images. Finally, with the degradation styles $\boxed{D}$ and image content $\boxed{C}$, the degraded image is reconstructed with the modulated convolution operation (MCBlock) in which the degradation styles serve as the convolutional weights to control the degradation process of the given image content [23]. With several cascaded MCBlocks, the final LQ result which is expected to have the similar degradation types with the given degradation representation can be synthesized. Since the degradation vector Ω should be a global representation without any spatial information, here we randomly crop the HQ image as the input of SynNet to alleviate the spatial dependency.

To introduce different scales of textures in the training phase, we adopt the random rotation, resampling, and cropping on face images in DegNet and SynNet, simultaneously. The proposed SynNet combined with DegNet constitutes our ReDegNet that can be jointly optimized in a supervised end-to-end manner.

3.3   Transferring Degradation to Natural Image

After training on face images, our ReDegNet can not only extract the real degradation representation from pairs of face images, but also generate the corresponding LQ image with the expected degradation styles. So as for general restoration, we store large amounts of degradation representations that are extracted from real-world LQ and their pseudo HQ face images, which will be sampled to imitate the real degradation process on natural HQ images (Fig. 2(c)). Here we also resample and rotate the LQ/HQ face pairs to augment the degradation space. Notably, our ReDegNet can be utilized in some specific restoration, in which the degradation types are not easy to synthesize with current degradation model. For the intractable old photos (e.g., Fig. 1) or old films, we can obtain their degradation representations with DegNet through the pairs of LQ face region within them and its pseudo HQ result. Then the HQ natural images can be utilized to generate the corresponding LQ image by SynNet to synthesize these degradation types of natural training pairs, which can be used to fine-tune the specific restoration on the whole image.

3.4   Learning Objective

Two types of loss functions are collaborated together to constrain the learning of our ReDegNet, i.e., (i) disentanglement loss that is introduced to extract the degradation-related representations, and (ii) reconstruction loss that is suggested to constrain the synthetic results close to the ground-truth.

Disentanglement Loss. The degradation representations Ω_f^{Rea} learned from face images are expected to perform on natural ones to control the degradation styles, so it should be degradation-aware and content-independent. To achieve this goal, we adopt contrastive learning [40,46] to minimize the distances of Ωs that are obtained from images with different content but have the same degradation parameters, and meanwhile maximize these negative pairs. To synthesize the degraded face and natural images with the same degradation parameters, we adopt the handcrafted degradation model from BSRGAN [56] to control the degradation process. To clarify the notations, we give a unified definition $I_\blacktriangledown^\blacktriangle$ in which $\blacktriangle \in \{SynL, ReaL, PseH, H\}$ denotes the handcrafted synthetic LQ image with BSRGAN [56], real-world LQ image, the restored pseudo HQ image, and real-world HQ image, respectively, $\blacktriangledown \in \{f, n\}$ represents the face and natural image, respectively. Denote these synthetic face and natural pairs with BSRGAN by $\{I_f^{PseH}, I_f^{SynL}\}$ and $\{I_n^H, I_n^{SynL}\}$. It should be noted that I_f^{SynL} and I_n^{SynL} are obtained from I_f^{PseH} and I_n^H with the same degradation sequence and parameters. As for these three types of pairs, *i.e.*, real-world LQ and HQ face pairs, synthetic LQ and HQ face pairs, as well as synthetic LQ and HQ natural pairs, their degradation representations can be formulated as:

$$\Omega_f^{Rea} = \mathcal{F}_{Deg}\left(I_f^{ReaL}, I_f^{PseH}; \Theta_{Deg}\right), \tag{4}$$

$$\Omega_f^{Syn} = \mathcal{F}_{Deg}\left(I_f^{SynL}, I_f^{PseH}; \Theta_{Deg}\right), \tag{5}$$

$$\Omega_n^{Syn} = \mathcal{F}_{Deg}\left(I_n^{SynL}, I_n^H; \Theta_{Deg}\right). \tag{6}$$

Then the disentanglement loss $\mathcal{L}_{disen}$ can be further formulated as:

$$\mathcal{L}_{disen} = \left\|\Omega_f^{Syn} - \Omega_n^{Syn}\right\|_2^2 + \frac{\lambda}{\|\Omega_f^{Syn} - \Omega_f^{Rea}\|_2^2 + \epsilon} + \frac{1}{2}\left\|\Theta_{Deg}\right\|_2^2, \tag{7}$$

where λ is the trade-off parameter. By minimizing the distance between Ω_f^{Syn} and Ω_n^{Syn} which share the same degradation process but have the different contents (*i.e.*, face and nature), we can constrain the extraction of degradation-aware and content-independent representations. On the contrary, by maximizing the distance between Ω_f^{Syn} and Ω_f^{Rea} which have the same contents (*i.e.*, I_f^{PseH}) but are corrupted with different degradation process, the degradation representation can be further constrained to the degradation-aware learning.

Reconstruction Loss. It mainly contains three terms, *i.e.*, i) mean square error loss $\mathcal{L}_{mse}$, ii) realistic loss $\mathcal{L}_{real}$, and iii) degradation-consistent loss $\mathcal{L}_{cons}$.

i) The MSE loss $\mathcal{L}_{mse}$ contains two terms and is formulated as:

$$\mathcal{L}_{mse} = \ell_{mse}(\hat{I}_f^L, I_f^{ReaL}) = \frac{1}{\mathcal{C}\mathcal{H}\mathcal{W}}\left\|\hat{I}_f^L - I_f^{ReaL}\right\|^2 + \sum_{i=1}^{4}\frac{0.1}{\mathcal{C}_i\mathcal{H}_i\mathcal{W}_i}\left\|\Phi_i(\hat{I}_f^L) - \Phi_i(I_f^{ReaL})\right\|^2 \tag{8}$$

where $\hat{I}_f^L$ is the generated LQ face image in Eq. 2 and I_f^{ReaL} is the collected real-world LQ image. $\mathcal{C}_*, \mathcal{H}_*, \mathcal{W}_*$ are the dimensions and Φ_i is the

i-th convolution layer of the pre-trained VGG-19 model [42]. This objective constrains the synthetic LQ images close to the real-world LQ images in both pixel and feature space [21].

ii) The realistic loss $\mathcal{L}_{real}$ mainly considers two types of constraints, *i.e.*, style loss [14] and adversarial loss [15]. The first one is computed with the Gram matrix on the feature spaces of VGG-19 model and can be formulated as:

$$\mathcal{L}_{style} = \sum_{i=1}^{4} \frac{1}{\mathcal{C}_i \mathcal{H}_i \mathcal{W}_i} \left\| \Phi_i(\hat{I}_f^L)^T \Phi_i(\hat{I}_f^L) - \Phi_i(I_f^{ReaL})^T \Phi_i(I_f^{ReaL}) \right\|^2, \qquad (9)$$

in which the variants have the same definitions as these in Eq. 8. The second one is the widely used adversarial loss which is effective in constraining the results within the natural manifold. In this paper, we adopt the discriminator from SNGAN [39] by incorporating the spectral normalization behind each convolutional layer. It is worth noting that the result $\hat{I}_f^L$ is expected to be a LQ image and visually blur in most cases, which is difficult for discriminator to distinguish whether it is a real LQ or fake LQ image due to the wider space of LQ types. So instead of only taking the synthetic result into the discriminator, we take the HQ image and their degradation representation as additional conditions [37]. The hinge version of adversarial loss [39,55] is given by:

$$\mathcal{L}_D = -\mathbb{E}[\min(0, -1 + D(I_f^{ReaL}, I_f^{PseH}, \Omega_f^{Rea}))] - \mathbb{E}[\min(0, -1 - D(\hat{I}_f^L, I_f^{PseH}, \Omega_f^{Rea}))] \tag{10}$$

$$\mathcal{L}_G = -\mathbb{E}[D(\mathcal{F}_{Syn}(I_f^{PseH}, \mathcal{F}_{Deg}(I_f^{ReaL}, I_f^{PseH}; \Theta_{Deg}); \Theta_{Syn}), I_f^{PseH}, \Omega_f^{Rea})]. \tag{11}$$

Combining the two terms together, the final realistic loss is formulated as:

$$\mathcal{L}_{real} = 0.1 \cdot \mathcal{L}_{style} + \mathcal{L}_G. \tag{12}$$

iii) The third one is the degradation-consistent loss. As analyzed before, the degradation representation Ω_f^{Syn} and Ω_n^{Syn} in Eqs. 5 and 6 are obtained from the face and natural pairs that are corrupted by the same degradation process. Therefore, switching Ω_f^{Syn} and Ω_n^{Syn} should have the same LQ results. Thus the degradation-consistent loss is suggested as:

$$\mathcal{L}_{cons} = \ell_{mse}(\mathcal{F}_{Syn}(I_n^H, \Omega_f^{Syn}; \Theta_{Syn}), I_n^{SynL}) + \ell_{mse}(\mathcal{F}_{Syn}(I_f^{PseH}, \Omega_n^{Syn}; \Theta_{Syn}), I_f^{SynL}), \tag{13}$$

where ℓ_{mse} is the MSE loss defined in Eq. 8. With the constraints on the degradation representation Ω_f^{Syn} (Ω_n^{Syn}) that is extracted from face (natural) images and performed on natural (face) ones, we can further optimize the disentanglement learning, and benefit the training process of the SynNet.

To sum up, the final learning objective is formulated as:

$$\mathcal{L} = \lambda_{disen}\mathcal{L}_{disen} + \lambda_{mse}\mathcal{L}_{mse} + \lambda_{real}\mathcal{L}_{real} + \lambda_{cons}\mathcal{L}_{cons}, \tag{14}$$

where λ_{disen}, λ_{mse}, λ_{real} and λ_{cons} are set to 5, 1, 0.1, and 2, respectively.

4   Experiments

Since our ReDegNet is proposed to design a degradation model for synthesizing LQ images, in this work, we mainly compare with three related works, *i.e.*, RealSR [19], BSRGAN [56] and Real-ESRGAN [48], in which RealSR synthesizes the LQ image with the estimated kernel and noise from the single real-world photograph, BSRGAN and Real-ESRGAN focus on handcrafted design of diverse degradation. These three methods and Ours adopt the same network (*i.e.*, ESRGAN [49]), so we can fairly compare with their released models. To evaluate the effectiveness of blind image super-resolution methods on handling the real-world LQ images, here we analyze the performance on two types of real-world images, *i.e.*, real-world pairs collected by digital camera, and real-world single LQ images. As for the quantitative evaluation, we use PSNR, SSIM, and LPIPS [58] to measure the distance between the result and ground-truth. Since real-world single LQ images do not have the ground-truth, we follow the competing methods [19,48,56] and adopt NIQE [38] to evaluate the non-reference image quality.

4.1   Dataset and Implementation Details

We collect real-world LQ face images from Internet, and then adopt GPEN [53] to obtain their pseudo HQ counterparts. These images cover diverse degradation types, from slightness to severeness, oldness to present, *etc*. Among them, 10,000 images are used for training, 1,000 images for validating, and the remaining 5,000 images for testing. Except these collected images, we also introduce the synthetic LQ face images from FFHQ [22] with common degradation, *e.g.*, blur, noise, JPEG compression, and downsampling operation, *etc*, to improve the generalization ability. During the inference, we conduct the degradation representation pool $\{\Omega_f^{ReaL}\}^N$ from these face pairs, which will be sampled to constitute the natural pairs for training our general restoration network (*i.e.*, F2N-ESRGAN).

As for the natural image, we follow BSRGAN [56], and adopt DIV2K [1], Flick2K [30,45] and FFHQ [22] for training our ReDegNet and F2N-ESRGAN. Adam optimizer [25] with $\beta_1 = 0.5$ and $\beta_2 = 0.999$ is adopted to train ReDegNet and F2N-ESRGAN. The initial learning rate is set to 2×10^{-4} and will decrease by 0.5 when the MSE loss $\mathcal{L}_{mse}$ on the validation set tends to be stable. All the experiments are implemented on a PC server with 4 T V100 GPUs.

4.2   Quantitative Comparison

Table 1 lists the quantitative results. One can see that (i) as for these real-world pairs (RealSR Canon and Nikon [3], and DRealSR [50]), although the PSNR and SSIM of Ours is comparable against others, the LPIPS of Ours obtains the best performance, which indicates that our results are more consistent with human perception [58]. The best LPIPS of Ours in turn validates the effectiveness of our ReDegNet in synthesizing the realistic training pairs. (ii) As for the non-reference image quality metric, we collect two groups of real-world images, *i.e.*, RealSRSet

Table 1. Quantitative comparison on two types of real-world LQ images.

| Methods | Real-world Pairs | | | | | | | | | Real-world LQ | |
| | RealSR-Canon | | | RealSR-Nikon | | | DRealSR | | | RealSRSet | RealLQSet |
	PSNR↑	SSIM↑	LPIPS↓	PSNR↑	SSIM↑	LPIPS↓	PSNR↑	SSIM↑	LPIPS↓	NIQE↓	NIQE↓
RealSR	<u>25.58</u>	.723	.458	**25.49**	.693	.459	**27.69**	**.759**	.438	**4.82**	5.62
BSRGAN	**25.61**	**.768**	<u>.363</u>	24.51	<u>.711</u>	.391	26.64	.744	.380	5.60	5.36
Real-ESRGAN	24.95	**.768**	.366	24.50	**.716**	<u>.388</u>	26.57	.753	<u>.374</u>	5.75	<u>5.24</u>
Ours	25.57	<u>.765</u>	**.362**	<u>25.43</u>	**.716**	**.385**	<u>26.91</u>	<u>.758</u>	**.373**	<u>4.85</u>	**4.93**
Ours (-D)	24.63	.749	.463	24.35	.684	.460	26.32	.740	.425	6.45	6.27
Ours (U)	25.05	.752	.428	24.72	.708	.421	26.35	.741	.404	5.81	5.93

Real-world Input   RealSR   BSRGAN   RealESRGAN   Ours

Fig. 3. Visual comparison of these competing methods on real-world LQ images.

proposed in BSRGAN [56], and RealLQSet that contains LQ images collected
from Internet and LQ frames extracted from 480P videos. We can see that results
of Ours are better than others in most cases, but inferior to RealSR [19] in
RealSRSet [56]. We analyze that the RealLQSet (1,000 images) covers more

| (a) Real-world LQ Image | (b) Inverse Halftone | (c) RealSR | (d) Real-ESRGAN |

| (e) BSRGAN | (f) BSRGAN* | (g) Ours | (h) Ours^s |

Fig. 4. Restoration results on real-world LQ image. Close-up on the right bottom of (a) is the face restoration result by GPEN [53]. BSRGAN* denotes the official BSRGAN model fine-tuned with the incorporation of halftone degradation [13]. Ours^s represents our general model (Ours) that is specifically fine-tuned with the synthetic natural pairs with the degradation representation from the face region. Best view it by zooming in.

types of common real-world LQ images than RealSRSet (only 20 images), which indicates RealLQSet is more suitable in evaluating the performance of super-resolving the real-world LQ images. The better NIQE of Ours may be attributed to the usage of degradation that are learned from real-world LQ face images.

4.3   Visual Comparison on Real-World LQ Images

Except the quantitative metrics, visual comparison appears to be critically important in evaluating the restoration performance, especially for these real-world LQ images. In this paper, we select these real-world LQ images from three types of datasets, *i.e.*, RealSRSet from BSRGAN [56], RealSR dataset [3], and the collected real-world LQ images from our RealLQSet. Visual results of the competing methods are shown in Fig. 3. One can see that results of Ours are much clearer than others, not only in the smooth regions (1*st* row), but also in these with rich and complex textures (2–4*th* rows). Due to the limited ability in predicting the kernel and noise from the real-world LQ images, RealSR [19] fails to generate plausible and photo-realistic textures when handling the input with complex degradation. Although BSRGAN [56] and Real-ESRGAN [48] show great generalization due to the wider handcrafted degradation spaces, our F2N-ESRGAN performs comparable against them with these degradation representations that are extracted from the real-world LQ face images, which indicates the effectiveness of our method in synthesizing the photo-realistic LQ images, and in turn contributes to the better restoration performance.

4.4   Fine-Tuning for Specific Restoration

Except the general super-resolution task mentioned above, our method can also fine-tune the restoration model on specific scenarios which have face images in

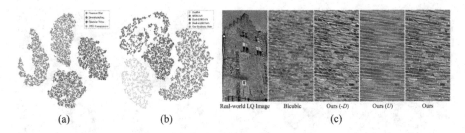

Fig. 5. (a) The t-SNE results of four groups degradation with only blur, downsampling, noise and JPEG compression. (b) The t-SNE results of the synthetic degradation by the competing methods. (c) Restoration comparison of different variants.

them. Figures 1 and 4 show the specific cases. We can observe that (1) although they are similar to the halftone degradation, the restoration result by the inverse halftone method [43] can not well handle it (see (b)) due to the complex degradation that these real-world LQ images usually suffer from. (2) The general restoration methods, *i.e.*, RealSR [19], BSRGAN [56], and Real-ESRGAN [48] also fail to generate plausible results on these unsynthesizable degradation (see (c–e)), while Ours perform favorable but still contain obvious artifacts (see (g)). (3) By fine-tuning BSRGAN with the synthetic halftone degradation [13], BSR-GAN* has slight improvement in reducing the artifacts, but still can not generate photo-realistic structures (see (f)). (4) By restoring the face region with GPEN [53] and synthesizing the similar degradation types on natural images (see our suppl.), results of Ours^s are much better than others, which indicates the effectiveness of our method in learning the degradation from face images and transferring to natural ones. Compared with BSRGAN and Real-ESRGAN, our method can not only handle the general restoration with limited real degradation, but also fine-tune the model for some specific scenarios that have face images, which are common in the consumer photography and old photos or films.

4.5   Ablation Study

Firstly, to illustrate the degradation extraction ability of our DegNet, we introduce t-SNE [35] to visualize the degradation representation Ω for different degradation types. To this end, we generate four groups of LQ face pairs by separately degrading 5,000 HQ test images with Gaussian blurring, downsampling, Gaussian noise and JPEG compression. Then DegNet is utilized to extract their degradation representations. The visualization of each group mapping to 2D space by t-SNE is shown in Fig. 5(a). We can observe that these four groups of degradation representations are embedded into four clusters completely, which indicates that our DegNet can well capture and distinguish the different degradation types.

Secondly, we explore the degradation space of these competing methods. With the 5,000 real-world test LQ and HQ face pairs, we synthesize the LQ images by utilizing the degradation models of RealSR [19], BSRGAN [56], Real-ESRGAN [48] and our ReDegNet on the pseudo HQ images. Among them, the kernel and noise of

RealSR are extracted from the real-world images. BSRGAN and Real-ESRGAN are used with their default settings from their released models. As for ours, we randomly sample from the degradation representation pool $\{\Omega_f^{ReaL}\}^N$ via Syn-Net to generate the LQ images. Note that $\{\Omega_f^{ReaL}\}^N$ have no overlap with the 5,000 test pairs. The visualization of the degradation representations of these five groups, *i.e.*, RealSR, BSRGAN, Real-ESRGAN, Ours and the real-world LQ/HQ pairs, is shown in Fig. 5(b). One can see that our synthetic LQ images are more consistent with the real-world LQ ones than the competing methods, indicating the effectiveness of our method in extracting the degradation from real pairs of face images. Albeit BSRGAN and Real-ESRGAN have more diversities due to the random/high orders and handcrafted degradation, only few LQ images are similar to the real-world LQ ones within 5,000 pairs.

Finally, to evaluate the necessities of the disentanglement loss and our pairs of LQ and HQ face images, we design two variants, *i.e.*, Ours (U) by using unpaired data which feeds only the LQ images into DegNet and random HQ images into SynNet, respectively, and adopts the discriminator to distinguish whether the result has the similar degradation with the LQ input or not, and Ours $(-D)$ by removing the disentanglement loss. The comparisons on real-world LQ images are shown in Table 1 and Fig. 5(c). We can see that compared with Ours (U), results of Ours are clearer and more photo-realistic, indicating the effectiveness of our supervised manner in predicting the real degradation from the pairs of face images. Besides, by removing the disentanglement loss, results of Ours $(-D)$ easily have distorted structures and obvious artifacts, which may be caused by the inaccurate degradation representation that may contain the face related content.

4.6   Limitations

This work is intuitively motivated by the observation that the face region usually shares the similar degradation with the non-face region. However, the background is sometimes out of the depth of field, which easily has the inconsistent degradation with face region, thereby bring limited benefits for the specific restoration. Besides, our general restoration model performs not obviously superior to the competing methods, especially on these camera captured test sets in Table 1. It is better to collect face images under the similar scenarios to augment the degradation space.

5   Conclusion

In this work, we made the first attempt to model the real degradation from the real-world LQ face images and their pseudo HQ counterparts, and transfer these real degradation processes to HQ natural images by disentangling the degradation-aware and content-independent representations. With the synthetic natural image pairs generated by our ReDegNet, the trained blind image super-resolution models (*i.e.*, F2N-ESRGAN) demonstrated competitive performance against SOTA methods, especially on real-world LQ images. Our method provided a new solution to synthesize more realistic LQ natural images with the degradation representation that are extracted from the facial regions within them, which are beneficial for restoring the details of non-facial regions. Experiments showed that our ReDegNet can well learn the real degradation from face images, and can effectively generate the photo-realistic LQ natural ones, thereby leading to promising performance in general and specific restoration.

Acknowledgment. This work is partially supported by the National Natural Science Foundation of China under grant No. U19A2073, the Major Key Project of PCL under grant No. PCL2021A12, and Hong Kong RGC RIF grant (R5001-18).

References

1. Agustsson, E., Timofte, R.: NTIRE 2017 challenge on single image super-resolution: dataset and study. In: CVPRW (2017)
2. Bell-Kligler, S., Shocher, A., Irani, M.: Blind super-resolution kernel estimation using an internal-GAN. In: NeurIPS (2019)
3. Cai, J., Zeng, H., Yong, H., Cao, Z., Zhang, L.: Toward real-world single image super-resolution: a new benchmark and a new model. In: ICCV (2019)
4. Chan, K.C., Wang, X., Xu, X., Gu, J., Loy, C.C.: GLEAN: generative latent bank for large-factor image super-resolution. In: CVPR (2021)
5. Chen, C., Li, X., Yang, L., Lin, X., Zhang, L., Wong, K.Y.K.: Progressive semantic-aware style transformation for blind face restoration. In: CVPR (2021)
6. Chen, J., Chen, J., Chao, H., Yang, M.: Image blind denoising with generative adversarial network based noise modeling. In: CVPR (2018)
7. Chen, Y., Tai, Y., Liu, X., Shen, C., Yang, J.: FSRNet: end-to-end learning face super-resolution with facial priors. In: CVPR (2018)
8. Chrysos, G.G., Zafeiriou, S.: Deep face deblurring. In: CVPRW (2017)
9. Chung, K.L., Wu, S.T.: Inverse halftoning algorithm using edge-based lookup table approach. IEEE TIP **14**, 1583–1589 (2005)
10. Elad, M., Feuer, A.: Restoration of a single superresolution image from several blurred, noisy, and undersampled measured images. IEEE TIP **16**, 1646–1658 (1997)
11. Freitas, P.G., Farias, M.C., Araújo, A.P.: Enhancing inverse halftoning via coupled dictionary training. Sig. Process. Image Commun. **49**, 1–8 (2016)
12. Fritsche, M., Gu, S., Timofte, R.: Frequency separation for real-world super-resolution. In: ICCVW (2019)
13. Gao, Q., Shu, X., Wu, X.: Deep restoration of vintage photographs from scanned halftone prints. In: ICCV (2019)
14. Gatys, L.A., Ecker, A.S., Bethge, M.: Image style transfer using convolutional neural networks. In: CVPR (2016)
15. Goodfellow, I., et al.: Generative adversarial nets. In: NeurIPS (2014)
16. Gu, J., Lu, Zuo, W., Dong, C.: Blind super-resolution with iterative kernel correction. In: CVPR (2019)
17. Guo, S., Yan, Z., Zhang, K., Zuo, W., Zhang, L.: Toward convolutional blind denoising of real photographs. In: CVPR (2019)
18. Huang, H., He, R., Sun, Z., Tan, T.: Wavelet-SRNet: a wavelet-based CNN for multi-scale face super resolution. In: ICCV (2017)

19. Ji, X., Cao, Y., Tai, Y., Wang, C., Li, J., Huang, F.: Real-world super-resolution via kernel estimation and noise injection. In: CVPRW (2020)
20. Jiang, J., Zhang, K., Timofte, R.: Towards flexible blind JPEG artifacts removal. In: ICCV (2021)
21. Johnson, J., Alahi, A., Fei-Fei, L.: Perceptual losses for real-time style transfer and super-resolution. In: Leibe, B., Matas, J., Sebe, N., Welling, M. (eds.) ECCV 2016. LNCS, vol. 9906, pp. 694–711. Springer, Cham (2016). https://doi.org/10.1007/978-3-319-46475-6_43
22. Karras, T., Laine, S., Aila, T.: A style-based generator architecture for generative adversarial networks. In: CVPR (2019)
23. Karras, T., Laine, S., Aittala, M., Hellsten, J., Lehtinen, J., Aila, T.: Analyzing and improving the image quality of styleGAN. In: CVPR (2020)
24. Kim, D., Kim, M., Kwon, G., Kim, D.S.: Progressive face super-resolution via attention to facial landmark. In: BMVC (2019)
25. Kingma, D.P., Ba, J.: Adam: a method for stochastic optimization. In: ICLR (2015)
26. Kite, T.D., Damera-Venkata, N., Evans, B.L., Bovik, A.C.: A fast, high-quality inverse halftoning algorithm for error diffused halftones. IEEE TIP 9, 1583–1592 (2000)
27. Li, X., Chen, C., Zhou, S., Lin, X., Zuo, W., Zhang, L.: Blind face restoration via deep multi-scale component dictionaries. In: Vedaldi, A., Bischof, H., Brox, T., Frahm, J.-M. (eds.) ECCV 2020. LNCS, vol. 12354, pp. 399–415. Springer, Cham (2020). https://doi.org/10.1007/978-3-030-58545-7_23
28. Li, X., Li, W., Ren, D., Zhang, H., Wang, M., Zuo, W.: Enhanced blind face restoration with multi-exemplar images and adaptive spatial feature fusion. In: CVPR (2020)
29. Li, X., Liu, M., Ye, Y., Zuo, W., Lin, L., Yang, R.: Learning warped guidance for blind face restoration. In: Ferrari, V., Hebert, M., Sminchisescu, C., Weiss, Y. (eds.) ECCV 2018. LNCS, vol. 11217, pp. 278–296. Springer, Cham (2018). https://doi.org/10.1007/978-3-030-01261-8_17
30. Lim, B., Son, S., Kim, H., Nah, S., Mu Lee, K.: Enhanced deep residual networks for single image super-resolution. In: CVPRW (2017)
31. Liu, C., Sun, D.: On Bayesian adaptive video super resolution. IEEE TPAMI 36, 346–360 (2013)
32. Lugmayr, A., Danelljan, M., Timofte, R.: Unsupervised learning for real-world super-resolution. In: ICCVW (2019)
33. Luo, J., De Queiroz, R., Fan, Z.: A robust technique for image descreening based on the wavelet transform. IEEE Trans. Signal Process. 46, 1179–1184 (1998)
34. Luo, Z., Huang, Y., Li, S., Wang, L., Tan, T.: Unfolding the alternating optimization for blind super resolution. In: NeurIPS (2020)
35. Van der Maaten, L., Hinton, G.: Visualizing data using t-SNE. J. Mach. Learn. Res. 9, 1–27 (2008)
36. Miceli, C.M., Parker, K.J.: Inverse halftoning. J. Electron. Imaging 1, 143–151 (1992)
37. Mirza, M., Osindero, S.: Conditional generative adversarial nets. arXiv preprint arXiv:1411.1784 (2014)
38. Mittal, A., Soundararajan, R., Bovik, A.C.: Making a "completely blind" image quality analyzer. IEEE SPL 20, 209–212 (2012)
39. Miyato, T., Kataoka, T., Koyama, M., Yoshida, Y.: Spectral normalization for generative adversarial networks. In: ICLR (2018)
40. Schroff, F., Kalenichenko, D., Philbin, J.: FaceNet: a unified embedding for face recognition and clustering. In: CVPR (2015)

41. Shocher, A., Cohen, N., Irani, M.: "Zero-shot" super-resolution using deep internal learning. In: CVPR (2018)
42. Simonyan, K., Zisserman, A.: Very deep convolutional networks for large-scale image recognition. In: ICLR (2015)
43. Son, C.H.: Inverse halftoning through structure-aware deep convolutional neural networks. Signal Process. **173**, 107591 (2020)
44. Stevenson, R.L.: Inverse halftoning via map estimation. IEEE TIP **6**, 574–583 (1997)
45. Timofte, R., Agustsson, E., Van Gool, L., Yang, M.H., Zhang, L.: NTIRE 2017 challenge on single image super-resolution: methods and results. In: CVPRW (2017)
46. Wang, L., et al.: Unsupervised degradation representation learning for blind super-resolution. In: CVPR (2021)
47. Wang, X., Li, Y., Zhang, H., Shan, Y.: Towards real-world blind face restoration with generative facial prior. In: CVPR (2021)
48. Wang, X., Xie, L., Dong, C., Shan, Y.: Real-ESRGAN: training real-world blind super-resolution with pure synthetic data. In: ICCVW (2021)
49. Wang, X., et al.: ESRGAN: enhanced super-resolution generative adversarial networks. In: Leal-Taixé, L., Roth, S. (eds.) ECCV 2018. LNCS, vol. 11133, pp. 63–79. Springer, Cham (2019). https://doi.org/10.1007/978-3-030-11021-5_5
50. Wei, P., et al.: Component divide-and-conquer for real-world image super-resolution. In: Vedaldi, A., Bischof, H., Brox, T., Frahm, J.-M. (eds.) ECCV 2020. LNCS, vol. 12353, pp. 101–117. Springer, Cham (2020). https://doi.org/10.1007/978-3-030-58598-3_7
51. Xia, M., Wong, T.-T.: Deep inverse halftoning via progressively residual learning. In: Jawahar, C.V., Li, H., Mori, G., Schindler, K. (eds.) ACCV 2018. LNCS, vol. 11366, pp. 523–539. Springer, Cham (2019). https://doi.org/10.1007/978-3-030-20876-9_33
52. Xiao, Y., Pan, C., Zhu, X., Jiang, H., Zheng, Y.: Deep neural inverse halftoning. In: International Conference on Virtual Reality and Visualization. IEEE (2017)
53. Yang, T., Ren, P., Xie, X., Zhang, L.: Gan prior embedded network for blind face restoration in the wild. In: CVPR (2021)
54. Yuan, Y., Liu, S., Zhang, J., Zhang, Y., Dong, C., Lin, L.: Unsupervised image super-resolution using cycle-in-cycle generative adversarial networks. In: CVPRW (2018)
55. Zhang, H., Goodfellow, I., Metaxas, D., Odena, A.: Self-attention generative adversarial networks. In: ICML (2019)
56. Zhang, K., Liang, J., Van Gool, L., Timofte, R.: Designing a practical degradation model for deep blind image super-resolution. In: ICCV (2021)
57. Zhang, K., Zuo, W., Zhang, L.: Deep plug-and-play super-resolution for arbitrary blur kernels. In: CVPR (2019)
58. Zhang, R., Isola, P., Efros, A.A., Shechtman, E., Wang, O.: The unreasonable effectiveness of deep features as a perceptual metric. In: CVPR (2018)
59. Zhou, R., Susstrunk, S.: Kernel modeling super-resolution on real low-resolution images. In: ICCV (2019)
60. Zhu, S., Liu, S., Loy, C.C., Tang, X.: Deep cascaded bi-network for face hallucination. In: Leibe, B., Matas, J., Sebe, N., Welling, M. (eds.) ECCV 2016. LNCS, vol. 9909, pp. 614–630. Springer, Cham (2016). https://doi.org/10.1007/978-3-319-46454-1_37

Towards Interpretable Video Super-Resolution via Alternating Optimization

Jiezhang Cao[1], Jingyun Liang[1], Kai Zhang[1(✉)], Wenguan Wang[1], Qin Wang[1], Yulun Zhang[1], Hao Tang[1], and Luc Van Gool[1,2]

[1] Computer Vision Lab, ETH Zürich, Zürich, Switzerland
{jiezhang.cao,jingyun.liang,kai.zhang,wenguan.wang,qin.wang,
yulun.zhang,hao.tang,vangool}@vision.ee.ethz.ch
[2] KU Leuven, Leuven, Belgium
https://github.com/caojiezhang/DAVSR

Abstract. In this paper, we study a practical space-time video super-resolution (STVSR) problem which aims at generating a high-framerate high-resolution sharp video from a low-framerate low-resolution blurry video. Such problem often occurs when recording a fast dynamic event with a low-framerate and low-resolution camera, and the captured video would suffer from three typical issues: i) motion blur occurs due to object/camera motions during exposure time; ii) motion aliasing is unavoidable when the event temporal frequency exceeds the Nyquist limit of temporal sampling; iii) high-frequency details are lost because of the low spatial sampling rate. These issues can be alleviated by a cascade of three separate sub-tasks, including video deblurring, frame interpolation, and super-resolution, which, however, would fail to capture the spatial and temporal correlations among video sequences. To address this, we propose an interpretable STVSR framework by leveraging both model-based and learning-based methods. Specifically, we formulate STVSR as a joint video deblurring, frame interpolation, and super-resolution problem, and solve it as two sub-problems in an alternate way. For the first sub-problem, we derive an interpretable analytical solution and use it as a Fourier data transform layer. Then, we propose a recurrent video enhancement layer for the second sub-problem to further recover high-frequency details. Extensive experiments demonstrate the superiority of our method in terms of quantitative metrics and visual quality.

Keywords: Video super-resolution · Motion blur · Motion aliasing

1 Introduction

Compared with existing space-time video super-resolution (STVSR) methods [55,56], we mainly focus on the more practical STVSR problem which aims at

Supplementary Information The online version contains supplementary material available at https://doi.org/10.1007/978-3-031-19797-0_23.

synthesizing a high space-time resolution (HSTR) clear video from a low space-time resolution (LSTR) blurry video. Although great progress has been made in existing STVSR methods, these methods mainly solve the video frame interpolation and video super-resolution tasks jointly, neglecting the motion blur and motion aliasing artifacts [39] that often occur in many real-world scenarios due to limited shutter speed and non-negligible exposure time. Different from exiting methods, we take above two temporal motion degradations into consideration and formulate it as a joint video restoration problem of the video frame interpolation, video deblurring and spatial video super-resolution.

To address the video restoration problem, one straightforward way is to directly combine a video frame interpolation (VFI) method (*e.g.*,SuperSloMo [15] and DAIN [3]), a video deblurring (VD) method (*e.g.*,EDVR [53] and CDVD-TSP [38]), and a video super-resolution (VSR) method (*e.g.*,IconVSR [6] and BasicVSR++ [7]) in a two-stage or three-stage manner, as shown in Fig. 1. For example, one can firstly interpolate missing intermediate video frames with VFI methods, then deblur the frames with VD methods, and finally super-resolve them with VSR methods. In this case, the VFI methods cannot eliminate motion blur nor motion aliasing because they only synthesize new blurry frames, while the VD methods cannot increase the framerate and resolve motion aliasing.

Alternatively, there are other combinations of VFI, VD and VSR methods, but solving these sub-tasks separately with multi-stage methods may suffer from the following limitations. First, ignoring the correlations among VFI, VD and VSR may lead to limited performance since these video restoration tasks are highly intra-related. As will be discussed in Sect. 3.1, the degradation from an HSTR clear video to an LSTR blurry video can be well-modelled by a single joint model. A "divide-and-conquer" strategy may not be able to benefit from the natural intra-relatedness and suffer from accumulated reconstruction errors from the first stage to the last stage. Second, as shown in Fig. 2, the composition of different methods may lead to expensive computational cost and a large number of parameters. This is because the overall runtime and parameter number are the summation of different standalone methods. Therefore, developing a one-stage unified model for the STVSR problem may a better choice.

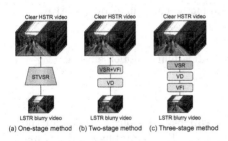

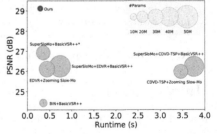

Fig. 1. Illustration of one-stage, two-stage and three-stage methods.

Fig. 2. Comparison on performance, runtime and parameter number.

To solve the above problem, in this paper, we propose a novel STVSR framework that exploits the correlation among different sub-tasks and boosts the overall efficiency significantly. We first reformulate this space-time video super-resolution problem as two sub-problems according to the half quadratic splitting algorithm, and solve them by an analytical solution and a deep learning-based neural network, respectively. More specifically, for the first sub-problem, we solve it based on the fast Fourier transform and propose a Fourier data transform layer to alleviate the motion blur and motion aliasing. For the second sub-problem, we propose a recurrent video enhancement layer with a multi-scale recurrent neural network to enhance the quality of the restored videos. Based on the alternating optimization, our end-to-end training method is able to jointly handle video frame interpolation, video deblurring and video super-resolution in STVSR.

The main contributions of this paper are summarized as follows:

- We formulate a more practical space-time video super-resolution (STVSR) problem by exploring the camera's intrinsic properties related to motion blur, motion aliasing and other spatial degradation.
- We make the first attempt to provide an analytical solution for the STVSR problem by leveraging the model-based methods and learning-based methods. With the help of the analytical solution, we develop a deep alternative video super-resolution network (DAVSR) to improve STVSR performance.
- We propose a new one-stage framework that can address video frame interpolation, video deblurring and video super-resolution simultaneously. By exploiting the correlation among the three sub-problems, our method is more effective than two-stage and three-stage methods.
- Our method achieves the state-of-the-art performance on both the REDS4 and Vid4 datasets. It is able to restore high-resolution and high-framerate videos even when the input videos have severe motion blur. Moreover, it only has a small number of parameters and has fast inference time.

2   Related Work

In this section, we discuss the related literature for video frame interpolation (VFI), video deblurring, video super-resolution (VSR) and other joint tasks as they are closely related to our practical STVSR problem.

Video frame interpolation (VFI) aims to synthesize intermediate frames between adjacent frames of the original frames. Recent VFI methods [28] propose to learn image matching or take local convolution over two input frames with a learned adaptive convolution kernel. Meyer et al. [30] propose a phase-based frame interpolation method which represents motion in the phase shift of individual pixels. In addition, flow-based video interpolation methods [3,4,15,27,35] propose to handle motions by estimating the optical flow. However, directly using VFI cannot reduce motion blur and motion aliasing [39]. This can become an potential issue in our STVSR problem setup as the input videos are blurry.

Video deblurring aims at removing the blur artifacts from the input videos. Depending on the number of required input frames, there are multiple-frame [13,16,18,21,23,33,46] and single-frame [20,46,49] deblurring methods. EDVR [53] restores high-quality deblurred frames by first extracting features of multiple inputs and then conducting feature alignment and fusion. To further exploit the temporal information, some recurrent mechanisms based video deblurring methods have been proposed [14,34,58,60]. Zhou et al. [62] propose a deblurring network based on filter adaptive convolutional layers. Recently, CDVD-TSP [38], a CNN-based video deblurring method, approaches the problem by optical flow estimation and latent frame restoration steps. To solve the STVSR problem, one can combine video deblurring methods with the traditional STVSR methods.

Video super-resolution reconstructs HR video frames from the corresponding LR frames. There are several VSR methods [5,23,41,48,52,57] that use optical flow for explicit temporal alignment. Recently, RBPN [12] combines ideas from single- and multiple-frame SR for VSR, and estimates inter-frame motion to generate SR frames. However, the estimated flow is often inaccurate, resulting in poor performance. To address this, DUF [17] synthesizes SR frames by generating dynamic upsampling filters and a residual image based on the local spatio-temporal neighborhood of each pixel without explicit motion estimation. TDAN [51] proposes deformable alignment at the feature level without computing optical flow. Based on TDAN, EDVR [53] aligns frames at the feature level using deformable convolution networks (DCN) in a coarse-to-fine manner, and proposes an attention module to fuse different frames both temporally and spatially. However, most of the above methods are computationally inefficient due to many-to-one frameworks. To ease this, recurrent neural networks (RNN) are adopted in VSR methods [6,7] for leveraging temporal information. BasicVSR and its extension (*i.e.*,IconVSR) [6] propose to improve the performance of feature alignment using bidirectional propagation. To improve the performance of BasicVSR, BasicVSR++ [7] proposes second-order grid propagation and flow guided deformable alignment. To address the STVSR problem, one can combine the above VFI, VD and VSR methods in a three-stage manner.

Space-time video super-resolution (STVSR) aims at synthesizing a high-resolution slow-motion video from a low-framerate and low-resolution video. Shechtman et al. [43] are among the first to extend SR methods to the space-time domain. Further STVSR methods based on Markov random field [31] and motion assisted steering kernel regression [47] are then proposed. In addition, Shahar et al. [42] explore the degree of the recurrences within natural videos. However, these methods are computationally expensive in practice. To address this, Xiang et al. [55] propose a one-stage STVSR network to directly learn the mapping from partial LR frames to HR frames. Different from our problem setting, traditional STVSR methods ignore the blur degradation from the camera, which can be critical in real-world applications.

Video frame interpolation and deblurring are a joint video restoration problem [2,11,36] that generates high-framerate clear videos from low-framerate

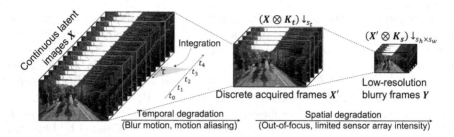

Fig. 3. Illustrations of our video degradation. Note that we show temporal and spatial degradation separately for clarity, although they occur simultaneously. Camera sensors capture discrete frames at the time step $t_i(i{\ge}0)$ by integrating the continuous latent images within an exposure time interval τ, leading to temporal degradation. Then, non-ideal imaging factors such as out-of-focus and limited sensor array intensity result in spatial degradation as well. These two degradations can be implemented by using a temporal kernel $\boldsymbol{K}_t$ and a spatial kernel $\boldsymbol{K}_s$ with the downsampling $\downarrow_{s_t}$ and $\downarrow_{s_h \times s_w}$.

blurry inputs. Recently, Shen et al. [44] propose a pyramid module and an inter-pyramid recurrent module to enhance the restoration quality and exploits the spatio-temporal information, respectively. Although these methods deal with motion blur and aliasing, spatial degradation is not considered as in STVSR. In addition, Pollak et al. [39] propose a deep internal learning approach by exploiting the recurrence within and across different spatio-temporal scales of the video. However, it is a zero-shot temporal-SR and is difficult to improve the SR performance without supervised information.

3 Proposed Method

3.1 Video Degradation Model

We present the video degradation model for the practical STVSR task, as shown in Fig. 3. In general, a sequence of video frames is captured by a camera with a periodically on-and-off shutter [44,50]. When the shutter is open, the camera sensors collect reflected photons and convert them into electrical signals. This can be formulated as an integration of luminous intensity over the exposure time, during which the motion blur may occur if the object moves or the camera shakes. Besides, due to limited shutter on-and-off frequency (framerate), motion aliasing may also occur when the temporal dynamic event frequency is beyond the Nyquist limit of framerate. In addition to above temporal degradation, video capturing also suffers from similar spatial degradation to single image capturing as a result of non-ideal imaging factors such as out-of-focus and limited sensor array intensity [24]. Formally, given a high spatio-temporal resolution (HSTR) video $\boldsymbol{X} \in \mathbb{R}^{T_h \times H_h \times W_h \times 3}$, a 3D blur kernel $\boldsymbol{K}$, a low spatio-temporal resolution (LSTR) video $\boldsymbol{Y} \in \mathbb{R}^{T_l \times H_l \times W_l \times 3}$ can be formulated as

$$\boldsymbol{Y} = (\boldsymbol{X} \otimes \boldsymbol{K}) \downarrow_{s_t \times s_h \times s_w} + \boldsymbol{N}, \tag{1}$$

where $\otimes$ represents the 3D convolution, and $\downarrow_{s_t \times s_h \times s_w}$ (abbreviated as $\downarrow_s$ in the rest of the paper for clarity) denotes the standard s-fold downsampling in three directions: temporal, vertical and horizontal directions. N is often assumed to be the additive white Gaussian noise with a noise level of σ. In addition, the sizes of X and Y satisfy $T_h = s_t T_l, H_h = s_h H_l$ and $W_h = s_w W_l$. In fact, some popular video restoration tasks, including spatial VSR, VFI and VD, *etc*, can be seen as special cases of the above degradation model. Note that Eq. (1) can also be used for bicubic degradation since it can be approximated by blur and downsampling with a center shift [59].

3.2   Problem Setting and Optimization Difficulty

Problem Formulation. The goal of practical STVSR is to solve the joint video restoration tasks, including video frame interpolation, video deblurring and super-resolution. Specifically, given a low-framerate and low-resolution (low spatio-temporal resolution) blurry video Y, a 3D blur kernel K and downsampling $\downarrow_s$, we propose to restore a high-framerate and high-resolution (high spatio-temporal resolution) video X. According to the Maximum A Posteriori (MAP) framework, we solve the problem by minimizing the energy function $E(X)$,

$$\widehat{X} = \arg\min_{X} E(X) := \frac{1}{2\sigma^2} \underbrace{\|Y - (X \otimes K) \downarrow_s\|^2}_{\text{data fidelity term}} + \lambda \underbrace{\Phi(X)}_{\text{prior term}}, \qquad (2)$$

where λ is a trade-off parameter, the data fidelity term is associated with the model likelihood for reconstruction, and the prior term is a regularization which is related to the prior information of the high spatio-temporal resolution video. However, the prior term is often unknown in practice, and thus it is intractable to directly compute an analytical solution to Problem (2). Compared with classic image SR problem, our task is more challenging since the high spatio-temporal resolution video lose high-frequency details in space and time.

Alternating Optimization. Based on the Half-Quadratic Splitting (HQS) algorithm [1,59], we introduce an auxiliary variable Z that is close to X, and we have a regularization $\|Z - X\|^2$ with a penalty parameter μ. Then, we reformulate Problem (2) as the following optimization problem:

$$E(X, Z) = \frac{1}{2\sigma^2} \|Y - (Z \otimes K) \downarrow_s\|^2 + \lambda \Phi(X) + \frac{\mu}{2} \|Z - X\|^2. \qquad (3)$$

Then, Problem (3) can be solved by alternately optimizing two sub-problems Eq. (4) (for Z) and Eq. (5) (for X) as follows

$$\begin{cases} Z_k = \arg\min_{Z} \|Y - (Z \otimes K) \downarrow_s\|^2 + \mu\sigma^2 \|Z - X_{k-1}\|^2, & (4) \\[2mm] X_k = \arg\min_{X} \frac{\mu}{2} \|Z_k - X\|^2 + \lambda \Phi(X). & (5) \end{cases}$$

With the help of the alternating optimization, we can calculate the closed-form solution to the sub-problem (4), and solve the sub-problem (5) as a video denoising problem. However, directly finding an analytic solution is time-consuming since it requires the inversion of a high dimensional matrix, whose computational complexity is $O(T_h^3 W_h^3 H_h^3)$. One can use simulation-based methods (*e.g.*,Markov Chain Monte Carlo [10]) to solve the problem, but it would still be computationally expensive for large videos. Inspired by existing image super-resolution methods [9,37,59], we take two additional challenging video problems, *i.e.*,dynamic blur removal and frame interpolation, into consideration, and derive a new analytical solution for the practical STVSR. Note that it is not a trivial issue for these methods to handle video problems because the practical STVSR suffers from more complex degradation such as motion blur and aliasing.

3.3   Analytical Solution

To solve the sub-problem (4), we propose to derive a theorem to compute an analytical solution for the practical STVSR problem. To develop the theorem, we introduce the Fourier transform to efficiently exploit intrinsic properties of the downsampling and the blur kernel in the frequency domain.

Theorem 1. *Let $\mathcal{F}$ and $\mathcal{F}^{-1}$ be the fast Fourier transform (FFT) and inverse FFT, and $\overline{\mathcal{F}}$ be the complex conjugate of $\mathcal{F}$. Assume the blur kernel $\boldsymbol{K}$ and the downsampling $\downarrow_s$ satisfy some properties [61]. Given a video $\boldsymbol{X}_{k-1}$ at the k-th iteration and a low-resolution video $\boldsymbol{Y}$, the solution to Eq. (4) can be computed using the following closed-form expression[1], i.e.,*

$$\boldsymbol{Z}_k = \mathcal{F}^{-1}\left(\frac{1}{\alpha_k}\left(\mathcal{F}(\boldsymbol{R}_{k-1}) - \overline{\mathcal{F}(\boldsymbol{K})}\left(\frac{(\mathcal{F}(\boldsymbol{K})\mathcal{F}(\boldsymbol{R}_{k-1}))\downarrow_s^a}{\left(s\alpha_k \boldsymbol{I} + \left(\mathcal{F}(\boldsymbol{K})\overline{\mathcal{F}(\boldsymbol{K})}\right)\downarrow_s^a\right)}\right)\uparrow_s^r \right) \right), \quad (6)$$

where $\boldsymbol{R}_{k-1} = \overline{\mathcal{F}(\boldsymbol{K})}\mathcal{F}(\boldsymbol{Y}\uparrow_s) - \alpha_k \boldsymbol{X}_{k-1}$ with $\alpha_k = \mu_k \sigma^2$, $\uparrow_s$ is a standard s-fold upsampler , i.e.,upsampling the spatial size by filling the new entries with zeros, $\uparrow_s^r$ is an upsampler by repeating the tensor the desired dimension, and $\downarrow_s^a$ is a distinct block downsampler, i.e.,averaging the $s_t \times s_h \times s_w$ distinct blocks.

In Theorem 1, we are able to derive an analytical solution to the sub-problem (4). Note that the assumptions are not strong and they are widely used in existing studies [40,45]. For example, the assumption of the blur kernel does not depend on the shape and it can be used in different kinds of blurring, such as motion blur and out-of-focus blur [61]. Different from USRNet [59], our theorem is more general and can be applied to more image or video restoration tasks, including classic image super-resolution, video frame interpolation, video deblurring and the space-time video super-resolution. Based on the analytical solution, we are able to further solve the next sub-problem (5).

---

[1] Please see the detailed proof in the supplementary materials.

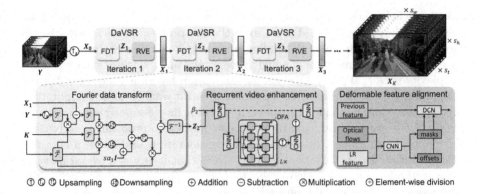

① ⓣ ⓦ Upsampling   ⓓ Downsampling   ⊕ Addition   ⊖ Subtraction   ⊗ Multiplication   ⊘ Element-wise division

Fig. 4. The overall architecture of the proposed method with K iterations. Our one-stage model is able to handle different video degradation (*i.e.*,Eq. (1)) in a joint way and synthesize HSTR frames by taking an LSTR blur video Y, scale factor s and blur kernel K as inputs. Specifically, the architecture consists of two main modules, including the FDT layer that reduces the blur degradation, and the RVE layer that makes HR synthesized videos cleaner.

Complexity Analysis. With the help of Theorem 1, we further analyze the complexity of calculating the analytical solution (6) and show that we are able to improve the effectiveness of computing the analytical solution to sub-problem (4). In the theorem, Eq. (6) requires three FFT computations and one inverse FFT computation, which are the most expensive parts in the implementation. Considering the computation complexities of FFT and inverse FFT, the computation complexity of Eq. (6) is $\mathcal{O}(T_h W_h H_h \log(T_h W_h H_h))$, which is much smaller than the computation complexity of directly solving Eq. (2) (*i.e.*,$\mathcal{O}(T_h^3 W_h^3 H_h^3)$) and can be computed efficiently on the modern GPU devices. More analyses can be found in the supplementary materials. With the efficient calculation of Z_k, we can deal with space-time blur (including motion and spatial blur, encoded in K) and space-time downsampling (including temporal and spatial downsampling, encoded in $\downarrow_s$) in a joint and analytical way. The blur is reduced and the details are restored gradually.

3.4   Deep Alternating Video Super-Resolution Network

In this paper, we propose to design a new video super-resolution network based on the alternating optimization, called DAVSR, which solves the sub-problems (4) and (5) alternately. To this end, we propose a Fourier data transform layer $\mathcal{T}$ and a recurrent video enhancement layer $\mathcal{R}$ to address the above two sub-problems, respectively. The overall architecture of our method is shown in Fig. 4. Specifically, the Fourier data transform layer aims to alleviate the video degradation, while the recurrent video enhancement layer aims to enhance synthesized videos by adding more high-frequency details.

Fourier Data Transform Layer. With the help of the analytical solution (4), we aim to reduce the video degradation from the LSTR blurry video. During the optimization, we propose to find a clearer HSTR video such that it minimizes a weighted combination of the data fidelity term and the quadratic regularization term. To this end, we propose a Fourier data transform (FDT) layer, as shown in Fig. 4. Specifically, given an LSTR blurry video $\boldsymbol{Y}$, the scale factor $\boldsymbol{s} = [s_t, s_h, s_w]$, blur kernel $\boldsymbol{K}$ and the parameters α_k, we calculate the video by using the analytical solution Eq. (6), i.e.,

$$\boldsymbol{Z}_k = \mathcal{T}(\boldsymbol{X}_{k-1}|\boldsymbol{Y}, \boldsymbol{K}, \boldsymbol{s}, \alpha_k). \tag{7}$$

Noted that the Fourier data transform is a model-based method and it has no trainable parameters. In this sense, this module has good generalization and it is able to generate meaningful data. In addition, this layer is differentiable since every sub-operation is differentiable. Compared with USRNet [59], this layer helps simultaneously synthesize high-frequency information in space and time.

Recurrent Video Enhancement Layer. For the sub-problem (5), we propose a recurrent video enhancement (RVE) layer to enhance the quality of videos and restore high-frequency sequential textures. Such sequential information is important in the continuous video frames, which, however, is neglected in the FDT layer and used in feature alignment. To address this, the RVE layer aims to model the sequential dependency and align the features of video frames. Specifically, given a video $\boldsymbol{Z}_k$ transformed by the FDT layer and the noise level β_k, the RVE model $\mathcal{R}$ restores a cleaner HSTR video, i.e.,

$$\boldsymbol{X}_k = \mathcal{R}(\boldsymbol{Z}_k|\beta_k), \quad \text{where } \beta_k = \sqrt{\lambda/\mu_k}. \tag{8}$$

Note that RVE is a learning-based model, and it is implemented by using deformable feature alignment (DFA) module, motivated by [7]. Specifically, we first use convolutional layers to extract low-level features $\{\boldsymbol{g}_k^1, \ldots, \boldsymbol{g}_k^{T_h}\}$ from the concatenation of $\boldsymbol{Z}_k$ and β_k. Then, we use DFA $\mathcal{G}$ to propagate and align the features $\widetilde{\boldsymbol{z}}_{k,j}^i$, and further use residual blocks $\mathcal{C}$ to fuse the features $\widehat{\boldsymbol{z}}_{k,j}^i$, i.e.,

$$\widetilde{\boldsymbol{z}}_{k,j}^i = \mathcal{G}\left(\boldsymbol{g}_k^i, \widehat{\boldsymbol{z}}_{k,j}^{i-1}, \widehat{\boldsymbol{z}}_{k,j}^{i-2}, \boldsymbol{f}_k^{i \to i-1}, \boldsymbol{f}_k^{i \to i-2}\right), \tag{9}$$

$$\widehat{\boldsymbol{z}}_{k,j}^i = \widetilde{\boldsymbol{z}}_{k,j}^i + \mathcal{C}\left([\widehat{\boldsymbol{z}}_{k,j-1}^i; \widetilde{\boldsymbol{z}}_{k,j}^i]\right), \tag{10}$$

where $\widehat{\boldsymbol{z}}_{k,j}^i$ is the feature at the i-th timestep in the j-th propagation branch at the k-th iteration, $\widehat{\boldsymbol{z}}_{k,0}^i = \boldsymbol{g}_k^i$, and $\boldsymbol{f}_k^{i_1 \to i_2}$ is the optical flow from i_1-th frame to the i_2-th frame at the k-th iteration, $[\cdot; \cdot]$ is a concatenation along the channel dimension. More details of $\mathcal{G}$ can be found in the supplementary. Last, we use convolutional layers to reconstruct $\boldsymbol{x}_k^i$ which is the i-th element of $\boldsymbol{X}_k$.

Loss Function and Algorithm. In the training, our goal is to train the model to minimize the distance between the HSTR video $\boldsymbol{X}_K$ at the last iteration and the ground-truth video $\boldsymbol{X}$. To this end, we use the following Charbonnier loss [8] because it can handle outliers, i.e.,

$$\mathcal{L} = \sqrt{\|\boldsymbol{X}_K - \boldsymbol{X}\|^2 + \epsilon^2}, \quad \text{where } \epsilon = 1 \times 10^{-3}. \tag{11}$$

Algorithm 1: Deep Alternating Video Super-Resolution

Input: LSTR video Y, blur kernel K, scale factor s, parameters α_k, β_k

1 Initialize number of iterations K, and initialize X_0 on Y in space and time;

2 **while** not convergent **do**

3   **for** $k \leftarrow 1$ **to** K **do**

4   Update Z_k by computing $Z_k = \mathcal{T}(X_{k-1}|Y, K, s, \alpha_k)$;

5   Update X_k by computing $X_k = \mathcal{R}(Z_k|\beta_k)$;

6   Update the RVE model $\mathcal{R}$ by minimize the training loss (11).

Algorithm 1 shows the detailed model optimization process. We alternately optimize two sub-problems (4) and (5), and update the RVE model by minimize the loss (11). Note that the FDT and RVE modules are differentiable during training. At the K-th iteration, the algorithm outputs the HSTR video.

4 Experiments

Implementation Details. We use Adam optimizer [19] with $\beta_1 = 0.9, \beta_2 = 0.99$, and use Cosine Annealing [29] to decay the learning rate of the main network from 1×10^{-4} to 10^{-7}. In the FAT layer, we use `torch.fft.fftn` and `torch.fft.ifftn` to calculate FFT and inverse FFT operators, respectively. The total number of iterations for training is 300K, and the number of iterations K for updating Z and X is 3. The batch size is 4 and the patch size of input LR frames is 64×64. The number of residual blocks for each branch is 7, and the number of feature channels is 64.

Datasets and Evaluation Metrics. REDS [32] is a realistic and dynamic scenes dataset, whose the version of "blur_bicubic" can be used for the practical time-space video super-resolution task. The dataset is synthesized by averaging five subsequent frames, and then downsampling these frames with 4× bicubic kernel. REDS contains 266 training clips (each with 100 LR frames and 500 GT frames) and 4 testing clips (000, 011, 015 and 020, denoted as REDS4) that have diverse scenes and motions. In addition, another widely used dataset Vid4 [25] is also used in our experiments. The same degradation model as REDS is used for Vid4 experiments. For the evaluation metrics, we use PSNR and SSIM [54] to measure the performance of VSR methods.

4.1 Comparison with State-of-the-Art Methods

To achieve STVSR, we compare with the following SOTA methods, including single-image SR model (*i.e.*,SwinIR [22]), two VFI approaches (*i.e.*,Super-SloMo [15] and DAIN [3]), two deblurring methods (*i.e.*,EDVR [53] and CDVD-TSP [38]), and four recent VSR models, EDVR [53], BasicVSR [6], IconVSR [6], and BasicVSR++ [7]. In addition, we also consider joint video restoration methods, including Zooming Slow-Mo [55] and BIN [44].

Table 1. Quantitative comparison of our results and two-stage/three-stage on REDS4. Red and **blue** indicates the best and the second best performance. The superscript * means that the model is trained on the "blur_bicubic" version of REDS, and the superscript † means the pre-trained video deblurring model.

Methods	Clip_000		Clip_011		Clip_015		Clip_020		Average	
	PSNR	SSIM	PSNR	SSIM	PSNR	SSIM	PSNR	SSIM	PSNR	SSIM
Bicubic+linear interpolation	23.57	0.606	21.75	0.587	25.59	0.739	20.19	0.564	22.78	0.624
BIN+EDVR	25.02	0.709	22.00	0.603	25.89	0.765	21.15	0.572	23.52	0.662
BIN+BasicVSR	25.69	0.716	22.49	0.622	26.33	0.789	21.74	0.583	24.06	0.678
BIN+IconVSR	25.80	0.735	22.65	0.632	26.52	0.792	21.99	0.590	24.24	0.687
BIN+BasicVSR++	26.01	0.752	22.82	0.638	26.69	0.799	22.23	0.654	24.44	0.711
CDVD-TSP+Zooming Slow-Mo	26.74	0.786	24.68	0.700	29.52	0.859	23.02	0.689	25.99	0.759
EDVR+Zooming Slow-Mo	26.89	0.791	24.72	0.710	29.68	0.861	23.19	0.695	26.12	0.764
DAIN+CDVD-TSP+SwinIR	25.00	0.705	24.23	0.689	28.22	0.812	22.59	0.672	25.01	0.720
DAIN+CDVD-TSP+EDVR	25.95	0.751	24.14	0.686	28.84	0.839	22.61	0.673	25.38	0.737
DAIN+CDVD-TSP+BasicVSR	26.32	0.777	24.23	0.688	29.11	0.849	22.79	0.681	25.61	0.748
DAIN+CDVD-TSP+IconVSR	26.40	0.782	24.37	0.691	29.32	0.855	22.86	0.684	25.74	0.753
DAIN+CDVD-TSP+BasicVSR++	26.58	0.793	24.45	0.691	29.57	0.860	23.02	0.689	25.90	0.758
DAIN+EDVR†+SwinIR	25.56	0.719	24.35	0.688	28.98	0.839	22.83	0.672	25.43	0.730
DAIN+EDVR†+EDVR	26.50	0.774	24.25	0.685	29.51	0.855	22.85	0.674	25.78	0.747
DAIN+EDVR†+BasicVSR	26.66	0.783	24.21	0.683	29.61	0.858	22.76	0.670	25.81	0.748
DAIN+EDVR†+IconVSR	26.75	0.787	24.25	0.685	29.77	0.863	22.80	0.672	25.89	0.752
DAIN+EDVR†+BasicVSR++	26.91	0.795	24.25	0.685	29.94	0.868	22.82	0.673	25.98	0.755
DAIN+EDVR*	26.29	0.760	24.53	0.699	29.32	0.848	22.96	0.682	25.77	0.747
DAIN+BasicVSR*	26.82	0.790	24.71	0.709	29.65	0.861	23.15	0.693	26.08	0.763
DAIN+IconVSR*	26.95	0.796	24.89	0.713	29.89	0.867	23.25	0.695	26.24	0.768
DAIN+BasicVSR++*	27.34	0.814	25.11	0.719	30.22	0.874	23.46	0.703	26.53	0.778
SuperSloMo+CDVD-TSP+SwinIR	25.26	0.709	24.20	0.686	28.82	0.835	22.76	0.675	25.26	0.726
SuperSloMo+CDVD-TSP+EDVR	26.22	0.753	24.18	0.686	29.32	0.845	22.75	0.674	25.62	0.739
SuperSloMo+CDVD-TSP+BasicVSR	26.70	0.779	24.29	0.689	29.57	0.855	22.97	0.683	25.88	0.752
SuperSloMo+CDVD-TSP+IconVSR	26.81	0.785	24.42	0.691	29.85	0.862	23.06	0.686	26.04	0.756
SuperSloMo+CDVD-TSP+BasicVSR++	27.06	0.797	24.53	0.692	30.12	0.868	23.24	0.691	26.24	0.762
SuperSloMo+EDVR†+SwinIR	25.86	0.726	24.32	0.687	29.36	0.844	22.87	0.672	25.60	0.732
SuperSloMo+EDVR†+EDVR	26.98	0.784	24.27	0.685	30.04	0.862	22.92	0.674	26.05	0.751
SuperSloMo+EDVR†+BasicVSR	27.12	0.793	24.24	0.683	30.07	0.864	22.82	0.670	26.06	0.753
SuperSloMo+EDVR†+IconVSR	27.24	0.798	24.27	0.685	30.28	0.870	22.86	0.672	26.16	0.756
SuperSloMo+EDVR†+BasicVSR++	27.41	0.805	24.28	0.685	30.46	0.874	22.88	0.673	26.26	0.759
SuperSloMo+EDVR*	26.66	0.769	24.60	0.700	29.83	0.855	23.11	0.684	26.05	0.752
SuperSloMo+BasicVSR*	27.35	0.803	24.78	0.710	30.16	0.868	23.35	0.696	26.41	0.769
SuperSloMo+IconVSR*	**27.52**	0.810	24.95	0.714	30.48	0.876	23.46	0.699	26.60	0.775
SuperSloMo+BasicVSR++*	28.00	0.829	25.19	0.720	30.83	0.883	23.70	0.707	26.93	0.785
DAVSR (Ours)	27.23	**0.820**	30.15	0.865	31.05	0.894	28.06	0.858	29.12	0.859

Quantitative Comparison. From Tables 1 and 2, we have the following observations. (1) Our method outperforms the two-stage and three-stage methods by a large margin on REDS4 and Vid4. Especially for fast motion videos (*e.g.*,clips 011 and 020), our method has the more significant improvements than these methods. It suggests that our one-stage network is able to exploit diverse spatio-temporal patterns and simultaneously handle VFI, VD and VSR. (2) The SOTA image SR method (*i.e.*,SwinIR [22]) performs worse than other VSR methods since it cannot handle sequential information of videos and cannot remove the motion blur. (3) The two-stage framework (*e.g.*,SuperSloMo+BasicVSR++*) is

Table 2. Quantitative comparison of our results and two-stage/three-stage methods on Vid4. Red and **blue** indicates the best and the second best performance.

Methods	Calendar		City		Foliage		Walk		Average	
	PSNR	SSIM	PSNR	SSIM	PSNR	SSIM	PSNR	SSIM	PSNR	SSIM
DAIN+CDCD-TSP+BasicVSR++	17.05	0.480	21.64	0.421	19.01	0.340	19.68	0.668	19.35	0.477
DAIN+EDVR†+BasicVSR++	17.35	0.497	21.80	0.433	19.22	0.350	19.91	0.687	19.57	0.492
DAIN+BasicVSR++*	18.05	0.522	**22.22**	**0.439**	20.08	**0.400**	**20.33**	**0.692**	20.17	0.513
SuperSloMo+CDCD-TSP+BasicVSR++	17.11	0.488	21.70	0.427	19.09	0.344	19.78	0.672	19.42	0.483
SuperSloMo+EDVR†+BasicVSR++	17.59	0.505	21.78	0.432	19.22	0.346	19.86	0.687	19.61	0.493
SuperSloMo+BasicVSR++*	**18.30**	**0.530**	22.21	0.439	**20.09**	0.398	20.30	0.692	**20.22**	**0.515**
DAVSR (Ours)	22.09	0.747	25.18	0.731	23.96	0.680	24.18	0.827	23.85	0.746

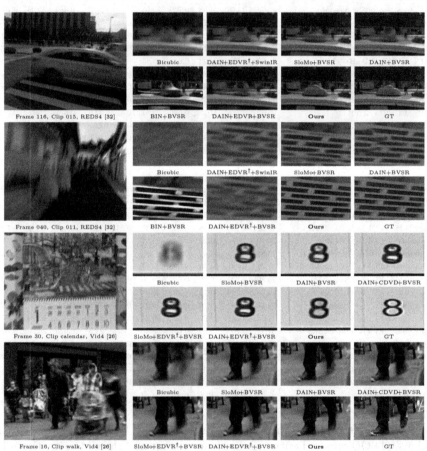

Fig. 5. Visual results of different methods on REDS4 and Vid4. Due to the space limitations of this figure, CDCD-TSP, SuperSloMo and BasicVSR++ are abbreviated as CDCD, SloMo and BVSR, respectively.

better than the three-stage framework because the reconstruction error propagates severely along the stages. (4) The performance of two-stage and three-

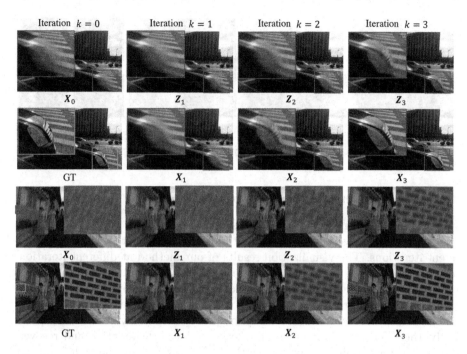

Fig. 6. Visualization of FDT and RVE at different iterations on REDS4.

stage methods are influenced by different motions. REDS4 has diverse scenes and motions, e.g.,Clip_000 has small motions and other video clips has more complex motions. Moreover, the VFI methods are sensitive to large motions. Thus, the performance of SuperSloMo+BasicVSR++* is better than that of our method on Clip_000, but is worse on other clips due to large motions.

Qualitative Comparison. Visual results of different methods are shown in Fig. 5. In this figure, our proposed method achieves significant visual improvements over two-stage and three-stage methods. This suggests that our one-stage framework is able to learn spatio-temporal information by exploring the natural intra-relatedness among the video interpolation, deblurring and super-resolution tasks. Compared with multi-stage methods, our method is able to synthesize high-quality HR video frames with clearer details and fewer blurring artifacts even for fast motion video sequences. Taking the second line (Frame 040, Clip 011) as an example, our method is able to restore textures which are very close to GT although Clip_011 has large motion. In contrast, multi-stage networks based on VFI methods (i.e.,Super-SloMo [15] and DAIN [3]) tend to suffer from severe motion blur in the synthesized HR video, because it is difficult for the VFI methods to handle large motions in the videos. More visual comparison results can be found in the supplementary materials.

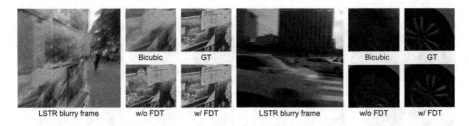

Fig. 7. Visual results of the RDT layer on the REDS4 dataset.

4.2 Visualization on Different Iterations

It is very interesting to investigate the synthesized outputs of the Fourier data transform (FDT) layer and the recurrent video enhancement (RVE) layer at different iterations. The visualization results of our method at different iterations are provided in Fig. 6. As one can see, the quality of synthesized video frames continuously improves as the iteration number increases. This shows that, given an LSTR blurry video frame, the FDT and RVE layers are able to cooperatively and alternately deblur and recover high-frequency details of video frames. Specifically, the FDT layer eliminates blur kernel induced degradation and recovers tiny structures and fine textures, then the RVE layer restores the high-frequency information in videos. The visualization results demonstrate that our proposed DAVSR provides an interpretable way to understand STVSR.

4.3 Model Size and Inference Time

We investigate model sizes and runtime of different networks, and the results are shown in Fig. 2. To synthesize HSTR clear frames, the composed two-stage or three-stage methods can lead to very large model sizes for frame reconstruction. In contrast, our one-stage model has much fewer parameters than the SOTA two-stage and three-stage networks. For example, it is more than 3× smaller than SuperSloMo+BasicVSR++*. With the help of the smaller model size, our model also achieves a fast inference time. More comparison results of model size and inference time can be found in the supplementary materials.

4.4 Ablation Study

We have already verified the superiority of our one-stage framework over two-stage and three-stage frameworks. To further demonstrate the effectiveness of our network, we propose to conduct a comprehensive ablation study on the Fourier data transform (FDT) layer and the recurrent video enhancement (RVE) layer. As shown in Table 3, the model

Table 3. Ablation study on the FDT and EVD layers. Here we use PSNR as the evaluation metric.

FDT	✗	✓	✓
EVD	✓	✗	✓
PSNR	27.25	23.05	**29.12**

without the FDT or RVE layer is worse than original model. Next, we show the visual results of the ablation study in Fig. 7. Here, we only conduct an ablation study on FDT because it contains no trainable parameters. If only the RVE layer is adopted without FDT, the synthesized SR video frames may suffer from blur artifacts. On the other hand, if the data module is used without the RVE layer, the network cannot recover the high-frequency textures. This suggests that the FDT and EVD layers are complementary to each other and both are important to the proposed alternating optimization-based model.

5 Conclusions

In this paper, we propose an alternating optimization for the practical space-time video super-resolution (STVSR) task by leveraging the model-based methods and learning-based methods. From an interpretable point of view, we first formulate the STVSR problem as two sub-problems related to the motion blur and motion aliasing. Specifically, we provide an analytical solution and propose a Fourier data transform layer to reduce the motion blur and motion aliasing for the first sub-problem. Then, we propose a recurrent video enhancement layer in the second sub-problem to enhance the quality of the synthesized video. By the alternating optimization, our method is able to jointly handle the video interpolation, video deblurring and video super-resolution. Extensive experiments demonstrate that our framework achieves the state-of-the-art performance and it is more effective yet efficient than existing multi-stage networks.

Acknowledgements. This work was partly supported by Huawei Fund and the ETH Zürich Fund (OK).

References

1. Afonso, M.V., Bioucas-Dias, J.M., Figueiredo, M.A.: Fast image recovery using variable splitting and constrained optimization. IEEE Trans. Image Process. **19**(9), 2345–2356 (2010)
2. Argaw, D.M., Kim, J., Rameau, F., Kweon, I.S.: Motion-blurred video interpolation and extrapolation. In: AAAI Conference on Artificial Intelligence, pp. 901–910 (2021)
3. Bao, W., Lai, W.S., Ma, C., Zhang, X., Gao, Z., Yang, M.H.: Depth-aware video frame interpolation. In: IEEE Conference on Computer Vision and Pattern Recognition, pp. 3703–3712 (2019)
4. Bao, W., Lai, W.S., Zhang, X., Gao, Z., Yang, M.H.: MEMC-Net: motion estimation and motion compensation driven neural network for video interpolation and enhancement. IEEE Trans. Pattern Anal. Mach. Intell. **43**(3), 933–948 (2019)
5. Caballero, J., et al.: Real-time video super-resolution with spatio-temporal networks and motion compensation. In: IEEE Conference on Computer Vision and Pattern Recognition, pp. 4778–4787 (2017)
6. Chan, K.C., Wang, X., Yu, K., Dong, C., Loy, C.C.: BasicVSR: the search for essential components in video super-resolution and beyond. In: IEEE Conference on Computer Vision and Pattern Recognition, pp. 4947–4956 (2021)

7. Chan, K.C., Zhou, S., Xu, X., Loy, C.C.: BasicVSR++: improving video super-resolution with enhanced propagation and alignment. In: IEEE Conference on Computer Vision and Pattern Recognition, pp. 5972–5981 (2022)
8. Charbonnier, P., Blanc-Feraud, L., Aubert, G., Barlaud, M.: Two deterministic half-quadratic regularization algorithms for computed imaging. In: International Conference on Image Processing, vol. 2, pp. 168–172 (1994)
9. Chiche, B.N., Frontera-Pons, J., Woiselle, A., Starck, J.L.: Deep unrolled network for video super-resolution. In: International Conference on Image Processing Theory, Tools and Applications, pp. 1–6 (2020)
10. Gilavert, C., Moussaoui, S., Idier, J.: Efficient Gaussian sampling for solving large-scale inverse problems using MCMC. IEEE Trans. Sig. Process. **63**(1), 70–80 (2014)
11. Gupta, A., Aich, A., Roy-Chowdhury, A.K.: ALANET: adaptive latent attention network forjoint video deblurring and interpolation. arXiv preprint arXiv:2009.01005 (2020)
12. Haris, M., Shakhnarovich, G., Ukita, N.: Recurrent back-projection network for video super-resolution. In: IEEE Conference on Computer Vision and Pattern Recognition, pp. 3897–3906 (2019)
13. Hyun Kim, T., Mu Lee, K.: Generalized video deblurring for dynamic scenes. In: IEEE Conference on Computer Vision and Pattern Recognition, pp. 5426–5434 (2015)
14. Hyun Kim, T., Mu Lee, K., Scholkopf, B., Hirsch, M.: Online video deblurring via dynamic temporal blending network. In: IEEE International Conference on Computer Vision, pp. 4038–4047 (2017)
15. Jiang, H., Sun, D., Jampani, V., Yang, M.H., Learned-Miller, E., Kautz, J.: Super SloMo: high quality estimation of multiple intermediate frames for video interpolation. In: IEEE Conference on Computer Vision and Pattern Recognition, pp. 9000–9008 (2018)
16. Jin, M., Meishvili, G., Favaro, P.: Learning to extract a video sequence from a single motion-blurred image. In: IEEE Conference on Computer Vision and Pattern Recognition, pp. 6334–6342 (2018)
17. Jo, Y., Oh, S.W., Kang, J., Kim, S.J.: Deep video super-resolution network using dynamic upsampling filters without explicit motion compensation. In: IEEE Conference on Computer Vision and Pattern Recognition, pp. 3224–3232 (2018)
18. Kim, T.H., Nah, S., Lee, K.M.: Dynamic video deblurring using a locally adaptive blur model. IEEE Trans. Pattern Anal. Mach. Intell. **40**(10), 2374–2387 (2017)
19. Kingma, D.P., Ba, J.: Adam: a method for stochastic optimization. In: International Conference on Learning Representations (2015)
20. Kupyn, O., Budzan, V., Mykhailych, M., Mishkin, D., Matas, J.: DeblurGAN: blind motion deblurring using conditional adversarial networks. In: IEEE Conference on Computer Vision and Pattern Recognition, pp. 8183–8192 (2018)
21. Liang, J., et al.: VRT: a video restoration transformer. arXiv preprint arXiv:2201.12288 (2022)
22. Liang, J., Cao, J., Sun, G., Zhang, K., Van Gool, L., Timofte, R.: Swinir: image restoration using swin transformer. In: IEEE International Conference on Computer Vision Workshops, pp. 1833–1844 (2021)
23. Liang, J., et al.: Recurrent video restoration transformer with guided deformable attention. arXiv preprint arXiv:2206.02146 (2022)
24. Liang, J., Sun, G., Zhang, K., Van Gool, L., Timofte, R.: Mutual affine network for spatially variant kernel estimation in blind image super-resolution. In: IEEE Conference on International Conference on Computer Vision, pp. 4096–4105 (2021)

25. Liu, C., Sun, D.: On Bayesian adaptive video super resolution. IEEE Trans. Pattern Anal. Mach. Intell. **36**(2), 346–360 (2013)
26. Liu, C., Sun, D.: On Bayesian adaptive video super resolution. IEEE Transactions on Pattern Anal. Mach. Intell. **36**(2), 346–360 (2013)
27. Liu, Z., Yeh, R.A., Tang, X., Liu, Y., Agarwala, A.: Video frame synthesis using deep voxel flow. In: IEEE International Conference on Computer Vision, pp. 4463–4471 (2017)
28. Long, G., Kneip, L., Alvarez, J.M., Li, H., Zhang, X., Yu, Q.: Learning image matching by simply watching video. In: Leibe, B., Matas, J., Sebe, N., Welling, M. (eds.) ECCV 2016. LNCS, vol. 9910, pp. 434–450. Springer, Cham (2016). https://doi.org/10.1007/978-3-319-46466-4_26
29. Loshchilov, I., Hutter, F.: SGDR: stochastic gradient descent with warm restarts. arXiv preprint arXiv:1608.03983 (2016)
30. Meyer, S., Wang, O., Zimmer, H., Grosse, M., Sorkine-Hornung, A.: Phase-based frame interpolation for video. In: IEEE Conference on Computer Vision and Pattern Recognition, pp. 1410–1418 (2015)
31. Mudenagudi, U., Banerjee, S., Kalra, P.K.: Space-time super-resolution using graph-cut optimization. IEEE Trans. Pattern Anal. Mach. Intell. **33**(5), 995–1008 (2010)
32. Nah, S., et al.: NTIRE 2019 challenge on video deblurring and super-resolution: dataset and study. In: IEEE Conference on Computer Vision and Pattern Recognition Workshops (2019)
33. Nah, S., Hyun Kim, T., Mu Lee, K.: Deep multi-scale convolutional neural network for dynamic scene deblurring. In: IEEE Conference on Computer Vision and Pattern Recognition, pp. 3883–3891 (2017)
34. Nah, S., Son, S., Lee, K.M.: Recurrent neural networks with intra-frame iterations for video deblurring. In: IEEE Conference on Computer Vision and Pattern Recognition, pp. 8102–8111 (2019)
35. Niklaus, S., Liu, F.: Context-aware synthesis for video frame interpolation. In: IEEE Conference on Computer Vision and Pattern Recognition, pp. 1701–1710 (2018)
36. Oh, J., Kim, M.: DeMFI: deep joint deblurring and multi-frame interpolation with flow-guided attentive correlation and recursive boosting. arXiv preprint arXiv:2111.09985 (2021)
37. Pan, J., Bai, H., Dong, J., Zhang, J., Tang, J.: Deep blind video super-resolution. In: IEEE International Conference on Computer Vision, pp. 4811–4820 (2021)
38. Pan, J., Bai, H., Tang, J.: Cascaded deep video deblurring using temporal sharpness prior. In: IEEE Conference on Computer Vision and Pattern Recognition, pp. 3043–3051 (2020)
39. Pollak Zuckerman, L., Naor, E., Pisha, G., Bagon, S., Irani, M.: Across scales & across dimensions: temporal super-resolution using deep internal learning. arXiv e-prints pp. arXiv-2003 (2020)
40. Robinson, M.D., Toth, C.A., Lo, J.Y., Farsiu, S.: Efficient Fourier-wavelet super-resolution. IEEE Trans. Image Process. **19**(10), 2669–2681 (2010)
41. Sajjadi, M.S., Vemulapalli, R., Brown, M.: Frame-recurrent video super-resolution. In: IEEE Conference on Computer Vision and Pattern Recognition, pp. 6626–6634 (2018)
42. Shahar, O., Faktor, A., Irani, M.: Space-time super-resolution from a single video. IEEE (2011)

43. Shechtman, E., Caspi, Y., Irani, M.: Increasing space-time resolution in video. In: Heyden, A., Sparr, G., Nielsen, M., Johansen, P. (eds.) ECCV 2002. LNCS, vol. 2350, pp. 753–768. Springer, Heidelberg (2002). https://doi.org/10.1007/3-540-47969-4_50

44. Shen, W., Bao, W., Zhai, G., Chen, L., Min, X., Gao, Z.: Blurry video frame interpolation. In: IEEE Conference on Computer Vision and Pattern Recognition, pp. 5114–5123 (2020)

45. Šroubek, F., Kamenický, J., Milanfar, P.: Superfast superresolution. In: IEEE International Conference on Image Processing, pp. 1153–1156 (2011)

46. Su, S., Delbracio, M., Wang, J., Sapiro, G., Heidrich, W., Wang, O.: Deep video deblurring for hand-held cameras. In: IEEE Conference on Computer Vision and Pattern Recognition, pp. 1279–1288 (2017)

47. Takeda, H., Beek, P.v., Milanfar, P.: Spatiotemporal video upscaling using motion-assisted steering kernel (mask) regression. In: Mrak, M., Grgic, M., Kunt, M. (eds.) High-Quality Visual Experience. Signals and Communication Technology, pp. 245–274. Springer (2010). https://doi.org/10.1007/978-3-642-12802-8_10

48. Tao, X., Gao, H., Liao, R., Wang, J., Jia, J.: Detail-revealing deep video super-resolution. In: IEEE International Conference on Computer Vision, pp. 4472–4480 (2017)

49. Tao, X., Gao, H., Shen, X., Wang, J., Jia, J.: Scale-recurrent network for deep image deblurring. In: IEEE Conference on Computer Vision and Pattern Recognition, pp. 8174–8182 (2018)

50. Telleen, J., et al.: Synthetic shutter speed imaging. In: Computer Graphics Forum, vol. 26, pp. 591–598 (2007)

51. Tian, Y., Zhang, Y., Fu, Y., Xu, C.: TDAN: temporally-deformable alignment network for video super-resolution. In: IEEE Conference on Computer Vision and Pattern Recognition, pp. 3360–3369 (2020)

52. Wang, L., Guo, Y., Lin, Z., Deng, X., An, W.: Learning for video super-resolution through HR optical flow estimation. In: Asian Conference on Computer Vision, pp. 514–529 (2018)

53. Wang, X., Chan, K.C., Yu, K., Dong, C., Change Loy, C.: EDVR: video restoration with enhanced deformable convolutional networks. In: IEEE Conference on Computer Vision and Pattern Recognition Workshops (2019)

54. Wang, Z., Bovik, A.C., Sheikh, H.R., Simoncelli, E.P.: Image quality assessment: from error visibility to structural similarity. IEEE Trans. Image Process. **13**(4), 600–612 (2004)

55. Xiang, X., Tian, Y., Zhang, Y., Fu, Y., Allebach, J.P., Xu, C.: Zooming slow-mo: fast and accurate one-stage space-time video super-resolution. In: IEEE Conference on Computer Vision and Pattern Recognition, pp. 3370–3379 (2020)

56. Xiao, Z., Xiong, Z., Fu, X., Liu, D., Zha, Z.J.: Space-time video super-resolution using temporal profiles. In: ACM International Conference on Multimedia, pp. 664–672 (2020)

57. Xue, T., Chen, B., Wu, J., Wei, D., Freeman, W.T.: Video enhancement with task-oriented flow. Int. J. Comput. Vis. **127**(8), 1106–1125 (2019)

58. Zamir, A.R., et al.: Feedback networks. In: IEEE Conference on Computer Vision and Pattern Recognition, pp. 1308–1317 (2017)

59. Zhang, K., Gool, L.V., Timofte, R.: Deep unfolding network for image super-resolution. In: IEEE Conference on Computer Vision and Pattern Recognition, pp. 3217–3226 (2020)

60. Zhang, K., Luo, W., Zhong, Y., Ma, L., Liu, W., Li, H.: Adversarial spatio-temporal learning for video deblurring. IEEE Trans. Image Process. **28**(1), 291–301 (2018)

61. Zhao, N., Wei, Q., Basarab, A., Dobigeon, N., Kouamé, D., Tourneret, J.Y.: Fast single image super-resolution using a new analytical solution for l2-l2 problems. IEEE Trans. Image Process. **25**(8), 3683–3697 (2016)
62. Zhou, S., Zhang, J., Pan, J., Xie, H., Zuo, W., Ren, J.: Spatio-temporal filter adaptive network for video deblurring. In: IEEE International Conference on Computer Vision, pp. 2482–2491 (2019)

Event-Based Fusion for Motion Deblurring with Cross-modal Attention

Lei Sun[1,2], Christos Sakaridis[2], Jingyun Liang[2], Qi Jiang[1], Kailun Yang[3],
Peng Sun[1], Yaozu Ye[1], Kaiwei Wang[1(✉)], and Luc Van Gool[2,4]

[1] Zhejiang University, Hangzhou, China
wangkaiwei@zju.edu.cn
[2] ETH Zürich, Zürich, Switzerland
[3] KIT, Karlsruhe, Germany
[4] KU Leuven, Leuven, Belgium

Abstract. Traditional frame-based cameras inevitably suffer from motion blur due to long exposure times. As a kind of bio-inspired camera, the event camera records the intensity changes in an asynchronous way with high temporal resolution, providing valid image degradation information within the exposure time. In this paper, we rethink the event-based image deblurring problem and unfold it into an end-to-end two-stage image restoration network. To effectively fuse event and image features, we design an event-image cross-modal attention module applied at multiple levels of our network, which allows to focus on relevant features from the event branch and filter out noise. We also introduce a novel symmetric cumulative event representation specifically for image deblurring as well as an event mask gated connection between the two stages of our network which helps avoid information loss. At the dataset level, to foster event-based motion deblurring and to facilitate evaluation on challenging real-world images, we introduce the Real Event Blur (REBlur) dataset, captured with an event camera in an illumination-controlled optical laboratory. Our Event Fusion Network (EFNet) sets the new state of the art in motion deblurring, surpassing both the prior best-performing image-based method and all event-based methods with public implementations on the GoPro dataset (by up to 2.47 dB) and on our REBlur dataset, even in extreme blurry conditions. The code and our REBlur dataset are available at https://ahupujr.github.io/EFNet/.

1 Introduction

Motion blur often occurs in images due to camera shake or object motion during the exposure time. The goal of deblurring is to recover a sharp image with clear edge structures and texture details from the blurry image. This is a highly ill-posed problem because of the infinitely many feasible solutions [2,10,53]. Traditional methods explicitly utilize natural image priors and various constraints

---

Supplementary Information The online version contains supplementary material available at https://doi.org/10.1007/978-3-031-19797-0_24.

[2, 11, 17, 18, 22, 23, 48]. To better generalize when addressing the deblurring problem, modern learning-based methods choose to train Convolutional Neural Networks (CNNs) on large-scale data to learn the implicit relationships between blurry and sharp images [13, 27, 40, 41, 52]. Despite their high performance on existing public datasets, these learning-based methods often fail when facing extreme or real-world blur. Their performance heavily relies on the quality and scale of the training data, which creates the need for a more general and reliable deblurring method.

Event cameras [5, 12, 30, 37] are bio-inspired asynchronous sensors with high temporal resolution (in the order of μs) and they operate well in environments with high dynamic range. Different from traditional frame-based cameras, event cameras capture the intensity change of each pixel (i.e. *event* information) independently, if the change surpasses a threshold. Event cameras encode the intensity change information within the exposure time of the image frame into an event stream, making it possible to deblur an image frame with events [28]. However, because of sensor noise and uncertainty in the aforementioned threshold, it is difficult to use a physical model to deblur images based solely on events. Thus, some methods [15, 24, 35] utilize CNNs to deal with noise corruption and threshold uncertainty. Nevertheless, these methods only achieve slight performance gains compared to image-only methods, due to rather ineffective event representations and fusion mechanisms between events and images.

In this paper, we first revisit the mechanism of motion blur and how event information is utilized in image reconstruction. To deal with the inherent defect of the event-based motion deblurring equation, we propose EFNet, an Event Fusion Network for image deblurring which effectively combines information from event and frame-based cameras for image deblurring. Motivated by the physical model of event-based image deblurring [28], we design a symmetric cumulative event representation (SCER) specifically for deblurring and formulate our network based on a two-stage image restoration model. Each stage of the model has a U-Net-like architecture [33]. The first stage consists of two branches, an image branch and an event branch, the features of which are fused at multiple levels. In order to perform the fusion of the two modalities, we propose an Event-Image Cross-modal Attention (EICA) fusion module, which allows to attend to the event features that are relevant for deblurring via a channel-level attention mechanism. To the best of our knowledge, this is the first time that a multi-head attention mechanism is applied to event-based image deblurring. We also enable information exchange between the two stages of our network by applying Event Mask Gated Connections (EMGC), which selectively transfer feature maps from the encoder and decoder of the first stage to the second stage. A detailed ablation study shows the effectiveness of our novel fusion module using cross-modal attention, our gated connection module and our multi-level middle fusion design. Additionally, we record a real-world event blur dataset named Real Event Blur (REBlur) in an optical laboratory with stable illumination and a high-precision electronically controlled slide-rail which allows various types of motion. We conduct extensive comparisons against state-of-the-art deblurring methods on the

GoPro dataset [27] with synthetic events and on REBlur with real events and demonstrate the superiority of our event-based image deblurring method.

In summary, we make the following main contributions:

- We design a novel event-image fusion module which applies cross-modal channel-wise attention to adaptively fuse event features with image features, and incorporate it at multiple levels of a novel end-to-end deblurring network.
- We introduce a novel symmetric cumulative event voxel representation for deblurring, which is inspired by the physical model that connects blurry image formation and event generation.
- We present REBlur, a real-world dataset consisting of tuples of blurry images, sharp images and event streams from an event camera, which provides a challenging evaluation setting for deblurring methods.
- Our deblurring network, equipped with our proposed modules and event representation, sets the new state of the art for image deblurring on the GoPro dataset and our REBlur dataset.

2   Related Work

Image Deblurring. Traditional approaches often formulate deblurring as an optimization problem [11,17,18,22,23,48]. Recently, with the success of deep learning, image deblurring has achieved impressive performance thanks to the usage of CNNs. CNN-based methods directly map the blurry image to the latent sharp image. Several novel components and techniques have been proposed, such as attention modules [39,42], multi-scale fusion [27,41], multi-stage networks [8,50], and coarse-to-fine strategies [9], improving the accuracy and robustness of deblurring. Despite the benefits they have shown for deblurring, all aforementioned deep networks operate solely on images, a modality which does not explicitly capture *motion* and thus inherently limits performance when facing real-world blurry images, especially in extreme conditions.

Event-Based Deblurring. Recently, events have been used for motion deblurring, due to the strong connection they possess with motion information. Pan *et al.* [28] proposed an Event Double Integral (EDI) deblurring model using the double integral of event data. They established a mathematical event-based model mapping blurry frames to sharp frames, which is a seminal approach to deblurring with events. However, limited by the sampling mechanism of event cameras, this method often introduces strong, accumulated noise. Jiang *et al.* [15] extracted motion information and sharp edges from events to assist deblurring. However, their early fusion approach, which merely concatenates events into the main branch of the network, does not account for higher-level interactions between frames and events. Lin *et al.* [24] fused events with the image via dynamic filters from STFAN [54]. In addition, Shang *et al.* [35] fused event information into a weight matrix that can be applied to any state-of-the-art network. To sum up, most of the above event-based learning methods did not use event information effectively, achieving only minor improvements compared to image-only methods on standard benchmarks.

Event Representation. Different from synchronous signals such as images from frame-based cameras, events are asynchronous and sparse. A key point in how to extract information from events effectively is the representation of the events. Event representation is an application-dependent problem and different tasks admit different solutions. The event-by-event method is suitable for spiking neural networks owing to its asynchronous architecture [29,34,46]. A Time Surface, which is a 2D map that stores the time value deriving from the timestamp of the last event, has proved suitable for event-based classification [1,21,36]. Some modern learning-based methods convert events to a 2D frame by counting events or accumulating polarities [25,26,35]. This approach is compatible with conventional computer vision tasks but loses temporal information. 3D space-time histograms of events, also called voxel grids, preserve the temporal information of events better by accumulating event polarity on a voxel [4,55]. For image deblurring, most works utilized 2D event-image pairs [35] or borrowed 3D voxel grids like Stacking Based on Time (SBT) from image reconstruction [43]. However, there still is no event representation specifically designed for motion deblurring.

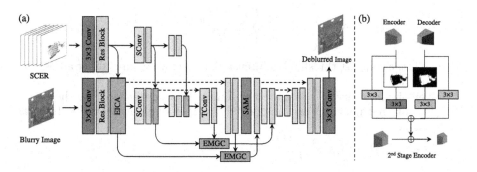

Fig. 1. (a): **The architecture of our Event Fusion Network (EFNet).** EFNet consists of two UNet-like backbones [33] and an event extraction branch. After each residual convolution block ("Res Block"), feature maps from the event branch and the image branch are fused. The second UNet backbone refines the deblurred image further. "SCER": symmetric cumulative event representation, "EICA": event-image cross-modal attention, "SConv": 4×4 strided convolution with stride 2, "TConv": 2×2 transposed convolution with stride 2, "SAM": supervision attention module [50]. (b): **The Event Mask Gated Connection module (EMGC)** transfers features across stages guided by an event mask.

3   Method

We first introduce the mathematical model for the formation of blurry images from sharp images that involves events in Sect. 3.1. Based on this model, we pose the event-based deblurring problem as a deblurring-denoising problem and base the high-level design of our network architecture on this formulation, as explained in Sect. 3.2. We present our symmetric cumulative representation for events, which constitutes a 3D voxel grid in which the temporal dimension is discretized, in Sect. 3.3. This event representation is provided as input together with the blurry image to our two-stage network. We then detail the two main novel components of our network: our novel event-image cross-modal attention fusion mechanism (Sect. 3.4), which adaptively fuses feature channels associated with events and images, and our event mask gated connection module between the two stages of our network (Sect. 3.5), which helps selectively forward to the second stage the features at sharp regions of the input from the encoder and the features at blurry regions from the decoder of the first stage.

3.1   Problem Formulation

For an event camera, the i-th event e_i is represented as a tuple $e_i = (x_i, y_i, t_i, p_i)$, where x_i, y_i and t_i represent the pixel coordinates and the timestamp of the event respectively, and $p_i \in \{-1, +1\}$ is the polarity of the event [5,30]. An event is triggered at time t only when the change in pixel intensity $\mathcal{I}$ surpasses the threshold compared to the pixel intensity at the time of the last trigger. This is formulated as

$$p_i = \begin{cases} +1, \text{if} \log \left(\frac{\mathcal{I}_t(x_i,y_i)}{\mathcal{I}_{t-\Delta t}(x_i,y_i)} \right) > c, \\ -1, \text{if} \log \left(\frac{\mathcal{I}_t(x_i,y_i)}{\mathcal{I}_{t-\Delta t}(x_i,y_i)} \right) < -c, \end{cases} \tag{1}$$

where c is the contrast threshold of intensity change, which may differ across the sensor plane.

Given the intensity of a latent sharp image $\mathbf{L}$, according to [28], the corresponding blurred image $\mathbf{B}$ can be derived by the Event-based Double Integral (EDI) model:

$$\begin{aligned} \mathbf{B} &= \frac{1}{T} \int_{f-T/2}^{f+T/2} \mathbf{L}(t) dt \\ &= \frac{\mathbf{L}(f)}{T} \int_{f-T/2}^{f+T/2} \exp \left(c \int_f^t p(s) ds \right) dt, \end{aligned} \tag{2}$$

where f is the middle point of the exposure time T, $p(s)$ is the polarity component of the event stream and $\mathbf{L}(f)$ is the latent sharp image corresponding to the blurred image $\mathbf{B}$. The discretized version of (2) can be expressed as

$$\mathbf{B} = \frac{\mathbf{L}(N)}{2N+1} \sum_{i=0}^{2N} \exp \left(c \operatorname{sgn}(i-N) \sum_{j:\, m \leq t_j \leq M} p_j \delta_{x_j y_j} \right), \tag{3}$$

where sgn is the signum function, $m = \min\{f+T/2(i/N-1), f\}$, $M = \max\{f+T/2(i/N-1), f\}$ and δ is the Kronecker delta, defined as

$$\delta_{kl}(m,n) = \begin{cases} 1, \text{ if } k = m \text{ and } l = n, \\ 0, \text{ otherwise.} \end{cases} \tag{4}$$

In (3), we partition the exposure time T into $2N$ equal intervals. Rearranging (3) yields:

$$\mathbf{L}(N) = \frac{(2N+1)\mathbf{B}}{\sum_{i=0}^{2N} \exp \left(c \operatorname{sgn}(i-N) \sum_{j:\, m \leq t_j \leq M} p_j \delta_{x_j y_j} \right)}. \tag{5}$$

3.2 General Architecture of EFNet

The formulation in (5) indicates that the latent sharp image can be derived from the blurred image combined with the set of events $\mathcal{E} = \{e_i = (x_i, y_i, t_i, p_i) : f - T/2 \leq t_i \leq f + T/2\}$ (i.e.., all the events which are triggered within the exposure time), when events in this set are accumulated over time. We propose to learn this relation with a deep neural network, named Event Fusion Network (EFNet), which admits as inputs the blurred image and the events and maps them to the sharp image. The generic form of the learned mapping is

$$\mathbf{L}_{\text{initial}} = f_3\left(f_1(\mathbf{B}; \Theta_1), f_2(\mathcal{E}; \Theta_2); \Theta_3\right), \qquad (6)$$

where the blurred image and the events are mapped individually to intermediate representations via f_1 and f_2 respectively and these intermediate representations are afterwards passed to a joint mapping f_3. Θ_1, Θ_2 and Θ_3 denote the respective parameters of the three mappings. The main challenges we need to address given this generic formulation of our model are (i) how to represent the set of events $\mathcal{E}$ in a suitable way for inputting it to the network, and (ii) how and when to fuse the intermediate representations that are generated for the blurred image by f_1 and for the events by f_2, i.e.., how to design f_3. We address the issue of how to represent the events in Sect. 3.3 and how to perform fusion in Sect. 3.4.

(3) is the ideal formulation for event-based motion image deblurring. However, in real-world settings, three factors make it impossible to restore the image simply based on this equation:

- Instead of being strictly equal to a fixed value, the values of threshold c for a given event camera are neither constant in time nor across the image [38,45].
- Intensity changes that are lower than the threshold c do not trigger an event.
- Spurious events occur over the entire image.

Most of the restoration errors come from the first two factors, which cause degradation of the restored image in regions with events. We denote these regions as R_e. Taking the above factors into account, we design our network so that it includes a final mapping of the initial deblurred image $\mathbf{L}_{\text{initial}}$ to a denoised version of it, which can correct potential errors in the values of pixels inside R_e:

$$\mathbf{L}_{\text{final}} = f_4(\mathbf{L}_{\text{initial}}; \Theta_4). \qquad (7)$$

Two-Stage Backbone. We design EFNet as a two-stage network to progressively restore sharp images from blurred images and event streams, where the first and second stage implement the generic mappings in (6) and (7) respectively. The detailed architecture of EFNet is illustrated in Fig. 1. Both stages of EFNet have an encoder-decoder structure, based on the UNet [33] architecture. Each stage consists of two down-sampling and two up-sampling layers. Between the encoder and decoder, we add a skip connection with 3×3 convolution. The residual convolution block in UNet consists of two 3×3 convolution layers and leaky ReLUs with a 1×1 convolution shortcut. Recently, the Supervised Attention

Module (SAM) in multi-stage methods proved successful in transferring features between different sub-networks [8,50]. Thus, we use SAM to connect the two stages of EFNet. In the first stage, we fuse features from the event branch and the image branch at multiple levels using a novel cross-modal attention-based block. Between the two stages, we design an Event Mask Gated Connection module to boost feature aggregation with blurring priors from events. The details of the two aforementioned components of EFNet are given in Sect. 3.4 and 3.5.

3.3   Symmetric Cumulative Event Representation

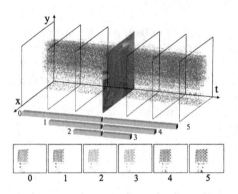

Fig. 2. Symmetric Cumulative Event Representation (SCER). Red/blue dots denote events with positive/negative polarity respectively. (Color figure online)

To feed the asynchronous events to our network, we design a representation specifically suited for deblurring. In (3), the accumulation of polarities via the inner sum on the right-hand side indicates the relative intensity changes between the target latent sharp image $\mathbf{L}(N)$ and each of the rest of latent sharp images in the exposure time. The accumulation via the outer sum on the right-hand side represents the sum of all latent sharp images. Based on this relationship, we propose the Symmetric Cumulative Event Representation (SCER). As Fig. 2 shows, the exposure time T of the blurry image is divided equally into $2N$ intervals. Assuming $2N + 1$ latent sharp images in T, the polarity accumulation from the central target latent image $\mathbf{L}(N)$ to a single latent image turns into a 2D tensor with dimensions (H, W):

$$\mathbf{SCER}_i = \text{sgn}(i - N) \sum_{j:\ m \leq t_j \leq M} p_j \delta_{x_j y_j}. \tag{8}$$

For $i = N$, $\mathbf{SCER}_N = 0$, so we discard this tensor. The remaining $2N$ tensors are concatenated together, forming a tensor which indicates intensity changes between the central latent sharp image $\mathbf{L}(N)$ and each of the $2N$ other latent images. In this way, $\mathbf{SCER} \in \mathbb{R}^{H \times W \times 2N}$ includes all the relative intensity values corresponding to the center latent sharp frame and it becomes suitable for feature extraction with our image deblurring model. As the accumulation limits change, our SCER also contains both information about the area in which blur occurs (channel 0 and channel $2N - 1$) and information about sharp edges (channel $N - 1$ and channel N).

Our method discretizes T into $2N$ parts, quantizing temporal information of events within the time interval $\frac{T}{2N}$. However, SCER still holds temporal information, as the endpoints of the time interval in which events are accumulated is different across channels. The larger N is, the less temporal information is lost. In our implementation, we fix $N = 3$.

3.4 Event-Image Cross-modal Attention Fusion

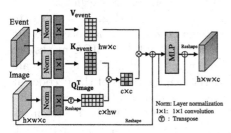

Fig. 3. The Event-Image Cross-modal Attention fusion module. The size of the attention map is $c \times c$.

Jointly extracting and fusing information from event streams and images is the key to event-based deblurring. Previous work [15,24] simply multiplies or concatenates low-resolution feature maps from the two modalities, but this fusion approach cannot model the long-range relations between events and images. Other methods estimate optical flow with events and use it for deblurring [35], but this estimation introduces errors.

We instead include a novel cross-modal attention block at multiple levels of EFNet. Contrary to self-attention blocks, in which the queries ($\mathbf{Q}$), keys ($\mathbf{K}$) and values ($\mathbf{V}$) all come from the same branch of the network, our Event-Image Cross-modal Attention (EICA) block admits as inputs the queries $\mathbf{Q}_{\text{image}}$ from the image branch and the keys $\mathbf{K}_{\text{event}}$ and values $\mathbf{V}_{\text{event}}$ from the event branch, as shown in Fig. 3. The input features from the two branches are fed to normalization and 1×1 convolution layers, where the latter have c output channels. We then apply cross-modal attention between vectorized features from the two modalities via

$$\text{Attention}(\mathbf{Q}_{\text{image}}, \mathbf{K}_{\text{event}}, \mathbf{V}_{\text{event}}) = \mathbf{V}_{\text{event}} \, \text{softmax}\left(\frac{\mathbf{Q}_{\text{image}}^T \mathbf{K}_{\text{event}}}{\sqrt{d_k}}\right). \quad (9)$$

We introduce the 1×1 convolution layer to reduce the spatial complexity of the above attention operation. In particular, c is chosen to be much smaller than hw, where h and w are the height and width of the input feature maps, and the soft indexing of $\mathbf{K}_{\text{event}}$ by $\mathbf{Q}_{\text{image}}$ is performed at the *channel* dimension instead of the spatial dimensions. Thus, the resulting soft attention map from (9) is $c \times c$ instead of $hw \times hw$, reducing the spatial complexity from $\mathcal{O}(h^2w^2)$ to $\mathcal{O}(c^2)$ and making the operation feasible even for features with high spatial resolution, as in our case. Finally, the output of the attention operation is added to the input image features and this sum is passed to a multi-layer perceptron consisting of two fully connected layers with a Gaussian Error Linear Unit (GELU) [14] in between. We use the EICA module at multiple levels of EFNEt to fuse event information aggregated across receptive fields of varying size.

3.5 Event Mask Gated Connection Module

Previous work [31] predicts a mask indicating which areas of an image are severely distorted, but this mask is not completely accurate. Apart from information about intensity changes, event data also contain spatial information about the blurred regions of the input image. Typically, regions in which events occur are more severely degraded in the blurry image. Motivated by this observation, we introduce an Event Mask Gated Connection (EMGC) between the two stages of our network to exploit the spatial information about blurred regions.

In particular, we binarize the sum of the first and last channel of SCER to obtain a binary event mask, in which pixels where an event has occurred are set to 0 and the rest are set to 1. As illustrated in Fig. 1(b), EMGC masks out the feature maps of the encoder at regions where the event mask is 0, which are expected to be more blurry, and masks out the feature maps of the decoder at regions where the event mask is 1 (using the complement of the event mask), which are expected to be less blurry. A skip connection is added beside the mask operation. Feature maps with less artifacts in the encoder and better restored feature maps are combined through the event mask gate. Besides, EMGC eases the flow of information through the network, as it creates a shortcut through which features can be transferred directly from the first to the second stage.

4   REBlur Dataset

Most event-based motion deblurring methods [6,15,24,35,47] train models on blurred image datasets, such as GoPro [27], with synthetic events from ESIM [32]. Although the contrast threshold c in the event simulator varies across pixels as in reality, a domain gap between synthetic and real events still exists because of the background activity noise, dark current noise, and false negatives in refractory period [3,38,45]. Recently, Jiang *et al.* [15] proposed BlurDVS by capturing an image plus events with slow motion, and then synthesizing motion blur by averaging multiple nearby frames. However, motion blur in the ground-truth images is inevitable in this setting and fast motion causes different events from slow motion because of the false negatives in the refractory period of event cameras [3,47]. Thus, a large-scale real-world dataset with blurry images, reliable corresponding events, and ground-truth sharp images is missing.

We present a new event-based dataset for deblurring, Real Event Blur (REBlur), to provide ground truth for blurry images in a two-shot way. To collect REBlur, we built an image collection system in a high-precision optical laboratory with very stable illumination. We fixed an Insightness Seem 1 event camera and a Dynamic and Active Pixel Vision Sensor (DAVIS) to the optical table, outputting time-aligned event streams and 260×360 gray images. To obtain blurry-sharp image pairs under high-speed motion, we also fixed a high-precision electronic-controlled slide-rail system to the optical table. In the first shot, we captured images with motion blur for the pattern on the slide-rail and corresponding event streams. In the second shot, according to the timestamp t_s of the blurry images, we selected events within the time range $[t_s - 125\mu s, t_s + 125\mu s]$ and visualized these events in the preview of the sharp image capture program. Referring to the edge information from high-temporal-resolution events, we could relocate the slide-rail to the coordinate corresponding to the timestamp t_s by an

Table 1. Comparison of motion deblurring methods on GoPro [27]. †: event-based methods, SRN+ and HINet+: event-enhanced versions of SRN [41] and HINet [8] using our SCER, percentages in brackets: relative reduction in error with EFNet.

Method	PSNR ↑	SSIM ↑
DeblurGAN [19]	28.70 (54.1%)	0.858 (80.3%)
BHA† [28]	29.06 (52.1%)	0.940 (53.3%)
Nah et al. [27]	29.08 (52.0%)	0.914 (67.4%)
DeblurGAN-v2 [20]	29.55 (49.4%)	0.934 (57.6%)
SRN [41]	30.26 (45.1%)	0.934 (57.6%)
SRN+† [41]	31.02 (40.0%)	0.936 (56.3%)
DMPHN [51]	31.20 (38.8%)	0.940 (53.3%)
D²Nets† [35]	31.60 (35.9%)	0.940 (53.3%)
LEMD† [15]	31.79 (34.5%)	0.949 (45.1%)
Suin et al. [39]	31.85 (34.0%)	0.948 (46.2%)
SPAIR [31]	32.06 (32.4%)	0.953 (40.4%)
MPRNet [50]	32.66 (27.6%)	0.959 (31.7%)
HINet [8]	32.71 (27.1%)	0.959 (31.7%)
Restormer [49]	32.92 (25.4%)	0.961 (28.2%)
ERDNet† [6]	32.99 (24.8%)	0.935 (56.9%)
HINet+† [8]	33.69 (18.4%)	0.961 (28.2%)
NAFNet [7]	33.69 (18.4%)	0.967 (15.2%)
EFNet (Ours)†	**35.46**	**0.972**

electronic-controlled stepping motor and then capture the latent sharp image. REBlur includes 12 kinds of linear and nonlinear motions for 3 different moving patterns and for the camera itself. It consists of 36 sequences and 1469 blurry-sharp image pairs with associated events, where 486 pairs are used for training and 983 for testing. The supplement includes more details on REBlur.

5 Experiments

5.1 Datasets and Settings

GoPro Dataset. We use the GoPro dataset [27], which is widely used in motion deblurring, for training and evaluation. It consists of 3214 pairs of blurry and sharp images with a resolution of 1280×720 and the blurred images are produced by averaging several high-speed sharp images. We use 2103 pairs for training and 1111 pairs for testing, following standard practice [27]. We use ESIM [32], an open-source event camera simulator, to generate simulated event data for GoPro. To make the results more realistic, we set the contrast threshold c randomly for each pixel, following a Gaussian distribution $N(\mu = 0.2, \sigma = 0.03)$.

REBlur Dataset. In order to close the gap between simulated events and real events, before evaluating models that are trained on GoPro on REBlur, we fine-tune them on the training set of REBlur. We then evaluate the fine-tuned models on the test set of REBlur. More details on this fine-tuning follow.

Implementation Details. Our network requires no pre-training. We train it on 256×256 crops of full images from GoPro. Full details about our network configuration (numbers of channels, kernel sizes *etc..*) are given in the supplement. For data augmentation, horizontal and vertical flipping, random noise and hot pixels in event voxels [38] are applied. We use Adam [16] with an initial learning rate of 2×10^{-4}, and the cosine learning rate strategy with a minimum learning rate of 10^{-7}. The model is trained with a batch size of 8 for 300k iterations on 4 NVIDIA Titan RTX GPUs, which take 41 h. Fine-tuning on REBlur involves 600 iterations and a single Titan RTX, the initial learning rate is 2×10^{-5} and other configurations are kept the same as for GoPro. We use the same training and fine-tuning settings for our method and other methods for a fair comparison.

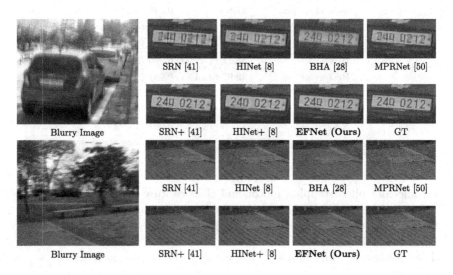

Fig. 4. Visual comparison on GoPro. SRN+ and HINet+: event-enhanced versions of SRN and HINet using SCER. Compared to image- and event-based state-of-the-art methods, our method restores fine texture and structures better.

Evaluation Protocol. All quantitative comparisons are performed using PSNR and SSIM [44]. Apart from these, we also report the relative reduction in error with the best-performing model compared to each method. This is done by first converting PSNR to RMSE (RMSE $\propto \sqrt{10^{-\text{PSNR}/10}}$) and SSIM to DSSIM (DSSIM $= (1 - \text{SSIM})/2$) and then computing the relative reduction in error.

5.2   Comparisons with State-of-the-Art Methods

We compare our method with state-of-the-art image-only and event-based deblurring methods on GoPro and REBlur. Since most learning-based methods using events do not have publicly available implementations, in the qualitative comparison part, apart from BHA [28], we compare our method with SRN [41] and HINet [8], the latter being the current best model on the GoPro benchmark. To have a fair comparison, we also include event-enhanced versions of these two models by concatenating event voxel grids and images in the input.

GoPro. We report deblurring results in Table 1. Compared to the best existing image-based [8] and event-based [6] methods, EFNet achieves 2.75 dB and 2.47 dB improvement in PSNR and 0.013 and 0.037 improvement in SSIM resp., with a low parameter count of 8.47M. Despite utilizing an extra modality, other learning-based methods using events such as D^2Nets, LEMD, and ERDNet do not improve significantly upon image-only methods. EFNet sets the new state of the art in image deblurring, showing that our principled architecture with attentive fusion leverages event information more effectively for this task. By simply including our SCER to HINet [8], the resulting enhanced version of it also surpasses the best previous event-based method [6]. We show qualitative results on GoPro in Fig. 4. Results of image-based methods are more blurry, losing sharp edge information. BHA [28] restores edges better but suffers from noise around them because of the factors described in Sect. 3.1. Learning-based methods using events cannot fully exploit the motion information from events. By inputting the concatenation of SCER with the image to SRN+ and HINet+, they both achieve large improvements. However, results from SRN+ include artifacts and noise due to the absence of a second stage in the network that would refine the result. HINet+ introduces more artifacts, indicating that concatenating events and images in the input is not sufficient. Based on the physical model for event deblurring, EFNet achieves sharp and faithful results. Both dominant structures and details are restored well thanks to our attentive fusion at multiple levels.

Table 2. Comparison of motion deblurring methods on REBlur. Read as Table 1.

Method	PSNR ↑	SSIM ↑	Params (M) ↓
SRN [41]	35.10 (29.4%)	0.961 (35.9%)	10.25
NAFNet [7]	35.48 (26.2%)	0.962 (34.2%)	67.89
Restormer [49]	35.50 (26.0%)	0.959 (39.0%)	26.13
HINet [8]	35.58 (25.4%)	0.965 (28.6%)	88.67
BHA[†] [28]	36.52 (16.8%)	0.964 (30.6%)	0.51
SRN+[†] [41]	36.87 (13.4%)	0.970 (16.7%)	10.43
HINet+[†] [8]	37.68 (4.9%)	0.973 (7.4%)	88.85
EFNet (Ours)[†]	**38.12**	**0.975**	8.47

REBlur. We report quantitative results on REBlur in Table 2. Our model outperforms all other methods in this challenging real-world setting. Figure 5 depicts qualitative results from the test set and the additional set. Even the best image-based method, HINet, does not perform well on these cases of severe real-world motion blur. Event-based methods are more robust to such adverse conditions and less prone to overfitting on synthetic training data. Results from BHA are sharper, but accumulation noise still exists. Simply adding events with our SCER representation to the state-of-the-art image-based method [8] improves performance significantly because of the physical basis of SCER, but still leads to artifacts and ghost structures. EFNet restores both smooth texture and sharp edges, demonstrating the utility of our two-stage architecture and our cross-modal attention for fusion. Thanks to the selective feature connection via EMGC, EFNet restores blurry regions well while also maintaining the content of sharp regions. More results, including failure cases, are provided in the supplement.

Table 3. Ablation study of various components of our method on GoPro [27]. "Early": fusion by concatenation of event voxel grid and image, "Multi-level": fusion with our proposed architecture. SCER is used to represent events.

	Architecture	Events	Fusion type	EMGC	Fusion module	PSNR ↑	SSIM ↑
1	1-Stage	✗	n/a	n/a	n/a	29.06	0.936
2	1-Stage	✓	Multi-level	n/a	EICA	34.90	0.968
3	2-Stage	✗	n/a	n/a	n/a	32.15	0.954
4	2-Stage	✓	Early	✗	n/a	33.68	0.960
5	2-Stage	✓	Early	✓	n/a	33.79	0.961
6	2-Stage	✓	Multi-level	✓	Concat	34.80	0.968
7	2-Stage	✓	Multi-level	✓	Multiply	34.86	0.968
8	2-Stage	✓	Multi-level	✓	Add	34.78	0.968
9	2-Stage	✓	Multi-level	✗	EICA	35.31	0.971
10	2-Stage	✓	Multi-level	✓	EICA	**35.46**	**0.972**

5.3   Ablation Study

Table 4. Comparison between different event representations on GoPro. "Stack": temporal event accumulation in a single channel.

Event representation	PSNR ↑	SSIM ↑
None (image-only)	32.15	0.954
Stack	31.90	0.950
SBT [43]	35.12	0.970
SCER (Ours)	**35.46**	**0.972**

We conduct two ablation studies on GoPro to analyze the contribution of different components of our network (Table 3) and our event representation (Table 4). First, our EICA fusion block fuses event and image features effectively, improving PSNR by 0.6 dB or more and SSIM by 0.4%

compared to simple strategies for fusion such as multiplication or addition (rows 6–8 and 10 of Table 3). Second, introducing middle fusion at multiple levels and using simple strategies for fusion yields an improvement of ∼1 dB in PSNR and 0.7% in SSIM over early fusion (rows 5–8), evidencing the benefit of using multi-level fusion in our EFNet. Third, adding events as input to the network via early fusion of our SCER voxel grids with the images improves PSNR by 1.53 dB and SSIM by 0.6% (rows 3–4), showcasing the informativeness of the event modality regarding motion, which leads to better deblurring. Fourth, adding a second stage in our network for progressive restoration benefits deblurring significantly, both in the image-only case (rows 1 and 3) and in the case where our fully-fledged EFNet is used (rows 2 and 10). Fifth, connecting the two stages of EFNet with our EMGC improves the selective flow of information between the two stages, yielding an improvement of 0.15 dB (rows 9–10). Finally, all our contributions together yield a substantial improvement of 6.4 dB in PSNR and 3.6% in SSIM over the image-only one-stage baseline, setting the new state of the art in motion deblurring.

Event Representation. Introducing events can improve performance due to the high temporal resolution of the event stream, which provides a vital signal for deblurring. Table 4 shows a comparison between SCER and other event representations, including SBT [43], which accumulates polarities in fixed time intervals. We use the same number of intervals (6) for SBT and SCER for a fair comparison. Based explicitly on physics, SCER utilizes event information for image deblurring more effectively than SBT. Note that simply accumulat-

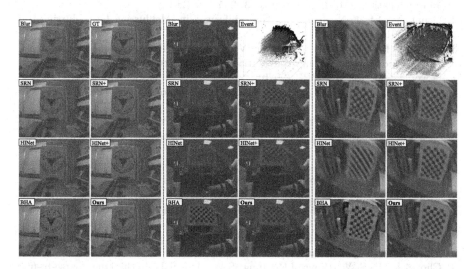

Fig. 5. Visual comparison on the REBlur dataset. The first two columns are from the test set of the REBlur dataset, and the rest are from the additional set, for which ground truth is not available. Our method shows superior performance in cases with severe blur both due to object motion and due to camera motion. Best viewed on a screen and zoomed in.

ing all events across the exposure time ("Stack") deteriorates the performance compared to not using events at all, which demonstrates that finding a suitable event representation for deblurring, such as SCER, is non-trivial.

6   Conclusion

In this work, we have looked into single-image motion deblurring from the perspective of event-based fusion. Based on the physical model which describes blurry image formation and event generation, we have introduced EFNet, an end-to-end motion deblurring network with attention-based event-image fusion applied at multiple levels of the network. In addition, we have proposed a novel event voxel representation for deblurring. We have captured a new real-world dataset, REBlur, including several cases of severe motion blur, which provides a challenging evaluation setting. EFNet significantly surpasses the prior state of the art in image deblurring, both on the GoPro dataset and on our new dataset.

Acknowledgments. This work was supported by the National Natural Science Foundation of China (NSFC) under Grant No.12174341, Sunny Optical Technology (group) co., Ltd, and the China Scholarship Council.

References

1. Ahad, M.A.R., Tan, J.K., Kim, H., Ishikawa, S.: Motion history image: its variants and applications. Mach. Vis. Appl. **23**, 255–281 (2012)
2. Bahat, Y., Efrat, N., Irani, M.: Non-uniform blind deblurring by reblurring. In: ICCV (2017)
3. Baldwin, R., Almatrafi, M., Asari, V., Hirakawa, K.: Event probability mask (EPM) and event denoising convolutional neural network (EDnCNN) for neuromorphic cameras. In: CVPR (2020)
4. Bardow, P., Davison, A.J., Leutenegger, S.: Simultaneous optical flow and intensity estimation from an event camera. In: CVPR (2016)
5. Brandli, C., Berner, R., Yang, M., Liu, S.C., Delbruck, T.: A 240 × 180 130 dB 3 μs latency global shutter spatiotemporal vision sensor. IEEE J. Solid-State Circ. **49**, 2333–2341 (2014)
6. Chen, H., Teng, M., Shi, B., Wang, Y., Huang, T.: Learning to deblur and generate high frame rate video with an event camera. arXiv preprint arXiv:2003.00847 (2020)
7. Chen, L., Chu, X., Zhang, X., Sun, J.: Simple baselines for image restoration. arXiv preprint arXiv:2204.04676 (2022)
8. Chen, L., Lu, X., Zhang, J., Chu, X., Chen, C.: HINet: Half instance normalization network for image restoration. In: CVPRW (2021)
9. Cho, S.J., Ji, S.W., Hong, J.P., Jung, S.W., Ko, S.J.: Rethinking coarse-to-fine approach in single image deblurring. In: ICCV (2021)
10. Cho, S., Lee, S.: Fast motion deblurring. In: ACM Transactions on Graphics (2009)
11. Fergus, R., Singh, B., Hertzmann, A., Roweis, S.T., Freeman, W.T.: Removing camera shake from a single photograph. In: ACM Transactions on Graphics (2006)

12. Gallego, G., et al.: Event-based vision: a survey. IEEE Trans. Pattern Anal. Mach. Intell. **44**, 154–180 (2022)
13. Gong, D., et al.: From motion blur to motion flow: a deep learning solution for removing heterogeneous motion blur. In: CVPR (2017)
14. Hendrycks, D., Gimpel, K.: Gaussian error linear units (GELUs). arXiv preprint arXiv:1606.08415 (2016)
15. Jiang, Z., Zhang, Y., Zou, D., Ren, J., Lv, J., Liu, Y.: Learning event-based motion deblurring. In: CVPR (2020)
16. Kingma, D.P., Ba, J.: Adam: a method for stochastic optimization. In: ICLR (2015)
17. Kotera, J., Šroubek, F., Milanfar, P.: Blind deconvolution using alternating maximum a posteriori estimation with heavy-tailed priors. In: CAIP (2013)
18. Krishnan, D., Tay, T., Fergus, R.: Blind deconvolution using a normalized sparsity measure. In: CVPR (2011)
19. Kupyn, O., Budzan, V., Mykhailych, M., Mishkin, D., Matas, J.: DeblurGAN: blind motion deblurring using conditional adversarial networks. In: CVPR (2018)
20. Kupyn, O., Martyniuk, T., Wu, J., Wang, Z.: DeblurGAN-v2: deblurring (orders-of-magnitude) faster and better. In: ICCV (2019)
21. Lagorce, X., Orchard, G., Galluppi, F., Shi, B.E., Benosman, R.B.: HOTS: a hierarchy of event-based time-surfaces for pattern recognition. IEEE Trans. Pattern Anal. Mach. Intell. **39**, 1346–1359 (2017)
22. Levin, A., Weiss, Y., Durand, F., Freeman, W.T.: Understanding and evaluating blind deconvolution algorithms. In: CVPR (2009)
23. Levin, A., Weiss, Y., Durand, F., Freeman, W.T.: Efficient marginal likelihood optimization in blind deconvolution. In: CVPR (2011)
24. Lin, S., Zhang, J., Pan, J., Jiang, Z., Zou, D., Wang, Y., Chen, J., Ren, J.: Learning event-driven video deblurring and interpolation. In: Vedaldi, A., Bischof, H., Brox, T., Frahm, J.-M. (eds.) ECCV 2020. LNCS, vol. 12353, pp. 695–710. Springer, Cham (2020). https://doi.org/10.1007/978-3-030-58598-3_41
25. Liu, M., Delbruck, T.: Adaptive time-slice block-matching optical flow algorithm for dynamic vision sensors. In: BMVC (2018)
26. Maqueda, A.I., Loquercio, A., Gallego, G., García, N., Scaramuzza, D.: Event-based vision meets deep learning on steering prediction for self-driving cars. In: CVPR (2018)
27. Nah, S., Hyun Kim, T., Mu Lee, K.: Deep multi-scale convolutional neural network for dynamic scene deblurring. In: CVPR (2017)
28. Pan, L., Scheerlinck, C., Yu, X., Hartley, R., Liu, M., Dai, Y.: Bringing a blurry frame alive at high frame-rate with an event camera. In: CVPR (2019)
29. Paredes-Vallés, F., Scheper, K.Y.W., de Croon, G.C.H.E.: Unsupervised learning of a hierarchical spiking neural network for optical flow estimation: From events to global motion perception. IEEE Trans. Pattern Anal. Mach. Intell. **42**, 2051–2064 (2020)
30. Patrick, L., Posch, C., Delbruck, T.: A 128×128 120 dB 15μ s latency asynchronous temporal contrast vision sensor. IEEE J. Solid-State Circuits **43**, 566–576 (2008)
31. Purohit, K., Suin, M., Rajagopalan, A.N., Boddeti, V.N.: Spatially-adaptive image restoration using distortion-guided networks. In: ICCV (2021)
32. Rebecq, H., Gehrig, D., Scaramuzza, D.: ESIM: an open event camera simulator. In: CoLR (2018)
33. Ronneberger, O., Fischer, P., Brox, T.: U-Net: convolutional networks for biomedical image segmentation. In: Navab, N., Hornegger, J., Wells, W.M., Frangi, A.F. (eds.) MICCAI 2015. LNCS, vol. 9351, pp. 234–241. Springer, Cham (2015). https://doi.org/10.1007/978-3-319-24574-4_28

34. Scheerlinck, C., Barnes, N., Mahony, R.: Continuous-time intensity estimation using event cameras. In: ACCV (2018)

35. Shang, W., Ren, D., Zou, D., Ren, J.S., Luo, P., Zuo, W.: Bringing events into video deblurring with non-consecutively blurry frames. In: ICCV (2021)

36. Sironi, A., Brambilla, M., Bourdis, N., Lagorce, X., Benosman, R.: HATS: histograms of averaged time surfaces for robust event-based object classification. In: CVPR (2018)

37. Stoffregen, T., Kleeman, L.: Event cameras, contrast maximization and reward functions: An analysis. In: CVPR (2019)

38. Stoffregen, T., et al.: Reducing the sim-to-real gap for event cameras. In: Vedaldi, A., Bischof, H., Brox, T., Frahm, J.-M. (eds.) ECCV 2020. LNCS, vol. 12372, pp. 534–549. Springer, Cham (2020). https://doi.org/10.1007/978-3-030-58583-9_32

39. Suin, M., Purohit, K., Rajagopalan, A.N.: Spatially-attentive patch-hierarchical network for adaptive motion deblurring. In: CVPR (2020)

40. Sun, J., Cao, W., Xu, Z., Ponce, J.: Learning a convolutional neural network for non-uniform motion blur removal. In: CVPR (2015)

41. Tao, X., Gao, H., Shen, X., Wang, J., Jia, J.: Scale-recurrent network for deep image deblurring. In: CVPR (2018)

42. Tsai, F.J., Peng, Y.T., Lin, Y.Y., Tsai, C.C., Lin, C.W.: BANet: blur-aware attention networks for dynamic scene deblurring. arXiv preprint arXiv:2101.07518 (2021)

43. Wang, L., I., S.M.M., Ho, Y., Yoon, K.: Event-based high dynamic range image and very high frame rate video generation using conditional generative adversarial networks. In: CVPR (2019)

44. Wang, Z., Bovik, A.C., Sheikh, H.R., Simoncelli, E.P.: Image quality assessment: from error visibility to structural similarity. IEEE Trans. Image Process. **13**, 600–612 (2004)

45. Wang, Z., Ng, Y., van Goor, P., Mahony, R.: Event camera calibration of per-pixel biased contrast threshold. In: ACRA (2019)

46. Weikersdorfer, D., Conradt, J.: Event-based particle filtering for robot self-localization. In: ROBIO (2012)

47. Xu, F., et al.: Motion deblurring with real events. In: ICCV (2021)

48. Xu, L., Zheng, S., Jia, J.: Unnatural L0 sparse representation for natural image deblurring. In: CVPR (2013)

49. Zamir, S.W., Arora, A., Khan, S., Hayat, M., Khan, F.S., Yang, M.H.: Restormer: efficient transformer for high-resolution image restoration. In: CVPR (2022)

50. Zamir, S.W., et al.: Multi-stage progressive image restoration. In: CVPR (2021)

51. Zhang, H., Dai, Y., Li, H., Koniusz, P.: Deep stacked hierarchical multi-patch network for image deblurring. In: CVPR (2019)

52. Zhang, J., et al.: Dynamic scene deblurring using spatially variant recurrent neural networks. In: CVPR (2018)

53. Zhang, K., Zuo, W., Chen, Y., Meng, D., Zhang, L.: Beyond a Gaussian denoiser: residual learning of deep CNN for image denoising. IEEE Trans. Image Process. **26**, 3142–3155 (2017)

54. Zhou, S., Zhang, J., Pan, J., Xie, H., Zuo, W., Ren, J.: Spatio-temporal filter adaptive network for video deblurring. In: ICCV (2019)

55. Zhu, A.Z., Yuan, L., Chaney, K., Daniilidis, K.: Unsupervised event-based learning of optical flow, depth, and egomotion. In: CVPR (2019)

Fast and High Quality Image Denoising via Malleable Convolution

Yifan Jiang[1]([✉]), Bartlomiej Wronski[2], Ben Mildenhall[2], Jonathan T. Barron[2], Zhangyang Wang[1], and Tianfan Xue[2]

[1] University of Texas at Austin, Austin, USA
yifanjiang97@utexas.edu
[2] Google Research, San Francisco, USA

Abstract. Most image denoising networks apply a single set of static convolutional kernels across the entire input image. This is sub-optimal for natural images, as they often consist of heterogeneous visual patterns. Dynamic convolution tries to address this issue by using per-pixel convolution kernels, but this greatly increases computational cost. In this work, we present **Malleable Conv**olution (**MalleConv**), which performs spatial-varying processing with minimal computational overhead. MalleConv uses a smaller set of spatially-varying convolution kernels, a compromise between static and per-pixel convolution kernels. These spatially-varying kernels are produced by an efficient predictor network running on a downsampled input, making them much more efficient to compute than per-pixel kernels produced by a full-resolution image, and also enlarging the network's receptive field compared with static kernels. These kernels are then jointly upsampled and applied to a full-resolution feature map through an efficient on-the-fly slicing operator with minimum memory overhead. To demonstrate the effectiveness of MalleConv, we use it to build an efficient denoising network we call **MalleNet**. MalleNet achieves high-quality results without very deep architectures, making it 8.9× faster than the best performing denoising algorithms while achieving similar visual quality. We also show that a single MalleConv layer added to a standard convolution-based backbone can significantly reduce the computational cost or boost image quality at a similar cost. More information are on our project page: https://yifanjiang.net/MalleConv.html.

Keywords: Image denoising · Dynamic kernel · Efficiency

1 Introduction

Image denoising is a fundamental problem to computational photography and computer vision. Recent advances in deep learning have sparked significant

---

Y. Jiang—This work was performed while Yifan Jiang worked at Google.

Supplementary Information The online version contains supplementary material available at https://doi.org/10.1007/978-3-031-19797-0_25.

S. Avidan et al. (Eds.): ECCV 2022, LNCS 13678, pp. 429–446, 2022.
https://doi.org/10.1007/978-3-031-19797-0_25

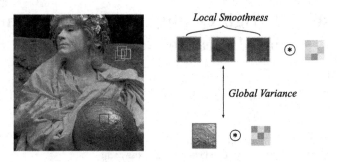

Fig. 1. Local smoothness and global variance in natural images. Our proposed MalleConv layer applies spatially-varying filters for features in different contexts and adopt similar filters in areas that are locally smooth, thus balancing the trade-off between global variance and local smoothness.

interest in learning an end-to-end mapping directly from corrupted observations to the unobserved clean signal, without an explicit model of signal corruptions. These networks appear to learn a prior over the appearance of "ground truth" noise-free images in addition to the statistical properties of the noise present in the inputs.

The performance of denoising networks has consistently been improved with deeper and wider layers, as they can extract richer representations and also increase the receptive field. However, deeper and wider layers also significantly amplify computational costs and the difficulty of optimization. One hurdle is that most of neural architectures only apply a single fixed set of convolutional kernels over the entire input, exploiting spatial equivariance for computational efficiency. However, natural images often contain spatially heterogeneous visual patterns, depriving the convolution of the ability to adapt to globally varying features.

One recent effort addresses this issue is a kernel prediction network (or "hypernetwork") [5,25,29,45,57,61], which generates spatially-varying kernels at each pixel location. Although applying per-pixel kernels increases representational power, it also greatly increases computational cost, as the number of kernels grows with the image resolution. This makes it particularly challenging for mobile cellphone cameras, which normally have about 12 megapixels, and very limited compute resources and power budget.

To achieve spatial-varying processing while maintaining low computational cost, we propose an efficient variant of spatially-varying kernels, dubbed Malleable Convolution (**MalleConv**). We draw inspiration from the trade-off between local smoothness and global spatial heterogeneity. Fundamentally, natural images contain spatially-varying patterns from a "global" perspective, which motivates the popularity of dynamic filters [25,29] and self-attention modules [38,56], but image content only changes slowly in a "local" neighborhood. Therefore, natural image patches tend to redundantly recur many times inside the image, both within the same scale and across different scales [20,48]. Natural image textures are also commonly represented as a fractal set with self-similarity

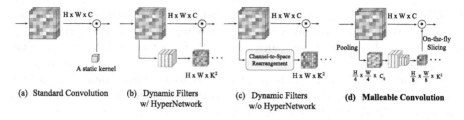

Fig. 2. Comparing MalleConv with static filter and other dynamic filters. (a) Standard convolution with a static kernel. (b) Generate dynamic filters using a Hyper-Network [25,29]. (c) Generate dynamic filters using a channel-to-space operation [36]. (d) Our Malleable convolution.

at all scales [32]. Examples in Fig. 1 also illustrate this phenomenon. The golden ball held by the man contains different patterns compared to the stone in the background, but the texture is locally consistent within a region of stone. Therefore, those similar content can share the same set of kernels to save compute.

Based on this observation, we proposed MalleConv, which scales per-pixel dynamic filter approach to a larger region. Specifically, unlike dynamic filters which take full-resolution input and generate full-resolution kernels, Malle-Conv only processes a downsampled representation, outputting location-specific dynamic filters at **a much smaller spatial resolution** compared with the original feature map (Fig. 2(d)). These kernels are later applied to the full-resolution feature map using a "slicing" strategy, which fuses on-the-fly bilinear interpolation and convolution into a single operator. This design has several advantages. First, comparing to the hypernetwork used in dynamic filters, our predictor network only takes a low-resolution feature map as input to keep it light-weight. Second, full resolution per-pixel kernels are calculated and applied in the same operation, without requiring additional memory I/O for storing and retrieving the high resolution kernel map. Together, these significantly reduce computational overhead compared to full-resolution dynamic filters. Moreover, by taking a downsampled image as input, the predictor network has a large receptive field without very deep structure.

Comprehensive experiments are conducted to demonstrate the effectiveness of the proposed method. We evaluate MalleNet on public synthetic and real image benchmarks (Synthetic: CBSD68, Kodak24, McMaster; Real: SIDD and DND). In addition, we conduct ablation study by injecting MalleConv into existing backbones, including DnCNN [67], UNet, and RDN [72], where the results show that MalleConv achives better quality-efficiency trade-off compared to other dynamic kernels.

In summary, our contributions are as follows:

- We propose Malleable Convolution (MalleConv), a new spatially-varying kernel layer that serves as a powerful variant of standard convolution. MalleConv largely benefits from an efficient predictor network, which incurs minimum additional cost to achieve a spatial-varying processing.

- We conduct a comprehensive ablation study by inserting MalleConv into various popular backbone architectures (including DnCNN, UNet, and RDN), where we show MalleConv can reduce runtime by up to **20×** with similar visual quality.
- We compare MalleConv with previous spatially-varying kernel architectures including HyperNetworks [25] and Involution [36]. MalleConv demonstrates a better quality-efficiency trade-off.
- We further design a new MalleNet architecture using the proposed MalleConv block, achieving faster performance and higher quality on both synthetic and real-world denoising benchmarks.

2   Related Work

2.1   Image Denoising

Traditional image denoising algorithms make use of information in local pixel neighborhoods [47,51] or sparse image prior [3,6,13,16,18,43]. Recently, deep convolutional networks have demonstrated success in many image restoration tasks [11,15,30,31,34,35,37,40,50,54,59,62,72]. For image denoising specifically, Burger et al. [7] proposed a plain multi-layer perception model that achieves comparable performance to BM3D. Chen et al. [10] proposed a trainable nonlinear reaction diffusion model that learns to remove additive white gaussian noise (AWGN) by unfolding a fixed number of inference steps. Many subsequent works further improved upon it by using more elaborate neural network architecture designs, including residual learning [67], dense networks [72], non-local modules [8,38,71], dilated convolutions [46], and more [9,12,64,65]. However, many of these approaches use heavy network architectures that are often impractical for mobile use cases. To tackle this issue, several recent works focus on fast image denoising, by either introducing a self-guidance network [22] or increasing the nonlinear model capacity [21]. In contrast, our approach relies on spatially-varying kernels, where parameters are dynamically generated by an efficient prediction network.

2.2   Dynamic Filters and Spatially Varying Kernels

Convolutional neural networks producing dynamic kernels have been widely studied for a variety of applications. The pioneering works [25,29] adopt a parameter-generating network to produce location-specific filters. These works directly produce spatially-varying weights for the whole convolutional layer, substantially increasing the latency and computational cost of their approaches. Wang et al. [57] designed a feature upsampling module (CARAFE) that generates kernels and reassembling features inside a predefined nearby region. However, CARAFE is designed as a feature upsampling operator instead of a variant of convolution. The context-gated convolution [41,73] adopts a gated module and channel/spatial interaction module to generate modified convolutional kernels. Although their filter weights are produced dynamically, they apply the

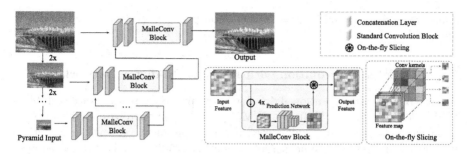

Fig. 3. Main architecture of MalleNet. MalleNet takes a 4-level image pyramid as input. Each layer consists of several Inverted Bottleneck Blocks with a MalleConv block inserted in between. Bottom middle shows the structure of MalleConv block, which consists of a small prediction network and a on-the-fly slicing operator. Bottom right shows details of on-the-fly slicing operator. For each input feature (red rectangle), four neighboring kernels are bilinearly combined and applied to that feature to generate the corresponding output feature. (Color figure online)

same filter at different spatial locations. Another line of work [36] avoids using a hypernetwork by employing a channel-to-space rearrangement to generate location-specific filters. Without the help of a hypernetwork, this approach can not capture the local information and image context. While previously described approaches mainly adopt dynamic filters inside multiple convolutional layers of a deep network, a different line of work [5] proposed to use a standard convolutional neural network to predict denoising kernels that are applied directly to the input to produce the target image. Mildenhall et al. [45] extended this approach to burst denoising by predicting a separate set of weights for each image in a temporal sequence. HDRNet [19] uses a deep neural network to process the low-resolution input and applies the produced spatially-varying affine matrix to the full-resolution input by slicing a predicted bilateral grid. In stead of processing the input image, our proposed Malleable Convolution applies an efficient predictor network to process a downsampled feature map, then constructs a deep spatially-varying network layer-by-layer.

3   Method

3.1   Preliminaries

A standard convolutional layer applies a kernel with weights $W \in \mathbb{R}^{C_{in} \times C_{out} \times K^2}$ to an input feature map sampled from a 2D tensor $X \in \mathbb{R}^{C_{in} \times H \times W}$. Here H, W are the height and width of the feature map, C_{in}, C_{out} denote the numbers of input and output channels, and K is the kernel size. This basic design struggles to capture global context information and cannot adapt to different regions of natural images that contain spatially heterogeneous patterns. Although previous works address this issue by adopting per-pixel dynamic filters [25,29,45] or generating spatial-agnostic filters via a channel-to-space permutation [36], their approaches either require large memory footprint or do not capture context information.

3.2 Malleable Convolution with Efficient Predictor Network

To overcome the aforementioned drawbacks, we propose a new operation, dubbed Malleable Convolution (MalleConv). MalleConv is equipped with an light-weight predictor network that significantly reduces the memory cost and runtime latency of previous dynamic kernel prediction [25,29,45]. The proposed predictor network first downsamples the input feature map X to $X' \in \mathbb{R}^{\frac{H}{4} \times \frac{W}{4} \times C}$ through a 4×4 average pooling. After that, we build a light-weight predictor network consists of multiple ResNet blocks [27] and max pooling layers [26] (see supplementary materials for detailed architecture). The predictor network outputs a feature map $Y \in \mathbb{R}^{\frac{H}{8} \times \frac{W}{8} \times C'}$, where $C' = K^2 \times C$. To formulate a spatially-varying filter, the learned representation Y is reshaped to a list of filters $\{W_{ij}\} \in \mathbb{R}^{K^2 \times C}$, where $i \in \{1, 2, ..., \frac{H}{8}\}$, $j \in \{1, 2, ..., \frac{W}{8}\}$. Each kernel in Y only has C channels, not $C_{in} \times C_{out}$, as we use depth-wise convolution [28] to further reduce the number of parameters. Finally, we upsample the learned spatially-varying filters $\{W_{ij}\}$ through bilinear interpolation to obtain per-pixel filters $\{W'_{ij}\} \in \mathbb{R}^{K^2 \times C}$, where $i \in \{1, 2, ..., H\}$, $j \in \{1, 2, ..., W\}$, and independently apply them to the corresponding input channels.

3.3 Efficient On-the-Fly Slicing

A naive way to implement malleable convolution is to first upsample the low-resolution filters to full-resolution using bilinear interpolation and then apply them to the full-resolution feature map. However, this introduces a large memory footprint since the high-resolution kernels are being precomputed and stored before their application.

To mitigate the memory issue, we combine these two steps into a on-the-fly slicing operator. It takes in a high-resolution feature map $X \in \mathbb{R}^{H \times W \times C}$ and low-resolution kernel maps $\{W_{ij}\} \in \mathbb{R}^{K^2 \times C}$ as input. The result of the on-the-fly slicing operator is a new feature map Z with the same resolution as X. For each pixel location, we first calculate the bilinear interpolated kernel weights from four neighboring kernels as (also illustrated in bottom right of Fig. 3)

$$W'_{x,y} = \sum_{i,j \in N(x,y)} \tau(r_x x - i)\tau(r_y y - j)W'_{i,j}, \qquad (1)$$

where τ is the linear interpolation operator $\tau(a) = max(1 - |a|, 0)$, r_x and r_y are the width and height ratios of the low-resolution filters w.r.t. the full resolution input feature map, and $N(x, y)$ is the four-neighborhood. Bias term $b'_{x,y}$ is sliced in the similar way. The output feature Z is then calculated as:

$$Z_{x,y}(c) = W'_{x,y}(c) \cdot X_{x,y}(c) + b'_{x,y}(c), \qquad (2)$$

Table 1. Comparing MalleNet with the state-of-the-art methods on three common benchmarks. We try our best to use the official implementation provided by the authors to calculate FLOPs and latency. "*" denotes that the original methods were trained with small-scale dataset and we retrain these networks with more training data and larger patch size, for fair comparison.

Method	Latency/(ms)	Flops/(G)	CBSD68			Kodak24			McMaster		
			$\sigma = 15$	$\sigma = 25$	$\sigma = 50$	$\sigma = 15$	$\sigma = 25$	$\sigma = 50$	$\sigma = 15$	$\sigma = 25$	$\sigma = 50$
BM3D [13]	41.56	-	33.52	30.71	27.38	34.28	32.15	28.46	34.06	31.66	28.51
FFDNet [69]	-	7.95	33.87	31.21	27.96	34.63	32.13	28.98	34.66	32.35	29.18
MalleNet-S	**4.62**	**2.93**	**33.90**	**33.22**	**27.97**	**34.66**	**32.16**	**29.00**	**34.68**	**32.35**	**29.20**
RPCNN [60]	95.11	-	-	31.24	28.06	-	32.34	29.25	-	32.33	29.33
DSNet [46]	-	-	33.91	31.28	28.05	34.63	32.16	29.05	34.67	32.40	29.28
IRCNN [68]	-	12.18	33.86	31.16	27.86	34.69	32.18	28.93	34.58	32.18	28.91
DnCNN [67]	21.69	68.15	33.90	31.24	27.95	34.60	32.14	28.95	33.45	31.52	28.62
DnCNN* [67]	21.69	68.15	34.02	31.34	28.11	34.62	32.18	29.11	35.18	32.73	29.49
MalleNet-M	**16.69**	**9.36**	**34.15**	**31.50**	**28.27**	**34.82**	**32.41**	**29.35**	**35.53**	**33.12**	**29.96**
BRDNet [55]	-	-	34.10	31.43	28.16	34.88	32.41	29.22	35.08	32.75	29.52
DRUNet [66]	-	102.91	34.30	31.69	28.51	**35.31**	**32.89**	**29.86**	35.40	33.14	30.08
MalleNet-L	**32.34**	**33.47**	**34.32**	**31.71**	**28.52**	34.93	32.58	29.50	**35.65**	**33.26**	**30.12**
RNAN [71]	-	774.67	-	-	28.27	-	-	29.58	-	-	29.72
RDN [72]	263.03	2001.86	-	-	28.31	-	-	29.66	-	-	-
RDN* [72]	263.03	2001.86	34.29	31.69	28.37	34.89	32.52	29.68	35.55	33.16	29.92
IPT [8]	-	938.66	-	-	28.39	-	-	29.64	-	-	29.98
SwinIR [38]	780.61	788.10	34.42	31.78	28.56	**35.34**	**32.89**	**29.79**	35.61	33/20	30.22
MalleNet-XL	**87.55**	**181.89**	**34.54**	**31.86**	**28.62**	35.07	32.67	29.61	**35.72**	**33.28**	**30.23**

where c is the channel index. Note that the sliced weight W' and bias b' are calculate on-the-fly without additional memory cost. We discuss more about the specific memory consumption in Sect. 4.4.

3.4 Malleable Network

As the goal of this work is to design an ultra-fast denoiser, current state-of-the-art algorithms such as the residual dense network [72] or transformer-based architectures [8,38] are sub-optimal to build an efficient backbone. Inspired by some recent pyramid-based approaches [22,39,64], we design a new backbone integrating the proposed malleable convolution, dubbed **MalleNet**.

MalleNet first builds a four-level pyramid using $2\times$ space-to-channel shuffle operations [53]. This allows us to extract multi-scale representations and increases the network's receptive field. In each stage, we stack several Inverted Bottleneck Blocks [52] with a fixed ratio and insert one $K \times K$ Malleable Convolution in-between to extract heterogeneous representations. At the end of the bottom stage, we upsample the feature map and concatenate it with the input of its upper stage. In the top stage, the representation extracted from different pyramids are aggregated to produce the final output. Compared to conventional encoder-decoder style architectures, the pyramid-based architecture reuses the extracted representation from each scale and thus can achieve faster inference speed. The whole network is shown in Fig. 3.

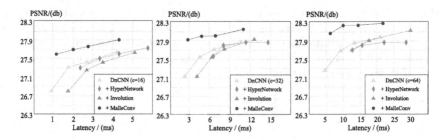

Fig. 4. Comparison between MalleConv and other dynamic filters in terms of runtime latency and PSNR value.

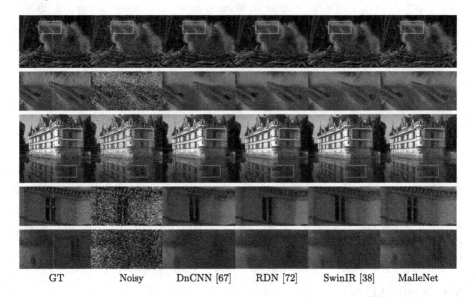

| GT | Noisy | DnCNN [67] | RDN [72] | SwinIR [38] | MalleNet |

Fig. 5. Visual comparison between MalleNet and previous approaches. More visual results are shown in the supplementary.

4   Experiments

We mainly evaluate the proposed module on the Additive White Gaussian Noise (AWGN) removal task. Following previous work [66], we construct a training dataset with 400 examples from the Berkeley Segmentation Dataset (BSD) [44], 4,744 examples from the Waterloo Exploration Database [42], 900 images from the DIV2K dataset [2], and 2,750 images from the Flick2K dataset [40]. We adopt 160×160 training patch size, which we augment through random cropping, rotations, and flipping. Other networks (e.g., IPT [8] and SwinIR [38]) are not able to be benefited from larger patch size, due to the heavy memory cost. We empirically choose kernels size 1×1 for MalleConv on AWGN removal tasks and kernel size 3×3 on real-world benchmarks, as that is observed to reach the best PSNR-to-Complexity trade-off. We adopt the Adam optimizer [33] with a batch

Fig. 6. Visual results by inserting MalleConv into a fast variant of DnCNN, with $\sigma = 50$.

size of 16 and a cosine learning rate scheduler. The initial learning rate is set to 0.001. The full training process takes 2.2M iterations. We adopt 3 common datasets as our testing set: CBSD68, kodak24 [17], and McMaster [70].

All of our experiments are conducted on 8 Nvidia V100 GPUs using the Tensorflow-2.6 platform. The FLOPs (floating point operations) and runtime are calculated on a 256 × 256 resolution RGB patches. We benchmar the inference speed on a single Nvidia P6000 GPU platform by setting batch size set to the maximum available number. For PyTorch-based implementations, we report the average latency of a single 256 × 256 × 3 input collected from 500 runs. For Tensorflow-based implementations, we report the latency time using the Tensorflow official profiler[1].

4.1   Comparing MalleConv with Other Dyanmic Kernels

To demonstrate the efficiency and effectiveness of the proposed MalleConv, we compare specific computational cost and performance of each individual network equipped with MalleConv and other dynamic filters, e.g., HyperNetwork [25] and Involution [36]. We adopt DnCNN [67] as our main backbone and replace the middle layer of DnCNN with a single dynamic filter operator. We evaluate three different DnCNN backbones with channel={16, 32, 64}. In each one, the number (depth) of DnCNN backbone are growing from 3, 6, 9, to 15. As shown in Fig. 4, MalleConv achieves the best performance-efficiency trade-off by significantly improving the PSNR with minimum additional runtime latency.

4.2   Comparing with State-of-the-Art Methods

To fairly compare the runtime speed between MalleNet and other baselines, we train 4 versions of MalleNet: -S, -M, -L, and -XL by increasing the number of

[1] https://www.tensorflow.org/guide/profiler.

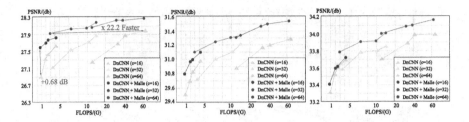

Fig. 7. PSNR-To-Complexity trade-off of DnCNN and DnCNN with a single MalleConv. We build DnCNN-families by setting depth = {3, 6, 9, 15} and channel = {16, 32, 64}. The three figures from left to right show experiments with σ = {50, 25, 15}.

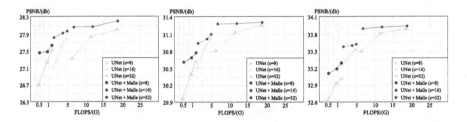

Fig. 8. PSNR-To-Complexity trade-off of UNet and UNet with a single MalleConv. We build UNet-families by setting the encoder-decoder block number = {2, 3, 4} and channel = {8, 16, 32}. The three figures show experiments with σ = {50, 25, 15}.

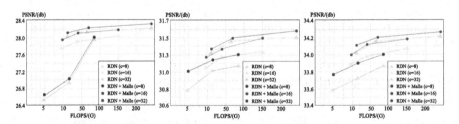

Fig. 9. PSNR-To-Complexity trade-off of RDN and RDN with a single MalleConv. We build RDN-families by setting the residual dense block number = {3, 6, 10} and channel = {8, 16, 32}. The three figures show experiments with σ = {50, 25, 15}.

channels from 16, 32, 64 to 144. We divide evaluated approaches into four categories according to their performance and runtime speed. As shown in Table 1, on these four categories, MalleNet achieves the best efficiency-performance trade-off and reaches state-of-the-art results among two of our main benchmark test sets. We show the PSNR-to-Complexity trade-off of each method in Fig. 12 left.

Table 2. Ablation study on the size of AvgPooling layer in MalleConv Operator. PSNR results are reported on the CBSD68 test set with $\sigma = 50$.

Depth	Metrics	AvgPooling Size			
		0	2	4	8
D=3	Latency/(ms)	13.19	7.08	5.62	5.18
	FLOPs/(G)	43.96	18.17	11.71	10.10
	PSNR/(dB)	27.91	**28.15**	28.07	28.01
D=6	Latency/(ms)	17.39	11.28	9.85	9.43
	FLOPs/(G)	62.05	36.26	29.81	28.19
	PSNR/(dB)	28.19	**28.24**	**28.24**	28.18
D=15	Latency/(ms)	30.09	23.98	22.53	22.09
	FLOPs/(G)	98.24	72.44	66.00	64.39
	PSNR/(dB)	28.25	28.28	**28.31**	28.28

4.3 MalleConv Layer with Alternative Backbones

To further demonstrate that the proposed Malleable Convolution can benefit wide variety of network architectures, we perform ablation studies by inserting MalleConv into existing well-known backbones as a plug-in operator. Here we choose three popular backbones as our main testbeds. Since most of original network structures are too heavy for edge devices, we also manually build a few cheaper variants by controlling the depth and channel variables. Using DnCNN as an example, the vanilla DnCNN architecture contains 15 layers with 64 channels. We construct its faster version by setting the depth = {3, 6, 9, 15} and channel = {16, 32, 64}, respectively, and obtain the architecture series of DnCNN with $3 \times 4 = 12$ variants.

Afterwards, we construct a number of better performing variants of these architecture series, **by replacing one standard convolution with a single** 1×1 **MalleConv operator**. We replace the middle layer of the network with a MalleConv block (detailed architectures are shown in the supplementary material). We conduct experiments on CBSD69 dataset and train these architectures using the same training recipes. As shown in Figs. 7, 8, and 9, a single MalleConv block brings significant improvement to all three backbones.

4.4 Visual Comparison and Interpretation

We first compare our best architecture MalleNet-XL with previous state-of-the-art approaches [38,38,67,72], as shown in Fig. 5. The examples produced by MalleNet preserve rich details and impressive textures while saving up to ×8.91 inference time compared to the best baseline, further demonstrating the effectiveness of our approach. Moreover, in the "ultra-fast" setting, we decrease the depth of DnCNN from 15 to 3 to obtain a much faster variant of DnCNN architecture. However, the image quality also degrades as shown in the bottom-left

Table 3. Comparing MalleNet with the State-of-the-art methods on real-world benchmark SIDD and DND. We try our best to use the official implementation provided by the authors to calculate the FLOPs cost and runtime speed.

Method	Latency	FLOPs/(G)	SIDD		DND	
			PSNR	SSIM	PSNR	SSIM
DnCNN [67]	21.69	68.15	23.66	0.583	32.43	0.79
BM3D [13]	41.56	–	25.78	0.685	34.51	0.851
WNNM [23]	–	–	25.78	0.809	34.67	0.865
CBDNet [24]	–	–	30.78	0.754	38.06	0.942
RIDNet [4]	98.13	–	38.71	0.914	39.26	0.953
VDN [63]	–	–	39.28	0.909	39.38	0.952
ACDA [58]	–	–	39.32	0.912	–	–
MPRNet [65]	–	573.50	39.71	0.958	39.80	0.954
NBNet [12]	37.44	88.70	39.75	0.973	39.89	0.955
MIRNet [64]	192.61	787.04	39.72	0.959	39.88	0.956
HINet [9]	32.83	170.71	39.99	0.958	–	–
MalleNet-R	**13.58**	**29.11**	39.56	0.941	39.21	0.949

of Fig. 6. In contrast, when replacing the middle layer of DnCNN with a single 1×1 MalleConv operator (DnCNN w/ MalleConv), it uses slightly more computational time, but achieves significantly better visual quality, as shown in the bottom-right of Fig. 6.

Furthermore, to illustrate how spatially-varying kernels in MalleConv capture heterogeneous visual patterns, we replace the spatially varying kernels in MalleNet with one selected kernel and apply it to the entire image. Figure 11 compares the default output of MalleNet (column 2) with the one that applies a selected kernel (columns 3 and 4). When a kernel generated from a sky region (column 3) is applied, the network is observed to denoise the rest of the image as if they are the sky. Similarly, using a kernel from a snowy-mountain patch will generate output that looks like snowy mountain (column 4). By combining kernels that are dedicated to different local image statistics together, MalleConv can better model the heterogeneous spatial patterns and yield better results.

4.5   Analysis of Runtime Latency and Memory Cost

In Fig. 10, we compare the memory cost of each operator during the training process. We conduct our testbed on three different modules: 1) The 1×1 MalleConv with input and output channel to be 16, 32, 64. MalleConv generates smaller-size of dynamic kernels and then applies it back to the full-resolution feature using on-the-fly slicing operator; 2) We directly upsample the generated dynamic kernel via an $8\times$ bilinear upsampling operator, to match the resolution of input features; 3) We remove the downsampling and maxpooling layers in the proposed efficient prediction network, thus it will generate per-pixel dynamic kernels and apply it to the feature map. As shown in Fig. 10, the memory cost of MalleConv is much smaller than other two counterparts, since it only needs to predict a smaller-size of filters compared to the per-pixel kernel prediction methods, and does not store the intermediate feature map of upsampled kernels compared to the bilinear interpolation operator.

Moreover, we conduct the ablation study on the downsampling ratio of the proposed efficient predictor network. Similar to the aforementioned setting, we set our testbed on DnCNN approach and examine three different architectures by setting depth = {3, 6, 15}. We evaluate the runtime speed, FLOPs cost, and PSNR value of four variants with the size of the AvgPooling layer equal to {0, 2, 4, 8}. As shown in Table 2, by processing a 4× downsampled feature map, our proposed efficient predictor network achieves a "win-win" in terms of both performance and efficiency. This demonstrates that applying the prediction network on a lower resolution feature map can not only improve the performance, due to a larger receptive field, but also save computations

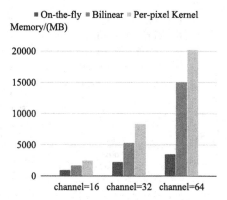

Fig. 10. cost comparison between the proposed method and per-pixel kernel prediction approaches (HyperNetwork).

4.6 Evaluation on Real Sensor Noise

To further demonstrate the generalization ability of MalleNet, we evaluate our approaches to real sensor noise. Similar to previous works [12,64], we adopt Smartphone Image Denoising Dataset (SIDD) [1] and Darmstadt Noise Dataset (DND) [49] as main benchmarks. We use training data from SIDD as our training set and evaluate our method on both two test sets. In the training process, We adopt Adam Optimizer with a batch size of 128, the weight decay is set to 0.03, and the learning rate is set to 2e-4. We randomly crop 256 × 256 patches and apply random rotation and flipping. We train a real denoiser MalleNet-R, by slightly modifing the channel/depth of MalleNet-M architecture and replace Inverse Bottleneck Block with standard residual block (see supplementary materials for details). As shown in Table 3, MalleNet-R achieves lower latency (**13.58 ms**) compared with other methods. In terms of image quality, MalleNet-R is able to reach similar PSNR/SSIM compared to most baselines, and only slightly behinds the approaches with very heavy computational cost or equipped with complex channel/spatial attention module. We show the PSNR-to-Complexity trade-off of each method in Fig. 12 right. More visual comparisons are included in the supplementary materials.

|Input|MalleConv|Selected kernel 1|Selected kernel 2|

Fig. 11. Comparison between default MalleConv output (column2) and outputs using two selected kernels (column 3 and 4).

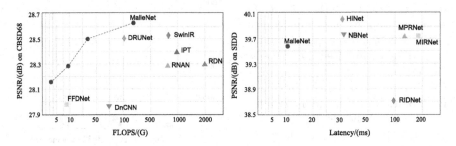

Fig. 12. Results on CBSD68 test set ($\sigma = 50$) and SIDD validation set. Our proposed MalleNet architecture achieves a better trade-off between quality and speed.

5   Conclusions

In this work, we propose Malleable Convolution (MalleConv), an efficient variant of spatially-varying convolution tailored for ultra-fast image denoising. Malle-Conv processes a low-resolution feature map and generates a much smaller set of spatially varying filters. The generated filters inherently fit the heterogeneous and spatially varying patterns presented in natural images, while taking little additional computational costs. Despite its effectiveness, we also observe that very deep or wide architectures benefit less from MalleConv, as they may also capture heterogenous image statistics in a less efficient way. Although in this work, we only evaluated MalleConv on image denoising, we believe MalleConv is also capable in other image processing tasks, like dehazing. Another future work is to combine MalleConv with attention mechanism [38] or deformable shape [14] to further improve its quality in applications with less computational constraints.

Acknowledgement. We would like to express our gratitude to the Google Research Luma team, in particular Zhengzhong Tu for generously providing us with the concrete training recipes on real-world denoising benchmarks.

References

1. Abdelhamed, A., Lin, S., Brown, M.S.: A high-quality denoising dataset for smartphone cameras. In: CVPR (2018)
2. Agustsson, E., Timofte, R.: Ntire 2017 challenge on single image super-resolution: dataset and study. In: CVPR Workshops (2017)
3. Aharon, M., Elad, M., Bruckstein, A.: K-SVD: an algorithm for designing overcomplete dictionaries for sparse representation. IEEE Trans. Signal Process. **54**, 4311–22 (2006)
4. Anwar, S., Barnes, N.: Real image denoising with feature attention. In: Proceedings of the IEEE/CVF International Conference on Computer Vision, pp. 3155–3164 (2019)
5. Bako, S., et al.: Kernel-predicting convolutional networks for denoising monte carlo renderings. ACM Trans. Graph. **36**, 1–14 (2017)
6. Buades, A., Coll, B., Morel, J.-M.: A non-local algorithm for image denoising. In: CVPR (2005)
7. Burger, H.C., Schuler, C.J., Harmeling, S.: Image denoising: can plain neural networks compete with bm3d? In: CVPR (2012)
8. Chen, H., et al.: Pre-trained image processing transformer. In: CVPR (2021)
9. Chen, L., Xin, L., Zhang, J., Chu, X., Chen, C.: Half instance normalization network for image restoration. In: CVPR (2021)
10. Chen, Y., Pock, T.: Trainable nonlinear reaction diffusion: a flexible framework for fast and effective image restoration. In: TPAMI (2016)
11. Chen, Z., Jiang, Y., Liu, D., Wang, Z.: CERL: a unified optimization framework for light enhancement with realistic noise. IEEE Trans. Image Process. **31**, 4162–4172 (2022)
12. Cheng, S., Wang, Y., Huang, H., Liu, D., Fan, H., Liu, S.: NBNet: noise basis learning for image denoising with subspace projection. In: CVPR (2021)
13. Dabov, K., Foi, A., Katkovnik, V., Egiazarian, K.: Image denoising by sparse 3-d transform-domain collaborative filtering. IEEE Trans. Image Process. **16**, 2080–2095 (2007)
14. Dai, J., et al.: Deformable convolutional networks. In: Proceedings of the IEEE International Conference on Computer Vision, pp. 764–773 (2017)
15. Dong, C., Loy, C.C., He, K., Tang, X.: Image super-resolution using deep convolutional networks. In: TPAMI (2015)
16. Elad, M., Aharon, M.: Image denoising via sparse and redundant representations over learned dictionaries. IEEE Trans. Image Process. **15**, 3736–3745 (2006)
17. Franzen, R.: Kodak lossless true color image suite (1999). source: http://r0k.us/graphics/kodak
18. Getreuer, P., et al.: Blade: filter learning for general purpose computational photography. In: 2018 IEEE International Conference on Computational Photography (ICCP), pp. 1–11. IEEE (2018)
19. Gharbi, M., Chen, J., Barron, J.T., Hasinoff, S.W., Durand, F.: Deep bilateral learning for real-time image enhancement. In: SIGGRAPH (2017)
20. Glasner, D., Bagon, S., Irani, M.: Super-resolution from a single image. In: ICCV (2009)
21. Gu, S., Li, W., Van Gool, L., Timofte, R.: Fast image restoration with multi-bin trainable linear units. In: ICCV (2019)
22. Gu, S., Li, Y., Van Gool, L., Timofte, R.: Self-guided network for fast image denoising. In: ICCV (2019)

23. Gu, S., Zhang, L., Zuo, W., Feng, X.: Weighted nuclear norm minimization with application to image denoising. In: CVPR (2014)
24. Guo, S., Yan, Z., Zhang, K., Zuo, W., Zhang, L.: Toward convolutional blind denoising of real photographs. In: Proceedings of the IEEE/CVF Conference on Computer Vision and Pattern Recognition, pp. 1712–1722 (2019)
25. Ha, D., Dai, A., Le, Q.V.: Hypernetworks. arXiv:1609.09106 (2016)
26. He, K., Zhang, X., Ren, S., Sun, J.: Delving deep into rectifiers: surpassing human-level performance on imagenet classification. In: ICCV (2015)
27. He, K., Zhang, X., Ren, S., Sun, J.: Deep residual learning for image recognition. In: CVPR (2016)
28. Howard, A.G.: Mobilenets: efficient convolutional neural networks for mobile vision applications. arXiv:1704.04861 (2017)
29. Jia, X., Brabandere, B.D., Tuytelaars, T., Gool, L.V.: Dynamic filter networks. In: NeurIPS (2016)
30. Jiang, Y., et al.: Enlightengan: deep light enhancement without paired supervision. IEEE Trans. Image Process. **30**, 2340–2349 (2021)
31. Jiang, Y., et al.: SSH: a self-supervised framework for image harmonization. In: Proceedings of the IEEE/CVF International Conference on Computer Vision, pp. 4832–4841 (2021)
32. Kataoka, H., et al.: Pre-training without natural images. In: ACCV (2020)
33. Kingma, D.P., Ba, J.: Adam: a method for stochastic optimization. In: ICLR (2015)
34. Kupyn, O., Budzan, V., Mykhailych, M., Mishkin, D., Matas, J.: Deblurgan: blind motion deblurring using conditional adversarial networks. In: CVPR (2018)
35. Kupyn, O., Martyniuk, T., Wu, J., Wang, Z.: Deblurgan-v2: deblurring (orders-of-magnitude) faster and better. In: ICCV (2019)
36. Li, D., et al.: Involution: inverting the inherence of convolution for visual recognition. In: CVPR (2021)
37. Li, S., et al.: Single image deraining: a comprehensive benchmark analysis. In: CVPR (2019)
38. Liang, J., Cao, J., Sun, G., Zhang, K., Van Gool, L., Timofte, R.: Swinir: image restoration using Swin transformer. In: ICCV (2021)
39. Liang, J., Zeng, H., Zhang, L.: High-resolution photorealistic image translation in real-time: a laplacian pyramid translation network. In: CVPR (2021)
40. Lim, B., Son, S., Kim, H., Nah, S., Lee, K.M.: Enhanced deep residual networks for single image super-resolution. In: CVPR Workshops (2017)
41. Lin, X., Ma, L., Liu, W., Chang, S.-F.: Context-Gated Convolution. In: Vedaldi, A., Bischof, H., Brox, T., Frahm, J.-M. (eds.) ECCV 2020. LNCS, vol. 12363, pp. 701–718. Springer, Cham (2020). https://doi.org/10.1007/978-3-030-58523-5_41
42. Ma, K., et al.: Waterloo exploration database: new challenges for image quality assessment models. IEEE Trans. Image Process. **26**, 1004–1016 (2016)
43. Mairal, J., Bach, F., Ponce, J., Sapiro, G., Zisserman, A.: Non-local sparse models for image restoration. In: ICCV (2009)
44. Martin, D., Fowlkes, C., Tal, D., Malik, J.: A database of human segmented natural images and its application to evaluating segmentation algorithms and measuring ecological statistics. In: Proceedings of the 8th International Conference on Computer Vision, vol. 2, pp. 416–423, July 2001
45. Mildenhall, B., Barron, J.T., Chen, J., Sharlet, D., Ng, R., Carroll, R.: Burst denoising with kernel prediction networks. In: CVPR (2018)
46. Peng, Y., Zhang, L., Liu, S., Wu, X., Zhang, Y., Wang, X.: Dilated residual networks with symmetric skip connection for image denoising. Neurocomputing **345**, 67–76 (2019)

47. Perona, P., Malik, J.: Scale-space and edge detection using anisotropic diffusion. In: TPAMI (1990)

48. Peyré, G., Bougleux, S., Cohen, L.: Non-local regularization of inverse problems. In: Forsyth, D., Torr, P., Zisserman, A. (eds.) ECCV 2008. LNCS, vol. 5304, pp. 57–68. Springer, Heidelberg (2008). https://doi.org/10.1007/978-3-540-88690-7_5

49. Plotz, T., Roth, S.: Benchmarking denoising algorithms with real photographs. In: Proceedings of the IEEE Conference on Computer Vision and Pattern Recognition, pp. 1586–1595 (2017)

50. Ren, D., Zuo, W., Qinghua, Hu., Zhu, P., Meng, D.: Progressive image deraining networks: a better and simpler baseline. In: CVPR (2019)

51. Rudin, L.I., Osher, S., Fatemi, E.: Nonlinear total variation based noise removal algorithms. Physica D **60**, 259–268 (1992)

52. Sandler, M., Howard, A., Zhu, M., Zhmoginov, A., Chen, L.-C.: Mobilenetv 2: inverted residuals and linear bottlenecks. In: CVPR (2018)

53. Shi, W., et al.: Real-time single image and video super-resolution using an efficient sub-pixel convolutional neural network. In: Proceedings of the IEEE Conference on Computer Vision and Pattern Recognition, pp. 1874–1883 (2016)

54. Tao, X., Gao, H., Shen, X., Wang, J., Jia, J.: Scale-recurrent network for deep image deblurring. In: CVPR (2018)

55. Tian, C., Xu, Y., Zuo, W.: Image denoising using deep CNN with batch renormalization. Neural Networks (2020)

56. Vaswani, A., et al.: Attention is all you need. In: NeurIPS (2017)

57. Wang, J., Chen, K., Rui, X., Liu, Z., Loy, C.C., Lin, D.: Carafe: content-aware reassembly of features. In: ICCV (2019)

58. Wang, Z., Miao, Z., Hu, J., Qiu, Q.: Adaptive convolutions with per-pixel dynamic filter atom. In: Proceedings of the IEEE/CVF International Conference on Computer Vision, pp. 12302–12311 (2021)

59. Wei, C., Wang, W., Yang, W., Liu, J.: Deep retinex decomposition for low-light enhancement. arXiv:1808.04560 (2018)

60. Xia, Z., Chakrabarti, A.: Identifying recurring patterns with deep neural networks for natural image denoising. In: WACV (2020)

61. Xu, Y.-S., Tseng, S.-Y.R., Tseng, Y., Kuo, H.-K., Tsai, Y.-M.: Unified dynamic convolutional network for super-resolution with variational degradations. In: CVPR (2020)

62. Yang, W., Tan, R.T., Wang, S., Fang, Y., Liu, J.: Single image deraining: from model-based to data-driven and beyond. In: TPAMI (2020)

63. Yue, Z., Yong, H., Zhao, Q., Zhang, L., Meng, D.: Variational denoising network: toward blind noise modeling and removal. arXiv preprint arXiv:1908.11314 (2019)

64. Zamir, S.W., et al.: Learning enriched features for real image restoration and enhancement. In: Vedaldi, A., Bischof, H., Brox, T., Frahm, J.-M. (eds.) ECCV 2020. LNCS, vol. 12370, pp. 492–511. Springer, Cham (2020). https://doi.org/10.1007/978-3-030-58595-2_30

65. Zamir, S.W., et al.: Multi-stage progressive image restoration. In: CVPR (2021)

66. Zhang, K., Li, Y., Zuo, W., Zhang, L., Van Gool, L., Timofte, R.: Plug-and-play image restoration with deep denoiser prior. In: TPAMI (2021)

67. Zhang, K., Zuo, W., Chen, Y., Meng, D., Zhang, L.: Beyond a gaussian denoiser: residual learning of deep CNN for image denoising. IEEE Trans. Image Process. **26**, 3142–3155 (2017)

68. Zhang, K., Zuo, W., Gu, S., Zhang, L.: Learning deep CNN denoiser prior for image restoration. In: CVPR (2017)

69. Zhang, K., Zuo, W., Zhang, L.: FFDNet: toward a fast and flexible solution for CNN-based image denoising. IEEE Trans. Image Process. **27**, 4608–4622 (2018)
70. Zhang, L., Wu, X., Buades, A., Li, X.: Color demosaicking by local directional interpolation and nonlocal adaptive thresholding. J. Electron. imaging **20**, 023016 (2011)
71. Zhang, Y., Li, K., Li, K., Zhong, B., Fu, Y.: Residual non-local attention networks for image restoration. arXiv:1903.10082 (2019)
72. Zhang, Y., Tian, Y., Kong, Y., Zhong, B., Fu, Y.: Residual dense network for image super-resolution. In: CVPR (2018)
73. Zhang, Y., Wei, D., Qin, C., Wang, H., Pfister, H., Fu, Y.: Context reasoning attention network for image super-resolution. In: ICCV (2021)

TAPE: Task-Agnostic Prior Embedding for Image Restoration

Lin Liu[1], Lingxi Xie[3], Xiaopeng Zhang[3], Shanxin Yuan[4], Xiangyu Chen[5,6],
Wengang Zhou[1,2], Houqiang Li[1,2], and Qi Tian[3(✉)]

[1] CAS Key Laboratory of Technology in GIPAS, EEIS Department,
University of Science and Technology of China, Hefei, China
[2] Institute of Artificial Intelligence, Hefei Comprehensive National Science Center,
Hefei, China
[3] Huawei Cloud BU, Shenzhen, China
`tian.qi1@huawei.com`
[4] Huawei Noah's Ark Lab, London, UK
[5] University of Macau, Zhuhai, China
[6] Shenzhen Institutes of Advanced Technology, CAS, Shenzhen, China

Abstract. Learning a generalized prior for natural image restoration is an important yet challenging task. Early methods mostly involved hand-crafted priors including normalized sparsity, ℓ_0 gradients, dark channel priors, etc. Recently, deep neural networks have been used to learn various image priors but do not guarantee to generalize. In this paper, we propose a novel approach that embeds a task-agnostic prior into a transformer. Our approach, named Task-Agnostic Prior Embedding (TAPE), consists of two stages, namely, task-agnostic pre-training and task-specific fine-tuning, where the first stage embeds prior knowledge about natural images into the transformer and the second stage extracts the knowledge to assist downstream image restoration. Experiments on various types of degradation validate the effectiveness of TAPE. The image restoration performance in terms of PSNR is improved by as much as 1.45 dB and even outperforms task-specific algorithms. More importantly, TAPE shows the ability of disentangling generalized image priors from degraded images, which enjoys favorable transfer ability to unknown downstream tasks.

1 Introduction

A good image prior can help to distinguish many kinds of noises from original image contents and improve the quality of images. Learning an image prior is important and challenging for image restoration tasks. Early studies explore specific degradation priors to achieve good performances on some low-level vision tasks, such as image dehazing [27,78], image deblurring [32,46], and image

Supplementary Information The online version contains supplementary material available at https://doi.org/10.1007/978-3-031-19797-0_26.

deraining [39, 77]. However, most priors are hand-crafted and mainly based on limited observations. With the popularity of deep learning, data-driven image priors estimated by combining conventional degradation properties with deep neural networks have been explored [11, 21, 23, 31, 34, 45, 71]. But these networks capturing task-specific priors, do not guarantee to generalize to unseen tasks.

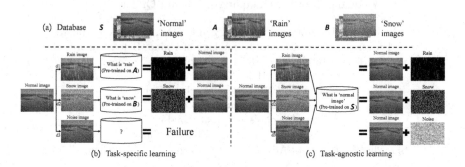

Fig. 1. The illustration of the differences of task specific learning and task-agnostic learning. Our method aims to learn 'what is normal image' instead of 'what are rain, snow or other degradation'.

Recently, there are also efforts in learning complicated priors for low-level vision tasks [10, 22, 38, 47, 56, 66]. These methods can be roughly grouped into two types. The first type [10, 38] learns specific priors for each task, *i.e.*, the priors formulate 'what is the distribution of specific noise'. Despite their effectiveness, these methods are often difficult to transfer across different tasks. The second type instead formulates generalized image priors, *i.e.*, 'what is the distribution of normal images'. For this purpose, these methods [22, 47, 60] often make use of scalable GANs [6] pre-trained on natural images, hence, the learned priors are often hidden in a latent feature space, making it difficult to disentangle the noise from image contents, especially in the scenarios of complex images.

In this paper, we propose Task-Agnostic Prior Embedding (TAPE), a novel kind of priors that are easily generalized to different low-level vision tasks. An intuitive comparison between TAPE and prior task-specific learning is illustrated in Fig. 1. TAPE absorbs the benefits of the aforementioned approaches: on the one hand, we learn the distribution of normal images from non-degraded natural images, which does not rely on any true or synthesized degradation; on the other hand, the priors are encoded in a simple prior learning module named PLM and the main network can decode them by transformer decoders (query embeddings). The training procedure of TAPE consists of two stages, namely, task-agnostic pre-training and task-specific fine-tuning, where a pixel-wise contrastive loss is designed in the first stage for unsupervised low-level representation learning.

In the experiment, we pre-train our model on four tasks (including deraining, deraindrop, denoising, and demoireing), fine-tune and test it on these four known tasks and four unknown tasks (desnowing, shadow removal, super-resolution, and deblurring). After the one-time learning, the generalized image prior (through pre-training) can be transferred to different tasks. Quantitative and qualitative experimental comparisons show that the proposed TAPE improves the performance for multiple tasks in both task-specific and task-agnostic settings. In particular, our method improves the PSNR by 1.45 dB, 1.03 dB, 0.84 dB, 0.49 dB, and 0.75 dB on the Rain200L, Rain200H, Raindrop800, SIDD, and TIP2018 datasets, respectively. The task-agnostic pre-training without touching the real noisy image on SIDD increases PSNR by 0.31 dB. For the unseen tasks in the pre-training, TAPE improves the PSNR by 0.91 dB, 0.29 dB, 0.41 dB and 0.48 dB on desnowing, shadow removal, super-resolution, and deblurring, respectively.

In summary, the contributions of our work are:

– The possibility and importance of learning task-agnostic and generalized image prior is addressed. As far as we know, TAPE is the first work to (explicitly) represent the universal prior that can be used in multiple image restoration tasks. We disentangle the generalized clean image prior of the corrupted images from the degrading objects/noises.
– We propose a two-stage method named TAPE for image restoration to learn the generalized degradation prior. The experiments demonstrate that our method can be easily applied to pre-train image restoration algorithms with other transformer backbones.
– We propose a pixel-wise contrastive loss in pre-training for learning better generalized features for PLM, which increases the generalization ability.

2   Related Work

Image Restoration. Image restoration is a general term for a series of low-level vision tasks, including denoising [24,70,72], deraining [37,39,77], deblurring [30, 34], demoireing [25,55,75], *etc.*. The aim of image restoration is to restore clean x from corrupted y. The corrupted image y can be formulated as, $y = Hx + v$, where H, x, and v are degradation matrix, underlying clean image, and noise, respectively. Before the deep learning era, studies design hand-crafted features of the degradation objects (*e.g.*, rain, snow, *etc.*) for different image restoration tasks. With the popularity of convolutional neural networks (CNNs), a handful of deep-learning based methods are proposed to handle one or multiple types of image restoration tasks. Most of these methods design task-specific models or loss functions to achieve better performances. For image super-resolution [17, 28], Dong *et al.* propose SRCNN [17] to obtain high-resolution images from the corresponding low-resolution images. For HDR imaging, solutions [15,35,74] are proposed for using multiple exposed images to reconstruct an HDR image. Fu *et al.* [20] introduce a ResNet-based CNN for image deraining. Li *et al.* and Yu *et al.*, propose FDRNet [38] and RL-Restore [66] to handle hybrid-distorted image restoration tasks. Zheng *et al.* [76] propose a learnable bandpass filter network for image demoireing. Different from these methods, we explore the power of pre-training to handle several image processing tasks.

Image Degradation Prior and Natural Image Prior. Since image restoration is ill-posed, the image prior can help to constrain the solution space. From the Bayesian perspective, the solution $\hat{x}$ can be obtained by optimizing:

$$\hat{\mathbf{x}} = \arg\min_{\mathbf{x}} \frac{1}{2}\|\mathbf{y} - \mathbf{H}\mathbf{x}\|^2 + \lambda\Phi(\mathbf{x}), \tag{1}$$

where the first term is the fidelity and the second term is the regularization. Deep-learning based methods try to learn the prior parameters Θ and a compact inference through an optimization of a loss function on a training dataset with corrupted-clean image pairs. Then Eqn. 1 can be refined as,

$$\min_{\Theta} \ell(\hat{\mathbf{x}}, \mathbf{x}) \quad \text{s.t.} \quad \hat{\mathbf{x}} = \arg\min_{\mathbf{x}} \frac{1}{2}\|\mathbf{y} - \mathbf{H}\mathbf{x}\|^2 + \lambda\Phi(\mathbf{x}; \Theta). \tag{2}$$

Image priors have been widely used in computer vision, including markov random fields [53,79], dark channel prior [27,46], low rank prior [14], and total variation [3,54]. He *et al.* [27] propose dark channel prior for image dehazing. It exploits the prior property that in an haze-free image there are pixels where at least one color channel is of low value. Chen *et al.* [14] propose a low-rank model to capture the spatial and temporal correlations between rain streaks. Different from these task-specific priors, we use a pre-trained network to extract more general priors from images. The prior queries are also being adjusted during end-to-end training. Recently, deep image prior (DIP) [56] shows that image statistics can be implicitly captured by the network's structure, which is also a kind of prior. Inspired by DIP, some attempts use a pre-trained GAN as a source of image statistics [8,19,22,47,52,60]. MGAN prior [22] utilizes multiple latent codes to increase the power of the pre-trained GAN model. DGP [47] fine-tunes the weights generator together with the latent code and use the discriminator to calculate the gap between the generated and real images.

Image Restoration Transformers. Transformer [57] is a new type of neural network framework of using mainly self-attention mechanism. It has achieved many successes in computer vision tasks, including object classification [18], objection detection [7,16,80], *etc.*. Recently, it's also been used in image restoration tasks [10,13,36,40,42,61,62,69]. Chen *et al.* [10] and Li *et al.* [36] develop pre-trained transformers IPT and EDT respectively for some low-level vision tasks. Wang *et al.* [61] and Zamir *et al.* [67] design novel transformer structures, named Uformer and Restormer respectively, and obtain good performance on several image restoration tasks. Most of these methods proposed new transformer-based backbones for image restoration, whereas the goal of our work is a new pre-training pipeline for image restoration. One can apply our method to pre-train an image restoration algorithm with other backbones. We make use of the strong fitting ability of transformers and the learning ability of the transformer decoder to embed prior information.

3   Proposed Method

In this section, we first illustrate why we need to learn a task-agnostic prior (Sect. 3.1). And then, the architecture (Sect. 3.2) and the pipeline (Sect. 3.3) of our method are presented. At last, we briefly discuss the relationship to prior work (Sect. 3.4).

3.1 Motivation

The motivation is shown in Fig. 1, where we assume that many image restoration tasks (*e.g.*, deraining, desnowing, *etc.*) are present. Most existing image restoration methods learn a specific model for each single task, trying to capture task-specific priors (*e.g.*, what patterns are likely to be rain and thus need to be removed). While the learning procedure is straightforward, the trained models are difficult to be applied to new restoration tasks because the degradation patterns may have changed significantly.

To alleviate the burden, we propose a different pipeline that is generalized across different restoration tasks. The key is to learn **task-agnostic priors** (*i.e.*, what patterns are likely to be from clean, non-degraded images) rather than the aforementioned, task-specific counterparts. For this purpose, we embed an explicit module, the prior learning module (PLM), into the network, and design a two-stage learning procedure that (i) pre-trains the architecture on multi-source clean images and then (ii) fine-tunes it on specific image restoration datasets. The second stage often occupies a small portion of computation, showing the advantage of our method.

3.2 Network Architecture

The TAPE-Net (see Fig. 2) consists of two components: backbone and prior learning module. The backbone has a transformer architecture, containing a CNN encoder for feature extraction, a transformer encoder, a transformer decoder, and a CNN decoder for mapping the deep features into restored images. With the self-attention mechanism, the transformer can separate the generalized prior from the corrupted images. Different from conventional transformer [18],

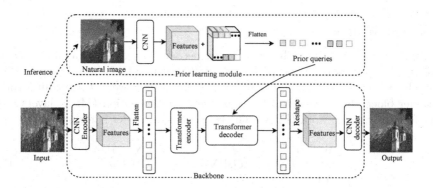

Fig. 2. The network architecture of our TAPE-Net. It consist of two parts: Backbone and prior learning module. With the input of natural images, PLM learns the features that natural images contain, not the features that noise contains. This makes our approach task-agnostic.

the decoder of our transformer takes additional prior queries, which comes from the prior learning module.

CNN Encoder and CNN Decoder. The CNN encoder consists of two 3×3 convolutional layers. The RGB image, $I \in \mathbb{R}^{3 \times H \times W}$, is the input of the CNN encoder, which generates a feature map $f_e \in \mathbb{R}^{64 \times H \times W}$ with 64 channels and with the same resolution as I. The CNN decoder also consists of two 3×3 convolutional layers. It generates a reconstructed image $O \in \mathbb{R}^{3 \times H \times W}$.

Transformer Encoder. The feature map f_e is firstly flattened into small patches $\{f_e^1, f_e^2, ..., f_e^N\}$, where $f_e^i \in \mathbb{R}^{64P^2} (i = 1, 2, ..., N)$, $N = \frac{HW}{P^2}$ is the total patch number and P is the patch size. A learnable position encoding PE_i with the same size of f_e^i is added to f_e^i and the sum (denoted as x_i) is sent into the transformer encoder. The transformer encoder has n transformer blocks ($n = 1$ in this work), each having a multi-head self-attention module and a feed forward network. The process of the transformer encoder can be formulated as,

$$x' = \text{MSA}\left(\text{LN}\left(x\right), \text{LN}\left(x\right), \text{LN}\left(x\right)\right) + x$$
$$o_e = \text{FFN}\left(\text{LN}\left(x'\right)\right) + x', \tag{3}$$

where MSA, FFN, and LN denote the multi-head self-attention module, feed forward network, and linear layer in the conventional transformer [57], respectively. $x = [x_1, x_2, ..., x_N]$ and $o_e = [o_{e_1}, o_{e_2}, ..., o_{e_N}]$ are the input and the output with the same size, respectively.

Prior Learning Module. The prior learning module (PLM) aims at providing additional prior queries to the transformer decoder. As shown in Fig. 2, PLM encodes an image into a feature map, and it can be formulated as $f_n = \text{G}_n(I_{gt})$, where f_n is a $64 \times H \times W$ feature map representing the deep natural image features and G_n is a VGG19 network to extract image features. Then f_n is flattened into a series of patches $[f_n^1, f_n^2, ..., f_n^N]$ and combined with learnable parameters $[e_1, e_2, ..., e_N]$ as follows,

$$Q = \left[e_1 + f_n^1, e_2 + f_n^2, ..., e_N + f_n^N\right], \tag{4}$$

where Q have the same length as o_e.

Transformer Decoder. The transformer decoder has a similar architecture as the transformer encoder except for an additional input of the prior queries Q (Similar with the object queries in [16]). In this paper, we use one transformer decoder block that consists of two multi-head self-attention (MSA) layers and one feed forward network (FFN). The transformer decoder is formulated as,

$$y = \text{MSA}\left(\text{LN}\left(o_e\right) + Q, \text{LN}\left(o_e\right) + Q, \text{LN}\left(o_e\right)\right) + o_e$$
$$y' = \text{MSA}\left(\text{LN}\left(y\right) + Q, \text{LN}\left(o_e\right), \text{LN}\left(o_e\right)\right) + y \tag{5}$$
$$o_d = \text{FFN}\left(\text{LN}\left(y'\right)\right) + y',$$

where $o_d = [o_{d_1}, o_{d_2}, ..., o_{d_N}]$ denotes the outputs of the transformer decoder. And then these patches are reshaped into f_d with the size of $64 \times H \times W$.

3.3 Optimization

3.3.1 The Training and Fine-tuning Pipeline

From Sect. 3.2, in our network design, PLM should extract statistics from the non-degraded (Ground truth) image and use the statistics to assist the main network for image restoration. However, ground truth is unavailable during the inference (test) stage. So PLM cannot extract statistics from it. To compensate, we train an auxiliary module (backbone ϕ in Fig. 3) to generate a pseudo GT from the degraded input. The pseudo GT, not being perfect, depicts the property of a non-degraded image to some extent. The pseudo GT is then fed into PLM for extracting general image priors, and the priors assist the main network (backbone θ) to generate the final output. As shown in Fig. 3, TAPE-Net has two stages: task-agnostic pre-training and task-specific fine-tuning.

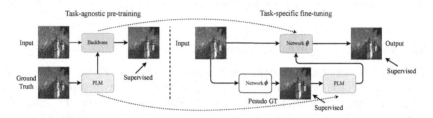

Fig. 3. The optimization procedure of TAPE. TAPE contains two stages: task-agnostic pre-training and task-specific fine-tuning. The dotted line means that the network trained in the previous stage is used to initialize the network in the next stage.

In the task-agnostic pre-training, multiple low-level vision tasks are trained together, using corresponding datasets $\{D_1, ..., D_m\}$, where $D_i, (i = 1, 2, ..., m)$ represents the dataset for task i. In each iteration, a pair of images (a corrupted image I_{cor} and its ground truth I_{gt}) are selected from one dataset D_i. The ground truth I_{gt} is sent into PLM to learn the prior queries, which are then sent to the backbone for end-to-end training. The combination of the L_1 loss and the proposed pixel-wise contrastive loss (see Sect. 3.3.2) is used to optimize the network (the weighting parameter is for the latter). Due to the task-agnostic pre-training, both the backbone and PLM are well optimized.

As shown in the right part of Fig. 3, in the task-specific fine-tuning, because we cannot take the ground truth as input as discussed above, we use an auxiliary module (network ϕ in Fig. 3) to generate a pseudo GT from the degraded input (Note that in our paper, the network ϕ can be any neural network or the backbone borrowed from the pre-training stage. For faster convergence, we use the network pre-trained in the first stage). And then, the pseudo GT generated by the network ϕ is served as the input of pre-trained PLM. The PLM outputs the prior queries and help the pre-trained network θ to predict better final result. With the estimated pseudo ground truth, PLM can capture the natural image priors better. There are two ways to optimize the parameters in the fine-tuning stage, namely: 1) The network ϕ is fine-tuned by loss between pseudo GT and GT firstly, and then fixed when fine-tuning other networks; 2) All components are fine-tuned simultaneously. In the supplementary material, we will show that these two optimization methods lead to similar performance.

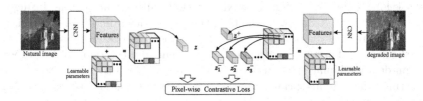

Fig. 4. The use of pixel-wise contrastive loss. z is selected from the prior queries of the natural image as 'query'. And z^+ and z_j^- are selected as the 'positive' and 'negative' elements in the contrastive loss, respectively.

3.3.2 Pixel-wise Contrastive Loss

PLM aims to estimate the distribution of natural patches. However, due to the limited amount of training data, learning from the loss between prediction and GT (unary term) is insufficient for accurate estimation. Inspired by some self-supervised learning for high-level semantics (*e.g.* MoCo [26] and SimCLR [12]) and image to image translation method [4,48], we propose a pixel-wise contrastive loss to offer another cue (binary terms) of estimation – the distance between the features of I_d and I_{gt} (from the same location) shall be smaller than that between features from different locations.

As shown in Fig. 4, in the task-agnostic pre-training stage, the degraded image I_d and the natural image I_{gt} are put into PLM, then Q^d and Q^{gt} are obtained as described in Sect. 3.2. We aim at minimizing the distance between the features of I_d and I_{gt} from the same location while maximizing the distance between features from different locations. For example, in Fig. 4, the roof without rain should be more closely associated with the roof contaminated by the rain than the other patches of the rainy input, such as other parts of the house or the blue sky.

Suppose that q_i^d is selected from $Q^d = \{q_1^d, q_2^d, ..., q_N^d\}$ as the 'query' element in the contrastive loss. q_i^{gt} and $q_{j_1}^{gt}, q_{j_2}^{gt}, ..., q_{j_m}^{gt}$ are selected from $Q^{gt} = \{q_1^{gt}, q_2^{gt}, ..., q_N^{gt}\}$ as the 'positive' and 'negative' elements in the contrastive loss, respectively. Thus, the contrastive loss is formulated as,

$$\mathcal{L} = \sum_{t=1}^{T} \ell_t \left(q_i^d, q_i^{gt}, q_j^{gt} \right), \tag{6}$$

$$\ell \left(q_i^d, q_i^{gt}, q_j^{gt} \right) = -\log \left[\frac{\exp\left(q_i^d \cdot q_i^{gt}/\tau\right)}{\exp\left(q_i^d \cdot q_i^{gt}/\tau\right) + \sum_{k=1}^{m} \exp\left(q_i^d \cdot q_{j_k}^{gt}/\tau\right)} \right], \tag{7}$$

where $T = 256$ is the feature number we randomly choose each time and the temperature τ is set to 0.07. The negative sample number m is set to 256 in our work.

3.4 Relationship to Prior Work

1) Compared with recent multiple degradation prior learning methods (e.g., IPT and EDT), our TAPE formulates generalized image priors, which means that our method can generalize well to the pre-training-unknown tasks. Recently, Air-Net [33] also has the ability to generalize to unknown tasks, but their learned representation contains the degraded information instead of normal image information through contrastive learning. 2) Different from the methods [5,22,47,60] where the learned image priors are hidden in the parameters of the generator, the learned prior of our model is explicit. It makes easy for our method to disentangle the unwanted noise from the image contents in some complex image restoration cases.

4 Experiments and Analysis

In this section, we evaluate the performance of TAPE on several low-level vision tasks and conduct an ablation study.

4.1 Tasks and Datasets

For pre-training, we use five datasets, each for one type of degradation. We also test on four more datasets for four tasks that are unknown in the pre-training stage. For both training and testing, we resize images into the resolution of 256×256, and then crop them into 64×64 patches for balancing the training procedure with different data sizes. Note that same resizing and cropping operations are also adopted for other models for a fair comparison. The evaluated tasks include denoising, deraining, deraindrop, demoireing, desnowing, shadow removal, super resolution and deblurring. As shown in Table 1 for details, the used datasets are: SIDD [1] for denoising, Rain200H and Rain200L [64] for deraining, Raindrop800 [49] for deraindrop, TIP2018 [55] for demoireing[1], Snow100K [43] for desnowing, ISTD [58] for shadow removal, DIV2K [2] for super resolution and REDS [44] for deblurring.

4.2 Implementation Details

Pre-training. We use one Nvidia Tesla V100 GPU to train our model using the Adam optimizer for 60×24000 iterations on the mixture of the five dataset (SIDD, Rain200L, Rain200H, Raindrop800, and TIP2018). The initial learning

---

[1] We select a subset of TIP2018 and Snow100K with 10000 training image pairs and 200 test pairs; 10000 training image pairs and 500 test pairs, respectively.

Table 1. Datasets' statistics (number of training and testing images) and quantitative comparison for two models (in terms of PSNR (dB)).

Dataset	Rain200L	Rain200H	Raindrop800	SIDD	TIP2018	Snow100K	ISTD	DIV2K	REDS
#Train/test images	1800/200	1800/200	800/60	96000/1280	10000/200	10000/500	1330/540	800/100	24000/3000
Baseline	31.72	22.81	26.85	37.41	26.77	25.42	26.28	31.25	32.46
TAPE-Net (Ours)	33.17	23.84	27.69	37.90	27.52	26.33	26.57	31.66	32.94
PSNR Gain	+1.45	+1.03	+0.84	+0.49	+0.75	+0.91	+0.29	+0.41	+0.48

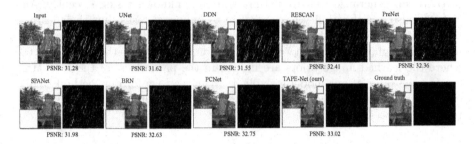

Fig. 5. Visual deraining comparison among our methods and SOTA deraining methods on Rain200L. The differences between the output and the ground truth are shown followed the predicted results.

rate is set as 0.0002 and decayed to 0.0001 in the 20 × 24000th iteration with batch size 4. In each iteration, we first randomly choose a dataset, from which one clean-corrupted image pair is randomly selected. **Fine-tuning.** After pre-training on all the datasets, we fine-tune the model on each desired task (*e.g.*, denoising). TAPE-Net is fine-tuned with 200 epochs and a learning rate of 2e-4 for task-specific fine-tuning.

4.3   Pre-training and Generalization Ability

In this subsection, we illustrate that our method has good generalization performance on both pre-training-known tasks and pre-training-unknown tasks.

Pre-training-Known Tasks, Corresponding Data. To illustrate the effectiveness of our task-agnostic pre-training, we compare our pre-trained model with the model without pre-training (denoted as 'Baseline' in Table 1). The TAPE-Net improve the PSNR by 1.45 dB, 1.03 dB, 0.84 dB, 0.49 dB and 0.75 dB on the Rain200L, Rain200H, Raindrop800, SIDD, and TIP2018 dataset, respectively. Please note that in image restoration, an 0.5 dB improvement is usually considered significant. It demonstrates the effectiveness of the pre-training and the superiority of our model.

Pre-training-Known Tasks, Different Data. And we also do experiments to explore the good generalization performance of our pre-trained model when transferred to different distributions of data in the pre-training-known task.

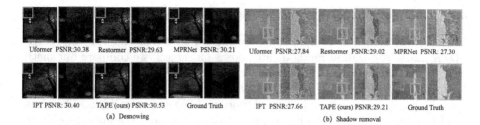

Uformer PSNR:30.38   Restormer PSNR:29.63   MPRNet PSNR: 30.21   Uformer PSNR:27.84   Restormer PSNR:29.02   MPRNet PSNR: 27.30

IPT PSNR: 30.40   TAPE (ours) PSNR:30.53   Ground Truth   IPT PSNR:27.66   TAPE (ours) PSNR:29.21   Ground Truth

(a) Desnowing   (b) Shadow removal

Fig. 6. Visual desnowing and shadow removal comparison among our methods and SOTA general image restoration methods on Snow100K and ISTD.

Table 2. Quantitative comparison with 4 SOTA general image restoration methods with similar model sizes (in terms of PSNR (dB)).

	Model size	Snow100K	ISTD	Rain200L	SIDD	Raindrop800
IPT	2.51M	26.26	26.34	32.67	38.80	27.86
Restormer	0.93M	26.80	26.42	33.61	38.91	27.98
UFormer	0.97M	26.50	26.27	32.66	38.84	27.70
MPRNet	1.11M	26.30	26.23	33.30	38.89	28.13
TAPE-Swin (Ours)	0.97M	**26.93**	26.61	**34.46**	38.98	29.15
TAPE-Restormer (Ours)	1.07M	26.91	**26.65**	34.28	**39.01**	**29.18**

Our experiments show that pre-training with synthetic Gaussian noises helps to restore the images corrupted by real noises (see Table 3). In practice, in the task-agnostic pre-training, we use ground truth in SIDD with added synthetic Gaussian noises as input, without touching the real noise images on the SIDD dataset. Then the pre-trained model is fine-tuned on SIDD (using real-noise/non-noise image pairs). The PSNRs increase by 0.19 dB, and 0.31 dB respectively when the σ of the added Gaussian noise (Sampled from $\mathcal{N}(0, \sigma)$) are in [5,20], and [1,50], respectively. When the range of the added Gaussian noise is larger, the generalization ability of the model in the pre-training stage is stronger, and the performance in the fine-tuning stage is better.

Pre-training-Unknown Tasks. To illustrate the generalization ability of our model, we conduct several experiments on the tasks that are unknown to the pre-training stage. In practice, we fine-tune the pre-trained model on four new low-level vision tasks: desnowing, shadow removal, super resolution and deblurring. As shown in Table 1, compared with the none-pre-trained model, TAPE-Net improves the PSNR by 0.91 dB, 0.29 dB, 0.41 dB and 0.48 dB, which demonstrates that the pre-trained model can capture more useful information and features from natural images. Learning task-agnostic priors and pixel-wise contrastive loss on pre-training stage can help the performance of fine-tuning on the unknown tasks.

4.4 Comparisons with State-of-the-Arts

In this subsection, the comparison between our methods and the very recent
SOTA image restoration methods are shown in Table 2. we compare our methods (TAPE-swin and TAPE-restormer) with the 4 SOTA methods (IPT [10],
Restormer [67], UFormer [61], MPRNet [68]) with the similar model parameters in 3 pre-training-known tasks and 2 pre-training-unknown tasks. The visual
results on two pre-training-unknown tasks (desnowing and shadow removal) are
shown in Fig. 6. Our method removes the artifacts more thoroughly and retains
more details. In the supplementary material, we compare our TAPE-Net with 12
state-of-the-art task-specific methods, including deraining methods (DDN [20],
SPANet [59], RESCAN [37], PreNet [51], BRN [50],SPDNet [65] and PCNet [29]);
demoireing methods (DMCNN [55], MopNet [25], FHDe2Net [25], HRDN [63],
WDNet [41] and MBCNN [76]); and denoising methods (DnCNN [70], FFD-
Net [72], RDN [73], and SADNet [9]) on PSNR. Qualitative results on deraining
are shown in Figs. 5 and 7(a), showing that our methods get cleaner images and
recover more details. The visual demoireing results are shown in Fig. 7(b). Ours
can remove moire patterns successfully and restore the underlying clean image.

In order to show the performance of our method on pre-training-unknown
tasks, we compare ours with the existing SOTA multi-task pre-training method,
IPT [10]. We fine-tuned and tested the official pre-trained model of IPT on three
unseen tasks, namely, desnowing, shadow removal and deblurring. We compared
the gain of PSNR with and without pre-training, because the training patches
and model size of IPT and ours are different. The pre-training stage of IPT boosts
PSNR by 0.07 dB, 0.19 dB and 0.08 dB, respectively, while the improvements of
TAPE (our method) are 0.91 dB, 0.29 dB and 0.48 dB, larger than that of IPT.

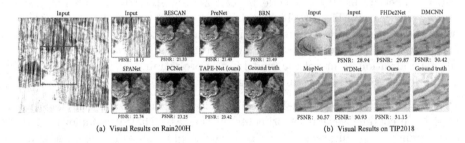

(a) Visual Results on Rain200H   (b) Visual Results on TIP2018

Fig. 7. Visual deraining comparison (a) and visual demoireing comparison (b) among
our methods and task-specific methods.

Table 3. Quantitative comparison on SIDD. It shows the good generalization performance of TAPE-Net when transferred to different distributions of data in the pre-training-known task.

TAPE-Net	W/o pre-train	Pre-train ($\sigma \in$ [5,20])	Pre-train ($\sigma \in$ [1,50])
PSNR	37.41	37.60	37.72

Table 4. Ablation study of the impact of the multi-task pre-training, which illustrates that adding more tasks will not harm the performance.

	Raindrop800	Rain200L	TIP2018	Snow100K
RD+RL+RH	27.71	33.20	27.56	26.17
RD+TIP+RL+RH	27.70	33.18	27.54	26.26
RD+TIP+RL+RH+S	27.69	33.17	27.52	26.33

Table 5. The ablation study of the importance of each pre-trained part on the Rain200H and the Raindrop-TestB dataset. '-' and '✓' in the first three columns mean that the model parameters are randomized and pre-trained respectively before the finetuning. '✗' means the corresponding part does not exist.

Name	Depth	Network ϕ	Network θ	PLM	Rain200H	Raindrop-TestB	Model size (M)
Baseline	3	✗	–	✗	25.57	26.13	0.76
With no-pre-trained all parts	2	–	–	–	25.46	25.96	1.12
With no-pre-trained ϕ	2	–	✓	✓	26.15	26.39	1.12
With no-pre-trained θ	2	✓	–	✓	25.96	26.35	1.12
With no-pre-trained θ and PLM	2	✓	–	–	25.73	26.17	1.12
Full model	2	✓	✓	✓	**26.18**	**26.41**	1.12

4.5   Ablation Study

Impact of the Multi-task Pre-training. We do ablation study to analyze the effect of the number of datasets in the pre-training. We pre-train our models on fewer datasets and compare with our original models. As shown in Table 4, RD, TIP, RL, RH, and S mean Raindrop800, TIP2018, Rain200L, Rain200H, and SIDD datasets respectively. '+' means we use these datasets in the pre-training stage. We do the experiments on three pre-trained-known datasets and the maximum PSNR difference is 0.04 dB. This PSNR difference is within a controllable error range. Increasing the dataset in the pre-training is meaningful. Compared with pre-training with 3 datasets, pre-training with 5 datasets increases the PSNR by 0.16 dB on Snow100K.

Importance of Pre-training of Each Component. In order to verify which component is more important with pre-training (network ϕ, network θ or PLM), we randomize the weights of corresponding parts of TAPE-Net before the finetuning stage. As shown in Table 5, we do ablation study on Rain200H and

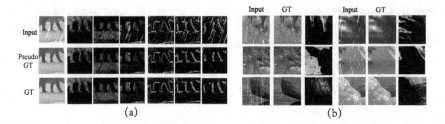

Fig. 8. The visualization of the PLM's output, Q. (a) The features of the pseudo GT and GT are very similar, but most of the features of input have the features of degraded objects. It means that the features of the pseudo GT is useful and can help the image restoration of the backbone. (b) The last lines are one of the predicted results of PLM.

Raindrop-TestB. All the modified models in this table have the same backbone, TAPE-Swin. Compared 'With no-pre-trained ϕ' and the 'Full model', we can see that the PSNRs drop slightly (0.03 dB and 0.02 dB). With no-pre-trained θ effects more than the network ϕ (the PSNRs drop by 0.22 dB and 0.06 dB). 'Without pre-training the network θ and PLM' also makes the PSNRs drop a lot. Thus, the last four lines in Table 5 demonstrate that the effectiveness of pre-training of θ and PLM. The first two lines in Table 5 show that even if the model size is larger than Baseline, the performance is not good without pre-training.

The ablation studies about the pixel-wise contrastive loss, optimization methods in task-specific fine-tuning can be see in the supplementary material.

4.6 Visualization Results

To validate that PLM learns useful and meaningful features with our proposed pipeline, we visualize the features learned by PLM on the deraining task. We put the input, pseudo GT and GT into PLM to get their respective output Q. As shown in Fig. 8(a), in the output features, some channels tend to preserve the information of shapes (the first three feature maps) and edges (the last three feature maps). The features of the pseudo GT and GT are very similar, but most of the features of input have the features of degraded objects. It means that the features of the pseudo GT is useful and can help the image restoration of the backbone. From Fig. 8(b), we can see that with the help of pre-training, the PLM module can correlate the information of similar textures or patches from a long distance. Thus, the transformer decoder of the backbone can utilize these long-distance similar areas/patches to restore the image.

5 Conclusions and Limitations

Conclusions. In this paper, we address the possibility and importance of learning task-agnostic and generalized image prior. We propose a pipeline named TAPE to learn task-agnostic prior embedding for image restoration. TAPE has two stages: task-agnostic pre-training and task-specific fine-tuning. Our task-agnostic training strategy is able to learn generalized natural image prior. It has good generalization performance when faced with pre-training-unknown tasks.

Limitations. Although our method shows generalized ability on a few image restoration tasks, the learned statistics in PLM are still difficult to explain, either in theory or by visualization results. Without these proofs, the PSNR and SSIM numbers are only side evidences of the effectiveness of the task-agnostic priors. In the future, we will continue exploring the possibility of disentangling the task-agnostic priors as well as finding more essential ways to evaluate cross-task image restoration. The pipeline may make the training time longer than the baseline. And the performance of TAPE on mixed degradation tasks needs to be explored.

Acknowledgements. This work was supported by the National Natural Science Foundation of China under Contract 61836011 and 62021001. It was also supported by the GPU cluster built by MCC Lab of Information Science and Technology Institution, USTC.

References

1. Abdelhamed, A., Lin, S., Brown, M.S.: A high-quality denoising dataset for smartphone cameras. In: CVPR (2018)
2. Agustsson, E., Timofte, R.: Ntire 2017 challenge on single image super-resolution: Dataset and study. In: CVPRW (2017)
3. Babacan, S.D., Molina, R., Katsaggelos, A.K.: Variational Bayesian blind deconvolution using a total variation prior. TIP **18**, 12–26 (2008)
4. Baek, K., Choi, Y., Uh, Y., Yoo, J., Shim, H.: Rethinking the truly unsupervised image-to-image translation. In: International Conference on Computer Vision (ICCV, 2021) (2021)
5. Bau, D., et al.: Semantic photo manipulation with a generative image prior. arXiv preprint arXiv:2005.07727 (2020)
6. Brock, A., Donahue, J., Simonyan, K.: Large scale GAN training for high fidelity natural image synthesis. In: ICLR (2018)
7. Carion, N., Massa, F., Synnaeve, G., Usunier, N., Kirillov, A., Zagoruyko, S.: End-to-end object detection with transformers. In: Vedaldi, A., Bischof, H., Brox, T., Frahm, J.-M. (eds.) ECCV 2020. LNCS, vol. 12346, pp. 213–229. Springer, Cham (2020). https://doi.org/10.1007/978-3-030-58452-8_13
8. Chan, K.C., Wang, X., Xu, X., Gu, J., Loy, C.C.: Glean: generative latent bank for large-factor image super-resolution. arXiv preprint arXiv:2012.00739 (2020)
9. Chang, M., Li, Q., Feng, H., Xu, Z.: Spatial-adaptive network for single image denoising. In: Vedaldi, A., Bischof, H., Brox, T., Frahm, J.-M. (eds.) ECCV 2020. LNCS, vol. 12375, pp. 171–187. Springer, Cham (2020). https://doi.org/10.1007/978-3-030-58577-8_11
10. Chen, H., et al.: Pre-trained image processing transformer. In: CVPR (2021)
11. Chen, L., Fang, F., Wang, T., Zhang, G.: Blind image deblurring with local maximum gradient prior. In: CVPR (2019)
12. Chen, T., Kornblith, S., Norouzi, M., Hinton, G.E.: A simple framework for contrastive learning of visual representations. In: ICML (2020)

462   L. Liu et al.

13. Chen, X., Wang, X., Zhou, J., Dong, C.: Activating more pixels in image super-resolution transformer. arXiv preprint arXiv:2205.04437 (2022)
14. Chen, Y.L., Hsu, C.T.: A generalized low-rank appearance model for spatio-temporally correlated rain streaks. In: ICCV (2013)
15. Dai, T., et al.: Wavelet-based network for high dynamic range imaging. arXiv preprint 2108.01434 (2021)
16. Dai, Z., Cai, B., Lin, Y., Chen, J.: Up-detr: unsupervised pre-training for object detection with transformers. In: CVPR (2021)
17. Dong, C., Loy, C.C., He, K., Tang, X.: Image super-resolution using deep convolutional networks. TPAMI **38**, 295–307 (2015)
18. Dosovitskiy, A., et al.: An image is worth 16x16 words: transformers for image recognition at scale. arXiv preprint arXiv:2010.11929 (2020)
19. El Helou, M., Süsstrunk, S.: BIGPrior: towards decoupling learned prior hallucination and data fidelity in image restoration. arXiv preprint arXiv:2011.01406 (2020)
20. Fu, X., Huang, J., Zeng, D., Huang, Y., Ding, X., Paisley, J.: Removing rain from single images via a deep detail network. In: CVPR (2017)
21. Golts, A., Freedman, D., Elad, M.: Unsupervised single image dehazing using dark channel prior loss. TIP **29**, 2692–2701 (2020)
22. Gu, J., Shen, Y., Zhou, B.: Image processing using multi-code GAN prior. In: CVPR (2020)
23. Guo, S., Liang, Z., Zhang, L.: Joint denoising and demosaicking with green channel prior for real-world burst images. arXiv preprint arXiv:2101.09870 (2021)
24. Guo, S., Yan, Z., Zhang, K., Zuo, W., Zhang, L.: Toward convolutional blind denoising of real photographs. In: CVPR (2019)
25. He, B., Wang, C., Shi, B., Duan, L.Y.: Mop moire patterns using mopnet. In: ICCV (2019)
26. He, K., Fan, H., Wu, Y., Xie, S., Girshick, R.: Momentum contrast for unsupervised visual representation learning. In: CVPR (2020)
27. He, K., Sun, J., Tang, X.: Single image haze removal using dark channel prior. TPAMI **33**, 2341–2353 (2010)
28. Isobe, T., et al.: Video super-resolution with temporal group attention. In: CVPR (2020)
29. Jiang, K., Wang, Z., Yi, P., Chen, C., Lin, C.W.: PCNet: progressive coupled network for real-time image deraining. In: TIP (2021)
30. Kupyn, O., Martyniuk, T., Wu, J., Wang, Z.: Deblurgan-v2: Deblurring (orders-of-magnitude) faster and better. In: ICCV (2019)
31. Lee, H., Sohn, K., Min, D.: Unsupervised low-light image enhancement using bright channel prior. IEEE Signal Process. Lett. **27**, 251–255 (2020)
32. Levin, A., Weiss, Y., Durand, F., Freeman, W.T.: Understanding and evaluating blind deconvolution algorithms. In: CVPR (2009)
33. Li, B., Liu, X., Hu, P., Wu, Z., Lv, J., Peng, X.: All-in-one image restoration for unknown corruption. In: CVPR (2022)
34. Li, L., Pan, J., Lai, W.S., Gao, C., Sang, N., Yang, M.H.: Blind image deblurring via deep discriminative priors. IJCV **127**, 1025–1043 (2019)
35. Li, W., et al.: Sj-hd^{2}r: Selective joint high dynamic range and denoising imaging for dynamic scenes. arXiv preprint 2206.09611 (2022)
36. Li, W., Lu, X., Lu, J., Zhang, X., Jia, J.: On efficient transformer and image pre-training for low-level vision. arXiv preprint arXiv:2112.10175

37. Li, X., Wu, J., Lin, Z., Liu, H., Zha, H.: Recurrent squeeze-and-excitation context aggregation net for single image deraining. In: Ferrari, V., Hebert, M., Sminchisescu, C., Weiss, Y. (eds.) ECCV 2018. LNCS, vol. 11211, pp. 262–277. Springer, Cham (2018). https://doi.org/10.1007/978-3-030-01234-2_16
38. Li, X., et al.: Learning disentangled feature representation for hybrid-distorted image restoration. In: Vedaldi, A., Bischof, H., Brox, T., Frahm, J.-M. (eds.) ECCV 2020. LNCS, vol. 12374, pp. 313–329. Springer, Cham (2020). https://doi.org/10.1007/978-3-030-58526-6_19
39. Li, Y., Tan, R.T., Guo, X., Lu, J., Brown, M.S.: Rain streak removal using layer priors. In: CVPR (2016)
40. Liang, J., Cao, J., Sun, G., Zhang, K., Van Gool, L., Timofte, R.: Swinir: image restoration using swin transformer. In: ICCVW 2021
41. Liu, L., et al.: Wavelet-based dual-branch network for image Demoiréing. In: Vedaldi, A., Bischof, H., Brox, T., Frahm, J.-M. (eds.) ECCV 2020. LNCS, vol. 12358, pp. 86–102. Springer, Cham (2020). https://doi.org/10.1007/978-3-030-58601-0_6
42. Liu, L., Yuan, S., Liu, J., Guo, X., Yan, Y., Tian, Q.: Siamtrans: zero-shot multi-frame image restoration with pre-trained siamese transformers. In: AAAI (2022)
43. Liu, Y.F., Jaw, D.W., Huang, S.C., Hwang, J.N.: Desnownet: context-aware deep network for snow removal. TIP **27**, 3064–3073 (2018)
44. Nah, S., et al.: Ntire 2019 challenge on video deblurring and super-resolution: Dataset and study. In: CVPRW (2019)
45. Pan, J., Bai, H., Tang, J.: Cascaded deep video deblurring using temporal sharpness prior. In: CVPR, 2020
46. Pan, J., Sun, D., Pfister, H., Yang, M.H.: Blind image deblurring using dark channel prior. In: CVPR (2016)
47. Pan, X., Zhan, X., Dai, B., Lin, D., Loy, C.C., Luo, P.: Exploiting deep generative prior for versatile image restoration and manipulation. In: Vedaldi, A., Bischof, H., Brox, T., Frahm, J.-M. (eds.) ECCV 2020. LNCS, vol. 12347, pp. 262–277. Springer, Cham (2020). https://doi.org/10.1007/978-3-030-58536-5_16
48. Park, T., Efros, A.A., Zhang, R., Zhu, J.-Y.: Contrastive learning for unpaired image-to-image translation. In: Vedaldi, A., Bischof, H., Brox, T., Frahm, J.-M. (eds.) ECCV 2020. LNCS, vol. 12354, pp. 319–345. Springer, Cham (2020). https://doi.org/10.1007/978-3-030-58545-7_19
49. Qian, R., Tan, R.T., Yang, W., Su, J., Liu, J.: Attentive generative adversarial network for raindrop removal from a single image. In: CVPR (2018)
50. Ren, D., Shang, W., Zhu, P., Hu, Q., Meng, D., Zuo, W.: Single image deraining using bilateral recurrent network. TIP **29**, 6852–6863 (2020)
51. Ren, D., Zuo, W., Hu, Q., Zhu, P., Meng, D.: Progressive image deraining networks: a better and simpler baseline. In: CVPR (2019)
52. Richardson, E., et al.: Encoding in style: a stylegan encoder for image-to-image translation. arXiv preprint arXiv:2008.00951 (2020)
53. Roth, S., Black, M.J.: Fields of experts: a framework for learning image priors. In: CVPR (2005)
54. Rudin, L.I., Osher, S., Fatemi, E.: Nonlinear total variation based noise removal algorithms. Physica D **60**, 259–268 (1992)
55. Sun, Y., Yu, Y., Wang, W.: Moiré photo restoration using multiresolution convolutional neural networks. TIP **27**, 4160–4172 (2018)
56. Ulyanov, D., Vedaldi, A., Lempitsky, V.: Deep image prior. In: CVPR (2018)
57. Vaswani, A., et al.: Attention is all you need. arXiv preprint arXiv:1706.03762 (2017)

58. Wang, J., Li, X., Yang, J.: Stacked conditional generative adversarial networks for jointly learning shadow detection and shadow removal. In: CVPR (2018)
59. Wang, T., Yang, X., Xu, K., Chen, S., Zhang, Q., Lau, R.W.: Spatial attentive single-image deraining with a high quality real rain dataset. In: CVPR (2019)
60. Wang, X., Li, Y., Zhang, H., Shan, Y.: Towards real-world blind face restoration with generative facial prior. In: CVPR (2021)
61. Wang, Z., Cun, X., Bao, J., Liu, J.: Uformer: a general u-shaped transformer for image restoration. arXiv preprint arXiv:2106.03106
62. Yang, F., Yang, H., Fu, J., Lu, H., Guo, B.: Learning texture transformer network for image super-resolution. In: CVPR (2020)
63. Yang, S., Lei, Y., Xiong, S., Wang, W.: High resolution demoire network. In: ICIP (2020)
64. Yang, W., Tan, R.T., Feng, J., Liu, J., Guo, Z., Yan, S.: Deep joint rain detection and removal from a single image. In: CVPR (2017)
65. Yi, Q., Li, J., Dai, Q., Fang, F., Zhang, G., Zeng, T.: Structure-preserving deraining with residue channel prior guidance. ICCV (2021)
66. Yu, K., Dong, C., Lin, L., Loy, C.C.: Crafting a toolchain for image restoration by deep reinforcement learning. In: CVPR (2018)
67. Zamir, S.W., Arora, A., Khan, S., Hayat, M., Khan, F.S., Yang, M.H.: Restormer: efficient transformer for high-resolution image restoration. In: CVPR (2022)
68. Zamir, S.W., et al.: Multi-stage progressive image restoration. In: CVPR (2021)
69. Zeng, Y., Fu, J., Chao, H.: Learning joint spatial-temporal transformations for video inpainting. In: Vedaldi, A., Bischof, H., Brox, T., Frahm, J.-M. (eds.) ECCV 2020. LNCS, vol. 12361, pp. 528–543. Springer, Cham (2020). https://doi.org/10.1007/978-3-030-58517-4_31
70. Zhang, K., Zuo, W., Chen, Y., Meng, D., Zhang, L.: Beyond a gaussian denoiser: residual learning of deep CNN for image denoising. TIP **26**, 3142–3155 (2017)
71. Zhang, K., Zuo, W., Gu, S., Zhang, L.: Learning deep CNN denoiser prior for image restoration. In: CVPR (2017)
72. Zhang, K., Zuo, W., Zhang, L.: FFDNet: toward a fast and flexible solution for CNN based image denoising. TIP **27**, 4608–4622 (2018)
73. Zhang, Y., Tian, Y., Kong, Y., Zhong, B., Fu, Y.: Residual dense network for image restoration. TPAMI **43**, 2480–2495 (2020)
74. Zheng, B., et al.: Domainplus: cross transform domain learning towards efficient high dynamic range imaging. In: ACM MM (2022)
75. Zheng, B., Yuan, S., Slabaugh, G., Leonardis, A.: Image demoireing with learnable bandpass filters. In: CVPR, 2020
76. Zheng, B., et al.: Learning frequency domain priors for image demoireing. TPAMI **44**, 7705–7717 (2021)
77. Zhu, L., Fu, C.W., Lischinski, D., Heng, P.A.: Joint bi-layer optimization for single-image rain streak removal. In: ICCV (2017)
78. Zhu, Q., Mai, J., Shao, L.: A fast single image haze removal algorithm using color attenuation prior. TIP **24**, 3522–3533 (2015)
79. Zhu, S.C., Mumford, D.: Prior learning and Gibbs reaction-diffusion. TPAMI **19**, 1236–1250 (1997)
80. Zhu, X., Su, W., Lu, L., Li, B., Wang, X., Dai, J.: Deformable detr: deformable transformers for end-to-end object detection. In: ICLR (2021)

Uncertainty Inspired Underwater Image Enhancement

Zhenqi Fu[1], Wu Wang[1], Yue Huang[1], Xinghao Ding[1(✉)], and Kai-Kuang Ma[2]

[1] Xiamen University, Fujian 361005, China
{fuzhenqi,23320170155546}@stu.xmu.edu.cn, {yhuang2010,dxh}@xmu.edu.cn
[2] Nanyang Technological University, Singapore 639798, Singapore
ekkma@ntu.edu.sg

Abstract. A main challenge faced in the deep learning-based Underwater Image Enhancement (UIE) is that the ground truth high-quality image is unavailable. Most of the existing methods first generate approximate reference maps and then train an enhancement network with certainty. This kind of method fails to handle the ambiguity of the reference map. In this paper, we resolve UIE into distribution estimation and consensus process. We present a novel probabilistic network to learn the enhancement distribution of degraded underwater images. Specifically, we combine conditional variational autoencoder with adaptive instance normalization to construct the enhancement distribution. After that, we adopt a consensus process to predict a deterministic result based on a set of samples from the distribution. By learning the enhancement distribution, our method can cope with the bias introduced in the reference map labeling to some extent. Additionally, the consensus process is useful to capture a robust and stable result. We examined the proposed method on two widely used real-world underwater image enhancement datasets. Experimental results demonstrate that our approach enables sampling possible enhancement predictions. Meanwhile, the consensus estimate yields competitive performance compared with state-of-the-art UIE methods. Code available at https://github.com/zhenqifu/PUIE-Net.

Keywords: Underwater image enhancement · Deep learning · Probabilistic network · Adaptive instance normalization · Conditional variational autoencoder

1 Introduction

Underwater images suffer from degradation due to the poor and complex lighting conditions in the water. The degradation of underwater images is mainly rooted in the wavelength-dependent light scattering and absorption, which reduces visibility, decreases contrast, and introduces unpleasant color casts. It is important and necessary to develop Underwater Image Enhancement (UIE) methods to adjust the degraded underwater signal so that the results are more suitable

© The Author(s), under exclusive license to Springer Nature Switzerland AG 2022
S. Avidan et al. (Eds.): ECCV 2022, LNCS 13678, pp. 465–482, 2022.
https://doi.org/10.1007/978-3-031-19797-0_27

for display or further analysis. In the past few years, deep learning-based UIE approaches have enabled tremendous progress. Commonly, this kind of method adopts corresponding pairs of clean and distorted images to learn a mapping between two quality levels [14,36,39,59].

UIE is an important low-level vision task. For underwater scenes with adverse visual conditions, it is difficult and impractical to capture the clean image to train a deep neural network directly. This is because the degradation of underwater images is non-reversible and very complex. To solve this problem, previous methods propose to generate approximate supervisors to train a deep neural network. For example, in [36] the authors applied several state-of-the-art algorithms to generate a set of potential reference images and manually select the best one as the ground truth. Benefiting from the large-scale dataset constructed in previous works, deep learning-based methods have made profound progress in learning the mapping from a degraded underwater image to the corresponding high-quality reference image [34]. Nonetheless, considering the progress of UIE under this pipeline, we would like to argue that this kind of method fails to capture the uncertainties in labeling the ground truth.

Although the reference image achieves high visual quality in existing UIE datasets, it is generated through an approximate approach (e.g., using exiting UIE algorithms [36]) and may be influenced by various factors, such as human-specific preference during subjective selection and different algorithm parameters. In this case, UIE suffers from uncertainty issues. For ambiguous labels, directly learning a mapping between the degraded underwater image and corresponding reference is inappropriate. There are many potential solutions for the same degraded underwater image because we cannot confidently know what a true clean image looks like. Nonetheless, most of the existing deep learning-based methods treat UIE as a point estimation problem. As a result, they have to make a compromise between possible solutions because they are following a deterministic learning pipeline.

In this paper, we propose the first probabilistic network for UIE, termed PUIE-Net. Instead of directly generating a single prediction (i.e., the point estimation), we are interested in how the network produces multiple results (i.e., the distribution estimation) so that the network can handle the uncertainty issue in UIE. Furthermore, once the distribution is estimated, we can perform a consensus process to capture a deterministic result based on a set of estimations. In this paper, we introduce two consensus processes to predict the final result named: Monte Carlo likelihood estimation (MC) [51] and Maximum Probability estimation (MP). Specifically, MC is calculated by taking the average of the likelihoods. While the sample with maximum probability is regarded as the final result in MP.

The proposed network structure is based on probabilistic adaptive instance normalization (PAdaIN), which combines conditional variational autoencoder (CVAE) [48] with adaptive instance normalization (AdaIN) [23] to construct the enhancement distribution. PAdaIN is motivated by AdaIN that is originally designed for style transfer. We extend AdaIN into PAdaIN via drawing style inputs from two posterior distributions constructed by conditional variational autoencoders. PAdaIN aims to transform the global enhancement statistics of input features. Therefore, diverse predictions can be achieved by sampling different enhancement attributes from the latent space. The whole pipeline of our method is trained following the standard training procedure of the CVAE. We conduct extensive experiments on two real-world UIE datasets to validate the effectiveness of our method.

Our main contributions are summarized as follows:

– We resolve UIE into distribution estimation and consensus process to handle the uncertainty issue in labeling the ground truth.
– We propose the first probabilistic network for UIE, which learns to approximate the posterior over meaningful appearance. Specifically, the enhancement distribution is constructed based on conditional variational autoencoder and adaptive instance normalization.
– We show that our method can generate diverse potential solutions. Besides, by inferring the consensus prediction based on a set of samples, our method achieves promising performance compared with state-of-the-art methods on two UIE datasets.

2   Related Work

2.1   Underwater Image Enhancement

According to the means of the modeling imaging process, the existing UIE methods can be roughly categorized into the following three types.

The first category is model-free methods, which enhance underwater images without considering the degradation process. Traditional contrast limited adaptive histogram equalization (CLAHE) [44], white balance (WB) [56], and Retinex [47] belong to this category. In [7], the authors proposed a fusion-based method for UIE, where the inputs and weight measures are derived only from the degraded image. An improvement version of [7] is presented in [5], which adopts a white balancing technique and a novel multi-scale fusion strategy to further promote the enhancement performance. Fu et al. [16] proposed a retinex-based UIE approach to enhance a single underwater image. Gao et al. [18] presented a teleost fish retina-guided underwater image enhancement approach to deal with the problems of nonuniform color shift and content blurring. Other relevant works can be found in [6,19].

The second category is prior-based methods, which enhance underwater images using physical imaging models and focus on accurately estimating the parameters of the defined physical model. Chiang et al. [12] proposed to enhance underwater images via a dehazing algorithm. Galdran et al. [17] proposed a variant of the Dark Channel Prior (DCP) [21] that uses red channel information to estimate the depth map of underwater images. Li et al. [33] proposed an underwater image dehazing algorithm and a contrast enhancement method based on a minimum information loss and histogram distribution prior. Berman et al. [11]

took into account multiple spectral profiles of different water types, in which the authors additionally estimated two global parameters, i.e., the attenuation ratios of the blue-red and blue-green color channels. Akkaynak et al. [3] developed a UIE method named Sea-thru based on a revised physical imaging model. Sea-thru takes RGBD images as the input and it first estimates backscatter using the darkest pixels and their known range map. Then it calculates the attenuation coefficient based on an estimation of the spatially varying illuminant. Other relevant works of prior-based UIE methods can be found in [2,10,35,42,43].

The third category is deep learning-based methods that automatically extract representations and learn an enhancement mapping based on numerous paired/unpaired training data. Li et al. [38] first proposed a generative adversarial network to generate synthetic underwater images in an unsupervised pipeline. Then the authors trained an enhancement network using these synthetic data. Li et al. [37] proposed a weakly supervised underwater image enhancement method that relaxes the need for paired data. Guo et al. [20] enhanced degraded underwater images using a multi-scale dense generative adversarial network. Li et al. [35] introduced a lightweight UIE model based on the underwater scene prior. Li et al. [36] constructed a large scale real-world UIE dataset. The reference image is generated by 12 existing UIE methods. Besides, based on this dataset, the authors proposed a gated fusion network for enhancing underwater images. Jamadandi et al. [25] proposed to enhance underwater images by augmenting the network with wavelet corrected transformations. To deal with the challenge of underwater image degradation diversity, Uplavikar et al. [53] trained a new deep neural network to learn the domain agnostic features for a given degraded underwater image, where the domain is the Jerlov water type of the image. Li et al. [34] presented an underwater image enhancement network called Ucolor by medium transmission-guided multi-color space embedding. Kar et al. [29] presented a zero-shot underwater and hazing image restoration method by leveraging a theoretically deduced property of degradation through the physical model. More relevant works of learning-based UIE methods can be found in [15,24,26,27,41,46,55,58].

2.2   VAE Based Deep Probabilistic Model

Variational autoencoder (VAE) and its conditional counterpart (CVAE) [48,51] have been widely used in various computer vision tasks. Rather than building an encoder that outputs a single value to describe each latent state attribute, VAE formulates the encoder to describe a probability distribution for each latent attribute. To train a VAE, a regularizer and a reconstruction loss are needed to penalize the disagreement of the posterior and prior distributions of the latent representation.

Despite not being explored to model ambiguities for underwater image enhancement, VAEs and CVAEs are utilized to sample diverse results from constructed posteriors. For example, in [32], the authors use VAEs to model the image background for salient object detection. In [57], the authors apply VAEs for learning motion sequence generation. In [30], a probabilistic U-Net based on

VAEs is proposed to learn a conditional distribution of medical image segmentation. [9] and [31] improve the diversity of samples in [30] via adopting a hierarchy of latent variables. In [1], a contrastive VAE is introduced which combines the benefits of contrastive learning with the power of VAEs to identify and enhance salient latent features. In [45], a VAE based denoising approach is developed by predicting a whole distribution of denoised images. In [8], the authors employ VAEs to predict multiple deprojected instances for images/videos collapsed along a dimension. In [60], the authors employ VAEs for RGB-D saliency detection by learning from the data labeling process. Other relevant works about VAEs for diverse solution sampling can be found in [4,13,52]

3   Method

In this section, we will introduce PUIE-Net in detail. PUIE-Net is based on PAdaIN that learns meaningful distributions of UIE. It is the first time that employs a probabilistic network to solve the UIE problem.

3.1   Motivation

Ambiguities for UIE. The main idea of PUIE-Net is to introduce ambiguities for UIE. This is because the true clean image is unavailable and there is a degree of uncertainties in recording approximate labels. Existing deterministic learning-guided methods fail to capture such uncertainty and have to make a compromise between possible results. We consider that as we cannot confidently know which of the possible clean image has given rise to the distorted underwater image at hand, estimating the distribution of possible interpretations may be an advisable solution. We use an implicit variable $\mathbf{z}$ to express the uncertainty. Here, $\mathbf{z}$ can be interpreted as human subjective preferences or camera/algorithm parameters in capturing the ground truth. Let $\mathbf{x}$ and $\mathbf{y}$ refer to the corrupted observation and the clean image, respectively. UIE under a probabilistic framework can be formulated as:

$$p(y\,|\mathbf{x}) \approx \frac{1}{S}\sum_{s=1}^{S} p\left(\mathbf{y}\,\Big|\mathbf{z}^{(s)},\mathbf{x}\right), \mathbf{z}^{(s)} \sim p(\mathbf{z}\,|\mathbf{x}) \tag{1}$$

where $p(\mathbf{z}\,|\mathbf{x})$ denotes the distribution of uncertainty. S represents the number of samples. Equation (1) not only allows us to generate multiple enhancement predictions but also gives a straightforward way to calculate a deterministic result, i.e., the MC estimation [51] that draws samples using the prior network and takes the average of the likelihoods. Apart from MC, the Maximum Probability estimation (MP) is also considered in this paper. MP takes the enhancement sample with the maximum probability as the final result. Mathematically, MP can be expressed as:

$$p(y\,|\mathbf{x}) \approx p(\mathbf{y}\,|\mathbf{z}_{\max},\mathbf{x}), \mathbf{z}_{\max} \sim p(\mathbf{z}\,|\mathbf{x}) \tag{2}$$

where $\mathbf{z}_{\max}$ denotes the sample with the maximum probability.

PAdaIN for Learning Appearance Distribution. Since the goal of UIE is to adjust the image appearance such as colors and contrasts, rather than the content, it is important to capture such information during the enhancement. Here, we adopt a modified AdaIN [23] to capture such features. AdaIN is originally developed for style transfer, which can be expressed as:

$$\text{AdaIN}\,(\mathbf{x}, \mathbf{y}) = \boldsymbol{\sigma}(\mathbf{y}) \left(\frac{\mathbf{x} - \boldsymbol{\mu}\,(\mathbf{x})}{\boldsymbol{\sigma}\,(\mathbf{x})} \right) + \boldsymbol{\mu}(\mathbf{y}) \tag{3}$$

where $\mathbf{x}$ denotes the features of the content image and $\mathbf{y}$ denotes the features of the style image. $\boldsymbol{\mu}$ and $\boldsymbol{\sigma}$ refer to the mean and standard deviation operations, respectively. AdaIN changes the appearance by adjusting the mean and standard deviation of features. We observe that UIE falls into the AdaIN paradigm. However, AdaIN relies on the known content and style images, it cannot be directly leveraged for UIE. To handle this problem, we propose PAdaIN, which can be formulated as:

$$\text{PAdaIN}\,(\mathbf{x}) = \boldsymbol{b} \left(\frac{\mathbf{x} - \boldsymbol{\mu}\,(\mathbf{x})}{\boldsymbol{\sigma}\,(\mathbf{x})} \right) + \boldsymbol{a} \tag{4}$$

where $\boldsymbol{b}$ and $\boldsymbol{a}$ are two random samples from the posterior distributions of the mean and standard deviation, respectively. Specifically, the posterior distributions can be learned with CVAEs, which will be detailed in the next subsection. Note that the proposed PAdaIN can be regarded as a generalized AdaIN.

3.2   Network Structure

The whole pipeline of PUIE-Net is illustrated in Fig. 1. The proposed network structure contains two branches. Both branches include a U-Net [49] based feature extractor. Specifically, the top branch aims to estimate the prior distribution of a single raw underwater image. While the goal of the bottom branch is to construct posterior distributions of UIE, it takes the raw underwater image and corresponding reference image as the input. In PUIE-Net, we simply modify the U-Net by adding SE-ResNet blocks [22]. This is useful to improve the network capacity of enhancement representations.

The core component of PUIE-Net is the PAdaIN after the feature extractor to encode the ambiguities. The prior/posterior block (i.e., Pr/Po block in Fig. 1) is designed to build the distribution of enhancement. We note that both Pr and Po need to construct a mean and a standard deviation distributions. After that, embeddings sampled form Pr/Po block are input to the AdaIN to transform the feature statistics. Let $\boldsymbol{f} \in \mathbb{R}^{B \times C \times H \times W}$ refers to the data matrix of Pr/Po block's input, where B, C, H, W indicate the batch size, number of channels, the height, and the width, respectively. First, we calculating the mean and standard deviation of each channel of $\boldsymbol{f}$. Then, we adopt 1×1 convolutions to obtain $\boldsymbol{\mu} \in \mathbb{R}^{B \times N \times 1 \times 1}$ and $\boldsymbol{\sigma} \in \mathbb{R}^{B \times N \times 1 \times 1}$ from the mean vector. Similarly, we adopt 1×1 convolutions to obtain $\boldsymbol{m} \in \mathbb{R}^{B \times N \times 1 \times 1}$ and $\boldsymbol{v} \in \mathbb{R}^{B \times N \times 1 \times 1}$ from the standard deviation vector. Finally, $\boldsymbol{\mu}$ and $\boldsymbol{\sigma}$ are applied to build the N-dimensional

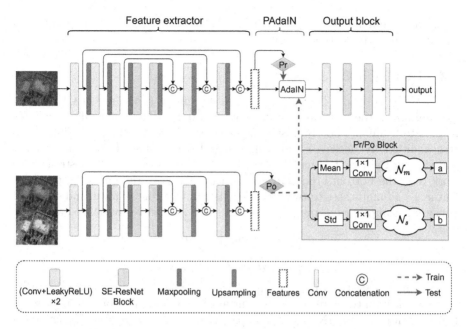

Fig. 1. The network architecture of PUIE-Net. The feature extractor is based on U-Net [49] that maps the input to representations. After the feature extractor is the PAdaIN module, which transforms the enhancement statistics of received deterministic features. **In the training phase,** features from the bottom branch are used to calculate the posterior distribution. Random samples from the posterior distributions are injected into AdaIN to transform the enhancement representation. **In the testing phase,** taking a single degraded image as the input, random samples from the Pr block are employed to generate the predictions.

Gaussian distribution of the mean ($\mathcal{N}_m$). m and v are applied to build the N-dimensional Gaussian distribution of the standard deviation ($\mathcal{N}_s$). As the two distributions are constructed, we extract random samples from them, which can be expressed as:

$$a \sim \mathcal{N}_m\left(\boldsymbol{\mu}\left(\mathbf{x}\right), \boldsymbol{\sigma}^2\left(\mathbf{x}\right)\right) \tag{5}$$

$$b \sim \mathcal{N}_s\left(\boldsymbol{m}\left(\mathbf{x}\right), \boldsymbol{v}^2\left(\mathbf{x}\right)\right) \tag{6}$$

where a and b are two random samples from the mean and standard deviation distributions, respectively. Note that, in the testing phase, the latent codes (a and b) are only dependent on the input image $\mathbf{x}$. While in the training phase we leverage input image $\mathbf{x}$ and corresponding reference image $\mathbf{y}$ to learn the posterior distributions, which will be described in the next subsection.

Random samples a and b are further injected into the AdaIN module to transform the statistics of received features. Typical AdaIN receives a content input and a style input, and simply aligns the mean and standard deviation of the content input to match those of the style input across channels. For UIE, the style input is unavailable in advance. Therefore, we propose to align the mean and standard deviation of received features based on random activations extracted from the learned distributions.

3.3 Training and Testing

PUIE-Net is trained following the standard training procedure of CVAE, i.e., by minimizing the variational lower bound (Eq. 12). The main difference with respect to training a deterministic enhancement model is that our training process additionally needs to find a meaningful embedding of the enhancement statistics in the latent space. This is addressed by introducing a posterior network (i.e., the bottom branch in Fig. 1), that learns to recognize the posterior features, and map those to two posterior distributions of the mean and standard deviation. Samples from the posterior distributions can be formalized as:

$$a \sim \mathcal{N}_\mathrm{m}\left(\boldsymbol{\mu}\left(\boldsymbol{y}, \mathbf{x}\right), \boldsymbol{\sigma}^2\left(\boldsymbol{y}, \mathbf{x}\right)\right) \tag{7}$$

$$b \sim \mathcal{N}_\mathrm{s}\left(\boldsymbol{m}\left(\boldsymbol{y}, \mathbf{x}\right), \boldsymbol{v}^2\left(\boldsymbol{y}, \mathbf{x}\right)\right) \tag{8}$$

where a and b are two random samples from the mean and standard deviation posterior distributions, respectively. During the training, random samples a and b are fed into the AdaIN module to predict the enhanced image. The enhancement loss L_e penalizes the differences between the output of PUIE-Net and the reference. L_e is formulated as:

$$L_\mathrm{e} = L_\mathrm{mse} + \lambda L_\mathrm{vgg16} \tag{9}$$

where L_mse denotes the mean square error loss and L_vgg16 denotes the perceptual loss explored by [28], λ refers to the weight.

Apart from minimizing the enhancement loss, Kullback-Leibler (KL) divergences are employed to assimilate the posterior distributions and the prior distributions:

$$L_m = D_\mathrm{KL}\left(\mathcal{N}_\mathrm{m}\left(\mathbf{x}\right) \| \mathcal{N}_\mathrm{m}\left(\boldsymbol{y}, \mathbf{x}\right)\right) \tag{10}$$

$$L_s = D_\mathrm{KL}\left(\mathcal{N}_\mathrm{s}\left(\mathbf{x}\right) \| \mathcal{N}_\mathrm{s}\left(\boldsymbol{y}, \mathbf{x}\right)\right) \tag{11}$$

where D_KL refers to the KL divergence between two distributions. Finally, the total loss function for training PUIE-Net is the weighted sum of above losses:

$$L = L_\mathrm{e} + \beta(L_m + L_s) \tag{12}$$

where β is the weight. In the testing phase, we apply the network n times to the same input image to predict n enhancement variants. Note that only PAdaIN and the output block need to be re-evaluated. Diverse enhancement solutions provide users with multiple alternative results for display or analysis. More importantly, a set of samples provide sufficient inferring data for the consensus process. In this paper, the default consensus processes are the Monte Carlo likelihood estimation (MC) and Maximum Probability estimation (MP). MC predicts a final result via averaging a group of possible samples. MP takes the enhancement sample with the maximum probability as the final estimation. Equations (1) and (2) in Sect. 3.1 describe the formulation of MC and MP, receptively.

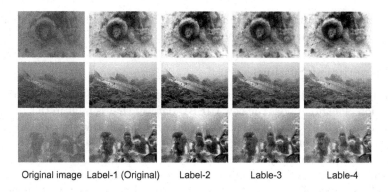

Original image Label-1 (Original)   Label-2   Lable-3   Lable-4

Fig. 2. Examples of our new UIE dataset. Label 2–4 denote the new labels generated by contrast adjustment, saturation adjustment, and gamma correction, respectively.

3.4   Training Data Generation

One obstacle before training our probabilistic network is that the existing UIE dataset generally only provides a single reference map for each degraded underwater image. To apply the probabilistic network, we re-build the existing UIE dataset by generating multiple reference images. Our new dataset is based on UIEBD [36], a real-world UIE dataset that contains 890 underwater images and corresponding reference maps. In the original UIEBD, the authors utilize 12 state-of-the-art enhancement algorithms to generate the potential ground truth. With raw underwater images and the 12 enhanced results, the authors invite volunteers to perform pairwise comparisons and subjectively select the best one among twelve candidates as the final reference image. Based on UIEBD, we create ambiguities by performing contrast and saturation adjustment, and gamma correction. We adopt these methods because the distortions of underwater images are mainly reflected in contrast, saturation, brightness, and colors. Note that we aim to generate ambiguous labels rather than significantly alter the original label. The contrast and saturation adjustment are performed via a simple linear transformation $y = (x - m) \times \alpha + x$, where x and y refer to the input and output, m denotes the mean of each channel. α is the adjustment coefficient. For contrast adjustment, α is the same for all pixels. For saturation adjustment, α is determined by each pixel itself. To generate a more reliable reference map, we first create two adjusted versions (i.e., over and under adjustment) per method and then choose the better one as the potential label. As a result, we obtain four reference maps (including the original label) for each raw underwater image, which can reflect the uncertainty during the ground truth recording. We show an example of the new dataset in Fig. 2.

4   Experiments

In this section, we will first show the detailed experimental settings including training and test datasets, performance criteria, compared methods, and the implementation details. Then, we quantitatively and qualitatively evaluate our method against several state-of-the-art algorithms on two UIE datasets.

4.1 Experiment Settings

Training and Testing Datasets: Two UIE datasets are used for performance verification. The first one is the new UIEBD dataset that is built in this paper. As described in Sect. 3.4, we create multiple labels for each raw underwater image. We use the first 700 original images and corresponding reference images for training, and the rest for testing. The second dataset is RUIE [39], which only contains raw underwater images. RUIE is a large-scale underwater dataset that contains three subsets, including an underwater image quality subset (3630 images), an underwater color cast subset (300 images), and an underwater higher-level task-driven subset (300 images). In this paper, we use the underwater image quality subset for testing since it contains different levels of image quality and various underwater scenes. Note that our model is trained on UIEBD and tested on both UIEBD and RUIE.

Performance Criteria: In the case of applying a probabilistic network for UIE, we not only want to compare a deterministic estimation with a unique reference image, but also we are interested in the distributions of enhancement. To analyze the learned distributions, we perform subjective comparisons by visualizing the latent space. To evaluate the enhancement performance, we adopt SSIM [54], PSNR, DeltaE (CIE2000 standard) [50], and NIQE [40] to measure the image quality objectively. SSIM, PSNR, and DeltaE are full-reference metrics calculated based on the original label in UIEBD for a fair comparison with existing methods. Note that DeltaE is used for color difference evaluation. NIQE is a no-reference metric and it does not need reference images. Additionally, we conduct subjective tests to understand how users prefer the results generated by each UIE method. We use Mean Opinion Score (MOS) to quantify the subjective evaluation. 20 participants (10 male and 10 female) are invited to join the subjective test. Raw and enhanced underwater images are simultaneously displayed on a screen. The subjective score of each image is rated on a five-level scale: 5 (excellent), 4 (good), 3 (fair), 2 (poor), and 1 (bad), according to the following measures: color distortion, contrast enhancement, naturalness preservation, brightness improvement, and artifacts. We note that since RUIE only contains raw underwater images, we adopt NIQE and MOS to measure the model performance.

Compared Methods: We compare PUIE-Net with 9 UIE methods, including three model-free methods (GC, Retinex [16] and Fusion [7]), three prior-based methods (IBLA [43], Histogram-Prior [33] and Haze-line [10]), and three deep learning-based approaches (Water-Net [36], Ucolor [34], and LC-Net [26]). We record the results of all competitors by conducting the same experiments using the original implementations provided by the authors for comparison fairness.

Implementation Details: PUIE-Net is implemented in the Pytorch framework and trained on an NVIDIA RTX 2080Ti GPU with ADAM optimizer. The

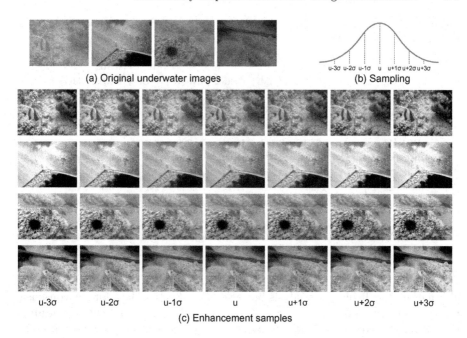

(a) Original underwater images   (b) Sampling

u-3σ   u-2σ   u-1σ   u   u+1σ   u+2σ   u+3σ

(c) Enhancement samples

Fig. 3. Visualization of the enhancement distribution of UIE. We show the original image in (a). The sampling scheme used for visualization is presented in (b) and the enhancement samples are shown in (c). μ and σ in (b) denote the mean and standard deviation of the distribution, respectively.

learning rate is 1×10^{-4}, the batch size is 4, and the patch size is 256×256. We augment the training data with rotation, flipping horizontally and vertically to promote network generalization. The dimension N of the latent space is 20. We adopt 1×1 convolutions to broadcast the samples to the desired number of channels before input to AdaIN. The parameter λ and β are empirically set as 1. The default kernel size of convolution layers is 3×3 and the number of channels is 64. The default sampling times for calculating MC estimations are 20.

4.2 Analysis of Enhancement Distribution

Although a lot of UIE algorithms have been developed, PUIE-Net is the first method that learns the distribution of enhancement and explicitly takes multi-solution into account. Figure 3 shows the original image and PUIE-Net samples. We manually control the sampling interval for better visualization. From Fig. 3, we can make the following observations: 1) Each PUIE-Net sample has a different but reasonable appearance. Enhanced samples with higher sampling probability show relatively mild enhancement. Enhanced samples with lower sampling probability show strong contrast and color adjustment. This demonstrates that our method can learn the meaningful distribution of UIE and can generate diverse enhancement predictions. 2) A set of enhanced samples not only provide multiple

Table 1. Quantitative comparison on UIEBD and RUIE datasets. The best result is highlighted in red and the second best one is in blue.

Method	UIEBD					RUIE	
	PSNR ↑	SSIM ↑	DeltaE ↓	NIQE ↓	MOS ↑	NIQE ↓	MOS ↑
GC	16.14	0.761	16.11	3.789	2.6	4.656	2.4
Retinex [16]	17.53	0.773	14.82	4.074	2.7	4.593	2.5
Fusion [7]	21.18	0.822	9.079	3.747	3.4	4.488	2.9
IBLA [43]	18.51	0.762	18.64	4.290	2.2	4.767	1.9
Histogram-Prior [33]	14.39	0.573	15.69	3.780	2.4	4.486	2.5
Water-Net [36]	19.31	0.830	10.14	3.879	3.3	4.491	3.3
Haze-line [10]	14.97	0.669	17.23	3.830	2.4	4.620	1.8
Ucolor [34]	21.65	0.840	8.646	3.786	3.7	4.755	3.0
LC-Net [26]	18.54	0.812	14.25	3.800	3.3	4.721	2.9
PUIE-Net (MC)	21.86	0.870	9.556	3.626	4.2	4.512	3.7
PUIE-Net (MP)	21.05	0.854	10.26	3.668	4.1	4.555	3.6

alternatives for display or analysis but also offer effective data for the consensus process to further obtain a robust and stable result. Compared with deterministic learning-based methods which have to make a compromise between possible results, our method is more flexible and can reduce the influence of biased labels in the existing UIE dataset.

4.3   Performance Comparison

Table 1 presents the quantitative comparisons on UIEBD and RUIE datasets. From Table 1, we can perceive that PUIE-Net achieves favorable performance and outperforms other methods. Specifically, prior-based approaches obtain relatively poor results since this kind of method is highly dependent on the used prior knowledge and the predefined imaging model. We found that the performance of MC is significantly better than the others. This is reasonable since averaging a set of samples can reduce enhancement bias in the testing phase. We further present visual comparisons in Fig. 4. As can be seen, although most of the methods can somehow enhance the contrast, severe visual defects caused by the unsatisfactory adjustment of colors or artifacts remain. For example, GC and Retinex show unnatural colors and saturation, smearing image details. Prior-based methods can improve the contrasts, however, the colors are seriously degraded in these cases. Water-Net and Ucolor tend to generate over/under-enhanced results. Our method works well on all these cases and the result looks more clean and natural with fine-grained textures.

4.4   Impact of Sampling Times

Since we apply the consensus process to obtain a deterministic result, it is necessary to analyze the influence of sampling times. We calculate the standard deviation of PSNR and SSIM under different sampling times on the UIEBD

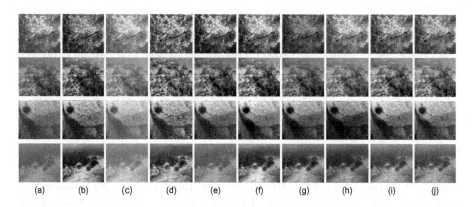

Fig. 4. Comparisons of visual results on UIEBD and RUIE datasets. (a) Original image. (b) Retinex. (c) GC. (d) Fusion. (e) IBLA. (f) Histogram-Prior. (g) Water-Net. (h) Ucolor. (i) PUIE-Net (MC). (j) PUIE-Net (MP).

Table 2. Impact of sampling times.

Sampling times	1	2	4	6	8	10	20	50
Mean std-PSNR	0.726	0.512	0.380	0.326	0.292	0.253	0.175	0.166
Mean std-SSIM	0.008	0.004	0.003	0.003	0.003	0.002	0.002	0.001

dataset. Note that we run the model 10 times to calculate the standard deviation of PSNR and SSIM (i.e., std-PSNR and std-SSIM) for each raw underwater image. The mean std-PSNR and std-SSIM of all test images are listed in Table 2. As can be observed, as the number of samples increases, the standard deviation of PSNR and SSIM first reduces and then becomes stable after 20 sampling times. This demonstrates that PUIE-Net can capture the diversity of enhanced images, and the consensus process can estimate a stable result based on multiple predictions. Note that increasing sampling times can further improve the stability of final predictions. In this paper, we set the default sampling times of MC estimation as 20 to better balance the stability and running time.

4.5   Discussion

Consensus Process The key idea of PUIE-Net is to learn the enhancement distribution and employ a consensus process to get the final prediction. Therefore, the effectiveness of the consensus process has a significant impact on the final results. In this paper, we have designed two consensus processes i.e., MC and MP. The former estimates an enhanced image by averaging a group of samples while the latter takes the image with the highest sampling probability as the final result. We consider that many other approaches can be applied to get the final result. For example, one can perform an image quality assessment method to select the best result according to the visual quality. In this case, both subjective and objective metrics can be used and the enhancement performance is highly dependent on the used evaluation method. Quality based selection can be expressed as:

$$p\left(y\left|\mathbf{x}\right.\right) \approx \max_{s} Q\left(p\left(\mathbf{y}\left|\mathbf{z}^{(s)},\mathbf{x}\right.\right),\mathbf{z}^{(s)} \sim p\left(\mathbf{z}\left|\mathbf{x}\right.\right)\right) \tag{13}$$

where Q denotes the subjective/objective image quality assessment function.

Relationship with Unsupervised Method The degradation of underwater images is non-reversible and complex, it is impracticable to record the ground truth for training a supervised UIE model directly. Therefore, we consider that unsupervised methods are more suitable for addressing the UIE problem. In this paper, instead of concentrating on developing an unsupervised method, we aim at making full use of the biased labels in existing UIE datasets. Biased reference maps of real-world underwater images are possible and cheap to obtain [34, 36]. With such reference maps, we proposed to leverage an AadIN module and a conditional variational autoencoder to learn the enhancement distribution. Therefore, the goal of both PUIE-Net and unsupervised UIE methods is to tackle the challenge of learning a UIE model without the ground truth. But our framework provides a new means to address the UIE problem i.e., resolving UIE into distribution estimation and consensus process based on biased reference maps, which is different from the unsupervised methods.

5   Conclusion

In this paper, we introduce PUIE-Net, a novel probabilistic network for underwater image enhancement. Specifically, we propose to learn the distribution of enhanced images rather than directly estimate a single result with certainty. This allows us to handle the label ambiguity issue of underwater image enhancement. The main idea is to leverage random style attributes from two posterior distributions constructed by conditional variational autoencoders, to transform the global enhancement statistics of input features. Moreover, with the consensus process, final enhancement results can be inferred via integrating a set of predictions. We demonstrate that PUIE-Net can effectively produce a set of reasonable results and the visual quality of the consensus estimation is highly competitive on two real-world UIE datasets. In the future, we plan to extend our method to other image enhancement tasks such as low-light image enhancement, dehazing, and denoising, where the ground truth image is difficult to obtain.

Acknowledgements. This study was partially supported by National Natural Science Foundation of China under Grants 82172033, 61971369, U19B2031, Science and Technology Key Project of Fujian Province 2019HZ020009, Fundamental Research Funds for the Central Universities 20720200003, Tencent Open Fund, and the State Scholarship Fund.

References

1. Abid, A., Zou, J.: Contrastive variational autoencoder enhances salient features. arXiv preprint arXiv:1902.04601 (2019)
2. Akkaynak, D., Treibitz, T.: A revised underwater image formation model. In: Proceedings of the IEEE Conference on Computer Vision and Pattern Recognition, pp. 6723–6732 (2018)
3. Akkaynak, D., Treibitz, T.: Sea-thru: a method for removing water from underwater images. In: Proceedings of the IEEE Conference on Computer Vision and Pattern Recognition (CVPR), pp. 1682–1691 (2019)
4. Aliakbarian, M.S., Saleh, F.S., Salzmann, M., Petersson, L., Gould, S., Habibian, A.: Learning variations in human motion via mix-and-match perturbation. arXiv preprint arXiv:1908.00733 (2019)
5. Ancuti, C.O., Ancuti, C., De Vleeschouwer, C., Bekaert, P.: Color balance and fusion for underwater image enhancement. IEEE Trans. Image Process. **27**(1), 379–393 (2017)
6. Ancuti, C.O., Ancuti, C., De Vleeschouwer, C., Sbert, M.: Color channel compensation (3c): a fundamental pre-processing step for image enhancement. IEEE Trans. Image Process. **29**, 2653–2665 (2019)
7. Ancuti, C., Ancuti, C.O., Haber, T., Bekaert, P.: Enhancing underwater images and videos by fusion. In: Proceedings of the IEEE Conference on Computer Vision and Pattern Recognition (CVPR), pp. 81–88 (2012)
8. Balakrishnan, G., Dalca, A.V., Zhao, A., Guttag, J.V., Durand, F., Freeman, W.T.: Visual deprojection: probabilistic recovery of collapsed dimensions. In: Proceedings of the IEEE International Conference on Computer Vision (ICCV), pp. 171–180 (2019)
9. Baumgartner, C.F., et al.: PHiSeg: capturing uncertainty in medical image segmentation. In: Shen, D., et al. (eds.) MICCAI 2019. LNCS, vol. 11765, pp. 119–127. Springer, Cham (2019). https://doi.org/10.1007/978-3-030-32245-8_14
10. Berman, D., Levy, D., Avidan, S., Treibitz, T.: Underwater single image color restoration using haze-lines and a new quantitative dataset. IEEE Trans. Pattern Anal. Mach. Intell. **43**(8), 2822–2837 (2020)
11. Berman, D., Treibitz, T., Avidan, S.: Diving into haze-lines: color restoration of underwater images. In: Proceedings of British Machine Vision Conference (BMVC), vol. 1 (2017)
12. Chiang, J.Y., Chen, Y.C.: Underwater image enhancement by wavelength compensation and dehazing. IEEE Trans. Image Process. **21**(4), 1756–1769 (2011)
13. Esser, P., Sutter, E., Ommer, B.: A variational u-net for conditional appearance and shape generation. In: Proceedings of the IEEE Conference on Computer Vision and Pattern Recognition (CVPR), pp. 8857–8866 (2018)
14. Fabbri, C., Islam, M.J., Sattar, J.: Enhancing underwater imagery using generative adversarial networks. In: Proceedings of the IEEE International Conference on Robotics and Automation (ICRA), pp. 7159–7165 (2018)
15. Fu, X., Cao, X.: Underwater image enhancement with global-local networks and compressed-histogram equalization. Sig. Process. Image Commun. **86**, 115892 (2020)
16. Fu, X., Zhuang, P., Huang, Y., Liao, Y., Zhang, X.P., Ding, X.: A retinex-based enhancing approach for single underwater image. In: 2014 IEEE International Conference on Image Processing (ICIP), pp. 4572–4576. IEEE (2014)

17. Galdran, A., Pardo, D., Picón, A., Alvarez-Gila, A.: Automatic red-channel under-water image restoration. J. Vis. Commun. Image Represent. **26**, 132–145 (2015)
18. Gao, S.B., Zhang, M., Zhao, Q., Zhang, X.S., Li, Y.J.: Underwater image enhancement using adaptive retinal mechanisms. IEEE Trans. Image Process. **28**(11), 5580–5595 (2019)
19. Ghani, A.S.A., Isa, N.A.M.: Underwater image quality enhancement through integrated color model with rayleigh distribution. Appl. Soft Comput. **27**, 219–230 (2015)
20. Guo, Y., Li, H., Zhuang, P.: Underwater image enhancement using a multiscale dense generative adversarial network. IEEE J. Oceanic Eng. **45**(3), 862–870 (2019)
21. He, K., Sun, J., Tang, X.: Single image haze removal using dark channel prior. IEEE Trans. Pattern Anal. Mach. Intell. **33**(12), 2341–2353 (2010)
22. Hu, J., Shen, L., Sun, G.: Squeeze-and-excitation networks. In: Proceedings of the IEEE Conference on Computer Vision and Pattern Recognition (CVPR), pp. 7132–7141 (2018)
23. Huang, X., Belongie, S.: Arbitrary style transfer in real-time with adaptive instance normalization. In: Proceedings of the IEEE International Conference on Computer Vision (ICCV), pp. 1501–1510 (2017)
24. Huo, F., Li, B., Zhu, X.: Efficient wavelet boost learning-based multi-stage progressive refinement network for underwater image enhancement. In: Proceedings of the IEEE/CVF International Conference on Computer Vision Workshops, pp. 1944–1952 (2021)
25. Jamadandi, A., Mudenagudi, U.: Exemplar-based underwater image enhancement augmented by wavelet corrected transforms. In: Proceedings of the IEEE/CVF Conference on Computer Vision and Pattern Recognition Workshops, pp. 11–17 (2019)
26. Jiang, N., Chen, W., Lin, Y., Zhao, T., Lin, C.W.: Underwater image enhancement with lightweight cascaded network. IEEE Trans. Multimedia **24**, 4301–4313 (2021)
27. Jiang, Q., Zhang, Y., Bao, F., Zhao, X., Zhang, C., Liu, P.: Two-step domain adaptation for underwater image enhancement. Pattern Recogn. **122**, 108324 (2022)
28. Johnson, J., Alahi, A., Fei-Fei, L.: Perceptual losses for real-time style transfer and super-resolution. In: Proceedings of the European Conference on Computer Vision (ECCV), pp. 694–711 (2016)
29. Kar, A., Dhara, S.K., Sen, D., Biswas, P.K.: Zero-shot single image restoration through controlled perturbation of koschmieder's model. In: Proceedings of the IEEE/CVF Conference on Computer Vision and Pattern Recognition, pp. 16205–16215 (2021)
30. Kohl, S., et al.: A probabilistic u-net for segmentation of ambiguous images. In: Advances in Neural Information Processing Systems (NeurIPS), pp. 6965–6975 (2018)
31. Kohl, S.A., et al.: A hierarchical probabilistic u-net for modeling multi-scale ambiguities. arXiv preprint arXiv:1905.13077 (2019)
32. Li, B., Sun, Z., Guo, Y.: Supervae: superpixelwise variational autoencoder for salient object detection. In: Proceedings of the AAAI Conference on Artificial Intelligence (AAAI), vol. 33, pp. 8569–8576 (2019)
33. Li, C.Y., Guo, J.C., Cong, R.M., Pang, Y.W., Wang, B.: Underwater image enhancement by dehazing with minimum information loss and histogram distribution prior. IEEE Trans. Image Process. **25**(12), 5664–5677 (2016)
34. Li, C., Anwar, S., Hou, J., Cong, R., Guo, C., Ren, W.: Underwater image enhancement via medium transmission-guided multi-color space embedding. IEEE Trans. Image Process. **30**, 4985–5000 (2021)

35. Li, C., Anwar, S., Porikli, F.: Underwater scene prior inspired deep underwater image and video enhancement. Pattern Recognit. **98**, 107038 (2020)
36. Li, C., et al.: An underwater image enhancement benchmark dataset and beyond. IEEE Trans. Image Process. **29**, 4376–4389 (2019)
37. Li, C., Guo, J., Guo, C.: Emerging from water: underwater image color correction based on weakly supervised color transfer. IEEE Sig. Process. Lett **25**(3), 323–327 (2018)
38. Li, J., Skinner, K.A., Eustice, R.M., Johnson-Roberson, M.: WaterGAN: unsupervised generative network to enable real-time color correction of monocular underwater images. IEEE Robot. Autom. Lett. **3**(1), 387–394 (2017)
39. Liu, R., Fan, X., Zhu, M., Hou, M., Luo, Z.: Real-world underwater enhancement: challenges, benchmarks, and solutions under natural light. IEEE Trans. Circ. Syst. Video Technol. **30**(12), 4861–4875 (2020)
40. Mittal, A., Soundararajan, R., Bovik, A.C.: Making a "Completely blind" image quality analyzer. IEEE Signal Process. Lett. **20**(3), 209–212 (2012)
41. Panetta, K., Kezebou, L., Oludare, V., Agaian, S.: Comprehensive underwater object tracking benchmark dataset and underwater image enhancement with GAN. IEEE J. Oceanic Eng. **47**(1), 59–75 (2021)
42. Peng, Y.T., Cao, K., Cosman, P.C.: Generalization of the dark channel prior for single image restoration. IEEE Trans. Image Process. **27**(6), 2856–2868 (2018)
43. Peng, Y.T., Cosman, P.C.: Underwater image restoration based on image blurriness and light absorption. IEEE Trans. Image Process. **26**(4), 1579–1594 (2017)
44. Pizer, S.M., Johnston, R.E., Ericksen, J.P., Yankaskas, B.C., Muller, K.E.: Contrast-limited adaptive histogram equalization: speed and effectiveness. In: Proceedings of the First Conference on Visualization in Biomedical Computing, pp. 337–345 (1990)
45. Prakash, M., Krull, A., Jug, F.: Divnoising: diversity denoising with fully convolutional variational autoencoders. arXiv preprint arXiv:2006.06072 (2020)
46. Qi, Q., et al.: Underwater image co-enhancement with correlation feature matching and joint learning. IEEE Trans. Circuits Syst. Video Technol. **32**(3), 1133–1147 (2021)
47. Rahman, Z.u., Jobson, D.J., Woodell, G.A.: Multi-scale retinex for color image enhancement. In: Proceedings of 3rd IEEE International Conference on Image Processing, vol. 3, pp. 1003–1006. IEEE (1996)
48. Rezende, D.J., Mohamed, S., Wierstra, D.: Stochastic backpropagation and approximate inference in deep generative models. In: Proceedings of the International Conference on Machine Learning (ICML), pp. 1278–1286 (2014)
49. Ronneberger, O., Fischer, P., Brox, T.: U-net: convolutional networks for biomedical image segmentation. In: Proceedings of the International Conference on Medical Image Computing and Computer-Assisted Intervention (MICCAI), pp. 234–241 (2015)
50. Sharma, G., Wu, W., Dalal, E.N.: The ciede2000 color-difference formula: implementation notes, supplementary test data, and mathematical observations. Color Res. Appl. **30**(1), 21–30 (2005)
51. Sohn, K., Lee, H., Yan, X.: Learning structured output representation using deep conditional generative models. Adv. Neural Inf. Process. Syst. (NeurIPS) **28**, 3483–3491 (2015)
52. Tan, Q., Gao, L., Lai, Y.K., Xia, S.: Variational autoencoders for deforming 3d mesh models. In: Proceedings of the IEEE Conference on Computer Vision and Pattern Recognition (CVPR), pp. 5841–5850 (2018)

53. Uplavikar, P.M., Wu, Z., Wang, Z.: All-in-one underwater image enhancement using domain-adversarial learning. In: CVPR Workshops, pp. 1–8 (2019)
54. Wang, Z., Bovik, A.C., Sheikh, H.R., Simoncelli, E.P.: Image quality assessment: from error visibility to structural similarity. IEEE Trans. Image Process. **13**(4), 600–612 (2004)
55. Xue, X., Hao, Z., Ma, L., Wang, Y., Liu, R.: Joint luminance and chrominance learning for underwater image enhancement. IEEE Signal Process. Lett. **28**, 818–822 (2021)
56. Liu, Y.C., Chan, W.H., Chen, Y.Q.: Automatic white balance for digital still camera. IEEE Trans. Consum. Electron. **41**(3), 460–466 (1995)
57. Yan, X., et al.: MT-VAE: learning motion transformations to generate multimodal human dynamics. In: Proceedings of the European Conference on Computer Vision (ECCV), pp. 265–281 (2018)
58. Yang, H.H., Huang, K.C., Chen, W.T.: Laffnet: a lightweight adaptive feature fusion network for underwater image enhancement. In: 2021 IEEE International Conference on Robotics and Automation (ICRA), pp. 685–692. IEEE (2021)
59. Yang, M., Hu, J., Li, C., Rohde, G., Du, Y., Hu, K.: An in-depth survey of underwater image enhancement and restoration. IEEE Access **7**, 123638–123657 (2019)
60. Zhang, J., et al.: UC-net: Uncertainty inspired RGB-D saliency detection via conditional variational autoencoders. In: Proceedings of the IEEE Conference on Computer Vision and Pattern Recognition (CVPR), pp. 8582–8591 (2020)

Hourglass Attention Network for Image Inpainting

Ye Deng[1], Siqi Hui[1], Rongye Meng[1], Sanping Zhou[1,2], and Jinjun Wang[1(✉)]

[1] Xi'an Jiaotong University, Xi'an, China
{dengye,huisiqi}@stu.xjtu.edu.cn, spzhou@xjtu.edu.cn,
jinjun@mail.xjtu.edu.cn
[2] Shunan Academy of Artificial Intelligence, Ningbo, China

Abstract. Benefiting from the powerful ability of convolutional neural networks (CNNs) to learn semantic information and texture patterns of images, learning-based image inpainting methods have made noticeable breakthroughs over the years. However, certain inherent defects (e.g. local prior, spatially sharing parameters) of CNNs limit their performance when encountering broken images mixed with invalid information. Compared to convolution, attention has a lower inductive bias, and the output is highly correlated with the input, making it more suitable for processing images with various breakage. Inspired by this, in this paper we propose a novel attention-based network (transformer), called hourglass attention network (HAN) for image inpainting, which builds an hourglass-shaped attention structure to generate appropriate features for complemented images. In addition, we design a novel attention called Laplace attention, which introduces a Laplace distance prior for the vanilla multi-head attention, allowing the feature matching process to consider not only the similarity of features themselves, but also distance between features. With the synergy of hourglass attention structure and Laplace attention, our HAN is able to make full use of hierarchical features to mine effective information for broken images. Experiments on several benchmark datasets demonstrate superior performance by our proposed approach. The code can be found at github.com/dengyecode/hourglassattention.

Keywords: Image inpainting · Attention · Transformer

1 Introduction

Image inpainting [3] is the process of filling missing areas of an image with reasonable content. It can support many applications such as removing objects, restoring old photos, image editing, etc. For image inpainting, it is most critical

Supplementary Information The online version contains supplementary material available at https://doi.org/10.1007/978-3-031-19797-0_28.

to be able to give plausible content to fill the target region based on the observed region and make the whole image consistent.

Traditional exemplar-based methods [1,2,21,26] usually match and copy background patches into missing areas or by propagating information from boundaries around the missing regions. These methods are quite effective for images with only a small portion of breakage or repeated patterns, while they often fail to generate reasonable results for images with large broken regions or complex structures due to the lack of higher-level semantic understanding of the image.

In recent years, benefiting from the advantages of convolution neural networks (CNNs) for representation learning, learning-based approaches [22,28,39, 58] have made noticeable breakthroughs. Nonetheless, CNNs have some limitations in complementing broken images. Firstly, each filter of CNNs spatially shares convolution kernel parameters when dealing with the broken input. For a single image with both broken and normal areas, each vanilla convolution operator allocates identical kernels for both valid, invalid as well as mixed (e.g. the ones located on broken border) features (pixels), which easily leads to structural distortions, texture blurring and artifacts, especially when the patterns are complex or the damaged regions are vast [30,59]. Secondly, CNNs that operate only within a local window are inefficient at modeling the long-range structure of an image, while in the processing of image inpainting, proper information within the entire image, sometimes far away from the corrupted regions, needs to be utilized for corrupted regions.

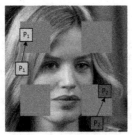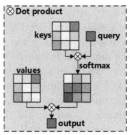

(a) Exemplar-based inpainting   (b) Attention mechanism

Fig. 1. Illustration of the connection between exemplar-based methods and attention mechanisms. Exemplar-based methods often try to find the appropriate content for broken regions in visible regions based on certain prior, while the result of the attention is obtained by weighting the "value" based on the similarity between the "query" and the "key". Thus we can consider the attention mechanism as a special exemplar-base method, where the "key-value" pairs play the role of exemplar.

To relieve the above limitation, we propose to learn an Hourglass Attention Network (HAN) for image inpainting, which builds an hourglass-shaped attention structure based on the powerful texture pattern learning capability of CNNs to mine the contextual information in the hierarchical features to generate appropriate feature maps for the reconstructed images. Compared to convolution, the attention module has a lower inductive bias and is able to generate different weights depending on the miscellaneous input, thus making it more suitable and flexible for images with multiple breakages in the inpainting tasks. Besides, there is a close connection between the attention based and the exemplar-based methods in terms of borrowing information from within the image. Specifically, exemplar-based approaches try to find the most plausible content to fill the target (unknown) areas based on the observed region of the image. As for the (dot-product) attention, the result is based on the relationship between the "query" and the "key-value" pairs, and we can consider the "key-value" as a special kind of exemplar, as shown in Fig. 1.

Our Hourglass Attention Network (HAN) consists of three parts, including a CNN encoder, a CNN decoder, and the hourglass attention structure. Particularly, the encoder is a stack of multiple convolution layers. It can be considered as a learnable feature extractor, which is responsible for the input images into the feature maps. The decoder, on the other hand, is similar in structure to the encoder and corresponds to the task of decoding the feature map into output images. As for the hourglass attention structure, it consists of attention blocks designed for feature sequences of different patch sizes stacked in a certain order, based on the property that a feature map can be divided into sequences of different patch sizes. To be specific, we divide the hourglass attention structure into two parts, the feature encoding and the feature decoding. In the feature encoding part, we employ the attention blocks from small to large according to the patch size, while in the feature decoding part we place the blocks from large to small. Therefore, the feature map resolution (number of patches) decreases gradually in the feature encoding phase and increases gradually in the feature decoding phase, which is similar to autoencoder or U-net [44]. Furthermore, since the dot-product attention is performed without considering the effect of the influence of features located in different locations. In contrast, early work on image restoration [8] emphasizes the impact of location. Therefore, we propose the Laplace attention, which introduces a new distance prior in the calculation of similarity and represents the effect of spatial location in the form of a Laplace distribution.

In summary, in this paper our contributions are summarized as follows:

- We propose a novel attention-based network (or transformer), called Hourglass Attention Network (HAN) for image inpainting, which combines the respective advantages of attention module and convolution to complete the image features.
- Our proposed hourglass result not only improves the quality of the inpainting image by using hierarchical feature information, but also reduces the computational complexity compared to the vanilla transformer structure.
- We propose Laplace attention, which considers not only the features themselves but also the effect of the distance between features located at different

locations when calculating the attention scores. The effect is also more efficient than the position encoding in transformer.

- Experiments on several datasets show that our proposed approach is effective and performs favorably against state of the art inpainting approaches.

2 Related Work

2.1 Image Inpainting

A variety of different approaches have been proposed for image inpainting, and in general these methods can be divided into the following two categories, namely traditional exemplar-based image inpainting methods and learning-based inpainting methods.

Traditional exemplar-based approaches [1–3,7,10] usually match and copy background patches into missing areas or by propagating information from boundaries around the missing regions. They perform pretty well on small holes or background inpainting tasks. Nonetheless, due to the low ability to obtain high-level semantic information, they cannot effectively complement images that have complex patterns or generate novel objects that are not present in the observed part.

Learning-based image inpainting approaches usually formulate inpainting as a conditional image generation problem based on CE (Context Encoders) [39], which is the first to introduce a generative adversarial network [14] framework in image inpainting fields and to use an autoencoder as its conditional image generator. Iizuka *et al.* [22] improve the quality of CE by designing a local-global discriminator. Then some researchers [32,46,50,55,58,62] propose a kind of contextual attention module to alleviate the deficiencies of CNNs in capturing long-range dependencies. Next for the problem of spatially sharing parameters, some researchers [30,51,53,54,59] modify convolution operation to adapt the difference between the damaged areas and non-damaged areas in images to obtain more accurate features comparing vanilla convolution. Due to the sparsity of the effective information caused by the broken image, some researchers have tried to guide generation of the missing content through other information of the image, such as edges [37], structure [16,27,31,43]. Finally, to extend the applicability of image inpainting, some researchers have started to focus on high-resolution large-area broken image inpainting [57,63,65], as well as diverse image inpainting [33,40,49,64,66].

2.2 Attention

The attention mechanism can be viewed as a way to bias the allocation of available computational resources towards the most informative components of a signal [20]. The transformer [48] constructed with attention as a cornerstone was firstly proposed for machine translation and has subsequently been proven

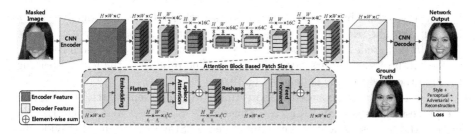

Fig. 2. Pipeline Overview. Our model consists of three parts including a CNN encoder, a CNN decoder, and an hourglass attention structure. The encoder is responsible for extracting features from the input image, and the decoder is used to render the features into an image. The hourglass attention structure is created by stacking designed attention blocks in an hourglass shape, which exploits the powerful long-range modeling capability of attention to fully mine the contextual information in hierarchical features.

successful in various down-stream natural language processing tasks. Carion *et al.* [5] started to introduce the transformer to the field of vision, and a series of transformer-based backbone networks [4,6,11,29,34,47,52] for high-level vision tasks were proposed. Moreover, because attention can model dense correlations between input elements well, some models have begun to explore transformer-based models for applications in low-level vision [56,61]. However, existing visual transformers often do not focus specifically on the effects of distance between features. Motivated by recent progress in self-attention approaches [15,18,25,42] for language modeling, we propose Laplace attention that remedies this deficiency.

3   Approach

The process of image inpainting is to predict the intact version (ground truth) I_g of a given corrupted image I_m by filling in the missing pixels. The overview of the proposed Hourglass Attention Network (HAN) is shown in Fig. 2. HAN contains a CNN encoder, CNN decoder, and the most critical hourglass attention structure. We will describe them in detail below.

3.1   Hourglass Attention Structure

Our hourglass attention structure is composed of tailored attention block based on feature patches of different sizes. The design of this attention block we refer to the encoder block in the vanilla transformer [48] and contains two sublayers. The first is a proposed Laplace attention layer, and the second is a simple feed-forward network (FFN). In addition, we adopt a residual connection [17] adhering to each of the sub-layers. Our hourglass attention structure consists of two processes, followed by feature encoding and feature decoding. In the process of feature encoding, we adopt a gradual reduction strategy to control the number of feature patches, and in the process of decoding, we adopt a gradual increase strategy.

Specifically, after the broken image is passed through the encoder, we get a feature map $F \in \mathbb{R}^{H \times W \times C}$. In the process of feature encoding, first we divide F into HW patches, each of size $1 \times 1 \times C$. Then we feed this patch sequence to the sub-layers of the first attention block. The process of the feature passing through the first module is denoted as "Stage E_1".

The procedure is repeated 3 more times with different patch sizes during the process of feature encoding, as "Stage E_2", "Stage E_3" and "Stage E_4". In brief in the process of feature encoding, in each "Stage E_i" we firstly divide the input feature map $F \in \mathbb{R}^{H \times W \times C}$ into $\frac{HW}{s_i^2}$ patches, and each of size $s_i \times s_i \times C$ (where $s_i = 1, 2, 4, 8$ in order). Then we feed these feature patches into the subsequent sub-layers of the attention block and output a new feature map with the same size as F. And as the network gets deeper, the number of patches will gradually decrease and the size of patches will gradually increase, which shares some similarities with T2T-ViT [60], PVT [52] and Swin [34]. In addition, the number of patches (spatial resolution) decreases progressively and the dimension of patches (number of channels) increases progressively, which is similar to the classical convolutional network design, such as VGG [45], Resnet [17].

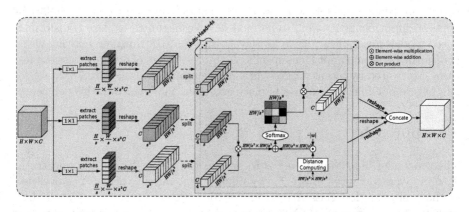

Fig. 3. Details of the proposed Laplace attention. Our proposed laplace prior adds a distance prior to the vanilla multi-head attention to capture the effects of distances located between different spatial locations. "Distance Computing" in the figure means calculating the taxicab geometry between feature patches.

As for the feature decoding process, it can be basically regarded as the inverse process of feature encoding. In each stage of feature decoding, we also divide the input feature $F \in \mathbb{R}^{H \times W \times C}$ into $\frac{HW}{s_i^2}$ patches, with size $s_i \times s_i \times C$ (where $s_i = 8, 4, 2, 1$ in order). Then similar to the feature encoding, these patches are feed to sub-layer of the attention block and obtain the corresponding feature map. The feature decoding process consists of four stages, in the order of "Stage D_4", "Stage D_3", "Stage D_2", and "Stage D_1". And as the network goes deeper, the number of patches (spatial resolution) increases and the dimension of patch (number of channels) decreases similar to classical generative networks, such as

DCGAN [41]. These proposed stages are arranged in our inpainting network as "Stage E_1, E_2, E_3, E_4, D_4, D_3, D_2, D_1", which jointly form a symmetric hourglass structure that generates a hierarchical feature representation as a classical autoencoder. They leverage the features information at multiple scales to fully exploit the contextual formation of the input and generate suitable features for the broken ares.

In summary, the hourglass attention structure allows our model to utilize multi-scale information, which not only allows our model to improve performance but also reduces computational complexity, as shown in Table 2 and Table 4.

3.2 Laplace Attention

Our Laplace attention can be regarded as a multi-head self-attention [48] with the special Laplace prior. Suppose that the patch size of the "Stage" where an attention located is s. First we embed a feature map $F \in \mathbb{R}^{H \times W \times C}$ into a query feature $Q \in \mathbb{R}^{H \times W \times C}$, a key feature $K \in \mathbb{R}^{H \times W \times C}$ and a value feature $V \in \mathbb{R}^{H \times W \times C}$ by different linear layers. Then we extract patches of shape $d = s \times s \times C$ from the query Q and we can get $l = H/s \times W/s$ patches. Next we flatten and reshape these patches into column vectors, and then merge the vectors into a matrix $Q \in \mathbb{R}^{d \times l}$, i.e. l d-dimensional patch sequences. Similar operations are performed for key K, value Q to obtain the corresponding $K \in \mathbb{R}^{d \times l}$, $V \in \mathbb{R}^{d \times l}$. Moreover, inspired by the language model [15,18,25,42], we introduce a Laplace prior on the similarity distribution (the softmax output in attention) to reflect the effect of distance in attention. Specifically, suppose the spatial coordinates c_i, c_j of patches q_i, k_j are (x_i, y_i), (x_j, y_j). For each q_i we introduce a two-dimensional spatial "isotropic" Laplace distribution $p_i(c) \sim \text{Laplace}(c \mid \mu_i, I)$ (where $\mu_i = (x_i, y_i)^\top$, and I is an identity matrix) as prior for the attention score (the value obtained after softmax). As shown in the Fig. 3, the attention output $o_i \in \mathbb{R}^d$ for i-th query patch $q_i \in \mathbb{R}^d$ in Q can be defined by:

$$
o_i = \text{Attention}\left(q_i, \{k_j\}_{j=1}^l, \{v_j\}_{j=1}^l\right)
$$

$$
= \sum_{j=1}^l \frac{p_i(c_j) \exp(q_i^\top k_j)}{\sum_{n=1}^l p_i(c_n) \exp(q_i^\top k_n)} v_j
$$

$$
= \sum_{j=1}^l \frac{\exp(-t_{ij}) \exp(q_i^\top k_j)}{\sum_{n=1}^l \exp(-t_{in}) \exp(q_i^\top k_n)} v_j \tag{1}
$$

$$
= \sum_{j=1}^l \text{softmax}_j(q_i^\top k_j - t_{ij}) v_j
$$

$$
\approx \sum_{j=1}^l \text{softmax}_j(q_i^\top k_j - |w| t_{ij}) v_j
$$

where $k_j \in \mathbb{R}^d$ is j-th key patch in K and $v_j \in \mathbb{R}^d$ is corresponding j-th value patch in V, $1 \leq i, j \leq l$, $t_{ij} = |x_i - x_j| + |y_i - y_j|$ and $|w|$ means a learnable parameter greater than 0. Since the variance of the Laplace distribution $p_i(c)$ will not always be I in real situations, we use $|w|$ to represent the variance here to enhance the flexibility of the model. Therefore, the incorporation of the taxicab geometry (l_1-distance) between the patches can also be seen as the Laplace prior when calculating the similarity.

Furthermore, revisiting the process of extracting patches from the feature $Q \in \mathbb{R}^{H \times W \times C}$, when we choose patches of larger size s, the dimension $d = s \times s \times c$ of the patch is also larger, and the length $l = H/s \times W/s$ of the patch sequences is smaller, so the size of the attention matrix $l \times l$ is smaller. Therefore, to alleviate parameter redundancy, we perform $4s$-heads attention in parallel, as:

$$O = \text{Concate}\left(\text{Head}_1, \ldots, \text{Head}_{4s}\right) \tag{2}$$

where $O \in \mathbb{R}^{H \times W \times C}$ and

$$\text{Head}_i = \text{Attention}\left(Q_i, K_i, V_i\right)$$

where $Q_i \in \mathbb{R}^{\frac{sC}{4} \times \frac{HW}{s^2}}$, $K_i \in \mathbb{R}^{\frac{sC}{4} \times \frac{HW}{s^2}}$, $V_i \in \mathbb{R}^{\frac{sC}{4} \times \frac{HW}{s^2}}$ are matrix stacked by the vectors $q_i \in \mathbb{R}^{\frac{sC}{4}}$, $k_i \in \mathbb{R}^{\frac{sC}{4}}$, $v_i \in \mathbb{R}^{\frac{sC}{4}}$, respectively.

In summary, with the help of multi-head and the distance prior, the Laplace attention, can effectively borrow relevant features from different regions, which better models the long range dependencies inside feature maps.

3.3 Loss Functions

The loss function L_{all} for training our HAN consists of four terms, containing the L_1 loss, the perceptual loss [23], the style loss [12] and the adversarial loss [14], as:

$$L_{\text{all}} = \alpha L_{\text{re}} + \beta L_{\text{perc}} + \gamma L_{\text{style}} + \lambda L_{\text{adv}} \tag{3}$$

where α, β, γ, and λ hyper-parameters. In our experimental procedure, we set $\alpha = 1$, $\beta = 1$, $\gamma = 250$, and $\lambda = 0.1$.

L_1 **Loss.** The L_1 loss refers to the value of the L_1-norm of the difference between the complementary images I_{out} and the real image I_g, :

$$L_{\text{re}} = \|I_{out} - I_g\|_1 \tag{4}$$

Perceptual Loss. The perceptual loss measures the feature map between the real image I_g and the output I_{out}, as:

$$L_{\text{perc}} = \mathbb{E}\left[\sum_i \frac{1}{N_i} \|\phi_i\left(I_{out}\right) - \phi_i\left(I_g\right)\|_1\right] \tag{5}$$

where ϕ_i is the feature map of the i-th layer of pre-trained VGG-19 [45]. And ϕ_i contains activation Relu1_1 [13], Relu2_1, Relu3_1, Relu4_1, and Relu_51 of the VGG-19.

Table 1. Numerical comparisons on the several datasets. The ↓ indicates lower is better, while ↑ indicates higher is better

DataSet		Paris street view				Celeba-HQ				Places2			
Mask ratio		10–20%	20–30%	30–40%	40–50%	10–20%	20–30%	30–40%	40–50%	10–20%	20–30%	30–40%	40–50%
FID↓	GC	20.68	39.48	58.66	82.51	2.54	4.49	6.54	9.83	18.91	30.97	45.26	61.16
	RFR	20.33	28.93	39.84	49.96	3.17	4.01	4.89	6.11	17.88	22.94	30.68	38.69
	DSN	16.28	29.39	42.02	53.66	1.91	3.18	4.70	6.20	13.64	22.74	31.97	41.14
	DTS	16.66	31.94	47.30	65.44	2.08	3.86	6.06	8.58	15.72	27.88	42.44	57.78
	Ours	**12.39**	**22.70**	**35.29**	**46.93**	**1.49**	**2.58**	**3.93**	**5.39**	**12.01**	**20.15**	**28.85**	**37.63**
PSNR↑	GC	32.28	29.12	26.93	24.80	32.25	29.10	26.71	24.78	28.55	25.22	22.97	21.24
	RFR	30.18	27.76	25.99	24.25	30.93	28.94	27.11	25.47	27.26	24.83	22.75	21.11
	DSN	31.06	28.05	25.92	24.05	32.72	29.53	27.15	25.34	28.39	25.03	22.69	20.97
	DTS	32.69	29.28	26.89	24.97	32.91	29.51	27.02	25.13	28.91	25.36	22.94	21.21
	Ours	**32.97**	**29.92**	**27.60**	**25.67**	**33.04**	**29.94**	**27.53**	**25.62**	**28.93**	**25.44**	**23.06**	**21.38**
SSIM↑	GC	0.960	0.925	0.872	0.800	0.979	0.959	0.931	0.896	0.944	0.891	0.824	0.742
	RFR	0.943	0.908	0.861	0.799	0.970	0.958	0.939	0.913	0.929	0.891	0.830	0.756
	DSN	0.952	0.914	0.859	0.791	0.981	0.963	0.939	0.910	0.946	0.894	0.827	0.749
	DTS	0.963	0.929	0.875	0.812	0.981	0.962	0.937	0.905	0.952	0.901	0.834	0.755
	Ours	**0.966**	**0.936**	**0.891**	**0.834**	**0.983**	**0.967**	**0.945**	**0.918**	**0.957**	**0.903**	**0.839**	**0.762**

Style Loss. The style loss is similar to perceptual loss, as:

$$L_{\text{style}} = \mathbb{E}_j \left[\left\| G_j^{\Phi}\left(\boldsymbol{I}_{out}\right) - G_j^{\Phi}\left(\boldsymbol{I}_g\right) \right\|_1 \right] \tag{6}$$

where G_j^{Φ} is a $C_j \times C_j$ Gram matrix formed by the corresponding feature maps ϕ_j. Here, ϕ_j contains the same layers as the ϕ_j in perceptual loss.

Adversarial Loss The adversarial loss is defined by:

$$L_{\text{adv}} = \mathbb{E}_{\boldsymbol{I}_g} \left[\log D\left(\boldsymbol{I}_g\right) \right] + \mathbb{E}_{\boldsymbol{I}_{out}} \log\left[1 - D\left(\boldsymbol{I}_{out}\right) \right] \tag{7}$$

where D is the a PatchGAN discriminator with spectral normalization [36].

4 Experiments

We evaluated our HAN on three public datasets, including Paris street view (Paris) [39], CelebA-HQ [24] and Places2 [67]. For data splitting, in CelebA-HQ we chose the first 2000 images as the test set and the rest as the training set. As for Paris and Places2, we used their original data splitting. The resolution of all images during experiment was resized to 256×256. In addition, we used the classical mask dataset [30] to determine the location of image breakage during the test.

Our proposed HAN was implemented based on Pytorch [38]. In the training process we used a RTX3090 (24 GB) and set the batch size to 6. We used an AdamW [35] optimizer with $\beta_1 = 0.5$, $\beta_2 = 0.9$ to train the model. At the start, a learning rate of 10^{-4} was used to train the model and then we used 10^{-5} for fine-tuning the model. Specifically, on CelebA-HQ and Paris, we trained 600,000 iterations and then fine-tuned 150,000 iterations. On the Places2 data set, we trained about 1.2 million iterations and then fine-tuned 400,000 iterations.

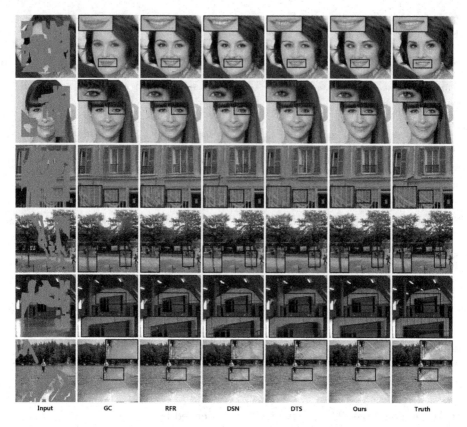

Fig. 4. Qualitative results with GC [59], RFR [28], DSN [51], DTS [16] and our models. The images in each of the two rows from top to the bottom are taken from CelebA-HQ, Paris street view, Places2 respectively. (Best viewed with zoom-in)

4.1 Baselines

We compare with the following baselines for their state-of-the-art performance:

- GC [59]: a two-stage inpainting model, which leverages the gated convolution and the contextual attention [58].
- RFR [28]: a recurrent inpainting model with a sepcial contextual attention which recurrently infers the hole and progressively strengthens the result.
- DSN [51]: an U-net inpainting model, which expands the receptive field of convolution based on deformable convolution [9] to skip those broken features and thus learns more valid information.
- DTS [16]: a dual U-net inpainting model, which recovers corrupted images by simultaneous modeling structure-constrained texture synthesis and texture-guided structure reconstruction.

4.2   Quantitative Comparison

We chose FID (Fréchet Inception Distance) [19], PSNR (peak signal-to-noise ratio), and SSIM (structural similarity index) to evaluate our model. SSIM and PSNR measure the similarity of pixels and structural information from paired images. SSIM and PSNR are widely used for image evaluation and measure the similarity of pixels and structural information from paired images to provide an appropriate approximation to human visual perception. Nonetheless, sometimes the results of inpainting are diverse from original images for the target areas (e.g. object removal described in [59]), while these metrics are limited to comparing with the original image content. Therefore we also adopted FID to indicate the perceptual quality of the results as generally adopted metric in image generation. As seen from Table 1, our proposed model achieves superior results compared with other baselines in almost all metrics. Meanwhile, favorable performance is achieved in our proposed method of filling irregular holes with various hole versus image ratios. It is worth noting that the advantage of our model tends to be more pronounced when the percentage of breakage is larger compared to other methods, which demonstrates the stronger adaptability of our proposed method to inputs mixed with invalid information with the addition of the hourglass attention structure.

Fig. 5. Fail results from Places2 with GC [59], RFR [28], DSN [51], DTS [16] and our models. when a large portion of the image got corrupted, our method is not able to obtain sufficient long term dependency information to assist reconstruction, and hence only the small handset wire part got restored. (Best viewed with zoom-in)

4.3   Qualitative Comparisons

Figure 4 shows qualitative results with previous state-of-art baselines to ours. GC [59] can get pretty credible results, but there is still some blurring on the completed images. The images predicted by RFR [28] are quite good in terms of detail texture, but the downside is that some artifacts appear on the generated images. The results generated by DSN [51] show fewer artifacts compared to RFR but are still not particularly desirable. The image produced by DTS [16] basically has no obvious artifacts, but when it recovers an image with complex patterns, the content filled is often not consistent with the original image, e.g., double eyelid on the left but single eyelid on the right in the second row of the Fig. 4. In contrast, our method generally does not bring significant artifacts when completing the image, and learns to represent structures and textures in a consistent formation. Note the last row of Fig. 4, when part of the stick can

Table 2. Ablation study on impact of the hourglass structure. The ↓ indicates lower is better, while ↑ indicates higher is better

Mask ratio	FID↓				PSNR↑				SSIM↑			
	10–20%	20–30%	30–40%	40–50%	10–20%	20–30%	30–40%	40–50%	10–20%	20–30%	30–40%	40–50%
W/ reverse	12.93	23.84	36.63	48.56	32.45	29.65	27.43	25.39	0.963	0.933	0.886	0.828
W/o hourglass	13.13	24.42	36.18	49.33	32.53	29.59	27.38	25.37	0.963	0.933	0.887	0.829
Ours	**12.39**	**22.70**	**35.29**	**46.93**	**32.97**	**29.92**	**27.60**	**25.67**	**0.966**	**0.936**	**0.891**	**0.834**

Table 3. Ablation study about the layer number of the hourglass attention. The ↓ indicates lower is better, while ↑ indicates higher is better

Mask ratio	FID↓				PSNR↑				SSIM↑			
	10–20%	20–30%	30–40%	40–50%	10–20%	20–30%	30–40%	40–50%	10–20%	20–30%	30–40%	40–50%
+0	16.08	32.22	48.27	68.21	31.66	28.63	26.07	23.87	0.956	0.918	0.854	0.771
+1	13.33	24.75	37.84	51.31	32.62	29.59	27.20	25.17	0.963	0.931	0.882	0.819
+2	13.09	23.69	36.55	49.71	32.73	29.71	27.43	25.26	0.964	0.933	0.886	0.824
+3	12.99	23.12	35.51	47.18	32.75	29.82	27.55	25.37	0.964	0.934	0.890	0.827
+4(ours)	**12.39**	**22.70**	**35.29**	**46.93**	**32.97**	**29.92**	**27.60**	**25.67**	**0.966**	**0.936**	**0.891**	**0.834**

be observed, our reconstructed portion shows a well connected stick structure, which also show the effectiveness by our method when non-local information can be modeled. In addition we show cases of failure of each model, as shown in Fig. 5. More qualitative comparisons are shown in the supplementary material.

5   Ablation Study

We explore the impact of our proposed module on the Paris dataset.

5.1   Effectiveness of Hourglass Attention Structure

Here we validate the role of the proposed hourglass attention structure, and the results are shown in Tables 2 and 3 respectively. In Table 2, we design two other attention structures to compare with our hourglass structure, including the standard structure (similar to the vanilla transformer, with patch size of the attention module all set to $s = 1$, i.e. without hourglass structure) and the spindle structure (i.e., reversing the order of the attention blocks in hourglass structure, as "Stage E_4, E_3, E_2, E_1, D_1, D_2, D_3, D_4", denoted by "reverse"). As we can see, compared to the standard structure, our hourglass structure utilizes multi-scale hierarchical feature information more helpful for image inpainting. Additionally, the hourglass structure from smallest to largest during encoding and largest to smallest during decoding is also more reasonable than the spindle structure with reversed order.

Further, we performed a series of experiments to demonstrate the effectiveness of hierarchical attention, as shown in Table 3. In the Table 3, S_0 represents no inclusion attention module, S_1 represents inclusion only "Stage E_1, D_1", then

S_2 represents inclusion "Stage E_1, E_2, D_2, D_1", and so on. We find that stacking more hierarchical attention can bring continuous improvements.

Finally, we show the advantage of the hourglass structure in terms of complexity and compare it with other baseline models, as shown in Table 4, where "MHA" represents the multi-headed attention (i.e., the vanilla transformer) without the hourglass structure. For a feature $F \in \mathbb{R}^{H \times W \times C}$, the complexity of attention can be simplified to $\mathcal{O}(CH^2W^2/s^2)$, where s is the size of the patch. It can be seen that due to the presence of the hourglass dividing the patches of larger size ($s = 1$ in the vanilla transformer), our hourglass structure improves the performance and reduces the complexity at the same time. In addition, it can be seen from the table that our inpainting model is able to maintain fewer model parameters and moderate computational effort while achieving a performance lead compared to other baseline models.

Table 4. Model complexity. Here we provide the FLoating-point OPerations (FLOPs) and parameters (Params) of the model

Model	GC	RFR	DSN	DTS	MHA	Ours
FlOPs	103.1G	206.1G	24.8G	75.9G	183.6G	137.7G
Params	16.0M	30.6M	99.3M	52.1M	19.4M	19.4M

Table 5. Ablation study on impact of the distance prior. The ↓ indicates lower is better, while ↑ indicates higher is better

Mask ratio	FID↓				PSNR↑				SSIM↑			
	10–20%	20–30%	30–40%	40–50%	10–20%	20–30%	30–40%	40–50%	10–20%	20–30%	30–40%	40–50%
W/Gus	12.94	23.50	35.38	48.26	32.90	29.81	27.52	25.59	0.965	0.934	0.889	0.831
W/Sin	13.06	23.55	36.39	48.17	32.79	29.76	27.52	25.52	0.964	0.934	0.889	0.832
W/o Lap	13.45	24.57	36.49	48.67	32.50	29.56	27.34	25.42	0.962	0.931	0.885	0.827
Ours	12.39	22.70	35.29	46.93	32.97	29.92	27.60	25.67	0.966	0.936	0.891	0.834

5.2   Effectiveness of Distance Prior

In our model we introduce a two-dimensional Laplace prior to represent the effect of the distance between feature patches located in different regions. On the other hand, many visual transformers [5,52] tend to represent this influence using an extension of the one-dimensional position encoding (of the vanilla transformer [48]) to two dimensions. Here we replace our proposed distance prior with a 2D position encoding (implemented by trigonometric functions, denoted "Tri") and the results show that the position encoding is less effective than the proposed distance prior, as shown in Table 5. Furthermore, we also compare the case of replacing the Laplace prior with a Gaussian prior (i.e. replacing the l_1-distance with a square of l_2-distance, denoted by "Gus"), removing the distance prior (denoted by "no"), and removing the variance coefficient $|w|$. From the Table 5, it can be seen that the Laplace prior, which makes the attention score decrease more slowly, is more suitable for image completion than the Gaussian prior. This may show that for inpainting, with features farther away from the target can still provide certain valid information for the target. Besides the variance coefficient $|w|$ makes the model more robust.

6 Conclusion

In this paper, we propose to learn the hourglass attention network (HAN) for image mapping, which builds an hourglass attention structure based on the powerful texture pattern learning capability of CNNs to mine the contextual information in hierarchical features to synthesize appropriate contents for the complemented images. Besides, we introduce a new distance prior to the attention mechanism, making the attention to consider not only the similarity of the features themselves, but also the influence of distance between the features. Quantitative and qualitative results show that our model is capable of generating more coherent and fine-detailed results.

Limitation. Similar to other learning-based inpainting models [16,28,51,59], it is still difficult for our HAN to handle images that have complex patterns suffering from extreme large breakage ratios.

Broader Impact. The proposed method will reflect the biases of the datasets they are trained on and may generate inexistent content. If deployed without careful consideration, inpainting methods (including but not limited to HAN) trained on research datasets like Celeba-HQ and Places2 may bring negative affect by propagating biases in the dataset. These issues warrant further research and consideration when building upon this work.

Acknowledgments. This work is jointly supported by the National Key Research and Development Program of China under Grant No. 2017YFA0700800, the General Program of China Postdoctoral Science Foundation under Grant No. 2020M683490, and the Youth program of Shaanxi Natural Science Foundation under Grant No. 2021JQ-054.

References

1. Ballester, C., Bertalmio, M., Caselles, V., Sapiro, G., Verdera, J.: Filling-in by joint interpolation of vector fields and gray levels. IEEE Trans. Image Process. **10**(8), 1200–1211 (2001). https://doi.org/10.1109/83.935036
2. Barnes, C., Shechtman, E., Finkelstein, A., Goldman, D.B.: PatchMatch: a randomized correspondence algorithm for structural image editing. ACM Trans. Graph. (Proc. SIGGRAPH) **28**(3), 24 (2009)

3. Bertalmio, M., Sapiro, G., Caselles, V., Ballester, C.: Image inpainting. In: Proceedings of the 27th Annual Conference on Computer Graphics and Interactive Techniques, SIGGRAPH 2000, pp. 417–424. ACM Press/Addison-Wesley Publishing Co., USA (2000). https://doi.org/10.1145/344779.344972

4. Cao, H., et al.: Swin-unet: Unet-like pure transformer for medical image segmentation. arXiv preprint arXiv:2105.05537 (2021)

5. Carion, N., Massa, F., Synnaeve, G., Usunier, N., Kirillov, A., Zagoruyko, S.: End-to-end object detection with transformers. In: Vedaldi, A., Bischof, H., Brox, T., Frahm, J.M. (eds.) Computer Vision, pp. 213–229. Springer International Publishing, Cham (2020)

6. Chen, J., et al.: TransUNet: transformers make strong encoders for medical image segmentation. arXiv preprint arXiv:2102.04306 (2021)

7. Criminisi, A., Pérez, P., Toyama, K.: Region filling and object removal by exemplar-based image inpainting. IEEE Trans. Image Process. **13**(9), 1200–1212 (2004)

8. Dabov, K., Foi, A., Katkovnik, V., Egiazarian, K.: Image denoising by sparse 3-d transform-domain collaborative filtering. IEEE Trans. Image Process. **16**(8), 2080–2095 (2007). https://doi.org/10.1109/TIP.2007.901238

9. Dai, J., et al.: Deformable convolutional networks. In: Proceedings of the IEEE International Conference on Computer Vision (ICCV), October 2017

10. Ding, D., Ram, S., Rodríguez, J.J.: Image inpainting using nonlocal texture matching and nonlinear filtering. IEEE Trans. Image Process. **28**(4), 1705–1719 (2019). https://doi.org/10.1109/TIP.2018.2880681

11. Dosovitskiy, A., et al.: An image is worth 16 x 16 words: transformers for image recognition at scale. In: International Conference on Learning Representations (2021)

12. Gatys, L.A., Ecker, A.S., Bethge, M.: Image style transfer using convolutional neural networks. In: Proceedings of the IEEE Conference on Computer Vision and Pattern Recognition (CVPR), June 2016

13. Glorot, X., Bordes, A., Bengio, Y.: Deep sparse rectifier neural networks. In: Gordon, G., Dunson, D., Dudík, M. (eds.) Proceedings of the Fourteenth International Conference on Artificial Intelligence and Statistics. Proceedings of Machine Learning Research, vol. 15, pp. 315–323. PMLR, Fort Lauderdale, FL, USA, 11–13 April 2011

14. Goodfellow, I., et al.: Generative adversarial nets. In: Ghahramani, Z., Welling, M., Cortes, C., Lawrence, N., Weinberger, K.Q. (eds.) Advances in Neural Information Processing Systems, vol. 27. Curran Associates, Inc. (2014)

15. Guo, M., Zhang, Y., Liu, T.: Gaussian transformer: a lightweight approach for natural language inference. In: Proceedings of the AAAI Conference on Artificial Intelligence, vol. 33, no. 01, pp. 6489–6496 (2019)

16. Guo, X., Yang, H., Huang, D.: Image inpainting via conditional texture and structure dual generation. In: Proceedings of the IEEE/CVF International Conference on Computer Vision (ICCV), pp. 14134–14143, October 2021

17. He, K., Zhang, X., Ren, S., Sun, J.: Deep residual learning for image recognition. In: Proceedings of the IEEE Conference on Computer Vision and Pattern Recognition (CVPR), June 2016

18. He, P., Liu, X., Gao, J., Chen, W.: {DEBERTA}: {DECODING}-{enhanced} {bert} {with} {disentangled} {attention}. In: International Conference on Learning Representations (2021)

19. Heusel, M., Ramsauer, H., Unterthiner, T., Nessler, B., Hochreiter, S.: GANs trained by a two time-scale update rule converge to a local Nash equilibrium. In: Guyon, I., et al. (eds.) Advances in Neural Information Processing Systems. vol. 30. Curran Associates, Inc. (2017)
20. Hu, J., Shen, L., Sun, G.: Squeeze-and-excitation networks. In: Proceedings of the IEEE Conference on Computer Vision and Pattern Recognition (CVPR), June 2018
21. Huang, J.B., Kang, S.B., Ahuja, N., Kopf, J.: Image completion using planar structure guidance. ACM Trans. Graph. (TOG) **33**(4), 1–10 (2014)
22. Iizuka, S., Simo-Serra, E., Ishikawa, H.: Globally and locally consistent image completion. ACM Trans. Graph. (Proc. of SIGGRAPH 2017) **36**(4), 107:1–107:14 (2017)
23. Johnson, J., Alahi, A., Fei-Fei, L.: Perceptual losses for real-time style transfer and super-resolution. In: Leibe, B., Matas, J., Sebe, N., Welling, M. (eds.) ECCV 2016. LNCS, vol. 9906, pp. 694–711. Springer, Cham (2016). https://doi.org/10.1007/978-3-319-46475-6_43
24. Karras, T., Aila, T., Laine, S., Lehtinen, J.: Progressive growing of GANs for improved quality, stability, and variation. In: International Conference on Learning Representations (2018). https://openreview.net/forum?id=Hk99zCeAb
25. Ke, G., He, D., Liu, T.Y.: Rethinking positional encoding in language pre-training. In: International Conference on Learning Representations (2021)
26. Komodakis, N., Tziritas, G.: Image completion using efficient belief propagation via priority scheduling and dynamic pruning. IEEE Trans. Image Process. **16**(11), 2649–2661 (2007). https://doi.org/10.1109/TIP.2007.906269
27. Li, J., He, F., Zhang, L., Du, B., Tao, D.: Progressive reconstruction of visual structure for image inpainting. In: Proceedings of the IEEE/CVF International Conference on Computer Vision (ICCV), October 2019
28. Li, J., Wang, N., Zhang, L., Du, B., Tao, D.: Recurrent feature reasoning for image inpainting. In: IEEE/CVF Conference on Computer Vision and Pattern Recognition (CVPR), June 2020
29. Li, Y., Zhang, K., Cao, J., Timofte, R., Van Gool, L.: LocalViT: bringing locality to vision transformers. arXiv preprint arXiv:2104.05707 (2021)
30. Liu, G., Reda, F.A., Shih, K.J., Wang, T.C., Tao, A., Catanzaro, B.: Image inpainting for irregular holes using partial convolutions. In: Proceedings of the European Conference on Computer Vision (ECCV), September 2018
31. Liu, H., Jiang, B., Song, Y., Huang, W., Yang, C.: Rethinking image inpainting via a mutual encoder-decoder with feature equalizations. In: Vedaldi, A., Bischof, H., Brox, T., Frahm, J.-M. (eds.) ECCV 2020. LNCS, vol. 12347, pp. 725–741. Springer, Cham (2020). https://doi.org/10.1007/978-3-030-58536-5_43
32. Liu, H., Jiang, B., Xiao, Y., Yang, C.: Coherent semantic attention for image inpainting. In: Proceedings of the IEEE/CVF International Conference on Computer Vision (ICCV), October 2019
33. Liu, H., Wan, Z., Huang, W., Song, Y., Han, X., Liao, J.: PD-GAN: Probabilistic diverse GAN for image inpainting. In: Proceedings of the IEEE/CVF Conference on Computer Vision and Pattern Recognition (CVPR), pp. 9371–9381, June 2021
34. Liu, Z., et al.: Swin transformer: Hierarchical vision transformer using shifted windows. In: Proceedings of the IEEE/CVF International Conference on Computer Vision (ICCV), pp. 10012–10022, October 2021
35. Loshchilov, I., Hutter, F.: Decoupled weight decay regularization. In: International Conference on Learning Representations (2019). https://openreview.net/forum?id=Bkg6RiCqY7

36. Miyato, T., Kataoka, T., Koyama, M., Yoshida, Y.: Spectral normalization for generative adversarial networks. In: International Conference on Learning Representations (2018). https://openreview.net/forum?id=B1QRgziT-
37. Nazeri, K., Ng, E., Joseph, T., Qureshi, F., Ebrahimi, M.: EdgeConnect: structure guided image inpainting using edge prediction. In: The IEEE International Conference on Computer Vision (ICCV) Workshops, October 2019
38. Paszke, A., et al.: PyTorch: an imperative style, high-performance deep learning library. In: Wallach, H., Larochelle, H., Beygelzimer, A., d' Alché-Buc, F., Fox, E., Garnett, R. (eds.) Advances in Neural Information Processing Systems. vol. 32. Curran Associates, Inc. (2019)
39. Pathak, D., Krahenbuhl, P., Donahue, J., Darrell, T., Efros, A.A.: Context encoders: Feature learning by inpainting. In: Proceedings of the IEEE Conference on Computer Vision and Pattern Recognition (CVPR), June 2016
40. Peng, J., Liu, D., Xu, S., Li, H.: Generating diverse structure for image inpainting with hierarchical VQ-VAE. In: Proceedings of the IEEE/CVF Conference on Computer Vision and Pattern Recognition (CVPR), pp. 10775–10784, June 2021
41. Radford, A., Metz, L., Chintala, S.: Unsupervised representation learning with deep convolutional generative adversarial networks. In: Bengio, Y., LeCun, Y. (eds.) 4th International Conference on Learning Representations, ICLR 2016, San Juan, Puerto Rico, 2–4 May 2016, Conference Track Proceedings (2016)
42. Raffel, C., et al.: Exploring the limits of transfer learning with a unified text-to-text transformer. J. Mach. Learn. Res. 21(140), 1–67 (2020)
43. Ren, Y., Yu, X., Zhang, R., Li, T.H., Liu, S., Li, G.: StructureFlow: image inpainting via structure-aware appearance flow. In: Proceedings of the IEEE/CVF International Conference on Computer Vision (ICCV), October 2019
44. Ronneberger, O., Fischer, P., Brox, T.: U-net: convolutional networks for biomedical image segmentation. In: Navab, N., Hornegger, J., Wells, W.M., Frangi, A.F. (eds.) MICCAI 2015. LNCS, vol. 9351, pp. 234–241. Springer, Cham (2015). https://doi.org/10.1007/978-3-319-24574-4_28
45. Simonyan, K., Zisserman, A.: Very deep convolutional networks for large-scale image recognition. In: Bengio, Y., LeCun, Y. (eds.) 3rd International Conference on Learning Representations, ICLR 2015, San Diego, CA, USA, 7–9 May 2015, Conference Track Proceedings (2015)
46. Song, Y., et al.: Contextual-based image inpainting: Infer, match, and translate. In: Proceedings of the European Conference on Computer Vision (ECCV), September 2018
47. Vaswani, A., Ramachandran, P., Srinivas, A., Parmar, N., Hechtman, B., Shlens, J.: Scaling local self-attention for parameter efficient visual backbones. In: Proceedings of the IEEE/CVF Conference on Computer Vision and Pattern Recognition (CVPR), pp. 12894–12904, June 2021
48. Vaswani, A., et al.: Attention is all you need. In: Guyon, I., Luxburg, U.V., et al. (eds.) Advances in Neural Information Processing Systems, vol. 30. Curran Associates, Inc. (2017)
49. Wan, Z., Zhang, J., Chen, D., Liao, J.: High-fidelity pluralistic image completion with transformers. In: Proceedings of the IEEE/CVF International Conference on Computer Vision (ICCV), pp. 4692–4701, October 2021
50. Wang, N., Li, J., Zhang, L., Du, B.: Musical: multi-scale image contextual attention learning for inpainting. In: Proceedings of the Twenty-Eighth International Joint Conference on Artificial Intelligence, IJCAI-19, pp. 3748–3754. International Joint Conferences on Artificial Intelligence Organization, July 2019. https://doi.org/10.24963/ijcai.2019/520

51. Wang, N., Zhang, Y., Zhang, L.: Dynamic selection network for image inpainting. IEEE Trans. Image Process. **30**, 1784–1798 (2021). https://doi.org/10.1109/TIP.2020.3048629
52. Wang, W., et al.: Pyramid vision transformer: a versatile backbone for dense prediction without convolutions. In: Proceedings of the IEEE/CVF International Conference on Computer Vision (ICCV), pp. 568–578, October 2021
53. Wang, Y., Chen, Y.-C., Tao, X., Jia, J.: VCNet: a robust approach to blind image inpainting. In: Vedaldi, A., Bischof, H., Brox, T., Frahm, J.-M. (eds.) ECCV 2020. LNCS, vol. 12370, pp. 752–768. Springer, Cham (2020). https://doi.org/10.1007/978-3-030-58595-2_45
54. Xie, C., et al.: Image inpainting with learnable bidirectional attention maps. In: Proceedings of the IEEE/CVF International Conference on Computer Vision (ICCV), October 2019
55. Yan, Z., Li, X., Li, M., Zuo, W., Shan, S.: Shift-net: image inpainting via deep feature rearrangement. In: Proceedings of the European Conference on Computer Vision (ECCV), September 2018
56. Yang, F., Yang, H., Fu, J., Lu, H., Guo, B.: Learning texture transformer network for image super-resolution. In: IEEE/CVF Conference on Computer Vision and Pattern Recognition (CVPR), June 2020
57. Yi, Z., Tang, Q., Azizi, S., Jang, D., Xu, Z.: Contextual residual aggregation for ultra high-resolution image inpainting. In: IEEE/CVF Conference on Computer Vision and Pattern Recognition (CVPR), June 2020
58. Yu, J., Lin, Z., Yang, J., Shen, X., Lu, X., Huang, T.S.: Generative image inpainting with contextual attention. In: Proceedings of the IEEE Conference on Computer Vision and Pattern Recognition (CVPR), June 2018
59. Yu, J., Lin, Z., Yang, J., Shen, X., Lu, X., Huang, T.S.: Free-form image inpainting with gated convolution. In: Proceedings of the IEEE/CVF International Conference on Computer Vision (ICCV), October 2019
60. Yuan, L., et al.: Tokens-to-Token ViT: training vision transformers from scratch on ImageNet. In: Proceedings of the IEEE/CVF International Conference on Computer Vision (ICCV), pp. 558–567, October 2021
61. Zeng, Y., Fu, J., Chao, H.: Learning joint spatial-temporal transformations for video inpainting. In: Vedaldi, A., Bischof, H., Brox, T., Frahm, J.-M. (eds.) ECCV 2020. LNCS, vol. 12361, pp. 528–543. Springer, Cham (2020). https://doi.org/10.1007/978-3-030-58517-4_31
62. Zeng, Y., Fu, J., Chao, H., Guo, B.: Learning pyramid-context encoder network for high-quality image inpainting. In: Proceedings of the IEEE/CVF Conference on Computer Vision and Pattern Recognition (CVPR), June 2019
63. Zeng, Yu., Lin, Z., Yang, J., Zhang, J., Shechtman, E., Lu, H.: High-resolution image inpainting with iterative confidence feedback and guided upsampling. In: Vedaldi, A., Bischof, H., Brox, T., Frahm, J.-M. (eds.) ECCV 2020. LNCS, vol. 12364, pp. 1–17. Springer, Cham (2020). https://doi.org/10.1007/978-3-030-58529-7_1
64. Zhao, L., et al.: UCTGAN: diverse image inpainting based on unsupervised cross-space translation. In: IEEE/CVF Conference on Computer Vision and Pattern Recognition (CVPR), June 2020
65. Zhao, S., et al.: Large scale image completion via co-modulated generative adversarial networks. In: International Conference on Learning Representations (2021)

66. Zheng, C., Cham, T.J., Cai, J.: Pluralistic image completion. In: Proceedings of the IEEE/CVF Conference on Computer Vision and Pattern Recognition (CVPR), June 2019
67. Zhou, B., Lapedriza, A., Khosla, A., Oliva, A., Torralba, A.: Places: a 10 million image database for scene recognition. IEEE Trans. Pattern Anal. Mach. Intell. **40**(6), 1452–1464 (2018). https://doi.org/10.1109/TPAMI.2017.2723009

Unfolded Deep Kernel Estimation for Blind Image Super-Resolution

Hongyi Zheng[1], Hongwei Yong[1], and Lei Zhang[1,2(✉)]

[1] The Hong Kong Polytechnic University, Hong Kong, People's Republic of China
{cshzheng,cshyong,cslzhang}@comp.polyu.edu.hk
[2] OPPO Research, Shenzhen, People's Republic of China

Abstract. Blind image super-resolution (BISR) aims to reconstruct a high-resolution image from its low-resolution counterpart degraded by unknown blur kernel and noise. Many deep neural network based methods have been proposed to tackle this challenging problem without considering the image degradation model. However, they largely rely on the training sets and often fail to handle images with unseen blur kernels during inference. Deep unfolding methods have also been proposed to perform BISR by utilizing the degradation model. Nonetheless, the existing deep unfolding methods cannot explicitly solve the data term of the unfolding objective function, limiting their capability in blur kernel estimation. In this work, we propose a novel unfolded deep kernel estimation (UDKE) method, which, for the first time to our best knowledge, explicitly solves the data term with high efficiency. The UDKE based BISR method can jointly learn image and kernel priors in an end-to-end manner, and it can effectively exploit the information in both training data and image degradation model. Experiments on benchmark datasets and real-world data demonstrate that the proposed UDKE method could well predict complex unseen non-Gaussian blur kernels in inference, achieving significantly better BISR performance than state-of-the-art. The source code of UDKE is available at https://github.com/natezhenghy/UDKE.

Keywords: Blind image super-resolution · Blur kernel estimation · Unfolding method

1 Introduction

Blind image super-resolution (BISR), which aims to reconstruct a high-resolution (HR) image from its low-resolution (LR) counterpart without knowing the degradation kernel and noise, is a very challenging computer vision problem [33]. The degradation process from an HR image to an LR image can be expressed as:

This work is supported by the Hong Kong RGC RIF grant (R5001-18) and the PolyU-OPPO Joint Innovation Lab.

Supplementary Information The online version contains supplementary material available at https://doi.org/10.1007/978-3-031-19797-0_29.

$$\mathbf{Y} = (\mathbf{K} \circledast \mathbf{X}) \downarrow_s + \mathbf{n} \tag{1}$$

where $\mathbf{X}$ is the HR image, $\mathbf{Y}$ is its observed LR counterpart, $\mathbf{K}$ is the blur kernel, $\circledast$ is the 2D convolution operator, $\downarrow_s$ is the downsampling operator with scaling factor s, and $\mathbf{n}$ is the additive white Gaussian noise.

A variety of classical methods have been proposed to tackle the BISR problem [14,22,26]. The interpolation-based methods, such as bilinear and bicubic interpolation, are efficient to implement, whereas they have poor results for BISR. Model based methods employ a degradation model (e.g., Eq. 1) to constrain the fidelity between the predicted SR image and the LR input, and exploit image priors to regularize the solution. Some representative methods include Maximum a Posterior [9], recurrence prior [12], etc. Learning based methods aim to learn image priors and mappings between the LR input and HR image from the training data, e.g., dictionary learning [30] and patch based learning [4].

With the rapid development of deep learning, the deep neural network (DNN) based methods have become prevalent in the research of super-resolution (SR) and shown highly competitive performance [11]. However, most of the existing DNN based methods focus on the non-blind SR tasks, where the degradation process is simply assumed to be bicubic downsampling [38], or direct downsampling after blurred by fixed isotropic Gaussian kernels [37]. In real-world applications, however, the image degradation process is much more complex due to the unknown varying blur kernels and the corrupted noise, and these non-blind SR methods often fail. Therefore, DNN based BISR methods have been later proposed. Zhou et al. [40] analyzed blur kernels in real LR images by using the dark channel priors [23], and built a BISR blur kernel dataset. The KGAN (Kernel-GAN) [5] employs a generative adversarial network (GAN), which is trained online during the inference stage, to estimate the blur kernel with some presumed priors, e.g., Gaussian prior. However, these methods rely heavily on training data and they do not consider the LR image degradation process. They often fail to handle images degraded with unseen kernels during inference.

To address the limitations of the above purely data-driven methods, some deep unfolding methods have been proposed to encode the degradation model into the learning process. With the input LR image $\mathbf{Y}$, the objective function of deep unfolding methods can be generally depicted as:

$$\min_{\{\mathbf{K},\mathbf{X}\}} \tfrac{1}{2\sigma^2} \|(\mathbf{K} \circledast \mathbf{X}) \downarrow_s - \mathbf{Y}\|_2^2 + \lambda_{\mathbf{X}} \psi(\mathbf{X}) + \lambda_{\mathbf{K}} \phi(\mathbf{K}) \tag{2}$$

where ψ and ϕ represent the priors on $\mathbf{X}$ and $\mathbf{K}$, $\lambda_{\mathbf{X}}$ and $\lambda_{\mathbf{K}}$ are the balance parameters, and σ is the noise level. Equation 2 can be divided into two components, namely data term ($\|(\mathbf{K} \circledast \mathbf{X}) \downarrow_s - \mathbf{Y}\|_2^2$) and prior term ($\lambda_{\mathbf{X}} \psi(\mathbf{X}) + \lambda_{\mathbf{K}} \phi(\mathbf{K})$). Typical deep unfolding methods include IKC [13] and DAN [20], which employ an iterative framework to unfold Eq. 2 and perform BISR. Nevertheless, the data term is difficult to solve under the deep learning framework, and these methods do not solve the data term explicitly in kernel estimation, which limits their BISR performance (please refer to Sect. 3.1 for more discussions).

In this work, we propose a novel unfolded deep kernel estimation method, namely UDKE, by explicitly solving the data term under the deep learning framework. Based on UDKE, we implement a BISR framework, which, to our best knowledge, is the first deep unfolding framework that fully unfolds the objective function in Eq. 2. UDKE effectively and efficiently encodes the knowledge of the image degradation model into the DNN architecture and learns priors of images and blur kernels jointly in an end-to-end manner. By explicitly solving the objective function of BISR with learned priors during inference, it can efficiently estimate the unseen complex non-Gaussian blur kernels, surpassing existing kernel estimation methods by a large margin.

We extensively evaluate the proposed UDKE based BISR framework on multiple BISR benchmarks as well as real-world data. It records new state-of-the-art BISR performance, while costs only 1% the inference time of leading online-learning based methods (*e.g.*, DIP-FKP [17]).

2   Related Work

Traditional BISR Methods. Traditional BISR methods can be categorized into model-based methods [14,19,22,26,29] and learning based methods [4,10]. The former adopts an image degradation model and image priors to estimate the desired HR image. He *et al.* [14] proposed a soft Maximum a Posteriori based method to alternatively perform blur kernel estimation and HR image reconstruction. Michaeli *et al.* [22] proposed a non-parametric BISR model that exploits the inherent recurrence property of image patches. Shao *et al.* [26] employed the convolution consistency prior to estimate the blur kernel. These methods follow the constraints of the degradation model and have good interpretability; however, their BISR performance is usually limited because of the relatively weak handcrafted priors.

Equipped with a training dataset, learning based methods aim to learn from it more effective image priors and/or LR-to-HR image mappings. Begin *et al.* [4] designed a framework to estimate camera parameters from the LR image, and estimate the HR image. Corduneanu *et al.* [10] proposed a spatial-variant BISR method, which learns a set of linear blur filters from the neighboring pixels. Liu *et al.* [19] developed a sparse representation based method for BISR, which utilizes the image self-similarity prior to learn an over-complete dictionary to represent the HR image. These methods, by learning from external training data, exhibit better BISR performance than model-based methods; however, their performance will drop a lot when the degradation parameters (*e.g.*, blur kernel) of test data are much different from that of the training data.

Direct DNN Based BISR Methods. DNN based methods have become the mainstream of BISR research, outperforming the traditional learning-based methods by a large margin. Many DNN based BISR methods directly perform BISR without performing blur kernel estimation. CinCGAN [34] converts the LR image with unknown degradation into the bicubic degradation domain and then performs non-blind SR. Degradation GAN [8] learns the degradation process implicitly via a GAN to assist SR task. DASR [28] learns abstract representations of various degradations, and then adopts a DNN to perform the SR task. Kligler *et al.* [5] proposed the KGAN method, which trains a GAN on the LR image to estimate the blur kernel based on Gaussian prior and patch recurrence property. Liang *et al.* [17] enhanced KGAN with flow-based prior, which works well when the blur kernel follows Gaussian assumption. These methods do not consider the image degradation process and largely rely on the training dataset in model learning. Their performance would deteriorate when encounter unseen degradation parameters (*e.g.*, blur kernel) in inference.

Deep Unfolding BISR Methods. To address the limitations of direct DNN based BISR methods, a few deep unfolding BISR methods have been proposed. These methods share an iterative framework to unfold the objective function in Eq. 2. By alternatively estimating the blur kernel and the super-resolved image, they aim to utilize the image degradation model to assist the BISR task. The early deep unfolding methods [3,25] utilize the maximum a posterior framework to perform the image denoising task. Zhang *et al.* [35] proposed a deep unfolding framework for non-blind SR by using the Half Quadratic Splitting algorithm to unfold the objective function. For BISR, Gu *et al.* [13] proposed the IKC method, which adopts a DNN to iteratively correct the blur kernel estimation in an implicit dimension-reduced space. Luo *et al.* [20] proposed a DAN approach, which iteratively estimates the blur kernel and super-resolved image with the help of conditional residual block.

However, all the previous unfolding deep methods do not explicitly solve the data term in kernel estimation, thus they do not fully unfold the objective. This limits their capability to estimate complex unseen kernels, and they fail to address the limits of direct DNN based methods properly. Actually, their performance might be even worse than those direct DNN based methods when encounter unseen kernels during inference (*e.g.*, IKC and DAN only work on Gaussian kernels). We propose an effective and efficient kernel estimation method by explicitly solving the data term and hence truly unfolding the whole objective function under the deep learning framework. Our proposed method can estimate more complex unseen non-Gaussian blur kernels in inference.

3 Methodology

3.1 Problems of Previous Deep Unfolding BISR Methods

As described in Eq. 2, the objective function of deep unfolding methods can be divided into the data term ($\| (\mathbf{K} \circledast \mathbf{X}) \downarrow_s -\mathbf{Y}\|_2^2$) and the prior term ($\lambda_{\mathbf{X}} \psi(\mathbf{X}) + \lambda_{\mathbf{K}} \phi(\mathbf{K})$). According to [35], the data term enforces physical constraints on the image degradation process, and it should be solved explicitly to enable an unfolding method to estimate unseen (different from those in training) blur kernels during inference. However, all the previous deep unfolding methods [13,20] employ DNNs to estimate the blur kernel implicitly without solving the data term explicitly. Therefore, they do not fully unfold the objective function to utilize the information embedded in the image degradation model. As a result, most of these methods simply assume Gaussian blur kernels in BISR and they have limited generalization capability to more complex non-Gaussian kernels.

The major reason that the previous methods do not explicitly unfold the data term lies in that the available solutions, which are developed in traditional unfolding methods, are hard to be incorporated into the deep learning framework. In traditional methods, the data term can be solved by either numerical methods or analytical methods. The numerical methods such as the Alternating Direction Method of Multipliers [7] solve the data term iteratively. Such iterative methods work well in traditional unsupervised BISR methods; however, they are too time-consuming to use in deep learning framework, which requires training on a large amount of data. On the other hand, the analytical methods such as the Least Squares Method (LSM) [1] can provide an analytical solution of the data term. However, the image-to-column (im2col) operation required in LSM would increase the memory-overhead by thousands of times, which is not acceptable in deep learning framework. One way to waive the im2col operation is to transform the original problem into the frequency domain by the Fast Fourier Transform. Such methods have been used in the non-blind SR task [35], where the blur kernel is known. In BISR, however, the support set of the unknown blur kernels is much smaller than that of images, making the explicit solution in frequency domain hard to achieve.

In this work, we investigate deeply this challenging problem, and propose an effective yet efficient method to explicitly solve the data term with minimal memory overhead under the deep learning framework.

3.2   Unfolded Deep Kernel Estimation Based BISR Framework

The framework of our proposed unfolded deep kernel estimation (UDKE) based BISR method is shown in Fig. 1. Suppose we are given N training triplets $\{\mathbf{Y}_i, \mathbf{Y}_i^{gt}, \mathbf{K}_i^{gt}\}$, where $\mathbf{Y}_i$ is the ith observed LR image, and $\mathbf{Y}_i^{gt}$ and $\mathbf{K}_i^{gt}$ are the ground-truth HR image and ground-truth blur kernel, respectively. In order to accommodate the unfolding objective in Eq. 2 into an end-to-end training framework, we rewrite it into a bi-level optimization problem as follows:

$$\min_{\{\theta_\psi, \theta_\phi\}} \frac{1}{N} \sum_{i=1}^{N} L_\mathbf{X}(\mathbf{X}_i, \mathbf{Y}_i^{gt}) + \gamma L_\mathbf{K}(\mathbf{K}_i, \mathbf{K}_i^{gt}) \tag{3a}$$

$$\text{s.t. } \{\mathbf{K}_i, \mathbf{X}_i\} = \operatorname{argmin}_{\mathbf{K},\mathbf{X}} \frac{1}{2\sigma_i^2} \|(\mathbf{K} \circledast \mathbf{X}) \downarrow_s - \mathbf{Y}_i\|_2^2 + \lambda_\mathbf{K}\phi(\mathbf{K}) + \lambda_\mathbf{X}\psi(\mathbf{X}) \tag{3b}$$

where $\mathbf{X}_i$ and $\mathbf{K}_i$ are the predicted HR image and blur kernel; $L_\mathbf{X}(\cdot, \cdot)$ and $L_\mathbf{K}(\cdot, \cdot)$ are the loss functions, γ is a trade-off parameter; θ_ψ and θ_ϕ denote the parameters of deep priors (*i.e.*, DNNs) ψ and ϕ.

In the above bi-level optimization problem, Eq. 3a describes its backward pass, where the parameters (of DNNs) θ_ψ and θ_ϕ implicitly embed the deep priors and they are updated based on the losses $L_\mathbf{X}$ and $L_\mathbf{K}$. Equation 3b describes the forward pass of the framework, which takes the LR observation $\mathbf{Y}_i$ as input to estimate the blur kernel $\mathbf{K}_i$ and the HR image $\mathbf{X}_i$ with the learned deep priors. For the convenience of expression, we omit the subscript "i" in the following development. Equation 3b can be split into the following two sub-problems by the Half Quadratic Splitting (HQS) algorithm:

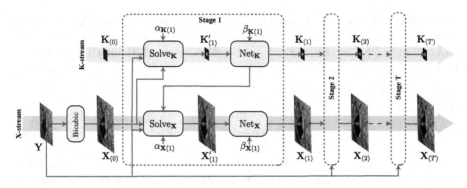

Fig. 1. The overall architecture of our UDKE based BISR framework.

$$\min_{\{\mathbf{X},\mathbf{X}'\}} \frac{1}{2\sigma^2} \|(\mathbf{K} \circledast \mathbf{X}') \downarrow_s -\mathbf{Y}\|_2^2 + \lambda_{\mathbf{X}}\psi(\mathbf{X}) + \frac{\mu_{\mathbf{X}}}{2}\|\mathbf{X} - \mathbf{X}'\|_2^2 \tag{4a}$$

$$\min_{\{\mathbf{K},\mathbf{K}'\}} \frac{1}{2\sigma^2} \|(\mathbf{K}' \circledast \mathbf{X}) \downarrow_s -\mathbf{Y}\|_2^2 + \lambda_{\mathbf{K}}\phi(\mathbf{K}) + \frac{\mu_{\mathbf{K}}}{2}\|\mathbf{K} - \mathbf{K}'\|_2^2 \tag{4b}$$

where $\mathbf{X}'$ and $\mathbf{K}'$ are auxiliary variables; $\mu_{\mathbf{X}}$ and $\mu_{\mathbf{K}}$ are penalty parameters.

Equations 4a and 4b can be solved iteratively. Particularly, in the t-th iteration we can solve the auxiliary variables $\mathbf{K}'_{(t)}$ and $\mathbf{X}'_{(t)}$ with analytical solutions, while the two mapping DNNs, denoted by $\text{Net}_{\mathbf{K}}$ and $\text{Net}_{\mathbf{X}}$, map the pre-priors $\mathbf{K}'_{(t)}$ and $\mathbf{X}'_{(t)}$ to post-priors $\mathbf{K}_{(t)}$ and $\mathbf{X}_{(t)}$ with the implicitly embedded priors:

$$\mathbf{K}'_{(t)} = \text{Solve}_{\mathbf{K}}(\mathbf{Y}, \mathbf{K}_{(t-1)}, \mathbf{X}_{(t-1)}, \alpha_{\mathbf{K}}) \tag{5a}$$
$$= \text{argmin}_{\mathbf{K}^\star} \tfrac{1}{2} \|(\mathbf{K}^\star \circledast \mathbf{X}_{(t-1)}) \downarrow_s -\mathbf{Y}\|_2^2 + \tfrac{\alpha_{\mathbf{K}}}{2}\|\mathbf{K}^\star - \mathbf{K}_{(t-1)}\|_2^2$$

$$\mathbf{K}_{(t)} = \text{Net}_{\mathbf{K}}(\mathbf{K}'_{(t)}, \beta_{\mathbf{K}}) = \text{argmin}_{\mathbf{K}^\star} \ \phi(\mathbf{K}^\star) + \tfrac{\beta_{\mathbf{K}}}{2}\|\mathbf{K}'_{(t)} - \mathbf{K}^\star\|_2^2 \tag{5b}$$

$$\mathbf{X}'_{(t)} = \text{Solve}_{\mathbf{X}}(\mathbf{Y}, \mathbf{K}_{(t)}, \mathbf{X}_{(t-1)}, \alpha_{\mathbf{X}}) \tag{5c}$$
$$= \text{argmin}_{\mathbf{X}^\star} \tfrac{1}{2} \|(\mathbf{K}_{(t)} \circledast \mathbf{X}^\star) \downarrow_s -\mathbf{Y}\|_2^2 + \tfrac{\alpha_{\mathbf{X}}}{2}\|\mathbf{X}^\star - \mathbf{X}_{(t-1)}\|_2^2$$

$$\mathbf{X}_{(t)} = \text{Net}_{\mathbf{X}}(\mathbf{X}'_{(t)}, \beta_{\mathbf{X}}) = \text{argmin}_{\mathbf{X}^\star} \ \psi(\mathbf{X}^\star) + \tfrac{\beta_{\mathbf{X}}}{2}\|\mathbf{X}'_{(t)} - \mathbf{X}^\star\|_2^2 \tag{5d}$$

where $\{\alpha_{\mathbf{K}}, \alpha_{\mathbf{X}}, , \beta_{\mathbf{K}}\beta_{\mathbf{X}}\} = \{\mu_{\mathbf{K}}\sigma^2, \mu_{\mathbf{X}}\sigma^2, \frac{\mu_{\mathbf{K}}}{\lambda_{\mathbf{K}}}, \frac{\mu_{\mathbf{X}}}{\lambda_{\mathbf{X}}}\}$.

The architecture of our UKDE based BISR framework is built from the unfolded equations Eqs. 5a–5d. It has two branches. The kernel estimation branch corresponds to Eqs. 5a–5b and is represented as the K-stream in Fig. 1, which will be discussed in Sect. 3.3. Equations 5c–5d super-resolve the HR image with the estimated kernel, and they are represented as the X-stream in Fig. 1, which will be discussed in Sect. 3.4.

3.3 K-stream: Unfolded Explicit Kernel Estimation

In this section, we elaborate in detail the proposed novel kernel estimation method, which corresponds to the K-stream in Fig. 1. The first step is to explicitly solve Eq. 5a (data term), which is represented as $\text{Solve}_{\mathbf{K}}$ in Fig. 1. It takes

$\mathbf{Y}$ and the estimations of $\mathbf{K}$ and $\mathbf{X}$ in previous stage as inputs, then explicitly solves Eq. 5a to update $\mathbf{K}'$. As the dimension of $\mathbf{K}$ is much lower than that of $\mathbf{X}$, this system is over-determined and can be solved by the LSM method [1]. Denote by $\boldsymbol{U}_a$ the im2col operator with block size a, and by $\boldsymbol{P}_{\frac{a-1}{2}}$ the circular padding operator with padding size of $\frac{a-1}{2}$. Let $\mathfrak{X} = U_k(\boldsymbol{P}_{\frac{a-1}{2}}(\mathbf{X}))$ and $\mathfrak{Y} = U_k(\mathbf{Y})$, then Eq. 5a can be written as:

$$\text{argmin}_{\mathbf{k}^\star} \ \tfrac{1}{2}\|\mathfrak{M}_s\mathfrak{X}\mathbf{k} - \mathfrak{Y}\|_2^2 + \tfrac{\alpha_\mathbf{K}}{2}\|\mathbf{k}^\star - \mathbf{k}\|_2^2 \tag{6}$$

where $\mathbf{k}^\star = \text{vec}(\mathbf{K}^\star)$, $\mathbf{k} = \text{vec}(\mathbf{K})$, $\text{vec}(\cdot)$ is the vectorization operator, and $\mathfrak{M}_s$ is the matrix representation of the downsampling operator $\downarrow_s$ with scale factor s.

By taking the derivative of Eq. 6 w.r.t. $\mathbf{k}^\star$ and letting the derivative be zero, we can obtain the closed-form solution of $\mathbf{K}'$ as follows:

$$\mathbf{K}' = \text{vec}^{-1}\{(\mathfrak{X}^T\mathfrak{M}_s^T\mathfrak{M}_s\mathfrak{X} + \alpha_\mathbf{K}\mathbf{I})^{-1}(\mathfrak{X}^T\mathfrak{M}_s^T\mathfrak{Y} + \alpha_\mathbf{K}\mathbf{k})\} \tag{7}$$

where $\text{vec}^{-1}(\cdot)$ reverses the vectorization operator $\text{vec}(\cdot)$. However, $\mathfrak{X}$ has a size of $C \times h \times w \times k \times k$, which is much larger than $\mathbf{X}$ of size $C \times h \times w$, where C, h, w, and k are channel number, height, width and blur kernel size of the super-resolved image. It is too memory-consuming to directly compute Eq. 7 in practice. In the rest of this section, we will elaborate the proposed memory-efficient solution to tackle this problem.

It can be seen that the size of $\mathfrak{X}^T\mathfrak{M}_s^T\mathfrak{M}_s\mathfrak{X}$ is $C \times k \times k \times k \times k$ and $k \ll h$, $k \ll w$. We propose an efficient solution to calculate $\mathfrak{X}^T\mathfrak{M}_s^T\mathfrak{M}_s\mathfrak{X}$ from $\mathbf{X}$ without storing $\mathfrak{X}$ or $\mathfrak{Y}$, reducing significantly the memory consumption. (Note that $\mathfrak{X}^T\mathfrak{M}_s^T\mathfrak{Y}$ can be regarded as a special case of $\mathfrak{X}^T\mathfrak{M}_s^T\mathfrak{M}_s\mathfrak{X}$, where $\mathfrak{Y} = \mathfrak{M}_s\mathfrak{X}$). Denote by $\boldsymbol{U}_k$ the im2col operator with block size k, and by $\boldsymbol{P}_{\frac{k-1}{2}}$ the circular padding operator with padding size $\frac{k-1}{2}$. The element at (x, y) in $\mathfrak{X}^T\mathfrak{M}_s^T\mathfrak{M}_s\mathfrak{X}$ can be calculated through dilated convolution between the xth and the yth im2col blocks in $\boldsymbol{U}_k \circ \boldsymbol{P}_{\frac{k-1}{2}}(\mathbf{X})$, where $\circ$ is the notation of function composition.

Unfortunately, calculating $h \times w$ elements in $\mathfrak{X}^T\mathfrak{M}_s^T\mathfrak{M}_s\mathfrak{X}$ requires $h \times w$ convolution operations, and each of them is based on a unique pair of kernel and feature maps, which is too time-consuming. Thus, we have to convert them into parallel operations to utilize the modern parallel computing library such as CUDA. This can be done by convolving $\boldsymbol{P}_{k-1}(\mathbf{X})$ with a series of dilated feature maps, each has a unique dilation pattern. Generally speaking, with the scale factor s, there are s^2 dilation patterns. We use 2-dimensional indices to arrange these dilated feature maps, denoted by $\hat{\mathbf{X}}^{(i,j)}$, by using the following rule:

$$\hat{\mathbf{X}}^{(i,j)} : \begin{cases} \hat{\mathbf{X}}^{(i,j)}_{(x,y)} = \mathbf{X}_{(x,y)} & x\%i = 0 \ \& \ y\%j = 0 \\ \hat{\mathbf{X}}^{(i,j)}_{(x,y)} = 0 & otherwise \end{cases} \tag{8}$$

where $\%$ is the modulo operator, $i = \{0, 1...s-1\}$ and $j = \{0, 1...s-1\}$. Convolution operations between $\boldsymbol{P}_{k-1}(\mathbf{X})$ and $\hat{\mathbf{X}}^{(i,j)}$ result in s^2 feature maps. Then we merge them into a single feature map, denoted by $\mathbf{F}$, with the help of a mapping function f. f and $\mathbf{F}$ are defined as follows:

$$f : (x,y) \rightarrow ((\lfloor \frac{k-1}{2} \rfloor - x)\%s, (\lfloor \frac{k-1}{2} \rfloor - y)\%s) \tag{9a}$$

$$\mathbf{F} : \mathbf{F}_{(x,y)} = (\hat{\mathbf{X}}^{f(x,y)} \circledast \mathbf{P}_{k-1}(\mathbf{X}))_{(x,y)} \tag{9b}$$

Equation 9 costs s^2 operations to solve, which is still time-consuming when s is large. With the help of pixel-shuffle operation, Eq. 9 can be further reduced into a constant number of operations as follows:

$$g : (x,y) \rightarrow x \times s + y \tag{10a}$$

$$\mathbf{F} = \mathbf{S}_s^{-1} \circ \mathbf{M}_{g \circ f \circ g^{-1}} \{ \mathbf{S}_s(\mathbf{X}) \circledast \mathbf{S}_s \circ \mathbf{P}_{k-1}(\mathbf{X}) \} \tag{10b}$$

where g is a mapping function, $\mathbf{S}_s$ and $\mathbf{S}_s^{-1}$ are the pixel shuffle/un-shuffle operations with scale factor s, and $\mathbf{M}$ reorders channels of a matrix according to mapping $g \circ f \circ g^{-1}$. The elements in the xth row of $\mathfrak{X}^T \mathfrak{M}_s^T \mathfrak{M}_s \mathfrak{X}$ will reside in the xth im2col block of $U_k(\mathbf{F})$. Finally, $\mathfrak{X}^T \mathfrak{M}_s^T \mathfrak{M}_s \mathfrak{X}$ can be computed as:

$$\mathfrak{X}^T \mathfrak{M}_s^T \mathfrak{M}_s \mathfrak{X} = \mathbf{R} \circ U_k(\mathbf{F}) \tag{11}$$

where $\mathbf{R}(\mathbf{A})$ flips each row of matrix $\mathbf{A}$.

The memory-efficient solution described in Eqs. 8–11 can reduce the memory consumption of solving blur kernels by a factor of $\frac{h \times w}{k \times k}$. For example, to super-resolve an image to 2K resolution (2048×1024) with $k = 11$, it can save over $17000\times$ memory overhead. The second step in the K-stream is to solve Eq. 5b to map pre-prior $\mathbf{K}'$ to post-prior $\mathbf{K}$, which is done by a DNN (Net$_\mathbf{K}$ in Fig. 1). The Net$_\mathbf{K}$ consists of 3 blocks, each of which is composed of two Convolutional (Conv) layers and one LeakyReLU layer. All Conv layers have 16 channels and all LeakyReLU layers have a negative slope of 0.01. A trailing ReLU layer is added to restrict the output estimation to be positive. The architecture graph is provided in the **Supplementary File**.

3.4 X-stream: Super-Resolved Image Estimation

The X-stream solves Eqs. 5c–5d to estimate the super-resolved image. Given the blur kernel estimated by UDKE, it reduces into a non-blind SR problem, which can be easily done in two steps. The first step takes $\mathbf{Y}$ and the estimations of $\mathbf{K}$ and $\mathbf{X}$ as inputs, then solves Eq. 5c to update $\mathbf{X}'$. According to [35], the closed-form solution of $\mathbf{X}'$ in Eq. 5c can be derived by the Fast Fourier Transform (FFT):

$$\mathbf{X}' = \frac{1}{\alpha_\mathbf{X}} \mathscr{F}^{-1} \{ \mathcal{Z} - \mathcal{K} \odot (\frac{(\bar{\mathcal{K}} \odot \mathcal{Z})}{\alpha_\mathbf{X} + (\bar{\mathcal{K}} \odot \mathcal{K})}) \} \tag{12}$$

where $\mathscr{F}(\cdot)$ and $\mathscr{F}^{-1}(\cdot)$ denote the 2D FFT and its inverse, $\mathcal{K} = \mathscr{F}(\mathbf{K})$, $\mathcal{X}^\star = \mathscr{F}(\mathbf{X}^\star)$, $\mathcal{Y} = \mathscr{F}(\mathbf{Y})$, $\mathcal{X} = \mathscr{F}(\mathbf{X})$, $\mathcal{Z} = \mathcal{K} \circ \mathcal{Y} + \alpha_\mathbf{X} \mathcal{X}$, $\bar{\mathcal{K}}$ is the complex conjugate of $\mathcal{K}$, $\odot$ and $\div$ are the 2D Hadamard product and division, respectively.

Algorithm 1: Overall unfolding process of our UDKE based BISR framework

---

Input   : LR image $\mathbf{Y}$, stages no. T, kernel size k, scale factor s, noise level σ
Output : Predicted HR image $\mathbf{X}^{pred}$, predicted blur kernel $\mathbf{K}^{pred}$
$\mathbf{X}_0 = \text{bic}_s(\mathbf{Y})$, $\mathbf{K}_0 = \frac{1}{k^2}$;
for $t = 1, ..., T$ **do**
$\quad \{\alpha_{\mathbf{X}(t)}, \alpha_{\mathbf{K}(t)}, \beta_{\mathbf{X}(t)}, \beta_{\mathbf{K}(t)}\} = \text{HyperNet}_{(t)}(s, \sigma)$;
$\quad \mathbf{K}'_{(t)} = \text{Solve}_{\mathbf{K}}(\mathbf{Y}, \mathbf{K}_{(t\text{-}1)}, \mathbf{X}_{(t\text{-}1)}, \alpha_{\mathbf{K}}(t))$;
$\quad \mathbf{K}_{(t)} = \text{Net}_{\mathbf{K}}(\mathbf{K}'_{(t)}, \beta_{\mathbf{K}(t)})$;
$\quad \mathbf{X}'_{(t)} = \text{Solve}_{\mathbf{X}}(\mathbf{Y}, \mathbf{K}_{(t)}, \mathbf{X}_{(t\text{-}1)}, \alpha_{\mathbf{X}(t)})$;
$\quad \mathbf{X}_{(t)} = \text{Net}_{\mathbf{X}}(\mathbf{X}'_{(t)}, \beta_{\mathbf{X}(t)})$;
$\mathbf{X}^{pred} = \mathbf{X}_T$;
$\mathbf{K}^{pred} = \mathbf{K}_T$;

The second step solves Eq. 5d and map pre-prior $\mathbf{X}'$ to post-prior $\mathbf{X}$. From the Bayesian perspective [35], this step can be exactly interpreted as a denoising problem and can be solved by a DNN $\text{Net}_{\mathbf{X}}$. For efficiency consideration, we adopt the U-Net [24] as the DNN following previous non-blind SR method [35]. $\text{Net}_{\mathbf{X}}$ consists of 7 blocks. The first 3 blocks downsample the feature maps through strided convolution, and the last 3 blocks upsample the feature maps by transposed convolution. Each block consists of 4 residual units, while each of them consists of 2 Conv layers with ReLU and a skip connection. The channel numbers of Conv layers in the first 4 blocks are 64, 128, 256, 512, respectively. The architecture graph is provided in the **Supplementary File**.

3.5   Summary of the Unfolding Process

The K-stream and X-stream work alternatively to estimate the blur kernel $\mathbf{K}$ and HR image $\mathbf{X}$ for T stages. The determination of T will be discussed in Sect. 4.1. In the first stage, the input $\mathbf{X}_0$ is initialized by $\text{bic}_s(\mathbf{Y})$, where bic_s is the bicubic upsampling operation with scale factor s, while all the elements of $\mathbf{K}_0$ are initialized to $\frac{1}{k^2}$. For each stage, a tiny 2-layer fully connected network, called HypaNet, which takes σ and s as inputs, is introduced to predict the hyperparameters. The architecture graph of HypaNet and is provided in the **Supplementary File**. Algorithm 1 depicts the overall unfolding process.

4   Experiments

4.1   Implementation Details

Training Data and Kernel Pool. Following previous BISR works [20,28,35], we use the DIV2K [2] and Flickr2K [18] datasets to train our UDKE based framework. The ground truth images $\mathbf{Y}^{gt}$ are obtained by randomly cropping patches of size 128×128 from the original images, and the LR images $\mathbf{Y}$ are obtained by randomly selecting kernels from the DEPD-training kernel pool [40]

Table 1. 2× BISR results (PSNR/SSIM). Best results are in red.

Datasets	Set5			BSD100			Urban100		
σ	0	2.55	7.65	0	2.55	7.65	0	2.55	7.65
Bicubic	26.56/.8196	26.53/.8111	25.87/.7569	24.95/.7071	24.79/.6402	24.49/.6402	22.18/.7032	22.07/.6895	21.86/.6327
RCAN	27.35/.8578	27.04/.8153	24.73/.6113	25.70/.7620	25.29/.7170	23.69/.5345	23.14/.7650	22.84/.7192	21.75/.5442
ZSSR	27.03/.8803	26.53/.8143	25.41/.5840	25.31/.7498	25.10/.7122	23.29/.5449	22.66/.7443	22.34/.7121	21.89/.5579
DASR	27.48/.8788	27.00/.8188	24.95/.6310	25.82/.7624	25.27/.7143	23.81/.5442	23.37/.7803	22.80/.7181	21.86/.5611
KGAN	25.70/.8448	24.56/.6748	19.50/.3765	24.02/.7540	22.67/.5776	18.56/.3149	21.85/.7575	21.14/.6007	18.02/.3706
KFKP	17.28/.5279	14.55/.2766	12.25/.1829	21.16/.6608	19.79/.4934	16.27/.2890	19.56/.6725	18.61/.5361	16.02/.3260
DFKP	27.42/.8795	26.16/.7633	21.44/.4464	25.60/.7968	24.79/.6925	19.99/.3687	22.91/.7860	22.63/.7155	19.76/.4414
IKC	27.02/.8807	26.36/.8095	24.81/.6199	25.42/.8029	25.26/.7141	23.75/.5412	23.28/.8030	22.86/.7168	21.79/.5539
DAN	27.40/.8705	27.01/.8163	24.93/.6277	25.70/.7620	25.29/.7179	23.79/.5438	23.14/.7647	22.84/.7201	21.79/.5500
Ours	30.50/.8964	30.11/.8786	28.93/.8416	27.68/.8282	27.29/.8017	26.46/.7516	25.51/.8341	25.19/.8138	24.57/.7748
UBound	34.65/.9424	33.01/.9145	31.07/.9004	30.02/.8840	29.11/.8754	27.94/.8433	28.01/.8468	27.45/.8371	25.87/.8210

Table 2. 4× BISR results (PSNR/SSIM). Best results are in red.

Datasets	Set5			BSD100			Urban100		
σ	0	2.55	7.65	0	2.55	7.65	0	2.55	7.65
Bicubic	23.05/.6844	22.93/.6782	22.70/.6335	22.60/.5680	22.58/.5622	22.35/.5231	19.70/.5524	19.69/.5452	19.56/.5043
RCAN	24.01/.7196	23.87/.7132	21.78/.4960	23.11/.5969	22.50/.5740	20.33/.4853	19.88/.5849	19.48/.5742	19.00/.4513
ZSSR	24.33/.7369	22.88/.6563	22.50/.5063	23.03/.6070	22.79/.5933	20.21/.5024	20.95/.6048	20.19/.5824	19.37/.4769
DASR	24.33/.7243	24.16/.7008	22.31/.5321	23.23/.6490	23.12/.6171	21.14/.5192	21.43/.6360	21.32/.6031	19.43/.4902
KGAN	22.65/.6613	22.03/.6325	17.4/3820	22.12/.6032	21.76/.5832	17.65/.3326	18.23/.6032	17.65/.4723	14.25/.3027
KFKP	15.32/.4859	14.21/.3332	12.75/.2199	18.23/.3765	17.65/.3321	15.64/.2818	17.64/.4083	17.53/.3125	15.13/.3022
DFKP	24.15/.7318	23.83/.6927	19.34/.4467	23.12/.6530	22.88/.6311	18.21/.3831	20.23/.6320	20.13/.5923	18.02/.3445
IKC	24.03/.7152	22.96/.6938	21.39/.5062	23.93/.6123	23.11/.6035	21.12/.4767	21.33/.6265	21.14/.6125	19.34/.4532
DAN	24.25/.7165	24.13/.6817	22.14/.5157	23.14/.6254	23.01/.5963	20.98/.4943	21.10/.6030	21.01/.5977	19.29/.4433
Ours	27.33/.8118	27.22/.8048	26.51/.7638	24.99/.6813	24.92/.6738	24.46/.6412	22.47/.6937	22.42/.6872	22.13/.6589
UBound	31.01/.8810	30.43/.8793	29.43/.8603	26.85/.7543	26.21/.7432	25.92/.7136	24.98/.7632	24.39/.7412	23.88/.6960

and applying the degradation model in Eq. 1. The DEPD kernel pool adopts dark channel priors [23] to analyze BISR kernels from real-world LR images captured by low-end camera phones. Specifically, the DEPD-training subset consists of 1,000 BISR kernels analyzed from photos captured by Blackberry Passport phone and Sony Xperia Z. The DEPD-evaluation subset consists of 300 BISR kernels analyzed from photos captured by iPhone 3GS.

Training Details. The L_1 loss is used as the loss function for each stage of UDKE. Following [39], the weight on the loss of the last stage is set as 1, and the weights on all the other stages are set as $\frac{1}{T-1}$. The Adam optimizer [16] is used for updating the parameters of Net$_\mathbf{K}$ and Net$_\mathbf{X}$. The batch size is 32. We train the network for 10^5 iterations. The learning rate starts from 10^{-4} and decays by a factor of 0.5 for every 2^4 iterations. In order to speed up and stabilize the training process, we first train a 1-stage model and reload its weights into the T-stage model for fine-tuning. All the T stages share the same parameters. The size k for BISR kernel is set to 11 and the scale factor s is set to $\{2, 3, 4\}$, following previous BISR methods [20, 28, 35]. For each scale factor, we train a model for all noise levels, which are set to $\{0, 2.55, 7.65\}$ as in [35].

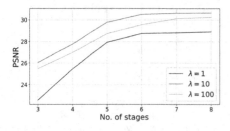

Fig. 2. Ablation study on λ and T.

Table 3. Kernel estimation results (PSNR). Best results are in red.

Scale	Datasets	Set5			BSD100			Urban100		
	σ	0	2.55	7.65	0	2.55	7.65	0	2.55	7.65
×2	KGAN	41.0	40.9	39.2	40.4	40.2	39.7	40.3	40.2	39.9
	KFKP	37.8	38.0	37.5	38.7	38.9	38.5	38.6	38.7	38.5
	DFKP	39.4	39.6	39.4	39.0	39.3	38.9	38.6	38.8	38.5
	Ours	51.0	49.7	48.9	49.3	47.2	47.3	48.8	47.7	47.0
×4	KGAN	40.1	39.1	37.1	39.0	38.2	37.2	38.7	37.1	36.9
	KFKP	37.7	37.2	36.8	37.3	36.4	36.1	37.0	36.0	35.8
	DFKP	39.1	38.4	37.7	37.8	37.8	37.1	37.1	36.8	36.2
	Ours	45.1	45.5	42.2	43.8	43.6	43.5	44.4	44.7	44.0

The Selection of λ and T. There are mainly two parameters to set in our method, the trade-off parameter λ and the no. of stages T. We perform ablation studies to select them. The ablation study is done on the Set5 [6] dataset with $s = 2$ and $\sigma = 0$. The PSNR results w.r.t. λ and T are illustrated in Fig. 2. It can be seen that the PSNR index increases with the increase of T, and the highest PSNR is achieved when $\lambda = 10$. However, the improvement becomes minor when $T = 6$. Hence, we set $\lambda = 10$ and $T = 6$ in all the following experiments.

4.2 Comparison with State-of-the-Arts

In this section, we compare the proposed UDKE based framework with state-of-the-art BISR methods. Three sets of experiments are conducted to comprehensively evaluate UDKE. First, we evaluate UDKE by using the DEPD-evaluation kernel pool, which is more complex than the widely used Gaussian kernels and more similar to the degradation in real-world images [40]. Second, we compare UDKE, which does not impose presumptions on blur kernels, with the methods that presume Gaussian blur kernels, by using just Gaussian kernels. Third, we evaluate UDKE on real-world images whose degradation kernels can be more complex than Gaussian kernels and those in the DEPD-evaluation kernel pool.

Experiments with DEPD-Evaluation Kernel Pool. Following prior works [17,20], the widely used Set5, BSD100 [21] and Urban100 [15] datasets are used in the experiments. Testing LR images are obtained by applying randomly selected BISR kernels from the DEPD-evaluation pool to HR images according to the degradation process described in Eq. 1. We compare our UDKE based framework with bicubic interpolation, SOTA non-blind SR method RCAN [38], SOTA direct DNN based BISR methods, including ZSSR [27], DASR [28], KGAN [5], DFKP (DIP-FKP) [17] and KFKP (KernelGAN-FKP) [17], and SOTA deep unfolding BISR methods, including IKC [13] and DAN [20]. Note that some methods (*e.g.*, KernelNet [32]) are inapplicable for comparison. This is because that their source code is not disclosed and we cannot reproduce them; and they reported performance on non-standard testing sets so that we cannot compare with the reported results either.

The experimental results of ×2 and ×4 BISR are shown in Tables 1–2, respectively. The experimental results of ×3 BISR are provided in the **Supplementary File**. We also provide an "upper bound" (UBound) of the BISR methods, which is obtained by feeding the ground truth kernel to the non-blind SISR method USRNet [35], yielding a non-blind "upper bound" as a reference for evaluating those blind BISR methods. Besides the PSNR/SSIM of the reconstructed image, for those BISR methods that estimate the blur kernels (*i.e.*, KGAN [5], DFKP [17], KFKP [17] and our UDKE), we also compute the PSNR of the estimated kernel (Kernel-PSNR), and list the results in Table 3.

It can be seen that UDKE based framework achieves the best PSNR, SSIM and Kernel-PSNR results under all experiment settings, significantly outperforming the competing methods. Both the direct DNN based methods (ZSSR, DASR, KGAN, KFKP, DFKP) and deep unfolding methods (IKC and DAN) do not surpass the non-blind method RCAN. This is mainly because these methods cannot encode effectively the information of the degradation process in their models, and hence they can not estimate the HR images with unseen degradation parameters during inference. In contrast, our proposed UDKE can estimate the degradation kernel very well (please see the Kernel-PSNR in Table 3) and consequently reproduce the original image with better quality. To further demonstrate the performance of UDKE, we also build several testing sets, each of them is built with a specific kernel from the DEPD-evaluation pool. The results are provided in the **Supplementary File** due to the limit of space.

Figure 3 visualizes the BISR results on an image by the competing methods. It can be seen that the image reconstructed by UDKE has the best visual quality with sharp edges and rich textures. Other methods generate blurry results as they fail to well estimate and exploit the BISR kernel information. KFKP, which enforces strong Gaussian priors on kernel estimation and employs unstable adversarial training, results in distorted image textures due to kernel mismatching. Figure 4 visualizes the predicted kernels by those BISR methods with explicit kernel estimation. It can be seen that only UDKE predicts the kernel with high fidelity, while others yield unreliable results because they generally impose the Gaussian-shape assumption on the kernels. More visualization results can be found in the **Supplementary File**.

Experiments with Gaussian Kernels. Although UDKE is not designed and trained for Gaussian kernel degradation, we also test its effectiveness on Gaussian kernels in comparison with those BISR methods designed and trained for Gaussian blur kernels, *i.e.*, DAN [20], KGAN [5], KFKP [17], and DFKP [17]. The Gaussian kernels are obtained by the process adopted in Gaussian BISR methods [5,17], which randomly samples the length and rotation angle to generate Gaussian kernels. The experiment is done on BSD100 set. Table 4 shows the BISR results on anisotropic Gaussian degradation. The isotropic Gaussian BISR results are provided in the **Supplementary File**. One can see that UDKE achieves competitive results with those Gaussian BISR methods but without hardcoding any Gaussian priors. With the increase of noise level, it can even surpass DFKP, showing better robustness to noise.

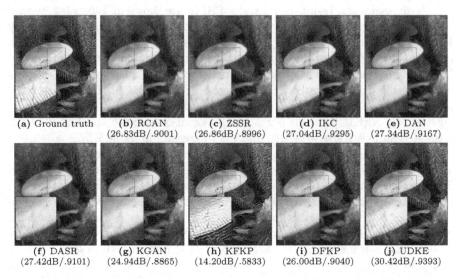

Fig. 3. Results on "208001" in BSD100 with $s = 2$ and $\sigma = 0$ (PSNR/SSIM).

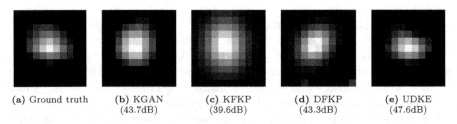

Fig. 4. Kernel estimation results on "208001" in BSD100 with $s = 2$ and $\sigma = 0$.

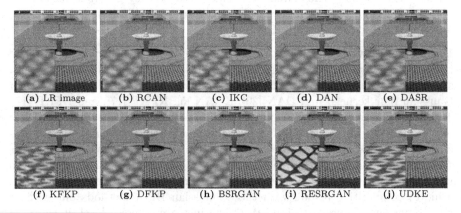

Fig. 5. Result on a real-world image (better viewed on screen).

Table 4. Anisotropic Gaussian BISR results (PSNR/SSIM/Kernel-PSNR).

s		$\sigma = 0$	$\sigma = 2.55$	$\sigma = 7.65$
2	DAN	28.12/.8557/-	27.13/.8028/-	26.35/.7443/–
	KGAN	26.33/.7751/44.3	26.01/.7432/43.8	25.79/.7026/42.1
	KFKP	27.62/.8512/49.1	27.11/.8010/46.9	26.34/.7450/45.2
	DFKP	28.42/.8863/49.8	27.32/.8218/47.2	26.71/.7570/45.8
	Ours	27.56/.8112/48.5	27.10/.8003/46.9	26.73/.7700/46.1
4	DAN	24.98/.6813/-	24.42/.6348/-	23.01/.5575/–
	KGAN	23.97/.6211/43.2	23.70/.5987/42.1	23.01/.5575/41.8
	KFKP	24.87/.6612/44.2	24.49/.6353/43.0	24.01/.5801/42.7
	DFKP	25.47/.7233/46.4	24.62/.6891/44.0	24.10/.6013/44.0
	Ours	24.89/.6612/44.3	24.52/.6348/43.1	24.32/.6187/44.0

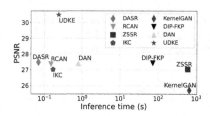

Fig. 6. Inference time v.s. PSNR.

Experiments on Real-World Images. We further test UDKE on real-world LR images whose degradation kernels can be more complex than Gaussian as well as the DEPD-evaluation pool. We add two state-of-the-art real-world SISR methods, *i.e.*, RESRGAN (Real-ESRGAN) [31] and BSRGAN [36], for more comprehensive comparison. The results are shown in Fig. 5. It can be seen that UDKE produces the best result, with not only superior perceptual quality but also more accurate fidelity (see the ground tiles). KFKP generates many noisy artifacts and distorted edges, while RESRGAN generates false patterns on the ground tiles. All the other competing methods output blurry results. This experiment demonstrates the robust kernel estimation capability of UDKE in real-world scenarios. More examples can be found in the **Supplementary File.**

Inference Time. We further compare the inference time of UDKE and the competing methods. The experiments are conducted on Set5 ($s = 2$ and $\sigma = 0$) with a GTX 2080Ti GPU. The results are shown in Fig. 6. It can be seen that UDKE is slightly slower than DASR and has a similar speed to RCAN and IKC. It is over ×100 times faster than the leading online training based BISR method DFKP, which trains a deep model during the inference, and ×1000 times faster than ZSSR and KGAN. Meanwhile, UDKE achieves significantly higher PSNR (about 3dB) than all competing methods.

5 Conclusion

We proposed a novel unfolded deep kernel estimation method, namely UDKE, to explicitly solve the data term of the unfolding objective function for effective BISR. Equipped with the designed memory-efficient algorithm, UDKE is free of the im2col operation required in traditional Least Squares Method and hence saves over 17000× memory overhead, providing an efficient solution to explicitly solve the data term under the deep learning framework. UDKE addresses the challenging BISR problem by efficiently utilizing the information of degradation model during inference. Extensive experiments on both synthetic and real-world images validated that UDKE could faithfully predict non-Gaussian blur kernels, and reproduce high quality images with sharp structures and rich textures, surpassing existing BISR methods by a large margin. Meanwhile, UDKE has good efficiency, making it an attractive choice for BISR in practice.

References

1. Abdi, H., et al.: The method of least squares. Encyclopedia Meas. Stat. **1**, 530–532 (2007)
2. Agustsson, E., Timofte, R.: Ntire 2017 challenge on single image super-resolution: dataset and study. In: The IEEE Conference on Computer Vision and Pattern Recognition (CVPR) Workshops, July 2017
3. Barbu, A.: Training an active random field for real-time image denoising. IEEE Trans. Image Process. **18**(11), 2451–2462 (2009)
4. Begin, I., Ferrie, F.: Blind super-resolution using a learning-based approach. In: Proceedings of the 17th International Conference on Pattern Recognition, 2004, ICPR 2004. vol. 2, pp. 85–89. IEEE (2004)
5. Bell-Kligler, S., Shocher, A., Irani, M.: Blind super-resolution kernel estimation using an internal-GAN. arXiv preprint arXiv:1909.06581 (2019)
6. Bevilacqua, M., Roumy, A., Guillemot, C., Alberi-Morel, M.L.: Low-complexity single-image super-resolution based on nonnegative neighbor embedding (2012)
7. Boyd, S., Parikh, N., Chu, E., Peleato, B., Eckstein, J., et al.: Distributed optimization and statistical learning via the alternating direction method of multipliers. Found. Trends® Mach. Learn. **3**(1), 1–122 (2011)
8. Bulat, A., Yang, J., Tzimiropoulos, G.: To learn image super-resolution, use a GAN to learn how to do image degradation first. In: Proceedings of the European Conference on Computer Vision (ECCV), pp. 185–200 (2018)
9. Capel, D., Zisserman, A.: Super-resolution enhancement of text image sequences. In: Proceedings 15th International Conference on Pattern Recognition, ICPR-2000, vol. 1, pp. 600–605. IEEE (2000)
10. Corduneanu, A., Platt, J.C.: Learning spatially-variable filters for super-resolution of text. In: IEEE International Conference on Image Processing 2005. vol. 1, pp. I-849. IEEE (2005)
11. Dong, C., Loy, C.C., He, K., Tang, X.: Learning a deep convolutional network for image super-resolution. In: Fleet, D., Pajdla, T., Schiele, B., Tuytelaars, T. (eds.) ECCV 2014. LNCS, vol. 8692, pp. 184–199. Springer, Cham (2014). https://doi.org/10.1007/978-3-319-10593-2_13
12. Glasner, D., Bagon, S., Irani, M.: Super-resolution from a single image. In: 2009 IEEE 12th International Conference on Computer Vision, pp. 349–356. IEEE (2009)
13. Gu, J., Lu, H., Zuo, W., Dong, C.: Blind super-resolution with iterative kernel correction. In: Proceedings of the IEEE/CVF Conference on Computer Vision and Pattern Recognition, pp. 1604–1613 (2019)
14. He, Y., Yap, K.H., Chen, L., Chau, L.P.: A soft map framework for blind super-resolution image reconstruction. Image Vis. Comput. **27**(4), 364–373 (2009)
15. Huang, J.B., Singh, A., Ahuja, N.: Single image super-resolution from transformed self-exemplars. In: Proceedings of the IEEE Conference on Computer Vision and Pattern Recognition, pp. 5197–5206 (2015)
16. Kingma, D.P., Ba, J.: Adam: a method for stochastic optimization. arXiv preprint arXiv:1412.6980 (2014)

17. Liang, J., Zhang, K., Gu, S., Van Gool, L., Timofte, R.: Flow-based kernel prior with application to blind super-resolution. In: Proceedings of the IEEE/CVF Conference on Computer Vision and Pattern Recognition, pp. 10601–10610 (2021)
18. Lim, B., Son, S., Kim, H., Nah, S., Mu Lee, K.: Enhanced deep residual networks for single image super-resolution. In: Proceedings of the IEEE Conference on Computer Vision and Pattern Recognition Workshops, pp. 136–144 (2017)
19. Liu, Y., Sun, W.: Blind super-resolution for single remote sensing image via sparse representation and transformed self-similarity. In: Journal of Physics: Conference Series, vol. 1575, p. 012115. IOP Publishing (2020)
20. Luo, Z., Huang, Y., Li, S., Wang, L., Tan, T.: Unfolding the alternating optimization for blind super resolution. arXiv preprint arXiv:2010.02631 (2020)
21. Martin, D., Fowlkes, C., Tal, D., Malik, J.: A database of human segmented natural images and its application to evaluating segmentation algorithms and measuring ecological statistics. In: Proceedings of 8th International Conference Computer Vision, vol. 2, pp. 416–423, July 2001
22. Michaeli, T., Irani, M.: Nonparametric blind super-resolution. In: Proceedings of the IEEE International Conference on Computer Vision, pp. 945–952 (2013)
23. Pan, J., Sun, D., Pfister, H., Yang, M.H.: Blind image deblurring using dark channel prior. In: Proceedings of the IEEE Conference on Computer Vision and Pattern Recognition, pp. 1628–1636 (2016)
24. Ronneberger, O., Fischer, P., Brox, T.: U-net: convolutional networks for biomedical image segmentation. In: Navab, N., Hornegger, J., Wells, W.M., Frangi, A.F. (eds.) MICCAI 2015. LNCS, vol. 9351, pp. 234–241. Springer, Cham (2015). https://doi.org/10.1007/978-3-319-24574-4_28
25. Samuel, K.G., Tappen, M.F.: Learning optimized map estimates in continuously-valued MRF models. In: 2009 IEEE Conference on Computer Vision and Pattern Recognition, pp. 477–484. IEEE (2009)
26. Shao, W.-Z., Elad, M.: Simple, accurate, and robust nonparametric blind super-resolution. In: Zhang, Y.-J. (ed.) ICIG 2015. LNCS, vol. 9219, pp. 333–348. Springer, Cham (2015). https://doi.org/10.1007/978-3-319-21969-1_29
27. Shocher, A., Cohen, N., Irani, M.: "Zero-shot" super-resolution using deep internal learning. In: Proceedings of the IEEE Conference on Computer Vision and Pattern Recognition, pp. 3118–3126 (2018)
28. Wang, L., et al.: Unsupervised degradation representation learning for blind super-resolution. In: Proceedings of the IEEE/CVF Conference on Computer Vision and Pattern Recognition, pp. 10581–10590 (2021)
29. Wang, Q., Tang, X., Shum, H.: Patch based blind image super resolution. In: Tenth IEEE International Conference on Computer Vision (ICCV'05) Volume 1, vol. 1, pp. 709–716. IEEE (2005)
30. Wang, S., Zhang, L., Liang, Y., Pan, Q.: Semi-coupled dictionary learning with applications to image super-resolution and photo-sketch synthesis. In: 2012 IEEE Conference on Computer Vision and Pattern Recognition, pp. 2216–2223. IEEE (2012)
31. Wang, X., Xie, L., Dong, C., Shan, Y.: Real-ESRGAN: training real-world blind super-resolution with pure synthetic data. In: International Conference on Computer Vision Workshops (ICCVW)
32. Yamac, M., Ataman, B., Nawaz, A.: KernelNet: a blind super-resolution kernel estimation network. In: Proceedings of the IEEE/CVF Conference on Computer Vision and Pattern Recognition, pp. 453–462 (2021)

33. Yang, W., Zhang, X., Tian, Y., Wang, W., Xue, J.H., Liao, Q.: Deep learning for single image super-resolution: a brief review. IEEE Trans. Multimedia **21**(12), 3106–3121 (2019)

34. Yuan, Y., Liu, S., Zhang, J., Zhang, Y., Dong, C., Lin, L.: Unsupervised image super-resolution using cycle-in-cycle generative adversarial networks. In: Proceedings of the IEEE Conference on Computer Vision and Pattern Recognition Workshops, pp. 701–710 (2018)

35. Zhang, K., Gool, L.V., Timofte, R.: Deep unfolding network for image super-resolution. In: Proceedings of the IEEE/CVF Conference on Computer Vision and Pattern Recognition, pp. 3217–3226 (2020)

36. Zhang, K., Liang, J., Van Gool, L., Timofte, R.: Designing a practical degradation model for deep blind image super-resolution. In: IEEE International Conference on Computer Vision, pp. 4791–4800 (2021)

37. Zhang, K., Zuo, W., Zhang, L.: Learning a single convolutional super-resolution network for multiple degradations. In: Proceedings of the IEEE Conference on Computer Vision and Pattern Recognition, pp. 3262–3271 (2018)

38. Zhang, Y., Li, K., Li, K., Wang, L., Zhong, B., Fu, Y.: Image super-resolution using very deep residual channel attention networks. In: Proceedings of the European Conference on Computer Vision (ECCV), pp. 286–301 (2018)

39. Zheng, H., Yong, H., Zhang, L.: Deep convolutional dictionary learning for image denoising. In: Proceedings of the IEEE/CVF Conference on Computer Vision and Pattern Recognition, pp. 630–641 (2021)

40. Zhou, R., Susstrunk, S.: Kernel modeling super-resolution on real low-resolution images. In: Proceedings of the IEEE/CVF International Conference on Computer Vision, pp. 2433–2443 (2019)

Event-guided Deblurring of Unknown Exposure Time Videos

Taewoo Kim[1], Jeongmin Lee[1], Lin Wang[2], and Kuk-Jin Yoon[1(✉)]

[1] Korea Advanced Institute of Science and Technology, Daejeon, South Korea
{intelpro,jeanmichel,kjyoon}@kaist.ac.kr
[2] AI Thrust, HKUST Guangzhou and Department of CSE, HKUST,
Hong Kong, China
linwang@ust.hk

Abstract. Motion deblurring is a highly ill-posed problem due to the loss of motion information in the blur degradation process. Since event cameras can capture apparent motion with a high temporal resolution, several attempts have explored the potential of events for guiding deblurring. These methods generally assume that the exposure time is the same as the reciprocal of the video frame rate. However, this is not true in real situations, and the exposure time might be unknown and dynamically varies depending on the video shooting environment (e.g., illumination condition). In this paper, we address the event-guided motion deblurring assuming dynamically variable unknown exposure time of the frame-based camera. To this end, we first derive a new formulation for event-guided motion deblurring by considering the exposure and readout time in the video frame acquisition process. We then propose a novel end-to-end learning framework for event-guided motion deblurring. In particular, we design a novel Exposure Time-based Event Selection (ETES) module to selectively use event features by estimating the cross-modal correlation between the features from blurred frames and the events. Moreover, we propose a feature fusion module to fuse the selected features from events and blur frames effectively. We conduct extensive experiments on various datasets and demonstrate that our method achieves state-of-the-art performance. Our project code and dataset are available at: https://intelpro.github.io/UEVD/

1 Introduction

Motion blur often occurs due to the non-negligible exposure time of the frame-based cameras. Any motion during the video recording makes the sensor observe an averaged signal from different points in the scene [23,44]. Motion deblurring is a task aiming at restoring sharp frame from the motion-blurred ones. This task is a highly ill-posed problem due to the loss of motion information in the blur degradation process, especially in the complex real-world scene [1,6,9].

Supplementary Information The online version contains supplementary material available at https://doi.org/10.1007/978-3-031-19797-0_30.

S. Avidan et al. (Eds.): ECCV 2022, LNCS 13678, pp. 519–538, 2022.
https://doi.org/10.1007/978-3-031-19797-0_30

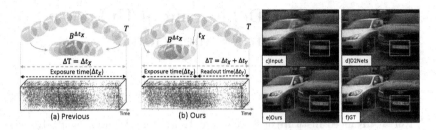

Fig. 1. (a–b)The motivation of our work. The figure shows the image formation setting assumed in (a) previous event-guided methods and (b) our work. Here, ΔT represents the shutter period. From above to bottom, continuous latent images, video frame acquisition, corresponding event streams($E^{\Delta T}$), respectively. Previous methods generally assume that the exposure time is the same as the reciprocal of the video frame rate, while ours considers the actual exposure time for selectively using events. (c–f) Results of deblurring on the unknown exposure time video frame. Our method restores a sharper frame than the existing event-guided deblurring methods, e.g., D2Nets [32], trained on the same dataset.

Recently, deep learning (DL)-based approaches have achieved great success in modeling general motion blur and recovering sharp frames from the motion-blurred frames [20,33,49,55]. However, they are limited to specific scenarios and may fail to recover the sharp frames for the severe motion blur. Event cameras are bio-inspired sensors that encode the per-pixel intensity change asynchronously with high temporal resolution.

Many endeavors have been engaged in reconstructing image/video from event streams [19,31,38–41,59]. However, the reconstructed results from the events may lose texture details. Consequently, several attempts have leveraged events for guiding motion deblurring [9,17,27,32,38,53], trying to take advantage of frame-based and event cameras. As shown in Fig. 1(a), these methods generally assume that the exposure time is the same as the reciprocal of the video frame rate and perform the deblurring guided by the events within the exposure time. However, this assumption may not be valid in real situations as the video frame acquisition process generally consists of two phases: exposure phase (X) and readout phase (Y) [5,55], as shown in Fig. 1(b). In the exposure phase, the camera's shutter opens and receives lights. In the readout phase, the camera clears charge from the serial register, and the pixel value is digitalized. The total time, reciprocal of the frame rate, is called the shutter period, not exposure time. Since the motion blur of the frame-based camera occurs only in the exposure phase rather than the readout phase, it is crucial to use the events during the exposure phase within the shutter period. However, the exposure time is not always known, and furthermore, it can dynamically vary depending on the imaging environments when the auto-exposure function turns on.

For that reason, we assume the exposure time is unknown when performing the event-guided motion deblurring, as shown in Fig. 1(b), to consider more practical situations. This assumption can lead to significant performance changes. If we apply the existing event-guided deblurring methods, e.g., [32], for unknown exposure time video frames, the performance degrades, as shown in Fig. 1(d).[1] Therefore, it is necessary to infer the actual exposure time to use events rightly for deblurring. Accordingly, we propose an end-to-end learning framework. As the exposure time is assumed to be unknown, we first propose an event selection module called the Exposure Time-based Event Selection (ETES). The proposed module extracts the relevant events within the shutter period by estimating the temporal correlation between events and blur frames features. As such, only the event features corresponding to the exposure time are automatically selected for guidance. Second, we propose a new module for events-frame feature fusion. Such a fusion module leads to more robust feature representation learning. Lastly, as a lack of publically available real-world event datasets for event-guided motion deblurring, we collect color images and event data in diverse real-world scenes using a DAVIS-346 color event camera. We then make a dataset by simulating dynamically variable exposure time using collected frames and real events for performing motion deblurring without exposure time information.

In summary, our contributions are four-fold. (I) We study and formulate an event-guided deblurring for unknown exposure time videos. (II) Based on the formulation, we design a novel event feature selection method within exposure time and propose a feature fusion module to use complementary information of events and frame features. (III) We build a novel large-scale dataset for event-guided motion deblurring, including RGB images and the real events in various scenes. (IV) We conduct various experiments on the synthetic event and our real-world event datasets and demonstrate that our method achieves new state-of-the-art performance.

2   Related Works

Image and Video Deblurring. DL has been broadly applied to image and video deblurring. Earlier works, *e.g.*, [34], utilized convolutional neural networks (CNNs) with frame alignment and merged multiple frames based on the homography for video deblurring. The baseline networks have been improved by applying more sophisticated network structures or learning methods, *e.g.*, recurrent neural networks (RNN) [7,21,28,36,44,56], multi-scale architecture [2,4,20], adversarial training [14,15,50–52], multi-stage approaches [3,48,49], video frame alignment [11,16,24,42,57] in an end-to-end learning manner.

Event-Guided Motion Deblurring. The event cameras show higher temporal resolution and HDR properties. To leverage the advantages of event cameras, recent works focus on event-guided deblurring. Pan *et al.* [26,27] first proposed a deblurring framework by formulating an event-based double integral model (EDI). Although they show the effectiveness of formulation, they often fail to reconstruct the scene details due to the noisy contrast threshold of the events. To solve the aforementioned issues, Jiang *et al.* [9] introduced a DL-based deblurring framework by using an RNN-based network architecture and a directional

---

[1] This result is obtained by using all the events during the shutter period without knowing the actual exposure time.

event filtering module. More recently, Lin *et al.* [17] proposed a CNN-based framework driven by an event-based physical model for deblurring and frame interpolation. Shang *et al.* [32] proposed an event-guided deblurring framework to exploit the non-consecutively blurry video frames. Concurrently, Xu *et al.* [47] proposed a self-supervised learning framework that utilizes real events to alleviate performance degradation due to the domain gap between real and synthetic data. These works generally assume the exposure time is the same as the shutter period. However, as aforementioned, this assumption is not valid in many real situations. *Unlike these works, we propose a novel framework for unknown exposure time videos.*

3   Method

3.1   Formulation

Event Selection. A video frame acquisition consists of the exposure phase X and readout phase Y, as depicted in Fig. 1. We denote the duration of the exposure phase as Δt_X and the readout phase as Δt_Y. The summation of two phases (shutter period), ΔT, represents the time to acquire one video frame. By the nature of frame-based cameras, motion blur only occurs during the exposure phase X. In contrast, events are generated in the exposure phase X and the readout phase Y. Therefore, it is imperative to use events during the exact duration of the exposure phase Δt_X only. The existing event-guided deblurring methods [17,27] generally assume that the exposure time is equal to the shutter period; $\Delta T = \Delta t_X$. By contrast, our goal is to estimate the temporal correlation between the motion-blurred frame and the event during ΔT to handle the unknown exposure time Δt_X. A motion-blurred frame can be expressed as the temporal average of N latent frames during the exposure time Δt_X as

$$B^{\Delta t_X}(x,y) \simeq \frac{1}{N} \sum_{i=1}^{N} L_{\tau_i}(x,y), \tag{1}$$

where $B^{\Delta t_X}(x,y)$ denotes a blurred frame, and $L_{\tau_i}(x,y)$ is the i-th latent frame at τ_i. For event cameras, an event is generated when the log intensity change exceeds a contrast threshold β.

$$E^t(x,y) = \begin{cases} +1, & if \ \log(\frac{I^t(x,y)}{I^{t-1}(x,y)}) \geq \beta \\ -1, & if \ \log(\frac{I^t(x,y)}{I^{t-1}(x,y)}) \leq -\beta \end{cases} \tag{2}$$

where $I^t(x,y)$ is the intensity value at timestamp t. Given two consecutive frames, $I^{t_1}(x,y)$ and $I^{t_2}(x,y)$, the events $E^t(x,y)$ are generated by intensity changes between them. Accordingly, we can derive the relationship between two intensity images based on event generation.

$$I^{t_2}(x,y) \simeq I^{t_1}(x,y) \cdot \exp(\sum_{t_1}^{t_2} \beta \cdot E^t(x,y)) = I^{t_1}(x,y)\tilde{R}(x,y) \tag{3}$$

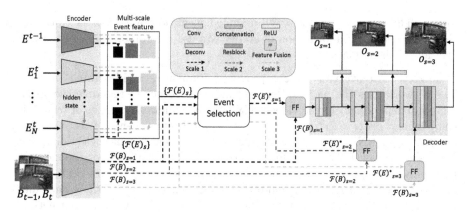

Fig. 2. Overview of the proposed framework. For the encoder, blue, yellow, and green boxes represent an event encoder for the past part, a shared RNN-based event encoder for the current part, and a blur-frame encoder, respectively. (Color figure online)

By combining Eq.(1) and Eq.(3), we can represent a blurred frame as follows:

$$B^{\Delta t_X}(x,y) \simeq I^t(x,y)(\frac{1}{N}\sum_{i=1}^{N}\tilde{R}_i(x,y)) = I^t(x,y)S(x,y) \tag{4}$$

where $I^t(x,y)$ denotes a latent frame, which is the result of deblurring, and $S(x,y)$ is the summation of residual matrix $\tilde{R}_i(x,y)$. According to Eq.(4), we need to estimate a $S(x,y)$ corresponding to the exposure time of the blurred frame. However, since the exact exposure time is assumed to be unknown, we aim at estimating the temporal correlation between the blurred frames and events during ΔT. That is, to estimate $S(x,y)$, we find a function f_{θ^*} that approximates a set of events $\{E^{\Delta t_X}\}$ based on $\{E^{\Delta T}\}$ and the blurred frame $B^{\Delta t_X}$ as

$$f_{\theta^*} \sim \{E^t \mid \psi(E^t, B^{\Delta t_X}) > 0\}; \quad t \in \{0, T\} \tag{5}$$

where $\psi(E^t, B^{\Delta t_X})$ is a conditional function obtained by calculating the temporal correlation between E^t and $B^{\Delta t}$. With respect to E^t, a function $\psi(E^t, B^{\Delta t_X})$ is true when the intensity change corresponding to E^t exists in the motion-blurred frame $B^{\Delta t_X}$ and vice versa. As such, only the events within the exposure time are selected as guidance.

Event-Guided Deblurring. Through the above formulation, we can select event streams $\{E^{\Delta t_X}\}$ among $\{E^{\Delta T}\}$ for the unknown exposure time Δt_X. Accordingly, we aim at recovering an intermediate sharp video frame from the motion-blurred ones $B^{\Delta t_X}$ using $\{E^{\Delta t_X}\}$.

3.2   The Proposed Framework

Based on the formulation, we propose a novel end-to-end learning framework. To feed event streams to DNNs, we need to embed them to the fixed size tensor-like format. The voxel grid [58] is a well-designed event representation as it preserves the spatio-temporal information of events. We use 16 temporal bins of the voxel grid for all the experiments.

Overview. An overview of the proposed framework is illustrated in Fig. 2. The network uses the past and current inputs together to reinforce the spatio-temporal dependency of the videos. The overall framework consists of *two* major components: *event selection* and *feature fusion*. First, we encode the embedded events via an RNN-based encoding network for event feature selection. Then, we propose a novel ETES module to select the event features corresponding to the unknown exposure time *without any supervision*. Second, in Sect. 3.4, we propose a new feature fusion module that efficiently exploits the complementary information of selected events and frames. After the two steps, our network processed fused feature in a coarse-to-fine manner using a pyramid structure.

3.3   Event Selection

Recurrent Encoding for Embedded Events. To extract features from events, recent works widely adopt 2D CNNs [17,58]; however, they are less effective in preserving temporal information for the event selection under unknown exposure time (Eq. 5). Specifically, we first divide the events into the past shutter period part $\{E^{t-1}\}$ and the current shutter period part $\{E^t\}$. We then use the current shutter-period events to infer unknown exposure time, and past information is only used for better deblurring. Therefore, we use different event encoders to allocate more channels to the current events for correctly estimating exposure time. For the past part $\{E^{t-1}\}$, we extract a feature pyramid $\{\mathcal{F}(E^{t-1})_s\} \in \mathbb{R}^{C_s^U \times H_s \times W_s}$, using a 2D CNN block with the scale index $s \in \{1,2,3\}$. Especially for the current part $\{E^t\}$, we devise a new RNN-cell based event encoder with shared weights to extract features for preserving temporal information inspired by recent frame-based video deblurring works [21,56] as shown in Fig. 2. Considering the temporal information of the current part, we first divide the voxel grid into N temporal units with an equal time interval Δt_{unit}. Thus, we get temporally divided event units $E_n^t \in \mathbb{R}^{2 \times H \times W}$ with the temporal index $n \in \{1, ..., N\}$. We then recursively update the hidden state of the RNN cell to reinforce temporal coherence between consecutive event units. As such, we generate N hierarchical feature maps at each scale index s for the current part $\{\mathcal{F}(E_1^t)_s, ..., \mathcal{F}(E_N^t)_s\}$. The extracted features of the current and past parts are concatenated to form a feature pyramid, denoted by $\{\mathcal{F}(E)_s\} \in \mathbb{R}^{(N+1) \times C_s^U \times H_s \times W_s}$, where C_s^U, H_s, W_s denotes the numbers of unit channels, height, and width at scale index s, respectively. For brevity, we denote $N + 1$ as T. The detailed network structures and RNN-based encoding methods are given in the supple. material.

Exposure Time-Based Event Selection (ETES) Module. Through encoding, we obtain the event and frame feature pyramids $\{\mathcal{F}(E)_s\}$ and $\{\mathcal{F}(B)_s\}$, respectively. To approximate Eq. (5), we now aim to select the beneficial event

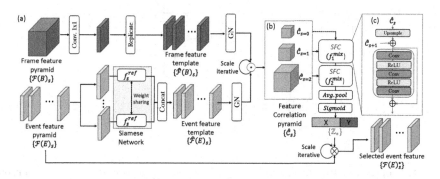

Fig. 3. The network structure of the proposed Exposure-Time based Event Selection Module. "GN" denotes the group normalization [46].

features corresponding to the dynamically varying unknown exposure time of the frame-based camera. However, there exist two crucial challenges. The first one is how to pre-process event features (with complete temporal information) and frame features (with missing temporal information). The second is how to better discover the cross-modal relationship between events and frames by aggregating the feature pyramid obtained from two different modalities. To this end, we propose a novel ETES module *without any supervision*, as depicted in Fig. 3. The main idea is to temporally mine the essential channels of event features based on the multi-scale cross-modal correlation. That is, we aim to suppress the event feature corresponding to the duration of the readout phase by calculating the similarity between the blur frame feature and the event feature along with the temporal flow. As depicted in Fig. 3(a), we first pre-process the event and frame features to calculate cross-modal correlation at multiple visual scales. For the frame features at scale s, we first compress them by applying the point-wise convolution to reduce spatial information loss. Then, we replicate the compressed frame features to have the same temporal dimension as the event features. The operations are formulated as:

$$\hat{\mathcal{F}}(B)_s = \xi(Conv_{1\times1,s}(\mathcal{F}(B)_s)), \tag{6}$$

where $Conv_{1\times1,s}$ is the point-wise convolution at scale s such that $\mathbb{R}^{C_s^U \times H_s \times W_s} \rightarrow \mathbb{R}^{C_{s=1}^U \times H_s \times W_s}$. Here, ξ denotes the replication operation along the temporal dimension to form frame template features $\hat{\mathcal{F}}(B)_s$ such that $\mathbb{R}^{C_{s=1}^U \times H_s \times W_s} \rightarrow \mathbb{R}^{T \times C_{s=1}^U \times H_s \times W_s}$. This allows calculating the cross-modal correlation in unit time interval Δt_{unit}. For the event features at scale s, we leverage a siamese network [13] to modulate them to effectively maintain the temporal information within Δt_{unit}, as shown in Fig. 3(a). We apply this w.r.t. each temporal unit of the event features, $f_s^{ref} : \mathbb{R}^{C_s^U \times H_s \times W_s} \rightarrow \mathbb{R}^{C_{s=1}^U \times H_s \times W_s}$. The features are concatenated along the temporal dimension to form event template features $\hat{\mathcal{F}}(E)_s$. We finally apply the group normalization [46] to these two template features to mitigate the extreme modality differences. Through preprocessing both the event and frame features, we can get two feature templates

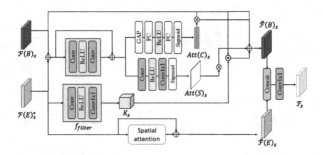

Fig. 4. Proposed feature fusion module. In the figure, ⊛ denotes dynamic convolution operation with a generated convolution filter.

at each scale s. As shown in Fig. 3(b), it is imperative to explore the correlations from the feature pyramids to select the most beneficial events. For this reason, we aggregate these two feature templates via the Hadamard product $\odot$ for all scales as

$$\hat{\mathcal{C}}_s = ReLU(\hat{\mathcal{F}}(E)_s \odot \hat{\mathcal{F}}(B)_s) \tag{7}$$

where the feature correlation $\hat{\mathcal{C}}_s \in \mathbb{R}^{T \times C_{s=1}^U \times H_s \times W_s}$ with ReLU for removing noisy correlation. Finally, we get a feature correlation pyramid $\{\mathcal{C}_s\}$ seen from multiple visual scales. As illustrated in Fig. 3(c), we merge the collection of correlation features by designing a scale-fusion convolutional (SFC) block. In particular, SFC aims to form a multi-scale temporal activation map $\{\mathbb{Z}_s\} \in \mathbb{R}^{T \times C_s^U \times 1 \times 1}$ in three steps. SFC upsamples the correlation features at scale s, followed by an element-wise addition with the features at scale $s + 1$. It then propagates the most beneficial correlation information in a top-down manner. In such a way, it effectively enables the merge of lower-level to a higher-level cross-modal correlation between the frame and event. Lastly, we squeeze the output tensor on the spatial dimension by global average-pooling followed by a sigmoid activation function. The output tensor is the condensed temporal activation map $\mathbb{Z}_{s=1} \in \mathbb{R}^{T \times C_{s=1}^U \times 1 \times 1}$. We then interpolate $\mathbb{Z}_{s=1}$ to get the temporal activation map at each scale s $\mathbb{Z}_s \in \mathbb{R}^{T \times C_s^U \times 1 \times 1}$ as

$$\mathcal{F}(E)_s^* = \mathbb{Z}_s \otimes \mathcal{F}(E)_s \tag{8}$$

where $\otimes$ denotes channel-wise multiplication. As such, the ETES module filters and selects the event features w.r.t. unknown exposure time of the frame, as shown in Fig. 7. Each of the selected event feature pyramids $\{\mathcal{F}(E)_s^*\}$ is fed into the feature fusion module of each scale, as depicted in Fig. 2.

3.4   Feature Fusion Module

The event features $\mathcal{F}(E)_s^*$ are selected via the event selection module. We notice that the blur frame features $\mathcal{F}(B)_s$ contain rich semantic and texture information, while the selected event features contain clear edge and motion cues.

Therefore, it is meaningful to leverage the information from event features to complement the frame features. It is possible to use existing feature fusion methods directly, *e.g.*, RGB-D [35,54]. However, as events are remarkably different from the frame, naively using these methods rather degrades the deblurring performance. Consequently, we propose a novel event-frame feature fusion module for deblurring, as depicted in Fig. 4. Our idea is to leverage the event features to mine the discriminative channels and spatial information from the blur frame features. That is, we first calibrate the frame and event features via element-wise summation. As a result, the frame features of blurry regions are highlighted through calibration due to the motion cues of the event features. We then employ the global average pooling (GAP) to obtain global statistics, which are fed into a fully connected (FC) layer to obtain a channel attention vector for the frame features $Att(C)_s \in \mathbb{R}^{T \times C_s \times 1 \times 1}$. Meanwhile, we extract spatial attention maps $Att(S)_s$ to attain the spatial statistics from calibrated features. As such, only the important blur frame features related to deblurring are highlighted, and the unnecessary information is suppressed. Moreover, we design a filter generation block f_{filter} (see Fig. 4) to generate a position-specific convolution filter $K_s = f_{\text{filter}}(\mathcal{F}(E)^*_s)$ from the selected event features $\mathcal{F}(E)^*_s$, inspired by kernel prediction networks [8,17,18,22]. The filtered features are formulated as:

$$\tilde{\mathcal{F}}(B)_s = \mathcal{F}(B)_s + Att(C)_s \otimes \mathcal{F}(B)_s + Att(S)_s \cdot \mathcal{F}(B)_s + K_s \circledast \mathcal{F}(B)_s$$

where $\circledast$ denotes convolution operation and $\otimes$ denotes channel-wise multiplication. For event features, we only apply spatial attention [45] from the selected event feature $\mathcal{F}(E)^*_s$. The fused features $\mathcal{F}_s$ at each scale are obtained by concatenating the enhanced event features $\tilde{\mathcal{F}}(E)_s$ and the filtered frame features $\tilde{\mathcal{F}}(B)_s$, followed by a 1×1 convolution. Lastly, the fused feature $\{\mathcal{F}_s\}$ are separately fed into the decoder to reconstruct a sharp video, as shown in Fig. 2. The outputs of the decoder consist of sharp video frames at each scale, represented as $\{O_s\}$. We use the charbonnier loss [10] for optimization, and the total loss is:

$$\mathcal{L}_{total} = \sum_{s=0}^{2} \lambda_s \sqrt{\|O_{gt,s} - O_s\|^2 + \varepsilon^2} \tag{9}$$

We empirically set to $\varepsilon = 10^{-3}$ for all experiments.

4   Experiments

4.1   Datasets and Implementation Details

Synthetic Event Datasets. We train and test our framework on the GoPro dataset [20], widely used for deblurring. We then test with the test split of the Adobe-240fps datasets [34] using the trained model on the GoPro dataset. For both datasets, we follow an official data split, and events are generated from the high frame rate video using the event simulator (ESIM) [30]. We synthesize blurry video by averaging the video frames. To mimic the real video frame acquisition, we follow the method in [55]. We discard several video frames to simulate the readout time. We denote the number of video frames of the exposure phase as m and that of the readout phase as n. We downsample the original video from 240 fps to 15 fps with $m + n = 16$. We set the frame number m of the exposure phase as an odd number $m = \{9, 11, 13, 15\}$. During training, we add random noise, $\epsilon \sim [--0.6n, 0.6n]$, to the readout interval for better generalization. Accordingly, we can simulate the random video frame acquisition process in training. As such, we get a synthetic dataset that simulates various exposure times. We denoted this dataset as "dataset-m-n".

Real-World Event Datasets. To evaluate our method on real-world events, we collected 53,601 sharp images of 59 different scenes with slow-motion using the DAVIS 346 color event camera that provides aligned events and RGB data(346×260 resolution). We attain the blurry video by averaging the sharp frames with the setting $m + n = 10$ for network training. We set the frame number of the exposure phase as an odd number $m = \{3, 5, 7, 9\}$. Similarly, we add a random noise $\epsilon \sim [--0.6n, 0.6n]$ to the read-out interval in the training phase. Finally, we generated training sets consisting of blur images and corresponding sharp ground truths images with events for 43 scenes. For testing, *we set the test set configuration differently from the composition of the training sets* by setting $m + n = 14$ and $m = \{9, 11, 13\}$ to confirm the generalization ability for the unseen video frame acquisition process. Finally, we generated a test set consisting of 3,588 blur and GT images with events for 16 scenes. In this manner, we conduct a quantitative evaluation with other methods. In addition, we collected real-world blurry videos by shooting various scenes with fast motion to evaluate our method on the real-world blurry videos qualitatively. For the real-world blurry video shooting, we set the exposure time as $\{15, 25, 35, 45, 55\}$ms or auto-exposure and the shutter period as 60ms. Then, we conducted experiments on real-world blurry videos at various unknown exposure times.

Implementation Details. Our frameworks are implemented using PyTorch [29]. For all datasets, we utilize the batch size of 8 and ADAM [12] optimizer to update weight using a multi-step scheduler with an initial learning rate $1e^{-4}$ and decay rate $\gamma = 0.5$. λ_s of Eq. (9) are set to $\{1, 0.1, 0.1\}$ for each scale. For data augmentation, we apply random cropping(256×256) to the event and frame for the same position. We adopt the dynamic convolution operation from the STFAN [57] implementation. For quantitative evaluation, we use common evaluation metrics PSNR and SSIM [43].

4.2   Experimental Results

We compare with Nah *et al.* [20] and DMPHN [49] by feeding the RGB frame with embedded events to the networks (denoted as Nah *et al.*[†], DMPHN[†]). For comparison of the SOTA event-guided video deblurring method D2Nets[†] [32], we used the official training code. In addition, we reimplement the other SOTA event-guided video deblurring methods [17](denoted as LEDVDI[†]) based on the

Table 1. Quantitative evaluation on a synthetic event dataset. Asterisk(*) means retraining our training dataset. † denotes the event-guided method. The **Bold** and _underline_ denote the best and the second-best performance, respectively. We trained our method on the GoPro dataset and directly applied it to the Adobe dataset. The same notation and typography are applied to the following tables.

Method	GoPro -15fps								Adobe-15fps							
	GoPro-9-7		GoPro-11-5		GoPro-13-3		GoPro-15-1		Adobe-9-7		Adobe-11-5		Adobe-13-3		Adobe-15-1	
	PSNR	SSIM	PSNR	SSIM	PSNR	SSIM	PSNR	SSIM	PSNR	SSIM	PSNR	SSIM	PSNR	SSIM	PSNR	SSIM
Nah et al. [20]	28.89	0.930	27.76	0.914	26.70	0.895	25.74	0.876	28.29	0.914	27.35	0.900	26.59	0.888	25.96	0.878
DMPHN [49]	31.21	0.946	30.39	0.936	28.75	0.914	26.83	0.880	29.17	0.920	28.22	0.905	27.21	0.888	26.31	0.872
Kupyn et al. [15]	30.18	0.932	29.10	0.918	28.11	0.903	27.21	0.888	29.81	0.924	28.85	0.913	28.09	0.903	27.51	0.894
DBGAN [51]	32.15	0.955	31.44	0.945	29.25	0.921	26.99	0.881	29.91	0.927	28.82	0.912	27.70	0.895	26.69	0.878
BANet [37]	33.02	0.961	32.38	0.956	30.89	0.941	28.93	0.915	31.01	0.943	29.96	0.929	28.84	0.913	27.90	0.898
MPRNet [48]	33.77	0.967	32.65	0.959	31.24	0.946	29.66	0.927	31.20	0.945	30.17	0.933	29.05	0.919	28.16	0.906
MIMO-UNet+ [4]	33.34	0.964	32.39	0.956	30.74	0.940	28.52	0.908	30.83	0.939	29.76	0.925	28.57	0.908	27.51	0.892
HINet [3]	33.60	0.965	32.86	0.960	31.26	0.945	29.09	0.917	31.06	0.944	30.08	0.932	28.90	0.915	27.91	0.901
ESTRNN* [56]	29.97	0.929	28.93	0.916	27.96	0.901	27.04	0.885	28.36	0.907	27.45	0.893	26.72	0.881	26.10	0.870
CDVD-TSP [25]	29.13	0.926	28.53	0.917	27.77	0.905	26.89	0.890	27.57	0.907	27.21	0.900	26.80	0.892	26.43	0.885
Nah et al.†* [20]	34.39	0.966	34.37	0.965	34.04	0.963	33.66	0.961	33.63	0.962	33.64	0.962	33.10	0.958	32.25	0.950
DMPHN† [49]	33.68	0.961	33.63	0.961	33.36	0.959	33.03	0.956	33.16	0.959	33.02	0.959	32.55	0.955	32.01	0.949
LEDVDI† [17]	33.39	0.958	33.57	0.959	33.68	0.959	32.81	0.953	32.92	0.958	32.92	0.958	33.18	0.953	31.91	0.949
D2Nets†* [32]	29.52	0.923	29.39	0.921	29.56	0.921	29.04	0.911	28.41	0.909	28.24	0.905	28.46	0.906	28.14	0.900
Ours-light†	34.91	0.969	34.61	0.968	_34.43_	_0.966_	_34.00_	_0.964_	_34.19_	_0.965_	_33.72_	_0.963_	_33.87_	_0.964_	_33.20_	_0.959_
Ours†	**36.22**	**0.976**	**35.93**	**0.974**	**35.67**	**0.973**	**35.28**	**0.971**	**35.52**	**0.973**	**35.24**	**0.971**	**35.11**	**0.970**	**34.67**	**0.968**

Table 2. Quantitative evaluation and complexity analysis on real event dataset. The inference time and FLOPs are measured using TITAN RTX GPU on 346 × 260 resolution images of test sets. ‡ means event-guided deblurring methods evaluated using the official pretrained model. As their official models only provide the result of a grayscale image input, we evaluate the performance of each model on the grayscale image input.

Methods	Real-world event dataset								Complexity FLOPs(G)/Runtime(ms)
	9-5		11-3		13-1		Avg.		
	PSNR	SSIM	PSNR	SSIM	PSNR	SSIM	PSNR	SSIM	
Nah et al.* [20]	29.74	0.8420	28.74	0.8207	27.96	0.8037	28.81	0.8221	245.40/154.65
DMPHN* [49]	29.76	0.8392	28.80	0.8188	28.03	0.8021	28.87	0.8200	56.99/27.99
CDVD-TSP* [25]	32.95	0.9077	31.73	0.8878	30.66	0.8683	31.78	0.8880	281.15/204.46
MPRNet* [48]	30.42	0.8596	29.22	0.8345	28.25	0.8136	29.30	0.8359	1247.17/151.9
MIMO-UNet+* [4]	30.32	0.8529	29.24	0.8309	28.37	0.8129	29.31	0.8322	112.44/44.0
e-SLNet‡ [38]	20.82	0.6379	21.39	0.6603	22.09	0.6872	21.43	0.6546	114.88/55.87
REDS‡ [47]	26.12	0.7399	30.20	0.8448	31.34	0.8542	29.22	0.8130	116.89/47.15
Nah et al.†* [20]	35.10	0.9326	32.84	0.9057	32.41	0.9016	33.45	0.9133	247.00/156.32
DMPHN† [49]	33.87	0.9069	33.09	0.8958	33.02	0.8957	33.33	0.8995	57.88/27.22
LEDVDI†* [17]	34.77	0.9258	33.83	0.9138	32.96	0.9047	33.86	0.9148	62.80/25.24
D2Nets†* [32]	31.36	0.8753	30.87	0.8663	29.90	0.8481	30.71	0.8632	283.86/243.9
Ours-light†	35.53	0.9342	34.58	0.9232	34.64	0.9248	34.92	0.9274	60.72/32.14
Ours†	**36.98**	**0.9487**	**36.10**	**0.9407**	**35.98**	**0.9404**	**36.35**	**0.9433**	237.77/75.07

code provided by the authors. We keep the original network architecture and with modification of the event representation [58].

Synthetic Event Datasets. For a fair comparison, we *retrain* the one frame-based video deblurring method [56] and four event-guided methods(D2Nets[†], LEDVDI[†] and Nah *et al.*[†] and DMPHN[†]) on our training dataset. Also, we compare with the SOTA frame-based methods using official pre-trained models provided by the authors [3,4,15,20,25,37,48,49,51]. As clearly shown in Table 1, our method surpasses the frame-based and event-guided methods by a large margin on the two datasets. Compared to the frame-based method, the avg. PSNR score of our method improves from 3.95 dB to 8.50 dB in the GoPro-15 fps, from 5.49 dB to 8.09 dB in the Adobe-15 fps. As we maximize the number of video frames corresponding to the exposure phase, the performance gap between our method and frame-based competitors widens from 5.62 dB to 9.5 4dB in the GoPro-15-1. This indicates our method achieves better results on challenging motion blur frames. Compared to the event-guided method, our method still shows better results from 1.66 dB to 6.40 dB in the GoPro-15 fps and 1.98 to 6.82 dB in the Adobe-15 fps.

Real-World Event Datasets. As mentioned above, the real-world datasets contain various scenes different from the synthetic event dataset, so we retrain the SOTA frame-based methods [4,20,25,48,49] and event-guided methods (LEDVDI[†], Nah *et al.*[†], DMPHN[†], D2Nets[†]) on our real-world event datasets. In addition, we evaluate the SOTA event-guided deblurring methods(e-SLNet[‡] [38], REDS[‡] [47]) using official pretrained model provided by the authors. In Table 2, we reported the deblurring performance of unseen and unknown exposure time videos compared with other methods. Compared to the frame-based methods, there is a performance gap(**4.57** to **7.54** dB) on avg. PSNR and SSIM (**0.0553** to **0.1233**). Moreover, our network records a significant performance improvement compared to the event-guided methods(retrained in our datasets) on avg. PSNR (**2.49** to **5.64** dB) and SSIM (**0.0285** to **0.0801**) with comparable test cost and running time. The "ours-light" network, the light version of our original network with reduced channels and res-blocks, has higher performance (1.06 dB to 4.21 dB) with low computational cost. Ours-light network shows the slight difference of test costs and running time with two light event-guided methods (DMPHN[†] [49], LEDVDI[†] [17]) and faster and lighter than the other two event-guided methods (D2Nets[†] [32], Nah *et al.*[†] [20]) with distinct performance differences. In Fig. 5, only our method effectively restores a detailed structure even under extreme non-linear motion.

Evaluation Results on Real-World Blurry Video Frames. Finally, we experiment generalization ability of our methods on real-world blurry videos. For testing, real-shot blurry video frames and corresponding events (in 1/(shutter speed) duration) are given to our model inputs. Then, we checked the results for the temporal activation map of our ETES module according to various unknown exposure times to confirm the inference ability of exposure time for deblurring. Specifically, we plot the average distribution of the activated event channels for

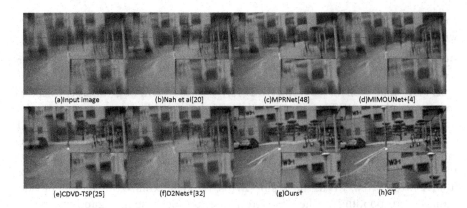

Fig. 5. Visual comparison on the test split of real-world event datasets.

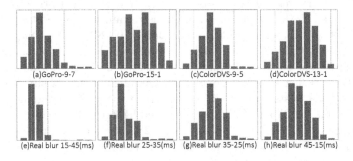

Fig. 6. Deblurring results on **real-world** unknown exposure time blurry video frames. From left to right: inputs, MIMO-UNet+ [4], D2Nets[†] [32], LEDVDI[†] [17], Ours[†].

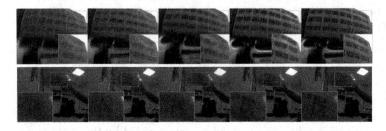

Fig. 7. The visualization of the average temporal activation map of the ETES module on various datasets, including real-shot blurry videos. The horizontal and vertical axes represent the temporal axis and the average amount of channel activation, respectively. The yellow and red dotted lines indicate the start and end of the exposure time, respectively. In the second row, the first and the last numbers indicate the exposure and readout time of real-world blurry videos. (Color figure online)

Table 3. The ablation study of the individual components.

RE			✓	✓	✓	✓	✓	✓
MS		✓		✓			✓	✓
ETES					✓	✓	✓	✓
FF						✓		✓
PSNR	34.45	34.93	34.96	35.42	35.77	36.09	_36.02_	**36.35**

each temporal unit of the ETES module by averaging over 200 real-world blurry frames for each video clip in Fig. 7(e)–(h). *We confirm all temporal activations are concentrated near the exposure phase even in the real-blurry video frames without exact exposure time information.* This indicates that event features are well selected based on cross-modality feature correlations according to real-world blurry videos' exposure time. Lastly, we performed qualitative comparisons with other methods(D2Nets[†] [32], LEDVDI[†] [17], MIMO-UNet+ [4]) as illustrated in Fig. 6. Only our method can restore the letters written on the box in the second row.

4.3 Ablation Study

We analyzed the performance contribution of our network modules. All ablation experiments are performed on the real-world event dataset with models trained for 2.5×10^5 iterations.

Recurrent Encoding (RE). To demonstrate the effectiveness of RE, we compare the model using 2D CNNs and the proposed shared-RNN cell for embedding event streams. From the 1st and 3nd rows of Table 3, we observe a performance gain (+0.51 db) when using RE. On the other hand, when using the 2D CNNs for encoding events, temporal information lying in the event streams is not well preserved, adversely affecting deblurring. Furthermore, if we use a multi-scale loss function(denoted as "MS"), we observe a performance gain (+0.46 db).

ETES Module. is the most crucial module in our method. We validate the deblurring performance with and without this module to verify the effectiveness. From the 3rd and 5th columns of Table 3, we observe a significant performance improvement (+0.81 db) in terms of the average PSNR. We plot the average distribution of the ETES module's output according to various unknown exposure times using all video frames of the test sets in the synthetic event datasets(Fig. 7(a), (b)) and real-world event datasets(Fig. 7(c), (d)). Here, we confirm that all activations are within the exposure phase and hardly activate at the readout phase, even in the different configuration in the training phase. This shows the *efficacy* of the ETES module.

Feature Fusion Module. For cross-modality feature fusion, the simplest way is to use a concatenation of two features to fuse two different modality features. In Table 3, by comparing 7rd and 8th columns, we can observe performance improvement (+0.33 db). The proposed feature fusion module can better utilize the complementary information from frame and event features.

5   Conclusion

This paper studied and formulated a new research problem of event-guided motion deblurring for unknown exposure time videos. To this end, we proposed a novel end-to-end framework. Specifically, we proposed a method of selectively using event features by estimating the feature correlation of different modalities of events and frames. Moreover, extensive experiments demonstrated our method significantly surpasses existing event-guided and frame-based deblurring methods on the various datasets, including real-world blurry videos.

Acknowledgements. This work was supported by Institute of Information and Communications Technology Planning & Evaluation(IITP) Grant funded by Korea Government (MSIT) (No. 2020-0-00440, Development of Artificial Intelligence Technology that Continuously Improves Itself as the Situation Changes in the Real World and No. 2014-3-00123, Development of High Performance Visual BigData Discovery Platform for Large-Scale Realtime Data Analysis) and the National Research Foundation of Korea(NRF) grant funded by the Korea government (MSIT) (NRF2022R1A2B5B03002636).

References

1. Argaw, D.M., Kim, J., Rameau, F., Kweon, I.S.: Motion-blurred video interpolation and extrapolation. In: Proceedings of the AAAI Conference on Artificial Intelligence. vol. 35, pp. 901–910 (2021)
2. Brehm, S., Scherer, S., Lienhart, R.: High-resolution dual-stage multi-level feature aggregation for single image and video deblurring. In: Proceedings of the IEEE/CVF Conference on Computer Vision and Pattern Recognition (CVPR) Workshops, June 2020
3. Chen, L., Lu, X., Zhang, J., Chu, X., Chen, C.: HiNet: half instance normalization network for image restoration. In: Proceedings of the IEEE/CVF Conference on Computer Vision and Pattern Recognition, pp. 182–192 (2021)
4. Cho, S.J., Ji, S.W., Hong, J.P., Jung, S.W., Ko, S.J.: Rethinking coarse-to-fine approach in single image deblurring. arXiv preprint arXiv:2108.05054 (2021)
5. Fellers, T., M.W., D.: Digital camera readout and frame rates. https://hamamatsu.magnet.fsu.edu/articles/readoutandframerates.html. Accessed 6 Apr 2020
6. Gao, H., Tao, X., Shen, X., Jia, J.: Dynamic scene deblurring with parameter selective sharing and nested skip connections. In: Proceedings of the IEEE/CVF Conference on Computer Vision and Pattern Recognition (CVPR), June 2019
7. Hyun Kim, T., Mu Lee, K., Scholkopf, B., Hirsch, M.: Online video deblurring via dynamic temporal blending network. In: Proceedings of the IEEE International Conference on Computer Vision, pp. 4038–4047 (2017)
8. Jia, X., De Brabandere, B., Tuytelaars, T., Gool, L.V.: Dynamic filter networks. Adv. Neural. Inf. aProcess. Syst. **29**, 667–675 (2016)

9. Jiang, Z., Zhang, Y., Zou, D., Ren, J., Lv, J., Liu, Y.: Learning event-based motion deblurring. In: Proceedings of the IEEE/CVF Conference on Computer Vision and Pattern Recognition, pp. 3320–3329 (2020)

10. Johnson, J., Alahi, A., Fei-Fei, L.: perceptual losses for real-time style transfer and super-resolution. In: Leibe, B., Matas, J., Sebe, N., Welling, M. (eds.) ECCV 2016. LNCS, vol. 9906, pp. 694–711. Springer, Cham (2016). https://doi.org/10.1007/978-3-319-46475-6_43

11. Kim, T.H., Sajjadi, M.S.M., Hirsch, M., Schölkopf, B.: Spatio-temporal transformer network for video restoration. In: Ferrari, V., Hebert, M., Sminchisescu, C., Weiss, Y. (eds.) ECCV 2018. LNCS, vol. 11207, pp. 111–127. Springer, Cham (2018). https://doi.org/10.1007/978-3-030-01219-9_7

12. Kingma, D.P., Ba, J.: Adam: a method for stochastic optimization. arXiv preprint arXiv:1412.6980 (2014)

13. Koch, G., et al.: Siamese neural networks for one-shot image recognition. In: ICML Deep Learning Workshop. vol. 2. Lille (2015)

14. Kupyn, O., Budzan, V., Mykhailych, M., Mishkin, D., Matas, J.:Deblurgan: Blind motion deblurring using conditional adversarial networks. In: Proceedings of the IEEE Conference on Computer Vision and Pattern Recognition (CVPR), June 2018

15. Kupyn, O., Martyniuk, T., Wu, J., Wang, Z.: Deblurgan-v2: deblurring (orders-of-magnitude) faster and better. In: The IEEE International Conference on Computer Vision (ICCV), October 2019

16. Li, D., et al.: ARVO: learning all-range volumetric correspondence for video deblurring. In: Proceedings of the IEEE/CVF Conference on Computer Vision and Pattern Recognition, pp. 7721–7731 (2021)

17. Lin, S., et al.: Learning event-driven video deblurring and interpolation. In: Vedaldi, A., Bischof, H., Brox, T., Frahm, J.-M. (eds.) ECCV 2020. LNCS, vol. 12353, pp. 695–710. Springer, Cham (2020). https://doi.org/10.1007/978-3-030-58598-3_41

18. Mildenhall, B., Barron, J.T., Chen, J., Sharlet, D., Ng, R., Carroll, R.: Burst denoising with kernel prediction networks. In: Proceedings of the IEEE Conference on Computer Vision and Pattern Recognition, pp. 2502–2510 (2018)

19. Mostafaviisfahani, S.M., Nam, Y., Choi, J., Yoon, K.J.: E2SRI: learning to super-resolve intensity images from events. IEEE Trans. Pattern Analy. Mach. Intell. 01, 1–1 (2021)

20. Nah, S., Hyun Kim, T., Mu Lee, K.: Deep multi-scale convolutional neural network for dynamic scene deblurring. In: Proceedings of the IEEE Conference on Computer Vision and Pattern Recognition, pp. 3883–3891 (2017)

21. Nah, S., Son, S., Lee, K.M.: Recurrent neural networks with intra-frame iterations for video deblurring. In: Proceedings of the IEEE/CVF Conference on Computer Vision and Pattern Recognition. pp. 8102–8111 (2019)

22. Niklaus, S., Mai, L., Liu, F.: Video frame interpolation via adaptive convolution. In: Proceedings of the IEEE Conference on Computer Vision and Pattern Recognition, pp. 670–679 (2017)

23. Noroozi, M., Chandramouli, P., Favaro, P.: Motion deblurring in the wild. In: Roth, V., Vetter, T. (eds.) GCPR 2017. LNCS, vol. 10496, pp. 65–77. Springer, Cham (2017). https://doi.org/10.1007/978-3-319-66709-6_6

24. Pan, J., Bai, H., Tang, J.: Cascaded deep video deblurring using temporal sharpness prior. In: Proceedings of the IEEE/CVF Conference on Computer Vision and Pattern Recognition (CVPR), June 2020

25. Pan, J., Bai, H., Tang, J.: Cascaded deep video deblurring using temporal sharpness prior. In: Proceedings of the IEEE/CVF Conference on Computer Vision and Pattern Recognition, pp. 3043–3051 (2020

26. Pan, L., Hartley, R., Scheerlinck, C., Liu, M., Yu, X., Dai, Y.: High frame rate video reconstruction based on an event camera. IEEE Trans. Pattern Anal. Mach. Intell. (2020)

27. Pan, L., Scheerlinck, C., Yu, X., Hartley, R., Liu, M., Dai, Y.: Bringing a blurry frame alive at high frame-rate with an event camera. In: Proceedings of the IEEE/CVF Conference on Computer Vision and Pattern Recognition, pp. 6820–6829 (2019)

28. Park, D., Kang, D.U., Kim, J., Chun, S.Y.: Multi-temporal recurrent neural networks for progressive non-uniform single image deblurring with incremental temporal training. In: Vedaldi, A., Bischof, H., Brox, T., Frahm, J.-M. (eds.) ECCV 2020. LNCS, vol. 12351, pp. 327–343. Springer, Cham (2020). https://doi.org/10.1007/978-3-030-58539-6_20

29. Paszke, A., et al.: Automatic differentiation in pytorch (2017)

30. Rebecq, H., Gehrig, D., Scaramuzza, D.: Esim: an open event camera simulator. In: Conference on Robot Learning, pp. 969–982. PMLR (2018)

31. Rebecq, H., Ranftl, R., Koltun, V., Scaramuzza, D.: High speed and high dynamic range video with an event camera. IEEE Trans. Pattern Anal. Mach. Intell. (2019)

32. Shang, W., Ren, D., Zou, D., Ren, J.S., Luo, P., Zuo, W.: Bringing events into video deblurring with non-consecutively blurry frames. In: Proceedings of the IEEE/CVF International Conference on Computer Vision (ICCV), pp. 4531–4540, October 2021

33. Shen, W., Bao, W., Zhai, G., Chen, L., Min, X., Gao, Z.: Blurry video frame interpolation. In: Proceedings of the IEEE/CVF Conference on Computer Vision and Pattern Recognition, pp. 5114–5123 (2020)

34. Su, S., Delbracio, M., Wang, J., Sapiro, G., Heidrich, W., Wang, O.: Deep video deblurring for hand-held cameras. In: Proceedings of the IEEE Conference on Computer Vision and Pattern Recognition, pp. 1279–1288 (2017)

35. Sun, P., Zhang, W., Wang, H., Li, S., Li, X.: Deep RGB-D saliency detection with depth-sensitive attention and automatic multi-modal fusion. In: Proceedings of the IEEE/CVF Conference on Computer Vision and Pattern Recognition, pp. 1407–1417 (2021)

36. Tao, X., Gao, H., Shen, X., Wang, J., Jia, J.: Scale-recurrent network for deep image deblurring. In: Proceedings of the IEEE Conference on Computer Vision and Pattern Recognition, pp. 8174–8182 (2018)

37. Tsai, F.J., Peng, Y.T., Lin, Y.Y., Tsai, C.C., Lin, C.W.: BaNet: blur-aware attention networks for dynamic scene deblurring. arXiv preprint arXiv:2101.07518 (2021)

38. Wang, B., He, J., Yu, L., Xia, G.-S., Yang, W.: Event enhanced high-quality image recovery. In: Vedaldi, A., Bischof, H., Brox, T., Frahm, J.-M. (eds.) ECCV 2020. LNCS, vol. 12358, pp. 155–171. Springer, Cham (2020). https://doi.org/10.1007/978-3-030-58601-0_10

39. Wang, L., Chae, Y., Yoon, K.J.: Dual transfer learning for event-based end-task prediction via pluggable event to image translation. In: ICCV (2021)

40. Wang, L., Chae, Y., Yoon, S.H., Kim, T.K., Yoon, K.J.: EvDistill: asynchronous events to end-task learning via bidirectional reconstruction-guided cross-modal knowledge distillation. In: Proceedings of the IEEE/CVF Conference on Computer Vision and Pattern Recognition, pp. 608–619 (2021)

41. Wang, L., Kim, T.K., Yoon, K.J.: Eventsr: From asynchronous events to image reconstruction, restoration, and super-resolution via end-to-end adversarial learning. In: CVPR, pp. 8315–8325 (2020)
42. Wang, X., Chan, K.C., Yu, K., Dong, C., Change Loy, C.: EDVR: video restoration with enhanced deformable convolutional networks. In: Proceedings of the IEEE/CVF Conference on Computer Vision and Pattern Recognition (CVPR) Workshops, June 2019
43. Wang, Z., Bovik, A.C., Sheikh, H.R., Simoncelli, E.P.: Image quality assessment: from error visibility to structural similarity. IEEE Trans. Image Process. **13**(4), 600–612 (2004)
44. Wieschollek, P., Hirsch, M., Scholkopf, B., Lensch, H.: Learning blind motion deblurring. In: ICCV, pp. 231–240 (2017)
45. Woo, S., Park, J., Lee, J.-Y., Kweon, I.S.: CBAM: convolutional block attention module. In: Ferrari, V., Hebert, M., Sminchisescu, C., Weiss, Y. (eds.) ECCV 2018. LNCS, vol. 11211, pp. 3–19. Springer, Cham (2018). https://doi.org/10.1007/978-3-030-01234-2_1
46. Wu, Y., He, K.: group normalization. In: Ferrari, V., Hebert, M., Sminchisescu, C., Weiss, Y. (eds.) ECCV 2018. LNCS, vol. 11217, pp. 3–19. Springer, Cham (2018). https://doi.org/10.1007/978-3-030-01261-8_1
47. Xu, F., et al.: Motion deblurring with real events. In: Proceedings of the IEEE/CVF International Conference on Computer Vision (ICCV), pp. 2583–2592, October 2021
48. Zamir, S.W., et al.: Multi-stage progressive image restoration. arXiv preprint arXiv:2102.02808 (2021)
49. Zhang, H., Dai, Y., Li, H., Koniusz, P.: Deep stacked hierarchical multi-patch network for image deblurring. In: Proceedings of the IEEE/CVF Conference on Computer Vision and Pattern Recognitio, pp. 5978–5986 (2019)
50. Zhang, K., Luo, W., Zhong, Y., Ma, L., Liu, W., Li, H.: Adversarial spatio-temporal learning for video deblurring. IEEE Trans. Image Process. (2018)
51. Zhang, K., et al.: Deblurring by realistic blurring. In: Proceedings of the IEEE/CVF Conference on Computer Vision and Pattern Recognition, pp. 2737–2746 (2020)
52. Zhang, K., et al.: Deblurring by realistic blurring. In: Proceedings of the EEE/CVF Conference on Computer Vision and Pattern Recognition (CVPR), June 2020
53. Zhang, L., Zhang, H., Zhu, C., Guo, S., Chen, J., Wang, L.: Fine-Grained video deblurring with event camera. In: Lokoč, J., et al. (eds.) MMM 2021. LNCS, vol. 12572, pp. 352–364. Springer, Cham (2021). https://doi.org/10.1007/978-3-030-67832-6_29
54. Zhang, L., Zhang, H., Zhu, C., Guo, S., Chen, J., Wang, L.: Fine-grained video deblurring with event camera. In: Lokoč, J., Skopal, T., Schoeffmann, K., Mezaris, V., Li, X., Vrochidis, S., Patras, I. (eds.) MMM 2021. LNCS, vol. 12572, pp. 352–364. Springer, Cham (2021). https://doi.org/10.1007/978-3-030-67832-6_29
55. Zhang, Y., Wang, C., Tao, D.: Video frame interpolation without temporal priors. In: 30th Proceedings Advances in Neural Information Processing Systems (2020)
56. Zhong, Z., Gao, Y., Zheng, Y., Zheng, B.: Efficient Spatio-temporal recurrent neural network for video deblurring. In: Vedaldi, A., Bischof, H., Brox, T., Frahm, J.-M. (eds.) ECCV 2020. LNCS, vol. 12351, pp. 191–207. Springer, Cham (2020). https://doi.org/10.1007/978-3-030-58539-6_12
57. Zhou, S., Zhang, J., Pan, J., Xie, H., Zuo, W., Ren, J.: Spatio-temporal filter adaptive network for video deblurring. In: Proceedings of the IEEE/CVF International Conference on Computer Vision (ICCV), October 2019

58. Zhu, A.Z., Yuan, L., Chaney, K., Daniilidis, K.: Unsupervised event-based learning of optical flow, depth, and egomotion. In: Proceedings of the IEEE/CVF Conference on Computer Vision and Pattern Recognition, pp. 989–997 (2019)
59. Zou, Y., Zheng, Y., Takatani, T., Fu, Y.: Learning to reconstruct high speed and high dynamic range videos from events. In: Proceedings of the IEEE/CVF Conference on Computer Vision and Pattern Recognition, pp. 2024–2033 (2021)

ReCoNet: Recurrent Correction Network for Fast and Efficient Multi-modality Image Fusion

Zhanbo Huang[1], Jinyuan Liu[2], Xin Fan[1(✉)], Risheng Liu[1,3], Wei Zhong[1], and Zhongxuan Luo[1]

[1] DUT-RU International School of Information Science and Engineering, Dalian University of Technology, Dalian, China
{xin.fan,rsliu,zhongwei,zxluo}@dlut.edu.cn
[2] School of Software Technology, Dalian University of Technology, Dalian, China
[3] Peng Cheng Laboratory, Shenzhen, China

Abstract. Recent advances in deep networks have gained great attention in infrared and visible image fusion (IVIF). Nevertheless, most existing methods are incapable of dealing with slight misalignment on source images and suffer from high computational and spatial expenses. This paper tackles these two critical issues rarely touched in the community by developing a recurrent correction network for robust and efficient fusion, namely ReCoNet. Concretely, we design a deformation module to explicitly compensate geometrical distortions and an attention mechanism to mitigate ghosting-like artifacts, respectively. Meanwhile, the network consists of a parallel dilated convolutional layer and runs in a recurrent fashion, significantly reducing both spatial and computational complexities. ReCoNet can effectively and efficiently alleviates both structural distortions and textural artifacts brought by slight misalignment. Extensive experiments on two public datasets demonstrate the superior accuracy and efficacy of our ReCoNet against the state-of-the-art IVIF methods. Consequently, we obtain a 16% relative improvement of CC on datasets with misalignment and boost the efficiency by 86%. The source code is available at https://github.com/dlut-dimt/reconet.

Keywords: Deep learning · Multi-modality image fusion

1 Introduction

Infrared and Visible Image Fusion (IVIF) generates a fused image presenting complementary characteristics and having richer information than either modality. The generated image is visually appealing and more importantly favorable for practical applications such as video surveillance [31], remote sensing [29,30], and autonomous driving [6,40].

Supplementary Information The online version contains supplementary material available at https://doi.org/10.1007/978-3-031-19797-0_31.

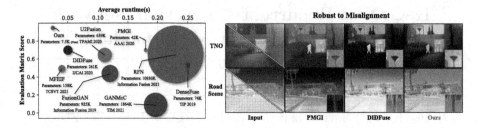

Fig. 1. Comparisons of computational complexity and robustness on the TNO and RoadScene datasets Our method outperforms all its counterparts with higher evaluation scores, lower average runtime, fewer training parameters, and is more robust to misalignment.

Conventional IVIF methods strive to find optimal representation of common features across modals and then to design appropriate weights for merging [17,28]. Recently, the community has witnessed the great success of deep learning in various artificial intelligent applications due to its strong ability in nonlinear fitting and feature extraction. Researchers employ deep networks to learn mutual features [21,23,26,27,41,44] or fusing strategies given training examples for IVIF [13,14,16,19]. These approaches can produce favorable fusion especially for human inspection in controlled scenarios, *e.g.*, fixed capturing devices and/or well-aligned input images [13,19]. Unfortunately, two vital issues still remain unresolved for existing IVIF methods in order to significantly foster subsequent Computer Vision (CV) tasks including object detection [24,46,47], tracking [2,12,43], and semantic segmentation [5,9,33].

First, existing IVIF approaches, either conventional [4,36] or deep-learning based ones [22,38,42], are typically sensitive to misalignment on input images. Slight shifts or deformations on one modality bring evident geometrical distortions on image structures and ghosting-like artifacts in the regions of textural details, as shown in Fig. 1, which substantially deteriorate downstream CV algorithms. Only a tiny fraction of works attempt to mitigate these unpleasant effects. Ma *et al.* [25] proposed total variation minimization that separately strengthens geometric structures in infrared images and preserves textures in visible inputs. However, these methods evidently smear details without exploiting complementary information between these two modalities. Additionally, its iterative optimizing process demands intensive gradient computations resulting in time-consuming fusion. Other deep-learning based methods [10,15,18–20] incorporate the attention/mask mechanism to bolster the misalignment's robustness, avoiding artifacts by reducing the weight of mismatched patches. Yet these attention/mask mechanisms have difficulty portraying correlations across different modalities, resulting in small, tiny artifacts in their fused results.

Second, the state-of-the-art methods demand a large space to store numerous network parameters and lag behind real time running, as illustrated in circles and time values in Fig. 1, though deep methods accelerate fusion with a large margin over conventional approaches. The major bottleneck lies in that these deep have to stack multiple layers of convolutional blocks to learn common features shared by infrared and visible images presenting significant differences on appearance. Meanwhile, training these huge networks require a large number of image pairs unavailable in practice.

This study addresses these two critical issues by developing a recurrent light network that effectively and efficiently corrects both structural distortions and textural artifacts brought by misalignment. Specifically, we train a micro registration module ($\mathcal{R}$) to predict deformation fields between input images. This module explicitly corrects distortions on geometrical structures caused by pixel shifts. We also learn attention maps from both modalities (σ_{ir} and σ_{vis}) that discover the salient regions in respective inputs. Hence, textures in the visible input weigh more in the fusion process while differentiate repeated patterns of high frequency caused by spatial offsets, thus implicitly attenuating ghosting artifacts. Catering for high efficiency, we design a parallel dilated convolutional layer (PDC) that learns contextual information with multiple scale receptive fields. We train one set of parameters of this simple PDC layer and recurrently run the network ($\mathcal{F}$) cascading the attention and lightweight PDC modules in the fusion workflow of Fig. 3. This recurrent process saves the space for network parameters and iteratively improves fusion quality. Figure 1 demonstrates that our approach achieves higher numerical scores, lower computation costs, and fewer parameters on two public available datasets compared with the state-of-the-art. We summarize the our main contributions as follows:

- To our best knowledge, this is the first work to jointly learn deep networks for both registration and fusion on mid-wave infrared and visible images, which enables generating images robust to misalignment of sources.
- We design a deformation module to explicitly compensate geometrical distortions and an attention mechanism to mitigate remaining ghosting-like artifacts. This design properly tackles two different types of undesired effects occurring in structural and textural regions of a given scene, respectively.
- We develop a parallel dilated convolutional layer and a recurrent mechanism, significantly reducing both spatial and computational complexities.

2 The Proposed Method

In this section, we will introduce our motivation and the network architecture of our ReCoNet. In addition, the loss function is also illustrated in the following.

2.1 Motivation

In real-life scenarios, pixel-level registered infrared and visible images are unavailable caused by insuperable internal and external factors. As illustrated in Fig. 2, we show three typical factors that frequently occur in genuine acquisitions. (i) In

Fig. 2. Three representative misalignment situations that occur in actual scenarios.

most of the encapsulated devices, supposing the internal systems have been work-ing for an extended period or in a high-temperature internal environment, the Complementary Metal-Oxide-Semiconductor (CMOS) produces noises into the image. (ii) For the server environments, *e.g.*, desert and tropical forest, the refrac-tion of hot airflow may cause severe distortion on the source images. (iii) The bumpy roads, fast-moving objects, or non-synchronous multi-vision cameras may degenerate the source images [45], *e.g.*, motion blur and transportation. Slight shifts or deformations on one modality bring evident geometrical distortions; few existing methods can overcome these issues because they only perform fusion on pixel-level registered pairs. Based on this observation, we raise a recurrent cor-rection network for realizing IVIF, which has sufficient capacity to deal with sight misalignment source inputs.

Apart from that, most previous fusion approaches take every effort to strengthen the network with a crease of depth and width, achieving state-of-the-art performance. However, these catastrophic increases of network layer may lead to a significant requirement of computation and memory, thus making them difficult to apply them in the follow-up high-level computer vision tasks, *e.g.*, object detection, depth estimation, and object tracking. Consequently, a parallel dilated convolutional layer and a recurrent learning mechanism are sophisticat-edly designed in our method to boost computational efficiency.

2.2 Micro Registration Module

The micro registration module $\mathcal{R}$ contributes to alleviate the slight misalignment errors cased by geometric distortions or scaling. It consist of two components: a deformation field prediction network $\mathcal{R}_\phi$ and a re-sampler layer $\mathcal{R}_S$. The defor-mation field ϕ is employ to represent the transformation, which allow our method to map images non-uniformly accurately.

Supposing given an infrared image x and a distorted visible image $\tilde{y}$, $\mathcal{R}_\phi$ aims to predict a deformation field $\phi_{\tilde{y}\to y} = \mathcal{R}_\phi(x, \tilde{y})$, describing how to align $\tilde{y}$

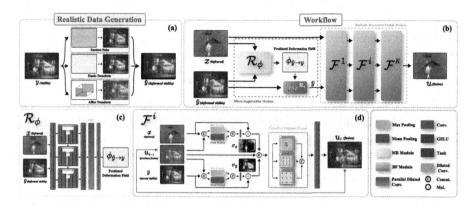

Fig. 3. Methodology framework: (a) pseudo-distortion data generation; (b) our ReCoNet workflow; (c) micro-registration (MR) module architecture; and (d) pipeline of biphasic-recurrent fusion (BF) module.

to y non-rigidly. The deformation field $\phi \in \mathbb{R}^{h \times w \times 2}$, in which each pair $\phi_{h,w} = (\Delta x_h, \Delta x_w) \in \mathbb{R}^2$ indicates the deformation offset for the (h, w) pixel $v_{h,w}$ in $\tilde{y}$. Our R mainly focuses on the fusion effect after registration, so that an U-Net like micro module is designed. The detailed architecture is given in the bottom-left conner of Fig. 3.

To apply geometric transformations to the image, we use a re-sampler layer $\mathcal{R}_S$ which takes the deformation field $\phi_{\tilde{y} \to y}$ generated by $\mathcal{R}_\phi$ and applies it to the distorted visible image $\tilde{y}$. The value of the transformed visible image $\bar{y}$ at pixel $v_{h,w}$ is calculated by the equation:

$$\bar{y}[v_{h,w}] = \tilde{y}\left[v_{h,w} + \phi_{h,w}^{\tilde{y} \to y}\right]. \tag{1}$$

2.3   Biphasic Recurrent Fusion Module

Contextual features (*e.g.*, edges, targets, and contours) play a vital role in the fusion process. However, with an increase of the network's depth, the contextual features degrade gradually, resulting in blurred targets and unclear details on the fusion results. To deal with this issue, previous works attempt to design various attention mechanisms or bring in enlarge the width of network (*e.g.*, adding dense or residual blocks). Actually, such aforementioned attention mechanisms have difficulty characterizing contextual features from the source images. The increasingly model architecture may lead to a significant requirement of computation and memory. Thus, we propose a biphasic recurrent fusion module to acquire high computational efficiency for sufficient contextual features representation at multiple scales.

Baphasic Attention Layer: To obtain the salient features and keep contextual consistency with the source images, a biphasic attention layer is proposed. It is composed of a max-pooling operation, an average-pooling operation, and a convolutional layer without bias. The maximum and average values of the pixels at each point of the two images are taken and combined as the input of the convolutional layer. Let $\mathcal{A}$ denote the biphasic attention layer, I_a and I_b as two input images, respectively, this process can be expressed as the following equation:

$$\mathcal{A}(I_a, I_b) = \theta_{\mathcal{A}} * [\max(I_a, I_b), \operatorname{avg}(I_a, I_b)],$$

where $*$ denotes the convolution operation, $\theta_{\mathcal{A}}$ denote the parameter of the convolutional layer in our attention layer, and we concat $\max(I_a, I_b)$ and $\operatorname{avg}(I_a, I_b)$ as the input of attention layer. As shown in Fig. 3, the network computes attention map σ_x and σ_y from input images group $\{x, u, \bar{y}\}$ according equation:

$$\sigma_{ir} = \mathcal{A}_x(x, u_i) \quad \sigma_{\bar{y}} = \mathcal{A}_{\bar{y}}(\bar{y}, u_i),$$

where $\mathcal{A}_x$ and $\mathcal{A}_y$ denote infrared and visible attention layer, respectively, while the u_i indicates the fused result of the last recurrence.

In addition, thanks to biphasic attention map, we can obtain more desired emphasis on contextual features and also make our method implicitly compatible with slight alignment errors by reducing the weight of the slightly distorted region such as non-smooth edge and ghosts.

Parallel Dilated Convolutional Layer: We develop a parallel dilated convolutional layer to extract features from the source images efficiently. A group of dilated convolutional layers with sawtooth wave-like dilated factors increases receptive field without losing neighboring information. Convolutions with the same kernel size 3×3 on three dilated paths have their receptive field with different dilated factors. As shown PDC in Fig. 3, the dilation rates are set as $1, 2, 3$ receptively. Thus, the three parallel convolutional paths have receptive fields of 3×3, 5×5, and 7×7.

To provide a formal description, let f_{in}^i denote the input for the dilated convolutional layers at the i-th recurrence. The output feature map f_{out}^i of the recurrent parallel dilated convolutional layers is gradually updated as follows:

$$f_{out}^i = \{\mathcal{C}^k(f_{in}^i)\}_{k \in \{1,2,3\}}, \mathcal{C}(f_{in}^i) = \theta_{\mathcal{C}}^k * f_{in}^i + \mathbf{b}_{\mathcal{C}}^k,$$

where $\theta_{\mathcal{C}}^k$ and $\mathbf{b}_{\mathcal{C}}^k$ denote the parameter and bias of the convolutional layer with dilation rate equaling k.

Recurrent Learning: We raise a recurrent architecture to replace time-consuming multi-layer convolution to extract contextual features from a coarse-to-fine manner. We can reduce the computational complexity overhead of building the graph by partially reusing the computational graph for dynamically graph network frameworks such as PyTorch [32]. As shown in Fig. 4, compared to a series network structure, we will spend a little more time in the first loop used to build the graph than the no-loop structure, but for each subsequent loop, we will save about 27% of the time. Overall, our recurrent architecture reduces about 15% of the time, 33% parameters, and 42% GPU memory. Such recurrent learning allows ReCoNet to extract image features from contextual information and meet real-time standards($\geq 25 fps$) [11]. Due to the parameters and memory reduction, our ReCoNet can be deployed on mobile devices.

2.4 Loss Functions

The total loss function $\mathcal{L}_{\text{total}}$ of our network is accomplished to two loss term, the fusion loss $\mathcal{L}_{\text{fuse}}$ and the registration loss $\mathcal{L}_{\text{reg}}$. The fusion loss ensures the network to generate the fused result with better effects and rich information, while the registration loss contributes to constrain and refine image distortion caused by misalignment. We train our network minimize the following loss function:

$$\mathcal{L}_{\text{total}} = \lambda\mathcal{L}_{\text{fuse}} + (1 - \lambda)\,\mathcal{L}_{\text{reg}}, \tag{2}$$

where λ is a trade-off parameter.

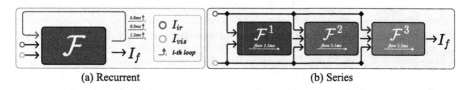

$$\text{(a) Recurrent} \qquad\qquad\qquad\qquad \text{(b) Series}$$

Fig. 4. Efficiency comparison of our recurrent and series architectures with the same floating point operations (FLOPs).

The fusion loss consists of two loss terms. Structure similarity $\mathcal{L}_{\text{SSIM}}$ is employed to maintain the over structure from light, contrast and structure information aspect, while $\mathcal{L}_{\text{pixel}}$ is used to balance the pixel intensity of the two source images. Therefore, $\mathcal{L}_{\text{fuse}}$ is expressed as:

$$\mathcal{L}_{\text{fuse}} = \gamma\mathcal{L}_{\text{SSIM}} + (1 - \gamma)\,\mathcal{L}_{\text{pixel}}, \tag{3}$$

where γ is the weight of two loss items. Specifically, we constrain our fused result to have the same fundamental architecture as the source images, and hence the $\mathcal{L}_{\text{SSIM}}$ loss is defined as:

$$\mathcal{L}_{\text{SSIM}} = (1 - SSIM\,(u, x)) + (1 - SSIM\,(u, y))\,. \tag{4}$$

Similarly, the fused results should balance the pixel intensity distribution from both infrared and visible images, and the pixel loss can be formulated as:

$$\mathcal{L}_{\text{pixel}} = \|u - x\|_1 + \|u - y\|_1\,, \tag{5}$$

where $\|\cdot\|_1$ denotes the $l1$-norm.

Apart from that, the registration loss $\mathcal{L}_{\text{reg}}$ also plays a key role in correcting the distortion, which can be expressed as:

$$\mathcal{L}_{\text{reg}} = \eta\mathcal{L}_{sim} + (1 - \eta)\,\mathcal{L}_{\text{smooth}}, \tag{6}$$

where $\mathcal{L}_{sim}$ denotes similarity loss, and $\mathcal{L}_{\text{smooth}}$ is a smoothing loss that targets ensure to generate a smooth deformation. η is trade-off parameter in balancing the two terms.

More precisely, $\mathcal{L}_{sim}$ is calculated as:

$$\mathcal{L}_{\text{sim}} = \|\phi_{\tilde{y}\to y} - (-\phi_{y\to\tilde{y}})\|_2^2, \tag{7}$$

where $\phi_{\tilde{y}\to y}$ denotes deformation field and $\phi_{y\to\tilde{y}}$ expresses the generated random deformation field, respectively. As our framework mainly focuses on the fusion effect after registration, the $-\phi_{y\to\tilde{y}}$ is roughly used as the ground truth of the deformation field for our register to converge. These slight errors introduced in this process will be eliminated in our recurrent fusion mechanism.

For each voxel p in 2D spatial domain Ω, the $\mathcal{L}_{smooth}$ can be specifically defined as:

$$\mathcal{L}_{\text{smooth}} = \sum_{p\in\Omega} \|\nabla\phi(p)\|_1^1, \tag{8}$$

where ∇ denotes the approximate spatial gradients using differences between neighboring voxels.

3   Experiments and Results

We first introduce the datasets, evaluation metrics and training details. Then we compare the proposed method against a broad range of the eight state-of-the-arts methods (*i.e.,* DenseFuse [13], FusionGAN [26], RFN [14], GANMcC [27], MFEIF [19], PMGI [44], DIDFuse [16] and U2Fusion [41]) on aligned/misaligned dataset, respectively. Besides, we also provide the complexity evaluation, the mean opinion score analysis and the extensive ablation experiments. All experiments are conducted with Pytorch on a computer with Nvidia V100 GPU.

3.1   Dataset and Preprocessing

Dataset: Both our aligned and misaligned fusion experiments are conducted on the TNO [37] and RoadScene [41] datasets. We generate infrared images with different degrees of distortion by randomly using deformation field. In each aligned/misaligned IVIF experiment, we randomly selected 20/180 pairs of images their corresponding TNO/RoadScene datasets as training samples.

Evaluation Metrics: We employ three existing statistical metrics including standard deviation (SD), entropy (EN) and correlation coefficient (CC), to comprehensively evaluates the quality of the fused images from different aspects.

Training Details: The λ, γ and η are set as 0.6, 0.28, and 0.78, respectively. The Adam optimizer updates the parameters with the learning rate of 0.001 and a total epoch of 300. The micro registration $\mathcal{R}_\phi$ and the biphasic recurrent fusion module $\mathcal{F}$ are jointly trained.

3.2   Results on Aligned Dataset

Qualitative Comparisons: Figure 5 shows eight representative fused images generated by different models. Visual inspection shows that, our method has obvious advantages over the comparative models. Although other methods achieve meaningful fused results, they still remain problems, such as unclear thermal targets (see the green box in the Fig. 5 of DenseFuse, RFN and U2Fusion), blurred details (see the red box in the Fig. 5 of GANMcC and DIDFuse). On the contrary, our method can generate visual-friendly fused results with clear target, distinct contrast and abundant details.

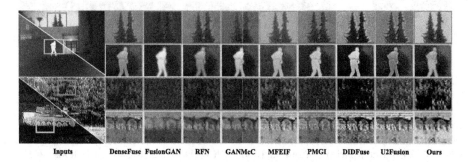

Fig. 5. Visual comparisons of our ReCoNet with state-of-the-art methods on the aligned TNO dataset. (Color figure online)

Quantitative Comparisons: Subsequently, the quantitative results on 15/40 image pairs of the TNO/RoadScene dataset are shown in Fig. 6. Obviously, our method reach the values for two metrics (SD and EN), followed by DIDFuse and U2Fusion. For the CC metric, our method only follows behind FGAN by a narrow margin on the TNO dataset.

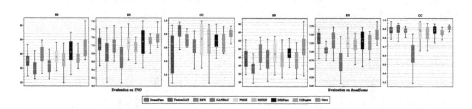

Fig. 6. Quantitative comparisons with eight IVIF methods on TNO and RoadScene datasets, respectively. In the boxes, the orange lines and the green tangles denote medium and mean values. (Color figure online)

3.3   Results on Slightly Misaligned Dataset

Qualitative Comparisons: As our method has the ability to fuse image pairs with slightly misalignment, we further test its fusion performance against other state-of-the-art methods on sight misaligned TNO and RoadScene datasets, respectively, which is shown in Fig. 7. Obviously, other methods suffer structural distortion or undesirable halos on their fused results. By comparison, our method overcomes the limitation of undesirable artifacts caused by misalignment in image pairs to a certain degree. This mainly benefits from the structure refinement and recurrent attention module in the training process.

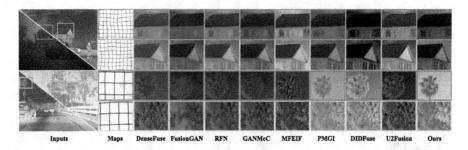

Fig. 7. Visual comparison of our method with eight state-of-the-art methods on the slightly misaligned TNO and Roadscene datasets.

Quantitative Comparisons: As shown in Fig. 8, we evaluated the CC metric of these methods on selected 20 images from TNO/RoadScene dataset with four different tranform: random noise, elastic transform, affine transform and mixed transform. It is easy to notice that as the transform applied to the input images, the scores of DenseFuse, PMGI, DIDFuse and U2Fusion drop down dramatically. As the MFEIF that uses the Attention mechanism, it exhibits some resistance to random noise. Since FusionGAN is a gradient transfer-based method, the elastic transform does not disturb it much. On the contrary, our method has a strong ability to deal with all four transforms.

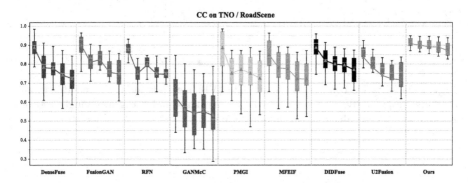

Fig. 8. CC matrix comparison with eight IVIF methods on the TNO and RoadScene dataset. The five scores in each method group represent, from left to right: original, datasets with random noise, with elastic transform, with affine transform dataset and with mixed transform dataset, respectively.

Table 1. Computational efficiency comparison with a series of completive CNN-based methods, the value is tested on GPU.

Methods	DenseFuse	FusionGAN	RFN	GANMcC	PMGI	MFEIF	DIDFuse	U2Fusion	Ours$_F$	Ours$_{R-F}$
SIZE(M)	0.074	0.925	10.93	1.864	0.042	0.158	0.261	0.659	**0.007**	0.209
FLOPs(G)	48.96	497.76	-	1002.56	745.21	25.32	18.71	366.34	**1.162**	12.54
TIME(s)	0.251	0.124	0.238	0.246	0.182	0.045	0.055	0.123	**0.024**	0.052

3.4   Computational Complexity Analysis

As shown in Table 1, a complexity evaluation is introduced to evaluate the efficiency of our method from three aspects, *i.e.*, training parameters, FLOPs and runtime. It worth to pointing that our method have the fastest average running speed and minimum size. This indicates the efficiency of our ReCoNet, which can serve practical vision tasks well.

3.5   Mean Opinion Score Analysis

We selected 20 typical image pairs from each dataset (*i.e.*, aligned/misaligned TNO/RoadScene) for the subjective experiment. Ten computer vision researchers rated the fused images' overall visual perception, target clarity, and detail richness. Figure 9 shows the sorted mean opinion score of all methods after normalization. Note that our method gets the highest rate for both groups, indicating the outstanding visual perception effects.

We conduct the additional subjective experiment on the aligned/misaligned TNO/Roadscene dataset of these eight IVIF methods, in which we select 20 typical image pairs from each dataset. The misaligned datasets are generated by transforming the infrared image with three kinds of transformation methods (*i.e.*, affine, elastic and both of them). We have found ten computer vision researchers, to provide a score from three aspects (*i.e.*, overall visual perception, target clarity and richness of details) for the fused image. Figure 9 shows the sorted mean opinion score (MOS) of all methods after normalization, in which

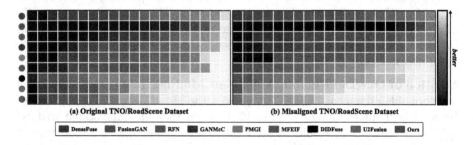

Fig. 9. Heat maps of MOS towards all methods on 20 typical image pairs from aligned and slightly misaligned datasets, respectively. Note that our method achieves more significant advantages when fusing the misaligned pairs.

the shade of the color indicates the level of the score (yellow: the best, purple: the worst). Note that our method acquires the highest score towards all the testing image pairs, which indicates our method is more in line with the human visual system.

3.6 Ablation Studies

Discuss the Iteration in Attention Module: Figure 10 exhibits the effect of iterations in recurrent attention learning the on the fusion result. According to the fused results, we discover that with the increase of the number of iteration in our attention module, the fused results tend to achieve a better visual effects.Both texture details and targets are become more clearly. This mainly benefits from the progressive recurrent attention module, which allows each iteration to have a positive effect on the fused result.

x y u_1 u_2 u_3

Fig. 10. A step-by-step visual result of our recurrent learning mechanism.

Ablation of Our Attention Mechanism. To validate the benefit of our attention module, we pick out the of attention and corresponding ablation study in Fig. 11. We can discover that our attention module perceive the most discriminative regions (*i.e.,* targets in the infrared image and details in the visible images) form the source images, and hence the fused results keep more meaningful information.

Ablation of Our Deformable Alignment Module: To investigate the effect of deformable alignment module, we present the visual results of with/without deformable alignment module in Fig. 12. Obvious that the unfavorable artifacts appears on the fusion result without the attention module (see road sign in the second row and flagpole in the bottom row). In contrast, our method can overcome ghosting halos and structure distortion to a certain degree.

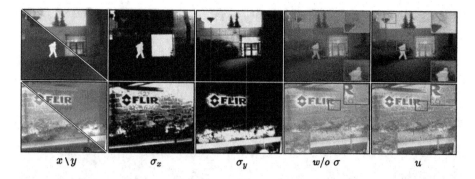

Fig. 11. Qualitative results on discussing biphasic attention layer.

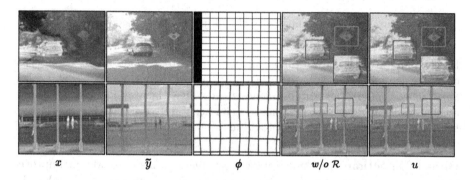

Fig. 12. Ablation study about the effect of our micro registration module.

3.7   Applications in Related Tasks

This section experiments with our ReCoNet in conjunction with a series of related follow-up applications on the RoadScene dataset covering day and night scenarios.

Salient Object Detection: Extracting critical information about a target scene under a harsh environment is a challenging task. We carry out our experiment based on U²-Net [34]. Taking an example from Fig. 13, the bright light from the opposite headlights causes the car to be invisible. Under poor lighting conditions, we confirm that the infrared information can detect more desirable areas, but some portion with low thermal radiation is easily ignored. Moreover, current methods focus more on infrared information(*e.g.,* PMGI), which cannot estimate the main natural object and visible details (*e.g.,* DIDFuse) that introduce unwanted artifacts. In contrast, our method estimates the whole region without artifacts.

Depth Estimation: Indeed, recent algorithms for depth estimation [8,39] are trained on daytime road datasets (*e.g.,* KITTI [7] and CityScapes [3]), resulting in a disconnect between daytime and nighttime sceneries. The second row of

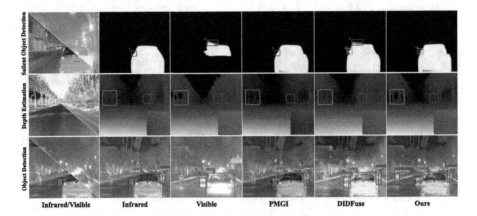

Fig. 13. Visual comparisons of multiple practical vision tasks.

Fig. 13 illustrates the depth maps calculated by MiDaS [35] on the recent efficiency fusion methods. Note that the depth maps from visible images and other approaches render apparent deficiencies, in which the wayside trees are misestimated. By comparison, our method can accurately estimate the depth map for diverse tree shapes, thereby providing a new auxiliary option for real-world depth estimation.

Object Detection: As a non-trivial byproduct, we also provide an improvement in our approach for detecting targets using the well-known YoloV4 [1]. In the last row of Fig. 13, our method accurately detects all three targets, and only our fusion results correctly detect the pedestrian on the left. These results demonstrate that our method significantly impacts the object detection task.

4   Conclusion

In this paper, we propose an innovative network based on biphasic recurrent attention learning, which robustly and efficiently realizes IVIF take in an end-to-end manner. We first design a micro registration module to coarse estimate the distortion caused by misalignment. Then, a biphasic recurrent learning network successfully merges the source images and removes other remaining ghosting halos or artifacts. Furthermore, we also employ the parallel dilated convolutional and share calculation graph in our recurrent network to achieve high computational efficiency. Both subjective and objective experimental results reveal that our ReCoNet has significant superiority against the state-of-the-art methods with high efficiency. In addition, our ReCoNet also can deal with misalignment image pairs to a certain degree.

Acknowledgments. This work is partially supported by the National Key R&D Program of China (2020YF-B1313503), the National Natural Science Foundation of China (Nos. 61922019, 61906029 and 62027826), and the Fundamental Research Funds for the Central Universities.

References

1. Bochkovskiy, A., Wang, C.Y., Liao, H.Y.M.: YOLOv4: optimal speed and accuracy of object detection. arXiv preprint arXiv:2004.10934 (2020)
2. Brasó, G., Leal-Taixé, L.: Learning a neural solver for multiple object tracking. In: IEEE CVPR, pp. 6247–6257 (2020)
3. Cordts, M., et al.: The cityscapes dataset for semantic urban scene understanding. In: Proceedings of the IEEE Conference on Computer Vision and Pattern Recognition (CVPR) (2016)
4. Du, Q., Xu, H., Ma, Y., Huang, J., Fan, F.: Fusing infrared and visible images of different resolutions via total variation model. Sensors **18**(11), 3827 (2018)
5. Fu, J., et al.: Dual attention network for scene segmentation. In: CVPR, pp. 3146–3154 (2019)
6. Gao, H., Cheng, B., Wang, J., Li, K., Zhao, J., Li, D.: Object classification using CNN-based fusion of vision and lidar in autonomous vehicle environment. IEEE Trans. Ind. Informat. **14**(9), 4224–4231 (2018)
7. Geiger, A., Lenz, P., Stiller, C., Urtasun, R.: Vision meets robotics: the KITTI dataset. Int. J. Rob. Res. **32**(11), 1231–1237 (2013)
8. Godard, C., Mac Aodha, O., Brostow, G.J.: Unsupervised monocular depth estimation with left-right consistency. In: CVPR (2017)
9. He, K., Gkioxari, G., Dollár, P., Girshick, R.: Mask R-CNN. In: Proceedings of the IEEE International Conference on Computer Vision, pp. 2961–2969 (2017)
10. Jiang, Z., Li, Z., Yang, S., Fan, X., Liu, R.: Target oriented perceptual adversarial fusion network for underwater image enhancement. IEEE Trans. Circ. Syst. Video Technol. **32**, 6584–6598 (2022)
11. Kristan, M., et al.: The visual object tracking vot2017 challenge results. In: Proceedings of the IEEE International Conference on Computer Vision Workshops, pp. 1949–1972 (2017)
12. Lan, X., et al.: Learning modality-consistency feature templates: a robust RGB-infrared tracking system. IEEE Tran. Ind. Enformat. **66**(12), 9887–9897 (2019)
13. Li, H., Wu, X.J.: DenseFuse: a fusion approach to infrared and visible images. IEEE Trans. Image Process. **28**(5), 2614–2623 (2018)
14. Li, H., Wu, X.J., Kittler, J.: RFN-nest: an end-to-end residual fusion network for infrared and visible images. Inf. Fus. **73**, 72–86 (2021)
15. Li, J., Huo, H., Li, C., Wang, R., Feng, Q.: AttentionfGAN: Infrared and visible image fusion using attention-based generative adversarial networks. IEEE Trans. Multimedia **23**, 1383–1396 (2020)
16. Li, P.: Didfuse: deep image decomposition for infrared and visible image fusion. In: Proceedings of the Twenty-Ninth International Conference on International Joint Conferences on Artificial Intelligence, pp. 976–976 (2021)
17. Li, S., Kang, X., Hu, J.: Image fusion with guided filtering. IEEE Trans. Image Process. **22**(7), 2864–2875 (2013)
18. Liu, J., et al.: Target-aware dual adversarial learning and a multi-scenario multi-modality benchmark to fuse infrared and visible for object detection. In: Proceedings of the IEEE/CVF Conference on Computer Vision and Pattern Recognition, pp. 5802–5811 (2022)
19. Liu, J., Fan, X., Jiang, J., Liu, R., Luo, Z.: Learning a deep multi-scale feature ensemble and an edge-attention guidance for image fusion. In: IEEE TCSVT (2021)

20. Liu, J., Shang, J., Liu, R., Fan, X.: Attention-guided global-local adversarial learning for detail-preserving multi-exposure image fusion. IEEE Trans. Circ. Syst. Video Technol. **32**, 5026–5040 (2022). https://doi.org/10.1109/TCSVT.2022.3144455

21. Liu, J., Wu, Y., Huang, Z., Liu, R., Fan, X.: SMOA: searching a modality-oriented architecture for infrared and visible image fusion. IEEE Signal Process. Lett. **28**, 1818–1822 (2021)

22. Liu, R., Liu, J., Jiang, Z., Fan, X., Luo, Z.: A bilevel integrated model with data-driven layer ensemble for multi-modality image fusion. IEEE Trans. Image Process. **30**, 1261–1274 (2021). https://doi.org/10.1109/TIP.2020.3043125

23. Liu, R., Liu, Z., Liu, J., Fan, X.: Searching a hierarchically aggregated fusion architecture for fast multi-modality image fusion. In: Proceedings of the 29th ACM International Conference on Multimedia, pp. 1600–1608 (2021)

24. Liu, W., et al.: SSD: single shot multibox detector. In: Leibe, B., Matas, J., Sebe, N., Welling, M. (eds.) ECCV 2016. LNCS, vol. 9905, pp. 21–37. Springer, Cham (2016). https://doi.org/10.1007/978-3-319-46448-0_2

25. Ma, J., Chen, C., Li, C., Huang, J.: Infrared and visible image fusion via gradient transfer and total variation minimization. Inf. Fus. **31**, 100–109 (2016)

26. Ma, J., Yu, W., Liang, P., Li, C., Jiang, J.: FusionGAN: a generative adversarial network for infrared and visible image fusion. Inf. Fus. **48**, 11–26 (2019)

27. Ma, J., Zhang, H., Shao, Z., Liang, P., Xu, H.: GANMcC:: a generative adversarial network with multiclassification constraints for infrared and visible image fusion. IEEE Trans. Instrum Meaure. **70**, 1–14 (2020)

28. Ma, J., Zhou, Z., Wang, B., Zong, H.: Infrared and visible image fusion based on visual saliency map and weighted least square optimization. Infr. Phys. Technol. **82**, 8–17 (2017)

29. Nencini, F., Garzelli, A., Baronti, S., Alparone, L.: Remote sensing image fusion using the curvelet transform. Inf. Fus. **8**(2), 143–156 (2007)

30. Palsson, F., Sveinsson, J.R., Ulfarsson, M.O.: Multispectral and hyperspectral image fusion using a 3-d-convolutional neural network. IEEE Geosci. Remote Sens. Lett. **14**(5), 639–643 (2017)

31. Paramanandham, N., Rajendiran, K.: Infrared and visible image fusion using discrete cosine transform and swarm intelligence for surveillance applications. Infrar. Phys. Technol. **88**, 13–22 (2018)

32. Paszke, A., et al.: An imperative style, high-performance deep learning library. In: Wallach, H., Larochelle, H., Beygelzimer, A., d'Alché-Buc, F., Fox, E., Garnett, R. (eds.) Advances in Neural Information Processing Systems, vol. 32, pp. 8024–8035. Curran Associates, Inc. (2019), http://papers.neurips.cc/paper/9015-pytorch-an-imperative-style-high-performance-deep-learning-library.pdf

33. Pu, M., Huang, Y., Guan, Q., Zou, Q.: GraphNet: learning image pseudo annotations for weakly-supervised semantaic segmentation. In: ACM MM, pp. 483–491. ACM (2018)

34. Qin, X., Zhang, Z., Huang, C., Dehghan, M., Zaiane, O., Jagersand, M.: U2-Net: going deeper with nested u-structure for salient object detection, vol. 106, p. 107404 (2020)

35. Ranftl, R., Lasinger, K., Hafner, D., Schindler, K., Koltun, V.: Towards robust monocular depth estimation: mixing datasets for zero-shot cross-dataset transfer. IEEE Trans. Pattern Anal. Mach. Intell. **44**, 1623–1637 (2020)

36. Shreyamsha Kumar, B.: Image fusion based on pixel significance using cross bilateral filter. Sig. Image Video. Process. **9**(5), 1193–1204 (2015)

37. Toet, A.: The tno multiband image data collection. Data Brief **15**, 249 (2017)
38. Wang, D., Liu, J., Fan, X., Liu, R.: Unsupervised misaligned infrared and visible image fusion via cross-modality image generation and registration. arXiv preprint arXiv:2205.11876 (2022)
39. Wang, L., Zhang, J., Wang, Y., Lu, H., Ruan, X.: CLIFFNet for monocular depth estimation with hierarchical embedding Loss. In: Vedaldi, A., Bischof, H., Brox, T., Frahm, J.-M. (eds.) ECCV 2020. LNCS, vol. 12350, pp. 316–331. Springer, Cham (2020). https://doi.org/10.1007/978-3-030-58558-7_19
40. Xiao, Y., Codevilla, F., Gurram, A., Urfalioglu, O., López, A.M.: Multimodal end-to-end autonomous driving. IEEE Trans. Intell. Trans. Syst. **23**, 537–547 (2020)
41. Xu, H., Ma, J., Jiang, J., Guo, X., Ling, H.: U2fusion: A unified unsupervised image fusion network. In: IEEE TPAMI (2020)
42. Xu, H., Ma, J., Yuan, J., Le, Z., Liu, W.: RfNet: unsupervised network for mutually reinforcing multi-modal image registration and fusion. In: Proceedings of the IEEE/CVF Conference on Computer Vision and Pattern Recognition, pp. 19679–19688 (2022)
43. Xu, T., Feng, Z.H., Wu, X.J., Kittler, J.: Learning adaptive discriminative correlation filters via temporal consistency preserving spatial feature selection for robust visual object tracking. IEEE Trans. Image Process. **28**(11), 5596–5609 (2019)
44. Zhang, H., Xu, H., Xiao, Y., Guo, X., Ma, J.: Rethinking the image fusion: A fast unified image fusion network based on proportional maintenance of gradient and intensity. In: AAAI. vol. 34, pp. 12797–12804 (2020)
45. Zhang, L., Zhu, X., Chen, X., Yang, X., Lei, Z., Liu, Z.: Weakly aligned cross-modal learning for multispectral pedestrian detection. In: Proceedings of the IEEE/CVF International Conference on Computer Vision, pp. 5127–5137 (2019)
46. Zhang, X., Ye, P., Leung, H., Gong, K., Xiao, G.: Object fusion tracking based on visible and infrared images: A comprehensive review. Inf. Fus. **63**, 166–187 (2020)
47. Zhao, J.X., Liu, J.J., Fan, D.P., Cao, Y., Yang, J., Cheng, M.M.: EgNet: edge guidance network for salient object detection. In: CVPR, pp. 8779–8788 (2019)

Content Adaptive Latents and Decoder for Neural Image Compression

Guanbo Pan[1], Guo Lu[2], Zhihao Hu[1], and Dong Xu[3]([✉])

[1] School of Software, Beihang University, Beijing, China
[2] School of Computer Science and Technology, Beijing Institute of Technology, Beijing, China
[3] Department of Computer Science, The University of Hong Kong, Hong Kong, China
dongxu@cs.hku.hk

Abstract. In recent years, neural image compression (NIC) algorithms have shown powerful coding performance. However, most of them are not adaptive to the image content. Although several content adaptive methods have been proposed by updating the encoder-side components, the adaptability of both latents and the decoder is not well exploited. In this work, we propose a new NIC framework that improves the content adaptability on both latents and the decoder. Specifically, to remove redundancy in the latents, our content adaptive channel dropping (CACD) method automatically selects the optimal quality levels for the latents spatially and drops the redundant channels. Additionally, we propose the content adaptive feature transformation (CAFT) method to improve decoder-side content adaptability by extracting the characteristic information of the image content, which is then used to transform the features in the decoder side. Experimental results demonstrate that our proposed methods with the encoder-side updating algorithm achieve the state-of-the-art performance.

Keywords: Neural image compression · Content adaptive coding

1 Introduction

Data compression has been studied for decades as an essential issue to alleviate data storage and transmission burden. The traditional codecs, such as JPEG [39], JPEG2000 [34], BPG [9] for image compression and H.264 [43], H.265 [36], H.266 [11] for video compression, still prevail nowadays. In recent years, neural image compression (NIC) has shown promising coding performance due to its powerful nonlinear transformation capability and end-to-end optimization strategy. The recent state-of-the-art NIC methods like [46] outperform the latest traditional compression standard Versatile Video Coding (VVC) [11]

Supplementary Information The online version contains supplementary material available at https://doi.org/10.1007/978-3-031-19797-0_32.

on various datasets including the Kodak [1] and Tecnick [4] datasets. These approaches generally reduce the redundancy of the images by using an autoencoder architecture, which learns a mapping between the RGB color space and the learned latent space. The latent representation of the image is then quantized into a discrete-valued version, which is further compressed by the lossless entropy coding methods.

Neural data compression methods learn a generalized model to ensure the coding performance during performance evaluation. However, domain shift between the training and testing data and lack of adaptability to the visual content degrade the performance when compressing unseen data samples. Therefore, some works [12,27,40,49] were proposed to improve the adaptability for neural image compression and neural video compression (NVC) by updating the encoder-side components. Those methods aim at generating more compressible latents and estimating more accurate entropy model parameters for each data instance by fine-tuning the latents [12,49], the encoder [27] or the input image [40]. However, such fine-tuning process is extremely time-consuming and the adaptability is still limited due to the fixed decoder.

To exploit the adaptability at the decoder, some full-model over-fitting methods [33] entropy encode and transmit the updates of the decoder parameters along with the quantized latents to the receiver side for better and consistent reconstruction. However, the design of additional model compression is quite complex and the updating approach is also time-consuming. Another limitation in NIC is that the number of channels of the latents is not adapted to the rate-distortion (RD) trade-offs and the image content. Most works train multiple models with the same network architecture based on different RD trade-offs for rate control, which generate the latents with the same channel number for different RD trade-offs and spatial locations. However, this leads to redundant elements in the latents.

In this work, we propose a content adaptive NIC framework to improve the adaptability on both latents and the decoder. To improve the adaptability on latent codes, we propose the content adaptive channel dropping (CACD) method, which selects the optimal quality level at each spatial location for the latents and drops redundant elements along the channel dimension. In order to improve decoder-side content adaptability, we propose the content adaptive feature transformation (CAFT) method for the decoder, which extracts characteristic information of the image content in the decoder side and utilizes it to adapt each upsampled feature to the image content by using the Spatial Feature Transform (SFT) [41] strategy.

The experiments demonstrate that our proposed methods improve the performance of the baseline framework [29] in terms of both latents and the decoder. Our proposed content adaptive methods are also complementary to those encoder-side updating methods. Experimental results on the Kodak dataset demonstrate that our framework equipped with the encoder-side updating method Stochastic Gumbel Annealing (SGA) [49] achieves comparable overall results to the recent state-of-the-art NIC methods [45,46] and outperforms them at high bit-rates. Additionally, the experimental results also indicate that our methods are general and can be readily applied to NVC for better coding performance. The contributions of our work are summarized as follows:

- We propose the content adaptive channel dropping (CACD) method to improve the adaptability of RD trade-offs and the image content for latent codes. Our CACD automatically selects the optimal quality level at each spatial location, and then drops redundant elements for bit-rate saving.
- To exploit the adaptability at the decoder side, our content adaptive feature transformation (CAFT) method modulates the output features at multiple levels by considering the characteristic information of the image content.
- Experimental results demonstrate that our methods improve the performance by adapting both latents and the decoder without any additional updating steps during performance evaluation, which are also complementary to the encoder-side updating methods.

2   Related Work

2.1   Neural Image Compression

In recent years, neural image compression (NIC) performance has been improved significantly, which are mostly based on recurrent neural networks (RNNs) [22, 37,38], convolutional neural networks (CNNs) [6,7,13,15,29,45,50], or invertible neural networks (INNs) [46]. In most works, CNN-based autoencoder is selected as the basic framework. Ballé et al. [6] proposed an end-to-end optimized image compression framework based on nonlinear transformation, the additive noise quantization proxy and the fully factorized entropy model. Subsequently, the researchers focus more on improving the accuracy of the estimated entropy model using hyperprior [7], auto-regressive context model [29] and Gaussian Mixture Model (GMM) [15]. Different transformations are also proposed to enhance the expression capability of the latent space, such as residual blocks with attention module [15] and INN [46]. Some works [22,24] applied the spatially variant bit allocation strategy as a post-process [22] or by using importance map [24]. Our method is also based on the convolutional autoencoder approach, but we improve the content adaptability of the baseline method [29].

2.2   Content Adaptive Data Compression

The effectiveness of neural data compression relies on the generalization capability to unseen data in the evaluation process. However, domain shift between training and testing data and lack of adaptability may degrade the coding performance when compressing various types of testing data. To solve this issue, a straightforward idea is to over-fit the encoder-side components. In this way, the model can adapt to test samples during performance evaluation, and does not affect the reconstruction quality because the encoder is not involved in the decoding process. To this end, Campos et al. [12] refined the latents by directly back propagating them, and Yang *et al.* [49] further closed the discretization gap by replacing the differentiable approximation for quantization with Stochastic Gumbel Annealing (SGA) when refining the latents. Moreover, Lu *et al.* [27] updated the encoder on each test frame for neural video compression (NVC), which generates content adaptive latent codes by using the over-fitted encoder. Recently, some full-model adaption methods for NVC have been proposed to adapt the decoder. The work in [33] updated both encoder and decoder when compressing I frames, and then transmitted the updates of the decoder parameters along with the compressed video sequences. These updating methods require hundreds or thousands of back propagation steps for each sample, which is extremely time-consuming. In summary, the encoder-side approaches do not utilize the adaptability of decoders and the full-model approach is often complex due to the additional model compression process.

Our proposed content adaptive methods adapt the latents and the decoder to the image content in a non-updating way. Our methods are also complementary to those encoder-side updating methods, which leads to a fully-adapted solution to address the issues of both domain shift and lack of adaptability.

2.3 Neural Video Compression

In recent years, significant progress has also been achieved for neural video compression (NVC). Increasing number of learning based approaches [3,14,16,17,19–21,25,28,44] have been proposed. Lu *et al.* [28] first proposed an end-to-end video compression framework DVC that follows the traditional hybrid coding framework and implements the key components with neural networks. Some subsequent works improved the motion compensation [3] or motion compression [19] for better optical flow based motion compensation. Recently, more works [16,17,21] were proposed to perform the operations in the feature space. Hu *et al.* [21] proposed the FVC framework where motion compensation and residual coding are performed in the feature space rather than the pixel space.

3   Proposed Method

3.1   Overall Architecture of Neural Image Compression

We use the state-of-the-art neural image compression (NIC) method [29] as our baseline method and apply our methods on top of both context version and the non-context version. The overview of the baseline framework is provided in Fig. 1(a). We also describe the details of the baseline method as follows.

At the encoder side, the input image x is first transformed into the latent representation y by using the encoder network, which consists of several convolution layers and uses the generalized divisive normalization (GDN) [5] layer as activation. The hyper-encoder captures the spatial dependencies of y and produces the hyperprior z. Then y and z are quantized into discrete-valued version $\hat{y}$ and $\hat{z}$ respectively by using the round operation, which is replaced by adding

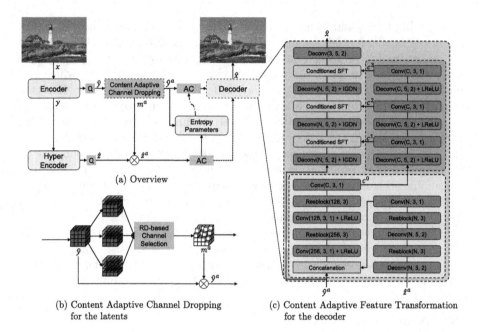

(a) Overview

(b) Content Adaptive Channel Dropping
for the latents

(c) Content Adaptive Feature Transformation
for the decoder

Fig. 1. Overview of our proposed framework based on [29] (a), the details in our content adaptive channel dropping (CACD) method for the latents (b) and the network architecture of our content adaptive feature transformation (CAFT) method for the decoder (c). For simplicity, the hyper-decoder and auto-regressive context model are denoted as "Entropy Parameters" and AC denotes arithmetic coding in the pipeline (a). The operation and modules with dashed container (*i.e.*, the CACD and the decoder in (a)) along with the dashed data flow are our newly proposed modules. In CACD (b), the features with different channel widths are firstly generated from the quantized latent representation $\hat{y}$. Then the rate-distortion (RD) based selection technique is applied to select the optimal channel number for each spatial location, which is stored in a binary mask m^a. Channel dropping is then completed by element-wise multiplication of the latents $\hat{y}$ and the mask m^a, which is also used to generate $\hat{z}^a$ (please see Sect. 3.2 for more details). In CAFT (c), we modulate each upsampled feature by using the Spatial Feature Transform (SFT) layer, which is conditioned on characteristic information of the image content. The multi-level characteristic information is generated by using the latents $\hat{y}^a$ and the hyperprior $\hat{z}^a$ (see Sect. 3.3 for more details). Conv(C, K, S) denotes the convolution layer with the output channel C, the kernel size $K \times K$ and the stride S. LReLU denotes the LeakyReLU activation for simplicity. The network architecture of Conditioned SFT and Resblock is illustrated in Fig. 3.

uniform noise [6] as an approximation during the training process. After that, the quantized features $\hat{y}$ and $\hat{z}$ are entropy coded into bit-stream. Each element in $\hat{z}$ is modeled as a factorized model $p_{\hat{z}}$ and each element in $\hat{y}$ is modeled as a Gaussian distribution $p_{\hat{y}|\hat{z}}$ conditioned on $\hat{z}$.

At the decoder side, the quantized hyperprior $\hat{z}$ is first entropy decoded and used to estimate the distribution of the quantized latent representation $\hat{y}$.

In the non-context version of [29], $\hat{z}$ is fed into the hyper-decoder to estimate the mean and standard deviation of $\hat{y}$. While in the context version, an auto-regressive context model is added to utilize the entropy-decoded parts of $\hat{y}$ for more accurate entropy parameter estimation. Finally, the decoder takes $\hat{y}$ as the input to generate the reconstructed image $\hat{x}$ by using several deconvolution layers and inverse generalized divisive normalization (IGDN) layers.

During the training process of NIC, a rate-distortion optimization (RDO) problem is formulated to minimize the bit-rate cost and the distortion between the original image x and its reconstruction image $\hat{x}$. A Lagrange multiplier λ is used to control the trade-off between the bit-rate cost and the distortion. The loss function is formulated as follows:

$$R + \lambda D = H(\hat{y}) + H(\hat{z}) + \lambda d(x, \hat{x}) \tag{1}$$

where $H(\hat{y})$ and $H(\hat{z})$ denote the bit costs to compress $\hat{y}$ and $\hat{z}$, $d(x, \hat{x})$ denotes the distortion between the reconstructed image and the input image, where mean squared error (MSE) is usually used.

In our approach, we propose new operations and modules for the latents and the decoder. The channel dropping algorithm selects the optimal quality level at each spatial location for the latents $\hat{y}$ by minimizing the rate-distortion (RD) value. Then the latents $\hat{y}$ and the hyperprior $\hat{z}$ are replaced with their channel-adapted version $\hat{y}^a$ and $\hat{z}^a$ before entropy coding for bit-rate saving, where the exceeding channels are dropped (see Sect. 3.2 for more details). In the decoder, we modulate the upsampled features after each IGDN layer by using the Spatial Feature Transform (SFT) [41] layer conditioned on characteristic information of the image content, which is extracted from the latents $\hat{y}^a$ and the hyperprior $\hat{z}^a$ (see Sect. 3.3 for more details).

3.2 Content Adaptive Channel Dropping for the Latents

In neural image compression, rate control is implemented by training the models with different trade-offs (i.e., different λ values) between bit-rate cost and reconstruction distortion. It is well-known that the more bits we use, the better reconstruction quality we can achieve. We also observe that the ability of converting extra bits to reconstruction quality (i.e., the quality gain when assigning similar additional bits) is different among image blocks. To this end, we quantify this ability as "bit conversion ratio", which is formulated as follows:

$$\eta(x, \lambda^l, \lambda^h)_i = \frac{PSNR(x, \lambda^h)_i - PSNR(x, \lambda^l)_i}{R(x, \lambda^h)_i - R(x, \lambda^l)_i} \tag{2}$$

where $PSNR(x, \lambda)$ denotes the peak signal-to-noise ratio (PSNR) between the input image x and its reconstructed image produced by the model trained with λ, $R(x, \lambda)$ denotes the bit-rate cost of the latents and the hyperprior generated by the model trained with λ, λ^l and λ^h denote the relatively lower and higher λ values respectively, and i denotes the ith spatial block of the image.

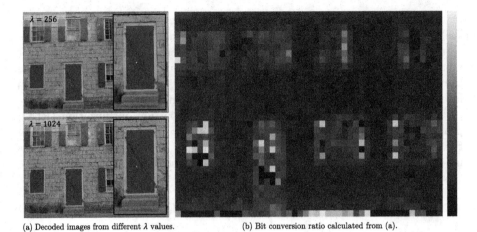

(a) Decoded images from different λ values.   (b) Bit conversion ratio calculated from (a).

Fig. 2. An example of bit conversion ratio calculation on an image from the Kodak dataset based on the existing method [29].

In Fig. 2, we provide a visualization example about bit conversion ratio on an image from the Kodak dataset [1]. Figure 2(a) visualizes two images decoded by [29] trained with two different λ values. It is observed that the grains of both woodwork (*i.e.*, the wooden door and windows) and the bricks are constructed with more details in the bottom image with high bit-rate. In Fig. 2(b), we observe that the bit conversion ratio of the wooden areas is much higher than that of the brick areas. To achieve better rate-distortion (RD) performance, it is therefore reasonable to assign more bits for the areas with higher bit conversion ratio. To this end, we aim at compressing each image block with the suitable quality level, at which the RD cost is minimal among all the alternative quality levels.

Before selecting the quality level at each spatial location for the latents $\hat{y}$, our content adaptive channel dropping (CACD) method need to enable multiple quality levels in one single model. For each λ value, we first decide the corresponding maximum channel number $g(\lambda)$ (also called the optimal channel width in this work), where the RD performance saturates at this channel width even if more number of channels is allowed for this λ value [48]. Then we train our model with multiple rate-distortion optimization (MRDO) loss [48]. Note that we only set the additional elements in the channel dimension as zero instead of directly reducing the number of channel as in the slimmable implementation [48]. Specifically, for the original target λ value, we have K λ values (*i.e.*, K quality levels) including its original λ value and $K-1$ smaller λ values (K is set as 3 in this work). A mask $m^{g(\lambda)}$ is generated by setting the value to zero for the channel locations exceeding the channel width $g(\lambda)$, and one otherwise. The latent representation with level λ is generated by the element-wise multiplication operation between the latents $\hat{y}$ and the corresponding mask $m^{g(\lambda)}$ (*i.e.*, $\hat{y}^{g(\lambda)} \leftarrow \hat{y} \odot m^{g(\lambda)}$), and the hyperprior is also mapped in the same way (*i.e.*, $\hat{z}^{g(\lambda)} \leftarrow \hat{z} \odot m^{g(\lambda)}$). The MRDO loss is then formulated as follows,

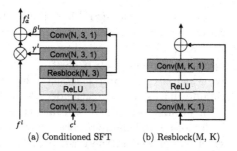

(a) Conditioned SFT   (b) Resblock(M, K)

Fig. 3. The network architecture of the conditioned SFT module (a) in our proposed content adaptive feature transformation and Resblock module (b). In each conditioned SFT, the extracted characteristic information c^l at level l is fed into the convolution layers to predict the adaptive parameters γ^l and β^l. In (b), Resblock(M, K) denotes the convolution layers with the output channel M and the kernel size $K \times K$.

$$\sum_{\lambda \in \Lambda} R(\hat{y}^{g(\lambda)}, \hat{z}^{g(\lambda)}) + \lambda D(\hat{y}^{g(\lambda)}) \tag{3}$$

where Λ denotes the set of K λ values, R and D denote the rate cost and the distortion in Eq.(1) respectively, and they are calculated by using the features with different quality levels.

As the model can compress the image with K quality levels, we adopt the block-based RD selection strategy, which selects the optimal channel width among alternatives for the smallest RD value at each spatial location. Specifically, at each spatial location, we calculate K RD values by using the features with the channel widths $g(\lambda)$ among alternative quality levels and store the channel width corresponding to the smallest RD value in the channel allocation vector a. We further generate the adaptation mask m^a by setting the value to zero for the channel locations exceeding the allocated channel width, and one otherwise. Then the adapted features are generated by the element-wise multiplication operation with the adaption mask m^a (*i.e.*, $\hat{y}^a \leftarrow \hat{y} \odot m^a$, $\hat{z}^a \leftarrow \hat{z} \odot m^a$). Therefore, our CACD method for the latents can automatically drop redundant elements at each spatial location and thus reduce the bit-rate cost.

3.3 Content Adaptive Feature Transformation for the Decoder

Domain shift between the training and testing data is a common problem for learning-based algorithms. Different from most tasks, the ground truth in neural image compression is exactly the same as the input image. Thus the model can be fine-tuned with the whole target domain dataset or even a target sample. Generally, only the encoder-side components are adapted because the change in the decoder will result in inconsistent reconstruction at the receiver side, which can not exploit the adaptability in the decoder. Although some works [33] synchronize the decoder to the receiver by transmitting the parameter changes, it is a non-trivial task to compress such parameter changes.

Recently, Spatial Feature Transform (SFT) [41] has shown efficient spatial adaptability for various vision tasks including image super-resolution [41], semantic image synthesis [32] and variable-rate image compression [35]. Inspired by these works, we propose the content adaptive feature transformation (CAFT) method for the decoder, which uses the SFT layers conditioned on the relatively high-level characteristic information to adapt the decoder to the image content.

As shown in Fig. 1(c), we first extract the characteristic information of the image content from the latents $\hat{y}$ and the hyperprior $\hat{z}$ by using the image characteristic extractor, which is denoted in the dashed cyan box (C is set as 192 in this work). To adapt the features with different resolutions, we then use the SFT layer after each IGDN layer, which is conditioned on the multi-level characteristic information c^l produced in the module denoted in the dashed purple box, where $l = 1...L$ (L is set as 3 in this work).

The detailed network structure of conditioned SFT is shown in Fig. 3(a). The conditioned SFT layer generates the affine transformation parameters (γ^l, β^l) by learning the mapping function $\Psi(c^l) \mapsto (\gamma^l, \beta^l)$. The input feature f^l is then transformed by using the learned parameters (γ^l, β^l) to produce the content adapted feature f_a^l:

$$f_a^l = f^l \odot \gamma^l + \beta^l \tag{4}$$

where $\odot$ denotes the element-wise multiplication operation. Our CAFT modulates the features by using the conditioned SFT layer whose condition is the relatively high-level characteristic information of the image content to improve decoder-side content adaptability.

4   Experiments

4.1   Experimental Setup

Datasets. We adopt the Flicker 2W dataset from [26] as our training dataset, which consists of 20,745 images. Each image is randomly cropped into 256×256 patches for data augmentation. The rate-distortion performance of our method is evaluated on the Kodak [1] and Tecnick [4] datasets.

Implementation Details. We apply our proposed content adaptive methods on both [29] and its non-context version. We train our models with seven λ values (*i.e.*, $\lambda = 128, 256, 512, 1024, 2048, 4096$ and 6144). We use $N = M = 192$ for the three lower λ values and $N = M = 320$ for the four higher values. We first train two models with higher λ values ($\lambda = 1024$ for low bit-rates and $\lambda = 8192$ for high bit-rates). Other models are then fine-tuned from its corresponding pretrained model with their λ values.

To train our model with content adaptive channel dropping (CACD), we first use the multi rate-distortion optimization (MRDO) technology (Eq. (3)) to

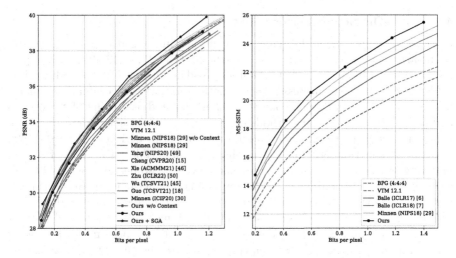

Fig. 4. Rate-distortion performance evaluation results on the Kodak dataset.

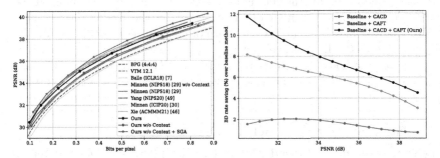

Fig. 5. Rate-distortion performance evaluation results on the Tecnick dataset.

Fig. 6. BD rate saving (%) of our CACD and CAFT methods on the Tecnick dataset. We use [29] without the auto-regressive context model as our baseline method.

achieve its original performance with multiple quality levels. Then the CACD module is activated to select the optimal channel width in the subsequent fine-tuning iterations.

We use the Adam [23] optimizer and set the batch size as 4. The initial learning rate is set as $5e-5$. Each fine-tuning step requires 1,000,000 iterations, which uses the initial learning rate for the first 500,000 iterations and $5e-6$ for the remaining iterations. For MS-SSIM [42] based rate-distortion performance evaluation, we further fine-tune our model with the learning rate of $5e-6$ for 500,000 iterations by using MS-SSIM as the distortion loss.

4.2   Rate-Distortion Performance

In Fig. 4, we report the performance of traditional image codecs [9, 31], the state-of-the-art image compression methods [15, 18, 29, 30, 45, 46, 49, 50] and our proposed methods (denoted as "Ours") on the Kodak dataset. VVC is evaluated by VTM-12.1 [2] on the CompressAI [8] evaluation platform. We evaluate our methods on both [29] and its non-context version (denoted as a suffix of "w/o Context"). We observe that our methods improve the rate-distortion performance on both versions of the baseline method in terms of both PSNR and MS-SSIM [42]. It is worth mentioning that our method is compatible with state-of-the-art updating-based adaption method Stochastic Gumbel Annealing (SGA) [49]. We also report the fully-adapted result by combining our methods and SGA, which is denoted as "Ours + SGA". It is obvious that our fully-adapted method achieves comparable results as the recent state-of-the-art methods [18, 45] and outperforms them at high bit-rates. For example, our fully-adapted method achieves 0.4dB improvement at 1.2bpp when compared with the current state-of-the-art methods Xie (ACMMM21) [46] and Wu (TCSVT21) [45].

In Fig. 5, we also report the coding performance of different methods on the Tecnick dataset. We have similar observations as on the Kodak dataset that our fully-adapted method achieves the state-of-the-art performance at all bit-rates and achieves 0.4 dB improvement at 0.7 bpp when compared with current state-of-the-art methods Minnen (ICIP20) [30] and Xie (ACMMM21) [46]. The experimental results clearly demonstrate the effectiveness of our proposed fully-adapted method.

4.3   Ablation Study and Model Analysis

Effectiveness of the Proposed Methods. To demonstrate the effectiveness of our proposed content adaptive methods for the latents and the decoder, we conduct ablation study on the Tecnick dataset. To fairly compare our work with the updating-based adaption method SGA [49], we take the non-context version of [29] as the baseline method. We provide the BD rate saving result of our proposed methods over the baseline method based on the piecewise BDBR [10] results. As shown in Fig. 6, the alternative method equipped with our content adaptive feature transformation (i.e., Baseline + CAFT) outperforms the baseline method with the BD rate saving from 4% to 8% at all bit-rates. Additionally, the alternative method equipped with our content adaptive channel dropping strategy (i.e., Baseline + CACD) generally achieves better performance than the baseline method. Our method equipped with both CAFT and CACD achieves the best performance and outperforms all other methods, which saves about 10% bit-rate in low PSNR range. When compared with the baseline method, we achieve the BDBR results of −1.51%, −5.90% and −7.78% for "Baseline + CACD", "Baseline + CAFT" and "Ours" respectively, which clearly demonstrates improvement of our proposed methods over the baseline method. The ablation study results demonstrate that our overall framework is able to adapt to the image content on both latents and the decoder for better compression performance.

Table 1. BDBR(%) results about the compatibility of our method and SGA [49] on different datasets. Negative values indicate bit-rate saving. We use [29] without the auto-regressive context model as the anchor method to calculate the BDBR results.

Methods	Kodak	Tecnick
SGA	−15.17	−18.72
Ours w/o Context	−6.64	−7.44
Ours w/o Context + SGA	−21.44	−24.50

Fig. 7. Qualitative comparison results of the traditional codes BPG [9], neural image compression method Minnen et al. [29] and our method.

Compatibility with Updating-based Method in the Encoder Side. Our methods adapt to the image content on both latents and the decoder, which is also compatible with the updating-based adaption method SGA [49]. To demonstrate the compatibility, we provide the BDBR [10] results on the Kodak and the Tecnick datasets in Table 1. Although our method (*i.e.*,"Ours w/o Context") saves less bit-rates than "SGA", our method in combination with SGA (*i.e.*,"Ours w/o Context + SGA") outperforms "SGA", which indicates that our content adaptive approach is complementary to SGA.

Qualitative Results. As shown in Fig. 7, we provide the visualization results of the reconstructed image *kodim14* from the Kodak dataset for qualitative comparison. It is observed that our method clearly improves the reconstruction quality over the baseline method [29] and achieves better performance than BPG. Our method preserves more details of the image content. For example, the artifacts

(a) Reconstructed image *kodim21* from the Kodak dataset.

(b) Visualization of the channel allocation results. Lighter color indicates more channels.

Fig. 8. Visualization of the channel width selection results by using our method CACD for the latents. In (b), the white, red, black colors represent the quality levels from the highest level (*i.e.*, the most channel number) to the lowest level (*i.e.*, the least channel number). (Color figure online)

can be clearly observed in both Minnen et al. [29] and BPG on the red life jacket, which are less obvious in our method. Additionally, the letters in front of the boat reconstructed by our proposed method are more clear than those reconstructed by other baseline algorithms with similar bit-rates.

Visualization of Content Adaptive Channel Dropping. In Fig. 8, we visualize the allocated channel number selected by our method CACD. Figure 8(a) is the reconstructed image of *kodim21* from the Kodak dataset and Fig. 8(b) visualizes the quality level selection results for the latents. The white, red, black colors represent three quality levels from high to low. It is observed that less channels are allocated in the sky area because the sky area is smooth and needs less bits for reconstruction, while full channels are allocated to preserve more details in the sharp areas like the rocks, houses and the lighthouse.

4.4   Experiments for Neural Video Compression

Datasets. We train our methods on the Vimeo-90k [47] dataset, which is used as the training dataset in DVC [28]. For performance evaluation, we use the video sequences from the HEVC Class B and Class C [36] datasets.

Implementation Details. We use an enhanced version of DVC [28] called "DVC*" as our baseline method, where the entropy models of both motion vector (MV) feature and residual feature are modeled by the mean-scale hyperprior. We train the models in a similar way as in neural image compression. We first pretrain a model with the λ value of 2048. The learning rate is set as 1e–4 for the first 1,800,000 steps and 1e–5 for the following 200,000 steps. Then we fine-tune the pretrained model with other λ values (*i.e.*, 256, 512 and 1024) for 500,000 steps. For the adapted decoder with content adaptive feature transformation, we fine-tune the baseline model for another 600,000 steps to adjust the decoder parameter with the learning rate as 1e–4 for the first 400,000 steps and 1e–5 for the remaining steps. We use the Adam [23] optimizer and set the batch size as 4 for all the training procedures.

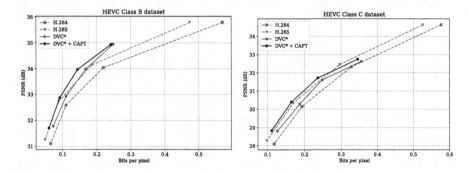

Fig. 9. Rate-distortion performance evaluation results on the HEVC Class B and Class C test sequences.

Rate-Distortion Performance. Figure 9 compares the rate-distortion performance between our method CAFT and the baseline method DVC*. It is observed that our method improves the PSNR by about 0.4 dB at three low bit-rates and by about 0.3 dB at the highest bit-rate on the HEVC Class C test sequence. Similar results can also be observed on the HEVC Class B test sequence, which has larger resolution than the HEVC Class C test sequence. The experimental results demonstrate that our CAFT is general and can be readily used for neural video compression.

5 Conclusions

In this work, we have proposed the content adaptive methods for both latents and the decoder to improve the content adaptability for neural image compression. Our newly proposed content adaptive channel dropping (CACD) method is able to adaptively compress different locations with different quality levels by dropping redundant channels for better bit-rate saving. Our newly proposed content adaptive feature transformation (CAFT) method in the decoder side can extract the characteristic information of the image content, which can be further regraded as the condition to transform the features in the decoder. Experimental results demonstrate that our content adaptive methods are general to different compression pipelines and are also complementary to the encoder-side updating-based content adaptive methods.

Acknowledgement. This work was supported by the National Key Research and Development Project of China (No. 2018AAA0101900).

References

1. Kodak lossless true color image suite. http://r0k.us/graphics/kodak/
2. VVC Official Test Model VTM. https://vcgit.hhi.fraunhofer.de/jvet/VVCSoftware_VTM/-/tree/VTM-12.1
3. Agustsson, E., Minnen, D., Johnston, N., Ballé, J., Hwang, S.J., Toderici, G.: Scale-space flow for end-to-end optimized video compression. In: 2020 IEEE/CVF Conference on Computer Vision and Pattern Recognition, CVPR 2020, Seattle, WA, USA, 13–19 June 2020, pp. 8500–8509. Computer Vision Foundation/IEEE (2020)
4. Asuni, N., Giachetti, A.: TESTIMAGES: a large-scale archive for testing visual devices and basic image processing algorithms. In: Giachetti, A. (ed.) Italian Chapter Conference 2014 - Smart Tools and Apps in computer Graphics, STAG 2014, Cagliari, Italy, 22–23 September 2014, pp. 63–70. Eurographics (2014)
5. Ballé, J., Laparra, V., Simoncelli, E.P.: Density modeling of images using a generalized normalization transformation. In: Bengio, Y., LeCun, Y. (eds.) 4th International Conference on Learning Representations, ICLR 2016, San Juan, Puerto Rico, 2–4 May 2016, Conference Track Proceedings (2016)
6. Ballé, J., Laparra, V., Simoncelli, E.P.: End-to-end optimized image compression. In: 5th International Conference on Learning Representations, ICLR 2017, Toulon, France, 24–26 April 2017, Conference Track Proceedings. OpenReview.net (2017)
7. Ballé, J., Minnen, D., Singh, S., Hwang, S.J., Johnston, N.: Variational image compression with a scale hyperprior. In: 6th International Conference on Learning Representations, ICLR 2018, Vancouver, BC, Canada, April 30–May 3, 2018, Conference Track Proceedings. OpenReview.net (2018)
8. Bégaint, J., Racapé, F., Feltman, S., Pushparaja, A.: Compressai: a pytorch library and evaluation platform for end-to-end compression research. arXiv preprint arXiv:2011.03029 (2020)
9. Bellard, F.: BPG image format. https://bellard.org/bpg (2015)
10. Bjontegaard, G.: Calculation of average PSNR differences between RD-curves. ITU-T VCEG-M33, April 2001 (2001)
11. Bross, B., et al.: Overview of the versatile video coding (VVC) standard and its applications. IEEE Trans. Circuits Syst. Video Technol. 31(10), 3736–3764 (2021)
12. Campos, J., Meierhans, S., Djelouah, A., Schroers, C.: Content adaptive optimization for neural image compression. In: IEEE Conference on Computer Vision and Pattern Recognition Workshops, CVPR Workshops 2019, Long Beach, CA, USA, 16–20 June 2019. p. 0. Computer Vision Foundation/IEEE (2019)
13. Chen, Z., Gu, S., Lu, G., Xu, D.: Exploiting intra-slice and inter-slice redundancy for learning-based lossless volumetric image compression. IEEE Trans. Image Process. 31, 1697–1707 (2022)
14. Chen, Z., Lu, G., Hu, Z., Liu, S., Jiang, W., Xu, D.: LSVC: a learning-based stereo video compression framework. In: Proceedings of the IEEE/CVF Conference on Computer Vision and Pattern Recognition, pp. 6073–6082 (2022)
15. Cheng, Z., Sun, H., Takeuchi, M., Katto, J.: Learned image compression with discretized gaussian mixture likelihoods and attention modules. In: 2020 IEEE/CVF Conference on Computer Vision and Pattern Recognition, CVPR 2020, Seattle, WA, USA, 13–19 June 2020, pp. 7936–7945. Computer Vision Foundation/IEEE (2020)

16. Djelouah, A., Campos, J., Schaub-Meyer, S., Schroers, C.: Neural inter-frame compression for video coding. In: 2019 IEEE/CVF International Conference on Computer Vision, ICCV 2019, Seoul, Korea (South), October 27–November 2, 2019, pp. 6420–6428. IEEE (2019)

17. Feng, R., Wu, Y., Guo, Z., Zhang, Z., Chen, Z.: Learned video compression with feature-level residuals. In: 2020 IEEE/CVF Conference on Computer Vision and Pattern Recognition, CVPR Workshops 2020, Seattle, WA, USA, 14–19 June 2020, pp. 529–532. Computer Vision Foundation/IEEE (2020)

18. Guo, Z., Zhang, Z., Feng, R., Chen, Z.: Causal contextual prediction for learned image compression. IEEE Trans. Circuits Syst. Video Technol. **32**(4), 2329–2341 (2022)

19. Hu, Z., Chen, Z., Xu, D., Lu, G., Ouyang, W., Gu, S.: Improving deep video compression by resolution-adaptive flow coding. In: Vedaldi, A., Bischof, H., Brox, T., Frahm, J.-M. (eds.) ECCV 2020. LNCS, vol. 12347, pp. 193–209. Springer, Cham (2020). https://doi.org/10.1007/978-3-030-58536-5_12

20. Hu, Z., Lu, G., Guo, J., Liu, S., Jiang, W., Xu, D.: Coarse-to-fine deep video coding with hyperprior-guided mode prediction. In: Proceedings of the IEEE/CVF Conference on Computer Vision and Pattern Recognition, pp. 5921–5930 (2022)

21. Hu, Z., Lu, G., Xu, D.: FVC: a new framework towards deep video compression in feature space. In: IEEE Conference on Computer Vision and Pattern Recognition, CVPR 2021, virtual, 19–25 June 2021, pp. 1502–1511. Computer Vision Foundation/IEEE (2021)

22. Johnston, N., et al.: Improved lossy image compression with priming and spatially adaptive bit rates for recurrent networks. In: 2018 IEEE Conference on Computer Vision and Pattern Recognition, CVPR 2018, Salt Lake City, UT, USA, 18–22 June 2018, pp. 4385–4393. Computer Vision Foundation/IEEE Computer Society (2018)

23. Kingma, D.P., Ba, J.: Adam: a method for stochastic optimization. In: Bengio, Y., LeCun, Y. (eds.) 3rd International Conference on Learning Representations, ICLR 2015, San Diego, CA, USA, 7–9 May 2015, Conference Track Proceedings (2015)

24. Li, M., Zuo, W., Gu, S., You, J., Zhang, D.: Learning content-weighted deep image compression. IEEE Trans. Pattern Anal. Mach. Intell. **43**(10), 3446–3461 (2021)

25. Lin, J., Liu, D., Li, H., Wu, F.: M-LVC: multiple frames prediction for learned video compression. In: 2020 IEEE/CVF Conference on Computer Vision and Pattern Recognition, CVPR 2020, Seattle, WA, USA, 13–19 June 2020, pp. 3543–3551. Computer Vision Foundation/IEEE (2020)

26. Liu, J., Lu, G., Hu, Z., Xu, D.: A unified end-to-end framework for efficient deep image compression. arXiv preprint arXiv:2002.03370 (2020)

27. Lu, G., et al.: Content adaptive and error propagation aware deep video compression. In: Vedaldi, A., Bischof, H., Brox, T., Frahm, J.-M. (eds.) ECCV 2020. LNCS, vol. 12347, pp. 456–472. Springer, Cham (2020). https://doi.org/10.1007/978-3-030-58536-5_27

28. Lu, G., Ouyang, W., Xu, D., Zhang, X., Cai, C., Gao, Z.: DVC: an end-to-end deep video compression framework. In: IEEE Conference on Computer Vision and Pattern Recognition, CVPR 2019, Long Beach, CA, USA, 16–20 June 2019, pp. 11006–11015. Computer Vision Foundation/IEEE (2019)

29. Minnen, D., Ballé, J., Toderici, G.: Joint autoregressive and hierarchical priors for learned image compression. In: Bengio, S., Wallach, H.M., Larochelle, H., Grauman, K., Cesa-Bianchi, N., Garnett, R. (eds.) Advances in Neural Information Processing Systems 31: Annual Conference on Neural Information Processing Systems 2018, NeurIPS 2018, 3–8 December 2018, Montréal, Canada, pp. 10794–10803 (2018)

30. Minnen, D., Singh, S.: Channel-wise autoregressive entropy models for learned image compression. In: IEEE International Conference on Image Processing, ICIP 2020, Abu Dhabi, United Arab Emirates, 25–28 October 2020, pp. 3339–3343. IEEE (2020)

31. Ohm, J.R., Sullivan, G.J.: Versatile video coding-towards the next generation of video compression. In: Picture Coding Symposium, vol. 2018 (2018)

32. Park, T., Liu, M., Wang, T., Zhu, J.: Semantic image synthesis with spatially-adaptive normalization. In: IEEE Conference on Computer Vision and Pattern Recognition, CVPR 2019, Long Beach, CA, USA, 16–20 June 2019, pp. 2337–2346. Computer Vision Foundation/IEEE (2019)

33. van Rozendaal, T., Huijben, I.A.M., Cohen, T.: Overfitting for fun and profit: Instance-adaptive data compression. In: 9th International Conference on Learning Representations, ICLR 2021, Virtual Event, Austria, 3–7 May 2021, OpenReview.net (2021)

34. Skodras, A., Christopoulos, C.A., Ebrahimi, T.: The JPEG 2000 still image compression standard. IEEE Sig. Process. Mag. 18(5), 36–58 (2001)

35. Song, M., Choi, J., Han, B.: Variable-rate deep image compression through spatially-adaptive feature transform. In: 2021 IEEE/CVF International Conference on Computer Vision, ICCV 2021, Montreal, QC, Canada, 10–17 October 2021, pp. 2360–2369. IEEE (2021)

36. Sullivan, G.J., Ohm, J., Han, W., Wiegand, T.: Overview of the high efficiency video coding (HEVC) standard. IEEE Trans. Circuits Syst. Video Technol. 22(12), 1649–1668 (2012)

37. Toderici, G., et al.: Variable rate image compression with recurrent neural networks. In: Bengio, Y., LeCun, Y. (eds.) 4th International Conference on Learning Representations, ICLR 2016, San Juan, Puerto Rico, 2–4 May 2016, Conference Track Proceedings (2016)

38. Toderici, G., et al.: Full resolution image compression with recurrent neural networks. In: 2017 IEEE Conference on Computer Vision and Pattern Recognition, CVPR 2017, Honolulu, HI, USA, 21–26 July 2017, pp. 5435–5443. IEEE Computer Society (2017)

39. Wallace, G.K.: The JPEG still picture compression standard. Commun. ACM 34(4), 30–44 (1991)

40. Wang, X., Jiang, W., Wang, W., Liu, S., Kulis, B., Chin, P.: Substitutional neural image compression. CoRR arXiv:2105.07512 (2021)

41. Wang, X., Yu, K., Dong, C., Loy, C.C.: Recovering realistic texture in image super-resolution by deep spatial feature transform. In: 2018 IEEE Conference on Computer Vision and Pattern Recognition, CVPR 2018, Salt Lake City, UT, USA, 18–22 June 2018, pp. 606–615. Computer Vision Foundation/IEEE Computer Society (2018)

42. Wang, Z., Simoncelli, E.P., Bovik, A.C.: Multiscale structural similarity for image quality assessment. In: The Thrity-Seventh Asilomar Conference on Signals, Systems & Computers, 2003. vol. 2, pp. 1398–1402. IEEE (2003)

43. Wiegand, T., Sullivan, G.J., Bjøntegaard, G., Luthra, A.: Overview of the H.264/AVC video coding standard. IEEE Trans. Circuits Syst. Video Technol. **13**(7), 560–576 (2003)

44. Wu, C.-Y., Singhal, N., Krähenbühl, P.: Video compression through image interpolation. In: Ferrari, V., Hebert, M., Sminchisescu, C., Weiss, Y. (eds.) ECCV 2018. LNCS, vol. 11212, pp. 425–440. Springer, Cham (2018). https://doi.org/10.1007/978-3-030-01237-3_26

45. Wu, Y., Li, X., Zhang, Z., Jin, X., Chen, Z.: Learned block-based hybrid image compression. IEEE Trans. Circuits Syst. Video Technol. **32**(6), 3978–3990 (2022)

46. Xie, Y., Cheng, K.L., Chen, Q.: Enhanced invertible encoding for learned image compression. In: Shen, H.T., et al. (eds.) MM 2021: ACM Multimedia Conference, Virtual Event, China, 20–24 October 2021, pp. 162–170. ACM (2021)

47. Xue, T., Chen, B., Wu, J., Wei, D., Freeman, W.T.: Video enhancement with task-oriented flow. Int. J. Comput. Vis. **127**(8), 1106–1125 (2019)

48. Yang, F., Herranz, L., Cheng, Y., Mozerov, M.G.: Slimmable compressive autoencoders for practical neural image compression. In: IEEE Conference on Computer Vision and Pattern Recognition, CVPR 2021, virtual, 19–25 June 2021, pp. 4998–5007. Computer Vision Foundation/IEEE (2021)

49. Yang, Y., Bamler, R., Mandt, S.: Improving inference for neural image compression. In: Larochelle, H., Ranzato, M., Hadsell, R., Balcan, M., Lin, H. (eds.) Advances in Neural Information Processing Systems 33: Annual Conference on Neural Information Processing Systems 2020, NeurIPS 2020, 6–12 December 2020, virtual (2020)

50. Zhu, Y., Yang, Y., Cohen, T.: Transformer-based transform coding. In: International Conference on Learning Representations (2022)

Efficient and Degradation-Adaptive Network for Real-World Image Super-Resolution

Jie Liang[1,2], Hui Zeng[2], and Lei Zhang[1,2(✉)]

[1] The HongKong Polytechnic University, Hung Hom, Hong Kong
[2] OPPO Research, Shenzhen, China
cslzhang@comp.polyu.edu.hk

Abstract. Efficient and effective real-world image super-resolution (Real-ISR) is a challenging task due to the unknown complex degradation of real-world images and the limited computation resources in practical applications. Recent research on Real-ISR has achieved significant progress by modeling the image degradation space; however, these methods largely rely on heavy backbone networks and they are inflexible to handle images of different degradation levels. In this paper, we propose an efficient and effective degradation-adaptive super-resolution (DASR) network, whose parameters are adaptively specified by estimating the degradation of each input image. Specifically, a tiny regression network is employed to predict the degradation parameters of the input image, while several convolutional experts with the same topology are jointly optimized to specify the network parameters via a non-linear mixture of experts. The joint optimization of multiple experts and the degradation-adaptive pipeline significantly extend the model capacity to handle degradations of various levels, while the inference remains efficient since only one adaptively specified network is used for super-resolving the input image. Our extensive experiments demonstrate that DASR is not only much more effective than existing methods on handling real-world images with different degradation levels but also efficient for easy deployment. Codes, models and datasets are available at https://github.com/csjliang/DASR.

Keywords: Real-world image super-resolution · Degradation-adaptive · Efficient super-resolution

1 Introduction

Single image super-resolution (SISR) [1–5] is an active research topic in low-level vision, aiming at reconstructing a high-resolution (HR) version of a degraded low-

This work is supported by the Hong Kong RGC RIF grant (R5001-18) and the PolyU-OPPO Joint Innovation Lab.

Supplementary Information The online version contains supplementary material available at https://doi.org/10.1007/978-3-031-19797-0_33.

resolution (LR) image. Since the seminal work of SRCNN [6], many convolutional neural network (CNN) based SISR methods [7–11] have been proposed, most of which assume a pre-defined degradation process (*e.g.*, bicubic down-sampling) from HR to LR images. Despite the great success, the performance of these non-blind SISR methods will deteriorate a lot when facing real-world images [12] because of the mismatch of degradation models between the training data and the real-world test data [13].

The blind image super-resolution (BISR) methods [12, 14–17] have been proposed to address the problems of non-blind SISR methods by considering more complex degradation kernels extracted from real-world images. However, the degradation space of these methods is actually restricted to a set of pre-collected kernels, such as the DPED kernel pool [17, 18]. For real-world images, their degradation space can be much larger, including more types and more complex kernels than the DPED kernel pool, more complex and stronger noise, and other degradation operations such as compression. Therefore, many recent researches have been focused on the real-world image super-resolution (Real-ISR) tasks [19–26] by modeling and synthesizing the complex degradation process of real-world images [27, 28]. The representative works include BSRGAN [13] and Real-ESRGAN [29], which introduce comprehensive degradation operations such as blur, noise, down-sampling, and JPEG compression, and control the severity of each operation by randomly sampling the respective hyper-parameters. Random shuffle of degradation orders [13] and second-order degradation [29] are also employed to better simulate the real-world complex degradations, respectively.

Despite the remarkable progress of BSRGAN [13] and Real-ESRGAN [29] on improving the image perceptual quality, they have several limitations for practical usage. On one hand, they are basically designed to work on severely degraded LR images. While BSRGAN and Real-ESRGAN can generate a certain amount of details on some tough LR images, they are difficult to generate fine details on mildly degraded LR inputs. It is highly anticipated to develop Real-ISR models which can handle images with different degradation levels. On the other hand, the BSRGAN and Real-ESRGAN methods rely on heavy backbone networks (*e.g.*, RRDB [2]), which make them difficult to be deployed on devices with limited computational resources [30–34]. It is also anticipated to develop efficient Real-ISR models to meet the requirement of high efficiency.

To tackle the above problems, in this paper, we propose a degradation-adaptive super-resolution (DASR) network whose parameters are adaptively specified to the given image according to its degradation. Our DASR consists of a tiny regression network to estimate the degradation parameters of the input image and multiple light-weight super-resolution experts, which are jointly optimized on a balanced degradation space. For each input image, an adaptive network is constructed via a non-linear mixture of experts, whose adaptive weighting factors are specified by the estimated degradation parameters. The multiple super-resolution experts and the degradation-aware mixture significantly improve the model capacity for handling images of different degradations. Meanwhile, the whole pipeline of DASR is highly efficient against existing methods to meet the requirement of Real-ISR tasks, as only one adaptive network is employed to super-resolve the image during inference and the cost of mixing experts is negligible.

The contributions of this paper are two-fold. First, we propose a degradation-adaptive super-resolution network, which significantly improves the model capacity to super-resolve images of various degradation levels. Second, the pipeline of our DASR network is highly efficient against existing methods, providing a good solution to perform Real-ISR in practical applications. Extensive experiments verified the effectiveness and efficiency of the proposed method.

2   Related Work

2.1   Real-World Image Super-Resolution

How to reproduce effectively and efficiently HR images from low-quality real-world LR images is a challenging issue in SISR research. The distribution of real-world images can differ dramatically due to the varying image degradation process, different imaging devices, and image signal processing methods [12,28]. Researchers [19,35] have tried to capture real-world HR-LR image pairs by adapting the focal length of the camera, yet the collection of data is tedious and this can only describe a limited subspace of image degradation. Some unsupervised methods [23,28] have also been proposed to explore the domain adaptation between the synthesized LR image and the real one, yet the domain gap is still big, deteriorating the SR performance [21,22].

Recently, several Real-ISR methods such as BSRGAN [13], Real-ESRGAN [29] and SwinIR [36] have achieved remarkable progress by introducing comprehensive degradation models to effectively synthesize real-world images. However, they rely on a heavy and computationally intensive backbone network, e.g., RRDB [2] and Swin transformer [37], and are not flexible to process images of different degradation levels. In this paper, we propose a degradation-adaptive framework to address this issue, targeting at an effective and efficient network for the challenging Real-ISR task.

2.2   Image Degradation Modeling

In many non-blind SISR methods [1–4,38–40], the degradation model is simply assumed as bicubic down-sampling or blurred down-sampling with a Gaussian kernel. The performance of these non-blind methods can be dramatically undermined when applied to images with different degradations [12]. As a remedy, SRMD [14], UDVD [41] and some other methods [42,43] extend the degradation space to cover more blur kernels and noise levels, and use the degradation map as additional input to perform conditional SISR. While these methods can handle multiple degradations with a single model, they rely on accurate degradation estimation, which itself is also a challenging task.

A few blind SISR methods have been proposed for handling unknown degradations [27,28,44–48]. In KMSR [17], a kernel pool is constructed from real photographs using generative adversarial network [49], and training pairs are synthesized in a more realistic way. Some methods like IKC [16] and VBSR [50] incorporate a blur kernel estimator into the SISR framework to be adaptive to images degraded with different blur kernels [15,51]. However, most of the blind SISR methods are trained with a pre-collected kernel pool [17,18], and hence they are not really blind and can hardly be generalized to real-world images.

Recent Real-ISR methods such as BSRGAN [13] and Real-ESRGAN [29] further extend the degradation modeling space by incorporating comprehensive degradation types with randomly sampled degradation parameters to enhance the variation. The larger degradation space helps the trained Real-ISR model to improve the perceptual quality of some tough LR inputs. However, the degradation parameter sampling in BSRGAN and Real-ESRGAN is unbalanced to train a flexible network, limiting the trained model in generating fine details, especially for inputs with mild degradations. In this work, we propose to balance the degradation space by partitioning it into three levels with balanced samplings. Such a balanced degradation space facilitates the optimization of our degradation-adaptive model on different degradation levels and brings a better approximation to the real-world LR images.

2.3   Mixture of Experts and Dynamic Convolution

The mixture of experts (MoE, [52–55]) is a long-standing method that calculates the weighted sum of multiple expert networks to improve the performance. A trainable gating network is employed to compute the weight for activating each expert [56], usually based on an explicit (*e.g.*, labeled classes) or implicit (content clustering) partition of the data. In this paper, we calculate the adaptive weight of experts according to the degradation of the image for the Real-ISR tasks. Besides, instead of activating all experts and calculating the weighted sum of outputs as in previous MoE methods [57], we adaptively mix the network parameters, resulting in only one adapted network for inference. Such a pipeline is effective and efficient due to the increased non-linearity and the fast inference.

Dynamic convolution [58,59] or conditional convolution [60,61] aims to enhance the feature representation capacity by making the convolutional parameters sample-adaptive. Most of the existing methods optimize multiple sets of convolutional parameters and learn feature self-attention to linearly combine the parameters. However, this pipeline introduces many computations to obtain self-attention, causing a trade-off between efficiency and effectiveness. In this paper, we achieve the non-linear mixture of experts via an adapted conditional convolution, where the conditions are the degradation parameters and the weighting factors are calculated once for all layers to keep efficiency.

3   Methodology

This section presents our degradation-adaptive network for real-world image super-resolution, *i.e.*, DASR. As shown in Fig. 1, DASR mainly consists of a degradation prediction network and a CNN-based SR network with multiple

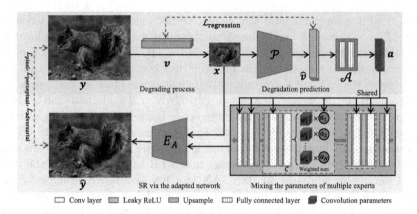

Fig. 1. Overall pipeline of the proposed DASR. Here, x, y and $\hat{y}$ denote the LR image, the ground truth HR image and the super-resolved result, respectively. For each convolution layer C, the parameters W_i^C of N experts are mixed according to the weighting factors in a. The input x is super-resolved to $\hat{y}$ by the adapted network E_A.

experts. In the following sections, we first provide the details of the proposed DASR framework and then introduce our degradation modeling to set degradation parameters and generate training pairs.

3.1   Degradation-Adaptive Super-Resolution

Degradation Prediction Network. To allow efficient and degradation-adaptive super-resolution, we propose to estimate the degradation parameters $v \in \mathbb{R}^{1 \times n}$ of each input x via a regression network $\mathcal{P}$, *i.e.*, $\hat{v} = \mathcal{P}(x)$, where $\hat{v}$ denotes the estimation of v. We employ a set of parameters v to elaborately describe the degradation space. The details of degradation space modeling will be discussed in Sect. 3.2. To make the estimation process efficient, we design a light-weighted network $\mathcal{P}$ to predict v. Specifically, $\mathcal{P}$ consists of 6 convolution layers with Leaky ReLU activation, followed by a global average pooling layer. We first use convolution layers to extract image spatial degradation features and then use the global average pooling layer to estimate the degradation parameters.

To optimize the network $\mathcal{P}$, we introduce a regression loss between the estimated degradation parameters $\hat{v}$ and the ground-truth v using the ℓ_1-norm distance as follows:

$$\mathcal{L}_{\text{regression}} = \|\hat{v} - v\|_1. \tag{1}$$

According to the degradation model, each parameter in v is randomly sampled to specify the degradation process to generate the LR-HR image pairs.

Image Super-Resolution Network. An ideal Real-ISR method is expected to be both effective and efficient. On one hand, in real-world SR tasks, the computation resources are usually limited, especially for edge devices. On the other hand, the model should be able to effectively handle images with various kinds of degradations. Nevertheless, most of the current SR methods [13,29, 36,38,62] can only trade-off between efficiency and effectiveness, and they are inflexible to handle images with different degradation types and levels.

To develop an effective and efficient Real-ISR model, we propose a degradation-adaptive SR network to boost the model capacity via non-linear mixture of experts (MoE), whose additional cost is negligible during inference. In specific, we employ N convolutional experts, denoted by $\boldsymbol{E} = [E_1, E_2, \cdots, E_N]$, where each expert E_i is a light-weighted SR network, e.g., SRResNet [38] or EDSR-M [62], with independent parameters $\boldsymbol{\Phi}_{E_i}$. All the E_i share the same network topology, and they are optimized jointly with the supervision of the same loss. Our idea is to implicitly train each expert to handle images falling into a sub-space of the degradation space so that they can work together to process images with various kinds of degradations in the whole space.

A vector of weighting factors $\boldsymbol{a} \in \mathbb{R}^{1 \times N}$, which is adaptive to the degradation of the input $\boldsymbol{x}$, is then calculated to adaptively mix the N experts. We calculate $\boldsymbol{a}$ conditioned on the estimated $\hat{\boldsymbol{v}}$ via a tiny network $\mathcal{A}$ with two fully-connected layers, i.e., $\boldsymbol{a} = \mathcal{A}(\hat{\boldsymbol{v}})$. As both $\hat{\boldsymbol{v}}$ and $\boldsymbol{a}$ are of low dimension ($n = 33$ and $N = 5$ in our experiments), the network $\mathcal{A}$ is highly efficient. Note that if $\boldsymbol{a}$ is constrained to be a one-hot vector, only one expert will be activated for super-resolving the input $\boldsymbol{x}$, and this will degrade our framework to a competitive MoE [56], which may perform well on tasks whose sample distribution space can be partitioned with clear boundaries, yet it can hardly work well for the Real-ISR task with a large and continuous degradation space.

With the multiple experts $\boldsymbol{E}$ and their adaptive weighting factors $\boldsymbol{a}$, we mix the experts adaptively in a non-linear manner. For each convolution layer C of the desired network, we employ the dynamic convolution technique [58,61] to parameterize the convolutional kernels as follows:

$$\boldsymbol{f}_{\text{output}} = \sigma((a_1 \cdot W_1^C + a_2 \cdot W_2^C + \cdots + a_N \cdot W_N^C) * \boldsymbol{f}_{\text{input}}). \tag{2}$$

where $\boldsymbol{f}_{\text{input}}$ and $\boldsymbol{f}_{\text{output}}$ denote the input and the output features, a_i indicates the ith value of $\boldsymbol{a}$, W_i^C denotes the layer C parameters for expert E_i and σ is the activation function. That is, we adaptively fuse the parameters of each layer among all experts, resulting in an adaptive network, denoted as E_A.

Note that in classic dynamic convolution, the weighting factor of each layer is calculated by an independent network conditioned on the feature map of the last layer, thus introducing non-negligible computational costs. In contrast, we learn a single set of degradation-adaptive weighting factors $\boldsymbol{a}$ for all convolution layers, which is very efficient. Our framework follows the spirit of MoE but in a non-linear manner due to the activation operation in intermediate layers. The non-linearity and the degradation-adaptive mixture of multiple experts significantly extend the model capacity to handle degradations of various levels.

Our DASR is very efficient. For each convolutional layer, the model only deploys one adapted network E_A in the inference stage, rather than deploying N models as done in the classic MoE methods [52,53]. The degradation prediction network $\mathcal{P}$ and the weighting module $\mathcal{A}$ are also very light-weighted. Therefore, the cost of inference is of the same order as one single expert network. The computational overhead caused by the mixture operation is negligible. Specifically, the mixture process consists of multiplications and additions operations on the parameters of N experts. For a light-weighted backbone network like SRResNet or EDSR-M, the number of parameters of each expert is only $1.52M$, and they are independent of the size of input images. Therefore, compared with the calculation of multiple feature maps, the complexity of the mixture of parameters is several orders of magnitude lower and thus can be neglected.

3.2 Degradation Modeling

Since high-quality real-world LR-HR pairs are hard to be collected due to the misalignment issue [19,35], the degradation modeling is very important to synthesize real-world LR inputs x from a given HR image y for Real-ISR model training. A degradation space, denoted by S, should be pre-defined to synthesize training pairs and perform degradation-adaptive optimization. The quality of an LR sample x in S is controlled by a degradation parameter vector $v = [v_1, v_2, \cdots, v_n]$, where v_i specifies the type or severity of a degrading operation and n denotes the number of degradation parameters. In our DASR, v also serves as the ground-truth for training the degradation prediction network.

The image degradation model has been recently improved significantly from the simple bicubic down-sampling [2,6] to shuffling [13] and second-order [29] pipelines. We adopt the degradation operations of blurring (both isotropic and anisotropic Gaussian blur), resizing (both down-sampling and up-sampling with area, and bilinear and bicubic operations), noise corruption (both additive Gaussian and Poisson noise), and JPEG compression in our modeling. In v, we use a one-hot code to quantify the degradation operation type and use a single value to record the degradation level normalized by its respective dynamic range.

It is worth mentioning that different from the methods [14,16] which quantify a blur kernel by its kernel coefficients, we quantify a blurring degradation by its kernel size s, the standard deviation σ_1, σ_2 along the two principal axes, and the rotation degree θ. In this way, the degradation parameters are more interpretable to specify the degradation types and levels, and can better support the degradation-aware mixture of experts. Meanwhile, the parameter vector $[s, \sigma_1, \sigma_2, \theta]$ has only 4 dimensions, while the kernel vector k will have much higher dimensions to estimate. Benefiting from the interpretability and compactness of the degradation space, our DASR allows explicit user control towards degradation parameters during inference. This can facilitate many user-interactive applications to customize the desired super-resolving effect.

Though the shuffling degradation method in BSRGAN [13] and the second-order degradation pipeline in Real-ESRGAN [29] can generate a sufficiently large degradation space, it is hard for them to train a model which can adaptively handle images with different levels of degradations. Our DASR is designed to be adaptive to a wide range of real-world inputs with multiple light-weight expert networks, each of which is expected to handle a subspace of images of different degradation levels. Therefore, we partition the whole degradation space S into 3 levels $[S_1, S_2, S_3]$ by specifying the parameters v accordingly. Among them, S_1 and S_2 are generated with first-order degradation with small and large parameter ranges, respectively, while S_3 is generated by the second-order degradation. Due to space limitation, more details of the degradation operations and the specification of $[S_1, S_2, S_3]$ are provided in the supplimentary material.

3.3 Training Losses

The learnable modules of our DASR network include $[E, P, A]$. As mentioned in Sect. 3.1, the $\mathcal{L}_{\text{regression}}$ loss is used to optimize P to predict the degradation parameters. To optimize the overall framework, following the many works in literature [2,13,29], we adopt the L_1-norm pixel-wise loss $\mathcal{L}_{\text{pixel}}$, the perceptual loss $\mathcal{L}_{\text{perceptual}}$ and the adversarial loss $\mathcal{L}_{\text{adversarial}}$. The total loss is defined as follows (more details are provided in the supplimentary material):

$$\mathcal{L}_{\text{total}} = \mathcal{L}_{\text{pixel}} + \lambda_1 \mathcal{L}_{\text{regression}} + \lambda_2 \mathcal{L}_{\text{perceptual}} + \lambda_3 \mathcal{L}_{\text{adversarial}}, \tag{3}$$

where λ_1, λ_2 and λ_3 denote the balancing parameters.

4 Experiments

4.1 Training Details

Following previous works [2,29], we employ DIV2K, Flickr2K, and OutdoorSceneTraining datasets for training our DASR model. For efficiency, we employ the SRResNet [38] as our backbone. The weights of the N experts are initialized by the model pre-trained with pixel-wise loss. The Adam [63] optimizer is employed to train the network. The learning rate is set to $1 \times e^{-4}$, the total batch size is 24 and the training iteration is set to $500K$. We balance the training loss with $\lambda_1 : \lambda_2 : \lambda_3 = 1 : 1 : 0.1$. Without loss of generality and for a fair comparison, we conduct Real-ISR experiments with the scale factor of 4 by following the setting in BSRGAN [13] and Real-ESRGAN [29]. In our experiment, the dimension of degradation parameters is $n = 33$ and the number of experts is $N = 5$. The LR patch size is set to 64×64.

4.2 Evaluation and Compared Methods

We evaluate our DASR method both quantitatively and qualitatively. For quantitative evaluation, as in BSRGAN [13] we synthesize 300 LR-HR pairs by applying the 3 levels of degradations to the 100 validation images in the DIV2K dataset, i.e., 100 LR-HR pairs for each level. We also make the comparison on the original DIV2K dataset with bicubic downsampling. An illustration of images with different degradations is shown in Fig. 2, where more samples are shown in the supplementary material. For qualitative evaluation, we also employ the images in the RealSRSet [13,29], where the input images are corrupted by various blur, noise, or other real degradation operations.

(a) HR	(b) Bicubic	(c) Level-I	(d) Level-II	(e) Level-III

Fig. 2. Sample images with different levels of degradations in our datasets.

We compare the proposed DASR with representative and state-of-the-art SR methods, including RRDB [2], ESRGAN [2], IKC [16], BSRGAN [13], Real-ESRGAN [29] and Real-SwinIR (-M and -L) [36]. Among them, RRDB is trained on bicubic degradation with pixel-wise loss; ESRGAN is trained on bicubic degradation with pixel-wise, perceptual and adversarial losses; IKC is a representative BISR method trained on various isotropic Gaussian blur kernels; BSRGAN and Real-ESRGAN are state-of-the-art Real-ISR methods with a heavy RRDB backbone; Real-SwinIR is trained on the degradation space of BSRGAN with the computationally expensive SwinIR backbone.

For a more comprehensive and fair comparison, we also re-train those commonly used backbone networks, including SRResNet, EDSR, RRDB, and SwinIR, with our constructed training dataset. Following the common practice [13,29], we employ PSNR (the larger the better) and LPIPS (learned perceptual image patch similarity, the smaller the better) to quantitatively compare the performance of different methods on synthetic datasets, and make visual comparisons on real-world images since there are no reference images.

4.3   Quantitative Comparison

Effectiveness. In Table 1 and Table 2, we quantitatively compare the performance of competing methods in terms of PSNR and LPIPS on datasets with different levels of degradations. Specifically, Table 1 compares the methods trained with their own degradation models, while Table 2 compares the methods re-trained on our proposed degradation space.

As shown in Table 1, existing methods can only achieve satisfactory performance on datasets with a specific type of degradation, yet show weakness in other cases. For example, RRDB and ESRGAN can respectively achieve good fidelity and perceptual quality on the bicubic-downsampled dataset, yet their performance drops dramatically when handling images with other degradations, even for the 'Level-I' degradation with mild noise and blurs. Real-ESRGAN, BSR-GAN, and Real-SwinIR perform well on the most severely degraded dataset. However, their performance deteriorates much on the other three datasets.

In contrast, our DASR achieves stable and significant improvement against other methods under the first three types of degradations, which cover the majority of real-world images, while achieving highly competitive (among the best two)

Table 1. Quantitative comparison of different methods on datasets with different degradations (D-Level). 'Bicubic' denotes the DIV2K validation set with bicubic degradation, while 'Level I', 'II', and 'III' denote the datasets with mild, medium, and severe degradations, respectively. For the compared methods, we employ their officially released pre-trained models. The PSNR is calculated on the Y channel of YCbCr space.

D-Level	Metric	RRDB	ESRGAN	IKC	BSRGAN	Real-ESRGAN	Real-SwinIR-M	Real-SwinIR-L	DASR
Bicubic	PSNR	30.92	28.17	28.01	27.32	26.65	26.83	27.21	28.55
	LPIPS	0.2537	0.1154	0.2695	0.2364	0.2284	0.2221	0.2135	0.1696
Level-I	PSNR	26.27	21.16	24.09	26.78	26.17	26.21	26.45	27.84
	LPIPS	0.3419	0.4727	0.3805	0.2412	0.2312	0.2247	0.2161	0.1707
Level-II	PSNR	26.46	22.77	25.39	26.75	26.16	26.12	26.39	27.58
	LPIPS	0.4441	0.4900	0.4531	0.2462	0.2391	0.2313	0.2213	0.2126
Level-III	PSNR	23.91	23.63	22.91	24.05	23.81	23.34	23.46	23.93
	LPIPS	0.7631	0.7314	0.7583	0.3995	0.3901	0.3844	0.3765	0.4144

results for the last type of degradation. For example, DASR outperforms Real-ESRGAN by about 1.7 dB in PSNR and 26% in LPIPS on the 'Level-I' dataset. On the 'Level-III' dataset with severely degraded images (as shown in Fig. 2(d)), DASR achieves almost the same PSNR and LPIPS indices as BSRGAN. These observations clearly demonstrate that our DASR can generalize well to images with a wide range of degradations.

To further validate the effectiveness of our degradation-adaptive strategy, in Table 2 we re-train the backbones of popular SR models on our proposed degradation space. Note that the heavy RRDB backbone is adopted in both BSRGAN and RealESRGAN, and the lightweight SRResNet is adopted in our DASR as the backbone. As can be seen from this table, with the same network topology and similar computational overhead, our DASR outperforms the baseline SRResNet on all datasets by a large margin, e.g., improving 0.5 db of PSNR on the bicubic-downsampled dataset and about 5% of LPIPS on the Level-II dataset. This demonstrates that the degradation-adaptive mixture of multiple experts can significantly extend the model capacity while keeping the efficiency.

Compared to RRDB and SwinIR backbones that are adopted in recent state-of-the-art methods [13,29,36], our DASR consumes much less computational resources, e.g., about 1/3 and 1/12 latency of RRDB and SwinIR, respectively. At the same time, DASR outperforms these heavy models in terms of reconstruction fidelity on all datasets, demonstrating its effectiveness of degradation-adaptive super-resolution and high efficiency to deploy in practice.

Efficiency. The inference efficiency is a crucial factor in Real-ISR tasks due to the limited computational resources in practical applications. We compare different backbone networks in terms of multiple efficiency-related metrics and depict the results in the bottom rows of Table 2.

As shown in the table, the computational overhead of different backbone networks differs dramatically. For example, RRDB [2], which is employed in recent Real-ISR methods [13,29], consumes about 7 times the FLOPs and more

Table 2. Quantitative comparison of different backbone networks re-trained on our proposed degradation space and the efficiency comparison (the bottom rows). The evaluation datasets are the same as in Table 1. For efficiency evaluation, the input-dependent metric FLOPs is calculated on images with 256×256 pixels; the Latency and Memory are the average inference time and the maximum GPU memory allocation on the DIV2K validation dataset (most LR inputs are with 510×339 pixels). Statistics are collected following the implementation of [64,65] by using an NVIDIA V100 GPU.

Data & Metrics		SRResNet	EDSR	SwinIR	RRDB	DASR
Bicubic	PSNR	28.05	28.26	28.28	27.92	28.55
	LPIPS	0.1747	0.1807	0.1488	0.1473	0.1696
Level-I	PSNR	27.60	27.79	27.78	27.84	27.84
	LPIPS	0.1772	0.1834	0.1531	0.1569	0.1707
Level-II	PSNR	27.34	27.53	27.45	27.29	27.58
	LPIPS	0.2228	0.2284	0.1854	0.1886	0.2126
Level-III	PSNR	23.71	23.87	23.60	23.54	23.93
	LPIPS	0.4419	0.4351	0.3869	0.3847	0.4144
Latency (ms)		113	105	1719	460	142
#FLOPs (G)		166	130	539	1176	184
#Params (M)		1.52	1.52	11.72	16.70	8.07
#Memory (M)		2359	2169	2699	2417	2452

than 4 times the inference time than SRResNet [38]. In other words, the RRDB based Real-ISR methods achieve superior performance at the price of applicability. The recent transformer-based method SwinIR has an acceptable number of FLOPs, however, it actually consumes much more inference time due to the heavy computation of attentions and frequent IO consumption.

Benefiting from the light SRResNet-based backbone and the efficient degradation prediction and parameter fusion, our DASR is very efficient against recent methods. In specific, the degradation prediction network $\mathcal{P}$ and the weighting module $\mathcal{A}$ consume 18G FLOPs, 18 ms latency, 0.47M parameters and 111M GPU memory in total for $N = 5$. Besides, the consumption on parameter fusion operation is negligible, as there are only $N \times 1.52$M multiplications and additions respectively and they can be calculated in parallel. Compared with the classical MoE methods that mix the feature maps of all experts [52,53,57,66], our DASR only conducts one forward pass. As a result, the computational cost increases slightly with a larger N, which supports a flexible extension of model capacity.

It is worth mentioning that although our model has more parameters, the maximum GPU memory consumption does not increase much as shown in the row of #Memory in Table 2, since the deployment of model parameters costs much less space than storing input-dependent feature maps. On the other hand, the increased model parameters do not demand much storage space, which is much easier to afford than the computing power.

4.4   Qualitative Comparison

Figure 3 shows the visual comparisons between different methods on images with different degradations. One can see that DASR can stably restore sharp and realistic details and remove artifacts for a wide range of degradations. In specific, the first sample image is degraded with bicubic downsampling and suffers from the aliasing issue. Both BSRGAN and Real-ESRGAN cannot generate satisfactory texture details even with the heavy RRDB backbone. This is because these two methods are trained on pairs with relatively severe degradations so that their denoising capacity is strengthened yet the detail-generation capacity is limited. Similar observations can be made on all the four samples in Fig. 3.

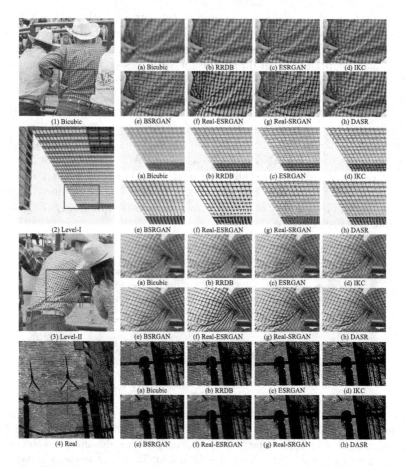

Fig. 3. Qualitative comparison of competing methods on images with different degradations. The results of (b–f) are generated by using the officially released models, while the output of (g) is obtained by re-training the SRResNet backbone with our proposed degradation model. Better zoom in for details.

The RRDB backbone trained with pixel-wise loss performs well on the first two samples in generating textures details, yet it cannot be generalized to the last two samples whose degradations are severe. This is reasonable since all its training pairs are generated by bicubic downsampling. In addition, the results of RRDB in the first and third samples are blurry, which is a well-known side-effect of pixel-wise loss. By applying perceptual and adversarial losses, ESRGAN achieves sharper results yet introduces many visual artifacts due to the instability of training generative adversarial networks. The ESRGAN also amplifies the noise as shown in the second sample. By considering different blur kernels, IKC can restore rich textures on most images, yet bring overshoot artifacts when facing unseen kernels in real-world images (the fourth sample). It also lacks the capacity to remove noise as shown in the second sample.

The results of Real-SRGAN are obtained by re-training the SRResNet on our proposed degradation space with the same loss as in Real-ESRGAN [29]. It can be observed that due to the insufficient feature representation capacity, Real-SRGAN cannot perform well on all the four samples compared to our DASR. In the first three samples, the Real-SRGAN generates messy details or artifacts, as the light-weighted model limits its capacity to achieve degradation-adaptive super-resolution. On the last sample, which is a real-world image, Real-SRGAN fails to reconstruct rich details. In contrast, DASR reproduces realistic details and inhibits artifacts. For hard cases in the real world that our degradation space may not cover, DASR would give a reasonable 'guess' on these images or regions (*e.g.*, synthesize less details to transit smoothly) rather than outputting fatal artifacts (*e.g.*, generate false structures or details), which may happen in other methods. The stability of DASR comes from its comprehensive degradation space and the fusing strategy.

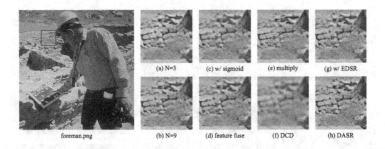

Fig. 4. Ablation study. (a) and (b) validate the models with different N; (c) appends a sigmoid layer to the weighting module $\mathcal{A}$; (d) conducts classical MoE [52,53,57,66] where the output of multiple experts are fused; (e) performs dynamic convolution with a single expert by learning a mapping matrix and multiplying it to the parameters; (f) conducts dynamic convolution following the work [59]; (g) applies EDSR-M backbone to DASR; (h) denotes our default DASR model.

4.5   Ablation Study

We conduct comprehensive ablation studies on our proposed DASR model by using real-world images and depict the visual results in Fig. 4. More results can be found in the supplementary material.

Effectiveness of N. Models in Figs. 4(a) and (b) evaluate the selection of N. It can be seen that using 3 experts leads to relatively smooth results, while models of $N = 5$ in (h) and $N = 9$ in (b) enhance the generation of details. As $N = 9$ shows similar visual quality to $N = 5$, we consider that $N = 5$ is sufficient to model the proposed degradation space.

Effectiveness of Model Design. Figures 4(c) and (d) validate the effectiveness of our model design. The result in (c) demonstrates that adding a sigmoid layer to the weighting module $\mathcal{A}$ cannot improve the performance. As we mix different experts in terms of model parameters, there is no need to ensure positive weights by a sigmoid layer. The experts in Fig. 4(d) are fused by following the strategy of classical MoE [52,53,57,66], where the outputs of all experts are fused. We can see that the result of classical MoE in (d) lacks fine details compared to (h), yet its computational cost is N times heavier than our DASR.

Fig. 5. Example of user-interactive super-resolution. (a) is the input image with bicubic upsampling; (b) is the result of DASR where the degradation parameters are estimated automatically by model $\mathcal{P}$; (c) and (d) are generated by manually increasing and decreasing the scale of blur kernel, respectively; (e) and (f) are the super-resolution results by manually increasing and decreasing the level of noise, respectively.

Effectiveness of Different Dynamic Convolutions. Figures 4(e) and (f) compare different dynamic convolutions [41,59] without introducing many additional parameters. While the inference latency and FLOPs are increased, the performance of those methods drops, e.g., the artifacts generated in (e). We believe it is the joint optimization of multiple experts and the degradation-adaptive mixture that make our DASR more effective than other methods.

Generalization to Different Backbone. Figure 4(g) applies the EDSR-M backbone to DASR. The satisfactory perceptual quality of (g) demonstrates the generalization capacity of our proposed DASR to different backbone networks.

4.6   User-Interactive Super-Resolution

One interesting advantage of our DASR over other Real-ISR methods is that it supports easy user-interactive super-resolution during inference, owing to its interpretable and compact degradation representation.

We depict an example of user-interactive super-resolution in Fig. 5. As can be seen, the proposed DASR allows explicit user control to customize the super-resolution effects. Manually setting larger values to the blur-related parameters (*e.g.*, kernel scale) leads to sharper super-resolution results, as shown in Fig. 5(c), while adjusting the level of noise can flexibly balance between image details and noise, as shown in Figs. 5(e) and (f). Such an advantage of flexible user control makes our DASR very attractive in practical Real-ISR tasks.

5   Conclusion

In this paper, we proposed an efficient degradation-adaptive network, namely DASR, for the real-world image super-resolution (Real-ISR) task. In order to improve the modeling capacity and flexibility of various degradation levels, we jointly learned multiple super-resolution experts and adaptively mixed them into one expert in a degradation-aware manner. The proposed DASR was not only degradation adaptive but also efficient during inference. Extensive quantitative and qualitative experiments were conducted. The results demonstrated that DASR not only achieved superior performance on images with a wide range of degradation levels but also kept good efficiency for easy deployment. In addition, DASR allowed easy user control for customized super-resolution results.

References

1. Johnson, J., Alahi, A., Fei-Fei, L.: Perceptual Losses for Real-Time Style Transfer and Super-Resolution. In: Leibe, B., Matas, J., Sebe, N., Welling, M. (eds.) ECCV 2016. LNCS, vol. 9906, pp. 694–711. Springer, Cham (2016). https://doi.org/10.1007/978-3-319-46475-6_43
2. Wang, X., et al.: ESRGAN: Enhanced Super-Resolution Generative Adversarial Networks. In: Leal-Taixé, Laura, Roth, Stefan (eds.) ECCV 2018. LNCS, vol. 11133, pp. 63–79. Springer, Cham (2019). https://doi.org/10.1007/978-3-030-11021-5_5
3. Zhang, Y., Li, K., Li, K., Wang, L., Zhong, B., Fu, Y.: Image super-resolution using very deep residual channel attention networks. In: Ferrari, V., Hebert, M., Sminchisescu, C., Weiss, Y. (eds.) ECCV 2018. LNCS, vol. 11211, pp. 294–310. Springer, Cham (2018). https://doi.org/10.1007/978-3-030-01234-2_18
4. Ma, C., Rao, Y., Cheng, Y., Chen, C., Lu, J., Zhou, J.: Structure-preserving super resolution with gradient guidance. In CVPR (2020)
5. Sun, J., Zongben, X., Shum, H.-Y.: Gradient profile prior and its applications in image super-resolution and enhancement. IEEE Trans. Image Process. **20**(6), 1529–1542 (2010)

6. Dong, C., Loy, C.C., He, K., Tang, X.: Learning a deep convolutional network for image super-resolution. In: Fleet, D., Pajdla, T., Schiele, B., Tuytelaars, T. (eds.) ECCV 2014. LNCS, vol. 8692, pp. 184–199. Springer, Cham (2014). https://doi.org/10.1007/978-3-319-10593-2_13

7. Sajjadi, M.S.M., Scholkopf, B., Hirsch, M.: EnhanceNet: single image super-resolution through automated texture synthesis. In: ICCV, (2017)

8. Kim, J., Lee, J.K., Lee, K.M.: Deeply-recursive convolutional network for image super-resolution, In : CVPR (2016)

9. Soh, J.W., Park, G.Y., Jo, J., Cho, N.I.: Natural and realistic single image super-resolution with explicit natural manifold discrimination, In: CVPR (2019)D

10. Zhang, Y., Tian, Y., Kong, Y., Zhong, B., Fu, Y.: Residual dense network for image super-resolution. In: CVPR (2018)

11. Jo, Y., Oh, S.W., Vajda, P., Kim, S.J.: Tackling the ill-posedness of super-resolution through adaptive target generation, In: CVPR (2021)

12. Liu, A., Liu, Y., Gu, J., Qiao, Y., Dong. C.: Blind image super-resolution: a survey and beyond. arXiv preprint arXiv:2107.03055 (2021)

13. Zhang, J., Liang, K., Van Gool, L., Timofte, R.: Designing a practical degradation model for deep blind image super-resolution. In : ICCV (2021)

14. Zhang, K., Zuo, W., Zhang, L.: Learning a single convolutional super-resolution network for multiple degradations. In: CVPR (2018)

15. Luo, Z., Huang, Y., Li, S., Wang, L., Tan, T.: Unfolding the alternating optimization for blind super resolution. In: NeurIPS (2020)

16. Gu, J., Lu, H., Zuo, W., Dong, C.: Blind super-resolution with iterative kernel correction. In: CVPR (2019)

17. Zhou, R., Susstrunk. Kernel modeling super-resolution on real low-resolution images. In: ICCV (2019)

18. Ignatov, A., Kobyshev, N., Timofte, R., Vanhoey, N., Van Gool, U.C.: DSLR-quality photos on mobile devices with deep convolutional networks. In ICCV (2017)

19. Cai, J., Zeng, H., Yong, H., Cao, Z., Zhang, L.: Toward real-world single image super-resolution: a new benchmark and a new model. In ICCV (2019)

20. Wei, P., et al.: Component divide-and-conquer for real-world image super-resolution. In: Vedaldi, A., Bischof, H., Brox, T., Frahm, J.-M. (eds.) ECCV 2020. LNCS, vol. 12353, pp. 101–117. Springer, Cham (2020). https://doi.org/10.1007/978-3-030-58598-3_7

21. Lugmayr, A., Danelljan, M., Timofte, R.: NTIRE 2020 challenge on real-world image super-resolution: methods and results. In: CVPRW (2020)

22. Lugmayr, A., et al:. AIM 2019 challenge on real-world image super-resolution: methods and results. In ICCVW (2019)

23. Fritsche, M., Gu, S., Timofte, R.: Frequency separation for real-world super-resolution. In: ICCVW (2019)

24. Lugmayr, A., Danelljan, M., Timofte, R.: Unsupervised learning for real-world super-resolution. In ICCVW (2019) D

25. Ji, X., Cao, Y., Tai, Y., Wang, C., Li, J., Huang, F.: Real-world super-resolution via kernel estimation and noise injection. In:: CVPRW (2020

26. Ji, X., Cao, Y., Tai, Y., Wang, C., Li, J., Huang, F.: Real-world super-resolution via kernel estimation and noise injection. In: CVPRW (2020)

27. Bulat, Adrian, Yang, Jing, Tzimiropoulos, Georgios: To learn image super-resolution, use a gan to learn how to do image degradation first. In: Ferrari, Vittorio, Hebert, Martial, Sminchisescu, Cristian, Weiss, Yair (eds.) ECCV 2018. LNCS, vol. 11210, pp. 187–202. Springer, Cham (2018). https://doi.org/10.1007/978-3-030-01231-1_12

28. Wei, Y., Gu, S., Li, Y., Timofte, R., Jin, L., Song, H.: Unsupervised real-world image super resolution via domain-distance aware training. In: CVPR (2021)

29. Wang, X., Xie, L., Dong, C., Shan, Y.: Real-ESRGAN: training real-world blind super-resolution with pure synthetic data. In: ICCVW (2021)

30. Dong, C., Loy, C.C., Tang, X.: Accelerating the super-resolution convolutional neural network. In: Leibe, B., Matas, J., Sebe, N., Welling, M. (eds.) ECCV 2016. LNCS, vol. 9906, pp. 391–407. Springer, Cham (2016). https://doi.org/10.1007/978-3-319-46475-6_25

31. Zhang, X., Zeng, H., Zhang, L.: Edge-oriented convolution block for real-time super resolution on mobile devices. In: ACM Multimedia (2021)

32. Ahn, N., Kang, B., Sohn, K.-A.: Fast, Accurate, and Lightweight Super-Resolution with Cascading Residual Network. In: Ferrari, V., Hebert, M., Sminchisescu, C., Weiss, Y. (eds.) ECCV 2018. LNCS, vol. 11214, pp. 256–272. Springer, Cham (2018). https://doi.org/10.1007/978-3-030-01249-6_16

33. Yang, W., Wang, W., Zhang, X., Sun, S., Liao, Q.: Lightweight feature fusion network for single image super-resolution. IEEE Signal Process. Lett. 26(4), 538–542 (2019)

34. Song, D., Wang, Y., Chen, H., Chang, X., Chunjing, X., Tao, D.: AdderSR: towards energy efficient image super-resolution. In: CVPR (2021)

35. Zhang, X., Chen, Q., Ng, R., Koltun, V.: Zoom to learn, learn to zoom. In: CVPR (2019)

36. Liang, J., Cao, J., Sun, G., Zhang, K., Van Gool, L., Timofte, R.: SwinIR: image restoration using swin transformer. In: ICCVW (2021)

37. Liu, Z., et al.: Swin transformer: hierarchical vision transformer using shifted windows. In: ICCV (2021)

38. Ledig, C., et al.: Photo-realistic single image super-resolution using a generative adversarial network. In: CVPR (2017)

39. Wang, X., Yu, K., Dong, C., Loy, C.C.: Recovering realistic texture in image super-resolution by deep spatial feature transform. In: CVPR (2018)

40. Fuoli, D., Van Gool, L., Timofte, R.: Fourier space losses for efficient perceptual image super-resolution. In: ICCV (2021)

41. Xu, Y-S., Roy Tseng, S.-Y., Tseng, Y., Kuo, H.-K., Tsai, Y.M Unified dynamic convolutional network for super-resolution with variational degradations In: CVPR (2020)

42. Zhang, K., Van Gool, L., Timofte, R.: Deep unfolding network for image super-resolution. In: CVPR (2020)

43. Zhang, K., Zuo, W., Zhang, L.: Deep plug-and-play super-resolution for arbitrary blur kernels. In: CVPR (2019)

44. Wang, L., et al.: Unsupervised degradation representation learning for blind super-resolution. In: CVPR (2021)

45. Hui, Z., Li, J., Wang, X., Gao, X.: Learning the non-differentiable optimization for blind super-resolution. In: CVPR (2021)

46. Liu, P., Zhang, H., Cao, Y., Liu, S., Ren, D., Zuo, W.: Learning cascaded convolutional networks for blind single image super-resolution. Neurocomputing 417, 371–383 (2020)

47. Maeda, S.: Unpaired image super-resolution using pseudo-supervision. In: CVPR (2020)

48. Yuan, Y., et al.: Unsupervised image super-resolution using cycle-in-cycle generative adversarial networks. In: CVPRW (2018)

49. Goodfellow, I., et al.: Generative adversarial nets. In: NeurIPS (2014)

50. Cornillere, V., Djelouah, A., Yifan, W., Sorkine-Hornung, O., Schroers, C.: Blind image super-resolution with spatially variant degradations. ACM Trans. Graph. **38**(6), 1–13 (2019)
51. Kim, S.Y., Sim, H., Kim, M.: KOALAnet: Blind super-resolution using kernel-oriented adaptive local adjustment. In: CVPR (2021)
52. Jacobs, R.A., Jordan, M.I., Nowlan, S.J., Hinton, G.E.: Adaptive mixtures of local experts. Neural Comput. **3**(1), 79–87 (1991)
53. Jordan, M.I., Jacobs, R.J.: Hierarchical mixtures of experts and the em algorithm. Neural Comput. **6**(2), 181–214 (1994)
54. Gross, S., Ranzato, M.A., Szlam, A.: Hard mixtures of experts for large scale weakly supervised vision. In: CVPR (2017)
55. Aljundi, R., Chakravarty, P., Tuytelaars, T.: Expert gate: lifelong learning with a network of experts. In: CVPR (2017)
56. Maeda, S.: Fast and flexible image blind denoising via competition of experts. In: CVPRW (2020)
57. Wang, Y., Wang, L., Wang, H., Li, P., Huchuan, L.: Blind single image super-resolution with a mixture of deep networks. Pattern Recogn. **102**, 107169 (2020)
58. Chen, Y., et al.: Dynamic convolution: attention over convolution kernels. In: CVPR (2020)
59. Li, Y., et al.: Revisiting dynamic convolution via matrix decomposition. In: ICLR (2021)
60. Li, C., Zhou, A., Yao, A.: Omni-dimensional dynamic convolution. In: ICLR (2021)
61. Yang, B., Bender, G., Le, Q.V., Ngiam, J.: CondConv: conditionally parameterized convolutions for efficient inference. In: NeurIPS (2019)
62. Lim, B., Son, S., Kim, H., Nah, S., Lee, K.M.: Enhanced deep residual networks for single image super-resolution. In: CVPRW (2017)
63. Kingma, D.P., Ba, J.: Adam: a method for stochastic optimization. arXiv preprint arXiv:1412.6980 (2014)
64. Zhang, K., et al.: AIM 2020 challenge on efficient super-resolution: methods and results. In: Bartoli, A., Fusiello, A. (eds.) ECCV 2020. LNCS, vol. 12537, pp. 5–40. Springer, Cham (2020). https://doi.org/10.1007/978-3-030-67070-2_1
65. Zhang, K., et al.: Aim 2019 challenge on constrained super-resolution: methods and results. In: ICCVW (2019)
66. Emad, M., Peemen, M., Corporaal, H.: MoESR: blind super-resolution using kernel-aware mixture of experts. In: WACV (2022)

Unidirectional Video Denoising by Mimicking Backward Recurrent Modules with Look-Ahead Forward Ones

Junyi Li[1], Xiaohe Wu[1(✉)], Zhenxing Niu[2], and Wangmeng Zuo[1]

[1] Harbin Institute of Technology, Harbin, China
csxhwu@gmail.com, wmzuo@hit.edu.cn
[2] Xidian University, Xi'an, China

Abstract. While significant progress has been made in deep video denoising, it remains very challenging for exploiting historical and future frames. Bidirectional recurrent networks (BiRNN) have exhibited appealing performance in several video restoration tasks. However, BiRNN is intrinsically offline because it uses backward recurrent modules to propagate from the last to current frames, which causes high latency and large memory consumption. To address the offline issue of BiRNN, we present a novel recurrent network consisting of forward and look-ahead recurrent modules for unidirectional video denoising. Particularly, look-ahead module is an elaborate forward module for leveraging information from near-future frames. When denoising the current frame, the hidden features by forward and look-ahead recurrent modules are combined, thereby making it feasible to exploit both historical and near-future frames. Due to the scene motion between non-neighboring frames, border pixels missing may occur when warping look-ahead feature from near-future frame to current frame, which can be largely alleviated by incorporating forward warping and proposed border enlargement. Experiments show that our method achieves state-of-the-art performance with constant latency and memory consumption. Code is avaliable at https://github.com/nagejacob/FloRNN.

Keywords: Video denoising · Recurrent neural networks · Temporal alignment

1 Introduction

Recent years have witnessed the great success of deep networks in video denoising [8,11,12,31,42–44,48,51]. Compare to image denoising, temporal information plays a pivotal role in video denoising, which is generally restricted by the spatial misalignment among consecutive frames. Self-similar spatial-temporal

Supplementary Information The online version contains supplementary material available at https://doi.org/10.1007/978-3-031-19797-0_34.

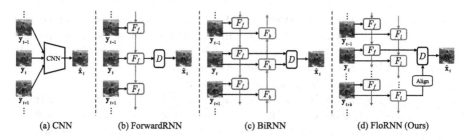

(a) CNN   (b) ForwardRNN   (c) BiRNN   (d) FloRNN (Ours)

Fig. 1. Illustration of representative deep network architectures for video denoising. When handling the current frame, (a) CNN cannot exploit long-term temporal information, and (b) ForwardRNN cannot exploit any future frames. (c) BiRNN is effective in exploiting the information from all frames, but can only be performed in an *offline* manner. In comparison, (d) FloRNN can leverage both the historical information and the crucial near-future frames, thereby being very appealing for *unidirectional* video denoising.

patch aggregation has been suggested for spatio-temporal modeling[12,44], but usually results in heavy computational cost. Other spatio-temporal alignment methods, *e.g.*, optical flow [41], deformable convolution [10], and kernel prediction network (KPN) [32], have also been studied and applied for video denoising [32,42,46,48,51]. Instead of explicit motion estimation and compensation, cascaded U-Net [43] and multi-stage recurrent network [31] are further suggested for the efficiency issue. Albeit the progress in deep video denoising, it remains a challenging issue to exploit historical and future frames for video denoising.

Bidirectional recurrent networks (BiRNN) provide a convenient way for temporal modeling and have been very appealing in several video restoration tasks [5,6,23,39,40,50]. In video super-resolution (VSR), BasicVSR [5] and its extension [6] have outperformed most state-of-the-art methods in terms of VSR performance and efficiency. Benefited from the forward and backward recurrent modules, BiRNN is effective in exploiting the information from all frames to restore the current frame. In comparison, convolutional network (CNN) takes neighborhood frames as inputs and only exploits short-term temporal information. However, BiRNN is intrinsically an offline approach where the backward recurrent module is deployed to propagate information from the last frame to current frame, and the restoration result of current frame cannot be obtained unless all video frames are processed. Meanwhile, hidden features of all frames have to be maintained in the memory during inference, which causes high memory consumption. The high latency and large memory consumption limit the practicability of BiRNN.

To address the offline issue of BiRNN, we present a novel recurrent network consisting of **F**orward and **lo**ok-ahead recurrent modules (*i.e.*, FloRNN) for unidirectional video denoising. From [5], the future frames are important to boost the denoising performance of current frame. Simply discarding backward modules from BiRNN (denote as ForwardRNN) hampers the use of future frames and results in inferior performance. Moreover, among all future frames, the near-future frames are most important to enhance the denoising results of current frame. To leverage future information while addressing offline issue, we present a look-ahead recurrent module for exploiting near-future frames. As shown in Fig. 1(d), our look-ahead module F_l adopts a forward recurrent architecture, but propagates k frames ahead of the forward module F_f. The look-ahead feature of the near-future frame (*i.e.*, $t + k$) is warped back to align with current frame (*i.e.*, t), and incorporated with the forward feature from F_f to produce current denoising results. Our FloRNN adopts a unidirectional propagation, yet extracts crucial near-future frames with F_l. Thus, it has the potential to approach the performance of BiRNN while maintaining constant latency and memory consumption. Furthermore, one can adjust k to meet the latency constraint, smaller k for real-time tasks, and larger k for better results.

Nonetheless, there remains a major issue to address for applying look-ahead module. As shown in Fig. 3(a), with an assumption of $k = 2$, the motion between the t-th and $(t+2)$-th frames makes that an amount of border pixels are lost when warping the look-ahead feature from $(t + 2)$-th frame back to t-th frame. Obviously, such insufficient utilization of near-future frames is harmful to denoising performance. To address this issue, we present to incorporate forward warping and border enlargement mechanism. As shown in Fig. 3(b), forward warping is adopted in the look-ahead module instead of backward warping. Meanwhile, we suggest to enlarge the border of look-ahead feature to a fixed ratio (*e.g.*, 10% in this work) during the forward warping. Due to that forward warping allows warped feature to splat out of border (*i.e.*, pixels out of the red box), we can save the missed border pixels when warping look-ahead feature to future frames, and recover them when aligning look-ahead feature back to the current frame. Our forward warping and border enlargement mechanism can largely reduce the amount of missed border pixels for better exploiting near-future frames and also benefiting denoising performance.

Extensive experiments are conducted to evaluate our FloRNN on commonly used video denoising benchmarks. Both synthetic additive white Gaussian noise (AWGN) and real-world noise are considered in our experiments. For AWGN, our method outperforms the second best competing method PaCNet [44] by a large margin (i.g., 0.76 dB by PSNR) on DAVIS. On real-world video datasets such as CRVD [51] and IOCV [27], FloRNN also achieves the best quantitative results than the competing methods. We also show that our look-ahead module could be applied to state-of-the-art BiRNN methods (*e.g.*, BasicVSR++ [6]), which forms a unidirectional counterpart and benefits from the advances in BiRNNs in the supplementary material.

To sum up, the main contribution of this work includes:

- A novel recurrent network (*i.e.*, FloRNN) is presented for unidirectional video denoising by incorporating forward and look-ahead recurrent modules.
- Forward warping and border enlargement are equipped in look-ahead recurrent module for better exploiting the near-future frames and also benefiting denoising performance.
- Experiments show that our method performs favorably against state-of-the-arts on various video denoising datasets.

2   Related Work

2.1   Image Denoising

With the observation that an image patch usually has many similar counterparts within the same image, many traditional methods are developed for joint modeling of a stack of similar patches to remove noise, such as non-local means (NLM) [3], BM3D [9], and WNNM [16]. Other methods use handcrafted priors on image patches, e.g., sparsity [14] and Gaussian Mixture [56]. Recently, CNN based methods have achieved favorable performance. DnCNN [52] incorporates residual learning [18] and batch normalization [20] for better convergence. FFD-Net [53] takes noise level map as input, and trains a single model for handling various noise levels. With the collected real-world denoising datasets [1,35], several methods [17,24,55] have also been suggested to handle real noise.

2.2   Video Denoising

For exploiting temporal information, traditional patch-based methods [2,4,30] search similar patches on volumetric data, and are very time consuming. By leveraging deep image denoising, several methods adopt two-stage scheme including spatial denoising and temporal fusion. ViDeNN [8] uses a plain CNN as fusion network, while DVDNet [42] assists the fusion with optical flow and warping neighbor frames to current frame. Temporal aggregation mechanisms have also been investigated and integrated into network design, e.g., non-local search [12,44], cascaded U-Net [43], kernel prediction network (KPN) [32,46,48], deformable convolution [51], and channel shifting [37]. However, these aggregation mechanisms either are complicated and inefficient, or cannot achieve state-of-the-art performance. EMVD [31] proposes a multi-stage recurrent architecture for mobile devices, but performs inferior when scaling to larger model on GPUs.

2.3   RNN in Video Restoration

RNN provides a convenient way for temporal modeling and thus can be readily applied to video restoration [7,19]. Taking VSR as an example, FRVSR [38] warps the $(t-1)$-th output to t-th frame, and use it as additional input to super-resolve the t-th frame. RLSP [15] introduces high-dimentional latent states for efficient propagation. RSDN [21] divides the input into structure and detail components to effectively exploit temporal correlation. BasicVSR [5] adopts bidirectional propagation and optical flow based alignment, achieving state-of-the-art VSR performance. BasicVSR++ [6] further improves BasicVSR with flow-guided deformable alignment and second order propagation. However, bidirectional propagation in BasicVSR [5] and its extension [6] makes them unable to be used for online video restoration. RNN has also been investigated for video deblurring [33,40,54], video inpainting [22,23], video frame interpolation [39,47], and video deraining [29,49,50].

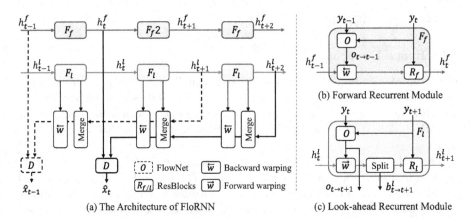

(a) The Architecture of FloRNN

(b) Forward Recurrent Module

(c) Look-ahead Recurrent Module

Fig. 2. Illustration of FloRNN. (a) FloRNN is mainly built with three components, *i.e.*, forward recurrent module F_f, look-ahead recurrent module F_l and decoder D. (b) F_f propagates from first to current frames which exploits all previous frames, (c) F_l propagates similarly to F_f in a forward manner, but k (*e.g.*, $k = 2$) frames ahead of F_f. The look-ahead feature is aligned back to current frame (details of split and merge operations are provided in Fig. 3 (b)) for exploiting crucial near-future frames. With the propagated historical and near-future information, FloRNN achieves compelling results while has constant latency and memory occupation.

3   Method

Given a video sequence consisting of T noisy frames $\{\mathbf{y}_t\}_{t=1}^{T}$, video denoising aims to produce the prediction $\{\hat{\mathbf{x}}_t\}_{t=1}^{T}$ for approximating its clean video $\{\mathbf{x}_t\}_{t=1}^{T}$. For better denoising of current frame $\mathbf{y}_t$, one favorable solution is to exploit all frames $\{\mathbf{y}_t\}_{t=1}^{T}$ to predict $\hat{\mathbf{x}}_t$. BasicVSR [5] originally suggested for VSR provides a bidirectional recurrent network (BiRNN, as shown in Fig. 1(c)) to leverage the information from all frames, and we empirically find that it is also very appealing for video denoising. However, due to the use of backward recurrent module, all the succeeding frames are required to produce backward hidden feature, making that BiRNN can only be performed in an offline manner.

To address the *offline* issue of BiRNN, we propose a novel recurrent network for *unidirectional* video denoising. As shown in Fig. 1(d), it consists of a **F**orward recurrent module as well as a **l**ook-ahead recurrent module, named as FloRNN. Analogous to BiRNN, FloRNN adopts the same forward recurrent module F_f for history frames propagation and decoder D for producing denoising results. The difference is that FloRNN substitutes the backward recurrent module of BiRNN with an elaborate look-ahead recurrent module F_l for exploiting near-feature frames. The look-ahead feature from F_l is then aligned and incorporated with forward feature from F_f to enhance the denoising results of current frame. To address the border missing issue during the alignment, we further introduce a border enlargement mechanism with forward warping. The details of our framework are illustrated in Fig. 2. In the following, we will describe the forward module, look-ahead module, forward warping and border enlargement, respectively.

3.1   Forward Recurrent Module

Analogous to BiRNN, we first introduce the forward recurrent module F_f to propagate information from the first to the current frames. As shown in Fig. 2(b), it adopts a recurrent manner by propagating the forward hidden feature $\mathbf{h}_{t-1}^f$ and combining it with the current frame $\mathbf{y}_t$ to obtain the hidden feature $\mathbf{h}_t^f$ at frame t.

$$\mathbf{h}_t^f = F_f(\mathbf{y}_t, \mathbf{y}_{t-1}, \mathbf{h}_{t-1}^f). \tag{1}$$

Nonetheless, $\mathbf{h}_{t-1}^f$ is aligned with $\mathbf{y}_{t-1}$ instead of $\mathbf{y}_t$. Following [5], we estimate the optical flow [41] from frame t to $t-1$, which is used to align and aggregate $\mathbf{h}_{t-1}^f$ with $\mathbf{y}_t$. Thus, the forward recurrent module in Eqn. (1) can be further written as,

$$\begin{aligned}
\mathbf{o}_{t \to t-1} &= O(\mathbf{y}_t, \mathbf{y}_{t-1}), \\
\mathbf{h}_{t-1 \to t}^f &= \overleftarrow{w}(\mathbf{h}_{t-1}^f, \mathbf{o}_{t \to t-1}), \\
\mathbf{h}_t^f &= R_f(\mathbf{y}_t, \mathbf{h}_{t-1 \to t}^f).
\end{aligned} \tag{2}$$

where $O(\cdot, \cdot)$ denotes an optical flow network, and $\mathbf{o}_{t \to t-1}$ denotes the estimated optical flow from t-th frame to $(t\text{-}1)$-th frame. $\overleftarrow{w}(\mathbf{h}_{t-1}^f, \mathbf{o}_{t \to t-1})$ stands for aligning $\mathbf{h}_{t-1}^f$ with $\mathbf{y}_t$ using backward warping [5] to obtain the warped hidden feature $\mathbf{h}_{t-1 \to t}^f$. R_f aggregates the warped hidden feature and current frame with multiple residual blocks to obtain the hidden feature $\mathbf{h}_t^f$ of t-th frame.

3.2   Look-Ahead Recurrent Module

To leverage the future information while addressing the offline issue, we propose the look-ahead recurrent module for exploiting near-future frames. As shown in Fig. 1(d), our look-ahead module adopts a specifically designed forward recurrent mechanism,

$$\mathcal{H}_{t+1}^l = F_l(\mathbf{y}_{t+1}, \mathbf{y}_t, \mathcal{H}_t^l). \tag{3}$$

Here we use $\mathcal{H}_{t+1}^l$ to indicate that the output of look-ahead module may contain hidden feature $\mathbf{h}_{t+1}^l$ and other variables. As the look-ahead module propagates k frames ahead of the forward module, $\mathbf{h}_{t+k}^l$ captures temporal information of k near-future frames. For restoring t-th frame, we align the look-ahead feature $\mathbf{h}_{t+k}^l$ back to t-th frame to produce the warped look-ahead feature $\mathbf{h}_{t+k \to t}^l$, which can be generally written as,

$$\mathbf{h}_{t+k \to t}^l = \text{Align}\left(\mathbf{h}_{t+k}^l, \cdots\right). \tag{4}$$

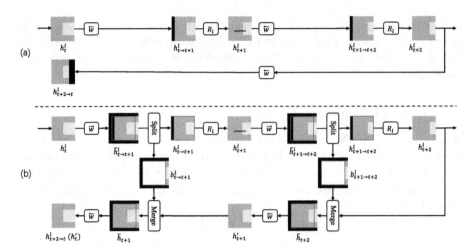

Fig. 3. Illustration of forward warping and border enlargement for our look-ahead recurrent module. (a) Aligning h_{t+2}^l to t-th frame with backward warping $\overleftarrow{w}$ suffers from border pixels missing problem. (b) Forward warping $\overrightarrow{w}$ allows the out of border pixels to splat to the enlarged border. We save the enlarged border when warping to future frames and recover it when warping back, which largely mitigates the border information missing problem.

With the forward feature $\mathbf{h}_t^f$ and the aligned look-ahead feature $\mathbf{h}_{t+k\to t}^l$, the denoising result at frame t can then be obtained by,

$$\hat{\mathbf{x}}_t = D(\mathbf{h}_t^f, \mathbf{h}_{t+k\to t}^l). \tag{5}$$

where the decoder D contains two convolution layers.

Note that F_l and Align$(\cdot, \cdots)$ can be implemented with different forms. For example, one can adopt the forward recurrent module defined in Eq. (2) to implement F_l. As for Align$(\cdot, \cdots)$, one direct solution is to compute the optical flow from $\mathbf{y}_{t+k}$ to $\mathbf{y}_t$, then warp $\mathbf{h}_{t+k}^l$ back to $\mathbf{y}_t$. In the following subsection, forward warping and border enlargement are presented as a reasonable implementation.

3.3   Forward Warping and Border Enlargement

As stated above, one straightforward way to implement the look-ahead module is adopting the forward recurrent module defined in Eq. (2) as F_l and aligning look-ahead feature to current frame by backward warping. However, as shown in Fig. 3(a), such a straightforward implementation suffers from border information missing issue when aligning look-ahead feature back to current frame (*i.e.*, black part exists in $\mathbf{h}_{t+2\to t}^l$). This is caused by scene motion between consecutive frames and backward warping mechanism in look-ahead module. To demonstrate this, we first give a brief introduction of backward warping. As shown in Fig. 4(a), taking warping $\mathbf{h}_t^l$ to $\mathbf{h}_{t\to t+1}^l$ as example, the value of $\mathbf{h}_{t\to t+1}^l$ at position (x, y) is sampled from $\mathbf{h}_t^l$ at position (x', y') according to backward

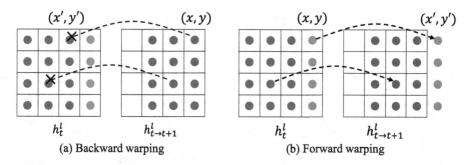

Fig. 4. Border pixels (colored in orange) in $\mathbf{h}_t^l$ are out of border in the $(t+1)$-th frame. (a) Backward warping ignores these border pixels in the warping result $\mathbf{h}_{t\to t+1}^l$, (b) forward warping splats these pixels to the outside of border, which can be preserved with border enlargement mechanism. (Color figure online)

optical flow $(x', y') = (\mathbf{o}_{t+1\to t})_{x,y}$. When scene motion exists, border pixels in $\mathbf{h}_t^l$ may have no correspondence in $\mathbf{h}_{t+1}^l$, and are implicitly dropped in the warped result. Along with the increase of timestamps, the part of lost information of current frame in look-ahead feature becomes larger. Consequently, when aligning $\mathbf{h}_{t+k}^l$ to current frame t, the lost information cannot be recovered (as shown in Fig. 3(a)). Such information missing leads to unexpected inferior performance.

To address the above issue, we replace backward warping in the look-ahead module with forward warping incorporated with border enlargement mechanism. As shown in Fig. 4(b), forward warping splats the value of $\mathbf{h}_t^l$ at position (x, y) to $\mathbf{h}_{t\to t+1}^l$ at position (x', y') according to forward optical flow $(x', y') = (\mathbf{o}_{t\to t+1})_{x,y}$. When scene motion exists, border pixels in $\mathbf{h}_t^l$ are splatted to positions out of the border. This offers an opportunity to save and reuse the out of border pixels by border enlargement mechanism as illustrated in Fig. 3(b). Specifically, forward flow is first calculated for aligning the $\mathbf{h}_t^l$ to $(t+1)$-th frame,

$$\mathbf{o}_{t\to t+1} = O(\mathbf{y}_t, \mathbf{y}_{t+1}). \tag{6}$$

To address the border missing issue, we first enlarge the border of the feature to a certain percent (*e.g.*, 10%) and then perform forward warping,

$$\tilde{\mathbf{h}}_{t\to t+1}^l = \overrightarrow{w}(\mathbf{h}_t^l, \mathbf{o}_{t\to t+1}). \tag{7}$$

The warped feature $\tilde{\mathbf{h}}_{t\to t+1}^l$ is further split into two separate parts,

$$\{\mathbf{b}_{t\to t+1}^l, \mathbf{h}_{t\to t+1}^l\} = Split(\tilde{\mathbf{h}}_{t\to t+1}^l). \tag{8}$$

$\mathbf{b}_{t\to t+1}^l$ denotes the enlarged border region that contains the pixels splatting out of border. $\mathbf{h}_{t\to t+1}^l$ denotes the within-frame region aligned with $(t+1)$-th frame, and is further aggregated with $\mathbf{y}_{t+1}$ to produce the hidden feature $\mathbf{h}_{t+1}^l$ with multiple residual blocks R_l,

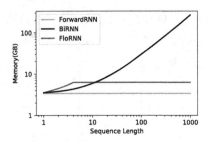 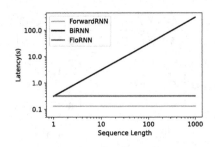

Fig. 5. Analysis of memory consumption (left) and latency (right) for three representative recurrent methods.

$$\mathbf{h}_{t+1}^l = R_l(\mathbf{y}_{t+1}, \mathbf{h}_{t \to t+1}^l). \tag{9}$$

In this manner, border pixels are preserved in the enlarged border $\mathbf{b}_{t \to t+1}^l$, which could be reused to recover the missed border region when aligning the look-ahead feature $\mathbf{h}_{t+k}^l$ to current frame. In particular, $\mathbf{h}_{t+k}^l$ is warped to t-th frame in a frame by frame manner. We first initialize $\mathbf{h}_{t+k}' = \mathbf{h}_{t+k}^l$. When warping from $(t+i)$-th frame to $(t+i\text{-}1)$-th frame, we first merge the border information $\mathbf{b}_{t+i-1 \to t+i}^l$ with $\mathbf{h}_{t+i}'$.

$$\bar{\mathbf{h}}_{t+i} = Merge(\mathbf{h}_{t+i}', \mathbf{b}_{t+i-1 \to t+i}^l) \tag{10}$$

Then, $\bar{\mathbf{h}}_{t+i}$ is aligned to $(t+i\text{-}1)$-th frame with backward warping,

$$\mathbf{h}_{t+i-1}' = \overleftarrow{w}(\bar{\mathbf{h}}_{t+i}, \mathbf{o}_{t+i-1 \to t+i}). \tag{11}$$

After k steps, the warped look-ahead feature can be obtained as,

$$\mathbf{h}_{t+k \to t}^l = \mathbf{h}_t'. \tag{12}$$

From Fig. 3(b), with the proposed border enlargement mechanism, the aligned look-ahead feature $h_{t+2 \to t}^l$ recovers the missed border information, which brings obvious performance gain. Moreover, we note that the optical flow $\mathbf{o}_{t+i-1 \to t+i}$ reuses the optical flow for forward warping in look-ahead module (*i.e.*, $\mathcal{H}_{t+1}^l = \{\mathbf{h}_{t+1}^l, \mathbf{b}_{t \to t+1}, \mathbf{o}_{t \to t+1}\}$), thereby being effective in improving consistency and efficiency in aligning look-ahead feature back.

4 Experiments

4.1 Experimental Settings

Datasets. To evaluate our method on both synthetic and real-world noisy videos, we conduct experiments on the following datasets,

- Set8 [42] and DAVIS [36] are two widely used synthetic Gaussian video denoising datasets.

Table 1. Quantitative comparison of three representative recurrent methods on Set8 [42], FloRNN performs close to BiRNN while maintaining unidirectional.

Model	Unidirectional	Online	PSNR/SSIM
ForwardRNN	✔	✔	33.12/0.9089
FloRNN	✔	✗	33.55/0.9153
BiRNN	✗	✗	33.74/0.9192

Table 2. Ablation study for look-ahead recurrent module on Set8 dataset [42].

(a) Effects on different alignment mechanism.

Warping	Border Enlargement	PSNR/SSIM
Backward warping	✗	33.44/.9132
Forward warping	✗	33.45/.9134
Forward warping	✔	33.55/.9153

(b) Effects on the number of near-future frames k.

k	0	1	2	3	4	5
PSNR	33.12	33.47	33.53	33.55	33.53	33.51

- CRVD [51] is a real-world video denoising dataset captured in raw domain. It contains 6 indoor scenes for training, 5 indoor scenes for testing, and 10 dynamic outdoor scenes without ground-truth for visual evaluation.
- IOCV [27] is a real-world video denoising test set in sRGB domain. Each noisy video is captured by a smartphone multiple times, and the mean video is taken as ground-truth.

Implementation Details. We adopt a pretrained PWC-Net [41] as our optical flow network and fix the parameters of flow network. We find that PWC-Net generalizes well on noisy data, perhaps benefiting from additive Gaussian noise data augmentation during training [13]. For raw videos, we use the demosaiced frames as inputs to PWC-Net. Training sequences are cropped at random spatial-temporal locations, with spatial patch size 96×96. The batch size is set to 16 and training length $T = 10$. We use ℓ_2 loss to train our network, and adopt Adam optimizer [25] with initial learning rate 10^{-4}. After 100k iterations, the learning rate is reduced to 10^{-5} until convergence. To train Gaussian denoising models, we synthesize noisy videos by adding AWGN of $\sigma \in [0, 55]$ to clean ones. For CRVD [51] dataset, as each training sequence only contains 7 frames, we mirror the training sequences to 14 frames to facilitate the model training, and crop patches with Bayer pattern preserving [28]. The evaluation is conducted on an RTX2080Ti.

Table 3. Quantitative comparison of PSNR/SSIM on the Set8 dataset [42] for Gaussian denoising. Hereinafter, red and blue indicate the best and the second best results, respectively. (Color figure online)

Set8	VBM4D [30]	VNLB [2]	DVDNet [42]	FastDVD [43]	VNLNet [12]	PaCNet [44]	FloRNN
$\sigma = 10$	36.05/–	37.26/–	36.08/.9510	36.44/.9540	37.28/.9606	37.06/.9590	37.57/.9639
$\sigma = 20$	32.19/–	33.72/–	33.49/.9182	33.43/.9196	34.02/.9273	33.94/.9247	34.67/.9379
$\sigma = 30$	30.00/–	31.74/–	31.68/.8862	31.68/.8889	–	32.05/.8921	32.97/.9138
$\sigma = 40$	28.48/–	30.39/–	30.46/.8564	30.46/.8608	30.72/.8622	30.70/.8623	31.75/.8911
$\sigma = 50$	27.33/–	29.24/–	29.53/.8289	29.53/.8351	–	29.66/.8349	30.80/.8696
Avg.	30.81/–	32.47/–	32.29/.8881	32.31/.8917	–	32.68/.8946	33.55/.9153

Table 4. Quantitative comparison of PSNR/SSIM on the DAVIS dataset [36] for Gaussian denoising.

DAVIS	VBM4D [30]	VNLB [2]	DVDNet [42]	FastDVD [43]	VNLNet [12]	PaCNet [44]	FloRNN
$\sigma = 10$	37.58/–	38.85/–	38.13/.9657	38.71/.9672	39.56/.9707	39.97/.9713	40.16/.9755
$\sigma = 20$	33.88/–	35.68/–	35.70/.9422	35.77/.9405	36.53/.9464	37.10/.9470	37.52/.9564
$\sigma = 30$	31.65/–	33.73/–	34.08/.9188	34.04/.9167	–	35.07/.9211	35.89/.9440
$\sigma = 40$	30.05/–	32.32/–	32.86/.8962	32.82/.8949	33.32/.8996	33.57/.8969	34.66/.9286
$\sigma = 50$	28.80/–	31.13/–	31.85/.8745	31.86/.8747	–	32.39/.8743	33.67/.9131
Avg	32.39/–	34.34/–	34.52/.9195	34.64/.9188	–	35.62/.9221	36.38/.9435

4.2   Ablation Study

We conduct the ablation study on the Set8 dataset [42] to assess the effectiveness of the proposed look-ahead recurrent module as well as its major components.

To demonstrate the effectiveness of FloRNN, we first compare it with two representative recurrent networks, *i.e.*, ForwardRNN and BiRNN. The main difference between the above three methods is how future frames are leveraged. ForwardRNN takes the forward recurrent module to propagate information from the first to the current frames, without leveraging any future information. BiRNN deploys a backward recurrent module to propagate all future frames from the last frame to current frame. Our FloRNN uses a look-ahead recurrent module for exploiting near-future frames. Table 1 and Fig. 5 show the quantitative comparison among them. From Table 1, FloRNN and BiRNN achieve better performance than ForwardRNN, witch demonstrates the importance of future information in video denoising. Although BiRNN exhibits better quantitative results (0.19 dB better than ours), it has a crucial issue that it can only be performed in an *offline* manner. As shown in Fig. 5, the memory consumption and latency of BiRNN grow linearly with respect to the sequence length. For example, denoising a 1000 frame sequence ($\sim$42 s at 24 fps), BiRNN consumes several hundred GB of memory, which limits its practicality for denoising long videos on common hardware. In comparison, both ForwardRNN and our FloRNN are unidirectional algorithms with constant memory consumption and latency. With the performance close to BiRNN, our FloRNN achieves much lower computation complexity and memory occupation, which demonstrates the effectiveness of our proposed look ahead recurrent module.

Table 5. Model complexity comparison on Set8 dataset [43].

	VBM4D [30]	VNLB [2]	DVDNet [42]	FastDVD [43]	VNLNet [12]	PaCNet [44]	FloRNN
PSNR	30.81	32.47	32.29	32.31	–	32.68	33.55
#.Frame	13	13	5	5	15	15	$T/2 + 3$
#. Param (M)	–	–	1.33	2.48	4.52	2.87	11.82
FLOPS (G)	–	–	1231.8	661.8	2.02×10^5	6.13×10^4	3002.8
Time (s)	420.0	156.0	2.51	0.08	1.65	35.24	0.31

Noisy(σ=40)   VBM4D   DVDNet   FastDVDNet

VNLNet   PaCNet   FloRNN(Ours)   GT

Fig. 6. Visual comparison for Gaussian denoising ($\sigma = 40$) on 'tractor' sequence of the DAVIS dataset [36].

Moreover, we explore the effects of two components in the look-ahead module, *i.e.*, (i) alignment mechanism, (ii) number of near-future frames k. Quantitative results are listed in the Table 2. Although backward warping is more popular in video restoration [5,6,42], from Table 2(a), forward warping and backward warping achieve similar performance. It can be explained that various splatting strategies [34] have been investigated to solve the conflict of target position in forward warping, and flow based feature warping in FloRNN may be robust to the hole problem of forward warping. Besides, incorporating forward warping and border enlargement significantly reduces the amount of lost border pixels during alignment, and achieves 0.1 dB performance gain. Table 2(b) analyzes the effect of k. When k increases, the benefit from near-future information first increases then becomes steady. In our following experiments, we set $k = 3$ for best performance and acceptable latency.

4.3 Results

We further compare our FloRNN with the state-of-the-art methods [2,12,26,30, 31,42–45,51] on both synthetic and real-world video denoising datasets. FloRNN shows appealing performance.

Table 6. Quantitative comparison of PSNR/SSIM on CRVD dataset [51] for real-world raw video denoising.

Method	RViDeNet [51]	FastDVDNet [43]	EMVD [31]	EDVR [45]	FloRNN
Raw	43.97/.9874	44.30/.9891	44.51/.9897	44.71/.9902	45.16/.9907
sRGB	39.95/.9792	39.91/.9812	–	40.89/.9838	41.01/.9843

Table 7. Quantitative comparison of PSNR/SSIM on IOCV dataset [27] for real-world video denoising in sRGB domain.

Method	Noisy	CVMSt-SVD [26]	VBM4D [30]	FastDVD [43]	VNLNet [12]	FloRNN
HUAWEI_BC	38.11/.9593	40.80/.9834	41.19/.9830	41.26/.9857	41.35/.9868	42.28/.9880
HUAWEI_FC	38.58/.9413	38.71/.9780	38.76/.9785	38.03/.9776	38.79/.9809	39.57/.9828
OPPO_BC	32.06/.9071	33.44/.9508	33.26/.9456	33.05/.9476	33.56/.9544	33.75/.9545
OPPO_FC	36.90/.9447	39.66/.9791	39.56/.9785	39.06/.9751	40.11/.9823	40.31/.9821

Gaussian Denoising on Set8 and DAVIS Datasets. Table 3 and 4 lists the quantitative comparison on Set8 [42] and DAVIS [36] datasets. From the table, our FloRNN outperforms the state-of-the-art methods by a large margin on both datasets in terms of PSNR/SSIM, which demonstrates its superiority on video denoising applications. We also analyse the model complexity of each method in Table 5, and found that FloRNN achieves good trade-off between performance and running time. Specifically, FloRNN surpasses non-local based PaCNet [44] by 0.87 dB on Set8, while hundred times faster. Compare to FastDVDNet [43] which is especially suggested for efficiency, the performance gain of FloRNN is promoted to 1.24 dB, with 4 times slower. Experiments on DAVIS dataset shows similar results, which demonstrates that FloRNN generates best results with good efficiency. Figure 6 illustrates the qualitative comparison on a dynamic scene with noise level $\sigma = 40$. Despite the large motion and severe noise, FloRNN could clearly recover the characters, which are hard to recognize in other results. More results are provided in the supplementary material.

Raw Domain Video Denoising on CRVD Dataset. We further evaluate our FloRNN on real-world video denoising datasets. On CRVD dataset [51], EMVD [31] adopts forward recurrent mechanism designed for mobile devices, but performs inferior due to lack of future information when scaling up on GPUs. EDVR [45] utilizes pyramid deformable convolution for alignment and achieves good results, but its multi-frame convolutional backbone limits the long term propagation. Instead, from Table 6, our FloRNN benefits both long term propagation of historical frames and near future information, and outperforms EDVR by 0.45 dB on raw domain. The performance on sRGB domain is calculated by rendering the raw results into sRGB ones with a pretrained ISP network. Our performance gain decreases on sRGB domain, which is possibly due to the inaccuracy of the ISP module.

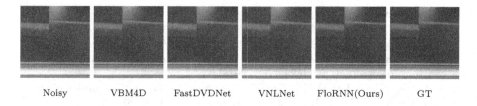

Noisy   VBM4D   FastDVDNet   VNLNet   FloRNN(Ours)   GT

Fig. 7. Visual comparison on the real-world IOCV dataset [27].

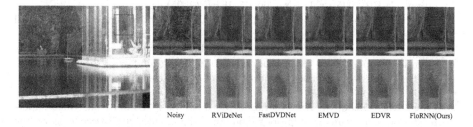

Noisy   RViDeNet   FastDVDNet   EMVD   EDVR   FloRNN(Ours)

Fig. 8. Visual comparison of an outdoor scene on the CRVD dataset [51], we render the results in raw domain to sRGB domain with a pretrained ISP.

sRGB Domain Video Denoising on IOCV Dataset. As IOCV [27] does not provide training sets, we apply our Gaussian denoising models for IOCV videos, and tune the noise level for each subset to get best results the same as [27]. Nonetheless, FloRNN achieves favorable results and surpasses competing methods (see Table 7). Visual comparison in Fig. 7 and Fig. 8 show that our FloRNN is able to remove the real-world video noise and recover fine-grained details.

5 Conclusion

In this paper, we propose a novel recurrent network for unidirectional video denoising. Look-ahead recurrent module is sufficient to exploit near-future frames in a forward manner. Combining with forward module, FloRNN achieves near BiRNN performance with constant memory occupation and latency. By analyzing backward and forward warping mechanisms, we found incorporating forward warping and border enlargement is favorable to address the border information missing problem during alignment. Experimental results demonstrate the superiority of the proposed method in removing both synthetic and real world noise. Our unidirectional video denoising algorithm is beneficial to various video applications, *e.g.*, video conference, live streaming, and could dynamically adjust the look-ahead step k for balance denoising results and latency.

Acknowledgement. This work is partially supported by the National Natural Science Foundation of China (NSFC) under Grant No.s 62006064 and U19A2073.

References

1. Abdelhamed, A., Lin, S., Brown, M.S.: A high-quality denoising dataset for smartphone cameras. In: Proceedings of the IEEE Conference on Computer Vision and Pattern Recognition, pp. 1692–1700 (2018)
2. Arias, P., Morel, J.M.: Video denoising via empirical bayesian estimation of spacetime patches. J. Math. Imaging and Vis. **60**(1), 70–93 (2018)
3. Buades, A., Coll, B., Morel, J.M.: A non-local algorithm for image denoising. In: 2005 IEEE Computer Society Conference on Computer Vision and Pattern Recognition (CVPR 2005), vol. 2, pp. 60–65. IEEE (2005)
4. Buades, A., Lisani, J.L., Miladinović, M.: Patch-based video denoising with optical flow estimation. IEEE Trans. Image Process. **25**(6), 2573–2586 (2016)
5. Chan, K.C., Wang, X., Yu, K., Dong, C., Loy, C.C.: Basicvsr: The search for essential components in video super-resolution and beyond. In: Proceedings of the IEEE/CVF Conference on Computer Vision and Pattern Recognition, pp. 4947–4956 (2021)
6. Chan, K.C., Zhou, S., Xu, X., Loy, C.C.: Basicvsr++: Improving video super-resolution with enhanced propagation and alignment. In: Proceedings of the IEEE/CVF Conference on Computer Vision and Pattern Recognition, pp. 5972–5981 (2022)
7. Chen, X., Song, L., Yang, X.: Deep rnns for video denoising. In: Applications of digital image processing XXXIX, vol. 9971, p. 99711T. International Society for)ptics and Photonics (2016)
8. Claus, M., van Gemert, J.: Videnn: Deep blind video denoising. In: Proceedings of the IEEE Conference on Computer Vision and Pattern Recognition Workshops (2019)
9. Dabov, K., Foi, A., Katkovnik, V., Egiazarian, K.: Image denoising by sparse 3-d transform-domain collaborative filtering. IEEE Trans. Image Process. **16**(8), 2080–2095 (2007)
10. Dai, J., et al.: Deformable convolutional networks. In: Proceedings of the IEEE International Conference on Computer Vision, pp. 764–773 (2017)
11. Davy, A., Ehret, T., Morel, J.M., Arias, P., Facciolo, G.: A non-local cnn for video denoising. In: 2019 IEEE International Conference on Image Processing (ICIP), pp. 2409–2413. IEEE (2019)
12. Davy, A., Ehret, T., Morel, J.M., Arias, P., Facciolo, G.: Video denoising by combining patch search and cnns. J. Math. Imaging Vis. **63**(1), 73–88 (2021)
13. Dosovitskiy, A., et al.: Flownet: Learning optical flow with convolutional networks. In: Proceedings of the IEEE International Conference on Computer Vision, pp. 2758–2766 (2015)
14. Elad, M., Aharon, M.: Image denoising via sparse and redundant representations over learned dictionaries. IEEE Trans. Image Process. **15**(12), 3736–3745 (2006)
15. Fuoli, D., Gu, S., Timofte, R.: Efficient video super-resolution through recurrent latent space propagation. In: 2019 IEEE/CVF International Conference on Computer Vision Workshop (ICCVW), pp. 3476–3485. IEEE (2019)
16. Gu, S., Zhang, L., Zuo, W., Feng, X.: Weighted nuclear norm minimization with application to image denoising. In: Proceedings of the IEEE Conference on Computer Vision and Pattern Recognition, pp. 2862–2869 (2014)
17. Guo, S., Yan, Z., Zhang, K., Zuo, W., Zhang, L.: Toward convolutional blind denoising of real photographs. In: Proceedings of the IEEE/CVF Conference on Computer Vision and Pattern Recognition, pp. 1712–1722 (2019)

18. He, K., Zhang, X., Ren, S., Sun, J.: Deep residual learning for image recognition. In: Proceedings of the IEEE Conference on Computer Vision and Pattern Recognition, pp. 770–778 (2016)
19. Huang, Y., Wang, W., Wang, L.: Video super-resolution via bidirectional recurrent convolutional networks. IEEE Trans. Pattern Anal. Mach. Intell. **40**(4), 1015–1028 (2017)
20. Ioffe, S., Szegedy, C.: Batch normalization: Accelerating deep network training by reducing internal covariate shift. In: International Conference on Machine Learning, pp. 448–456. PMLR (2015)
21. Isobe, T., Jia, X., Gu, S., Li, S., Wang, S., Tian, Q.: Video super-resolution with recurrent structure-detail network. In: Vedaldi, A., Bischof, H., Brox, T., Frahm, J.-M. (eds.) ECCV 2020. LNCS, vol. 12357, pp. 645–660. Springer, Cham (2020). https://doi.org/10.1007/978-3-030-58610-2_38
22. Kim, D., Woo, S., Lee, J.Y., Kweon, I.S.: Deep video inpainting. In: Proceedings of the IEEE/CVF Conference on Computer Vision and Pattern Recognition, pp. 5792–5801 (2019)
23. Kim, D., Woo, S., Lee, J.Y., Kweon, I.S.: Recurrent temporal aggregation framework for deep video inpainting. IEEE Trans. Pattern Anal. Mach. Intell. **42**(5), 1038–1052 (2019)
24. Kim, Y., Soh, J.W., Park, G.Y., Cho, N.I.: Transfer learning from synthetic to real-noise denoising with adaptive instance normalization. In: Proceedings of the IEEE/CVF Conference on Computer Vision and Pattern Recognition, pp. 3482–3492 (2020)
25. Kingma, D.P., Ba, J.: Adam: A method for stochastic optimization. arXiv preprint arXiv:1412.6980 (2014)
26. Kong, Z., Yang, X.: Color image and multispectral image denoising using block diagonal representation. IEEE Trans. Image Process. **28**(9), 4247–4259 (2019)
27. Kong, Z., Yang, X., He, L.: A comprehensive comparison of multi-dimensional image denoising methods. arXiv preprint arXiv:2011.03462 (2020)
28. Liu, J., et al.: Learning raw image denoising with bayer pattern unification and bayer preserving augmentation. In: Proceedings of the IEEE/CVF Conference on Computer Vision and Pattern Recognition Workshops (2019)
29. Liu, J., Yang, W., Yang, S., Guo, Z.: Erase or fill? deep joint recurrent rain removal and reconstruction in videos. In: Proceedings of the IEEE Conference on Computer Vision and Pattern Recognition, pp. 3233–3242 (2018)
30. Maggioni, M., Boracchi, G., Foi, A., Egiazarian, K.: Video denoising, deblocking, and enhancement through separable 4-d nonlocal spatiotemporal transforms. IEEE Trans. Image Process. **21**(9), 3952–3966 (2012)
31. Maggioni, M., Huang, Y., Li, C., Xiao, S., Fu, Z., Song, F.: Efficient multi-stage video denoising with recurrent spatio-temporal fusion. In: Proceedings of the IEEE/CVF Conference on Computer Vision and Pattern Recognition, pp. 3466–3475 (2021)
32. Mildenhall, B., Barron, J.T., Chen, J., Sharlet, D., Ng, R., Carroll, R.: Burst denoising with kernel prediction networks. In: Proceedings of the IEEE Conference on Computer Vision and Pattern Recognition, pp. 2502–2510 (2018)
33. Nah, S., Son, S., Lee, K.M.: Recurrent neural networks with intra-frame iterations for video deblurring. In: Proceedings of the IEEE/CVF Conference on Computer Vision and Pattern Recognition, pp. 8102–8111 (2019)
34. Niklaus, S., Liu, F.: Softmax splatting for video frame interpolation. In: Proceedings of the IEEE/CVF Conference on Computer Vision and Pattern Recognition, pp. 5437–5446 (2020)

35. Plotz, T., Roth, S.: Benchmarking denoising algorithms with real photographs. In: Proceedings of the IEEE Conference on Computer Vision and Pattern Recognition, pp. 1586–1595 (2017)
36. Pont-Tuset, J., et al.: The 2017 davis challenge on video object segmentation. arXiv preprint arXiv:1704.00675 (2017)
37. Rong, X., Demandolx, D., Matzen, K., Chatterjee, P., Tian, Y.: Burst denoising via temporally shifted wavelet transforms. In: Vedaldi, A., Bischof, H., Brox, T., Frahm, J.-M. (eds.) ECCV 2020. LNCS, vol. 12358, pp. 240–256. Springer, Cham (2020). https://doi.org/10.1007/978-3-030-58601-0_15
38. Sajjadi, M.S., Vemulapalli, R., Brown, M.: Frame-recurrent video super-resolution. In: Proceedings of the IEEE Conference on Computer Vision and Pattern Recognition, pp. 6626–6634 (2018)
39. Shen, W., Bao, W., Zhai, G., Chen, L., Min, X., Gao, Z.: Blurry video frame interpolation. In: Proceedings of the IEEE/CVF Conference on Computer Vision and Pattern Recognition, pp. 5114–5123 (2020)
40. Son, H., Lee, J., Lee, J., Cho, S., Lee, S.: Recurrent video deblurring with blur-invariant motion estimation and pixel volumes. ACM Trans. Graph. (TOG) 40(5), 1–18 (2021)
41. Sun, D., Yang, X., Liu, M.Y., Kautz, J.: Pwc-net: Cnns for optical flow using pyramid, warping, and cost volume. In: Proceedings of the IEEE Conference on Computer Vision and Pattern Recognition, pp. 8934–8943 (2018)
42. Tassano, M., Delon, J., Veit, T.: Dvdnet: A fast network for deep video denoising. In: 2019 IEEE International Conference on Image Processing (ICIP), pp. 1805–1809. IEEE (2019)
43. Tassano, M., Delon, J., Veit, T.: Fastdvdnet: Towards real-time deep video denoising without flow estimation. In: IEEE/CVF Conference on Computer Vision and Pattern Recognition (CVPR) (June 2020)
44. Vaksman, G., Elad, M., Milanfar, P.: Patch craft: Video denoising by deep modeling and patch matching. In: Proceedings of the IEEE/CVF International Conference on Computer Vision (ICCV), pp. 2157–2166 (October 2021)
45. Wang, X., Chan, K.C., Yu, K., Dong, C., Change Loy, C.: Edvr: Video restoration with enhanced deformable convolutional networks. In: Proceedings of the IEEE/CVF Conference on Computer Vision and Pattern Recognition Workshops (2019)
46. Xia, Z., Perazzi, F., Gharbi, M., Sunkavalli, K., Chakrabarti, A.: Basis prediction networks for effective burst denoising with large kernels. In: Proceedings of the IEEE/CVF Conference on Computer Vision and Pattern Recognition, pp. 11844–11853 (2020)
47. Xiang, X., Tian, Y., Zhang, Y., Fu, Y., Allebach, J.P., Xu, C.: Zooming slow-mo: Fast and accurate one-stage space-time video super-resolution. In: Proceedings of the IEEE/CVF Conference on Computer Vision and Pattern Recognition, pp. 3370–3379 (2020)
48. Xu, X., Li, M., Sun, W., Yang, M.H.: Learning spatial and spatio-temporal pixel aggregations for image and video denoising. IEEE Trans. Image Process. 29, 7153–7165 (2020)
49. Yang, W., Liu, J., Feng, J.: Frame-consistent recurrent video deraining with dual-level flow. In: Proceedings of the IEEE/CVF Conference on Computer Vision and Pattern Recognition, pp. 1661–1670 (2019)
50. Yang, W., Tan, R.T., Feng, J., Wang, S., Cheng, B., Liu, J.: Recurrent multi-frame deraining: Combining physics guidance and adversarial learning. IEEE Trans. Pattern Anal. Mach. Intell. 44, 8569–858 (2021)

51. Yue, H., Cao, C., Liao, L., Chu, R., Yang, J.: Supervised raw video denoising with a benchmark dataset on dynamic scenes. In: IEEE/CVF Conference on Computer Vision and Pattern Recognition (CVPR) (June 2020)
52. Zhang, K., Zuo, W., Chen, Y., Meng, D., Zhang, L.: Beyond a gaussian denoiser: Residual learning of deep cnn for image denoising. IEEE Trans. Image Process. **26**(7), 3142–3155 (2017)
53. Zhang, K., Zuo, W., Zhang, L.: Ffdnet: Toward a fast and flexible solution for cnn-based image denoising. IEEE Trans. Image Process. **27**(9), 4608–4622 (2018)
54. Zhong, Z., Gao, Y., Zheng, Y., Zheng, B.: Efficient spatio-temporal recurrent neural network for video deblurring. In: Vedaldi, A., Bischof, H., Brox, T., Frahm, J.-M. (eds.) ECCV 2020. LNCS, vol. 12351, pp. 191–207. Springer, Cham (2020). https://doi.org/10.1007/978-3-030-58539-6_12
55. Zhuo, S., Jin, Z., Zou, W., Li, X.: Ridnet: Recursive information distillation network for color image denoising. In: Proceedings of the IEEE/CVF International Conference on Computer Vision Workshops (2019)
56. Zoran, D., Weiss, Y.: From learning models of natural image patches to whole image restoration. In: 2011 International Conference on Computer Vision, pp. 479–486. IEEE (2011)

Self-supervised Learning for Real-World Super-Resolution from Dual Zoomed Observations

Zhilu Zhang[1], Ruohao Wang[1], Hongzhi Zhang[1(✉)], Yunjin Chen[1,2], and Wangmeng Zuo[1,2]

[1] Harbin Institute of Technology, Harbin, China
zhanghz0451@gmail.com, wmzuo@hit.edu.cn
[2] Peng Cheng Laboratory, Shenzhen, China

Abstract. In this paper, we consider two challenging issues in reference-based super-resolution (RefSR), (i) how to choose a proper reference image, and (ii) how to learn real-world RefSR in a self-supervised manner. Particularly, we present a novel self-supervised learning approach for real-world image SR from observations at dual camera zooms (SelfDZSR). Considering the popularity of multiple cameras in modern smartphones, the more zoomed (telephoto) image can be naturally leveraged as the reference to guide the SR of the lesser zoomed (short-focus) image. Furthermore, Self-DZSR learns a deep network to obtain the SR result of short-focus image to have the same resolution as the telephoto image. For this purpose, we take the telephoto image instead of an additional high-resolution image as the supervision information and select a center patch from it as the reference to super-resolve the corresponding short-focus image patch. To mitigate the effect of the misalignment between short-focus low-resolution (LR) image and telephoto ground-truth (GT) image, we design an auxiliary-LR generator and map the GT to an auxiliary-LR while keeping the spatial position unchanged. Then the auxiliary-LR can be utilized to deform the LR features by the proposed adaptive spatial transformer networks (AdaSTN), and match the Ref features to GT. During testing, SelfDZSR can be directly deployed to super-solve the whole short-focus image with the reference of telephoto image. Experiments show that our method achieves better quantitative and qualitative performance against state-of-the-arts. Codes are available at https://github.com/cszhilu1998/SelfDZSR.

Keywords: Reference-based super-resolution · Self-supervised learning · Real world

1 Introduction

Image super-resolution (SR) aiming to recover a high-resolution (HR) image from its low-resolution (LR) counterpart is a severely ill-posed inverse problem with

---

Supplementary Information The online version contains supplementary material available at https://doi.org/10.1007/978-3-031-19797-0_35.

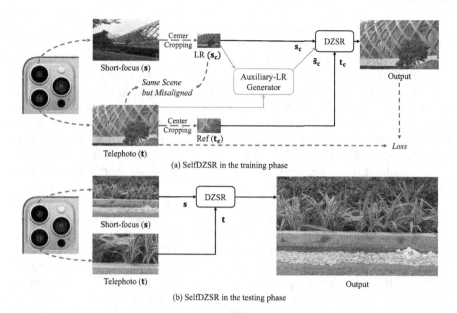

(a) SelfDZSR in the training phase

(b) SelfDZSR in the testing phase

Fig. 1. Overall pipeline of proposed SelfDZSR in the training and testing phase.

many practical applications. To relax the ill-posedness of the SR, reference-based image SR (RefSR) has recently been suggested to super-resolve the LR image with more accurate details by leveraging a reference (Ref) image containing similar content and texture with the HR image. Albeit progress has been made in RefSR, it remains a challenging issue to choose a proper reference image for each LR image.

Fortunately, advances and popularity of imaging techniques make it practically feasible to collect images of a scene at two different camera zooms (*i.e.*, dual zoomed observations). For example, asymmetric cameras with different fixed-focal lenses have been equipped in modern smartphones. In these practical scenarios, the more zoomed (telephoto) image can be naturally leveraged as the reference to guide the SR of the lesser zoomed (short-focus) image. Image SR from dual zoomed observations (DZSR) can thus be regarded as a special case of RefSR, in which Ref has the same scene as the center part of the LR image but is with higher resolution. While conventional RefSR methods [19,27,33,46,47,54] usually use synthetic (*e.g.*, bicubic) degraded LR images for training and evaluation, DZSR should cope with real-world LR short-focus images and no ground-truth HR images are available in training. To bridge the domain gap between synthetic and real-world LR images, dual-camera super-resolution (DCSR) [38] suggests self-supervised real-image adaptation (SRA) involving a degradation preserving and a detail transfer terms. However, DCSR only attains limited success, due to that the two loss terms in SRA cannot well address the gap between the synthetic and real-world LR degradation as well as the misalignment between short-focus and telephoto images.

In this work, we aim at super-resolving the real world short-focus image with the reference of the corresponding telephoto image. Different from DCSR [38] requiring to pre-train on synthetic images, we adopt self-supervised learning to train DZSR model (*i.e.*, SelfDZSR) from scratch directly on short-focus and telephoto images without additional high-resolution images. As shown in Fig. 1(a), instead of the whole images, during training we crop the center part of the short-focus and telephoto image respectively as the input LR and Ref, and use the whole telephoto image as the ground-truth (GT). In the testing phase, by using the whole short-focus and telephoto images respectively as LR and Ref, Self-DZSR can be directly deployed to super-solve the whole short-focus image, as shown in Fig. 1(b).

However, when training SelfDZSR, the cropped short-focus image generally cannot be accurately aligned with the telephoto GT image, making the learned model prone to producing blurry SR results [51,55]. Matching the Ref to LR will also result in the warped Ref being not aligned with the GT, bringing more uncertainty to network training. To handle the misalignment issue, we map GT to an auxiliary-LR while keeping the spatial position unchanged, and utilize the auxiliary-LR as the target position image for deforming LR and Ref features during training. During testing, given that GT is unavailable, the auxiliary-LR should be replaced by LR. Specifically, we propose an auxiliary-LR generator network constrained by position preserving loss and content preserving loss. The position preserving loss constrains that the auxiliary-LR is aligned with GT, so that the warped LR and Ref features are aligned with GT during training. The content preserving loss constrains that the auxiliary-LR has similar contents as LR, so that the auxiliary-LR can be replaced by LR safely during testing.

Moreover, for aligning LR with GT, we propose adaptive spatial transformer networks (AdaSTN) that takes the auxiliary-LR and LR images for estimating the offsets between them to deform the LR features. AdaSTN implicitly aligns contents between LR and auxiliary-LR by minimizing the reconstruction loss of SelfDZSR. When training is done, the auxiliary-LR generator and the offset estimator of AdaSTN can be safely detached. That is, the estimated offsets of AdaSTN can be set to default, bringing no extra cost in the test phase. For the matching of Ref image, instead of searching corresponding contents from Ref to LR features in most existing RefSR methods [19,27,38,47,54], we perform it from Ref to auxiliary-LR features. Finally, the warped LR and warped Ref features can be regarded as aligned with GT, which are then combined and fed into the restoration module.

Extensive experiments are conducted on the Nikon camera from the DRealSR dataset [42] as well as the CameraFusion dataset [38]. The results demonstrate the effectiveness and practicability of our SelfDZSR for real-world image SR from dual zoomed observations. In comparison to the state-of-the-art SR and RefSR methods, our SelfDZSR performs favorably in terms of both quantitative metrics and perceptual quality.

To sum up, the main contributions of this work include:

– An effective self-supervised learning approach, *i.e.*, SelfDZSR, is presented to super-resolve the real-world images from dual zoomed observations.

- The adverse effect of image misalignment for self-supervised learning and Ref matching is alleviated by the proposed auxiliary-LR and adaptive spatial transformer networks (AdaSTN), while bringing no extra inference cost.
- Quantitative and qualitative results on Nikon camera and CameraFusion show that our method outperforms the state-of-the-art methods.

2   Related Work

2.1   Blind Image Super-Resolution

With the development of deep networks, single image super-resolution (SISR) methods based on fixed and known degradation have achieved great success in terms of both performance [10,22,25,49,52] and efficiency [16,21,26,36,45]. However, these methods perform poorly when applying to images with an unknown degradation, and may cause some artifacts. Thus, blind super-resolution comes into being to bridge the gap.

On the one hand, some works estimate the blur kernel or degradation representation for LR and feed it into the SR reconstruction network. IKC [13] performed kernel estimation and SR reconstruction processes iteratively, while DAN [30] conducted it in an alternating optimization scheme. KernelGAN [1] utilized the image patch recurrence property to estimate an image-specific kernel, and FKP [24] learned a kernel prior based on normalization flow [9] at test time. To relaxing the assumption that blur kernels are spatially invariant, MANet [23] estimated spatially variant kernel by suggesting mutual affine convolution. Different from the above explicit methods of estimating kernel, DASR [37] introduced contrastive learning [14] to extract discriminative representations to distinguish different degradations. On the other hand, Hussein *et al.* [17] modified the LR to a pre-defined degradation (*e.g.*, bicubic) type by a closed-form correction filter. BSRGAN [48] and Real-ESRGAN [39] designed more complex degradation models to generate LR data for training the networks, making the networks generalize well to many real-world degradation scenarios.

2.2   Real-World Image Super-Resolution

Although blind SR models trained on synthetic data have shown appreciable generalization capacity, the formulated degradation assumption limits the performance on real-world images with much more complicated and changeable degradation. Thus, image SR directly towards real-world scenes has also received much attention. On the one hand, given unpaired real LR an HR, several real-world SR methods [2,41,43] attempt to approximate real degradation and generate the auxiliary-LR image from HR, and then learn to super-resolve the auxiliary-LR in a supervised manner. On the other hand, some methods [3,5,28,29,42] construct paired datasets by adjusting the focal length of a camera, in which the image with a long focal and short focal length is regarded as GT and LR, respectively. Among these methods, LP-KPN [3] presented a kernel prediction network based on the Laplacian pyramid. CDC [42] considered reconstruction difficulty of different components, and performed image SR in a divide-and-conquer manner.

In addition, the misalignment of data pairs is a universal problem in real scenes, and it may cause blurry SR result. The above methods based on paired datasets pre-execute complex alignment or even manual selection, which are generally laborious and time-consuming. Different from them, CoBi [51] loss offered an effective way to deal with misalignment during SR training. Zhang *et al.* [55] incorporated global color mapping and optical flow [35] to explicitly align the data pairs with severe color inconsistency. Nevertheless, optical flow is limited in handling complicated misalignment. In this work, we further propose AdaSTN to handle the complicated misalignment after pre-alignment with optical flow.

2.3   Reference-Based Image Super-Resolution

RefSR aims to take advantage of a high-resolution reference image that has similar content and texture as LR for super-resolution. It relaxes the ill-posedness of SISR and facilitates the generation of more accurate details. The features extracting and matching between LR and Ref is the research focus of most RefSR methods. Among them, Zheng *et al.* [56] proposed a correspondence network to extract features for matching, and an HR synthesis network with the input of the matched Ref. SRNTT [54] calculated the correlation between pre-trained VGG features of LR and Ref at multiple levels for matching them. Zhang *et al.* [53] extended the scaling factor of RefSR methods from 4× to 16×. Furthermore, TTSR [47] and FRM [46] developed an end-to-end training framework and proposed learnable feature extractors. Recently, C^2-Matching [19] performed a more accurate match by the teacher-student correlation distillation while MASA-SR [27] reduced the computational cost by coarse-to-fine correspondence matching. Besides, CrossNet [57] and SEN [33] respectively introduced optical flow [11] and deformable convolution [6,58] to align Ref with LR. However, optical flow is limited in handling large and complicated motions while deformable convolution is limited in modeling long-distance correspondence. In this work, we follow [19] to perform patch-wise matching.

Additionally, the RefSR methods mentioned above are all based on the bicubic down-sampling. DCSR [38] explores an adaptive fine-tuning strategy on real-world images based on the pre-trained model with synthetic data. In this work, we propose a fully self-supervised learning framework directly on weakly aligned dual zoomed observations.

3   Proposed Method

In this section, we first give a description of our self-supervised learning framework for super-resolution from dual zoomed observations. Then we detail the solutions for handling the misalignment problem, including the generation of auxiliary-LR, alignment between LR and auxiliary-LR by AdaSTN, alignment between Ref and (auxiliary-)LR. Finally, the design of the restoration module is introduced, and the learning objective is provided.

3.1   Self-supervised Learning Framework

Denote by **s** and **t** the short-focus image and the telephoto image, respectively. Super-resolution based on dual zoomed observations aims to super-resolve the short-focus image **s** with the reference telephoto image **t**, which can be written as,

$$\hat{\mathbf{y}} = \mathcal{Z}(\mathbf{s}, \mathbf{t}; \Theta_{\mathcal{Z}}), \tag{1}$$

where $\hat{\mathbf{y}}$ has the same field-of-view as **s** and the same resolution as **t**, $\mathcal{Z}$ denotes the zooming network with the parameter $\Theta_{\mathcal{Z}}$.

However, in real-world scenarios, the GT of $\hat{\mathbf{y}}$ is hard or almost impossible to acquire. A simple alternative solution is to leverage synthetic data for training, but the domain gaps between the degradation model in training and that in real-world images prevent it from working well. DCSR [38] tries to bridge the gaps by fine-tuning the trained model using an SRA strategy, but the huge difference in the field of view between the output and the target telephoto image limits it in achieving satisfying results.

In contrast to the above methods, we propose a novel self-supervised dual-zooms super-resolution (SelfDZSR) framework, which can be trained from scratch solely on the short-focus and telephoto image (see Fig. 1(a)), and be directly deployed to the real-world dual zoomed observations (see Fig. 1(b)). During training, we first crop the central area of the telephoto and short-focus images,

$$\mathbf{s_c} = \mathcal{C}(\mathbf{s}; r), \qquad \mathbf{t_c} = \mathcal{C}(\mathbf{t}; r), \tag{2}$$

where $\mathcal{C}$ denotes the center cropping operator, r is the focal length ratio of **t** and **s**. Note that $\mathbf{t_c}$ has the same scene and higher resolution with $\mathcal{C}(\mathbf{s_c}; r)$, *i.e.*, the central area of $\mathbf{s_c}$. Moreover, **t** and $\mathbf{s_c}$ have the same scene, while the resolution is different by r times. Thus, $\mathbf{s_c}$ and $\mathbf{t_c}$ can be naturally used as LR and Ref respectively, while **t** can be regarded as the GT. Then we can define DZSR as,

$$\Theta_{\mathcal{Z}} = \arg\min_{\Theta_{\mathcal{Z}}} \mathcal{L}\left(\mathcal{Z}(\mathbf{s_c}, \mathbf{t_c}; \Theta_{\mathcal{Z}}), \mathbf{t}\right) \tag{3}$$

where $\mathcal{L}$ denotes the self-supervised learning objective.

Nonetheless, GT **t** is not spatially aligned with LR $\mathbf{s_c}$, bringing adverse effects on self-supervised learning and Ref $\mathbf{t_c}$ matching. To handle the misalignment issue, we hope to construct an auxiliary-LR to guide the deformation of LR and Ref towards the GT. For this purpose, the elaborate design on network architecture and loss terms is essential for SelfDZSR, which is introduced below.

3.2   Generation of Auxiliary-LR for Alignment

For SelfDZSR during training, the LR image $\mathbf{s_c}$ and GT image **t** are captured from the different camera lenses, and thus are misaligned in space. It has been shown in recent works [51,55] that the spatial misalignment of data pairs will cause the network to produce blurry results. Off-the-shelf optical flow [35] offers a probable solution in dealing with this issue. However, limited to the offset diversity [4] of optical flow, images after registration are still slightly misaligned

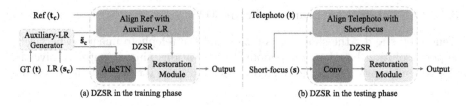

(a) DZSR in the training phase   (b) DZSR in the testing phase

Fig. 2. The pipeline of proposed DZSR model. (a) DZSR in the training phase. The auxiliary-LR is generated to guide the deformation of LR and Ref towards the GT. The aligned LR and Ref features are fed into the restoration module. (b) DZSR in the testing phase. The short-focus and telephoto image can be regarded as LR and Ref, respectively. The auxiliary-LR generator is detached and AdaSTN is simplified to a convolution layer.

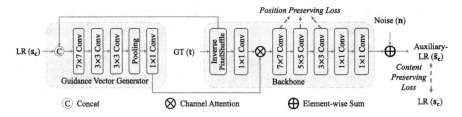

Fig. 3. Illustration of the auxiliary-LR generator. The position preserving loss constraints the kernel weight to ensure the alignment between auxiliary-LR and GT, while content preserving loss constraints that auxiliary-LR has similar contents as LR.

in some complex circumstances and explicit perfect alignment is very difficult. Moreover, the misalignment will result in the warped Ref features being not aligned with GT after matching Ref to LR, bringing more uncertainty to network training. To handle the above issues, we construct an auxiliary-LR $\tilde{s}_c$ from the GT **t** while keeping the spatial position unchanged, and take it to guide the alignment of LR and Ref towards GT (see Fig. 2(a)). Noted that the auxiliary-LR cannot be used in testing, and it should be substituted by the short-focus **s** (see Fig. 2(b)).

Thus, the auxiliary-LR $\tilde{s}_c$ is required to satisfy two prerequisites. (i) $\tilde{s}_c$ can be substituted by **s** during testing. (ii) The spatial position of $\tilde{s}_c$ should keep the same as **t**. For the first point, The auxiliary-LR should have similar contents and degradation types as LR, so that it can be substituted safely during testing. In particular, we design an auxiliary-LR generator network and constrain the contents of auxiliary-LR to be similar with these of LR, as shown in Fig. 3. For the second point, inspired by KernelGAN [1], we take advantage of the position preserving loss to constrain the centroid of the local convolution kernel in the center of space. The position preserving loss $\mathcal{L}_p$ can be defined as,

$$\mathcal{L}_p(\mathbf{W}^l) = \|\sum_{i=0}^{k-1}\sum_{j=0}^{k-1}(i - \frac{k}{2} + 0.5)w_{i,j}^l\|_1 + \|\sum_{i=0}^{k-1}\sum_{j=0}^{k-1}(j - \frac{k}{2} + 0.5)w_{i,j}^l\|_1, \quad (4)$$

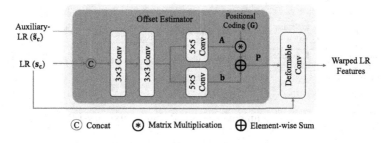

Fig. 4. Illustration of AdaSTN.

where $\mathbf{W}^l$ denotes the kernel weight parameters of the l-th convolution layer in the backbone of the auxiliary-LR generator, k is odd and denotes the kernel size, $w_{i,j}^l$ denotes the value in the (i,j) position of $\mathbf{W}^l$. In addition, LR $\mathbf{s_c}$ can be used to generate a conditional guidance vector for modulating features of $\mathbf{t}$ globally. Noted that the global modulation does not affect the preservation of spatial position. In short, the auxiliary-LR can be represented as,

$$\tilde{\mathbf{s}}_{\mathbf{c}} = \mathcal{D}(\mathbf{t}, \mathbf{s_c}; \Theta_{\mathcal{D}}) + \mathbf{n}, \tag{5}$$

where $\mathcal{D}$ denotes the auxiliary-LR generator network with the parameter $\Theta_{\mathcal{D}}$, $\mathbf{n}$ denotes the noise detailed in the suppl. Furthermore, $\Theta_{\mathcal{D}}$ can be written as,

$$\Theta_{\mathcal{D}} = \arg\min_{\Theta_{\mathcal{D}}} \|(\tilde{\mathbf{s}}_{\mathbf{c}} - \mathbf{n}) - \mathbf{s_c}\|_1 + \lambda_p \sum_{l=1}^{L} \mathcal{L}_{\mathrm{p}}(\mathbf{W}^l), \tag{6}$$

where we set λ_p to 100.

3.3 Alignment Between LR and GT by AdaSTN

Given LR and auxiliary-LR, we suggest implicitly aligning LR to auxiliary-LR (aligned with GT). We can estimate the offsets between them and then deform the LR features to align with GT. Deformable convolution [6] is a natural choice, but the direct estimation of the offsets may bring instability to the network training. Inspired by [12], we propose adaptive spatial transformer networks (AdaSTN) that offset is obtained indirectly by estimating the pixel-level affine transformation matrix and translation vector, as shown in Fig. 4. For every pixel, the estimated offset of AdaSTN can be written as,

$$\mathbf{P} = \mathbf{AG} + \mathbf{b}, \tag{7}$$

where $\mathbf{A} \in \mathbb{R}^{2 \times 2}$ is a predicted affine transformation matrix and $\mathbf{b} \in \mathbb{R}^{2 \times 1}$ is the translation vector. $\mathbf{G}$ is a positional coding represented by

$$\mathbf{G} = \begin{bmatrix} -1 & -1 & -1 & 0 & 0 & 0 & 1 & 1 & 1 \\ -1 & 0 & 1 & -1 & 0 & 1 & -1 & 0 & 1 \end{bmatrix}. \tag{8}$$

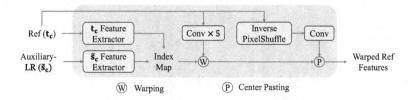

Fig. 5. Alignment between Ref and auxiliary-LR.

Thus, the deformable convolution of AdaSTN can be formulated as,

$$\mathbf{y}(\mathbf{q}) = \sum\nolimits_{k=0}^{8} \mathbf{w}_k \mathbf{x}(\mathbf{q} + \mathbf{p}_k),\tag{9}$$

where $\mathbf{x}$ and $\mathbf{y}$ represent the input and output features, respectively. $\mathbf{w}_k$ denotes the kernel weight and $\mathbf{p}_k$ denotes the k-th column value of $\mathbf{P}$. AdaSTN can be regarded as a variant of STN [18], which is from a global mode to a pixel-wise mode. In comparison to deformable convolution [6], AdaSTN is more stable in estimating the offsets. During experiments, we stack 3 AdaSTNs to align LR and auxiliary-LR progressively.

Note that auxiliary-LR is not available in the testing phase. A feasible way is to replace auxiliary-LR with LR. Actually, there is no need to estimate the offsets for AdaSTN. We can set $\mathbf{P} = \mathbf{0}$ directly, which means that the deformable convolution of AdaSTN can only observe the input value at the center point of the kernel and AdaSTN degenerates into $1{\times}1$ convolution (see Fig. 2(b)). However, this way may produce some artifacts in the results due to the gap between training and testing. In order to bridge this gap, for each AdaSTN, we randomly set $\mathbf{P} = \mathbf{0}$ with probability p (*e.g.*, 0.3) during training. For each training sample, the probability p^3 (*e.g.*, 0.027) that 3 AdaSTNs are all set to $\mathbf{P} = \mathbf{0}$ is low, so it has little impact on the learning of the overall framework.

3.4   Alignment Between Ref and (Auxiliary-) LR

Previous RefSR methods generally perform matching by calculating cosine similarity between Ref and LR features. For SelfDZSR during training, the misalignment between LR and GT will result in the warped Ref features being not aligned with GT after matching Ref to LR. To handle the issue, we instead calculate the correlation between Ref and auxiliary-LR features (see Fig. 2(a)). And the auxiliary-LR $\tilde{\mathbf{s}}_c$ can be substituted by the short-focus $\mathbf{s}$ during testing (see Fig. 2(b)). Figure 5 shows the alignment between Ref and auxiliary-LR. The index map is obtained by calculating the cosine similarity between Ref and auxiliary-LR features that are extracted by pre-trained feature extractors. Then the Ref is warped according to the index map. In addition, for SelfDZSR, the central part of LR has the same scene as Ref. Taking this property into account, we can rearrange Ref elements by an inverse PixelShuffle [32] layer, and then paste it to the center area of the warped Ref features.

3.5   Restoration Module and Learning Objective

Restoration Module. After getting the aligned LR and aligned Ref features, we concatenate and feed them into the backbone of the restoration module consisting of 16 residual blocks [25]. The concatenated features are also fed into an encoder to generate condition vectors for global modulation of the backbone features. The role of modulation is to make better use of Ref information and relieve the color inconsistency between LR and GT images. The details of restoration module will be introduced in the suppl.

Learning Objective for DZSR. The sliced Wasserstein (SW) distance has exhibited outstanding merit for training deep generative networks [8,44]. Recently, SW loss has been successfully applied in texture synthesis [15], image enhancement [7] and *etc.*. Here, we also use SW loss $\mathcal{L}_{\mathrm{SW}}$ to optimize DZSR, the detailed description will be given in the suppl. The loss term of DZSR can be written as,

$$\mathcal{L}_{\mathrm{DZSR}}(\hat{\mathbf{y}}, \mathbf{t}) = \|\hat{\mathbf{y}} - \mathbf{t}\|_1 + \lambda_{SW}\mathcal{L}_{\mathrm{SW}}(\phi(\hat{\mathbf{y}}), \phi(\mathbf{t})), \tag{10}$$

where ϕ denotes the pre-trained VGG-19 [34] network, and we set $\lambda_{SW} = 0.08$.

4   Experiments

4.1   Experimental Setup

Datasets. Experiments are conducted on Nikon camera images from DRealSR dataset [42] and the CameraFusion dataset [38]. The training patches of DRealSR have been manually and carefully selected for mitigating the alignment issue, which is laborious and time-consuming. Instead, we take the original captured data without manual processing for training, making the whole process fully automated. In particular, each scene of the orginal data contains four different focal-length images. We adopt the longest focal-length image as the telephoto input and the shortest focal-length image as the short-focus input, which forms a ×4 DZSR dataset. There are 163 image pairs for training and 20 images for evaluation. In the CameraFusion [38] dataset, the telephoto and short-focus images are from two lenses with different focal lengths of a smartphone. The focal length ratio between the telephoto and short-focus images is ∼2. Thus, it can constitute a ×2 DZSR dataset. For this dataset, we use 112 image pairs for training and 12 images for evaluation.

Data Pre-processing. We first crop the center area of the short-focus image as LR. Then the brightness and color matching are employed between the LR and the telephoto images. Next, we use PWC-Net [35] to calculate the optical flow between the LR and the telephoto images, and warp the telephoto image. The warped telephoto image is used as GT and the center patch of it can be seen as Ref. Note that misalignment can still occur after registration, and our SelfDZSR is suggested to learn deep DZSR model while alleviating the adverse effect of misalignment.

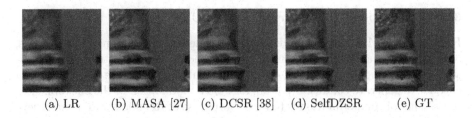

(a) LR   (b) MASA [27]   (c) DCSR [38]   (d) SelfDZSR   (e) GT

Fig. 6. Visual comparison on Nikon camera images.

Table 1. Quantitative results on Nikon camera images. Best results are highlighted by red. The models trained only with ℓ_1 (or ℓ_2) loss are marked in gray. RefSR† represents that the RefSR methods are trained in our self-supervised learning manner.

	Method	# Param (M)	Full-Image PSNR↑ / SSIM↑ / LPIPS↓	Corner-Image PSNR↑ / SSIM↑ / LPIPS↓
SISR	EDSR [25]	43.1	27.26 / 0.8364 / 0.362	27.29 / 0.8345 / 0.363
	RCAN [52]	15.6	27.30 / 0.8344 / 0.383	27.33 / 0.8323 / 0.383
	CDC [42]	39.9	27.20 / 0.8306 / 0.412	27.24 / 0.8283 / 0.412
	BSRGAN [48]	16.7	26.91 / 0.8151 / 0.279	26.96 / 0.8135 / 0.278
	Real-ESRGAN [39]	16.7	25.96 / 0.8076 / 0.272	26.00 / 0.8063 / 0.271
RefSR†	SRNTT-ℓ_2 [54]	5.5	27.30 / 0.8387 / 0.359	27.33 / 0.8366 / 0.359
	SRNTT [54]	5.5	27.31 / 0.8242 / 0.286	27.35 / 0.8223 / 0.283
	TTSR-ℓ_1 [47]	7.3	25.83 / 0.8272 / 0.369	25.80 / 0.8259 / 0.369
	TTSR [47]	7.3	25.31 / 0.7719 / 0.282	25.27 / 0.7708 / 0.282
	C^2-Matching-ℓ_1 [19]	8.9	27.19 / 0.8402 / 0.362	27.23 / 0.8381 / 0.362
	C^2-Matching [19]	8.9	26.79 / 0.8141 / 0.327	26.81 / 0.8123 / 0.325
	MASA-ℓ_1 [27]	4.0	27.27 / 0.8372 / 0.339	27.30 / 0.8352 / 0.339
	MASA [27]	4.0	27.32 / 0.7640 / 0.273	27.37 / 0.7615 / 0.274
	DCSR-ℓ_1 [38]	3.2	27.73 / 0.8274 / 0.355	27.72 / 0.8275 / 0.349
	DCSR [38]	3.2	27.69 / 0.8232 / 0.276	27.68 / 0.8232 / 0.272
Ours	SelfDZSR-ℓ_1	3.2	28.93 / 0.8572 / 0.308	28.67 / 0.8457 / 0.328
	SelfDZSR	3.2	28.67 / 0.8356 / 0.219	28.42 / 0.8238 / 0.231

Training Configurations. We augment the training data with random horizontal flip, vertical flip and 90° rotation. The batch size is 16, and the patch size for LR is 48×48. The model is trained with the Adam optimizer [20] by setting $\beta_1 = 0.9$ and $\beta_2 = 0.999$ for 400 epochs. The learning rate is initially set to 1×10^{-4} and is decayed to 5×10^{-5} after 200 epochs. The experiments are conducted with PyTorch [31] on an Nvidia GeForce RTX 2080Ti GPU.

Evaluation Configurations. There is no GT when inputting the original short-focus and telephoto images directly, so we also use the processed LR and Ref as input and warped telephoto as GT to compare the various methods by rule and line. Three common metrics (*i.e.*, PSNR, SSIM [40] and LPIPS [50]) on RGB channels are computed. Noted that the scene of the Ref is the same as the center area of LR. In addition to calculating the metrics on the full image (marked as *Full-Image*), we also calculate the metrics of the area excluding the center (marked as *Corner-Image*). And all patches for visual comparison are selected from the area excluding the center of the whole image.

4.2   Results on Nikon Camera

We compare results with SISR (*i.e.*, EDSR [25], RCAN [52], CDC [42], BSR-GAN [48] and Real-ESRGAN [39]) and RefSR (*i.e.*, SRNTT [54], TTSR [47], MASA [27], C^2-Matching [19] and DCSR [38]) methods. The results of BSR-GAN and Real-ESRGAN are generated via the officially released model, other methods are retrained using our processed data for a fair comparison. Among them, RefSR methods are trained in our self-supervised learning manner and each method has two models, obtained by minimizing ℓ_1 (or ℓ_2) loss and all loss terms that are used in their papers.

Table 2. tative results on CameraFusion dataset. Best results are highlighted by red. The models trained only with ℓ_1 (or ℓ_2) loss are marked in gray. RefSR† represents that the RefSR methods are trained in our self-supervised learning manner.

	Method	# Params (M)	Full-Image PSNR↑ / SSIM↑ / LPIPS↓	Corner-Image PSNR↑ / SSIM↑ / LPIPS↓
SISR	EDSR [25]	43.1	25.43 / 0.8041 / 0.356	25.25 / 0.8007 / 0.349
	RCAN [52]	15.6	25.31 / 0.8034 / 0.355	25.14 / 0.8004 / 0.349
	CDC [42]	39.9	24.31 / 0.7811 / 0.380	24.11 / 0.7771 / 0.374
	BSRGAN [48]	16.7	25.09 / 0.7779 / 0.272	24.92 / 0.7749 / 0.266
	Real-ESRGAN [39]	16.7	25.13 / 0.7788 / 0.261	24.90 / 0.7755 / 0.255
RefSR†	SRNTT-ℓ_2 [54]	5.5	24.78 / 0.7781 / 0.333	24.49 / 0.7737 / 0.331
	SRNTT [54]	5.5	23.69 / 0.7740 / 0.230	23.38 / 0.7700 / 0.229
	TTSR-ℓ_1 [47]	7.3	24.42 / 0.7937 / 0.375	24.12 / 0.7901 / 0.372
	TTSR [47]	7.3	23.05 / 0.7879 / 0.303	22.74 / 0.7854 / 0.300
	C^2-Matching-ℓ_1 [19]	8.9	25.24 / 0.7992 / 0.346	25.07 / 0.7971 / 0.340
	C^2-Matching [19]	8.9	24.18 / 0.7252 / 0.252	24.06 / 0.7254 / 0.245
	MASA-ℓ_1 [27]	4.0	25.78 / 0.8063 / 0.335	25.52 / 0.8026 / 0.331
	MASA [27]	4.0	25.42 / 0.7543 / 0.194	25.27 / 0.7524 / 0.190
	DCSR-ℓ_1 [38]	3.2	25.80 / 0.7974 / 0.300	25.48 / 0.7932 / 0.298
	DCSR [38]	3.2	25.51 / 0.7890 / 0.209	25.20 / 0.7847 / 0.211
Ours	SelfDZSR-ℓ_1	3.2	26.35 / 0.8276 / 0.262	25.67 / 0.8040 / 0.292
	SelfDZSR	3.2	26.03 / 0.8008 / 0.158	25.37 / 0.7740 / 0.174

Benefiting from the implicit alignment of the data pairs and better utilization of Ref information, SelfDZSR exceeds all competing methods on all metrics from Table 1. As shown in Fig. 6, our visual result restores much more details. More visual results and the evaluation of generalization capacity on other cameras will be given in the suppl.

4.3   Results on CameraFusion Dataset

Different from the Nikon camera images which scale factor of SR is ×4, it is ×2 for the CameraFusion dataset. Other settings of experiments on the CameraFusion dataset are the same as those on the Nikon camera images. Table 2 shows the comparison of quantitative results on the CameraFusion dataset, and we still achieve the best results among SISR and RefSR methods. The qualitative comparison will be given in the suppl.

5   Ablation Study

In this section, we conduct ablation experiments for assessing the effect of self-supervised learning, auxiliary-LR for alignment and AdaSTN. Unless otherwise stated, experiments are carried out on the Nikon camera images [42], and the metrics are evaluated on full images.

5.1   Effect of Self-supervised Learning

In order to verify the effectiveness of our proposed self-supervised approach, we conduct experiments on different training strategies. First, we remove the auxiliary-LR generator and AdaSTN in SelfDZSR. Then we replace the real LR and auxiliary-LR images with the bicubic downsampling HR image, and retrain the network. Finally, for a fair comparison, we take the self-supervised real-image adaptation (SRA) [38] and our self-supervised strategy to fine-tune the above model, respectively. As can be seen from Table 3, when evaluating on real-world images, our proposed self-supervised method achieves the better results. The PSNR metric is 0.27 dB higher than the model based on SRA fine-tuning. And our visual result is sharper and clearer.

Moreover, for the CameraFusion dataset, DCSR [38] model trained by our self-supervised approach obtains a 0.31 dB PSNR gain in comparison to the officially released model. In a word, it can be seen that even if the misalignment between LR and GT is not handled, our self-supervised method is still better than SRA [38] strategy.

Table 3. Ablation study on training strategies.

Training strategy	Bicubic degradation	SRA fine-tuning [38]	Our fine-tuning
PSNR↑ / LPIPS↓	28.07/0.398	28.26/0.278	28.53/0.223

Table 4. Ablation study on alignment methods. Data pairs are pre-aligned by [35]. '×' represents replacing auxiliary-LR with LR.

Align LR with auxiliary-LR	Align Ref with auxiliary-LR	PSNR↑ / LPIPS↓
×	×	28.48/0.222
✓	×	28.67/0.224
×	✓	28.61/0.220
✓	✓	28.67/0.219

5.2   Effect of Auxiliary-LR for Alignment

In order to evaluate the effect of our alignment methods, we experiment on the role of auxiliary-LR in alignment by replacing auxiliary-LR with LR during the training, which corresponds to Sect. 3.3 and Sect. 3.4. We consider the model that does not leverage auxiliary-LR as the baseline, which also means that the training data is only pre-aligned by optical flow [35]. When aligning LR with auxiliary-LR only, the PSNR increases by 0.19 dB against the baseline, as shown in Table 4. Coupled with the alignment between Ref and auxiliary-LR, better quantitative results can be further attained.

In addition, we conduct an experiment that replaces auxiliary-LR with bicubically down-sampled GT, and PSNR drops by 0.47 dB, LPIPS gets worse by 0.165. The result shows the auxiliary-LR generator is necessary and effective. We also conduct experiments on different coefficients (*i.e.*, λ_p) of position preserving loss, as shown in Table 5. In order to bring auxiliary-LR into play better on alignment and obtain better SR performance, we take a trade-off between content preserving loss and position preserving loss, and set λ_p to 100.

Table 5. Ablation study on loss terms of auxiliary-LR generator. λ_p denotes the coefficient of position preserving loss in Eqn. (6).

λ_p	0	1	100	10000
PSNR↑ / LPIPS↓	28.22/0.225	28.47/0.221	28.67/0.219	28.28/0.222

Table 6. Ablation study on AdaSTN.

Method	PSNR↑ / LPIPS↓
Baseline	28.48/0.222
Baseline + Deformable Conv [6]	28.52/0.225
Baseline + STN [18]	28.57/0.219
Baseline + AdaSTN	28.67/0.219

5.3 Effect of AdaSTN

We regard the model only using flow-based alignment [35] as the baseline. We modify the proposed AdaSTN to deformable convolution [6] and STN [18] to verify the effect of AdaSTN. For deformable convolution, instead of calculating the offset by estimating the affine transformation matrix and vector according to Eq. (7), we estimate the offset directly. For STN, we replace the pixel-level offset with a global affine transformation. The PSNR gain of taking AdaSTN is 0.15 dB compared with deformable convolution and 0.1 dB compared with STN, as shown in Table 6. In addition, for the image with the size of $1445{\times}945$, setting $\mathbf{P} = \mathbf{0}$ (see Eq. (7)) for AdaSTNs increases the average inference speed by $\sim0.2\,$s without performance dropping.

6 Conclusion

Real-world image super-resolution from dual zoomed observations (DZSR) is an emerging topic, which aims to super-resolve the short focal length image with the reference of telephoto image. To circumvent the problem that ground-truth is unavailable, we present an effective self-supervised learning method, named SelfDZSR. To mitigate the adverse effect of image misalignment during training, the auxiliary-LR that is aligned with GT is generated to guide the alignment of LR and Ref towards GT. And with the help of auxiliary-LR, we propose adaptive spatial transformer networks (AdaSTN) to align LR with GT. Experiments show that our proposed method can achieve better performance against the state-of-the-art methods both quantitatively and qualitatively.

Acknowledgement. This work was supported by Alibaba Group through Alibaba Innovative Research Program, the Major Key Project of Peng Cheng Laboratory (PCL2021A12), and the National Natural Science Foundation of China (NSFC) under Grants No.s 61872118 and U19A2073.

References

1. Bell-Kligler, S., Shocher, A., Irani, M.: Blind super-resolution kernel estimation using an internal-gan. In: NeurIPS, pp. 284–293 (2019)
2. Cai, J., Gu, S., Timofte, R., Zhang, L.: Ntire 2019 challenge on real image super-resolution: Methods and results. In: CVPR Workshops (2019)
3. Cai, J., Zeng, H., Yong, H., Cao, Z., Zhang, L.: Toward real-world single image super-resolution: A new benchmark and a new model. In: ICCV, pp. 3086–3095 (2019)
4. Chan, K.C., Wang, X., Yu, K., Dong, C., Loy, C.C.: Understanding deformable alignment in video super-resolution. In: AAAI, pp. 973–981 (2021)
5. Chen, C., Xiong, Z., Tian, X., Zha, Z.J., Wu, F.: Camera lens super-resolution. In: CVPR, pp. 1652–1660 (2019)
6. Dai, J., Qi, H., Xiong, Y., Li, Y., Zhang, G., Hu, H., Wei, Y.: Deformable convolutional networks. In: ICCV, pp. 764–773 (2017)

7. Delbracio, M., Talebi, H., Milanfar, P.: Projected distribution loss for image enhancement. arXiv preprint arXiv:2012.09289 (2020)
8. Deshpande, I., Zhang, Z., Schwing, A.G.: Generative modeling using the sliced wasserstein distance. In: CVPR, pp. 3483–3491 (2018)
9. Dinh, L., Sohl-Dickstein, J., Bengio, S.: Density estimation using real nvp. In: ICLR (2017)
10. Dong, C., Loy, C.C., He, K., Tang, X.: Image super-resolution using deep convolutional networks. IEEE PAMI **38**(2), 295–307 (2015)
11. Dosovitskiy, A., et al.: Flownet: Learning optical flow with convolutional networks. In: ICCV, pp. 2758–2766 (2015)
12. Geng, Z., Sun, K., Xiao, B., Zhang, Z., Wang, J.: Bottom-up human pose estimation via disentangled keypoint regression. In: CVPR, pp. 14676–14686 (2021)
13. Gu, J., Lu, H., Zuo, W., Dong, C.: Blind super-resolution with iterative kernel correction. In: CVPR, pp. 1604–1613 (2019)
14. He, K., Fan, H., Wu, Y., Xie, S., Girshick, R.: Momentum contrast for unsupervised visual representation learning. In: CVPR, pp. 9729–9738 (2020)
15. Heitz, E., Vanhoey, K., Chambon, T., Belcour, L.: A sliced wasserstein loss for neural texture synthesis. In: CVPR, pp. 9412–9420 (2021)
16. Hui, Z., Gao, X., Yang, Y., Wang, X.: Lightweight image super-resolution with information multi-distillation network. In: ACM MM, pp. 2024–2032 (2019)
17. Hussein, S.A., Tirer, T., Giryes, R.: Correction filter for single image super-resolution: Robustifying off-the-shelf deep super-resolvers. In: CVPR, pp. 1428–1437 (2020)
18. Jaderberg, M., Simonyan, K., Zisserman, A., et al.: Spatial transformer networks. In: NeurIPS, pp. 2017–2025 (2015)
19. Jiang, Y., Chan, K.C., Wang, X., Loy, C.C., Liu, Z.: Robust reference-based super-resolution via c2-matching. In: CVPR, pp. 2103–2112 (2021)
20. Kingma, D.P., Ba, J.: Adam: A method for stochastic optimization. In: ICLR (2015)
21. Kong, X., Zhao, H., Qiao, Y., Dong, C.: Classsr: A general framework to accelerate super-resolution networks by data characteristic. In: CVPR, pp. 12016–12025 (2021)
22. Ledig, C., et al.: Photo-realistic single image super-resolution using a generative adversarial network. In: CVPR, pp. 4681–4690 (2017)
23. Liang, J., Sun, G., Zhang, K., Van Gool, L., Timofte, R.: Mutual affine network for spatially variant kernel estimation in blind image super-resolution. In: ICCV, pp. 4096–4105 (2021)
24. Liang, J., Zhang, K., Gu, S., Van Gool, L., Timofte, R.: Flow-based kernel prior with application to blind super-resolution. In: CVPR, pp. 10601–10610 (2021)
25. Lim, B., Son, S., Kim, H., Nah, S., Mu Lee, K.: Enhanced deep residual networks for single image super-resolution. In: CVPR Workshops, pp. 136–144 (2017)
26. Liu, M., Zhang, Z., Hou, L., Zuo, W., Zhang, L.: Deep adaptive inference networks for single image super-resolution. In: Bartoli, A., Fusiello, A. (eds.) ECCV 2020. LNCS, vol. 12538, pp. 131–148. Springer, Cham (2020). https://doi.org/10.1007/978-3-030-66823-5_8
27. Lu, L., Li, W., Tao, X., Lu, J., Jia, J.: Masa-sr: Matching acceleration and spatial adaptation for reference-based image super-resolution. In: CVPR, pp. 6368–6377 (2021)
28. Lugmayr, A., Danelljan, M., Timofte, R.: Ntire 2020 challenge on real-world image super-resolution: Methods and results. In: CVPR Workshops, pp. 494–495 (2020)

29. Lugmayr, A., Danelljan, M., Timofte, R., Fritsche, M., et al.: Aim 2019 challenge on real-world image super-resolution: Methods and results. In: ICCV Workshops, pp. 3575–3583. IEEE (2019)
30. Luo, Z., Huang, Y., Li, S., Wang, L., Tan, T.: Unfolding the alternating optimization for blind super resolution. In: NeurIPS (2020)
31. Paszke, A., et al.: Pytorch: An imperative style, high-performance deep learning library. In: NeurIPS, pp. 8024–8035 (2019)
32. Shi, W., et al.: Real-time single image and video super-resolution using an efficient sub-pixel convolutional neural network. In: CVPR, pp. 1874–1883 (2016)
33. Shim, G., Park, J., Kweon, I.S.: Robust reference-based super-resolution with similarity-aware deformable convolution. In: CVPR, pp. 8425–8434 (2020)
34. Simonyan, K., Zisserman, A.: Very deep convolutional networks for large-scale image recognition. In: ICLR (2014)
35. Sun, D., Yang, X., Liu, M.Y., Kautz, J.: Pwc-net: Cnns for optical flow using pyramid, warping, and cost volume. In: CVPR, pp. 8934–8943 (2018)
36. Wang, L., et al.: Exploring sparsity in image super-resolution for efficient inference. In: CVPR, pp. 4917–4926 (2021)
37. Wang, L., et al.: Unsupervised degradation representation learning for blind super-resolution. In: CVPR, pp. 10581–10590 (2021)
38. Wang, T., Xie, J., Sun, W., Yan, Q., Chen, Q.: Dual-camera super-resolution with aligned attention modules. In: ICCV, pp. 2001–2010 (2021)
39. Wang, X., Xie, L., Dong, C., Shan, Y.: Real-esrgan: Training real-world blind super-resolution with pure synthetic data. In: ICCV Workshops, pp. 1905–1914 (2021)
40. Wang, Z., Bovik, A.C., Sheikh, H.R., Simoncelli, E.P.: Image quality assessment: from error visibility to structural similarity. IEEE TIP **13**(4), 600–612 (2004)
41. Wei, P., et al.: AIM 2020 challenge on real image super-resolution: methods and results. In: Bartoli, A., Fusiello, A. (eds.) ECCV 2020. LNCS, vol. 12537, pp. 392–422. Springer, Cham (2020). https://doi.org/10.1007/978-3-030-67070-2_24
42. Wei, P., et al.: Component divide-and-conquer for real-world image super-resolution. In: Vedaldi, A., Bischof, H., Brox, T., Frahm, J.-M. (eds.) ECCV 2020. LNCS, vol. 12353, pp. 101–117. Springer, Cham (2020). https://doi.org/10.1007/978-3-030-58598-3_7
43. Wei, Y., Gu, S., Li, Y., Timofte, R., Jin, L., Song, H.: Unsupervised real-world image super resolution via domain-distance aware training. In: CVPR, pp. 13385–13394 (2021)
44. Wu, J., et al.: Sliced wasserstein generative models. In: CVPR, pp. 3713–3722 (2019)
45. Xie, W., Song, D., Xu, C., Xu, C., Zhang, H., Wang, Y.: Learning frequency-aware dynamic network for efficient super-resolution. In: ICCV, pp. 4308–4317 (2021)
46. Xie, Y., Xiao, J., Sun, M., Yao, C., Huang, K.: Feature representation matters: End-to-end learning for reference-based image super-resolution. In: Vedaldi, A., Bischof, H., Brox, T., Frahm, J.-M. (eds.) ECCV 2020. LNCS, vol. 12349, pp. 230–245. Springer, Cham (2020). https://doi.org/10.1007/978-3-030-58548-8_14
47. Yang, F., Yang, H., Fu, J., Lu, H., Guo, B.: Learning texture transformer network for image super-resolution. In: CVPR, pp. 5791–5800 (2020)
48. Zhang, K., Liang, J., Van Gool, L., Timofte, R.: Designing a practical degradation model for deep blind image super-resolution. In: ICCV, pp. 4791–4800 (2021)
49. Zhang, K., Zuo, W., Zhang, L.: Learning a single convolutional super-resolution network for multiple degradations. In: CVPR, pp. 3262–3271 (2018)

50. Zhang, R., Isola, P., Efros, A.A., Shechtman, E., Wang, O.: The unreasonable effectiveness of deep features as a perceptual metric. In: CVPR, pp. 586–595 (2018)
51. Zhang, X., Chen, Q., Ng, R., Koltun, V.: Zoom to learn, learn to zoom. In: CVPR, pp. 3762–3770 (2019)
52. Zhang, Y., Li, K., Li, K., Wang, L., Zhong, B., Fu, Y.: Image super-resolution using very deep residual channel attention networks. In: Ferrari, V., Hebert, M., Sminchisescu, C., Weiss, Y. (eds.) ECCV 2018. LNCS, vol. 11211, pp. 294–310. Springer, Cham (2018). https://doi.org/10.1007/978-3-030-01234-2_18
53. Zhang, Y., Zhang, Z., DiVerdi, S., Wang, Z., Echevarria, J., Fu, Y.: Texture hallucination for large-factor painting super-resolution. In: Vedaldi, A., Bischof, H., Brox, T., Frahm, J.-M. (eds.) ECCV 2020. LNCS, vol. 12352, pp. 209–225. Springer, Cham (2020). https://doi.org/10.1007/978-3-030-58571-6_13
54. Zhang, Z., Wang, Z., Lin, Z., Qi, H.: Image super-resolution by neural texture transfer. In: CVPR, pp. 7982–7991 (2019)
55. Zhang, Z., Wang, H., Liu, M., Wang, R., Zhang, J., Zuo, W.: Learning raw-to-srgb mappings with inaccurately aligned supervision. In: ICCV, pp. 4348–4358 (2021)
56. Zheng, H., et al.: Learning cross-scale correspondence and patch-based synthesis for reference-based super-resolution. In: BMVC, vol. 1, p. 2 (2017)
57. Zheng, H., Ji, M., Wang, H., Liu, Y., Fang, L.: Crossnet: An end-to-end reference-based super resolution network using cross-scale warping. In: Ferrari, V., Hebert, M., Sminchisescu, C., Weiss, Y. (eds.) ECCV 2018. LNCS, vol. 11210, pp. 87–104. Springer, Cham (2018). https://doi.org/10.1007/978-3-030-01231-1_6
58. Zhu, X., Hu, H., Lin, S., Dai, J.: Deformable convnets v2: More deformable, better results. In: CVPR, pp. 9308–9316 (2019)

Secrets of Event-Based Optical Flow

Shintaro Shiba[1,2][(✉)] [iD], Yoshimitsu Aoki[1], and Guillermo Gallego[2,3] [iD]

[1] Department of Electronics and Electrical Engineering, Faculty of Science
and Technology, Keio University, Kanagawa, Japan
`sshiba@keio.jp`
[2] Department of EECS, Technische Universität Berlin, Berlin, Germany
[3] Einstein Center Digital Future and SCIoI Excellence Cluster, Berlin, Germany

Abstract. Event cameras respond to scene dynamics and offer advantages to estimate motion. Following recent image-based deep-learning achievements, optical flow estimation methods for event cameras have rushed to combine those image-based methods with event data. However, it requires several adaptations (data conversion, loss function, etc.) as they have very different properties. We develop a principled method to extend the Contrast Maximization framework to estimate optical flow from events alone. We investigate key elements: how to design the objective function to prevent overfitting, how to warp events to deal better with occlusions, and how to improve convergence with multi-scale raw events. With these key elements, our method ranks first among unsupervised methods on the MVSEC benchmark, and is competitive on the DSEC benchmark. Moreover, our method allows us to expose the issues of the ground truth flow in those benchmarks, and produces remarkable results when it is transferred to unsupervised learning settings. Our code is available at https://github.com/tub-rip/event_based_optical_flow.

1 Introduction

Event cameras are novel bio-inspired vision sensors that naturally respond to motion of edges in image space with high dynamic range (HDR) and minimal blur at high temporal resolution (on the order of μs) [3,35]. These advantages provide a rich signal for accurate motion estimation in difficult real-world scenarios for frame-based cameras. However such a signal is, by nature, asynchronous and sparse, which is not compatible with traditional computer vision algorithms. This poses the challenge of rethinking visual processing [12,23]: motion patterns (i.e., *optical flow*) are no longer obtained by analyzing the intensities of images captured at regular intervals, but by analyzing the stream of events (per-pixel brightness changes) produced by the event camera.

Multiple methods have been proposed for event-based optical flow estimation. They can be broadly categorized in two: (*i*) model-based methods, which investigate the principles and characteristics of event data that enable optical

Supplementary Information The online version contains supplementary material available at https://doi.org/10.1007/978-3-031-19797-0_36.

(a) Frame (reference)   (b) Events (zero flow)   (c) Warped events, IWE   (d) Estimated flow

Fig. 1. Two test sequences (interlaken_00_b, thun_01_a) from the DSEC dataset [17]. Our optical flow estimation method produces sharp images of warped events (IWE) despite the scene complexity, the large pixel displacement and the high dynamic range. The examples utilize 500k events on an event camera with 640×480 pixels.

flow estimation, and (*ii*) learning-based methods, which exploit correlations in the data and/or apply the above-mentioned principles to compute optical flow. One of the challenges of event-based optical flow is the lack of ground truth flow in real-world datasets (at µs resolution and HDR) [12], which makes it difficult to evaluate and compare the methods properly, and to train supervised learning-based ones. Ground truth (GT) in de facto standard datasets [17,55] is given by the *motion field* [49] using additional depth sensors and camera information. However, such data is limited by the field-of-view (FOV) and resolution (spatial and temporal) of the depth sensor, which do not match those of event cameras. Hence, it is paramount to develop interpretable optical flow methods that exploit the characteristics of event data, and that do not need expensive-to-collect and error-prone ground truth.

Among prior work, Contrast Maximization (CM) [13,14] is a powerful framework that allows us to tackle multiple motion estimation problems (rotational motion [15,20,22], homographic motion [14,30,34], feature flow estimation [39,44,53,54], motion segmentation [27,32,42,52], and also reconstruction [14,36,51]). It maximizes an objective function (e.g., contrast) that measures the alignment of events caused by the same scene edge. The intuitive interpretation is to estimate the motion by recovering the sharp (motion-compensated) image of edge patterns that caused the events. Preliminary work on applying CM to estimate optical flow has reported a problem of overfitting to the data, producing undesired flows that warp events to few pixels or lines [57] (i.e., event collapse [41]). This issue has been tackled by changing the objective function, from contrast to the energy of an average timestamp image [21,33,57], but this loss is not straightforward to interpret and makes training difficult to converge [13].

Given the state-of-the-art performance of CM in low-DOF motion problems and its issues in more complex motions (dense flow), we think prior work may have rushed to use CM in unsupervised learning of complex motions. There is a gap in understanding how CM can be sensibly extended to estimate dense optical flow accurately. In this paper we fill this gap and learn a few "secrets" that are also applicable to overcome the issues of previous approaches.

We propose to extend CM for dense optical flow estimation via a tile-based approach covering the image plane. We present several distinctive contributions:

1. A *multi-reference* focus loss function to improve accuracy and discourage overfitting (Sect. 3.2).
2. A principled *time-aware flow* to better handle occlusions, formulating event-based optical flow as a transport problem via differential equations (Sect. 3.3).
3. A *multi-scale* approach on the raw events to improve convergence to the solution and avoid getting trapped in local optima (Sect. 3.4).

The results of our experimental evaluation are surprising: the above design choices are key to our simple, model-based tile-based method (Fig. 1) achieving the best accuracy among all state-of-the-art methods, including supervised-learning ones, on the de facto benchmark of MVSEC indoor sequences [56]. Since our method is interpretable and produces better event alignment than the ground truth flow, both qualitatively and quantitatively, the experiments also expose the limitations of the current "ground truth". Finally, experiments demonstrate that the above key choices are transferable to unsupervised learning methods, thus guiding future design and understanding of more proficient Artificial Neural Networks (ANNs) for event-based optical flow estimation.

Because of the above, we believe that the proposed design choices deserve to be called "secrets" [46]. To the best of our knowledge, they are novel in the context of event-based optical flow estimation, e.g., no prior work considers constant flow along its characteristic lines, designs the multi-reference focus loss to tackle overfitting, or has explicitly defined multi-scale (i.e., multi-resolution) contrast maximization on the raw events.

2   Prior Work on Event-Based Optical Flow Estimation

Given the identified advantages of event cameras to estimate optical flow, extensive research on this topic has been carried out. Prior work has proposed adaptations of frame-based approaches (block matching [26], Lucas-Kanade [4]), filter-banks [6,31], spatio-temporal plane-fitting [1,3], time surface matching [29], variational optimization on voxelized events [2], and feature-based contrast maximization [14,43,53]. For a detailed survey, we refer to [12].

Current state-of-the-art approaches are ANNs [10,18,21,24,56,57], largely inspired by frame-based optical flow architectures [37,48]. Non-spiking–based approaches need to additionally adapt the input signal, converting the events into a tensor representation (event frames, time surfaces, voxel grids, etc. [7,16]). These learning-based methods can be classified into supervised, semi-supervised or unsupervised (to be used in Table 1). In terms of architectures, the three most common ones are U-Net [56], FireNet [57] and RAFT [18].

Supervised methods train ANNs in simulation and/or real-data [16,18,45]. This requires accurate ground truth flow that matches the space-time resolution of event cameras. While this is no problem in simulation, it incurs in a performance gap when trained models are used to predict flow on real data [45]. Besides, real-world datasets have issues in providing accurate ground truth flow.

Semi-supervised methods use the grayscale images from a colocated camera (e.g., DAVIS [47]) as a supervisory signal: images are warped using the flow predicted by the ANN and their photometric consistency is used as loss function [10,24,56]. While such supervisory signal is easier to obtain than real-world ground truth flow, it may suffer from the limitations of frame-based cameras (e.g., low dynamic range and motion blur), consequently affecting the trained ANNs. These approaches were pioneered by EV-FlowNet [56].

Unsupervised methods rely solely on event data. Their loss function consists of an event alignment error using the flow predicted by the ANN [21,33,50,57]. Zhu et al. [57] extended EV-FlowNet [56] to the unsupervised setting using a motion-compensation loss function in terms of average timestamp images. This approach has been used and improved in [21,33]. Paredes-Vallés et al. [33] also proposed FireFlowNet, a lightweight ANN producing competitive results.

Similar to the works in the unsupervised category, our method produces dense optical flow and does not need ground truth or additional supervisory signals. In contrast to prior work, we adopt a more classical modeling perspective to gain insight into the problem and discover principled solutions that can subsequently be applied to the learning-based setting. Stemming from an accurate and spatially-dependent contrast loss (the gradient magnitude [13]), we model the problem using a tile of patches and propose solutions to several problems: overfitting, occlusions and convergence. To the best of our knowledge, (i) no prior work has proposed to estimate dense optical flow from a CM model-based perspective, and (ii) no prior unsupervised learning approach based on motion compensation has succeeded in estimating optical flow without the average timestamp image loss.

3 Method

3.1 Event Cameras and Contrast Maximization

Event cameras have independent pixels that operate continuously and generate "events" $e_k \doteq (\mathbf{x}_k, t_k, p_k)$ whenever the logarithmic brightness at the pixel increases or decreases by a predefined amount, called contrast sensitivity. Each event e_k contains the pixel-time coordinates $(\mathbf{x}_k, t_k)$ of the brightness change and its polarity $p_k = \{+1, -1\}$. Events occur asynchronously and sparsely on the pixel lattice, with a variable rate that depends on the scene dynamics.

The CM framework [14] assumes events $\mathcal{E} \doteq \{e_k\}_{k=1}^{N_e}$ are generated by moving edges, and transforms them geometrically according to a motion model $\mathbf{W}$, producing a set of warped events $\mathcal{E}'_{t_{\mathrm{ref}}} \doteq \{e'_k\}_{k=1}^{N_e}$ at a reference time t_{ref}:

$$e_k \doteq (\mathbf{x}_k, t_k, p_k) \;\mapsto\; e'_k \doteq (\mathbf{x}'_k, t_{\mathrm{ref}}, p_k). \tag{1}$$

The warp $\mathbf{x}'_k = \mathbf{W}(\mathbf{x}_k, t_k; \boldsymbol{\theta})$ transports each event from t_k to t_{ref} along the motion curve that passes through it. The vector $\boldsymbol{\theta}$ parametrizes the motion curves. Transformed events are aggregated on an image of warped events (IWE):

$$I(\mathbf{x}; \mathcal{E}'_{t_{\text{ref}}}, \boldsymbol{\theta}) \doteq \sum_{k=1}^{N_e} \delta(\mathbf{x} - \mathbf{x}'_k), \tag{2}$$

where each pixel $\mathbf{x}$ sums the number of warped events $\mathbf{x}'_k$ that fall within it. The Dirac delta δ is approximated by a Gaussian, $\delta(\mathbf{x} - \boldsymbol{\mu}) \approx \mathcal{N}(\mathbf{x}; \boldsymbol{\mu}, \epsilon^2 \text{Id})$ with $\epsilon = 1$ pixel. Next, an objective function $f(\boldsymbol{\theta})$ is built from the transformed events, such as the contrast of the IWE (2), given by the variance

$$\text{Var}(I(\mathbf{x}; \boldsymbol{\theta})) \doteq \frac{1}{|\Omega|} \int_\Omega (I(\mathbf{x}; \boldsymbol{\theta}) - \mu_I)^2 d\mathbf{x}, \tag{3}$$

with mean $\mu_I \doteq \frac{1}{|\Omega|} \int_\Omega I(\mathbf{x}; \boldsymbol{\theta}) d\mathbf{x}$. The objective function measures the goodness of fit between the events and the candidate motion curves (warp). Finally, an optimization algorithm iterates the above steps until convergence. The goal is to find the motion parameters that maximize the alignment of events caused by the same scene edge. Event alignment is measured by the strength of the edges of the IWE, which is directly related to image contrast [19].

Dense Optical Flow. In the task of interest, the warp used is [21,33,57]:

$$\mathbf{x}'_k = \mathbf{x}_k + (t_k - t_{\text{ref}}) \mathbf{v}(\mathbf{x}_k), \tag{4}$$

where $\boldsymbol{\theta} = \{\mathbf{v}(\mathbf{x})\}_{\mathbf{x} \in \Omega}$ is a flow field on the image plane at a set time, e.g., t_{ref}.

3.2   Multi-reference Focus Objective Function

Zhu et al. [57] report that the contrast objective (variance) overfits to the events. This is in part because the warp (4) can describe very complex flow fields, which can push the events to accumulate in few pixels [41]. To mitigate overfitting, we reduce the complexity of the flow field by dividing the image plane into a tile of non-overlapping patches, defining a flow vector at the center of each patch and interpolating the flow on all other pixels (we show the tiles in Sect. 3.4).

However, this is not enough. Additionally, we discover that warps that produce sharp IWEs *at any* reference time t_{ref} have a regularizing effect on the flow field, discouraging overfitting. This is illustrated in Fig. 2. In practice we compute the *multi-reference* focus loss using 3 reference times: t_1 (min), $t_{\text{mid}} \doteq (t_1 + t_{N_e})/2$ (midpoint) and t_{N_e} (max). The flow field is defined only at one reference time.

Furthermore, we measure event alignment using the magnitude of the IWE gradient because: (*i*) it has top accuracy performance among the objectives in [13], (*ii*) it is sensitive to the arrangement (i.e., permutation) of the IWE pixel values, whereas the variance of the IWE (3) is not, (*iii*) it converges more easily than other objectives we tested, (*iv*) it differs from the Flow Warp Loss (FWL) [45], which is defined using the variance (3) and will be used for evaluation.

Finally, letting the (squared) gradient magnitude of the IWE be

$$G(\boldsymbol{\theta}; t_{\text{ref}}) \doteq \frac{1}{|\Omega|} \int_\Omega \|\nabla I(\mathbf{x}; t_{\text{ref}})\|^2 d\mathbf{x}, \tag{5}$$

the proposed multi-reference focus objective function becomes the average of the G functions of the IWEs at multiple reference times:

$$f(\boldsymbol{\theta}) \doteq \big(G(\boldsymbol{\theta}; t_1) + 2G(\boldsymbol{\theta}; t_{\text{mid}}) + G(\boldsymbol{\theta}; t_{N_e})\big) / 4G(\mathbf{0}; -), \tag{6}$$

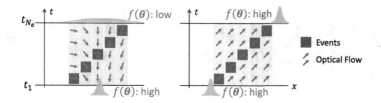

Fig. 2. *Multi-reference focus loss.* Assume an edge moves from left to right. Flow estimation with single reference time (t_1) can overfit to the data, warping all events into a single pixel, which results in a maximum contrast (at t_1). However, the same flow would produce low contrast (i.e., a blurry image) if events were warped to time t_{N_e}. Instead, we favor flow fields that produce high contrast (i.e., sharp images) at any reference time (here, $t_{\text{ref}} = t_1$ and $t_{\text{ref}} = t_{N_e}$). See results in Fig. 7.

normalized by the value of the G function with zero flow (identity warp). The normalization in (6) provides the same interpretation as the FWL: $f < 1$ implies the flow is worse than the zero flow baseline, whereas $f > 1$ means that the flow produces sharper IWEs than the baseline.

Remark: Warping to two reference times (min and max) was proposed in [57], but with important differences: (*i*) it was done for the average timestamp loss, hence it did not consider the effect on contrast or focus functions [13], and (*ii*) it had a completely different motivation: to lessen a back-propagation scaling problem, so that the gradients of the loss would not favor events far from t_{ref}.

3.3 Time-Aware Flow

State-of-the-art event-based optical flow approaches are based on frame-based ones, and so they use the warp (4), which defines the flow $\mathbf{v}(\mathbf{x})$ as a function of $\mathbf{x}$ (i.e., a pixel displacement between two given frames). However, this does not take into account the space-time nature of events, which is the basis of the CM approach, because not all events at a pixel $\mathbf{x}_0$ are triggered at the same timestamp t_k. They do not need to be warped with the same velocity $\mathbf{v}(\mathbf{x}_0)$. Figure 3 illustrates this with an occlusion example taken from the slider_depth sequence [28]. Instead of $\mathbf{v}(\mathbf{x})$, the *event-based flow* should be a function of space-time, $\mathbf{v}(\mathbf{x}, t)$, i.e., *time-aware*, and each event e_k should be warped according to the flow defined at $(\mathbf{x}_k, t_k)$. Let us propose a more principled warp than (4).

To define a space-time flow $\mathbf{v}(\mathbf{x}, t)$ that is compatible with the propagation of events along motion curves, we are inspired by the method of characteristics [11]. Just like the brightness constancy assumption states that brightness is constant along the true motion curves in image space, we assume the flow is constant along its streamlines: $\mathbf{v}(\mathbf{x}(t), t) = \text{const}$ (Fig. 3). Differentiating in time and applying the chain rule gives a system of partial differential equations (PDEs):

$$\frac{\partial \mathbf{v}}{\partial \mathbf{x}} \frac{d\mathbf{x}}{dt} + \frac{\partial \mathbf{v}}{\partial t} = \mathbf{0}, \tag{7}$$

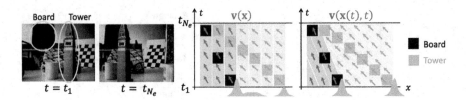

Fig. 3. *Time-aware Flow.* Traditional flow (4), inherited from frame-based approaches, assumes per-pixel constant flow $\mathbf{v}(\mathbf{x})$ = const, which cannot handle occlusions properly. The proposed space-time flow assumes constancy along streamlines, $\mathbf{v}(\mathbf{x}(t), t)$ = const, which allows us to handle occlusions more accurately. (See results in Fig. 8).

where, as usual, $\mathbf{v} = d\mathbf{x}/dt$ is the flow. The boundary condition is given by the flow at say $t = 0$: $\mathbf{v}(\mathbf{x}, 0) = \mathbf{v}^0(\mathbf{x})$. This system of PDEs essentially states how to propagate (i.e., *transport*) a given flow $\mathbf{v}^0(\mathbf{x})$, from the boundary $t = 0$ to the rest of space $\mathbf{x}$ and time t. The PDEs have advection terms and others that resemble those of the inviscid Burgers' equation [11] since the flow is transporting itself. We parametrize the flow at $t = t_{\mathrm{mid}}$ (boundary condition), and then propagate it to the volume that encloses the current set of events $\mathcal{E}$. We develop two explicit methods to solve the PDEs, one with upwind differences and one with a conservative scheme adapted to Burgers' terms [40]. Each event e_k is then warped according to a flow $\hat{\mathbf{v}}$ given by the solution of the PDEs at $(\mathbf{x}_k, t_k)$:

$$\mathbf{x}'_k = \mathbf{x}_k + (t_k - t_{\mathrm{ref}})\,\hat{\mathbf{v}}(\mathbf{x}_k, t_k). \tag{8}$$

3.4   Multi-scale Approach

Inspired by classical estimation methods, we combine our tile-based approach with a multi-scale strategy. The goal is to improve the convergence of the optimizer in terms of speed and robustness (i.e., avoiding local optima).

Some learning-based works [33,56,57] also have a multi-scale component, inherited from the use of a U-Net architecture. However, they work on discretized event representations (voxel grid, etc.) to be compatible with CNNs. In contrast, our tile-based approach works directly on raw events, without discarding or quantizing the temporal information in the event stream. While some prior work outside the context of optical flow has considered multi-resolution on raw events [25], there is no agreement on the best way to perform multi-resolution due to the sparse and asynchronous nature of events.

Our multi-scale CM approach is illustrated in Fig. 4. For an event set $\mathcal{E}_i$, we apply the tile-based CM in a coarse-to-fine manner (e.g., $N_\ell = 5$ scales). There are $2^{l-1} \times 2^{l-1}$ tiles at the l-th scale. We use bilinear interpolation to upscale between any two scales. If there is a subsequent set $\mathcal{E}_{i+1}$, the flow estimated from $\mathcal{E}_i$ is used to initialize the flow for $\mathcal{E}_{i+1}$. This is done by downsampling the finest flow to coarser scales. The coarsest scale initializes the flow for $\mathcal{E}_{i+1}$. For finer scales, initialization is computed as the average of the upsampled flow from the coarser scale of $\mathcal{E}_{i+1}$ and the same-scale flow from $\mathcal{E}_i$.

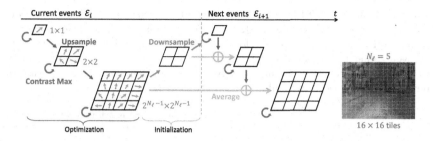

Fig. 4. *Multi-scale Approach* using tiles (rectangles) and raw events.

Composite Objective. To encourage additional smoothness of the flow, even in regions with few events, we include a flow regularizer $\mathcal{R}(\boldsymbol{\theta})$. The flow is obtained as the solution to the problem with the composite objective:

$$\boldsymbol{\theta}^* = \arg\min_{\theta}\big(1/f(\boldsymbol{\theta}) + \lambda\mathcal{R}(\boldsymbol{\theta})\big), \tag{9}$$

where, $\lambda > 0$ is the regularizer weight, and we use the total variation (TV) [38] as regularizer. We choose $1/f$ instead of simply $-f$ because it is convenient for ANN training, as we will apply in Sec 4.6.

4   Experiments

4.1   Datasets, Metrics and Hyper-parameters

We evaluate our method on sequences from the MVSEC dataset [55,56], which is the de facto dataset used by prior works to benchmark optical flow. It provides events, grayscale frames, IMU data, camera poses, and scene depth from a LiDAR [55]. The dataset was extended in [56] to provide ground truth optical flow, computed as the motion field [49] given the camera velocity and the depth of the scene. The event camera has 346×260 pixel resolution [47]. In total, we evaluate on 63.5 million events spanning 265 s.

We also evaluate on a recent dataset that provides ground truth flow: DSEC [18]. It consists of sequences recorded with Prophesee Gen3 event cameras, of higher resolution (640×480 pixels), mounted on a car. Optical flow is also computed as the motion field, with the scene depth from a LiDAR. In total, we evaluate on 3 billion events spanning the 208 s of the test sequences.

The metrics used to assess optical flow accuracy are the average endpoint error (AEE) and the percentage of pixels with AEE greater than 3 pixels (denoted by "% Out"), both are measured over pixels with valid ground-truth and at least one event in the evaluation intervals. We also use the FWL metric (the IWE variance relative to that of the identity warp) to assess event alignment [45].

In all experiments our method uses $N_\ell = 5$ resolution scales, $\lambda = 0.0025$ in (9), and the Newton-CG optimization algorithm with a maximum of 20 iterations/scale. The flow at t_{mid} is transported to each side via the upwind or

Table 1. Results on MVSEC dataset [56]. Methods are sorted according to how much data they need: supervised learning (SL) requires ground truth flow; semi-supervised learning (SSL) uses grayscale images for supervision; unsupervised learning (USL) uses only events; and model-based (MB) needs no training data. Bold is the best among all methods; underlined is second best. Nagata et al. [29] evaluate on shorter time intervals; for comparison, we scale the errors to $dt = 1$.

		indoor_flying1		indoor_flying2		indoor_flying3		outdoor_day1	
		AEE ↓	%Out ↓	AEE ↓	%Out ↓	AEE ↓	%Out ↓	AEE ↓	%Out ↓
$dt = 1$									
SL	EV-FlowNet-EST [16]	0.97	0.91	1.38	8.20	1.43	6.47	-	-
	EV-FlowNet+ [45]	0.56	1.00	<u>0.66</u>	<u>1.00</u>	<u>0.59</u>	1.00	0.68	0.99
	E-RAFT [18]	-	-	-	-	-	-	**0.24**	1.70
SSL	EV-FlowNet (original) [56]	1.03	2.20	1.72	15.10	1.53	11.90	0.49	0.20
	Spike-FlowNet [24]	0.84	-	1.28	-	1.11	-	0.49	-
	Ziluo et al. [10]	0.57	0.10	0.79	1.60	0.72	1.30	0.42	**0.00**
USL	EV-FlowNet [57]	0.58	**0.00**	1.02	4.00	0.87	3.00	0.32	**0.00**
	EV-FlowNet (retrained) [33]	0.79	1.20	1.40	10.90	1.18	7.40	0.92	5.40
	FireFlowNet [33]	0.97	2.60	1.67	15.30	1.43	11.00	1.06	6.60
	ConvGRU-EV-FlowNet [21]	0.60	0.51	1.17	8.06	0.93	5.64	0.47	0.25
MB	Nagata et al. [29]	0.62	-	0.93	-	0.84	-	0.77	-
	Akolkar et al. [1]	1.52	-	1.59	-	1.89	-	2.75	-
	Brebion et al. [5]	<u>0.52</u>	0.10	0.98	5.50	0.71	2.10	0.53	0.20
	Ours (w/o time aware)	**0.42**	<u>0.09</u>	**0.60**	**0.59**	**0.50**	<u>0.29</u>	<u>0.30</u>	0.11
	Ours (Upwind)	**0.42**	0.10	**0.60**	**0.59**	**0.50**	**0.28**	<u>0.30</u>	<u>0.10</u>
	Ours (Burgers')	**0.42**	0.10	**0.60**	**0.59**	**0.50**	**0.28**	<u>0.30</u>	<u>0.10</u>
$dt = 4$									
SSL	EV-FlowNet (original) [56]	2.25	24.70	4.05	45.30	3.45	39.70	1.23	<u>7.30</u>
	Spike-FlowNet [24]	2.24	-	3.83	-	3.18	-	<u>1.09</u>	-
	Ziluo et al. [10]	1.77	14.70	<u>2.52</u>	26.10	<u>2.23</u>	22.10	**0.99**	**3.90**
USL	EV-FlowNet [57]	2.18	24.20	3.85	46.80	3.18	47.80	1.30	9.70
	ConvGRU-EV-FlowNet [21]	2.16	21.51	3.90	40.72	3.00	29.60	1.69	12.50
MB	Ours (w/o time aware)	**1.68**	**12.79**	**2.49**	<u>26.31</u>	**2.06**	**18.93**	1.25	9.19
	Ours (Upwind)	<u>1.69</u>	<u>12.83</u>	**2.49**	26.37	**2.06**	<u>19.02</u>	1.25	9.23
	Ours (Burgers')	<u>1.69</u>	12.95	**2.49**	26.35	**2.06**	19.03	1.25	9.21

Burgers' PDE solver (using 5 bins for MVSEC, 40 for DSEC), and used for event warping (8) (see Suppl. Mat.). In the optimization, we use 30k events for MVSEC indoor sequences, 40k events for outdoors, and 1.5M events for DSEC.

4.2   Results on MVSEC

Table 1 reports the results on the MVSEC benchmark. The different methods (rows) are compared on three indoor sequences and one outdoor sequence (columns). This is because many learning-based methods train on the other outdoor sequence, which is therefore not used for testing. Following Zhu et al., outdoor_day1 is tested only on specified 800 frames [56]. The top part of Table 1 reports the flow corresponding to a time interval of $dt = 1$ grayscale frame (at ≈ 45 Hz, i.e., 22.2 ms), and the bottom part corresponds to $dt = 4$ frames (89 ms).

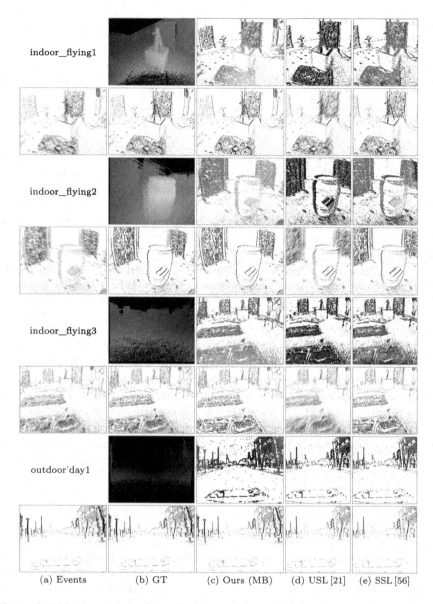

indoor_flying1

indoor_flying2

indoor_flying3

outdoor·day1

(a) Events   (b) GT   (c) Ours (MB)   (d) USL [21]   (e) SSL [56]

Fig. 5. *MVSEC comparison* ($dt = 4$) of our method and two state-of-the-art baselines: ConvGRU-EV-FlowNet (USL) [21] and EV-FlowNet (SSL) [56]. For each sequence, the upper row shows the flow masked by the input events, and the lower row shows the IWE using the flow. Our method produces the sharpest motion-compensated IWEs. Note that learning-based methods crop input events to center 256 × 256 pixels, whereas our method does not. Black points in ground truth (GT) flow maps indicate the absence of LiDAR measurements. The optical flow color wheel is in Fig. 1.

Table 2. Results on DSEC test sequences [18]. For the calculation of FWL, we use events within 100 ms. More sequences are provided in the supplementary material.

	thun_01_a			thun_01_b			zurich_city_15_a		
	AEE ↓	%Out ↓	FWL ↑	AEE ↓	%Out ↓	FWL ↑	AEE ↓	%Out ↓	FWL ↑
E-RAFT [18]	**0.65**	**1.87**	1.20	**0.58**	**1.52**	1.18	**0.59**	**1.30**	1.34
Ours	2.12	17.68	**1.24**	2.48	23.56	**1.24**	2.35	20.99	**1.41**

Our methods provide the best results among all methods in all indoor sequences and are the best among the unsupervised and model-based methods in the outdoor sequence. The errors for $dt = 4$ are about four times larger than those for $dt = 1$, which is sensible given the ratio of time interval sizes. We observe no significant differences between the three versions of the method tested (warp models, see also Sec. 4.5), which can be attributed to the fact that the MVSEC dataset does not comprise large pixel displacements or occlusions.

Qualitative results are shown in Fig. 5, where we compare our method against the state of the art. Our method provides sharper IWEs than the baselines, without overfitting, and the estimated flow resembles the ground truth one.

Ground truth (GT) is not available on the entire image plane (see Fig. 5), such as in pixels not covered by the LiDAR's range, FOV, or spatial sampling. Additionally, there may be interpolation issues in the GT, since the LiDAR works at 20 Hz and the GT flow is given at frame rate (45 Hz). In the outdoor sequences, the GT from the LiDAR and the camera motion cannot provide correct flow for independently moving objects (IMOs). These issues of the GT are noticeable in the IWEs: they are not as sharp as expected. In contrast, the IWEs produced by our method are sharp. Taking now into account the GT quality on the comparison Table 1, it is remarkable that our method outperforms the state-of-the-art baselines on the indoor sequences, where GT has the best quality (with more points in the valid LiDAR range and no IMOs).

4.3   Results on DSEC

Table 2 gives quantitative results on the DSEC Optical Flow benchmark. Currently only the method that proposed the benchmark reports values [18]. As expected, this supervised learning method is better than ours in terms of flow accuracy because (*i*) it has additional training information (GT labels), and (*ii*) it is trained using the same type of GT signal used in the evaluation. Nevertheless, our method provides competitive results and is better in terms of FWL, which exposes similar GT quality issues as those of MVSEC: pixels without GT (LiDAR's FOV and IMOs). Qualitative results are shown in Fig. 6. Our method provides sharp IWEs, even for IMOs (car) and the road close to the camera.

We observe that the evaluation intervals (100 ms) are large for optical flow standards. In the benchmark, 80% of the GT flow has up to 22px displacement, which means that 20% of the GT flow is larger than 22px (on VGA resolution). The apparent motion during such intervals is sufficiently large that it breaks the classical assumption of scene points flowing in linear trajectories.

| (a) Events | (b) IWE (Ours) | (c) Flow (Ours) | (d) IWE (SL) [18] | (e) Flow (SL) [18] |

Fig. 6. *DSEC results* on the interlaken_00_b test sequence (no GT available). Since GT is missing at IMOs and points outside the LiDAR's FOV, the supervised method [18] may provide inaccurate predictions around IMOs and road points close to the camera, whereas our method produces sharp edges. For visualization, we use 1M events.

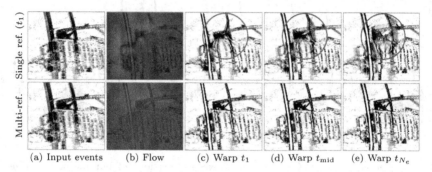

| (a) Input events | (b) Flow | (c) Warp t_1 | (d) Warp t_{mid} | (e) Warp t_{N_e} |

Fig. 7. *Effect of the multi-reference focus loss.*

4.4 Effect of the Multi-reference Focus Loss

The effect of the proposed multi-reference focus loss is shown in Fig. 7. The single-reference focus loss function can easily overfit to the only reference time, pushing all events into a small region of the image at t_1 while producing blurry IWEs at other times (t_{mid} and t_{N_e}). Instead, our proposed multi-reference focus loss discourages such overfitting, as the loss favors flow fields which produce sharp IWEs at *any* reference time. The difference is also noticeable in the flow: the flow from the single-reference loss is irregular, with a lot of spatial variability in terms of directions (many colors, often in opposite directions of the color wheel). In contrast, the flow from the multi-reference loss is considerably more regular.

4.5 Effect of the Time-Aware Flow

To assess the effect of the proposed time-aware warp (8), we conducted experiments on MVSEC, DSEC and ECD [28] datasets. Accuracy results are already reported in Tables 1 and 2. We now report values of the FWL metric in Table 3. For MVSEC, $dt = 1$ is a very short time interval, with small motion and therefore few events, hence the sharpness of the IWE with or without motion compensation are about the same (FWL ≈ 1). Instead, $dt = 4$ provides more events, and larger FWL values (1.1–1.3), which means that the contrast of the motion-compensated IWE is better than that of the zero flow baseline. All three methods provide sharper IWEs

Table 3. FWL (IWE sharpness) results on MVSEC, DSEC, and ECD. Higher is better.

	MVSEC ($dt = 4$)				ECD	DSEC	
	indoor1	indoor2	indoor3	outdoor1	slider_depth	thun_00_a	zurich_city_07_a
Ground truth	1.09	1.20	1.12	1.07	_	1.01	1.042
Ours: w/o time aware	**1.17**	**1.30**	**1.23**	**1.11**	1.88	1.39	1.57
Ours: Upwind	**1.17**	**1.30**	**1.23**	**1.11**	1.92	1.40	1.60
Ours: Burgers'	**1.17**	**1.30**	**1.23**	**1.11**	**1.93**	**1.42**	**1.63**

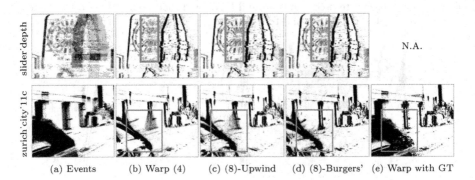

(a) Events   (b) Warp (4)   (c) (8)-Upwind   (d) (8)-Burgers'   (e) Warp with GT

Fig. 8. *Time-aware flow.* Comparison between 3 versions of our method: Burgers', upwind, and no time-aware (4). At occlusions (dartboard in slider_depth [28] and garage door in DSEC [17]), upwind and Burgers' produce sharper IWEs. Due to the smoothness of the flow conferred by the tile-based approach, some small regions are still blurry.

than ground truth. The advantages of the time-aware warp (8) over (4) to produce better IWEs (higher FWL) are most noticeable on sequences like slider_depth [28] and DSEC (see Fig. 8) because of the occlusions and larger motions. Notice that FWL differences below 0.1 are significant [45], demonstrating the efficacy of time-awareness.

4.6   Application to Deep Neural Networks (DNN)

The proposed secrets are not only applicable to model-based methods, but also to unsupervised-learning methods. We train EV-FlowNet [56] in an unsupervised manner, using (9) as data-fidelity term and a Charbonnier loss [8] as the regularizer. Since the time-aware flow does not have a significant influence on the MVSEC benchmark (Table 1), we do not port it to the learning-based setting. We convert 40k events into the voxel-grid representation [57] with 5 time bins. The network is trained for 50 epochs with a learning rate of 0.001 with Adam optimizer and with 0.8 learning rate decay. To ensure generalization, we train our network on indoor sequences and test on the outdoor_day1 sequence.

Table 4 shows the quantitative comparison with unsupervised-learning methods. Our model achieves the second best accuracy, following [57], and the best

Table 4. Results of unsupervised learning on MVSEC's outdoor_day1 sequence.

	$dt = 1$			$dt = 4$		
	AEE ↓	%Out ↓	FWL ↑	AEE ↓	%Out ↓	FWL ↑
EV-FlowNet [57]	**0.32**	**0.00**	-	**1.30**	**9.70**	-
EV-FlowNet (retrained) [33]	0.92	5.4	-	-	-	-
ConvGRU-EV-FlowNet [21]	0.47	0.25	0.94	1.69	12.50	0.94
Our EV-FlowNet using (9)	0.36	0.09	**0.96**	1.49	11.72	**1.11**

sharpness (FWL) among the existing methods. Notice that [57] was trained on the outdoor_day2 sequence, which is a similar driving sequence to the test one, while the other methods were trained on drone data [9]. Hence [57] might be overfitting to the driving data, while ours is not, by the choice of training data.

4.7   Limitations

Like previous unsupervised works [21,57], our method is based on the brightness constancy assumption. Hence, it struggles to estimate flow from events that are not due to motion, such as those caused by flickering lights. SL and SSL methods may forego this assumption, but they require high quality supervisory signal, which is challenging due to the HDR and high speed of event cameras.

Like other optical flow methods, our approach can suffer from the aperture problem. The flow could still collapse (events may be warped to too few pixels) if tiles become smaller (higher DOFs), or without proper regularization or initialization. Optical flow is also difficult to estimate in regions with few events, such as homogeneous brightness regions and regions with small apparent motion. Regularization fills in the homogeneous regions, whereas recurrent connections (like in RNNs) could help with small apparent motion.

5   Conclusion

We have extended the CM framework to estimate dense optical flow, proposing principled solutions to overcome problems of overfitting, occlusions and convergence without performing event voxelization. The comprehensive experiments show that our method achieves the best accuracy among all methods in the MVSEC indoor benchmark, and among the unsupervised and model-based methods in the outdoor sequence. It is also competitive in the DSEC optical flow benchmark. Moreover, our method delivers the sharpest IWEs and exposes the limitations of the benchmark data. Finally, we show how our method can be ported to the unsupervised setting, producing remarkable results. We hope our work unlocks future optical flow research on stable and interpretable methods.

Acknowledgements. We thank Prof. A. Yezzi and Dr. A. Zhu for useful discussions. Funded by the German Academic Exchange Service (DAAD), Research Grant - Binationally Supervised Doctoral Degrees/Cotutelle, 2021/22 (57552338). Funded by the Deutsche Forschungsgemeinschaft (DFG, German Research Foundation) under Germany's Excellence Strategy - EXC 2002/1 "Science of Intelligence" - project number 390523135.

References

1. Akolkar, H., Ieng, S.H., Benosman, R.: Real-time high speed motion prediction using fast aperture-robust event-driven visual flow. IEEE Trans. Pattern Anal. Mach. Intell. **44**(1), 361–372 (2022). https://doi.org/10.1109/TPAMI.2020. 3010468

2. Bardow, P., Davison, A.J., Leutenegger, S.: Simultaneous optical flow and intensity estimation from an event camera. In: IEEE Conference on Computer Vision and Pattern Recognition (CVPR), pp. 884–892 (2016). https://doi.org/10.1109/CVPR. 2016.102

3. Benosman, R., Clercq, C., Lagorce, X., Ieng, S.H., Bartolozzi, C.: Event-based visual flow. IEEE Trans. Neural Netw. Learn. Syst. **25**(2), 407–417 (2014). https:// doi.org/10.1109/TNNLS.2013.2273537

4. Benosman, R., Ieng, S.H., Clercq, C., Bartolozzi, C., Srinivasan, M.: Asynchronous frameless event-based optical flow. Neural Netw. **27**, 32–37 (2012). https://doi.org/ 10.1016/j.neunet.2011.11.001

5. Brebion, V., Moreau, J., Davoine, F.: Real-time optical flow for vehicular perception with low- and high-resolution event cameras. IEEE Trans. Intell. Transport. Syst. **23**, 1–13 (2021). https://doi.org/10.1109/TITS.2021.3136358

6. Brosch, T., Tschechne, S., Neumann, H.: On event-based optical flow detection. Front. Neurosci. **9**, 137 (2015). https://doi.org/10.3389/fnins.2015.00137

7. Cannici, M., Ciccone, M., Romanoni, A., Matteucci, M.: A differentiable recurrent surface for asynchronous event-based data. In: Vedaldi, A., Bischof, H., Brox, T., Frahm, J.-M. (eds.) ECCV 2020. LNCS, vol. 12365, pp. 136–152. Springer, Cham (2020). https://doi.org/10.1007/978-3-030-58565-5_9

8. Charbonnier, P., Blanc-Feraud, L., Aubert, G., Barlaud, M.: Deterministic edge-preserving regularization in computed imaging. IEEE Trans. Image Process. **6**(2), 298–311 (1997). https://doi.org/10.1109/83.551699

9. Delmerico, J., Cieslewski, T., Rebecq, H., Faessler, M., Scaramuzza, D.: Are we ready for autonomous drone racing? the UZH-FPV drone racing dataset. In: IEEE International Conference on Robotics and Automation (ICRA), pp. 6713–6719 (2019). https://doi.org/10.1109/ICRA.2019.8793887

10. Ding, Z., et al.: Spatio-temporal recurrent networks for event-based optical flow estimation. In: AAAI Conference on Artificial intelligence, vol. 36(1), pp. 525–533 (2022)

11. Evans, L.C.: Partial Differential Equations. Graduate Studies in Mathematics. American Mathematical Society (2010)

12. Gallego, G., et al.: Event-based vision: A survey. IEEE Trans. Pattern Anal. Mach. Intell. **44**(1), 154–180 (2022). https://doi.org/10.1109/TPAMI.2020.3008413

13. Gallego, G., Gehrig, M., Scaramuzza, D.: Focus is all you need: Loss functions for event-based vision. In: IEEE Conference on Computer Vision and Pattern Recognition (CVPR), pp. 12272–12281 (2019). https://doi.org/10.1109/CVPR.2019.01256

14. Gallego, G., Rebecq, H., Scaramuzza, D.: A unifying contrast maximization framework for event cameras, with applications to motion, depth, and optical flow estimation. In: IEEE Conference on Computer Vision and Pattern Recognition (CVPR), pp. 3867–3876 (2018). https://doi.org/10.1109/CVPR.2018.00407

15. Gallego, G., Scaramuzza, D.: Accurate angular velocity estimation with an event camera. IEEE Robot. Autom. Lett. **2**(2), 632–639 (2017). https://doi.org/10.1109/LRA.2016.2647639

16. Gehrig, D., Loquercio, A., Derpanis, K.G., Scaramuzza, D.: End-to-end learning of representations for asynchronous event-based data. In: Conference on Computer Vision (ICCV), pp. 5632–5642 (2019). https://doi.org/10.1109/ICCV.2019.00573

17. Gehrig, M., Aarents, W., Gehrig, D., Scaramuzza, D.: DSEC: A stereo event camera dataset for driving scenarios. IEEE Robot. Autom. Lett. **6**(3), 4947–4954 (2021). https://doi.org/10.1109/LRA.2021.3068942

18. Gehrig, M., Millhäusler, M., Gehrig, D., Scaramuzza, D.: E-RAFT: Dense optical flow from event cameras. In: International Conference on 3D Vision (3DV), pp. 197–206 (2021). https://doi.org/10.1109/3DV53792.2021.00030

19. Gonzalez, R.C., Woods, R.E.: Digital Image Processing. Pearson Education (2009)

20. Gu, C., Learned-Miller, E., Sheldon, D., Gallego, G., Bideau, P.: The spatio-temporal Poisson point process: A simple model for the alignment of event camera data. In: International Conference on Computer Vision (ICCV), pp. 13495–13504 (2021). https://doi.org/10.1109/ICCV48922.2021.01324

21. Hagenaars, J.J., Paredes-Valles, F., de Croon, G.C.H.E.: Self-supervised learning of event-based optical flow with spiking neural networks. In: Advances in Neural Information Processing Systems (NeurIPS). vol. 34, pp. 7167–7179 (2021). https://doi.org/10.48550/arXiv.2106.01862

22. Kim, H., Kim, H.J.: Real-time rotational motion estimation with contrast maximization over globally aligned events. IEEE Robot. Autom. Lett. **6**(3), 6016–6023 (2021). https://doi.org/10.1109/LRA.2021.3088793

23. Lagorce, X., Orchard, G., Gallupi, F., Shi, B.E., Benosman, R.: HOTS: A hierarchy of event-based time-surfaces for pattern recognition. IEEE Trans. Pattern Anal. Mach. Intell. **39**(7), 1346–1359 (2017). https://doi.org/10.1109/TPAMI.2016.2574707

24. Lee, C., Kosta, A.K., Zhu, A.Z., Chaney, K., Daniilidis, K., Roy, K.: Spike-flownet: Event-based optical flow estimation with energy-efficient hybrid neural networks. In: Vedaldi, A., Bischof, H., Brox, T., Frahm, J.-M. (eds.) ECCV 2020. LNCS, vol. 12374, pp. 366–382. Springer, Cham (2020). https://doi.org/10.1007/978-3-030-58526-6_22

25. Li, H., Li, G., Shi, L.: Super-resolution of spatiotemporal event-stream image. Neurocomputing **335**, 206–214 (2019). https://doi.org/10.1016/j.neucom.2018.12.048

26. Liu, M., Delbruck, T.: Adaptive time-slice block-matching optical flow algorithm for dynamic vision sensors. In: British Machine Vision Conference (BMVC), pp. 1–12 (2018)

27. Mitrokhin, A., Fermuller, C., Parameshwara, C., Aloimonos, Y.: Event-based moving object detection and tracking. In: IEEE/RSJ International Conference on Intelligent Robots and Systems (IROS), pp. 1–9 (2018). https://doi.org/10.1109/IROS.2018.8593805

28. Mueggler, E., Rebecq, H., Gallego, G., Delbruck, T., Scaramuzza, D.: The event-camera dataset and simulator: Event-based data for pose estimation, visual odometry, and SLAM. Int. J. Robot. Research **36**(2), 142–149 (2017). https://doi.org/10.1177/0278364917691115

29. Nagata, J., Sekikawa, Y., Aoki, Y.: Optical flow estimation by matching time surface with event-based cameras. Sensors 21(4) (2021). https://doi.org/10.3390/s21041150
30. Nunes, U.M., Demiris, Y.: Robust event-based vision model estimation by dispersion minimisation. IEEE Trans. Pattern Anal. Mach. Intell. (2021). https://doi.org/10.1109/TPAMI.2021.3130049
31. Orchard, G., Benosman, R., Etienne-Cummings, R., Thakor, N.V.: A spiking neural network architecture for visual motion estimation. In: IEEE Biomedical Circuits and Systems Conference (BioCAS), pp. 298–301 (2013). https://doi.org/10.1109/biocas.2013.6679698
32. Parameshwara, C.M., Sanket, N.J., Singh, C.D., Fermüller, C., Aloimonos, Y.: 0-MMS: Zero-shot multi-motion segmentation with a monocular event camera. In: IEEE International Conference on Robotics and Automation (ICRA), pp. 9594–9600 (2021). https://doi.org/10.1109/ICRA48506.2021.9561755
33. Paredes-Vallés, F., de Croon, G.C.H.E.: Back to event basics: Self-supervised learning of image reconstruction for event cameras via photometric constancy. In: IEEE Conference on Computer Vision and Pattern Recognition (CVPR), pp. 3445–3454 (2021). https://doi.org/10.1109/CVPR46437.2021.00345
34. Peng, X., Gao, L., Wang, Y., Kneip, L.: Globally-optimal contrast maximisation for event cameras. IEEE Trans. Pattern Anal. Mach. Intell. 44(7), 3479–3495 (2022). https://doi.org/10.1109/TPAMI.2021.3053243
35. Posch, C., Serrano-Gotarredona, T., Linares-Barranco, B., Delbruck, T.: Retinomorphic event-based vision sensors: Bioinspired cameras with spiking output. Proc. IEEE 102(10), 1470–1484 (2014). https://doi.org/10.1109/jproc.2014.2346153
36. Rebecq, H., Gallego, G., Mueggler, E., Scaramuzza, D.: EMVS: Event-based multiview stereo–3D reconstruction with an event camera in real-time. Int. J. Comput. Vis. 126(12), 1394–1414 (2018). https://doi.org/10.1007/s11263-017-1050-6
37. Ronneberger, O., Fischer, P., Brox, T.: U-Net: Convolutional networks for biomedical image segmentation. In: Navab, N., Hornegger, J., Wells, W.M., Frangi, A.F. (eds.) MICCAI 2015. LNCS, vol. 9351, pp. 234–241. Springer, Cham (2015). https://doi.org/10.1007/978-3-319-24574-4_28
38. Rudin, L.I., Osher, S., Fatemi, E.: Nonlinear total variation based noise removal algorithms. Physica D 60(1–4), 259–268 (1992). https://doi.org/10.1016/0167-2789(92)90242-F
39. Seok, H., Lim, J.: Robust feature tracking in dvs event stream using Bezier mapping. In: IEEE Winter Conference on Applications of Computer Vision (WACV), pp. 1647–1656 (2020). https://doi.org/10.1109/WACV45572.2020.9093607
40. Sethian, J.: Level Set Methods and Fast Marching Methods: Evolving Interfaces in Computational Geometry, Fluid Mechanics, Computer Vision, and Materials Science. Cambridge University Press, Cambridge Monographs on Applied and Computational Mathematics (1999)
41. Shiba, S., Aoki, Y., Gallego, G.: Event collapse in contrast maximization frameworks. Sensors 22(14), 1–20 (2022). https://doi.org/10.3390/s22145190
42. Stoffregen, T., Gallego, G., Drummond, T., Kleeman, L., Scaramuzza, D.: Event-based motion segmentation by motion compensation. In: International Conference on Computer Vision (ICCV), pp. 7243–7252 (2019). https://doi.org/10.1109/ICCV.2019.00734
43. Stoffregen, T., Kleeman, L.: Simultaneous optical flow and segmentation (SOFAS) using Dynamic Vision Sensor. In: Australasian Conference on Robotics and Automation (ACRA) (2017)

44. Stoffregen, T., Kleeman, L.: Event cameras, contrast maximization and reward functions: an analysis. In: IEEE Conference on Computer Vision and Pattern Recognition (CVPR), pp. 12292–12300 (2019). https://doi.org/10.1109/CVPR.2019.01258

45. Stoffregen, T., et al.: Reducing the sim-to-real gap for event cameras. In: Vedaldi, A., Bischof, H., Brox, T., Frahm, J.-M. (eds.) ECCV 2020. LNCS, vol. 12372, pp. 534–549. Springer, Cham (2020). https://doi.org/10.1007/978-3-030-58583-9_32

46. Sun, D., Roth, S., Black, M.J.: A quantitative analysis of current practices in optical flow estimation and the principles behind them. Int. J. Comput. Vis. **106**(2), 115–137 (2013). https://doi.org/10.1007/s11263-013-0644-x

47. Taverni, G., et al.: Front and back illuminated Dynamic and Active Pixel Vision Sensors comparison. IEEE Trans. Circuits Syst. II **65**(5), 677–681 (2018). https://doi.org/10.1109/TCSII.2018.2824899

48. Teed, Z., Deng, J.: RAFT: Recurrent all pairs field transforms for optical flow. In: Vedaldi, A., Bischof, H., Brox, T., Frahm, J.-M. (eds.) ECCV 2020. LNCS, vol. 12347, pp. 402–419. Springer, Cham (2020). https://doi.org/10.1007/978-3-030-58536-5_24

49. Trucco, E., Verri, A.: Introductory Techniques for 3-D Computer Vision. Prentice Hall PTR, Upper Saddle River, NJ, USA (1998)

50. Ye, C., Mitrokhin, A., Parameshwara, C., Fermüller, C., Yorke, J.A., Aloimonos, Y.: Unsupervised learning of dense optical flow, depth and egomotion with event-based sensors. In: IEEE/RSJ International Conference on Intelligent Robots and Systems (IROS), pp. 5831–5838 (2020). https://doi.org/10.1109/IROS45743.2020.9341224

51. Zhang, Z., Yezzi, A., Gallego, G.: Image reconstruction from events. Why learn it? arXiv e-prints (2021). https://doi.org/10.48550/arXiv.2112.06242

52. Zhou, Y., Gallego, G., Lu, X., Liu, S., Shen, S.: Event-based motion segmentation with spatio-temporal graph cuts. IEEE Trans. Neural Netw. Learn. Syst. 1–13 (2021). https://doi.org/10.1109/TNNLS.2021.3124580

53. Zhu, A.Z., Atanasov, N., Daniilidis, K.: Event-based feature tracking with probabilistic data association. In: IEEE International Conference on Intelligent Robots and Systems (ICRA), pp. 4465–4470 (2017). https://doi.org/10.1109/ICRA.2017.7989517

54. Zhu, A.Z., Atanasov, N., Daniilidis, K.: Event-based visual inertial odometry. In: IEEE Conf. Comput. Vis. Pattern Recog. (CVPR). pp. 5816–5824 (2017). https://doi.org/10.1109/CVPR.2017.616

55. Zhu, A.Z., Thakur, D., Ozaslan, T., Pfrommer, B., Kumar, V., Daniilidis, K.: The multivehicle stereo event camera dataset: An event camera dataset for 3D perception. IEEE Robot. Autom. Lett. **3**(3), 2032–2039 (2018). https://doi.org/10.1109/lra.2018.2800793

56. Zhu, A.Z., Yuan, L., Chaney, K., Daniilidis, K.: EV-FlowNet: Self-supervised optical flow estimation for event-based cameras. In: Robotics: Science and Systems (RSS) (2018). https://doi.org/10.15607/RSS.2018.XIV.062

57. Zhu, A.Z., Yuan, L., Chaney, K., Daniilidis, K.: Unsupervised event-based learning of optical flow, depth, and egomotion. In: IEEE Conference on Computer Vision and Pattern Recognition (CVPR), pp. 989–997 (2019). https://doi.org/10.1109/CVPR.2019.00108

Towards Efficient and Scale-Robust Ultra-High-Definition Image Demoiréing

Xin Yu[1], Peng Dai[1], Wenbo Li[2], Lan Ma[3], Jiajun Shen[3], Jia Li[4],
and Xiaojuan Qi[1(✉)]

[1] The University of Hong Kong, Hong Kong, China
xjqi@eee.hku.hk
[2] The Chinese University of Hong Kong, Hong Kong, China
[3] TCL AI Lab, Hong Kong, China
[4] Sun Yat-sen University, Guangzhou, China

Abstract. With the rapid development of mobile devices, modern widely-used mobile phones typically allow users to capture 4K resolution (i.e., ultra-high-definition) images. However, for image demoiréing, a challenging task in low-level vision, existing works are generally carried out on low-resolution or synthetic images. Hence, the effectiveness of these methods on 4K resolution images is still unknown. In this paper, we explore moiré pattern removal for ultra-high-definition images. To this end, we propose the first ultra-high-definition demoiréing dataset (UHDM), which contains 5,000 real-world 4K resolution image pairs, and conduct a benchmark study on current state-of-the-art methods. Further, we present an efficient baseline model ESDNet for tackling 4K moiré images, wherein we build a semantic-aligned scale-aware module to address the scale variation of moiré patterns. Extensive experiments manifest the effectiveness of our approach, which outperforms state-of-the-art methods by a large margin while being much more lightweight. Code and dataset are available at https://xinyu-andy.github.io/uhdm-page.

Keywords: Image demoiréing · Image restoration · Ultra-high-definition

1 Introduction

When photographing the contents displayed on the digital screen, an inevitable frequency aliasing between the camera's color filter array (CFA) and the screen's LCD subpixel widely exists. The captured images are thus mixed with colorful stripes, named moiré patterns, which severely degrade the perceptual quality of images. Currently, efficiently removing moiré patterns from a single moiré image is still challenging and receives growing attention from the research community.

Recently, several image demoiréing methods [8,12,13,20,22,29,40,46] have been proposed, yielding a plethora of dedicated designs such as moiré pattern

---

Supplementary Information The online version contains supplementary material available at https://doi.org/10.1007/978-3-031-19797-0_37.

S. Avidan et al. (Eds.): ECCV 2022, LNCS 13678, pp. 646–662, 2022.
https://doi.org/10.1007/978-3-031-19797-0_37

classification [12], frequency domain modeling [22,46], and multi-stage framework [13]. Apart from FHDe^{2}Net [13] which is specially designed for high-definition images, most of the research efforts have been devoted to studying low-resolution images [29] or synthetic images [40]. However, the fast development of mobile devices enables modern mobile phones to capture ultra-high-definition images, so it is more practical to conduct research on 4K image demoiréing for real applications. Unfortunately, the highest resolution in current public demoiréing datasets (see Table 1) is 1080p [13] (1920 × 1080). Whether methods investigated on such datasets can be trivially transferred into the 4K scenario is still unknown due to the data distribution change and dramatically increased computational cost.

Under this circumstance, we explore the more practical yet more challenging demoiréing scenario, i.e., ultra-high-definition image demoiréing. To evaluate the demoiréing methods in this scenario, we build the first large-scale real-world ultra-high-definition demoiréing dataset (UHDM), which consists of 4,500 training image pairs and 500 testing image pairs with diverse scenes (see Fig. 1).

Benchmark Study and Limitation Analysis: Based upon our dataset, we conduct a benchmark study on state-of-the-art methods [8,12,13,22,29,46]. Our empirical study reveals that most methods [8,29,46] struggle to remove moiré patterns with a much wider range of scales in 4K images while simultaneously tolerating the growing demands for computational cost (see Fig. 3) or fine image detail [13] (see Fig. 2). We attribute their deficiencies to the lack of an effective multi-scale feature extraction strategy. Concretely, existing methods attempting to address the scale challenge can be coarsely categorized into two lines of research. One line of research develops multi-stage models, such as FHDe^{2}Net [13], to process large moiré patterns at a low-resolution stage and then refines the textures at a high-resolution stage, which however incurs huge computational cost when applied to 4K images (see Fig. 3: FHDe^{2}Net). Another line of research utilizes features from different depths of a network to build multi-scale representations, in which the most representative work [46] achieves a better trade-off between accuracy and efficiency (see Fig. 3: MBCNN), yet still cannot be generally scale-robust (see Fig. 2 and Fig. 5). We note that the extracted multi-scale features are from different semantic levels which may result in misaligned features when fused together, potentially limiting its capabilities. Detailed study and analysis are unfolded in Sect. 3.2.

To this end, inspired by HRNet [33], we propose a plug-and-play semantic-aligned scale-aware module (SAM) to boost the network's capability in handling moiré patterns with diverse scales without incurring too much computational cost, serving as a supplement to existing methods. Specifically, SAM incorporates a pyramid context extraction module to effectively and efficiently extract multi-scale features aligned at the same semantic level. Further, a cross-scale dynamic fusion module is developed to selectively fuse multi-scale features where the fusion weights are learned and dynamically adapted to individual images.

Equipped with SAM, we develop an efficient and scale-robust network for 4K image demoiréing, named ESDNet. ESDNet adopts a simple encoder-decoder network with skip-connections as its backbone and stacks SAM at different semantic levels to boost the model's capability in addressing scale variations of 4K moiré images. ESDNet is easy to implement while achieving state-of-the-art performance (see Fig. 5 and Table 2) on the challenging ultra-high-definition image demoiréing dataset and three other public demoiréing datasets [13, 29, 40]. In particular, ESDNet exceeds multi-stage high-resolution method FHDe^{2}Net, **1.8dB** in terms of PSNR while being **300× faster (5.620s vs 0.017s)** in the UHDM dataset. Our major contributions are summarized as follows:

- We are the first to explore the ultra-high-definition image demoiréing problem, which is more practical yet more challenging. To this end, we build a large-scale real-world 4K resolution demoiréing dataset UHDM.
- We conduct a benchmark study for the existing state-of-the-art methods on this dataset, summarizing several challenges and analyses. Motivated by these analyses, we propose an efficient baseline model ESDNet for ultra-high-definition image demoiréing.
- Our ESDNet achieves state-of-the-art results on the UHDM dataset and three other public demoiréing datasets, in terms of quantitative evaluation and qualitative comparisons. Moreover, ESDNet is lightweight and can process standard 4K (3840 × 2160) resolution images at 60 fps.

2   Related Work

Image Demoiréing: To remove moiré patterns caused by the frequency aliasing, Liu et al. [20] propose a synthetic dataset by simulating the camera imaging process and develop a GAN-based [10] framework. Further, a large-scale synthetic dataset [40] is proposed and promotes many follow-up works [8, 40, 46]. However, it is difficult for models trained on synthetic data to handle real-world scenarios due to the sim-to-real gap. For real-world image demoiréing, Sun et al. [29] propose the first real-world moiré image dataset (i.e., TIP2018) and develop a multi-scale network (DMCNN). To distinguish different types of moiré patterns, He et al. [12] manually annotate moiré images with category labels to train a moiré pattern classification model. Frequency domain methods [22, 46] are also studied for moiré removal. To deal with high-resolution images, He et al. [13] construct a high-definition dataset FHDMi and develop the multi-stage framework FHDe^{2}Net. Although significant progress has been achieved, the above methods either cannot achieve satisfactory results [8, 12, 29, 46] or suffer from heavy computational cost [8, 12, 13, 46]. More importantly, the highest resolution of existing image demoiréing datasets is FHDMi [13] with 1080p resolution, which is not suitable for practical use considering the ultra-high-definition (4K) images captured by current mobile cameras. We focus on developing a lightweight model that can process ultra-high-definition images.

Image Restoration: To this point, plenty of learning-based image restoration models have been proposed. For instance, residual learning [14] and dense connection [15] are widely used to develop very deep neural networks for different low-level vision tasks [1, 17, 19, 43, 45]. In order to capture multi-scale information, encoder-decoder [25] structures or hierarchical architectures are frequently exploited in image restoration tasks [9,41,42]. Inspired by iterative solvers, some methods utilize recurrent structures [9,31] to gradually recover images while reducing the number of parameters. To preserve structural and semantic information, many works [21,28,30,34,36,37] adopt the perceptual loss [16] or generative loss [2,10,11] to guide the training procedure. In our work, we also take advantage of the well-designed dense blocks for efficient feature reuse and the perceptual loss for semantically guided optimization.

Multi-Scale Network: The multi-scale network has been widely adopted in various tasks [4,6,33,38,47] due to its ability to leverage features with different receptive fields. U-Net [25], as one representative multi-scale network, extracts multi-scale information using an encoder-decoder structure, and enhances features in decoder with skip-connections. To preserve the high-resolution representation, the full resolution residual network [24] extends the U-Net by introducing an extra stream containing information of the full resolution, and similar operations can be found in the HRNet [33]. Considering that the extracted multi-scale features have different semantic meanings, the question of how to fuse features with different meanings is also important and has been widely studied in many works [3,5,7]. In this work, we design a semantic-aligned scale-aware module to handle moiré patterns with diverse scales without incurring too great a computational cost, which renders our method highly practical for 4K images.

3   UHDM Dataset

We study ultra-high-definition image demoiréing, which has more practical applications. For the training of 4K demoiréing models and the evaluation of existing methods, we collect a large-scale ultra-high-definition demoiréing dataset (UHDM). Dataset collection and benchmark study are elaborated upon below.

3.1   Data Collection and Selection

To obtain the real-world 4K image pairs, we first collect high-quality images with resolutions ranging from 4K to 8K from the Internet. We note that Internet resources lack document scenes, which also constitute a vital application scenario (e.g., slides, papers), so we manually generate high-quality text images and make sure they maintain 3000 dpi (Dots Per Inch). Finally, the collected moiré-free images cover a wide range of scenes (see Fig. 1), such as landscapes, sports, video clips, and documents. Given these high-quality images, we generate diverse real-world moiré patterns elaborated upon below.

First, to produce realistic moiré images and ease the difficulties of calibrations, we shoot the clean pictures displayed on the screen with a camera phone fixed on a DJI OM 5 smartphone gimbal, which allows us to conveniently and flexibly adjust the camera view through its control button, as shown in Fig. 1. Second, we note that the characteristics of moiré patterns highly are highly

Fig. 1. Upper left: Our dataset contains diversified scenarios. Upper right: we capture the moiré image with a DJI OM 5 smartphone gimbal. Lower: moiré images in our dataset show a wide range of scale variations.

dependent upon the geometric relationship between the screen and the camera (see supplement for more details). Therefore, during the capturing process, we continuously adjust the viewpoint every ten shots to produce diverse moiré patterns. Third, we adopt multiple < mobile phone, screen > (i.e., three mobile phones and three digital screens, see supplement for more details) combinations to cover various device pairs, since they will also have an impact on the styles of moiré patterns. Finally, to obtain aligned pairs, we utilize RANSAC algorithm [32] to estimate the homography matrix between the original high-quality image and the captured moiré screen image. Since it is difficult to ensure accurate pixel-wise calibration due to the camera's internal nonlinear distortions and perturbations of moiré artifacts, manual selection is performed to rule out severely misaligned image pairs, thereby ensuring quality.

Our dataset contains 5,000 image pairs in total. We randomly split them into 4,500 for training and 500 for validation. As we collect moiré images using various mobile phones, the resolution can either be 4032 × 3024 or 4624 × 3472. Comparisons with other existing datasets are shown in Table 1, and the characteristics of our dataset are summarized as below.

- **Ultra-high resolution** UHDM is the first 4K resolution demoiréing dataset, consisting of 5,000 image pairs in total.
- **Diverse image scenes** The dataset includes diverse scenes, such as landscapes, sports, video clips, and documents.
- **Real-world capture settings** The moiré images are generated following practical routines, with different device combinations and viewpoints to produce diverse moiré patterns.

Table 1. Comparisons of different demoiréing datasets; our dataset is the first ultra-high-definition dataset ("London's Buildings" is not available currently).

Dataset	Avg. Resolution	Size	Diversity	Real-world
TIP18 [29]	256 × 256	135,000	No text scenes	✓
LCDMoiré [40]	1024 × 1024	10,200	Only text scenes	×
FHDMi [13]	1920 × 1080	12,000	Diverse scenes	✓
London's Buildings [22]	2100 × 1700	460	Only urban scenes	✓
UHDM	**4328 × 3248**	**5,000**	**Diverse scenes**	✓

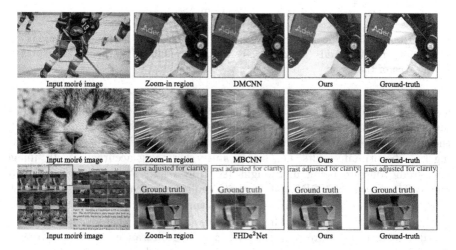

Fig. 2. Limitations of current methods: they are often unable to remove the moiré pattern with a wider scale range or lose high-frequency details.

3.2 Benchmark Study on 4K Demoiréing

As the image resolution is increased to the 4K resolution, the scale of moiré patterns has a very wide range, from very large moiré patterns to small ones (see Fig. 1). This poses a major challenge to demoiréing methods as they are required to be scale-robust. Furthermore, increased image resolution also leads to dramatically increased computational cost and high requirements of detail restoration/preservation. Here, we carry out a benchmark study on the existing state-of-the-art methods [8,12,13,22,29,46] on our 4K demoiréing dataset to evaluate their effectiveness. Main results are summarized in Fig. 2 and Fig. 3: existing methods are mostly not capable of achieving a good balance of accuracy and computational efficiency. More detailed results are shown in Sect. 5.

Analysis and Discussions: Although existing methods also attempt to address the scale challenge by developing multi-scale strategies, they still have several deficiencies regarding computational efficiency and restoration quality when applied to 4K high-resolution images (see Fig. 2). One line of methods,

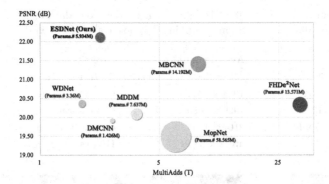

Fig. 3. Comparisons of computational cost of different methods: The x-axis and the y-axis denote the MultiAdds (T) and PSNR (dB). The number of parameters is expressed by the area of the circle.

such as DMCNN [29] and MDDM [8], fuses multi-scale features harvested from multi-resolution inputs only at the output stage, which potentially prohibits the intermediate features from interacting with and refining each other, leading to sub-optimal results, i.e., significantly sacrificing accuracy on 4K image demoiréing despite being lightweight (see Fig. 3 and Fig. 2). Another line of methods, such as MBCNN [46], exploits multi-scale features at different network depths following a U-Net-like architecture. Compared with other existing methods, although it achieves the best trade-off between accuracy and efficiency, it still suffers from moiré patterns with a wide-scale range (the second row of Fig. 2 and Fig. 5). One possible issue is that the combined multi-scale features come from different semantic levels [33], prohibiting a specific feature level to harvest multi-resolution representations [33], which could also be an important cue for image demoiréing. On the other hand, FHDe²Net [13] designs a coarse-to-fine two-stage model to simultaneously address the scale and detail challenge. It suffers, however, from heavy computational cost when applied to 4K images (see Fig. 3) yet is still not sufficient to remove moiré patterns (see Fig. 5) or recover fine image detail (see Fig. 2 and Fig. 5).

4   Proposed Method

Motivated by observations in Sect. 3.2, we introduce a baseline approach to advance 4K resolution image demoiréing, aimed towards a more scale-robust and efficient model. In the following, we first present an overview of our pipeline and then elaborate on our core semantic-aligned scale-aware module (SAM).

4.1   Pipeline

The overall architecture is shown in Fig. 4, where a pre-processing head is utilized to enlarge the receptive field, followed by an encoder-decoder architecture for image demoiréing. The pre-processing head adopts pixel shuffle [26] to

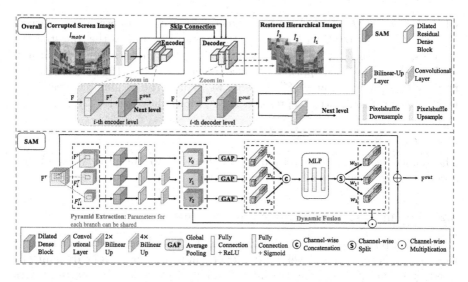

Fig. 4. The pipeline of our ESDNet and the proposed semantic-aligned scale-aware module (SAM).

downsample the image by two times and a 5×5 convolution layer to further extract low-level features. Then, the extracted low-level features are fed into an encoder-decoder backbone architecture that consists of three downsampling and upsampling levels. Note that the encoder and decoder are connected via skip-connections to allow features containing high-resolution information to facilitate the restoration of corresponding moiré-free images. At each decoder level, the network would produce intermediate results through a convolution layer and a pixelshuffle upsampling operation (see the upper part of Fig. 4), which are also supervised by the ground-truth, serving the purpose of deep supervision to facilitate training. Specifically, each encoder or decoder level (see Fig. 4) contains a dilated residual dense block [14,15,39,45] for refining the input features (as detailed below) and a proposed semantic-aligned multi-scale module (SAM) for extracting and dynamically fusing multi-scale features at the same semantic level (as elaborated in Sect. 4.2).

Dilated Residual Dense Block: For each level $i \in \{1, 2, 3, 4, 5, 6\}$ (i.e., three encoder levels and three decoder levels), the input feature F_i first goes through a convolutional block, i.e., dilated residual dense block, for refining input features. It incorporates the residual dense block (RDB) [14,15,45] and dilated convolution layers [39] to process the input features and output refined ones. Specifically, given an input feature F_i^0 to the i-th level encoder or decoder, the cascaded local features from each layer inside the block can be formulated as Eq. (1):

$$F_i^l = C^l([F_i^0, F_i^1, ..., F_i^{l-1}]), (l = 1, 2, ..., L) \tag{1}$$

where $[F_i^0, F_i^1, ..., F_i^{l-1}]$ denotes the concatenation of all intermediate features inside the block before layer l, and C^l is the operator to process the concatenated features, consisting of a 3×3 Conv with dilated rate d^l and a rectified linear unit (ReLU). After that, we apply a 1×1 convolution to keep the output channel number the same as that of F_i^0. Finally, we exploit the residual connection to produce the refined feature representation F_i^r, formulated as Eq.(2):

$$F_i^r = F_i^0 + \text{Conv}_{1\times1}(F_i^L). \tag{2}$$

The refined feature representation F_i^r is then fed to our proposed SAM for semantic-aligned multi-scale feature extraction.

4.2   Semantic-Aligned Scale-Aware Module

Given the input feature F_i^r, the SAM is intended to extract multi-scale features within the same semantic level i and allow them to interact and be dynamically fused, significantly improving the model's ability to handle moiré patterns with a wide range of scales. As demonstrated in Table 3, SAM enables us to develop a lightweight network while still being more effective in comparison with existing methods. In the following, we detail the design of SAM which encompasses two major modules: pyramid feature extraction and cross-scale dynamic fusion.

Pyramid Context Extraction: Given an input feature map $F^r \in \mathbb{R}^{H \times W \times C}$ (we simplify F_i^r by F^r in the following discussion), we first produce pyramid input features $F^r \in \mathbb{R}^{H \times W \times C}, F_\downarrow^r \in \mathbb{R}^{\frac{H}{2} \times \frac{W}{2} \times C}$ and $F_{\downarrow\downarrow}^r \in \mathbb{R}^{\frac{H}{4} \times \frac{W}{4} \times C}$ through bilinear interpolation, then feed them into a corresponding convolutional branch with five convolution layers to yield pyramid outputs Y_0, Y_1, Y_2 (see the lower part of Fig. 4):

$$Y_0 = E_0(F^r), \quad Y_1 = E_1\left(F_\downarrow^r\right), \quad Y_2 = E_2\left(F_{\downarrow\downarrow}^r\right), \tag{3}$$

where we build E_0, E_1, and E_2 via the dilated dense block, followed by a 1×1 convolution layer. In addition, the up-sampling operations will be performed in E_1, E_2 to align the size of three outputs, i.e., $Y_i \in \mathbb{R}^{H \times W \times C}, (i = 0, 1, 2)$.

Note that, as the internal architectures of E_0, E_1, and E_2 are identical, their corresponding learnable parameters can be shared to lower the cost of parameter number. In fact, as proven in Sect. 5, the improvement primarily comes from the pyramid architecture instead of additional parameters.

Cross-Scale Dynamic Fusion: Given the pyramid features Y_0, Y_1, Y_2, the cross-scale dynamic fusion module fuses them together to produce fused multi-scale features for the next level to process. The insight for this module is that scale of moiré patterns vary from image to image and thus the importance of different scale features would also vary across images. Therefore, we develop the following cross-scale dynamic fusion module to make the fusion process dynamically adjusted and adapted to each image. Specifically, we learn dynamic weights to fuse Y_1, Y_2, Y_3.

Given $Y_i \in \mathbb{R}^{H \times W \times C} (i = 0, 1, 2)$, we first apply global average pooling in the spatial dimension of each feature map to obtain the 1D global feature $v_i \in \mathbb{R}^C$ for each scale i following Eq. (4).

$$v_i = \frac{1}{H \times W} \sum_{s=1}^{H} \sum_{t=1}^{W} Y_i(s, t) \tag{4}$$

Then, we concatenate them along the channel dimension and learn the dynamic weights through an MLP module as:

$$[w_0, w_1, w_2] = \text{MLP}([v_0, v_1, v_2]) \tag{5}$$

where "MLP" consists of three fully connected layers and outputs $w_0, w_1, w_2 \in \mathbb{R}^C$ to fuse Y_1, Y_2, Y_3 dynamically. Finally, with fusion weights, we channel-wisely fuse the pyramid features with the input-adaptive weights, and then add the input feature F^r to get the final output of SAM:

$$F^{\text{out}} = F^r + w_0 \odot Y_0 + w_1 \odot Y_1 + w_2 \odot Y_2 \tag{6}$$

where $\odot$ denotes the channel-wise multiplication, and the output F^{out} will go through the next level $(i \rightarrow i + 1)$ for further feature extraction and image reconstruction.

Comparisons and Analysis: Existing methods [22, 46] utilize features from different depths to obtain multi-scale representations. However, features at different depths have different levels of semantic information. Thus, they are incapable of representing multi-scale information at the same semantic level, which might provide important cues for boosting the model's multi-scale modeling capabilities, as indicated in [33]. We offer SAM as a supplement to existing methods as Y_0, Y_1, Y_2 include semantic-aligned information with different local receptive fields. The dynamic fusion methods further make the module adaptive to different images and boost its abilities. This strategy can also be treated as an implicit classifier compared with the explicit one in MopNet [12], which is more efficient and avoids the ambiguous hand-craft attribute definition. We include more detailed analysis in our supplementary file.

4.3 Loss Function

To boost optimization, we adopt the deep supervision strategy, which has been proven useful in [46]. As shown in Fig. 4, in each decoder level, the network will produce hierarchical predictions $\hat{I}_1, \hat{I}_2, \hat{I}_3$, which are also supervised by ground-truth images. We note that moiré patterns disrupt image structures since they generate new strip-shaped structures. Therefore, we adopt the perceptual

Table 2. Quantitative comparisons between our model and state-of-the-art methods on four datasets. (↑) denotes the larger the better, and (↓) denotes the smaller the better. Red: best and Blue: second-best.

Dataset	Metrics	Input	DMCNN [29]	MDDM [8]	WDNet [22]	MopNet [12]	MBCNN [46]	FHDe^{2}Net [13]	ESDNet	ESDNet-L
UHDM	PSNR↑	17.117	19.914	20.088	20.364	19.489	21.414	20.338	22.119	22.422
	SSIM↑	0.5089	0.7575	0.7441	0.6497	0.7572	0.7932	0.7496	0.7956	0.7985
	LPIPS↓	0.5314	0.3764	0.3409	0.4882	0.3857	0.3318	0.3519	0.2551	0.2454
FHDMi	PSNR↑	17.974	21.538	20.831	–	22.756	22.309	22.930	24.500	24.882
	SSIM↑	0.7033	0.7727	0.7343	–	0.7958	0.8095	0.7885	0.8351	0.8440
	LPIPS↓	0.2837	0.2477	0.2515	–	0.1794	0.1980	0.1688	0.1354	0.1301
TIP2018	PSNR↑	20.30	26.77	–	28.08	27.75	30.03	27.78	29.81	30.11
	SSIM↑	0.738	0.871	–	0.904	0.895	0.893	0.896	0.916	0.920
LCDMoiré	PSNR↑	10.44	35.48	42.49	29.66	–	44.04	41.40	44.83	45.34
	SSIM↑	0.5717	0.9785	0.9940	0.9670	–	0.9948	–	0.9963	0.9966
–	Params (M)	–	1.426	7.637	3.360	58.565	14.192	13.571	5.934	10.623

loss [16] for feature-based supervision. At each level, we build our loss function by combining the pixel-wise L_1 loss and the feature-based perceptual loss L_p. Hence, the final loss function is formulated as:

$$\mathcal{L}_{total} = \sum_{i=1}^{3} \mathcal{L}_1(I_i, \hat{I}_i) + \lambda \times \mathcal{L}_p(I_i, \hat{I}_i) \tag{7}$$

For the perceptual loss, we extract features from conv3_3 (after ReLU) using a pre-trained VGG16 [27] network and compute the L_1 distance in the feature space; we simply set $\lambda = 1$ during training. We find that this perceptual loss is effective in removing moiré patterns.

5   Experiments

Datasets and Metrics: We conduct experiments on the proposed UHDM dataset and three other public datasets: FHDMi [13], TIP2018 [29] and LCD-Moiré [40]. In our UHDM dataset, we keep the original two resolutions (see Sect. 3) and models are trained with cropped patches. During the evaluation phase, we do center crop from the original images to obtain test pairs with a resolution of 3840 × 2160 (standard 4K size). We adopt the widely used PSNR, SSIM [35] and LPIPS [44] metrics for quantitative evaluation. It has been proven that LPIPS is more consistent with human perception and suitable for measuring demoiréing quality [13]. Note that existing methods only report PSNR and SSIM on the TIP2018 and LCDMoiré, so we follow this setup for comparisons.

Implementation Details: We implement our algorithm using PyTorch on an NVIDIA RTX 3090 GPU card. During training, we randomly crop a 768 × 768 patch from the ultra-high-definition images, and set the batch size to 2. The model is trained for 150 epochs and optimized by Adam [18] with $\beta_1 = 0.9$ and $\beta_2 = 0.999$. The learning rate is initially set to 0.0002 and scheduled by cyclic cosine annealing [23]. Details for implementations on other benchmarks are unfolded in the supplementary file. We also train other methods on our dataset faithfully and sufficiently and unfold details in the supplementary file.

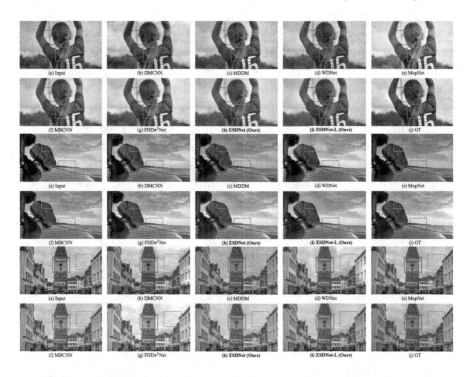

Fig. 5. Qualitative comparisons with state-of-the-art methods on the UHDM dataset. Please zoom in for a better view. More results are given in the supplementary file.

5.1 Comparisons with State-of-the-Art Methods

We provide two versions of our model: ESDNet and ESDNet-L. ESDNet is the default lightweight model and ESDNet-L is a larger model, stacking one more SAM in each network level.

Quantitative Comparison: Table 2 shows quantitative performance of existing approaches. The proposed method achieves state-of-the-art results on all four datasets. Specifically, both of our two models outperform other methods by a large margin in the ultra-high-definition UHDM dataset and high-definition FHDMi dataset, demonstrating the effectiveness of our method in high-resolution scenarios. It is worthwhile to note that our ESDNet, though possessing far fewer parameters, already shows competitive performance.

Qualitative Comparison: We present visual comparisons between our algorithm and existing methods in Fig. 5. Apparently, our method obtains more perceptually satisfactory results. In comparison, MDDM [8], DMCNN [29] and WDNet [22] often fail to remove moiré patterns, while MBCNN [46] and Mop-Net [12] cannot handle large-scale patterns well. Though performing better than other methods (except for ours), FHDe^{2}Net [13] usually suffers from severe loss of details. All these facts manifest the superiority of our method.

Table 3. Ablation study of the proposed SAM. "A" represents the baseline model. "A$^+$" denotes a stronger baseline which is of similar model capacity compared to our full model "E". "B" adds the pyramid context extraction with shared weights across all branches to "A" while "D" adopts adaptive weights. "C" and "E" add the cross-scale dynamic fusion based on "B" and "D", respectively.

Dataset	Metrics	A	A$^+$	B	C	D	E
UHDM	PSNR↑	20.646	20.860	21.176	21.958	21.300	**22.119**
	SSIM↑	0.7899	0.7908	0.7937	0.7938	0.7947	**0.7956**
	LPIPS↓	0.2750	0.2626	0.2683	0.2596	0.2623	**0.2551**
	Params (M)	2.705	5.978	2.705	3.014	5.625	5.934

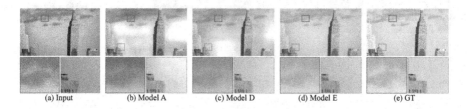

(a) Input   (b) Model A   (c) Model D   (d) Model E   (e) GT

Fig. 6. Qualitative effects of different components in SAM.

Computational Cost: As shown in Fig. 3, our method strikes a sweet point of balancing the parameter number, computation cost (MACs), and demoiréing performance. Also, we test the inference speed of our method on an NVIDIA RTX 3090 GPU. Surprisingly, our ESDNet only needs 17 ms (i.e., 60 fps) to process a standard 4K resolution image, almost 300× faster than FHDe^{2}Net. The competitive performance and low computational cost render our method highly practical in the 4K scenario.

5.2   Ablation Study

In this section, we tease apart which components of our network contribute most to the final performance on the UHDM dataset. As shown in Table 3, we start from the baseline model (model "A"), which ablates the pyramid context extraction and the cross-scale dynamic fusion strategies. To make a fair comparison, we further build a stronger baseline model (model "A$^+$") that is comparable to our full model (model "E") in terms of the model capacity.

Pyramid Context Extraction: We construct two variants (model "B" and model "D") for exploring the effectiveness of this design. Compared with the baseline (model "A"), we observe that the proposed pyramid context extraction can significantly boost the model performance. To validate whether the improvement comes from more parameters in the additional two sub-branches, we exploit a weight-sharing strategy across all branches (model "B"). The observations in Table 3 demonstrate that the performance gain mainly stems from the pyramid

Table 4. Ablation study of the loss function. The left and the right of "/" denote results trained by the pixel-wise L_1 loss and trained by our loss, respectively.

Dataset	Metrics	DMCNN	MDDM	Ours
UHDM	PSNR↑	**19.914**/19.911	20.088/**20.333**	21.489/**22.119**
	SSIM↑	**0.7575**/0.7212	**0.7441**/0.7412	0.7893/**0.7956**
	LPIPS↓	0.3764/**0.3089**	0.3409/**0.2986**	0.3330/**0.2551**

design rather than the increase of parameters. Further, as shown in Fig. 6, we find our pyramid design can successfully remove the moiré patterns that are not well addressed in the baseline model.

Cross-Scale Dynamic Fusion: To verify the importance of the proposed dynamic fusion scheme, we increasingly add this design to model "B" and model "D", resulting in model "C" and model "E". We observe consistent improvements for both models, especially on PSNR. Also, Fig. 6 shows that the artifacts retained in model "D" are totally removed in the result of model "E", achieving a more harmonious color style.

Loss Function: Through our experiments, we find the perceptual loss plays an essential role in image demoiréing. As shown in Table 4, when replacing our loss function with a single L_1 loss, we notice obvious performance drops in our method, especially on LPIPS. Also, we make further exploration by applying our loss function to other state-of-the-art methods [8,29]. The significant improvements on LPIPS illustrate the importance of the loss design in yielding a higher perceptual quality of recovered images. We suggest our loss is more robust to address the large-scale moiré patterns and the misaligned issue in the real-world datasets [13,29]. More discussions are included in the supplementary file.

6   Conclusion

In this paper, to explore the more practical yet challenging 4K image demoiréing scenario, we propose the first real-world ultra-high-definition demoiréing dataset (UHDM). Based upon this dataset, we conduct a benchmark study and limitation analysis of current methods, which motivates us to build a lightweight semantic-aligned scale-aware module (SAM) to strengthen the model's multiscale ability without incurring much computational cost. By leveraging SAM in different depths of a simple encoder-decoder backbone network, we develop ESDNet to handle 4K high-resolution image demoiréing effectively. Our method is computationally efficient and easy to implement, achieving state-of-the-art results on four benchmark demoiréing datasets (including our UHDM). We hope our investigation could inspire future research in this more practical setting.

Acknowledgements. This work is partially supported by HKU-TCL Joint Research Center for Artificial Intelligence, Hong Kong Research Grant Council - Early Career Scheme (Grant No. 27209621), National Key R&D Program of China (No.2021YFA1001300), and Guangdong-Hong Kong-Macau Applied Math Center grant 2020B1515310011.

References

1. Anwar, S., Barnes, N.: Densely residual laplacian super-resolution. IEEE Trans. Pattern Anal. Mach. Intell. **44**, 1192–1204 (2020)
2. Arjovsky, M., Chintala, S., Bottou, L.: Wasserstein generative adversarial networks. In: International conference on machine learning. PMLR, pp. 214–223 (2017)
3. Cao, D., Chen, Z., Gao, L.: An improved object detection algorithm based on multi-scaled and deformable convolutional neural networks. Human-centric Computing and Information Sciences **10**(1), 1–22 (2020). https://doi.org/10.1186/s13673-020-00219-9
4. Chen, C., Chen, Q., Xu, J., Koltun, V.: Learning to see in the dark. In: Proceedings of the IEEE Conference on Computer Vision and Pattern Recognition, pp. 3291–3300 (2018)
5. Chen, L.C., Papandreou, G., Kokkinos, I., Murphy, K., Yuille, A.L.: DeepLab: semantic image segmentation with deep convolutional nets, atrous convolution, and fully connected CRFs. IEEE Trans. Pattern Anal. Mach. Intell. **40**(4), 834–848 (2017)
6. Chen, Q., Koltun, V.: Photographic image synthesis with cascaded refinement networks. In: Proceedings of the IEEE international conference on computer vision, pp. 1511–1520 (2017)
7. Chen, Y., Wang, Z., Peng, Y., Zhang, Z., Yu, G., Sun, J.: Cascaded pyramid network for multi-person pose estimation. In: Proceedings of the IEEE conference on computer vision and pattern recognition, pp. 7103–7112 (2018)
8. Cheng, X., Fu, Z., Yang, J.: Multi-scale dynamic feature encoding network for image demoiréing. In: 2019 IEEE/CVF International Conference on Computer Vision Workshop (ICCVW), pp. 3486–3493. IEEE (2019)
9. Gao, H., Tao, X., Shen, X., Jia, J.: Dynamic scene deblurring with parameter selective sharing and nested skip connections. In: Proceedings of the IEEE/CVF Conference on Computer Vision and Pattern Recognition, pp. 3848–3856 (2019)
10. Goodfellow, I., et al.: Generative adversarial nets. In: Advances in neural information processing systems, vol. 27 (2014)
11. Gulrajani, I., Ahmed, F., Arjovsky, M., Dumoulin, V., Courville, A.: Improved training of wasserstein GANs. arXiv preprint arXiv:1704.00028 (2017)
12. He, B., Wang, C., Shi, B., Duan, L.Y.: Mop moire patterns using mopnet. In: Proceedings of the IEEE/CVF International Conference on Computer Vision, pp. 2424–2432 (2019)
13. He, B., Wang, C., Shi, B., Duan, L.-Y.: FHDe^{2}Net: full high definition demoireing network. In: Vedaldi, A., Bischof, H., Brox, T., Frahm, J.-M. (eds.) ECCV 2020. LNCS, vol. 12367, pp. 713–729. Springer, Cham (2020). https://doi.org/10.1007/978-3-030-58542-6_43
14. He, K., Zhang, X., Ren, S., Sun, J.: Deep residual learning for image recognition. In: Proceedings of the IEEE conference on computer vision and pattern recognition, pp. 770–778 (2016)

15. Huang, G., Liu, Z., Van Der Maaten, L., Weinberger, K.Q.: Densely connected convolutional networks. In: Proceedings of the IEEE conference on computer vision and pattern recognition, pp. 4700–4708 (2017)
16. Johnson, J., Alahi, A., Fei-Fei, L.: Perceptual losses for real-time style transfer and super-resolution. In: Leibe, B., Matas, J., Sebe, N., Welling, M. (eds.) ECCV 2016. LNCS, vol. 9906, pp. 694–711. Springer, Cham (2016). https://doi.org/10. 1007/978-3-319-46475-6_43
17. Kim, J., Lee, J.K., Lee, K.M.: Accurate image super-resolution using very deep convolutional networks. In: Proceedings of the IEEE conference on computer vision and pattern recognition, pp. 1646–1654 (2016)
18. Kingma, D.P., Ba, J.: Adam: A method for stochastic optimization. arXiv preprint arXiv:1412.6980 (2014)
19. Lim, B., Son, S., Kim, H., Nah, S., Mu Lee, K.: Enhanced deep residual networks for single image super-resolution. In: Proceedings of the IEEE conference on computer vision and pattern recognition workshops, pp. 136–144 (2017)
20. Liu, B., Shu, X., Wu, X.: Demoir\'eing of camera-captured screen images using deep convolutional neural network. arXiv preprint arXiv:1804.03809 (2018)
21. Liu, G., Reda, F.A., Shih, K.J., Wang, T.C., Tao, A., Catanzaro, B.: Image inpainting for irregular holes using partial convolutions. In: Proceedings of the European Conference on Computer Vision (ECCV), pp. 85–100 (2018)
22. Liu, l, et al.: Wavelet-based dual-branch network for image demoiréing. In: Vedaldi, A., Bischof, H., Brox, T., Frahm, J.-M. (eds.) ECCV 2020. LNCS, vol. 12358, pp. 86–102. Springer, Cham (2020). https://doi.org/10.1007/978-3-030-58601-0_6
23. Loshchilov, I., Hutter, F.: SGDR: Stochastic gradient descent with warm restarts. arXiv preprint arXiv:1608.03983 (2016)
24. Pohlen, T., Hermans, A., Mathias, M., Leibe, B.: Full-resolution residual networks for semantic segmentation in street scenes. In: Proceedings of the IEEE conference on computer vision and pattern recognition, pp. 4151–4160 (2017)
25. Ronneberger, O., Fischer, P., Brox, T.: U-Net: convolutional networks for biomedical image segmentation. In: Navab, N., Hornegger, J., Wells, W.M., Frangi, A.F. (eds.) MICCAI 2015. LNCS, vol. 9351, pp. 234–241. Springer, Cham (2015). https://doi.org/10.1007/978-3-319-24574-4_28
26. Shi, W., et al.: Real-time single image and video super-resolution using an efficient sub-pixel convolutional neural network. In: Proceedings of the IEEE conference on computer vision and pattern recognition, pp. 1874–1883 (2016)
27. Simonyan, K., Zisserman, A.: Very deep convolutional networks for large-scale image recognition. arXiv preprint arXiv:1409.1556 (2014)
28. Song, Y., et al.: Contextual-based image inpainting: Infer, match, and translate. In: Proceedings of the European Conference on Computer Vision (ECCV), pp. 3–19 (2018)
29. Sun, Y., Yu, Y., Wang, W.: Moiré photo restoration using multiresolution convolutional neural networks. IEEE Trans. Image Process. **27**(8), 4160–4172 (2018)
30. Suvorov, R., et al.: Resolution-robust large mask inpainting with fourier convolutions. arXiv preprint arXiv:2109.07161 (2021)
31. Tao, X., Gao, H., Shen, X., Wang, J., Jia, J.: Scale-recurrent network for deep image deblurring. In: Proceedings of the IEEE Conference on Computer Vision and Pattern Recognition, pp. 8174–8182 (2018)
32. Vedaldi, A., Fulkerson, B.: Vlfeat: An open and portable library of computer vision algorithms. In: Proceedings of the 18th ACM International Conference on Multimedia, pp. 1469–1472 (2010)

33. Wang, J., et al.: Deep high-resolution representation learning for visual recognition. IEEE Trans. Pattern Anal. Mach. Intell. **43**(10), 3349–3364 (2020)

34. Wang, Yi., Chen, Ying-Cong., Tao, Xin, Jia, Jiaya: VCNet: a robust approach to blind image inpainting. In: Vedaldi, Andrea, Bischof, Horst, Brox, Thomas, Frahm, Jan-Michael. (eds.) ECCV 2020. LNCS, vol. 12370, pp. 752–768. Springer, Cham (2020). https://doi.org/10.1007/978-3-030-58595-2_45

35. Wang, Z., Bovik, A.C., Sheikh, H.R., Simoncelli, E.P.: Image quality assessment: from error visibility to structural similarity. IEEE Trans. Image Process. **13**(4), 600–612 (2004)

36. Xie, C., et al.: Image inpainting with learnable bidirectional attention maps. In: Proceedings of the IEEE/CVF International Conference on Computer Vision, pp. 8858–8867 (2019)

37. Yang, C., Lu, X., Lin, Z., Shechtman, E., Wang, O., Li, H.: High-resolution image inpainting using multi-scale neural patch synthesis. In: Proceedings of the IEEE conference on computer vision and pattern recognition, pp. 6721–6729 (2017)

38. Yeh, R., Chen, C., Lim, T.Y., Hasegawa-Johnson, M., Do, M.N.: Semantic image inpainting with perceptual and contextual losses. arXiv preprint arXiv:1607.07539 2(3) (2016)

39. Yu, F., Koltun, V.: Multi-scale context aggregation by dilated convolutions. arXiv preprint arXiv:1511.07122 (2015)

40. Yuan, S., et al.: Aim 2019 challenge on image demoireing: Methods and results. In: 2019 IEEE/CVF International Conference on Computer Vision Workshop (ICCVW), pp. 3534–3545. IEEE (2019)

41. Zamir, S.W., et al.: Multi-stage progressive image restoration. In: Proceedings of the IEEE/CVF Conference on Computer Vision and Pattern Recognition, pp. 14821–14831 (2021)

42. Zhang, H., Dai, Y., Li, H., Koniusz, P.: Deep stacked hierarchical multi-patch network for image deblurring. In: Proceedings of the IEEE/CVF Conference on Computer Vision and Pattern Recognition, pp. 5978–5986 (2019)

43. Zhang, K., Zuo, W., Chen, Y., Meng, D., Zhang, L.: Beyond a gaussian denoiser: residual learning of deep CNN for image denoising. IEEE Trans. Image Process. **26**(7), 3142–3155 (2017)

44. Zhang, R., Isola, P., Efros, A.A., Shechtman, E., Wang, O.: The unreasonable effectiveness of deep features as a perceptual metric. In: Proceedings of the IEEE Conference on Computer Vision and Pattern Recognition, pp. 586–595 (2018)

45. Zhang, Y., Tian, Y., Kong, Y., Zhong, B., Fu, Y.: Residual dense network for image super-resolution. In: Proceedings of the IEEE Conference on Computer Vision and Pattern Recognition, pp. 2472–2481 (2018)

46. Zheng, B., Yuan, S., Slabaugh, G., Leonardis, A.: Image demoireing with learnable bandpass filters. In: Proceedings of the IEEE/CVF Conference on Computer Vision and Pattern Recognition, pp. 3636–3645 (2020)

47. Zhou, T., Tucker, R., Flynn, J., Fyffe, G., Snavely, N.: Stereo magnification: Learning view synthesis using multiplane images. arXiv preprint arXiv:1805.09817 (2018)

ERDN: Equivalent Receptive Field Deformable Network for Video Deblurring

Bangrui Jiang[1,2], Zhihuai Xie[2(✉)], Zhen Xia[2], Songnan Li[2], and Shan Liu[2]

[1] Tsinghua Shenzhen International Graduate School,
Tsinghua University, Beijing, China
[2] Tencent Media Lab, Shenzhen, China
{zhihuaixie,zhenxia,sunnysnli,shanl}@tencent.com

Abstract. Video deblurring aims to restore sharp frames from blurry video sequences. Existing methods usually adopt optical flow to compensate misalignment between reference frame and each neighboring frame. However, inaccurate flow estimation caused by large displacements will lead to artifacts in the warped frames. In this work, we propose an equivalent receptive field deformable network (ERDN) to perform alignment at the feature level without estimating optical flow. The ERDN introduces a dual pyramid alignment module, in which a feature pyramid is constructed to align frames using deformable convolution in a cascaded manner. Specifically, we adopt dilated spatial pyramid blocks to predict offsets for deformable convolutions, so that the theoretical receptive field is equivalent for each feature pyramid layer. To restore the sharp frame, we propose a gradient guided fusion module, which incorporates structure priors into the restoration process. Experimental results demonstrate that the proposed method outperforms previous state-of-the-art methods on multiple benchmark datasets. The code is made available at: https://github.com/TencentCloud/ERDN.

Keywords: Video deblurring · Deformable convolution · Receptive field

1 Introduction

The goal of video deblurring is to recover high quality consecutive frames from their blurry counterparts. Camera shake and object motion, which are common when capturing videos with hand-held devices, serve as the main causes of video blur. Video deblurring is a fundamental problem in the community of computer vision and can be beneficial to many high-level tasks including video segmentation and video understanding. However, it is an ill-posed problem since each blurry frame may have multiple sharp solutions.

Compared to image deblurring, video deblurring can use neighboring frames for restoration. A vital issue in video deblurring is how to align the neighboring frames with the reference frame, since the neighboring frames may not be

© The Author(s), under exclusive license to Springer Nature Switzerland AG 2022
S. Avidan et al. (Eds.): ECCV 2022, LNCS 13678, pp. 663–678, 2022.
https://doi.org/10.1007/978-3-031-19797-0_38

naturally aligned due to motions of objects. Previous methods [9,12,18,21,29] usually exploit optical flow to predict motion fields, which can be used to warp neighboring frames to the reference frame. However, these methods perform flow estimation explicitly and wrap frames at the image level, which may introduce artifacts in regions with large displacements. ARVo [12] further estimates pairwise image correspondence to compensate misalignment caused by inaccurate flow estimation, while extra computational cost and storage space are required.

Besides flow-based alignment, deformable convolution [7] is widely adopted as another alignment method and achieve remarkable performance in video restoration [13,24,26]. When deformable convolution is applied in temporal alignment, the displaced kernels on neighboring frames will be used to align intermediate features from several locations, while optical flow only samples from one location. Because of the diverse sampling, deformable convolution tends to perform better than flow-based alignment [3]. However, existing works [24,26] usually predict offsets in a limited receptive field, which leads to relatively local offset predictions and fail to achieve comparable performance.

To alleviate the problem, we propose an equivalent receptive field deformable network (ERDN) that performs temporal alignment using deformable convolution. A dual pyramid alignment module is developed to construct a feature pyramid for reference frame and each neighboring frame. In particular, the module first aligns high level features with coarse offset estimations and then propagates the offsets and the aligned features to lower levels, in which way the offsets can be refined in a coarse-to-fine manner. However, different from [26], we propose a novel dilated spatial pyramid block to predict offsets for each feature pyramid layer. The block uses dilated convolution to guarantee each layer having equivalent receptive field, with the principle that the offset refinement is more effective to be performed in an equivalent region. To compensate information loss caused by dilated convolution, the block further concatenates several convolution layers with different dilation rates, which constitute a spatial receptive field pyramid.

In order to preserve structures for further enhancing the deblurring performance, we introduce a gradient guided fusion module, in which a gradient branch converts the gradient maps of blurry frames to the sharp ones. The recovered gradients can be integrated into the deblurring branch with a series of Spatial Feature Transform (SFT) layers [25], allowing our method to incorporate structure priors. To the best of our knowledge, we are the first to introduce gradient branch in video deblurring and achieve success.

The main contributions can be summarized as follows:

1. We propose a novel equivalent receptive field deformable network (ERDN) for video deblurring, which performs alignment using deformable convolution without optical flow estimation.
2. To handle large displacement, we propose a dual pyramid alignment module, which predicts offsets in a cascaded manner within equivalent receptive field.
3. We introduce a gradient branch to incorporate structure priors as a guidance for the frame restoration.
4. Extensive experiments show that our method achieves superior performance over previous state-of-the-art methods quantitatively and qualitatively.

2   Related Works

2.1   Video Deblurring

Early video deblurring approaches [1, 20, 28] mostly estimate blur kernels and restore sharp frames by applying deconvolution with the estimated kernels. Some works [1, 28] utilize segmentation map for blur kernel estimation, and process blur caused by moving objects. More recently, [20] propose a pixel-wise non-linear kernel model, where the blur kernel is estimated from optical flow. However, estimating spatially-varying blur kernels is a severely ill-posed problem. These approaches may fail when applied to videos that include complex blur.

To overcome the above problems, several methods explicitly align frames using optical flow. [21] restore the deblurred frame using channel-concatenated neighboring frames, which are aligned by an external optical flow module. [18] plug an optical flow estimation module into an end-to-end model while using temporal sharpness prior. Based on [18], [12] further incorporate a correlation volume pyramid to learn spatial correspondence between pixel pairs in the feature space. The spatial correspondence can serve as a complement to the optical flow alignment. Most of the optical flow-based methods align frames at the image level, while incorrect flow estimation may introduce image artifacts.

By contrast, a few methods adopt implicitly alignment using Recurrent Neural Network (RNN) for its excellent performance on time-series signal [5, 23]. [27] introduce a novel recurrent encoder-decoder network and transfer temporal feature between subsequent iterations. [10] incorporate a dynamic temporal blending mechanism that enable adaptive information propagation. The recent method [31] uses a recurrent cell based on residual dense blocks and a global spatio-temporal attention module. The above works have achieved considerable success, but are still insufficient to deal with fast motion and large displacement. In this work, we alternatively use deformable convolution for implicitly temporal alignment.

2.2   Deformable Convolution

[7] first propose deformable convolution, which is originally applied to high-level vision tasks, such as object detection [2] and crowd understanding [14]. By learning an additional offset, deformable convolution has spatial flexibility to obtain information from several locations. Due to its sampling diversity, deformable convolution has been creatively utilized in low-level video restoration. In video super-resolution, [24] first adopt deformable convolution to align frames at the feature level. [30] successfully apply deformable alignment to video denoising. [13] further integrate optical flow into deformable convolution in order to add explicit motion constraints.

However, deformable convolution is rarely explored in video deblurring. [26] propose a pyramid deformable architecture for video super-resolution, and attempt to transfer it into video deblurring without specific designs. Since the offsets are predicted by typical convolution layers in [26], the theoretical receptive field is limited, which may lead to performance drop in occurrence of fast motion and large displacement. In contrast, our work develops a well-designed deblurring framework based on deformable convolution, and proposes a novel dual pyramid alignment module that introduces a larger receptive field.

3 Method

3.1 Overview

Let $I_t \in \mathbb{R}^{H \times W \times C}$ be the t-th blurry video frame and $I_t^s \in \mathbb{R}^{H \times W \times C}$ be the ground-truth sharp frame, where $H \times W$ denotes the frame size, and C refers to channel number. Our goal is to restore the sharp video frame I_t^r from the consecutive $2N + 1$ frames $\{I_i\}_{i=t-N}^{t+N}$. I_t^r should be as similar to I_t^s as possible.

The overall framework is depicted as Fig. 1. It consists of two modules: 1) Dual pyramid alignment module that aligns neighboring frames with reference frame. 2) Gradient guided fusion module that reconstructs the sharp frame.

3.2 Dual Pyramid Alignment Module

Motivation: Cascading refinement has been well-established in optical flow estimation and achieves remarkable performance [8,11,22]. In PWC-Net [22], the main principle for optical flow refinement can be summarized as three steps: warping, cost volume computation and optical flow estimation. The PWC-Net first warps features of the target image toward the reference image using the coarse optical flow. Next, a cost volume, which stores the matching costs for associating a pixel with its corresponding pixels, is constructed between features of the reference image and warped features of the target image. Finally, a refined optical flow is estimated based on the cost volume and the coarse optical flow. The cost volume is explicitly computed to indicate errors of coarse estimation.

However, the principle of cascading refinement has not been thoroughly studied in the deformable alignment, which serves as another important alignment method in video restoration [26,30]. The EDVR [26] predicts offsets at each pyramid level using several convolution layers. Then, the offsets predicted at higher level will be propagated to lower level, and fused with offsets from lower level. During the whole procedure, refinements are conducted via the fusion of offsets from different levels. However, the offsets of higher level are predicted in relatively larger receptive fields compare to those of lower level, which may lead to inconsistency of offset scales. Therefore, the refinement may fail since offsets in larger scale can not facilitate offset estimation in smaller scale.

In this work, we guarantee equivalent receptive field in different levels so that offset in deeper level can guide offset prediction in lower level. In other words, our framework first detect region with similar structure, then detect area with similar details among that region. More details are described in the following.

Alignment in Feature Pyramid: The alignment module aims to align neighboring frames to reference frame, while pre-deblurring the reference frame. The proposed module constructs a feature pyramid and aligns features in each layer

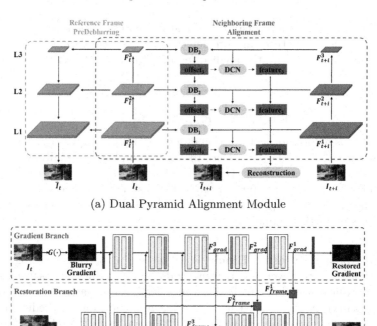

(a) Dual Pyramid Alignment Module

(b) Gradient Guided Fusion Module

Fig. 1. Overall framework of our ERDN method. The dual pyramid alignment module aims to align neighboring frames using deformable convolution in a cascaded manner. The module adopts dilated spatial pyramid blocks (DB) to predict offsets within equivalent receptive fields. A gradient guided fusion module is utilized to restore frame, taking reference frame and aligned neighboring frames as input. For simplicity, we only present the feature pyramid with three layers.

using deformable convolution. As for a deformable convolution kernel with K sample positions, we note the learned offsets for location p as $\Delta P_{t+i}(p)_k$. Then aligned feature F_{t+i}^a can be obtained using deformable convolution:

$$F_{t+i}^a(p) = \sum_{k=1}^{K} \omega_k \cdot F_{t+i}(p + p_k + \Delta P_{t+i}(p)_k) \tag{1}$$

where F_{t+i} represents features extracted from neighboring frame I_{t+i}, while ω_k and p_k represent weight and pre-specified offset respectively. The learned offsets ΔP_{t+i} can be predicted from the features of reference frame F_t and the features of neighboring frame F_{t+i}.

Inspired by [26,30], we align frames in a cascaded manner. As shown in Fig. 1, we use strided convolution with factor 2 to generate F_{t+i}^l at the l-th level, obtaining a four-level pyramid of feature representation. At the l-th level, offsets and aligned features are predicted using the l-th features together with the upsampled offsets and the aligned features from the $(l+1)$-th level:

$$\Delta P_{t+i}^l = DB([F_{t+i}^l, F_t^l], (\Delta P_{t+i}^{l+1})^{\uparrow 2}) \tag{2}$$

$$(F_{t+i}^a)^l = f(DCN(F_{t+i}^l, \Delta P_{t+i}^l), ((F_{t+i}^a)^{l+1})^{\uparrow 2}) \tag{3}$$

where DCN is deformable convolution described in Eq. 1 and f represent several convolution layers, while $(\cdot)^{\uparrow 2}$ refers to $\times 2$ upsampling. Specially, we utilize a dilated spatial pyramid block (DB) to predict offsets for each layer. After cascaded alignment, $(F_{t+i}^a)^1$ is further applied into several residual blocks to reconstruct aligned frame $\bar{I}_{t+i}$, while a decoder is used to restore reference frame to obtain pre-deblurring frame $\bar{I}_t$.

Dilated Spatial Pyramid Block: A vital step in the cascaded alignment is offset refinement. However, previous methods [26,30] predict offsets using several convolution layers at different levels, which leads to inconsistency of receptive fields, as shown in Fig. 2 (a). Due to the inconsistency, offsets predicted at the higher level may exceed receptive field at the lower level, so that the offsets will not be refined at lower levels.

A simple solution is to replace typical convolution with dilation convolution for offset prediction, making each level to have equivalent receptive field. However, for a pixel p in a dilated convolution layer, the information that contributes to pixel p comes from a nearby $k_d \times k_d$ region centered at p. Since dilated convolution introduces zeros in the convolution kernel, the actual pixels that participate in the computation from the $k_d \times k_d$ region are just $k \times k$. As a result, pixel p can only view information from limited location which can be irrelevant across large distances, and lose a large portion of information.

To overcome the previous issue, we propose a dilated spatial pyramid block, which concatenates several convolution layers with different dilation rates.

A dilated layer is defined as follows:

$$C_i(F) = DConv_d(Conv_k(F)) \tag{4}$$

where $DConv_d$ represents dilated convolution with dilation rate d and kernel size 3×3, and $Conv_k$ represents typical convolution with kernel size $k \times k$.

In this work, we adopt 3×3 convolution layers with stride 2 for downsampling. Therefore, a $k \times k$ theoretical receptive field at the l-th level correspond to $(2k+2) \times (2k+2)$ theoretical receptive field at the $(l-1)$-th level. In practice, we use receptive field with size $(2k+3) \times (2k+3)$. Therefore, we set d and k in Eq. 4 as $d = k = 2^i - 1$, where the theoretical receptive field is $(2^{i+1} + 2^i - 3) \times (2^{i+1} + 2^i - 3)$.

At l-th level of a N-layer feature pyramid, the dilated spatial pyramid block is built as:

$$DB_l(F, \Delta P) = f([Conv_1([C_1(F), \cdots, C_{N-l+1}(F)]), \Delta P]) \tag{5}$$

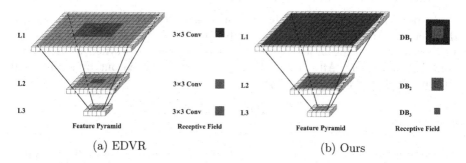

Fig. 2. EDVR predicts offsets using 3×3 convolution at every scales, which will lead to inconsistency of receptive fields due to downsample operation as shown in (a). The proposed method introduces dilated spatial pyramid blocks, which guarantees predicting offsets within equivalent receptive field. The dilated spatial pyramid block constructs a receptive field spatial pyramid as shown in (b). The receptive fields of DB_3, DB_2 and DB_1 are 3×3, 9×9 and 21×21 respectively.

where f represents several convolution layers and $[\cdot]$ represents concatenation.

Similar to ASPP [4] and RFB [15], the dilated spatial pyramid block makes use of multi-branch pooling with varying kernels corresponding to receptive fields of different sizes. Specially, the proposed dilated spatial pyramid block (DB) compensates inconsistency of receptive field, as shown in Fig. 2 (b).

3.3   Gradient Guided Fusion Module

The target of the fusion network is to restore sharp frame from the aligned neighboring frames and the pre-deblurred reference frame. Inspired by [16], we introduce a simple but effective gradient branch, which is to translate gradient maps from the blurry modality to the sharp one. The gradient map for an image I is obtained by computing the difference between adjacent pixels:

$$G_x(\mathbf{x}) = I(x+1, y) - I(x-1, y)$$
$$G_y(\mathbf{x}) = I(x, y+1) - I(x, y-1)$$
$$G(I) = \sqrt{G_x^2 + G_y^2} \tag{6}$$

where $G(\cdot)$ stands for the operation to extract gradient map for pixels with coordinates $\mathbf{x} = (x, y)$. As shown in Fig. 1, the proposed module first extracts gradient map from reference frame, which is applied to gradient branch. The gradient branch incorporates several intermediate features from the restoration branch, because the restoration branch carries structure information which is beneficial to the restoration of gradient maps. Then, several spatial feature transform layers are utilized to effectively incorporate structure priors, which can implicitly reflect whether a region should be sharp or smooth. Specially, the gradient information is integrated in different scales, taking into account both structure information at high level and detailed texture information at low level.

In our task, both gradient branch and restoration branch adopt encoder-decoder structures. In each scale, we integrate gradient features $\boldsymbol{F}_{grad}$ using a pair of affine transformation parameters (α, β), which is learned using several convolutional layers. After that, the modulation is carried out by scaling and shifting the frame feature $\boldsymbol{F}_{frame}$:

$$\alpha, \ \beta = f_1(\boldsymbol{F}_{grad}), \ f_2(\boldsymbol{F}_{grad})$$
$$\boldsymbol{F}_{output} = SFT(\boldsymbol{F}_{frame}|\alpha, \beta) = \alpha \odot \boldsymbol{F}_{frame} + \beta \tag{7}$$

Although gradient branch has been used in [16], the original gradient map in video deblurring is more difficult to be reconstructed due to the blur structure. The proposed gradient branch has a more effective structure, which performs feature fusion at three scales, taking into account local texture information and global structural information, and adopts SFT for feature fusion.

3.4 Training Strategy

Cascaded Training: Following [18] and [12], we train the proposed method using a cascaded strategy. At stage n, we restore the frame $I_{t,n}^r$ from three consecutive frames $\{I_{i,n-1}^r\}_{i=t-1}^{t+1}$, which are the outputs of stage $n-1$. In particular, the proposed method takes $\{I_i\}_{i=t-1}^{t+1}$ and outputs $I_{t,1}^r$ for the first stage. Therefore, a N stage training strategy will take $2N+1$ blurry frames as input.

Then, the overall loss function $L_{overall}$ for N stage strategy can be formulated as follows:

$$L_{overall} = \sum_{n=1}^{N} \sum_{i=t-N+n}^{t+N-n} L_{stage}(\{I_{j,n-1}^r\}_{j=i-1}^{i+1}, I_i^s) \tag{8}$$

where L_{stage} represents loss function for recovering center frames from three consecutive frames and the final restoration result is $I_{t,N}^r$.

In this work, we use five consecutive frames for restoration with two stages as the trade-off between efficiency and performance. Then the overall loss function can be specified as:

$$L_{overall} = \sum_{i=t-1}^{t+1} L_{stage}(\{I_j\}_{j=i-1}^{i+1}, I_i^s) + L_{stage}(\{I_{j,1}^r\}_{j=t-1}^{t+1}, I_t^s) \tag{9}$$

Loss Functions: The training objective L_{stage} consists of reconstruction loss L_{rec}, alignment loss L_{align} and gradient loss L_{grad}.

We adopt the widely-used L1 loss as our reconstruction loss, defined as follows:

$$L_{rec} = \|I_t^r - I_t^s\|_1 \tag{10}$$

To stabilize the training of dual pyramid alignment module, we add an additional alignment loss:

$$L_{align} = \frac{1}{2N+1} \sum_{i=t-1}^{t+1} \|\bar{I}_i - I_i^s\|_1 \tag{11}$$

Specially, we argue that the alignment module is used to align neighboring frames with sharp target frame rather than blurry reference counterpart.

We further design a gradient loss to penalize the difference between reconstructed gradient map and gradient map of sharp frame:

$$L_{grad} = \|G_t - G(I_t^s)\|_1 \qquad (12)$$

where G_t represents recovered gradient maps by gradient branch. The overall objective is defined as follows:

$$L_{stage} = L_{rec} + L_{grad} + \lambda L_{align} \qquad (13)$$

where λ represents weight of alignment loss.

4 Experiments

4.1 Implementation Details

Datasets and Evaluation Metrics: Following previous deblurring method [12,18,32], we adopt Peak Signal-to-Noise Ratio (PSNR) and Structural Similarity (SSIM) as the evaluation metrics. We evaluate the proposed method DVD [21], GOPRO [17] and HFR-DVD [12]. We provide a brief introduction here.

- *DVD* contains 71 videos (6,708 pairs) captured at 240 fps, splitting into 61 training videos (5708 pairs) and 10 testing videos (1000 pairs).
- *GOPRO* is composed of 33 videos (3214 frame pairs) captured at 240 fps, of which 22 videos (2103 pairs) are used for training and 11 videos (1111 pairs) are used for testing.
- *HFR* contains 120 videos for training and 30 videos for testing, each with 90 frames. It is a newly released dataset that captures videos at 1000 fps.

Training Details: As for the trade-off between performance and efficiency, we use a four-layer feature pyramid in the dual pyramid alignment module. We apply patches of size 256×256 for training, while adopting flip and rotation as data augmentation. Our method is implemented on Pytorch [19]. We set the training rate as 1×10^{-4} and reduce it to half every 200 epochs.

4.2 Comparisons with the State-of-the-Art

Quantitative Comparison: We compare our method quantitatively with previous video deblurring methods including EDVR [26], STFAN [32], CDVD-TSP [18] and ARVo [12]. Results of PSNR and SSIM values are presented in Table 1. In each row, the best result is highlighted in red while the second best is in blue. In all datasets, our proposed method achieves the best performance using five frames, while achieving the second best performance in most metrics using three frames. In comparison with the CDVD-TSP and ARVo on the

Table 1. Quantitative comparison with state-of-the-art methods. The best performance is denoted in red, while second best performance in blue.

Dataset	Metric	EDVR [26] (7 Frames)	STFAN [32] (2 Frames)	TSP [18] (5 Frames)	ARVo [12] (5 Frames)	Ours (3 Frames)	**Ours** **(5 Frames)**
DVD	PSNR	28.51	31.15	32.13	32.80	32.91	33.31
	SSIM	0.8637	0.9049	0.9268	0.9352	0.9334	0.9395
GOPRO	PSNR	26.83	28.59	31.67	–	32.20	32.48
	SSIM	0.8426	0.8608	0.9279	–	0.9288	0.9329
HFR	PSNR	29.15	28.48	29.71	31.15	32.01	32.14
	SSIM	0.8733	0.8560	0.8822	0.9063	0.9156	0.9173

(a) Blurry Input   (b) EDVR [26]   (c) TSP [18]   (d) Ours   (e) GT

Fig. 3. Qualitative comparisons on the DVD-HFR dataset [12].

(a) Blurry Input   (b) EDVR [26]   (c) TSP [18]   (d) Ours   (e) GT

Fig. 4. Qualitative comparisons on the GOPRO dataset [17].

DVD dataset, the ERDN yields significant improvements with 1.18 dB and 0.51 dB increases in the PSNR, respectively. On the GOPRO dataset, our ERDN achieves a 1.17 dB improvement in the PSNR and a tiny margin of improvement in the SSIM. Notably, compared with the ARVo on both the PSNR and SSIM metrics, the ERDN achieves considerable improvements of 0.99 dB and 0.011 on the HFR dataset, respectively. The results demonstrate that the ERDN has superior robustness.

Specifically, the EDVR is originally designed for video super-resolution and transferred to video deblurring without specific design. The method first applies downsampling to the input frames, which will lead to significant information loss. The TSP aligns frames using optical flow at the image level, which is less effective in occurrence of fast object motions. The ARVo learns spatial correspondence between pixel pairs as a complement to optical flow-based alignment. However, artifacts caused by inaccurate flow will affect the performance of the whole model. In contrast, our model adopts deformable convolution for better alignment at the feature level without estimating optical flow. With the well-designed dual pyramid alignment module, the proposed model can predict offsets in a larger receptive field, which is effective to handle large displacement.

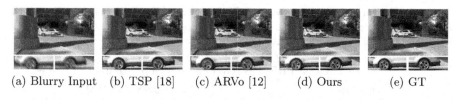

(a) Blurry Input   (b) TSP [18]   (c) ARVo [12]   (d) Ours   (e) GT

Fig. 5. Qualitative comparisons on the DVD dataset [21].

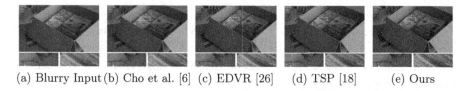

(a) Blurry Input (b) Cho et al. [6] (c) EDVR [26]   (d) TSP [18]   (e) Ours

Fig. 6. Qualitative comparisons on the real blurry frames from [6].

(a) Frame 1   (b) Frame 2   (c) Frame 3   (d) Frame 3   (e) Frame 4

Fig. 7. Qualitative comparisons on consecutive frames from DVD dataset [21].

Qualitative Comparison: We also conduct visual comparison on the three datasets, as shown in Figs. 3, 4 and 5. We observe that previous methods generate obvious artifacts and suffer from incomplete deblurring. In contrast, the proposed method is capable to restore clearer frames. Specially, since the HFR dataset [12] exhibits more fast motions, our method outperforms previous methods more significantly, which exhibits the strength of handling fast motions.

To further evaluate the effectiveness of our proposed method, we conduct experiment on the real video deblurring dataset released by [6]. As shown in Fig. 6, our method restores better detailed structure with sharper outlines, which demonstrates promising generalization ability to handle real-world blurry videos.

As the temporal consistency property is very important for video deblurring, we also present deblurring results on a series of consecutive frames as shown in Fig. 7. It is obvious that inconsistent bands and artifacts appear near edges in TSP [18], while our proposed method demonstrates better consistency.

Table 2. Network ablation analysis on DVD dataset [21]. DCN, ERF, DB and GB represent deformable convolution, equivalent receptive field, dilated spatial pyramid block and gradient branch respectively.

	DCN	ERF	DB	GB	PSNR	SSIM	Param
Baseline					32.13	0.9268	16.19M
Net-1	✓				32.82	0.9328	16.33M
Net-2	✓	✓			33.02	0.9359	16.33M
Net-3	✓	✓	✓		33.17	0.9378	17.54M
Net-4	✓	✓	✓	✓	**33.31**	**0.9395**	**22.84M**

Table 3. Effects of using different layers of feature pyramids on the video deblurring result. The final setting is highlighted.

Layers	1	2	3	4	5
PSNR	31.89	32.41	33.05	**33.31**	33.20
SSIM	0.9168	0.9256	0.9359	**0.9395**	0.9382

4.3 Ablation Studies

We conduct more experiments on different models to validate the necessity of each part in our proposed framework. Since we adopt the architecture of CDVD-TSP [18], we use it as the baseline model. The Net-1 replaces the optical flow estimation module with deformable convolution architecture similar to EDVR [26]. Compared to the Net-1, the Net-2 replaces typical convolution with dilated convolution without increasing parameters. The Net-3 adopts dilated spatial pyramid block instead of a single dilation convolution layer. The Net-4 further incorporates gradient branch. Quantitative comparison is presented in Table 2.

Effects of the Dual Pyramid Alignment Module: As shown in Table 2, the replacement of flow-based alignment with deformable alignment significantly improves deblurring performance, which reveals the effectiveness of deformable convolution for alignment in video deblurring. Furthermore, we enlarge receptive field with dilated convolution at low level, achieving an improvement of 0.2 dB without any extra parameters. The improvement of performance straightly demonstrates that refinement of offsets can be conducted more effectively within equivalent receptive field. With our proposed dilated spatial pyramid block, the Net-3 is nearly 0.2 dB better than the Net-2, since features in the receptive field is better explored compared to a single dilated convolution layer.

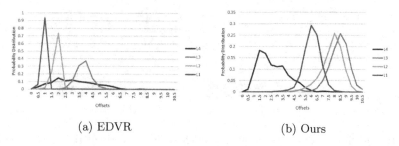

(a) EDVR (b) Ours

Fig. 8. Quantitative comparison of the offset distribution on video with fast motion. L1, L2, L3 and L4 represent offsets predicted at different feature pyramid levels, denoted the same as Fig. 1. Both the proposed method and EDVR predict offsets in a cascaded manner. Due to the inconsistency of receptive field, EDVR fails to refine offsets as shown in (a), while offsets in lower level are significantly smaller than those at higher level. Our method otherwise holds comparable offsets for each level.

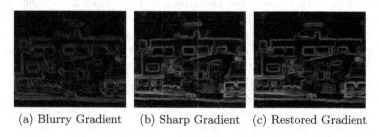

(a) Blurry Gradient (b) Sharp Gradient (c) Restored Gradient

Fig. 9. Visualization of gradient maps. The sharp gradient map has larger intensity than the blurry counterparts. Our gradient branch is capable to recover gradient map with pleasant structures.

We further analyse the offsets using different methods quantitatively in Fig. 8. In EDVR, offsets predicted at different layers have different scales obviously, which reveals the failure of offset refinement when processing video with fast motion. In contrast, our method holds comparable offset scale and samples in a significant larger region at $L1$ layer. The major difference is that previous method predicts offsets with several convolution layers, while our method adopts dilated spatial pyramid block with larger receptive field at lower level.

We propose to construct a feature pyramid for alignment at different scales. To analyze the effect, we conduct experiments with different numbers of pyramid layers. As shown in Table 3, we observe that the restoration quality achieves improvement by adding pyramid layers. This is because enlarging receptive field helps to capture large displacement. However, we notice a little performance drop when using pyramid with five layers. This probably implies that the receptive field is too large to capture useful information.

(a) w/o GB   (b) GB

Fig. 10. Qualitative comparison of the models with and without the gradient branch. Frame restored by the model with gradient branch is clearer with detailed structures.

Effects of the Gradient Branch: As shown in Table 2, the model with gradient branch achieves better results. This is because the gradient branch incorporates structure priors into restoration process as an implicitly guidance.

In order to further reveal the effectiveness of the gradient branch, we visualize the gradient maps in Fig. 9. The gradient map extracted from the blurry frame commonly have thick outlines, while the gradient map from the sharp counterpart have clear outlines and larger intensity. From the output gradient map in Fig. 9, we can see that the proposed gradient branch successfully recover gradient map similar to the sharp gradient map.

Moreover, the restoration results are shown in Fig. 10. The boundaries restored by the complete model are more sharper than those recovered by the model without gradient branch. The change of detailed textures reveals that the gradient branch can help preserve structure.

5   Conclusion

In this paper, we propose an effective model for video deblurring using deformable alignment. The model develops a novel dual pyramid alignment module, which constructs a feature pyramid to align frames using deformable convolution in a coarse-to-fine manner. Based on the feature pyramid, we further incorporate dilated spatial pyramid blocks to predict offsets within equivalent receptive fields for every feature pyramid layers, which guarantee temporal compensatory information can be sampled in a large region from the neighboring frames. To restore sharp frame, we introduce a gradient guided fusion module providing implicit structure guidance to alleviate geometric distortion. The proposed model has shown its effectiveness and outperforms previous state-of-the-art methods on several benchmarks.

References

1. Bar, L., Berkels, B., Rumpf, M., Sapiro, G.: A variational framework for simultaneous motion estimation and restoration of motion-blurred video. In: 2007 IEEE 11th International Conference on Computer Vision. IEEE, pp. 1–8 (2007)

2. Bertasius, G., Torresani, L., Shi, J.: Object detection in video with spatiotemporal sampling networks. In: Proceedings of the European Conference on Computer Vision. ECCV, pp. 331–346 (2018)

3. Chan, K.C., Wang, X., Yu, K., Dong, C., Loy, C.C.: Understanding deformable alignment in video super-resolution. In: Proceedings of the AAAI Conference on Artificial Intelligence **35**, 973–981 (2021)

4. Chen, L.C., Papandreou, G., Schroff, F., Adam, H.: Rethinking atrous convolution for semantic image segmentation. arXiv preprint arXiv:1706.05587 (2017)

5. Cho, K., et al.: Learning phrase representations using rnn encoder-decoder for statistical machine translation. arXiv preprint arXiv:1406.1078 (2014)

6. Cho, S., Wang, J., Lee, S.: Video deblurring for hand-held cameras using patch-based synthesis. ACM Transactions on Graphics (TOG) **31**(4), 1–9 (2012)

7. Dai, J., et al:. Deformable convolutional networks. In: Proceedings of the IEEE International Conference on Computer Vision, pp. 764–773 (2017)

8. Hui, T.W., Tang, X., Loy, C.C.: Liteflownet: A lightweight convolutional neural network for optical flow estimation. In: Proceedings of the IEEE Conference on Computer Vision and Pattern Recognition, pp. 8981–8989 (2018)

9. Hyun Kim, T., Mu Lee, K.: Generalized video deblurring for dynamic scenes. In: Proceedings of the IEEE Conference on Computer Vision and Pattern Recognition, pp. 5426–5434 (2015)

10. Hyun Kim, T., Mu Lee, K., Scholkopf, B., Hirsch, M.: Online video deblurring via dynamic temporal blending network. In: Proceedings of the IEEE International Conference on Computer Vision, pp. 4038–4047 (2017)

11. Ilg, E., Mayer, N., Saikia, T., Keuper, M., Dosovitskiy, A., Brox, T.: Flownet 2.0: Evolution of optical flow estimation with deep networks. In: Proceedings of the IEEE Conference on Computer Vision and Pattern Recognition, pp. 2462–2470 (2017)

12. Li, D., et al.: Learning all-range volumetric correspondence for video deblurring. In: Proceedings of the IEEE Conference on Computer Vision and Pattern Recognition, pp. 7721–7731 (2021)

13. Lin, J., Huang, Y., Wang, L.: Fdan: Flow-guided deformable alignment network for video super-resolution. arXiv preprint arXiv:2105.05640 (2021)

14. Liu, N., Long, Y., Zou, C., Niu, Q., Pan, L., Wu, H.: Adcrowdnet: An attention-injective deformable convolutional network for crowd understanding. In: Proceedings of the IEEE Conference on Computer Vision and Pattern Recognition, pp. 3225–3234 (2019)

15. Liu, S., Huang, D., et al.: Receptive field block net for accurate and fast object detection. In: Proceedings of the European Conference on Computer Vision (ECCV), pp. 385–400 (2018)

16. Ma, C., Rao, Y., Cheng, Y., Chen, C., Lu, J., Zhou, J.: Structure-preserving super resolution with gradient guidance. In: Proceedings of the IEEE Conference on Computer Vision and Pattern Recognition, pp. 7769–7778 (2020)

17. Nah, S., Hyun Kim, T., Mu Lee, K.: Deep multi-scale convolutional neural network for dynamic scene deblurring. In: Proceedings of the IEEE Conference on Computer Vision and Pattern Recognition, pp. 3883–3891 (2017)

18. Pan, J., Bai, H., Tang, J.: Cascaded deep video deblurring using temporal sharpness prior. In: Proceedings of the IEEE Conference on Computer Vision and Pattern Recognition, pp. 3043–3051 (2020)

19. Paszke, A., et al.: Automatic differentiation in pytorch (2017)

20. Ren, W., Pan, J., Cao, X., Yang, M.H.: Video deblurring via semantic segmentation and pixel-wise non-linear kernel. In: Proceedings of the IEEE International Conference on Computer Vision, pp. 1077–1085 (2017)
21. Su, S., Delbracio, M., Wang, J., Sapiro, G., Heidrich, W., Wang, O.: Deep video deblurring for hand-held cameras. In: Proceedings of the IEEE Conference on Computer Vision and Pattern Recognition, pp. 1279–1288 (2017)
22. Sun, D., Yang, X., Liu, M.Y., Kautz, J.: Pwc-net: Cnns for optical flow using pyramid, warping, and cost volume. In: Proceedings of the IEEE Conference on Computer Vision and Pattern Recognition, pp. 8934–8943 (2018)
23. Sutskever, I., Vinyals, O., Le, Q.V.: Sequence to sequence learning with neural networks. In: Advances in Neural Information Processing Systems, pp. 3104–3112 (2014)
24. Tian, Y., Zhang, Y., Fu, Y., Xu, C.: Tdan: Temporally-deformable alignment network for video super-resolution. In: Proceedings of the IEEE Conference on Computer Vision and Pattern Recognition, pp. 3360–3369 (2020)
25. Wang, X., Yu, K., Dong, C., Loy, C.C.: Recovering realistic texture in image super-resolution by deep spatial feature transform. In: Proceedings of the IEEE Conference on Computer Vision and Pattern Recognition, pp. 606–615 (2018)
26. Wang, X., Chan, K.C., Yu, K., Dong, C., Change Loy, C.: Edvr: Video restoration with enhanced deformable convolutional networks. In: Proceedings of the IEEE/CVF Conference on Computer Vision and Pattern Recognition Workshops, pp. 0–0 (2019)
27. Wieschollek, P., Hirsch, M., Scholkopf, B., Lensch, H.: Learning blind motion deblurring. In: Proceedings of the IEEE International Conference on Computer Vision, pp. 231–240 (2017)
28. Wulff, J., Black, M.J.: Modeling Blurred Video with Layers. In: Fleet, D., Pajdla, T., Schiele, B., Tuytelaars, T. (eds.) ECCV 2014. LNCS, vol. 8694, pp. 236–252. Springer, Cham (2014). https://doi.org/10.1007/978-3-319-10599-4_16
29. Xiang, X., Wei, H., Pan, J.: Deep video deblurring using sharpness features from exemplars. IEEE Transactions on Image Processing **29**, 8976–8987 (2020)
30. Yue, H., Cao, C., Liao, L., Chu, R., Yang, J.: Supervised raw video denoising with a benchmark dataset on dynamic scenes. In: Proceedings of the IEEE Conference on Computer Vision and Pattern Recognition, pp. 2301–2310 (2020)
31. Zhong, Z., Gao, Y., Zheng, Y., Zheng, B.: Efficient Spatio-Temporal Recurrent Neural Network for Video Deblurring. In: Vedaldi, A., Bischof, H., Brox, T., Frahm, J.-M. (eds.) ECCV 2020. LNCS, vol. 12351, pp. 191–207. Springer, Cham (2020). https://doi.org/10.1007/978-3-030-58539-6_12
32. Zhou, S., Zhang, J., Pan, J., Xie, H., Zuo, W., Ren, J.: Spatio-temporal filter adaptive network for video deblurring. In: Proceedings of the IEEE International Conference on Computer Vision, pp. 2482–2491 (2019)

Rethinking Generic Camera Models for Deep Single Image Camera Calibration to Recover Rotation and Fisheye Distortion

Nobuhiko Wakai[1]([✉]) [iD], Satoshi Sato[1] [iD], Yasunori Ishii[1] [iD],
and Takayoshi Yamashita[2] [iD]

[1] Panasonic Holdings, Osaka, Japan
{wakai.nobuhiko,sato.satoshi,ishii.yasunori}@jp.panasonic.com
[2] Chubu University, Aichi, Japan
{takayoshi@isc.chubu.ac.jp}

Abstract. Although recent learning-based calibration methods can predict extrinsic and intrinsic camera parameters from a single image, the accuracy of these methods is degraded in fisheye images. This degradation is caused by mismatching between the actual projection and expected projection. To address this problem, we propose a generic camera model that has the potential to address various types of distortion. Our generic camera model is utilized for learning-based methods through a closed-form numerical calculation of the camera projection. Simultaneously to recover rotation and fisheye distortion, we propose a learning-based calibration method that uses the camera model. Furthermore, we propose a loss function that alleviates the bias of the magnitude of errors for four extrinsic and intrinsic camera parameters. Extensive experiments demonstrated that our proposed method outperformed conventional methods on two large-scale datasets and images captured by off-the-shelf fisheye cameras. Moreover, we are the first researchers to analyze the performance of learning-based methods using various types of projection for off-the-shelf cameras.

Keywords: Camera calibration · Fisheye camera · Rectification

1 Introduction

Learning-based perception methods are widely used for surveillance, cars, drones, and robots. These methods are well established for many computer vision tasks. Most computer vision tasks require undistorted images; however, fisheye images have the superiority of a large field of view (FOV) in visual surveillance [18], object detection [51], pose estimation [11], and semantic segmentation [41]. To

---

Supplementary Information The online version contains supplementary material available at https://doi.org/10.1007/978-3-031-19797-0_39.

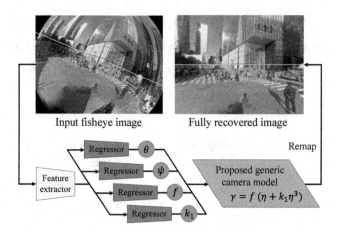

Fig. 1. Concept illustrations of our work. Our network predicts parameters in our proposed generic camera model to obtain fully recovered images using remapping. Red lines indicate horizontal lines in each of the images, for which we used [46] (Color figure online).

use fisheye cameras by removing distortion, camera calibration is a desirable step before perception. Camera calibration is a long-studied topic in areas of computer vision, such as image undistortion [37,66], image remapping [60], virtual object insertion [24], augmented reality [3], and stereo measurement [43]. In camera calibration, we cannot escape the trade-off between accuracy and usability that we need a calibration object; hence, tackling the trade-off has been an open challenge, which we explain further in the following.

Calibration methods are classified into two categories: geometric-based and learning-based methods. Geometric-based calibration methods achieve high accuracy but require a calibration object, such as a cube [59] or a plane [68], to obtain a strong geometric constraint. By contrast, learning-based methods can calibrate cameras without a calibration object from a general scene image [8,13,34,37,45,60,66], which is called deep single image camera calibration. Although learning-based methods do not require a calibration object, the accuracy of these methods is degraded for fisheye images because of the mismatch between the actual projection and expected projection in conventional methods. In particular, calibration methods [45,60] that predict both camera rotation and distortion have much room for improvement regarding addressing complex fisheye distortion. López-Antequera's method [45] was designed for non-fisheye cameras with radial distortion and cannot process fisheye distortion. Although four standard camera models are used for fisheye cameras, Wakai's method [60] supports only one fisheye camera model.

Based on the observations above, we propose a new generic camera model for various fisheye cameras. The proposed generic camera model has the potential to address various types of distortion. For the generic camera model, we propose a learning-based calibration method that predicts extrinsic parameters (tilt and roll angles), focal length, and a distortion coefficient simultaneously from a single image, as shown in Fig. 1. Our camera model is utilized for learning-based methods through a closed-form numerical calculation of camera projection. To improve the prediction accuracy, we use a joint loss function composed of each loss for the four camera parameters. Unlike heuristic approaches in conventional methods, our loss function makes considerable progress; that is, we can determine the optimal joint weights based on the magnitude of errors for these camera parameters instead of the heuristic approaches.

To evaluate the proposed method, we conducted extensive experiments on two large-scale datasets [12, 46] and images captured by off-the-shelf fisheye cameras. This evaluation demonstrated that our method meaningfully outperformed nine conventional geometric-based [2, 55] and learning-based [8, 13, 34, 37, 45, 60, 66] methods. The major contributions of our study are summarized as follows:

– We propose a learning-based calibration method for recovering camera rotation and fisheye distortion using the proposed generic camera model that has an adaptive ability for off-the-shelf fisheye cameras. To the best of our knowledge, we are the first researchers to calibrate extrinsic and intrinsic parameters of generic camera models addressing various types of projection in off-the-shelf fisheye cameras from a single image.
– We propose a new loss function that alleviates the bias of the magnitude of errors between the ground-truth and predicted camera parameters for four extrinsic and intrinsic parameters to obtain accurate camera parameters.
– We first analyze the performance of learning-based methods using off-the-shelf fisheye cameras consisting of four types of fisheye projection: stereographic projection, equidistance projection, equisolid angle projection, and orthogonal projection.

2   Related Work

Camera Calibration: Camera calibration estimates parameters composed of extrinsic parameters (rotation and translation) and intrinsic parameters (image sensor and distortion parameters). Geometric-based calibration methods have been developed using a strong constraint based on a calibration object [59,68], line detection [2,7,10,19,55,67], or vanishing points [44,49]. This constraint explicitly represents the relation between world coordinates and image coordinates to achieve stable calibration optimization. By contrast, learning-based methods using convolutional neural networks calibrate cameras from a single image in the wild. In this study, we focus on learning-based calibration methods and describe them below.

Calibration methods for only extrinsic parameters have been proposed that are aimed at narrow view cameras [27,48,56,57,62,63] and panoramic 360° images [16]. These methods cannot calibrate intrinsic parameters; that is, they cannot remove distortion. For extrinsic parameters and focal length, narrow-view camera calibration was developed with depth estimation [14,22] and room layout [52]. These methods are not suitable for fisheye cameras with over 180° FOV because fisheye distortion is not negligible.

Calibration methods for only undistortion have been proposed using regressors or generators. These regressors predicted camera parameters of polynomial models [35], division distortion models [25, 39, 53], unified spherical models [8], or generic camera models using fisheye projection [36, 64, 66]. These camera models have room for improvement in learning-based methods because the models were originally designed for geometric-based calibration methods. By contrast, the generators predicted undistorted images using multi-scale information [65] or discriminators [13, 38] in generative adversarial networks (GAN) [20]. Only undistortion methods cannot recover camera rotation.

To calibrate both extrinsic and intrinsic parameters, López-Antequera *et al.* [45] proposed a pioneering method for non-fisheye cameras. This method estimated distortion using a polynomial function model of perspective projection similar to Brown's quartic polynomial model [9]. This polynomial function against the distance from a principal point has two coefficients for the second- and fourth-order terms. The method is only trainable for the second-order coefficient, and the fourth-order coefficient is calculated using a quadratic function of the second-order one. This method does not calibrate fisheye cameras effectively because the camera model does not represent fisheye camera projection. Additionally, Wakai *et al.* [60] proposed a calibration method for extrinsic parameters and focal length in fisheye cameras. Although four types of standard fisheye projection are used for camera models, for example, equisolid angle projection, Wakai's method [60] only expects equisolid angle projection. Li *et al.* [34] proposed image transformation for rotation and distortion. Images with rotation and distortion degrade accuracy because this method needs to employ rotation and distortion transformation separately. As discussed above, conventional learning-based calibration methods do not fully calibrate extrinsic and intrinsic parameters of generic camera models from a single image.

Exploring Loss Landscapes: To optimize networks effectively, loss landscapes have been explored after training [15, 21, 33] and during training [23]. In learning-based calibration methods, we have the problem that joint weights are difficult to determine before training. The joint loss function was often defined to stabilize training or to merge heterogeneous loss components [37, 45, 60, 66]. However, these joint weights were defined using experiments or the same values, that is, unweighted joints. These joint weights are hyperparameters that depend on networks and datasets. A hyperparameter search method was proposed by Akiba *et al.* [1]. However, hyperparameter search tools require high computational costs because they execute various conditions. Additionally, to analyze optimizers, Goodfellow *et al.* [21] proposed an examination method for loss landscapes using linear interpolation from the initial network weights to the final weights. To overcome the saddle points of loss landscapes, Dauphin *et al.* [15] proposed an optimization method based on Newton's method. Furthermore, Li *et al.* [33] developed an approach for visualizing loss landscapes. Although these methods can explore high-order loss landscapes, the optimal values of joint loss weights have not been determined in learning-based calibration methods. Moreover, the aforementioned methods cannot explore loss landscapes before training because they require training results.

3   Proposed Method

First, we describe our proposed camera model based on a closed-form solution for various fisheye cameras. Second, we explain our learning-based calibration method for recovering rotation and fisheye distortion. Finally, we introduce a new loss function, with its notation and mechanism.

3.1   Generic Camera Model

Camera models are composed of extrinsic parameters [$\mathbf{R} \mid \mathbf{t}$] and intrinsic parameters, and these camera models represent the mapping from world coordinates $\tilde{\mathbf{p}}$ to image coordinates $\tilde{\mathbf{u}}$ in homogeneous coordinates. This projection can be expressed for radial distortion of perspective projection [6,9,17,50] and fisheye projection [5,30,58] as

$$\tilde{\mathbf{u}} = \begin{bmatrix} \gamma/d_u & 0 & c_u \\ 0 & \gamma/d_v & c_v \\ 0 & 0 & 1 \end{bmatrix} [\ \mathbf{R} \mid \mathbf{t}\ ]\,\tilde{\mathbf{p}}, \tag{1}$$

where γ is distortion, (d_u, d_v) is an image sensor pitch, (c_u, c_v) is a principal point, $\mathbf{R}$ is a rotation matrix, and $\mathbf{t}$ is a translation vector. The subscripts of u and v denote the horizontal and vertical direction, respectively.

The generic camera model including fisheye lenses [30] is defined as

$$\gamma = \tilde{k}_1\eta + \tilde{k}_2\eta^3 + \cdots, \tag{2}$$

where $\tilde{k}_1, \tilde{k}_2, \ldots$ are distortion coefficients and η is an incident angle. Note that the focal length is not defined explicitly; that is, the focal length is set to 1 mm, and the distortion coefficients represent distortion and implicit focal length.

3.2   Proposed Camera Model

Many off-the-shelf fisheye cameras have 180° FOV and more. To calibrate them, camera models need to support over 180° FOV; that is, the models require fisheye projection defined by a distortion function against η. In accordance with the FOV range, we select fisheye projection rather than perspective projection for our camera model. A generic camera model with high order has the potential to achieve high calibration accuracy. However, this high-order function leads to unstable optimization, particularly for learning-based methods. Considering this problem, we propose a generic camera model for learning-based fisheye calibration using explicit focal length, given by

$$\gamma = f(\eta + k_1\eta^3), \tag{3}$$

where f is the focal length and k_1 is a distortion coefficient.

Table 1. Comparison of absolute errors in fisheye camera models.

Reference model[1]	Mean absolute error [pixel]			
	STG	EQD	ESA	ORT
Stereographic (STG)	–	9.33	13.12	93.75
Equidistance (EQD)	9.33	–	3.79	23.58
Equisolid angle (ESA)	13.12	3.79	–	14.25
Orthogonal (ORT)	93.75	23.58	14.25	–
Unified spherical model [5]	0.71	0.19	0.00	0.51
Proposed generic model	**0.54**	**0.00**	**0.02**	**0.35**

[1] Each reference model is compared with other fisheye models

Evaluating our Camera Model: Our generic camera model is a third-order polynomial function corresponding to the Taylor series expansion of the trigonometric function in fisheye cameras, that is, stereographic projection, equidistance projection, equisolid angle projection, and orthogonal projection. In the following, we show that our model can express trigonometric function models with slight errors.

To evaluate camera models using fisheye projection and a few parameters, we compared the projection function, $\gamma = g(\eta)$, of the four trigonometric function models, the unified spherical model [5], and our generic camera model, as shown in Table 1. All the camera models have two or fewer intrinsic camera parameters for fisheye projection. In this comparison, we calculated the mean absolute errors ϵ between pairs of the projection function g_1 and g_2. We defined the errors as $\epsilon = 1/(\pi/2) \int_0^{\pi/2} |g_1(\eta) - g_2(\eta)| \, d\eta$. These mean absolute errors simply represent mean distance errors in image coordinates. Overall, our model is useful for various fisheye models because our model had small mean absolute errors, as shown in Table 1.

Calculation Easiness: For our generic camera model, it is easy to calculate back-projection, which converts image coordinates to corresponding incident angles. When using back-projection, we must solve the generic camera model against incident angles η in Eq. (3). Practically, we can solve equations on the basis of iterations or closed forms. Non-fisheye cameras often use the iteration approaches [4]. By contrast, we cannot use the iteration approaches for fisheye cameras because large distortion prevents us from obtaining the initial values close to solutions. We, therefore, use a closed-form approach because the Abel-Ruffini theorem [70] shows that fourth-order or less algebraic equations are solvable. Refer to the supplementary material for the details of our model.

3.3   Proposed Calibration Method

To calibrate various fisheye cameras, we propose a learning-based calibration method that uses our generic camera model. We use DenseNet-161 [26] pretrained on ImageNet [54] to extract image features and details as follows: First, we convert the image features using global average pooling [40] for regressors. Second, four individual regressors predict the normalized parameters (from 0 to

1) of a tilt angle θ, a roll angle ψ, focal length f, and a distortion coefficient k_1. Each regressor consists of a 2208-channel fully connected (FC) layer with Mish activation [47] and a 256-channel FC layer with sigmoid activation. Batch normalization [29] uses these FC layers. Finally, we predict a camera model by recovering the ranges of the normalized camera parameters to their original ranges. Following conventional studies [24,45,60], we scale the input images to 224×224 pixels.

3.4   Harmonic Non-grid Bearing Loss

Unlike a loss function based on image reconstruction, Wakai *et al.* proposed the non-grid bearing loss function L [60] based on projecting image coordinates to world coordinates as

$$L_\alpha = \frac{1}{n} \sum_{i=1}^{n} \mathrm{Huber}(\|\mathbf{p}_{\alpha i} - \hat{\mathbf{p}}_i\|_2), \tag{4}$$

where n is the number of sampling points; α is a parameter, $\alpha = \{\theta, \psi, f, k_1\}$; $\mathbf{p}_\alpha$ is a projected world coordinate using a predicted parameter α and ground-truth values for the remaining parameters; and $\hat{\mathbf{p}}$ is the ground-truth value of world coordinates $\mathbf{p}_\alpha$. The Huber ($\bullet$) denotes the Huber loss function with $\delta = 1$ [28]. The loss function L_θ uses a predicted θ and ground-truth parameters for ψ, f, and k_1. Additionally, L_ψ, L_f, and L_{k_1} are determined in the same manner. We obtain the world coordinates $\mathbf{p}_\alpha$ from the image coordinates in sampled points. The sampled points are projected from a unit sphere. For sampling on the unit sphere, we use uniform distribution within valid incident angles that depend on k_1. The loss function achieved stable optimization using the unit sphere. The joint loss is defined as

$$L = w_\theta L_\theta + w_\psi L_\psi + w_f L_f + w_{k_1} L_{k_1}, \tag{5}$$

where w_θ, w_ψ, w_f, and w_{k_1} are the joint weights of θ, ψ, f, and k_1, respectively. Although this loss function can effectively train networks, we need to determine the joint weights for each camera parameter. Wakai *et al.* [60] and López-Antequera *et al.* [45] used joint weights set to the same values. To determine the optimal joint weights, they needed to repeat training and validation. However, they did not search for the optimal joint weights because of high computational costs.

To address this problem, we surprisingly found that numerical simulations instead of training can analyze loss landscapes. This loss function can be divided into two steps: predicting camera parameters from an image and projecting sampled points using camera parameters. The latter step requires only the sampled points and camera parameters. Therefore, we focused on the latter step independent of input images. Figure 2 (a) shows the loss landscapes for camera parameters along normalized camera parameters. The landscapes express that the magnitude of loss values of the focal length is the smallest among θ, ψ, f, and k_1, and the focal length is relatively hard to train. Our investigation suggests that the optimal joint loss weights w are estimated as follows: We calculate

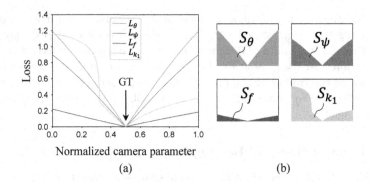

Fig. 2. Difference between the non-grid bearing loss functions [60] for the camera parameters. (a) Each loss landscape along the normalized camera parameters using a predicted camera parameter with a subscript parameter and ground-truth parameters for the remaining parameters, and the ground-truth values are set to 0.5. (b) Areas S calculated using the integral of L with respect to θ, ψ, f, and k_1 from 0 to 1.

areas S under the loss function L for θ, ψ, f, and k_1. Assuming practical conditions, we set the ground-truth values to 0.5, which means that the center of the normalized parameter ranges from 0 to 1 in Fig. 2 (a). This area S is calculated using the integral of L from 0 to 1, as illustrated in Fig. 2 (b) and is given by

$$S_\alpha = \int_0^1 L_\alpha d\alpha = \int_0^1 \frac{1}{n} \sum_{i=1}^n \mathrm{Huber}(||\mathbf{p}_{\alpha i} - \hat{\mathbf{p}}_i||_2)\, d\alpha, \qquad (6)$$

These areas S represent the magnitude of each loss for θ, ψ, f, and k_1. Therefore, we define the joint weights w in Eq. (5) using normalization as follows:

$$w_\alpha = \tilde{w}_\alpha\ /\ W, \qquad (7)$$

where $\tilde{w}_\alpha = 1/S_\alpha$ and $W = \sum_\alpha \tilde{w}_\alpha$. We call a loss function using the weights in Eq. (7) "harmonic non-grid bearing loss (HNGBL)." As stated above, our joint weights can alleviate the bias of the magnitude of the loss for camera parameters. Remarkably, we determine these weights before training.

4   Experiments

To validate the adaptiveness of our method to various types of fisheye cameras, we conducted massive experiments using large-scale synthetic images and off-the-shelf fisheye cameras.

4.1   Datasets

We used two large-scale datasets of outdoor panoramas called the StreetLearn dataset (Manhattan 2019 subset) [46] and the SP360 dataset [12]. First, we

Table 2. Distribution of the camera parameters for our train set.

Parameters	Distribution	Range or values[1]
Pan ϕ	Uniform	[0, 360)
Tilt θ	Mix	Normal 70%, Uniform 30%
	Normal	$\mu = 0, \sigma = 15$
	Uniform	[−90, 90]
Roll ψ	Mix	Normal 70%, Uniform 30%
	Normal	$\mu = 0, \sigma = 15$
	Uniform	[−90, 90]
Aspect ratio	Varying	{1/1 9%, 5/4 1%, 4/3 66%, 3/2 20%, 16/9 4%}
Focal length f	Uniform	[6, 15]
Distortion k_1	Uniform	[−1/6, 1/3]
Max angle η_{max}	Uniform	[84, 96]

[1]Units: ϕ, θ, ψ, and η_{max} [deg]; f [mm]; k_1 [dimensionless]

Table 3. Off-the-shelf fisheye cameras with experimental IDs.

ID	Camera body	Camera lens
1	Canon EOS 6D	Canon EF8-15mm F4L Fisheye USM
2	Canon EOS 6D	Canon EF15mm F2.8 Fisheye
3	Panasonic LUMIX GM1	Panasonic LUMIX G FISHEYE 8mm F3.5
4	FLIR BFLY-U3-23S6C	FIT FI-40
5	FLIR FL3-U3-88S2	FUJIFILM FE185C057HA-1
6	KanDao QooCam8K	Built-in

divided each dataset into train and test sets following in [60]: 55,599 train and 161 test images for StreetLearn, and 19,038 train and 55 test images for SP360. Second, we generated image patches, with 224-pixel image height (H_{img}) and image width ($W_{img} = H_{img} \cdot A$), where A is the image aspect ratio, from panorama images: 555,990 train and 16,100 test image patches for StreetLearn, and 571,140 train and 16,500 test image patches for SP360. Table 2 shows the random distribution of the train set when we generated image patches using camera models with the maximum incident angle η_{max}. The test set was generated using the uniform distribution instead of the mixed and varying distribution applied to the train set. During the generation step, we set the minimum image circle diameter to the image height, assuming practical conditions. Note that each generated camera parameter means the ground-truth parameter. Refer to the supplementary material for the details of the camera parameter ranges.

4.2 Off-the-Shelf Fisheye Cameras

We evaluated off-the-shelf fisheye cameras because fisheye cameras have complex lens distortion, unlike narrow-view cameras. Table 3 shows various fisheye cameras that we used for evaluation. Note that we only used the front camera in the QooCam8K camera, which has front and rear cameras. Using the off-the-shelf cameras, we captured outdoor fisheye images in Kyoto, Japan.

4.3 Parameter and Network Settings

To simplify the camera model, we fixed $d_u = d_v$ and the principal point (c_u, c_v) as the image center following in [45,60]. Because the scale factor depends on the focal length and the image sensor size, which is arbitrary for undistortion, we assumed that the image sensor height was 24 mm, which corresponds to a full-size image sensor. We ignored the arbitrary translation vector **t**. Because the origin of the pan angle is arbitrary, we provided the pan angle for training

Table 4. Feature summarization of the conventional methods and our method.

Method	DL[1]	Rot[1]	Dist[1]	>180° FOV[1]	Projection	Network
Alemán-Flores [2]			✓		Perspective	–
Santana-Cedrés [55]			✓		Perspective	–
Liao [37]	✓		✓		Perspective	Regressor
Yin [66]	✓		✓	✓	Generic camera [30]	Regressor
Chao [13]	✓		✓	–	–	Generator (GAN)
Bogdan [8]	✓		✓	✓	Unified spherical model [5]	Regressor
Li (GeoNetS-$\mathcal{B}$) [34]	✓		✓	–	–	Generator
López-Antequera [45]	✓	✓	✓		Perspective	Regressor
Wakai [60]	✓	✓	✓	✓	Equisolid angle	Regressor
Ours	✓	✓	✓	✓	Proposed generic camera	Regressor

[1] DL denotes learning-based method; Rot denotes rotation; Dist denotes distortion; ">180° FOV" denotes supporting over 180° FOV

Table 5. Comparison of the absolute parameter errors and reprojection errors on the test set for our generic camera model.

Method	StreetLearn					SP360				
	Mean absolute error ↓				REPE ↓	Mean absolute error ↓				REPE ↓
	Tilt θ [deg]	Roll ψ [deg]	f [mm]	k_1	[pixel]	Tilt θ [mm]	Roll ψ [deg]	f [mm]	k_1	[pixel]
López-Antequera [45]	27.60	44.90	2.32	–	81.99	28.66	44.45	3.26	–	84.56
Wakai [60]	10.70	14.97	2.73	–	30.02	11.12	17.70	2.67	–	32.01
Ours w/o HNGBL[1]	7.23	7.73	0.48	0.025	12.65	6.91	8.61	0.49	0.030	12.57
Ours	**4.13**	**5.21**	**0.34**	**0.021**	**7.39**	**3.75**	**5.19**	**0.39**	**0.023**	**7.39**

[1] "Ours w/o HNGBL" refers to replacing HNGBL with non-grid bearing loss [60]

and evaluation. Therefore, we focused on four trainable parameters, that is, a tilt angle θ, a roll angle ψ, focal length f, and a distortion coefficient k_1, in our method. Note that we considered camera rotation based on the horizontal line, unlike calibration methods [31,32] under the Manhattan world assumption.

We optimized our network for a 32 mini-batch size using a rectified Adam optimizer [42], whose weight decay was 0.01. We set the initial learning rate to 1×10^{-4} and multiplied the learning rate by 0.1 at the 50th epoch. Additionally, we set the joint weights in Eq. (5) using $w_\theta = 0.103$, $w_\psi = 0.135$, $w_f = 0.626$, and $w_{k_1} = 0.136$.

4.4   Experimental Results

In Table 4, we summarize the features of the conventional methods. We implemented the methods according to the corresponding papers, except that StreetLearn [46] and SP360 [12] were used for training. Note that we trained Yin's method [66] using ADE20K [69] following Yin's implementation because the method requires semantic segmentation data. In Li's methods [34], we selected GeoNetS-$\mathcal{B}$, which is the single-model distortion network to remove barrel distortion. For Alemán-Flores's [2] and Santana-Cedrés's [55] methods, we excluded test images with few lines because they require many lines for calibration.

Table 6. Comparison of mean PSNR and SSIM on the test set for our generic camera model.

Method	StreetLearn						SP360					
	PSNR ↑			SSIM ↑			PSNR ↑			SSIM ↑		
	Diag[1]	Circ[1]	All	Diag	Circ	All	Diag	Circ	All	Diag	Circ	All
Alemán-Flores [2]	14.79	11.70	13.25	0.354	0.271	0.313	14.57	11.03	12.82	0.408	0.311	0.360
Santana-Cedrés [55]	16.27	13.17	14.65	0.384	0.306	0.341	16.06	12.38	14.26	0.438	0.343	0.390
Liao [37]	13.92	13.48	13.71	0.355	0.369	0.362	14.08	13.61	13.85	0.401	0.408	0.404
Yin [66]	14.24	13.57	13.91	0.344	0.354	0.349	14.37	13.68	14.03	0.389	0.391	0.390
Chao [13]	17.36	14.89	16.13	0.439	0.378	0.409	17.23	14.86	15.88	0.480	0.417	0.449
Bogdan [8]	14.81	14.32	14.57	0.360	0.353	0.356	17.82	16.20	17.02	0.517	0.459	0.488
Li (GeoNetS-B) [34]	18.77	15.15	16.98	0.529	0.410	0.470	18.76	15.13	16.97	0.572	0.452	0.513
López-Antequera [45]	19.17	16.58	17.88	0.547	0.449	0.499	17.72	14.73	16.24	0.542	0.429	0.486
Wakai [60]	21.12	22.04	21.57	0.604	0.640	0.622	21.03	20.93	20.98	0.640	0.637	0.639
Ours w/o HNGBL[2]	27.12	27.70	27.41	0.801	0.801	0.801	25.93	27.07	26.49	0.790	0.812	0.801
Ours	**28.39**	**29.63**	**29.01**	**0.828**	**0.847**	**0.838**	**27.19**	**29.03**	**28.10**	**0.819**	**0.852**	**0.835**

[1] Diag denotes evaluation using only diagonal fisheye images; Circ denotes evaluation using only circumferential fisheye images
[2] "Ours w/o HNGBL" refers to replacing HNGBL with non-grid bearing loss [60]

Parameter and Reprojection Errors. To validate the accuracy of the predicted camera parameters, we compared methods that can predict rotation and distortion parameters. We evaluated the mean absolute errors of the camera parameters and the mean reprojection errors (REPE) on the test set for our generic camera model. We did not compare the focal length in Bogdan's method [8] because the unified spherical model [5] has ambiguity between the focal length and the distortion parameter [8]. Table 5 shows that our method achieved the lowest mean absolute errors and REPE among all methods. This REPE reflected the errors of both extrinsic and intrinsic parameters. To calculate the REPE, we generated $32,400$ uniform world coordinates on a unit sphere within less than $90°$ incident angles because of the lack of calibration points for image-based calibration methods. López-Antequera's method [45] did not seem to work well because it expects non-fisheye input images. Our method substantially reduced focal length errors and camera rotation errors (tilt and roll angles) by 86% and 66%, respectively, on average for the two datasets compared with Wakai's method [60]. Furthermore, our method reduced the REPE by 76% on average for the two datasets compared with Wakai's method [60]. Therefore, our method predicted accurate extrinsic and intrinsic camera parameters.

We also evaluated our method, referred to as "Ours w/o HNGBL," replacing our loss function with non-grid bearing loss [60] to analyze the performance of our loss function, as shown in Table 5. This result demonstrates that our loss function effectively reduced the rotation errors in the tilt and roll angles by $3.05°$ on average for the two datasets compared with the "Ours w/o HNGBL" case. In addition to rotation errors, the REPE for our method with HNGBL was 5.22 pixels on average for the two datasets smaller than that for "Ours w/o HNGBL." These results suggest that our loss function enabled networks to accurately predict not only focal length but also other camera parameters.

Comparison Using PSNR and SSIM. Comparison using PSNR and SSIM. To demonstrate validity and effectiveness in images, we used the peak signal-to-noise ratio (PSNR) and the structural similarity (SSIM) [61] for intrin-

Table 7. Comparison of mean PSNR on the test set for the trigonometric function models.

Method	StreetLearn					SP360				
	Stereo-graphic	Equi-distance	Equisolid angle	Ortho-gonal	All	Stereo-graphic	Equi-distance	Equisolid angle	Ortho-gonal	All
Alemán-Flores [2]	13.23	12.25	11.70	9.72	11.72	12.89	11.69	10.99	8.53	11.03
Santana-Cedrés [55]	14.68	13.20	12.49	10.29	12.66	14.25	12.57	11.77	9.34	11.98
Liao [37]	13.63	13.53	13.52	13.74	13.60	13.76	13.66	13.67	13.92	13.75
Yin [66]	13.81	13.62	13.59	13.77	13.70	13.92	13.74	13.72	13.94	13.83
Chao [13]	15.86	15.12	14.87	14.52	15.09	15.60	15.02	14.83	14.69	15.03
Bogdan [8]	14.55	14.43	14.46	14.71	14.54	16.92	16.34	16.14	15.65	16.26
Li (GeoNetS-B) [34]	16.37	15.41	15.07	14.58	15.36	16.22	15.33	15.04	14.72	15.33
López-Antequera [45]	17.84	16.84	16.43	15.15	16.57	15.72	14.94	14.68	14.52	14.97
Wakai [60]	22.39	23.62	22.91	17.79	21.68	22.29	22.65	21.79	17.54	21.07
Ours w/o HNGBL[1]	26.49	29.08	28.56	**23.97**	27.02	25.35	28.53	28.26	23.85	26.50
Ours	**26.84**	**30.10**	**29.69**	23.70	**27.58**	**25.74**	**29.28**	**28.95**	**23.93**	**26.98**

[1] "Ours w/o HNGBL" refers to replacing HNGBL with non-grid bearing loss [60]

sic parameters. When performing undistortion, extrinsic camera parameters are arbitrary because we consider only intrinsic camera parameters, image coordinates, and incident angles. Table 6 shows the performance of undistortion on the test set for our generic camera model. We verified that circumferential fisheye images did not degrade the accuracy of our method because our camera model supports over 180° FOV. By contrast, the circumferential fisheye images degraded the performance of methods using perspective projection in Alemán-Flores [2], Santana-Cedrés [55], and López-Antequera [45]. Note that the comparison of camera projection is shown in Table 4. Our method notably improved the image quality of undistortion by 7.28 for the PSNR and 0.206 for the SSIM on average for the two datasets compared with Wakai's method [60], as shown in Table 6 (*All*). Therefore, our method outperformed conventional methods on both diagonal and circumferential fisheye images.

To validate the dependency of the four types of fisheye camera models, we also evaluated the performance on the trigonometric function models in Table 7. Although orthogonal projection decreased the PSNR, our method addressed all the trigonometric function models; hence, our method had the highest PSNR in all cases. This suggests that our generic camera model precisely behaved like a trigonometric function model. Therefore, our method has the potential to calibrate images from various fisheye cameras.

Qualitative Evaluation. We evaluated the performance of undistortion and full recovery for not only synthetic images but also off-the-shelf cameras to describe the image quality after calibration.

Synthetic Images: Figure 3 shows the qualitative results on the test set for our generic camera model. Our results are the most similar to the ground-truth images in terms of undistortion and fully recovering rotation and fisheye distortion. Our method worked well for various types of distortion and scaling. By contrast, it was difficult to calibrate circumferential fisheye images with large distortion using Alemán-Flores's [2], Santana-Cedrés's [55], Liao's [37],

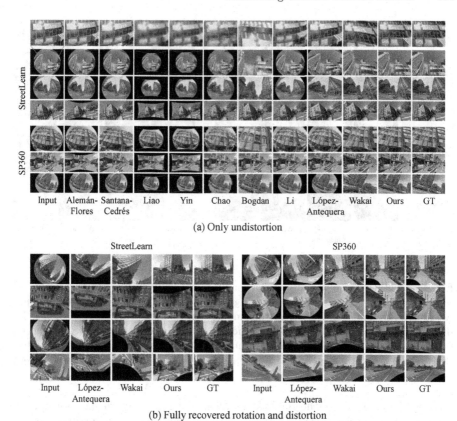

Fig. 3. Qualitative results on the test images for our generic camera model. (a) Undistortion results shown in the input image, results of the compared methods (Alemán-Flores [2], Santana-Cedrés [55], Liao [37], Yin [66], Chao [13], Bogdan [8], Li (GeoNetS-$\mathcal{B}$) [34], López-Antequera [45], and Wakai [60]), our method, and the ground-truth image from left to right. (b) Fully recovered rotation and distortion shown in the input image, results of the compared methods (López-Antequera [45] and Wakai [60]), our method, and the ground-truth image from left to right.

Yin's [66], Chao's [13], and Li's (GeoNetS-$\mathcal{B}$) [34] method. Furthermore, López-Antequera's [45] and Wakai's [60] methods did not remove distortion, although the scale was close to the ground truth. When fully recovering rotation and distortion, López-Antequera's [45] and Wakai's [60] methods tended to predict camera rotation with large errors in the tilt and roll angles. As shown in Fig. 3, our synthetic images consisted of zoom-in images of parts of buildings and zoom-out images of skyscrapers. Our method processed both types of images; that is, it demonstrated scale robustness.

Off-the-Shelf Cameras: We also validated calibration methods using off-the-shelf fisheye cameras to analyze the performance of actual complex fisheye dis-

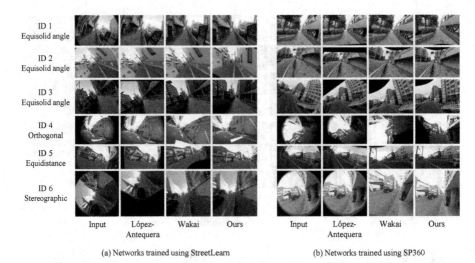

ID 1
Equisolid angle

ID 2
Equisolid angle

ID 3
Equisolid angle

ID 4
Orthogonal

ID 5
Equidistance

ID 6
Stereographic

Input   López-   Wakai   Ours   Input   López-   Wakai   Ours
         Antequera   Antequera

(a) Networks trained using StreetLearn   (b) Networks trained using SP360

Fig. 4. Qualitative results of fully recovering rotation and fisheye distortion for the off-the-shelf cameras shown in the input image, results of the compared methods (López-Antequera [45] and Wakai [60]), and our method from left to right for each image. The IDs correspond to IDs in Table 3, and the projection names are attached to the IDs from specifications (ID: 3–5) and our estimation (ID: 1, 2, and 6). Qualitative results of the methods trained using StreetLearn [46] and SP360 [12] in (a) and (b), respectively.

tortion. Figure 4 shows the qualitative results of fully recovering rotation and fisheye distortion for methods that can predict extrinsic and intrinsic camera parameters. These methods were trained using the StreetLearn [46] or SP360 [12] datasets. The results for López-Antequera's method had rotation and/or distortion errors. Our method outperformed Wakai's method [60], which often recovered only distortion for all our cameras. Our fully recovered images demonstrated the effectiveness of our method for off-the-shelf fisheye cameras with four types of projection: stereographic projection, equidistance projection, equisolid angle projection, and orthogonal projection.

In all the calibration methods, images captured by off-the-shelf cameras seemingly degraded the overall performance in the qualitative results compared with synthetic images. This degradation probably occurred because of the complex distortion of off-the-shelf fisheye cameras and the dataset domain mismatch between the two panorama datasets and our captured images. Overall, our method outperformed the conventional methods in the qualitative evaluation of off-the-shelf cameras. As described above, our method precisely recovered both rotation and fisheye distortion using our generic camera model. Refer to the supplementary material for error distribution and additional calibration results.

5   Conclusion

We proposed a learning-based calibration method using a new generic camera model to address various types of camera projection. Additionally, we introduced a novel loss function that has optimal joint weights determined before training. These weights can alleviate the bias of the magnitude of each loss for four camera parameters. As a result, we enabled networks to precisely predict both extrinsic and intrinsic camera parameters. Extensive experiments demonstrated that our method substantially outperformed conventional geometric-based and learning-based methods on two large-scale datasets. Moreover, we demonstrated that our method fully recovered rotation and distortion using off-the-shelf fisheye cameras consisting of stereographic projection, equidistance projection, equisolid angle projection, and orthogonal projection. To improve the calibration performance in off-the-shelf cameras, in future work, we will study the dataset domain mismatch.

References

1. Akiba, T., Sano, S., Yanase, T., Ohta, T., Koyama, M.: Optuna: A next-generation hyperparameter optimization framework. In: Proceedings of International Conference on Knowledge Discovery and Data Mining (KDD), pp. 2623–2631 (2019). https://doi.org/10.1145/3292500.3330701
2. Alemán-Flores, M., Alvarez, L., Gomez, L., Santana-Cedrés, D.: Automatic lens distortion correction using one-parameter division models. Image Process. On Line (IPOL) **4**, 327–343 (2014). https://doi.org/10.5201/ipol.2014.106
3. Alhaija, H.A., Mustikovela, S.K., Mescheder, L., Geiger, A.: Augmented reality meets computer vision: efficient data generation for urban driving scenes. Int. J. Comput. Vision (IJCV) **126**(9), 961–972 (2018). https://doi.org/10.1007/s11263-018-1070-x
4. Alvarez, L., Gómez, L., Sendra, J.: An algebraic approach to lens distortion by line rectification. J. Math. Imaging Vision (JMIV) **35**(1), 36–50 (2009). https://doi.org/10.1007/s10851-009-0153-2
5. Barreto, J.: A unifying geometric representation for central projection systems. Comput. Vision Image Understanding (CVIU) **103**(3), 208–217 (2006). https://doi.org/10.1016/j.cviu.2006.06.003
6. Basu, A., Licardie, S.: Modeling fish-eye lenses. In: Proceedings of IEEE/RSJ International Conference on Intelligent Robots and Systems (IROS). vol. 3, pp. 1822–1828 (1993). https://doi.org/10.1109/IROS.1993.583883
7. Benligiray, B., Topal, C.: Blind rectification of radial distortion by line straightness. In: Proceedings of European Signal Processing Conference (EUSIPCO), pp. 938–942 (2016). https://doi.org/10.1109/EUSIPCO.2016.7760386
8. Bogdan, O., Eckstein, V., Rameau, F., Bazin, J.C.: DeepCalib: A deep learning approach for automatic intrinsic calibration of wide field-of-view cameras. In: Proceedings of SIGGRAPH European Conference on Visual Media Production (CVMP) (2018). https://doi.org/10.1145/3278471.3278479
9. Brown, D.: Close-range camera calibration. Photogram. Eng. **37**(8), 855–866 (1971)
10. Bukhari, F., Dailey, M.: Automatic radial distortion estimation from a single image. J. Math. Imaging Vision (JMIV) **45**, 31–45 (2013). https://doi.org/10.1007/s10851-012-0342-2

11. Cao, Z., Simon, T., Wei, S., Sheikh, Y.: Realtime multi-person 2D pose estimation using part affinity fields. In: Proceedings of IEEE Conference on Computer Vision and Pattern Recognition (CVPR), pp. 1302–1310 (2017). https://doi.org/10.1109/CVPR.2017.143

12. Chang, S., et al.: Generating 360 outdoor panorama dataset with reliable sun position estimation. In: Proceedings of SIGGRAPH Asia, pp. 1–2 (2018). https://doi.org/10.1145/3283289.3283348

13. Chao, C., Hsu, P., Lee, H., Wang, Y.: Self-supervised deep learning for fisheye image rectification. In: Proceedings of IEEE International Conference on Acoustics, Speech, and Signal Processing (ICASSP), pp. 2248–2252 (2020). https://doi.org/10.1109/ICASSP40776.2020.9054191

14. Chen, Y., Schmid, C., Sminchisescu, C.: Self-supervised learning with geometric constraints in monocular video: Connecting flow, depth, and camera. In: Proceedings of IEEE International Conference on Computer Vision (ICCV), pp. 7062–7071 (2019). https://doi.org/10.1109/ICCV.2019.00716

15. Dauphin, Y.N., Pascanu, R., Gulcehre, C., Cho, K., Ganguli, S., Bengio, Y.: Identifying and attacking the saddle point problem in high-dimensional non-convex optimization. In: Proceedings of Advances in Neural Information Processing Systems (NeurIPS). vol. 2, pp. 2933–2941 (2018). arXiv:1406.2572

16. Davidson, B., Alvi, M., Henriques, J.F.: 360° Camera alignment via segmentation. In: Proceedings of European Conference on Computer Vision (ECCV), pp. 579–595 (2020). https://doi.org/10.1007/978-3-030-58604-1_35

17. Fitzgibbon, A.: Simultaneous linear estimation of multiple view geometry and lens distortion. In: Proceedings of IEEE Conference on Computer Vision and Pattern Recognition (CVPR). vol. 1, pp. I-I (2001). https://doi.org/10.1109/CVPR.2001.990465

18. Fu, Z., Liu, Q., Fu, Z., Wang, Y.: Template-free visual tracking with space-time memory networks. In: Proceedings of IEEE/CVF Conference on Computer Vision and Pattern Recognition (CVPR) pp. 13774–13783 (2021). https://doi.org/10.1109/CVPR46437.2021.01356

19. González-Aguilera, D., Gómez-Lahoz, J., Rodríguez-Gonzálvez, P.: An automatic approach for radial lens distortion correction from a single image. IEEE Sensors J. (JSEN) 11(4), 956–965 (2011). https://doi.org/10.1109/JSEN.2010.2076403

20. Goodfellow, I.J., et al.: Generative adversarial nets. In: Proceedings of Advances in Neural Information Processing Systems (NeurIPS). vol. 2, pp. 2672–2680 (2014). arXiv:1406.2661

21. Goodfellow, I.J., Vinyals, O., Saxe, A.M.: Qualitatively characterizing neural network. In: Proceedings of International Conference on Learning Representations (ICLR), pp. 1–20 (2015). arXiv:1412.6544

22. Gordon, A., Li, H., Jonschkowski, R., Angelova, A.: Depth from videos in the wild: Unsupervised monocular depth learning from unknown cameras. In: Proceedings of IEEE/CVF International Conference on Computer Vision (ICCV), pp. 8976–8985 (2019). https://doi.org/10.1109/ICCV.2019.00907

23. Groenendijk, R., Karaoglu, S., Gevers, T., Mensink, T.: Multi-loss weighting with coefficient of variations. In: Proceedings of IEEE Winter Conference on Applications of Computer Vision (WACV), pp. 1468–1477 (2021). https://doi.org/10.1109/WACV48630.2021.00151

24. Hold-Geoffroy, Y., et al.: A perceptual measure for deep single image camera calibration. In: Proceedings of IEEE/CVF Conference on Computer Vision and Pattern Recognition (CVPR), pp. 2354–2363 (2018). https://doi.org/10.1109/CVPR.2018.00250

25. Hosono, M., Simo-Serra, E., Sonoda, T.: Self-supervised deep fisheye image rectification approach using coordinate relations. In: Proceedings of IEEE International Conference on Machine Vision and Applications (MVA), pp. 1–5 (2021). https://doi.org/10.23919/MVA51890.2021.9511349

26. Huang, G., Liu, Z., Van Der Maaten, L., Weinberger, K.Q.: Densely connected convolutional networks. In: Proceedings of IEEE Conference on Computer Vision and Pattern Recognition (CVPR), pp. 2261–2269 (2017). https://doi.org/10.1109/CVPR.2017.243

27. Huang, Z., Xu, Y., Shi, J., Zhou, X., Bao, H., Zhang, G.: Prior guided dropout for robust visual localization in dynamic environments. In: Proceedings of IEEE/CVF International Conference on Computer Vision (ICCV), pp. 2791–2800 (2019). https://doi.org/10.1109/ICCV.2019.00288

28. Huber, P.J.: Robust estimation of a location parameter. Annals Math. Stat. 35(1), 73–101 (1964). https://doi.org/10.1214/aoms/1177703732

29. Ioffe, S., Szegedy, C.: Batch Normalization: Accelerating deep network training by reducing internal covariate shift. In: Proceedings of International Conference on Machine Learning (ICML). vol. 37, pp. 448–456 (2015). arXiv:1502.03167

30. Kannala, J., Brandt, S.S.: A generic camera model and calibration method for conventional, wide-angle, and fish-eye lenses. IEEE Trans. Pattern Analysis Mach. Intell. (PAMI) 28(8), 1335–1340 (2006). https://doi.org/10.1109/TPAMI.2006.153

31. Lee, J., Go, H., Lee, H., Cho, S., Sung, M., Kim, J.: CTRL-C: Camera calibration TRansformer with line-classification. In: Proceedings of IEEE/CVF International Conference on Computer Vision (ICCV), pp. 16228–16237 (2021). https://doi.org/10.1109/ICCV48922.2021.01592

32. Lee, J., Sung, M., Lee, H., Kim, J.: Neural geometric parser for single image camera calibration. In: Proceedings of European Conference on Computer Vision (ECCV), pp. 541–557 (2020). https://doi.org/10.1007/978-3-030-58610-2_32

33. Li, H., Xu, Z., Taylor, G., Studer, C., Goldstein, T.: Visualizing the loss landscape of neural nets. In: Proceedings of Advances in Neural Information Processing Systems (NeurIPS), pp. 6391–6401 (2018). arXiv:1712.09913

34. Li, X., Zhang, B., Sander, P.V., Liao, J.: Blind geometric distortion correction on images through deep learning. In: Proceedings of IEEE/CVF Conference on Computer Vision and Pattern Recognition (CVPR), pp. 4855–4864 (2019). https://doi.org/10.1109/CVPR.2019.00499

35. Liao, K., Chunyu, L., Liao, L., Zhao, Y., Lin, W.: Multi level curriculum for training a distortion-aware barrel distortion rectification model. In: Proceedings of IEEE/CVF International Conference on Computer Vision (ICCV), pp. 4369–4378 (2021). https://doi.org/10.1109/ICCV48922.2021.00435

36. Liao, K., Lin, C., Wei, Y., Li, F., Yang, S., Zhao, Y.: Towards complete scene and regular shape for distortion rectification. In: Proceedings of IEEE/CVF International Conference on Computer Vision (ICCV), pp. 14549–14558 (2021). https://doi.org/10.1109/ICCV48922.2021.01430

37. Liao, K., Lin, C., Zhao, Y.: A deep ordinal distortion estimation approach for distortion rectification. IEEE Trans. Image Process. (TIP) 30, 3362–3375 (2021). https://doi.org/10.1109/TIP.2021.3061283

38. Liao, K., Lin, C., Zhao, Y., Gabbouj, M.: DR-GAN: automatic radial distortion rectification using conditional GAN in real-time. IEEE Trans. Circ. Syst. Video Technol. (TCSVT) 30(3), 725–733 (2020). https://doi.org/10.1109/TCSVT.2019.2897984

39. Liao, K., Lin, C., Zhao, Y., Xu, M.: Model-free distortion rectification framework bridged by distortion distribution map. IEEE Trans. Image Process. (TIP) **29**, 3707–3718 (2020). https://doi.org/10.1109/TIP.2020.2964523

40. Lin, M., Chen, Q., Yan, S.: Network in network. In: Proceedings of International Conference on Learning Representations (ICLR), pp. 1–10 (2014). arXiv:1312.4400

41. Liu, C., et al.: Auto-DeepLab: Hierarchical neural architecture search for semantic image segmentation. In: Proceedings of IEEE/CVF Conference on Computer Vision and Pattern Recognition (CVPR), pp. 82–92 (2019). https://doi.org/10.1109/CVPR.2019.00017

42. Liu, L., et al.: On the variance of the adaptive learning rate and beyond. In: Proceedings of International Conference on Learning Representations (ICLR), pp. 1–14 (2020). arXiv:1908.03265

43. Locher, A., Perdoch, M., Gool, L.V.: Progressive prioritized multi-view stereo. In: Proceedings of IEEE Conference on Computer Vision and Pattern Recognition (CVPR), pp. 3244–3252 (2016). https://doi.org/10.1109/CVPR.2016.353

44. Lochman, Y., Dobosevych, O., Hryniv, R., Pritts, J.: Minimal solvers for single-view lens-distorted camera auto-calibration. In: Proceedings of IEEE Winter Conference on Applications of Computer Vision (WACV). pp. 2886–2895 (2021). https://doi.org/10.1109/WACV48630.2021.00293

45. López-Antequera, M., Marí, R., Gargallo, P., Kuang, Y., Gonzalez-Jimenez, J., Haro, G.: Deep single image camera calibration with radial distortion. In: Proceedings of IEEE/CVF Conference on Computer Vision and Pattern Recognition (CVPR), pp. 11809–11817 (2019). https://doi.org/10.1109/CVPR.2019.01209

46. Mirowski, P., et al.: The StreetLearn environment and dataset. arXiv preprint arXiv:1903.01292 (2019)

47. Misra, D.: Mish: A self regularized non-monotonic neural activation function. In: Proceedings of British Machine Vision Conference (BMVC), pp. 1–14 (2020). arXiv:1908.08681

48. Nie, Y., Han, X., Guo, S., Zheng, Y., Chang, J., Zhang, J.J.: Total3DUnderstanding: Joint layout, object pose and mesh reconstruction for indoor scenes from a single image. In: Proceedings of IEEE/CVF Conference on Computer Vision and Pattern Recognition (CVPR), pp. 52–61 (2020). https://doi.org/10.1109/CVPR42600.2020.00013.

49. Pritts, J., Kukelova, Z., Larsson, V., Chum, O.: Radially-distorted conjugate translations. In: Proceedings of IEEE/CVF Conference on Computer Vision and Pattern Recognition (CVPR), pp. 1993–2001 (2018). https://doi.org/10.1109/CVPR.2018.00213

50. Puskorius, G., Feldkamp, L.: Camera calibration methodology based on a linear perspective transformation error model. In: Proceedings of IEEE International Conference on Robotics and Automation (ICRA). vol. 3, pp. 1858–1860 (1988). https://doi.org/10.1109/ROBOT.1988.12340

51. Redmon, J., Divvala, S., Girshick, R., Farhadi, A.: You Only Look Once: Unified, real-time object detection. In: Proceedings of IEEE Conference on Computer Vision and Pattern Recognition (CVPR), pp. 779–788 (2016). https://doi.org/10.1109/CVPR.2016.91

52. Ren, L., Song, Y., Lu, J., Zhou, J.: Spatial geometric reasoning for room layout estimation via deep reinforcement learning. In: Proceedings of European Conference on Computer Vision (ECCV), pp. 550–565 (2020). https://doi.org/10.1007/978-3-030-58583-9_33

53. Rong, J., Huang, S., Shang, Z., Ying, X.: Radial lens distortion correction using convolutional neural networks trained with synthesized images. In: Proceedings of Asian Conference on Computer Vision (ACCV). vol. 10113, pp. 35–49 (2017). https://doi.org/10.1007/978-3-319-54187-7_3

54. Russakovsky, O., et al.: ImageNet large scale visual recognition challenge. Int. J. Comput. Vision (IJCV) **115**(3), 211–252 (2015). https://doi.org/10.1007/s11263-015-0816-y

55. Santana-Cedrés, D., et al.: An iterative optimization algorithm for lens distortion correction using two-parameter models. Image Processing OnLine (IPOL) **6**, 326–364 (2016). https://doi.org/10.5201/ipol.2016.130

56. Saputra, M.R.U., Gusmao, P., Almalioglu, Y., Markham, A., Trigoni, N.: Distilling knowledge from a deep pose regressor network. In: Proceedings of IEEE/CVF International Conference on Computer Vision (ICCV), pp. 263–272 (2019). https://doi.org/10.1109/ICCV.2019.00035

57. Sha, L., Hobbs, J., Felsen, P., Wei, X., Lucey, P., Ganguly, S.: End-to-End camera calibration for broadcast videos. In: Proceedings of IEEE/CVF Conference on Computer Vision and Pattern Recognition (CVPR), pp. 13624–13633 (2020). https://doi.org/10.1109/CVPR42600.2020.01364

58. Shah, S., Aggarwal, J.K.: A simple calibration procedure for fish-eye (high distortion) lens camera. In: Proceedings of IEEE International Conference on Robotics and Automation (ICRA). vol. 4, pp. 3422–3427 (1994). https://doi.org/10.1109/ROBOT.1994.351044

59. Tsai, R.Y.: A versatile camera calibration technique for high-accuracy 3D machine vision metrology using off-the-shelf TV cameras and lenses. IEEE J. Robot. Autom. (JRA) **3**(4), 323–344 (1987). https://doi.org/10.1109/JRA.1987.1087109

60. Wakai, N., Yamashita, T.: Deep single fisheye image camera calibration for over 180-degree projection of field of view. In: Proceedings of IEEE/CVF International Conference on Computer Vision Workshops (ICCVW), pp. 1174–1183 (2021). https://doi.org/10.1109/ICCVW54120.2021.00137

61. Wang, Z., Bovik, A.C.: Image quality assessment: from error visibility to structural similarity. IEEE Trans. Image Process. (TIP) **13**(4), 600–612 (2004). https://doi.org/10.1109/TIP.2003.819861

62. Xian, W., Li, Z., Snavely, N., Fisher, M., Eisenman, J., Shechtman, E.: UprightNet: Geometry-aware camera orientation estimation from single images. In: Proceedings of IEEE/CVF International Conference on Computer Vision (ICCV), pp. 9973–9982 (2019). https://doi.org/10.1109/ICCV.2019.01007

63. Xue, F., Wang, X., Yan, Z., Wang, Q., Wang, J., Zha, H.: Local supports global: Deep camera relocalization with sequence enhancement. In: Proceedings of IEEE/CVF International Conference on Computer Vision (ICCV), pp. 2841–2850 (2019). https://doi.org/10.1109/ICCV.2019.00293

64. Xue, Z., Xue, N., Xia, G., Shen, W.: Learning to calibrate straight lines for fisheye image rectification. In: Proceedings of IEEE/CVF Conference on Computer Vision and Pattern Recognition (CVPR), pp. 1643–1651 (2019). https://doi.org/10.1109/CVPR.2019.00174

65. Yang, S., Lin, C., Liao, K., Zhang, C., Zhao, Y.: Progressively complementary network for fisheye image rectification using appearance flow. In: Proceedings of IEEE/CVF Conference on Computer Vision and Pattern Recognition (CVPR), pp. 6344–6353 (2021). https://doi.org/10.1109/CVPR46437.2021.00628

66. Yin, X., Wang, X., Yu, J., Zhang, M., Fua, P., Tao, D.: FishEyeRecNet: a multi-context collaborative deep network for fisheye image rectification. In: Ferrari, V., Hebert, M., Sminchisescu, C., Weiss, Y. (eds.) ECCV 2018. LNCS, vol. 11214, pp. 475–490. Springer, Cham (2018). https://doi.org/10.1007/978-3-030-01249-6_29

67. Zhang, M., Yao, J., Xia, M., Li, K., Zhang, Y., Liu, Y.: Line-based multi-label energy optimization for fisheye image rectification and calibration. In: Proceedings of IEEE Conference on Computer Vision and Pattern Recognition (CVPR), pp. 4137–4145 (2015). https://doi.org/10.1109/CVPR.2015.7299041

68. Zhang, Z.: A flexible new technique for camera calibration. IEEE Trans. Pattern Analysis Mach. Intell. (PAMI) **22**(11), 1330–1334 (2000). https://doi.org/10.1109/34.888718

69. Zhou, B., Zhao, H., Puig, X., Fidler, S., Barriuso, A., Torralba, A.: Scene parsing through ADE20K dataset. In: Proceedings of IEEE Conference on Computer Vision and Pattern Recognition (CVPR), pp. 5122–5130 (2017). https://doi.org/10.1109/CVPR.2017.544

70. Żołądek, H.: The topological proof of Abel-Ruffini theorem. Topological Methods Nonlinear Analysis **16**, 253–265 (2000)

ART-SS: An Adaptive Rejection Technique for Semi-supervised Restoration for Adverse Weather-Affected Images

Rajeev Yasarla$^{(\boxtimes)}$ ⓘ, Carey E. Priebe, and Vishal M. Patel ⓘ

Johns Hopkins University, Baltimore, MD 21218, USA
{ryasarl1,cep,vpatel36}@jhu.edu

Abstract. In recent years, convolutional neural network-based single image adverse weather removal methods have achieved significant performance improvements on many benchmark datasets. However, these methods require large amounts of clean-weather degraded image pairs for training, which is often difficult to obtain in practice. Although various weather degradation synthesis methods exist in the literature, the use of synthetically generated weather degraded images often results in sub-optimal performance on the real weatherdegraded images due to the domain gap between synthetic and real world images. To deal with this problem, various semi-supervised restoration (SSR) methods have been proposed for deraining or dehazing which learn to restore clean image using synthetically generated datasets while generalizing better using unlabeled real-world images. The performance of a semi-supervised method is essentially based on the quality of the unlabeled data. In particular, if the unlabeled data characteristics are very different from that of the labeled data, then the performance of a semi-supervised method degrades significantly. We theoretically study the effect of unlabeled data on the performance of an SSR method and develop a technique that rejects the unlabeled images that degrade the performance. Extensive experiments and ablation study show that the proposed sample rejection method increases the performance of existing SSR deraining and dehazing methods significantly. Code is available at: https://github.com/rajeevyasarla/ART-SS.

Keywords: Semi-supervision · Deraining · Dehazing · Rejection technnique

1 Introduction

Images captured in weather degradations like rain or fog conditions are of poor quality, leading to a loss of situational awareness and a general decrease in use-

This work was supported by an ARO grant W911NF–21–1–0135.

Supplementary Information The online version contains supplementary material available at https://doi.org/10.1007/978-3-031-19797-0_40.

fulness. Hence, it is very important to compensate for the visual degradation in images caused by these weather degradations. Additionally, such weather degraded images also reduce the performance of down-stream computer vision tasks such as detection, segmentation and recognition [3,17,29]. The main objective Single image restoration (SIR) of weather degraded image, is to restore the clean image y, given a weather degraded image x, in-order to improve performance of such down-stream tasks. Extensive research on methods to remove such weather degradation effects like rain and haze.

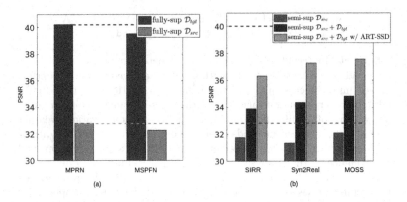

Fig. 1. Cross-domain deraining experiment where Rain800 [55] is used as the synthetic source dataset $\mathcal{D}_{src}$, and SPA-data [38] is used as the real rain target dataset $\mathcal{D}_{tgt}$. Here, MPRN [52] and MSPFN [14] are fully-supervised methods and SIRR [40], Syn2Real [48] and MOSS [13] are semi-supervised methods. Fully-supervised methods are supervised using the corresponding labeled clean images and semi-supervised images are trained using a labeled source data $\mathcal{D}_{src}$ and an unlabeled target data $\mathcal{D}_{tgt}$. (a) Blue and Red bars show the target only and source only performance of MSPFN and MPRN, respectively. We can see a drop in performance of supervised methods when they are trained on $\mathcal{D}_{src}$ and tested on $\mathcal{D}_{tgt}$. (b) Semi-supervised methods such as SIRR, Syn2Real and MOSS perform better than the supervised methods by leveraging the information from unlabeled images. However, with the help of ART-SS, we are able improve the performance of semi-supervised restoration (SSR) methods even further by rejecting the unlabeled images that are not helpful in semi-supervision. (Color figure online)

In recent years, various convolutional neural network-based methods have been proposed for deraining [7,8,23,25,28,37,38,43,58], dehazing [5,19,41,54, 56,57]. These fully-supervised methods require large amounts of clean-weather degraded image pairs for training. Since collecting real world weather degraded-clean image pairs of data is difficult, most existing supervised methods rely on synthetically generated data to train the network. However, the use of synthetically generated weather degraded images often results in sub-optimal performance on the real world images due to the domain difference between synthetic and real world images. For example when we consider deraining task, this can be clearly seen in Fig. 1 (a), where we train two fully-supervised SID networks, MPRN [52] and MSPFN [14], on a synthetic source dataset $\mathcal{D}_{src}$ from Rain800 [55] and test them on a real rain target dataset $\mathcal{D}_{src}$ from SPA-data [38]. From Fig. 1 (a), we can observe that the performance of fully-supervised methods degrades significantly when trained on Rain800 [55] and tested on SPA-data [38] compared to target only performance which corresponds to the case where the methods are trained and tested on SPA-data [38].

To address this domain gap between source and target datasets, Wei *et al.* [40] initially attempted to address the semi-supervised deraining task by leveraging the rain information in unlabeled target dataset while training the network. In proposed method, the authors model rain residuals by imposing a likelihood term on Gaussian Mixture Models (GMMs) for both labeled and unlabeled datasets, and minimize the Kullback-Leibler (KL) divergence between the obtained GMMs of labeled and unlabeled images to enforce the consistency that distribution of labeled rainy data should be close to that of the unlabeled data. Later following this approach, Yasarla *et al.* [48] proposed a non-parametric model for semi-supervised deraining where they project labeled and unlabeled rainy images to a latent space and formulate a joint Gaussian distribution to generate pseudo labels for the unlabeled images. Recently, Huang *et al.* [13] proposed a memory-based encoder-decoder network where the memory module learns rain information from synthetic and real rainy images in a self-supervised manner using Exponential Moving Average (EMA) updates. On the other hand, to address the semi-supervised dehazing Li *et al.* [18] proposed to leverage hazy information from unlabeled images using dark channel priors based gradient updates while training the network. Later, Shao *et al.* [33] proposed a bi-directional translations method that minimizes the gap between synthetic and real hazy domains using adversarial loss and dark channel priors.

One major drawback of these semi-supervised restoration(SSR) techniques is that they don't account for the effect of unlabeled images on the overall semi-supervised performance. Not all images in the unlabeled target dataset are useful in improving the SSR performance. If the unlabeled image characteristics are very different from that of in the source data, then there is a good chance that SSR performance will converge to unsupervised deraining performance instead of converging towards fully-supervised. We explore theoretical evidence for this behavior, and also conduct cross-domain experiments to empirically show that unlabeled observations which are different from the labeled source images might not be beneficial in improving the SSR performance.

In particular, we theoretically understand why a few unlabeled observations might have an adverse effect on the performance of an SSR method, and propose a novel technique called adaptive rejection technique for semi-supervision (ART-SS), that selects unlabeled observations which are useful in improving the SSD performance. In Syn2real [48] and MOSS [13], authors project the unlabeled and labeled images to a latent space and express latent vector of each image using either latent basis vector representations or labeled latent-space vectors. Additionally, these works perform supervision at the defined latent space level in unlabeled trainning phase of semi-supervised training. Following these works, we use the latent representation of the labeled or unlabeled images and compute similarity index (ψ) for each image that indicates how similar is the given image to the labeled images. Note as the unlabeled images can be easy or hard samples, and network might produce errors in computing the latent representations, thus we compute the variance σ (aleotoric uncertainty [16,46,47]) that indicates a measure of how confident the network is about computing the latent representation. Hence, we use proposed theorem and corollaries in our theoretical study, and come up with a novel selection criterion for ART-SS method using ψ and σ measures, to decide whether the given unlabeled image is helpful for improving the SSR performance. Note, using variance σ (aleotoric uncertainty) makes the ART-SS method robust to error in the networks latent-space representations. In this way given unlabeled image, we compute ψ and σ measures for the unlabeled image, and using the criterion to decide whether the unlabeled image is similar or dis-similar (*i.e.* might have adverse affect on SSR performance) to source domain, and can be used for updating the weights of a SSR method or not. For example using proposed ART-SS, we are able to significantly boost the performance of existing SSR deraining methods [13,40,48] (see Fig. 1(b)).

In summary, this paper makes the following contributions:

- We theoretically study how unlabeled images can affect the performance of an semi-supervised restoration(SSR) method.
- We propose a novel rejection technique, called ART-SS, to select images that are useful in improving the SSR performance.
- Extensive cross-domain experiments and ablation study are conducted to show the significance of the proposed method. In particular, our simple rejection technique is shown to boost the performance of the existing deraining [13,40,48], and dehazing [18,33] methods.

2   Related Work

Various single image restoration methods have been proposed for adverse weather removal problems like deraining [11,12,15,21,22,24,26,34–36,39,44,45, 49–51], dehazing [1,6,10,20,30,31]. Here, we mainly focus on SSR tasks in deraining, and dehazing.

Deraining. Jiang *et al.* [14] proposed a fusion network called MSPFN that fuses hierarchical deep features in a progressive manner for deraining. Zamir *et al.* [52] proposed a multi-stage architecture that incorporates the information exchange between different stages in retrieving the derained image. As these methods are trained on synthetic rainy-clean pairs, these methods might obtain sub-optimal performances when tested on real rainy images since there is domain gap between synthetic and real rainy images. To this end, semi-supervised approaches have been proposed Wei *et al.* [40] (GMM based), Yasarla *et al.* [48] (Gaussian process based pesudo-GT generation), Huang *et al.* [13] (mean student teacher learning) to address the domain gap between synthetic and real rainy images to improve SSR performance.

Dehazing. Ren *et al.* [31] pre-processed a hazy image to generate multiple input images, hence introducing color distortions to perform dehazing. Qu *et al.* [27] proposed an enhanced image-to-image translation based dehazing method trained using adversarial loss. Although these achieve better performance on synthetic hazy images, might fail to restore high quality clean image given real hazy image. To this end, [18,33] proposed semi-supervised dehazing approaches using dark channel priors, and total-variation loss to reduce domain gap between synthetic and real hazy images.

These SSR methods don't account for the effect of unlabeled image on semi-supervised performance and might suffer to obtain optimal semi-supervised performance gains. Inspired by Yang and Priebe [42], we theoretically study the effect of unlabeled data on the SSR performance and develop a rejection technique that rejects unlabeled images which are not beneficial in improving the SSR performance.

3   Preliminaries

In this section, we define notations and key concepts regarding specified and misspecified models and present a semi-supervised degradation theorem.

3.1   Model and Notations

Given, a weather-degraded image x, our objective is to obtain a restored image $\hat{y} = f(x)$, where $f(.)$ is a function with parameters θ that performs the restoration(deraining or dehazing) task. This function can be any deep learning-based model or a GMM-based model. Let us denote the collection of all possible restoration functions $\{f(.)\}$ in the parametric model $\mathcal{F}$ whose parameters expressed as $\Theta_{\mathcal{F}}$ by a dashed circle. Let $f_{opt}(.)$ denote the best possible deraining function in $\mathcal{F}$, i.e.,

$$f_{opt} = \arg \min_{f \in \mathcal{F}} L(f), \tag{1}$$

where $L(.)$ is used to denote the error for the function $f(.)$ in the restoration task. Bayes error (the lowest possible error that can be achieved and is the same as irreducible error) is expressed as L^* and the corresponding function as f^*. Let $\hat{f}$ be the learned restoration function with parameters $\hat{\theta}$. The model bias is measured by $L(f_{opt}) - L^*$ and the estimation error is $L(\hat{f}) - L(f_{opt})$. Now let us define the limits depending on whether we are learning the restoration task in supervised fashion, $(L^*_{sup}, f^*_{sup}, \theta^*_{sup})$ or unsupervised fashion $(L^*_{unsup}, f^*_{unsup}, \theta^*_{unsup})$. We denote error for the fully-supervised method using labeled data as L_ℓ, and semi-supervised method using labeled and unlabeled as $L_{\ell+u}$.

We denote the labeled source dataset as $\mathcal{D}_{src}$, and the target unlabeled dataset as $\mathcal{D}_{tgt}$. Following Syn2real [48] and MOSS [13], we project the labeled and unlabeled datasets onto a latent space which is defined as the output of an encoder. That is, every image $x_i^l \in \mathcal{D}_{src}$ is passed through the encoder network to obtain $z_i^l = g(x_i^l)$. Similarly, $z_i^u = g(x_i^u)$ is obtained for every image $x_i^u \in \mathcal{D}_{tgt}$.

Note that encoder and decoder of a restoration network are represented using functions $g(.)$ and $h(.)$, with corresponding parameters θ^{enc} and θ^{dec}, respectively. For the sake of simplicity, let us assume that all the labeled latent vectors, $Z_{src} = \{z_i^l\}$ can be spanned by a set of vectors $\{\{s_i\}_{i=1}^{M_l}, \{c_j\}_{j=1}^{M_c}\}$, $i.e. z_i^l \in span(\{\{s_i\}_{i=1}^{M_l}, \{c_j\}_{j=1}^{M_c}\})$ or $z_i^l = \sum_{v_i \in \{\{s_i\}_{i=1}^{M_l}, \{c_j\}_{j=1}^{M_c}\}} \alpha_i v_i$ and we represent this vector space as $\mathcal{V}_{src}$. Similarly, all unlabeled latent vectors, $Z_{tgt} = \{z_i^u\}$ can be spanned by a set vectors $\{\{t_i\}_{i=1}^{M_u}, \{c_j\}_{j=1}^{M_c}\}$, $i.e. z_i^u \in span(\{\{t_i\}_{i=1}^{M_u}, \{c_j\}_{j=1}^{M_c}\})$ or $z_i^u = \sum_{v_i \in \{\{t_i\}_{i=1}^{M_u}, \{c_j\}_{j=1}^{M_c}\}} \alpha_i v_i$ and we represent this vector space as $\mathcal{V}_{tgt}$. Note that we have assumed that the labeled vector space $\mathcal{V}_{src}$ and the unlabeled vector space $\mathcal{V}_{tgt}$, have common basis vectors $V_c = \{c_j\}_{j=1}^{M_c}$ (because of similarities between labeled and unlabeled images). In addition, these vector spaces $\mathcal{V}_{src}$ and $\mathcal{V}_{tgt}$ have different basis vectors $V_s = \{\{s_i\}_{i=1}^{M_l}$ and $V_t = \{\{t_i\}_{i=1}^{M_u}$ respectively (this is due to differences or domain gap between the labeled and unlabeled weather-degraded images).

3.2 Correct Parametric Model (specified)

If $f^* \in \mathcal{F}$, then the model bias is 0, $i.e.$, $L(f_{opt}) - L^* = 0$. The estimation error is the only thing that contributes to the regression error of the weather removal task. In other words, $V_s = \{s_i\}_{i=1}^{M_l} = \emptyset$ and $V_t = \{t_i\}_{i=1}^{M_u} = \emptyset$, where $\emptyset$ denotes the empty set. In other words, model $\mathcal{F}$ is good enough in learning the weather removal function $f(.)$ that minimizes the difference between labeled and unlabeled weather-degraded images. In the parametric setting, if we use Mean Squared Error (MSE) on the parameter space $\Theta_{\mathcal{F}}$, then we have

$$MSE(\hat{\theta}) = \mathbf{E}\left[\left(\hat{\theta} - \theta\right)^2\right] = \left(\mathbf{E}[\hat{\theta}] - \theta\right)^2 + Var(\hat{\theta}). \tag{2}$$

The term $\left(\mathbf{E}[\hat{\theta}] - \theta\right)^2$ is a form of bias. In a correct parametric model, fully-supervised and semi-supervised deep learning models converge to the same parameter value θ^*. In other words, both fully-supervised error and semi-supervised error tends to L^*, $i.e. L_l \to L^*$, and $L_{l+u} \to L^*$, as $N_\ell \to \infty$ and $\frac{N_\ell}{N_u} \to 0$, where N_ℓ and N_u represent the number of labeled and unlabeled images.

3.3 Incorrect Parametric Model (misspecified)

If $f^* \notin \mathcal{F}$, then $L(f_{opt}) - L^* > 0$. In this case we change the training set from $\mathcal{D}_{src}$ (labeled) to $\mathcal{D}_{src} + \mathcal{D}_{tgt}$. However, this will only change the estimation error (in Eq. 2). Adding unlabeled observations reduces the estimation variance. Nonetheless, fully-supervised and semi-supervised deep learning models may converge to different parameter values. In other words, model $\mathcal{F}$ isn't good enough to learn a deraining function $f(.)$ that minimizes labeled and unlabeled weather-degraded images. There exists domain gap between latent labeled and unlabeled vectors, and $V_s \neq \emptyset$ and $V_t \neq \emptyset$. Given a fixed number of weather-degraded images in the labeled training set, increasing the unlabeled observations may cause a larger estimation bias, *i.e.*

$$\left(\mathbf{E}[\hat{\theta}_{l+u}] - \theta \right)^2 > \left(\mathbf{E}[\hat{\theta}_l] - \theta \right)^2, \tag{3}$$

where $\hat{\theta}_l$ and θ_{l+u} are the parameters of fully-supervised and semi-supervised methods. In this case, semi-supervised performance would be degraded if the increase in estimation bias is more significant than the decrease in the estimation variance.

3.4   Semi-supervised Degradation Theorem

Before discussing about a lemma and a theorem for the degradation in semi-supervised (SS) performance, we construct a few idealizations that are required. Let $L(\hat{f})$ be the regression error of a learned restoration function $\hat{f}(\in \mathcal{F})$, and $KL(f_{\theta^*_{sup}} || \hat{f})$ be the Kullback-Leibler divergence between fully-supervised limit density and the estimated $\hat{f}$. Here, we assume that $L^*_{sup}, f^*_{sup}, \theta^*_{sup}$ is the best possible fully-supervised parameters that can be learned given the model $\mathcal{F}$. Similarly, $L^*_{unsup}, f^*_{unsup}, \theta^*_{unsup}$ denote the best possible unsupervised parameters that can be learned given the model $\mathcal{F}$.

Lemma. *For any fixed finite N_ℓ or $N_\ell \to \infty$, as $\frac{N_\ell}{N_u} \to 0$, the limit of the maxima of semi-supervised likelihood function reaches the unsupervised limit θ^*_{unsup}. That is, let $\hat{\theta}_{l+u}$ denote the parameters of a learned SS method when the number of labeled and unlabeled images are N_ℓ and N_u, then as $\frac{N_\ell}{N_u} \to 0$,*

$$\left\{ \hat{\theta}_{(l+u)} \right\}_u \xrightarrow{p} \theta^*_{unsup} \quad \forall N_\ell \tag{4}$$

Proof. In semi-supervised learning the samples are drawn from a collection $\mathcal{D}_{src} + \mathcal{D}_{tgt}$ which implies that the probability of drawn realization being labeled image is $\lambda = \frac{N_\ell}{N_\ell + N_u}$, and being unlabeled image is $1 - \lambda = \frac{N_u}{N_\ell + N_u}$. The optimization involved in learning the parameters $\hat{\theta}$, is as follows,

$$\arg\max_\theta \left(\lambda \mathbf{E}_{f(x,y)}[\log f(x, y \mid \theta)] + (1 - \lambda)\mathbf{E}_{f(x,y)}[\log f(x \mid \theta)] \right), \tag{5}$$

which is a convex combination of the fully-supervised and unsupervised expected log-likelihood functions. For an arbitrary finite value of N_ℓ, as $\frac{N_\ell}{N_u} \to 0$, $\lambda = \frac{N_\ell}{N_\ell + N_u} \to 0$, indicating the above optimization in $\hat{\theta}$, maximizes $\mathbf{E}_{f(x,y)}[\log f(x \mid \theta)]$, which by definition is θ^*_{unsup}. Thus the learned semi-supervised parameters, $\left\{ \hat{\theta}_{(l+u)} \right\}_u \xrightarrow{p} \theta^*_{unsup} \quad \forall N_\ell$. $\qquad \square$

Theorem. *If* $L(f_{\theta^*_{sup}}) < L(f_{\theta^*_{unsup}})$, *then for fixed* N_ℓ *or* $N_\ell \to \infty$, *as* $\frac{N_\ell}{N_u} \to 0$,

$$\mathbb{K}\left\{L\left(f_{\hat{\theta}_\ell}\right) < L\left(f_{\hat{\theta}_{(\ell+u)}}\right)\right\} - \mathbb{K}\left\{KL\left(f_{\theta^*_{sup}}\|f_{\hat{\theta}_\ell}\right) < KL\left(f_{\theta^*_{sup}}\|f_{\hat{\theta}_{\ell+u}}\right)\right\} \xrightarrow{p} 0$$

and we have

$$\lim_{N_\ell \to \infty, \frac{N_\ell}{N_u} \to 0} P\left\{L\left(f_{\hat{\theta}_\ell}\right) < L\left(f_{\hat{\theta}_{(\ell+u)}}\right)\right\} = \lim_{N_\ell \to \infty} P\left\{KL\left(f_{\theta^*_{sup}}\|f_{\hat{\theta}_\ell}\right) < KL\left(f_{\theta^*_{sup}}\|f_{\theta^*_{unsup}}\right)\right\}.$$

Proof. Please refer to the supplementary document for the proof. We use these theoretical results, and come-up with the following corollaries. □

Corollary 1. *If* $L(f_{\theta^*_{sup}}) < L(f_{\theta^*_{unsup}})$, *then for the misspecified model,* $\exists \ell$, *s.t.*

$$\lim_{N_u \to \infty} P\left\{L\left(f_{\hat{\theta}_\ell}\right) < L\left(f_{\hat{\theta}_{(\ell+u)}}\right)\right\} > 0.$$

i.e. semi-supervised task yields degradation with positive probability as $N_u \to \infty$

Proof. Please refer to the supplementary document for proof. □

Corollary 2. *If for a subset of unlabeled images* $\mathcal{T}_1 \subset \mathcal{D}_{tgt}$, $\exists$ *very small* $\epsilon > 0$, *s.t.* $|L(f_{\theta^*_{sup}}) - L(f_{\theta^*_{unsup}, \mathcal{T}_1})| < \epsilon$, *then*

$$\left\{\hat{\theta}_{(l+u)}\right\}_{u \in \mathcal{T}_1} \xrightarrow{p} \theta^*_{sup} \quad \forall N_\ell. \tag{6}$$

In other words, model $\mathcal{F}$ *behaves nearly like a specified model on the labeled images in* $\mathcal{D}_{src}$, *and unlabeled images in* $\mathcal{T}_1$, *since the unlabeled images from subset* $\mathcal{T}_1$ *are very similar to the labeled images in* $\mathcal{D}_{src}$.

Proof. From Eq. 5, the optimization for learning parameters $\hat{\theta}$ is $\arg\max_\theta$ $(\lambda \mathbf{E}_{sup} + (1-\lambda)\mathbf{E}_{unsup})$, where $\mathbf{E}_{sup} = \mathbf{E}_{f(x,y)}[\log f(x, y \mid \theta)]$, and $\mathbf{E}_{unsup} = \mathbf{E}_{f(x,y)}[\log f(x \mid \theta)]$. We rewrite, $\mathbf{E}_{unsup} = \mathbf{E}_{\mathcal{T}_1} + \mathbf{E}_{\mathcal{D}_{tgt}-\mathcal{T}_1}$, where $\mathbf{E}_{\mathcal{T}_1} = \mathbf{E}_{f(x,y)}[\log f(x \mid \theta, x \in \mathcal{T}_1)]$ and $\mathbf{E}_{\mathcal{D}_{tgt}-\mathcal{T}_1} = \mathbf{E}_{f(x,y)}[\log f(x \mid \theta, x \in \mathcal{D}_{tgt} - \mathcal{T}_1)]$. Thus optimization for learning parameters $\hat{\theta}$ is,

$$\arg\max_\theta \left(\lambda \mathbf{E}_{sup} + (1-\lambda)(\mathbf{E}_{\mathcal{T}_1} + \mathbf{E}_{\mathcal{D}_{tgt}-\mathcal{T}_1})\right)$$

if we learn parameter $\hat{\theta}$ for a semi-supervision task using only $\mathcal{T}_1$ and $\mathcal{D}_{src}$. That is, rejecting unlabeled observations from $\mathcal{D}_{tgt} - \mathcal{T}_1$ while learning $\hat{\theta}$. Thus the resultant optimization for learning parameters $\hat{\theta}$ is

$$\arg\max_\theta \left(\lambda \mathbf{E}_{sup} + (1-\lambda)\mathbf{E}_{\mathcal{T}_1}\right) \approx \arg\max_\theta \left(\lambda \mathbf{E}_{sup} + (1-\lambda)\mathbf{E}_{sup}\right). \tag{7}$$

Since $|L(f_{\theta^*_{sup}}) - L(f_{\theta^*_{unsup,\mathcal{T}_1}})| < \epsilon$, or unlabeled images from $\mathcal{T}_1$ are similar to the labeled images $\mathcal{D}_{src}$, and have similar error, we approximate the optimization for $\hat{\theta}$ to $\mathbf{E}_{sup} = \mathbf{E}_{f(x,y)}[\log f(x, y \mid \theta)]$. Thus, $\left\{\hat{\theta}_{(l+u)}\right\}_{u\in\mathcal{T}_1} \xrightarrow{p} \theta^*_{sup}$.

The key takeaway from the above theorem and Corollaries is that if the SSR is misspecified, then as increasing the unlabeled images might degraded the SSR performance. In such cases, to boost the SSR performance we can create subset of unlabeled images($\mathcal{T}_1$) by rejecting the unlabeled images that are adversely effecting SSR performance. By doing this SSR will nearly act like a specified model on $\mathcal{T}_1$ and $\mathcal{D}_{src}$, and semi-supervised performance of SSR tends towards fully-supervised performance. ☐

4   Proposed Method

Let an SSR method $f_{\hat{\theta}} \in \mathcal{F}$, leveraging weather information from unlabeled and labeled images to learn the parameters $\hat{\theta}$. As discussed in the previous section, if the model $\mathcal{F}$ is missepcified, then a domain gap can exist between the unlabeled and labeled images. In other words, the projected latent labeled and unlabeled vectors can have some different basis vectors, implying $V_s = \{s_i\}_{i=1}^{M_l} \neq \emptyset$ and $V_t = \{t_i\}_{i=1}^{M_u} \neq \emptyset$. For example in the Fig. 2 t-SNE plot of Syn2Real [48] for cross-domain experiment with $\mathcal{D}_{src} = $ Rain800 and $\mathcal{D}_{tgt} = $ SPA-data, we can see some unlabeled images are similar or close to labeled images and others are not. In such cases we can use Corollary 2 and approximate the model $\mathcal{F}$ as a specified model by training on the labeled dataset $\mathcal{D}_{src}$ and on a subset of unlabeled images $\mathcal{T}_1 \subset \mathcal{D}_{tgt}$. In this way, we make the model $\mathcal{F}$ behave as nearly specified model on $\mathcal{D}_{src} + \mathcal{T}_1$, and can boost the performance of a SSR method, i.e. training SSR on $\mathcal{D}_{src}+\mathcal{T}_1$ improves SSR performance towards fully-supervised performance. To this end, we propose ART-SS that rejects unlabeled images that are not similar to labeled images or adversely effecting the SSR performance while training the SSR method.

4.1   Adaptive Rejection Technique

Figure 3 gives an overview of the proposed method where we introduce a rejection module in order to carefully reject the unlabeled observations in $\mathcal{D}_{tgt}$ that are effecting the performance of SSD methods. In our ART-SS method, we project labeled and unlabeled images from $\mathcal{D}_{src}$ and $\mathcal{D}_{tgt}$, to obtain latent vectors Z_{src} and Z_{tgt} respectively. Note [13,48] express the latent vectors of labeled and unlabeled images using either fixed number of basis latent vectors [13] or using nearest labeled latent vectors [48]. So, we can define error function L for every image with help of similarity index(ψ), i.e. $L = -\psi$. Here, similarity index (ψ) for each image is computed as, $\psi = \frac{1}{M_{NN}}\sum_{z^k \in NN(z)} \frac{\langle z, z^k \rangle}{|z||z^k|}$, where $NN(z)$ nearest neighbor of z and M_{NN} number of nearest neighbors. Figure 4 shows sample normalized histogram graphs corresponding to ψ. In Fig. 4, we can observe that there is some domain gap between labeled and unlabeled images. We can also deduce the fact from Fig. 4 that a few unlabeled images are similar to the labeled images that will help to improve the SSR performance and a few unlabeled images may hurt the SSR performance. According to Corollary 2 to make a SSR method specified we should create subset $\mathcal{T}_1$, where unlabeled images in $\mathcal{T}_1$ should satisfy $|L_u - L_l| < \epsilon$ and ϵ is small positive number.

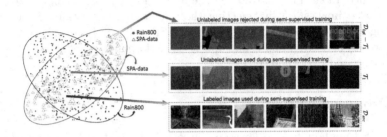

Fig. 2. t-SNE plot of Syn2Real [48] for cross-domain experiment with $\mathcal{D}_{src} = $ Rain800 and $\mathcal{D}_{tgt} = $ SPA-data. Here, we can see SSR is misspecified since $V_s = \{s_i\}_{i=1}^{M_l} \neq \emptyset$ and $V_t = \{t_i\}_{i=1}^{M_u} \neq \emptyset$. In order to boost Syn2Real performance we need to create $\mathcal{T}_1$, and train using $\mathcal{D}_{src} + \mathcal{T}_1$, *i.e.* not using unlabeled images from $\mathcal{D}_{tgt} - \mathcal{T}_1$. Rain streaks in $\mathcal{D}_{tgt} - \mathcal{T}_1$ are very different, for example in images 1,3 and 6 rain streaks are curved or look like irregular patches or rain streaks pointing in all directions. On the other hand unlabeled images from $\mathcal{T}_1$ are similar to $\mathcal{D}_{src}$

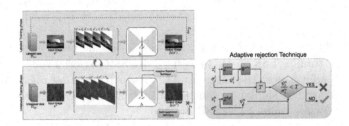

Fig. 3. Overview of the proposed adaptive rejection technique. In our rejection, labeled and unlabeled images are projected to the latent space to obtain $z^l \in Z_{src}$ and $z^u \in Z_{tgt}$. Given z_u, Z_{tgt}, Z_{src}, we use a rejection module to decide whether to update the network weights f_θ using x_u or not. Note that the semi-supervised technique in this figure can be one of [13,40,48]. Here "tick" in green means perform SSD using x_i^u unlabeled image, and "red x" in means don't perform SSR using x_i^u. (Color figure online)

Hence, one can come up with a rejection rule to reject the unlabeled images that might hurt the SSR performance. To this end, we propose a novel rejection technique where we adaptively update the threshold T using ψ values and aelotoric uncertainity [16]. Note, we compute aleotoric uncertainty [16] variance σ that makes ART-SS robust to network's errors in latent representations, since σ indicates how confident the network is about the computed latent representation vector z. By re-scalinng ψ values with σ, we will be giving higher importance to highly confident or less importance to less confident image samples while computing threshold T and rejecting the unnlabeled images.

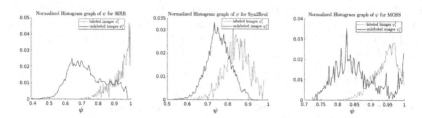

Fig. 4. Normalized histogram graphs of ψ for a cross-domain experiment where $\mathcal{D}_{src}$ is Rain800 [55] and $\mathcal{D}_{tgt}$ is SPA-data [38]. Three graphs correspond to three different SSD methods [13,40,48].

In our adaptive rejection technique, we project every labeled image x_i^l and unlabeled image x_i^u to a latent space and obtain z_i^l, σ_i^l and z_i^u, σ_i^u respectively using aleotoric uncertainity. For more details on how to compute σ, please refer to the supplementary document. Thus, we obtain $Z^{src}, \{\sigma^l\}^{src}$ and $Z^{tgt}, \{\sigma^u\}^{tgt}$. Having obtained $Z^{src}, \{\sigma^l\}^{src}$ and $Z^{tgt}, \{\sigma^u\}^{tgt}$ values, we compute ψ_i^l and ψ_i^u for each labeled x_i^l and unlabeled x_i^u image respectively. We define the threshold, T, as a weighted mean ψ_i^l values of the labeled images, i.e.,

$$\Psi^{src} = \left\{ \psi_i^l : \psi_i^l = \frac{1}{M_{NN}} \sum_{z^k \in NN(z_i^l)} \frac{\langle z_i^l, z^k \rangle}{|z_i^l||z^k|}, z_i^l = g_\theta(x_i^l), \forall x_i^l \in \mathcal{D}_{src} \right\}, T = \frac{1}{N_\ell} \sum_{\Psi^{src}, \{\sigma^l\}^{src}} \frac{\psi_i^l}{\sigma_i^l}, \tag{8}$$

where $g_\theta(.)$ is the encoder of the network f_θ, and we use σ_i^l values implying higher importance is given to highly confident samples in deciding the threshold T. During semi-supervised training of network f_θ, we will reject the unlabeled image, if $\frac{\psi_i^u}{\sigma_i^u} < T$. Figure 3 gives the overview of the proposed adaptive rejection technique. We also provide a pseudo algorithm for the proposed rejection technique in the supplementary document.

Thus, following [13,18,33,40,48] we train a semi-supervised network in two phases: (i) labeled training phase, and (ii) unlabeled training phase. In the labeled training phase, we learn the network weights f_θ using the labeled images $x_i^l \in \mathcal{D}_{src}$ in a fully-supervised fashion. Additionally, we compute $\{\psi_i^l\}$ and $\{\sigma_i^l\}$ for all the labeled images,i.e. we compute Ψ^{src} and decide threshold T as explained earlier. In the unlabeled training phase, given an unlabeled images $x_i^u \in \mathcal{D}_{tgt}$, we compute $\{\psi_i^u\}$ and $\{\sigma_i^u\}$ values For each unlabeled image, we check the criterion: $\frac{\psi_i^u}{\sigma_i^u} < T$, and decide whether to use unlabeled image for updating the network weights f_θ using $\mathcal{L}_{unsup}$. Note that $\mathcal{L}_{unsup}$ can be an unsupervised loss proposed in corresponding SSR method [13,13,18,33,40,48].

5   Experiments

To show the effectiveness of ART-SS we conduct experiments on existing SSR methods [13,18,33,40,48] showing that ART-SS boosts their performance. We conduct cross-domain experiments which cover 1) synthetic-to-synthetic experiments (where $\mathcal{D}_{src}$ and $\mathcal{D}_{tgt}$ contains synthetic rain images) and 2) synthetic-to-real (where $\mathcal{D}_{src}$ contains synthetic rain and $\mathcal{D}_{tgt}$ contains real rain).

5.1   Datasets and Metrics

Synthetic Deraining Datasets. (i) Rain800 proposed by Zhang *et al.* [55] which contains 700 synthetic paired training images and 100 synthetic paired test images. (ii) Rain200H dataset published by Yang *et al.* [43] which contains synthetic 1,800 paired training images and 200 paired test images. (iii) Rain1400 proposed by Fu *et al.* [7] which contains 9,100 synthetic pairs for training and 1,400 pairs in the test set. (iv) Rain1200 introduced by Zhang *et al.* [54] which consists of 12,000 synthetic pairs for training, and 1,200 pairs in the test set.

Real Rainy Image Datasets. Wang *et al.* [38] constructed a real rainy image dataset, called SPA-data, which contains paired 342 high resolution real rain frames extracted from videos for training. SPA-data contains 1,000 real rainy image pairs in the test set.

Wei *et al.* [40] created the DDN-SIRR dataset which has both labeled synthetic(9100 training images from Rain1400) and unlabeled (147 real-world rainy images) for training of semi-supervised deraining methods. Furthermore, a test set for DDN-SIRR is created using 10 dense and 10 sparse rain streak images.

Dehazing Datasets. Following [18,33], we create training source ($\mathcal{D}_{src}$) and target dataset($\mathcal{D}_{tgt}$) using RESIDE [17] (contains ITS (Indoor Training Set), OTS (Outdoor Training Set), SOTS (Synthetic Object Testing Set), URHI (Unlabeled real Hazy Images), and RTTS (Real Task-driven Testing Set)). Labeled training set(Syn-haze) is constructed using randomly selecting 3000 from ITS and 3000 from OTS. 2000 random images from URHI are used as unlabeled training set.

Metrics. We use peak-signal-to-noise ratio (PSNR) and structural similarity index measure (SSIM) to compare the performance of different methods.

5.2   Implementation

We performed our experiments on three existing SSD methods [13,40,48]. We follow the same instructions and settings provided in the corresponding papers to train their SSD model in a semi-supervision fashion.

SIRR. The authors use a DerainNet [7] to perform deraining. We extract the 16th layer output and define it as the latent vector z. For more details about the labeled and unlabeled training phases please refer [40]. Additionally, we compute $\{z_i^l, \sigma_i^l, \psi_i^l\}$, and threshold T in labeled training phase. In unlabeled training phase we model GMM_{real} using the unlabeled images that follow the criterion in Sect. 4.1 to while modelling GMM_{real}. Finally, KL divergence is used to minimize the distribution difference between GMM_{syn} and GMM_{real}.

Syn2Real. The authors use an encoder-decoder network constructed using Res2Block [9] to perform deraining. We use encoder output as the latent vector z. In the labeled training phase authors perform L1-norm minimization using paired images from $\mathcal{D}_{src}$. In the unlabeled training phase, we apply the proposed ART-SS method and compute the pseudo-ground truths (pseudo-GTs) using Gaussian process for the images which follow the criterion in Sect. 4.1. Finally, we update the network weights using these computed pseudo-GTs using $\mathcal{L}_{unsup}$ Please refer to [48] for more training details.

MOSS. The authors constructed a UNet-based [32] deraining network using an encoder and a decoder with residual blocks. We use the encoder output as the latent vector z. Obtaining the latent vectors for the labeled and unlabeled images (z_i^l and z_i^u respectively) we apply our rejection technique, to reject the unlabeled images that are hurting the semi-supervised performance of MOSS. For more details about the labeled and unlabeled training phases refer to [13].

Li *et al.* and DAID. For Li *et al.* [18] we define 15th layer output as latent z. On the other hand, for DAID [33] we define 12th layer output as latent z. Please refer [18,33] for corresponding labeled and unlabeled training phases details. Given the latent labeled and unlabeled vectors obtained from the network, we apply our ART-SS and use the unlabeled images that follow the criterion in Sect. 4.1 during unlabeled training phase.

Note that we compute $\{z_i^l, \sigma_i^l, \psi_i^l\}$, $\{z_i^u, \sigma_i^u, \psi_i^u\}$, (every iteration) and threshold T (every epoch) in order to apply our ART-SS to these SSR methods.

5.3   Comparisons

DDN-SIRR. Following the protocol introduced by [40], in this experiment, we train the SSR methods [13,40,48] where we set $\mathcal{D}_{src}$ as the synthetic labeled data of DDN-SIRR, and $\mathcal{D}_{tgt}$ as the real rainy image unlabeled data of DDN-SIRR. On the other hand, fully-supervised methods [4,7,14,28,43,52] only use $\mathcal{D}_{src}$, synthetic labeled data of DDN-SIRR for training. Table 1 shows the quantitative results on the synthetic test set of DDN-SIRR. We can observe that SSR methods [13,40,48] outperform fully-supervised methods [4,7,14,28,43,52], since they leverage information from unlabeled images in $\mathcal{D}_{tgt}$ during training. However, there is still a room for improving the performance of these SSR methods [13,40,48]. As can be seen from Table 1, when we use the proposed rejection method to reject samples from the unlabeled target domain, we observe a significant improvement in the performance of these SSR methods. Results are shown in Table 1 . We also provide qualitative results on one example from the synthetic test set of DDN-SIRR, and two real rain examples, in Fig. 5. As can be seen from this figure, the output images [13,40,48] without ART-SS still contain some rain streaks and are of low-quality (see the highlighted red box where the network under-performed). On the other hand, [13,40,48] with ART-SS achieve better quality derained output images.

De-haze Experiments. Following the protocol introduced in [18,33], we train SSR methods [18,33] using Syn-Haze (as labeled $\mathcal{D}_{src}$) and URHI(as unlabeled $\mathcal{D}_{tgt}$). We use SOTS and HazeRD test sets for comparing SSR methods [18,33] performance. Table 2 shows the proposed ART-SS improved the SSR [18,33] performance by around 1.4dB in PSNR. Figure 6 shows the qualitative comparisons on real haze images from RTTS, we can see visual quality of dehazed images by SSR [18,33] improved when trained with ART-SS.

Table 1. Quantitative gains obtained for SSD methods [13,40,48] using our ART-SS method on DDN-SIRR dataset. Here synthetic labeled images of DDN-SIRR dataset are used as $\mathcal{D}_{src}$, and real rainy images as $\mathcal{D}_{tgt}$. Note gains are indicated in the brackets.

Dataset	Input	Methods that use only synthetic dataset						Methods that use synthetic and real-world dataset								
		JORDER [43] (CVPR '17)	DDN [7] (CVPR '17)	PReNet [28] (CVPR '19)	MSPFN [14] (CVPR '20)	DRD [4] (CVPR '20)	MPRN [52] (CVPR '21)	SIRR [40] (CVPR '19)			Syn2Real [48] (CVPR'20)			MOSS [13] (CVPR '21)		
								w/o SSD	SSD w/o ART-SS	SSD w/ ART-SS	w/o SSD	SSD w/o ART-SS	SSD w/ ART-SS	w/o SSD	SSD w/o ART-SS	SSD w/ ART-SS
Dense	17.95	18.75	19.90	20.65	19.54	20.34	20.87	20.01	21.60(1.59)	22.16(2.15)	20.24	22.36(2.12)	22.67(2.43)	20.29	22.91(2.62)	23.32(3.02)
Sparse	24.14	24.22	26.88	26.40	26.47	26.04	26.28	26.90	26.98(0.08)	27.21(0.31)	26.15	27.12(0.97)	27.48(1.33)	25.90	27.78(1.88)	28.16(2.26)

Table 2. PSNR/SSIM comparisons for SSR methods [18,33] using our ART-SS method. Here synthetic labeled images of Syn-haze are used as $\mathcal{D}_{src}$, and real hazy images of URHI as $\mathcal{D}_{tgt}$.

Test set	Haze	DCP [10]	DehazeNet [2]	DPCDN [53]	GFN [31]	EPDN [27]	Li et al. [18]		DAID [33]	
							w/o ART-SS	w/ ART-SS	w/o ART-SS	w/ ART-SS
SOTS	13.95/0.64	15.49/0.64	21.14/0.85	19.39/0.65	22.30/0.88	23.82/0.89	24.44/0.89	25.56/0.92	27.76/0.93	29.15/0.95
HazeRD	14.01/0.39	14.01/0.39	15.54/0.41	16.12/0.34	13.98/0.37	17.37/0.56	16.55/0.47	18.17/0.56	18.07/0.63	19.50/0.66

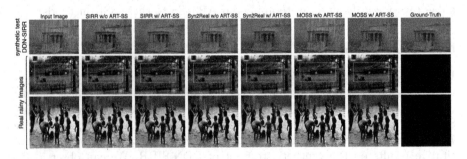

Fig. 5. Qualitative comparisons showing the benefits of using ART-SS technique for SSR methods [13,40,48]. First, second, third rows: $\mathcal{D}_{src}$ = synthetic labeled images from DDN-SIRR, and $\mathcal{D}_{tgt}$ = real unlabeled images from DDN-SIRR.

Input Image   DAID w/o ART-SS   DAID w/ ART-SS   Li et al. w/o ART-SS   Li et al. w/ ART-SS

Fig. 6. Qualitative comparisons showing the benefits of using ART-SS for SSR methods [18,33] using real hazy images from RTTS.

Cross-Domain Experiments. In Table 4, we set $\mathcal{D}_{src}$ as Rain800, and $\mathcal{D}_{tgt}$ as Rain1400, Rain200L, and SPA-data to train the SSD methods [13,40,48]. In Table 3, we set $\mathcal{D}_{src}$ as Rain1400, and $\mathcal{D}_{tgt}$ as Rain800, Rain200L, and SPA-data. From Tables 3, and 4, we can clearly see that SSR methods [13,40,48] with ART-SS outperform methods without rejection with huge margin in PSNR and SSIM. Furthermore, from Tables 3 and 4, it is evident that ART-SS is beneficial in improving the performance of [13,40,48], even in variations in the dataset sizes of $\mathcal{D}_{src}$ and $\mathcal{D}_{tgt}$, and different synthetic and real rain datasets.

Table 3. Cross-domain experiment with $\mathcal{D}_{src}$ as Rain1400, and $\mathcal{D}_{tgt}$ as Rain800, Rain200L and SPA-data. Note gains are indicated in the brackets. We highlight gains obtained using our ART-SS rejection technique for SSD methods [13,40,48] with blue.

Source dataset $\mathcal{D}_{src}$	SSD method	SIRR						Syn2Real						MOSS					
	Target dataset $\mathcal{D}_{tgt}$	Rain800		Rain200L		SPA-data		Rain800		Rain200L		SPA-data		Rain800		Rain200L		SPA-data	
		PSNR	SSIM	PSNR	SSIM	PSNR	SSIM	PSNR	SSIM	PSNR	SSIM	PSNR	SSIM	PSNR	SSIM	PSNR	SSIM	PSNR	SSIM
$\mathcal{D}_{src}$ = Rain1400	Source only $\mathcal{D}_{src}$ w/o SSD	22.17	0.828	24.82	0.867	33.28	0.941	22.59	0.845	27.08	0.907	31.58	0.955	21.80	0.824	25.77	0.881	32.01	0.948
	SSD w/o ART-SS $\mathcal{D}_{src}+\mathcal{D}_{tgt}$	22.62 (0.45)	0.833 (0.005)	26.75 (1.93)	0.882 (0.015)	34.07 (0.79)	0.950 (0.009)	22.87 (0.28)	0.846 (0.001)	27.97 (0.89)	0.929 (0.022)	34.24 (2.66)	0.962 (0.007)	22.56 (0.76)	0.831 (0.007)	27.09 (1.32)	0.896 (0.015)	34.56 (2.55)	0.960 (0.012)
	SSD w/ ART-SS $\mathcal{D}_{src}+\mathcal{D}_{tgt}$	23.42 (1.25)	0.841 (0.012)	29.38 (4.56)	0.910 (0.043)	36.12 (2.84)	0.962 (0.021)	23.85 (1.26)	0.863 (0.018)	30.76 (3.68)	0.948 (0.041)	37.36 (5.78)	0.974 (0.019)	24.32 (2.52)	0.870 (0.046)	30.42 (4.65)	0.939 (0.059)	37.94 (5.93)	0.983 (0.035)

Table 4. Cross-domain experiment with $\mathcal{D}_{src}$ as Rain800, and $\mathcal{D}_{tgt}$ as Rain1400, Rain200L and SPA-data. We highlight gains obtained using our ART-SS rejection technique for SSD methods [13,40,48] with blue.

Source dataset $\mathcal{D}_{src}$	SSD method	SIRR						Syn2Real						MOSS					
	Target dataset $\mathcal{D}_{tgt}$	Rain1400		Rain200L		SPA-data		Rain1400		Rain200L		SPA-data		Rain1400		Rain200L		SPA-data	
		PSNR	SSIM	PSNR	SSIM	PSNR	SSIM	PSNR	SSIM	PSNR	SSIM	PSNR	SSIM	PSNR	SSIM	PSNR	SSIM	PSNR	SSIM
$\mathcal{D}_{src}$ = Rain800	Source only $\mathcal{D}_{src}$ w/o SSD	24.64	0.871	24.78	0.881	31.75	0.937	25.17	0.903	27.02	0.923	31.36	0.959	24.98	0.888	26.75	0.923	32.09	0.946
	SSD w/o ART-SS $\mathcal{D}_{src}+\mathcal{D}_{tgt}$	26.17 (1.53)	0.889 (0.018)	26.56 (1.78)	0.897 (0.016)	33.89 (2.14)	0.946 (0.009)	26.38 (1.21)	0.911 (0.008)	27.65 (0.63)	0.930 (0.007)	34.16 (2.80)	0.966 (0.007)	26.84 (1.86)	0.904 (0.016)	27.67 (0.92)	0.928 (0.005)	34.82 (2.73)	0.962 (0.016)
	SSD w/ ART-SS $\mathcal{D}_{src}+\mathcal{D}_{tgt}$	26.98 (2.34)	0.903 (0.032)	29.10 (4.32)	0.918 (0.037)	36.32 (4.57)	0.962 (0.025)	27.84 (2.67)	0.922 (0.019)	30.41 (3.39)	0.944 (0.021)	37.28 (5.92)	0.981 (0.022)	29.01 (4.03)	0.919 (0.031)	31.02 (4.27)	0.951 (0.028)	37.56 (5.47)	0.982 (0.036)

Table 5. Ablation study for ART-SS. Note, "RS" mean random sampling, "NR" means no rejection *i.e.* using all unlabeled images from $\mathcal{D}_{tgt}$.

Source dataset	Target dataset	Metrics	Syn2Real					MOSS				
			w/o SSD	SSD w/ NR	SSD w/ RS	SSD w/ ψ	SSD w/ ART-SS	w/o SSD	SSD w/ NR	SSD w/ RS	SSD w/ ψ	SSD w/ ART-SS
$\mathcal{D}_{src}$ = Rain800	$\mathcal{D}_{tgt}$ = SPA-data	PSNR	31.36	34.16	34.94	35.99	37.28	32.09	34.82	35.38	35.86	37.56
		SSIM	0.959	0.966	0.970	0.973	0.981	0.946	0.962	0.968	0.970	0.982

5.4 Ablation Study

We perform an ablation study to show the improvements of ART-SS over random-sampling or nearest neighbors. In this experiment, we train [13,48] with Rain800 as $\mathcal{D}_{src}$ and SPA-data as $\mathcal{D}_{tgt}$, in five different settings, (i) without semi-supervision (*i.e.* training with only $\mathcal{D}_{src}$), w/o SSD, (ii) with semi-supervision using all the images from $\mathcal{D}_{tgt}$ and $\mathcal{D}_{src}$, SSD w/ NR, (iii) semi-supervision using all the images from $\mathcal{D}_{src}$ but randomly sampling N_T images from $\mathcal{D}_{tgt}$ for training, SSD w/ RS, (iv) semi-supervision using all the images from $\mathcal{D}_{src}$, and rejecting unlabeled images using the just similarity index ψ between unlabeled image and nearest neighbors, (v) semi-supervision using ART-SS, *i.e.* computing T using ψ and σ values, and rejecting unlabeled image x_i^u from $\mathcal{D}_{tgt}$ using T and corresponding $\{\psi_i^u, \sigma_i^u\}$ values, SSD w/ ART-SS. Ablation experiment results are shown in Table 5. From these results, we can notice that SSR w/ ART-SS produces significant improvements for both SSR methods [13,48], when compared to other rejection techniques.

6   Conclusion

We theoretically study the effect of unlabeled weather-degraded observations on semi-supervised performance, and develop a novel technique called ART-SS, that rejects the unlabeled images which are not beneficial for improving the semi-supervised performance. We conduct extensive cross-domain experiments on different datasets to show the effectiveness of proposed ART-SS technique in improving the performance of [13,18,33,40,48].

References

1. Berman, D., et al.: Non-local image dehazing. In: Proceedings of the IEEE conference on computer vision and pattern recognition, pp. 1674–1682 (2016)
2. Cai, B., Xu, X., Jia, K., Qing, C., Tao, D.: Dehazenet: an end-to-end system for single image haze removal. IEEE Trans. Image Process. 25(11), 5187–5198 (2016)
3. Chen, L.-C., Zhu, Y., Papandreou, G., Schroff, F., Adam, H.: Encoder-decoder with atrous separable convolution for semantic image segmentation. In: Ferrari, V., Hebert, M., Sminchisescu, C., Weiss, Y. (eds.) ECCV 2018. LNCS, vol. 11211, pp. 833–851. Springer, Cham (2018). https://doi.org/10.1007/978-3-030-01234-2_49
4. Deng, S., et al.: Detail-recovery image deraining via context aggregation networks. In: Proceedings of the IEEE/CVF Conference on Computer Vision and Pattern Recognition, pp. 14560–14569 (2020)

5. Dong, H., et al.: Multi-scale boosted dehazing network with dense feature fusion. In: Proceedings of the IEEE/CVF Conference on Computer Vision and Pattern Recognition, pp. 2157–2167 (2020)

6. Fattal, R.: Dehazing using color-lines. ACM Trans. Graph. (TOG) **34**(1), 1–14 (2014)

7. Fu, X., Huang, J., Zeng, D., Huang, Y., Ding, X., Paisley, J.: Removing rain from single images via a deep detail network. In: Proceedings of the IEEE Conference on Computer Vision and Pattern Recognition, pp. 3855–3863 (2017)

8. Fu, X., Qi, Q., Zha, Z.J., Zhu, Y., Ding, X.: Rain streak removal via dual graph convolutional network. In: Proceedings AAAI Conference on Artificial Intelligence, pp. 1–9 (2021)

9. Gao, S., Cheng, M.M., Zhao, K., Zhang, X.Y., Yang, M.H., Torr, P.H.: Res2net: a new multi-scale backbone architecture. IEEE Transactions on Pattern Analysis and Machine Intelligence (2019)

10. He, K., Sun, J., Tang, X.: Single image haze removal using dark channel prior. IEEE Trans. Pattern Anal. Mach. Intell. **33**(12), 2341–2353 (2010)

11. Hu, X., Fu, C.W., Zhu, L., Heng, P.A.: Depth-attentional features for single-image rain removal. In: Proceedings of the IEEE/CVF Conference on Computer Vision and Pattern Recognition, pp. 8022–8031 (2019)

12. Huang, D.A., Kang, L.W., Wang, Y.C.F., Lin, C.W.: Self-learning based image decomposition with applications to single image denoising. IEEE Trans. Multimedia **16**(1), 83–93 (2013)

13. Huang, H., Yu, A., He, R.: Memory oriented transfer learning for semi-supervised image deraining. In: Proceedings of the IEEE/CVF Conference on Computer Vision and Pattern Recognition (CVPR), pp. 7732–7741 (2021)

14. Jiang, K., et al.: Multi-scale progressive fusion network for single image deraining. In: Proceedings of the IEEE/CVF Conference on Computer Vision and Pattern Recognition, pp. 8346–8355 (2020)

15. Kang, L.W., Lin, C.W., Fu, Y.H.: Automatic single-image-based rain streaks removal via image decomposition. IEEE Trans. Image Process. **21**(4), 1742–1755 (2011)

16. Kendall, A., Gal, Y.: What uncertainties do we need in Bayesian deep learning for computer vision? arXiv preprint arXiv:1703.04977 (2017)

17. Li, B., et al.: Benchmarking single-image dehazing and beyond. IEEE Trans. Image Process. **28**(1), 492–505 (2018)

18. Li, L., et al.: Semi-supervised image dehazing. IEEE Trans. Image Process. **29**, 2766–2779 (2019)

19. Li, P., Tian, J., Tang, Y., Wang, G., Wu, C.: Deep retinex network for single image dehazing. IEEE Trans. Image Process. **30**, 1100–1115 (2020)

20. Li, R., Pan, J., Li, Z., Tang, J.: Single image dehazing via conditional generative adversarial network. In: Proceedings of the IEEE Conference on Computer Vision and Pattern Recognition, pp. 8202–8211 (2018)

21. Li, R., Cheong, L.F., Tan, R.T.: Heavy rain image restoration: Integrating physics model and conditional adversarial learning. In: Proceedings of the IEEE/CVF Conference on Computer Vision and Pattern Recognition, pp. 1633–1642 (2019)

22. Li, R., Tan, R.T., Cheong, L.F.: All in one bad weather removal using architectural search. In: Proceedings of the IEEE/CVF Conference on Computer Vision and Pattern Recognition, pp. 3175–3185 (2020)

23. Li, X., Wu, J., Lin, Z., Liu, H., Zha, H.: Recurrent squeeze-and-excitation context aggregation net for single image deraining. In: Ferrari, V., Hebert, M., Sminchis-

escu, C., Weiss, Y. (eds.) ECCV 2018. LNCS, vol. 11211, pp. 262–277. Springer, Cham (2018). https://doi.org/10.1007/978-3-030-01234-2_16

24. Li, Y., Tan, R.T., Guo, X., Lu, J., Brown, M.S.: Rain streak removal using layer priors. In: Proceedings of the IEEE Conference on Computer Vision and Pattern Recognition, pp. 2736–2744 (2016)

25. Lin, H., Li, Y., Fu, X., Ding, X., Huang, Y., Paisley, J.: Rain o'er me: Synthesizing real rain to derain with data distillation. IEEE Trans. Image Process. **29**, 7668–7680 (2020)

26. Luo, Y., Xu, Y., Ji, H.: Removing rain from a single image via discriminative sparse coding. In: Proceedings of the IEEE International Conference on Computer Vision, pp. 3397–3405 (2015)

27. Qu, Y., Chen, Y., Huang, J., Xie, Y.: Enhanced pix2pix dehazing network. In: Proceedings of the IEEE/CVF Conference on Computer Vision and Pattern Recognition, pp. 8160–8168 (2019)

28. Ren, D., Zuo, W., Hu, Q., Zhu, P., Meng, D.: Progressive image deraining networks: a better and simpler baseline. In: Proceedings of the IEEE/CVF Conference on Computer Vision and Pattern Recognition, pp. 3937–3946 (2019)

29. Ren, S., He, K., Girshick, R., Sun, J.: Faster R-CNN: towards real-time object detection with region proposal networks. In: Advances in neural information processing systems 28 (2015)

30. Ren, W., Liu, S., Zhang, H., Pan, J., Cao, X., Yang, M.-H.: Single image dehazing via multi-scale convolutional neural networks. In: Leibe, B., Matas, J., Sebe, N., Welling, M. (eds.) ECCV 2016. LNCS, vol. 9906, pp. 154–169. Springer, Cham (2016). https://doi.org/10.1007/978-3-319-46475-6_10

31. Ren, W., et al.: Gated fusion network for single image dehazing. In: Proceedings of the IEEE Conference on Computer Vision and Pattern Recognition, pp. 3253–3261 (2018)

32. Ronneberger, O., Fischer, P., Brox, T.: U-Net: convolutional networks for biomedical image segmentation. In: Navab, N., Hornegger, J., Wells, W.M., Frangi, A.F. (eds.) MICCAI 2015. LNCS, vol. 9351, pp. 234–241. Springer, Cham (2015). https://doi.org/10.1007/978-3-319-24574-4_28

33. Shao, Y., Li, L., Ren, W., Gao, C., Sang, N.: Domain adaptation for image dehazing. In: Proceedings of the IEEE/CVF Conference on Computer Vision and Pattern Recognition, pp. 2808–2817 (2020)

34. Tu, Z., et al.: Maxim: Multi-axis MLP for image processing. In: Proceedings of the IEEE/CVF Conference on Computer Vision and Pattern Recognition, pp. 5769–5780 (2022)

35. Wang, G., Sun, C., Sowmya, A.: ERL-Net: entangled representation learning for single image de-raining. In: Proceedings of the IEEE/CVF International Conference on Computer Vision, pp. 5644–5652 (2019)

36. Wang, H., Xie, Q., Zhao, Q., Meng, D.: A model-driven deep neural network for single image rain removal. In: Proceedings of the IEEE/CVF Conference on Computer Vision and Pattern Recognition, pp. 3103–3112 (2020)

37. Wang, H., Yue, Z., Xie, Q., Zhao, Q., Zheng, Y., Meng, D.: From rain generation to rain removal. In: Proceedings of the IEEE/CVF Conference on Computer Vision and Pattern Recognition, pp. 14791–14801 (2021)

38. Wang, T., Yang, X., Xu, K., Chen, S., Zhang, Q., Lau, R.W.: Spatial attentive single-image deraining with a high quality real rain dataset. In: Proceedings of the IEEE/CVF Conference on Computer Vision and Pattern Recognition, pp. 12270–12279 (2019)

39. Wang, Y., Song, Y., Ma, C., Zeng, B.: Rethinking image deraining via rain streaks and vapors. In: Vedaldi, A., Bischof, H., Brox, T., Frahm, J.-M. (eds.) ECCV 2020. LNCS, vol. 12362, pp. 367–382. Springer, Cham (2020). https://doi.org/10.1007/978-3-030-58520-4_22

40. Wei, W., Meng, D., Zhao, Q., Xu, Z., Wu, Y.: Semi-supervised transfer learning for image rain removal. In: Proceedings of the IEEE/CVF Conference on Computer Vision and Pattern Recognition, pp. 3877–3886 (2019)

41. Wu, H., et al.: Contrastive learning for compact single image dehazing. In: Proceedings of the IEEE/CVF Conference on Computer Vision and Pattern Recognition, pp. 10551–10560 (2021)

42. Yang, T., Priebe, C.E.: The effect of model misspecification on semi-supervised classification. IEEE Trans. Pattern Anal. Mach. Intell. **33**(10), 2093–2103 (2011)

43. Yang, W., Tan, R.T., Feng, J., Liu, J., Guo, Z., Yan, S.: Deep joint rain detection and removal from a single image. In: Proceedings of the IEEE Conference on Computer Vision and Pattern Recognition, pp. 1357–1366 (2017)

44. Yasarla, R., Patel, V.M.: Uncertainty guided multi-scale residual learning-using a cycle spinning CNN for single image de-raining. In: Proceedings of the IEEE/CVF Conference on Computer Vision and Pattern Recognition, pp. 8405–8414 (2019)

45. Yasarla, R., Patel, V.M.: Confidence measure guided single image de-raining. IEEE Trans. Image Process. **29**, 4544–4555 (2020)

46. Yasarla, R., Patel, V.M.: Learning to restore images degraded by atmospheric turbulence using uncertainty. In: 2021 IEEE International Conference on Image Processing (ICIP), pp. 1694–1698. IEEE (2021)

47. Yasarla, R., Patel, V.M.: CNN-based restoration of a single face image degraded by atmospheric turbulence. Behavior, and Identity Science, IEEE Transactions on Biometrics (2022)

48. Yasarla, R., Sindagi, V.A., Patel, V.M.: Syn2real transfer learning for image deraining using gaussian processes. In: Proceedings of the IEEE/CVF Conference on Computer Vision and Pattern Recognition (CVPR) (2020)

49. Yasarla, R., Sindagi, V.A., Patel, V.M.: Unsupervised restoration of weather-affected images using deep gaussian process-based cyclegan. arXiv preprint arXiv:2204.10970 (2022)

50. Yasarla, R., Valanarasu, J.M.J., Patel, V.M.: Exploring overcomplete representations for single image deraining using CNNs. IEEE J. Select. Top. Sig. Process. **15**(2), 229–239 (2020)

51. Zamir, S.W., Arora, A., Khan, S., Hayat, M., Khan, F.S., Yang, M.H.: Restormer: efficient transformer for high-resolution image restoration. In: Proceedings of the IEEE/CVF Conference on Computer Vision and Pattern Recognition, pp. 5728–5739 (2022)

52. Zamir, S.W., et al.: Multi-stage progressive image restoration. In: Proceedings of the IEEE/CVF Conference on Computer Vision and Pattern Recognition, pp. 14821–14831 (2021)

53. Zhang, H., Patel, V.M.: Densely connected pyramid dehazing network. In: Proceedings of the IEEE conference on Computer Vision and Pattern Recognition, pp. 3194–3203 (2018)

54. Zhang, H., Patel, V.M.: Density-aware single image de-raining using a multi-stream dense network. In: Proceedings of the IEEE conference on computer vision and pattern recognition, pp. 695–704 (2018)

55. Zhang, H., Sindagi, V., Patel, V.M.: Image de-raining using a conditional generative adversarial network. IEEE Trans. Circuits Syst. Video Technol. **30**(11), 3943–3956 (2019)

56. Zhang, H., Sindagi, V., Patel, V.M.: Joint transmission map estimation and dehazing using deep networks. IEEE Trans. Circuits Syst. Video Technol. **30**(7), 1975–1986 (2019)
57. Zhang, J., et al.: Hierarchical density-aware dehazing network. IEEE Transactions on Cybernetics (2021)
58. Zhou, M., et al.: Image de-raining via continual learning. In: Proceedings of the IEEE/CVF Conference on Computer Vision and Pattern Recognition, pp. 4907–4916 (2021)

Fusion from Decomposition:
A Self-Supervised Decomposition
Approach for Image Fusion

Pengwei Liang[1], Junjun Jiang[1(✉)], Xianming Liu[1], and Jiayi Ma[2]

[1] Harbin Institute of Technology, Harbin 150001, China
{jiangjunjun,csxm}@hit.edu.cn
[2] Wuhan University, Wuhan 430072, China

Abstract. Image fusion is famous as an alternative solution to generate one high-quality image from multiple images in addition to image restoration from a single degraded image. The essence of image fusion is to integrate complementary information or best parts from source images. The current fusion methods usually need a large number of paired samples or sophisticated loss functions and fusion rules to train the supervised or unsupervised model. In this paper, we propose a powerful image decomposition model for fusion task via the self-supervised representation learning, dubbed **De**composition for **Fusion** (**DeFusion**). Without any paired data or sophisticated loss, DeFusion can decompose the source images into a feature embedding space, where the common and unique features can be separated. Therefore, the image fusion can be achieved within the embedding space through the jointly trained reconstruction (projection) head in the decomposition stage even without any fine-tuning. Thanks to the development of self-supervised learning, we can train the model to learn image decomposition ability with a brute but simple pretext task. The pretrained model allows for learning very effective features that generalize well: the DeFusion is a unified versatile framework that is trained with an image fusion irrelevant dataset and can be directly applied to various image fusion tasks. Extensive experiments demonstrate that the proposed DeFusion can achieve comparable or even better performance compared to state-of-the-art methods (whether supervised or unsupervised) for different image fusion tasks.

Keywords: Image fusion · Self-supervised learning · Image decomposion

1 Introduction

The scene perception is a long-standing goal of machine vision, in which the scene is digitized by multiple hardware sensors. Each sensor can capture only parts of

Supplementary Information The online version contains supplementary material available at https://doi.org/10.1007/978-3-031-19797-0_41.

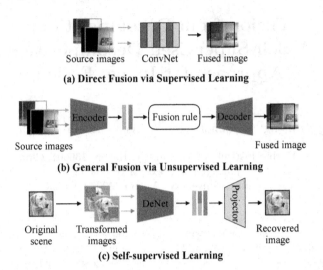

(a) Direct Fusion via Supervised Learning

(b) General Fusion via Unsupervised Learning

(c) Self-supervised Learning

Fig. 1. Paradigms of different image fusion methods. Most existing image fusion methods based on deeplearning can be classified into (a) and (b). We draw the insights from the essence of image fusion and propose a new image fusion framework based on self-supervised learning.

information from the scene at a time due to hardware limitations. In order to represent the scene accurately and effectively, image fusion is pushed forward to integrate the complementary features of multiple source views in the same scene, thus generating a high-quality image for the downstream high-level tasks or human perception [43]. For example, the multi-exposure fusion (MEF) utilizes multiple low dynamic range (LDR) images to obtain a single high dynamic range (HDR) image [23,52]; the multi-focus fusion (MFF) combines multiple images with different focus areas into a single all-in-focus image [53]. An essential step in image fusion methods is to effectively represent the source images. In the early years, some classical feature representation and decomposition methods have been introduced into image fusion, such as wavelet [26], pyramid [37], edge-preserving filter [14], sparse coding and dictionary learning [42]. Driving from the signal processing perspective, these manually designed feature representation approaches poorly understand the semantic knowledge of images, which limits the generalizability of those models.

Recently, deep learning has been introduced to address the limitations by adaptively learning image representations from large-scale dataset, and push forward the frontier of image fusion research. In the pioneer works, researchers simply regard the network as an optimizer, which is used to model the relationship between the source images and the target fusion result, and we called the framework 'direct fusion via supervised learning' as shown in Fig. 1a. Obviously, these models exhibit a major flaw: obtaining the paired source images and ground-truth fused image would be difficult [3], if not impossible, in some scenario, e.g., infrared-visible image fusion [18]. An alternative solution is to abandon the supervision information and carefully design some auxiliary losses to maintain the consistency between the fused image and source images [47]; or leverage tailored fusion rules to perform fusion at the semantic bottleneck layer of some pretrained networks (such as AutoEncoder [13,33]), as shown in Fig. 1b. Although these advancements expand the applicable scenarios, they still suffer from a serious flaw: their performance seriously depends on the human knowledge about the auxiliary loss and fusion rule.

To address the aforementioned issues, we propose a self-supervised learning framework for image fusion, dubbed **DeFusion**, without needing sophisticated loss functions or fusion rules shown in Fig. 1c. We can learn from the definition of image fusion that the essence of image fusion is to integrate the complementary information of multiple source images. Therefore, if we can decompose the source images into the unique component and the shared common component of all images, the target fusion image can be generated by simply combining the components. The remaining question is: *how to decompose the source images to obtain the unique and common components without any supervision?*

Given the source images, it is very hard for us to obtain the supervision information to guide the prediction of the unique and common components. In this paper, we design a pretext task, called common and unique decomposition (CUD), to perform image decomposition under a self-supervised learning framework. We are dedicated to decomposing the multiple source images into unique and common feature representations to accomplish the unsupervised image fusion (*i.e., fusion from decomposition*). As shown in Fig. 2, we design a specific image augmentation strategy that will replace some patches of the original scene x with noise to generate two 'source images', x^1 and x^2. Afterwards, they are fed into the decomposition network DeNet to get the common features f_c, and the unique features f_u^1 and f_u^2 corresponding to x^1 and x^2. Acquiring the embedding features, we then apply two projection heads, the common projection head P_c and the unique projection head P_u, to produce the common and unique images (parts) of the source images x^1 and x^2. Under the specific image augmentation strategy, we can easily generate the supervision of the projected common and unique images. In addition, the combined features f_c, f_u^1, f_u^2 are also fed into a reconstruction projection head P_r to reconstruct the original scene x. In the inference phase, we can decompose the source images into common and unique semantic representations and reconstruct the fused images from the combined features, as shown in Fig. 3. In this way, the combination of decomposed common and unique features provides explainable information for fused images and bypasses the difficulties of developing sophisticated loss functions or fusion rules.

In summary, we can summarize our contributions as follows: (i) We propose a novel image fusion method called DeFusion by decomposing the source image based on a self-supervised learning framework. (ii) We design a pretext task, called CUD, for image fusion, which does not rely on the existing supervised image fusion dataset, sophisticated loss functions and fusion rules. (iii) The proposed DeFusion is trained only with the COCO dataset and can be used as a unified and versatile framework for various image fusion tasks without any further fine-tuning or introducing an additional fusion rule. It achieves comparable or even better performance compared to the most competitive image fusion methods (including supervised ones) on various types of fusion tasks.

2   Related Work

2.1   Deep Learning-Based Image Fusion

In the past decades, image fusion based on deep learning has gained much spotlight in research community. Liu *et al.* [17] first trained a binary classification convolutional neural network for the multi-focus image fusion task. Inspired by this, many multi-focus image fusion methods via supervised-learning had been proposed [9,40,54]. Specifically, Zhang *et al.* [54] proposed an end-to-end fusion method called IFCNN that used RBG image and the corresponding depth image to simulate training samples. However, these methods are hard to transfer into the multi-modal image fusion task, *e.g.*, infrared-visual image fusion, in which ground truth does not naturally exist.

Rather than simulating training data from ground truths, unsupervised methods focus on designing fusion rules and loss functions [13,19,20,33,38]. Typically, the DeepFuse [33], DenseFuse [13] employed the fusion rule (addition strategy) into the extracted features on the bottleneck of autoencoder. The U2fusion [38], MEFNet [21], PMGI [47] designed multiple losses with considerable variation for the same fusion task. However, the design of sophisticated losses requires the human knowledge, which limits its generalizability. In this work, we decompose the multiple images into semantic embeddings via self-supervised learning, and thus avoiding the design of fusion rules and sophisticated losses.

2.2   Image Decomposition Model

In traditional image fusion methods, the image decomposition model is one of mainstream fusion strategy. A typical option of image decomposition is to use a set of predefined basis functions, *e.g.*, wavelets [26], conventional pyramids [2,32], to represent the images. In addition, the average filter is employed to decompose the images into base layer and detail layer [14]. Nevertheless, the decomposed components still rely on manually tailored fusion rules to extract the useful information, in which the distortion information may incorrectly be retained into fused results [39]. Different with the traditional image decomposition model, the CU-Net [6] used a coupled dictionary learning algorithm to jointly decompose multiple source inputs into necessary features and avoid designing the fusion rules. The DRF [39] decomposed the visible and infrared images into scene and sensor modality representations to alleviate the disadvantage of fusion with fusion rules. However, since the supervision of decomposed components is insufficient during training, these methods may fall into a trivial solution that the decomposed components may be meaningless. Instead of regarding the decomposition components as intermediate procedures (byproducts) and only focusing on the prediction results, we focus on decomposing the multiple source images into unique and common feature representations to assist the image fusion task.

2.3 Self-Supervised Learning

Self-supervised learning is a paradigm to obtain the useful representations from large unlabeled data [16]. Practically, useful representations are extracted by specific pretext task [8]. The pretext tasks are designed to solve the complementary prediction task where we remove part inherent attributes of the image (*e.g.*, the color) to recover it. Recently, a large body of novel pretext tasks had been proposed and had made great progress. One class of pretext is to exploit the geometric transformations of image, such as solving jigsaw puzzles [27,29], recognizing image orientation [12], learning to count [28], image colorization [49]. The others is to leverage multi-modal information (*e.g.*, predicting depth from RGB [34,50], detecting misalignment between audio and visual streams [30]).

3 Method

In this section, we first introduce the self-supervised learning pipeline for image fusion in Sect. 3.1. Next, we elaborate on a carefully designed pretext task (*i.e.*, CUD) for self-supervised image decomposition and fusion in Sect. 3.2. Finally, the implementation details are presented in Sect. 3.3.

3.1 Self-supervised Learning for Image Fusion

Self-supervised Learning Pipeline. Suppose that we are given an unlabeled image dataset D. For each image $x \in \mathbb{R}^{H \times W \times 3}$ in D, we apply a random data augmentation from a set of image transformations $\mathcal{T}$ into x to generate the distorted views x^i. The distorted view will be fed into a convolution network to obtain corresponding embeddings. To generate a powerful embedding representation, the convolution network needs to be trained in solving pretext tasks, such as predicting image rotations [12], image colorization [49], and jigsaw puzzles [24]. After pre-training by the pretext task, the embedding representation can be used for downstream tasks.

Image Fusion by Self-supervised Learning. According to the type of sensor that obtains the source images, we can further classify the image fusion into single-modal fusion and multi-modal fusion. For single modality fusion, the observed images are generated from the same type of sensor but with different settings. For multi-modal fusion, the source images come from different types of sensors with different imaging mechanisms, such as infrared-visible. Although the source images exhibit obvious discrepancies, whether the single-modal or the multi-modal cases, they all are transformed from the same scene and represent different (complementary) parts of the scene. Moreover, the goal of image fusion is to retain the vivid information of the multiple inputs to generate the fused image. The procedure of *original scene* ↦ *source images* ⇉ *fused image* is similar to the pipeline of embedding representation in self-supervised learning. Therefore, similar to the self-supervised learning pipeline, we assign the source images to represent the distorted views which will be fed into $\phi_\theta(\cdot)$ to extract the embeddings, and then apply the embeddings to produce the final fused image via a projection head. In the following, we will present how to practice self-supervised learning of the procedure *original scene* $\rightarrow$ *source images* $\rightrightarrows$ *fused image*.

3.2   Details of CUD Pretext Task

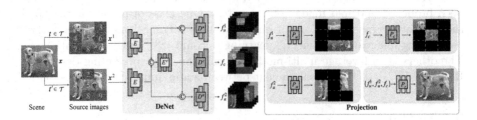

Fig. 2. An overview of our proposed self-supervised image decomposition and fusion method.

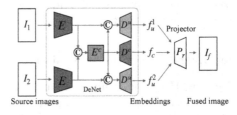

Fig. 3. The testing pipeline of the DeFusion method.

In the typical self-supervised learning paradigm, the learned embeddings have strong representation ability by training with some pretext tasks and can be used for downstream tasks by fine-tuning with limited supervision. However, as for the image fusion task, in some cases there is not always supervisory information available. Therefore, we hope that the fusion result can be obtained after the pre-training, without the need for additional supervision information to fine-tune.

Motivated by these observations, we carefully design a specific pretext task, common and unique decomposition (CUD), for image decomposition and image fusion. The CUD task follows a generally acknowledged definition of data fusion to simulate the fusion process, where the goal of image fusion is to combine complementary information from different source images into a synthetic image. For each source image, it shares parts of the scene information with other source images while retaining some unique information. Therefore, the CUD pretext task will force each source image to be decomposed into two parts: the unique features and the common features. After pre-training, the obtained common and unique embeddings can be directly used for the image fusion task.

As discussed in Sect. 3.1, the unlabeled image x corresponds to the original scene in image fusion. Note that we conjecture that the scene in the image fusion involves the most comprehensive information while each observed degraded views x^i only can reflect part of original scene. In CUD, we use a random mask M_i and Gaussian noise n to simulate the degraded transformation $\mathcal{T}$:

$$x^i = M_i(x) + \bar{M}_i(n), \tag{1}$$

where $\bar{M}_i$ is the logical negation operator of mask M_i. To simplify notations, we only focus on the case where the number of source images is 2:

$$x^1 = M_1(x) + \bar{M}_1(n), x^2 = M_2(x) + \bar{M}_2(n),$$
$$s.t. \quad M_1 + M_2 \succ 0.$$

The constraint is used to ensure that all information in the original scene is included in the augmented images. Different from the traditional inpainting-based pretext tasks [7,31], which remove the remaining regions, here we fill the remaining with random noise, and this will guarantee that the unique information of one image is independent with the counterpart of the other image.

We show a simple example of the transformed images in Fig. 2. The simulated images x^1, x^2 are fed into the DeNet $\phi_\theta(\cdot)$ to generate the embedding:

$$f_c, f_u^1, f_u^2 = \phi_\theta(x^1, x^2), \tag{2}$$

where f_c denotes the common embedding of source images, f_u^1, and f_u^2 represent the unique embeddings of the x^1 and x^2, respectively. Similar to the self-supervised learning pipeline [5], we also introduce some projection heads to project the embeddings into the image space. For the common embedding f_c, the projection $\hat{x}_c = P_c(f_c)$ in the image space should be close to the intersection regions of source images $x_c = M_1(x) \cap M_2(x)$. In a similar vein, $x_u^1 = M_1(x) \cap \bar{M}_2(x)$ and $x_u^2 = \bar{M}_1(x) \cap M_2(x)$ are the ground truths corresponding to the projection of embeddings, $P_u(f_u^1)$ and $P_u(f_u^2)$, respectively. Since the embeddings have encoded the whole semantic information of scene, the projection of embeddings $P_r(f_c, f_u^1, f_u^2)$ should be corresponding to the original scene x. As a consequence, our loss function computes the mean absolute error (MAE) between the four projected results and the corresponding original images or masked regions in the pixel space.

3.3 Implementation Details

Details of the Network. The overall network $\phi_\theta(\cdot)$ is similar to the bottleneck structure, which can prevent a trivial identity mapping from being learned. The $\phi_\theta(\cdot)$ can be split into three parts: the encoder $E_\theta(\cdot)$, the ensembler $E_\theta^c(\cdot)$, and the decoder $D_\theta(\cdot) = \{D_\theta^u(\cdot), D_\theta^c(\cdot)\}$. As shown in Fig. 2, the $E_\theta(\cdot)$ includes three maxpool layers and residual layers [45] to obtain the compressive representations whose feature maps size is $\frac{H}{8} \times \frac{W}{8} \times k$. Subsequently, the representations $E_\theta(x^1)$

and $E_\theta(x^2)$ are jointly fed into the $E_\theta^c(\cdot)$ to extract abstract common representation in which the $E_\theta^c(\cdot)$ is composed of only a residual layer. Afterwards, the $D_\theta(\cdot)$ which is composed of several upsample layers and residual layers is applied to generate the corresponding embeddings with the different outputs of the $E_\theta(\cdot)$ and $E_\theta^c(\cdot)$. For instance, the embeddings f_u^1 are extracted by the $D_\theta^u(\cdot)$ with the input $[E_\theta(x^1); E_\theta^c[E_\theta(x^1); E_\theta(x^2)]]$ where $[;]$ is the concatenation operator; and similarly for the embeddings $f_u^2 = D_\theta^u[E_\theta(x^2); E_\theta^c[E_\theta(x^1); E_\theta(x^2)]]$; For the embedding f_c, it only takes the $E_\theta^c[E_\theta(x^1); E_\theta(x^2)]$ as input. In addition to the convolution network $\phi_\theta(\cdot)$, the projection heads $P_c(\cdot), P_u(\cdot), P_r(\cdot)$ that consist of upsample layers and ResNest layers with learned parameters. More details are shown in the supplementary materials.

Training Details. We train the convolution network $\phi_\theta(\cdot)$ and projection heads for the CUD pretext task on scenes from large-scale dataset, *i.e.*, COCO dataset [15]. We select 50k images from it to build up the training dataset. During the training phase, our model is trained with an Adam optimizer [11], 50 epochs, batch size 8, and the initial learning rate is set to $1e$-3 that decreased by half each 10 epochs. As for data augmentation, we randomly reshape and crop the images to 256×256. To better simulate degraded process, the M in Eq. 1 is designed as the combination of two random masks with different resolution.

4   Experiments

In this section, we evaluate the DeFusion on multiple tasks such as multi-exposure image fusion, multi-focus image fusion, and visible infrared image fusion. The qualitative and quantitative experiment results demonstrate that DeFusion achieves comparable or even better performance compared to the state-of-the-art (SoTA) methods. In the next subsection, we only show a few examples for each fusion task, the more quantitative fused results can be found in the supplementary materials.

4.1   Comparisons on Different Fusion Tasks

Multi-Exposure Image Fusion. We compare the DeFusion with six SoTA methods, including unified fusion methods, *i.e.*, CU-Net [6], U2Fusion [38], IFCNN [54], PMGI [47], specific-task fusion methods, *i.e.*, DeepFuse [33], MEFNet [21]. For a fair and comprehensive comparison, we evaluate comparison methods on the most comprehensive MEFB benchmark [52] and the largest SICE dataset [3]. Note that the MEFB benchmark contains 100 image pairs collected from multiple public datasets [22,33,44].

Qualitative results on the MEFB benchmark are reported in Fig. 4, where we highlight two regions in each example. As can be seen, the CU-Net suffers random shadowy artifacts, and the IFCNN shows color distortion across the whole images in the first example. The MEFNet shows poor performance on the fusion of semantic information, resulting in inconsistent background with

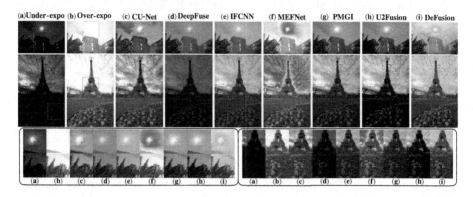

Fig. 4. Qualitative comparison of the DeFusion with 7 SoTA methods on 2 multi-exposure image pairs on the MEFB benchmark. (Color figure online)

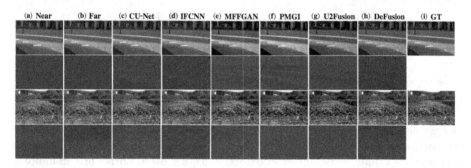

Fig. 5. Qualitative comparisons of multi-focus images fusion results. We provide the enhanced residual maps for each result of comparison and input images to highlight the difference with GT.

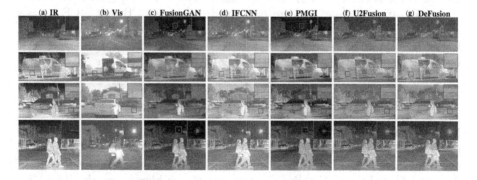

Fig. 6. Qualitative comparisons of visible and infrared image fusion results. (Color figure online)

Table 1. Quantitative results on MEFB [52] and SICE [3] datasets for multi-exposure image fusion. The best, **second best** and the third best results are marked with red, bold, and underlined.

Method	MEFB [52]						SICE [3]					
	CE	QCV	SSIM	MEF-SSIM	IS	LPIPS	CE	QCV	SSIM	MEF-SSIM	IS	LPIPS
CU-Net	4.800	425.5	0.547	0.794	6.470	0.359	4.728	345.6	0.486	0.742	7.564	0.389
DeepFuse	4.993	363.0	0.544	0.796	6.346	0.380	5.262	189.3	0.523	0.797	**8.391**	0.322
IFCNN	4.943	247.7	0.573	0.818	6.776	0.335	4.551	290.2	0.492	0.697	8.453	0.372
MEFNet	**4.257**	593.4	**0.593**	0.796	6.432	0.321	5.102	505.7	**0.526**	0.711	8.068	0.358
PMGI	4.698	293.9	0.547	**0.822**	6.521	0.336	5.556	294.7	0.480	0.740	7.973	0.375
U2Fusion	4.526	**253.8**	0.526	0.815	**3.438**	**6.745**	0.332	209.5	0.488	**0.796**	8.314	0.346
DeFusion	2.881	262.3	0.608	0.827	6.587	0.332	2.830	207.7	0.571	0.788	7.869	0.353

Table 2. Quantitative results on the dataset collected by [53] and the Real-MFF [48] for multi-focus image fusion.

	Method	Dataset[53]		Real-MFF noref [48]		Real-MFF [48]	
		SSIM	PSNR	SSIM	PSNR	SSIM	PSNR
Super-vised	IFCNN	**0.905**	**26.91**	**0.964**	**32.93**	0.983	36.92
Unsupervised	CU-Net	0.874	24.88	0.900	26.66	0.938	29.17
	MFFGAN	0.879	24.30	0.811	22.81	0.850	24.14
	PMGI	0.865	20.88	0.890	24.09	0.903	24.66
	U2Fusion	0.815	21.94	0.849	23.99	0.880	25.26
	DeFusion	0.928	28.13	0.969	33.61	**0.971**	**33.88**

Table 3. Quantitative results on TNO [36] and RoadScene [38] datasets for visible-infrared image fusion.

Method	TNO [36]				RoadScene [38]			
	CE	QCV	SSIM	CC	CE	QCV	SSIM	CC
FusionGAN	2.489	954.7	0.631	0.461	1.723	1225.6	0.595	0.561
IFCNN	1.746	340.2	0.701	0.519	0.989	509.8	0.707	0.627
PMGI	1.751	481.0	0.696	0.534	1.277	1024.1	0.668	0.591
U2Fusion	**1.549**	586.1	0.727	0.552	**0.786**	908.2	**0.723**	**0.635**
DeFusion	1.487	425.3	**0.715**	**0.539**	0.767	647.5	0.727	0.652

heavy halo effects. In addition, the DeepFuse, PMGI and U2Fusion convert the RGB into YCbCr color space and just focus on fusing the Y channel, which may suffer the color shift issue. For example, in the highlighted region of the second sample, the generated flowers of those methods are painted orange, while the original color of the flowers is yellow. The results generated by DeFusion perform are visually pleasant, whose fused objects show a consistent and uniform appearance while avoiding artifacts and distortions. For instance, as shown in the second sample, the DeFusion introduces the details of under-exposed image into fused image while remaining the brightness of over-exposed image rather than the under-exposed image. It demonstrates that the DeFusion can fuse the source images at the semantic feature level by using the embedding representations.

Quantitative comparisons are performed on the MEFB and SICE dataset in Table 1. We introduce six commonly used metrics, *i.e.*, cross entropy (CE), QCV [4], SSIM, MEF-SSIM [22], IS [35], and LPIPS [51] to measure the quality of fused images. Since the ground truths are unavailable, all metrics are computed by comparing with the two source images as in many previous works. As can be seen, DeFusion ranks first in terms of CE and SSIM on all datasets, and achieves comparable results in terms of QCV, LPIPS and MEF-SSIM.

Multi-Focus Image Fusion. We compare the DeFusion with the following five SoTA methods: CU-Net [6], IFCNN [17], MFFGAN [46], PMGI [47], and U2Fusion [38]. All comparison methods are evaluated on the Real-MFF dataset [48] and dataset in [53]. To the best of our knowledge, the Real-MFF is the biggest realistic public dataset which provides the realistic source images with corresponding ground truth captured by a light field camera. In addition to the Real-MFF dataset, we also use the collected dataset by Zhang [53], which includes three MFIF datasets, *i.e.*, the Lytro dataset [25], the MFI-WHU dataset [46] and the MFFW dataset [41].

The qualitative results on the Real-MFF are shown in Fig. 5. The results of quantitative comparison on the dataset [53] and Real-MFF [48] are shown in Table 2. From these reported results, we can learn that the performance of DeFusion goes beyond the other unsupervised methods, and has achieved comparable performance to the IFCNN that is trained via the supervised learning.

Infrared Visible Image Fusion. We compare DeFusion with four SoTA methods: IFCNN [54], FusionGAN [20], PMGI [47], and U2Fusion [38]. For infrared visible image fusion, TNO [36] is a widely used dataset, and RoadScene [38] is a challenging dataset whose infrared images show rich thermal textures. We employ them to explore the performance of comparison methods.

Some qualitative results of the RoadScene dataset are shown in Fig. 6. Due to the physical differences, the source images captured by two different cameras are quite different, which may cause the fusion methods fail to distinguish the object from the background. For example, FusionGAN mixes up the object of visible image and background of infrared image, resulting in the object disappears in the fused result, as shown in the highlighted region of first example. In the second example of Fig. 6, IFCNN, FusionGAN, and PMGI just preserve the edge of stripe and miss the key filled color information in their fused results. A similar phenomenon shows in the third example where the textual information is not well preserved by FusionGAN and IFCNN. In addition, it is of paramount importance for the fusion task to preserve useful information into fused results. However, U2fusion is inclined to preserve excessive infrared information, which may remain some noise of infrared image into the fused image shown in the fourth example. In contrast, our method can well balance these effects and preserve much semantic information.

Quantitative comparisons are shown in Table 3 where we use four metrics, *i.e.*, CE, QCV, SSIM, and CC to evaluate all comparison methods. On the RoadScene dataset, the DeFusion ranks first on the CE, SSIM, and CC, indicating that the generated fused results are higher similarity to the source images. For QCV, DeFusion also achieves comparable results. In addition, the results of the TNO dataset show similar performances to those of RoadScene.

4.2   Visualizing Feature Embeddings

In this section, we will demonstrate the unique and common representation ability of our method by some toy and read examples. We take some images from Set5 [1] dataset as the original scenes and apply several image augmentation strategies to them. In principle, the strategies can be classified into toy examples, *i.e.*, the 1st-3rd rows, and real examples, *i.e.*, 4th-5th rows.

| (a) Source1 | (b) Source2 | (c) f_u^1 | (d) f_u^2 | (e) f_c | (f) Unique1 | (g) Unique2 | (h) Common | (i) Fusion |

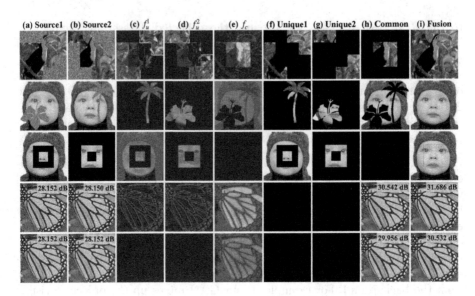

Fig. 7. Visualization of feature embeddings intermediate results for some toy and real examples.

Toy Experiments. As shown in Fig. 7, for the first example, the image augmentation is similar to the one defined in Eq. 1. In this sample, the common and unique components are accurately decomposed from the two source images by the pretrained network. To further verify the generalization of the proposed model, we also demonstrate the results with other image augmentation methods that are different with the one in Eq. 1. In the second example, we change the mask shape to an arbitrary shape with increasing difficulty and ignore the constraint in Eq. 3.2 to allow the region of noise to be overlapped. Although more difficult, the decomposition and fusion results do not lose too much information. In addition, we replace the noise with zeros to generate the source images, as shown in the third example. We can see that the pretrained network can also extract appropriate semantic features and project them into image space. Note that the final fused result shows edge information around the mask, and this is due to the information diffusion caused by the convolution. From these toy examples, we can learn that our network pretrained by the CUD pretext has learned the ability to extract the semantic information to some extent.

Some Real Results. Instead of synthesizing with specific masks, we add the additive white Gaussian noise into the original image twice, which can be seen as the two augmented source images of the original scene, to see whether our model can obtain the common (*i.e.*, the denoised image) and unique components. In the fourth example, we add two different noises ($\sigma = 10$) to the 'butterfly' image to generate two source images. As can be seen, only the common component is projected into the image while the unique components are deactivated. It is worth noting that both the fused image and common image are denoised images.

In the last example, we feed two identical noisy images with $\sigma = 10$ into our network, and the noise of fused image and common image can be also removed. It demonstrates that our network avoids the trivial mapping between the input and output, and is able to adaptively preserve the scene semantic information.

We also visualize the intermediate embedding representation in real image fusion tasks, as shown in Fig. 8. Taking the first multi-exposure sample as an example, the over-exposed image shows abundant details in the room and meaningless brightness on the windows, while the under-exposed image exhibits landscape outside the window and furnishings with lower sharpness energy in the room. After the DeFusion embeds the multi-exposure image pair, we find that the windows regions are not activated in the over-exposed unique embedding, but are activated in the under-exposure unique embedding. It demonstrates that unique embeddings can adaptively distinguish the effective unique information from meaningless image contents. Moreover, in this case, the common embedding is slightly activated at the edges of the window and lamp, indicating that those edges are salient in both images.

(a) Source1	(b) Source2	(c) Unique1	(d) Unique2	(e) Common

Fig. 8. Feature embedding visualization on multi-exposure image fusion (first two rows) and multi-focus image fusion (last two rows).

In particular, for the multi-focus fusion task, we intuitively infer that the unique useful information should be related with the focus region of the images. However, it is hard to determine which regions should be related to the common information of source images. Interestingly, the statistics of feature representations is consistent with our guess. To vividly describe the statistics, we show a representative example in the second row of Fig. 8. In this case, the unique representations of source images have higher activation values than the corresponding common representations. Moreover, the focused regions are always corresponding to the activated regions. Note that the common region of multi-focus example shown in Fig. 8(e) is totally black, which may indicate that there are no regions with same amount of defocus in both images.

5   Discussion and Broader Impact

Discussion and Limitation. We design an image decomposition model following the essence of image fusion, which is to integrate complementary information from multiple source images and fuse them. Since there are no natural image decomposition components in image fusion, we design a brute but simple pretext task using masks with Gaussian noise to generate the common or unique supervised information. Note that we do not ask the training source images to be strictly aligned with the multiple input images of image fusion task, as our goal is to train the network to learn the ability of decomposing source images into common and unique components. We believe that the obtained decomposed feature embeddings can make the image fusion easier, so that the fused images are generated by a simple convolutional layer called projector, which just likes the last linear layer for classification in general self-supervised learning [10]. Compared to the various pretext tasks for classification in the self-supervised learning, the proposed pretext task for image fusion is **simple and far from a perfect pretext task**. However, the present idea provides a new paradigm for learning multi-source image features jointly, which may provide new directions and considerations for multi-source pre-training. We hope that the new paradigm will inspire more work in the image fusion community.

Broader Impact. Recently, the image inpainting-like pretext, *masked autoencoding*, based network pretraining has achieved great success [7,31] in NLP and computer vision. Our DeFusion takes inspirations from these previous works. It can be seen as an extension of these previous single-view masked autoencoding to the multi-view masked autoencoding. Therefore, it provides a paradigm for learning multi-view image features jointly, which may provide new directions and considerations for multi-view pre-training.

6   Conclusion

We present a unified and versatile image fusion framework, *fusion from decomposition*, for multiple image fusion tasks. To obtain an effective representations of the source images, we design pretext task based on the common and unique decomposition (CUD), which can be trained in a self-supervised way and is friendly with our image fusion task. The proposed method achieves comparable or even better performance than previous unsupervised as well as supervised methods. The feature embedding and generalizability of the model have also been verified.

Acknowledgements. The research was supported by the National Natural Science Foundation of China (61971165, 61922027), and also is supported by the Fundamental Research Funds for the Central Universities.

References

1. Bevilacqua, M., Roumy, A., Guillemot, C., Alberi-Morel, M.L.: Low-complexity single-image super-resolution based on nonnegative neighbor embedding. In: Proceedings of the British Machine Vision Conference, pp. 135.1-135.10. BMVA press (2012)
2. Burt, P.J., Kolczynski, R.J.: Enhanced image capture through fusion. In: Proceedings of IEEE International Conference on Computer Vision, pp. 173–182. IEEE (1993)
3. Cai, J., Gu, S., Zhang, L.: Learning a deep single image contrast enhancer from multi-exposure images. IEEE Trans. Image Process. **27**(4), 2049–2062 (2018)
4. Chen, H., Varshney, P.K.: A human perception inspired quality metric for image fusion based on regional information. Inf. Fusion **8**(2), 193–207 (2007)
5. Chen, T., Kornblith, S., Norouzi, M., Hinton, G.: A simple framework for contrastive learning of visual representations. In: Proceedings of the International Conference on Machine Learning, pp. 1597–1607. PMLR (2020)
6. Deng, X., Dragotti, P.L.: Deep convolutional neural network for multi-modal image restoration and fusion. IEEE Trans. Pattern Anal. Mach. Intell. **43**, 3333–3348 (2020)
7. Devlin, J., Chang, M.W., Lee, K., Toutanova, K.: BERT: pre-training of deep bidirectional transformers for language understanding. In: Proceedings of the Conference of the North American Chapter of the Association for Computational Linguistics: Human Language Technologies. Association for Computational Linguistics (2019)
8. Doersch, C., Gupta, A., Efros, A.A.: Unsupervised visual representation learning by context prediction. In: Proceedings of the IEEE International Conference on Computer Vision, pp. 1422–1430 (2015)
9. Guo, X., Nie, R., Cao, J., Zhou, D., Mei, L., He, K.: FuseGAN: learning to fuse multi-focus image via conditional generative adversarial network. IEEE Trans. Multimed. **21**(8), 1982–1996 (2019)
10. He, K., Chen, X., Xie, S., et al.: Masked autoencoders are scalable vision learners. arXiv (2021)
11. Kingma, D.P., Ba, J.: Adam: a method for stochastic optimization. In: Proceedings of the International Conference on Learning Representations (2015)
12. Komodakis, N., Gidaris, S.: Unsupervised representation learning by predicting image rotations. In: Proceedings of the International Conference on Learning Representations (2018)
13. Li, H., Wu, X.J.: DenseFuse: a fusion approach to infrared and visible images. IEEE Trans. Image Process. **28**(5), 2614–2623 (2018)
14. Li, S., Kang, X., Hu, J.: Image fusion with guided filtering. IEEE Trans. Image Process. **22**(7), 2864–2875 (2013)
15. Lin, T.-Y., et al.: Microsoft COCO: common objects in context. In: Fleet, D., Pajdla, T., Schiele, B., Tuytelaars, T. (eds.) ECCV 2014. LNCS, vol. 8693, pp. 740–755. Springer, Cham (2014). https://doi.org/10.1007/978-3-319-10602-1_48
16. Liu, X., et al.: Self-supervised learning: generative or contrastive. IEEE Trans. Knowl. Data Eng. (2021)
17. Liu, Y., Chen, X., Peng, H., Wang, Z.: Multi-focus image fusion with a deep convolutional neural network. Inf. Fusion **36**, 191–207 (2017)
18. Ma, J., Ma, Y., Li, C.: Infrared and visible image fusion methods and applications: a survey. Inf. Fusion **45**, 153–178 (2019)

19. Ma, J., Tang, L., Fan, F., Huang, J., Mei, X., Ma, Y.: Swinfusion: cross-domain long-range learning for general image fusion via swin transformer. IEEE/CAA J. Automatica Sinica **9**(7), 1200–1217 (2022)
20. Ma, J., Yu, W., Liang, P., Li, C., Jiang, J.: FusionGAN: a generative adversarial network for infrared and visible image fusion. Inf. Fusion **48**, 11–26 (2019)
21. Ma, K., Duanmu, Z., Zhu, H., Fang, Y., Wang, Z.: Deep guided learning for fast multi-exposure image fusion. IEEE Trans. Image Process. **29**, 2808–2819 (2019)
22. Ma, K., Zeng, K., Wang, Z.: Perceptual quality assessment for multi-exposure image fusion. IEEE Trans. Image Process. **24**(11), 3345–3356 (2015)
23. Mertens, T., Kautz, J., Van Reeth, F.: Exposure fusion. In: 15th Pacific Conference on Computer Graphics and Applications (PG'07), pp. 382–390. IEEE (2007)
24. Misra, I., Maaten, L.v.d.: Self-supervised learning of pretext-invariant representations. In: Proceedings of the IEEE Conference on Computer Vision and Pattern Recognition, pp. 6707–6717 (2020)
25. Nejati, M., Samavi, S., Shirani, S.: Multi-focus image fusion using dictionary-based sparse representation. Inf. Fusion **25**, 72–84 (2015)
26. Nikolov, S., Hill, P., Bull, D., Canagarajah, N.: Wavelets for image fusion. In: Petrosian, A.A., Meyer, F.G. (eds.) Wavelets in signal and image analysis, pp. 213–241. Springer, Dordrecht (2001). https://doi.org/10.1007/978-94-015-9715-9_8
27. Noroozi, M., Favaro, P.: Unsupervised learning of visual representations by solving jigsaw puzzles. In: Leibe, B., Matas, J., Sebe, N., Welling, M. (eds.) ECCV 2016. LNCS, vol. 9910, pp. 69–84. Springer, Cham (2016). https://doi.org/10.1007/978-3-319-46466-4_5
28. Noroozi, M., Pirsiavash, H., Favaro, P.: Representation learning by learning to count. In: Proceedings of the IEEE International Conference on Computer Vision, pp. 5898–5906 (2017)
29. Noroozi, M., Vinjimoor, A., Favaro, P., Pirsiavash, H.: Boosting self-supervised learning via knowledge transfer. In: Proceedings of the IEEE Conference on Computer Vision and Pattern Recognition, pp. 9359–9367 (2018)
30. Owens, A., Efros, A.A.: Audio-visual scene analysis with self-supervised multisensory features. In: Proceedings of the European Conference on Computer Vision, pp. 631–648 (2018)
31. Pathak, D., Krahenbuhl, P., Donahue, J., Darrell, T., Efros, A.A.: Context encoders: feature learning by inpainting. In: Proceedings of the IEEE conference on Computer Vision and Pattern Recognition, pp. 2536–2544 (2016)
32. Petrovic, V.S., Xydeas, C.S.: Gradient-based multiresolution image fusion. IEEE Trans. Image Process. **13**(2), 228–237 (2004)
33. Ram Prabhakar, K., Sai Srikar, V., Venkatesh Babu, R.: Deepfuse: a deep unsupervised approach for exposure fusion with extreme exposure image pairs. In: Proceedings of the IEEE International Conference on Computer Vision, pp. 4714–4722 (2017)
34. Ren, Z., Lee, Y.J.: Cross-domain self-supervised multi-task feature learning using synthetic imagery. In: Proceedings of the IEEE Conference on Computer Vision and Pattern Recognition, pp. 762–771 (2018)
35. Salimans, T., Goodfellow, I., Zaremba, W., Cheung, V., Radford, A., Chen, X.: Improved techniques for training GANs. In: Proceedings of the Advances in Neural Information Processing Systems 29 (2016)
36. Toet, A.: TNO Image Fusion Dataset (2014). https://doi.org/10.6084/m9.figshare.1008029.v1. https://figshare.com/articles/dataset/TNO_Image_Fusion_Dataset/1008029

37. Wang, W., Chang, F.: A multi-focus image fusion method based on Laplacian pyramid. J. Comput. **6**(12), 2559–2566 (2011)
38. Xu, H., Ma, J., Jiang, J., Guo, X., Ling, H.: U2Fusion: a unified unsupervised image fusion network. IEEE Trans. Pattern Anal. Mach. Intell. 44, 502–518 (2020)
39. Xu, H., Wang, X., Ma, J.: DRF: disentangled representation for visible and infrared image fusion. IEEE Trans. Instrum. Meas. **70**, 1–13 (2021)
40. Xu, K., Qin, Z., Wang, G., Zhang, H., Huang, K., Ye, S.: Multi-focus image fusion using fully convolutional two-stream network for visual sensors. KSII Trans. Internet Inf. Syst. (TIIS) **12**(5), 2253–2272 (2018)
41. Xu, S., Wei, X., Zhang, C., Liu, J., Zhang, J.: MFFW: a new dataset for multi-focus image fusion. arXiv preprint arXiv:2002.04780 (2020)
42. Yang, B., Li, S.: Multifocus image fusion and restoration with sparse representation. IEEE Trans. Instrum. Meas. **59**(4), 884–892 (2009)
43. Yang, C., Zhang, J.Q., Wang, X.R., Liu, X.: A novel similarity based quality metric for image fusion. Inf. Fusion **9**(2), 156–160 (2008)
44. Zeng, K., Ma, K., Hassen, R., Wang, Z.: Perceptual evaluation of multi-exposure image fusion algorithms. In: 2014 Sixth International Workshop on Quality of Multimedia Experience (QoMEX), pp. 7–12. IEEE (2014)
45. Zhang, H., et al.: ResNeSt: split-attention networks. arXiv preprint arXiv:2004.08955 (2020)
46. Zhang, H., Le, Z., Shao, Z., Xu, H., Ma, J.: MFF-GAN: an unsupervised generative adversarial network with adaptive and gradient joint constraints for multi-focus image fusion. Inf. Fusion **66**, 40–53 (2021)
47. Zhang, H., Xu, H., Xiao, Y., Guo, X., Ma, J.: Rethinking the image fusion: a fast unified image fusion network based on proportional maintenance of gradient and intensity. In: Proceedings of the AAAI Conference on Artificial Intelligence, vol. 34, pp. 12797–12804 (2020)
48. Zhang, J., Liao, Q., Liu, S., Ma, H., Yang, W., Xue, J.H.: Real-MFF: a large realistic multi-focus image dataset with ground truth. Pattern Recogn. Lett. **138**, 370–377 (2020)
49. Zhang, R., Isola, P., Efros, A.A.: Colorful image colorization. In: Leibe, B., Matas, J., Sebe, N., Welling, M. (eds.) ECCV 2016. LNCS, vol. 9907, pp. 649–666. Springer, Cham (2016). https://doi.org/10.1007/978-3-319-46487-9_40
50. Zhang, R., Isola, P., Efros, A.A.: Split-brain autoencoders: unsupervised learning by cross-channel prediction. In: Proceedings of the IEEE Conference on Computer Vision and Pattern Recognition, pp. 1058–1067 (2017)
51. Zhang, R., Isola, P., Efros, A.A., Shechtman, E., Wang, O.: The unreasonable effectiveness of deep features as a perceptual metric. In: Proceedings of the IEEE Conference on Computer Vision and Pattern Recognition, pp. 586–595 (2018)
52. Zhang, X.: Benchmarking and comparing multi-exposure image fusion algorithms. Inf. Fusion (2021)
53. Zhang, X.: Deep learning-based multi-focus image fusion: a survey and a comparative study. IEEE Trans. Pattern Anal. Mach. Intell. 44, 4819–4838 (2021)
54. Zhang, Y., Liu, Y., Sun, P., Yan, H., Zhao, X., Zhang, L.: IFCNN: a general image fusion framework based on convolutional neural network. Inf. Fusion **54**, 99–118 (2020)

Learning Degradation Representations for Image Deblurring

Dasong Li[1], Yi Zhang[1], Ka Chun Cheung[2], Xiaogang Wang[1,4],
Hongwei Qin[3(✉)], and Hongsheng Li[1,4,5(✉)]

[1] MMLab, CUHK, Hong Kong, China
dasongli@link.cuhk.edu.hk, hsli@ee.cuhk.edu.hk
[2] NVIDIA AI Technology Center, Santa Clara, USA
[3] SenseTime Research, Hong Kong, China
qinhongwei@sensetime.com
[4] Centre for Perceptual and Interactive Intelligence Limited, Hong Kong, China
[5] Xidian University, Xi'an, China

Abstract. In various learning-based image restoration tasks, such as image denoising and image super-resolution, the degradation representations were widely used to model the degradation process and handle complicated degradation patterns. However, they are less explored in learning-based image deblurring as blur kernel estimation cannot perform well in real-world challenging cases. We argue that it is particularly necessary for image deblurring to model degradation representations since blurry patterns typically show much larger variations than noisy patterns or high-frequency textures. In this paper, we propose a framework to learn spatially adaptive degradation representations of blurry images. A novel joint image reblurring and deblurring learning process is presented to improve the expressiveness of degradation representations. To make learned degradation representations effective in reblurring and deblurring, we propose a Multi-Scale Degradation Injection Network (MSDI-Net) to integrate them into the neural networks. With the integration, MSDI-Net can handle various and complicated blurry patterns adaptively. Experiments on the GoPro and RealBlur datasets demonstrate that our proposed deblurring framework with the learned degradation representations outperforms state-of-the-art methods with appealing improvements. The code is released at https://github. com/dasongli1/Learning_degradation.

Keywords: Image deblurring · Degradation representations

Supplementary Information The online version contains supplementary material available at https://doi.org/10.1007/978-3-031-19797-0_42.

1   Introduction

Image restoration is required to handle various and complicated degradation patterns produced in different degradation processes. The degradation representations act as a crucial component to model the degradation processes and handle complicated degradation patterns, such as different noise levels in image denoising [8,21,51] and different combinations of Gaussian blurs and motion blurs in blind super-resolution [41]. However, the degradation representations are less exploited in learning-based deblurring methods and have not been well integrated into state-of-the-art deblurring networks.

The general blurring process can be formulated as

$$y = F(x, k) + \eta, \tag{1}$$

where x and y are sharp image and blurry image respectively. $F(x, k)$ is usually modeled as a blurring operator with kernel k. η represents the Gaussian noise.

A popular paradigm for image deblurring is based on the Maximum A Posterior (MAP) estimate framework,

$$(k, x) = \arg\max \mathbb{P}(y|x, k)\mathbb{P}(x)\mathbb{P}(k), \tag{2}$$

where $\mathbb{P}(x)$ and $\mathbb{P}(k)$ model the priors of the clean images and the blur kernels. Many handcrafted priors for modeling $\mathbb{P}(x)$ and $\mathbb{P}(k)$ have been proposed [1,11, 18,26]. But most of them are insufficient in characterizing the clean images and blur kernels accurately. Furthermore, the operator F is generally modeled as a convolution operation in conventional MAP frameworks, which does not hold in practice and causes unpleasing artifacts in real-world challenging cases.

Based on the limitations of kernel-based blurring modeling, a series of kernel-free approaches [3,4,6,38,47] are proposed to directly learn the mapping from blurry images to corresponding sharp images. While those methods outperform previous deblurring methods significantly, their performances are still limited in complicated blurry patterns, due to the lack of explicit modeling of the degradation process. This is because, unlike denoising methods, where the noise level might be similar across different images, blurring of different images generally have totally different patterns and cannot be well handled by fixed-weight networks without considering the degradation process. To combine the modeling of degradation and learning-based deblurring, recent works [29,39] propose to learn explicit degradation representations by using Deep Image Prior (DIP) [40] to reparameterize the kernel k and the sharp image x. This inevitably involves the time-consuming iterative inverse optimization and hyperparameter tuning of DIP to adapt the deblurring process. Moreover, degradation representations have not been taken as a common component in SOTA deblurring methods [3,47].

In this paper, we propose to learn explicit degradation representations with a novel joint sharp-to-blurry image reblurring and blurry-to-sharp image deblurring learning framework. Specifically, the degradation representations are learned in the process of sharp-to-blurry image reblurring. The process takes as input a blurry image and learns the degradation representations as a multi-channel spatial latent map to encode the spatially varying blur patterns in replacement of the conventional convolutional blur kernels or the DIP prior. A reblurring generator then takes as input the latent degradation map and the original sharp image and reblurs the sharp image back to its corresponding blurry image.

To effectively integrate the learned degradation representations into the reblurring process, we introduce a multi-scale degradation injection network (MSDI-Net) for achieving conditional image reblurring. The network adopts a U-Net like architecture [31]. The sharp image is fed into the encoder of the U-Net but the degradation is input into the encoder-decoder via the skip-connections to modulate the shortcut encoder feature maps. Specifically, the latent degradation map is gradually upsampled via nearest-neighbor interpolation and a convolution layer to multiple resolutions and are then used to predict spatially varying weighting and bias parameters of the shortcut feature maps at each corresponding resolution. In this way, the learning of the latent degradation representation is supervised by the original blurry image for sharp-to-blurry image reblurring.

To make the learned degradation representations contributing to image deblurring, another blurry-to-sharp image generator network is also introduced, which shares the same MSDI-Net architecture but does not share weights with the reblurring generator. The learned degradation representations are processed similarly to deblur a blurry input image. Specifically, its encoder takes the blurry image as input, while the latent degradation representations are used to modulate the blurry image's encoder-decoder shortcut feature maps at multiple resolutions. With the help of learned degradation map, the deblurring generator can handle complicated spatially varying blurry patterns, which are adaptively learned from the data to optimize both reblurring and deblurring tasks.

The main contributions of this work are two-fold: 1) We propose a novel joint framework for learning both sharp-to-blurry image reblurring and blurry-to-sharp image deblurring to adaptively encode spatially varying degradations and model the image blurring process, which in turn, benefits the image deblurring performance. 2) The proposed joint reblurring and deblurring framework outperforms state-of-the-art image deblurring methods on the widely used GoPro [24] and RealBlur [30] datasets.

2   Related Work

In this section, we briefly talk about the related works of image restoration with degradation representations and different image deblurring methods.

Image Restoration with Degradation Representations. Image restoration tasks are usually required to handle different and complicated degradations in real-world applications. The degradation representations have been exploited and taken as one crucial component in several image restoration tasks, such as image denoising and image super-resolution. In image denoising, [8,21,51] take the noise variance as one network input to adaptively handle various noise strengths. Several practical denoising methods stabilize the noise variance caused by various ISO [43] and the property of Poisson-Gaussian distribution [15,35].

Similarly, image blind super-resolution is required to handle various degradations (different Gaussian blurs, motion blurs, and noises) in real-world applications. [41] proposes an unsupervised learning scheme for learning degradation representations based on the assumption that the degradation is the same in an image but can vary for different images. However, this assumption does not hold in image deblurring.

Optimization-Based Deblurring. A popular approach for image deblurring is based on the Maximum A Posterior (MAP). Most MAP-based methods focus on finding good priors for sharp images and blur kernels. Many priors are designed to model clean images and blur kernels. They include total variation (TV) [1], hyper-Laplacian prior [11], l_0-norm gradient prior [46] and sparse image priors [14]. They all assume the blur kernel is linear and uniform and can be represented as a convolution kernel. However, this assumption does not hold for real-world blurring with the non-uniform kernels. Some non-uniform deblurring methods [5,23,33,44] are proposed based on the assumption that the blur is locally uniform. They are not practical even with high computational costs.

Learning-Based Deblurring. Many deep deblurring models have been proposed over the past few years. Earlier attempts [32,37] utilize deep convolution neural networks to facilitate blur kernel estimation. However, there are several limitations [24] in estimating kernels. 1) Simple kernel convolution is not practical in real-world challenging cases. 2) The incorrect kernel estimations, caused by noise and large motions, may cause unpleasing artifacts. 3) Estimating spatially varying kernels requires a huge amount of computation. To avoid the above limitations, a series of kernel-free methods [3,4,6,12,13,24,27,36,38,47,49,52] are proposed with much better performances. Nah et al. [24] propose a multi-scale network for image deblurring. Similarly, Tao et al. [38] propose a scale-recurrent structure for image deblurring. Adversarial training is also introduced in image deblurring [12,13]. Chen *et al.* [2] introduces a reblur2deblur framework for video deblurring. Zhang *et al.* [52] proposes a reblurring network to synthesize additional blurry training images. The reblurring network and deblurring network are separate in both two methods. In this work, we combine reblurring network and deblurring network in learning the degradation representations. Recently, multistage approaches [3,36,47,49] achieve impressive performance against previous methods. While those deblurring networks outperform the traditional deblurring methods significantly, their performances are still limited due to the lack of explicit degradation modeling.

Learning Blurring Degradation Representations. While the explicit degradation representations have shown convincing improvements on many low-level vision tasks, it is rarely explored in learning-based deblurring methods. SelfDeblur [29] introduces the Deep Image Prior (DIP) [40] to model the clean images and the kernels separately. But, it assumes the blur kernels are linear and uniform, which is not practical in complicated real-world scenes. Tran *et al.* [39] address the limitation by introducing the explicit representation for the blur kernels and the blur operators and reparameterizing the degradation and

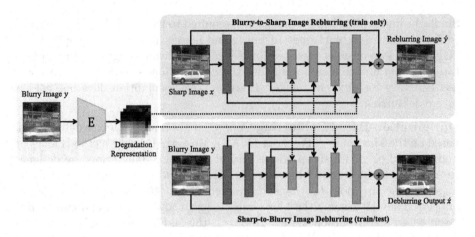

Fig. 1. Learning degradation representations with reblurring and deblurring.

the sharp image by using DIP. This inevitably involves alternative optimization, which is time-consuming. The learned representations cannot improve the performance of existing deblurring networks directly and their application is limited to time-consuming DIP-based optimization methods.

3   Methodology

In this section, we first introduce a joint learning framework for both sharp-to-blurry image reblurring and blurry-to-sharp image deblurring to encode latent spatially varying degradation representations from blurry images. A blur-aware loss is introduced to enhance the image deblurring performance. To more effectively integrate the latent degradation representations for reblurring and deblurring, a multi-scale degradation injection network is proposed for both tasks.

3.1   Learning Degradation Representations from Joint Reblurring and Deblurring

Most existing deblurring methods [1,11,18,26,32] take the blur kernels as the degradation representations and model the blurring process as a convolution on the input image. However, the simple kernel convolution is not practical in real-world challenging cases and it is usually difficult to estimate the blur kernels in large motions and spatially varying blurring cases. We propose to encode latent degradation representations from blurry images via the joint learning of image reblurring and deblurring. As shown in Fig. 1, we introduce an encoder E to encode the blurry image y into the degradation representations $E(y)$, which is modeled as a multi-channel latent map encoding 2D spatially varying blurring degradation in a latent space. Then an image reblurring generator G_r and an image deblurring generator G_d are introduced to generate the reblurred image

$\acute{y}$ and the deblurred image $\acute{x}$, respectively. The degradation representations do not only help the reblurring generator G_r model the degradation process, but also help the deblurring network handle complicated spatially varying degradation patterns. The joint training of reblurring and deblurring strengthens the expressiveness of learned degradation representations.

Sharp-to-Blurry Image Reblurring. Different from modeling the blurring process as a convolution, our generator G_r models the degradation process via learning to generate the blurry image $\acute{y}$, given the sharp image x and the corresponding degradation representations $E(y)$. In addition, instead of generating the whole blurry image from scratch, the reblurring generator G_r learns to predict the residual between the sharp image x and the blurry image y. The learning of the blurring degradation process in our framework is therefore formulated as generating a blurry image $\acute{y}$ from its clean image x as

$$\acute{y} = x + G_r(x, E(y)), \tag{3}$$

where $\acute{y}$ is the reblurred image conditioned on the sharp image x and degradation representation $E(y)$. With the residual learning, the encoder E is encouraged to neglect the contents of the blurry image and to focus on disentangling the content-independent degradation representation $E(y)$ from the blurry image y.

Note that most existing encoder-decoder networks, such as VAE [10], can also learn implicit image representations via image reconstruction. They aim at encoding the whole-image contents into the latent representations. However, our framework aims at encoding only the degradation information by predicting the residuals between the sharp and blurry images. Such a task actually has a lower difficulty level than reconstructing all contents of an input image and therefore leads to encoding better blurring degradation representations.

We first tried the mainstream L_1 distance as the loss function. But, as shown later in our supplementary, the L_1 loss function merely measures the pixel-wise distance and cannot properly describe the similarity of the blurry patterns of two images. Then the reblurring generator G_r cannot well generate the blurry images with L_1 loss, which harms the learning of degradation representation. Therefore, we further resort to perceptual loss [9] and adversarial training [7] to distinguish different degradation patterns in training. Adversarial loss is applied on the output of the generator G_r to distinguish real and fake blurry images so that the decoder can well model the blurring process and improve the expressiveness of degradation representation. We take the hinge loss [17,22,28,48] as the adversarial loss to help the reblurring generator G_r model the degradation (blurring) process and improve the expressiveness of learned degradation representations. We train the reblurring generator G_r to generate the blurry images with the multi-scale discriminator D used in [42]. The training objective for image reblurring is formulated as

$$L_G = -E_{x \sim p_{\text{data}}} D(x, \acute{y}) + \lambda_1 L_{\text{perceptual}}(y, \acute{y}),$$
$$L_D = -E_{(x,y) \sim p_{\text{data}}}[\min(0, -1 + D(x, y))] - E_{x \sim p_{\text{data}}}[\min(0, -1 - D(x, \acute{y}))], \tag{4}$$

where λ_1 balances the L_1 loss and the discriminator loss for image reblurring, and the discriminator D is a conditional discriminator conditioning on the sharp image x. Conditioning on the sharp image x, the conditional discriminator D can focus on whether the reblurred image $\acute{y}$ has the same image contents with the corresponding sharp image x. The reblurring helps extract content-independent degradation information (shown in Fig), which is different with the content-dependent conditional networks [45,50,53].

Blurry-to-Sharp Image Deblurring. To make the learned degradation representations contributing to image deblurring, we also model the image deblurring process with the image reblurring process jointly. The image deblurring generator G_d follows a similar design to that of G_r. The deblurring generator G_d is only required to learn the deblurring residuals between the blurry image y and its corresponding sharp image x, and the learned degradation representations $E(y)$. The blurry-to-sharp image deblurring is modeled as

$$\acute{x} = y + G_d(y, E(y)). \tag{5}$$

Thanks to the 2D learnable degradation representations, the image deblurring generator G_d is aware of the spatially varying blurry patterns and thus can adaptively handle various and complicated degradation patterns. The learning of image deblurring makes the learned degradation representations adapted to the deblurring task. The loss function for image deblurring is formulated as

$$L_(x, \acute{x}) = \lambda_2 L_1(x, \acute{x}). \tag{6}$$

Discussion of the Learned Degradation Representation. The learned degradation representation has two main advantages against conventional kernel modeling: 1) Our degradation representations can learn non-uniform spatially varying degradations effectively. Figures 1 and 6 show that the encoder can distinguishe different degradation representations. 2) Interpolating on the latent space of representations can generate blurry images with controllable blurry levels (as shown in Fig. 5). The representations are also content-independent (as shown in Fig. 6), which is different from previous conditional networks [45,50,53]. Built on this latent space, the representations show better interpretability and expressiveness.

3.2   Image Deblurring with Learned Degradation Representations

After obtaining the pre-trained encoder E, we freeze the pre-trained encoder and re-train the deblurring generator G_d to illustrate that our improvement is not from the complicated framework but the learned degradation representations. To further demonstrate the generality of learned degradation representations, we also train the deblurring generator G_d on the RealBlur dataset [30] with the encoder trained on the GoPro dataset [24].

Following HINet [3], we select the Peak Signal-to-Noise Ratio (PSNR) loss as the main supervision. We also utilize a blur-aware loss function as extra supervision. The well-trained encoder E should be quite sensitive to capture

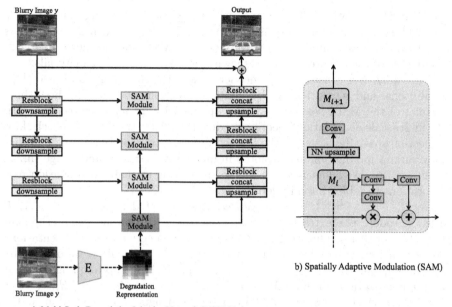

a) Multi-Scale Degradation Injection Network (MSDI-Net)

b) Spatially Adaptive Modulation (SAM)

Fig. 2. The network structure of multi-scale degradation injection network for image deblurring. Image reblurring shares the same structure.

various and even subtle blur patterns. We, therefore, define the blur-aware loss as the distance between degradation encoder features of the ground-truth sharp image x and the estimated sharp image $\acute{x}$. The deviation between the encoder feature maps $\|E(x) - E(\acute{x})\|_1$ of images x and $\acute{x}$ can give more weights on the remaining blurry regions of the network output $\acute{x}$. Similar to perceptual loss [9], the L_1 distances between the encoder feature maps can be calculated at multiple scales. The blur-aware loss L_{blur} is therefore formulated as

$$L_{\text{blur}}(\acute{x}, x) = \sum_{i=1}^{N} \frac{1}{|E^{(i)}|}[\|E^{(i)}(\acute{x}) - E^{(i)}(x)\|_1], \qquad (7)$$

where $E^{(i)}$ denotes the i-th layer of the encoder E and $|E^{(i)}|$ denotes the number of pixels in feature map $E^{(i)}(x)$. Using the blur-aware loss makes the deblurring generator G_d pay more attention to the remaining blurry regions of the network output $\acute{x}$. Then the deblurring objective is formulated as

$$L(x, \acute{x}) = \text{PSNR}(x, \acute{x}) + \lambda_2 L_{\text{blur}}(x, \acute{x}). \qquad (8)$$

3.3 Multi-scale Degradation Injection Network

To effectively integrate the degradation $E(y)$ to predict the reblurring and deblurring residuals, we propose a multi-scale degradation injection network

(MSDI-Net) for both reblurring and deblurring. Our reblurring generator G_r and deblurring generator G_d consists of two MSDI-Nets, which are stacked as HINet [3] does. for simplicity, the overview of a MSDI-Net is shown in Fig. 2. The details of the architectures are shown in the supplementary materials.

The MSDI-Net consists of an encoder, a decoder, concatenation-based skip-connections, and a multi-scale degradation injection module. The first three modules of the MSDI-Net are widely adopted in U-Net like architectures [31]. The multi-scale degradation injection module modulates the feature of each skip-connection spatially, based on the learned degradation representation. The spatially variant modulation are explored in image synthesis [28] and image super-resolution [16]. We adopt it as the key to connecting learnable degradation representations to reblurring and deblurring.

Let $f_i \in \mathbb{R}^{C_i \times H_i \times W_i}$ denote the features extracted at scale $i = 1, \dots, 5$ in the encoder. The extracted feature f_i is passed to the decoder at the skip connection of scale i. Our MSDI-Net integrates the degradation representations into concatenation-based skip-connections of scale i. At scale i, we obtain the degradation map $M_i \in \mathbb{R}^{C_i \times H_i \times W_i}$ by a convolution-based upsampling block on the original degradation map $M_{i-1} \in \mathbb{R}^{C_{i-1} \times H_{i-1} \times W_{i-1}}$ ($H_i = 2 \times H_{i-1}, W_i = 2 \times W_{i-1}$), which is implemented by a nearest-neighbor interpolation and a convolution layer to avoid checkerboard artifacts [25]. Then we utilize a spatially adaptive modulation (SAM) module to modulate the skip-connection feature f_i at scale i. The spatially adaptive modulation modulates the feature map channels in a spatially varying manner with both predicted scaling and additions. At the skip connection of scale i, we use several convolution (3×3) layers on the degradation map M_i to predict the modulating parameters $\gamma_i \in \mathbb{R}^{C_i \times H_i \times W_i}$ and $\beta_i \in \mathbb{R}^{C_i \times H_i \times W_i}$ respectively, which modulate the feature map f_i as

$$F_i = \gamma_i \odot f_i + \beta_i, \tag{9}$$

where F_i is the modulated skip-connection features. Since the modulation parameters are predicted from the degradation representations, the learnable modulation of the feature channels makes the deblurring network aware of spatially varying degradations. The degradation-aware feature F_i is then concatenated with the decoder feature at scale i and the last decoder layer predicts the image residuals for both image reblurring and deblurring.

Injecting the degradation representations enables the networks to handle various and complicated degradation patterns adaptively. Injection at multiple scales improves the expressiveness of degradation representations by strengthening the connections between the degradation representations and two generators.

4 Experiments

4.1 Dataset and Implementation Details

We train and evaluate our method on the GoPro [24] and RealBlur datasets [30]. The GoPro dataset consists of 2,103 pairs of blurry and sharp images for training and 1,111 pairs for testing. The RealBlur dataset consists of 3,758 pairs for

Table 1. Deblurring comparisons on GoPro [24] dataset. Best and second best scores are **highlighted** and underlined.

Method	Reference	PSNR	SSIM
DeblurGAN [12]	CVPR'18	28.70	0.858
DeblurGAN-v2 [13]	ICCV'19	29.55	0.934
SRN [38]	CVPR'18	30.26	0.934
Gao et al. [6]	CVPR'19	30.90	0.935
DBGAN [52]	CVPR'20	31.10	0.942
MT-RNN [27]	ECCV'20	31.15	0.945
DMPHN [49]	CVPR'19	31.20	0.940
Suin et al. [36]	CVPR'20	31.85	0.948
MIMO-UNet [4]	ICCV'21	32.45	0.957
MPRNet [47]	CVPR'21	32.66	0.959
HINet [3]	CVPRW'21	32.71	0.959
MPRNet-patch256 [47]	CVPR'21	<u>32.96</u>	<u>0.961</u>
Ours	ECCV'22	**33.28**	**0.964**

Table 2. Detailed comparisons of MPRNet [47] and our method on GoPro test dataset [24]. MACs are estimated with the input size of $3 \times 256 \times 256$.

Model	Blurriest 10%	Sharpest 10%	All	MACs (G)
MPRNet-patch256 [47]	29.31	35.52	32.96	760.11
Ours	**29.65**	**35.58**	**33.28**	336.43

training and 980 pairs for testing. We first train the framework of reblurring and deblurring on GoPro dataset [24]. We apply horizontal flipping and rotation as data augmentation and crop image patch of size 256×256 from the dataset for training. λ_1 is set as 30 and λ_2 is set as 10. The networks of whole framework are trained with a batch size of 32 for 200k iterations. Then we freeze the weights of well-trained encoder E and train the deblurring generator G_d on the GoPro dataset [24] and the RealBlur dataset [30] respectively. λ_3 is set as 1. The deblurring generator G_d is trained with a batch size of 64 for 400k iterations. We use the Adam optimizer and the learning rate is set as 3×10^{-4} at the beginning and decreased to 1×10^{-7} following the cosine annealing strategy [19].

4.2 Performance Comparison

We compare our method with state-of-the-art deblurring methods [3,4,47] on the GoPro test dataset [24]. The quantitative results are reported in Table 1. For testing, we slice the whole image into several 256×256 patches and test all patches to report the results of HINet [3], MPRNet-patch256 [47] and our

Fig. 3. Visual comparisons for image deblurring on the GoPro test dataset [24]. From left-top to right-bottom: blurry images, ground-truth images, and results obtained by MIMO-UNet [4], HINet [3], MPRNet [47] and our proposed method.

method. Our method achieves 0.45 dB improvement in terms of PSNR over the previous best-performing method HINet [3]. To evaluate effectiveness and generality of learned degradation representations, we also evaluate our method on the RealBlur dataset. As listed in Table 3, our method achieves the best performance in terms of PSNR and SSIM. Since HINet [3] does not release the model for RealBlur dataset [30], we train the HINet model on RealBlur dataset based on their released training code. Note that we apply the degradation representations trained on GoPro dataset [24] directly on RealBlur dataset [30]. Our method outperforms the previous SOTA HINet [3] by 0.23 dB PSNR, which demonstrate the generality of learnable degradation representations.

In Table 2, we provide detailed comparisons between our method and MPR-Net [47]. We divide the whole gopro dataset into blurriest 10% and sharpest 10% as [34] does. It is observed that the main improvement of our method is the improvement of 0.34dB PSNR in the blurriest 10%, which demonstrates the advantage of proposed degradation learning. What's more, our method's computational cost is less than 50% of MPRNet's [47].

Figures 3 and 4 show example deblurred results from the GoPro [24] and Real-Blur [30] test sets by the evaluated approaches. Our method produces sharper images and recovers more details in the regions of texts and moving objects, compared with other methods.

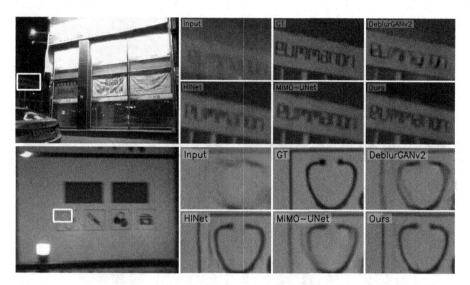

Fig. 4. Visual comparisons for image deblurring on the RealBlur test dataset [30]. From left-top to right-bottom: blurry images, ground-truth images and resuls obtained by DeblurGANv2, HINet [3], MIMO-UNet [4], our proposed method.

Table 3. Deblurring comparisons on the RealBlur test dataset [30].

Method	Reference	PSNR	SSIM
DeblurGAN-v2 [13]	ICCV'19	29.69	0.870
SRN [38]	CVPR'18	31.38	0.909
MPRNet [47]	CVPR'21	31.76	<u>0.922</u>
MIMO-UNet [4]	ICCV'21	32.05	0.921
HINet [3]	CVPRW'21	<u>32.12</u>	0.921
Ours	ECCV'22	**32.35**	**0.923**

4.3 Interpolation and Decoupleness of Degradation Representations

To demonstrate the effectiveness of learned degradation representations, we study the interpolation and decoupleness of learned degradation representations. Given a blurry image y and its corresponding sharp image x, we can obtain two degradation representations $E(y)$ and $E(x)$. Then we obtain several intermediate degradation representations by interpolating from $E(y)$ to $E(x)$. The corresponding output of the decoder changes smoothly from sharp to blurry images. The blur interpolation in Fig. 5 shows that our degradation representations are built on the latent space and accurately aware of different degradations. We empirically validate the decoupleness of blur and image contents on GoPro dataset. We divide the GoPro test dataset into 555 pairs of images. For each pair of sharp images $\{A, B\}$, the corresponding blurry images are $\{\text{blur}(A), \text{blur}(B)\}$

Fig. 5. Generating blurry images with linearly interpolated degradation representations. From left to right: the blurry level from sharp to blur.

Fig. 6. Reblurring A_1, A_2, A_3 with the degradation representation of $\mathrm{Blur}(B)$.

and the degradation representations are obtained as $\{\deg_A, \deg_B\}$. The sharp image A can be reblurred according to $\deg_B$ to obtain $\mathrm{ReBlur}(A, \deg_B)$. We use the average contextual similarity CX [20] to measure pairwise image similarity. We have $\mathrm{CX}(\mathrm{blur}(A), A) = 2.72$, $\mathrm{CX}(\mathrm{ReBlur}(A, \deg_B), A) = 2.65$, $\mathrm{CX}(\mathrm{blur}(A), B) = 5.43$, and $\mathrm{CX}(\mathrm{ReBlur}(A, \deg_B), B) = 5.39$, averaging over all the pairs. The similarities empirically show that $\mathrm{ReBlur}(A, \deg_B)$ has similar contents with A (the former two equations) but doesn't have similar contents with B (the latter two equations). The visual examples on degradation decoupleness are provided in Fig. 6. The decoupleness of learned degradation representations shows our difference with the content-dependent conditional networks [45,50,53] and the capacity of being a general operator to replace conventional blurring process.

4.4   Ablation Study

We evaluate the effectiveness of learning degradation representations and the multi-scale degradation injection network by revising one of the components of

Table 4. The ablation study of image deblurring on GoPro test dataset [24].

Model	PSNR
Ours w/o degradation	32.81
Ours w/o reblurring	33.09
Ours w/o blur loss	33.21
Our injection w/o multi-scale	32.80
Our input w/ concat	32.98
Ours w/ concat injection	33.05
Ours	**33.28**

our model at a time. Table 4 lists the performances of different settings on the GoPro test set [24]. We first remove the degradation encoder for learning the degradation representations and make G_d only takes as input the blurry image (denoted as "Ours w/o degradation"). The performance suffers a large drop of 0.47dB PSNR. Then we remove the generator of image reblurring and reserve the encoder to provide additional encoding from the blurry images (denoted as "Our w/o reblurring"), this operation causes a drop of 0.19 dB PSNR, demonstrating that reblurring indeed contributes to the learning of better degradation representations. Then we remove the blur-aware loss function (Eq. (7)). The training objective for deblurring becomes only the PSNR loss (denoted as "Ours w/o blur loss"). The performance drops slightly by about 0.07 PSNR. We further experiment with different ways of integrating degradation representations into the generators. When we remove the injection at multiple scales, the degradation representation is integrated just at the lowest resolution skip connection (denoted as "Our injection w/o multi-scale"). The performance suffers a significant drop of 0.48 PSNR, which means that injecting the degradation representation into a single scale would affect the deblurring performance significantly. Then we replace the modulation and test on concatenating latent degradation map with skip-connection feature maps (denoted as "Our w/ concat injection"). For fair comparisons of computational cost, we add two-layer residual blocks after the feature concatenation. The operation causes a drop of 0.23 PSNR. We also remove the integration totally and concatenate the upsampling degradation maps with the blurry images at the network entrance with the blurry image (denoted as "Ours input w/ concat"), which is the mainstream design in image denoising [8,21,51]. Its performance drops by about 0.3 PSNR. All the ablation studies demonstrate the effectiveness of our proposed learnable degradation representations and MSDI-Net for image deblurring.

5   Conclusions

In this paper, we propose a framework for learning degradation representation with image reblurring and image deblurring. We first utilize an encoder to learn the degradation representations explicitly. Then we propose a multi-scale degradation injection network to effectively integrate the degradation representations for reblurring and deblurring. With the degradation representations, our networks can be aware of and handle spatially varying degradation patterns adaptively. The experimental results demonstrate that our method outperforms other methods with a clear margin.

Acknowledgments. This work is supported in part by Centre for Perceptual and Interactive Intelligence Limited, in part by the General Research Fund through the Research Grants Council of Hong Kong under Grants (Nos. 14204021, 14207319, 14203118, 14208619), in part by Research Impact Fund Grant No. R5001-18, in part by CUHK Strategic Fund.

References

1. Chan, T., Wong, C.K.: Total variation blind deconvolution. IEEE Trans. Image Process. **7**(3), 370–375 (1998)
2. Chen, H., Gu, J., Gallo, O., Liu, M.Y., Veeraraghavan, A., Kautz, J.: Reblur2Deblur: deblurring videos via self-supervised learning. In: 2018 IEEE International Conference on Computational Photography (ICCP), pp. 1–9 (2018)
3. Chen, L., Lu, X., Zhang, J., Chu, X., Chen, C.: HiNet: half instance normalization network for image restoration. In: Proceedings of the IEEE/CVF Conference on Computer Vision and Pattern Recognition (CVPR) Workshops, pp. 182–192 (2021)
4. Cho, S.J., Ji, S.W., Hong, J.P., Jung, S.W., Ko, S.J.: Rethinking coarse-to-fine approach in single image deblurring. In: Proceedings of the IEEE/CVF International Conference on Computer Vision (ICCV), pp. 4641–4650 (2021)
5. Cho, S., Matsushita, Y., Lee, S.: Removing non-uniform motion blur from images. In: 2007 IEEE 11th International Conference on Computer Vision, pp. 1–8 (2007)
6. Gao, H., Tao, X., Shen, X., Jia, J.: Dynamic scene deblurring with parameter selective sharing and nested skip connections. In: Proceedings of the IEEE Conference on Computer Vision and Pattern Recognition, pp. 3848–3856 (2019)
7. Goodfellow, I., et al.: Generative adversarial nets. In: Ghahramani, Z., Welling, M., Cortes, C., Lawrence, N., Weinberger, K.Q. (eds.) Advances in Neural Information Processing Systems, vol. 27. Curran Associates, Inc. (2014)
8. Guo, S., Yan, Z., Zhang, K., Zuo, W., Zhang, L.: Toward convolutional blind denoising of real photographs. In: 2019 IEEE Conference on Computer Vision and Pattern Recognition (CVPR) (2019)
9. Johnson, J., Alahi, A., Fei-Fei, L.: Perceptual losses for real-time style transfer and super-resolution. In: European Conference on Computer Vision (2016)
10. Kingma, D.P., Welling, M.: Auto-Encoding Variational Bayes. In: 2nd International Conference on Learning Representations, ICLR 2014, Banff, AB, Canada, April 14–16, 2014, Conference Track Proceedings (2014)
11. Krishnan, D., Fergus, R.: Fast image deconvolution using hyper-laplacian priors. In: Bengio, Y., Schuurmans, D., Lafferty, J., Williams, C., Culotta, A. (eds.) Advances in Neural Information Processing Systems, vol. 22. Curran Associates, Inc. (2009)
12. Kupyn, O., Budzan, V., Mykhailych, M., Mishkin, D., Matas, J.: DeblurGAN: blind motion deblurring using conditional adversarial networks. In: CVPR, pp. 8183–8192. Computer Vision Foundation/IEEE Computer Society (2018)

13. Kupyn, O., Martyniuk, T., Wu, J., Wang, Z.: DeblurGAN-v2: deblurring (orders-of-magnitude) faster and better. In: ICCV, pp. 8877–8886. IEEE (2019)
14. Levin, A., Weiss, Y., Durand, F., Freeman, W.T.: Understanding and evaluating blind deconvolution algorithms. In: 2009 IEEE Conference on Computer Vision and Pattern Recognition, pp. 1964–1971 (2009)
15. Li, D., Zhang, Y., Law, K.L., Wang, X., Qin, H., Li, H.: Efficient burst raw denoising with variance stabilization and multi-frequency denoising network. Int. J. Comput. Vis. **130**(8), 2060–2080 (2022)
16. Liang, J., Sun, G., Zhang, K., Van Gool, L., Timofte, R.: Mutual affine network for spatially variant kernel estimation in blind image super-resolution. In: IEEE International Conference on Computer Vision (2021)
17. Lim, J.H., Ye, J.C.: Geometric GAN (2017). arXiv:1705.02894
18. Liu, G., Chang, S., Ma, Y.: Blind image deblurring using spectral properties of convolution operators. IEEE Trans. Image Process. **23**(12), 5047–5056 (2014)
19. Loshchilov, I., Hutter, F.: SGDR: stochastic gradient descent with warm restarts. In: 5th International Conference on Learning Representations, ICLR 2017, Toulon, France, April 24–26, 2017, Conference Track Proceedings (2017)
20. Mechrez, R., Talmi, I., Zelnik-Manor, L.: The contextual loss for image transformation with non-aligned data. arXiv preprint arXiv:1803.02077 (2018)
21. Mildenhall, B., Barron, J.T., Chen, J., Sharlet, D., Ng, R., Carroll, R.: Burst denoising with kernel prediction networks. In: CVPR (2018)
22. Miyato, T., Kataoka, T., Koyama, M., Yoshida, Y.: Spectral normalization for generative adversarial networks. In: International Conference on Learning Representations (2018)
23. Nagy, J.G., O'Leary, D.P.: Restoring images degraded by spatially variant blur. SIAM J. Sci. Comput. **19**(4), 1063–1082 (1998)
24. Nah, S., Kim, T.H., Lee, K.M.: Deep multi-scale convolutional neural network for dynamic scene deblurring. In: The IEEE Conference on Computer Vision and Pattern Recognition (CVPR) (2017)
25. Odena, A., Dumoulin, V., Olah, C.: Deconvolution and checkerboard artifacts. Distill (2016)
26. Pan, J., Sun, D., Pfister, H., Yang, M.H.: Blind image deblurring using dark channel prior. In: 2016 IEEE Conference on Computer Vision and Pattern Recognition (CVPR), pp. 1628–1636 (2016)
27. Park, D., Kang, D.U., Kim, J., Chun, S.Y.: Multi-temporal recurrent neural networks for progressive non-uniform single image deblurring with incremental temporal training. In: Vedaldi, A., Bischof, H., Brox, T., Frahm, J.-M. (eds.) ECCV 2020. LNCS, vol. 12351, pp. 327–343. Springer, Cham (2020). https://doi.org/10.1007/978-3-030-58539-6_20
28. Park, T., Liu, M.Y., Wang, T.C., Zhu, J.Y.: Semantic image synthesis with spatially-adaptive normalization. In: Proceedings of the IEEE Conference on Computer Vision and Pattern Recognition (2019)
29. Ren, D., Zhang, K., Wang, Q., Hu, Q., Zuo, W.: Neural blind deconvolution using deep priors. In: 2020 IEEE/CVF Conference on Computer Vision and Pattern Recognition (CVPR), pp. 3338–3347. IEEE Computer Society, Los Alamitos, CA, USA (2020)
30. Rim, J., Lee, H., Won, J., Cho, S.: Real-world blur dataset for learning and benchmarking deblurring algorithms. In: Vedaldi, A., Bischof, H., Brox, T., Frahm, J.-M. (eds.) ECCV 2020. LNCS, vol. 12370, pp. 184–201. Springer, Cham (2020). https://doi.org/10.1007/978-3-030-58595-2_12

31. Ronneberger, O., Fischer, P., Brox, T.: U-Net: convolutional networks for biomedical image segmentation. In: Navab, N., Hornegger, J., Wells, W.M., Frangi, A.F. (eds.) Medical Image Computing and Computer-Assisted Intervention - MICCAI 2015 (2015)

32. Schuler, C.J., Hirsch, M., Harmeling, S., Schölkopf, B.: Learning to deblur. IEEE Trans. Pattern Anal. Mach. Intell. **38**, 1439–1451 (2016)

33. Shan, Q., Xiong, W., Jia, J.: Rotational motion deblurring of a rigid object from a single image. In: 2007 IEEE 11th International Conference on Computer Vision, pp. 1–8 (2007)

34. Son, H., Lee, J., Lee, J., Cho, S., Lee, S.: Recurrent video deblurring with blur-invariant motion estimation and pixel volumes. ACM Trans. Graph. (TOG) 40(5) (2021)

35. Starck, J.L., Murtagh, F., Bijaoui, A.: Image Processing and Data Analysis. Cambridge University Press, Cambridge (1998)

36. Suin, M., Purohit, K., Rajagopalan, A.N.: Spatially-attentive patch-hierarchical network for adaptive motion deblurring. In: CVPR, pp. 3603–3612. Computer Vision Foundation/IEEE (2020)

37. Sun, J., Cao, W., Xu, Z., Ponce, J.: Learning a convolutional neural network for non-uniform motion blur removal. In: 2015 IEEE Conference on Computer Vision and Pattern Recognition (CVPR), pp. 769–777 (2015)

38. Tao, X., Gao, H., Shen, X., Wang, J., Jia, J.: Scale-recurrent network for deep image deblurring. In: IEEE Conference on Computer Vision and Pattern Recognition (CVPR) (2018)

39. Tran, P., Tran, A., Phung, Q., Hoai, M.: Explore image deblurring via encoded blur kernel space. In: Proceedings of the In: IEEE Conference on Computer Vision and Pattern Recognition (CVPR) (2021)

40. Ulyanov, D., Vedaldi, A., Lempitsky, V.: Deep image prior. In: Proceedings of the In: IEEE Conference on Computer Vision and Pattern Recognition (CVPR) (2018)

41. Wang, L., et al.: Unsupervised degradation representation learning for blind super-resolution. In: CVPR (2021)

42. Wang, T.C., Liu, M.Y., Zhu, J.Y., Tao, A., Kautz, J., Catanzaro, B.: High-resolution image synthesis and semantic manipulation with conditional GANs. In: Proceedings of the IEEE Conference on Computer Vision and Pattern Recognition (2018)

43. Wang, Y., Huang, H., Xu, Q., Liu, J., Liu, Y., Wang, J.: Practical deep raw image denoising on mobile devices. In: Vedaldi, A., Bischof, H., Brox, T., Frahm, J.-M. (eds.) ECCV 2020. LNCS, vol. 12351, pp. 1–16. Springer, Cham (2020). https://doi.org/10.1007/978-3-030-58539-6_1

44. Whyte, O., Sivic, J., Zisserman, A., Ponce, J.: Non-uniform deblurring for shaken images. In: 2010 IEEE Computer Society Conference on Computer Vision and Pattern Recognition, pp. 491–498 (2010)

45. Xintao Wang, Ke Yu, C.D., Loy, C.C.: Recovering realistic texture in image super-resolution by deep spatial feature transform. In: IEEE Conference on Computer Vision Pattern Recognition (CVPR) (2018)

46. Xu, L., Zheng, S., Jia, J.: Unnatural L0 sparse representation for natural image deblurring. In: 2013 IEEE Conference on Computer Vision and Pattern Recognition, pp. 1107–1114 (2013)

47. Zamir, S.W.,et al.: Multi-stage progressive image restoration. In: CVPR (2021)

48. Zhang, H., Goodfellow, I., Metaxas, D., Odena, A.: Self-attention generative adversarial networks. In: Chaudhuri, K., Salakhutdinov, R. (eds.) Proceedings of the 36th

International Conference on Machine Learning. Proceedings of Machine Learning Research, vol. 97, pp. 7354–7363. PMLR (2019)

49. Zhang, H., Dai, Y., Li, H., Koniusz, P.: Deep stacked hierarchical multi-patch network for image deblurring. In: CVPR, pp. 5978–5986. Computer Vision Foundation/IEEE (2019)

50. Zhang, J., et al.: Dynamic scene deblurring using spatially variant recurrent neural networks. In: 2018 IEEE/CVF Conference on Computer Vision and Pattern Recognition, pp. 2521–2529 (2018)

51. Zhang, K., Zuo, W., Zhang, L.: FFDNet: toward a fast and flexible solution for CNN based image denoising. IEEE Transactions on Image Processing (2018)

52. Zhang, K., et al.: Deblurring by realistic blurring. In: CVPR, pp. 2734–2743. Computer Vision Foundation/IEEE (2020)

53. Zhou, S., Zhang, J., Pan, J., Xie, H., Zuo, W., Ren, J.: Spatio-temporal filter adaptive network for video deblurring. In: Proceedings of the IEEE International Conference on Computer Vision (2019)

Author Index